PENGUIN REFERENCE

THE PENGUIN A–Z THESAURUS

Rosalind Fergusson was born in Liverpool in 1953 and obtained her degree in French from Exeter University. From here she took a teaching certificate and became an assistant teacher at a school in West Sussex. From 1978 to 1984 she worked for Market House Books where she trained as an assistant editor and lexicographer and rose to the position of Senior Editor. During this time she worked on a range of reference books. Since leaving Market House Books she has worked as a freelance editor.

Her other publications include *The Penguin Dictionary of Proverbs* (1983), *The Penguin Rhyming Dictionary* (1985), *Choose your Baby's Name* (1987), *The Hamlyn Dictionary of Quotations* (1989), *Chambers Dictionary of Foreign Words and Phrases* (1995), *Cassell Dictionary of English Idioms* (1999) and *The New Penguin Dictionary of Abbreviations* (2000). Rosalind Fergusson has also edited and co-edited a number of dictionaries and reference books, and has contributed to *The Bloomsbury Good Word Guide* (1988) and *Brewer's Dictionary of 20th-Century Phrase and Fable* (1991), among others.

Rosalind Fergusson is married and lives in Kent. Her leisure interests include walking, sailing and music.

THE PENGUIN A–Z THESAURUS

(previously published as THE PENGUIN DICTIONARY OF SYNONYMS AND ANTONYMS)

EDITED BY ROSALIND FERGUSSON,
MARKET HOUSE BOOKS LIMITED

PENGUIN BOOKS

PENGUIN BOOKS

Published by the Penguin Group
Penguin Books Ltd, 80 Strand, London WC2R 0RL, England
Penguin Putnam Inc., 375 Hudson Street, New York, New York 10014, USA
Penguin Books Australia Ltd, Ringwood, Victoria, Australia
Penguin Books Canada Ltd, 10 Alcorn Avenue, Toronto, Ontario, Canada M4V 3B2
Penguin Books India (P) Ltd, 11 Community Centre, Panchsheel Park, New Delhi – 110 017, India
Penguin Books (NZ) Ltd, Cnr Rosedale and Airborne Roads, Albany, Auckland, New Zealand
Penguin Books (South Africa) (Pty) Ltd, 24 Sturdee Avenue, Rosebank 2196, South Africa

Penguin Books Ltd, Registered Offices: 80 Strand, London WC2R 0RL, England

www.penguin.com

The Nuttall Dictionary of English Synonyms and Antonyms, a revised edition,
first published by Frederick Warne & Co. Ltd 1943
A fully revised and updated edition,
under the title *The New Nuttall Dictionary of English Synonyms and Antonyms*,
first published by Viking 1986
Published under the title *The Penguin Dictionary of Synonyms and Antonyms* in Penguin Books 1992
Reprinted under the present title 2001
2

Printed in England by Clays Ltd, St Ives plc

Preface

This classic work, formerly entitled *The Nuttall Dictionary of English Synonyms and Antonyms,* was last revised in 1943. It was reprinted twenty-eight times, indicating that it had found a substantial and continuing market. For this entirely new edition the dictionary has been updated and considerably enlarged, both in the selection of words covered and in the range of synonyms and antonyms offered. In the last half-century many words and senses have changed their meaning, and many new ones have appeared. This edition reflects these changes in the English language without altering the essential flavour of the book, although it has now been computerized and typeset using the latest technology.

The aim of this edition, as with earlier versions, is to collect together groups of words of similar meaning, enabling the user to avoid repetition in both writing and speaking and to find quickly and easily the most appropriate word for any occasion. English has a uniquely prolific vocabulary reflecting the multiplicity of its sources – the Anglo-Saxon of its early inhabitants, the enrichment provided by its Roman, Viking, and Norman invaders, the borrowings from all parts of the globe acquired by generations of seafarers, and the two-way trade in vocabulary from the Empire and Colonies. The result is a language more precise than any other in its ability to differentiate shades and nuances of meaning; for the users of such an affluent language a dictionary of synonyms becomes a near-necessity.

While it is probable that there are no true synonyms – that few words can really be interchanged in all contexts without any shift of connotation – on many occasions memories need to be nudged for the appropriate near-synonym to complete a sentence or paragraph without repetition. To provide this service, this dictionary consists of a single alphabetical list of headwords, each followed by a selection of synonyms grouped together according to the various senses of the word and the different shades of meaning within each sense. Clearly a book of this size cannot list all the words in the language, but what it does provide is a broad selection of the words in the general language. Concrete nouns with simple synonyms, such as **car**, **automobile**, and **radio**, **wireless**, have not been included. Our aim, like those of the original editors of the book, has been to cover the more interesting semantic areas of abstract nouns and adjectives, especially those with metaphorical senses.

In addition to the synonym lists, for many of the entries an antonym is given in small capital letters at the end of the entry. (Further antonyms may be obtained by seeking the antonyms of words listed as synonyms.)

Where the derived form of a word is not given as an independent headword, its synonyms may be formed from those given for its stem. For example, from the entry

sad, unhappy, sorrowful, downcast, dejected, depressed, despondent, etc.

both

sadly, unhappily, sorrowfully, dejectedly, despondently,

and

sadness, unhappiness, sorrow, dejection, depression, despondency, etc.

may be derived.

Part-of-speech labels are given where necessary to distinguish between the different senses of a headword or between headwords with identical spelling. They are abbreviated as follows:

adj	adjective
adv	adverb
conj	conjunction
interj	interjection
n	noun
prep	preposition
v	verb
vi	intransitive verb
vt	transitive verb

The label (*inf*), as an abbreviation of the word 'informal', has been introduced to designate synonyms that may be unacceptable in formal usage.

Finally we would like to thank Commander F. Val. Jones, who, with his late wife, made many helpful suggestions for bringing this book up to date.

R.F.
1985

A

aback backwards, rearwards, behind, aft.
taken aback, surprised, startled, dumbfounded, nonplussed, disconcerted.

abandon *v*, desert, leave, forsake, jilt, discard, get rid of, drop.
quit, vacate, evacuate, withdraw from.
give up, forgo, yield, surrender, cede, relinquish, renounce, abdicate, resign. RETAIN
n, unrestraint, dash, verve, impulsiveness, wantonness, lawlessness. RESTRAINT

abandoned deserted, forsaken, left, discarded, cast away, rejected, forlorn, derelict. KEPT
unrestrained, uninhibited, wanton, dissolute, shameless, impenitent, licentious, depraved, corrupt, sinful. VIRTUOUS

abase lower, reduce, depress, degrade, disgrace, dishonour, humiliate, humble, demean, demote, debase, belittle. EXALT

abasement degradation, lowering, disgrace, dishonour, ignominy, shame, humiliation, mortification. EXALTATION

abash confound, confuse, disconcert, discompose, discomfit, embarrass, shame, humble, humiliate, daunt, overawe, intimidate.

abashment confusion, discomposure, discomfiture, chagrin, embarrassment, shame, humiliation.

abate lessen, reduce, decrease, diminish, attenuate, alleviate, ease, moderate, assuage, soothe, calm, pacify, appease, quell, subside, let up, ebb, decline, wane, slacken, remit. INCREASE
deduct, subtract, discount.

abatement decrease, diminution, lessening, reduction, decline, easing, moderation, alleviation, relief. INCREASE
suppression, termination, control, restraint, limitation.
deduction, subtraction, discount, reduction, rebate.

abbey monastery, friary, priory, nunnery, convent, cloister, church, minster.

abbreviate condense, shorten, curtail, abridge, cut, reduce, contract, compress, paraphrase, summarize, précis. LENGTHEN

abbreviation shortening, abridgment, reduction, contraction, compression, condensation, summary, résumé, synopsis. EXTENSION

abdicate resign, renounce, give up, relinquish, cede, surrender, vacate, retire, quit.

abdomen belly, paunch, stomach, tummy (*inf*), gut, intestines.

abdominal intestinal, visceral, gastric, stomachic, ventral.

abduct kidnap, carry off, seize, remove, run off with, appropriate. RESTORE

abduction kidnapping, seizure, appropriation. RESTORATION

aberrant irregular, abnormal, eccentric, peculiar, untypical, anomalous, unusual, singular, odd. REGULAR
deviant, wandering, deviating, divergent, rambling.
erroneous, wrong, perverse, perverted, corrupt.

aberration deviation, divergence, irregularity, abnormality, peculiarity, anomaly. REGULARITY
delusion, vagary, mental disorder, hallucination.

abet aid, assist, help, succour, sustain, support, back, condone, favour, sanction, encourage, advocate, incite, urge, egg on. OPPOSE

abettor accomplice, accessory, henchman, partner in crime, assistant, helper, associate, confederate, instigator, adviser. OPPONENT

abeyance suspension, intermission, deferment, postponement, reservation, dormancy. REVIVAL
in abeyance, suspended, put aside, shelved, pending, hanging fire, on ice (*inf*).

abhor abominate, loathe, detest, execrate, shrink from, hate. ADORE

abhorrence abomination, loathing, execration, detestation, odium, repugnance, horror, aversion, antipathy, hate, hatred. LOVE

abhorrent loathsome, detestable, execrable, abominable, obnoxious, repugnant, odious, hateful, horrid. ADORABLE

abide *vt*, bear, tolerate, put up with, suffer, stand, brook, endure, sustain, accept, submit to.
vi, remain, last, endure, persist, continue, survive. PERISH
dwell, reside, live, lodge, sojourn, settle, rest, tarry, stay. DEPART
abide by, comply with, conform to, observe, obey, submit to, fulfil, carry out, keep to. BREAK

abiding lasting, permanent, durable, enduring, eternal, changeless, unchanging, steadfast. CHANGING

ability capacity, capability, competence, efficiency, proficiency, skill, aptitude, cleverness, talent, gift, knack, flair, potential, power, might, force. INABILITY

abject contemptible, despicable, base, vile, mean, low, ignoble, worthless, degraded, sordid, servile, grovelling, cringing, slavish. HONOURABLE
miserable, wretched, forlorn, dejected, pitiable, pathetic.

abjectness abjection, baseness, dishonour, degradation, vileness, meanness, worthlessness, servility.
destitution, forlornness, wretchedness, misery, humiliation.

abjure retract, recant, withdraw, disclaim, forswear, disavow. ACKNOWLEDGE
renounce, reject, repudiate, discard, disown, abandon, forsake, abstain from.

able capable, competent, fit, efficient, accomplished, qualified, adept, proficient, adroit, skilful, clever, talented, expert, masterly, powerful, strong. INCAPABLE

ablution washing, cleansing, bathing, purification.

abnegate deny, renounce, abstain from, abjure, forgo, reject.

abnegation denial, renunciation, abjuration, surrender, self-denial, abstinence.

abnormal irregular, unusual, uncommon, extraordinary, singular, eccentric, aberrant divergent, atypical, exceptional, monstrous, peculiar, strange, odd, curious, weird, queer. NORMAL

abnormality anomaly, irregularity, deformity, monstrosity, aberration, peculiarity, idiosyncrasy, strangeness, oddity. NORMALITY

aboard on board, afloat, on, in, inside, within.

abode dwelling, home, domicile, residence, habitation, lodging, house, seat, quarters.

abolish destroy, do away with, annihilate, nullify, annul, abrogate, eradicate, terminate, end, put an end to, suppress, revoke, cancel, erase, obliterate, eliminate. RETAIN

abolition destruction, annihilation, annulment, abrogation, eradication, end, suppression, cancellation, obliteration, elimination.

abominable detestable, loathsome, horrible, hateful, execrable, odious, obnoxious, foul, vile, repulsive, repugnant, hellish, damnable, accursed, terrible, unpleasant. LOVABLE

abominate abhor, detest, loathe, execrate, hate. ADORE

abomination abhorrence, loathing, detestation, aversion, hatred. LOVE
plague, torment, nuisance, annoyance, bugbear, curse, pest. BLESSING
evil, villainy, wickedness, corruption, pollution.

aboriginal original, first, earliest, primary, autochthonous, native, indigenous, primitive, primeval. ALIEN

aborigine native, indigene, aboriginal, autochthon.

abort miscarry, terminate, halt, stop, check, arrest, go wrong, fail. ACHIEVE

abortion miscarriage, termination of pregnancy, stillbirth, aborticide, feticide.
failure, disappointment, fiasco, mishap, misadventure, blunder. ACHIEVEMENT

abortive fruitless, vain, unavailing, ineffectual, futile, failed, failing. SUCCESSFUL
immature, incomplete, imperfect, rudimentary, stunted, untimely, premature.

abound teem, swarm, flow, overflow, be plentiful, proliferate, flourish, thrive.

about *prep*, concerning, relating to, regarding, touching, with respect to.
near, close to, around, nearby, nigh.
around, encircling, surrounding, on all sides, throughout, all over.
adv, approximately, roughly, more or less, circa, around, almost, nearly, well-nigh. PRECISELY

about to, on the point of, soon to, ready to, on the verge of.

above *prep*, over, on top of, higher than, exceeding, beyond, superior to. BELOW
adv, overhead, atop, aloft, higher, earlier, before, previously. BELOW

aboveboard frank, honest, truthful, open, candid, forthright, ingenuous, artless. DISHONEST

abrasion attrition, erosion, wearing down, rubbing, scraping, scouring.
scratch, graze, scrape.

abrasive *adj*, rough, scratching, grating, harsh.

irritating, annoying, biting, caustic, sharp.
n, scourer, abradant, emery, pumice, sandpaper, grindstone, rasp, file.

abreast beside, alongside, side by side, aligned, level.
informed, knowledgeable, conversant, familiar, up to date, *au courant*.

abridge condense, shorten, compress, contract, cut, reduce, abbreviate, summarize, cut down, curtail, lessen, diminish. EXPAND

abridgment shortening, condensation, abbreviation, summary, précis, abstract, digest, synopsis, outline, résumé, compendium. EXPANSION

abroad overseas, in foreign parts, out of the country.
away, out, elsewhere, at large, apart, dispersed, far, widely, publicly. NEAR

abrogate repeal, revoke, countermand, annul, nullify, cancel, expunge, quash, overrule, invalidate, abolish, terminate. ENACT

abrupt sudden, unexpected, unanticipated, unforeseen, hasty, precipitate, rash.
steep, sheer, precipitous. GRADUAL
curt, brusque, short, unceremonious, gruff, blunt, impolite, rude. COURTEOUS
broken, jagged, rough, uneven, disconnected, jerky.

abscess sore, boil, ulcer, inflammation, festering.

abscond flee, fly, run away, run off, elope, decamp, bolt, escape, leave, withdraw, beat it (*inf*), clear off (*inf*), disappear, hide. APPEAR

absence nonattendance, nonappearance. PRESENCE
lack, want, need, deficiency, default, unavailability.

absent *adj*, away, off, missing, out, abroad, gone, lacking, wanting, nonexistent. PRESENT
inattentive, preoccupied, distracted, oblivious, unaware, dreaming, faraway. ATTENTIVE

absent oneself, *v*, stay away, play truant, leave, depart, withdraw, abscond.

absent-minded forgetful, distracted, preoccupied, absorbed, absent, faraway, oblivious, unthinking, unconscious.

absolute complete, entire, utter, total, unlimited, unrestricted, unconditional, unqualified, perfect, pure, unadulterated, unalloyed, unmixed. PARTIAL
despotic, autocratic, tyrannical, authoritative, dictatorial, supreme, arbitrary.
undoubted, real, genuine, actual, veritable, certain, unquestionable. DUBIOUS

absolutely completely, entirely, utterly, totally, wholly, perfectly, categorically. PARTIALLY
really, unquestionably, definitely, indeed, positively, certainly, indubitably. POSSIBLY

absolution remission, forgiveness, pardon, acquittal, discharge, dispensation, amnesty, liberation, deliverance. CONDEMNATION

absolve forgive, pardon, excuse, acquit, exonerate, clear, exculpate, release, discharge, liberate, free, remit. CONDEMN

absorb consume, assimilate, incorporate, imbibe, soak up, suck up, take in, swallow, engulf. EXUDE
engross, fascinate, enthral, engage, preoccupy, monopolize.

absorbent porous, permeable, pervious, spongy, blotting, receptive, assimilative. IMPERMEABLE

absorbing engrossing, fascinating, riveting, gripping, interesting. DULL

abstain refrain, forbear, desist, decline, refuse, forgo, renounce, give up, shun, avoid, withhold. INDULGE

abstemious abstinent, temperate, moderate, sober, teetotal, continent, self-denying, ascetic, sparing, frugal. GREEDY

abstinence teetotalism, sobriety, temperance, moderation, abstemiousness, continence, self-denial. SELF-INDULGENCE

abstract *adj*, theoretical, hypothetical, unreal, spiritual, vague, conceptual, imaginary, indefinite, abstruse, recondite, profound, philosophical. CONCRETE
n, abridgment, summary, synopsis, digest, outline, précis, résumé.
v, separate, detach, remove, isolate, dissociate, extract, take out. UNITE
abbreviate, condense, shorten, abridge, epitomize, summarize. EXPAND

abstracted preoccupied, inattentive, absent-minded, faraway, daydreaming, unaware, distracted. ATTENTIVE

abstraction inattention, preoccupation, reverie, absence, brown study, absorption. ATTENTION

concept, idea, notion, theory, hypothesis, generality.
separation, isolation, removal, withdrawal, disconnection. UNION

abstruse obscure, recondite, abstract, vague, esoteric, arcane, occult, mysterious, perplexing, incomprehensible, unfathomable, profound, remote, subtle. CLEAR

absurd ridiculous, preposterous, irrational, incongruous, unreasonable, foolish, silly, asinine, crazy, stupid, ludicrous, nonsensical, senseless, laughable, farcical. SENSIBLE

abundance plenty, plentifulness, copiousness, profusion, exuberance, luxuriance, ampleness, fullness, bounty, affluence, richness, wealth, flood, overflow, surfeit, glut, excess. SCARCITY

abundant plentiful, copious, profuse, luxuriant, ample, bountiful, lavish, rich, replete, overflowing, teeming. SCARCE

abuse *v*, misuse, misapply, misemploy, pervert, exploit, take advantage of.
maltreat, harm, injure, hurt, ill-treat, persecute.
insult, slander, revile, disparage, defame, calumniate, malign, vilify, reproach, upbraid. PRAISE
n, misuse, misapplication, exploitation, perversion.
maltreatment, ill-treatment, injury, damage, persecution.
slander, calumny, insults, defamation, invective, disparagement. PRAISE

abusive insulting, offensive, defamatory, slanderous, rude, derogatory, derisive. COMPLIMENTARY

abut adjoin, touch, meet, join, impinge, border on, end at.

abyss gulf, gorge, chasm, crevasse, ravine, abysm, bottomless pit, void.

academic scholarly, learned, erudite, highbrow, intellectual, scholastic, literary, collegiate.
abstract, theoretical, hypothetical, speculative, artificial, unreal, irrelevant, unimportant. REAL

academy school, college, university, institution, institute, seminary.

accede agree, concur, assent, acquiesce, accept, consent, grant, concede, comply. DISAGREE
attain, succeed, inherit, assume, ascend, enter upon.

accelerate hasten, quicken, speed up, hurry, expedite, urge on, spur, stimulate, advance. RETARD

accent *n*, stress, accentuation, emphasis, force, beat, rhythm, cadence, pitch, tone, intonation, modulation, pronunciation, inflection.
v, accentuate, emphasize, stress.

accentuate accent, stress, emphasize, underline, highlight, draw attention to.

accept take, receive, gain, acquire, obtain. REFUSE
agree to, accede to, assent to, admit, acknowledge, acquiesce, allow, affirm, avow. REPUDIATE
tolerate, put up with, bear, stand, suffer.

acceptable satisfactory, adequate, passable, tolerable, all right, not bad, so-so. UNACCEPTABLE
welcome, agreeable, gratifying, pleasant, pleasing, delightful. UNWELCOME

acceptance acknowledgment, receipt, accepting, taking, reception. REFUSAL
approval, approbation, favour, sanction, assent, agreement, ratification.

accepted approved, authorized, usual, customary, normal, standard, conventional, traditional, established. UNCONVENTIONAL

access admission, admittance, approach, entrance, door, entry, way, passage, path.
attack, onset, fit, paroxysm, spasm, seizure, outburst.

accessible approachable, reachable, getatable (*inf*), obtainable, available, to hand. INACCESSIBLE
affable, cordial, friendly, approachable, genial. UNFRIENDLY

accession succession, inheritance, attainment, arrival, inauguration, investiture, installation.
addition, augmentation, increase, enlargement, extension, expansion. DECREASE

accessory *n*, supplement, subsidiary, component, element, minor part, detail, appendage, addition, attachment. ESSENTIAL
accomplice, abettor, confederate, partner, helper, assistant.
adj, subsidiary, supplementary, auxiliary, subordinate, additional, extra, minor. CHIEF

accident mishap, misadventure, mischance, casualty, calamity, chance, fluke, fortuity, contingency.
accidental casual, fortuitous, chance, unintentional, unplanned, contingent, unforeseen, unexpected. PLANNED
accidentally by accident, by mistake, inadvertently, unintentionally, by chance.
acclaim *v*, cheer, hail, welcome, applaud, praise, extol. DENOUNCE
n, praise, applause, acclamation.
acclamation applause, cheers, shouting, acclaim, praise, tribute, homage. DENUNCIATION
acclimatize habituate, familiarize, inure, season.
acclivity ascent, upward slope, rising ground, elevation, incline, hill. DECLIVITY
accommodate adapt, adjust, fit, suit, settle, compose, reconcile, harmonize.
oblige, help, aid, serve, provide, supply, give. DISOBLIGE
lodge, house, put up, billet, receive, hold, contain.
accommodating obliging, conciliatory, adaptable, yielding, compliant, considerate, kind, friendly, unselfish, polite. UNFRIENDLY
accommodation lodgings, housing, quarters, digs (*inf*), service, advantage, provision, supply, convenience.
adjustment, adaptation, conformity, harmonization.
accompaniment appendage, adjunct, appurtenance, attachment, accessory, attendant.
accompany escort, go with, attend, wait on, conduct, chaperon, convoy, follow. DESERT
accomplice accessory, abettor, partner in crime, conspirator, collaborator, associate, confederate, helper. OPPONENT
accomplish complete, finish, achieve, effect, execute, perform, do, perfect, fulfil, consummate.
accomplished talented, skilled, expert, experienced, proficient, competent, able, qualified, educated, refined, polished, cultured, sophisticated. UNSKILLED
finished, consummated, done, completed. UNFINISHED
accomplishment achievement, exploit, feat, attainment, success, completion, perfection, consummation. FAILURE
accord *v*, grant, concede, yield, give, award, allow, vouchsafe. DENY
agree, consent, concur, correspond, tally, harmonize, be in unison, match. DIFFER
n, harmony, concord, agreement, unanimity. DISCORD
accordance accord, agreement, conformity, harmony, unison. DIFFERENCE
accordant agreeing, harmonious, consonant, suitable. DISCORDANT
accordingly correspondingly, agreeably, suitably, in accordance.
consequently, therefore, so, thus.
accost confront, approach, greet, address, hail, stop, buttonhole, waylay, assail. AVOID
account *v*, judge, esteem, deem, regard, consider, think, reckon.
account for, explain, elucidate, justify, be responsible for, answer for.
n, narrative, narration, tale, story, description, report, statement, explanation, exposition, record, chronicle.
reckoning, bill, invoice, statement, ledger, tally, score, calculation, count.
consideration, importance, note, consequence, repute, worth, profit, advantage. UNIMPORTANCE
accountable responsible, answerable, liable, amenable.
accoutrements equipment, paraphernalia, gear, trappings, dress, apparel, attire.
accredit attribute, credit, ascribe, assign.
endorse, guarantee, certify, attest, vouch for. REPUDIATE
authorize, appoint, sanction, commission, delegate, entrust.
accretion growth, increase, enlargement, accumulation, agglomeration. DISPERSION
accrue result, come, proceed, issue, accumulate, amass, increase. DIMINISH
accumulate *v*, gather, collect, assemble, heap, amass, hoard, store, increase, grow, accrue, multiply. DISPERSE
accumulation hoard, store, heap, pile, mass, accretion, build-up, collection, assembly, aggregation. DISPERSION
accuracy accurateness, exactness, exactitude, precision, correctness, veracity, truth. INACCURACY
accurate exact, precise, spot-on (*inf*), correct, unerring, true, veracious, careful, scrupulous, rigorous, nice. INACCURATE
accursed doomed, ill-fated, damned.

execrable, damnable, diabolical, obnoxious, despicable, wretched. BLESSED

accusation charge, allegation, indictment, impeachment, incrimination, arraignment. VINDICATION

accuse charge, indict, incriminate, impeach, arraign, summon, cite, inculpate, censure, blame, denounce, impute. EXCULPATE

accuser plaintiff, complainant, prosecutor, blamer, informer. DEFENDANT

accustom familiarize, acquaint, habituate, acclimatize, make used (to), inure, train, drill.

accustomed customary, usual, habitual, routine, regular. UNUSUAL

ace *n*, expert, adept, master, dab hand (*inf*), professional, pro (*inf*).
adj, excellent, first-rate, first-class, outstanding, superb. TERRIBLE

acerbity sourness, bitterness, acidity, acridity, pungency, sharpness, harshness, roughness, asperity, acrimony. SWEETNESS

ache *v*, hurt, pain, throb, be sore, be in pain, suffer, sorrow, grieve.
n, pain, soreness, hurt, discomfort, throb, pang, agony, suffering, anguish, distress, grief, sorrow.

achieve accomplish, complete, finish, conclude, consummate, perfect, do, perform, execute, carry out, realize, effect, get, acquire, reach, attain, obtain, win, earn, gain.

achievement accomplishment, completion, perfection, attainment, execution, realization, performance, exploit, feat, deed, act. FAILURE

acid sour, bitter, tart, sharp, pungent, acerbic, acidulous, vinegary. SWEET
biting, cutting, sarcastic, caustic, sharp, hurtful, trenchant, vitriolic. MILD

acknowledge recognize, admit, grant, own, concede, allow, confess, accept, acquiesce, declare, profess. DENY
answer, reply to, respond to, give thanks for.
greet, address, hail, recognize, notice. IGNORE

acknowledgment recognition, admission, acceptance, declaration, avowal. DENIAL
reply, answer, response, reaction, thanks.

acme top, summit, peak, pinnacle, apex, vertex, zenith, crown, climax, culmination. BASE

acolyte follower, admirer, attendant, assistant.

acquaint inform, tell, advise, let know, notify, apprise, teach, familiarize.

acquaintance friend, companion, colleague, associate.
familiarity, awareness, knowledge, understanding, experience. IGNORANCE

acquainted familiar, conversant, knowledgeable, aware, informed, privy. IGNORANT

acquiesce assent, agree, accede, concur, consent, conform, comply, submit, yield. OBJECT

acquiescence assent, agreement, consent, compliance, submission, yielding. OBJECTION

acquire obtain, get, procure, buy, purchase, pick up, gain, secure, achieve, attain, win, earn, appropriate. LOSE

acquisition possession, property, purchase, prize.
acquirement, achievement, attainment, gaining, procurement, appropriation, purchase. LOSS

acquisitive avid, grasping, greedy, avaricious, rapacious, covetous.

acquit free, release, liberate, pardon, forgive, excuse, absolve, exonerate, exculpate, clear, discharge. CONDEMN
repay, settle, discharge.

acquittal release, deliverance, liberation, exoneration, pardon, discharge.

acrid pungent, sharp, biting, caustic, acid, tart, harsh, cutting, acrimonious, sarcastic, sardonic. SWEET

acrimonious bitter, sour, tart, sharp, caustic, astringent, harsh, acrid, acerbic, trenchant, cutting, mordant, sarcastic, spiteful, virulent, malignant, petulant, peevish, testy, crabbed, snappish, cross, ill-tempered. AMICABLE

acrimony bitterness, sourness, acridity, astringency, harshness, severity, trenchancy, virulence, asperity, peevishness, churlishness, spleen. MILDNESS

across crosswise, transversely, athwart, astride, over, opposite. ALONG

act *v*, do, perform, carry out, execute, operate, work, function, behave.

pretend, assume, feign, counterfeit, simulate, play, represent, portray, pose, mimic, impersonate, enact, stage.

act on, follow, obey, carry out, comply with.

n, action, deed, feat, exploit, achievement, accomplishment, performance, execution, operation.

statute, law, ordinance, edict, decree, judgment, ruling, enactment, measure, bill.

action act, deed, feat, exploit, enterprise, undertaking.

movement, motion, gesture, gesticulation.

operation, exertion, exercise, performance, agency, movement.

activity, energy, force, effort, liveliness, vigour, vim. INACTION

battle, skirmish, encounter, fight, fighting, conflict, warfare, engagement.

lawsuit, case, litigation, prosecution.

active operative, efficient, potent, effective, functioning, working, running, in action. INACTIVE

busy, industrious, diligent, hard-working, occupied, on the go (*inf*). INDOLENT

agile, nimble, quick, alert, prompt, ready, energetic, lively, vigorous. SLUGGISH

activity bustle, movement, stir, action, animation, industry. IDLENESS

undertaking, venture, hobby, pastime, pursuit, enterprise, endeavour, act, deed, job, work.

actor actress, performer, player, Thespian, entertainer, star.

actual real, true, veritable, genuine, positive, absolute, certain, definite, factual, physical, substantial, present, existent. FALSE

actually really, truly, indeed, in fact, in truth, veritably.

actuate motivate, stimulate, prompt, inspire, instigate, urge, impel, drive, incite, encourage, spur. DETER

activate, trigger, switch on, set in motion, animate.

acumen keenness, shrewdness, insight, perspicacity, astuteness, perception, discernment, ingenuity, sagacity, wisdom, sharpness, acuteness. STUPIDITY

acute sharp, keen, quick, astute, shrewd, perspicacious, perceptive, discerning, penetrating, sagacious. OBTUSE

intense, sharp, cutting, stabbing, piercing, excruciating, violent, severe, distressing, poignant. DULL

adage saying, proverb, maxim, saw, aphorism, precept, dictum, byword, apophthegm.

adamant unyielding, inflexible, rigid, firm, unbending, intransigent, determined, resolute, stubborn, obdurate. FLEXIBLE

adapt adjust, accommodate, fit, conform, suit, match, harmonize, coordinate, prepare, alter, modify, familiarize, acclimatize.

adaptable adjustable, convertible, alterable, versatile, flexible, pliant, amenable, compliant, easy-going. INFLEXIBLE

adaptation adjustment, accommodation, conformity, modification, alteration, acclimatization, familiarization.

add join, attach, append, affix, annex, connect, adjoin, combine. REMOVE

add up, sum up, total, reckon, tot up. SUBTRACT

add to, increase, enlarge, augment, supplement, aggravate, intensify.

addendum addition, adjunct, appendage, appendix, supplement, codicil, postscript, tag.

addict *v*, accustom, habituate, devote, dedicate.

n, drug addict, dope fiend (*inf*), junkie (*inf*), pothead (*inf*).

enthusiast, devotee, fan, buff (*inf*).

addicted dependent, hooked (*inf*), devoted, dedicated, habituated, prone, inclined.

addiction dependence, craving, habit, obsession, enslavement.

addition adding, joining, attachment, increase, extension, augmentation, enlargement. DECREASE

addendum, adjunct, appendage, affix, extra, supplement, appurtenance, accessory, increment.

in addition, also, as well, too, besides, moreover, additionally.

additional supplementary, extra, added, further, more, new, fresh.

address *n*, domicile, abode, lodging, residence, home, location, whereabouts.

speech, discourse, talk, lecture, oration, presentation, harangue, sermon.

skill, dexterity, adroitness, expertness, ability, cleverness, ingenuity, tact, art. CLUMSINESS

v, greet, hail, accost, approach, speak to, talk to, invoke, entreat, appeal to, direct, apply. IGNORE

adduce cite, quote, mention, name, give, offer, present, advance, allege.

adept *adj*, proficient, skilled, expert, masterly, adroit, versed, practised, accomplished, experienced, able, clever, talented. INCOMPETENT
n, expert, master, dab hand (*inf*), genius, professional, specialist.

adequacy sufficiency, adequateness, completeness, capacity, acceptability, competence. INADEQUACY

adequate enough, sufficient, fit, suitable, satisfactory, acceptable, passable, fair. INADEQUATE

adhere stick, cohere, glue, fix, hold fast, cling, cleave, attach, unite. SEPARATE

adhere to, follow, observe, heed, keep, respect, comply with, abide by, be faithful to.

adherent *n*, disciple, follower, supporter, admirer, fan, partisan, ally. OPPONENT
adj, adhering, clinging, attached, sticking, adhesive.

adhesion adhesiveness, stickiness, sticking, cohesion, attachment.
adherence, devotion, attachment, constancy, fidelity, loyalty, allegiance.

adhesive *n*, glue, gum, paste, mucilage, cement, plaster.
adj, sticky, gummed, tacky, viscous, glutinous, tenacious, clinging.

adieu *interj*, goodbye, farewell, so long (*inf*). HELLO
n, farewell, valediction, parting, leave-taking. GREETING

adjacent adjoining, contiguous, touching, bordering, connecting, neighbouring, next-door, near, close. DISTANT

adjoin abut, touch, border on, be next to, join, attach, unite, combine, add, annex. SEPARATE

adjourn postpone, put off, defer, suspend, interrupt, delay, procrastinate, prorogue. COMPLETE

adjournment postponement, deferral, suspension, interruption, delay, procrastination. COMPLETION

adjudge pronounce, declare, decree, judge, adjudicate, decide, award, allot, assign.

adjudicate judge, arbitrate, determine, decide, settle, umpire, referee.

adjudication judgment, judging, arbitration, decision, verdict, ruling, sentence, award.

adjunct appendage, addition, attachment, addendum, appurtenance, accessory, supplement, auxiliary. ESSENTIAL

adjure charge, command, enjoin, invoke, appeal to, entreat, implore, beseech, beg, pray, supplicate.

adjust alter, adapt, modify, change, rectify, fix, regulate, trim, fit, suit, accommodate, harmonize, arrange, dispose, acclimatize, habituate, become accustomed.

adjustment alteration, adaptation, modification, change, regulation, arrangement, acclimatization, habituation.

ad-lib *v*, improvise, make up, extemporize.
adj, improvised, impromptu, extempore, unrehearsed, off-the-cuff (*inf*), spontaneous. PREPARED
adv, spontaneously, freely, extempore, off the cuff (*inf*).

administer manage, control, conduct, direct, govern, superintend, supervise, oversee, run.
distribute, dispense, supply, give, contribute, apply, mete out, perform, execute.

administration management, government, running, direction, supervision, control, ministry, executive.
distribution, dispensing, supply, application, execution.

admirable excellent, fine, superb, wonderful, laudable, praiseworthy, commendable. DESPICABLE

admiration esteem, regard, respect, reverence, awe, wonder, approval, liking, love. CONTEMPT

admire esteem, respect, value, revere, venerate, wonder at, adore, love, like, approve, appreciate, prize, extol, praise. DESPISE

admirer devotee, fan, aficionado, supporter, follower, disciple, adherent, worshipper.
suitor, beau, boyfriend, lover, sweetheart.

admissible allowable, acceptable, permissible, lawful, just, fair, right, proper, reasonable, justifiable. INADMISSIBLE

admission acknowledgment, confession, avowal, declaration, affirmation, allowance, concession. DENIAL
admittance, introduction, access, entrance, entry. EXCLUSION

admit acknowledge, confess, own, declare, avow, divulge, accept, allow, grant, concede. DENY
let in, give access to, allow to enter, receive, welcome. EXCLUDE
admittance entrance, admission, right of entry, access, passage, reception, welcome, introduction. EXCLUSION
admonish warn, caution, advise, counsel, instruct, urge, enjoin.
scold, rebuke, reprove, chide, upbraid, reprimand, tell off (*inf*), censure. COMMEND
admonition warning, caution, advice, counsel.
reprimand, rebuke, reproof, remonstrance, scolding. PRAISE
ado fuss, bustle, commotion, hubbub, flurry, stir, tumult, turmoil, excitement, to-do, bother, trouble. TRANQUILLITY
adolescence youth, teens, minority, pubescence, boyhood, girlhood, immaturity. MATURITY
adolescent *adj*, teenage, young, youthful, immature, juvenile, growing. MATURE
n, teenager, youth, youngster, minor, juvenile. ADULT
adopt foster, take in, affiliate, father, mother. ABANDON
assume, appropriate, choose, select, accept, take on, endorse, approve. REJECT
adorable delightful, divine, wonderful, lovely, captivating, charming, lovable. ABOMINABLE
adoration devotion, worship, veneration, reverence, homage, admiration, esteem, love, passion. ABOMINATION
adore love, dote on, worship, idolize, venerate, revere, esteem, admire. DESPISE
adorn decorate, ornament, embellish, deck, garnish, trim, gild, beautify, enhance, enrich. STRIP
adornment decoration, ornament, embellishment, trimming, frill, accessory.
adrift drifting, floating, afloat, unanchored, loose, astray, amiss. SECURE
adroit dexterous, skilful, adept, able, clever, ingenious, masterly, expert, handy, nimble. CLUMSY
adulation flattery, blandishment, cajolery, compliment, sycophancy, fawning, servility, obsequiousness. OBLOQUY
adulatory flattering, fawning, sycophantic, servile, obsequious.
adult *n*, grown-up, man, woman. CHILD
adj, mature, fully grown, fully developed, grown-up, of age. IMMATURE
adulterate debase, vitiate, alloy, water down, tamper with, contaminate, pollute. PURIFY
adulterated debased, vitiated, watered down, impure, contaminated. PURE
adultery infidelity, unfaithfulness, affair, unchastity. FIDELITY
adumbrate outline, sketch, delineate, silhouette.
foreshadow, presage, forecast, predict, denote, represent, indicate, hint, suggest.
darken, obscure, overshadow, bedim, eclipse, conceal, hide. REVEAL
advance *vt*, push forward, hasten, spur, propel, send onward.
promote, further, improve, strengthen, increase, augment, foster, support. RETARD
suggest, allege, put forward, proffer, propose, propound. WITHDRAW
lend, loan, pay, give.
vi, go on, go forward, progress, proceed, continue, improve, rise, thrive, flourish, prosper. RETREAT
n, advancement, rise, promotion, development, progress, headway, improvement, breakthrough, innovation. RETROGRESSION
loan, retainer, deposit, down payment.
proposal, offer, proposition, approach.
in advance, ahead, beforehand, earlier, previously.
advanced forward, ahead, avant-garde, progressive, precocious. RETARDED
advantage help, assistance, avail, convenience, benefit, gain, profit, boon, blessing. DISADVANTAGE
superiority, ascendancy, power, upper hand, edge.
advantageous beneficial, profitable, helpful, convenient, useful. PREJUDICIAL
advent arrival, coming, approach, visitation, appearance, onset. DEPARTURE
adventitious accidental, casual, fortuitous, unexpected, incidental, extrinsic, extraneous, superfluous.
adventure *n*, venture, undertaking, enterprise, exploit, incident, event, occurrence, risk, hazard, experiment, trial, speculation.
v, venture, risk, hazard, imperil, endanger.

adventurous daring, bold, enterprising, venturesome, brave, intrepid, fearless, foolhardy, rash, dangerous. TIMID

adversary opponent, antagonist, enemy, foe, rival, competitor. ALLY

adverse unfavourable, hostile, inimical, antagonistic, opposing, contrary, conflicting, harmful, injurious, unfortunate, unlucky. FAVOURABLE

adversity misfortune, ill-luck, affliction, trouble, woe, misery, hardship, suffering, distress, calamity, disaster, ruin, desolation. PROSPERITY

advertise announce, declare, proclaim, publicize, broadcast, promulgate, make known, promote, praise, plug (*inf*). CONCEAL

advertisement announcement, notice, placard, poster, bill, circular, commercial, advert, ad (*inf*), promotion, plug (*inf*).

advice counsel, admonition, caution, warning, guidance, instruction, recommendation, opinion, view.
information, notification, news, intelligence, word.

advisable prudent, sensible, judicious, wise, recommended, expedient, advantageous, proper, appropriate, fit. INADVISABLE

advise counsel, recommend, suggest, guide, persuade, urge, admonish, caution. DETER
inform, tell, notify, apprise, acquaint.

adviser counsellor, mentor, confidant, consultant, tutor, teacher, guide, aide, helper.

advocacy support, advancement, recommendation, backing, sponsorship, endorsement, defence. OPPOSITION

advocate *v*, support, recommend, advise, endorse, favour, countenance, maintain, uphold, defend, plead for, champion, promote. OPPOSE
n, supporter, backer, sponsor, champion, defender, promoter, upholder, apologist. OPPONENT
lawyer, counsel, barrister, attorney, solicitor.

aegis support, patronage, sponsorship, protection, auspices.

aerial high, lofty, empyrean, airy, gaseous, ethereal, light.

aeronaut pilot, aviator, airman, flyer, balloonist.

aeronautics aviation, flying, flight, ballooning, aerostatics.

aeroplane plane, aircraft, airliner, glider, jet.

aesthetic tasteful, beautiful, artistic, classic, cultured, refined. UGLY

afar far off, far away, yonder, away, abroad. NEARBY

affable amicable, friendly, congenial, cordial, complaisant, approachable, easygoing, open, sociable, amiable, mild, kind, kindly, good-natured, benign, benevolent, obliging, gracious, civil, urbane, suave, polite, courteous. HAUGHTY

affair matter, subject, question, business, concern, interest, duty.
incident, event, circumstance, episode, occurrence, happening.
liaison, intrigue, amour, relationship.

affairs business, concerns, finances, interests, activities.

affect influence, alter, modify, change, act on, relate to, concern, interest.
move, touch, impress, stir, upset, disturb.
feign, simulate, assume, adopt, fake, counterfeit.

affectation pretence, sham, display, artifice, insincerity, hypocrisy, affectedness, mannerism, airs. NATURALNESS

affected artificial, unnatural, studied, insincere, sham, put-on, feigned, mannered, pretentious. NATURAL
moved, touched, altered, changed. UNAFFECTED

affection love, devotion, caring, fondness, liking, inclination, partiality, tenderness, kindness, warmth, feeling, passion. DISLIKE

affectionate loving, devoted, attached, doting, caring, fond, tender, warm, friendly. COLD

affiance betroth, engage, bind, pledge, promise.

affidavit declaration, statement, deposition, testimony, evidence.

affiliate join, unite, combine, amalgamate, incorporate, annex, adopt. SEVER

affiliation amalgamation, annexation, incorporation, alliance, coalition, union, relationship, adoption. SEVERANCE

affinity attraction, liking, inclination, partiality, rapport, sympathy. ANTIPATHY relationship, kinship, connection, correspondence, correlation, analogy, resemblance, similarity, likeness.

affirm assert, declare, state, profess, aver, maintain, attest, ratify, confirm, vouch for, uphold, certify, endorse. DENY

affirmation assertion, declaration, statement, avowal, testimony, ratification, confirmation. DENIAL

affirmative asserting, confirming, declaratory, positive, agreeing, favourable. NEGATIVE

affix *v*, attach, join, fasten, stick, connect, subjoin, add, append, annex. DETACH
n, appendage, addition, prefix, suffix.

afflict trouble, distress, hurt, pain, grieve, torment, harass, vex, plague, persecute. CONSOLE

affliction trouble, distress, suffering, anguish, pain, torment, agony, grief, sorrow, misery, woe, trial, tribulation, adversity, misfortune, calamity, scourge, plague, disease. COMFORT

afflictive distressing, painful, grievous, sorrowful, wretched, miserable, harrowing, piteous, deplorable, tragic, dire.

affluence abundance, plenty, opulence, wealth, riches, fortune, prosperity. POVERTY

affluent wealthy, rich, opulent, prosperous, well-off, well-heeled (*inf*), loaded (*inf*), moneyed.
abundant, profuse, copious, plentiful, luxuriant, exuberant. SCARCE

afford spare, give, bestow, supply, provide, furnish, produce, yield, support. DENY

affray brawl, mêlée, fight, fray, scrap, scuffle, fracas, rumpus, disturbance, tumult, contest, conflict, quarrel, strife. ORDER

affront *v*, insult, abuse, outrage, slight, offend, annoy, vex, irritate, provoke, pique, anger. PACIFY
n, insult, offence, slight, outrage, indignity, wrong.

afire ablaze, alight, aflame, burning, blazing, on fire, ignited. EXTINGUISHED
aglow, aroused, passionate, fervent. INDIFFERENT

afloat floating, drifting, loose, abroad, at sea, flooded. AGROUND

afoot astir, about, abroad, in circulation, in motion, going on, up, in operation.

aforesaid aforementioned, above-mentioned, above-named, described above, preceding.

afraid frightened, scared, terrified, fearful, alarmed, anxious, uneasy, apprehensive, timid. BOLD

afresh again, anew, once more, newly.

aft astern, abaft, back, behind, rearward. FORWARD

after *prep*, following, behind, succeeding, below. BEFORE
adv, afterwards, later, subsequently, behind.

aftermath results, consequences, aftereffects, repercussions, issue, outcome, upshot, effect.

afterthought reflection, second thought, addition, appendix, postscript.

afterwards after, subsequently, later, thereafter. BEFORE

again anew, afresh, once more, another time.
besides, moreover, also, furthermore.

against hostile to, opposing, counter, resisting, versus, opposite to.
facing, abutting, touching, on, in contact with.

agape gaping, yawning, wide open.
open-mouthed, spellbound, dumbfounded, thunderstruck, astonished, amazed, stupefied, dazed, agog, eager.

age *n*, epoch, era, eon, period, span, time, duration, date, generation.
old age, maturity, senility, antiquity, seniority. YOUTH
v, grow old, mature, ripen, season, decline.

aged old, elderly, senescent, ancient, antiquated. YOUNG

agency organization, business, bureau, office, institution.
action, operation, influence, power, force, means, medium, instrumentality, intervention.

agenda list, schedule, programme, plan, calendar, timetable.

agent representative, deputy, substitute, middleman, go-between, envoy, factor, delegate, broker, salesman.
executor, doer, operator, performer.
instrument, cause, force, means, vehicle.

agglomerate gather, cluster, collect, accumulate, conglomerate, mass, amalgamate. DISPERSE

agglomeration mass, lump, heap, pile, accumulation, gathering, cluster, clump.

agglutinate adhere, fuse, unite, stick, glue, paste, cement, bond, weld, solder, attach, cling. DETACH

agglutination adhesion, bonding, attachment, union, conglomeration, mass, group.

aggrandize magnify, enlarge, amplify, augment, inflate, exaggerate, exalt, promote, elevate, advance, ennoble. DEBASE

aggravate worsen, make worse, exacerbate, increase, heighten, intensify, magnify, exaggerate. MITIGATE
irritate, annoy, provoke, exasperate, vex, nettle, irk, tease. SOOTHE

aggravation exacerbation, increase, heightening, intensification. MITIGATION
irritation, annoyance, exasperation, vexation.

aggregate *v*, collect, gather, accumulate, amass, heap, pile, agglomerate, cluster. DISPERSE
adj, total, collected, massed, composite, collective, corporate.
n, total, sum, amount, whole, totality, mass, lump, collection, assemblage, group, agglomeration. UNIT

aggregation collection, gathering, accumulation, cluster, clump, heap, pile, mass. DISTRIBUTION

aggression attack, onslaught, assault, invasion, encroachment, offence. RESISTANCE
aggressiveness, hostility, belligerence, pugnacity, militancy. PASSIVITY

aggressive attacking, pugnacious, belligerent, hostile, militant, quarrelsome. PEACEFUL
assertive, vigorous, bold, forceful, dynamic, energetic, enterprising, pushy (*inf*). PASSIVE

aggressor attacker, assailant, assaulter, invader, instigator, enemy, foe.

aggrieve trouble, distress, afflict, torment, grieve, hurt, injure, wound, annoy, aggravate, vex, wrong, abuse, maltreat. SOOTHE

aghast horrified, appalled, terrified, frightened, shocked, dismayed. RELIEVED
astounded, astonished, stunned, dumbfounded, thunderstruck, amazed, stupefied.

agile nimble, active, spry, sprightly, lively, brisk, quick, fleet, lithe, supple, prompt, ready, alert, smart. CLUMSY

agility nimbleness, sprightliness, activity, liveliness, briskness, quickness, litheness, suppleness, acumen, alertness. CLUMSINESS

agitate stir, disturb, shake up, churn, beat, toss.
excite, stir up, arouse, provoke, incite, disturb, trouble, ruffle, fluster, disconcert, perturb. CALM
discuss, debate, talk over, consider, examine, ventilate, moot. SETTLE

agitated nervous, jumpy, unsettled, fidgety, ruffled, uneasy, worked-up.

agitation excitement, arousal, trouble, disturbance, upheaval, commotion, disquiet, discomposure, upset, flurry, fluster. CALMNESS
discussion, debate, examination, consideration.

agitator demagogue, instigator, *agent provocateur*, revolutionary, firebrand, rabble-rouser, troublemaker.

agnostic sceptic, doubter, unbeliever, cynic, phenomenalist, freethinker, pagan, heathen. BELIEVER

ago past, gone by, earlier, before now, in the past.

agog eager, avid, keen, impatient, excited, expectant, on tenterhooks, curious. COOL

agonize *vi*, suffer, writhe, be in agony, worry, labour, struggle, strive.
vt, torture, torment, pain, afflict, distress, grieve. SOOTHE

agony torment, torture, pain, anguish, distress, misery, suffering, pangs. ECSTASY

agree concur, coincide, conform, settle, correspond, tally, match, suit, fit, harmonize, accord. DIFFER
assent, consent, acquiesce, accede, comply, concede, yield, grant, allow, permit, promise, engage. REFUSE

agreeable pleasant, pleasing, attractive, acceptable, gratifying, delightful, delicious, charming, amiable. OBNOXIOUS
suitable, consistent, appropriate, harmonious, in keeping, in accord.

agreement accord, concord, unison, unanimity, harmony, amity, correspondence, conformity, congruity, settlement. DISAGREEMENT contract, undertaking, obligation, bond, treaty, pact, compact, covenant, deal, transaction.

agriculture farming, husbandry, cultivation, tillage, agronomy, agronomics.

aground grounded, ashore, beached, stranded, high and dry. AFLOAT

ahead in front, leading, in advance, before, onwards, forwards. BEHIND

aid *v*, help, assist, abet, support, back, second, encourage, facilitate, serve, relieve, subsidize, succour. IMPEDE
n, help, assistance, support, backing, encouragement, service, relief, subsidy, benefit, alms. HINDRANCE
helper, aider, assistant, abettor, supporter, second, colleague, ally, associate, aide-de-camp. OPPONENT

ail *vt*, afflict, trouble, distress, pain, upset.
vi, be ill, suffer, be unwell, pine, ache.

ailing sick, ill, unwell, indisposed, poorly, off colour, under the weather (*inf*), suffering, diseased, infirm, weak, sickly. WELL

ailment illness, sickness, disorder, complaint, affliction, infirmity, malady.

aim *v*, point, direct, level.
intend, propose, mean, plan, design, aspire, strive.
n, intention, purpose, plan, design, end, target, objective, mark, goal.
direction, sighting, bearing.

aimless purposeless, pointless, useless, futile, random, chance, haphazard, wayward, wandering, stray. PURPOSEFUL

air *n*, atmosphere, sky, heavens, breeze, draught.
manner, aspect, look, appearance, demeanour, bearing, behaviour, mien, attitude, character, aura, impression.
tune, melody, strain, theme, song, lay.
v, ventilate, freshen, cool, fan, aerate.
display, exhibit, expose, publicize, show, reveal. CONCEAL

aircraft aeroplane, plane, airliner, jet, glider, helicopter, chopper (*inf*), balloon, airship, rocket.

airiness lightness, buoyancy, weightlessness, ethereality, incorporeality. HEAVINESS
liveliness, gaiety, vivacity, levity, sprightliness, jauntiness, blitheness. SULLENNESS
grace, gracefulness, suppleness, flexibility. AWKWARDNESS

airing ventilation, aeration, drying, freshening.
stroll, walk, outing, excursion, jaunt, drive, ride.

airless close, heavy, muggy, oppressive, sultry, stifling, stuffy. BREEZY

airs affectation, affectedness, pretension, superciliousness, haughtiness, pomposity.

airtight sealed, impermeable, unassailable, invulnerable, indisputable.

airy breezy, draughty, exposed, ventilated, open, spacious, uncluttered. AIRLESS
light, buoyant, insubstantial, weightless, ethereal, incorporeal, flimsy. HEAVY
lively, gay, sprightly, jaunty, vivacious, blithe. SULLEN
graceful, supple, lithe, nimble. AWKWARD

aisle passageway, gangway, corridor, passage, path, lane.

ajar unclosed, partly open, gaping, open. SHUT

akin related, kindred, cognate, consanguineous, homogeneous, analogous, allied, similar, like, corresponding. UNRELATED

alacrity quickness, promptness, readiness, willingness, eagerness, zeal, enthusiasm, alertness, agility, sprightliness, liveliness. RELUCTANCE

alarm *v*, frighten, scare, startle, terrify, dismay, daunt, intimidate, unnerve. REASSURE
n, fear, fright, terror, panic, dread, apprehension, trepidation, dismay, anxiety, consternation. REASSURANCE
siren, tocsin, alarm-bell, danger signal, alert.

alarming frightening, terrifying, ominous, daunting, intimidating, distressing, unnerving, disturbing, terrible, dreadful, appalling, shocking. REASSURING

albeit although, even though, notwithstanding that.

album book, folder, scrapbook, file, collection.
record, LP, disc.

alchemy magic, sorcery, witchcraft, thaumaturgy.

alcohol spirits, liquor, intoxicant, booze (*inf*), hard stuff (*inf*).

alcoholic *adj*, intoxicating, spirituous, inebriant.
n, drunk, drunkard, dipsomaniac, inebriate, boozer (*inf*), wino (*inf*).

alcove recess, niche, nook, cubbyhole, bay, bower, arbour, retreat.

alert *adj*, watchful, vigilant, attentive, observant, on guard, wide-awake, wary, circumspect, heedful, ready, prepared, prompt.
agile, nimble, active, lively, spry, brisk, smart. LETHARGIC
n, alarm, warning, signal, siren.
v, warn, signal, notify, inform, tell.

alertness vigilance, watchfulness, attention, wariness, caution, circumspection.
agility, liveliness, sprightliness, activity, briskness. LETHARGY

alias *adv*, also called, otherwise, formerly.
n, pseudonym, assumed name, pen name, *nom de plume*, stage name.

alibi defence, excuse, pretext, reason, explanation, justification.

alien *adj*, foreign, strange, unfamiliar, incongruous, outlandish, exotic, remote, estranged. NATIVE
opposed, hostile, repugnant, contrary, conflicting, differing. HARMONIOUS
n, foreigner, immigrant, stranger, outsider, newcomer. NATIVE

alienate estrange, separate, disaffect, set against, divert, turn away, break off, withdraw. CONCILIATE

alienation estrangement, separation, disaffection, withdrawal, breaking off, rupture, breach, division. CONCILIATION

alight[1] *v*, get off, disembark, dismount, descend, land, settle, perch, come to rest. ASCEND

alight[2] *adj*, lit, illuminated, bright, burning, on fire. EXTINGUISHED

align straighten, range, line up, even up, make parallel, adjust, regulate, arrange.
affiliate, associate, ally, join, sympathize.

alike *adj*, similar, resembling, like, allied, related, akin, analogous, corresponding, same, identical. UNLIKE
adv, the same, similarly, equally.

aliment food, nourishment, nutriment, sustenance, alimentation, subsistence, fare, provisions, bread, meat.

alive living, live, breathing, animate, existent, extant, active, operative, in force. DEAD
lively, brisk, sprightly, alert, quick, smart, prompt, animated, vivacious, spirited, cheerful. SLUGGISH

all *adj*, whole, entire, complete, total, every, each. SOME
adv, wholly, entirely, completely, totally, altogether, quite, fully. PARTLY
n, whole, total, aggregate, entirety, totality, everything, everybody. NOTHING

allay soothe, alleviate, ease, relieve, lessen, reduce, mitigate, moderate, mollify, abate, restrain, subdue, quiet, still, calm, appease, pacify, assuage, repress, quell, check. AGGRAVATE

allegation assertion, statement, declaration, affirmation, avowal, deposition, accusation, charge. DENIAL

allege assert, state, declare, maintain, affirm, profess, claim, plead, put forward, advance. DENY

alleged supposed, assumed, doubtful, unlikely, dubious, so-called.

allegiance loyalty, faithfulness, fidelity, constancy, devotion, obedience, duty, fealty, homage. DISLOYALTY

allegorical metaphorical, figurative, symbolic, representative, typical. LITERAL

allegory fable, parable, apologue, story, tale, myth, symbol, illustration, metaphor, analogy.

allergy sensitivity, hypersensitivity, susceptibility, antipathy, aversion, hostility.

alleviate allay, soothe, relieve, ease, palliate, assuage, mitigate, lessen, diminish, moderate, mollify, soften, quell, dull, deaden, abate. INTENSIFY

alleviation soothing, relief, easing, palliation, mitigation, dulling, deadening. INTENSIFICATION

alley alleyway, passage, path, footpath, way, walk, lane, back street.

alliance treaty, pact, compact, agreement, contract, union, league, confederacy, confederation, coalition, bloc, affiliation, partnership, cooperation, merger, association, combination, marriage. DISUNION
affinity, correspondence, relationship, similarity, connection.

allied united, joined, confederate, amalgamated, cooperating.
related, akin, cognate, alike, similar, analogous. UNRELATED

allocate assign, allot, apportion, designate, earmark, set aside, divide, distribute, share out.

allocation portion, share, quota, ration, allowance.

allot allocate, apportion, assign, designate, set aside, distribute, divide, deal, mete, dispense, grant, administer. WITHHOLD

allotment allocation, apportionment, portion, quota, share, allowance, dole.
plot, strip of land, patch, garden.

allow permit, let, authorize, approve, sanction, tolerate, suffer, bear, put up with, endure. FORBID
acknowledge, concede, grant, admit, confess, own. DENY
apportion, allot, allocate, assign, set aside, deduct, give, grant, let have, provide. WITHHOLD

allow for, consider, take into account, provide for, keep in mind.

allowable permissible, admissible, justifiable, warrantable, lawful, legitimate, proper, right, acceptable. INADMISSIBLE

allowance ration, share, allocation, grant, pension, subsidy, discount, rebate, concession.
authorization, approval, permission, leave, consent, sanction, licence, toleration. PROHIBITION

alloy *n*, compound, mixture, blend, amalgam, composite.
admixture, combination, adulteration, debasement.
v, mix, combine, blend, amalgamate, compound. SEPARATE
adulterate, debase, impair, diminish, depreciate. PURIFY

all right *adj*, acceptable, satisfactory, OK (*inf*), adequate, passable, fair. UNACCEPTABLE
well, healthy, sound, safe, unharmed, unhurt, unbroken.
adv, satisfactorily, well enough, acceptably, passably.

allude refer, touch upon, mention, suggest, hint, insinuate, imply.

allure *v*, tempt, entice, lure, seduce, bait, attract, beguile enchant, cajole, coax, inveigle, persuade. REPEL
n, attraction, appeal, charm, enchantment, lure, allurement, temptation, enticement.

alluring tempting, enticing, seductive, beguiling, captivating, fascinating, attractive, charming. REPULSIVE

allusion reference, mention, suggestion, hint, insinuation, innuendo, implication.

allusive suggestive, hinting, insinuating, referential, indicative, symbolic, figurative.

ally *v*, unite, unify, join, marry, combine, league, confederate, associate, collaborate. SEPARATE
n, confederate, associate, colleague, partner, friend, accomplice, abettor, assistant, helper, coadjutor. ENEMY

almanac calendar, register, yearbook, annual, ephemeris.

almighty all-powerful, omnipotent, supreme, absolute. IMPOTENT

almost nearly, well-nigh, virtually, practically, just about, all but, not quite.

alms charity, bounty, dole, gift, donation, handout, gratuity.

aloft above, overhead, high up, on high, skyward, up. BELOW

alone solitary, lone, single, only, sole, isolated, apart, detached, lonely, forsaken, deserted, unaccompanied, solo, unaided, single-handed. TOGETHER

along *prep*, beside, alongside, by, through. ACROSS
adv, lengthwise, longitudinally, beside, parallel with.
together, in company, simultaneously.
forward, onward, ahead.

aloof distant, detached, apart, remote, unapproachable, forbidding, cool, haughty, supercilious, standoffish, unfriendly, reserved, uninterested. FRIENDLY

aloud audibly, distinctly, clearly, out loud, loudly, noisily. SILENTLY

already by now, by this time, before, previously, yet.

also as well, too, in addition, besides, furthermore, moreover.

altar shrine, sanctuary, holy of holies, holy table.

alter change, modify, adjust, adapt, amend, revise, vary, transform, convert, turn. MAINTAIN

alteration change, modification, adjustment, amendment, adaptation, transformation, conversion, variation, difference. CONSERVATION

altercation quarrel, argument, dispute, wrangle, row, disagreement, difference, dissension, controversy, contention, strife. AGREEMENT

alternate *v*, rotate, interchange, take turns, reciprocate, substitute.

adj, alternating, every other, in rotation, successive, consecutive, reciprocal.

alternative *n*, choice, option, recourse, substitute.
adj, different, other, second.

although though, even though, even if, notwithstanding, despite the fact that, albeit.

altitude height, elevation, loftiness, tallness. DEPTH

altogether completely, entirely, wholly, fully, utterly, totally, quite, thoroughly, absolutely. PARTIALLY
in all, in sum, all told, *in toto*, with everything included.
collectively, all in all, on the whole, in general, all things considered.

altruistic unselfish, philanthropic, public-spirited, charitable, benevolent. SELFISH

always continually, incessantly, unceasingly, perpetually, forever, eternally, everlastingly, constantly, regularly, every time, without exception. NEVER

amalgam compound, alloy, composite, mixture, combination, blend.

amalgamate unite, join, fuse, combine, mix, mingle, blend, compound, alloy, incorporate, integrate, merge, consolidate. SEPARATE

amalgamation mixture, combination, compound, union, fusion, joining, incorporation, merger. SEPARATION

amanuensis secretary, copyist, scribe, transcriber, clerk.

amass gather, collect, accumulate, heap up, pile up, assemble, aggregate, agglomerate. SCATTER

amateur nonprofessional, layman, dilettante, dabbler, novice, learner.
beginner, tyro. EXPERT

amateurish unprofessional, inexpert, unskilled, incompetent, bungling, crude, inferior, second-rate. PROFESSIONAL

amatory amorous, passionate, sensual, erotic, romantic, tender.

amaze astonish, astound, stun, stupefy, flabbergast (*inf*), dumbfound, stagger, daze, nonplus, bewilder, confound.

amazement astonishment, incredulity, surprise, wonder, awe, stupefaction, bewilderment.

amazing astonishing, astounding, remarkable, striking, prodigious, extraordinary, stupendous, marvellous. ORDINARY

ambassador diplomat, envoy, emissary, plenipotentiary, legate, deputy, representative, consul, minister.

ambience atmosphere, surroundings, setting, milieu, mood, aura, feeling, vibrations (*inf*).

ambient surrounding, encircling, encompassing, enfolding.

ambiguity vagueness, obscurity, uncertainty, doubtfulness, equivocation, *double entendre*. LUCIDITY

ambiguous vague, obscure, unclear, uncertain, indefinite, indeterminate, cryptic, enigmatic, doubtful, dubious, equivocal. CLEAR

ambition aspiration, desire, yearning, dream, goal, objective, target, enterprise, drive, energy, eagerness, get-up-and-go (*inf*).

ambitious aspiring, desirous, intent, eager, avid, enterprising, go-ahead, pushy (*inf*), zealous, bold. LETHARGIC
challenging, exacting, arduous, strenuous, formidable. EASY

ambivalence uncertainty, irresolution, indecision, doubt, hesitation, wavering, conflict, contradiction, clash, opposition.

ambivalent uncertain, unsure, doubtful, hesitant, in two minds, conflicting, contradictory, opposing.

amble dawdle, saunter, stroll, meander, ramble, mosey (*inf*), walk. HURRY

ambush *n*, ambuscade, surprise attack, hiding-place, cover, concealment, retreat, trap, snare, pitfall.
v, ambuscade, lie in wait, lurk, surprise, waylay, trap, ensnare, lure.

ameliorate improve, better, amend, advance, promote, raise, elevate. DETERIORATE

amelioration improvement, betterment, amendment, advancement, promotion. DETERIORATION

amenable agreeable, persuadable, open to suggestion, flexible, pliant, susceptible, tractable, docile. OBSTINATE
liable, accountable, answerable, responsible.

amend alter, change, modify, revise, improve, ameliorate, correct, rectify, repair. MAR

amendment alteration, change, modification, reform, revision, correction, improvement, amelioration.
addition, appendage, attachment, addendum.

amends recompense, compensation, atonement, reparation, satisfaction, indemnity, redress, apology. INJURY
make amends, compensate, recompense, conciliate, atone, make good, repay, apologize.

amenity facility, convenience, service, advantage.
pleasantness, agreeableness, mildness, affability, amiability, graciousness, politeness, courtesy, suavity. AUSTERITY

amiable pleasant, agreeable, likeable, friendly, affable, amicable, hearty, genial, good-natured, kind, kindly, warm, benign, benevolent, outgoing, unreserved, sociable, attractive, charming, polite, cordial. DISAGREEABLE

amicable friendly, cordial, congenial, amiable, neighbourly, civil, sociable, harmonious, peaceable, polite. HOSTILE

amid amidst, among, amongst, between, surrounded by, with.

amiss *adj*, wrong, incorrect, inaccurate, erroneous, untoward, improper, faulty, false, untrue. RIGHT
adv, wrong, awry, astray, wrongly, incorrectly, erroneously, badly, improperly, falsely.

amity friendship, friendliness, amicableness, cordiality, accord, harmony, understanding, good will, peacefulness, comradeship, fellowship. HOSTILITY

ammunition munitions, armaments, shells, cartridges, bullets, rounds, powder, explosives, missiles, rockets.

amnesty pardon, forgiveness, absolution, acquittal, remission, reprieve, immunity, dispensation, clemency, indulgence. CONDEMNATION

among amongst, amid, amidst, surrounded by, between, with, out of.

amorous fond, affectionate, loving, tender, amatory, passionate, impassioned, ardent, lustful, erotic. COLD

amorphous shapeless, formless, unformed, unstructured, inchoate, irregular, vague, nebulous, confused, chaotic. ORDERED

amount *n*, quantity, number, measure, total, sum, aggregate, whole.
amount to, *v*, add up to, come to, total, reach, equal, correspond with, become, develop into.

ample sufficient, abundant, plentiful, copious, rich, lavish, unrestricted, liberal, large, great, broad, big, spacious, capacious, extensive. SCANTY

amplification expansion, enlargement, extension, augmentation, increase, dilation, broadening, development, fleshing out, addition, supplement, appendix. REDUCTION

amplify expand, enlarge, extend, augment, increase, magnify, boost, intensify, broaden, develop, flesh out, expatiate. REDUCE

amplitude ampleness, abundance, profusion, copiousness, magnitude, dimensions, size, bulk, mass, volume, capaciousness, bigness, largeness, width, breadth, extent, range, scope, sweep, compass.

amputate cut off, sever, lop, clip, prune, remove, separate, curtail, truncate.

amuse entertain, divert, interest, please, cheer, gladden, charm, delight, regale, enliven, gratify, tickle. BORE

amusement entertainment, diversion, pastime, hobby, game, sport, recreation, prank, lark, joke, fun, enjoyment, pleasure, delight, merriment, mirth, laughter.

amusing entertaining, diverting, funny, droll, comical, humorous, witty, pleasing, pleasant, delightful, interesting. BORING

anaemic bloodless, colourless, pale, pallid, wan, ashen, sickly, weak, feeble, languid.

analogous similar, like, alike, resembling, corresponding, homologous, equivalent, comparable. DIFFERENT

analogy similarity, likeness, resemblance, comparison, parallel, correspondence, agreement, equivalence. DIFFERENCE

analyse examine, investigate, interpret, explain, break down, separate, dissect, anatomize.

analysis examination, investigation, interpretation, breakdown, separation, dissection, partition, decomposition, resolution. SYNTHESIS

analytic analytical, inquiring, questioning, investigative, critical, detailed, logical, systematic, organized, interpretative, problem-solving, diagnostic.

anarchic lawless, riotous, disorderly, disorganized, confused, chaotic, rebellious, revolutionary. ORDERED

anarchist rebel, insurgent, revolutionary, rabble-rouser, agitator, terrorist, radical, nihilist.

anarchy lawlessness, disorder, confusion, chaos, riot, tumult, mayhem, revolution, rebellion, insurgence, misrule. ORDER

anathema curse, imprecation, malediction, excommunication, denunciation, ban, proscription. BLESSING
aversion, antipathy, enemy, bugbear, bane, *bête noire*.

anatomize dissect, vivisect, analyse, examine, scrutinize, study, investigate, probe, sift.

anatomy structure, skeleton, framework, composition.
analysis, dissection, examination, scrutiny.

ancestor forebear, forefather, progenitor, predecessor, parent, forerunner, precursor, prototype. DESCENDANT

ancestral inherited, hereditary, patrimonial.

ancestry ancestors, family, house, line, lineage, pedigree, race, stock, descent, parentage, extraction, genealogy, origin, heritage, background. POSTERITY

anchor *n*, security, stay, mainstay, defence, support.
v, fasten, secure, fix, make fast, attach. LOOSEN

anchorage mooring, wharf, quay, harbour, dock, port.
refuge, shelter, sanctuary.

anchorite anchoress, recluse, hermit, solitary.

ancient old, aged, hoary, olden, bygone, antique, antiquated, archaic, obsolete, outmoded, old-fashioned, primitive, primeval, primordial, prehistoric. MODERN

ancillary subsidiary, auxiliary, accessory, secondary, additional, supplementary, extra, contributory, helping, subordinate, subservient. ESSENTIAL

and plus, in addition, including, along with, also, furthermore.

androgynous hermaphrodite, hermaphroditic, bisexual, epicene, gynandrous.

anecdote story, tale, yarn, sketch, illustration, narrative, memoir, reminiscence, incident, occurrence.

anew afresh, again, newly, once more, over again.

anfractuous winding, sinuous, tortuous, devious, meandering, intricate, convoluted, circuitous. STRAIGHT

angel seraph, cherub, archangel, spirit, divine messenger, guardian angel. DEVIL
paragon, saint, darling, treasure, gem, beauty.

angelic seraphic, cherubic, divine, celestial, heavenly, ethereal.
adorable, delightful, entrancing, beautiful, lovely, pure, virtuous, saintly. DIABOLIC

anger *n*, rage, wrath, ire, fury, choler, exasperation, annoyance, irritation, vexation, displeasure, indignation, resentment, passion, temper, spleen. COMPOSURE
v, enrage, infuriate, incense, outrage, madden, exasperate, annoy, irritate, provoke, antagonize, rile, rouse, vex, nettle, irk, displease. APPEASE

angle[1] *n*, corner, bend, crook, hook, elbow, knee, nook, niche, recess.
viewpoint, position, standpoint, aspect, outlook, slant, approach, perspective.

angle[2] *v*, fish, hook, catch.
angle for, fish for, look for, invite, solicit, be after (*inf*), scheme, contrive.

angry furious, irate, mad (*inf*), enraged, infuriated, livid, fuming, wrathful, vexed, exasperated, riled, inflamed, annoyed, indignant, displeased, piqued, chafed, hot, passionate, cross, irritable, moody, bad-tempered, irascible, choleric. CALM

anguish *n*, agony, torture, torment, pain, pang, distress, suffering, woe, misery, heartache, grief. ECSTASY
v, afflict, distress, torture, torment, agonize, hurt, pain, wound. SOOTHE

angular bony, lean, rangy, scrawny, lanky, gaunt, awkward, ungainly, stiff, austere.

animadversion censure, rebuke, reproof, blame, condemnation, disapproval, stricture, aspersion, criticism, comment. PRAISE

animal *n*, creature, beast, brute, monster, barbarian.
adj, bestial, brutal, brutish, carnal, fleshly, bodily, physical, sensual. SPIRITUAL

animate *v*, enliven, vitalize, stimulate, invigorate, vivify, activate, quicken, encourage, waken, rouse, excite, goad, provoke, stir, inspire, incite, embolden. DEPRESS
adj, alive, living, breathing, moving. INANIMATE

animated lively, spirited, vigorous, dynamic, brisk, vivacious, gay, blithe, buoyant, elated, excited, ebullient, enthusiastic, zestful, fervent, aroused, passionate. DULL

animation liveliness, activity, spirit, vitality, energy, vigour, vivacity, zest, ardour, buoyancy, elation, ebullience, zeal, passion.

animosity hatred, hate, aversion, loathing, dislike, virulence, spleen, antipathy, hostility, enmity, malice, ill will, malignity, bitterness, acrimony, rancour, resentment, grudge, antagonism. LOVE

animus animosity, hate, antipathy, dislike, hostility, ill will, rancour, malice. LOVE
intention, aim, purpose, will, motive, spirit, inclination, disposition.

annals archives, records, chronicles, registers, rolls, journals, memoirs, memorials, history.

annex add, append, adjoin, attach, affix, fasten, join, subjoin, connect, unite. DETACH
appropriate, acquire, occupy, seize, take over.

annexation addition, appending, attachment, union, connection. SEPARATION
appropriation, conquest, seizure, takeover, confiscation.

annexe extension, wing, attachment, appendage, addition.

annihilate abolish, exterminate, wipe out, obliterate, efface, extinguish, blast, raze, destroy, kill, decimate, liquidate, nullify.
annul, extirpate, eradicate, uproot, root out. PRESERVE

annihilation abolition, extermination, obliteration, extinction, eradication, extirpation, destruction, decimation, liquidation. PRESERVATION

annotate comment on, commentate, interpret, explain, gloss, elucidate, illustrate.

annotation note, explanation, exegesis, footnote, gloss, illustration, comment, observation, remark, interpretation, commentary.

announce declare, proclaim, publish, make known, broadcast, publicize, advertise, promulgate, propound, report, divulge, intimate, reveal, disclose. CONCEAL
herald, signal, presage, portend.

announcement declaration, proclamation, bulletin, notice, statement, report, publication, revelation, disclosure, advertisement, promulgation, broadcast. SUPPRESSION

annoy vex, irritate, irk, nettle, exasperate, enrage, anger, infuriate, bother, trouble, disturb, harass, pester, hector, badger, tease, torment, provoke, rile, madden. SOOTHE

annoyance vexation, irritation, pique, exasperation, displeasure, anger.
nuisance, pest, bother, affliction, pain (*inf*), bore, bind (*inf*). PLEASURE

annual yearly, every year, once a year.

annually yearly, per annum, each year.

annul nullify, abolish, invalidate, render null and void, repeal, revoke, abrogate, cancel, countermand, overrule, quash, rescind, eliminate, annihilate, extinguish, obliterate. CONFIRM

annular circular, ring-shaped, round.

annulment nullification, invalidation, cancellation, repeal, revocation, abrogation, negation, abolition.

anodyne *adj*, pain-killing, analgesic, anaesthetic, narcotic, palliative, lenitive, sedative, assuasive.
n, pain-killer, analgesic, narcotic, opiate, palliative, sedative. STIMULANT

anoint rub, smear, spread, daub, embrocate, oil.
consecrate, sanctify, bless, anele.

anomalous abnormal, irregular, unusual, unnatural, incongruous, deviating, aberrant, eccentric, peculiar, exceptional, singular. NORMAL

anomaly irregularity, abnormality, incongruity, inconsistency, deviation, aberration, exception, eccentricity, peculiarity, quirk, oddity.

anon soon, shortly, presently, before long, forthwith.

anonymous nameless, unnamed, unidentified, incognito, unsigned, unacknowledged.

answer *v*, reply, respond, acknowledge, retort, rejoin.
satisfy, fulfil, suffice, serve, suit, measure up to, conform.
n, reply, response, acknowledgment, retort, riposte, rejoinder, solution, defence, plea. QUESTION

answerable liable, responsible, accountable, amenable.

antagonism hostility, animosity, enmity, opposition, contradiction, conflict, discord, disharmony, rivalry, competition, contention. AMITY

antagonist opponent, adversary, enemy, foe, rival, competitor, contender. ALLY

antagonistic opposed, opposing, opposite, adverse, hostile, unfriendly, inimical, conflicting, rival, dissonant, disharmonious. FRIENDLY

antecedence precedence, priority, anteriority.

antecedent *adj*, prior, preceding, previous, earlier, anterior, foregoing, precursory. FOLLOWING
n, precursor, forerunner, harbinger, herald.

antedate predate, precede, forego, forestall, anticipate.

antediluvian antiquated, antique, archaic, ancient, age-old, old-fashioned, out-of-date, obsolete, prehistoric, primeval, primordial. MODERN

anterior front, fore, forward. POSTERIOR
prior, preceding, earlier, previous, foregoing, former, introductory.

anteroom antechamber, hall, lobby, vestibule, foyer, waiting room.

anthem hymn, song, psalm, canticle, chorale, chant.

anthology collection, compilation, compendium, treasury, miscellany, selection, excerpts, extracts.

anticipate expect, foresee, forecast, await, prepare for, hope for, look forward to, reckon on.
forestall, intercept, prevent, antedate.

anticipation expectation, prospect, foresight, presentiment, premonition, forecast, foretaste, expectancy, hope, apprehension.

antics pranks, tricks, jokes, mischief, capers, larks, skylarking, frolics, tomfoolery, buffoonery.

antidote remedy, cure, corrective, restorative, neutralizer, antivenin, antitoxin, antibody. POISON

antipathy aversion, loathing, hatred, abhorrence, detestation, repugnance, disgust, dislike, hostility, animosity. SYMPATHY

antiquated archaic, ancient, antediluvian, antique, superannuated, aged, fossilized, bygone, obsolete, old-fashioned, out-of-date, outmoded, old hat (*inf*). MODERN

antique *adj*, old, ancient, early, primitive, antiquated, archaic, old-fashioned, outdated. MODERN
n, curio, *objet d'art*, rarity, heirloom, fossil, relic, antiquity.

antiseptic *adj*, aseptic, sterile, hygienic, germ-free, sanitary, clinical, clean, pure, uncontaminated. POLLUTED
n, disinfectant, germicide, bactericide.

antisocial unsociable, uncommunicative, withdrawn, reserved, unfriendly, misanthropic, asocial, hostile, antagonistic, disruptive. FRIENDLY

antithesis opposition, contrast, opposite, reverse, converse, contrary.

anxiety uneasiness, worry, concern, disquiet, misgiving, foreboding, apprehension, fear, dread, trouble, care, solicitude, distress. TRANQUILLITY

anxious worried, troubled, concerned, fretful, uneasy, on edge, nervous, apprehensive, fearful. CALM

anyway in any case, at any rate, nevertheless, however, anyhow.

apace quickly, rapidly, swiftly, fast, speedily, hastily, hurriedly, without delay. SLOWLY

apart separately, aside, away, aloof, alone.
asunder, in pieces. TOGETHER

apart from, besides, other than, excluding, not counting, save.

apartment room, chamber, quarters, accommodation, lodging, suite, flat.

apathetic indifferent, unconcerned, uninterested, impassive, unfeeling, unresponsive, unmoved, insensible, cold, cool, callous, soulless, dull, listless, languid, passive, lethargic, torpid, sluggish. ENTHUSIASTIC

apathy indifference, unconcern, impassivity, insensibility, coldness, unfeelingness, listlessness, passiveness, lethargy, torpor. ENTHUSIASM

ape *n*, anthropoid, monkey, gorilla, baboon, gibbon, chimpanzee, orang-utan.
mimic, imitator, copycat (*inf*).

v, imitate, mimic, copy, counterfeit, parody, echo, mirror.

aperture opening, hole, perforation, gap, chink, cleft, crack, rift, slit, slot, mouth, orifice, eye, eyelet, space, passage.

apex top, summit, pinnacle, peak, vertex, apogee, acme, zenith, culmination, height. BASE

aphorism proverb, maxim, dictum, axiom, adage, apophthegm, saying, saw, byword, precept.

apiece each, individually, separated, severally. COLLECTIVELY

apish foolish, stupid, silly, affected, foppish, imitative, mimicking.

aplomb poise, assurance, self-assurance, confidence, self-confidence, self-possession, composure, collectedness, sang-froid, equanimity. AGITATION

apocalypse revelation, disclosure, manifestation, unveiling.

apocalyptic revelatory, prophetic, oracular, predictive, ominous, warning, threatening.

apocryphal unauthentic, unsubstantiated, dubious, doubtful, questionable, spurious, legendary, fictitious, false, untrue. AUTHENTIC

apologetic sorry, regretful, remorseful, contrite, penitent, repentant. UNREPENTANT

defensive, vindicative, justificatory, exculpatory.

apologist supporter, defender, advocate, champion, vindicator. ADVERSARY

apologize beg pardon, say sorry, regret, be sorry.

defend, plead, support, maintain, vindicate, excuse.

apologue allegory, fable, parable, moral tale, story.

apology explanation, excuse, justification, defence, plea, vindication, confession, acknowledgment, expression of regret. ACCUSATION

apophthegm adage, saying, saw, proverb, aphorism, maxim, precept, dictum, axiom.

apostasy desertion, abandonment, dereliction, defection, backsliding, disloyalty, perfidy, treason, faithlessness. LOYALTY

apostate *n*, deserter, renegade, turncoat, backslider, defector, traitor. LOYALIST

adj, disloyal, perfidious, unfaithful, false, treacherous, traitorous, heretical, backsliding. LOYAL

apostle messenger, missionary, preacher, evangelist, crusader, pioneer, champion, advocate, supporter.

apotheosis deification, elevation, exaltation, glorification, idealization.

appal horrify, outrage, shock, harrow, dismay, daunt, unnerve, alarm, frighten, terrify, petrify, astound, stun. REASSURE

appalling dreadful, frightful, awful, dire, terrible, horrifying, horrific, shocking, ghastly, hideous. WONDERFUL

apparatus equipment, tools, utensils, device, instrument, appliance, contrivance, mechanism.

apparel clothes, clothing, attire, dress, garments, wear, garb, outfit, costume, robes, habit, trappings.

apparent obvious, evident, patent, plain, clear, conspicuous, manifest, visible, perceptible, discernible, distinct. HIDDEN

seeming, ostensible, external, outward, superficial. ACTUAL

apparently obviously, evidently, patently, clearly, unmistakeably, plainly, perceptibly.

seemingly, ostensibly, outwardly, on the face of it, allegedly. ACTUALLY

apparition ghost, spirit, spectre, phantom, spook (*inf*), vision, illusion, chimera, hallucination.

appearance, manifestation, presence, materialization.

appeal *n*, entreaty, plea, prayer, petition, request, suit, address.

attraction, allure, attractiveness, charm, fascination. UNATTRACTIVENESS

v, entreat, implore, beg, beseech, plead, petition, invoke, solicit, request, address.

attract, engage, interest, fascinate, captivate, charm, entice, tempt. REPEL

appear emerge, arrive, arise, dawn, loom up, come into view, be present, turn up (*inf*). DISAPPEAR

seem, look.

appearance emergence, arrival, advent, coming, presence, debut, manifestation, publication. DISAPPEARANCE

look, aspect, demeanour, manner, air, bearing, mien, expression, semblance, pretence, show.

appease pacify, calm, assuage, moderate, mitigate, lull, still, soothe, allay, tranquillize, alleviate, ease, lessen, abate, compose, placate, propitiate, conciliate, satisfy, quell. AGGRAVATE

appellation name, title, designation, cognomen, sobriquet, term, denomination.

append add, attach, affix, annex, join, fasten, hang, subjoin, tag on, tack on. DETACH

appendage attachment, adjunct, addition, appendix, supplement, addendum, accessory. ESSENTIAL

appendant attached, affixed, added, annexed, appended, supplementary, additional, attendant, associated, consequential. SEPARATE

appendix appendage, adjunct, annexation, addition, addendum, supplement, postscript, epilogue.

appertain belong, pertain, refer, relate, touch, concern, apply, be connected.

appetite desire, want, craving, longing, hunger, thirst, passion, relish, liking, affinity, inclination, propensity. INDIFFERENCE

appetizing tempting, inviting, appealing, savoury, delicious, mouthwatering, tasty. UNAPPETIZING

applaud clap, cheer, praise, laud, acclaim, extol, approve, commend, encourage, congratulate, compliment. DENOUNCE

applause clapping, ovation, cheers, praise, acclamation, acclaim, laudation, plaudit, accolade, eulogy, approbation, approval, commendation. DENUNCIATION

appliance device, machine, mechanism, contrivance, gadget, instrument, tool, implement, utensil, apparatus, piece of equipment.

application, use, exercise, practice.

applicable appropriate, apt, suitable, fitting, suited, proper, apposite, apropos, relevant, pertinent, adjustable, useful, convenient. INAPPROPRIATE

applicant candidate, aspirant, suitor, petitioner, claimant.

application request, petition, appeal, suit, claim, demand, inquiry.

relevance, pertinence, value, purpose, use, function.

assiduity, industry, diligence, perseverance, commitment, attention, dedication, effort, study. INDOLENCE

apply *vt*, use, utilize, employ, put to use, exercise, practise, execute, bring to bear, assign, administer. NEGLECT

devote, commit, dedicate, direct, address. DIVERT

vi, be relevant, be appropriate, pertain, appertain, fit, refer, relate.

request, appeal, solicit, claim, seek, inquire.

appoint assign, designate, nominate, name, elect, select, install. DISMISS

fix, arrange, settle, establish, ordain, prescribe, decree. CANCEL

furnish, equip, fit out, supply.

appointment arrangement, engagement, assignation, tryst, meeting, rendezvous, date, interview.

office, post, position, job, situation, place.

appointing, nomination, election, selection, designation, ordainment.

fixture, fitting, furnishing, appurtenance, accoutrement.

apportion allot, assign, allocate, divide, share, administer, dispense, distribute, deal out. RETAIN

apportionment allocation, allotment, division, sharing, distribution, dispensing.

apposite apt, appropriate, fitting, fit, suitable, proper, relevant, pertinent, applicable, germane, apropos. INAPPROPRIATE

appraisal appraisement, evaluation, valuation, estimate, assessment, judgment.

appraise evaluate, assess, inspect, survey, value, price, rate, estimate, judge.

appreciable noticeable, perceptible, detectable, discernible, marked, obvious, evident, substantial, considerable. IMPERCEPTIBLE

appreciate *vt*, value, prize, rate highly, esteem, respect, acknowledge, be grateful for. SCORN

recognize, perceive, comprehend, realize, be aware of.

vi, rise in value, increase, grow, multiply, gain, intensify. DEPRECIATE

appreciation value, esteem, respect, admiration, acknowledgment, gratitude, thanks. SCORN

recognition, perception, comprehension, awareness.

apprehend seize, catch, capture, arrest, take into custody, nick (*inf*), run in (*inf*). RELEASE

understand, comprehend, perceive, grasp, recognize, realize, appreciate, conceive, imagine.
dread, fear, anticipate.

apprehension fear, foreboding, dread, trepidation, anxiety, misgiving, disquiet, uneasiness, mistrust, suspicion. COMPOSURE
arrest, seizure, capture.
understanding, comprehension, grasp, perception, conception, concept, notion, view, belief. MISAPPREHENSION

apprehensive fearful, anxious, worried, troubled, uneasy, afraid, scared, suspicious, mistrustful. COMPOSED

apprentice novice, beginner, tyro, learner, student, pupil, probationer. MASTER

apprise acquaint, inform, tell, notify, make aware, advise, warn.

approach *v*, near, come near, draw near, advance, move towards, accost, address, broach, embark on. RECEDE
approximate, resemble, come close to.
n, advent, coming, nearing, advance, arrival.
access, passage, entrance, way, road, path. EXIT
method, procedure, technique, means, attitude, manner.

approbation approval, sanction, assent, consent, recognition, praise, commendation, acclaim, encouragement, support. CENSURE

appropriate *adj*, fitting, suitable, adapted, apt, proper, seemly, becoming, befitting, timely, apposite, pertinent, relevant, germane. INAPPROPRIATE
v, seize, take over, commandeer, annex, confiscate, impound.
assign, allot, apportion, earmark, set aside.

appropriateness suitability, fitness, aptness, propriety, timeliness, relevance, pertinence.

appropriation seizure, capture, arrogation, confiscation, impounding. RETURN
allocation, apportionment, allotment, assignment.

approval approbation, appreciation, recommendation, praise, commendation, acclaim, admiration, esteem. CENSURE
sanction, consent, assent, agreement, acquiescence, endorsement, encouragement, support. DISAPPROVAL

approve appreciate, praise, commend, admire, esteem, value, prize. DISAPPROVE
sanction, authorize, assent, consent, agree, endorse, bless, uphold, support, encourage, recommend. OPPOSE

approximate *adj*, rough, inexact, imprecise, loose, near, close. EXACT
v, approach, come near, resemble. DIFFER

approximately roughly, about, around, more or less, nearly, almost. PRECISELY

approximation estimate, guess, guesstimate (*inf*), conjecture, rough idea, approach, semblance.

appurtenance appendage, adjunct, accessory, attachment, addition, supplement, incidental, concomitant. ESSENTIAL

appurtenances equipment, paraphernalia, trappings, belongings.

appurtenant pertaining, connected, related, relevant, belonging, attached, supplementary, incidental.

apropos *adj*, appropriate, apt, timely, opportune, suitable, fit, proper. INOPPORTUNE
adv, appropriately, aptly, timely, opportunely, to the purpose.
apropos of, regarding, with reference to, in respect of.

apt appropriate, suitable, fitting, proper, opportune, timely, apropos, apposite, pertinent, relevant. INAPPROPRIATE
disposed, inclined, prone, liable, subject, given, likely.
quick, sharp, able, dexterous, clever, bright, intelligent, gifted, adroit, expert, adept. SLOW

aptitude ability, disposition, faculty, gift, talent, knack, flair, intelligence, cleverness, inclination, leaning, aptness, readiness, competence. INCOMPETENCE

aptness appropriateness, suitability, fitness, timeliness, appositeness, relevance, pertinence. UNSUITABILITY
aptitude, disposition, inclination, ability, faculty.

aquiline eagle-like, hooked, bent, curved, Roman. STRAIGHT

arable cultivable, tillable, farmable, ploughable, fertile, fruitful, productive.

arbiter judge, adjudicator, arbitrator, referee, umpire, controller, governor, ruler, sovereign, master, lord.

arbitrament decision, verdict, judgment, decree, award, sentence.

arbitrary capricious, whimsical, random, chance, subjective, discretionary, wilful, unreasonable. REASONED
despotic, dictatorial, autocratic, absolute, tyrannical, imperious, magisterial, domineering, overbearing.

arbitrate settle, decide, determine, judge, adjudicate, mediate, intervene, negotiate, conciliate.

arbitration judgment, adjudication, decision, settlement, mediation, intervention, negotiation, conciliation.

arbitrator judge, arbiter, adjudicator, mediator, negotiator, peacemaker, go-between.

arbour bower, retreat, recess, shelter, pergola.

arc bend, curve, bow, arch, crescent.

arcade colonnade, peristyle, portico, cloister, gallery, loggia, passageway, precinct.

arcane mysterious, abstruse, occult, esoteric, recondite, secret, hidden.

arch[1] *n*, curve, bend, arc, vault, span, archway, dome.

arch[2] *adj*, chief, main, principal, leading, first, greatest. MINOR
shrewd, knowing, cunning, artful, roguish, waggish, mischievous, playful.

archaic ancient, old, bygone, obsolete, outdated, obsolescent, old-fashioned, antiquated, superannuated. MODERN

arched curved, domed, vaulted, bowed, concave. STRAIGHT

archetype type, model, pattern, paradigm, original, prototype, precursor, example, paragon, ideal.

architect designer, planner, draughtsman, builder, constructor, maker, creator, author, contriver, instigator.

architecture design, planning, building, construction, structure, framework.

archives records, annals, chronicles, registers, rolls, documents, papers.

arctic northern, boreal, polar, hyperborean. ANTARCTIC
cold, freezing, glacial, icy, wintry, chilly, bleak. HOT

ardent intense, fervent, passionate, impassioned, burning, hot, fiery, keen, eager, avid, enthusiastic, spirited, zealous, vehement, fierce. COOL

ardour intensity, fervour, passion, feeling, warmth, heat, eagerness, enthusiasm, spirit, zeal, vehemence. APATHY

arduous difficult, hard, laborious, onerous, tiring, exhausting, toilsome, strenuous, rigorous, gruelling, formidable, harsh, severe, steep, uphill. EASY

area district, region, locality, zone, territory, realm, domain, sphere, field, expanse, surface, space, extent, scope, range.
part, section, portion, tract, sector. WHOLE
yard, enclosure, plot.

arena enclosure, amphitheatre, ring, stage, stadium, ground, field, track.

argue debate, discuss, moot, reason, maintain, contend, persuade, plead.
dispute, disagree, quarrel, wrangle, squabble, bicker, row. AGREE
denote, indicate, betoken, demonstrate, show, suggest, imply.

argument dispute, disagreement, quarrel, altercation, row, squabble, wrangle, conflict, clash. AGREEMENT
discussion, debate, polemic, controversy.
defence, case, evidence, reason, reasoning, grounds, proof.
summary, outline, abstract, gist, plot, theme, subject, topic.

argumentative contentious, quarrelsome, disputatious, contrary, belligerent, combative.

arid dry, parched, barren, sterile, dreary, dull, uninteresting, boring. FERTILE

aridity aridness, dryness, barrenness, sterility, dreariness, dullness. FERTILITY

arise originate, proceed, begin, spring, issue, flow, emerge, appear, emanate, result, ensue. END
rise, get up, stand up, ascend, go up, mount, soar. SINK

aristocracy nobility, gentry, peerage, ruling class, upper class, elite.

aristocrat noble, nobleman, patrician, gentleman, lady, lord, earl, peer. PLEBEIAN

aristocratic noble, titled, patrician, blue-blooded, genteel, highborn, elite, upper-class. LOWBORN
elegant, stylish, refined, sophisticated, well-bred, ladylike, dignified, haughty, snobbish, arrogant. VULGAR

arm[1] *n*, limb, appendage, branch, bough, offshoot, division, department.
inlet, channel, strait, sound, estuary, firth, cove.

power, authority, might, strength.

arm[2] *v*, equip, provide, supply, furnish, fit out, prepare, fortify, strengthen, guard, protect. DISARM

armada fleet, flotilla, squadron, navy.

armament arms, weapons, weaponry, munitions, materiel.

armistice truce, ceasefire, peace, reprieve, suspension, intermission.

armoury arsenal, magazine, ammunition dump, depot, depository, warehouse.

arms weapons, weaponry, munitions, armament, materiel, firearms, guns, ammunition.
shield, crest, escutcheon, insignia, blazonry, armorial bearings.

army military, soldiers, troops, armed forces.
multitude, host, crowd, throng, horde.

aroma odour, smell, scent, redolence, fragrance, perfume, bouquet, savour.

aromatic fragrant, scented, perfumed, balmy, redolent, sweet-smelling, spicy, pungent.

around *prep*, round, surrounding, encircling, about. AMID
roughly, approximately, about, circa.
adj, on all sides, everywhere, all over, throughout, about, here and there.
near, nearby, at hand, close by.

arouse awaken, stir, excite, stimulate, whet, spur, provoke, rouse.
agitate, animate, instigate, kindle, incite, inflame. PACIFY

arraign summon, accuse, charge, indict, impeach, incriminate, denounce. CONDONE

arraignment summons, accusation, charge, indictment, impeachment, incrimination, denunciation.

arrange order, dispose, array, assort, distribute, group, classify, class, marshal, organize, range, place, position. DISARRANGE
adjust, settle, agree to, fix, contrive, devise, prepare, plan, organize.
adapt, orchestrate, score.

arrangement order, disposition, array, grouping, classification, organization.
plan, preparation, provision, measure, schedule.
agreement, settlement, understanding, compact, contract.
adaptation, interpretation, version, orchestration, score.

arrant utter, downright, out-and-out, thorough, absolute, veritable, undisguised, blatant, rank, gross.
infamous, notorious, vile, atrocious, monstrous.

array *v*, dress, clothe, attire, adorn, deck, bedeck, equip, fit out, supply. STRIP
marshal, dispose, arrange, draw up, order, place, rank, line up. DISARRANGE
n, display, collection, parade, show, exhibition, arrangement, disposition, line-up, order, formation. DISARRAY
dress, attire, apparel, clothing, finery, regalia.

arrears arrearage, debt, liabilities, amount overdue, deficiency.
in arrears, overdue, behind, late, in debt, in the red.

arrest *v*, seize, capture, take prisoner, apprehend, take into custody, detain, nick (*inf*), run in (*inf*), bust (*inf*). RELEASE
check, restrain, hold, halt, stop, interrupt, inhibit, slow, delay, retard, hinder, obstruct. STIMULATE
attract, rivet, engage, occupy, absorb, engross, fascinate. BORE
n, seizure, capture, apprehension, detention. RELEASE
check, restraint, halt, stoppage, cessation, blockage, obstruction, delay, slowing, inhibition, suppression.

arresting striking, conspicuous, impressive, remarkable, noticeable, extraordinary.

arrival advent, coming, appearance, entrance. DEPARTURE
newcomer, visitor, caller, guest.

arrive come, land, turn up, appear, show up (*inf*). DEPART
occur, happen, befall.
succeed, make it (*inf*), thrive, prosper. FAIL
arrive at, reach, get to, attain, realize.

arrogance pride, haughtiness, loftiness, hauteur, self-importance, conceit, superciliousness, disdain, contemptuousness, pomposity, lordliness, insolence, self-assurance, self-assertion. HUMILITY

arrogant proud, haughty, self-important, conceited, disdainful, supercilious, contemptuous, overbearing, lordly, pompous, insolent, self-assured. MODEST

arrogate appropriate, assume, claim, usurp, commandeer, demand. WAIVE
assign, impute, attribute, ascribe.

arrow shaft, dart, bolt, missile.
pointer, marker, indicator.

arsenal armoury, magazine, store, depot, depository, warehouse.

art skill, dexterity, adroitness, aptitude, address, cleverness, ingenuity, facility, knack, flair, expertise, mastery. CLUMSINESS
artfulness, shrewdness, astuteness, slyness, cunning, guile, deceit, duplicity, artifice, craft, trickery. HONESTY

artful cunning, sly, wily, subtle, shrewd, astute, sharp, knowing, crafty, insidious, deceitful, tricky, clever, skilful, dexterous, adroit. ARTLESS

article item, thing, object, commodity, component, part, portion, section, piece, division.
essay, composition, paper, feature, treatise, story, column, report, review, commentary.

articulate *v*, pronounce, enunciate, utter, speak, say, voice, express.
join, unite, connect, link, hinge, joint. SEVER
adj, clear, distinct, coherent, intelligible, audible, eloquent, well-spoken, fluent. INARTICULATE

articulation pronunciation, enunciation, diction, delivery, presentation, elocution, expression, inflection.
connection, joint, linkage, hinge, coupling.

artifice trick, stratagem, wile, deception, fraud, subterfuge, machination, contrivance, device, manoeuvre, ruse, dodge.
cunning, artfulness, deceit, duplicity, trickery, guile, craft, craftiness, slyness. HONESTY
skill, art, cleverness, dexterity, finesse, invention, ingenuity, facility. INCOMPETENCE

artificer maker, creator, craftsman, artisan, designer, inventor, mechanic.

artificial unnatural, man-made, synthetic, manufactured, ersatz, simulated, imitation, mock, sham, phoney (*inf*), counterfeit, fake, spurious. GENUINE
affected, insincere, forced, contrived, assumed, feigned, pretended. SINCERE

artillery guns, gunnery, cannon, cannonry, ordnance, battery, enginery.

artisan craftsman, master, artificer, handicraftsman, skilled workman, technician, mechanic.

artist painter, sculptor, designer, master, adept, expert.

artistic tasteful, exquisite, beautiful, stylish, refined, aesthetic, sensitive, creative, imaginative, decorative, ornamental. TASTELESS

artless simple, unaffected, natural, unpretentious, guileless, honest, truthful, straightforward, sincere, open, frank, forthright, candid, plain, naive, unsophisticated, ingenuous, innocent. ARTFUL
awkward, clumsy, inexpert, inept, untaught, ignorant, rude, primitive. REFINED

as *conj*, while, when, just as.
like, in the manner that, in the same way that.
since, because, seeing that, considering that.
for example, for instance, such as, like.
prep, being, in the role of.

ascend go up, climb, scale, rise, mount, soar, slope upwards. DESCEND

ascendancy superiority, advantage, authority, upper hand, control, power, sway, influence, mastery, supremacy, dominion, command, sovereignty, rule, domination. SERVITUDE

ascendant *n*, ascendancy, superiority, dominance, dominion, supremacy, control, rule, command, power.
adj, rising, ascending, climbing, mounting. DESCENDING
dominant, prevailing, superior, powerful, commanding, ruling, authoritative, influential. SUBORDINATE

ascent ascension, ascending, rising, rise, climbing, climb, mounting, scaling. DESCENT
gradient, incline, slope, acclivity, rising ground, ramp, elevation, height, eminence.

ascertain discover, find out, determine, verify, make certain, confirm, settle, establish, resolve. SURMISE

ascetic *n*, abstainer, self-denier, recluse, hermit, anchorite, monk, nun.
adj, abstemious, abstinent, self-denying, continent, celibate, temperate, moderate, austere, puritanical, severe, rigorous, harsh, stern. LAX

ascribe attribute, assign, credit, charge, impute, put down, refer.

ashamed abashed, shamefaced, conscience-stricken, mortified, embarrassed, humiliated, sheepish, guilty, remorseful, sorry, chagrined, distressed, crestfallen, bashful, shy. PROUD

ashen ashy, pale, pallid, wan, livid, ghastly, colourless, pasty, grey. COLOURED

ashore on shore, to the shore, on land, aground, beached, stranded. AFLOAT

aside away, apart, aloof, separately, on one side, in reserve, out of the way.
beside, alongside, laterally.

asinine stupid, foolish, idiotic, absurd, senseless, doltish, thickheaded, brainless, obstinate, stubborn. CLEVER

ask inquire, question, quiz, interrogate. REPLY
request, seek, demand, expect, require, desire, crave, petition, sue, solicit, entreat, beg, implore, beseech, supplicate.
invite, bid, summon.

askance awry, obliquely, aslant, sideways, indirectly. STRAIGHT
suspiciously, mistrustfully, dubiously.

askew awry, crooked, aslant, oblique, askance, lopsided, off-centre. STRAIGHT

asleep sleeping, slumbering, dozing, napping, resting, dormant, inactive, numb, insensible. AWAKE

aspect look, appearance, bearing, demeanour, mien, attitude, air, expression.
outlook, prospect, direction, situation, position, viewpoint, view.
side, angle, slant, feature, facet, part, phase.

asperity harshness, roughness, ruggedness, sharpness, tartness, bitterness, acerbity, acrimony, sourness, moroseness, sullenness, churlishness, crabbedness, peevishness, irascibility, severity, virulence. MILDNESS

asperse slander, calumniate, defame, abuse, vilify, traduce, slur, besmirch, defile, smear, disparage, impugn. EULOGIZE

aspersion slander, calumny, defamation, abuse, vilification, disparagement, censure, obloquy, slur, smear. COMMENDATION

asphyxiate suffocate, smother, stifle, choke, strangle, throttle.

aspirant aspirer, seeker, hopeful, suitor, postulant, claimant, applicant, candidate, competitor.

aspiration longing, yearning, hope, desire, craving, dream, goal, ambition, aim, objective, eagerness, zeal, endeavour, enterprise. APATHY

aspire long, yearn, hope, desire, crave, seek, dream, aim, rise, mount, soar.

ass donkey, jackass, dolt, blockhead, simpleton, fool, idiot, nincompoop, dope (*inf*), dunce, halfwit, twit (*inf*).

assail attack, assault, beset, set upon, invade. RESIST
abuse, slander, calumniate, defame, vilify, malign, asperse, revile, impugn, vituperate, attack, berate, criticize, deride, ridicule. VINDICATE

assailable vulnerable, sensitive, unprotected, defenceless, lame, weak. UNASSAILABLE

assailant attacker, assaulter, assailer, aggressor, invader, antagonist, opponent. PROTECTOR

assassin killer, murderer, slayer, liquidator, gunman, hit man (*inf*), cut-throat, executioner.

assassinate kill, slay, murder, liquidate, eliminate (*inf*), dispatch, execute.

assassination murder, killing, dispatch, execution, liquidation, elimination.

assault *v*, attack, assail, set upon, invade, charge, beset, molest, rape. DEFEND
n, attack, onslaught, onset, charge, strike, invasion, aggression, offensive. DEFENCE

assay *v*, test, try, prove, analyse, examine, inspect, investigate, assess.
n, test, trial, analysis, examination, inspection, investigation, assessment.

assemblage assembly, gathering, meeting, rally, throng, crowd, group, conclave, congregation, body, collection, combination, union, aggregation, mass, cluster, accumulation. DISPERSION

assemble collect, gather, muster, congregate, convene, rally, come together, bring together, convoke, summon, call. DISPERSE
put together, join, connect, make, fabricate, manufacture, build, erect, construct. DISMANTLE

assembly gathering, meeting, rally, conference, congress, council, conclave, congregation,. assemblage, group, body, crowd, throng, collection.
construction, fabrication, manufacture.

assent *v*, agree, acquiesce, concur, accept, go along with, approve, consent, accord, grant. DISSENT *n*, agreement, acquiescence, concurrence, acceptance, approval, consent, compliance, accord. OPPOSITION

assert declare, affirm, aver, avow, asseverate, maintain, state, pronounce, predicate, allege, claim, emphasize, insist upon, uphold, support. DENY

assertion declaration, statement, pronouncement, affirmation, averment, asseveration, insistence. DENIAL

assertive positive, decided, confident, self-assured, emphatic, dogmatic, insistent, pushy (*inf*), strong-willed, demanding, forceful, aggressive, overbearing. HESITANT

assess estimate, gauge, value, rate, appraise, evaluate, compute, determine, fix, impose, levy, tax.

assessment evaluation, appraisal, review, estimation, estimate, valuation, rating, rate, charge, levy, tax, duty, toll.

asset advantage, benefit, boon, blessing, resource, help. DISADVANTAGE

assets property, goods, possessions, estate, capital, wealth, resources. LIABILITIES

asseverate declare, affirm, assert, state, pronounce, avow, maintain, attest, aver, predicate. DENY

asseveration declaration, affirmation, assertion, statement, pronouncement, attestation, averment. DENIAL

assiduity assiduousness, industry, diligence, application, devotion, constancy, sedulousness, effort, labour, exertion, pains, persistence, tirelessness, perseverance, care, attention. INDOLENCE

assiduous industrious, hard-working, diligent, sedulous, persistent, persevering, studious, painstaking, attentive, untiring, tireless, indefatigable, constant, steady. INDOLENT

assign appoint, designate, select, choose, delegate, charge, commission. DISMISS
allot, allocate, apportion, appropriate, set aside, fix, determine, specify, give, distribute, dispense.
attribute, ascribe, accredit, put down.

assignation meeting, rendezvous, appointment, tryst, date.

assignment task, mission, job, duty, obligation, post, appointment, commission.
allotment, allocation, apportionment, distribution, designation, appointment, specification, determination, attribution, ascription.

assimilate digest, absorb, incorporate, take in, learn. REJECT
adjust, adapt, acclimatize, accustom, naturalize, blend, mingle, merge, conform.

assist help, aid, abet, support, back, sustain, second, reinforce, promote, further, expedite, work with, cooperate, collaborate, relieve, succour. HINDER

assistance help, aid, service, support, backing, cooperation, collaboration, relief, succour. HINDRANCE

assistant helper, helpmate, aider, aide, right-hand man, ally, accomplice, abettor, partner, colleague, collaborator, auxiliary, accessory, second, supporter. OPPONENT

associate *v*, link, join, connect, relate, unite, combine, affiliate, ally. DISSOCIATE
consort, fraternize, team up, befriend, mix, keep company, go around.
n, colleague, co-worker, partner, confederate, ally, accomplice, fellow, mate, comrade, friend, companion, intimate. ENEMY

association society, union, company, partnership, corporation, confederation, alliance, consortium, syndicate, body, group, organization, club, fraternity, guild, lodge.
friendship, companionship, fraternization, intimacy.
connection, relation, relationship, correlation, bond, tie, linking, union. DISSOCIATION

assort *vt*, arrange, sort, group, classify, rank, distribute, dispose, array.
vi, match, suit, coordinate.

assorted mixed, varied, various, miscellaneous, heterogeneous, diverse, different, motley, sundry. HOMOGENEOUS

assortment mixture, variety, miscellany, medley, pot-pourri, hotchpotch, jumble, selection, collection, array.
class, type, sort, group, category, set, batch, lot.
arrangement, distribution, classification, sorting.

assuage mitigate, soothe, moderate, lessen, ease, alleviate, tranquillize, pacify, appease, calm, relieve, quell, abate, allay, mollify, soften. AGGRAVATE

assuagement mitigation, moderation, alleviation, pacification, appeasement, relief, easing, abatement. AGGRAVATION

assume suppose, presume, surmise, infer, postulate, believe, think, take for granted. KNOW
affect, feign, pretend, counterfeit, simulate.
take on, undertake, adopt, acquire, appropriate, seize, usurp, arrogate. DISCARD
assumed false, fictitious, bogus, phoney (*inf*), made-up, counterfeit, spurious, feigned, affected. GENUINE
assuming presumptuous, arrogant, imperious, overbearing, haughty, conceited, forward, brazen, bold, audacious. MODEST
assumption supposition, presumption, conjecture, guess, hypothesis, theory, postulate, surmise, inference. KNOWLEDGE
arrogance, presumption, conceit, self-importance, forwardness, boldness. MODESTY
assuming, taking, undertaking, acceptance, adoption, appropriation, seizure, usurpation.
assurance pledge, promise, vow, oath, guarantee, assertion, affirmation, declaration. EQUIVOCATION
certainty, conviction, confidence, courage, boldness, nerve, assuredness, sureness, self-confidence, poise, security, belief, persuasion. DOUBT
arrogance, presumption, conceit, effrontery, impertinence, impudence. MODESTY
assure promise, guarantee, warrant, aver, pledge, vow, attest, affirm, confirm, give one's word, clinch, make certain. EQUIVOCATE
convince, persuade, encourage, reassure, comfort, hearten, embolden.
assured indubitable, unquestionable, certain, sure, guaranteed, secure. DOUBTFUL
self-confident, self-possessed, self-assured, positive, complacent, assertive, pushy (*inf*), audacious, bold. TIMID
astir active, on the move, in motion, afoot, alert, stirring, roused, awake, up and about. IDLE
astonish amaze, astound, stagger, dumbfound, flabbergast (*inf*), stupefy, stun, daze, startle, confound. BORE
astonished amazed, astounded, flabbergasted (*inf*), dumbfounded, stunned, surprised, open-mouthed, bowled over (*inf*).
astonishing amazing, astounding, staggering, surprising, stunning, impressive, breathtaking. ORDINARY
astonishment amazement, stupefaction, surprise, awe, wonder, bewilderment, confusion.
astound amaze, astonish, stagger, dumbfound, flabbergast (*inf*), stupefy, stun, daze, startle, confound. BORE
astral starry, starlike, stellar, sidereal.
astray wrong, off course, straying, wandering, loose, adrift, amiss, abroad, missing, absent. SAFE
astringent harsh, severe, rigorous, strict, stringent, austere, acerbic, caustic, sharp. LAX
contractive, styptic, binding, constrictive.
astute shrewd, cunning, crafty, wily, artful, subtle, knowing, perceptive, intelligent, discerning, sharp, keen, penetrating, adroit, clever, ingenious. SLOW
astuteness shrewdness, perception, insight, intelligence, subtlety, artfulness, guile, craftiness, cunning, sharpness, keenness, acumen, cleverness. SLOWNESS
asunder apart, to bits, in pieces. TOGETHER
asylum sanctuary, refuge, haven, shelter, retreat, safety.
institution, home, hospital, mental hospital, mad house (*inf*), loony bin (*inf*).
atheist unbeliever, disbeliever, sceptic, doubter, freethinker, infidel, heathen, pagan. BELIEVER
athlete sportsman, sportswoman, competitor, contestant, runner, gymnast, player.
athletic strong, muscular, sinewy, robust, sturdy, powerful, lusty, stalwart, energetic, fit, able-bodied, active. WEAK
athwart *adv*, across, crosswise, transversely, awry, askew, aslant, obliquely. STRAIGHT
prep, across, over. ALONG
against, in opposition to, counter to, versus.
atmosphere air, climate, sky, heavens.
mood, tone, character, feeling, ambience, aura, environment, milieu, surroundings, setting.
atom molecule, particle, jot, iota, scrap, whit, bit, mite, shred, crumb, morsel, trace.
atone expiate, redeem, appease, recompense, make up, redress, do penance, make amends. OFFEND

atonement expiation, reparation, satisfaction, propitiation, amends, recompense, compensation, redress, penance. OFFENCE

atrocious monstrous, abominable, infamous, nefarious, outrageous, heinous, horrible, infernal, diabolical, cruel, brutal, inhuman, savage, vicious, ruthless, vile, wicked, villainous. NOBLE
appalling, terrible, awful, horrible, detestable, shocking, horrifying. EXCELLENT

atrocity outrage, brutality, monstrosity, enormity, horror, crime, act of cruelty.
atrociousness, barbarity, savagery, inhumanity, monstrousness, heinousness, vileness, wickedness, ruthlessness, fiendishness. NOBILITY

atrophy *n*, decline, wasting, degeneration, decay, diminution, emaciation, shrivelling, withering.
v, decline, wither, shrivel, waste away, decay, diminish, dwindle, dry up. FLOURISH

attach join, fasten, affix, connect, append, tie, bind, tack, hitch, fix, stick, adhere. DETACH
assign, attribute, ascribe, accredit, associate, impute.

attached fond, loving, affectionate, devoted, enamoured.
engaged, spoken for, married. UNATTACHED

attachment fastening, joint, connection, bond, clamp, coupling, link, tie.
appendage, adjunct, accessory, appurtenance, addition, extra, fitting, extension. ESSENTIAL
affection, fondness, love, tenderness, liking, partiality, regard, affinity, attraction, bond, fidelity, devotion. HATRED

attack *v*, assault, assail, storm, beset, raid, charge, invade, violate, set upon, lay into (*inf*). DEFEND
abuse, berate, vilify, calumniate, impugn, malign, censure, blame. PRAISE
n, assault, onslaught, onset, raid, charge, invasion, incursion, aggression, offensive. DEFENCE
bout, spasm, access, fit, paroxysm, seizure.

attacker assailant, aggressor, invader, intruder, raider. DEFENDER

attain achieve, realize, accomplish, fulfil, arrive at, get to, reach, grasp, secure, get, obtain, acquire, gain, win, earn. LOSE

attainable achievable, realizable, reachable, within reach, accessible, at hand, possible, likely, feasible, practicable. IMPOSSIBLE

attainment achievement, accomplishment, feat, exploit, qualification, talent, ability.
realization, success, fulfilment, achievement, acquisition. FAILURE

attempt *v*, try, endeavour, have a go, strive, seek, venture, undertake, tackle.
n, try, effort, endeavour, undertaking, venture, experiment, trial, go, stab (*inf*), crack (*inf*).

attend be present, go to, frequent, visit.
accompany, follow, escort, guard, serve, wait on, minister to, care for, tend, look after. DESERT
listen, heed, pay attention, observe, mark, note. IGNORE

attendance presence, attending, appearance. ABSENCE
audience, turnout, house, gate, number present.
service, aid, assistance, care, ministration. NEGLECT

attendant escort, companion, servant, maid, waiter, waitress, valet, footman, steward, aide, assistant, usher, guide.
consequence, result, accompaniment, concomitant.

attention heed, heedfulness, alertness, observation, awareness, regard, notice, thought, consideration, concentration, application, intentness, deliberation. INATTENTION
care, concern, ministration, treatment, service, respect, courtesy, civility, deference, politeness, compliment, address. NEGLECT

attentive heedful, alert, mindful, careful, observant, aware, intent, concentrating, diligent, sedulous. INATTENTIVE
considerate, thoughtful, kind, obliging, civil, gallant, chivalrous, polite, courteous. NEGLECTFUL

attenuate thin, extend, draw out, rarefy, diminish, reduce, lessen, weaken, dilute.

attenuation thinning, rarefaction, diminution, reduction, lessening, weakening, dilution.
thinness, slenderness, fineness, elongation.

attest affirm, adjure, aver, confirm, corroborate, verify, witness, testify, certify, ratify, endorse, vouch for. DENY

show, exhibit, manifest, display, demonstrate, prove, bear out.
attestation testimony, evidence, witness, statement.
affirmation, confirmation, endorsement, ratification, averment. DENIAL
attic[1] *n*, loft, garret, mansard. BASEMENT
attic[2] *adj*, classic, classical, elegant, tasteful, refined, polished, pure, simple, delicate. VULGAR
attire *v*, dress, clothe, robe, array, apparel, rig out, equip. STRIP
n, dress, clothing, clothes, garments, wear, apparel, costume, outfit, garb, finery, vestments, robes.
attitude opinion, point of view, stance, position, outlook, view, perspective, approach, disposition, frame of mind.
pose, posture, position, stance, air, demeanour, bearing, manner.
attorney agent, deputy, substitute, proctor, factor, lawyer.
attract draw, pull, allure, entice, engage, win, charm, fascinate, captivate. REPEL
attraction draw, pull, magnetism, affinity, appeal, allure, lure, bait, enticement, temptation, inducement, fascination, charm, captivation, attractiveness. REPULSION
attractive appealing, pleasing, lovely, beautiful, pretty, fetching, prepossessing, winsome, charming, engaging, winning, seductive, tempting, inviting. UNATTRACTIVE
attributable ascribable, assignable, imputable, chargeable, traceable.
attribute *v*, ascribe, assign, credit, impute, charge, blame, put down.
n, quality, virtue, characteristic, trait, feature, property, peculiarity, quirk, idiosyncrasy, mark, note, sign, indication.
attrition abrasion, friction, wear, wearing down, rubbing, scraping, erosion. ACCRETION
attune harmonize, accord, coordinate, adjust, adapt, acclimatize. DISTURB
auburn reddish-brown, copper-coloured, chestnut, henna, russet, rust-coloured, Titian red, bronze, tawny.
audacious bold, daring, fearless, intrepid, dauntless, venturesome, courageous, brave, valiant, rash, foolhardy, reckless. TIMID
forward, shameless, brazen, impertinent, impudent, cheeky, insolent, arrogant, presumptuous, assuming. MODEST
audacity boldness, fearlessness, guts (*inf*), nerve, courage, valiance, bravery, rashness, recklessness, foolhardiness. TIMIDITY
forwardness, shamelessness, effrontery, impertinence, gall, cheek, nerve, impudence, insolence, arrogance, presumption. MODESTY
audible perceptible, discernible, distinct, clear, hearable. INAUDIBLE
audience assembly, congregation, crowd, turnout, house, onlookers, spectators, viewers, listeners, patrons, public.
interview, hearing, reception, meeting.
audit *v*, examine, inspect, scrutinize, check, verify.
n, examination, inspection, scrutiny, checking, verification.
audition hearing, test, trial.
augment increase, enlarge, magnify, amplify, swell, expand, add to, boost, strengthen, extend, raise, enhance. DECREASE
augmentation increase, enlargement, amplification, expansion, addition, extension, boost, rise. DECREASE
augur *v*, predict, foretell, prophesy, portend, presage, foreshadow, signify.
n, prophet, soothsayer, seer, oracle.
augury divination, soothsaying, prophecy, prediction.
omen, sign, portent, presage, prophecy, harbinger.
august dignified, majestic, imposing, lofty, grand, magnificent, noble regal, venerable, exalted, solemn, stately. HUMBLE
aura air, atmosphere, ambience, feeling, mood, quality, aroma, scent, emanation, odour.
auspice augury, omen, portent, sign, presage.
auspices patronage, backing, sponsorship, favour, influence, protection, aegis, support, guidance.
auspicious favourable, happy, bright, rosy, promising, propitious, opportune, timely, encouraging, hopeful, successful, fortunate, lucky. INAUSPICIOUS
austere stern, severe, harsh, strict, firm, inflexible, unbending, rigid, stringent,

grim, solemn, grave, serious, cold, unfeeling. LENIENT
abstemious, ascetic, self-denying, self-disciplined, Spartan, abstinent, sober, puritanical, chaste, pure, simple, unadorned. LUXURIOUS

austerity severity, harshness, strictness, firmness, rigidity, solemnity, coldness. LENIENCY
abstemiousness, asceticism, self-denial, self-discipline, abstinence, economy, privation, hardship. LUXURY

authentic genuine, true, veritable, real, pure, legitimate, valid, reliable, dependable, trustworthy, accurate, faithful, bona fide, authoritative. SPURIOUS

authenticate verify, prove, substantiate, validate, certify, confirm, seal, endorse, guarantee, attest, vouch for. DISPROVE

author writer, novelist, storyteller, biographer, essayist, poet, playwright, dramatist, composer, lyricist.
creator, originator, parent, inventor, designer, architect, producer, perpetrator.

authoritarian *adj*, despotic, dictatorial, domineering, strict, severe, disciplinarian, absolute, imperious, autocratic. LENIENT
n, disciplinarian, despot, dictator, autocrat.

authoritative official, legitimate, approved, authentic, reliable, true, definitive, decisive, conclusive, certain, sure, positive, imperative, ruling.
dictatorial, imperious, dogmatic, peremptory, commanding, assertive, arrogant. SUBORDINATE

authority power, dominion, supremacy, ascendancy, sway, sovereignty, rule, control, command, influence, direction, government. SUBORDINATION
permission, sanction, authorization, right, justification, warrant, licence, permit. BAN
expert, master, scholar, connoisseur, specialist, professional. NOVICE
evidence, testimony, say-so (*inf*), avowal, declaration.

authorize empower, commission, accredit, enable, entitle, license, legalize, sanction, ratify, permit, allow, warrant. FORBID

autocracy dictatorship, despotism, absolutism, tyranny, totalitarianism. DEMOCRACY

autocrat dictator, despot, tyrant, absolute ruler.

autocratic dictatorial, despotic, absolute, unlimited, all-powerful, tyrannical, totalitarian, oppressive, domineering, overbearing, imperious. DEMOCRATIC

automatic mechanical, self-activating, automated, mechanized, push-button. MANUAL
involuntary, unconscious, instinctive, reflex, spontaneous, mechanical, uncontrolled. DELIBERATE

autonomous self-governing, self-ruling, self-reliant, independent, free, unfettered. DEPENDENT

autonomy self-government, home rule, self-rule, independence, freedom. DEPENDENCE

autopsy post mortem, necropsy, dissection.

auxiliary *adj*, supplementary, accessory, ancillary, subsidiary, additional, extra, secondary, reserve, supporting, assisting, helping. ESSENTIAL
n, assistant, accessory, subordinate, aide, helper, right-hand man, second, supporter, partner, ally, confederate, associate. OPPONENT

avail *v*, benefit, profit, advantage, help, serve, be of use. HINDER
avail oneself of, use, exploit, make use of, take advantage of. WASTE
n, use, service, efficacy, benefit, good, profit, advantage, help.

available obtainable, accessible, to hand, attainable, handy, ready, convenient, at one's disposal. UNAVAILABLE

avalanche landslide, deluge, flood, inundation.

avant-garde experimental, innovative, progressive, unconventional, way-out (*inf*), modernistic. OLD-FASHIONED

avarice greed, greediness, cupidity, rapacity, covetousness, acquisitiveness, miserliness, parsimony, close-fistedness, meanness. LIBERALITY

avaricious greedy, rapacious, grasping, covetous, acquisitive, miserly, niggardly, parsimonious, close-fisted, mean, stingy. LIBERAL

avenge revenge, vindicate, retaliate, requite, repay, get even (*inf*), punish. PARDON

avenue approach, access, entrance, entry, way, path, passage, alley, drive, road, route, street, boulevard.

aver assert, affirm, asseverate, avow, predicate, state, declare, pronounce, say, allege, maintain. DENY

average *n*, mean, medium, norm, standard, rule. EXTREME
adj, mean, medium, median, middling, mediocre, passable, fair, not bad, indifferent, moderate, tolerable, normal, typical, usual, ordinary, commonplace, run-of-the-mill. EXCEPTIONAL
v, equate, even out, balance out, proportion.

averment assertion, affirmation, asseveration, avowal, statement, declaration, pronouncement, allegation. DENIAL

averse unwilling, indisposed, disinclined, reluctant, loath, opposed, hostile, inimical, adverse. READY

aversion loathing, repugnance, abhorrence, detestation, disgust, horror, antipathy, hatred, dislike, distaste, revulsion, opposition, hostility, reluctance, indisposition, unwillingness. LOVE

avert turn away, divert, deflect. DIRECT
ward off, avoid, forestall, prevent, preclude, fend off. ENCOURAGE

aviation flight, flying, aeronautics.

aviator aviatrix, airman, airwoman, flier, pilot, aeronaut.

avid keen, eager, enthusiastic, fervent, passionate, ardent, zealous, fanatical. APATHETIC
greedy, rapacious, acquisitive, avaricious, grasping.

avidity keenness, eagerness, impatience, longing, enthusiasm, ardour, zeal. APATHY
greed, greediness, rapacity, avarice, acquisitiveness, cupidity.

avocation hobby, pastime, recreation, amusement, diversion.
calling, vocation, trade, occupation, job, business, profession, employment, work.

avoid evade, elude, dodge, shun, shirk, refrain from, eschew, escape, avert, circumvent, steer clear of, keep away from. CONFRONT

avow affirm, assert, asseverate, aver, state, declare, proclaim, admit, acknowledge, recognize, confess. DENY

avowal assertion, affirmation, proclamation, declaration, averment, admission, acknowledgment, confession, profession, oath, testimony, deposition. DENIAL

await wait for, abide, expect, anticipate, look forward to, be ready for, be in store.

awake *v*, wake up, rouse, awaken, arouse, excite, stimulate, kindle, provoke, stir up, activate. LULL
adj, astir, waking, aware, conscious, alert, attentive, vigilant, watchful, lively, active. ASLEEP

awaken arouse, excite, stimulate, spur, kindle, rouse, provoke, incite, stir up, activate, animate. LULL

award *v*, give, grant, bestow, present, endow, confer, assign, allot, appoint, apportion, adjudge, decree. WITHDRAW
n, prize, trophy, medal, decree, verdict, endowment, grant, gift, bestowal, conferment.

aware conscious, sensible, cognizant, enlightened, apprised, informed, knowledgeable, mindful, awake, alert, appreciative, acquainted, familiar, conversant. UNAWARE

awareness perception, understanding, recognition, enlightenment, knowledge, cognizance, consciousness, sensibility, acquaintance, familiarity. IGNORANCE

away *adj*, absent, out, not present, elsewhere, abroad, gone, distant, remote. PRESENT
adv, off, hence, abroad, apart, far, at a distance, aside. NEAR
continuously, incessantly, relentlessly, interminably.

awe *n*, admiration, wonder, respect, reverence, amazement, dread, fear, terror. CONTEMPT
v, impress, amaze, overwhelm, daunt, intimidate, cow, subdue, frighten, alarm, dismay. REASSURE

awesome awe-inspiring, impressive, breathtaking, overwhelming, majestic, magnificent, venerable, formidable, daunting, intimidating, frightening, dreadful, fearsome. CONTEMPTIBLE

awful dreadful, terrible, fearful, dire, abominable, appalling, ghastly, horrendous, frightful, nasty, unpleasant, bad. WONDERFUL

awhile briefly, for a moment, for a short time.

awkward ungainly, graceless, clumsy, maladroit, inept, bungling, unskilful,

hamfisted, gauche, lumbering, uncouth, coarse, rough, crude, unpolished, oafish. DEXTEROUS
unwieldy, unmanageable, cumbersome, difficult, troublesome, inconvenient, inopportune, untimely, embarrassing.
perverse, trying, vexatious, stubborn, unhelpful, bloody-minded (*inf*). OBLIGING

awning canopy, tarpaulin, tilt, baldachin.

awry *adv*, askew, askance, amiss, wrongly, obliquely, off-centre, to one side, crookedly.
adj, askew, askance, amiss, wrong, oblique, slanting, off-centre, crooked, distorted, skew-whiff (*inf*). STRAIGHT

axe *n*, chopper, hatchet, cleaver, pickaxe.
v, cut, chop, fell, hew.
cancel, terminate, dismiss, discharge, cut back.

axiom truism, postulate, maxim, adage, aphorism, apophthegm, precept, dictum.

axiomatic self-evident, absolute, certain, manifest, unquestioned, indubitable, assumed, understood.

azure blue, sky-blue, cerulean, ultramarine.

B

babble *v*, prattle, gibber, blab, gossip, mutter, chatter, gabble, jabber, prate, mumble, murmur.
n, chatter, prattle, gabble, gibberish, drivel, nonsense, murmur, whisper.

babbler chatterbox, prattler, gabbler, gossip, blabbermouth.

babe baby, infant, nursling, suckling. ADULT
babe in arms, innocent, ingénue, novice, beginner.

babel hubbub, din, clamour, uproar, tumult, confusion, disorder, pandemonium, hullabaloo. QUIET

baby *n*, infant, babe, newborn, suckling, nursling, child, toddler, tot, youngest. ADULT
adj, tiny, miniature, minute, dwarf, small, little. GIANT
v, coddle, mollycoddle, pamper, pet, cosset, indulge, spoil.

babyish childish, infantile, puerile, immature, silly, foolish. ADULT

bacchanalia revelry, revel, orgy, saturnalia, carousal, debauch, spree, merrymaking, festival.

bacchanalian riotous, wild, drunken, orgiastic, debauched, licentious, unrestrained, merry, festive. SOBER

back *n*, rear, stern, reverse, posterior, end, hindquarters. FRONT
v, support, encourage, second, sustain, help, aid, assist, abet, finance, sponsor, subsidize, advocate, endorse, favour, countenance. OBSTRUCT
go back, move back, reverse, retreat, retire, recoil, withdraw. ADVANCE
back out, abandon, give up, withdraw, retreat, renege, chicken out (*inf*).
adj, rear, hind, hindmost, end, last. FRONT
earlier, former, past, bygone, previous, elapsed, overdue.
adv, backward, rearward, to the rear, behind. ONWARD

backbite malign, revile, defame, vilify, asperse, denigrate, run down, slander, calumniate, traduce, attack, abuse. PRAISE

backbiting defamation, denigration, aspersion, slander, calumny, malice, spitefulness, bitchiness (*inf*), vilification, mudslinging, gossip, scandalmongering. PRAISE

backbone spine, spinal column, vertebral column, vertebrae.
stamina, fortitude, mettle, courage, nerve, pluck, determination, resolution, firmness, character, moral fibre. WEAKNESS

backer patron, sponsor, benefactor, promotor, supporter, advocate, well-wisher. OPPONENT

background setting, context, environment, milieu, circumstances, breeding, upbringing, education, qualifications, experience, grounding, preparation.
in the background, unobtrusive, inconspicuous, behind the scenes, unnoticed, out of sight.

backhanded indirect, oblique, equivocal, ambiguous, double-edged, ironic, sarcastic.

backing support, aid, help, assistance, sponsorship, patronage, advocacy, endorsement, approval. OPPOSITION

backslide relapse, regress, revert, lapse, go wrong, go astray, sin, fall from grace.

backslider apostate, renegade, deserter, recreant, recidivist. ADHERENT

backward *adj*, slow, retarded, underdeveloped, dull, stupid, behind, tardy, late. ADVANCED
reluctant, hesitant, unwilling, averse, disinclined, loath, bashful, shy. FORWARD
adv, backwards, rearwards, behind, in reverse, retrogressively, back to front. FORWARDS

bad wicked, evil, villainous, immoral, depraved, corrupt, sinful, dishonest, criminal. VIRTUOUS
harmful, injurious, pernicious, detrimental, deleterious, unwholesome, noxious, vile. GOOD
inferior, poor, defective, imperfect, substandard, faulty, unsatisfactory.
rotten, mouldy, putrid, rancid, off, spoiled, tainted, contaminated.
naughty, mischievous, disobedient. WELL-BEHAVED
unpleasant, disagreeable, distressing, discouraging, unwelcome, unfortunate, adverse, serious, grave, severe, harsh. SPLENDID
sick, ill, unwell, miserable, wretched. WELL
not bad, fair, average, all right, passable, tolerable, so-so (*inf*), OK (*inf*).

badge emblem, device, insignia, sign, mark, token, stamp, brand.

badger harass, torment, plague, harry, persecute, worry, trouble, tease, bait, vex, annoy, try, hector, pester, nag.

badinage banter, raillery, teasing, chaff, repartee, persiflage.

baffle perplex, bewilder, confuse, confound, puzzle, mystify. ENLIGHTEN
frustrate, foil, balk, check, thwart, hinder, defeat. ABET

bag sack, pouch, container, receptacle, satchel, handbag, case, purse.

baggage luggage, suitcases, bags, belongings, effects, paraphernalia, things, gear, equipment.

baggy loose, ill-fitting, billowing, puffed out, bulging, slack, floppy, shapeless, lumpish. TIGHT

bail *n*, surety, security, bond, guarantee, warranty, pledge.
bail out, *v*, release, rescue, aid, assist, help, relieve.

bait *n*, lure, decoy, snare, enticement, allurement, temptation, inducement, incentive, bribe.
v, badger, tease, persecute, torment, harry, harass, hector, plague, worry, try, vex, annoy, bother.
lure, entice, tempt, seduce, beguile. REPEL

bake cook, braise, roast, scorch, sear, dry, parch, harden.

balance *v*, weigh, estimate, compare, consider, ponder.
poise, stabilize, adjust, level, square, match, equalize, counterbalance, offset, counteract, neutralize, compensate, make up for. UPSET
n, equilibrium, equipoise, evenness, symmetry, parity, equivalence.
equanimity, composure, self-possession, self-control, poise, aplomb, stability. AGITATION
remainder, rest, surplus, excess, residue, difference.

balcony terrace, veranda, loggia, gallery, upper circle.

bald hairless, bare, naked, uncovered, barren, bleak, plain, unadorned, simple, unvarnished, undisguised, outright, straightforward, blunt.

balderdash rubbish, nonsense, drivel, rot, trash, humbug, poppycock (*inf*), claptrap (*inf*), bombast, verbiage. WISDOM

bale bundle, package, pack, parcel, truss, bunch.

baleful harmful, injurious, ruinous, disastrous, pernicious, noxious, malevolent, menacing, ominous, sinister, evil. BENIGN

balk hesitate, shrink from, recoil, flinch, jib, stop, refuse, demur.
thwart, frustrate, baffle, hinder, confound, defeat, foil, check, prevent, disappoint. ABET

ball[1] sphere, globe, globule, drop.
bullet, pellet, shot, projectile.

ball[2] dance, hop (*inf*), party, soirée, social.

ballast weight, packing, filling, stabilizer, balance, counterweight, equilibrium, stability.

ballot poll, vote, election, referendum.

balm ointment, unguent, lotion, salve, cream, oil, liniment, embrocation. IRRITANT
comfort, consolation, solace, remedy, cure.

balmy mild, pleasant, clement, temperate, sweet, fragrant, scented, aromatic, soothing, mitigating, assuasive, sedative, healing. HARSH

bamboozle cheat, defraud, deceive, mislead, trick, hoax, dupe, hoodwink, con (*inf*), confuse, baffle, perplex, mystify.

ban *v*, prohibit, forbid, proscribe, interdict, outlaw, disallow, exclude, bar. PERMIT
n, prohibition, embargo, interdiction, proscription, taboo, proclamation, edict, decree. PERMISSION

banal trite, commonplace, everyday, clichéd, hackneyed, unoriginal, humdrum, ordinary, stereotyped. ORIGINAL

banality platitude, commonplace, cliché, truism, bromide (*inf*).

band[1] *n*, group, company, body, troop, gang, crew, party, society, association, club, horde, crowd. INDIVIDUAL
v, join, unite, combine, merge, affiliate, ally, confederate, gather, group. SEPARATE

band[2] *n*, strip, belt, girdle, ribbon, bandage, tie, cord, ligament, ligature, strap, bond, binding.

bandage *n*, ligature, dressing, compress, tourniquet, gauze, plaster, band, fillet.
v, dress, bind, swathe, wrap.

bandit brigand, outlaw, robber, thief, marauder, pirate, hijacker, gangster, desperado, highwayman, footpad.

bandy *v*, exchange, interchange, swap, trade, toss, throw, pass.
adj, bent, crooked, bowed, bow-legged. STRAIGHT

bane woe, misery, affliction, curse, plague, scourge, torment, pest, nuisance, blight, ruin, calamity, disaster, injury, harm. DELIGHT
poison, venom, toxin.

bang *n*, explosion, boom, shot, report, burst, thud, thump, crash, clap, peal, clash, clang.
blow, knock, stroke, hit, bump, thump, whack, slap.
v, knock, hit, bump, strike, bash (*inf*), thump, rap, hammer, pound.
boom, explode, crash, thump, clatter, echo, resound, ring, peal.
adv, precisely, directly, straight, headlong, smack (*inf*), suddenly, abruptly.

banish expel, eject, exile, deport, expatriate, outlaw, cast out, dismiss, repudiate, spurn, exclude, ostracize, abandon, dispel, get rid of. HARBOUR

banishment exile, deportation, expatriation, expulsion, repudiation, exclusion.

bank[1] *n*, shore, margin, border, edge, brink, side.
heap, pile, mound, knoll, ridge, embankment.

bank[2] *n*, depository, storehouse, hoard, store, stock, fund, reserve, savings, accumulation.

bank on, *v*, depend on, count on, rely on, trust, expect.

bankrupt insolvent, broke (*inf*), in debt, ruined, destitute, impoverished, depleted, lacking, deficient. AFFLUENT

bankruptcy insolvency, liquidation, ruin, failure, disaster, depletion, deficiency. AFFLUENCE

banner standard, flag, colours, ensign, streamer, pennant, banderole.

banquet feast, dinner, repast, revel, celebration, entertainment, regalement, treat, spread (*inf*).

banter *v*, chaff, tease, rib (*inf*), twit, ridicule, mock, jeer, deride, make fun of.
n, badinage, raillery, chaff, repartee, joking, mockery, ridicule, derision.

bar *n*, rod, rail, pole, shaft, crosspiece.
barrier, obstacle, barricade, hindrance, impediment, ban, prohibition, injunction, embargo, boycott. AID
counter, saloon, lounge, pub (*inf*), inn, tavern, hotel.
tribunal, bench, court.
v, prohibit, forbid, ban, hinder, obstruct, impede, stop, prevent, deter, restrain, exclude, ostracize. ALLOW

barb point, bristle, spine, quill, thorn, prickle.

barbarian *n*, savage, brute, ruffian, boor, ignoramus, philistine.
adj, primitive, savage, barbarous, uncivilized, unsophisticated, uncouth, boorish, vulgar. CIVILIZED

barbaric savage, brutal, cruel, inhuman, barbarous, uncivilized, wild, primitive, barbarian. HUMANE

barbarity cruelty, brutality, savagery, inhumanity, ruthlessness, viciousness. HUMANITY
barbarism, outrage, atrocity, enormity.
coarseness, vulgarity, crudity, rudeness. REFINEMENT

barbarous uncivilized, primitive, barbarian, uncouth, ignorant, uncultured, rough, rude, coarse, vulgar, crude. CIVILIZED brutal, savage, barbaric, cruel, inhuman, ferocious, vicious, ruthless. HUMANE

bare naked, nude, unclothed, undressed, stripped, denuded, uncovered, exposed, unprotected. CLOTHED
plain, simple, stark, bald, unadorned, unfurnished, empty, barren. ORNAMENTED

barefaced impudent, brazen, shameless, audacious, bold, undisguised, unconcealed, manifest, glaring, blatant, palpable, flagrant. CONCEALED

barely scarcely, only just, no more than, hardly, merely, just.

bargain *n*, agreement, arrangement, contract, compact, stipulation, deal, transaction, understanding, promise, pledge.
discount, reduction, giveaway, snip (*inf*), good buy.
v, haggle, barter, deal, trade, traffic.
agree, arrange, contract, pledge, promise.
bargain for, anticipate, expect, foresee, contemplate, imagine.

bark *v*, yelp, yap, bay, howl, snap, snarl, growl, shout, yell, bawl.
n, yelp, yap, howl, woof, snarl.

barmy crazy, idiotic, insane, daft, nuts (*inf*), silly, foolish, stupid. SENSIBLE

barrage bombardment, battery, volley, hail, deluge, torrent, plethora.

barrel cask, keg, vat, tank, vessel, container.

barren infertile, sterile, infecund, childless, unfruitful, unproductive, bare, arid, desolate, empty. FERTILE
futile, useless, fruitless, unprofitable, ineffectual, unavailing, vain. USEFUL

barricade *n*, barrier, obstruction, blockade, bulwark, obstacle, hindrance.
v, obstruct, block, blockade, bar, fortify, protect, defend, shut in.

barrier barricade, obstacle, obstruction, bar, blockade, fence, railing, wall, rampart, ditch, moat. GATE
hindrance, impediment, stumbling block, obstruction, obstacle, hurdle, limitation, restriction, restraint, difficulty. AID

barrister lawyer, counsel, solicitor, advocate.

barrow handcart, truck, wheelbarrow, handbarrow.

barter exchange, trade, swap, deal, traffic, haggle, bargain.

base[1] *n*, bottom, foot, foundation, support, stand, pedestal. TOP
basis, core, heart, essence, root, principal.
home, settlement, camp, headquarters, starting point.
v, establish, found, build, rest, hinge, depend.
station, locate, post.

base[2] *adj*, low, mean, despicable, vile, wicked, bad, evil, contemptible, abject, ignoble, dishonourable, disgraceful, shameful, depraved, immoral, worthless, wretched, miserable, pitiful, sorry, menial, lowly. NOBLE
false, fake, spurious, counterfeit, alloyed, impure, debased, cheap, inferior, poor. REFINED

baseless groundless, unfounded, unsubstantiated, unreasonable, unjustifiable. REASONABLE

bashful shy, timid, timorous, coy, diffident, modest, reserved, reticent, shrinking, sheepish, abashed, shamefaced. BOLD

bashfulness shyness, timidity, coyness, diffidence, modesty, reserve, reticence, constraint. BOLDNESS

basic fundamental, essential, intrinsic, inherent, underlying, primary, elementary. SUBSIDIARY

basics fundamentals, essentials, rudiments, brass tacks (*inf*), hard facts, practicalities, nitty-gritty (*inf*).

basis base, foundation, bottom, ground, cause, reason, principle, fundamental, essence, core, root.

bask revel, bathe, luxuriate, wallow, indulge oneself, enjoy, delight, savour, relish, lounge, lie, relax, laze.

bass deep, low, grave, sonorous, resonant. TREBLE

bastard *adj*, illegitimate, natural, baseborn. LEGITIMATE
abnormal, irregular, imperfect, inferior, impure, adulterated, counterfeit, fake, spurious.
n, illegitimate child, love child, natural child.
villain, rogue, scoundrel, wretch, cad, heel (*inf*), rotter (*inf*).

bastion citadel, fortress, stronghold, bulwark, support, prop, mainstay.

bat stick, club, mallet, racquet, cudgel.

batch set, lot, quantity, amount, group, bunch, collection, crowd, aggregation.

bath *n*, wash, washing, bathing, ablution, soak, scrub, shower, douche.

v, wash, bathe, scrub, soak, shower.

bathe wash, cleanse, rinse, immerse, soak, steep, wet, moisten, suffuse.
swim, float, paddle.

bathos anticlimax, comedown, triteness, superficiality, shallowness, sentimentality, mawkishness.

baton stick, wand, rod, staff, club, truncheon.

batten fatten, grow fat, flourish, thrive, prosper, gain.

batter beat, pound, pummel, thrash, lash, buffet, smite, hit, strike, assault, attack, hurt, injure, wear, bruise, deface, mar, shatter, smash, demolish, destroy.

battle *n*, fight, combat, engagement, skirmish, encounter, contest, action, war, hostilities. PEACE
conflict, campaign, struggle, strife, clash, dispute, debate.
v, fight, struggle, contest, combat, contend, strive, dispute, argue. AGREE

bauble trinket, trifle, toy, gewgaw, bagatelle, knick-knack, ornament.

bawdy obscene, blue, lewd, indecent, coarse, vulgar, rude, risqué, salacious, filthy, dirty, smutty. DECOROUS

bawl yell, shout, cry, vociferate, roar, bellow, howl. WHISPER
wail, lament, cry, weep, sob, blubber.

bay[1] *n*, cove, inlet, gulf, bight, sound, estuary.

bay[2] *n*, recess, alcove, niche, compartment.

bay[3] *v*, bark, yelp, howl, cry.

bazaar market, market-place, mart, exchange.
fête, fair, sale.

be exist, live, breathe.
occur, happen, take place, come about.
survive, persist, remain, stay, continue, endure, last.

beach shore, seashore, strand, sands, shingle, coast, seaside, littoral, margin, brink, rim.

beached aground, ashore, wrecked, grounded, stranded, marooned, high and dry, deserted, forsaken, abandoned.

beacon signal, flare, rocket, lighthouse, bonfire, warning, sign, mark, landmark, guidepost.

bead drop, droplet, globule, bubble, blob, spherule, pellet, ball.

beads necklace, necklet, pearls, choker, pendant, chaplet, rosary.

beak bill, mandible, nib, prow, bow, stem.

beaker cup, glass, mug, goblet, tankard.

beam *n*, plank, board, rafter, girder, support, joist.
ray, streak, shaft, flash, gleam, glint, glimmer.
v, shine, gleam, glitter, glisten, radiate, emit, transmit.
smile, grin. FROWN

beaming bright, brilliant, gleaming, shining, radiant, sunny, smiling, grinning, cheerful, joyful. DULL

bear carry, convey, transport, take, bring, move, waft. DROP
support, sustain, hold up, lift, shoulder, uphold.
endure, stand, tolerate, suffer, abide, brook, stomach, allow, permit, admit, submit to, put up with. RESIST
harbour, cherish, hold, maintain, keep, entertain. DISCARD
give birth to, bring forth, beget, engender, produce, generate, yield.

bear on, affect, concern, regard, relate to, pertain to.

bear out, confirm, substantiate, corroborate, prove, justify, vindicate.

bearable tolerable, supportable, endurable, admissible, passable. UNBEARABLE

beard *n*, whiskers, stubble, bristles.
v, confront, face, defy, oppose, brave.

bearer carrier, porter, messenger, agent, conveyor, courier, holder, incumbent, beneficiary, payee.

bearing behaviour, conduct, deportment, carriage, manner, attitude, posture, mien, demeanour, air, aspect.
relevance, connection, relation, pertinence.
direction, course, aim, position, location.

bearish surly, gruff, churlish, boorish, clumsy, rough, coarse, uncouth, rude. POLITE

beast brute, animal, creature, savage, monster, ogre, barbarian, swine.

beastly unpleasant, vile, nasty, mean, rotten, foul, loathsome, abominable, terrible, awful, disagreeable. SPLENDID
brutal, bestial, cruel, inhuman, savage, coarse, depraved. HUMANE

beat *v*, strike, hit, thrash, whip, flog, lash, cane, whack, batter, bash, pound, pummel,

hammer, knock, thump, cudgel, maul. CARESS
defeat, overcome, subdue, quell, vanquish, trounce, rout, conquer, outstrip, surpass, excel.
whisk, whip, blend, stir.
throb, pulsate, pound, thump, palpitate.
n, throb, pulsation, pulse, accent, rhythm.
blow, stroke, hit, lash, thump.
round, circuit, course, route, zone, area.
beaten defeated, conquered, subdued, baffled, thwarted. VICTORIOUS
trampled, trodden, worn, well-used. UNTRODDEN
beatific ecstatic, glorious, joyful, blissful, serene, heavenly, enchanting, rapturous. WOEFUL
beating defeat, conquest, rout, overthrow, downfall, ruin. SUCCESS
thrashing, spanking, flogging, whipping, caning, pasting (*inf*).
beatitude ecstasy, delight, joy, happiness, bliss, blissfulness, felicity, blessedness, saintliness, beatification.
beau admirer, suitor, escort, sweetheart, boyfriend, lover.
dandy, fop, ladies' man, popinjay.
beautiful attractive, lovely, fair, elegant, graceful, seemly, handsome, pretty, comely, good-looking, ravishing, stunning (*inf*). UGLY
beautify adorn, embellish, titivate, ornament, bedeck, array, enhance, garnish, gild, embroider, decorate. DISFIGURE
beauty comeliness, attractiveness, fairness, loveliness, prettiness, elegance, grace, glamour, charm. UGLINESS
belle, Venus, goddess, good-looker (*inf*).
advantage, benefit, attraction, boon, asset. DISADVANTAGE
because as, since, for, seeing that.
because of, owing to, on account of, thanks to, as a result of.
beck nod, signal, gesture, wave, summons.
beckon summon, invite, bid, signal, wave, gesticulate.
entice, lure, tempt, attract.
becloud dim, bedim, darken, obscure, befog, cloud, veil, confuse, obfuscate. ILLUMINATE
become grow, turn, get, develop into, change into, come to be.
suit, grace, enhance, embellish, befit.
becoming attractive, comely, pretty, pleasing, suitable, appropriate, fitting, seemly, in keeping. UNBECOMING
bed bunk, couch, divan, berth, cot, cradle, hammock.
bottom, base, foundation, layer, stratum, seam.
bedaub daub, smear, plaster, besmear, bespatter, splash, stain, smirch, deface, mar.
bedding bedclothes, covers, sheets, linen, blankets.
litter, straw, hay.
bedeck array, adorn, deck, festoon, ornament, embellish, decorate, garnish. STRIP
bedevil harass, torment, pester, plague, annoy, irritate, vex, confuse, muddle, confound.
bedew moisten, dampen, sprinkle, spray, wet.
bedim dim, darken, cloud, becloud, shadow, obscure, befog. ILLUMINATE
bedlam uproar, pandemonium, hubbub, clamour, chaos, confusion, commotion. QUIET
bedraggled untidy, unkempt, dishevelled, grimy, sodden, drenched, dripping. NEAT
beetle *v*, jut, project, overhang, protrude, stick out.
adj, overhanging, beetling, jutting, projecting, prominent.
befall *vi*, happen, occur, take place, supervene, chance, transpire, ensue.
vt, happen to, overtake, betide.
befitting suitable, appropriate, fitting, right, proper, seemly, becoming. UNSUITABLE
befog obscure, confuse, muddle, perplex, obfuscate, blur. CLARIFY
befool fool, dupe, trick, hoodwink, deceive, cheat, beguile, bamboozle, mislead, delude.
before *prep*, in front of, ahead of, prior to, earlier than. AFTER
adv, previously, formerly, beforehand, earlier, sooner, ahead, in advance. AFTERWARDS
befriend assist, help, aid, defend, protect, look after, stand by, support, encourage, patronize, favour, advocate. OPPOSE
befuddle confuse, muddle, perplex, bewilder, intoxicate, inebriate.

beg ask, request, entreat, beseech, pray, plead, supplicate, implore, crave, solicit, petition.
cadge, scrounge (*inf*), sponge off, solicit alms, seek charity.

beget father, sire, breed, generate, procreate, engender, create, produce, cause.

beggar *n*, pauper, down-and-out, mendicant, tramp, vagrant, cadger, scrounger (*inf*), sponger (*inf*), parasite.
v, impoverish, ruin, bankrupt. ASSIST
surpass, exceed, challenge, defy.

beggarly destitute, impoverished, poor, indigent, needy, wretched, miserable, pitiful, contemptible, abject, paltry, inadequate, meagre, mean, shabby, vile.

begin start, commence, arise, come into being, originate, inaugurate, institute, initiate, embark on, set about. END

beginner novice, learner, tyro, neophyte, recruit, initiate, pupil, apprentice, trainee, student, amateur. EXPERT

beginning start, commencement, opening, outset, dawn, birth, origin, source, creation, inception, initiation, inauguration. END

begrime soil, dirty, foul, sully, defile, tarnish, besmirch, blacken, bedaub, smear, spatter. CLEANSE

begrudge envy, grudge, resent.

beguile delude, deceive, cheat, trick, hoodwink, mislead, dupe, fool.
charm, delight, enchant, amuse, entertain, divert, cheer, solace.

behalf interest, benefit, advantage, good, part, side, sake.

behave act, function, operate, perform, work.
comport, conduct, bear, deport.
be good, toe the line, mind one's manners, obey. MISBEHAVE

behaviour conduct, deportment, comportment, demeanour.
manners, actions, habits, ways.

behead decapitate, decollate, guillotine, execute.

behest injunction, command, order, instruction, mandate, precept, demand, bidding, request, wish.

behind *prep*, after, following, later than, at the back of. BEFORE
supporting, on the side of, backing. AGAINST
adv, in the rear, following, after, afterwards, next. AHEAD
behindhand, late, in arrears, overdue, in debt.

behold *v*, see, look at, observe, eye, contemplate, view, regard, survey, watch, witness, discern, perceive. MISS
interj, look, see, mark, watch, observe.

beholden obliged, indebted, bound, obligated, grateful. UNGRATEFUL

behove befit, become, be fitting, be necessary, be incumbent upon.

being existence, actuality, reality, living, animation, presence. NONEXISTENCE
essence, substance, soul, spirit, nature.
creature, animal, thing, individual, body.

belabour beat, strike, hit, thrash, batter, pound, pummel.
attack, criticize, censure, berate, lay into. PRAISE

belated late, overdue, behindhand, tardy, delayed, postponed. PROMPT

belch burp (*inf*), eruct, eructate, hiccup.
emit, discharge, eject, spew, gush, disgorge, expel.

beleaguer besiege, surround, encompass, hem in, blockade, beset, assail. RELIEVE
harass, badger, plague, pester, bother, annoy, vex.

belie contradict, disprove, gainsay, deny, negate. CONFIRM
misrepresent, falsify, disguise, distort, gloss over.

belief faith, believing, conviction, confidence, assurance, trust, credence, view, opinion, notion, theory, feeling, impression. DISBELIEF
creed, doctrine, dogma, faith, ideology, religion.

believe be convinced, have faith, have confidence, trust, credit, accept, rely on, depend on. DOUBT
think, reckon, maintain, hold, opine, suppose, assume, imagine, gather, understand.

belittle disparage, decry, deprecate, depreciate, underestimate, undervalue, deride, scorn, sneer at, detract, diminish, minimize. EXTOL

bellicose aggressive, belligerent, pugnacious, warlike, militant, combative, contentious, quarrelsome. GENIAL

belligerent warlike, martial, militant, bellicose, hostile, antagonistic, aggressive, pugnacious, argumentative, quarrelsome. PEACEFUL

bellow roar, bawl, yell, cry, shout, blare, trumpet, howl, screech. WHISPER

belly abdomen, paunch, stomach, tummy (*inf*), gut.

belong be owned by, be the property of, be part of, be a member of, be associated with, relate to, go with, fit.

belongings possessions, property, effects, chattels, things (*inf*), stuff (*inf*), gear, paraphernalia.

beloved dear, dearest, darling, favourite, pet, cherished, treasured, precious, loved, adored, worshipped. HATED

below *prep*, under, underneath, beneath. ABOVE
less than, lower than, inferior to, subordinate to.
unbefitting, unworthy of, unbecoming.
adv, under, underneath, beneath, down, lower. ABOVE

belt band, girdle, sash, cummerbund, waistband.
zone, region, area, tract.

bemire soil, dirty, muddy, bedaub, begrime, spatter, smear, sully, defile. CLEANSE

bemoan lament, mourn, grieve over, bewail, deplore, regret, moan, wail. REJOICE

bemuse bewilder, baffle, confuse, muddle, perplex, puzzle, daze, stupefy, stun, overwhelm, amaze.

bench settle, form, pew, stall, seat.
workbench, trestle table, board, counter.
court, tribunal, judiciary, judge, magistrate.

bend *v*, curve, bow, crook, flex, deflect, deviate, diverge, veer, swerve, twist, contort, turn. STRAIGHTEN
stoop, crouch, squat, bow, incline, lean.
yield, submit, give way, bow, concede, agree. RESIST
mould, influence, dispose, sway, subdue, overwhelm.
n, curve, bow, arc, angle, turn, twist, zigzag, crook, hook.

beneath *prep*, below, under, underneath. ABOVE
unworthy of, unbefitting, undignified for.
lower than, inferior to, subordinate to, less than.
adv, below, under, underneath, down, lower. ABOVE

benediction blessing, grace, consecration, prayer, invocation, thanksgiving. CURSE

benefaction donation, contribution, gift, present, bequest, legacy, endowment, grant, alms, boon.
generosity, philanthropy, charity, beneficence, benevolence. AVARICE

benefactor patron, sponsor, donor, backer, supporter, helper, friend, well-wisher.

benefice living, office, sinecure, stipend, emolument.

beneficence generosity, liberality, bounty, charity, benevolence, kindness, unselfishness, altruism. AVARICE
gift, donation, benefaction, aid, relief.

beneficent generous, liberal, munificent, charitable, benevolent, benign, kind, helpful. HARD

beneficial helpful, useful, valuable, advantageous, profitable, favourable, good, wholesome, salutary, salubrious, healthy. UNWHOLESOME

benefit *n*, good, sake, interest, advantage, profit, gain, avail, use, service, help, aid, boon, blessing. LOSS
v, help, aid, avail, serve, profit, improve, promote, further, advantage. DAMAGE

benevolence kindness, compassion, goodwill, humanity, philanthropy, altruism, charity, beneficence, liberality. MALEVOLENCE

benevolent kind, kindly, benign, compassionate, humane, kind-hearted, good, unselfish, charitable, philanthropic, beneficent, bountiful, liberal. MALEVOLENT

benighted unenlightened, uncivilized, primitive, ignorant, backward. SOPHISTICATED

benign kind, kindly, benevolent, sympathetic, gentle, compassionate, genial, amiable, friendly, obliging, gracious. COLD
favourable, propitious, beneficial, advantageous, good, lucky. UNFAVOURABLE

bent *adj*, crooked, twisted, curved, bowed, arched, stooped, hunched. STRAIGHT
determined, set, resolved, decided, fixed, inclined, disposed.
n, inclination, tendency, disposition, leaning, aptitude, forte, flair, faculty, talent, predilection, partiality, liking, fondness, predisposition.

benumb deaden, numb, anaesthetize, blunt, stupefy, paralyse. STIMULATE
bequeath leave, will, bestow, endow, pass on, hand down, transmit, impart, grant, give.
bequest legacy, inheritance, endowment, settlement, trust, gift.
berate reprove, reprimand, chide, scold, rebuke, upbraid, castigate, tell off (*inf*), censure, vituperate, revile. COMMEND
bereave deprive, rob, dispossess, strip, divest, despoil. RESTORE
bereavement loss, deprivation, distress, affliction, misfortune, tribulation. CONSOLATION
bereft deprive, cut off, parted from, lacking, devoid, stripped, destitute.
berserk frenzied, insane, mad, enraged, violent, raging, rabid, wild, crazy, maniacal, uncontrollable. SUBDUED
berth bed, bunk, billet.
mooring, anchorage, harbour, dock, quay, wharf.
post, position, appointment, situation, job, employment.
v, dock, anchor, moor, land, tie up.
beseech implore, beg, entreat, pray, plead, supplicate, petition, adjure, crave, solicit, ask.
beset beleaguer, surround, encircle, encompass, assail, attack, harass, trouble, bother, badger, plague, perplex. RELIEVE
beside next to, alongside, adjacent to, near, close to.
compared with, next to, in contrast with.
besides *prep*, apart from, other than, except, excepting, in addition to, over and above.
adv, moreover, furthermore, in addition, as well, too, also.
besiege surround, encompass, hem in, blockade, lay siege to, beleaguer, beset, importune, harass, plague, hound. RELIEVE
besmear besmirch, smear, daub, bedaub, soil, dirty, spatter, begrime, defile, sully, stain, tarnish.
besotted infatuated, doting, smitten, intoxicated, befuddled, stupefied, foolish, confused, muddled.
bespatter splash, spatter, daub, bedaub, soil, dirty, begrime, besmear, besmirch, defile, sully.
bespeak order, engage, solicit, request, ask for.
denote, signify, indicate, betoken, suggest, imply, reveal, show, exhibit, display.
besprinkle sprinkle, scatter, strew, dust, dredge, bedew, moisten, spray, spatter.
best *adj*, finest, outstanding, excellent, first-rate, highest, supreme, leading, unsurpassed, perfect, superlative. WORST
n, choice, pick, flower, élite, cream, prime.
bestial brutish, beastly, brutal, savage, barbaric, inhuman, depraved, degraded, carnal, sensual, vile, sordid, low.
bestir stir, rouse, awaken, animate, get going (*inf*), activate, stimulate, exert, bustle, hasten, hurry. RESTRAIN
bestow confer, give, grant, accord, present, award, impart, bequeath, endow. WITHHOLD
bestrew strew, scatter, sprinkle, spread, sow, disseminate, broadcast. GATHER
bestride straddle, bridge, span, extend across, step over, dominate, tower over.
bet *v*, wager, stake, put money on, pledge, gamble, risk, speculate, hazard.
n, wager, gamble, ante, stake, pledge.
betide befall, chance, happen, occur, crop up, supervene, come to pass, ensue, transpire.
betoken denote, indicate, signify, represent, show, manifest, betray, proclaim, declare, bespeak, presage, augur, portend, bode. HIDE
betray inform on, double-cross, be disloyal, be treacherous, sell out (*inf*).
disclose, reveal, divulge, expose, tell, give away, let slip, show, exhibit, manifest, display. CONCEAL
conceive, mislead, delude, beguile, ensnare, trap, lure, seduce, lead astray, corrupt, undo.
abandon, desert, walk out on, forsake, jilt.
betroth engage, affiance, plight, pledge, promise.
betrothal engagement, marriage contract, plighting, troth, promise, pledge, vow.
better *adj*, superior, finer, surpassing, greater, preferable, more desirable. WORSE
improving, recovering, on the mend (*inf*), fitter, well, healthy. ILL
v, improve, ameliorate, advance, promote, further, amend, correct, rectify, reform. WORSEN
surpass, exceed, outstrip, beat, improve on.

betterment improvement, amelioration, edification. DETERIORATION

between mid, amidst, in the middle of, betwixt, among.

bevel angle, cant, chamfer, oblique, slant, slope, incline.

beverage drink, potable, potation, libation, draught.

bevy flock, swarm, flight, pack, troop, group, company, throng, bunch, collection, band, troupe, party.

bewail lament, mourn, bemoan, grieve for, deplore, regret, sorrow, wail, moan. REJOICE

beware take care, watch out, look out, be careful, mind, take heed, avoid, steer clear of, guard against.

bewilder confuse, puzzle, perplex, confound, muddle, distract, bemuse, baffle, mystify, daze, stupefy. ENLIGHTEN

bewilderment confusion, perplexity, puzzle, muddle, bafflement, mystification, stupefaction. ENLIGHTENMENT

bewitch enchant, spellbind, fascinate, captivate, entrance, hypnotize, charm, beguile, allure, enrapture, transport. REPEL

beyond above, over, past, further than, apart from, out of reach of, more than, over and above. WITHIN

bias *n*, tendency, inclination, proclivity, predisposition, bent, propensity, leaning, predilection, partiality, prejudice, favouritism, one-sidedness. IMPARTIALITY
v, influence, predispose, incline, sway, prejudice.

bibulous alcoholic, boozy (*inf*), intemperate. TEETOTAL

bicker quarrel, squabble, wrangle, row, fight, spar, argue, dispute, disagree. AGREE

bid *v*, offer, tender, proffer, propose, submit.
command, order, demand, require, direct, instruct, summon, enjoin, invite, request, ask. FORBID
say, wish, tell.
n. offer, tender, proposal, submission, price, amount, sum.
attempt, try, endeavour.

bidding order, command, behest, injunction, instruction, summons, invitation, request.

big large, great, huge, massive, enormous, immense, colossal, gigantic, vast, spacious, voluminous, burly, hulking, bulky, fat, gross. SMALL
important, significant, prominent, influential, notable, famous, principal, main. INSIGNIFICANT
generous, magnanimous, unselfish, altruistic, gracious, benevolent. MEAN
arrogant, boastful, pompous, conceited, inflated, pretentious. HUMBLE

bigot fanatic, zealot, dogmatist, sectarian, racialist, sexist, chauvinist.

bigoted intolerant, narrow-minded, illiberal, dogmatic, opinionated, obstinate, prejudiced, biased. TOLERANT

bigotry prejudice, one-sidedness, bias, discrimination, narrow-mindedness, intolerance, dogmatism, obstinacy. TOLERANCE

bile anger, spleen, ill humour, irritability, irascibility, peevishness, rancour, bitterness, resentment, indignation.

bilious queasy, sick, nauseated, liverish.
bad-tempered, irritable, peevish, cross, grumpy, testy, touchy. AFFABLE

bilk thwart, balk, frustrate, foil.
deceive, cheat, defraud, trick, bamboozle.
elude, dodge, escape.

bill[1] account, statement, invoice, reckoning, tally, score, charge, fee.
poster, notice, placard, advertisement, bulletin, circular, leaflet.
list, agenda, programme, schedule.

bill[2] beak, nib, mandible.

billet *n*, quarters, accommodation, lodgings, rooms, barracks.
v, quarter, accommodate, lodge, assign station.

billow *v*, roll, surge, swell, heave, puff out, balloon.
n, wave, breaker, roller, surge, swell, deluge, rush, outpouring.

billowy rolling, heaving, surging, swelling, rippling, undulating, swirling. SMOOTH

bin receptacle, container, box, can, case, crate.

bind *v*, tie, tie up, truss, secure, fasten, strap, lace, lash, wrap, bandage, encircle, gird. LOOSE
restrict, confine, restrain, hamper, encumber. LIBERATE
oblige, force, compel, constrain, obligate, require, prescribe.

n, nuisance, bore, predicament, quandary, dilemma.

binding *adj*, obligatory, compulsory, imperative, irrevocable.
n, cover, covering, fastening, band.

biography life, history, life story, memoir, profile, account.

birth childbirth, parturition, delivery, confinement.
nativity, genesis, origin, beginning, source, creation, emergence, appearance. DEATH
ancestry, descent, extraction, line, lineage, family, blood, race, stock, pedigree, parentage, background, breeding.

bisect halve, cut in two, divide, split, intersect, cross. UNITE

bisexual androgynous, hermaphrodite, hermaphroditic, epicene, gynandrous, AC /DC (*inf*).

bishop prelate, patriarch, suffragan, overseer.

bishopric diocese, see, episcopacy, episcopate.

bit morsel, crumb, scrap, sliver, fragment, piece, particle, jot, iota, atom, mite, whit, tittle, speck, grain, drop, trace, hint. LOT

bite *v*, chew, gnaw, champ, munch, crunch, nibble, nip, snap, tear, rend, pierce, wound.
smart, sting, tingle, burn, corrode, eat into.
grip, hold, grasp, clutch, clasp.
n, nip, sting, wound.
morsel, mouthful, taste, snack.

biting piercing, keen, nipping, sharp, piquant, pungent, penetrating, cold, freezing. MILD
stinging, caustic, cutting, incisive, mordant, trenchant, sarcastic, scathing. GENIAL

bitter acrid, pungent, biting, harsh, sharp, sour, acid, tart, vinegary. SWEET
acrimonious, resentful, embittered, sour, morose, hostile, sullen, crabbed.
intense, severe, harsh, fierce, virulent, piercing, biting, stinging, cruel. MILD
distressing, sore, painful, grievous, poignant, harrowing, heartbreaking. CHEERY

bitterness acridity, pungency, harshness, sharpness, sourness, tartness. SWEETNESS
acrimony, resentment, malice, rancour, spleen, pique, grudge, hostility, animosity, asperity.
intensity, severity, harshness, fierceness, cruelty, virulence. MILDNESS

bizarre strange, odd, weird, extraordinary, grotesque, peculiar, unusual, fantastic, outlandish, eccentric. NORMAL

blab divulge, reveal, let slip, tell, tattle, prate, prattle, gossip.

black dark, inky, sooty, swarthy, dusky, ebony, jet, pitchy. WHITE
murky, dingy, dark, sombre, gloomy, dismal, depressing, mournful, forbidding, ominous. BRIGHT
dirty, filthy, soiled, grubby, grimy. CLEAN
evil, villainous, heinous, nefarious, wicked, atrocious, horrible. GOOD

blacken soil, begrime, dirty, darken, cloud, obscure.
defame, slander, calumniate, besmear, besmirch, sully, defile, vilify, traduce, malign, denigrate. VINDICATE

blackguard scoundrel, rogue, rascal, villain, wretch, knave, bounder (*inf*). GENTLEMAN

blacklist exclude, ban, bar, black, boycott, reject, repudiate, proscribe, ostracize. ACCEPT

blackmail *n*, extortion, exaction, hush money (*inf*), bribe, ransom, protection (*inf*), tribute.
v, extort, exact, bribe, milk, squeeze, bleed (*inf*), coerce, compel, force.

blamable culpable, blameworthy, in the wrong, guilty, liable, answerable, responsible. BLAMELESS

blame *v*, censure, condemn, criticize, find fault with, disapprove, reproach, reprove, chide, rebuke. PRAISE
accuse, charge, hold responsible, ascribe, attribute. VINDICATE
n, censure, condemnation, disapproval, criticism, reproach, reproof. APPROVAL
accusation, charge, incrimination, responsibility, culpability, fault, guilt. VINDICATION

blameless inculpable, innocent, guiltless, in the clear, above suspicion, unimpeachable, irreproachable, unsullied, unblemished, spotless, immaculate, perfect, faultless, virtuous. BLAMEWORTHY

blameworthy reprehensible, inexcusable, indefensible, discreditable, shameful, blamable. BLAMELESS

blanch whiten, bleach, fade, pale, blench. COLOUR

bland mild, gentle, soft, soothing, benign, suave, affable, amiable, agreeable. HARSH dull, boring, uninteresting, insipid, nondescript, unexciting. PIQUANT

blandishments flattery, blarney, compliments, cajolery, coaxing, wheedling, fawning, ingratiation.

blank *adj*, empty, void, unfilled, bleak, plain, unadorned, bare, unmarked, spotless. FILLED

expressionless, deadpan, poker-faced (*inf*), impassive, uninterested, indifferent, apathetic. ALERT

confused, confounded, at a loss, perplexed, disconcerted, dumbfounded, uncomprehending.

outright, absolute, utter, complete, unqualified, unmitigated. PARTIAL

n, void, emptiness, vacuum, space, gap.

blanket *n*, cover, rug, carpet, cloak, mantle, sheet, wrapping, envelope, coating, layer, film.

v, cover, overlie, envelop, coat, cloak, mask, conceal. UNCOVER

blare proclaim, broadcast, trumpet, blast, roar, bellow, resound, clamour, sound, blow, toot.

blarney flattery, blandishments, compliments, cajolery, soft soap (*inf*), fawning, adulation. BLUNTNESS

blasé satiated, surfeited, cloyed, jaded, hardened, bored, weary, apathetic, indifferent, offhand, nonchalant, unmoved. EXCITED

blaspheme swear, curse, execrate, damn, revile, abuse, profane, desecrate. WORSHIP

blasphemous impious, profane, sacrilegious, irreligious, irreverent, ungodly. REVERENT

blasphemy impiety, profanity, swearing, execration, sacrilege, irreverence. REVERENCE

blast *v*, explode, blow up, burst, shatter, demolish, destroy, annihilate, ruin.

blight, wither, shrivel, kill.

n, explosion, discharge, burst, eruption, boom, bang, roar, thunder.

blare, honk, toot, bellow, peal, clang.

gust, squall, flurry, gale, storm.

blight, pestilence, infestation, affliction.

blatant conspicuous, obvious, glaring, flagrant, brazen, bald, naked, sheer, outright. CONCEALED

clamorous, noisy, obstreperous, vociferous, loud, deafening. QUIET

blaze *v*, flame, burn, flare up, flash, shine, gleam.

n, flame, fire, inferno, conflagration.

glow, glimmer, flash, flare, glare, light, radiance, brilliance.

outburst, eruption, storm, blast, torrent, flare-up.

blazon proclaim, broadcast, publicize, blaze, herald, trumpet. SUPPRESS

bleach blanch, whiten, etiolate, fade, lighten. DARKEN

bleak bare, exposed, open, unsheltered, barren, desolate, windswept, cold, raw, chilly. SHELTERED

gloomy, dismal, dreary, cheerless, depressing, hopeless, discouraging. CHEERFUL

bleary blurred, hazy, dim, indistinct, watery, rheumy.

bleed *vt*, draw blood, drain, sap, exhaust, extract, milk, extort.

vi, lose blood, exude, ooze, trickle, flow, spurt, gush.

blemish *n*, defect, fault, imperfection, spot, mark, speck, stain, scratch, blotch.

v, flaw, impair, deface, mark, spot, stain, taint, sully, tarnish, spoil, mar.

blench shrink, recoil, flinch, shy, shudder, quail, cower, hesitate, falter, shirk, avoid, evade, shun. FACE

blend *v*, mix, mingle, intermingle, combine, amalgamate, fuse, coalesce, merge, unite. SEPARATE

harmonize, go with, suit, fit, complement. CLASH

n, mixture, combination, compound, amalgamation, synthesis.

bless praise, extol, glorify, magnify, hallow, sanctify, consecrate, dedicate, anoint. CURSE

bestow, endow, grant, give, favour.

blessed sacred, holy, hallowed, divine, revered, adored, beatified.

happy, blissful. joyful, contented. SAD

favoured, fortunate, lucky, endowed. WRETCHED

blessing benediction, grace, thanksgiving, invocation, prayer, praise, honour, glory. CURSE

approval, sanction, consent, favour, good wishes.

boon, advantage, benefit, godsend, bounty, gain, profit, favour, good fortune.

blight *n*, disease, infestation, pestilence, canker, fungus, scourge, plague, bane, curse, woe, affliction.
v, blast, wither, shrivel, destroy, crush, ruin, wreck, dash, frustrate, disappoint, damage, mar.

blind *adj*, sightless, unseeing, unsighted, eyeless. SEEING
ignorant, unaware, unconscious, uninformed, unenlightened, oblivious, neglectful, thoughtless, inconsiderate, heedless, inattentive. AWARE
injudicious, unreasoning, unthinking, rash, reckless, hasty, impetuous, careless, mindless. CAREFUL
closed, shut, blocked, without exit. OPEN
n, shade, screen, curtain, shutter, cover.
mask, cloak, camouflage, disguise, feint, façade, stratagem, ruse.

blink *v*, wink, nictitate, flutter, bat, squint, peer.
flicker, twinkle, glitter, gleam, sparkle.
blink at, ignore, disregard, overlook, turn a blind eye to, condone.
n, glance, glimpse, wink, flutter.
twinkle, gleam, flash, glimmer.

bliss blissfulness, ecstasy, happiness, joy, rapture, elation, felicity, gladness. MISERY

blissful happy, joyful, ecstatic, euphoric, elated. MISERABLE

blister pustule, vesicle, bleb, boil, carbuncle, abscess, ulcer, cyst, wen, sore, bubble, swelling.

blithe merry, gay, jolly, cheerful, carefree, joyful, happy, vivacious, lively, animated, buoyant, sprightly, jaunty. DEJECTED
heedless, indifferent, casual, nonchalant, thoughtless.

blitz attack, bombardment, onslaught, offensive.

bloat swell, puff up, inflate, balloon, distend, dilate, enlarge. SHRINK

blob drop, globule, bead, ball, bubble, pearl, lump, mass, spot, dab.

block *n*, lump, mass, chunk, piece, cake, bar, brick.
blockage, obstruction, hindrance, impediment, bottleneck, jam, stoppage, obstacle, barrier, blockade. PASSAGE
v, obstruct, impede, blockade, check, stop, halt, arrest, thwart, deter, clog, plug. CLEAR

blockade barrier, obstacle, impediment, restriction, closure, siege.
block, obstruct, close, besiege.

blockhead dunce, simpleton, dolt, idiot, fool, numbskull, nitwit, noodle, dope, half-wit, ignoramus.

blond blonde, light, fair, flaxen, fair-haired. BRUNETTE

blood gore, life fluid, plasma.
ancestry, descent, family, extraction, lineage, race, stock, kinship, kindred, relations.
feeling, temper, spirit, temperament, disposition.

bloodcurdling terrifying, horrifying, fearful, hair-raising, spine-chilling, appalling, frightening.

bloodless pale, wan, pallid, pasty, sickly, anaemic, ashen. RUDDY
listless, languid, sluggish, torpid, unfeeling, cold, indifferent.

bloodshed carnage, slaughter, butchery, murder, massacre.

bloodthirsty murderous, savage, ferocious, vicious, cruel, inhuman, brutal, barbaric, ruthless.

bloody gory, sanguinary, bleeding, bloodstained.
bloodthirsty, murderous, savage, ferocious, cruel.

bloom *n*, blossom, flower, inflorescence, bud, efflorescence, flowering.
freshness, beauty, radiance, flush, lustre, prime, heyday, health, vigour. DECADENCE
v, blossom, flower, bud, burgeon, blow, open. WITHER
flourish, prosper, thrive, grow, wax. FADE

blossom *n*, bloom, flower, bud, floret, flowers.
v, bloom, flower, burgeon, bud, blow. WITHER
develop, mature, bloom, thrive, flourish. DECLINE

blot *n*, spot, stain, smudge, mark, blotch.
blemish, taint, stain, flaw, blur, disgrace.
v, absorb, dry, soak up.
sully, spot, soil, mar, spoil, disfigure, tarnish, disgrace, dishonour. CLEAR
blot out, cancel, erase, expunge, obliterate, efface, destroy, eliminate, obscure, darken, shadow. PERPETUATE

blotch patch, spot, splodge, smudge, blot, mark, stain, blemish.

blow[1] *v*, breathe, exhale, expel, pant, puff.

waft, fan, drive, move, sweep, whirl, spread.
sound, blast, whistle, toot, play.
blow out, extinguish, snuff, douse, put out.
blow up, explode, go off, detonate, burst, shatter, bomb.
exaggerate, enlarge, distend, inflate, swell.
n, blast, gust, puff, breath.
blow[2] *n*, hit, stroke, knock, thump, buffet, slap, punch, rap, whack, bang.
shock, calamity, disaster, bombshell, disappointment, setback, misfortune, affliction.
blubber sob, cry, weep, wail, whine.
bludgeon *n*, cudgel, club, truncheon.
v, coerce, force, bully, hector, browbeat.
blue azure, sapphire, cobalt, turquoise, aquamarine, ultramarine, navy.
dejected, depressed, unhappy, sad, melancholy, gloomy, glum, downcast, downhearted, despondent. CHEERFUL
obscene, indecent, coarse, risqué, bawdy, smutty, dirty, near the knuckle (*inf*).
blueprint design, pattern, model, template, prototype, plan, sketch, draft.
blues depression, dejection, melancholy, despondency, doldrums, dumps (*inf*). ELATION
bluff[1] *v*, mislead, deceive, delude, pretend, sham, feign.
n, deceit, fraud, pretence, feint, show, bravado, bluster.
bluff[2] *adj*, hearty, genial, good-natured, open, blunt, frank. RESERVED
n, cliff, ridge, crag, scarp, headland, promontory, bank.
blunder *v*, stumble, flounder, err, bungle, botch, miss, misjudge, mistake. SUCCEED
n, error, mistake, oversight, slip, gaffe, faux pas, clanger (*inf*), indiscretion.
blunt *adj*, dull, unsharpened, rounded, worn, pointless. SHARP
bluff, unceremonious, plain, frank, open, candid, straightforward, tactless, outspoken, rude, impolite, abrupt, brusque, curt. TACTFUL
v, dull, deaden, numb, weaken, soften, alleviate. SHARPEN
blur *v*, dim, obscure, becloud, befog, make indistinct. CLARIFY
blot, stain, spot, smear, smudge, sully, tarnish, mar.
n, haze, fog, confusion, obscurity, indistinctness. CLARITY
blot, stain, spot, smear, smudge, blemish.
blurred hazy, fuzzy, blurry, indistinct, vague, unclear, out of focus. CLEAR
blush *v*, redden, flush, colour, go red, glow. BLANCH
n, flush, reddening, colour, rosiness, glow. PALLOR
bluster *v*, swagger, boast, vaunt, brag, roar, storm, bully, domineer, hector.
n, boasting, bravado, swaggering, bluff, boisterous, tumult, commotion. RETICENCE
blustery windy, gusty, squally, stormy, tempestuous, wild, blusterous, boisterous. QUIET
board *n*, plank, panel, slat, lath, timber.
food, meals, provisions, victuals.
committee, council, panel, directors.
v, get on, embark, mount, enter, go aboard. ALIGHT
lodge, house, put up, accommodate, feed.
boast *v*, brag, vaunt, crow, exaggerate, swagger, bluster, flaunt, show off, swank (*inf*).
n, brag, vaunt, bragging, bluster, gasconade, rodomontade. MODESTY
pride, treasure, gem, pride and joy.
boastful bragging, vaunting, vain, conceited, egotistical, cocky, swollen-headed, swanky (*inf*). MODEST
boat vessel, craft, yacht, dinghy, canoe, barge, ferry, ship.
bob bounce, jerk, nod, duck, quiver, waggle.
bob up, emerge, pop up, appear, materialize.
bode presage, portend, betoken, signify, augur, import, predict, foretell, foreshadow.
bodily *adj*, physical, corporeal, material, carnal, fleshly, sensual, actual, tangible. SPIRITUAL
adv, wholly, entirely, completely, altogether, collectively, en masse.
body trunk, torso, physique, build, figure.
corpse, cadaver, carcass, stiff (*inf*).
person, individual, being, creature, mortal.
crowd, throng, multitude, group, collection, party, company, band, association, corporation, confederation. INDIVIDUAL
substance, mass, whole, bulk, essence, majority. PART

density, solidity, firmness, substance, consistency.

bog swamp, marsh, quagmire, fen, morass, slough.

boggle start, take fright, shy, be alarmed, be surprised.
hesitate, falter, vacillate, waver, shrink from, demur.

bogus false, counterfeit, sham, fake, phoney (*inf*), spurious. GENUINE

boil[1] *v*, seethe, bubble, foam, froth, simmer, stew. COOL
fume, rage, storm, be angry.

boil[2] *n*, furuncle, carbuncle, tumour, ulcer, pustule, blister, gathering, sore.

boisterous lively, unruly, unrestrained, rowdy, noisy, loud, vociferous, obstreperous, clamorous, riotous, uproarious. QUIET
tumultuous, tempestuous, stormy, blustery, raging, turbulent. CALM

bold brave, fearless, valiant, lion-hearted, daring, dauntless, courageous, intrepid, heroic, audacious, adventurous. TIMID
insolent, rude, brazen, brash, shameless, impudent, pert, cheeky, forward, confident.
prominent, striking, conspicuous, eye-catching. FAINT

boldness bravery, valiance, courage, audacity, bravura. TIMIDITY
insolence, rudeness, shamelessness, impudence, cheek, forwardness. MODESTY
prominence, conspicuousness. FAINTNESS

bolster *v*, support, prop up, brace, hold up, maintain, reinforce, strengthen, boost, aid, help.
n, pillow, cushion, pad.

bolt *n*, bar, latch, catch, lock, fastening, rod, pin, peg.
arrow, dart, shaft, missile, projectile.
vt, fasten, secure, latch, lock, bar. UNBOLT
gulp, devour, wolf, gobble, cram, stuff.
vi, abscond, flee, escape, run away, fly, dash, rush. STAY

bomb *n*, explosive, torpedo, mine, shell, grenade.
v, shell, bombard, torpedo, strafe.

bombard attack, assail, barrage, pelt, harass, pester.

bombast pomposity, grandiloquence, magniloquence, rant, bluster, bravado, braggadocio, fustian.

bombastic pompous, grandiloquent, magniloquent, grandiose, fustian, pretentious, high-flown, turgid, flatulent, verbose, ranting, declamatory.

bond *n*, cord, oand, ligament, ligature, tie, fastening, chain, fetter, manacle, shackle.
link, tie, connection, affinity, attachment, union.
contract, compact, agreement, obligation, pledge, guarantee, promise.
v, bind, fasten, fuse, connect. SEPARATE

bondage slavery, servitude, captivity, imprisonment, confinement, duress, subjugation. FREEDOM

bonny fair, pretty, comely, beautiful, handsome, sweet, lovely, fine. UGLY
chubby, plump, bouncing, round, healthy, buxom.
cheerful, blithe, merry, joyful, gay, jolly. MISERABLE

bonus award, reward, gift, bounty, premium, extra, dividend, honorarium, gratuity, commission, perquisite, perk (*inf*).

booby dunce, fool, simpleton, idiot, blockhead.

book *n*, volume, tome, tract, text, novel, manual, work, publication.
v, reserve, engage, charter, schedule, programme.
register, enter, record, log, put down.

bookish studious, learned, erudite, scholarly, intellectual, academic, pedantic. ILLITERATE

boom *v*, resound, reverberate, roar, thunder, bang, blast.
prosper, thrive, flourish, develop, increase, gain. DECLINE
n, roar, thunder, crash, blast, bang.
rise, increase, development, upsurge, boost. DECLINE

boon blessing, benefit, advantage, godsend, grant, favour, gift, present. DRAWBACK

boor lout, oaf, churl, bumpkin, rustic, clodhopper, peasant, barbarian, philistine.

boorish loutish, oafish, clumsy, awkward, rustic, uncouth, coarse, ill-bred, vulgar, uncivilized, churlish, gruff, rude. REFINED

boost *v*, promote, advertise, publicize, plug (*inf*), encourage, raise, lift, increase, expand, support, assist, further, improve, push.

n, encouragement, help, support, promotion, improvement, increase, rise, push, thrust.

bootless unavailing, useless, futile, vain, fruitless, ineffective, worthless, abortive. USEFUL

booty spoils, plunder, pillage, loot, haul (*inf*), swag (*inf*), takings.

booze drink, alcohol, liquor, beer, wine, spirits.

border *n*, boundary, frontier, limit, bound, edge, margin, fringe, rim, hem, skirt, verge, brink. CENTRE
v, adjoin, abut, impinge, touch, join, connect.

border on, verge on, approach, resemble, come close to.

bore[1] *v*, drill, mine, pierce, perforate, penetrate.
n, hole, tunnel, shaft, calibre.

bore[2] *v*, tire, weary, fatigue, jade, vex, annoy, bother. EXCITE
n, pest, nuisance, bother, drag (*inf*), pain (*inf*).

boredom weariness, dullness, tedium, monotony, ennui, apathy. EXCITEMENT

boring dull, tedious, monotonous, repetitious, routine, humdrum, flat, unvaried, tiresome, wearisome. EXCITING

borough town, township, municipality.

borrow take, cadge, scrounge, appropriate, adopt, usurp, pirate, steal, plagiarize, imitate. LEND

bosh nonsense, balderdash, rubbish, rot.

bosom chest, breast, bust.
heart, soul, mind, spirit, emotions, feelings.
centre, heart, core, depths, recesses, midst, protection, shelter.

boss[1] *n*, employer, supervisor, superintendent, overseer, manager, director, foreman, master, leader, chief, governor (*inf*). EMPLOYEE
v, employ, supervise, direct, manage, command, control.

boss around, bully, domineer, oppress, tyrannize.

boss[2] *n*, stud, knob, protuberance, umbo.

bossy domineering, overbearing, authoritarian, imperious, arrogant. MEEK

botch *v*, bungle, spoil, mar, muff, mismanage, mess up, screw up (*inf*), blunder. ACCOMPLISH
mend, patch, cobble.
n, mess, hash, miscarriage, failure, blunder, bungle. SUCCESS

both the two. NEITHER

bother *v*, trouble, annoy, irritate, vex, pester, harass, plague, worry, disturb, upset, perplex, perturb. COMFORT
n, trouble, annoyance, vexation, irritation, nuisance, inconvenience, upset, problem, difficulty, fuss, flurry.

bottom *n*, base, foot, floor, ground, bed, depths, foundation, basis. TOP
underside, underpart, underneath, sole. TOPSIDE
seat, rump, buttocks, rear, posterior, backside (*inf*), behind (*inf*), bum (*inf*), fundament.
origin, root, source, root, essence, core, heart.
adj, lowest, last, basic, fundamental. TOP

bottomless unfathomable, abysmal, deep, immeasurable, infinite, boundless, unlimited.

bough branch, limb, stem, stalk, shoot, twig. TRUNK

bounce *v*, rebound, recoil, spring, jump, leap, bound, bob.
n, springiness, elasticity, give, resilience.
spring, leap, jump, bound.
vitality, energy, liveliness, go (*inf*), pep. LETHARGY

bound[1] *adj*, tied, fastened, shackled, fettered. FREE
certain, sure, destined, fated. UNLIKELY
obliged, forced, compelled, constrained, required.

bound[2] *v*, spring, leap, jump, vault, bounce, skip, hop, prance, caper.
n, spring, leap, jump, vault, bounce, hop.

bound[3] *n*, limit, boundary, border, confine, margin.
v, limit, restrict, confine, border, enclose, surround, circumscribe, demarcate.

boundary border, perimeter, circumference, limit, confine, bound, barrier, pale, frontier, margin, edge, extremity, termination.

boundless unlimited, infinite, endless, immense, vast, immeasurable, untold. LIMITED

bountiful plentiful, abundant, ample, copious, profuse, lavish, luxuriant. MEAGRE
generous, liberal, bounteous, princely, beneficent, munificent, magnanimous, benevolent. MISERLY

bounty generosity, liberality, charity, beneficence, philanthropy, almsgiving. MEANNESS
largess, gift, present, donation, grant, award, bonus, premium, reward.

bouquet bunch, posy, nosegay, spray, corsage, garland, wreath.

bourgeois middle class, conservative, conventional, traditional, unimaginative, materialistic. ARISTOCRATIC

bout fight, contest, conflict, encounter, match.
spell, period, session, spree, turn, fit.

bow[1] *v*, salaam, kowtow, bob, curtsy, genuflect, kneel, nod.
incline, stoop, bend, curve, flex, arch, warp, droop. STRAIGHTEN
submit, yield, surrender, give in, accept, comply. RESIST
subdue, crush, conquer, vanquish, depress, weigh down.
n, salaam, bob, curtsy, genuflection, nod.

bow[2] *n*, prow, beak, stem.

bowels intestines, entrails, guts, viscera, innards (*inf*), insides (*inf*).
depths, interior, belly, core. SURFACE

bower arbour, alcove, recess, grotto, shelter, summerhouse.

bowl basin, receptacle, vessel, dish, plate, saucer.

box[1] *n*, carton, package, case, chest, trunk, casket, receptacle, container.
v, encase, pack, wrap, confine.

box[2] *v*, spar, fight.
cuff, buffet, strike, hit.
n, cuff, buffet, stroke, blow.

boy lad, youth, youngster, stripling. MAN

boycott ostracize, shun, refuse, spurn, reject, black, blacklist, blackball, ban, prohibit, proscribe, embargo, bar, exclude.

boyfriend beau, date, young man, lover, sweetheart, suitor, admirer.

boyish young, youthful, juvenile, childish, immature, puerile. ADULT

brace *v*, support, prop, steady, reinforce, strengthen, fortify, bind, fasten, tie, tighten.
n, support, prop, strut, spar, truss, bracket.
pair, couple.

bracing invigorating, stimulating, restorative, tonic, refreshing, exhilarating, crisp, brisk. RELAXING

bracket support, prop, corbel, console, shelf, brace.
group, category, division, class, status.

brackish salty, briny, saline.

brag *v*, boast, vaunt, crow, swagger, bluster, gasconade, flaunt, flourish.
n, boast, boasting, vaunt, bluster, gasconade. MODESTY

braggart brag, braggadocio, boaster, show-off, big mouth (*inf*), blusterer, swaggerer.

braid weave, interweave, plait, twine, intertwine, lace, interlace. UNRAVEL

brainless stupid, foolish, thoughtless, witless, senseless, idiotic. WISE

brains mind, sense, intellect, reason, intelligence, understanding, shrewdness, common sense. STUPIDITY

brainy clever, intelligent, smart, bright. STUPID

brake *n*, curb, rein, restraint, control, check.
v, slow down, decelerate, moderate, check, halt, stop. ACCELERATE

branch *n*, limb, bough, arm, shoot, ramification, spray.
offshoot, tributary, affluent, channel.
division, subdivision, section, department, wing, office.
v, ramify, diverge, fork. CONVERGE

branch out, expand, extend, develop, diversify.

brand *n*, kind, sort, type, grade, quality, make.
mark, stamp, emblem, label, trademark, symbol.
stigma, disgrace, infamy, blot, stain, taint. HONOUR
v, mark, label, stamp, burn.
stigmatize, denounce, disgrace, discredit.

brandish flourish, wield, swing, wave, shake, flaunt, exhibit, display.

brash rash, hasty, precipitate, reckless, foolhardy, impulsive, impetuous. CAUTIOUS
insolent, impudent, rude, audacious, bold, forward, brassy, brazen, cheeky, saucy. MODEST

brass audacity, cheek, gall, nerve (*inf*), boldness, effrontery, impertinence, impudence, assurance, presumption.

brat urchin, guttersnipe, child, kid (*inf*), youngster, rascal, whippersnapper.

bravado brag, braggadocio, boast, boasting, swagger, vaunting, bluster, bombast. MODESTY

brave *adj*, courageous, valiant, heroic, gallant, dauntless, daring, fearless, intrepid, bold, plucky. COWARDLY
v, confront, face, defy, challenge, dare.

bravery courage, valour, heroism, gallantry, daring, fearlessness, boldness, mettle, pluck, guts (*inf*). COWARDICE

brawl *v*, fight, wrangle, tussle, scuffle, wrestle, scrap (*inf*), dispute, argue, quarrel, bicker, squabble, row. AGREE
n, fight, wrangle, scrap (*inf*), punch-up (*inf*), fracas, fray, affray, broil, row, rumpus, uproar, tumult, quarrel, dispute, altercation.

brawny strong, powerful, muscular, sinewy, strapping, lusty, sturdy, robust, stalwart, athletic, herculean. WEAK

bray heehaw, neigh, whinny, call, roar, blare, hoot, bellow.

brazen bold, audacious, forward, brassy, brash, barefaced, shameless, immodest, impudent, insolent, saucy, pert, impertinent. MODEST

breach rupture, fracture, break, crack, fissure, rift, gap, opening, chasm.
violation, infringement, infraction, contravention, transgression, trespass. OBSERVANCE
separation, schism, alienation, estrangement, dissension, difference, variance, disagreement, quarrel. RECONCILIATION

bread nourishment, nutriment, sustenance, food, fare, provisions, aliment.
money, cash, funds, dough (*inf*).

breadth width, broadness, span, spread. LENGTH
magnitude, amplitude, vastness, expanse, extent, range, scope, size, measure, dimensions. NARROWNESS
latitude, liberality, freedom, openness, broad-mindedness.

break fracture, snap, crack, rend, sever, split, divide, separate, smash, shatter, shiver, splinter, disintegrate, demolish, destroy, wreck. MEND
violate, infringe, disobey, breach. OBEY
weaken, enervate, enfeeble, tame, cow, subdue, impair, cripple. STRENGTHEN
discontinue, break off, interrupt, halt, stop, suspend, pause, rest. CONTINUE
appear, emerge, erupt, dawn, burst forth.
reveal, disclose, divulge, let out, betray, tell, inform, impart.

break down, collapse, fall apart, fail, stop working, go to pieces, crack up (*inf*).

break in, train, accustom, habituate, condition, initiate, prepare.
interrupt, butt in, intrude, enter, invade, barge in.

break out, begin, start, commence, emerge, erupt.

break through, penetrate, pass, get past, succeed, achieve.

break up, divide, separate, dissolve, dismantle, split, part, disband, disperse, scatter, end, terminate. UNITE
n, fracture, crack, split, gap, breach, rupture, rift, opening, fissure.
pause, hiatus, interruption, recess, respite, suspension, intermission.
opportunity, advantage, chance, stroke of luck.

breakdown collapse, downfall, failure, ruin. RESTORATION
analysis, itemization, dissection, review, summary.

breakthrough advance, development, progress, step forward, discovery, invention.

breakwater mole, groyne, jetty, sea wall.

breast chest, front, thorax, bosom, bust, udder, teat, tit (*inf*), boob (*inf*).
heart, soul, emotions, feelings, conscience.

breath respiration, breathing, inhalation, exhalation, air, gasp, pant, wheeze.
odour, aroma, whiff, vapour.
pause, respite, rest, breather, break.
hint, suggestion, whisper, murmur, sigh, gust, puff, waft.
animation, life, vitality, existence.

breathe respire, inhale, exhale, gasp, wheeze, pant, puff, sigh.
exist, live, be alive.
say, utter, articulate, voice, whisper, murmur.
imbue, instil, infuse, impart.

breathless gasping, panting, winded, out of breath, exhausted, spent.
eager, agog, excited, open-mouthed, amazed, thunderstruck, anxious, on tenterhooks.

breathtaking awesome, awe-inspiring, impressive, magnificent, stunning (*inf*), exciting, thrilling. UNINSPIRING

breed *v*, bear, produce, bring forth, engender, beget, procreate, propagate, reproduce, generate.

rear, raise, bring up, nurture, foster, educate, train, teach, school, instruct, discipline.
create, produce, generate, originate, cause, bring about, arouse.
n, race, stock, strain, variety, kind, sort, type, species, pedigree, lineage, progeny, family, extraction.

breeding reproduction, propagation, procreation, bearing, begetting.
training, education, upbringing, development, background, ancestry, manners, bearing, conduct, refinement, culture, civility, politeness.

breeze light wind, zephyr, gust, flurry, waft, puff, breath of air, draught. HURRICANE

breezy windy, fresh, airy, blowy. CALM
carefree, casual, light-hearted, cheerful, blithe, buoyant, sprightly, lively, vivacious, jaunty.

brevity conciseness, terseness, succinctness, pithiness. PROLIXITY
briefness, shortness, transience, ephemerality.

brew ferment, infuse, boil, stew, steep, soak, prepare, make.
plot, hatch, contrive, devise, concoct, design, plan.

bribe *v*, suborn, corrupt, square, tempt, entice, lure, reward.
n, inducement, enticement, reward, backhander (*inf*), graft, hush money (*inf*).

bridal nuptial, conjugal, matrimonial, marital, connubial, wedding, marriage.

bridge *n*, span, arch, flyover, viaduct, overpass.
v, span, traverse, cross, connect, unite, join. DIVIDE

bridle *n*, curb, restraint, check, control, halter.
v, curb, restrain, check, control, govern, master. RELEASE
bristle, be indignant, raise one's hackles, get angry.

brief *adj*, short, fleeting, transitory, transient, ephemeral, momentary, temporary. LONG
concise, terse, succinct, pithy, laconic, curt, abrupt, brusque. LENGTHY
n, abstract, synopsis, outline, summary, epitome, digest.
v, instruct, inform, fill in (*inf*), enlighten, explain, prepare, advise.

briefly in brief, in short, in a nutshell, concisely.
momentarily, in passing, fleetingly, hurriedly.

brigade group, party, troop, squad, unit, team, crew, corps, company.

brigand bandit, robber, outlaw, ruffian, thug, desperado, gangster, marauder, plunderer.

bright luminous, shining, brilliant, radiant, gleaming, glittering, sparkling, flashing, glowing, glossy, lustrous, resplendent, glorious, dazzling, vivid, intense. DULL
intelligent, clever, smart, acute, keen, sharp, astute, quick-witted. STUPID
cheerful, happy, gay, merry, jolly, genial, lively, vivacious. MISERABLE
favourable, auspicious, promising, encouraging, rosy.
clear, transparent, translucent, lucid, limpid. MUDDY

brighten illuminate, lighten, clear, grow bright, shine, polish, enhance. DARKEN
enliven, cheer, gladden, hearten, encourage, perk up, buck up (*inf*). DISHEARTEN

brilliance brightness, radiance, brilliancy, lustre, sheen, glitter, sparkle, splendour, magnificence. DULLNESS
excellence, distinction, talent, genius, wisdom, cleverness. MEDIOCRITY

brilliant bright, radiant, shining, sparkling, glittering, lustrous, intense, vivid, dazzling, splendid, magnificent. DULL
excellent, outstanding, exceptional, distinguished, illustrious, eminent, famous, accomplished, expert, talented, gifted, intelligent, clever, bright, brainy. MEDIOCRE

brim rim, lip, edge, brink, margin, verge. CENTRE

brindled mottled, speckled, patched, spotted, dappled, streaked, tabby.

brine salt water, sea water, sea, saline solution, pickle.

bring bear, carry, convey, conduct, lead, usher, escort, accompany, take, fetch. REMOVE
cause, engender, produce, result in.
draw, pull, attract, prompt, force, compel.
bring about, cause, effect, occasion, accomplish, achieve, realize.
bring in, yield, fetch, return, produce, profit, earn.

bring up, raise, rear, nurture, train, educate, teach.
propose, put forward, raise, mention, introduce, broach.

brink border, edge, rim, margin, verge, threshold, bank, shore, boundary, limit. CENTRE

brisk lively, active, animated, vigorous, energetic, agile, nimble, spry, quick, alert. SLUGGISH
sharp, keen, crisp, fresh, invigorating, bracing. OPPRESSIVE

bristle *n*, hair, whisker, barb, spine, prickle.
v, stand up, rise, prickle.
be indignant, be angry, bridle, seethe, flare up.
swarm, teem, crawl, be alive, abound.

brittle fragile, frail, delicate, crisp, breakable, frangible, crumbly, friable. FLEXIBLE

broach introduce, suggest, mention, bring up, open, propose, advance.
open, tap, pierce, uncork, break into. SEAL

broad wide, ample, vast, large, extensive, spacious, roomy, capacious. NARROW
wide-ranging, full, comprehensive, sweeping, all-embracing, universal, general. LIMITED
vulgar, coarse, indecent, blue, gross.

broadcast *v*, transmit, relay, show, air, publish, proclaim, announce, advertise, disseminate, spread.
n, show, programme, transmission.

broaden widen, enlarge, amplify, expand, swell, develop, augment, increase. RESTRICT

broad-minded liberal, tolerant, indulgent, permissive, unbiased, dispassionate, open-minded, catholic. NARROW-MINDED

broadside attack, assault, bombardment, criticism, censure, abuse.

brochure leaflet, pamphlet, booklet, handbill, circular, advertisement.

broil *n*, quarrel, dispute, row, brawl, scuffle, wrangle, fray, fracas.
v, quarrel, dispute, brawl, wrangle.

broke penniless, insolvent, bankrupt, ruined, skint (*inf*). RICH

broken shattered, smashed, fractured, ruptured, torn, rent, separated, destroyed. MENDED
imperfect, defective, feeble, weakened, spent, exhausted, run-down, demoralized, beaten.
discontinuous, interrupted, disconnected, fragmentary, intermittent, spasmodic. CONTINUOUS
halting, imperfect, hesitant, disjointed, stammering. FLUENT

brokenhearted inconsolable, desolate, sorrowful, grief-stricken, miserable, wretched, heartbroken, crestfallen, disappointed. DELIGHTED

broker agent, middleman, intermediary, factor, dealer.

brooch pin, clasp.

brood *v*, ponder, muse, meditate, reflect, ruminate, dwell on.
n, litter, clutch, offspring, family, young, progeny, issue.

brook[1] *n*, stream, beck, rivulet, rill, burn.

brook[2] *v*, bear, endure, suffer, stand, abide, tolerate, put up with (*inf*), allow.

brother sibling, kinsman, comrade, mate, companion, friend, colleague, associate, partner. SISTER

brotherhood fraternity, society, association, club, league, union, guild.
brotherliness, comradeship, friendliness, fellowship, camaraderie.

brotherly fraternal, friendly, affectionate, kind, sympathetic, benevolent, philanthropic. UNKIND

brow forehead, temple, front, eyebrow, face, countenance, appearance.
brink, verge, edge, rim, crown, summit, peak, top.

browbeat bully, intimidate, cow, overbear, domineer, badger, hector.

brown chestnut, bronze, copper, rust, auburn, ginger, tan, tawny, chocolate, coffee, hazel, umber, brunette.
tanned, bronzed, sunburnt. PALE

browse scan, glance at, skim, dip into, leaf through, peruse, look around.
nibble, crop, feed, graze.

bruise *v*, contuse, injure, damage, batter, pound, crush, mark, discolour, blacken.
offend, injure, wound, hurt.
n, contusion, discoloration, mark, blemish, injury.

brunt shock, force, full force, impact, violence, stress, strain.

brush[1] *n*, broom, besom, hairbrush, paintbrush.
skirmish, clash, encounter, engagement, contest, fight, scrap (*inf*).
v, sweep, wipe, clean, dust, groom.

touch, graze, stroke, kiss, scrape.
brush up, relearn, revise, study, polish.
brush² *n*, scrub, thicket, undergrowth, bushes, copse.
brush-off rejection, snub, slight, rebuff, cold shoulder.
brusque curt, abrupt, short, gruff, bluff, blunt, rude, unceremonious. POLITE
brutal cruel, inhuman, pitiless, merciless, savage, ferocious, vicious, barbarous, ruthless, remorseless. HUMANE
harsh, severe, gruff, rude, uncivil, callous, heartless, unfeeling. GENTLE
coarse, crude, gross, vulgar, brutish, uncouth, carnal, sensual. REFINED
brutality cruelty, inhumanity, savagery, ferocity, harshness, severity, barbarism, atrocity, pitilessness, ruthlessness. HUMANITY
brute *n*, animal, beast, creature.
barbarian, savage, monster, ogre, devil, fiend, swine.
adj, physical, bodily, carnal, sensual, bestial, savage, brutish, coarse, rude, uncivilized.
instinctive, mindless, unthinking.
bubble *n*, blob, drop, bead, globule, blister, vesicle.
v, foam, froth, seethe, boil, fizz, effervesce.
gurgle, burble, babble, murmur.
buccaneer pirate, corsair, freebooter, privateer, sea-rover.
buck spring, jump, leap, prance, jerk, throw, unseat.
buck up, cheer up, encourage, brighten, hearten.
hasten, hurry, speed up, get a move on.
buckle *n*, clasp, clip, fastener, catch, hasp.
v, bow, bend, warp, distort, contort, twist, bulge, crumple, collapse, cave in.
fasten, secure, close, clasp.
bud *n*, shoot, germ, sprout, burgeon.
v, sprout, shoot, burgeon, germinate, grow, develop, burst forth. WITHER
budge move, stir, go, shift, push, dislodge, give way.
budget *n*, estimate, statement, cost, funds, resources, allocation, allowance.
v, plan, cost, estimate, allocate.
buffer bumper, shock absorber, cushion, fender, shield, guard.
buffet¹ *n*, cafeteria, snack bar, counter, bar, table, sideboard.
buffet² *v*, knock, bump, batter, pound, strike, hit, beat, box, thump, slap.
n, knock, bump, stroke, slap, cuff, hit, blow, thump.
buffoon jester, clown, harlequin, fool, comic, comedian, joker, wag.
buffoonery clowning, jesting, drollery, tomfoolery, silliness, nonsense. WISDOM
bug *n*, germ, virus, bacterium, infection, disease.
flaw, defect, error, fault, imperfection.
v, irritate, annoy, vex, bother, pester, harass, plague.
eavesdrop, tap, listen in.
bugbear bogey, hobgoblin, ogre, nightmare, bane, pet hate, *bête noire*, anathema.
build *v*, erect, put up, raise, construct, make, fabricate, assemble, put together, form. DEMOLISH
base, establish, found, originate, institute.
build up, develop, increase, expand, amplify, intensify, strengthen, reinforce.
n, physique, body, figure, form, shape.
building edifice, erection, construction, structure, house, pile.
bulbous rounded, swollen, bloated, bulging.
bulge *v*, swell, expand, dilate, distend, balloon, protrude, stick out.
n, swelling, lump, bump, protuberance, protrusion, projection. HOLLOW
bulk size, volume, mass, magnitude, dimensions, substance, largeness, immensity, bulkiness.
majority, preponderance, greater part, lion's share, body, mass, most. MINORITY
bulky large, big, massive, huge, enormous, colossal, unwieldy, cumbersome, unmanageable, awkward. SMALL
bulletin announcement, news flash, statement, report, communiqué, dispatch.
bully *n*, browbeater, ruffian, tough, hector, tormentor, persecutor, oppressor, intimidator.
v, browbeat, intimidate, overbear, domineer, hector, coerce, terrorize, torment, persecute, harass, tyrannize.
bulwark rampart, fortification, redoubt, bastion, outwork, buttress.
buffer, guard, security, support, mainstay.
bump *v*, knock, bang, strike, hit, collide, crash.
jostle, bounce, jolt, jar.

bump into, come across, meet, encounter, run into, chance upon.
n, blow, knock, bang, crash, collision, impact, shock, jar, jolt.
swelling, lump, protuberance.
bumper generous, abundant, plentiful, excellent, exceptional, large, jumbo (*inf*), whopping (*inf*), massive. MEAGRE
bumpkin rustic, peasant, yokel, clown, oaf, boor, lubber, clod.
bumptious conceited, vain, arrogant, self-assertive, pushy (*inf*), overbearing, cocky. MODEST
bunch cluster, clump, collection, assortment, group, bundle, sheaf, bouquet, tuft, batch, lot, heap, pile, mass.
bundle bunch, sheaf, collection, batch, parcel, package, pack, packet, bale, heap, pile, stack.
bungle botch, mismanage, mess up, spoil, mar, screw up (*inf*). ACCOMPLISH
bungler botcher, fumbler, incompetent, novice, dunce, duffer (*inf*), butterfingers (*inf*). ADEPT
bungling awkward, clumsy, maladroit, gauche, incompetent, inept, ham-fisted (*inf*). ADROIT
bunker container, bin, chest, tank.
obstacle, hazard.
bunkum nonsense, claptrap, balderdash, rubbish, twaddle, bunk (*inf*), rot (*inf*), poppycock (*inf*).
buoy *n*, float, marker, signal, beacon, guide.
v, cheer, hearten, encourage, sustain, support. DEPRESS
buoyancy lightness, weightlessness, floatability. HEAVINESS
cheerfulness, joy, high spirits, gaiety, liveliness, animation. DESPONDENCY
buoyant light, weightless, floating, floatable. HEAVY
cheerful, gay, bright, breezy, light-hearted, lively, vivacious, animated, carefree, blithe. DESPONDENT
burden *n*, load, weight, millstone, onus, responsibility, encumbrance, impediment, trouble, affliction, trial, worry, strain, sorrow.
cargo, freight, load, capacity, tonnage.
v, load, weigh down, saddle, oppress, overload, afflict, trouble, encumber, tax. RELIEVE
bureau desk, chest, dresser.
department, office, agency, branch, division.
burglar housebreaker, robber, thief, picklock, safe-cracker.
burial burying, interment, inhumation, entombment, funeral, obsequies. EXHUMATION
burlesque *n*, caricature, parody, satire, lampoon, travesty, take-off (*inf*).
adj, caricatural, parodic, ludicrous, comic, mocking, satirical, ironical, mock-heroic, hudibrastic.
burly sturdy, stout, stocky, thickset, well-built, strong, powerful, hefty, strapping. FRAIL
burn flame, blaze, flare, flicker, glow, smoulder.
ignite, light, set on fire, kindle, incinerate. EXTINGUISH
scorch, char, singe, sear, toast, parch, scald.
smart, sting, tingle.
burning flaming, blazing, fiery, hot, glowing, ardent, fervent, intense, passionate, vehement, earnest. COOL
urgent, pressing, crucial, vital, essential. UNIMPORTANT
burnish polish, shine, buff, furbish, glaze, brighten. DULL
burrow *n*, tunnel, hole, den, lair, retreat.
v, dig, excavate, scoop out, tunnel.
bursar treasurer, cashier.
burst *v*, explode, blow up, puncture, split, crack, rupture, break, bust (*inf*), shatter.
erupt, rush, gush, spout, surge.
n, explosion, blast, blasting, break, split, rupture, breach.
eruption, outburst, torrent, gush, outbreak, spate, fit.
bury inter, inhume, entomb, lay to rest. EXHUME
cover, conceal, hide, secrete.
sink, embed, submerge, engulf, immerse, engross.
bush shrub, hedge, thicket, undergrowth, brush, scrub.
bushy thick, shaggy, luxuriant, fuzzy, bristly.
business occupation, trade, craft, profession, employment, work, job, vocation, calling, pursuit, career. LEISURE
company, firm, organization, concern, partnership.
commerce, trade, dealings, industry, transaction.

affair, concern, problem, matter, issue, responsibility, duty, function.

businesslike efficient, orderly, methodical, systematic, thorough, assiduous, correct, professional.

bust chest, bosom, breast.

bustle *v*, hurry, rush, scamper, scurry, scuttle, stir, fuss, flutter.
n, fuss, flurry, activity, commotion, stir, ado, hurry, haste. CALM

busy occupied, engaged, employed, engrossed, involved. FREE
industrious, diligent, sedulous, assiduous, active, energetic, on the go (*inf*), bustling, astir. IDLE
nosy, inquisitive, fussy, officious, interfering, meddling.

busybody meddler, snooper, nosy parker (*inf*), eavesdropper, gossip, scandalmonger.

but *conj*, yet, still, on the contrary, however, nevertheless.
prep, except, save, barring, notwithstanding.
adv, only, merely, just, simply.

butcher *v*, slaughter, massacre, kill, slay, murder, assassinate, mutilate, destroy.
n, slaughterer, killer, murderer, assassin, destroyer.

butchery slaughter, massacre, carnage, blood bath, murder, bloodshed.

butt[1] *n*, stock, shaft, handle, end, stub.

butt[2] *n*, target, object, subject, victim, laughing stock.

butt[3] *v*, push, shove, ram, poke, prod, bump, knock.
butt in, interfere, meddle, intrude, interrupt, chip in (*inf*).

butt[4] *n*, cask, barrel.

buttocks rump, hindquarters, rear, posterior, seat, behind (*inf*), bottom, bum (*inf*).

buttonhole accost, waylay, catch, grab, detain, importune, bore.

buttress support, stay, prop, strut, brace, shore.

buxom plump, healthy, lusty, ample, full-bosomed, voluptuous, hearty, lively, jolly, attractive, comely, bonny. THIN

buy purchase, pay for, procure, obtain, acquire, get. SELL
bribe, corrupt, suborn.

buzz hum, murmur, drone, ring, purr, whisper, hiss.

by *prep*, through, via, over, past, along, beside, near, next to, at, on, before.
adv, near, aside, past, beyond.

bygone past, gone by, departed, former, erstwhile, previous, ancient, of old. FUTURE

bypass *v*, avoid, get round, circumvent, overlook, neglect, ignore.

bystander onlooker, spectator, observer, witness, watcher, viewer, passer-by.

byword slogan, motto, epithet, saying, proverb, maxim, adage, aphorism, precept.

C

cab taxi, taxicab, minicab, hackney.

cabal clique, coterie, faction, junta, league, party, gang, coalition, confederacy.
plot, intrigue, conspiracy, scheme.

cabaret show, floor show, entertainment, nightclub, club, discotheque, disco (*inf*).

cabbalistic mystic, occult, secret, mysterious, cryptic, obscure, esoteric. PATENT

cabin shed, hut, cottage, shack, chalet, lodge, shanty, hovel.
room, apartment, compartment, berth.

cabinet dresser, commode, cupboard, chiffonier, chest, locker, case.
council, assembly, ministry, administration, committee.

cable line, wire, rope, cord.
cablegram, telegram, message.

cache hiding place, repository, store, hoard, stockpile, supply, reserve.

cackle cluck, crow, squawk, quack.
chuckle, giggle, snigger, titter, laugh.
chatter, gabble, jabber, prattle, prate, babble.

cacophonous discordant, dissonant, inharmonious, jarring, harsh, strident, grating, raucous, cacophonic. HARMONIOUS

cacophony discord, dissonance, stridency, jarring, jar, caterwauling. CONCORD

cad scoundrel, rogue, rascal, knave, rotter (*inf*), heel (*inf*), bounder (*inf*).

cadaver corpse, body, remains, stiff (*inf*).

cadaverous deathly, deathlike, ghastly, pallid, pale, ashen, wan, haggard, gaunt, emaciated. RUDDY

cadence intonation, tone, modulation, inflection, accent, rhythm, lilt, swing.

cadre nucleus, core, key group, framework, infrastructure.

café cafeteria, snack bar, bistro, restaurant, teashop, tearoom, coffee bar.

cage *n*, enclosure, pen, pound, box, aviary.
v, confine, fence in, coop up, impound, imprison, incarcerate, restrain, restrict. FREE

cagey cautious, guarded, wary, discreet, noncommittal, evasive. FRANK

cajole coax, wheedle, persuade, beguile, tempt, entice, lure, entrap, inveigle, flatter, blandish, dupe.

cajolery coaxing, wheedling, persuasion, beguilement, temptation, enticement, flattery, blandishments, blarny, soft soap (*inf*), sweet talk (*inf*).

cake *n*, lump, block, bar, slab, piece, mass.
pastry, bun, tart, patisserie, gâteau, biscuit.
v, solidify, congeal, harden, bake, encrust.

calamitous disastrous, catastrophic, dire, devastating, ruinous, ill-starred, ill-fated, unfortunate, unlucky, adverse, deplorable, dreadful, tragic, woeful. FORTUNATE

calamity disaster, catastrophe, misfortune, adversity, hardship, affliction, trouble, setback, reverse, blow, trial, tribulation, distress, woe. BLESSING

calculate compute, reckon, work out, count, enumerate, measure, gauge, estimate, value, assess, weigh, consider.

calculated aimed, adapted, designed, planned, intended, considered, intentional, deliberate, premeditated.

calculating crafty, scheming, devious, cunning, sly, shrewd, sharp, cautious, wary, politic, circumspect, far-sighted. DIRECT

calculation computation, reckoning, working out, estimation, forecast, valuation, assessment.
foresight, forethought, prudence, care, caution, discretion, circumspection, wariness, deliberation. RASHNESS

calendar almanac, chronology, list, schedule, register, agenda.

calibre gauge, diameter, bore.
capacity, ability, faculty, talent, gifts, endowment, distinction, merit, worth, quality.

call *v*, shout, cry, yell, exclaim, call out. WHISPER
name, dub, christen, entitle, designate, label, term, style, proclaim, announce.
summon, invite, bid, convene, convoke, muster, assemble. DISMISS
ring, ring up, telephone, phone.
rouse, arouse, waken, wake up, awaken.
call for, demand, require, necessitate, involve, entail.
fetch, pick up, collect.
call off, cancel, abandon, postpone.
call on, visit, look up, drop in on.
invoke, appeal to, call upon, request.
n, shout, cry, exclamation, yell, scream.
summons, signal, appeal, request, invitation, command, claim, demand.
need, cause, occasion, grounds, excuse, reason, justification.

calling vocation, mission, career, profession, occupation, métier, trade, craft, business, job, work, pursuit.

callous unfeeling, insensible, insensitive, hard, hardened, obdurate, cold, unsympathetic, indifferent, uncaring, apathetic, hard-hearted, heartless. TENDER

callow green, inexperienced, naive, ingenuous, jejune, immature, simple, unsophisticated, guileless. EXPERIENCED

calm *adj*, serene, tranquil, peaceful, still, smooth, quiet, mild. STORMY
placid, composed, self-possessed, collected, unruffled, unexcited, unmoved, cool, impassive, relaxed, sedate, imperturbable. AGITATED
v, pacify, placate, appease, mollify, still, quiet, hush, lull, allay, assuage, soothe, alleviate, compose, relax, sedate, tranquillize. AGITATE
n, calmness, peace, serenity, tranquillity, stillness, lull, smoothness, quiet, hush. STORM

calmness calm, peacefulness, serenity, tranquillity, quietness, stillness. DISTURBANCE
composure, self-possession, placidity, coolness, equanimity, poise, sang-froid. AGITATION

calumniate slander, libel, defame, vilify, malign, asperse, denigrate, blacken, traduce, detract, revile, abuse, insult. EULOGIZE

calumnious slanderous, libellous, defamatory, derogatory, aspersive, abusive, scurrilous, insulting, vituperative. COMPLIMENTARY

calumny slander, libel, misrepresentation, defamation, aspersion, slur, smear, denigration, vituperation, abuse, insult, vilification, obloquy, revilement. EULOGY

camaraderie comradeship, companionship, fellowship, brotherhood, brotherliness, friendliness, esprit de corps. ENMITY

camber curve, arch, curvature, convexity.

camouflage *n*, disguise, mask, cloak, screen, veil, blind, guise, front, covering, concealment, subterfuge, deception.
v, disguise, mask, screen, veil, cover, conceal, hide. EXPOSE

camp[1] *n*, encampment, cantonment, bivouac, tents, cabins, quarters.
faction, clique, party, group, set, sect.
v, encamp, pitch one's tent, settle, lodge.

camp[2] *adj*, effeminate, gay (*inf*), limp-wristed, mannered, affected, studied, extravagant, ostentatious, posing, posturing, theatrical.

campaign operation, exercise, expedition, crusade, drive, fight, battle, attack, offensive.

can *n*, container, receptacle, tin, jar.
v, tin, preserve.

canaille populace, masses, mob, rabble, proletariat, plebs, hoi polloi, riffraff, scum. NOBILITY

canal channel, waterway, watercourse.
duct, tube, pipe, passage.

cancel annul, nullify, revoke, repeal, rescind, countermand, abrogate, quash, call off. CONFIRM
obliterate, erase, delete, expunge, cross out, efface, eliminate, abolish, do away with. RETAIN
neutralize, counterbalance, compensate for, offset, make up for.

cancellation annulment, repeal, revocation, abrogation, deletion, obliteration, elimination, abolition. CONFIRMATION

cancer tumour, carcinoma, malignancy, growth, canker, blight, evil, scourge, corruption.

candid frank, open, straightforward, honest, truthful, sincere, plain, blunt, forthright, outspoken, unreserved, fair, unbiased, impartial, guileless, artless, naive, ingenuous. DEVIOUS

candidate aspirant, applicant, claimant, suitor, nominee, contestant, competitor, contender, entrant, runner.

candle taper, light, torch.

candour frankness, openness, straightforwardness, honesty, sincerity, plainness, bluntness, forthrightness, fairness, impartiality, artlessness, naiveté, ingenuousness. DEVIOUSNESS

cane *n*, stick, staff, rod.
v, beat, thrash, flog, whip, strike.

canker *n*, abscess, ulcer, infection, lesion, sore, chancre.
blight, bane, evil, corruption, rot, curse, scourge, pestilence.
v, infect, blight, corrupt, pollute, poison, envenom, rot, corrode, erode, eat away. PURIFY

cannonade bombardment, shelling, battery, barrage, assault, broadside, volley, salvo.

canny astute, shrewd, knowing, perspicacious, discerning, sharp, acute, subtle, sagacious, prudent, cautious, circumspect.

canon law, rule, decree, edict, precept, statute, formula, standard, principle, criterion.
catalogue, list, roll.

canonical authorized, accepted, approved, recognized, orthodox. UNORTHODOX

canopy awning, baldachin, shade, cover, tarpaulin, tester, tilt.

cant[1] hypocrisy, insincerity, lip service, false piety, sanctimoniousness, platitudes.
jargon, lingo, argot, slang, patter.

cant[2] inclination, slope, slant, tilt, angle, bevel.

cantankerous irascible, testy, crabby, bad-tempered, peevish, irritable, crotchety (*inf*), grumpy, ill-humoured, perverse, contrary, quarrelsome, argumentative. AFFABLE

canteen cafeteria, snack bar, restaurant, dining room.
bottle, flask, canister.

canter amble, trot, jog, lope, gallop.

canticle hymn, song, psalm, poem.

canting hypocritical, insincere, two-faced, sanctimonious.

canvas sailcloth, tarpaulin, ticking, drill, painting, tent.

canvass *v*, electioneer, solicit votes, campaign, poll, survey.
examine, sift, scrutinize, investigate, study, inspect.
debate, discuss, dispute, air.

n, inspection, scrutiny, examination, investigation, study, survey, poll.

canyon ravine, gulch, gully, gorge, chasm.

cap *n*, hat, headgear, beret, bonnet, covering, cover, lid.
top, peak, summit, apex, acme. FOOT
v, cover, top, surmount, crown, complete, perfect, surpass, exceed, excel, outdo.

capability ability, capacity, faculty, means, potential, power, proficiency, skill, aptitude. INCAPABILITY

capable able, competent, proficient, adequate, fitted, suited, qualified, adept, clever, skilful, gifted, intelligent, efficient, accomplished. INCOMPETENT

capacious spacious, roomy, ample, wide, broad, large, vast, immense, voluminous, extensive, comprehensive. NARROW

capaciousness spaciousness, roominess, ampleness, vastness, immensity. NARROWNESS

capacitate enable, empower, qualify, authorize, sanction. PREVENT

capacity volume, dimensions, size, magnitude, amplitude, scope, extent, range, compass.
ability, capability, competence, aptitude, faculty, power, strength, talent, gift, skill, genius, intelligence, cleverness, readiness, facility. INABILITY
position, office, post, function, role, sphere, province, duty, service.

cape headland, promontory, peninsula, point.

caper *v*, frolic, gambol, frisk, romp, hop, skip, jump, leap, bound, spring, dance, cavort, prance.
n, frolic, romp, hop, skip, jump, leap, bound, spring.
prank, practical joke, stunt, antic, escapade, sport, jest, lark (*inf*).

capital *adj*, principal, chief, main, leading, major, key, cardinal, first, primary, foremost, paramount, prime, important. MINOR
excellent, first-rate, splendid, fine, superb. POOR
n, assets, funds, cash, finance, investments, stock, principal, resources, means, wealth, property.

capitalist financier, investor, banker, tycoon.

capitalize take advantage of, profit by, turn to account, exploit, realize.

capitulate yield, surrender, submit, give in, relent. RESIST

capitulation yielding, surrender, submission, acquiescence. RESISTANCE

caprice whim, whimsy, vagary, notion, impulse, fancy, humour, crotchet, freak, quirk, oddity.

capricious fickle, inconstant, changeable, mercurial, whimsical, fanciful, freakish, impulsive, wayward, odd, queer, erratic, fitful, irresolute, uncertain. FIRM

capsize upturn, overturn, upset, keel over, turn turtle (*inf*), turn over, tip over.

capsule lozenge, tablet, pill.
case, sheath, covering, shell, pod, seed vessel, receptacle.

captain commander, leader, head, chief, chieftain, pilot, skipper, master, officer.

caption title, heading, legend, inscription, explanation, note, comment.

captious carping, cavilling, hypercritical, censorious, fault-finding, nit-picking (*inf*). APPRECIATIVE
cantankerous, touchy, irritable, testy, peevish, crabbed, waspish, acrimonious, cross. AFFABLE

captivate fascinate, charm, enchant, bewitch, enthral, entrance, enamour, delight, transport, attract, allure, seduce, win. REPEL

captivating fascinating, charming, enchanting, delightful, attractive, winning. REPULSIVE

captive prisoner, hostage, slave, convict, detainee.

captivity imprisonment, incarceration, confinement, custody, detention, internment, duress, bondage, slavery, servitude, thraldom. FREEDOM

capture *v*, catch, take, seize, collar (*inf*), arrest, apprehend, take prisoner. RELEASE
n, catching, seizure, arrest, apprehension. RELEASE

car automobile, vehicle, motorcar, cab, limousine, jalopy (*inf*), wheels (*inf*).

carafe flask, decanter, bottle, flagon, jug, pitcher.

carcass corpse, body, cadaver, remains, stiff (*inf*).
structure, framework, skeleton, hulk, shell.

cardinal principal, chief, main, capital, vital, essential, fundamental, central, key, primary, first, leading, foremost, paramount, important. SECONDARY

care *n*, concern, anxiety, trouble, worry, affliction, distress, sorrow, pressure, strain, burden, responsibility. INDIFFERENCE
attention, heed, caution, prudence, pains, carefulness, regard, consideration, watchfulness, vigilance, circumspection, forethought. CARELESSNESS
protection, keeping, custody, guardianship, charge, control, supervision.
v, worry, be concerned, mind, bother, give a damn (*inf*).

care for, tend, nurse, minister to, attend, mind, look after, protect. NEGLECT
like, enjoy, be fond of, fancy, want, desire.

career *n*, calling, vocation, occupation, profession, work, job, livelihood.
progress, path, course, passage.
v, rush, dash, hurtle, speed, race, tear, bolt.

carefree cheerful, light-hearted, buoyant, blithe, untroubled, happy-go-lucky, nonchalant, breezy. ANXIOUS

careful cautious, wary, prudent, circumspect, judicious, vigilant, watchful, heedful, mindful. INCAUTIOUS
attentive, thoughtful, conscientious, painstaking, meticulous, scrupulous, thorough, precise. CARELESS

careless negligent, remiss, heedless, unmindful, thoughtless, unthinking, forgetful, imprudent, rash, hasty, inattentive, unguarded. PRUDENT
neglectful, sloppy, slipshod, untidy, disorderly, slapdash, offhand, lackadaisical, nonchalant, unconcerned, casual, indifferent. CAREFUL

carelessness inattention, neglect, negligence, heedlessness, thoughtlessness, imprudence, rashness. CARE

caress *n*, pat, stroke, touch, fondling, hug, cuddle, embrace, kiss.
v, stroke, fondle, pet, pat, touch, hug, cuddle, embrace, kiss. PUNISH

caretaker janitor, curator, custodian, keeper, warden, porter.

cargo load, lading, burden, freight, consignment, shipment, goods, merchandise.

caricature cartoon, representation, lampoon, burlesque, parody, take-off (*inf*), send-up (*inf*), travesty, satire, distortion.

carnage butchery, slaughter, massacre, holocaust, blood bath, bloodshed, mass murder.

carnal sensual, fleshly, voluptuous, licentious, lascivious, prurient, salacious, lewd, lecherous, lustful, libidinous, wanton, impure, base. CHASTE
physical, human, corporeal, natural, unspiritual, worldly, earthly, temporal, secular, profane. SPIRITUAL

carnality sensuality, voluptuousness, lust, lechery, prurience, salaciousness, lewdness.
earthliness, worldliness, corporeality, secularity.

carnival festival, fair, gala, jamboree, celebration, festivity, revel, masquerade, merrymaking, revelry.

carol *n*, song, hymn, canticle, noel, chorus, ditty, lay.
v, sing, chant, troll, warble, chirp.

carousal revel, revelry, merrymaking, carouse, spree, bacchanalia, drinking bout, booze-up (*inf*), binge (*inf*), debauch, orgy, saturnalia.

carouse drink, booze (*inf*), make merry, revel, roister, wassail.

carp cavil, censure, hypercriticize, find fault, quibble, complain, nag, reproach. PRAISE

carpenter joiner, woodworker, cabinet-maker.

carping cavilling, hypercritical, critical, captious, fault-finding, censorious, hard to please, nit-picking (*inf*). APPRECIATIVE

carriage carrying, conveyance, transport, transportation, freight, delivery.
vehicle, conveyance, coach, cab, car.
bearing, demeanour, mien, air, posture, deportment, conduct, behaviour.

carry bear, take, transport, convey, transmit, transfer, move, bring, fetch.
support, sustain, uphold, hold up, bear, maintain, shoulder. DROP
impel, drive, urge, spur, propel, influence. DETER
extend, reach, spread.
win, secure, gain, accomplish, effect. LOSE

carry on, continue, go on, persist, persevere, keep going. STOP
conduct, run, administer, manage, operate.

carry out, perform, execute, effect, implement, discharge, fulfil, complete, accomplish, achieve, realize.

cart wagon, barrow, handcart, vehicle, carriage.
carton box, container, case, packet, pack, package.
cartoon caricature, lampoon, satire, sketch, line drawing, comic strip.
cartridge capsule, cylinder, case, magazine, cassette, container.
carve cut, chisel, sculpt, fashion, mould, form, whittle, incise, engrave, etch, hew, slice, divide.
carving sculpture, model, engraving, etching.
cascade waterfall, cataract, torrent, deluge, flood.
case[1] instance, occurrence, occasion, example, illustration, specimen.
situation, state, event, circumstance, condition, predicament, plight.
action, suit, lawsuit, dispute, cause, trial, process, proceedings, testimony, evidence, plea.
case[2] box, chest, trunk, crate, carton, package, container, receptacle.
covering, capsule, sheath, shell, pod, envelope, wrapper, jacket, holder, socket.
cash money, coin, specie, currency, ready money, banknotes, coins, change, payment.
cashier[1] *n*, teller, bank clerk, bursar, banker, treasurer, accountant.
cashier[2] *v*, dismiss, discharge, expel, drum out, reject, discard.
casino gaming house, gambling den, club.
cask barrel, vat, keg, vessel, container.
casket box, chest, coffer, case, receptacle.
cast *v*, throw, fling, pitch, sling, hurl, toss, chuck, launch, send, drive, thrust, impel. KEEP
radiate, diffuse, emit, spread, scatter, distribute, direct.
shed, drop, throw off, discard, reject. RETAIN
shape, mould, form, model.
compute, calculate, reckon, figure.
n, throw, toss, fling, thrust.
mould, shape, form, stamp, style, tone, look, air, manner, bearing, mien, demeanour.
tinge, shade, touch, trace, suggestion.
actors, players, performers, characters, dramatis personae, company, troupe.
castaway *n*, outcast, exile, wanderer, vagabond, discard, cast-off.
adj, shipwrecked, adrift, marooned, stranded, discarded, rejected.
caste class, order, rank, status, position, station, race, lineage.
castigate chastise, rebuke, reprimand, censure, berate, upbraid, correct, discipline, punish, whip, beat, cane, flog, thrash, lash. CARESS
castigation chastisement, rebuke, censure, upbraiding, correction, discipline, punishment, beating, flogging, caning, thrashing.
castle citadel, keep, fortress, stronghold, palace, mansion, chateau.
castrate geld, emasculate, neuter, spay, unman, weaken.
expurgate, censor, bowdlerize, purge.
castration gelding, emasculation, orchidectomy, oophorectomy.
casual accidental, chance, fortuitous, unexpected, unforeseen, unplanned, incidental, occasional, contingent, random, irregular. DELIBERATE
informal, unceremonious, offhand, nonchalant, easy-going, relaxed, blasé, indifferent, apathetic, unconcerned. FORMAL
casualty victim, sufferer, fatality, loss, injured person, dead person. SURVIVOR
accident, mishap, misfortune, disaster, calamity, catastrophe, blow. BLESSING
casuistry sophistry, sophism, quibbling, equivocation, subtlety, chicanery, speciousness.
cataclysm upheaval, convulsion, debacle, collapse, catastrophe, disaster, calamity, deluge, flood, inundation, avalanche.
catacomb crypt, tomb, vault, sepulchre, ossuary.
catalogue list, inventory, register, roll, record, file, index, directory, schedule.
catapult *n*, sling, ballista, trebuchet.
v, hurl, propel, shoot, launch, pitch, toss.
cataract cascade, waterfall, falls, rapids, deluge, downpour.
catastrophe disaster, calamity, cataclysm, blow, reverse, misfortune, affliction, adversity, distress, tragedy, mishap, trouble, trial, failure, fiasco, flop (*inf*). TRIUMPH

culmination, climax, dénouement, debacle, end, conclusion, termination, finale, upshot, issue. BEGINNING

catastrophic disastrous, calamitous, dire, terrible, tragic, distressing.

catcall boo, hiss, whistle, raspberry, hoot, cry, jeer.

catch *v*, take, seize, snatch, grab, grasp, grip, clutch. DROP
capture, nab (*inf*), arrest, apprehend, snare, ensnare, trap, entrap, entangle, hook, net. RELEASE
captivate, charm, fascinate, enchant, bewitch. REPEL
reach, catch up, intercept, overtake, pass.
discover, find out, detect, surprise, expose, unmask.
contract, develop, succumb to, go down with.
hear, discern, perceive, grasp, take in, understand, catch on, twig (*inf*).
n, clasp, fastener, clip, hook, hasp, bolt, latch.
snag, drawback, stumbling block, hitch, trap, trick.
take, haul (*inf*), bag, trophy, prize.

catching infectious, contagious, communicable, transmittable.
captivating, winning, charming, fascinating, enchanting, bewitching, fetching, attractive, taking. REPULSIVE

catchword slogan, motto, byword, refrain, cliché.

catechism interrogation, questioning, examination, drill, instruction.

catechize interrogate, question, examine, drill.

catechumen pupil, learner, beginner, novice, initiate, neophyte, tyro, proselyte, convert. MASTER

categorical positive, emphatic, unqualified, unconditional, absolute, unreserved, downright, direct, explicit, plain, unequivocal, unambiguous. VAGUE

category class, classification, division, section, heading, grouping, group, grade, order, rank, sort, kind, type.

cater provide, furnish, supply, purvey.
cater to, indulge, humour, gratify, oblige, satisfy, pamper, coddle, spoil.

caterwaul yell, howl, scream, screech, shriek, bawl.

catharsis purification, cleansing, purging, purgation.

cathartic purgative, cleansing, purifying.

catholic general, universal, world-wide, global, comprehensive, all-inclusive, liberal, tolerant, broad-minded, unbiased. NARROW

cattle cows, bulls, livestock, stock, animals.

cauldron pot, kettle, boiler, copper, crock.

causation production, creation, origination, causality.

cause *n*, source, origin, root, spring, agent, creator, maker, producer. EFFECT
reason, basis, justification, grounds, occasion, motive, inducement, incentive, object, purpose, aim, end.
matter, topic, subject, principle, ideal, purpose, enterprise, undertaking, attempt.
lawsuit, action, case.
v, occasion, bring about, engender, generate, originate, create, produce, effect, precipitate, provoke, begin, give rise to, result in.
compel, induce, make, force, constrain.

caustic burning, corrosive, acid, keen, pungent, acrid, mordant, biting, sharp, cutting, trenchant, stinging, scathing, sarcastic, severe, acrimonious, bitter, virulent. MILD

cauterize burn, sear, scorch, singe.

caution *n*, carefulness, care, wariness, heedfulness, heed, vigilance, watchfulness, discretion, prudence. RASHNESS
admonition, warning, advice, counsel, injunction.
v, warn, forewarn, admonish, advise, urge, enjoin.

cautious careful, wary, heedful, vigilant, watchful, prudent, judicious, discreet, guarded. RASH

cavalcade procession, parade, march-past, array, spectacle, train, cortege.

cavalier *n*, knight, gentleman, gallant, escort, beau.
adj, arrogant, haughty, disdainful, supercilious, proud, insolent, curt, offhand. MEEK

cave cavern, grotto, den, hollow, cavity, pothole.

cavern cave, grotto, hollow, underground chamber.

cavernous hollow, sunken, deep-set, concave, yawning.

cavil *v*, carp, censure, hypercriticize, quibble, complain, object, find fault. PRAISE
n, objection, quibble, criticism, carping, censure, hypercriticism.

cavilling carping, captious, hypercritical, quibbling, fault-finding, nit-picking (*inf*). APPRECIATIVE

cavity hole, hollow, pit, crater, fissure, gap.

cease stop, end, finish, terminate, conclude, discontinue, halt, desist, refrain, leave off. BEGIN

ceaseless unceasing, continuous, constant, unremitting, nonstop, endless, unending, continual, perpetual, eternal, everlasting. FITFUL

cede yield, surrender, relinquish, abandon, abdicate, resign, transfer, hand over, convey, grant, allow, concede. RETAIN

celebrate honour, commemorate, observe, keep, glorify, extol, praise, applaud, toast, drink to, proclaim, rejoice, make merry. IGNORE

celebrated famous, distinguished, eminent, noted, acclaimed, illustrious, renowned, notable, well-known, popular. UNKNOWN

celebration festivity, festival, gala, carnival, party, revelry, merrymaking, carousal.
commemoration, observance, remembrance, anniversary, ceremony, rite, performance.

celebrity star, personality, lion, hero, heroine, personage, dignitary, VIP, bigwig (*inf*), big shot (*inf*), somebody. NOBODY
fame, distinction, renown, note, eminence, glory, honour, reputation, repute, prominence, popularity, stardom. IGNOMINY

celerity speed, swiftness, rapidity, quickness, haste, promptness, dispatch, velocity, pace. SLOWNESS

celestial heavenly, divine, angelic, seraphic, immortal, eternal, ethereal, empyrean, astral, spiritual, supernatural. EARTHLY

celibacy continence, abstinence, self-denial, chastity, virginity, purity, singleness, bachelorhood.

celibate *adj*, single, unmarried, continent, abstinent, chaste, virginal. MARRIED
n, bachelor, spinster, single person, virgin, monk, nun.

cell chamber, room, cubicle, compartment, stall, recess, cavity, cage, dungeon.

cellar basement, vault, storeroom, larder. ATTIC

cellular alveolated, honeycombed, open, porous.

cement *v*, unite, join, connect, attach, cleave, cohere, bind, stick, glue, gum, paste, bond. SEPARATE
n, mortar, plaster, adhesive, glue, gum, paste, sealant, bond.

cemetery graveyard, churchyard, necropolis, burial ground, God's acre.

cenotaph monument, memorial, shrine.

censor *v*, expurgate, cut, bowdlerize, purge, edit, delete.
n, inspector, examiner, reviewer, critic.

censorious critical, fault-finding, hypercritical, captious, carping, cavilling, disapproving, disparaging. APPRECIATIVE

censurable blamable, blameworthy, at fault, guilty, culpable, reprehensible. BLAMELESS

censure *v*, blame, condemn, denounce, criticize, reprove, rebuke, reproach, reprimand, chide, castigate, upbraid, disapprove. PRAISE
n, condemnation, denunciation, disapproval, disapprobation, blame, criticism, stricture, reproof, reproach. APPROVAL

central middle, median, mid, inner, interior. EXTREME
key, focal, chief, cardinal, main, essential, principal, fundamental, primary. PERIPHERAL

centralize concentrate, converge, congregate, collect, focus, consolidate, amalgamate, compact, unify. DECENTRALIZE

centre *n*, middle, midst, midpoint, focus, hub, pivot, core, heart, nucleus.
v, focus, converge, concentrate.

century centenary, hundred years, hundred, era, period, age.

cereal grain, corn, wheat, oats, barley, maize, rye, grass, crop, seed, meal.

ceremonial *adj*, formal, solemn, ritual, stately, imposing, dignified, majestic, official, functional, liturgical. CASUAL
n, ceremony, solemnity, ritual, rite, formality, etiquette.

ceremonious formal, precise, punctilious, exact, stiff, starchy (*inf*), courteous, civil, polite. UNCEREMONIOUS
stately, dignified, solemn. INFORMAL

ceremony rite, ritual, ceremonial, observance, service, sacrament, commemoration, parade, show.
formality, pomp, stateliness, protocol, etiquette, form, decorum. INFORMALITY
certain sure, positive, convinced, confident, assured. DOUBTFUL
unquestionable, indubitable, undoubted, indisputable, incontestable, incontrovertible, irrefutable, absolute, conclusive, positive, manifest, plain. UNCERTAIN
bound, destined, sure, inevitable. UNLIKELY
definite, decided, settled, determined, fixed, established.
infallible, unfailing, reliable, dependable, stable, constant. UNRELIABLE
particular, specific, special, precise, express, individual.
certainly undoubtedly, unquestionably, without doubt, positively, absolutely, plainly.
willingly, surely, of course, by all means, definitely.
certainty conviction, sureness, confidence, assurance, certitude, trust, faith. DOUBT
fact, reality, truth, actuality. POSSIBILITY
unquestionableness, indubitableness, irrefutability, incontestability, incontrovertibility, positiveness, plainness. UNCERTAINTY
certificate credential, testimonial, diploma, document, licence, warrant, authorization, voucher.
certify attest, testify, witness, avow, aver, corroborate, confirm, verify, validate, declare, guarantee, vouch for, endorse, prove, show. DENY
certitude certainty, confidence, assurance, conviction. DOUBT
cessation ceasing, ending, stop, termination, discontinuance, arrest, stoppage, halt, pause, stay, suspension, intermission, interval, abeyance, respite, remission, rest, let-up (*inf*). CONTINUANCE
cession surrender, yielding, capitulation, submission, abandonment, relinquishment, renunciation, transfer, conveyance, grant, concession. RETENTION
chafe rub, warm, wear, scrape, scratch, rasp, grate, inflame, irritate, vex, annoy, exasperate, anger, incense, gall, fume, rage, provoke, offend, fret, worry, trouble. SOOTHE
chaff[1] *n*, husks, hulls, remains, dregs, refuse, waste, rubbish.
chaff[2] *v*, tease, banter, rib (*inf*), mock, ridicule, taunt, jeer, scoff, deride.
n, banter, raillery, teasing, joking, badinage, persiflage.
chaffer haggle, bargain, negotiate.
chagrin *n*, irritation, vexation, annoyance, exasperation, anger, displeasure, mortification, embarrassment, discomfiture, disquiet, discomposure, humiliation. PLEASURE
v, irritate, vex, annoy, exasperate, anger, displease, mortify, embarrass, discomfit, humiliate. PLEASE
chain *n*, bond, restraint, fetter, shackle, manacle.
series, succession, progression, sequence, string, train.
v, restrain, confine, tether, fasten, tie, bind, shackle, fetter, enslave. LOOSE
chair *n*, seat, stool, bench, pew, throne.
professorship, professorate.
v, preside over, lead, direct, supervise, manage, control.
chairman chairwoman, chairperson, speaker, director, president, master of ceremonies, MC (*inf*), toastmaster.
chalice goblet, cup, bowl.
challenge *v*, dare, defy, invite, summon, brave, beard, confront, accost.
arouse, stimulate, test, tax.
question, dispute, dissent, oppose, protest. PASS
n, dare, defiance, ultimatum, confrontation, provocation, summons, invitation, test, trial.
question, protest, objection, dissension, disputation.
chamber room, hall, apartment, bedroom, cell, cubicle.
cavity, hollow, compartment, recess.
assembly, council, judicature, legislature.
champ chew, gnaw, bite, munch, crunch.
champion *n*, winner, title-holder, victor, conqueror, hero, defender, protector, upholder, guardian, patron, backer, supporter, advocate. RENEGADE
v, back, promote, support, defend, fight for, advocate, uphold. OPPOSE

chance *n*, luck, fortuity, fortune, providence, fate, destiny, accident, contingency. DESIGN
opportunity, opening, occasion, time.
possibility, likelihood, prospect, probability. CERTAINTY
risk, gamble, hazard, peril, jeopardy, uncertainty.
v, happen, occur, befall, come about, betide.
risk, hazard, venture, gamble, speculate, jeopardize.
adj, accidental, unintentional, fortuitous, unforeseen, incidental, casual, random. INTENTIONAL

change *v*, alter, vary, modify, transform, convert, transmute, shift, veer, alternate, fluctuate, vacillate. REMAIN
replace, substitute, exchange, swap, trade, barter, commute. RETAIN
n, alteration, variation, modification, transformation, conversion, metamorphosis, mutation, shift, difference. IMMUTABILITY
variety, innovation, novelty, revolution, alternation, fluctuation, vicissitude. CONSERVATION

changeable variable, inconstant, fickle, capricious, irregular, fluctuating, wavering, vacillating, unsteady, unstable, shifting, mobile, fitful, mercurial, volatile, unpredictable, unreliable. STEADFAST

changeless steadfast, constant, unchanging, immutable, unvarying, consistent, unalterable, permanent, fixed, regular, steady, reliable, abiding, perpetual, everlasting. CHANGEABLE

channel *n*, duct, conduit, passage, canal, strait, gutter, groove, furrow.
approach, way, avenue, route, course, path.
v, direct, guide, conduct, convey.
groove, flute, carve.

chant *n*, song, psalm, cantata, canticle, carol, plainsong, intonation, melody, tune, chorus, incantation.
v, sing, carol, intone, chorus, recite.

chaos disorder, confusion, anarchy, turmoil, tumult, havoc, pandemonium. ORDER

chaotic disordered, confused, disorganized, topsy-turvy, anarchic, lawless, riotous, tumultuous. ORDERED

chap[1] *v*, crack, split, open, redden, roughen.

chap[2] *n*, boy, man, fellow, bloke (*inf*), guy (*inf*), character, type, sort.

chaperon *n*, escort, companion, duenna, governess, attendant, protector, shepherd.
v, escort, accompany, watch over, protect, shepherd, attend.

chapfallen crestfallen, despondent, dejected, downcast, dispirited, disheartened, discouraged, sad, depressed, downhearted. HAPPY

chaplet wreath, garland, coronal, circlet.

chapter division, section, part, episode, phase, period, stage.

char burn, scorch, singe, sear, carbonize, cauterize.

character personality, temperament, disposition, nature, individuality, attributes, constitution, cast, complexion, quality.
reputation, repute, status, position, honour, integrity, uprightness, rectitude. DISREPUTE
person, individual, sort, type, fellow, eccentric, oddity, card (*inf*).
role, part, persona, portrayal, characterization.
symbol, letter, type, mark, device, emblem, sign, figure.

characteristic *adj*, distinctive, peculiar, special, individual, specific, representative, typical. GENERAL
peculiarity, idiosyncrasy, trait, feature, quality, attribute, property, mark.

characterize mark, distinguish, brand, stamp, identify, designate, indicate, represent, describe, portray.

charade travesty, pretence, pantomime, farce.

charge *v*, accuse, impeach, arraign, impute, indict, incriminate. CLEAR
attack, assault, assail, rush, storm. RETREAT
entrust, commit, load, burden, afflict. RELIEVE
demand, ask, levy, price.
command, enjoin, bid, direct, order, instruct, require.
fill, suffuse, permeate, imbue.
n, accusation, imputation, indictment, allegation. PLEA
attack, assault, onset, onslaught, sortie, raid. RETREAT
responsibility, duty, office, trust, commission, custody, care, safekeeping, ward.
burden, load, cargo, freight.

price, payment, fee, rate, levy, cost, outlay, expense.
command, order, injunction, direction, instruction, mandate.

chargeable liable, accountable, imputable, attributable, blamable, imposable, taxable, rateable.

charger war-horse, mount, steed, horse.

charily cautiously, carefully, warily, guardedly, circumspectly, heedfully. RECKLESSLY
sparingly, frugally, prudently, judiciously.

charitable kind, benevolent, beneficent, philanthropic, generous, liberal, bountiful. MEAN
lenient, considerate, compassionate, gracious, magnanimous, indulgent, tolerant, understanding, humane, forgiving. HARSH

charity alms, almsgiving, benefaction, relief, assistance, donation, contribution, gift.
kindness, benevolence, compassion, love, goodness, humanity, generosity, bounty. SELFISHNESS

charlatan quack, mountebank, cheat, swindler, con man (*inf*), impostor, pretender, fraud.

charm *v*, enchant, fascinate, captivate, bewitch, mesmerize, entrance, delight, please, win, allure, attract, transport, enrapture, enamour. REPEL
n, attractiveness, allure, appeal, desirability, fascination, magic, enchantment, spell, sorcery. REPULSION
amulet, talisman, trinket.

charming attractive, fetching, delightful, pleasing, lovely, appealing, engaging, alluring, enchanting, bewitching, fascinating, captivating. REPULSIVE

chart plan, diagram, graph, map, table.

charter *n*, licence, permit, franchise, concession, authority, privilege, right, prerogative, document, deed, bond.
v, lease, hire, rent, commission, sanction, authorize.

chary cautious, prudent, careful, circumspect, heedful, wary, guarded, slow, reluctant, shy. RECKLESS
sparing, frugal, thrifty, parsimonious, mean, niggardly.

chase *v*, pursue, follow, run after, hunt, track, hound, drive away, send packing, put to flight.
n, pursuit, hunt, hunting, race.

chasm abyss, gorge, crevasse, ravine, gulf, rift, cleft, fissure, cavity, crater, opening, gap, hiatus.

chaste pure, undefiled, unsullied, immaculate, vestal, virginal, virtuous, innocent, modest, decent, simple, unaffected. CORRUPT

chasten correct, discipline, chastise, castigate, repress, humble, subdue, tame, curb. PAMPER

chastise correct, discipline, punish, castigate, beat, flog, lash, whip, cane, spank, thrash, scourge, berate, upbraid, scold. REWARD

chastisement discipline, punishment, castigation, beating, flogging, caning, spanking, thrashing, censure, scolding. PRAISE

chastity purity, virtue, virginity, maidenhood, celibacy, continence, modesty, decency, innocence, simplicity. CORRUPTION

chat *v*, talk, natter, gossip, chatter, prattle, confabulate, converse.
n, conversation, talk, natter, gossip, confab (*inf*), tête-à-tête, chinwag (*inf*).

chattels goods, belongings, property, effects, furniture, movables.

chatter *v*, chat, natter, gossip, prattle, prate, tattle, babble, jabber, gab (*inf*).
n, prattle, talk, gossip, babbling, prating, chit-chat.

chatterbox chatterer, babbler, gossip, blabbermouth, prattler, windbag (*inf*).

chatty talkative, loquacious, garrulous, babbling, prating. RESERVED
gossipy, newsy, informal, friendly, familiar, colloquial. FORMAL

cheap inexpensive, low-priced, cut-price, reduced, reasonable, economical. EXPENSIVE
shoddy, inferior, second-rate, poor, indifferent, paltry, worthless, common, vulgar. SUPERIOR
mean, shabby, contemptible, despicable, low. NOBLE

cheapen debase, devalue, lower, depreciate, belittle, disparage, demean. APPRECIATE

cheat *v*, deceive, delude, beguile, hoodwink, bamboozle, dupe, fool, trick, hoax, defraud, swindle, con (*inf*), diddle (*inf*), rip off (*inf*), do (*inf*), double-cross.

n, swindler, con man (*inf*), fraud, impostor, liar, deceiver, rogue, trickster, sharper, cheater, charlatan.
deception, hoax, fraud, swindle, rip-off (*inf*), trick, imposture, artifice.

check *v*, examine, inspect, scrutinize, look over, test, verify, confirm, compare, investigate, enquire into, probe.
curb, restrain, control, bridle, repress, inhibit, hinder, impede, obstruct, retard, halt, stop, arrest, pause. ADVANCE
chide, rebuke, reprove, reprimand, scold. ENCOURAGE
n, examination, inspection, scrutiny, test, trial, comparison, verification, confirmation, investigation, probe.
criterion, norm, yardstick, standard, model.
curb, restraint, control, inhibition, hindrance, impediment, obstruction, barrier, bar, stoppage.

checkmate *n*, defeat, rout, conquest, victory.
stalemate, deadlock, halt, stoppage, arrest, check.
v, frustrate, foil, thwart, overcome, conquer, defeat, vanquish, beat.

cheek impertinence, impudence, effrontery, sauce (*inf*), insolence, disrespect, nerve, gall, audacity, temerity. RESPECT

cheer *v*, applaud, clap, acclaim, shout, yell, encourage, spur, urge. BOO
gladden, hearten, brighten, cheer up, comfort, console, solace, encourage, enliven, animate, inspirit, exhilarate, uplift. DEPRESS
n, cheerfulness, gladness, happiness, joy, gaiety, merriment, comfort, solace, hope, hopefulness, buoyancy, animation, liveliness. DEJECTION
shout, yell, cry, hurrah, applause, acclamation. BOO

cheerfulness happiness, joy, joyfulness, gaiety, merriment, cheer, buoyancy, blitheness, good spirits, hopefulness, enthusiasm. DEJECTION

cheerless dreary, dull, gloomy, dismal, dark, sombre, bleak, depressing, melancholy, mournful, doleful, dejected, depressed, despondent, miserable, sad, disconsolate, forlorn, desolate, morose, pessimistic. CHEERFUL

cheery cheering, cheerful, joyous, gay, merry, sprightly, blithe, lively, hearty, jovial, sunny, breezy, carefree. GLUM

chequered varied, diverse.
variegated, multicoloured, checked, tartan.

cherish treasure, prize, hold dear, love, cling to, harbour, entertain, nurture, nourish, nurse, cosset, foster, support, promote. ABANDON

cherub angel, child, baby, innocent, darling.

chest box, case, trunk, coffer, casket.
breast, bosom, bust, thorax.

chew masticate, munch, champ, grind, crunch, gnaw, bite, nibble.

chew over, ponder, ruminate, consider, deliberate, mull over, meditate.

chic fashionable, modish, trendy (*inf*), stylish, smart, elegant.

chicanery trickery, artifice, subterfuge, chicane, sophistry, deception, duplicity, wiles, stratagems, intrigue, underhandedness. HONESTY

chide rebuke, scold, reprimand, admonish, upbraid, tick off (*inf*), tell off (*inf*), reprove, reproach, berate, censure, criticize, blame. PRAISE

chief *n*, leader, head, chieftain, ruler, captain, commander, master, governor, principal, boss (*inf*), director, manager. SUBORDINATE
adj, principal, cardinal, capital, main, leading, first, foremost, primary, prime, supreme, paramount, grand, key, essential, vital, prevailing, predominant. MINOR

chiefly especially, above all, principally, mainly, mostly, predominantly, on the whole, primarily.

chieftain chief, head, leader, ruler, commander.

child baby, infant, toddler, youngster, youth, juvenile, boy, girl, offspring, progeny, issue, suckling, nursling, nipper (*inf*), brat, kid (*inf*). ADULT

childbirth confinement, accouchement, lying-in, labour, delivery, parturition.

childhood babyhood, infancy, youth, minority, boyhood, girlhood. ADULTHOOD

childish babyish, infantile, puerile, juvenile, immature, boyish, girlish, silly, foolish, trivial, trifling, simple, young, tender. MATURE

childlike innocent, artless, guileless, naive, ingenuous, credulous, gullible, trustful, trusting.

chill *adj*, chilly, cool, cold, bleak, frigid. WARM

v, cool, refrigerate, freeze. HEAT
depress, discourage, dishearten, dampen. ENCOURAGE
n, cold, coldness, chilliness, coolness, bleakness, frigidity, rawness, nip, bite. WARMTH

chilly chill, cool, cold, bleak, frosty, freezing, raw, wintry, nippy, fresh, crisp. WARM
unfriendly, cool, frigid, hostile, unwelcoming, unresponsive. FRIENDLY

chime toll, sound, strike, peal, ring, clang, dong, tinkle.
harmonize, accord, agree, blend, coordinate, complement. CLASH

chimera hallucination, fantasy, dream, delusion, fancy, illusion, phantom, spectre, nightmare, monster. REALITY

chimerical illusory, fanciful, imaginary, hallucinatory, visionary, unreal, wild, fantastic. REAL

china porcelain, ceramics, pottery, earthenware, crockery, tableware, service, dishes.

chink[1] *n*, crack, fissure, cleft, rift, cranny, crevice, gap, opening, aperture.

chink[2] *v*, jingle, ring, clink, tinkle, jangle.
n, clink, jingle, tinkle, ring.

chip *n*, piece, fragment, flake, sliver, splinter, shard, shaving, scrap, bit.
dent, scratch, nick, flaw, defect.
v, chisel, whittle, nick, scratch, gash, cut, hew.
chip in, contribute, donate, pay.
interrupt, interpose, break in.

chirography calligraphy, handwriting, hand, penmanship.

chiromancy palmistry, fortune-telling, prediction, divination.

chirp chirrup, cheep, twitter, tweet, warble, trill, pipe, peep.

chisel carve, sculpt, cut, hew, engrave, incise, chase, shape, model.

chit chitty, memo, memorandum, note, slip, voucher, receipt.

chivalrous knightly, heroic, courageous, valiant, brave, bold, intrepid, gallant, courtly, courteous, gentlemanly, generous, magnanimous, noble, high-minded. COWARDLY

chivalry knighthood, heroism, courage, valour, bravery, gallantry, courtesy, nobility.

chock block, wedge, stop.

choice *n*, option, alternative, selection, pick, variety, adoption, election, preference.
adj, select, hand-picked, elite, excellent, superior, prime, rare, uncommon, unusual, exquisite, dainty, exclusive, special, valuable, precious. INFERIOR

choke *v*, throttle, strangle, stifle, suffocate, smother, asphyxiate, block, obstruct, congest, clog, dam, suppress, overcome, overpower.
vi, gag, retch, gasp, cough.

choler anger, ire, wrath, fury, rage, indignation. MILDNESS

choleric irritable, bad-tempered, testy, irascible, touchy, petulant, angry, fiery, hot, passionate. PLACID

choose select, pick, elect, adopt, cull, single out, settle on, opt for, prefer, fancy, desire, wish, see fit. REJECT

choosy discriminating, selective, particular, fussy, faddy, finicky, exacting, fastidious.

chop cut, hew, fell, axe, lop, shear, hack, slice, dice, cube, mince, chop up.

choppy rough, ruffled, broken, uneven, squally, blustery, tempestuous, turbulent.

chops jaws, jowls, mouth, muzzle.

chore job, task, duty, burden, bother, drag (*inf*), fag (*inf*).

chortle chuckle, snigger, cackle, crow.

chorus choir, choristers, singers, ensemble.
refrain, burden, response. VERSE
song, carol, ballad, hymn, anthem, tune, melody.
accord, unison, harmony, concert, unity, concord. DISCORD

christen baptize, name, call, dub, designate, entitle, style, term.

chronic inveterate, habitual, confirmed, deep-seated, deep-rooted, ingrained, persistent, constant, incessant, permanent, incurable, recurring, perennial, lingering.
appalling, dreadful, awful, atrocious. EXCELLENT

chronicle *n*, journal, diary, log, record, register, history, annals, account, narrative, story, saga.
v, record, register, enter, set down, relate, tell, recount, narrate.

chronicler historian, historiographer, annalist, diarist, recorder, narrator, reporter.

chronological consecutive, sequential, in sequence, ordered, progressive, historical.
chronometer timepiece, watch, clock.
chubby plump, tubby, podgy, round, portly, rotund, flabby, fleshy, buxom. LEAN
chuck throw, toss, hurl, cast, pitch, sling, discard, reject, abandon, forsake, quit, give up.
chuckle giggle, titter, chortle, snigger, laugh, crow, cackle, grin, smile.
chum friend, companion, comrade, crony, pal (*inf*), mate (*inf*).
chunk lump, block, hunk, slab, wedge, mass, piece.
church chapel, cathedral, abbey, temple, meeting-house, mosque, synagogue, sanctuary.
denomination, faith, congregation, parish, clergy.
churchyard graveyard, cemetery, necropolis, burial ground.
churl boor, lout, oaf, rustic, peasant, bumpkin, clodhopper, yokel. GENTLEMAN
niggard, miser, skinflint, Scrooge.
churlish rude, impolite, uncivil, brusque, surly, waspish, crabbed, sullen, morose, rough, harsh, vulgar, uncouth, crass, boorish, oafish, loutish. POLITE
miserly, niggardly, mean, stingy, close-fisted, illiberal, inhospitable, unneighbourly. GENEROUS
churlishness rudeness, impoliteness, brusqueness, surliness, sullenness, roughness, uncouthness, boorishness. POLITENESS
meanness, miserliness, parsimony, illiberality, inhospitality. GENEROSITY
churn agitate, stir, beat, whip, foam, froth, convulse, toss, shake, disturb, upset.
chute channel, trough, groove, gutter, shaft, slide, slope, ramp.
cicerone guide, courier, escort, pilot.
cigarette smoke, cig (*inf*), ciggy (*inf*), fag (*inf*), coffin nail (*inf*), cancer stick (*inf*), joint, reefer.
cincture belt, girdle, band, border.
cinder ash, ember, coal, clinker, remnant.
cinema pictures, movies, flicks (*inf*), films, motion pictures, big screen (*inf*).
cinereous cineritious, ashy, ashen, greyish.
cipher code, cryptograph, symbol, character, figure, number, numeral, device, logo, monogram.
nil, zero, nought, nothing, nonentity, nobody.
circle ring, round, hoop, loop, disc, globe, sphere, orb, cycle, revolution, circumference, periphery.
coterie, club, clique, set, society, fraternity, group, company.
domain, province, realm, sphere, orbit, range, compass, field, area, region, circuit, bounds.
circuit revolution, round, lap, orbit, tour, course, journey, perambulation.
circle, boundary, circumference, ambit, limit, compass, district, region.
circuitous roundabout, indirect, devious, tortuous, winding, serpentine, meandering, rambling. DIRECT
circular *adj*, round, annular, ring-shaped, discoid, spherical, globular. SQUARE
n, notice, advertisement, handbill, broadsheet, leaflet, pamphlet, brochure.
circulate distribute, spread, propagate, publish, promulgate, broadcast, disseminate, diffuse, send round. RETAIN
rotate, revolve, gyrate, move round, pass round, flow, radiate. STAGNATE
circulation dissemination, spread, spreading, promulgation, propagation, diffusion, transmission. RETENTION
flow, movement, motion, circling, rotation. STAGNATION
circumference periphery, circuit, perimeter, outline, border, edge, rim, verge, fringe, boundary, limits, extremity. DIAMETER
circumlocution periphrasis, verbosity, long-windedness, prolixity, indirectness, euphemism, ambiguity. TERSENESS
circumlocutory periphrastic, verbose, long-winded, prolix, indirect, roundabout, euphemistic, ambiguous. TERSE
circumscribe surround, encircle, encompass, enclose, bound, limit, confine, restrict, hem in, restrain, define, demarcate, delineate, mark off.
circumspect cautious, wary, careful, vigilant, watchful, heedful, attentive, scrupulous, discreet, prudent, judicious, politic. RASH

circumspection caution, wariness, care, vigilance, prudence, discretion, attention. RASHNESS

circumstance incident, event, occurrence, happening, element, factor, detail, particular, point, item, condition.

circumstances situation, condition, position, state, state of affairs, means, resources, status, surroundings, background.

circumstantial inferential, conjectural, presumed, implied, indirect, hearsay, incidental, contingent. POSITIVE
detailed, elaborate, particular, specific, minute, precise. VAGUE

circumvent bypass, get round, evade, elude, avoid, steer clear of, sidestep. CONFRONT
outwit, beguile, dupe, cheat, deceive, trick, delude, bamboozle, hoodwink, mislead.
ensnare, entrap, encircle, surround, hem in, thwart, foil, checkmate.

circumvention evasion, avoidance, sidestepping, dodge.
deception, deceit, cheating, fraud, imposture, chicanery, trickery, duplicity. HONESTY

cistern tank, reservoir, well, vat, sink, tub.

citadel fortress, stronghold, castle, keep, tower, bastion.

citation quoting, quotation, passage, excerpt, extract, source, reference.
commendation, award, mention, honour.

cite quote, name, mention, allude to, refer to, adduce, enumerate.
summon, call, subpoena.

citizen townsman, inhabitant, dweller, resident, householder, ratepayer, voter, burgher, burgess, freeman, denizen, subject, native. OUTSIDER

city metropolis, municipality, town, conurbation.

civic municipal, community, communal, public, borough, civil. RURAL

civil civic, municipal, domestic, home, internal, political.
polite, courteous, well-mannered, respectful, civilized, refined, urbane, suave, gracious, complaisant, obliging, accommodating. CHURLISH

civility politeness, courtesy, urbanity, graciousness, complaisance. CHURLISHNESS

civilization refinement, sophistication, cultivation, culture, education, development, advancement, progress. BARBARISM
society, nation, people, customs, way of life.

civilize refine, sophisticate, cultivate, educate, enlighten, polish, improve.
humanize, domesticate, tame, school, teach. BARBARIZE

clack click, clatter, crack, rap.
chatter, jabber, gabble, prattle, babble, prate.

claim *v*, demand, call for, require, request, ask for, exact, requisition, commandeer, appropriate, usurp, take. WAIVE
assert, maintain, insist, allege, profess, declare.
n, demand, call, requirement, requisition, request, petition, application, privilege, right, title, pretension.
assertion, allegation, affirmation, profession, declaration.

claimant applicant, supplicant, petitioner, pretender, candidate.

clairvoyant *adj*, psychic, extrasensory, second-sighted, telepathic, prescient, prophetic, oracular.
n, fortune-teller, soothsayer, seer, prophet, prophetess, augur, diviner, oracle.

clamber climb, scramble, crawl, scale, shin.

clammy damp, moist, wet, sticky, viscous, slimy, sweaty, dank, close, humid. DRY

clamorous vociferous, noisy, loud, deafening, uproarious, riotous, boisterous, unruly, obstreperous. QUIET

clamour *n*, noise, din, racket, hullabaloo, uproar, outcry, shouting, vociferation, hubbub, commotion, fuss. QUIET
v, shout, cry, yell, vociferate, demand, insist.

clamp *n*, vice, brace, clasp, grip, bracket.
v, secure, fix, brace, grip, fasten, press, impose, inflict.

clan family, sept, tribe, race, house, group, set, band, company, clique, coterie, fraternity, brotherhood, sect, faction.

clandestine furtive, surreptitious, sly, secret, private, hidden, concealed, stealthy, underhand, cloak-and-dagger, underground, covert. OPEN

clang *v*, ring, resound, reverberate, toll, chime, clank, clash, jangle.

n, clank, clash, clangour, reverberation.

clangour clang, clash, reverberation, clamour, din, uproar, racket.

clank clash, clang, clink, chink, rattle, clatter.

clannish cliquish, exclusive, select, insular, sectarian, parochial, narrow.

clap *v*, applaud, cheer, acclaim. HISS
slap, slam, whack, bang, pat, strike, thrust.
n, applause, ovation, acclaim.
burst, peal, explosion, slap, bang, slam.

claptrap bombast, cant, rodomontade, humbug, nonsense, rubbish, bunk (*inf*), drivel (*inf*), flannel (*inf*), blarney, insincerity, hypocrisy.

clarification explanation, illumination, elucidation, simplification, interpretation, exposition. MYSTIFICATION

clarify explain, elucidate, elaborate, make clear, simplify, illuminate, enlighten, clear up, resolve, shed light on. OBSCURE
purify, refine, cleanse, filter, strain. POLLUTE

clarity clearness, limpidity, transparency, purity. MURKINESS
lucidity, precision, definition, distinctness, comprehensibility, intelligibility, obviousness, simplicity. OBSCURITY

clash *n*, collision, crash, conflict, disagreement, discord, opposition, brush, confrontation, fight, struggle, showdown. HARMONY
clang, clank, crash, clatter.
v, conflict, jar, collide, disagree, differ, quarrel, cross swords. AGREE
crash, bang, clang, clank, clatter, jangle.

clasp *v*, grasp, clutch, hold, grip, seize, press, squeeze, hug, embrace, enfold. RELEASE
fasten, join, connect, concatenate, link, unite. DETACH
n, fastener, hook, catch, hasp, button, buckle, clip, pin, brooch.
grasp, clutch, hold, grip, hug, embrace.

class *n*, set, collection, group, division, classification, category, section, grade, rank, order, degree, league, status, caste, kind, sort, type, genre, species, genus.
form, year, pupils, students, lesson, seminar.
v, classify, rank, grade, order, dispose, group, categorize, designate.

classic *adj*, first-rate, excellent, masterly, consummate, outstanding. INFERIOR
standard, model, archetypal, definitive, ideal, time-honoured, traditional, usual.
n, masterpiece, exemplar, paradigm, prototype, model, standard.

classical Greek, Attic, Grecian, Roman, Latin, Augustan.
pure, chaste, refined, polished, elegant, harmonious, symmetrical. VULGAR

classification arrangement, grouping, organization, codification, categorization, sorting. MUDDLE
category, group, class, division, set, collection.

classify arrange, sort, group, class, rank, rate, grade, categorize, pigeonhole, assort, dispose, distribute, tabulate, catalogue, file. MUDDLE

clatter rattle, crash, clash, clank, clang.

clause provision, proviso, article, stipulation, specification, condition, term, rider, addendum, codicil.
section, passage, paragraph, part, chapter, division, heading.

claw *n*, nail, talon, pincer.
v, scratch, tear, lacerate, rip, gouge, dig, scrape, scrabble.

clean *adj*, spotless, immaculate, unsullied, unsoiled, washed, laundered, scrubbed, dusted. DIRTY
pure, unadulterated, uncontaminated, unpolluted, sterile, antiseptic, hygienic, sanitary. CONTAMINATED
unblemished, flawless, faultless, perfect, whole, entire, complete. IMPERFECT
neat, tidy, elegant, graceful, simple, uncluttered. UNTIDY
innocent, chaste, virginal, decent, respectable, honourable, virtuous, moral. INDECENT
v, cleanse, purify, wash, launder, rinse, scrub, scour, dust, vacuum, sweep, mop, wipe. SOIL
adv, completely, utterly, altogether, entirely, fully, quite.

cleanse clean, wash, scrub, rinse, bathe, purify, clear, absolve. POLLUTE

cleanser soap, detergent, solvent, scourer, disinfectant, purifier.

clear *adj*, bright, light, sunny, cloudless, fine, luminous, undimmed. DULL
transparent, see-through, crystalline, glossy, unclouded, pellucid, limpid, translucent. CLOUDY

plain, distinct, coherent, intelligible, comprehensible, obvious, evident, conspicuous, visible, apparent, patent, manifest, palpable, unquestionable, indisputable, unmistakable, unequivocal, unambiguous, explicit, clear-cut. INDISTINCT
open, free, empty, unobstructed, unencumbered, unhindered, unimpeded, unhampered. BLOCKED
clean, pure, spotless, unsullied, immaculate, innocent, guiltless, unblemished, untarnished, faultless, flawless. TARNISHED
certain, sure, convinced, confident, positive. UNSURE
v, clean, cleanse, sweep, wipe, erase, tidy, refine, purify. POLLUTE
brighten, lighten, clear up, clarify. DARKEN
liberate, free, emancipate, release, discharge, let go, absolve, acquit, exonerate, vindicate, justify. CHARGE
evacuate, empty, disencumber, unload, rid, disentangle, extricate, free, loosen, unblock, remove. ENCUMBER
settle, square, pay off, discharge.
jump, leap, vault, pass over, miss. HIT
authorize, pass, sanction, permit, approve. BAR
clear out, leave, withdraw, depart, go away, beat it (*inf*), clear off (*inf*), decamp.
clear up, clarify, elucidate, explain, solve, resolve.

clearance permission, consent, sanction, authorization, green light, go-ahead.
headroom, leeway, margin, gap, allowance.

cleave[1] split, divide, separate, part, open, sunder, rend, crack, sever, hew, chop, slash. UNITE

cleave[2] cling, adhere, stick, cohere, hold, hold fast, remain faithful, be devoted, stand by. LEAVE

cleft *n*, rift, fissure, crevice, crack, chink, cranny, fracture, break, breach, chasm, hole, gap, opening.
adj, split, divided, separated, parted, rent, torn, cloven, branched, forked.

clemency mercy, leniency, forgiveness, indulgence, tolerance, compassion, tenderness, kindness, humanity, mildness, moderation. HARSHNESS

clement merciful, lenient, forgiving, forbearing, indulgent, tolerant, compassionate, tender, soft-hearted, kind, kind-hearted, benevolent. HARSH
mild, temperate, moderate, balmy, fair, fine.

clench close, shut, grit, tighten, grip, grasp, hold. RELAX

clergyman cleric, churchman, ecclesiastic, divine, minister, vicar, parson, pastor, rector, curate, priest, padre, chaplain, preacher, man of God. LAYMAN

clerical ecclesiastical, priestly, sacerdotal, pastoral, ministerial. LAY
secretarial, office, clerkly, book-keeping, white-collar.

clerk secretary, typist, office worker, junior, recorder, registrar, book-keeper, scribe, pen-pusher.

clever bright, intelligent, brainy (*inf*), quick-witted, smart, astute, sharp, knowledgeable, gifted, talented, able, adroit, apt, skilful, expert, dexterous, capable, ingenious, resourceful, shrewd, cunning, sly. STUPID

cleverness brightness, intelligence, brains, smartness, talent, flair, gift, ability, adroitness, skill, dexterity, ingenuity, resourcefulness, shrewdness, cunning. STUPIDITY

cliché platitude, commonplace, truism, banality, bromide, saw, maxim.

click snap, clack, crack, clink, tick, beat, clap.

client patron, regular, customer, buyer, consumer, user, patient, protégé, dependant.

clientele clients, patrons, regulars, customers, market, business, trade, following.

cliff crag, bluff, precipice, scar, escarpment, headland.

climate weather, clime, temperature, region, area, place, country.
feeling, mood, ambience, atmosphere, trend, tendency.

climax culmination, acme, peak, height, top, head, zenith, high spot (*inf*), crisis, turning point.

climb ascend, mount, scale, go up, shin, clamber, scramble, rise, soar. DESCEND

clinch *v*, secure, fasten, fix, rivet, bolt, clamp, hold, grip, clutch. LOOSE
settle, decide, conclude, complete, cap, close, sew up (*inf*).
n, hold, grip, clasp, clutch.

cling hold fast, cleave, stick, adhere, clasp, clutch, grip, hug, embrace, remain faithful, be devoted. SEPARATE

clinical cold, dispassionate, unemotional, detached, objective, impersonal, scientific, analytic. SUBJECTIVE
clink ring, jingle, chink, tinkle.
clip[1] *v*, trim, cut, snip, prune, pare, crop, shear, shorten, curtail, abridge. ELONGATE
strike, hit, smack, cuff, box, thump.
n, hit, blow, smack, cuff, box, thump.
speed, pace, rate, lick (*inf*).
clip[2] *v*, fasten, fix, pin, hold, attach. DETACH
clipping cutting, excerpt, extract, snippet, piece.
clique set, coterie, gang, clan, party, faction, group, fraternity, club.
cloak *v*, hide, conceal, cover, veil, screen, mask, disguise, camouflage. EXPOSE
n, cape, mantle, wrap, shawl.
cover, screen, mask, veil, blind, front, pretext.
clock timepiece, chronometer, timer, dial, speedometer, taximeter, mileometer.
clod lump, mass, sod, turf, earth.
fool, blockhead, dolt, dunce, clodpoll, clodpate.
clodhopper lout, oaf, clown, yokel, rustic, bumpkin, peasant.
clog *v*, block, obstruct, choke, congest, jam, hamper, hinder, impede, encumber, burden, load, restrain, shackle, fetter. FREE
n, obstruction, hindrance, impediment, burden, encumbrance, drag, restraint, handicap.
cloister colonnade, arcade, piazza, gallery, covered walk, corridor.
monastery, priory, abbey, convent, nunnery.
cloistered cloistral, secluded, sequestered, restricted, confined, sheltered, shielded, reclusive, solitary, monastic, withdrawn. SOCIABLE
close *v*, shut, seal, fasten, secure, lock, bar, stop, block, obstruct, clog, plug. OPEN
finish, end, cease, terminate, conclude, complete, wind up. BEGIN
join, come together, grapple, connect, unite, coalesce, merge, fuse. SEPARATE
close in, approach, draw near, encircle, surround, hem in.
n, end, finish, conclusion, cessation, termination, completion. BEGINNING
courtyard, quadrangle, enclosure, grounds, road, cul-de-sac.
adj, near, nearby, adjacent, adjoining, neighbouring, nigh, imminent, impending, at hand. DISTANT
dense, solid, compact, compressed, tight, packed, crowded.
stuffy, oppressive, stifling, confined, airless, heavy, muggy, humid, stale, stagnant. FRESH
mean, niggardly, miserly, tight-fisted, stingy, near, parsimonious, illiberal, ungenerous. GENEROUS
secret, hidden, concealed, private, secretive, reticent, reserved, taciturn, uncommunicative. OPEN
accurate, exact, precise, faithful, conscientious, true, strict, literal. IMPRECISE
dear, intimate, familiar, devoted, attached, inseparable, loving. DISTANT
intense, keen, fixed, concentrated, earnest, intent, assiduous, thorough, painstaking, dogged.
closet cupboard, cabinet, recess, room, chamber.
closure close, closing, stoppage, end, finish, conclusion. START
stopper, plug, cork, cap, lid, top.
clot *n*, lump, mass, concretion, thrombus, coagulation, clotting.
fool, buffoon, blockhead, dolt, ass, idiot, dope (*inf*), nincompoop.
v, coagulate, congeal, thicken, curdle.
cloth fabric, textile, material, stuff, rag.
clothe dress, attire, array, apparel, garb, robe, deck, fit out, rig out, cover, enwrap, drape, swathe, endow, invest. STRIP
clothes clothing, garments, attire, dress, apparel, vestments, habits, garb, wear, wardrobe, costume, outfit, get-up (*inf*), rig-out (*inf*), gear (*inf*), togs (*inf*).
cloud *n*, haze, mist, vapour, fog, nebulosity, obscurity, darkness, gloom, pall, shroud, blur, smudge.
mass, crowd, horde, throng, host, multitude, swarm, shower, flock.
v, dim, darken, obscure, shadow, overshadow, blur, veil, shroud, eclipse, conceal. CLEAR
cloudy overcast, dark, grey, gloomy, lowering, sunless, murky, muddy, dull, lustreless. BRIGHT
dim, obscure, confused, blurred, indistinct, vague, indefinite. CLEAR
clown buffoon, jester, fool, harlequin, pierrot, joker, comedian.

boor, lout, oaf, clodhoppper, yokel, peasant, bumpkin, dolt. GENTLEMAN

clownish foolish, awkward, clumsy, ungainly, coarse, rough, loutish, boorish, churlish. GENTEEL

cloy surfeit, sate, satiate, pall, glut, gorge, sicken, nauseate.

club *n*, society, association, organization, company, group, circle, clique, coterie, set, fraternity, brotherhood, guild, league, union.
cudgel, truncheon, bludgeon, stick, bat, staff, mace.
v, beat, cudgel, bludgeon, batter, cosh, bash, hammer, strike.
unite, combine, join, amalgamate, confederate, affiliate. SEPARATE

clue hint, guide, indication, tip, tip-off, lead, pointer, sign, key, inkling, suggestion, trace, suspicion.

clump *n*, bunch, cluster, group, collection, mass, bundle, gathering, assemblage.
v, clomp, stomp, stamp, thump, thud, tramp, plod, trudge, lumber.
cluster, gather, bunch, agglutinate, assemble. DISPERSE

clumsy awkward, maladroit, bungling, blundering, unskilful, inexpert, ham-fisted (*inf*), lumbering, ungainly, gauche, ungraceful, ponderous, heavy, unwieldy. ADROIT

cluster *n*, clump, bunch, knot, gathering, collection, group, accumulation, aggregation, agglomeration.
v, bunch, gather, collect, flock, throng, crowd, aggregate, agglomerate, accumulate. DISPERSE

clutch *v*, grasp, grip, hold, clasp, seize, snatch, grab.
n, grasp, grip, hold, clasp.

clutches power, control, keeping, custody, possession, hands, claws, talons.

clutter *v*, strew, scatter, litter, disorder, disarrange, mess.
clatter, rattle, bustle, chatter, gabble.
n, litter, mess, jumble, disorder, disarray, confusion, muddle, hotchpotch, rubbish, lumber.

coach *n*, bus, vehicle, car, carriage.
tutor, instructor, trainer, teacher, manager.
v, train, drill, exercise, instruct, teach, cram (*inf*).

coagulate clot, thicken, curdle, congeal, jell, harden, set.

coalesce unite, combine, incorporate, integrate, amalgamate, blend, mix, merge, fuse, consolidate. SEPARATE

coalition alliance, confederation, confederacy, affiliation, league, bloc, union, compact, amalgamation, merger, fusion, combination. SEPARATION

coarse rough, crude, impure, unrefined, unpolished, unfinished, uneven, scaly, bristly, thick. FINE
rude, vulgar, impolite, indecent, earthy, dirty, smutty, gross, indelicate, immodest, inelegant, lewd, ribald, bawdy. POLITE
uncivil, boorish, uncouth, crass, unsophisticated, brutish. REFINED

coast *n*, seaside, shore, beach, strand, seaboard.
v, sail, glide, cruise, drift, freewheel.

coat *n*, jacket, blazer, overcoat, fur, mackintosh, cape, mantle.
covering, coating, layer, film, sheet, blanket, cover.
hair, fur, pelt, hide, fleece, wool.
v, cover, spread, paint, apply.

coating coat, layer, film, blanket, covering, glaze, varnish, finish.

coax cajole, wheedle, persuade, induce, entice, lure, flatter, soft-soap (*inf*), urge, implore. COERCE

cobble mend, patch, botch, bungle.

cock *n*, rooster, cockerel, chanticleer, male bird. HEN
tap, valve, spigot, stopcock.
v, raise, prick, stick up, stand up, perk up.

cockeyed crooked, askew, awry, lopsided, aslant, skew-whiff (*inf*), crazy, absurd, insane, ludicrous, preposterous.

cocksure overconfident, arrogant, cocky, presumptuous, bumptious, pushy (*inf*). HUMBLE

cocky vain, conceited, egotistical, proud, swollen-headed, arrogant, cocksure. MODEST

coddle pamper, indulge, humour, cosset, mollycoddle, baby, spoil, pet. HARDEN

code system, canon, maxim, rule, regulation, guideline, ethics, morals, custom, convention, etiquette, manners.
cipher, cryptograph, secret writing.

codicil supplement, addendum, addition, rider, postscript, appendix.

codify systematize, organize, classify, catalogue, order, tabulate, collect, summarize, condense, digest.

coerce force, constrain, compel, press, drive, impel, bulldoze (*inf*), browbeat, bully, intimidate. COAX

coercion force, constraint, compulsion, pressure, duress, browbeating, bullying, intimidation. COAXING

coeval coetaneous, coexistent, contemporary, contemporaneous, simultaneous, synchronous, concurrent.

coexistent coetaneous, coeval, contemporary, contemporaneous, simultaneous, synchronous, concurrent.
compatible, cooperating, symbiotic.

coffer chest, trunk, case, box, casket, repository, treasury, safe, strongbox.

coffin casket, sarcophagus, box.

cogency force, strength, conviction, power, potency. WEAKNESS

cogent forceful, strong, convincing, persuasive, potent, powerful, weighty, influential, effective, compelling, irresistible, conclusive. WEAK

cogitate ponder, ruminate, meditate, muse, reflect, contemplate, consider, think, speculate, deliberate, mull over.

cogitation meditation, rumination, reflection, contemplation, consideration, thought, deliberation.

cognate related, akin, kindred, connected, allied, affiliated, analogous, alike, similar. UNRELATED

cognition perception, awareness, discernment, intuition, insight, reasoning, intelligence, comprehension, understanding, knowledge, cognizance.

cognizance knowledge, acquaintance, perception, cognition, recognition, acknowledgment, notice, apprehension. IGNORANCE

cognizant aware, informed, knowledgeable, conscious, acquainted, familiar, conversant. IGNORANT

cognize perceive, comprehend, recognize, know, notice, discern.

cognomen surname, title, name, nickname, sobriquet.

cohere stick, adhere, cling, cleave, join, unite, fuse, coalesce. PART
be consistent, be connected, follow, make sense, hang together, hold good, correspond, agree.

coherence consistency, connection, agreement, congruity, unity, harmony, logic, intelligibilty, comprehension. INCOHERENCE

coherent consistent, connected, congruous, logical, orderly, rational, articulate, intelligible, comprehensible. INCOHERENT

cohesion adhesion, adherence, union, fusion, coalescence, accretion, consolidation. DISINTEGRATION

cohort band, company, troop, legion, squadron, regiment.

coil *n*, spiral, helix, convolution, curl, loop.
v, wind, twine, twist, curl, loop, spiral, convolute, convolve, wreathe, entwine. UNCOIL

coin *v*, devise, invent, create, formulate, make up, originate, fabricate, make, mould, stamp, mint, forge, counterfeit.
n, money, specie, cash, change, silver, copper.

coincide agree, concur, correspond, tally, harmonize, match, square. CLASH
synchronize, be concurrent, coexist, happen together, occur simultaneously.

coincidence chance, accident, fluke, fortuity, stroke of luck. DESIGN
correspondence, harmony, concurrence, agreement. DIFFERENCE
synchronism, coexistence, simultaneity, concomitance.

coincident corresponding, agreeing, concurring, coinciding, harmonious, coordinate. DIFFERING
synchronous, simultaneous, concurrent, concomitant, contemporaneous, coexistent.

coincidental chance, fortuitous, casual, accidental, unplanned, unforeseen. PLANNED

cold *adj*, cool, chill, chilly, frigid, gelid, freezing, icy, frozen, frosty, arctic, polar, wintry, raw, bitter, biting, nippy. HOT
unfeeling, unsympathetic, unresponsive, impassive, indifferent, apathetic, unmoved, unconcerned, distant, stand offish, aloof, frigid, glacial, stony, lukewarm, unfriendly, inhospitable. WARM
n, coldness, chill, chilliness, frigidity, iciness, frost. HEAT

cold-blooded cruel, inhuman, barbarous, brutal, savage, vicious, ruthless, merciless, heartless, callous, unfeeling. HUMANE

collaborate cooperate, work together, join forces, team up. COMPETE

collaborator partner, associate, confederate, colleague, contributor, participant. RIVAL
traitor, turncoat, double-dealer, collaborationist, quisling. PATRIOT

collapse *v*, subside, cave in, give way, crumble, fall, break down, founder, fail, fold, faint. RECOVER
n, subsidence, breakdown, fall, downfall, failure, faint, exhaustion, prostration. RECOVERY

collar *n*, ruff, gorget, neckband, collarette, band, necklace.
v, grab, seize, catch, capture, apprehend, arrest. RELEASE

collate compare, analogize, check, verify, collect, gather, sort, collocate.

collateral *n*, security, surety, deposit, pledge, assurance, guarantee.
adj, parallel, indirect, related, subordinate, secondary, supporting.

collation comparison, verification, collocation, collection.
snack, bite, light meal.

colleague partner, associate, co-worker, teammate, workmate, helper, aider, assistant, auxiliary, ally, confederate, collaborator, cooperator, friend, companion, comrade. OPPONENT

collect gather, muster, assemble, amass, accumulate, aggregate, congregate, cluster, agglomerate, heap, pile, glean, hoard, save, stockpile. DISPERSE
fetch, pick up, call for.

collection gathering, muster, assembly, crowd, congregation, cluster, group, assortment, set, accumulation, heap, pile, hoard, store, anthology, compilation. DISPERSION
offering, offertory, alms, donation, contribution, whip-round (*inf*).

college school, polytechnic, university, academy, institution, department, faculty.
association, society, guild, league, body, company, corporation.

collide crash, smash, bump, encounter, clash, conflict.

colligate connect, link, tie, fasten, bind, join, unite, combine, relate.

collision crash, smash, impact, bump, encounter, accident, pile-up.
clash, conflict, opposition. ACCORD

collocate arrange, order, dispose, classify, tabulate, sort, place, group, put together, collate.

collocation grouping, order, arrangement, organization, sorting, placing, allocation.

colloquial conversational, idiomatic, vernacular, informal, casual, familiar, everyday. FORMAL

colloquy conversation, discourse, talk, dialogue, debate, discussion, conference.

collude connive, conspire, plot, intrigue, scheme, machinate, collaborate, abet.

collusion connivance, conspiracy, complicity, intrigue, cahoots (*inf*), plot, scheme.

collusive conniving, scheming, deceitful, fraudulent, dishonest. HONEST

colony settlement, community, group, district, quarter, province, dependency, dominion, territory.

colossal enormous, huge, gigantic, immense, massive, mammoth, vast, mountainous, herculean, titanic, prodigious, tremendous. TINY

colour *n*, tint, hue, shade, tinge, tincture, dye, paint, pigment, colorant, colouring, complexion, tone.
rosiness, ruddiness, flush, blush, glow, bloom. PALLOR
disguise, pretence, guise, semblance, front, façade, appearance, pretext, excuse.
vt, dye, stain, paint, tint, tinge.
distort, pervert, garble, falsify, disguise, varnish, exaggerate.
vi, blush, flush, redden, go crimson. BLANCH

colourful bright, vivid, rich, intense, brilliant, multicoloured, psychedelic, kaleidoscopic. COLOURLESS

colourless achromatic, hueless, uncoloured, blanched, bleached, washed out, anaemic, wan, ashen, pale, pallid, pasty, livid. COLOURFUL
dull, dreary, dry, insipid, vapid, monotonous, boring, uninteresting, characterless. EXCITING

colours banner, ensign, standard, flag.
nature, character, personality, identity, attitude, breed, strain, stamp.

colt foal, youngster, novice, beginner, junior.

coltish frisky, frolicsome, playful, lively, spirited, sportive, unruly. LETHARGIC

column pillar, post, shaft, support, upright, obelisk, monolith, caryatid.
list, file, row, line, string, procession, train.
article, feature, editorial, review.

coma stupor, unconsciousness, oblivion, torpor, lethargy, somnolence. CONSCIOUSNESS

comatose unconscious, insensible, drugged, stupefied, torpid, drowsy, sleepy, somnolent, sluggish, lethargic. LIVELY

comb *v*, disentangle, untangle, groom, curry, smooth, arrange, dress.
sift, search, rake, rummage, scour.

combat *v*, fight, oppose, resist, withstand, defy, battle, contest, contend, struggle, strive. SURRENDER
n, war, battle, action, fight, conflict, encounter, contest, engagement, skirmish, struggle, strife. PEACE

combatant fighter, soldier, adversary, opponent, enemy, contestant, competitor, champion. NEUTRAL

combination mixture, blend, compound, synthesis, amalgamation, composite.
fusion, conjunction, blending, coalescence, mixing, mingling. SEPARATION
association, union, combine, alliance, coalition, confederacy, league, consortium, cabal, conspiracy.

combine *v*, mix, blend, compound, synthesize, mingle, amalgamate, put together, incorporate, integrate, unite, join, fuse, bond, marry, link, connect, pool, merge. SEPARATE
n, association, alliance, coalition, league, confederacy.

combustible inflammable, flammable, ignitable, incendiary.

combustion burning, incineration, cremation, ignition.

come approach, advance, near, move towards, arrive, reach, turn up (*inf*), appear. DEPART
occur, happen, take place, befall, come about, transpire.
issue, originate, proceed, flow, emanate, result, ensue, arise, spring.
come across, find, discover, stumble upon, chance upon, meet, encounter, run into, bump into (*inf*).
come at, attack, assault, assail, charge, rush, fall upon, fly at. RESIST
come by, obtain, get, acquire, procure.
come in, enter, cross the threshold, penetrate, arrive, appear, show up (*inf*). LEAVE
come round, relent, submit, yield, bend, mellow, soften, acquiesce, concede, allow.
come to, recover, revive, regain consciousness, come round, stir. FAINT
come up with, advance, propose, put forward, suggest, submit, present, produce, provide, supply.

comedian comic, wit, humorist, joker, clown, jester.

comedown decline, humiliation, deflation, reverse, blow, disappointment, anticlimax.

comedy farce, satire, slapstick, sitcom, pantomime, burlesque, revue.
wit, drollery, humour, fun, joking, badinage, witticisms, buffoonery.

comeliness prettiness, beauty, fairness, attractiveness, loveliness, grace, elegance. UGLINESS

comely pretty, good-looking, attractive, beautiful, handsome, fair, lovely, winsome, elegant, graceful. UGLY

comfort *v*, console, solace, cheer, encourage, hearten, gladden, inspirit, enliven, reassure, relieve, ease, alleviate, soothe, assuage, calm, revive, refresh, strengthen, invigorate. TROUBLE
n, consolation, compensation, solace, cheer, encouragement, reassurance, relief, ease, alleviation, help, aid, succour. DISTRESS
well-being, ease, contentment, satisfaction, peace, snugness, cosiness, luxury, opulence, plenty. NEED

comfortable snug, cosy, comfy (*inf*), agreeable, pleasant, luxurious, ample, easy, relaxing, restful, convenient, commodious. UNCOMFORTABLE
relaxed, at ease, satisfied, contented, cheerful, serene, tranquil, well-off, prosperous, affluent. UNEASY

comfortless dismal, bleak, cheerless, dreary, cold, inhospitable. COMFORTING
disconsolate, forlorn, wretched, miserable, woebegone. CHEERFUL

comic *adj*, humorous, witty, droll, zany, amusing, funny, farcical, slapstick, comical. SERIOUS
n, comedian, humorist, wit, joker, clown, jester.

comical funny, amusing, entertaining, diverting, comic, droll, ludicrous, ridiculous, absurd, laughable, hilarious, side-splitting. SERIOUS

coming *adj*, approaching, near, at hand, imminent, impending, in store, forthcoming, future, next. PAST
n, arrival, advent, approach. DEPARTURE

comity civility, courtesy, politeness, urbanity, suavity, affability. INCIVILITY

command *v*, order, enjoin, bid, direct, charge, require, instruct, compel, demand. OBEY
govern, rule, control, lead, head, supervise, dominate.
n, order, injunction, bidding, behest, charge, direction, instruction, decree, commandment, edict, precept, demand, requirement, mandate. ENTREATY
government, rule, control, authority, mastery, power, sway, charge, leadership, dominion, domination. SUBORDINATION

commandeer seize, take, usurp, appropriate, requisition, expropriate, hijack, confiscate, sequester, impound. SURRENDER

commander captain, chief, leader, head, ruler, governor, boss, director, commanding officer.

commanding dominant, superior, advantageous, dominating, overlooking.
impressive, imposing, forceful, assertive, compelling, authoritative, imperious, peremptory. MEEK

commemorate celebrate, observe, keep, mark, honour, solemnize, immortalize, perpetuate, memorialize, remember, pay tribute to, salute. FORGET

commemoration celebration, observance, memorial service, ceremony, remembrance, tribute, memoralization, perpetuation.

commemorative memorial, celebratory, dedicatory, perpetuating, acknowledging, marking, in remembrance, in memory, in honour.

commence begin, start, embark on, open, inaugurate, institute, initiate, originate, instigate. END

commencement beginning, start, opening, outset, inauguration, institution, initiation, origin, dawn, birth. END

commend praise, extol, laud, applaud, acclaim, eulogize, speak highly of, compliment, approve, recommend, promote, endorse, advocate. CENSURE
entrust, commit, hand over, yield, give, deliver, consign, confide.

commendable laudable, praiseworthy, admirable, exemplary, noble, estimable, worthy, deserving, creditable. DEPLORABLE

commendation praise, compliment, tribute, approval, approbation, eulogy, panegyric, encomium, acclaim, applause, encouragement. CONDEMNATION

commensurate corresponding, proportionate, to scale, equal, coextensive, equivalent, comparable, appropriate, due, fit, in accord, compatible, adequate, sufficient.

comment *v*, remark, observe, say, point out, mention, note, annotate, explain, interpret, criticize, illustrate.
n, remark, observation, statement, note, annotation, explanation, commentary, exposition, criticism, illustration.

commentary narration, comments, remarks, notes, annotation, exposition, explanation, interpretation, analysis, critique, review, dissertation, essay, record, chronicle, journal.

commentator reporter, broadcaster, sportscaster, narrator, commenter, interpreter, annotator, critic.

commerce trade, business, traffic, barter, dealing, exchange, merchandising.
communication, intercourse, relations, dealings, interchange, communion.

commercial trading, mercantile, business, saleable, marketable, profit-making, mercenary.

commingle mingle, intermingle, mix, commix, intermix, blend, combine, amalgamate, join, unite. SEPARATE

comminute break, shatter, splinter, fragment, pulverize, triturate, grind.

commiserate sympathize, condole, pity, feel sorry for, feel for, grieve, console, comfort, solace.

commiseration sympathy, condolence, pity, compassion, fellow feeling, consolation, comfort, solace.

commission *n*, errand, duty, task, mission, assignment, appointment, job, function, employment, charge, mandate, authority, warrant, permit.
committee, board, delegation, deputation, council.
allowance, dividend, percentage, cut, share, rake-off (*inf*), fee, brokerage.

perpetration, committal, execution, performance.
v, authorize, empower, nominate, appoint, delegate, depute, assign, detail, engage, contract, order.

commissioner agent, deputy, delegate, representative, envoy, ambassador, official, officer.

commit do, perform, perpetrate, enact, execute, carry out.
entrust, consign, deliver, confide, hand over, charge, commend.
engage, align, pledge, obligate, bind, implicate, compromise.
confine, imprison, jail, intern, incarcerate. RELEASE

commitment pledge, engagement, promise, guarantee, vow, undertaking, obligation, duty, responsibility, liability.
dedication, involvement, loyalty, devotion.

committal consignment, delivery, entrustment, assignment, commission, delegation.
perpetration, commission, execution, performance.
imprisonment, confinement, custody, detention, incarceration.

committee board, council, panel, commission, jury, working party.

commodious spacious, ample, roomy, capacious, large, extensive, vast, expansive, comfortable, convenient. NARROW

commodities goods, wares, produce, merchandise, products, stock.

common universal, general, public, communal, joint, shared, mutual. PRIVATE
ordinary, everyday, usual, average, standard, customary, habitual, regular, plain, simple, workaday, run-of-the-mill, widespread, general, familiar, popular, conventional. RARE
trite, hackneyed, stale, commonplace, inferior, vulgar, cheap, low, coarse, undistinguished. REFINED

commonplace *adj*, ordinary, everyday, common, undistinguished, humdrum, trite, obvious, banal, hackneyed, stale, threadbare. DISTINCTIVE
n, cliché, platitude, truism, banality.

common-sense *adj*, common-sensical, sensible, sound, wise, practical, reasonable, realistic, prudent, judicious, level-headed, shrewd, astute, down-to-earth, matter-of-fact. FOOLISH
n, intelligence, good sense, mother wit, prudence, practicality, wisdom, discernment, gumption (*inf*), nous (*inf*). FOLLY

commonwealth empire, realm, state, nation, people, republic.

commotion turmoil, tumult, upheaval, disorder, disturbance, fuss, ado, furore, agitation, perturbation, bustle, uproar, hullabaloo, to-do, riot, rumpus, brouhaha. CALM

communal public, common, shared, collective, joint. PRIVATE

commune[1] *v*, communicate, converse, talk, confer, discourse, discuss, confide.

commune[2] *n*, community, collective, cooperative, kibbutz.

communicable transferable, transmittable, infectious, contagious, catching.

communicate impart, transmit, inform, tell, declare, announce, divulge, disclose, reveal, disseminate, spread, pass on, bestow, confer, convey. WITHHOLD
converse, talk, commune, correspond, ring up, call, be in contact, get in touch.
connect, adjoin.

communication announcement, declaration, disclosure, communiqué, dispatch, news, information, report, account, statement, bulletin, message.
conversation, discourse, intercourse, correspondence, contact, touch, link, connection.
dissemination, spreading, transmission, conveyance.

communicative open, unreserved, forthcoming, expansive, frank, candid, talkative, voluble, loquacious, chatty, sociable. RESERVED

communion intercourse, exchange, conversation, dialogue, rapport, sympathy, affinity, participation, intimacy, closeness, togetherness, harmony, accord, concord, agreement, unity. ESTRANGEMENT
Eucharist, Lord's Supper, Sacrament, Mass.

communist Marxist, Bolshevik, collectivist, socialist, leftist, radical, Red (*inf*). FASCIST

community society, general public, nation, state, people, populace, brotherhood, association, company, colony, village, township, district, neighbourhood, parish.
similarity, likeness, affinity, agreement.

commute exchange, barter, substitute, switch, replace, change, alter.
reduce, shorten, curtail, remit, mitigate, alleviate.

compact[1] *adj*, close, dense, thick, impenetrable, impermeable, solid, firm, compressed, condensed, packed, tight, small, neat, portable. LOOSE
short, terse, concise, brief, succinct, pithy, laconic. LENGTHY
v, compress, condense, pack, cram, stuff, consolidate, fuse, bind, join, unite. DIFFUSE

compact[2] *n*, contract, covenant, treaty, concordat, alliance, pact, entente, bond, agreement, arrangement, bargain, deal.

companion associate, comrade, colleague, partner, consort, fellow, counterpart, mate, accomplice, ally, friend, acquaintance. FOE
attendant, escort, chaperon, duenna, aide, assistant, squire.

companionship fellowship, friendship, amity, brotherhood, fraternity, comradeship, camaraderie, esprit de corps, rapport, conviviality, company, togetherness, society, association. LONELINESS

company business, firm, corporation, association, syndicate, partnership, concern, establishment, house.
assembly, assemblage, gathering, concourse, convention, meeting, collection, group, band, troop, troupe, body, party, ensemble, gang, set, circle, association, crowd, congregation.
companionship, fellowship, society, visitors, guests, callers, party.

comparable like, similar, akin, related, alike, resembling, corresponding, equivalent, commensurate, approximate, tantamount, as good as, equal, on a par. INCOMPARABLE

comparative relative, by comparison, qualified, approximate, near. ABSOLUTE

compare liken, equate, correlate, relate, parallel, match, juxtapose, contrast, collate, balance, weigh.
resemble, equal, correspond, be on a par, approximate, approach, compete, vie.

comparison likeness, resemblance, similarity, relation, correlation, comparability, likening, parallel, analogy, simile. CONTRAST
juxtaposition, collation, contrast, distinction.

compartment partition, division, section, part, space, area, department. WHOLE
locker, cubbyhole, pigeonhole, booth, cubicle, cell, alcove, niche.

compass *n*, range, scope, extent, reach, stretch, circumference, bound, boundary, limit, sphere, realm, zone, field, area, enclosure.
v, encircle, encompass, surround, circumscribe, environ, gird, enclose, hem in, besiege, beset.
attain, achieve, accomplish, realize, fulfil, effect, perform, execute, obtain, procure. FAIL

compassion sympathy, commiseration, pity, tenderness, kindliness, kindness, clemency, mercy, humanity, charity. CRUELTY

compassionate kind, kindly, tender, sympathetic, benign, understanding, humane, soft-hearted, indulgent, clement, lenient, merciful, charitable, benevolent, magnanimous. HARSH

compatible congruous, consistent, accordant, reconcilable, in keeping, consonant, harmonious, in harmony, agreeable, like-minded, at one. INCOMPATIBLE

compatriot fellow countryman, fellow citizen.

compeer peer, equal, mate, fellow, counterpart, companion, comrade. SUPERIOR

compel force, coerce, drive, impel, urge, make, oblige, constrain, require, exact, necessitate. COAX
subdue, overpower, crush, bow.

compelling enthralling, gripping, riveting, spellbinding, hypnotic. BORING
forceful, convincing, irrefutable, cogent, weighty, powerful. WEAK

compendious concise, succinct, brief, short, terse, abridged, condensed, compressed, compact, pithy, comprehensive, summary. EXTENDED

compendium synopsis, summary, digest, abstract, epitome, abridgment, condensation, résumé, précis, syllabus, prospectus. AMPLIFICATION

compensate recompense, reimburse, refund, repay, remunerate, reward, requite, indemnify, satisfy, atone, make amends, make good, make up for, redress. INJURE offset, balance, counterbalance, cancel out, neutralize, nullify.

compensation recompense, reimbursement, repayment, refund, remuneration, reward, indemnity, reparation, damages, satisfaction, atonement, amends. INJURY

compete contest, contend, vie, rival, emulate, challenge, oppose, struggle, strive, fight, participate. ALLY

competence ability, capability, capacity, adequacy, fitness, suitability, qualification, skill, expertise, proficiency, mastery. INCOMPETENCE

sufficiency, enough, subsistence, means, wherewithal, livelihood. POVERTY

competent able, capable, adequate, sufficient, fit, suitable, equal, qualified, expert, proficient, masterful, skilled, skilful, adept, knowledgeable. INCOMPETENT

competition contest, tournament, match, championship, race, game, quiz.

rivalry, emulation, one-upmanship (*inf*), contention, strife, conflict, opposition. ALLIANCE

competitive rival, competing, vying, combative, aggressive, cutthroat, striving, ambitious.

competitor rival, opponent, adversary, antagonist, opposition, competition, emulator, challenger, contestant, contender, entrant, candidate, aspirant. PARTNER

compilation collection, anthology, treasury, assortment, selection, compendium.

compiling, gathering, assembly, combination, accumulation.

compile collect, gather, garner, cull, amass, accumulate, assemble, put together, prepare, compose, organize, arrange.

complacency self-satisfaction, smugness, contentment, pleasure, satisfaction, gratification, ease, tranquillity. UNEASINESS

complacent self-satisfied, smug, contented, pleased, satisfied, serene, tranquil, at ease, placid, unconcerned. UNEASY

complain grumble, moan, groan, grouse, gripe (*inf*), bellyache (*inf*), beef (*inf*), bewail, bemoan, lament, deplore, murmur, carp, find fault, cavil. REJOICE

complainant accuser, claimant, plaintiff, petitioner. DEFENDANT

complaint grumble, grievance, grouse, plaint, lament, moan, quibble, cavil, criticism, accusation, charge, remonstrance, protest.

ailment, disorder, malady, affliction, indisposition, illness, sickness, disease. HEALTH

complaisance deference, compliance, obligingness, acquiescence, agreeableness, graciousness, urbanity, suavity, politeness, courtesy, civility. CHURLISHNESS

complaisant deferential, compliant, obliging, acquiescent, agreeable, accommodating, gracious, urbane, polite, civil, courteous. CHURLISH

complement *n*, quota, total, totality, aggregate, full number, capacity, entirety, whole. PART

counterpart, companion, match, coordinate, supplement, accessory, finishing touch.

v, complete, supplement, add to, make up, round off, crown, set off. CLASH

complementary completing, perfecting, consummating, corresponding, reciprocal, correlative, interdependent, matched. CONFLICTING

complete *adj*, entire, whole, total, full, integral, unabridged, undivided, unimpaired, perfect. INCOMPLETE

completed, finished, ended, concluded, fulfilled, accomplished, achieved, done. UNFINISHED

absolute, utter, thorough, downright, total, out-and-out, perfect, consummate. PARTIAL

v, finish, end, conclude, terminate, fulfil, realize, achieve, attain, accomplish, perform, do, execute, perfect, consummate, crown, cap. BEGIN

completion conclusion, end, finish, termination, close, fulfilment, realization, achievement, fruition, accomplishment, performance, execution, perfection, consummation. BEGINNING

complex manifold, multiple, composite, compound, mingled, mixed, elaborate, intricate, involved, knotty, tangled, complicated, tortuous, labyrinthine. SIMPLE

complexion colour, colouring, skin tone, pigmentation, cast, appearance, aspect, countenance, look, character, nature, angle, light.

complexity intricacy, complication, ramification, involvement, entanglement, network, labyrinth. SIMPLICITY

compliance acquiescence, yielding, concession, concurrence, consent, assent, agreement, complaisance, submission, docility, obedience, cooperation, conformity. RESISTANCE

compliant acquiescent, yielding, obliging, accommodating, complaisant, agreeable, submissive, docile, obedient, cooperative. OBSTINATE

complicate confuse, involve, entangle, muddle, confound. SIMPLIFY

complicated confused, involved, complex, intricate, elaborate, convoluted, tangled, knotty, perplexing, labyrinthine. SIMPLE

complication complexity, intricacy, confusion, tangle, entanglement, web, network. SIMPLICITY
difficulty, problem, drawback, snag, obstacle.

complicity collusion, conspiracy, connivance, collaboration, abetment.

compliment *v*, praise, speak highly of, commend, acclaim, laud, extol, flatter, congratulate, felicitate. INSULT
n, praise, commendation, eulogy, encomium, tribute, honour, flattery, admiration, congratulations. ABUSE

complimentary flattering, congratulatory, laudatory, eulogistic, commendation, appreciative, approving, adulatory. INSULTING
free, gratis, on the house.

compliments greetings, respects, regards, good wishes.

comply obey, conform, accede, abide by, observe, respect, defer, submit, yield, acquiesce, agree, consent, fulfil, discharge, perform, execute, meet, satisfy. REFUSE

component *n*, constituent, element, part, ingredient, unit, item, piece, factor. WHOLE
adj, constituent, integral, intrinsic.

comport agree, tally, correspond, harmonize, accord, match, suit, square, coincide. DIFFER
behave, conduct, act, demean, carry, bear, acquit.

compose form, make, put together, construct, build, comprise, constitute, make up, invent, create, contrive, devise, write, frame, produce.
adjust, arrange, organize, settle, resolve, regulate. DISORGANIZE
pacify, calm, soothe, assuage, appease, still, quiet, quell, control, collect. DISTURB

composed calm, tranquil, serene, sedate, cool, collected, self-possessed, unruffled, poised, imperturbable, placid, relaxed, at ease, untroubled. AGITATED

composite *adj*, compound, complex, intricate, manifold, multiple, mixed, combined, synthesized, hybrid. SIMPLE
n, compound, blend, mixture, synthesis, combination.

composition formation, make-up, structure, arrangement, organization, form, constitution.
making, creation, production, manufacture, fabrication, formulation.
work, essay, opus, piece, exercise.

compost fertilizer, manure, muck, dung, mulch.

composure calmness, tranquillity, serenity, coolness, self-possession, sang-froid, poise, aplomb, imperturbability, placidity, ease, equanimity. AGITATION

compound *v*, mix, blend, combine, mingle, intermingle, amalgamate, unite, synthesize, fuse. SEPARATE
intensify, augment, heighten, aggravate, exacerbate, complicate. LESSEN
arrange, settle, agree, compromise.
n, mixture, blend, combination, composite, synthesis, amalgam, alloy, medley, composition.
adj, composite, complex, complicated, intricate, multiple, combined. SIMPLE

comprehend understand, fathom, apprehend, grasp, see, perceive, conceive, discern, make out, assimilate, take in.
include, comprise, embrace, involve, contain. EXCLUDE

comprehensible understandable, intelligible, clear, coherent, explicit, plain, distinct, articulate. INCOMPREHENSIBLE

comprehension understanding, apprehension, grasp, perception, conception, discernment, awareness, sense, intelligence, intellect, knowledge, wisdom. INCOMPREHENSION
compass, scope, range, extent, reach, field, limits.

comprehensive wide, broad, large, extensive, sweeping, full, encyclopedic, inclusive, all-inclusive, all-embracing, exhaustive, thorough, universal, catholic. LIMITED

compress compact, concentrate, press, squeeze, squash, crush, cram, pack, constrict, contract, condense, abbreviate, shorten, summarize, abridge. EXPAND

compression contraction, constriction, pressure, squeezing, condensation, abbreviation, shortening. EXPANSION

comprise include, contain, embrace, comprehend, consist of. EXCLUDE
form, compose, constitute, make up.

compromise *v*, agree, concede, settle, compose, adjust, accommodate, meet halfway, give and take. DIFFER
imperil, endanger, jeopardize, hazard, expose, implicate, prejudice, discredit, weaken. PROTECT
n, agreement, settlement, concession, give-and-take, adjustment, accommodation, middle ground, happy medium, balance.

compulsion force, constraint, coercion, obligation, duress, pressure. COAXING
urge, drive, need, obsession, preoccupation.

compulsive compelling, urgent, driving, overwhelming, uncontrollable, obsessive, habitual, inveterate.

compulsory obligatory, binding, imperative, mandatory, necessary, requisite, unavoidable. VOLUNTARY

compunction remorse, regret, contrition, repentance, penitence, qualm, misgiving, hesitation, reluctance, sorrow, guilt, embarrassment. SATISFACTION

compunctious remorseful, regretful, sorry, apologetic, contrite, repentant, penitent, hesitant, reluctant, sorrowful, ashamed, embarrassed.

computation calculation, reckoning, estimation, valuation, measurement, adding up, counting, enumeration.

compute calculate, work out, reckon, figure, estimate, rate, total, add up, count, enumerate, measure. GUESS

comrade companion, associate, mate, fellow, compeer, colleague, partner, ally, friend, pal (*inf*). ENEMY

con *v*, swindle, defraud, deceive, dupe, cheat, hoodwink, mislead, rip off (*inf*).
n, swindle, fraud, deception, trick, hoax, rip-off (*inf*).

concatenate join, connect, link, unite, couple, string, chain. SEVER

concatenation chain, series, succession, sequence, continuity, connection, linking, link, nexus, coupling.

concave hollow, hollowed, sunken, depressed, cupped, scooped, excavated. CONVEX

conceal hide, secrete, disguise, dissemble, screen, cloak, mask, camouflage, veil, obscure, cover, bury, suppress. REVEAL

concealment hiding, disguise, camouflage, masking, screening, cover-up, blind, cover, hideaway, shelter, retreat, privacy. REVELATION

concede admit, acknowledge, grant, allow, recognize, accept, yield, surrender, cede, relinquish, hand over, deliver. DENY

conceit vanity, egotism, vainglory, pride, self-esteem, self-love, narcissism, boastfulness, swagger, arrogance, complacency. MODESTY
notion, fancy, idea, thought, belief, concept, whim.

conceited vain, egotistical, vainglorious, arrogant, proud, cocky, bigheaded (*inf*), boastful, smug, complacent, self-important, narcissistic. MODEST

conceivable possible, imaginable, thinkable, picturable, believable, credible. INCONCEIVABLE

conceive imagine, think, picture, envisage, fancy, suppose, comprehend, understand, perceive, apprehend, grasp, fathom, see.
devise, contrive, invent, think up, formulate, design, plan, project.

concentrate focus, converge, centre, centralize, localize, cluster, conglomerate, congregate, assemble, muster, amass, collect. DISPERSE
condense, reduce, distil, purify, intensify, thicken, compress, compact. DILUTE
meditate, ponder, ruminate, think, be engrossed, pay attention.

concentration attention, application, absorption, heed, deliberation, meditation. DISTRACTION
convergence, focus, centralization, intensification, consolidation, collection, gathering, conglomeration, cluster, aggregation, accumulation, mass. DISPERSAL

concept conception, idea, notion, thought, abstraction, impression, hypothesis, theory.

conception idea, notion, concept, thought, theory, design, plan.
impression, picture, image, perception, understanding, comprehension, inkling, clue.
fertilization, fecundation, impregnation, insemination.
beginning, origin, birth, inception, genesis, outset, inauguration, invention. TERMINATION

concern interest, affect, involve, relate to, touch, regard, bear on, apply to.
disturb, trouble, distress, worry, disquiet, perturb, bother.
n, affair, business, duty, responsibility, field, matter, interest, importance, consequence, bearing, relevance.
anxiety, worry, care, solicitude, sympathy, regard, heed, attention, distress, disquiet, sorrow, grief. INDIFFERENCE
company, firm, business, enterprise, establishment, corporation, house.

concerning about, touching, regarding, respecting, re, with reference to, relating to, apropos of. DISREGARDING

concert *n*, performance, entertainment, recital, symphony, concerto, festival, gig (*inf*).
agreement, accord, concord, harmony, unison, unanimity, concensus, cooperation. DISAGREEMENT
v, arrange, contrive, devise, design, concoct, plan, plot, scheme.

concerted combined, united, joint, mutual, cooperative, collaborative, prearranged, planned. INDIVIDUAL

concession yielding, surrender, admission, acknowledgment, assent, grant, licence, permit, right, privilege, boon, exemption, dispensation, indulgence, allowance, adjustment, compromise. REFUSAL

conciliate win, win over, placate, appease, propitiate, pacify, mollify, reconcile, reunite, mediate, negotiate. ALIENATE

conciliation appeasement, propitiation, placation, peace, pacification, reconciliation. ESTRANGEMENT

conciliatory placatory, pacifying, appeasing, propitiative, pacific, peaceable, disarming, winning, friendly.

concise brief, short, terse, to the point, compact, pithy, succinct, laconic, condensed, compressed, summary, compendious, epigrammatic. LENGTHY

conclave council, assembly, meeting, session, cabinet, synod, convention, conference.

conclude close, end, terminate, finish, complete, wind up (*inf*), wrap up (*inf*). BEGIN
settle, resolve, decide, determine, negotiate, effect, accomplish, pull off (*inf*), clinch (*inf*).
infer, deduce, construe, surmise, guess, assume, suppose, gather, reckon, judge, decide.

conclusion close, end, ending, termination, finish, completion, outcome, issue, result, upshot. BEGINNING
inference, deduction, surmise, guess, assumption, supposition, opinion, judgment, decision, resolution, verdict.

conclusive final, definitive, ultimate, definite, positive, decisive, convincing, clinching, indisputable, irrefutable, unanswerable. INCONCLUSIVE

concoct contrive, devise, invent, think up, cook up (*inf*), brew, hatch, plot, plan, prepare, project, design, make up, formulate.

concoction mixture, compound, blend, brew, potion.

concomitant attendant, accompanying, associative, connected, concurrent, synchronous, coincident, contemporaneous. INDEPENDENT

concord harmony, agreement, accord, concert, unanimity, consensus, concordance, amity, unity, peace, rapport, friendship, good will. DISCORD
treaty, compact, concordant, entente, convention, pact, agreement.

concordant harmonious, in agreement, consonant, agreeing, accordant, unanimous, at one. DISCORDANT

concordat covenant, agreement, bond, compact, treaty, pact, convention, settlement, bargain.

concourse assembly, assemblage, gathering, meeting, collection, crowd, throng, mob, multitude, horde, crush, cluster, convergence, confluence.

concrete *n*, cement, mortar.
adj, real, material, tangible, substantial, physical, actual, factual. ABSTRACT
specific, particular, precise, explicit, definite. VAGUE

firm, solid, solidified, consolidated, compressed, compact, petrified, calcified. FLUID

concubine mistress, paramour, courtesan, kept woman, odalisque.

concupiscence desire, passion, lust, lechery, lasciviousness, prurience, randiness (*inf*). CONTINENCE

concur agree, assent, acquiesce, accede, accord, harmonize, coincide, cooperate, combine, collaborate. DISSENT

concurrence agreement, assent, accord, harmony, unity, coincidence, simultaneity, cooperation, collaboration, alliance, combination. DISAGREEMENT

concurrent simultaneous, synchronous, contemporaneous, parallel, coincident, concomitant, attendant.
convergent, confluent, intersecting. DIVERGENT
agreeing, accordant, harmonious, consentient, in agreement, unanimous, at one. DISCORDANT

concussion collision, crash, impact, shock, clash, blow, jolt, jarring.
shaking, agitation.

condemn doom, damn, sentence, convict, find guilty. ACQUIT
censure, blame, disapprove, rebuke, upbraid, reproach, reprove, reprobate, denounce, proscribe, prohibit, ban, bar. PRAISE

condemnation conviction, sentence, judgment, doom, damnation. ACQUITTAL
censure, blame, disapproval, disapprobation, reproof, reproach, reprobation, denunciation, proscription, banning, prohibition. PRAISE

condemnatory accusatory, incriminating, damning, imputative, denunciatory, censorious, critical, disapproving, reproachful, defamatory, deprecatory. LAUDATORY

condensation contraction, compression, reduction, abridgment, abbreviation, curtailment, diminution, concentration, consolidation, crystallization, precipitation, distillation, liquefaction. AMPLIFICATION
digest, epitome, summary, abridgment, synopsis, précis, résumé, abstract.

condense contract, compress, reduce, compact, encapsulate, abridge, abbreviate, curtail, shorten, diminish, concentrate, consolidate, solidify, coagulate, thicken, boil down, precipitate, crystallize, liquefy. AMPLIFY

condescend deign, stoop, vouchsafe, see fit, unbend, descend, lower oneself, humble oneself, patronize, talk down.

condescending patronizing, disdainful, supercilious, pompous, lofty, haughty, arrogant, snobbish, toffee-nosed (*inf*). HUMBLE

condescension stooping, patronage, disdain, snobbery, airs, haughtiness, loftiness, superciliousness. HUMILITY
favour, grace, deference, graciousness, indulgence, civility, courtesy.

condign fitting, suitable, appropriate, just, fair, deserved, merited. UNDESERVED

condiment sauce, relish, seasoning, flavouring, dressing, spice.

condition *n*, state, situation, position, circumstances, case, plight, predicament.
stipulation, proviso, provision, term, clause, qualification, restriction, requirement, necessity.
estate, rank, station, standing, position, class, caste.
shape, order, fitness, fettle, health.
v, habituate, accustom, inure, adapt, prepare, equip, educate, train.

conditional provisional, qualified, restricted, dependent, relative, subject to, contingent. ABSOLUTE

condole commiserate, sympathize, feel for, console, grieve, lament. REJOICE

condolence commiseration, sympathy, pity, fellow feeling, compassion, consolation, comfort, solace.

condonation pardon, forgiveness, dispensation, amnesty, remission, excusing, ignoring, overlooking. PUNISHMENT

condone pardon, forgive, excuse, overlook, ignore, disregard, wink at, turn a blind eye to. PUNISH

conduce lead, tend, contribute, aid, help, advance, promote, forward. HINDER

conducive leading, tending, contributory, helpful, useful, instrumental, favourable, advantageous, productive.

conduct *n*, behaviour, bearing, manners, mien, demeanour, attitude, deportment, comportment, carriage, ways, actions, habits.
leadership, management, administration, control, handling, direction, guidance, running, operation, supervision.

v, lead, guide, direct, usher, steer, pilot, escort, accompany, bring, convey, transmit.
control, manage, run, direct, administer, handle, supervise, preside over.
act, behave, comport, acquit, bear, carry.

conductor leader, guide, director, official, maestro.
transmitter, carrier, bearer.

conduit duct, passage, pipe, tube, channel, canal.

confabulate converse, talk, chat, gossip, natter, chatter, prate, prattle.

confection making, manufacture, production, composition.
sweet, sweetmeat, candy, comfit, preserve, confectionery.

confederacy league, confederation, federation, coalition, union, alliance, bloc.

confederate *adj*, allied, combined, united, federal, confederated. OPPOSED
n, ally, associate, partner, colleague, abettor, accomplice, accessory. OPPONENT
v, ally, combine, unite, merge, amalgamate, federate. SEPARATE

confederation alliance, federation, confederacy, league, union, coalition.

confer *vt*, bestow, grant, award, present, accord, vouchsafe, give. WITHDRAW
vi, converse, talk, consult, parley, deliberate.

conference meeting, congress, convention, council, forum, symposium, seminar, discussion, talk, parley, consultation, debate.

confess acknowledge, admit, own, own up (*inf*), come clean (*inf*), grant, concede, recognize, aver, assert, affirm, avow, declare, profess, attest, confirm. DENY

confession acknowledgment, admission, declaration, avowal, disclosure, revelation, recognition. DENIAL

confide trust, depend, rely, have faith, believe. DISTRUST
disclose, reveal, divulge, tell, impart, confess, admit. CONCEAL
entrust, commit, commend, consign.

confidence trust, faith, reliance, dependence, belief, assurance, conviction. DOUBT
self-assurance, self-reliance, aplomb, poise, courage, nerve, boldness, audacity. TIMIDITY

confident sure, positive, certain, assured, convinced, satisfied. DOUBTFUL
self-assured, self-reliant, self-possessed, assured, bold, courageous, dauntless. TIMID

confidential private, secret, personal, intimate, privy, classified, restricted, hush-hush (*inf*). PUBLIC
trusty, trustworthy, reliable, dependable, faithful. UNRELIABLE

confidentially in confidence, between ourselves, off the record, sub rosa, in camera, behind closed doors, secretly, privately. PUBLICLY

configuration figure, form, shape, cast, outline, contour, formation, structure, arrangement.

confine *v*, restrict, limit, circumscribe, straiten, hem in, bound, bind, restrain, hold back, imprison, cage, incarcerate, immure, impound, pen, intern. RELEASE
n, limit, boundary, border, frontier, edge.

confinement imprisonment, incarceration, internment, detention, custody, duress, restraint, restriction. LIBERATION
childbirth, lying-in, *accouchement*, labour, parturition, delivery.

confirm verify, corroborate, substantiate, validate, bear out, prove, endorse, ratify, sanction, approve, affirm. REFUTE
strengthen, reinforce, fortify, fix, establish, settle, clinch, assure. ANNUL

confirmation verification, corroboration, substantiation, proof, evidence, ratification, endorsement, sanction, approval, affirmation. REFUTATION

confirmed habitual, chronic, inveterate, dyed-in-the-wool, hardened, seasoned, established, ingrained.

confiscate seize, sequester, sequestrate, dispossess, distrain, impound, appropriate, expropriate. RESTORE

conflagration fire, blaze, inferno, holocaust.

conflict *v*, clash collide, disagree, differ, be at variance, interfere, oppose, contest, contend, struggle, fight.
n, clash, collision, disagreement, difference, discord, dispute, variance, friction, opposition, antagonism, strife, struggle, battle, fight, combat, contest, contention, encounter, engagement. AGREEMENT

confluence conflux, convergence, junction, meeting, union, concurrence. DIVERGENCE
concourse, assembly, assemblage, crowd, throng, host, multitude, congregation.

confluent meeting, converging, merging, mingling, blending. DIVERGENT

conform comply, yield, submit, obey, follow, consent, adapt, adjust, reconcile. REBEL

agree, correspond, tally, match, accord, harmonize, suit, square, fit. DISAGREE

conformity compliance, yielding, submission, obedience, observance, allegiance, orthodoxy, conventionality. NONCONFORMITY

agreement, correspondence, likeness, resemblance, similarity, harmony, accord, congruity, compatibility. DISCORD

confound astound, amaze, surprise, stun, dumbfound, astonish, perplex, bewilder, nonplus, mystify, confuse, embarrass, disconcert.

defeat, annihilate, destroy, ruin, overwhelm, upset, quash, contradict, refute.

confounded miserable, wretched, accursed, damnable, blasted, abominable, execrable, detestable, odious. BLESSED

confront face, encounter, challenge, defy, brave, beard, tackle, face up to, accost, oppose, resist, stand up to. EVADE

confrontation encounter, conflict, contest, battle, crisis, showdown (*inf*).

defiance, opposition, challenge, resistance.

confuse bewilder, perplex, puzzle, mystify, baffle, bemuse, nonplus. ENLIGHTEN

muddle, mix up, mistake, confound, jumble, disorder, garble, disarrange, derange, mingle, intermingle, blend.

abash, mortify, shame, embarrass, disconcert, discomfit, discompose, fluster.

confusion bewilderment, perplexity, puzzlement, mystification, bafflement. ENLIGHTENMENT

muddle, mess, disorder, disarray, jumble, garble, chaos, anarchy, turmoil, tumult, commotion, upheaval. ORDER

abashment, mortification, shame, embarrassment, chagrin, discomfiture, discomposure.

confute refute, disprove, rebut, invalidate, belie, contradict, controvert, overthrow, overcome. PROVE

congeal coagulate, clot, curdle, thicken, set, jell, stiffen, harden, solidify, freeze.

congenial pleasant, agreeable, friendly, genial, affable, complaisant, kindly, sympathetic, kindred, compatible, suited, well-matched, congruous, consonant, favourable. DISAGREEABLE

congenital inherent, innate, inborn, inbred, connate, natural, ingrained, inveterate.

congested blocked, clogged, jammed, full, crowded, packed, crammed, stuffed, overflowing, teeming. CLEAR

congestion crowding, jam, bottleneck, blocking, clogging, packing, cramming, surfeit, repletion. CLEARANCE

conglomerate *v*, cluster, gather, amass, accumulate, aggregate, agglomerate. DISPERSE

n, conglomeration, mass, aggregate, agglomerate.

multinational, corporation, merger, cartel.

conglomeration cluster, mass, conglomerate, aggregate, aggregation, agglomeration, accumulation, assortment, medley, miscellany.

congratulate compliment, felicitate, acclaim, praise.

congratulations felicitations, compliments, best wishes, good wishes, well done, bravo.

congregate collect, gather, assemble, muster, convene, meet, rally, mass, throng, flock. DISPERSE

congregation gathering, assembly, assemblage, muster, meeting, host, crowd, throng.

parish, flock, parishioners, fellowship, brethren, laity.

congress meeting, conference, convention, assembly, council, conclave, convocation, legislature, parliament, senate.

congruity congruence, agreement, accord, concord, correspondence, consistency, harmony, compatibility, suitability, fitness, appropriateness. INCONGRUITY

congruous agreeing, accordant, concordant, corresponding, congruent, consonant, consistent, harmonious, compatible, suitable, fit, appropriate. INCONGRUOUS

conjectural hypothetical, theoretical, academic, speculative, supposed, putative, surmised, guessed, suspected. PROVEN

conjecture *v*, guess, surmise, suppose, suspect, assume, infer, imagine, fancy, theorize, hypothesize, postulate. PROVE

n, guess, surmise, supposition, assumption, inference, speculation, theory, hypothesis, conclusion, judgment, belief, suspicion, fancy, divination. PROOF

conjoin join, connect, link, unite, tie, bind, fasten, hitch, combine, associate, league, merge, confederate. SEVER

conjugal connubial, matrimonial, married, wedded, marital, nuptial, bridal, hymeneal. CELIBATE

conjunction joining, connection, link, union, combination, association, junction, juxtaposition, concurrence, coincidence. SEPARATION

conjuncture juncture, stage, pass, point, turning point, crisis, crossroads, emergency, exigency, predicament, dilemma, quandary.

conjuration incantation, chant, invocation, spell, charm, magic, sorcery, enchantment.

conjure perform magic, juggle, do tricks. enchant, bewitch, charm, fascinate, cast a spell, invoke, call up, summon, rouse.

beseech, implore, appeal to, entreat, crave, adjure, beg, pray, supplicate. ORDER

conjure up, evoke, call to mind, bring to mind, recall, recollect.

conjurer magician, sorcerer, wizard, juggler, illusionist.

connate inborn, congenital, innate, natural, inherent.

akin, related, cognate, allied, similar, associated.

connect join, link, tie, fasten, bind, unite, couple, affix, adhere, combine, associate, relate, ally, adjoin, communicate. SEVER

connected joined, linked, bound, united, combined, associated, related, akin, allied, adjoining, adjacent. UNCONNECTED

coherent, intelligible, comprehensible, fluent, consecutive. DISCONNECTED

connection junction, union, link, tie, attachment, bond, alliance, association, relationship, liaison, correspondence, communication, intercourse, commerce.

contact, acquaintance, friend, associate, ally.

relative, relation, kin, kindred, family.

connivance conspiracy, intrigue, collusion, complicity, abetment, consent, approval, condonation.

connive conspire, intrigue, plot, scheme, collude.

connive at, overlook, disregard, blink at, wink at, turn a blind eye to, let pass, condone. OPPOSE

connoisseur expert, authority, specialist, savant, devotee, buff (*inf*), judge, arbiter, critic, epicure, gourmet, aesthete.

connotation implication, significance, meaning, nuance, undertone, suggestion, inference, association, allusion, reference.

connote imply, suggest, infer, hint at, signify, mean, betoken, indicate, involve, implicate.

connubial conjugal, matrimonial, married, wedded, marital, nuptial, bridal, hymeneal. CELIBATE

conquer defeat, vanquish, beat, surmount, overcome, overpower, master, subdue, crush, quell, suppress, subjugate, rout, checkmate, humble, humiliate. SURRENDER

triumph, prevail, succeed, win, gain, achieve, obtain, acquire, occupy, annex, seize. LOSE

conqueror victor, winner, champion, master, lord, conquistador, hero. VICTIM

conquest victory, triumph, success, mastery, defeat, vanquishment, overthrow, rout, subjugation, humiliation, invasion, occupation, annexation, coup. SURRENDER

seduction, enchantment, captivation, allurement, enticement, enthralment. REPULSION

catch, prize, trophy, booty, plunder, spoils.

consanguinity kinship, blood tie, family tie, common ancestry, relationship, affinity, association, connection.

conscience scruples, principles, morals, ethics, moral sense, integrity, honesty, conscientiousness.

conscientious diligent, painstaking, assiduous, scrupulous, meticulous, thorough, exact, precise, strict, faithful, careful. CARELESS

honest, upright, just, fair, incorruptible, scrupulous, principled, moral, high-minded, good, honourable. UNPRINCIPLED

conscious aware, awake, alert, cognizant, mindful, sensible, sentient, alive, knowing, percipient, thinking, reasoning, rational. UNCONSCIOUS

deliberate, intentional, planned, premeditated, calculated, wilful. UNINTENTIONAL

consciousness awareness, realization, recognition, cognizance, perception, apprehension, mindfulness, knowledge. IGNORANCE

consecrate sanctify, bless, anoint, hallow, dedicate, devote, assign, ordain, venerate, honour, exalt. DESECRATE

consecutive sequential, successive, serial, following, continuous, uninterrupted, orderly, logical. DISCONTINUOUS

consensus agreement, concurrence, unanimity, common consent, harmony, concord, accord, unity. DISSENSION

consent *v*, agree, concur, assent, accede, acquiesce, concede, submit, yield, comply, permit, allow, approve, grant. REFUSE
n, agreement, concurrence, assent, acquiescence, permission, sanction, approval, go-ahead (*inf*), green light (*inf*). REFUSAL
accord, harmony, unison, unanimity, consensus, agreement. DISSENSION

consequence result, outcome, issue, effect, end, event, upshot, aftermath, repercussion. CAUSE
importance, significance, moment, weight, note, concern, matter, value, influence, distinction, standing, repute, notability, eminence. INSIGNIFICANCE

consequent resultant, consequential, ensuing, following, subsequent, successive, sequential. PRECEDING

consequential important, significant, momentous, weighty, substantial, serious. INSIGNIFICANT
pompous, self-important, conceited, vain, proud, arrogant, bumptious, supercilious, pretentious. MODEST

conservation preservation, maintenance, upkeep, protection, custody, keeping, perpetuation, saving, economy. ABOLITION

conservative cautious, moderate, sober, middle-of-the-road, conventional, traditional, old-fashioned, hidebound, die-hard. right-wing, Tory, reactionary. LIBERAL

conserve preserve, maintain, keep, protect, save, spare, go easy on (*inf*). SQUANDER

consider contemplate, deliberate, reflect, ponder, meditate, ruminate, cogitate, muse, mull over, study, examine, weigh, chew over.
deem, think, believe, judge, regard, rate, estimate.
respect, have regard for, care for, heed, bear in mind, mark, remember, take into account. IGNORE

considerable large, great, substantial, sizable, marked, appreciable, ample, abundant, plentiful, much. TRIFLING
important, significant, noteworthy, remarkable, distinguished, renowned, influential, venerable. INSIGNIFICANT

considerate thoughtful, kind, charitable, unselfish, benevolent, compassionate, attentive, solicitous, obliging, mindful, tactful, discreet, patient, forbearing. INCONSIDERATE

consideration contemplation, meditation, deliberation, reflection, rumination, thought, attention, notice, regard, heed, study, examination, scrutiny. DISREGARD
thoughtfulness, kindness, unselfishness, benevolence, compassion, concern, solicitude, tact, discretion, patience, forbearance. THOUGHTLESSNESS
issue, factor, circumstance, concern, point.
payment, fee, recompense, reward, remuneration, perquisite, tip, gratuity.
esteem, estimation, respect, regard, admiration.

consign commit, entrust, hand over, deliver, transfer, convey, transmit, send, dispatch, ship.

consignment committal, commitment, handing over, delivery, transferral, conveyance, dispatch.
load, shipment, batch.

consignor sender, shipper, merchant, seller.

consist accord, harmonize, agree, be compatible, conform, be consistent. CLASH
consist of, comprise, be composed of, include, contain, incorporate, embody, involve, amount to.

consistency accordance, harmony, agreement, correspondence, consonance, correlation, compatibility, congruity. INCONSISTENCY
viscosity, firmness, thickness, density, coherence.

consistent accordant, harmonious, agreeing, corresponding, consonant, coherent, congruous, compatible. INCONSISTENT
regular, constant, persistent, unchanging, steady, dependable, faithful, loyal. ERRATIC

consolation comfort, solace, cheer, encouragement, ease, relief, help, support. DISTRESS

console comfort, solace, cheer, encourage, soothe, calm, relieve, support. UPSET

consolidate unite, join, conjoin, combine, fuse, amalgamate, coalesce, condense, compact, compress, congeal, harden, solidify. DISINTEGRATE
strengthen, fortify, reinforce, stabilize. WEAKEN

consonance congruity, consistency, agreement, harmony, unison, accord, concord, conformity, correspondence. DISCORD

consonant consistent, congruous, accordant, harmonious, in agreement, concordant, correspondent, compatible. DISCORDANT

consort *n*, companion, partner, mate, spouse, husband, wife, associate, fellow, friend, comrade.
v, associate, fraternize, keep company, mix, mingle, go around with.

conspectus outline, synopsis, summary, résumé, précis, abstract, digest, compendium, survey.

conspicuous obvious, evident, plain, clear, patent, manifest, visible, marked, prominent, outstanding, noticeable, discernible, perceptible, apparent. INCONSPICUOUS
blatant, flagrant, garish, loud, showy. SUBDUED
remarkable, striking, impressive, eminent, notable, distinguished, celebrated, famous, illustrious. INSIGNIFICANT

conspiracy intrigue, plot, scheme, cabal, league, collaboration, collusion, connivance, machination, treason, treachery.

conspire plot, plan, scheme, intrigue, machinate, collude, combine, concur, collaborate, cooperate.

constancy steadfastness, resolution, perseverance, tenacity, firmness, determination, decision, inflexibility, permanence, stability, regularity, uniformity, steadiness, faithfulness, fidelity, loyalty, devotion. FICKLENESS

constant regular, uniform, unchanging, invariable, fixed, permanent, stable, steady, firm. CHANGEABLE
perpetual, continuous, incessant, unending, interminable, nonstop, uninterrupted, unbroken, unrelenting, sustained, persistent. INTERMITTENT
faithful, loyal, steadfast, devoted, staunch, dependable, trusty, true. FICKLE

constellation galaxy, cluster, collection, group, assemblage, gathering.

consternation dismay, distress, alarm, shock, fear, terror, fright, anxiety, trepidation, panic, confusion, bewilderment, astonishment, amazement. RELIEF

constituent *adj*, component, integral, composing, constituting, elemental, basic, essential.
n, component, ingredient, element, part, unit, factor. WHOLE
voter, elector.

constitute compose, make up, comprise, form.
found, establish, set up, create. ABOLISH
appoint, nominate, depute, ordain, empower, commission, authorize.

constitution composition, structure, formation, organization, establishment, creation, foundation.
physique, build, make-up, health, disposition, temper, temperament, character, nature, spirit.
code, charter, rules, laws.

constitutional *adj*, inherent, innate, inborn, inbred, organic, congenital, natural, connate.
lawful, legitimate, legal, statutory, chartered, vested, authorized. UNCONSTITUTIONAL
n, stroll, walk, airing, promenade.

constrain compel, force, oblige, make, coerce, drive, impel, urge, press.
restrain, confine, curb, check, restrict, limit, hem in, cage. FREE

constraint compulsion, force, obligation, coercion, necessity, pressure.
restraint, confinement, restriction, repression, suppression, inhibition, limitation, check, hindrance, obstruction, deterrent. FREEDOM

constrict squeeze, tighten, contract, narrow, shrink, compress, cramp, pinch, choke, strangle, restrict, limit, inhibit, restrain. EXPAND

constriction tightness, narrowing, stricture, pressure, cramp, strangulation, restriction, knot, lump, blockage, impediment, restraint, constraint, inhibition, limitation. EXPANSION

construct build, erect, raise, put up, assemble, fabricate, make, form, fashion, shape, create, design, invent, frame, compose. DESTROY

construction building, erection, structure, edifice, assembly, fabrication, formation, creation, design, composition. DEMOLITION
interpretation, explanation, rendering, reading, analysis, inference.

constructive positive, useful, helpful, practical, productive, valuable. DESTRUCTIVE

construe interpret, translate, render, analyse, parse, expound, explain, read, take, deduce, infer.

consult ask, question, interrogate, canvass, confer, discuss, deliberate, refer to, turn to, seek advice from.
consider, regard, respect, take into account. IGNORE

consultation conference, deliberation, examination, consideration, council, parley, powwow, colloquy, dialogue, discussion, interview, hearing, meeting, session.

consume devour, eat, drink, swallow, bolt, put away (*inf*).
use, use up, exhaust, expend, drain, dissipate, waste, squander, lavish, fritter away, spend, deplete, absorb, devour, eat up, swallow up. CONSERVE
destroy, devastate, ravage, raze, gut, demolish, lay waste.
engross, absorb, preoccupy, obsess, monopolize, rivet, fascinate, enthral.

consumer buyer, purchaser, shopper, user, customer, client. PRODUCER

consummate *v*, accomplish, fulfil, achieve, compass, peform, execute, complete, finish, conclude, perfect, crown. ABORT
adj, accomplished, skilled, masterly, proficient, practised, polished, perfect, excellent, superb, supreme, utter, complete, absolute, total, unqualified, matchless.

consummation perfection, completion, finish, end, conclusion, culmination, fulfilment, achievement, realization. FRUSTRATION

consumption use, expenditure, depletion, reduction, dissipation, exhaustion, waste, destruction, decay. CONSERVATION
tuberculosis, emaciation, decline, wasting, atrophy.

contact *n*, communication, connection, touch, union, junction, contiguity, juxtaposition, association, conjunction. ISOLATION
acquaintance, connection.
v, call, ring, phone, write to, communicate with, get in touch with, approach, reach, get hold of.

contagion infection, transmission, communication, spread, contamination, corruption, pollution, pestilence, plague.

contagious infectious, catching, communicable, transmissible, transferable, spreading, epidemic, pestilential.

contain hold, include, comprise, consist of, embody, embrace, comprehend, incorporate, accommodate, seat, admit, enclose.
restrain, curb, control, repress, hold back, suppress. RELEASE

container receptacle, holder, vessel, repository, box, case, tin, jar, pot, bowl.

contaminate pollute, adulterate, debase, infect, poison, corrupt, vitiate, deprave, soil, defile, sully, taint, tarnish. CLEANSE

contamination pollution, adulteration, infection, poisoning, contagion, corruption, vitiation, defilement, debasement, impurity, foulness. PURIFICATION

contemn scorn, despise, disdain, spurn, slight, deride, shun, hold in contempt. RESPECT

contemplate consider, deliberate, ponder, think about, reflect, muse, meditate, ruminate, mull over, study, examine.
behold, regard, observe, watch, eye, look at, stare at, gaze at, view, survey, scrutinize, inspect. IGNORE
intend, plan, mean, propose, envisage, have in mind.

contemplation reflection, meditation, rumination, consideration, deliberation, cogitation, thought, reverie.
observation, scrutiny, examination, inspection, viewing, surveying.
purpose, intention, plan, project, prospect, anticipation, expectation, ambition, aspiration.

contemplative thoughtful, meditative, reflective, ruminative, pensive, intent, rapt, lost in thought.

contemporary contemporaneous, coexistent, coexisting, coeval, coetaneous, concurrent, synchronous.
modern, up-to-date, fashionable, newfangled, latest, recent, current, present, present-day. ANCIENT

contempt scorn, derision, mockery, disdain, disregard, disrespect, condescension, superciliousness, contemptuousness. RESPECT

contemptible despicable, derisory, base, mean, abject, low, vile, paltry, worthless, disreputable, shabby, ignominious, detestable, wretched, miserable, pitiful. NOBLE

contemptuous scornful, disdainful, supercilious, haughty, condescending, arrogant, derisive, insulting, insolent, cynical, sneering. RESPECTFUL

contend struggle, strive, compete, vie, combat, fight, contest, grapple, wrestle, cope. SURRENDER
debate, dispute, argue, maintain, hold, aver, assert, affirm, claim, allege, declare. DISCLAIM

content[1] *v*, satisfy, gratify, appease, mollify, placate, humour, indulge, gladden, delight, please.
adj, contented, satisfied, at ease, comfortable, pleased, happy, glad, willing, agreeable. DISSATISFIED
n, contentment, satisfaction, gratification, ease, comfort, peace of mind. DISCONTENT

content[2] *n*, matter, substance, essence, gist, pith, meaning, significance, text, subject, matter, topics, ideas, themes.
capacity, volume, size, measure, dimensions, magnitude, scope.

contented content, satisfied, gratified, at ease, comfortable, complacent, placid, glad, happy, pleased. DISCONTENTED

contention struggle, strife, rivalry, competition, conflict, discord, dispute, debate, dissension, controversy, wrangle, quarrel, squabble, altercation. AGREEMENT
claim, assertion, affirmation, declaration, view, opinion, belief, argument, point.

contentious quarrelsome, argumentative, pugnacious, combative, disputatious, bickering, querulous, peevish, captious, perverse, petulant. OBLIGING
controversial, litigious, debatable, disputable.

contentment content, contentedness, satisfaction, gratification, ease, comfort, complacency, equanimity, happiness, pleasure. DISCONTENT

contents ingredients, constituents, filling, load, content, chapters, topics, subjects.

contest *n*, competition, match, tournament, game, race.
struggle, battle, fight, combat, conflict, discord, dispute, dissension, contention, quarrel, altercation. AGREEMENT
v, dispute, argue, litigate, oppose, challenge, question, contend.
fight, battle, contend, struggle, strive, vie, compete.

contestant competitor, contender, entrant, participant, player, aspirant, candidate.

context background, framework, connection, relation, meaning, substance.
conditions, circumstances, situation, state of affairs, facts.

contiguity contiguousness, juxtaposition, adjacency, nearness, proximity, contact, meeting.

contiguous meeting, touching, in contact, abutting, adjoining, conterminous, bordering, beside, next to, adjacent, juxtaposed, neighbouring, near. REMOTE

continence self-restraint, self-control, moderation, temperance, sobriety, restraint, abstinence, chastity, celibacy, asceticism, austerity, self-denial. LICENTIOUSNESS

continent self-restrained, self-controlled, moderate, temperate, sober, abstinent, abstemious, chaste, celibate, ascetic, austere. LICENTIOUS

contingency possibility, eventuality, event, occasion, occurrence, incident, happening, chance, fortuity, uncertainty, accident, casualty, emergency, situation, circumstance, case, juncture, factor, aspect, detail.

contingent *adj*, dependent, depending, subject to, conditional, provisional, possible, uncertain.
accidental, incidental, casual, chance, fortuitous, random, haphazard, unforeseen.
n, group, body, band, party, company, faction, deputation, detachment, section, batch, quota, portion.

continual recurrent, regular, repeated, frequent, persistent, perpetual, sustained, constant, nonstop, incessant, continuous, uninterrupted, unremitting. INTERMITTENT

continually constantly, incessantly, forever, always, all the time, repeatedly, persistently. OCCASIONALLY

continuance continuation, constancy, permanence, persistence, perseverance, duration, term, period.

continuation sequel, addition, supplement, postscript, epilogue, appendix, extension, protraction, prolongation.
resumption, perpetuation, maintenance, continuance. CESSATION

continue persist, carry on, go on, persevere, sustain, keep up, maintain, prolong, extend, draw out, protract, perpetuate. STOP
resume, recommence, carry on, proceed, advance. INTERRUPT
remain, last, endure, abide, stay, persist, survive. CEASE

continuity connection, interrelationship, cohesion, flow, progression, sequence, succession, continuousness. INTERRUPTION

continuous unbroken, uninterrupted, connected, prolonged, extended, constant, endless, unending, incessant, ceaseless, eternal, everlasting, nonstop, sustained, perpetual, continual. BROKEN

contort distort, deform, misshape, twist, warp, gnarl, convolute, writhe, squirm. STRAIGHTEN

contortion distortion, deformity, twist, warp, convolution, convulsion, grimace.

contour outline, silhouette, profile, relief, shape, form, figure, line, curve.

contraband *n*, smuggling, trafficking, bootlegging, gunrunning.
adj, smuggled, illegal, illicit, unlawful, banned, prohibited, black-market, hot (*inf*). LAWFUL

contract *v*, shrink, reduce, lessen, diminish, condense, compress, shorten, abbreviate, abridge, curtail, epitomize, narrow, constrict, squeeze, tighten, purse, shrivel, wrinkle. EXPAND
agree, stipulate, covenant, pledge, engage, enter into, undertake, commit oneself, bargain, negotiate, come to terms.
catch, get, acquire, develop, go down with (*inf*).
n, agreement, pact, compact, treaty, covenant, bond, pledge, bargain, deal (*inf*), settlement, stipulation, commitment, arrangement, understanding.

contraction shrinkage, reduction, diminution, lessening, compression, shortening, abbreviation, narrowing, constriction, tightening, shrivelling. EXPANSION

contradict deny, controvert, gainsay, dispute, oppose, challenge, refute, disprove, negate, confute, dissent, belie, contravene, be at variance. CONFIRM

contradiction denial, opposition, negation, refutation, confutation, dissension, contravention. AGREEMENT
inconsistency, incongruity, variance, conflict, clash. HARMONY

contradictory contrary, opposite, at variance, antagonistic, irreconcilable, repugnant, incompatible, inconsistent, paradoxical, antithetical, incongruous. AFFIRMATIVE

contraption contrivance, device, gadget, rig, gear, apparatus, mechanism, appliance.

contrariety opposition, contrast, disagreement, antagonism, repugnance, contradiction, inconsistency. HARMONY

contrary *adj*, opposed, opposite, counter, hostile, adverse, antagonistic, repugnant, inimical, contradictory, discordant, conflicting, at variance. LIKE
perverse, awkward, difficult, obstinate, stubborn, froward, intractable, refractory, self-willed, headstrong. OBLIGING
n, opposite, reverse, converse, antithesis.

contrast *v*, differentiate, distinguish, oppose, compare, differ, stand out, set off. LIKEN
n, difference, distinction, contrariety, opposition, polarity, dissimilarity, disparity, differentiation, comparison. SIMILARITY

contravene infringe, break, violate, disobey, transgress. KEEP
dispute, contradict, refute, oppose, cross, counteract, hinder, obstruct, impede, thwart, frustrate, nullify, annul, abrogate. ASSIST

contravention infringement, violation, transgression, trespass, disobedience.
contradiction, opposition, antagonism, obstruction, frustration, nullification, abrogation.

contretemps mishap, accident, mistake, blunder, gaffe, difficulty, predicament.

contribute supply, furnish, provide, give, donate, bestow, grant, afford, subscribe, chip in (*inf*). WITHHOLD
conduce, lead, tend, add, influence, help, advance, be instrumental in, have a hand in, be responsible for.

contribution donation, gift, offering, addition, grant, subscription.

contributor donor, giver, subscriber, backer, patron, supporter.
writer, freelance, reporter, correspondent, journalist.

contributory instrumental, accessory, conducive, helpful.

contrite penitent, repentant, sorry, regretful, remorseful, conscience-stricken, chastened, humble. UNREPENTANT

contrition penitence, repentance, sorrow, regret, remorse, self-reproach, compunction, shame, embarrassment, humiliation. IMPENITENCE

contrivance device, invention, contraption, gadget, machine, mechanism, apparatus, appliance, implement, tool.
scheme, plan, plot, ruse, stratagem, artifice, design, expedient.

contrive devise, invent, frame, design, create, concoct, fabricate, improvise, construct.
engineer, manoeuvre, arrange, manage, effect, bring about.
scheme, plot, brew, hatch, conspire, intrigue.

contrived artificial, forced, unnatural, elaborate, recherché. SPONTANEOUS

control *v*, rule, govern, reign over, command, direct, lead, conduct, supervise, manage, dominate, boss, discipline.
restrain, curb, check, subdue, master, bridle, hold back, contain, confine, limit, constrain, suppress.
regulate, monitor, verify.
n, management, mastery, direction, guidance, government, rule, authority, command, discipline, supervision, charge.
restraint, check, curb, restriction, constraint, limitation, regulation.
lever, switch, instrument, dial, knob, handle.

controversial contentious, disputed, debatable, controvertible, disputable, at issue, contended, questionable, polemic, dialectic. INDISPUTABLE

controversy dispute, debate, polemic, discussion, argument, wrangle, quarrel, altercation, disagreement, contention, dissension, strife. AGREEMENT

controvert deny, refute, oppose, counter, challenge, contest, dispute, contend, contradict. AFFIRM
debate, discuss, argue, wrangle.

contumacious stubborn, obstinate, perverse, contrary, froward, refractory, recalcitrant, rebellious, insubordinate, obdurate, intractable, headstrong, tenacious, wilful. DOCILE

contumacy stubbornness, obstinacy, perverseness, recalcitrance, rebelliousness, mutiny, disobedience, insubordination, resistance, contempt, intractability, obduracy, tenacity, wilfulness. DOCILITY

contumelious insulting, abusive, rude, humiliating, scornful, disdainful, contemptuous, supercilious, arrogant, overbearing. RESPECTFUL

contumely insult, affront, abuse, invective, obloquy, opprobrium, reproach, contempt, scorn, derision, disdain, arrogance, superciliousness, insolence, rudeness. RESPECT

contuse bruise, discolour, injure, knock, bump.

contusion bruise, discoloration, mark, injury, bump, lump, swelling.

conundrum riddle, puzzle, poser, brainteaser (*inf*), enigma, mystery, problem.

convalesce recover, recuperate, improve, mend, get well, get better. DETERIORATE

convalescence recovery, recuperation, improvement, restoration, cure, rehabilitation.

convalescent recovering, recuperating, improving, on the mend, getting better. DETERIORATING

convene gather, congregate, assemble, muster, meet, collect, rally, convoke, summon, call. DISBAND

convenience suitability, appropriateness, fitness, opportuneness, availability, accessibility, utility, usefulness, handiness. INCONVENIENCE
advantage, benefit, aid, help, assistance, service, use, facility, amenity, comfort, ease, accommodation. HINDRANCE

convenient suitable, fit, appropriate, timely, seasonable, opportune, adapted,

handy, useful, serviceable, helpful, beneficial, advantageous. INCONVENIENT
accessible, available, at hand, handy, nearby, within reach. INACCESSIBLE

convent nunnery, cloister, abbey, priory, religious community, school.

convention meeting, assembly, conference, congress, council, convocation.
agreement, contract, treaty, entente, concordat, compact, arrangement, pact.
custom, tradition, practice, protocol, etiquette, usage, formality.

conventional accepted, approved, proper, formal, orthodox, traditional, customary, standard, regular, normal, usual, habitual, ordinary, common. UNCONVENTIONAL

converge meet, join, unite, merge, blend, mingle, focus, concentrate, coincide, concur, come together, approach, tend. DIVERGE

convergence meeting, junction, merging, mingling, conflux, confluence, focus, concentration, coincidence, concurrence, approach. DIVERGENCE

conversable communicative, sociable, affable, open, out-going, expansive, unreserved, talkative, loquacious. RESERVED

conversant familiar, acquainted, *au fait*, versed, knowledgeable, experienced, skilled, proficient, practised. UNFAMILIAR

conversation talk, discussion, dialogue, communication, discourse, intercourse, colloquy, exchange, conference, parley, powwow, chat, gossip, confabulation, confab (*inf*), chinwag (*inf*), tête-à-tête.

conversational colloquial, informal, chatty, communicative, conversable, open, unreserved.

converse[1] *v*, talk, speak, chat, confabulate, discourse, commune.
n, conversation, talk, chat, dialogue, discourse.

converse[2] *n*, opposite, reverse, contrary, antithesis. SAME
adj, opposite, contrary, reversed, transposed.

conversion change, transformation, metamorphosis, transfiguration, alteration, modification, adaptation, remodelling, reconstruction. CONSERVATION
reformation, rebirth, regeneration, proselytization, proselytism.

convert change, transform, transfigure, transmute, alter, modify, adapt, revise, remodel, restyle, transpose, interchange.
proselytize, reform, convince, win over, regenerate, baptize.

convex bulging, rounded, gibbous, protuberant. CONCAVE

convey carry, take, transfer, transport, bear, conduct, bring, fetch.
transmit, send, communicate, impart, reveal, disclose, tell.

conveyance transport, transportation, carriage, movement, conveying, transfer, transference, transmission.
vehicle, transport, car, cab, carriage, van, lorry, bus, coach.

convict *v*, condemn, sentence, find guilty. ACQUIT
n, criminal, felon, culprit, malefactor, crook (*inf*), prisoner, jailbird, con (*inf*).

conviction sentence, condemnation, judgment, punishment.
assurance, confidence, certainty, certitude, persuasion, trust, belief, faith, opinion, view, principle, tenet. DOUBT

convince persuade, satisfy, assure, prove to, win over, bring round, sway.

convincing plausible, credible, probable, likely, cogent, persuasive, conclusive, powerful, impressive. UNCONVINCING

convivial sociable, jovial, festive, jolly, gay, merry, cheerful, hearty, genial, friendly. GLOOMY

convocation assembly, meeting, convention, congress, council, synod, congregation, concourse.

convoke call, summon, convene, muster, assemble, gather, collect. DISBAND

convolution coil, curl, twist, loop, spiral, helix, roll, fold, undulation.
intricacy, complexity, complication, involvement, entanglement, tortuousness.

convoy *n*, escort, guard, protection, attendance, entourage, fleet, company, line, file, train.
v, escort, accompany, attend, guard, protect, usher, pilot, lead, direct.

convulse disturb, agitate, shake, churn, heave, toss, discompose, derange. COMPOSE

convulsion spasm, paroxysm, contraction, cramp, seizure, stroke, fit, tremor.
agitation, disturbance, upheaval, commotion, turbulence, tumult, turmoil. CALM

cook *v*, boil, fry, roast, toast, poach, grill, stew, bake.
cook up, concoct, devise, invent, contrive, prepare, fabricate, improvise, plot, scheme.
n, chef, baker, pastry cook, confectioner.

cool *adj*, chilly, chill, cold, nippy, breezy, fresh, chilled. WARM
composed, calm, collected, unruffled, unperturbed, placid, quiet, serene, self-possessed, dispassionate. AGITATED
unfriendly, cold, frigid, chilly, lukewarm, uninviting, unresponsive, uncommunicative, reserved, aloof, distant, standoffish, indifferent, unconcerned, unenthusiastic. FRIENDLY
audacious, bold, presumptuous, impudent, shameless, brazen.
v, chill, refrigerate, freeze. WARM
moderate, temper, dampen, quench, calm, assuage, abate, lessen, quiet. EXCITE

coop *n*, cage, pen, enclosure, box.
v, cage, pen, imprison, confine. LIBERATE

cooperate help, aid, assist, abet, conspire, collaborate, combine, unite, join forces, work together, contribute, pitch in, participate, go along, play ball (*inf*). OPPOSE

cooperation help, assistance, collaboration, interaction, teamwork, combined effort, give and take, participation. OPPOSITION

cooperative helpful, obliging, accommodating. REBELLIOUS
collective, combined, joint, united, concerted. INDIVIDUAL

coordinate *v*, organize, systematize, categorize, arrange, integrate, harmonize, match, correspond, mesh, synchronize.
adj, equal, equivalent, tantamount, synonymous, correspondent, correlative.

cope manage, get by, survive, hold one's own.
contend, deal, grapple, struggle, handle, dispatch, take care of.

copious abundant, plentiful, plenteous, ample, profuse, exuberant, luxuriant, lavish, rich, overflowing, full, bountiful, unstinted. SCANTY

copiousness abundance, plenty, amplitude, exuberance, richness, fullness, bounty. SPARSENESS

copse coppice, thicket, grove, wood.

copulation mating, coupling, coition, coitus, sexual intercourse, sex, lovemaking, carnal knowledge.

copulative linking, joining, connecting, uniting.

copy *v*, duplicate, replicate, reproduce, photocopy, transcribe, plagiarize, crib (*inf*), counterfeit. ORIGINATE
imitate, mimic, ape, echo, mirror, simulate, follow.
n, duplicate, replica, reproduction, facsimile, transcription, photocopy, print, carbon, representation, counterfeit, forgery, likeness, imitation. ORIGINAL

coquet flirt, philander, dally, trifle, tease, ogle, make eyes at, vamp.

coquetry flirtation, philandering, dalliance, trifling, ogling, vamping.

cord line, string, twine, rope, braid.
bond, tie, link, connection.

cordial friendly, warm, courteous, affectionate, genial, amiable, affable, hearty, sincere, heartfelt, earnest, ardent, wholehearted. DISTANT

cordiality friendliness, warmth, affection, geniality, affability, heartiness, sincerity, wholeheartedness. HOSTILITY

core centre, heart, kernel, nucleus, essence, gist, nub. EXTERIOR

corner *n*, angle, bend, crook, knee, elbow, joint, junction.
niche, recess, nook, cranny, hole, retreat.
v, trap, bring to bay.
monopolize, hog (*inf*).

corny trite, banal, hackneyed, old-fashioned, mawkish, sentimental, feeble.

corollary inference, deduction, conclusion, consequence, result.

corporal bodily, fleshly, physical, carnal, corporeal. MENTAL

corporation association, company, partnership, corporate body, council.
paunch, spare tyre, potbelly.

corporeal physical, material, bodily, flesly, tangible, substantial. SPIRITUAL

corps body, company, band, crew, troupe, troop, regiment, squadron, unit, squad, platoon, division, detachment, contingent.

corpse body, cadaver, carcass, remains, stiff (*inf*).

corpulence fatness, stoutness, plumpness, tubbiness, rotundity, portliness, *embonpoint*, obesity, fleshiness. THINNESS

corpulent fat, stout, plump, tubby, rotund, portly, large, big, obese, overweight, bulky, burly, strapping. THIN

correct *adj*, accurate, true, right, faultless, unerring, exact, precise, strict, spot on (*inf*). INCORRECT
proper, fitting, seemly, accepted, appropriate, conventional. IMPROPER
v, rectify, redress, amend, emend, reform, adjust, put right, remedy, improve.
discipline, punish, chasten, castigate, admonish, reprove, reprimand, chide, scold, rebuke. INDULGE

correction rectification, amendment, modification, improvement, remedy, reparation.
discipline, punishment, castigation, chastisement, admonition, reproof, reprimand, scolding. INDULGENCE

corrective remedial, therapeutic, restorative, rectifying, improving. DETRIMENTAL
disciplinary, punitive, reformatory, penal.

correctness accuracy, truth, faultlessness, exactness, exactitude, precision, strictness, fidelity. INCORRECTNESS
propriety, correctitude, decorum, etiquette, civility, good manners, *bon ton*. IMPROPRIETY

correlate compare, contrast, equate, associate, correspond, connect, relate, tie in.

correlation correspondence, equivalence, interrelationship, reciprocity, mutuality, interdependence, connection. INDEPENDENCE

correlative corresponding, reciprocal, mutual, complementary, interrelated. INDEPENDENT

correspond agree, accord, harmonize, conform, tally, coincide, match, square, fit, correlate, reciprocate, complement. DIFFER
communicate, write, keep in touch.

correspondence agreement, accord, harmony, concurrence, conformity, coincidence, correlation, match, similarity, analogy, comparison, congruity. DIFFERENCE
letters, mail, post, communication, writing.

correspondent *n*, journalist, reporter, contributor.
writer, letter writer, pen friend, pen pal.
adj, corresponding, analogous, comparable, similar, reciprocal, parallel, equivalent, matching, accordant. DIFFERENT

corridor passage, passageway, hall, hallway, aisle, gallery, cloister.

corrigible tractable, submissive, yielding, compliant, amenable, docile. INTRACTABLE

corroborate confirm, support, ratify, substantiate, verify, validate, bear out, endorse, document, establish, uphold, sustain, back up. INVALIDATE

corroboration confirmation, ratification, substantiation, verification, validation, endorsement. INVALIDATION

corrode rust, oxidize, erode, eat away, wear away, consume, gnaw, impair, destroy, ruin, crumble, waste. RESTORE

corrosion rust, oxidation, erosion, attrition, wearing, deterioration, destruction, crumbling.

corrosive corroding, erosive, gnawing, wearing, acid, biting, caustic, mordant, acrid, trenchant, cutting, incisive.

corrugate wrinkle, pucker, crinkle, ruffle, rumple, crumple, crease, furrow, groove, ridge. SMOOTH

corrupt *adj*, dishonest, unscrupulous, unprincipled, bent (*inf*), bribable, venal, crooked, untrustworthy. HONEST
immoral, depraved, degenerate, abandoned, dissolute, profligate, wicked, evil. VIRTUOUS
rotten, putrid, contaminated, polluted, tainted, adulterated, impure, defiled, infected. PURE
v, deprave, debauch, pervert, bribe, suborn, square (*inf*), lure, entice, seduce. EDIFY
contaminate, defile, debase, vitiate, pollute, infect, putrefy, adulterate, doctor, taint, spoil. PURIFY

corruption dishonesty, unscrupulousness, bribery, venality, fraud, deception, deceit. HONESTY
immorality, depravity, vice, iniquity, turpitude, sin, degeneracy, decadence, dissolution, profligacy, evil, wickedness. VIRTUE
contamination, adulteration, pollution, debasement, vitiation, rot, decay, putrefaction. PURIFICATION

corsair pirate, privateer, buccaneer, freebooter, sea rover.

corset girdle, foundation, stays, corselet, bodice, belt.

cortege procession, cavalcade, train, suite, retinue.

coruscate sparkle, flash, gleam, scintillate, glitter, twinkle, glisten, glimmer, glint.

coruscation sparkle, flash, gleam, scintillation, glimmer, ray, beam, glint.

cosmopolitan universal, global, catholic, widely distributed.
broad-minded, urbane, sophisticated, worldly.

cosmos world, universe, nature, creation, macrocosm.
order, harmony.

cosset pamper, coddle, mollycoddle, baby, pet, caress, fondle, hug, cuddle. NEGLECT

cost *n*, price, charge, rate, expense, outlay, expenditure, payment, amount, figure, worth, value.
loss, penalty, sacrifice, damage, detriment, suffering, pain, injury, harm.
v, sell for, amount to, set back (*inf*).
necessitate, require.

costly dear, expensive, valuable, priceless, extortionate, excessive, exorbitant, steep (*inf*). INEXPENSIVE
sumptuous, lavish, splendid, fine, luxurious, rich, opulent, precious. POOR

costume uniform, livery, robes, dress, apparel, garb, habit, outfit, attire, clothes, clothing.

cosy snug, comfortable, comfy (*inf*), warm, sheltered, homely, intimate, easy, relaxed. UNCOMFORTABLE

coterie clique, set, gang, group, circle, clan, fraternity, club, society, association, company.

cottage lodge, cabin, chalet, hut, shack, shanty.

couch *n*, sofa, settee, divan, bed, chaise longue, chesterfield.
v, utter, express, phrase, word, frame.
lie down, recline, loll, lounge, repose.

council assembly, congress, committee, board, panel, cabinet, chamber, parliament, ministry, diet, synod, conclave, convention.

counsel *n*, advice, guidance, admonition, warning, caution, instruction, direction, recommendation, suggestion, opinion, consultation, deliberation, discussion.
advocate, lawyer, solicitor, barrister, attorney.
v, advise, guide, urge, exhort, instruct, warn, admonish, suggest, recommend, advocate. DISCOURAGE

counsellor adviser, mentor, confidant, guide, tutor, teacher.

count *v*, enumerate, number, calculate, reckon, add up, sum up, total, tally, compute, estimate.
include, take into account, number among.
consider, regard, deem, judge, esteem, hold, look upon.
matter, signify, rate, tell, weigh, carry weight.
count on, depend on, rely on, bank on, trust, take for granted.
n, enumeration, reckoning, calculation, computation, sum, total, tally, score.

countenance *n*, face, visage, features, physiognomy, expression, aspect, appearance, look, mien, air.
approval, support, sanction, favour, endorsement, backing, encouragement, aid, assistance. DISAPPROVAL
v, support, encourage, endorse, sanction, approve, back, aid, help, promote, champion. OPPOSE
tolerate, endure, brook, stand for (*inf*), put up with (*inf*), permit, allow. FORBID

counter[1] *adv*, against, versus, in opposition, at variance.
adj, contrary, opposite, opposed, opposing, conflicting, contrasting. LIKE
v, retaliate, parry, hit back, respond, answer, return, offset, dispute, contend.

counter[2] *n*, table, board, bar, stall.
disc, token, marker, piece, man.

counteract neutralize, annul, nullify, counterbalance, offset, negate, foil, frustrate, thwart, defeat, check, resist, oppose, contravene. ASSIST

counteraction opposition, resistance, contravention, check, frustration, negation, neutralization, annulment, nullification.

counterbalance balance, equilibrate, offset, compensate, counterpoise, countervail, make up for.

counterfeit *v*, forge, fake, sham, pretend, feign, simulate, copy, imitate, impersonate.
adj, forged, fake, sham, false, mock, spurious, feigned, simulated, imitation, ersatz, bogus, phoney (*inf*), fraudulent. GENUINE
n, forgery, fake, copy, reproduction, imitation, sham, fraud, phoney (*inf*).

countermand revoke, rescind, repeal, abrogate, annul, cancel, retract, withdraw. CONFIRM

counterpart fellow, match, double, twin, mate, partner, opposite number, equivalent, complement, supplement, correlative, copy, duplicate, likeness.

counterpoise *v*, counterbalance, balance, compensate, equalize, countervail, offset, neutralize.
n, counterweight, counterbalance, balance, equilibrium.

countless innumerable, incalculable, myriad, legion, numberless, untold, immeasurable, infinite, endless. FEW

country *n*, nation, people, state, kingdom, realm, commonwealth, homeland, fatherland, motherland.
region, territory, land, terrain, area, district.
countryside, farmland, provinces, rural areas, sticks (*inf*), backwoods, outback, bush, wilds. TOWN
adj, rural, rustic, pastoral, countrified, bucolic, provincial, Aracadian, agrarian, agricultural. URBAN
uncouth, unrefined, unpolished, unsophisticated, rough, rude. POLISHED

countryman rustic, provincial, yokel, bumpkin, peasant, farmer. TOWNSMAN
compatriot, fellow citizen, native, indigene. FOREIGNER

countryside country, farmland, rural areas, green belt, outdoors, scenery, panorama, view, landscape. TOWN

coup feat, exploit, master stroke, tour de force, accomplishment, deed, action, manoeuvre, stunt. FAILURE
coup d'état, rebellion, revolution, uprising, putsch, takeover, overthrow, seizure.

couple *n*, pair, brace, team, duo, twosome.
v, connect, join, conjoin, unite, yoke, bracket, link, pair, marry, wed, mate. SEPARATE

coupon voucher, certificate, slip, ticket, card.

courage bravery, valour, fearlessness, boldness, audacity, pluck, nerve, mettle, intrepidity, daring, grit, spunk (*inf*), guts (*inf*), bottle (*inf*), heroism, gallantry, fortitude, resolution. COWARDICE

courageous brave, valiant, valorous, fearless, dauntless, unafraid, bold, audacious, plucky, intrepid, daring, heroic, gallant, resolute, indomitable, lion-hearted. COWARDLY

courier messenger, bearer, carrier, runner, herald, envoy, emissary, representative, guide.

course *n*, progression, series, sequence, order, succession, continuity, progress, advance, march, flow, development.
duration, period, time, term, season, spell, lapse, passage.
route, path, road, track, way, channel, direction, line, trajectory, circuit, orbit, round, beat.
policy, procedure, programme, plan, regimen, mode, method, conduct, behaviour, deportment.
classes, lectures, lessons, studies, curriculum, programme, schedule.
of course, certainly, surely, by all means, obviously, naturally, undoubtedly, definitely. MAYBE
v, race, dash, rush, speed, bolt, charge, surge, gush, run, flow. DAWDLE
chase, pursue, hunt, follow.

court *n*, courtyard, yard, quadrangle, square, plaza, cloister.
retinue, train, entourage, cortege, attendants, royal household, palace, castle.
tribunal, bar, bench, assize, trial, session.
homage, deference, attention, addresses, respects, civilities, suit.
v, woo, make love to, date, take out, go out with, go steady (*inf*).
invite, solicit, seek, provoke, ask for, prompt, attract. AVOID
flatter, blandish, wheedle, cajole, curry favour with, fawn on, pander to, butter up (*inf*).

courteous polite, well-mannered, respectful, civil, gracious, gallant, courtly, ladylike, gentlemanly, urbane, debonair, ceremonious, complaisant, affable, obliging, attentive. IMPOLITE

courtesan prostitute, whore, harlot, paramour, kept woman, mistress, call girl, *fille de joie*.

courtesy politeness, respect, good manners, civility, graciousness, gallantry, courtliness, urbanity, refinement, polish, cordiality, affability. RUDENESS
consent, favour, indulgence, generosity, kindness, benevolence.

courtly refined, polished, well-bred, dignified, decorous, ceremonious, stately, gallant, chivalrous, gentlemanly, polite, well-mannered, respectful, gracious, affable. CHURLISH

courtship wooing, suit, romance, dating, engagement.
courtyard court, quadrangle, quad (*inf*), yard, enclosure, area, peristyle.
cove bay, bight, inlet, creek, firth, sound.
covenant agreement, contract, compact, pact, treaty, convention, concordat, promise, pledge, bond, commitment, bargain, deal, stipulation.
cover *v*, cloak, veil, mask, screen, shroud, conceal, hide, disguise, camouflage, secrete. UNCOVER
coat, spread, daub, plaster, overlay, blanket, mantle, carpet, clothe, envelop, invest, wrap. STRIP
protect, shield, shelter, guard, defend, watch over, fortify. EXPOSE
include, embrace, incorporate, embody, contain, comprise, comprehend, encompass, involve, deal with. EXCLUDE
replace, substitute, stand in, fill in, relieve, take over.
traverse, cross, pass through, travel over.
cover up, suppress, conceal, repress, hush up (*inf*), keep secret, whitewash (*inf*). REVEAL
n, covering, lid, top, wrapper, jacket, sheath, case, envelope, blanket, bedspread.
cloak, veil, mask, screen, shroud, disguise, camouflage, façade, front, cover-up, smokescreen.
defence, protection, shield, guard, shelter, refuge, camouflage, hiding place, undergrowth, woods.
covering cover, top, protection, shelter, wrapper, blanket, mantle, coating, layer, film.
covert *adj*, clandestine, secret, concealed, hidden, disguised, surreptitious, furtive, stealthy, underhand, sly, insidious. OPEN
n, undergrowth, thicket, bushes, shrubbery, woodland.
shelter, cover, protection, refuge, sanctuary, asylum, retreat, den, lair.
covet desire, long for, hanker after, crave, lust for, yearn for, aspire to, dream of, fancy, envy. DESPISE
covetous jealous, envious, desirous, acquisitive, grasping, avaricious, greedy, rapacious, eager, avid, craving.
covetousness desire, avarice, greed, rapacity, cupidity, avidity, yearning, craving.
covey brood, flock, group, party, set, company.
cow frighten, awe, overawe, daunt, unnerve, intimidate, browbeat, bully, oppress, subdue, break, discourage, dishearten, dismay. ENCOURAGE
coward craven, poltroon, dastard, baby, sissy, weakling, chicken (*inf*), scaredy-cat (*inf*), yellow-belly (*inf*). HERO
cowardice cowardliness, pusillanimity, timidity, timorousness, fear, faint-heartedness, cold feet (*inf*). BRAVERY
cowardly timid, timorous, fearful, scared, afraid, craven, pusillanimous, faint-hearted, lily-livered, spineless, yellow (*inf*), chicken (*inf*), dastardly. BRAVE
cower cringe, shrink, recoil, flinch, quail, tremble, crouch, stoop, fawn, grovel, skulk, slink. CONFRONT
coxcomb dandy, fop, prig, beau, popinjay, swell (*inf*), poser (*inf*).
coy shy, bashful, diffident, reserved, retiring, timid, shrinking, modest, demure, arch, coquettish, flirtatious. FORWARD
cozen cheat, trick, dupe, deceive, swindle, defraud, con (*inf*), take for a ride (*inf*), beguile, inveigle, hoodwink.
crabbed crabby, irritable, bad-tempered, testy, touchy, waspish, crusty, cantankerous, captious, perverse, peevish, petulant, surly, morose, sour, tart, acrid, acrimonious, harsh. GENIAL
crabbedness ill humour, bad temper, irritability, spleen, captiousness, peevishness, petulance, surliness, moroseness, sourness, acrimony. GENIALITY
crack *v*, break, split, cleave, burst, shatter, chip, splinter, shatter, craze, chap. MEND
snap, pop, clap, crash, crackle, burst, explode.
yield, succumb, break down, collapse, go to pieces, crack up (*inf*). RESIST
decipher, solve, unravel, work out, fathom, decode.
n, fissure, gap, rift, split, break, breach, crevice, cleft, chink, cranny, hole, aperture.
snap, pop, clap, crash, burst, explosion, report.
joke, quip, wisecrack, witticism, jibe, dig (*inf*).
cracked broken, chipped, split, crazed, damaged, imperfect, faulty.
crazy, mad, insane, crackers (*inf*), nuts (*inf*), round the bend (*inf*). SANE
crackle snap, crack, pop, crepitate.

cradle *n*, cot, bed, crib, bassinet.
source, origin, fountainhead, birthplace.
v, hold, rock, lull, nurse, nurture, foster, tend.

craft skill, ability, dexterity, aptitude, talent, knack, flair, cleverness, art, expertness, mastery. INCOMPETENCE
guile, cunning, artfulness, deceitfulness, wiliness, craftiness, subtlety, deceit, duplicity, trickery, artifice, wiles, stratagem, subterfuge. ARTLESSNESS
trade, vocation, calling, occupation, employment, business, work, pursuit, handicraft, art.
vessel, boat, ship, barque, plane, aircraft.

craftsman artisan, artificer, master, technician, skilled worker.

crafty cunning, sly, artful, guileful, wily, foxy, subtle, sharp, shrewd, astute, canny, calculating, designing, scheming, tricky, insidious, deceitful, fraudulent, crooked. ARTLESS

craggy rough, uneven, broken, rugged, jagged, rocky. SMOOTH

cram stuff, fill, press, ram, shove, force, pack, crowd, jam, choke, squeeze, crush, compress.
gorge, stuff, overeat, guzzle, glut, gormandize.
coach, study, revise, swot, mug up (*inf*).

cramp[1] *v*, hinder, obstruct, impede, encumber, hamper, check, restrain, restrict, confine, constrain, shackle, inhibit. LOOSE

cramp[2] *n*, spasm, contraction, convulsion, twinge, pang, stitch, crick, ache, pain.

crank *n*, lever, arm, shaft, handle.
eccentric, oddity, crackpot (*inf*), nut (*inf*), maniac, enthusiast, devotee, fanatic.
v, start, turn over, turn, rotate, spin.

cranky eccentric, odd, strange, peculiar, bizarre, queer. NORMAL

cranny chink, crevice, fissure, rift, cleft, crack, breach, gap, opening, interstice.

crapulent crapulous, drunk, inebriated, intoxicated, tipsy, tight (*inf*). SOBER

crash *v*, smash, shatter, shiver, splinter, dash, break, fracture. MEND
collide, bump, bang, hit, drive, wreck.
clatter, clash, clang, bang, boom, roar, thunder.
fall, topple, tumble, collapse, fold, crumble, fail. SOAR
rush, hurtle, precipitate, dash. AMBLE
n, bang, clatter, clash, clang, boom, thunder, racket, din, clangour.
collision, bump, accident, pile-up (*inf*), smash, wreck.
collapse, downfall, ruin, failure, bankruptcy.

crass stupid, dense, thick, asinine, obtuse, oafish, boorish, indelicate, insensitive, gross, coarse, unrefined.

crate case, box, container, chest, basket, hamper.

crave desire, long for, yearn for, hanker after, hunger for, thirst for, want, covet, fancy, need, require, cry out for. SPURN
beseech, entreat, implore, ask, beg, plead, pray, petition, solicit, supplicate.

craven *adj*, cowardly, pusillanimous, timorous, fearful, dastardly, base, fainthearted, yellow (*inf*). BRAVE
n, coward, poltroon, dastard, yellow-belly (*inf*), chicken (*inf*). HERO

craving longing, yearning, hunger, thirst, desire, yen (*inf*), lust, hankering.

crawl creep, inch, steal, slink, worm, slither, move slowly. RACE
swarm, team, be overrun.
grovel, cringe, fawn, toady, abase oneself.

craze *n*, fashion, fad, vogue, rage, mania, passion, enthusiasm, obsession, infatuation.
v, madden, derange, unbalance, unhinge, drive crazy, enrage, inflame. CALM

crazy mad, deranged, demented, insane, lunatic, daft, nuts (*inf*), barmy (*inf*), round the bend (*inf*), potty (*inf*). SANE
silly, foolish, absurd, idiotic, inane, senseless, ludicrous, asinine, half-baked (*inf*), impractical, unwise, imprudent, reckless. SENSIBLE
strange, bizarre, fantastic, odd, peculiar. NORMAL
infatuated, enamoured, wild, passionate, ardent, enthusiastic, fanatical. INDIFFERENT

creak squeak, grate, rasp, scrape, grind, squeal, groan.

crease *v*, fold, ridge, wrinkle, crumple, pucker, corrugate, crinkle.
n, fold, wrinkle, ridge, furrow, line, groove, pucker, pleat, tuck.

create invent, originate, coin, concoct, devise, formulate, design, make, fashion, produce, generate, beget, spawn, hatch. DESTROY appoint, invest, install, constitute, establish, set up. ABOLISH

cause, occasion, bring about, start, lead to.

creation invention, conception, design, origination, start, beginning, generation, genesis, inception, foundation, production, making, formation, construction. DESTRUCTION

universe, cosmos, world, earth, nature, life.

creative inventive, artistic, imaginative, inspired, original, ingenious, clever, talented, skilled. UNIMAGINATIVE

creator maker, inventor, originator, author, architect, designer, founder, father, prime mover, God.

creature being, living thing, animal, beast, brute, person, human being, individual, mortal, body, soul, character.

wretch, cur, rascal, minion, lackey, parasite, hanger-on, dependant, puppet, tool, hireling.

credence belief, acceptance, credit, faith, trust, reliance, confidence, assurance. DISBELIEF

credentials certificate, diploma, licence, warrant, authorization, authority, docket, pass, passport, testimonial, letter of introduction, reference, deed, title.

credible believable, probable, likely, plausible, conceivable, imaginable, thinkable, tenable. INCREDIBLE

trustworthy, trusty, reliable, dependable, honest, truthful. UNRELIABLE

credit *n*, praise, commendation, recognition, acknowledgment, honour, merit, acclaim, glory, tribute. BLAME

belief, credence, faith, trust, confidence. DISBELIEF

reputation, standing, status, influence, regard, esteem, name, character.

reliability, credibility, trustworthiness, integrity, probity, honesty.

on credit, on account, by instalments, by hire-purchase, by deferred payment, on tick (*inf*), on the slate (*inf*).

v, ascribe, attribute, accredit, assign, impute.

believe, accept, trust, have faith in, buy (*inf*), swallow (*inf*). DISBELIEVE

creditable praiseworthy, admirable, estimable, meritorious, laudable, commendable, worthy, reputable, honourable, respectable. SHAMEFUL

credulous gullible, naive, green, trustful, trusting, unsuspicious, unsuspecting, deceivable, simple, soft. SUSPICIOUS

creed belief, faith, dogma, doctrine, tenet, principles, credo, canon, catechism, articles of faith.

creek inlet, bay, bight, cove, firth, sound, estuary.

stream, brook, rivulet, watercourse.

creep steal, sneak, tiptoe, slink, slither, wriggle, glide, worm, insinuate, crawl, inch, edge. RUSH

fawn, grovel, cringe, crawl, toady, kowtow, bootlick (*inf*).

creepy eerie, weird, ghoulish, macabre, ghostly, frightening, scary (*inf*), gruesome, nightmarish, sinister, ominous.

crepitate crackle, rattle, snap, crack.

crest top, apex, summit, pinnacle, peak, ridge, crown, head. FOOT

tuft, mane, comb, topknot, plume, tassel.

bearings, arms, device, badge, emblem, symbol, insignia, charge.

crestfallen dejected, discouraged, dispirited, disheartened, downcast, depressed, downhearted, despondent, sad, melancholy, disconsolate, gloomy. ELATED

crevasse chasm, abyss, ravine, gorge, fissure, cleft.

crevice chink, crack, slit, cranny, cleft, rift, fissure, gap, breach, split.

crew company, team, squad, corps, gang, party, band, group, troupe, crowd, horde, throng, mob, pack.

crib *n*, cot, cradle, bassinet, bed.

rack, manger, box, bin, stall, pen.

v, steal, pilfer, purloin, plagiarize, pirate, copy, cheat.

confine, pen, enclose, imprison, cage, coop up, shut in, restrict. FREE

crick cramp, spasm, twinge.

crime felony, misdemeanour, offence, violation, misdeed, trespass, transgression, atrocity, fault.

wrongdoing, misconduct, lawbreaking, vice, wrong, sin, iniquity, villainy, corruption, delinquency.

criminal *n*, felon, offender, lawbreaker, malefactor, wrongdoer, delinquent, recidivist, villain, crook (*inf*), transgressor, sinner, culprit, convict, jailbird (*inf*).

adj, illegal, unlawful, illicit, wrong, felonious, culpable, guilty, crooked (*inf*), cor-

rupt, iniquitous, wicked, nefarious, villainous, heinous. LAWFUL
deplorable, scandalous, senseless, preposterous, ridiculous.

crimp flute, curl, wave, ridge, corrugate, crinkle, pucker, press, crease.

cringe shrink, flinch, cower, recoil, duck, shy, quail, blench, wince, tremble.
fawn, grovel, crawl, creep, toady, truckle, kowtow, stoop, bend, bow, crouch.

cringing servile, obsequious, fawning, toadying, sycophantic, bootlicking (*inf*).

crinkle crimp, rumple, crumple, wrinkle, crease, pucker, furrow, fold, flute, corrugate, curl. SMOOTH
rustle, crackle, whisper, swish.

cripple lame, disable, maim, mutilate, hamstring, incapacitate, paralyse, injure, impair, damage, handicap, enfeeble, weaken, mar, ruin, spoil.

crisis emergency, exigency, dilemma, quandary, plight, strait, predicament, disaster, catastrophe.
turning point, crux, climax, height, juncture, pass.

crisp brittle, friable, crumbly, crunchy, dry, firm, fresh. PLIABLE
bracing, invigorating, fresh, brisk, stimulating, refreshing. SULTRY
terse, short, brusque, abrupt, brief, succinct, pithy, incisive. LENGTHY

criterion standard, norm, test, rule, measure, touchstone, benchmark, yardstick, canon, principle, guide, model, example.

critic judge, arbiter, reviewer, commentator, analyst, authority, expert, connoisseur, specialist.
censurer, censor, faultfinder, carper, attacker, knocker (*inf*), detractor, Momus.

critical faultfinding, carping, cavilling, censorious, captious, nit-picking (*inf*), disparaging, derogatory. FLATTERING
analytical, diagnostic, perceptive, discerning, penetrating, fastidious, accurate, precise, exact, scrupulous.
crucial, all-important, decisive, vital, essential, momentous, urgent, pressing, serious, grave. UNIMPORTANT
dangerous, perilous, risky, touch-and-go. SAFE

criticism judgment, evaluation, appraisal, assessment, analysis, examination, review, notice, commentary, critique.
censure, animadversion, condemnation, disapproval, objection, stricture, disparagement, brickbat, slating (*inf*), flak (*inf*). PRAISE

criticize censure, find fault, carp, cavil, disparage, disapprove, condemn, denounce, knock (*inf*), slate (*inf*), pan (*inf*). PRAISE
judge, appraise, evaluate, review, analyse, comment on.

croak grunt, squawk, groan, murmur, gasp.
complain, grumble, grouse, moan, mutter.

crockery pottery, earthenware, china, dishes, crocks, pots.

crone hag, witch, old woman, old bag (*inf*), old bat (*inf*).

crony friend, companion, chum, pal (*inf*), mate, associate, ally, sidekick (*inf*). ENEMY

crook *n*, bend, angle, hook, bow, curve, turn.
criminal, thief, robber, swindler, rogue, villain, cheat.
v, bend, curve, bow, flex, turn, twist. STRAIGHTEN

crooked bent, curved, bowed, hooked, twisted, winding, tortuous, zigzag, askew, lopsided, awry, oblique, distorted, deformed, misshapen, irregular, asymmetric. STRAIGHT
dishonest, fraudulent, criminal, illegal, unlawful, underhand, deceitful, dubious, shady (*inf*), unscrupulous, bent (*inf*), corrupt. HONEST

crop *n*, harvest, yield, produce, gathering.
assortment, collection, batch, lot, group.
v, cut, trim, clip, shear, mow, lop, pare, prune, shorten, curtail.

cross *n*, crucifix, rood, X.
burden, affliction, trial, trouble, woe, vexation, misfortune.
hybrid, mongrel, crossbreed, blend, combination, mixture.
v, traverse, pass over, go across, ford, span, bridge.
intersect, crisscross, interweave, entwine, lace.
interbreed, crossbreed, hybridize, mix, blend.
hinder, impede, obstruct, frustrate, foil, thwart, oppose, resist. HELP
cross out, delete, cancel, strike out, blue-pencil.
adj, angry, annoyed, vexed, ill-tempered, grumpy, irritable, testy, touchy, fractious,

peevish, petulant, crusty, snappy, waspish, cantankerous, short, shirty (*inf*). AFFABLE
transverse, crosswise, oblique, athwart.
contrary, adverse, unfavourable, opposing. FAVOURABLE

cross-examine interrogate, question, grill (*inf*), quiz, catechize, pump.

cross-grained stubborn, obdurate, perverse, headstrong, wilful, cantankerous, peevish, wayward, refractory, intractable, awkward, difficult. OBLIGING

crotch crutch, groin, angle, fork.

crotchet notion, whim, whimsy, caprice, fancy, fad, quirk, vagary.

crotchety cross, irritable, peevish, crusty, testy, touchy, grumpy, crabby, irascible, bad-tempered, cantankerous, contrary, awkward. AFFABLE
capricious, whimsical, fanciful, fitful, erratic, fickle.

crouch stoop, hunch, bend, bow, duck, squat, kneel.
cower, cringe, fawn, grovel, truckle.

crow brag, boast, vaunt, gloat, swagger, bluster, exult, triumph, rejoice.

crowd *n*, host, multitude, throng, mob, rabble, horde, pack, herd, swarm, assembly, concourse, congregation, company, group, bunch.
v, throng, swarm, flock, herd, congregate, gather, cluster, huddle. DISPERSE
press, pack, cram, squeeze, compress, congest, fill, stuff, shove, push, jostle.

crown *n*, diadem, coronet, coronal, circlet, tiara, chaplet, wreath, garland.
reward, award, prize, trophy, laurels, kudos, honour.
sovereign, monarch, ruler, king, queen, royalty, monarchy.
top, head, summit, brow, crest, apex, pinnacle, peak, acme, zenith, culmination. FOOT
v, adorn, honour, decorate, reward, invest, endow, install.
perfect, consummate, cap, top, surmount, complete, fulfil, round off, finish, conclude. BEGIN

crucial critical, decisive, central, pivotal, vital, all-important, momentous, essential, imperative, urgent, pressing. TRIVIAL

crucify torture, torment, persecute, rack, harrow.
overcome, subdue, mortify.
execute, put to death.

crude rude, vulgar, ribald, smutty, tasteless, gross, lewd, obscene, indecent, coarse, uncouth, crass, boorish.
raw, rough, unrefined, coarse, unfinished, unpolished, unprocessed, natural, primitive, rudimentary, sketchy, incomplete. REFINED

crudeness crudity, rawness, roughness, coarseness, vulgarity, rudeness, indecency, indelicacy, obscenity, ribaldry, impropriety. REFINEMENT

cruel savage, barbarous, brutal, ferocious, bloodthirsty, vicious, sadistic, merciless, pitiless, unrelenting, ruthless, harsh, severe, heartless, inhuman, unfeeling, unkind, callous, hard-hearted, cold-blooded, implacable. HUMANE

cruelty barbarity, brutality, savagery, ferocity, sadism, mercilessness, ruthlessness, harshness, severity, inhumanity, callousness. COMPASSION

cruise *n*, voyage, trip, sail.
v, sail, travel, journey, voyage, coast, drift, rove.

crumb scrap, morsel, bit, fragment, mite, shred, particle, speck, grain, sliver, bite, *soupçon*, atom, snippet.

crumble *vi*, disintegrate, fall apart, break up, fragment, decompose, perish. ENDURE
vt, crush, bruise, pulverize, pound, grind, triturate.

crumple rumple, wrinkle, crinkle, crease, corrugate, ruffle, crush, pucker, screw up. SMOOTH
collapse, fall, cave in, give way, break down, go to pieces, shrivel, shrink.

crunch munch, gnaw, chew, champ, grind, masticate.

crusade campaign, movement, cause, struggle, drive.

crush squeeze, squash, compress, pinch, break, smash, crumble, pound, pulverize, mash, grind, triturate, bruise, contuse, crumple, wrinkle, crease, demolish, raze, flatten.
overpower, subdue, overcome, overwhelm, suppress, quash, quell, put down, vanquish, conquer. RESIST
abash, humiliate, mortify, shame, chagrin, put down (*inf*).

crust covering, coating, layer, film, surface, skin, rind, shell, incrustation, scab.

crusty peevish, touchy, testy, crabbed, fractious, captious, bad-tempered, irritable, waspish, cantankerous, surly, curt, gruff, brusque, short. AFFABLE

cry *v*, sob, weep, wail, bawl, whine, whimper, snivel, blubber, lament, keen. LAUGH
call, shout, exclaim, vociferate, ejaculate, yell, shriek, scream, roar, bellow, holler (*inf*). WHISPER
proclaim, announce, broadcast, trumpet, blazon, noise, advertise, hawk.
cry down, disparage, belittle, denigrate, run down, decry.
n, sob, sobbing, weep, weeping, wail, bawl, blubber, lamentation, crying. LAUGH
call, shout, exclamation, ejaculation, yell, shriek, scream, roar, bellow, outcry. WHISPER
proclamation, announcement, slogan.
plea, entreaty, appeal, supplication, prayer, request.

crypt vault, tomb, catacomb, burial chamber, sepulchre.

cryptic secret, hidden, occult, esoteric, arcane, abstruse, obscure, vague, oracular, cabbalistic, enigmatic, mysterious, puzzling.

cuddle embrace, hug, clasp, fondle, caress, snuggle, nestle.

cudgel *n*, club, bludgeon, truncheon, cosh, stick, bastinado.
v, beat, batter, pound, baste, drub, club, bludgeon, thrash.

cue signal, sign, indication, nod, wink, hint, suggestion, intimation, reminder, prompt, catchword.

cuff *v*, strike, hit, box, slap, smack, buffet, punch, belt (*inf*).
n, blow, box, slap, smack, buffet, punch.

cuisine cookery, cooking, menu, food, fare.

cull pick, choose, select, single out, pluck, gather, collect, glean.

culminate end, finish, close, conclude, terminate, result, climax, come to a head. START

culmination climax, zenith, meridian, acme, height, peak, top, summit, pinnacle, crown, consummation, conclusion, completion, close, finishing touch, finale. BEGINNING

culpable blameworthy, blamable, censurable, wrong, reprehensible, at fault, guilty, sinful. INNOCENT

culprit offender, guilty party, wrongdoer, malefactor, criminal, felon, miscreant, delinquent, sinner.

cult sect, clique, faction, party, school, belief, faith, religion, denomination.
worship, homage, veneration, adoration, devotion, idolization.
craze, fashion, fad.

cultivate till, work, farm, plant, plough, fertilize.
promote, foster, nurture, further, support, encourage, help, aid. IMPEDE
improve, better, ameliorate, develop, refine, civilize, enrich, polish, train, educate. NEGLECT

cultivation agriculture, agronomy, farming, husbandry, tillage, gardening.
civilization, culture, refinement, polish, breeding, education, training, development, enlightenment, improvement. NEGLECT
promotion, support, encouragement, furtherance, patronage, advocacy, nurture, help, aid.

cultural edifying, enriching, instructive, educational, enlightening, civilizing, artistic, elevating.

culture refinement, sophistication, polish, cultivation, urbanity, gentility, breeding, education, enlightenment, edification. BARBARITY
civilization, society, customs, way of life, life style, mores.
agriculture, farming, cultivation, husbandry, agronomy.

cultured refined, sophisticated, civilized, polished, well-bred, genteel, urbane, educated, knowledgeable, erudite, scholarly, enlightened. BARBAROUS

cumbersome awkward, unwieldy, bulky, heavy, burdensome, oppressive, inconvenient, incommodious. LIGHT

cumulative increasing, snowballing, accumulative, collective, accruing, growing. DECREASING

cunning *adj*, artful, crafty, sly, wily, foxy, sharp, shrewd, astute, canny, arch, subtle, devious, calculating, designing, deceitful, dishonest, shifty. ARTLESS
ingenious, skilful, clever, deft, dexterous.
n, artfulness, craft, craftiness, slyness, wiliness, guile, sharpness, shrewdness, subtlety, trickery, deception. ARTLESSNESS

ingenuity, skill, dexterity, cleverness, ability, art.

cup chalice, goblet, beaker, mug, trophy.

cupboard cabinet, locker, closet, sideboard, wardrobe.

cupidity avarice, greed, acquisitiveness, rapacity, covetousness, desire, lust, longing, hankering, thirst, hunger.

cur hound, dog, mongrel, mutt (*inf*).
scoundrel, blackguard, wretch, rotter (*inf*), cad, villain, rat (*inf*).

curative healing, restorative, therapeutic, medicinal, remedial, salutary, healthy. NOXIOUS

curb *v*, restrain, check, control, bridle, repress, muzzle, hold back, suppress, moderate, restrict. ENCOURAGE
n, restraint, check, control, bridle, rein, moderation, restriction, limitation.

curdle coagulate, congeal, thicken, curd, clot, go sour, turn.

cure *v*, heal, restore, remedy, make well, correct, ease, alleviate, relieve, treat. AGGRAVATE
preserve, dry, salt, smoke, pickle.
n, remedy, antidote, restorative, treatment, therapy, medicine, drug, panacea, corrective, healing, restoration, recovery.

curiosity inquisitiveness, nosiness (*inf*), snooping, prying, interest, questioning. INDIFFERENCE
oddity, rarity, novelty, curio, phenomenon, freak, spectacle, sight, marvel, wonder.

curious inquisitive, inquiring, questioning, interested, prying, snooping, meddlesome, nosy (*inf*). INDIFFERENT
odd, strange, queer, unusual, uncommon, extraordinary, peculiar, singular, bizarre, rare, exotic, unexpected. ORDINARY

curl *v*, twist, wind, coil, spiral, snake, twine, convolute, bend, curve, loop, wave, crimp, frizz. STRAIGHTEN
n, coil, spiral, whorl, curlicue, convolution, loop, kink, wave, ringlet, lock, tress.

curmudgeon miser, skinflint, churl, bear, crosspatch (*inf*), sourpuss (*inf*), grumbler, grouch (*inf*).

currency money, cash, notes, coins, legal tender.
circulation, transmission, acceptance, prevalence, popularity, vogue, fashion, publicity, exposure.

current *adj*, present, ongoing, prevailing, in progress, latest, up-to-date, contemporary, fashionable, popular. OBSOLETE
widespread, rife, circulating, general, common, prevalent.
n, flow, stream, tide, drift, trend, course, progression.

curse *n*, oath, expletive, swearword, blasphemy, profanity, obscenity.
execration, imprecation, anathema, malediction, malison, denunciation, excommunication, damnation, incantation, charm, spell, jinx, voodoo. BENEDICTION
scourge, bane, affliction, trouble, torment, plague, vexation, burden, misfortune, evil. BLESSING
v, swear, blaspheme, cuss (*inf*).
execrate, imprecate, anathematize, denounce, damn, blast, fulminate, excommunicate. BLESS
blight, destroy, plague, scourge, afflict, vex, torment.

cursory superficial, perfunctory, summary, hasty, rapid, hurried, brief, slight, passing, fleeting, careless, slapdash. THOROUGH

curt terse, short, brief, concise, succinct, laconic, blunt, brusque, abrupt, rude, unceremonious, gruff.

curtail shorten, cut short, abridge, abbreviate, cut, lop, reduce, decrease, diminish, lessen, contract. LENGTHEN

curtailment shortening, abridgment, abbreviation, reduction, cutting, docking, retrenchment, diminution, contraction. EXTENSION

curtain *n*, hanging, shade, screen, blind, drape, veil.
v, conceal, hide, shut off, screen, veil, shroud. EXPOSE

curvature curve, incurvation, flexure, bend, bending.

curve *v*, bend, turn, twist, wind, inflect, arch, hook, bow, curl, coil, spiral. STRAIGHTEN
n, bend, arc, arch, camber, vault, turn, hook, loop, crescent, curvature.

cushion *n*, pad, bolster, pillow, hassock, headrest, buffer.
v, protect, support, bolster, brace.
lessen, stifle, muffle, soften, deaden, suppress.

cusp point, tip, apex, angle.

custodian guardian, keeper, warden, warder, protector, curator, caretaker, watchman.

custody care, protection, keeping, safekeeping, charge, ward, tutelage, guardianship, trusteeship, supervision, watch, auspices, aegis.
arrest, confinement, imprisonment, detention, duress. RELEASE

custom convention, usage, habit, wont, routine, policy, rule, practice, use, formality, etiquette, fashion, way, manner, procedure, ritual.

customary usual, habitual, wonted, accustomed, regular, routine, conventional, traditional, normal, ordinary, common, popular, familiar. UNUSUAL

customer client, patron, buyer, purchaser, shopper, consumer. SELLER

cut *v*, sever, cut off, slice, chop, carve, divide, cut up, cleave, gash, slash, score, nick, lacerate, wound. JOIN
trim, shear, mow, lop, crop, dock, prune, fell, hew, cut down, pare, shave.
shorten, abridge, edit, abbreviate, curtail, reduce, retrench, cut back, cut down, lessen, lower, decrease. EXTEND
snub, ignore, cold-shoulder, avoid, spurn, slight, rebuff. ACKNOWLEDGE
cut in, interpose, interrupt, butt in, intervene.
cut off, intercept, interrupt, discontinue, stop, halt, suspend, disconnect.
cut out, delete, eliminate, exclude, remove, extract, excise.
cut short, break off, halt, suspend, interrupt, abort, terminate, end, stop.
n, incision, gash, wound, laceration, slash, nick.
reduction, cutback, decrease, lowering, fall.
share, percentage, slice, portion, piece.
style, shape, form, fashion, mode.

cute sweet, appealing, attractive, delightful, pretty, charming. REPULSIVE
clever, shrewd, astute, canny, sharp. DULL

cutting *adj*, keen, sharp, trenchant, piercing, biting, caustic, acid, mordant, incisive, acerbic, sardonic, sarcastic, cruel, bitter, hurtful, stinging. SOOTHING
n, clipping, excerpt, abstract, piece, slip, snippet.

cycle circle, revolution, rotation, round, series, succession.
period, era, aeon, age, epoch.

cyclone tornado, typhoon, whirlwind, hurricane, tempest, storm.

cynical pessimistic, misanthropic, sceptical, distrustful, suspicious, unbelieving, contemptuous, scornful, derisive, sardonic, sarcastic, ironic, mocking, sneering.

cynosure focus, focal point, centre, attraction, centre of attention, polestar, leading light, paragon, ideal.

cyst blister, sac, vesicle, bladder, bleb.

D

dab *v*, pat, tap, touch, daub, spot, blot.
n, spot, drop, speck, touch, bit, trace.
pat, tap, stroke, blow, touch.
dab hand, expert, master, adept, ace (*inf*), dabster.

dabble dip, paddle, splash, spatter, sprinkle, moisten, wet.
potter, tinker, trifle, dally, toy with, play at, dip into.

daft silly, foolish, stupid, idiotic, simple, soft (*inf*), crazy, absurd, senseless, lunatic, insane, crackers (*inf*), potty (*inf*), nuts (*inf*). SENSIBLE

dagger dirk, stiletto, poniard, skean, knife, blade.

dainty delicate, fine, elegant, refined, exquisite, charming, pretty, beautiful, graceful, petite, neat, trim. CLUMSY
delicious, tasty, tender, choice, savoury, luscious, delectable, toothsome, palatable. LOATHSOME
scrupulous, fastidious, squeamish, particular, fussy, finicky, choosy.

dale valley, vale, dell, dingle, glen. HILL

dalliance dawdling, dilly-dallying, idling, loafing, delay, procrastination, pottering, trifling, dabbling. HASTE

dally dawdle, loiter, linger, dilly-dally, tarry, delay, waste time, hang around. HURRY
trifle, toy, play, sport, flirt, fool around, tease, caress, pet, fondle.

damage *n*, harm, injury, hurt, suffering, mischief, impairment, detriment, loss, destruction, ruin. REPARATION
v, harm, hurt, injure, impair, tamper with, mar, spoil, ruin, wreck, deface, mutilate. REPAIR

damages compensation, satisfaction, reparation, indemnity, costs, expenses, fine, penalty.

dame lady, noblewoman, peeress, baroness, matron, dowager.

damn *v*, condemn, denounce. censure, criticize, berate, vituperate, vilify, slate (*inf*). EXTOL
curse, swear, blaspheme, blast, cuss (*inf*), anathematize, imprecate. BLESS
doom, sentence, condemn, convict. ACQUIT
n, trifle, jot, whit, iota, hoot (*inf*), brass farthing.
give a damn, care, mind, be concerned.

damnable abominable, execrable, odious, detestable, accursed, despicable, horrible, atrocious. SPLENDID

damnation condemnation, denunciation, objurgation, excommunication, proscription, exile, ban, doom, anathema, curse. BLESSING

damp *adj*, moist, dewy, wet, dank, humid, muggy, clammy, soggy, sodden, misty, drizzly. DRY
n, dampness, moisture, humidity, fog, mist, vapour, dankness, dew. DRYNESS
v, moisten, dampen, wet, bedew, humidify. DRY
check, curb, restrain, moderate, abate, allay, temper, dull, deaden, blunt, cool, inhibit, stifle, muffle, discourage, dishearten, depress, deject. ENCOURAGE

dampen damp, wet, moisten, bedew, humidify. DRY
moderate, restrain, temper, dull, blunt, deaden, stifle, discourage, depress, damp. ENCOURAGE

damper obstacle, hindrance, impediment, hitch, check, restraint, discouragement, pall, cloud, wet blanket, kill-joy.

dance *v*, caper, skip, hop, jig, swing, rock, prance, frolic, gambol.
n, ball, social, hop (*inf*), disco (*inf*).

dandle caress, pet, fondle, rock, cradle, amuse.

dandy *n*, beau, fop, coxcomb, swell (*inf*), popinjay, ladies' man.
adj, fine, excellent, splendid, first-rate.

danger peril, risk, jeopardy, hazard, vulnerability, precariousness, threat, menace. SAFETY

dangerous perilous, risky, hazardous, unsafe, chancy, hairy (*inf*), vulnerable, insecure, precarious, ominous, threatening, menacing. SAFE

dangle hang, suspend, swing, droop, trail, sway, oscillate.
flaunt, brandish, wave, flourish.

dank damp, clammy, moist, dewy, humid, wet, chilly. DRY

dapper smart, spruce, neat, trim, natty, chic, elegant. SLOVENLY
nimble, spry, brisk, agile, lively, sprightly, active, quick. SLOW

dappled mottled, variegated, spotted. speckled, brindled, piebald, pied, brindled, dapple.

dare *v*, challenge, defy, provoke, goad, taunt, brave, confront.
risk, hazard, venture, endanger, gamble, stake, attempt, presume. QUAIL
n, challenge, provocation, ultimatum, gauntlet.

daring *adj*, bold, brave, adventurous, venturesome, intrepid, dauntless, fearless, courageous, plucky, rash, reckless, daredevil, foolhardy, death-defying. TIMOROUS
n, boldness, audacity, bravery, intrepidity, courage, valour, nerve, mettle, pluck, guts (*inf*), bottle (*inf*), temerity, rashness, recklessness. TIMOROUSNESS

dark *adj*, dim, unlit, sunless, shadowy, dingy, murky, cloudy, overcast, dusky, swarthy, black, ebony, sable, pitchy. LIGHT
sombre, drab, dismal, gloomy, cheerless, bleak, mournful, discouraging. BRIGHT
dour, sullen, morose, glowering, threatening, forbidding, ominous, menacing, sinister. CHEERFUL
ignorant, unenlightened, benighted, uneducated. ENLIGHTENED
secret, hidden, abstruse, recondite, cryptic, incomprehensible, unintelligible, obscure, mysterious, enigmatic, occult, arcane. PLAIN
infernal, hellish, satanic, nefarious, infamous, evil, wicked, vile, atrocious, horrible. GOOD
n, darkness, dimness, blackness, gloom, obscurity, murkiness, dusk, twilight, evening. night. LIGHT
ignorance, blindness, secrecy, concealment. ENLIGHTENMENT

darken dim, obscure, eclipse, shade, shadow, overshadow, cloud, blacken, make dark, go dark. LIGHTEN deject, depress, dishearten, discourage, oppress, sadden, make gloomy. BRIGHTEN

darkness *n*, dark, gloom, murkiness, murk, dimness, obscurity, shadows, dusk, night, blackness. BRIGHTNESS

ignorance, blindness, secrecy, concealment. ENLIGHTENMENT

darling *n*, dear, sweetheart, beloved, pet, love, favourite.

adj, dear, beloved, precious, cherished, adored, loved, treasured, pet, favourite.

charming, lovely, sweet, adorable, enchanting. REPULSIVE

darn mend, repair, stitch, sew, patch.

dart *vi*, shoot, dash, race, sprint, fly, run, scoot, tear, rush. AMBLE

vt, hurl, throw, fling, cast, pitch, sling, propel.

dash *v*, rush, run, race, dart, hurry, hasten, fly, bolt, sprint. AMBLE

hurl, throw, cast, fling, strike, crash, break, shatter, splinter.

frustrate, thwart, foil, ruin, destroy.

n, dart, rush, spurt, sprint, onset.

tinge, touch, trace, *soupçon*, hint, drop, bit, pinch, grain, smack, sprinkling.

élan, flair, style, flourish, panache, vigour, spirit.

dashing lively, spirited, impetuous, dynamic, gallant, valiant, plucky. LETHARGIC

showy, flamboyant, brilliant, dazzling, elegant, chic, stylish, dapper, jaunty.

dastard coward, craven, poltroon, cur, worm, mouse.

dastardly dastard, cowardly, craven, faint-hearted, timorous, pusillanimous, yellow (*inf*). BRAVE

base, mean, despicable, low, underhand. NOBLE

data facts, information, input, figures, statistics.

date *n*, age, period, era, epoch, time, day, month, year, century.

appointment, engagement, assignation, tryst, rendezvous.

escort, boyfriend, girlfriend, lover, steady (*inf*).

out of date, old-fashioned, outmoded, dated, passé, obsolete, antiquated, superannuated. MODERN

expired, invalid, lapsed. CURRENT

up to date, modern, fashionable, trendy (*inf*), up-to-the-minute, current, contemporary. DATED

v, take out, go out with, court.

obsolesce, become old-fashioned.

dated out of date, old-fashioned, outmoded, passé, old hat, antiquated, obsolescent. MODERN

daub *v*, smear, paint, plaster, cover, bedaub, spatter, smudge, soil, begrime, deface, sully, stain.

n, smear, smudge, spot, blot, smirch.

daunt intimidate, unnerve, dismay, alarm, scare, frighten, terrify, appal, cow, overawe.

discourage, dispirit, deter, put off, stop, check, thwart. ENCOURAGE

dauntless undaunted, bold, daring, brave, fearless, intrepid, valiant, doughty, indomitable, courageous, stout-hearted, heroic. COWARDLY

dawdle lag, loiter, dilly-dally (*inf*), dally, waste time, idle, trifle, potter. HURRY

dawdler laggard, loiterer, snail, slowcoach (*inf*), idler.

dawn *n*, daybreak, sunrise, sun-up, cockcrow, aurora, daylight, morning. SUNSET

beginning, start, outset, origin, birth, genesis, inception, advent, onset, emergence. END

v, break, gleam, grow light, brighten.

begin, start, appear, emerge, rise, open, originate. CLOSE

day daylight, daytime, sunshine. NIGHT

generation, age, period, epoch, era, lifetime, heyday, prime.

daybreak dawn, sunrise, sun-up, cockcrow, first light, morning. NIGHTFALL

daydream *n*, dream, reverie, woolgathering, fancy, pipe dream, fantasy, castle in the air.

v, dream, muse, fantasize, stargaze, imagine.

daylight sunshine, sunlight, day, daytime, light of day. NIGHT

daze *v*, stun, stupefy, shock, dumbfound, amaze, astonish, flabbergast (*inf*), bewilder, confuse, blind, dazzle.

n, stupor, trance, confusion, distraction, bewilderment.

dazzle *v*, blind, bedazzle, daze, stun, stagger, amaze, astonish, strike dumb, impress, overawe, bowl over (*inf*), fascinate. BORE *n*, brilliance, splendour, magnificence, sparkle, flash. DULLNESS

dead *adj*, lifeless, defunct, deceased, late, departed, gone, extinct, inanimate. ALIVE
numb, insensitive, unresponsive, unfeeling, cold, frigid, lukewarm, indifferent, apathetic, spiritless, torpid, dull.
inactive, inert, still, inoperative, not working.
complete, utter, downright, total, absolute, thorough.
n, midst, depth, darkness, coldness, stillness.
adv, completely, utterly, totally, absolutely, entirely.

deaden damp, dampen, muffle, blunt, subdue, weaken, moderate, diminish, lessen, abate, alleviate, dull, numb, anaesthetize, paralyse. INTENSIFY

deadlock stalemate, impasse, standstill, halt, cessation, tie, draw.

deadly mortal, fatal, lethal, malignant, pernicious, noxious, venomous, destructive, baleful, murderous, savage, sanguinary, implacable.
pale, ashen, deathly, deathlike, wan, ghostly, livid. RUDDY
boring, dull, tedious, monotonous, tiresome. ENTHRALLING

deaf unhearing, stone deaf, hard of hearing.
heedless, oblivious, insensitive, unmoved, indifferent. AWARE

deafen make deaf, din, drown out, muffle.

deafening ear-splitting, piercing, thunderous, resounding, intense. QUIET

deal *v*, distribute, dispense, mete, dole, bestow, give, divide, share, allot, apportion.
trade, traffic, bargain, negotiate, do business.
act, behave, conduct oneself.
deal with, handle, manage, cope with, see to, take care of, attend to, treat.
n, agreement, bargain, transaction, contract, pact, understanding.
quantity, amount, degree, extent.

dealer merchant, trader, tradesman, wholesaler, retailer, vendor, trafficker.

dealings business, commerce, trade, traffic.
action, behaviour, relations.

dear *adj*, beloved, darling, precious, cherished, treasured, prized, favourite. LOATHSOME
expensive, costly, pricey (*inf*). CHEAP
n, darling, beloved, treasure, love, precious.

dearth lack, deficiency, scarcity, shortage, insufficiency, want, need, famine, poverty, absence. ABUNDANCE

death decease, demise, expiration, dying, passing, departure, quietus, exit, end, cessation, dissolution. BIRTH
destruction, annihilation, extermination, extinction, eradication.

deathless immortal, undying, imperishable, everlasting, eternal, unceasing, timeless. MORTAL

deathly deathlike, ghastly, livid, pale, wan, gaunt, haggard, cadaverous.

debacle rout, defeat, overthrow, ruin, collapse, downfall, break-up, wreck, havoc, devastation, catastrophe.

debar bar, exclude, shut out, blackball, proscribe, prohibit, restrain, impede, hinder, obstruct, thwart, stop. ADMIT

debase degrade, lower, abase, reduce, humble, humiliate, shame, disgrace, dishonour, demean, devalue, depreciate, deteriorate. RAISE
adulterate, vitiate, contaminate, deprave, corrupt, taint, defile, pollute, sully, alloy, impair. PURIFY

debasement degradation, lowering, abasement, humiliation, disgrace, dishonour, depreciation, reduction, deterioration, adulteration, contamination, pollution, corruption, depravation.

debatable disputable, questionable, unsettled, undecided, moot, contestable, controversial, doubtful, dubious, uncertain. CERTAIN

debate *v*, discuss, dispute, argue, contend, question, moot, wrangle, controvert. AGREE
deliberate, consider, ponder, reflect, mull over. DECIDE
n, discussion, dispute, disputation, polemic, controversy, wrangle, altercation, contention, contest. AGREEMENT

debauch *v*, deprave, corrupt, debase, demoralize, pervert, vitiate, defile, deflower, violate, seduce, lead astray. PURIFY
n, spree, orgy, fling, revel, carousal, saturnalia, binge (*inf*), bout.

debauched depraved, corrupt, licentious, degenerate, dissolute, dissipated, immoral, abandoned, wanton. ASCETIC
debauchery depravity, dissipation, dissoluteness, lust, licentiousness, intemperance, incontinence, indulgence, excess, revelry, debauch. RESTRAINT
debilitate enfeeble, weaken, enervate, sap, exhaust, prostrate, incapacitate, undermine. STRENGTHEN
debility feebleness, weakness, enervation, prostration, exhaustion, infirmity, decrepitude, frailty, languor, lassitude, incapacity. STRENGTH
debonair affable, gracious, courteous, polite, suave, urbane, refined, elegant, dashing, jaunty, sprightly, buoyant, cheery, sunny, breezy, light-hearted, gay.
debris remains, ruins, wreckage, detritus, fragments, pieces, rubble, rubbish, litter.
debt liability, obligation, due, duty, debit, arrears, deficit, bill, account, score. ASSET
in debt, owing, liable, accountable, beholden, in arrears, in the red.
debut beginning, launch, premiere, coming out, introduction, presentation, entrance, first appearance.
decadence decay, decline, degeneration, deterioration, wane, fall, retrogression, debasement, corruption, dissipation, dissolution. RISE
decadent depraved, dissolute, dissipated, self-indulgent, immoral, corrupt, degenerate.
decaying, declining, waning, deteriorating. RISING
decamp abscond, bolt, fly, flee, run away, make off, escape, scarper (*inf*), do a bunk (*inf*).
decapitate behead, guillotine, execute.
decay *v*, decline, deteriorate, waste away, wither, crumble, atrophy, degenerate, wane, decrease, dwindle. FLOURISH
rot, decompose, spoil, perish, go bad, putrefy.
n, decline, deterioration, decadence, wasting, atrophy, degeneration, wane, collapse, downfall. GROWTH
rot, decomposition, spoilage, putrefaction, caries, gangrene, mould.
decease death, demise, dying, expiration, passing, departure, exit, release. BIRTH
deceased dead, lifeless, defunct, departed, gone, late, former. ALIVE
deceit fraud, deception, guile, duplicity, cheating, trickery, artifice, deceitfulness, dishonesty. HONESTY
trick, ruse, stratagem, wile, subterfuge, pretence, imposture, fraud, swindle, lie, falsehood.
deceitful dishonest, untruthful, mendacious, hollow, false, insincere, hypocritical, fraudulent, crooked, treacherous, wily, scheming, tricky, guileful, artful, deceptive. HONEST
deceive mislead, cheat, trick, fool, beguile, dupe, hoodwink, cozen, delude, hoax, swindle, con (*inf*), bamboozle (*inf*), double-cross (*inf*), take in (*inf*), take for a ride (*inf*).
deceiver cheat, fraud, impostor, swindler, sharper, con man (*inf*), hypocrite, liar, charlatan.
decency propriety, modesty, decorum, correctness, respectability, seemliness, etiquette. IMPROPRIETY
decent proper, seemly, fitting, appropriate, seemly, becoming, decorous, nice, polite, pure, modest, respectable. INDECENT
adequate, passable, fair, reasonable, not bad, acceptable, tolerable.
obliging, accommodating, kind, generous, thoughtful, courteous. UNKIND
deception deceit, fraud, cheating, guile, artifice, duplicity, hypocrisy, trickery, cunning, treachery, deceitfulness, dishonesty. HONESTY
trick, ruse, wile, fraud, imposture, swindle, hoax, lie, bluff, sham, illusion.
deceptive misleading, deceiving, unreliable, illusory, illusive, delusive, fallacious, ambiguous, fraudulent, false, fake, counterfeit, dishonest, deceitful. TRUE
decide determine, settle, adjudicate, judge, rule, decree, resolve, make up one's mind, choose, elect, conclude, terminate, end. WAVER
decided determined, resolute, unwavering, firm, decisive, unhesitating. IRRESOLUTE
certain, unquestionable, indisputable, unmistakable, unequivocal, positive, distinct, clear, definite, categorical. DUBIOUS
decipher solve, unravel, decode, translate, interpret, explain, construe, read, make out. ENCODE

decision resolution, conclusion, verdict, judgment, ruling, settlement, finding.
determination, resolution, resolve, firmness, decisiveness, purpose. INDECISION
decisive conclusive, deciding, definitive, absolute, categorical, final, emphatic, momentous, crucial, influential. INCONCLUSIVE
resolute, decided, determined, firm, unwavering. INDECISIVE
deck adorn, bedeck, array, clothe, dress, attire, decorate, trim, ornament, embellish. STRIP
declaim orate, harangue, perorate, hold forth, rant, proclaim, speak, enunciate, recite, spout.
declaim against, criticize, attack, denounce, decry, inveigh against, rail at.
declamation harangue, tirade, recitation, oration, speech, address, lecture, oratory, grandiloquence.
declamatory rhetorical, bombastic, grandiloquent, magniloquent, fustian, turgid, orotund, pompous, theatrical, stilted.
declaration statement, affirmation, avowal, assertion, asseveration, averment, acknowledgment, testimony, deposition, profession. DENIAL
proclamation, announcement, notice, publication, manifesto, pronouncement, notification.
declare state, affirm, avow, assert, attest, aver, say, maintain, claim, swear, testify, certify. DENY
proclaim, announce, broadcast, trumpet, pronounce, decree.
declension decline, fall, deterioration, decay, decadence, degeneracy. RISE
declination inclination, slope, descent, declivity, deviation, divergence, departure.
decline *v*, refuse, turn down, reject, forgo, deny. ACCEPT
decrease, diminish, lessen, dwindle, wane, ebb, sink, fall, fail, deteriorate, weaken, droop, languish, pine, degenerate, decay, waste away. FLOURISH
descend, sink, dip, slope, incline. ASCEND
n, decrease, diminution, lessening, recession, wane, deterioration, failing, weakening, degeneration, decay, senility, decrepitude.
declivity, slope, incline, descent. ASCENT
declivity descent, declination, downward slope, decline, incline, hill. ACCLIVITY
decompose rot, go bad, putrefy, decay, crumble, fall apart, break up.
disintegrate, dissolve, break down, analyse, dissect, atomize, distil, separate, resolve.
decomposition rotting, putrefaction, putrescence, decay, corruption.
disintegration, analysis, dissection, dissolution, separation, resolution. SYNTHESIS
decorate embellish, ornament, adorn, deck, bedeck, trim, beautify. MAR
paint, wallpaper, renovate, do up (*inf*).
cite, honour.
decoration embellishment, ornament, ornamentation, adornment, trimming, garnish, flourish, frill, bauble.
medal, ribbon, badge, order, award, citation.
decorous proper, seemly, decent, becoming, fitting, appropriate, suitable, correct, mannerly, dignified, sedate, refined, elegant, polite. UNSEEMLY
decorum propriety, correctness, seemliness, decency, etiquette, protocol, breeding, good manners, politeness, dignity, respectability. IMPROPRIETY
decoy *v*, lure, allure, entice, tempt, bait, inveigle, seduce, deceive, mislead, ensnare, entrap.
n, lure, enticement, bait, trap, pretence, fake.
decrease *v*, lessen, diminish, reduce, dwindle, decline, lower, wane, subside, ebb, fall, drop, abate, ease, cut down, curtail, shrink, contract. INCREASE
n, lessening, diminution, reduction, decline, lowering, decrement, ebb, recession, wane, fall, abatement, cutback, retrenchment, curtailment, shrinkage, contraction. INCREASE
decree *n*, edict, order, command, precept, law, enactment, statute, mandate, rule, regulation, injunction, dictum, ordinance.
v, order, command, adjudge, ordain, rule, enact, appoint, proclaim, pronounce, decide, determine.
decrement decrease, diminution, decline, reduction. INCREMENT
decrepit infirm, enfeebled, feeble, weak, frail, crippled, incapacitated, aged, doddering, tottering. YOUTHFUL
dilapidated, ramshackle, broken-down, run-down, rickety, worn-out, antiquated, superannuated.

decrial disparagement, condemnation, denunciation, depreciation, belittlement. APPRECIATION

decry disparage, belittle, deprecate, depreciate, underrate, undervalue, discredit, run down, abuse, criticize, condemn, denounce, rail against, defame, vilify. APPRECIATE

dedicate devote, pledge, commit, assign, give.
consecrate, sanctify, hallow, bless, set apart. DESECRATE
inscribe, address.

dedication devotion, commitment, wholeheartedness, allegiance, loyalty, fidelity.
consecration, sanctification, hallowing, ordination, blessing. DESECRATION
inscription, address.

deduce conclude, infer, gather, understand, derive, reason, presume, surmise. GUESS

deduct subtract, take away, dock, withdraw, remove, take off. ADD

deduction conclusion, inference, corollary, finding, reasoning, result, assumption. GUESS
subtraction, reduction, decrease, withdrawal, removal, allowance, discount. ADDITION

deed action, act, feat, exploit, achievement, accomplishment, performance, doing.
title, document, contract, indenture.

deem consider, judge, hold, regard, think, imagine, believe, estimate, account, suppose.

deep *adj*, profound, bottomless, unfathomable, immeasurable, broad, wide, extensive, cavernous, yawning. SHALLOW
abstruse, obscure, difficult, mysterious, arcane, recondite, esoteric, incomprehensible. PLAIN
learned, intellectual, astute, shrewd, knowing, discerning, intelligent, sagacious, wise.
engrossed, absorbed, preoccupied, rapt, immersed, involved.
grave, great, intense, extreme, profound.
dark, rich, intense, vivid, full. LIGHT
low, bass, sonorous, resonant, rumbling. HIGH
n, sea, ocean, main.
depth, bottom, vastness, midst, dead, still.

deepen dig, hollow, excavate, scoop out, dredge, mine, sink.
intensify, increase, amplify, augment, strengthen, enhance. LESSEN

deface disfigure, mar, spoil, deform, blemish, flaw, mutilate, vandalize, sully, tarnish. BEAUTIFY

defacement disfigurement, injury, damage, mutilation, vandalism, blemish, flaw. BEAUTIFICATION

de facto *adj*, real, actual, existing.
adv, in fact, in reality, in effect, actually, really.

defalcation misappropriation, embezzlement, deficit, shortage, deficiency, default.

defamation aspersion, calumny, abuse, slander, libel, traducement, obloquy, scandal, smear, backbiting, vilification, denigration, disparagement. PRAISE

defamatory calumnious, abusive, slanderous, libellous, injurious, scandalous, insulting, denigrating, maledictory, disparaging. COMPLIMENTARY

defame calumniate, asperse, slander, libel, traduce, denigrate, vilify, discredit, dishonour, malign, speak ill of, abuse, smear, besmirch, disparage, belittle. PRAISE

default *n*, failure, omission, neglect, lapse, oversight, want, lack, absence, deficiency, deficit, nonpayment.
v, fail, neglect, dodge, evade, cheat, bilk, welsh (*inf*).

defaulter offender, delinquent, nonpayer, embezzler, cheat.

defeat *v*, beat, conquer, vanquish, overcome, rout, worst, overpower, subdue, quell, crush, thrash. SURRENDER
thwart, foil, frustrate, discomfit, checkmate, balk, check, baffle, confound.
n, conquest, overthrow, beating, rout, vanquishment, subjugation, trouncing. VICTORY
frustration, reverse, setback, discomfiture, checkmate, failure, disappointment.

defecate excrete, egest, evacuate, move the bowels.
purge, cleanse, purify, clarify, refine. POLLUTE

defecation excretion, egestion, evacuation, bowel movement.
purification, cleansing, clarification, purge. POLLUTION

defect *n*, imperfection, flaw, blemish, spot, fault, error, failing, weakness, shortcoming, deficiency, omission, default, lack, want. PERFECTION
v, desert, abandon, forsake, change sides, apostatize, tergiversate, go over, rebel, mutiny.

defection desertion, abandonment, dereliction, backsliding, apostasy, disloyalty, mutiny, conversion.

defective faulty, imperfect, flawed, impaired, broken, out of order, not working, inadequate, incomplete, deficient, lacking, wanting, short. PERFECT

defence resistance, protection, guard, shelter, cover, shield, screen, fortification, bulwark, barricade. ATTACK
vindication, justification, excuse, plea, apology, argument. ACCUSATION

defenceless unprotected, unguarded, unarmed, exposed, vulnerable, wide open, weak, helpless. PROTECTED

defend resist, protect, guard, safeguard, shield, screen, shelter, preserve, fortify, arm. ATTACK
support, endorse, uphold, maintain, vindicate, justify, plead, argue for, champion, stick up for, represent. ACCUSE

defendant accused, offender, prisoner, respondent. PLAINTIFF

defender protector, guard, escort, bodyguard, keeper, guardian. ASSAILANT
champion, advocate, supporter, upholder, backer, vindicator. ACCUSER

defensive defending, protective, opposing, watchful, on the defensive, on guard. ATTACKING

defer[1] delay, postpone, put off, adjourn, shelve, prorogue, suspend, hold over, procrastinate, temporize. HASTEN

defer[2] comply, yield, submit, bow, accede, capitulate, give in. RESIST

deference compliance, submission, yielding, capitulation, acquiescence, complaisance, obedience, nonresistance. RESISTANCE
respect, regard, esteem, honour, reverence, homage, consideration, courtesy, politeness. DISRESPECT

deferential submissive, compliant, obeisant, obsequious, complaisant, obedient, respectful, considerate, courteous, polite. DEFIANT

deferment deferral, delay, postponement, suspension, adjournment, moratorium, abeyance, procrastination.

defiance resistance, opposition, confrontation, challenge, insubordination, disobedience, rebelliousness, contumacy, disregard, contempt. COMPLIANCE

defiant antagonistic, resistant, aggressive, belligerent, challenging, provocative, audacious, bold, daring, insolent, disobedient, insubordinate, recalcitrant, contumacious, stubborn, unyielding. COMPLIANT

deficiency lack, shortage, want, insufficiency, dearth, deficit, scarcity, inadequacy, absence. ABUNDANCE
weakness, failing, shortcoming, imperfection, defect, flaw. PERFECTION

deficient lacking, short, wanting, insufficient, inadequate, scarce, scant, scanty. ABUNDANT
defective, imperfect, incomplete, flawed, faulty, infirm, weak. PERFECT

deficit shortage, shortfall, deficiency, loss, arrears. SURPLUS

defile pollute, soil, dirty, befoul, contaminate, sully, taint, tarnish, corrupt, poison, vitiate, besmirch, disgrace, degrade, debase. PURIFY
profane, desecrate, molest, violate, rape, deflower, debauch.

definable specific, determinable, perceptible, describable, definite. INDEFINABLE

define describe, explain, interpret, spell out, specify, determine, designate, fix, lay down.
delineate, outline, demarcate, limit, bound, circumscribe.

definite certain, fixed, settled, positive, sure, decided, determined. POSSIBLE
clear, clear-cut, explicit, exact, precise, specific, marked, particular, plain, obvious, unambiguous. VAGUE

definition description, explanation, meaning, interpretation, exposition.
distinctness, clarity, sharpness, precision, contrast, focus. BLURREDNESS
demarcation, delineation, delimitation, determination, specification, fixing, settling.

definitive final, conclusive, decisive, ultimate, authoritative, exhaustive, complete, perfect, absolute, positive.

deflate collapse, let down, flatten, empty, shrink, contract, puncture. INFLATE chasten, humble, humiliate, mortify, squash, dash, discourage, dispirit. BOOST

deflect deviate, diverge, veer, swerve, bend, turn, twist, divert, sidetrack, shy, turn aside.

deflection deviation, divergence, declination, refraction, aberration, diversion, bend, turn, twist, swerve.

deflower rape, ravish, violate, despoil, defile, mar, molest, assault, debauch, corrupt, seduce.

deform distort, misshape, contort, twist, warp, malform, disfigure, deface, mar, injure, maim, cripple.

deformity malformation, abnormality, misshapenness, distortion, disfigurement, ugliness, monstrosity.

defraud cheat, swindle, fleece, rook (*inf*), cozen, dupe, deceive, beguile, trick, hoodwink, bamboozle (*inf*), rip off (*inf*), diddle (*inf*), do (*inf*), con (*inf*).

defray meet, pay, cover, clear, discharge, settle, liquidate.

deft adept, dexterous, adroit, skilful, clever, able, expert, proficient, handy, neat, agile, nimble, brisk. CLUMSY

defunct dead, gone, deceased, departed, extinct. LIVING
obsolete, expired, invalid, inoperative, not functioning.

defy flout, disregard, ignore, scorn, spurn, slight, disobey, challenge, brave, dare, confront, provoke, resist, oppose. OBEY
elude, frustrate, foil, baffle, withstand.

degeneracy dissoluteness, dissipation, depravity, decadence, corruption, immorality, debasement, degradation, meanness, lowness, inferiority, baseness. REFINEMENT
decline, deterioration, degeneration, decay, descent, decrease, retrogression. AMELIORATION

degenerate *v*, decline, deteriorate, decay, retrogress, sink, lapse, slip, fall. IMPROVE
adj, dissolute, debauched, depraved, corrupt, decadent, fallen, immoral, low, mean, base, debased, degraded, inferior. SUPERIOR

degeneration decline, deterioration, degeneracy, decay, descent, decrease, retrogression, depravation, debasement, degradation, dissolution. AMELIORATION

degradation disgrace, dishonour, humiliation, mortification, shame, ignominy, discredit, demotion. HONOUR
degeneration, abasement, decline, deterioration, decadence, debasement.

degrade disgrace, dishonour, lower, abase, humiliate, demean, cheapen, debase, corrupt, pervert, vitiate, deprave, defame, disparage, depreciate, deteriorate. EXALT
demote, downgrade, cashier, depose. PROMOTE

degree grade, rank, class, order, standing, status, station, position.
stage, step, rung, gradation, mark, notch, division, interval.
extent, measure, amount, intensity, range, scope, level, standard, rate.

dehydrate dry, parch, desiccate, exsiccate, drain, evaporate. MOISTEN

deify elevate, exalt, ennoble, glorify, idolize, apotheosize, immortalize, venerate, idolize, worship. DEBASE

deign condescend, stoop, lower oneself, see fit, consent. REFUSE

deity god, goddess, immortal, divine being, divinity, godhead. MORTAL

deject dishearten, dispirit, depress, cast down, sadden, demoralize, dismay, discourage. CHEER

dejected downcast, despondent, disconsolate, downhearted, dispirited, disheartened, crestfallen, depressed, sad, unhappy, miserable, doleful, woebegone, gloomy, glum, melancholy, blue. CHEERFUL

dejection despondency, downheartedness, depression, sadness, gloom, low spirits, melancholy, sorrow, blues, dumps (*inf*). CHEERFULNESS

delay *v*, defer, postpone, put off, suspend, shelve, hold over, procrastinate, temporize, stall. ADVANCE
obstruct, hinder, impede, hold back, slow down, retard, set back, detain, arrest, stop, halt. HASTEN
dawdle, linger, loiter, lag, dilly-dally (*inf*). HURRY
n, deferment, postponement, suspension, procrastination.
lull, interlude, pause, wait, break, breather, hiatus, interval. CONTINUATION
obstruction, hindrance, impediment, stoppage, setback, hold-up.

dawdling, lingering, loitering, dalliance, hesitation. HASTE

delectable delightful, delicious, choice, luscious, ambrosial, scrumptious (*inf*), tasty, dainty, appetizing, inviting, adorable, charming, agreeable, pleasant. REPULSIVE

delectation delight, enjoyment, pleasure, gratification, ecstasy, rapture, joy, amusement, entertainment, refreshment, relish.

delegate *n*, representative, envoy, ambassador, agent, deputy, commissioner.
v, depute, appoint, commission, authorize, empower, nominate, elect, ordain, charge, commit, entrust, assign, devolve, transfer.

delegation deputation, contingent, committee, embassy, legation, mission.
assignment, devolvement, authorization, commissioning, appointment, nomination.

delete cross out, strike out, obliterate, efface, cancel, expunge, remove, erase, cut out, edit, blue-pencil. INSERT

deleterious harmful, noxious, injurious, hurtful, pernicious, destructive, damaging, detrimental, unwholesome, bad, noisome. BENEFICIAL

deliberate *v*, consider, ponder, ruminate, reflect, think, cogitate, meditate, mull over, weigh, evaluate, debate. DECIDE
adj, intentional, premeditated, calculated, planned, designed, purposeful, conscious, meant, wilful, studied. ACCIDENTAL
cautious, careful, circumspect, thoughtful, methodical, unhurried, slow, leisurely, measured. HASTY

deliberately intentionally, on purpose, wilfully, knowingly. ACCIDENTALLY

deliberation consideration, rumination, reflection, thought, cogitation, meditation, study, scrutiny, speculation, discussion, debate, consultation.
care, caution, circumspection, wariness, prudence. RASHNESS

delicacy fineness, daintiness, fragility, flimsiness, slightness, slenderness, lightness, exquisiteness, subtlety. COARSENESS
tact, sensitivity, sensibility, scrupulousness, fastidiousness, discrimination, refinement, finesse, elegance, nicety, purity, precision, accuracy. INDELICACY
frailty, weakness, debility, infirmity. ROBUSTNESS
morsel, titbit, dainty, sweetmeat, luxury, treat.

delicate fine, dainty, exquisite, choice, elegant, graceful, flimsy, slender, slight, fragile, tender. ROBUST
weak, frail, infirm, ailing, sickly. HEALTHY
faint, muted, subdued, soft, subtle, pastel. GARISH
sensitive, tactful, diplomatic, scrupulous, fastidious, discriminating, refined, pure. INDELICATE
critical, precarious, difficult, ticklish, sensitive.

delicious tasty, appetizing, luscious, scrumptious (*inf*), ambrosial, toothsome, succulent, mouthwatering, savoury, palatable, delectable, dainty, choice. UNPALATABLE
delightful, exquisite, charming, agreeable, nice, pleasant, enjoyable. LOATHSOME

delight *v*, charm, enchant, ravish, thrill, transport, enrapture, please, gratify, cheer. DISAPPOINT
delight in, enjoy, love, like, relish, savour, revel in. DISLIKE
n, charm, enchantment, ecstasy, rapture, transport, elation, felicity, joy, delectation, pleasure, gratification, enjoyment. DISGUST

delighted enchanted, elated, overjoyed, ecstatic, thrilled, jubilant, joyous, pleased, happy. DISAPPOINTED

delightful charming, enchanting, ravishing, captivating, engaging, attractive, heavenly, lovely, delectable, agreeable, pleasant, enjoyable, gratifying. NASTY

delineate describe, depict, portray, picture, draw, sketch, outline, trace, design, chart, map out.

delineation description, representation, depiction, portrayal, portrait, picture, drawing, sketch, draft, outline, profile, diagram, chart, account, narration.

delinquency crime, offence, misdeed, misdemeanour, misconduct, wrongdoing, dereliction, negligence.

delinquent offender, wrongdoer, criminal, malefactor, miscreant, lawbreaker, culprit.

delirious raving, incoherent, demented, deranged, insane, mad, crazy, hysterical, frenzied, frantic, wild, ecstatic, carried away. SANE

delirium madness, insanity, derangement, raving, incoherence, hallucination,

frenzy, passion, fever, hysteria, ecstasy. SANITY
deliver transfer, entrust, commit, hand over, consign, give, grant, surrender, relinquish, yield, cede. APPROPRIATE
send, transmit, convey, transport, bear, carry, bring.
release, liberate, set free, emancipate, acquit, discharge, free, rescue, save, redeem. CAPTURE
utter, speak, present, give, declare, announce, proclaim.
direct, deal, administer, inflict, throw, launch.
deliverance release, liberation, emancipation, rescue, salvation. CAPTURE
delivery conveyance, transmission, consignment, dispatch, shipment, transfer, surrender, handing over, distribution.
articulation, enunciation, elocution, intonation, diction, utterance, speech.
childbirth, parturition, confinement, labour, accouchement.
delude deceive, mislead, misguide, dupe, beguile, cheat, fool, trick, cozen, take in, hoodwink, bamboozle (*inf*), con (*inf*).
deluge *n*, flood, inundation, cataclysm, downpour, cloudburst, overflow, rush, torrent, spate, avalanche. DROUGHT
v, flood, inundate, soak, drench, overrun, overwhelm, swamp, engulf, drown, submerge.
delusion illusion, hallucination, fancy, mirage, vision, dream, misapprehension, misconception, error, mistake, fallacy, self-deception. REALITY
trick, artifice, ruse, deception, deceit, imposture, fraud, hoax.
delusive misleading, deceptive, fallacious, illusive, illusory, imaginary. REAL
delve dig, burrow, ferret out, unearth, probe, search, rummage, penetrate, investigate, look into.
demand *v*, request, ask for, solicit, claim, insist on, order, exact. WAIVE
require, need, necessitate, call for, involve. OBVIATE
ask, question, interrogate, inquire, query. REPLY
n, request, claim, order, requisition, command, direction, charge, bidding, behest.
requirement, need, want, necessity.
question, query, inquiry, interrogation. ANSWER
demanding challenging, trying, difficult, hard, tough, exacting, taxing, tiring. EASY
demarcation distinction, differentiation, division, separation, delimitation, definition, boundary, border, limit, bound, confine.
demean lower, humble, abase, descend, stoop, debase, degrade. EXALT
demeanour behaviour, conduct, bearing, manner, air, mien, carriage, deportment.
demented insane, deranged, unhinged, unbalanced, mad, crazy, idiotic, lunatic, daft (*inf*), barmy (*inf*), nuts (*inf*). SANE
demerit fault, misdeed, crime, offence, delinquency.
demesne estate, land, property, realm, domain.
demise *n*, death, decease, expiration, passing. BIRTH
collapse, downfall, failure, ruin, end, termination.
transfer, conveyance, transmission, alienation.
v, bequeath, leave, will, transfer, convey.
democratic egalitarian, republican, autonomous, self-governing, popular, representative. AUTOCRATIC
demolish destroy, raze, level, flatten, bulldoze, tear down, break down, dismantle, take down. BUILD
wreck, ruin, destroy, devastate, undo, crush, overturn, annihilate, obliterate.
demolition destruction, razing, bulldozing, devastation, ruin, wrecking. BUILDING
demon fiend, devil, goblin, imp, evil spirit. ANGEL
rogue, villain, scoundrel, knave, fiend, monster, ogre.
demonic demoniac, demoniacal, fiendish, diabolic, diabolical, devilish, satanic, hellish, infernal. ANGELIC
frenzied, frenetic, frantic, hectic, maniacal, rabid, feverish, delirious, crazed, demented, mad.
demonstrate show, display, exhibit, manifest, evince, indicate, prove, substantiate, establish. DISPROVE
explain, illustrate, describe, show how.
protest, march, rally, strike, picket.
demonstration display, exhibition, manifestation, showing, show, evidence, proof, substantiation, testimony, confirmation. CONCEALMENT

explanation, exposition, presentation, experiment, trial, illustration, example.
march, rally, parade, protest, sit-in.

demonstrative open, unreserved, expressive, communicative, loving, affectionate. RESERVED
illustrative, indicative, symptomatic, explanatory.
indisputable, convincing, conclusive, absolute, certain, sure. DEBATABLE

demoralize dishearten, dispirit, discourage, depress, deject, daunt, unnerve, weaken, enfeeble, crush, subdue. ENCOURAGE
corrupt, deprave, pervert, debase, debauch, vitiate. IMPROVE

demote downgrade, degrade, cashier, depose, relegate, humble. PROMOTE

demulcent soothing, lenitive, mild, calming, sedative, emollient, softening, mollifying. IRRITANT

demur *v*, object, protest, dispute, take exception, be reluctant, scruple, hesitate, balk, cavil. CONSENT
n, demurral, objection, dissent, hesitation, qualm, scruple.

demure modest, diffident, shy, reserved, unassuming, sedate, staid, sober, grave, discreet, decorous, prudish, strait-laced, prim. WANTON

den lair, hole, cavern, cave, haunt, shelter.
study, retreat, hideaway, sanctuary, cloister, snuggery.

denial contradiction, negation, refutation, disavowal, disclaimer, repudiation, retraction, renunciation, abjuration. CONFIRMATION
refusal, rejection, rebuff, veto, proscription prohibition. CONSENT

denigrate disparage, belittle, defame, run down, slander, besmirch, blacken, traduce, vilify, malign, speak ill of. PRAISE

denizen citizen, resident, occupant, inhabitant, dweller. ALIEN

denominate designate, name, style, entitle, dub, christen, call, term.

denomination sect, school, creed, faith, persuasion, religion.
class, group, kind, sort, type, category.
grade, unit, value.
designation, appellation, name, style, title.

denote indicate, betoken, signify, mean, imply, stand for, represent, designate, mark.

denouement climax, culmination, conclusion, finale, termination, resolution, solution, outcome, issue, result, upshot.

denounce condemn, decry, denunciate, deplore, arraign, attack, censure, revile, impugn, upbraid, rebuke, castigate. EXTOL
accuse, charge, impeach, vilify, defame, brand, stigmatize.

dense thick, compressed, compact, condensed, heavy, solid, thickset, close, close-knit, packed, crowded, impenetrable. THIN
stupid, obtuse, dull, slow, thick (*inf*), stolid, crass, blockish. CLEVER

density denseness, thickness, solidity, bulk, mass, closeness, compactness, impenetrability.
stupidity, obtuseness, dullness, slowness, stolidity, crassness. CLEVERNESS

dent *v*, indent, dint, press in, chip, notch, groove, hollow.
n, hollow, depression, dint, pit, concavity, hole, impression, indentation, notch, chip.

denude strip, divest, bare, expose, uncover, denudate. CLOTHE

denunciation condemnation, denouncement, fulmination, censure, animadversion, obloquy, reproof, castigation, vituperation, accusation, arraignment. EULOGY

deny contradict, dispute, gainsay, controvert, negate, refute, disprove, oppose, disagree. CONFIRM
refuse, withhold, reject, turn down, prohibit, forbid, veto, proscribe. ALLOW
disown, disavow, renounce, abjure, disclaim, recant, repudiate. AVOW

depart go, leave, start, set out, decamp, abscond, escape, go away, disappear, vanish, exit, quit, withdraw, retire. ARRIVE
deviate, diverge, digress, veer, swerve, differ, vary.

department branch, division, subdivision, section, office, bureau, unit.
sphere, realm, domain, province, line, station, function, responsibility.

departure exit, going, leaving, disappearance, withdrawal, retirement. ARRIVAL
deviation, divergence, digression, variation, difference, novelty, innovation.

depend rely, count, bank, trust, confide.
be dependent, hang, hinge, turn, rest, be contingent, be subject to.

dependable reliable, trusty, trustworthy, sure, steady, faithful, true. UNRELIABLE

dependant child, minor, relative, hanger-on, protégé, minion, retainer, henchman.

dependence reliance, trust, faith, confidence.
subordination, subjection, helplessness, weakness, attachment, addiction. INDEPENDENCE

dependent relying, reliant, counting, clinging, helpless, weak, defenceless, vulnerable, immature, subordinate, subject. INDEPENDENT
contingent, conditional, subject to, depending.

depict delineate, portray, sketch, draw, paint, outline, picture, illustrate, represent, describe, characterize, detail.

deplete empty, drain, evacuate, exhaust, use up, spend, consume, reduce, lessen, decrease. FILL

depletion emptying, evacuation, exhaustion, using up, consumption, reduction, decrease.

deplorable lamentable, grievous, regrettable, pitiable, wretched, miserable, pathetic, distressing, unfortunate, disastrous, calamitous. AUSPICIOUS
scandalous, disgraceful, shameful, reprehensible, opprobrious, despicable. COMMENDABLE

deplore lament, mourn, regret, bemoan, bewail, grieve for, sorrow over. WELCOME
condemn, denounce, censure, abhor, disapprove of. EXTOL

deploy dispose, arrange, position, station, spread out, distribute, use, utilize.

deport expel, banish, exile, expatriate, extradite, transport, remove.
conduct, behave, comport, bear, carry, acquit.

deportment carriage, bearing, posture, air, mien, demeanour, behaviour, conduct, comportment, manner.

depose dethrone, oust, displace, unseat, dismiss, cashier, demote, degrade. ENTHRONE
declare, testify, asseverate.

deposit *v*, lay, drop, place, put, set down, settle, precipitate.
save, store, hoard, bank, lodge, consign, entrust. WITHDRAW
n, sediment, precipitate, deposition, silt, alluvium, dregs, lees.
security, pledge, stake, warranty, retainer, down payment.

depositary trustee, guardian, steward, fiduciary.

deposition affidavit, statement, declaration, testimony, evidence.
dethronement, ousting, displacement, dismissal, demotion, removal. ENTHRONEMENT

depository depot, storehouse, warehouse, repository, safe.

depot storehouse, warehouse, depository, repository, magazine, arsenal.
bus station, terminus, garage.

deprave corrupt, vitiate, debauch, subvert, demoralize, pervert, lead astray, seduce, debase, degrade, degenerate. IMPROVE

depraved corrupt, immoral, debauched, demoralized, degenerate, dissolute, abandoned, licentious, profligate, perverted, warped, wicked, evil, vicious, sinful, shameless, wanton. VIRTUOUS

depravity corruption, immorality, debauchery, degeneracy, turpitude, depravation, demoralization, profligacy, perversion, vice, evil, iniquity, sin. VIRTUE

deprecate deplore, condemn, denounce, censure, inveigh against, frown on, disapprove of, object to, protest. COMMEND
belittle, disparage, depreciate. PRAISE

depreciate devalue, devaluate, deflate, reduce, lower, lose value, fall, decline. APPRECIATE
disparage, belittle, deprecate, malign, traduce, underrate, undervalue, underestimate, decry, deride, slight. PRAISE

depreciation devaluation, deflation, depression, decline, fall, drop, slump. APPRECIATION
disparagement, belittlement, deprecation, detraction, derogation, underestimation. PRAISE

depredation plunder, pillage, spoliation, rapine, robbery, theft, marauding, raid, inroad, devastation.

depredator robber, thief, plunderer, looter, pillager, marauder, raider, despoiler.

depress deject, sadden, dishearten, discourage, dispirit, cast down, damp, chill. CHEER
weaken, debilitate, enfeeble, exhaust, drain, sap. FORTIFY
depreciate, devalue, devaluate, cheapen, reduce, lower, diminish, downgrade. RAISE

depressed dejected, dispirited, blue, glum, low, despondent, downcast, morose, gloomy, pessimistic, miserable, sad, melancholy. ELATED
poor, needy, disadvantaged. deprived, distressed, run-down. AFFLUENT

depression dejection, gloom, despondency, melancholy, sadness, low spirits, despair, blues, dumps (*inf*). ELATION
indentation, concavity, hollow, pit, dent, dint, dimple, hole, cavity. MOUND
recession, slump, decline, hard times, stagnation, inactivity. BOOM

deprivation privation, need, want, hardship, distress, disadvantage, loss, bereavement.
dispossession, expropriation, removal, denial, deprival, withholding. ENDOWMENT

deprive strip, divest, dispossess, rob, bereave. ENDOW
deny, withhold, refuse, debar. PROVIDE

depth deepness, profoundness, profundity, extent, measure, drop. SHALLOWNESS
wisdom, sagacity, penetration, discernment, astuteness, shrewdness, perspicacity.
middle, midst, innermost part, deep, bowels, pit, abyss, chasm. SURFACE
intensity, vividness, strength, richness.

depurate cleanse, purify, clarify.

deputation delegation, embassy, legation, commission, committee.
appointment, designation, nomination, authorization, assignment.

depute appoint, nominate, designate, commission, delegate, deputize, authorize, empower, entrust, charge. DISMISS

deputy agent, representative, delegate, envoy, ambassador, commissioner, legate, surrogate, substitute, proxy, vicegerent, nuncio, lieutenant, assistant.

deracinate uproot, extirpate, eradicate, exterminate, stamp out.

derange disorder, disarrange, displace, disturb, upset, ruffle, discompose, disconcert, confuse. ORDER
unhinge, unbalance, madden, craze, drive mad.

derangement disorder, disarray, disarrangement, disturbance, upset, confusion.
madness, insanity, lunacy, dementia, unbalance, loss of reason, mania, delirium. SANITY

derelict *adj*, abandoned, forsaken, deserted, discarded, neglected, dilapidated, ruined.
remiss, negligent, neglectful, lax.
n, tramp, vagrant, down-and-out, outcast, wastrel, ne'er-do-well.

dereliction neglect, negligence, laxity, delinquency, default, omission, nonperformance, fault, failure. OBSERVANCE
abandonment, desertion, forsaking, relinquishment, abdication, renunciation, rejection.

deride mock, ridicule, scoff, jeer, laugh at, taunt, chaff, scorn, disdain, sneer at, contemn, lampoon, satirize, disparage, belittle, knock (*inf*), insult, abuse. RESPECT

derision mockery, ridicule, scoffing, jeer, taunt, raillery, scorn, contempt, disrespect, contumely, satire, lampoon, irony, abuse, insult. RESPECT

derisive scornful, contemptuous, disdainful, mocking, jeering, sarcastic, insulting. RESPECTFUL
derisory, contemptible, laughable, ridiculous, ludicrous.

derivation source, origin, etymology, root, spring, foundation, beginning, cause, rise, ancestry, descent, extraction.

derivative *adj*, derived, acquired, borrowed, unoriginal, secondary.
n, derivation, offshoot, by-product, spin-off.

derive draw, extract, get, obtain, gain, acquire, procure, receive, elicit, glean, collect, gather.
deduce, infer, trace, track.
originate, arise, spring, flow, proceed, come.

derogate disparage, run down, belittle, decry, depreciate, cheapen, lessen, diminish, devalue, defame, denigrate, malign, discredit, degrade, debase. EXTOL

derogation disparagement, detraction, belittlement, depreciation, defamation, denigration, discredit. PRAISE

derogatory disparaging, belittling, detracting, depreciative, defamatory, insulting, offensive, abusive, injurious, damaging, unfavourable, opprobrious. FLATTERING

descant *v*, discourse, dilate, expatiate, discuss, elaborate, enlarge, amplify.
n, melody, tune, counterpoint, variation.

discourse, dissertation, discussion, commentary.

descend go down, sink, fall, drop, plunge, slope downwards. ASCEND
dismount, alight, disembark, get off. EMBARK
originate, derive, issue, spring.
stoop, condescend, lower oneself, degenerate, deteriorate.

descendants offspring, issue, progeny, seed, posterity, family, children. ANCESTORS

descent fall, drop, plunge, dip, declination, declivity. ASCENT
ancestry, parentage, extraction, stock, heredity, genealogy, lineage, origin, derivation.
decline, deterioration, degeneration, decadence, degradation.
attack, assault, onslaught, incursion, raid, invasion, foray.

describe delineate, portray, depict, picture, illustrate, characterize, detail, explain, tell, narrate, relate, recount, define, specify.

description delineation, portrayal, depiction, explanation, account, narration, report, explanation, sketch, representation.
sort, kind, type, variety, breed, genre, ilk.

descry discern, make out, distinguish, espy, detect, perceive, discover, see, observe, notice. MISS

desecrate profane, defile, violate, pollute, pervert, abuse, misuse, blaspheme. CONSECRATE

desecration profanation, defilement, sacrilege, blasphemy, impiety, violation, outrage, abuse. CONSECRATION

desert[1] *n*, wilderness, wasteland, wilds, dust bowl.
adj, barren, infertile, arid, parched, uncultivated, desolate, bare, wild, uninhabited, waste. FERTILE

desert[2] *v*, abandon, leave, forsake, quit, jilt, strand, renounce, relinquish, defect, abscond, decamp.

desert[3] due, right, reward, recompense, retribution, come-uppance (*inf*).
worth, value, merit, virtue.

deserted abandoned, derelict, forsaken, empty, vacant, unoccupied, uninhabited, desolate, lonely, solitary, isolated, forlorn, bereft. POPULOUS

deserter runaway, truant, absconder, fugitive, defector, renegade, apostate, turncoat, traitor, rat (*inf*).

desertion abandonment, dereliction, defection, apostasy, flight, escape, relinquishment, renunciation.

deserve earn, win, merit, be worthy of, be entitled to, justify, warrant.

deserved merited, due, rightful, just, fair, fitting, suitable, appropriate, condign. UNDESERVED

deserving worthy, meritorious, estimable, commendable, laudable, good, righteous. UNDESERVING

desiccate dry, parch, exsiccate, dehydrate, drain, evaporate. MOISTEN

desideratum need, want, lack, essential, aspiration, goal, aim, objective, hope, dream.

design *v*, plan, plot, scheme, intend, purpose, mean, aim, devise, contrive.
sketch, outline, delineate, draft, draw, trace.
invent, originate, conceive, think up, create.
n, sketch, draft, drawing, plan, model, blueprint, prototype.
style, form, shape, configuration, arrangement, motif, pattern.
plan, plot, scheme, project, proposal, aim, intention, purpose, point, objective.

designate name, call, style, term, dub, christen, entitle.
indicate, denote, make, show, specify, particularize, pinpoint, earmark, define, describe.
appoint, assign, nominate, choose, depute, allot.

designation name, title, denomination, appellation, epithet, label.
indication, specification, particularization, description.
appointment, nomination, delegation, selection.

designing artful, crafty, wily, foxy, sly, scheming, tricky, cunning, Machiavellian, intriguing, astute, treacherous, insidious, crooked (*inf*), dishonest, deceitful. ARTLESS

desirable profitable, advantageous, beneficial, advisable, enviable, sought-after, eligible, popular, good, pleasing, attractive, captivating, seductive, sexy (*inf*). UNDESIRABLE

desire *v*, crave, long for, covet, hanker after, yearn for, fancy, wish for, want. ABHOR
ask, request, solicit, petition, entreat.
n, craving, longing, yearning, yen (*inf*), wish, want, aspiration, inclination, appetite. AVERSION
lust, passion, libido, lechery, lasciviousness.
request, solicitation, petition, entreaty.

desirous eager, avid, longing, yearning, craving, wishing, hopeful, anxious, impatient. APATHETIC

desist stop, cease, break off, discontinue, suspend, abstain, refrain from, forbear, give up. PERSIST

desolate *adj*, deserted, uninhabited, desert, wild, waste, barren, bare, bleak, dreary, empty, lonely, isolated. POPULOUS
forlorn, forsaken, abandoned, bereft, lonely, friendless, despondent, sad, cheerless, comfortless, wretched, miserable. CHEERFUL
v, destroy, devastate, lay waste, pillage, plunder, despoil, depopulate. CULTIVATE
depress, dishearten, deject, sadden, grieve, distress, dismay, daunt. CHEER

desolation destruction, devastation, ruin, ravage, pillage, depopulation. CULTIVATION
barrenness, bleakness, desolateness, wildness, dreariness, loneliness, isolation.
gloom, gloominess, despondency, dejection, despair, sadness, grief, anguish, sorrow, distress, misery, melancholy. JOY

despair *n*, hopelessness, desperation, despondency, gloom, dejection, distress, wretchedness, anguish, discouragement, resignation. HOPE
v, lose hope, lose heart, give up, despond.

desperado ruffian, thug, gangster, criminal, cutthroat, hoodlum, mugger, bandit, outlaw.

desperate rash, reckless, daring, audacious, impetuous, precipitate, madcap, foolhardy, dangerous, risky, frantic, wild. CAUTIOUS
grave, critical, urgent, dire, acute, extreme.
despairing, hopeless, despondent, forlorn, wretched, inconsolable, irretrievable, irredeemable. HOPEFUL

desperation recklessness, rashness, impetuosity, madness, frenzy, fury, rage. COOLNESS
despair, despondency, hopelessness, anxiety, anguish, distress, wretchedness. HOPE

despicable contemptible, low, mean, base, abject, ignominious, vile, sordid, disreputable, pitiful, wretched, worthless. ADMIRABLE

despise scorn, contemn, disdain, spurn, slight, disregard, flout, deride, dislike, detest, abhor. ADMIRE

despite in spite of, notwithstanding, even with, regardless of, against, in defiance of.

despoil pillage, plunder, loot, ravage, rifle, rob, deprive, strip, denude, divest, devastate, desolate, wreck, lay waste.

despond despair, lose hope, lose heart, give up, be depressed, mope, grieve. HOPE

despondency depression, dejection, gloom, melancholy, downheartedness, low spirits, discouragement, hopelessness, despair. CHEERFULNESS

despondent depressed, dejected, gloomy, miserable, doleful, downcast, downhearted, discouraged, glum, sad, melancholy, blue. CHEERFUL

despot tyrant, autocrat, dictator, oppressor. DEMOCRAT

despotic tyrannical, tyrannous, autocratic, dictatorial, oppressive, imperious, absolute, arbitrary, authoritarian. DEMOCRATIC

despotism tyranny, autocracy, dictatorship, absolutism, totalitarianism. DEMOCRACY

dessert sweet, pudding, afters (*inf*).

destination goal, objective, end, target, ambition, aim, purpose.
terminus, stop, station, harbour, haven, journey's end. START

destine ordain, design, intend, purpose, appoint, assign, allot, designate, earmark, consecrate, devote.

destined bound, heading, en route, directed.
fated, doomed, foreordained, predestined, certain, sure, unavoidable, inescapable, bound, meant, intended.

destiny lot, fate, fortune, doom, karma, kismet.

destitute impoverished, penurious, penniless, poverty-stricken, impecunious, indigent, poor, needy, down and out, distressed, ruined, hard up (*inf*). RICH
devoid, bereft, without, deficient, lacking, wanting, deprived.

destitution penury, pennilessness, beggary, indigence, poverty, need, privation, distress, dire straits. WEALTH

destroy demolish, raze, gut, ruin, wreck, devastate, overturn, crush, smash, shatter, annihilate, eradicate, extirpate, extinguish, wipe out, slay, kill. CREATE

destruction demolition, ruin, devastation, havoc, wreckage, crushing, shattering, annihilation, eradication, end, extinction, liquidation, massacre, slaughter. CREATION

destructive pernicious, noxious, baneful, harmful, damaging, hurtful, injurious, detrimental, deleterious, deadly, fatal, lethal, ruinous, devastating, catastrophic. BENEFICIAL

negative, adverse, contrary, unfavourable, hostile, disparaging, derogatory. CONSTRUCTIVE

desuetude disuse, obsolescence, discontinuance. USE

desultory random, haphazard, irregular, unmethodical, unsystematic, unconnected, spasmodic, fitful, discursive, rambling, roving, erratic, capricious. METHODICAL

detach separate, disconnect, uncouple, unfasten, disengage, disjoin, cut off, sever, divide, isolate, free. ATTACH

detached separate, unconnected, disconnected, discrete, free, isolated. ATTACHED

aloof, uninvolved, objective, impartial, disinterested, dispassionate, neutral. INVOLVED

detachment separation, disconnection, disunion, disengagement, division. CONNECTION

aloofness, indifference, unconcern, objectivity, impartiality, disinterestedness, neutrality. INVOLVEMENT

squad, unit, party, detail, force.

detail *n*, particular, item, component, element, factor, point, feature, aspect, circumstance.

detachment, squad, unit, party, group.

v, list, catalogue, enumerate, recount, narrate, describe, particularize, itemize, specify, delineate. SUMMARIZE

appoint, assign, delegate, commission, charge.

detailed comprehensive, exhaustive, thorough, minute, meticulous, precise, blow-by-blow, involved, elaborate, intricate. CURSORY

detain delay, hold up, retard, slow, hinder, impede, stay, keep back, stop, check, restrain, hold, confine, arrest. FREE

detect discover, perceive, discern, observe, notice, descry, sense, ascertain, expose, reveal, uncover, unmask, find, trace.

detection discovery, exposure, revelation, observation, perception.

detective investigator, private eye, sleuth (*inf*), policeman, copper (*inf*).

detention custody, confinement, imprisonment, incarceration, duress, restraint. RELEASE

deter discourage, put off, dissuade, warn, daunt, disincline, inhibit, restrain, prevent, stop, check, hinder, thwart. ENCOURAGE

detergent *adj*, cleansing, detersive, abstergent, depurative.

n, cleanser, cleaner, solvent, depurative, soap powder.

deteriorate decline, degenerate, worsen, depreciate, debase, degrade, impair, vitiate, decay, fall apart, go to pot (*inf*), go downhill (*inf*). IMPROVE

deterioration decline, degeneration, worsening, depreciation, debasement, degradation, vitiation, retrogression, slump, lapse, fall, erosion, decay. IMPROVEMENT

determinate fixed, definite, established, settled, positive, certain, absolute, conclusive, limited, precise, explicit. INDETERMINATE

determination resolution, resolve, resoluteness, firmness, constancy, conviction, single-mindedness, persistence, perseverance, drive, doggedness, tenacity, willpower. IRRESOLUTION

decision, conclusion, result, solution, settlement, verdict, judgment, purpose, resolve.

determine settle, decide, resolve, conclude, terminate, judge, arbitrate.

ascertain, detect, find out, discover, learn, establish, verify, fix.

decide, resolve, purpose, choose, elect, make up one's mind. WAVER

influence, affect, shape, condition, lead, incline, govern, control, dictate.

determined resolute, firm, single-minded, set, fixed, intent, dogged, persevering, persistent, tenacious, purposeful, strong-willed. IRRESOLUTE

deterrent impediment, hindrance, obstacle, discouragement, disincentive, restraint, curb, check. ENCOURAGEMENT

detest abhor, loathe, abominate, execrate, hate, despise. LOVE

detestable abhorrent, loathsome, abominable, execrable, hateful, odious, repugnant, repulsive, abnoxious, despicable, vile, accursed, disgusting, heinous. ADORABLE

detestation abhorrence, loathing, abomination, execration, odium, repugnance, hate, aversion, antipathy, disgust. LOVE

dethrone depose, uncrown, unseat, oust. ENTHRONE

detonate explode, set off, go off, blow up, blast.

detour diversion, deviation, bypass, roundabout way, circuitous route, indirect course.

detract diminish, lessen, reduce, devaluate, depreciate. ENHANCE
divert, avert, deflect, distract, sidetrack.

detraction disparagement, depreciation, belittlement, derogation, aspersion, denigration, defamation, vilification, abuse, calumny, slander, traducement. FLATTERY

detriment damage, harm, injury, hurt, loss, mischief, disadvantage, prejudice. BENEFIT

detrimental damaging, harmful, injurious, hurtful, deleterious, pernicious, prejudicial, disadvantageous, adverse, unfavourable. BENEFICIAL

devastate desolate, despoil, ravage, lay waste, destroy, demolish, raze, wreck, ruin, pillage, plunder, sack.
overwhelm, confound, disconcert, take aback, nonplus, floor.

devastation desolation, despoliation, destruction, demolition, havoc, ravages, ruin, waste, wreckage, pillage, plunder.

develop advance, grow, evolve, mature, ripen, progress, flourish, foster, cultivate. STUNT
elaborate, amplify, expand, enlarge, enhance, unfold, disclose. ABRIDGE
acquire, contract, begin, start, invent, create, generate, originate.

development growth, evolution, advance, advancement, progress, increase, maturation, maturity, unfolding, blossoming. RETROGRESSION
amplification, expansion, enlargement, elaboration. ABRIDGMENT
incident, occurrence, event, happening, circumstance, situation, change.

deviate veer, diverge, wander, stray, err, depart, digress, swerve, turn aside, deflect, differ, vary, change.

deviation divergence, aberration, departure, digression, deflection, shift, variation, difference, declination, disparity, discrepancy.

device contrivance, contraption (*inf*), gadget, tool, machine, instrument, implement, utensil, appliance.
ruse, wile, stratagem, artifice, plan, design, scheme, ploy, expedient, manoeuvre, shift.
emblem, symbol, design, motif, figure, motto, legend, crest, badge, logo.

devil demon, fiend, evil spirit, prince of darkness, Satan, Lucifer, Beelzebub, Old Nick. ANGEL
rogue, scoundrel, villain, demon, imp, beast, monster, ogre.

devilish diabolic, demonic, demoniacal, satanic, fiendish, hellish, infernal, evil, wicked, accursed, damnable, atrocious, execrable. ANGELIC

devious underhand, deceitful, surreptitious, sly, tricky, wily, scheming, calculating, evasive, shifty. STRAIGHTFORWARD
rambling, circuitous, roundabout, indirect, tortuous, crooked, meandering, wandering, deviating, erratic. DIRECT

devise invent, contrive, scheme, plan, project, design, concoct, create, think up, formulate, work out.

devoid destitute, bereft, barren, void, empty, lacking, wanting, deficient, without, free from. FULL

devolve delegate, depute, transfer, commission, fall upon, rest with.

devote dedicate, consecrate, give, pledge, assign, allot, reserve, commit, apply. WITHHOLD

devoted ardent, zealous, dedicated, committed, devout, faithful, loyal, true, fond, loving, affectionate. INDIFFERENT

devotee enthusiast, fanatic, fan, admirer, aficionado, addict, buff (*inf*), zealot, adherent, disciple, votary.

devotion dedication, commitment, consecration, loyalty, allegiance, fidelity, passion, zeal, ardour, enthusiasm, attachment, affection, love, fondness. APATHY

devoutness, piety, holiness, sanctity, godliness, saintliness. IMPIETY
prayer, worship, service, observance.
devotional devout, pious, holy, sacred, religious, spiritual. PROFANE
devour consume, eat, gorge, gobble, bolt, wolf, gulp, swallow.
destroy, consume, ravage, annihilate, waste, wipe out, engulf, overwhelm, absorb.
devout pious, godly, saintly, holy, religious, reverent, devotional. IMPIOUS
sincere, genuine, heartfelt, earnest, fervent, ardent, intense, profound. INSINCERE
dexterity skill, skilfulness, adroitness, handiness, cleverness, ability, aptitude, expertise, proficiency, mastery, finesse, deftness, knack, facility, art, address, agility, nimbleness. CLUMSINESS
dexterous deft, adroit, adept, skilled, skilful, apt, able, clever, expert, proficient, masterly, agile, nimble, handy. CLUMSY
diabolic devilish, demonic, demoniacal, satanic, fiendish, infernal, hellish, nefarious, evil, wicked, monstrous. ANGELIC
diabolical outrageous, appalling, atrocious, dreadful, shocking, excruciating, vile, damnable.
diadem crown, coronet, circlet, tiara, chaplet, wreath.
diagnosis analysis, investigation, examination, interpretation, conclusion, opinion, verdict.
diagram plan, chart, drawing, sketch, representation, outline, figure, graph.
dialect language, idiom, vernacular, patois, jargon, localism, provincialism, regionalism, accent, speech, tongue.
dialectic *adj*, dialectical, logical, rational, analytic, polemical, argumentative.
n, argumentation, disputation, polemics, logic, reasoning.
dialogue conversation, confabulation, colloquy, interlocution, discourse, converse, talk, chat, communication, discussion, conference.
diametric diametrical, opposite, opposed, contrary, counter, antithetical, antipodal.
diaphanous translucent, pellucid, gauzy, gossamer, silken, fine, delicate, sheer, transparent, clear. OPAQUE
diary chronicle, journal, log, record, appointment book.
diatribe tirade, philippic, invective, abuse, harangue, criticism, denunciation, vituperation. EULOGY
dictate *v*, say, speak, utter.
command, order, direct, enjoin, decree, bid, prescribe, impose.
n, command, order, decree, injunction, ordinance, bidding, behest, mandate, edict.
principle, rule, code, precept, law, dictum.
dictator tyrant, despot, autocrat, oppressor, ruler.
dictatorial tyrannnical, tyrannous, despotic, autocratic, absolute, arbitrary, imperious, oppressive, overbearing, domineering, authoritarian. DEMOCRATIC
diction speech, language, vocabulary, phraseology, usage, style, intonation, pronunciation, articulation, enunciation, elocution, delivery, eloquence, oratory, rhetoric.
dictionary lexicon, glossary, vocabulary, wordbook, encyclopedia.
dictum decree, pronouncement, edict, fiat.
saying, maxim, adage, proverb, saw, axiom, aphorism.
didactic instructive, informative, educational, preceptive, moralistic, edifying, homiletic.
die expire, decease, perish, depart, pass away, snuff it (*inf*), kick the bucket (*inf*). LIVE
dwindle, fade, ebb, subside, abate, die down, wane, decline, sink, wither, fail, peter out, disappear, vanish, end, stop. GROW
diet[1] *n*, food, fare, nourishment, nutriment, sustenance, subsistence, aliment, comestibles, provisions, victuals.
regimen, regime, dietary, fast, abstinence.
v, slim, lose weight, reduce, fast, abstain.
diet[2] *n*, parliament, congress, council, assembly, legislature.
differ vary, diverge, contrast, be different, contradict. COINCIDE
disagree, argue, contend, dispute, demur, clash, oppose, be at variance. AGREE
difference dissimilarity, unlikeness, contrast, disparity, discrepancy, divergence, deviation, variation, alteration, change. SIMILARITY
disagreement, argument, contention, wrangle, dispute, strife, discord, conflict,

variance, altercation, clash, quarrel, bickering, tiff. AGREEMENT
balance, remainder, residue, rest.
different dissimilar, unlike, contrasting, disparate, discrepant, divergent, deviating, at variance, altered, changed. SIMILAR
varied, various, diverse, miscellaneous, assorted, sundry.
unusual, unique, distinctive, out of the ordinary, new, novel. ORDINARY
differentiate distinguish, set apart, separate, tell apart, discriminate, tell the difference.
difficult hard, arduous, demanding, uphill, laborious, strenuous, wearisome, formidable. EASY
intricate, involved, complex, complicated, abstruse, obscure, baffling, perplexing, knotty, thorny, ticklish. SIMPLE
awkward, unaccommodating, unamenable, intractable, unmanageable, refractory, obstreperous, trying, demanding, fussy, finicky, rigid, unyielding. TRACTABLE
difficulty arduousness, laboriousness, strenuousness, strain, hardship, trouble, trial, tribulation. EASE
problem, perplexity, dilemma, quandary, predicament, plight, fix (*inf*), trouble, hot water, exigency, embarrassment.
obstacle, hurdle, hindrance, impediment, problem, complication, objection.
diffidence shyness, bashfulness, timidity, backwardness, hesitation, reluctance, sheepishness, modesty, self-effacement, constraint, reserve, insecurity. CONFIDENCE
diffident shy, bashful, timid, backward, hesitant, reluctant, sheepish, modest, shrinking, self-effacing, constrained, self-conscious, reserved, withdrawn, insecure. CONFIDENT
diffuse *v*, spread, scatter, disperse, disseminate, propagate, circulate, dispense, distribute. GATHER
adj, wordy, prolix, verbose, long-winded, rambling, discursive, circumlocutory, vague, loose. CONCISE
scattered, spread out, dispersed. CONCENTRATED
diffusion dispersion, scattering, spread, dissemination, radiation, propagation, circulation, distribution. AGGLOMERATION
verbosity, prolixity, wordiness, rambling, long-windedness, discursiveness, circumlocution. TERSENESS
dig *v*, excavate, scoop, gouge, burrow, tunnel, quarry, mine, till, work, turn over, break up, delve, probe.
poke, prod, jab, thrust, drive, force.
dig up, discover, find, expose, unearth, exhume.
n, poke, prod, jab, punch, thrust.
gibe, taunt, jeer, insult, quip, crack (*inf*).
digest *v*, assimilate, absorb, dissolve, break down.
take in, grasp, assimilate, master, comprehend, understand, ponder, meditate, reflect, consider, study.
systematize, codify, classify, order, methodize, tabulate.
abridge, condense, summarize, shorten. AMPLIFY
n, abridgment, summary, compendium, abstract, synopsis, résumé, précis, epitome.
digit figure, numeral, symbol.
finger, toe.
dignified stately, grand, majestic, august, noble, honourable, distinguished, lofty, imposing, solemn, grave, staid, formal, decorous. LOWLY
dignify ennoble, honour, exalt, elevate, raise, advance, promote, aggrandize, adorn, grace. DEGRADE
dignitary notable, personage, celebrity, public figure, VIP (*inf*), bigwig (*inf*).
dignity nobility, stateliness, majesty, grandeur, loftiness, eminence, elevation, greatness, importance, standing, rank, status, station, honour, respectability, solemnity, gravity, propriety, decorum, formality, pride, self-esteem. LOWLINESS
digress deviate, diverge, wander, stray, depart, drift, ramble, go off at a tangent.
digression deviation, divergence, departure, wandering, detour, apostrophe, aside, footnote.
dilapidated ramshackle, tumble-down, ruined, broken-down, shabby, battered, neglected, decayed, decaying, crumbling, decrepit, run-down. RESTORED
dilapidation ruin, decay, deterioration, disintegration, disrepair, downfall, collapse. RENOVATION
dilate expand, extend, stretch, enlarge, widen, broaden, spread, swell, distend, inflate, puff out. CONTRACT
develop, amplify, enlarge, expatiate, descant, dwell on. ABRIDGE

dilation dilatation, expansion, extension, enlargement, increase, widening, broadening, distension, inflation, amplification. CONTRACTION

dilatory dawdling, lagging, lingering, slow, sluggish, tardy, behindhand, procrastinating, delaying, backward. PROMPT

dilemma quandary, predicament, plight, fix (*inf*), spot (*inf*), difficulty, problem, perplexity, strait.

dilettante dabbler, amateur, nonprofessional.
aesthete, art lover, connoisseur.

diligence assiduity, assiduousness, application, industry, intentness, care, attention, heed, perseverance, persistence, tenacity, sedulousness. CARELESSNESS

diligent assiduous, industrious, hardworking, sedulous, painstaking, thorough, attentive, careful, intent, persistent, persevering, tireless, busy, active. LAZY

dilly-dally loiter, lag, dawdle, dally, linger, delay, potter, falter, hesitate, waver, vacillate. HURRY

dilute adulterate, attenuate, water down, cut, thin, weaken, reduce. CONCENTRATE

dim *adj*, dark, dusky, shadowy, tenebrous, gloomy, dingy, dull, grey, cloudy, overcast. BRIGHT
obscure, indistinct, vague, blurred, hazy, faint, ill-defined, confused. CLEAR
dense, obtuse, slow, thick, stupid, doltish. CLEVER
v, darken, dull, obscure, cloud, tarnish, lower, fade, pale, blur. BRIGHTEN

dimension measurement, measure, extent, size, capacity, volume, bulk, mass, magnitude, range, scope, importance, scale, proportion.

diminish lessen, decrease, reduce, lower, shrink, contract, shorten, retrench, curtail, abate, weaken, subside, decline, wane, dwindle. INCREASE
disparage, belittle, deprecate, depreciate, devalue, cheapen. APPRECIATE

diminution decrease, reduction, lessening, lowering, contraction, shortening, retrenchment, cutback, abatement, weakening, decline, ebb. INCREASE

diminutive tiny, minute, small, little, wee, pygmy, midget, dwarfish, miniature, mini, Lilliputian, undersized, puny. LARGE

din noise, clangour, clamour, uproar, racket, row, crash, clatter, commotion, hullabaloo, bedlam, pandemonium. SILENCE

dine eat, sup, feast, banquet, lunch.

dingy dull, dark, dim, dusky, sombre, gloomy, murky, obscure, drab, colourless, faded, shabby, seedy, dirty, grimy. BRIGHT

dinner supper, lunch, main meal, meal, repast, spread, feast, banquet.

dint dent, impression, indentation, pit, hollow, depression.
means, use, force, power, virtue.

diocese see, bishopric, episcopate, province, jurisdiction.

dip *v*, plunge, immerse, duck, submerge, souse, douse, dunk, bathe, dive.
descend, sink, lower, drop, decline, slope, incline, droop, sag, subside. RISE
n, plunge, ducking, bathe, swim.
incline, slope, hollow, depression, basin, decline, fall, slump.

diplomacy tact, discretion, subtlety, finesse, skill. TACTLESSNESS
statecraft, statesmanship, negotiation, politics.

diplomat ambassador, envoy, plenipotentiary, consul, politician, negotiator, mediator, conciliator, diplomatist.

diplomatic tactful, discreet, sensitive, judicious, prudent, politic, subtle. TACTLESS

dire direful, dreadful, terrible, frightful, fearful, shocking, appalling, awful, horrible, disastrous, calamitous, catastrophic. SPLENDID
desperate, urgent, pressing, imperative, critical, crucial.

direct *adj*, straight, unswerving, undeviating, uninterrupted, through, shortest. CIRCUITOUS
straightforward, honest, frank, candid, blunt, open, sincere, plain, unambiguous, explicit, categorical, absolute. EQUIVOCAL
immediate, first-hand, face-to-face, personal. INDIRECT
v, manage, control, run, govern, rule, regulate, administer, lead, superintend.
command, order, enjoin, bid, instruct.
guide, lead, conduct, show, usher. MISLEAD
aim, point, level, fix, focus, steer, destine, address.

direction way, course, route, path, line, bearing, orientation, trend, tendency, aim.

instruction, guidance, guideline, recommendation, injunction, order, command, directive.
management, control, administration, running, leadership, supervision, guidance, charge, rule.

directly immediately, straightaway, at once, without delay, instantly, quickly, promptly, forthwith, soon, in a moment, presently. LATER

director manager, executive, administrator, governor, head, chief, boss (*inf*), supervisor, controller.

dirge requiem, elegy, lament, threnody, coronach.

dirt filth, grime, muck, excrement, mud, dust, stain, smudge, pollution, impurity, dirtiness, foulness. CLEANNESS
earth, soil, clay.

dirty *adj*, filthy, grimy, soiled, mucky, grubby, unwashed, foul, polluted, cloudy, muddy, murky. CLEAN
obscene, salacious, indecent, blue, smutty, risqué, suggestive, pornographic.
mean, low, contemptible, abject, base, vile, nasty, despicable, shabby, sordid, squalid, ignominious, unscrupulous, unsporting, unfair, dishonest. HONOURABLE
v, soil, begrime, befoul, stain, smear, muddy, foul, pollute, sully, defile. CLEAN

disability handicap, infirmity, affliction, disorder, disablement, incapacity, inability, impotency, unfitness, incompetence, disqualification. FITNESS

disable cripple, lame, incapacitate, prostrate, handicap, paralyse, immobilize, hamstring, impair, damage, weaken, enfeeble. STRENGTHEN

disabuse undeceive, enlighten, correct, set right, disillusion. DECEIVE

disadvantage drawback, snag, flaw, hindrance, impediment, handicap, inconvenience, trouble, nuisance, privation, weakness. ADVANTAGE
detriment, harm, prejudice, disservice, injury, hurt, loss. BENEFIT

disadvantageous detrimental, prejudicial, deleterious, injurious, damaging, harmful, adverse, unfavourable, inconvenient, ill-timed, inopportune, troublesome. ADVANTAGEOUS

disaffect estrange, alienate, disunite, divide, antagonize, embitter. WIN

disaffected disloyal, unfaithful, estranged, alienated, antagonistic, hostile, dissatisfied, disgruntled, mutinous, rebellious. LOYAL

disaffection estrangement, alienation, breach, disagreement, disloyalty, hostility, animosity, bad blood, dissatisfaction, dislike, aversion. LOYALTY

disagree dissent, debate, dispute, contend, contest, object, differ, argue, wrangle, quarrel, bicker, fall out (*inf*), oppose. AGREE
conflict, clash, differ, vary, contradict, diverge, deviate, be at variance. CORRESPOND

disagreeable unpleasant, offensive, nasty, obnoxious, objectionable, repugnant, repulsive, disgusting, distasteful. PLEASANT
unfriendly, brusque, churlish, surly, ill-tempered, cross, rude, impolite, unpleasant. AGREEABLE

disagreement argument, dispute, wrangle, bickering, quarrel, tiff (*inf*), altercation, dissension, contention, strife, conflict, clash, discord, debate, controversy, misunderstanding. HARMONY
difference, variance, deviation, divergence, dissimilarity, disparity, discrepancy, incompatibility, discord, incongruity. SIMILARITY

disallow forbid, prohibit, ban, proscribe, bar, veto. SANCTION
reject, repudiate, disclaim, disavow, abjure, disown, rebuff, shun. ACCEPT

disannul annul, nullify, void, invalidate, quash, cancel, rescind, abrogate, repeal, abolish. CONFIRM

disappear vanish, fade, melt, dissolve, evaporate, perish, cease, die, ebb, recede, withdraw, go, depart, flee. APPEAR

disappoint fail, let down, dissatisfy, disillusion, disenchant, delude, deceive, vex, sadden. SATISFY
frustrate, foil, thwart, defeat, confound, baffle, balk, hamper, disconcert. GRATIFY

disappointment frustration, disenchantment, chagrin, regret, dissatisfaction, discontent, distress, discouragement. SATISFACTION
letdown, setback, failure, defeat, misfortune, blow.

disapprobation disapproval, displeasure, censure, blame, condemnation, reproof. APPROBATION
disapproval disapprobation, displeasure, dissatisfaction, censure, criticism, condemnation, reproof, objection, exception. APPROVAL
disapprove censure, condemn, frown on, discountenance, deplore, deprecate, object to, criticize, dislike. APPROVE
disallow, veto, turn down, refuse. SANCTION
disarm disable, unman, unarm, demilitarize, demobilize. ARM
win over, persuade, set at ease, appease, conciliate.
disarrange derange, disorder, confuse, disorganize, disturb, unsettle, discompose, untidy, mess up, tousle, jumble. ARRANGE
disarray disorder, disarrangement, confusion, muddle, jumble, disorganization, derangement, discomposure, untidiness, mess, chaos. ORDER
disaster calamity, catastrophe, tragedy, stroke, blow, misfortune, accident, mishap, reverse, adversity, ruin, trouble, affliction. BLESSING
disastrous calamitous, catastrophic, dire, ruinous, destructive, cataclysmic, devastating, terrible, dreadful, tragic, adverse, unfortunate, untoward, unlucky, ill-fated, hapless. AUSPICIOUS
disavow deny, repudiate, reject, disown, disclaim, retract, contradict, abjure. ACKNOWLEDGE
disband disperse, break up, dissolve, scatter, separate, part company, dismiss, demobilize. MUSTER
disbelief unbelief, incredulity, doubt, scepticism, distrust, mistrust, rejection. BELIEF
disbelieve discredit, reject, discount, mistrust, suspect, doubt. BELIEVE
disburden unburden, disencumber, unload, relieve, free, ease, discharge. ENCUMBER
disburse spend, pay out, expend, fork out (*inf*). SAVE
disc plate, circle, ring, counter.
record, recording, single, LP, album.
discard reject, abandon, cast aside, shed, throw away, get rid of, drop, dispose of, dispense with, jettison, scrap. RETAIN
discern perceive, descry, make out, see, observe, notice, espy, detect, discover, recognize. MISS
differentiate, distinguish, discriminate, judge.
discernible perceptible, noticeable, apparent, obvious, plain, visible, conspicuous, distinct, palpable, detectable, recognizable. IMPERCEPTIBLE
discerning discriminating, critical, judicious, wise, perceptive, perspicacious, clear-sighted, astute, shrewd, intelligent. DULL
discernment discrimination, perspicacity, perception, judgment, sagacity, astuteness, shrewdness, sharpness, insight, ingenuity, intelligence, clear-sightedness. DULLNESS
discharge *v*, release, free, liberate, loose, absolve, acquit, exonerate, clear. DETAIN
expel, eject, oust, dismiss, fire (*inf*), sack (*inf*). APPOINT
emit, exude, eject, excrete, disembogue, release, gush, ooze, leak, empty. ABSORB
fire, shoot, detonate, explode, set off.
unload, unburden, disburden, relieve, remove. LOAD
perform, execute, carry out, fulfil, accomplish, do. NEGLECT
n, liberation, release, acquittal, exoneration. DETENTION
dismissal, congé, sack (*inf*). RECRUITMENT
emission, secretion, suppuration, excretion, voidance, ejection. ABSORPTION
blast, volley, salvo, shot, report, explosion, detonation.
performance, execution, fulfilment, accomplishment. NEGLECT
disciple follower, adherent, partisan, votary, devotee, supporter, believer, student, scholar, pupil, convert, proselyte, apostle.
discipline *n*, training, routine, drill, exercise, instruction, schooling, practice.
regulation, control, order, rule, government, restraint, check. INDISCIPLINE
punishment, chastisement, castigation, correction. INDULGENCE
v, train, drill, break in, exercise, teach, instruct, school.
control, restrain, check, govern, regulate.
punish, castigate, chastise, correct, reprimand, reprove. INDULGE
disclaim deny, abjure, abnegate, renounce, disown, abandon, disavow, retract, repudiate. CONFESS

disclaimer denial, abjuration, repudiation, retraction, disavowal, contradiction, renunciation, disowning, rejection. CONFESSION

disclose divulge, let slip, confess, reveal, make known, tell, impart, communicate, broadcast. SUPPRESS
expose, lay bare, reveal, uncover, unveil, show, bring to light. CONCEAL

disclosure divulgence, revelation, confession, admission, announcement, broadcast, discovery, exposure. SUPPRESSION

discolour stain, tarnish, taint, tinge, mark, streak, bruise, fade, bleach, soil, mar.

discomfit embarrass, fluster, ruffle, abash, unsettle, perturb, discompose, disconcert, confuse, perplex, confound.
thwart, frustrate, foil, baffle. ASSIST

discomfiture embarrassment, abashment, chagrin, unease, discomposure, disconcertion, confusion. EASE
frustration, undoing, failure, disappointment.

discomfort uneasiness, disquiet, trouble, distress, affliction, malaise, pain, ache, irritation, annoyance, vexation, nuisance, inconvenience. EASE

discommode trouble, inconvenience, incommode, bother, disturb, annoy.

discompose disconcert, ruffle, discomfit, fluster, perturb, agitate, disquiet, fret, worry, vex, annoy, irritate, nettle, perplex, confuse, unsettle, disturb, upset. CALM

discomposure disconcertion, discomfiture, perturbation, agitation, disquiet, vexation, annoyance, irritation, perplexity, confusion, disturbance. EASE

disconcert discompose, ruffle, discomfit, fluster, unsettle, perturb, perplex, bewilder, nonplus, take aback, abash, worry, agitate, trouble, upset. REASSURE
frustrate, thwart, balk, baffle, confuse, defeat, undo. ASSIST

disconnect disengage, uncouple, separate, part, divide, sever, detach, cut off, unplug. CONNECT

disconnected confused, garbled, disjointed, rambling, illogical, unconnected, incoherent, unintelligible. COHERENT

disconnection separation, division, severance, discontinuity, interruption, cessation, detachment, disunion. UNION

disconsolate forlorn, unhappy, sad, desolate, dejected, heartbroken, inconsolable, woeful, wretched, miserable, melancholy. JOYFUL

discontent discontentment, dissatisfaction, displeasure, uneasiness, impatience, envy, fretfulness, vexation, restlessness. CONTENT

discontented discontent, dissatisfied, disgruntled, fed up, cheesed off (*inf*), fretful, exasperated, unhappy, miserable, displeased. CONTENTED

discontinue stop, terminate, end, cease, halt, suspend, interrupt, abandon, drop. CONTINUE

discontinuous broken, interrupted, intermittent, fitful, spasmodic, disjointed, disconnected. CONTINUOUS

discord dissonance, disharmony, cacophony, harshness, jarring, jangle. HARMONY
discordance, dissension, strife, contention, friction, conflict, dispute, disagreement, variance, difference, wrangling, disunity, breach, rupture. ACCORD

discordant dissonant, inharmonious, cacophonous, unmelodious, atonal, harsh, jarring, grating, strident. HARMONIOUS
conflicting, incompatible, incongruous, contrary, different, divergent, disagreeing, contradictory, at variance. CONCORDANT

discount *n*, reduction, rebate, allowance, concession, deduction, cut price. PREMIUM
v, disregard, ignore, overlook, pass over.
deduct, take off, reduce, lower, mark down.

discountenance embarrass, abash, chagrin, discompose, discomfit, disconcert, perturb, shame, humiliate.
disapprove, disfavour, discourage, frown on, condemn, object to, oppose, veto. COUNTENANCE

discourage damp, dampen, dishearten, dispirit, cow, daunt, intimidate, unnerve, dismay, deject, depress. INSPIRE
deter, dissuade, put off, check, curb, prevent, inhibit, hinder. ENCOURAGE
disapprove, disfavour, discountenance, frown on, oppose. SANCTION

discourse *n*, conversation, confabulation, talk, chat, discussion, dialogue, converse.
speech, sermon, homily, lecture, address, dissertation, essay, treatise.

v, converse, talk, speak, hold forth, expatiate, discuss, confer, confabulate, debate.

discourteous rude, bad-mannered, unmannerly, impolite, uncivil, ill-bred, disrespectful, curt, short, abrupt, brusque. COURTEOUS

discourtesy rudeness, bad manners, impoliteness, incivility, disrespect, insolence, curtness, brusqueness. COURTESY

discover find, come across, happen upon, unearth, dig up, ferret out, locate, bring to light, uncover, disclose, reveal. CONCEAL

ascertain, find out, learn, determine, see, discern, perceive, notice, descry, detect. MISS

discovery find, finding, location, uncovering, revelation, detection, ascertainment, perception, realization.

discredit *v*, disbelieve, doubt, question, dispute, challenge, distrust, mistrust. BELIEVE

dishonour, disgrace, degrade, defame, vilify, smear, denigrate, slur, slander, disparage. HONOUR

invalidate, refute, disprove. PROVE

n, disbelief, doubt, scepticism, distrust, mistrust. BELIEF

dishonour, disgrace, shame, ignominy, disrepute, obloquy, scandal, reproach, odium, opprobrium, ill-repute. CREDIT

discreditable dishonourable, disgraceful, shameful, ignoble, degrading, ignominious, scandalous, blameworthy, reprehensible, improper, unworthy. HONOURABLE

discreet tactful, politic, diplomatic, guarded, reserved, cautious, wary, careful, circumspect, prudent, sagacious, judicious, wise, thoughtful, considerate. INDISCREET

discrepancy difference, variation, variance, inconsistency, disagreement, conflict, disparity, incongruity, dissimilarity, divergence, contrariety, discordance. CORRESPONDENCE

discrepant different, at variance, inconsistent, conflicting, disagreeing, discordant, contrary, incongruous. CONSISTENT

discrete separate, distinct, individual, detached, disjunct, discontinuous.

discretion tact, diplomacy, prudence, judgment, wisdom, sagacity, judiciousness, caution, circumspection, wariness, care, consideration, thoughtfulness, discrimination, discernment. RASHNESS

liberty, freedom, will, wish, option, choice, liking, inclination, disposition.

discretionary discretional, optional, elective, arbitrary, voluntary, unrestricted, open. MANDATORY

discriminate distinguish, differentiate, discern, separate, isolate, segregate, single out, judge, assess.

discriminating discerning, selective, critical, particular, fastidious, sensitive, astute.

discrimination distinction, differentiation, prejudice, bigotry, intolerance, bias, favouritism, racism, sexism.

discernment, judgment, acumen, shrewdness, astuteness, perception, refinement, taste, subtlety, insight, penetration, wisdom, sagacity.

discriminatory discriminative, biased, prejudiced, one-sided, partisan, unjust, preferential, racist, sexist. UNBIASED

discriminating, discerning, perceptive, critical, analytical.

discursive rambling, wandering, roving, desultory, digressive, prolix, wordy, circuitous, roundabout, circumlocutory, long-winded, verbose, diffuse. TERSE

discuss debate, talk about, confer, argue, thrash out, consider, deliberate, examine, review, sift.

discussion debate, argument, conference, talk, conversation, consultation, consideration, deliberation, examination, review, analysis.

disdain *v*, scorn, spurn, contemn, despise, deride, belittle, slight, ignore, disregard. RESPECT

n, scorn, contempt, contumely, superciliousness, haughtiness, arrogance, indifference, derision, sneering, dislike. ADMIRATION

disdainful scornful, contemptuous, contumelious, supercilious, haughty, proud, arrogant, sneering, derisive, insolent. RESPECTFUL

disease sickness, illness, complaint, malady, ailment, affliction, disorder, ill health, indisposition, infirmity, infection, contagion. HEALTH

diseased infected, contaminated, sick, ill, sickly, ailing, unwell, unhealthy, unsound. HEALTHY

disembark land, go ashore, alight, get off, dismount. EMBARK

disembarrass relieve, ease, clear, rid, free, disburden, disencumber, extricate, disentangle.

disembodied spiritual, incorporeal, bodiless, immaterial, intangible, ghostly.

disembowel eviscerate, gut, draw.

disenable disable, incapacitate, cripple, enfeeble, disqualify, prevent, hinder, impede, hamstring. ENABLE

disenchant disillusion, disabuse, undeceive, bring down to earth, disappoint.

disencumber disburden, unburden, disembarrass, unload, discharge, unhamper, relieve, free. ENCUMBER

disengage release, free, liberate, loose, unloose, unfasten, untie, unfetter, extricate. ENGAGE
detach, sever, separate, disjoin, divide, undo, disunite, disconnect, uncouple. JOIN

disengaged free, loose, separate, detached, unattached, unoccupied, at leisure, not busy. ENGAGED

disentangle disembroil, extricate, release, free, loose, disengage, untangle, unsnarl, undo, unravel, unknot. ENTANGLE
resolve, work out, sort out, clarify, clear up. EMBROIL

disenthral liberate, free, release, emancipate, manumit, enfranchise, unfetter, loose. ENSLAVE

disfavour *n*, disapproval, disapprobation, displeasure, dislike, disrespect, disesteem, discredit, disgrace. APPROVAL
disservice, bad turn, affront, offence. FAVOUR
v, disapprove, dislike, disesteem. APPROVE

disfigure deface, mutilate, scar, distort, deform, spoil, mar, damage, blemish, disfeature. EMBELLISH

disfigurement defacement, mutilation, scar, deformity, blemish, defect, ugliness. EMBELLISHMENT

disgorge vomit, spew, belch, eject, expel, empty, discharge.
surrender, yield, relinquish, resign, cede, give up, renounce, hand over. RETAIN

disgrace *v*, dishonour, discredit, shame, degrade, debase, humiliate, sully, taint, stain, tarnish, slur, defame, disparage, depreciate, lower. HONOUR
n, shame, dishonour, discredit, humiliation, disesteem, obloquy, disfavour, disrepute, ignominy, infamy, odium, opprobrium, reproach, disparagement, depreciation, defamation, slur, scandal. ESTEEM

disgraceful shameful, scandalous, ignominious, discreditable, dishonourable, infamous, opprobrious, low, degrading, disreputable, reprehensible, bad, shocking, outrageous, unworthy. HONOURABLE

disgruntled discontented, malcontent, displeased, dissatisfied, sulky, peevish, put out, annoyed, irritated, grumpy, fed up (*inf*). CONTENTED

disguise *v*, conceal, hide, mask, veil, shroud, cloak, muffle, gloss over, dissemble, misrepresent, falsify, camouflage, screen, cover. REVEAL
n, camouflage, incognito, mask, costume, concealment, cover, screen, blind, façade, pretence, guise, semblance, front.

disgust *v*, sicken, nauseate, revolt, repel, offend, displease, shock, appal, scandalize, outrage. PLEASE
n, distaste, nausea, repulsion, repugnance, disrelish, loathing, abhorrence, dislike, displeasure, aversion, hatred, antipathy, abomination. RELISH

disgusting sickening, nauseating, revolting, repulsive, repugnant, obnoxious, nasty, foul, noisome, odious, abhorrent, loathsome, unpleasant, outrageous, shocking, scandalous. DELIGHTFUL

dish *n*, plate, saucer, platter, bowl, vessel, receptacle.
food, fare, recipe, serving, helping, course.
v, ruin, spoil, wreck.

dish out, distribute, dole out, mete out, inflict.

dish up, serve, present, ladle, spoon.

dishearten discourage, dispirit, damp, dampen, depress, cast down, sadden, deject, crush, dismay, daunt, disconcert. ENCOURAGE

dishevelled unkempt, uncombed, bedraggled, untidy, disarranged, disordered, tousled. TIDY

dishonest fraudulent, deceitful, lying, untruthful, mendacious, false, crooked (*inf*), perfidious, knavish, tricky, unscrupulous, treacherous, corrupt, unfair, unlawful, untrustworthy, faithless. HONEST

dishonesty fraudulence, cheating, deceit, mendacity, duplicity, falsity, perfidy, trickery, unscrupulousness, treachery, corruption, crime, chicanery, improbity, fraud, criminality, crookedness. HONESTY

dishonour *n*, disgrace, shame, disrepute, discredit, ignominy, infamy, scandal, obloquy, opprobrium, reproach, degradation, abasement, disesteem, disfavour. ESTEEM
v, disgrace, discredit, shame, degrade, debase, abase, lower, humiliate, defame, sully. HONOUR
deflower, rape, seduce, ravish, molest, violate, defile, pollute, debauch.

dishonourable discreditable, disgraceful, shameful, scandalous, infamous, ignominious, despicable, contemptible, low, base, disreputable, unscrupulous, shameless. HONOURABLE

disillusion disenchant, disabuse, undeceive, enlighten, bring down to earth, disappoint.

disinclined reluctant, unwilling, indisposed, averse, loath, opposed, antipathetic. WILLING

disinfect fumigate, sterilize, sanitize, decontaminate, purify, cleanse. CONTAMINATE

disingenuous insincere, deceitful, dishonest, lying, two-faced, false, insidious, artful, guileful, sly, shifty, crafty. INGENUOUS

disinherit dispossess, deprive, cut off, disown, repudiate, oust.

disintegrate crumble, break up, fall apart, separate, shatter, splinter, decompose, decay, rot.

disinter exhume, disentomb, dig up, unearth, bring to light, expose, uncover. BURY

disinterested impartial, unbiased, objective, dispassionate, neutral, impersonal, uninvolved, detached, equitable, fair, just, unselfish, honest, candid. BIASED

disjoin detach, separate, disconnect, disunite, sever, divide, split. JOIN

disjointed disconnected, unconnected, fitful, rambling, incoherent, desultory, loose, aimless, disordered, confused. COHERENT
dislocated, displaced, dismembered, disunited, divided, split.

disjunction separation, disconnection, severance, disunion, disjuncture, detachment, split. UNION

dislike *v*, hate, detest, loathe, abhor, disapprove, disfavour, disrelish, object to, mind, despise. LIKE
n, hate, hatred, detestation, loathing, abhorrence, aversion, antipathy, disgust, repugnance, hostility, disfavour, disapproval, disrelish, displeasure. LIKING

dislocate disjoint, displace, luxate, disarticulate, disengage, unhinge, disconnect, derange, disorder, disrupt, misplace.

dislocation luxation, displacement, disarticulation, disconnection, derangement, disorder, disarray, disorganization, disruption, disturbance.

dislodge remove, displace, uproot, extricate, oust, expel, eject, evict. PLACE

disloyal unfaithful, faithless, perfidious, treacherous, false, untrue, apostate, recreant, disaffected. LOYAL

disloyalty unfaithfulness, faithlessness, infidelity, perfidy, treachery, treason, falseness, inconstancy, apostasy, disaffection. LOYALTY

dismal gloomy, dreary, cheerless, sombre, dull, dark, drab, bleak, depressing, melancholy, lugubrious, doleful, sad, joyless, wretched, miserable, dolorous, funereal, forlorn, grim, gruesome. CHEERFUL

dismantle disassemble, take apart, demolish, raze, strip, divest. ASSEMBLE

dismay *n*, consternation, alarm, apprehension, dread, fear, terror, horror, panic, anxiety, trepidation, agitation, misgiving, disappointment, discouragement, chagrin. REASSURANCE
v, alarm, frighten, scare, perturb, upset, disconcert, daunt, intimidate, terrify, horrify, appal, discourage, dishearten, depress, sadden, disappoint, chagrin. REASSURE

dismember dissect, cut up, anatomize, disjoint, divide, sever, amputate, mutilate.

dismiss discharge, send away, banish, disband, disperse, demobilize, release, free, let go, remove, oust, cashier, lay off, sack (*inf*), fire (*inf*). RETAIN
discard, reject, dispel, banish, set aside, shelve, drop.

dismissal discharge, release, freedom, expulsion, removal, notice, sack (*inf*).

dismount descend, alight, get off, get down, disembark. MOUNT

disobedience insubordination, noncompliance, wilfulness, contumacy, recalcitrance, defiance, indiscipline, mutiny, infraction. OBEDIENCE

disobedient insubordinate, noncompliant, contrary, wayward, contumacious, refractory, defiant, undisciplined, naughty, unruly, wilful, mutinous, rebellious. OBEDIENT

disobey infringe, violate, contravene, transgress, break, disregard, ignore, defy, flout. OBEY

disoblige displease, annoy, bother, trouble, disturb, put out, inconvenience, discommode, offend, affront, slight, insult. OBLIGE

disobliging unaccommodating, uncooperative, awkward, unhelpful, unpleasant, disagreeable, rude, discourteous, offensive, unkind, unfriendly. OBLIGING

disorder *n*, disarray, confusion, muddle, jumble, mess, chaos, disarrangement, derangement, disorderliness, disorganization, turmoil, tumult, riot, commotion, disturbance. ORDER
ailment, complaint, malady, illness, disease, affliction, indisposition, sickness.
v, disarrange, derange, disorganize, disturb, upset, confuse, muddle, jumble, mess up, turn upside down, discompose, unsettle. ARRANGE

disorderly untidy, disordered, disorganized, disarranged, confused, chaotic, irregular, unsystematic. NEAT
unruly, unmanageable, lawless, riotous, boisterous, disruptive, obstreperous, rebellious, wild. ORDERLY

disorganize disarrange, derange, disorder, disrupt, disturb, upset, confuse, muddle, jumble. ORGANIZE

disorientated disoriented, confused, perplexed, bewildered, lost, all at sea, astray, unsettled, mixed up, unbalanced.

disown repudiate, disclaim, abandon, reject, cast off, renounce, deny, disavow, ignore, disinherit, cut off. ACKNOWLEDGE

disparage belittle, depreciate, underrate, undervalue, underestimate, decry, derogate, run down, deprecate, denigrate, vilify, defame, traduce, malign, discredit, degrade, debase, asperse, criticize. EXTOL

disparagement belittlement, depreciation, underestimation, derogation, deprecation, denigration, vilification, defamation, discredit, disdain, contempt, scorn, aspersion, slander. APPRECIATION

disparate distinct, different, contrasting, unlike, dissimilar, diverse. IDENTICAL

disparity difference, inequality, discrepancy, incongruity, disproportion, gap, contrast, dissimilarity, unlikeness. EQUALITY

dispassionate objective, impartial, unbiased, disinterested, neutral, detached, impersonal, candid, fair, just. BIASED
composed, calm, collected, cool, unruffled, imperturbable, serene, poised, impassive, placid, unexcited. EXCITABLE

dispatch *v*, send, post, mail, transmit, remit, consign, ship, forward, expedite, hasten, hurry, accelerate. RETAIN
conclude, finish, complete, discharge, perform, dispose of.
murder, kill, slay, assassinate, execute, put to death, slaughter.
n, promptness, alacrity, speed, rapidity, celerity, haste, swiftness, quickness. SLOWNESS
communication, message, report, bulletin, communiqué, missive, note, letter, story, account.

dispel disperse, scatter, dismiss, banish, expel, dissipate, dissolve, rout, drive away. COLLECT

dispensable expendable, disposable, unnecessary, nonessential, superfluous, needless, redundant. ESSENTIAL

dispensation distribution, apportionment, allotment, assignment, allocation, bestowal, endowment. WITHHOLDING
management, administration, direction, regulation, control, system, order, scheme, plan, arrangement.
exemption, immunity, indulgence, licence, permission, privilege, exception, relaxation, reprieve, remission.

dispense distribute, give out, apportion, share, allot, assign, allocate, dole out, mete out. WITHHOLD
administer, apply, implement, enforce, discharge, execute.
exempt, excuse, release, except, reprieve, let off (*inf*).

dispense with, dispose of, get rid of, do away with, abolish, cancel. RETAIN
do without, abstain, forgo, give up, renounce.

disperse scatter, dispel, dissipate, broadcast, spread, disseminate, diffuse, dissolve, separate, break up, disband, dismiss, rout, disappear, vanish. GATHER

dispirit dishearten, discourage, damp, dampen, depress, deject, cast down, deter, disincline. ENCOURAGE

dispirited downhearted, downcast, disheartened, discouraged, depressed, dejected, crestfallen, despondent, glum. BLITHE

displace move, shift, disturb, derange, transpose, relocate, dislodge, dislocate. FIX
remove, depose, dismiss, discharge, cashier, sack (*inf*), fire (*inf*), oust, supplant, replace. RETAIN
eject, evict, force out, exile, banish.

display *v*, show, exhibit, demonstrate, manifest, betray, evince, reveal, expose, present. DISGUISE
parade, flaunt, show off, flourish, vaunt. CONCEAL
unfold, unfurl, spread out, open out, extend, expand.
n, show, exhibition, demonstration, exposition, presentation, array, revelation, exposure.
parade, spectacle, pageant, pomp, ceremony, ostentation, splash (*inf*).

displease offend, annoy, vex, irritate, nettle, pique, anger, incense, provoke, exasperate, aggravate (*inf*), disgust, dissatisfy, upset, hurt. PLEASE

displeasure offence, annoyance, irritation, anger, exasperation, wrath, disgust, disfavour, disapproval, dislike, dissatisfaction, resentment.

disport *vt*, amuse, entertain, divert, cheer, beguile, delight. BORE
vi, frolic, gambol, caper, frisk, romp, play, sport. WORK

disposal arrangement, array, disposition, order, grouping, placing.
removal, clearance, scrapping, dumping, discarding, ejection.
conveyance, transfer, dispensation, bestowal, bequest, consignment, assignment.
control, command, discretion, direction, regulation, power, authority.

dispose arrange, group, place, set, put, array, order, marshal, range, rank, organize, regulate, settle, adjust. DERANGE
incline, lead, move, prompt, tempt, induce, predispose, bias, influence, adapt, condition.

dispose of, get rid of, discard, throw away, scrap, dump (*inf*), destroy. RETAIN
settle, determine, decide, deal with, end.
distribute, allocate, transfer, bestow, make over, sell.

disposed apt, liable, subject, likely, given, inclined, prone, ready.

disposition character, nature, temperament, constitution, temper, humour, spirit.
inclination, tendency, turn, leaning, proneness, predisposition, proclivity, propensity, readiness.
disposal, arrangement, distribution, grouping, order, placement.

dispossess deprive, divest, strip, take away, confiscate, expropriate.
evict, expel, eject, oust, turn out, drive out. HOUSE

dispraise *v*, censure, criticize, reproach, condemn, denounce, disparage, discredit, disapprove. PRAISE
n, censure, criticism, animadversion, condemnation, disparagement, obloquy, disapproval, disapprobation, disgrace.

disproof confutation, refutation, rebuttal, negation, denial, disproval, invalidation. PROOF

disproportion disparity, inequality, discrepancy, difference, imbalance, unevenness, asymmetry. EQUALITY

disproportionate unequal, uneven, unbalanced, out of proportion, top-heavy, incommensurate, excessive, extreme, inordinate. COMMENSURATE

disprove confute, refute, rebut, negate, invalidate, controvert, contradict, discredit, expose, overturn. PROVE

disputable debatable, arguable, moot, controversial, questionable, doubtful, dubious, uncertain. INDISPUTABLE

disputant debater, arguer, wrangler, contender, opponent, adversary, antagonist, litigant. ADVOCATE

disputatious argumentative, contentious, captious, polemical, controversial, quarrelsome, irascible, cantankerous, litigious. GENIAL

dispute *v*, argue, debate, discuss, quarrel, wrangle, squabble, brawl, bicker, altercate. AGREE
question, challenge, contest, controvert, contradict, deny, impugn, resist. UPHOLD
n, argument, debate, discussion, disputation, controversy, contest, conflict, strife, wrangle, quarrel, altercation, row, disagreement. AGREEMENT

disqualify incapacitate, disable, injure, invalidate.
preclude, debar, disenable, disentitle, prohibit, exclude, rule out, eliminate. QUALIFY

disquiet *n*, disquietude, anxiety, worry, concern, foreboding, uneasiness, restlessness, unrest, fear, alarm, distress, trouble, fretfulness, agitation, disturbance, discomposure. CALM
v, worry, concern, unsettle, fret, perturb, agitate, discompose, distress, upset, disturb, annoy, irritate, bother, harass. APPEASE

disquisition dissertation, essay, treatise, thesis, paper, discourse, discussion, exposé.

disregard *v*, ignore, overlook, neglect, pass over, discount, take no notice of, disobey. HEED
slight, snub, cold-shoulder (*inf*), contemn, disdain, disparage.
n, inattention, neglect, oversight, heedlessness, indifference, slight, disrespect, disdain, contempt.

disrelish *v*, dislike, disfavour, loathe, detest. LIKE
n, aversion, antipathy, dislike, distaste, repugnance, loathing. LIKING

disrepair dilapidation, decay, deterioration, collapse, ruination, decrepitude.

disreputable discreditable, shameful, disgraceful, opprobrious, ignominious, base, abject, dishonourable, despicable, contemptible, mean, low, notorious, infamous, shady, unscrupulous, unprincipled. RESPECTABLE
scruffy, shabby, bedraggled, dishevelled, disorderly, seedy, threadbare. SMART

disrepute discredit, disesteem, disgrace, dishonour, shame, infamy, ignominy, ill repute. ESTEEM

disrespect rudeness, discourtesy, impoliteness, incivility, irreverence, insolence, impertinence, disregard, neglect, contempt. RESPECT

disrespectful rude, discourteous, impolite, uncivil, bad-mannered, cheeky, insolent, impudent, impertinent, irreverent, contemptuous. POLITE

disrobe undress, unclothe, doff, shed, strip, divest, denude, bare, uncover. DRESS

disrupt disturb, upset, disorganize, disorder, unsettle, agitate, confuse, break up, interrupt, intrude, interfere with.

disruption disturbance, disorder, confusion, disarray, interruption, interference.
rupture, split, breach, cleft, rift, cleavage, separation, division.

dissatisfaction discontent, displeasure, dislike, unhappiness, uneasiness, disquiet, disappointment, dismay, distress, chagrin, annoyance, exasperation, frustration, disapproval, resentment. SATISFACTION

dissatisfied discontented, displeased, disgruntled, put out, unhappy, annoyed, frustrated, disappointed, unfulfilled, uneasy, restless. SATISFIED

dissect anatomize, cut up, dismember, analyse, scrutinize, examine, investigate, study, explore, sift, probe.

dissemble hide, conceal, cloak, mask, camouflage, dissimulate. REVEAL
pretend, feign, simulate, affect, sham, fake, counterfeit.

disseminate disperse, diffuse, spread, scatter, distribute, circulate, broadcast, promulgate, propagate, publish, proclaim, publicize, preach. SUPPRESS

dissemination dispersion, diffusion, spread, distribution, circulation, broadcasting, promulgation, propagation, publication. SUPPRESSION

dissension disagreement, discord, strife, conflict, quarrel, contention, dissent, dispute, variance, difference. AGREEMENT

dissent *v*, disagree, differ, dispute, object, protest, reject, refuse, abjure. ASSENT
n, disagreement, discord, dissidence, dissension, difference, opposition, disaffection, nonconformity.

dissenter dissident, nonconformist, objector, protestant, sectarian. CONFORMIST

dissentient dissenting, disagreeing, dissident, conflicting, opposing, objecting, unorthodox. COMPLIANT

dissertation discourse, treatise, essay, thesis, disquisition, exposition.

disservice disfavour, wrong, bad turn, ill turn, injury, harm, injustice, unkindness. FAVOUR

dissever sever, sunder, cleave, disunite, separate, disjoin, disjoint, part, dissociate. UNITE

dissident dissenter, protester, rebel, nonconformist.

dissimilar unlike, different, divergent, disparate, unrelated, heterogeneous, diverse, various. ALIKE

dissimilarity dissimilitude, difference, unlikeness, divergence, disparity, heterogeneity, diversity. SIMILARITY

dissimulation dissembling, concealment, disguise, feigning, sham, pretence, deception, deceit, hypocrisy, duplicity. HONESTY

dissipate spend, expend, consume, drain, deplete, burn up, waste, squander, fritter away, lavish, indulge oneself. HOARD
scatter, disperse, diffuse, dispel, disappear, vanish, evaporate, dissolve. COLLECT

dissipated debauched, dissolute, licentious, profligate, abandoned, intemperate, self-indulgent.

dissipation debauchery, profligacy, licentiousness, dissoluteness, abandonment, depravity, self-indulgence, intemperance.
expenditure, squandering, wastefulness, waste, extravagance, excess, lavishness, prodigality. FRUGALITY
dispersion, diffusion, dissemination, dissolution, evaporation, disappearance. ACCUMULATION

dissociate separate, disunite, sever, detach, break off, disconnect, disjoin, divorce, set apart, isolate. JOIN

dissociation separation, disunion, severance, detachment, division, disjunction, divorce, parting, isolation. UNION

dissolute dissipated, debauched, wanton, depraved, loose, profligate, abandoned, licentious, lewd, corrupt, degenerate, rakish, intemperate, unrestrained. AUSTERE

dissolution disintegration, decomposition, breaking up, separation, resolution, parting, division, dispersion. CONSOLIDATION
termination, end, conclusion, finish, discontinuation, divorce, dismissal, dispersal, destruction, overthrow, ruin, annihilation, extinction, death.
dissolving, liquefaction, solution, evaporation, disappearance.

dissolve liquefy, melt, thaw, deliquesce, fuse. SOLIDIFY
disintegrate, crumble, collapse, decompose, disperse, diffuse, dissipate, evaporate, fade, dwindle, vanish, disappear. ENDURE
terminate, end, wind up, discontinue, dismiss, break up, destroy, overthrow, ruin.
sever, disunite, separate, part, divorce, divide, break up. UNITE

dissonance discord, discordance, cacophony, harshness, stridency, jarring, jangle. HARMONY
disagreement, difference, discrepancy, inconsistency, incongruity, variance, disparity. ACCORD

dissonant discordant, inharmonious, unmelodious, cacophonous, harsh, strident, jarring, grating, raucous. HARMONIOUS
inconsistent, incongruous, discrepant, at variance, disagreeing, differing, divergent. CONGRUOUS

dissuade deter, discourage, disincline, put off, talk out of, advise against, expostulate, remonstrate. URGE

distance space, interval, gap, remove, separation, extent, range, span, reach, length, width, remoteness, farness.
reserve, coolness, aloofness, constraint, stiffness. CORDIALITY

distant far, remote, outlying, faraway, far-flung, removed, separate, apart. NEAR
reserved, cool, frigid, aloof, stiff, formal, haughty, standoffish, unfriendly, unapproachable. AFFABLE
faint, indistinct, obscure, slight. CLEAR

distaste dislike, disrelish, disgust, repugnance, aversion, loathing, revulsion, antipathy, displeasure. RELISH

distasteful unpleasant, disagreeable, undesirable, offensive, repugnant, disgusting, loathsome, hateful, abhorrent, repulsive, uninviting, unsavoury, unpalatable, nauseating. PLEASANT

distend dilate, enlarge, expand, swell, inflate, bloat, puff out, balloon, stretch, extend. CONTRACT

distension dilation, dilatation, enlargement, expansion, swelling, inflation, intumescence, extension. CONTRACTION

distil condense, vaporize, sublimate, evaporate, purify, refine, brew, extract, draw out, separate.
drip, drop, dribble, trickle.

distinct clear, sharp, clear-cut, well-defined, plain, obvious, apparent, evident, definite, unmistakable, marked, conspicuous, noticeable, palpable, patent, lucid, unambiguous. INDISTINCT
separate, detached, individual, discrete, unconnected, different, dissimilar, unlike.

distinction differentiation, discrimination, discernment, separation, difference, dissimilarity, contrast.

characteristic, peculiarity, individuality, feature, quality, mark.
fame, renown, repute, reputation, eminence, note, prominence, celebrity, honour, credit, importance, account, merit, worth, superiority, greatness, excellence. INSIGNIFICANCE

distinctive distinguishing, characteristic, individual, particular, unique, idiosyncratic, notable, remarkable, different, unusual.

distinguish differentiate, tell apart, discriminate, judge, separate, divide, categorize, classify, single out, characterize, mark, set apart.
discern, perceive, see, descry, make out, detect, recognize.
honour, ennoble, dignify, celebrate, immortalize, make famous.

distinguished eminent, illustrious, notable, renowned, famous, well-known, celebrated, noted. UNKNOWN
dignified, august, stately, majestic, lordly, aristocratic, noble.
marked, conspicuous, striking, outstanding, signal.

distort deform, twist, contort, buckle, warp, misshape, bend, turn, wrest. STRAIGHTEN
falsify, misrepresent, pervert, colour, slant, misinterpret, garble.

distortion deformation, deformity, contortion, crookedness, twist, bend, buckle.
falsification, misrepresentation, perversion, misinterpretation, colouring, slant, bias.

distract divert, deflect, sidetrack, turn aside, draw away. FOCUS
amuse, entertain, occupy, engage, engross, absorb. BORE
confuse, perplex, bewilder, confound, disturb, discompose, harass, torment, derange, madden, craze. COMPOSE

distracted confused, perplexed, bewildered, troubled, agitated, flustered, harassed, overwrought, distraught, frantic, mad, deranged, crazy, insane. COMPOSED

distraction confusion, bewilderment, perplexity, discomposure, agitation, turmoil, abstraction, aberration, derangement, frenzy, desperation, delirium, madness, mania, lunacy, insanity. COMPOSURE
amusement, entertainment, diversion, pastime, recreation.
interruption, disturbance, diversion, interference, disruption.

distrait absent-minded, forgetful, abstracted, preoccupied, distracted, inattentive, oblivious.

distraught agitated, anxious, upset, overwrought, distracted, worked up, beside oneself, frantic, hysterical, wild, mad. CALM

distress *v*, upset, grieve, sadden, afflict, pain, harrow, disturb, trouble, worry, bother, torment, agonize, vex, harass. PLEASE
n, grief, sorrow, heartache, anguish, suffering, affliction, pain, agony, trouble, worry, anxiety, desolation, torment. JOY
adversity, hardship, privation, poverty, destitution, misfortune, disaster, calamity, trial, straits. RELIEF

distribute dispense, dole out, mete out, allot, share, divide, apportion, allocate, administer, give, assign. WITHHOLD
deliver, hand out, issue, pass round, circulate, disseminate, spread, scatter, disperse, diffuse. COLLECT
classify, sort, order, arrange, class, group.

distribution dispensation, dole, sharing, division, apportionment, allotment, allocation, assignment, administration.
circulation, spread, dissemination, dispersal, diffusion, scattering.
classification, grouping, arrangement, organization, location, disposition, situation.

district region, quarter, area, section, locality, community, neighbourhood, sector, ward, borough, zone.

distrust *v*, doubt, mistrust, disbelieve, question, suspect, be wary of. BELIEVE
n, doubt, mistrust, disbelief, suspicion, wariness, misgiving, scepticism. TRUST

distrustful suspicious, mistrustful, doubtful, dubious, sceptical, cynical, disbelieving, chary, wary. TRUSTFUL

disturb disrupt, interrupt, rouse, inconvenience, put out, bother, pester, harass, trouble, annoy, vex.
disarrange, derange, upset, disorder, unsettle, muddle, confuse. ARRANGE
worry, concern, trouble, agitate, upset, distress, alarm, perturb, discompose, ruffle, shake. CALM

disturbance disruption, upheaval, interruption, distraction, intrusion, inconvenience, bother, nuisance.

commotion, disorder, turmoil, tumult, riot, brawl, fray, fracas, uproar, hubbub, noise, racket. PEACE
agitation, confusion, discomposure, perturbation, derangement, upset. CALM

disunite separate, part, disjoin, disconnect, sever, split, sunder, detach, disengage, dissociate. JOIN
estrange, alienate, set at odds, embroil. UNITE

disuse desuetude, nonuse, neglect, abandonment, discontinuance. USE

ditch *n*, trench, dyke, channel, furrow, moat, drain, gully.
v, discard, get rid of, scrap, jettison, abandon, dump (*inf*).

dither waver, vacillate, hesitate, falter, shillyshally (*inf*). DECIDE
shiver, tremble, shake, quiver, shudder.

diurnal daily, quotidian, circadian, daytime, day-to-day.

dive plunge, submerge, dip, duck, plummet, descend, fall, drop, swoop, pitch, lunge, dart, jump.

diverge divide, separate, split, fork, branch, divaricate, part, spread, radiate, open. CONVERGE
deviate, digress, wander, stray, swerve, depart, veer, drift.
differ, vary, conflict, disagree, be at variance. AGREE

divergence division, separation, forking, branching, divarication, ramification, spreading. CONVERGENCE
deviation, digression, divagation, departure, deflection, difference, variation, disagreement.

divergent diverging, separating, branching, radial, spreading. CONVERGENT
different, conflicting, diverse, variant, disagreeing, differing, separate. CONCORDANT

divers sundry, various, different, manifold, multifarious, some, several, numerous, many.

diverse different, varied, assorted, mixed, miscellaneous, separate, distinct, discrete, unlike, dissimilar, divergent, varying. SIMILAR

diversify vary, variegate, chequer, assort, change, alter, modify, branch out.

diversion detour, deviation, digression, departure, deflection, alteration, variation.
amusement, entertainment, distraction, sport, play, recreation, pastime, relaxation, fun, pleasure, enjoyment. WORK

diversity variety, assortment, medley, miscellany, multiplicity, difference, variation, divergence, dissimilarity, unlikeness. SIMILARITY

divert deflect, turn aside, avert, sidetrack, distract, switch, redirect, shift, change.
amuse, entertain, distract, interest, occupy, beguile, delight, regale. BORE

divest strip, deprive, dispossess, denude, unclothe, undress, disrobe, doff, shed, take off. CLOTHE

divide separate, split, part, sever, cleave, disunite, cut, bisect, disjoin, detach, disconnect, divert, branch, fork. JOIN
share, apportion, distribute, dispense, deal out, allot, allocate, parcel out. COLLECT
alienate, estrange, come between, disunite, split, set at odds. UNITE
categorize, classify, group, arrange, sort, dispose.

dividend share, portion, cut (*inf*), surplus, gain, bonus, extra.

divination prophecy, prediction, augury, divining, soothsaying, fortune-telling, clairvoyance.

divine *adj*, godlike, godly, supernatural, superhuman, spiritual, angelic, heavenly, celestial, transcendent, mystical. EARTHLY
holy, sacred, religious, consecrated, hallowed, sanctified. PROFANE
lofty, exalted, supreme, rapturous, ecstatic, blissful, beatific.
splendid, wonderful, excellent, gorgeous, beautiful, perfect. DRFADFUL
v, predict, foretell, prophesy, prognosticate, surmise, guess, conjecture, suspect, intuit, discern, perceive.

diviner prophet, seer, soothsayer, clairvoyant, fortune-teller, augur, oracle, astrologer.

divinity god, goddess, deity, spirit, angel, godhead, godhood, godliness, holiness.
theology, religion.

division section, part, segment, portion, group, class, category, branch, department, sector, compartment, partition, border, boundary.
separation, parting, partition, dividing, disunion, disconnection, detachment, severance, split. UNION

distribution, sharing, apportionment, allotment. COLLECTION
breach, rupture, split, feud, discord, variance, disagreement, disunion, estrangement. UNITY
divorce *v*, separate, divide, part, split up, split, disunite, sever, dissociate, detach. JOIN
n, dissolution, annulment, split, disunion, separation, break-up. MARRIAGE
divulge disclose, reveal, make known, communicate, tell, impart, leak, betray, let slip, confess, declare, proclaim, expose, uncover, publish, broadcast. CONCEAL
dizzy giddy, light-headed, reeling, vertiginous, shaky, unsteady, faint, woozy (*inf*).
confused, bewildered, bemused, dazed, befuddled. CLEAR-HEADED
foolish, silly, scatterbrained, fickle, flighty, capricious. RELIABLE
do *v*, perform, execute, carry out, fulfil, attain, accomplish, achieve, effect, complete, conclude, finish, end, work at, practice. NEGLECT
act, behave, comport oneself, conduct oneself.
suffice, serve, be adequate, satisfy, suit, answer.
prepare, make, fix, arrange, organize, see to, look after, produce, create, cause.
cheat, swindle, defraud, diddle (*inf*), con (*inf*), dupe, deceive, hoax.
manage, get along, proceed, fare, make out.
do away with, get rid of, dispose of, dispense with, discard, abolish, remove, eliminate, destroy, kill, murder.
do in, tire, exhaust, weary, fatigue, shatter (*inf*).
kill, murder, slay, slaughter, eliminate (*inf*), bump off (*inf*).
do up, tie, lace, fasten, wrap, pack, enclose.
renovate, restore, modernize, redecorate, refurbish, adorn, beautify.
do without, forgo, abstain from, give up, dispense with.
n, party, function, soirée, gathering, event, affair.
do's and don'ts, rules, regulations, customs, etiquette, code, policy.
docile tractable, manageable, amenable, compliant, submissive, yielding, ductile, pliant, obedient, biddable, meek, passive. OBSTINATE
docility tractability, manageability, amenability, compliance, submissiveness, obedience, meekness, passiveness. OBSTINACY
dock[1] *v*, clip, crop, cut off, shorten, curtail, reduce, diminish, decrease, lessen, deduct, subtract. INCREASE
dock[2] *n*, wharf, pier, quay, harbour.
v, moor, berth, anchor, tie up, land.
doctor *n*, physician, GP, locum, medic (*inf*), surgeon, specialist, consultant.
v, alter, tamper with, falsify, distort, fudge, adulterate, cut.
fix, repair, mend, patch up.
doctrinaire dogmatic, insistent, opinionated, overbearing, inflexible, intolerant. AMENABLE
theoretical, hypothetical, speculative, unrealistic, impractical. REALISTIC
doctrine dogma, creed, tenet, principle, precept, teaching, canon, belief, opinion, conviction.
document *n*, paper, certificate, instrument, record, charter, deed, credential.
v, support, back up, substantiate, corroborate, authenticate, validate.
doddering weak, feeble, shaky, infirm, unsteady, tottering, decrepit, aged, senile. ROBUST
dodge *v*, evade, elude, avoid, shirk, hedge, equivocate, parry, fend off, duck, dart, sidestep, swerve. FACE
n, artifice, trick, ruse, wile, stratagem, ploy, device.
dodgy risky, dangerous, delicate, dicey (*inf*), difficult, tricky, uncertain, unreliable. SAFE
doer performer, agent, operator, achiever, entrepreneur, go-getter (*inf*), dynamo (*inf*). IDLER
doff raise, lift, take off, remove, shed, cast off, disrobe, undress, strip, divest. DON
dog *n*, hound, cur, mongrel, whelp, pup, puppy, bitch, canine, mutt (*inf*), pooch (*inf*).
v, follow, pursue, trail, track, hound, plague, haunt, trouble.
dogged determined, resolute, intent, tenacious, firm, steadfast, persevering, persistent, unwavering, indefatigable, set, wilful, headstrong, stubborn, obstinate, inflexible, unyielding. APATHETIC
dogma doctrine, creed, principle, tenet, code, precept, teaching, belief, opinion, article of faith.

dogmatic assertive, opinionated, obdurate, emphatic, positive, insistent, doctrinaire, arbitrary, overbearing, imperious, authoritative, categorical, peremptory, dictatorial, arrogant, intolerant. AMENABLE

doing action, act, deed, exploit, achievement, accomplishment, work, handiwork, performance, event, concern, affair, dealing, transaction.

dole *n*, allowance, benefit, grant, subsidy, handout (*inf*), charity, alms, donation, gift. WAGE

share, portion, quota, allotment, allocation, apportionment, distribution, dispensation, division.

v, distribute, dispense, apportion, allot, assign, share, divide, deal, mete, administer. WITHHOLD

doleful gloomy, melancholy, sad, miserable, unhappy, sorrowful, woebegone, dejected, depressed, dismal, dreary, cheerless, lugubrious, mournful, wretched, dolorous, pitiful, pathetic. JOYFUL

dolorous painful, harrowing, grievous, distressing, doleful, melancholy, mournful, sad, miserable, woebegone, wretched. HAPPY

dolt fool, idiot, simpleton, blockhead, ass, dunce, dullard, ignoramus, clot (*inf*), dope (*inf*), nincompoop. GENIUS

doltish foolish, idiotic, simple, blockish, asinine, dull, halfwitted, brainless, dense, thick, dopey (*inf*), dumb (*inf*). CLEVER

domain dominion, kingdom, realm, empire, land, territory, demesne, estate, province, region.

area, field, sphere, department, concern, specialty, discipline, jurisdiction, authority.

domestic *adj*, home, family, household, domiciliary, private, home-loving. PUBLIC

domesticated, tame, pet, house-trained. WILD

internal, civil, native, indigenous, home-grown, home-made. FOREIGN

n, servant, maid, housekeeper, charwoman, help, menial, drudge.

domesticate tame, house-train, train, break in, habituate, familiarize, accustom, acclimatize, naturalize.

domicile abode, home, residence, dwelling, house, habitation, quarters, lodgings, address.

dominant commanding, controlling, ruling, governing, supreme, paramount, predominant, prevailing, prevalent, principal, chief, main, primary, leading, ascendant, assertive, authoritative. SUBORDINATE

dominate control, rule, govern, reign, command, direct, master, domineer, subdue, tyrannize, subjugate, crush, suppress, monopolize, prevail, predominate, override, overshadow, eclipse.

bestride, tower above, overlook, survey, loom over.

domination power, authority, dominion, ascendancy, supremacy, sway, rule, control, influence, mastery.

tyranny, despotism, oppression, subjugation, subjection, subordination. SUBMISSION

domineer tyrannize, oppress, overbear, dominate, browbeat, intimidate, bully, hector. SUBMIT

domineering overbearing, imperious, tyrannical, authoritarian, dictatorial, lordly, magisterial, high-handed, masterful, bossy (*inf*), haughty, arrogant. MEEK

dominion power, authority, domination, ascendancy, supremacy, sway, rule, control, mastery, command, jurisdiction.

domain, country, territory, province, realm, kingdom, empire.

don put on, get into, slip on, dress in, wear. DOFF

donate give, bestow, bequeath, grant, confer, present, contribute, subscribe. RECEIVE

donation gift, present, grant, bequest, contribution, offering, subscription, benefaction, alms, charity.

done finished, over, through, ended, completed, concluded, accomplished. UNFINISHED

cooked, ready.

exhausted, spent, drained, depleted.

conventional, acceptable, proper.

done for, ruined, wrecked, broken, destroyed, lost, foiled, dashed, beaten, defeated, undone, finished.

done in, tired out, exhausted, worn out, all in (*inf*), dead beat (*inf*), knackered (*inf*).

donkey ass, mule, jackass, dunce, fool, blockhead, dolt, simpleton, dullard, dope (*inf*), nincompoop. GENIUS

donor giver, donator, benefactor, contributor. RECIPIENT

doom *v*, destine, ordain, fate, damn, condemn, sentence, judge, decree.
n, fate, destiny, fortune, lot, ruin, destruction, death.
judgment, verdict, decision, sentence, condemnation.

door entrance, exit, doorway, opening, hatch, gate, portal.

dope *n*, drug, narcotic, opiate, barbiturate, sedative, stimulant.
dolt, nincompoop, blockhead, fool, idiot, simpleton, dunce. GENIUS
facts, information, details, news, gen (*inf*), info (*inf*).
v, sedate, drug, narcotize, anaesthetize, stupefy.

dormant sleeping, asleep, hibernating, resting, quiescent, latent, inactive, inert, sluggish, torpid. ACTIVE

dose draught, measure, portion, quantity, dosage, drench.

dot *n*, point, spot, speck, mark, fleck, jot, iota, atom.
on the dot, punctually, promptly, precisely, exactly, on time.
v, spot, speckle, fleck, stud, pepper, sprinkle, scatter.

dotage senility, caducity, old age, decrepitude, feebleness, imbecility, second childhood. YOUTH

dote idolize, adore, love, treasure, hold dear, indulge, pamper, spoil. LOATHE

double *adj*, twice, twofold, dual, duplex, coupled, paired, twin, doubled. SINGLE
deceitful, false, insincere, hypocritical, two-faced, dishonest. HONEST
v, duplicate, fold, repeat, multiply, enlarge, magnify, increase. HALVE
n, twin, duplicate, copy, counterpart, replica, clone, look-alike, Doppelgänger, dead ringer (*inf*), spitting image (*inf*).
at the double, quickly, briskly, posthaste, without delay, immediately. SLOWLY

double-cross cheat, hoodwink, trick, swindle, defraud, betray.

doublet jacket, jerkin, waistcoat.

doubt *vt*, suspect, question, query, mistrust, distrust, disbelieve, discredit. TRUST
vi, waver, vacillate, hesitate, demur, be uncertain, scruple, lack conviction. RESOLVE
n, suspicion, mistrust, distrust, misgiving, qualm, uncertainty, hesitation, vacillation, irresolution, indecision, dubiety, doubtfulness, disbelief, scepticism. TRUST

doubtful uncertain, unsure, undecided, irresolute, wavering, vacillating, distrustful, suspicious, sceptical. CERTAIN
dubious, questionable, debatable, unlikely, improbable, vague, obscure, ambiguous, equivocal, unsettled, problematic. DEFINITE

doubtless certainly, surely, indisputably, undoubtedly, assuredly, clearly, of course, without doubt. MAYBE
probably, most likely, apparently, seemingly, presumably.

doughty brave, bold, valiant, valourous, courageous, heroic, intrepid, fearless, dauntless, hardy, resolute, redoubtable, gallant. TIMOROUS

dour sullen, morose, sour, gloomy, grim, forbidding.
hard, inflexible, austere, rigorous, harsh, strict, severe, unyielding, obstinate.

douse souse, dip, plunge, duck, immerse, submerge, soak, drench.
extinguish, snuff, put out, blow out. LIGHT

dowdy shabby, untidy, slovenly, drab, dingy, frumpish, frowzy, old-fashioned. SMART

dower estate, property, legacy, inheritance, bequest, provision, settlement, dowry.
gift, talent, faculty, knack, endowment.

down[1] *adv*, downwards, low, below, beneath, under, to the ground. UP
adj, depressed, dejected, downcast, sad, miserable, unhappy, low, blue. CHEERFUL
down and out, destitute, impoverished, penniless, derelict. WEALTHY
n, descent, drop, fall, decline, reverse. RISE
v, prostrate, fell, knock down, floor, bring down, overthrow, subdue.
drink, swallow, gulp, put away.

down[2] *n*, feathers, fluff, fur, fuzz.

downcast dejected, downhearted, depressed, discouraged, disheartened, dispirited, crestfallen, unhappy, sad, miserable, despondent. HAPPY

downfall fall, ruin, destruction, collapse, debacle, overthrow, undoing. RISE

downgrade degrade, demote, humble, lower. UPGRADE
denigrate, disparage, belittle, depreciate, run down, decry. PRAISE

downhearted discouraged, disheartened, dispirited, despondent, depressed, dejected, downcast, crestfallen, sad, unhappy, miserable. CHEERFUL

downpour cloudburst, deluge, torrent, flood, inundation, pouring rain.

downright absolute, positive, utter, categorical, outright, complete, total, thorough, sheer, unqualified, clear, plain, unequivocal.
candid, frank, open, honest, blunt, straightforward, forthright, plain-spoken, sincere. EVASIVE

downward descending, declining, slipping, sliding, down. UPWARD

dowry dot, marriage portion, marriage settlement, gift, endowment.

doze *v*, drowse, nap, catnap, snooze (*inf*), sleep, slumber. WAKE
n, nap, catnap, forty winks (*inf*), snooze (*inf*), siesta.

drab dull, dingy, dreary, flat, colourless, grey, lacklustre, dark, gloomy, cheerless, dismal. BRIGHT

draft *v*, draw, sketch, outline, delineate, draw up, put together, prepare, frame, plan, compose, formulate, write.
n, sketch, outline, plan, rough, delineation, skeleton.
bill of exchange, cheque, money order.

drag *v*, draw, pull, haul, heave, lug, tug, tow, trail. PUSH
crawl, shuffle, creep, inch, plod, trudge, lag, linger, loiter, dawdle. HURRY
prolong, protract, spin out, draw out, lengthen, stretch out, extend.
n, bore, nuisance, bother, annoyance, pain (*inf*).

draggle bedraggle, begrime, drabble, soil, dirty, befoul, trail.
lag, dawdle, straggle, trail, dilly-dally (*inf*). HURRY

dragoon force, compel, coerce, drive, impel, constrain, bully, browbeat. COAX

drain *v*, empty, draw off, pump out, remove, evacuate, dry, strain, tap, bleed, milk. FILL
exhaust, sap, deplete, consume, expend.
drip, trickle, seep, leak, exude, discharge, flow out.
n, channel, culvert, duct, conduit, pipe, gutter, ditch, sewer, outlet.
depletion, exhaustion, strain, reduction, expenditure.

drama play, show, piece, work, dramatization.
acting, theatre, dramaturgy, stagecraft, histrionics, dramatics, theatrics, scene, spectacle, excitement, crisis.

dramatic theatrical, Thespian, histrionic, dramaturgic.
striking, vivid, effective, impressive, spectacular, breathtaking, powerful, exciting, sensational, melodramatic, sudden, startling. UNIMPRESSIVE

drape hang, cover, clothe, dress, adorn, deck, festoon, array, shroud, cloak, wrap. DIVEST
drop, hang, droop, dangle, suspend.

drastic extreme, radical, violent, forceful, powerful, strong, severe, intensive, desperate. MODERATE

draught breath, puff, air current, movement, flow, breeze.
drink, potion, dose, drench, quantity, cup.
pulling, drawing, haulage, traction.

draw *v*, pull, drag, haul, tow, tug, heave. PUSH
attract, allure, entice, invite, tempt, induce, persuade, influence, elicit, call forth, evoke. REPEL
sketch, delineate, map out, outline, trace, depict, portray, represent.
extract, pull out, take out.
inhale, breathe in, inspire, suck, drain, siphon, draw off.
move, go, come, proceed, advance, approach.
deduce, infer, conclude, derive, glean, get, take.
pick, choose, select, take.
draw back, recoil, shrink, retreat, withdraw, retract.
draw out, protract, extend, prolong, drag out, spin out, stretch, lengthen.
draw up, draft, compose, formulate, prepare.
halt, stop, pull up.
n, attraction, pull, lure, influence, magnetism, charisma.
tie, stalemate, dead heat.
raffle, lottery, sweepstake.

drawback disadvantage, snag, hitch, hindrance, impediment, obstacle, flaw, fault, imperfection, defect, difficulty, problem, detriment, shortcoming, deficiency. ADVANTAGE

drawing sketch, picture, delineation, outline, diagram, plan, illustration, cartoon, representation, portrait.

drawl drag, protract, draw out, prolong, lengthen, drone, twang. GABBLE
dread *v*, fear, quail, tremble, shudder, apprehend, anticipate.
n, fear, terror, horror, fright, alarm, apprehension, trepidation, misgiving, qualm. CONFIDENCE
adj, dreaded, dreadful, fearful, awful, terrible, alarming, frightful, dire.
dreadful awful, terrible, frightful, horrible, dire, appalling, shocking, alarming, ghastly, horrendous, monstrous, atrocious, distressing, tragic, formidable, tremendous, terrific. WONDERFUL
dream *n*, vision, illusion, delusion, hallucination, fantasy, trance, reverie, daydream, fancy, notion, nightmare. REALITY
ambition, goal, target, aspiration, hope, wish.
v, imagine, envisage, visualize, fancy, conceive, think, conjure up, fantasize, hallucinate, daydream.
dream up, invent, create, devise, concoct, think up, hatch.
dreamer visionary, idealist, utopian, daydreamer, romancer, fantast. REALIST
dreary dull, flat, drab, colourless, monotonous, boring, tedious, uninteresting, wearisome, routine, humdrum. EXCITING
gloomy, sombre, dark, cheerless, comfortless, bleak, dismal, uninviting, depressing, chilling. BRIGHT
dregs sediment, residue, lees, grounds, draff, dross, refuse, waste, deposit, scum, leavings, remains.
rabble, riffraff, *canaille*, good-for-nothings, scum.
drench soak, wet, saturate, steep, douse, souse, submerge, inundate, drown. DRY
dress *v*, clothe, garb, rig, fit, turn out, attire, robe, drape, cover, array, deck, adorn, decorate. STRIP
arrange, dispose, adjust, straighten, align, prepare, groom, comb. DISARRANGE
treat, bandage, plaster, strap up, attend to. NEGLECT
n, frock, gown, costume, suit, outfit.
clothes, clothing, attire, garb, apparel, garments, wardrobe, costume, guise, habit, vestments, gear (*inf*), togs (*inf*).
dressing sauce, relish, condiment, garnish.
bandage, plaster, compress, covering.
manure, fertilizer, compost, dung, muck.
dribble trickle, drip, drop, ooze, seep, run.
drool, slaver, slobber, drivel.
driblet scrap, bit, morsel, fragment, piece, dash, trace, drop.
drift *v*, wander, meander, stray, digress, float, coast, waft.
accumulate, pile up, amass, gather, drive, bank up.
n, trend, tendency, bearing, course, direction, flow, movement, current, rush, sweep, drive.
meaning, intention, purpose, aim, design, tenor, gist, implication, significance, import.
bank, mound, pile, heap, mass, accumulation.
drill *v*, teach, instruct, train, coach, rehearse, exercise, discipline, school.
bore, pierce, perforate, puncture, penetrate.
n, instruction, training, coaching, exercise, practice, repetition, discipline.
borer, bit, gimlet, rotary tool.
drink *vt*, imbibe, quaff, sup, swallow, gulp, swig (*inf*), sip, drain, absorb, take in, assimilate.
vi, tipple, tope, indulge, booze (*inf*), carouse, revel.
drink to, toast, pledge, salute, drink the health of.
n, potion, beverage, liquid, refreshment.
draught, sip, gulp, glass, cup.
alcohol, liquor, spirits, booze (*inf*).
drip *v*, drop, dribble, trickle, filter, percolate, seep, ooze, sprinkle.
n, drop, trickle, dribble.
weakling, milksop, weed (*inf*), wet (*inf*), bore.
drive *v*, propel, push, thrust, send, hurl, impel, herd, shepherd, pilot, steer, direct, guide, control, handle, operate, ride, motor.
force, oblige, constrain, urge, coerce, press, compel, dragoon, goad, spur, motivate. DETER
n, ride, jaunt, outing, excursion, journey, trip, run, spin (*inf*).
vigour, energy, effort, enterprise, initiative, ambition, get-up-and-go (*inf*). APATHY
campaign, crusade, effort, appeal, action.
drivel *v*, dribble, slaver, slobber, drool.
prate, babble, jabber, chatter, ramble, waffle (*inf*).

n, nonsense, gibberish, twaddle, balderdash, rubbish, rot (*inf*). SENSE
slaver, slobber, dribble, saliva.
drizzle *n*, mist, spray, light rain.
v, spit, spot, rain, sprinkle, spray.
droll comical, amusing, funny, humorous, clownish, ridiculous, ludicrous, laughable, farcical, zany, whimsical, quaint, odd. SERIOUS
drollery comedy, humour, fun, buffoonery, farce, wit, waggishness.
drone[1] *n*, parasite, leech, sponger (*inf*), shirker, idler, loafer, sluggard, lounger. WORKER
drone[2] *v* + *n*, hum, buzz, whirr, purr, murmur, thrum.
drool dribble, slaver, slobber, drivel, salivate.
droop sag, sink, drop, bow, bend, hang, wilt, fade, wither, languish, weaken, faint, flag, decline, slump. FLOURISH
drop *v*, fall, sink, droop, decline, lower, diminish, lessen, subside, descend, dive, plummet, plunge, tumble. RISE
drip, trickle, dribble.
abandon, desert, forsake, relinquish, give up, discontinue, cease, forbear, quit. CONTINUE
discharge, deposit, set down, unload, let off, leave.
drop off, fall asleep, drowse, doze, catnap, nod off, snooze (*inf*).
decline, decrease, lessen, dwindle, fall off.
n, bead, pearl, globule, drip, droplet, blob, driblet, spot, dash, trickle, trace, bit, sip, tot, draught, nip.
fall, decline, slump, fall-off, decrease, reduction, diminution, deterioration. RISE
dross scum, waste, dregs, lees, scoria, refuse, recrement.
drought aridity, dryness, parchedness, dehydration. DELUGE
shortage, deficiency, dearth, scarcity, lack, want. GLUT
drove herd, flock, pack, swarm, crowd, mob, horde, multitude, throng.
drown submerge, immerse, sink, go under, engulf, inundate, flood, deluge, swamp.
overwhelm, overpower, overcome, muffle, stifle, suppress, silence, obliterate, wipe out.
drowse be sleepy, be drowsy, doze, nap, sleep, slumber, snooze (*inf*). WAKE
drowsy sleepy, tired, dozy, somnolent, comatose, lethargic, sluggish, torpid, heavy, dull, dazed, dopey (*inf*), groggy (*inf*). ALERT
soporific, hypnotic, dreamy, soothing, restful.
drub beat, club, cudgel, pound, pummel, cane, flog, thrash, whack, hit, strike.
defeat, beat, trounce, rout, lick (*inf*), hammer (*inf*).
drudge *v*, toil, slave, labour, plod, work. IDLE
n, toiler, plodder, labourer, slave, factotum, dogsbody (*inf*), menial, hack. IDLER
drudgery toil, hard work, labour, chore, slog, fag (*inf*), grind (*inf*), slavery.
drug *n*, medicine, medication, medicament, remedy, cure, physic.
narcotic, opiate, barbiturate, amphetamine, sedative, stimulant, dope (*inf*).
v, sedate, stupefy, dope (*inf*), narcotize, anaesthetize, deaden, benumb, dull.
drum *n*, tambour, tabor, kettledrum, tympanum, tom-tom.
v, beat, tap, thrum, hammer.
drum into, instil, drive home, reiterate, harp on, din into.
drum out, cashier, discharge, expel, dismiss, oust.
drum up, obtain, round up, canvass, solicit, petition.
drunk *adj*, drunken, boozy (*inf*), inebriated, intoxicated, tipsy, tiddly (*inf*), merry (*inf*), tight (*inf*), plastered (*inf*), well-oiled (*inf*), blotto (*inf*). SOBER
n, drunkard, inebriate, alcoholic, dipsomaniac, boozer (*inf*), wino (*inf*).
drunkard drunk, drinker, inebriate, tippler, toper, sot, alcoholic, dipsomaniac, boozer (*inf*), wino (*inf*). TEETOTALLER
drunkenness inebriety, intoxication, intemperance, alcoholism, dipsomania. TEMPERANCE
dry *adj*, arid, parched, thirsty, dehydrated, desiccated, waterless, barren. WET
dull, flat, boring, tedious, tiresome, uninteresting, plain, dreary, vapid, insipid, jejune. INTERESTING
witty, droll, sharp, keen, cutting, ironic, sarcastic, satirical.
v, parch, dehydrate, exsiccate, desiccate, drain. SOAK
sponge, towel, wipe, blot, mop. WET

dual double, twofold, duplex, binary, twin, paired. SINGLE

dub name, christen, entitle, designate, denominate, nickname, style, call, term.

dubious doubtful, uncertain, hesitant, wavering, vacillating, undecided, unsettled, sceptical, suspicious. CERTAIN
questionable, debatable, ambiguous, equivocal, suspect, unreliable, untrustworthy, shady (*inf*), fishy (*inf*). TRUSTWORTHY

duck dip, dunk, immerse, plunge, dive, submerge, douse, souse.
bob, crouch, stoop, bow, bend. STRAIGHTEN
dodge, avoid, evade, shirk, parry, sidestep. FACE

duct conduit, pipe, tube, canal, channel, passage.

ductile malleable, plastic, flexible, pliant, extensible.
compliant, yielding, tractable, docile, amenable, accommodating, passive. OBDURATE

dudgeon anger, wrath, ire, indignation, resentment.
in high dudgeon, angry, irate, vexed, indignant, resentful.

due *adj*. owing, owed, payable, unpaid, outstanding, in arrears. PAID
rightful, fitting, proper, apposite, appropriate, apt, justified, merited, deserved, requisite, obligatory. UNDUE
adequate, sufficient, enough, ample. INSUFFICIENT
scheduled, expected, anticipated.
n, right, prerogative, just deserts, comeuppance (*inf*).

duel combat, contest, fight, affair of honour.

dulcet sweet, pleasant, agreeable, delightful, charming, melodious, harmonious, euphonious, mellifluous, soothing, soft. RAUCOUS

dull *adj*, gloomy, dark, drab, murky, grey, overcast, cloudy, opaque, faded, dim, dismal, cheerless. BRIGHT
blunt, dulled, muted, subdued, indistinct, muffled. SHARP
obtuse, stolid, stupid, slow, thick, dense, witless, unintelligent. CLEVER
boring, uninteresting, dry, dreary, vapid, jejune, plain, flat, humdrum, prosaic, insipid. INTERESTING
insensitive, numb, callous, dead, unfeeling, insensible, apathetic, listless, sluggish, lethargic, torpid, slow, heavy, inactive, inert. LIVELY
v, blunt, alleviate, assuage, mitigate, lessen, soften, moderate, reduce, ease. AGGRAVATE
benumb, deaden, paralyse, stupefy, sedate, drug.
depress, deject, dispirit, dishearten, discourage, dampen. CHEER
dim, fade, cloud, obscure, tarnish, stain. BRIGHTEN

dullard dunce, simpleton, ignoramus, dolt, blockhead, dope (*inf*). GENIUS

duly rightly, properly, fittingly, appropriately, accordingly. UNDULY

dumb silent, mute, speechless, voiceless, inarticulate, tongue-tied. ARTICULATE
stupid, foolish, unintelligent, dull, thick, dense, ignorant. INTELLIGENT

dumbfound astonish, astound, amaze, stun, stagger, take aback, bowl over (*inf*), flabbergast (*inf*), nonplus, confuse, bewilder.

dummy figure, model, mannequin.
sham, counterfeit, substitute, imitation, copy, duplicate, sample.
dolt, dullard, blockhead, fool, simpleton, dunce.

dump *v*, drop, deposit, throw down, discharge, unload, empty out, tip.
scrap, jettison, get rid of, dispose of. KEEP
n, tip, rubbish heap, junkyard.
hovel, pigsty, slum, hole (*inf*).

dun urge, press, importune, pester.

dunce ignoramus, dullard, simpleton, idiot, fool, blockhead, dolt, halfwit, dimwit (*inf*). GENIUS

dung muck, excrement, ordure, manure, fertilizer.

dungeon cell, cage, oubliette, prison, jail, donjon, keep.

dupe *v*. cheat, deceive, hoodwink, trick, fool, cozen, beguile, delude, outwit, overreach, bamboozle (*inf*), con (*inf*).
n, victim, fool, simpleton, sucker (*inf*), pushover (*inf*).

duplicate *v*, copy, replicate, clone, reproduce, photocopy, double, repeat, echo.
adj, identical, twin, matching, double, duplex, twofold.

n, copy, replica, facsimile, carbon, photocopy, transcript, reproduction, clone, twin, double, look-alike. ORIGINAL

duplicity deceit, deception, double-dealing, guile, trickery, fraud, artifice, chicanery, hypocrisy, dissimulation, dishonesty. HONESTY

durable lasting, enduring, abiding, persistent, resistant, long-lasting, strong, stout, sturdy, substantial, firm, stable, constant, reliable, permanent. PERISHABLE

duration continuance, term, spell, period, time, span, stretch, length, extent, course.

duress constraint, coercion, compulsion, pressure, force.
imprisonment, detention, confinement, incarceration, captivity, restraint. FREEDOM

during throughout, in, through, over.

dusk twilight, nightfall, sunset, evening, eventide, gloaming, gloom, shade, darkness, obscurity. DAWN

dusky swarthy, dark, dark-skinned. PALE
dark, dim, gloomy, shadowy, murky, cloudy, overcast, obscure, tenebrous. LIGHT

dust *n*, powder, particles, dirt, earth, soil.
v, sprinkle, dredge, sift, scatter, spread, powder.
clean, wipe, sweep, brush.

dutiful obedient, respectful, deferential, filial, conscientious, faithful, devoted, submissive, docile, compliant, obliging. DISOBEDIENT

duty obligation, responsibility, onus, trust, charge, role, part, function, task, business, mission, calling, office, assignment, commission, service.
respect, deference, obedience, allegiance, loyalty.
tax, impost, excise, customs, toll, tariff.

dwarf *n*, midget, pygmy, manikin, homunculus, runt. GIANT
v, dominate, overshadow, bestride, tower over, rise above, diminish.
stunt, retard, check.

dwarfish stunted, undersized, pygmy, miniature, small, little, tiny, diminutive, Lilliputian. GIGANTIC

dwell live, reside, inhabit, lodge, abide, sojourn, tarry, stay, remain, settle, stop. MOVE
expatiate, elaborate, harp, descant, linger.

dwelling abode, residence, house, home, lodgings, quarters, domicile, habitation.

dwindle diminish, decrease, lessen, shrink, wane, ebb, decline, fade, peter out, shrivel, wither, waste away. INCREASE

dye *n*, colour, colouring, pigment, tint, stain, tinge, hue, shade.
v, stain, tint, colour.

dying moribund, expiring, fading, sinking, going, at death's door, *in extremis*, last, final.

dynamic forceful, powerful, energetic, vigorous, lively, spirited, driving, go-ahead, electric. LETHARGIC

dynasty house, line, succession, empire, ascendancy, dominion, rule, sway, government, sovereignty.

E

each *pron*, every one, one and all.
adj, every, individual, separate.
adv, apiece, per person, per capita, individually, singly, respectively.

eager desirous, longing, yearning, impatient, avid, ardent, earnest, fervent, keen, enthusiastic, anxious, agog, vehement, zealous. INDIFFERENT

eagerness longing, yearning, impatience, avidity, ardour, earnestness, fervour, keenness, enthusiasm, vehemence, zeal. INDIFFERENCE

ear heed, attention, notice, regard, consideration.
sensitivity, discrimination, taste, appreciation.

early *adj*, premature, forward, advanced, precocious, untimely. LATE
primitive, primordial, primeval, ancient, initial, first. LATEST
adv, in advance, beforehand, too soon, prematurely. LATE

earn gain, get, obtain, procure, acquire, achieve, win, deserve, merit. FORFEIT
make, yield, bring in, gross, net, take home (*inf*). PAY

earnest[1] *adj*, serious, intent, determined, resolute, fixed, passionate, fervent, ardent, eager, avid, keen, dedicated, committed. CASUAL
sincere, serious, solemn, heartfelt, profound, warm. FLIPPANT

n, seriousness, earnestness, sincerity, truth, reality, determination, resolution.

earnest² pledge, promise, assurance, security, deposit, guarantee.

earnings pay, wages, salary, remuneration, emolument, stipend, income, profits, receipts, proceeds, return. EXPENDITURE

earth land, ground, soil, dirt, clay, loam, turf, sod.
world, globe, planet, sphere, orb, mankind, people.

earthly terrestrial, tellurian, worldly, mundane, temporal, material, materialistic, physical, fleshly, carnal. SPIRITUAL

earthy coarse, crude, lusty, robust, uninhibited, ribald, bawdy, vulgar, rude, rough, down-to-earth, unsophisticated. REFINED

ease *v*, alleviate, allay, assuage, soothe, mitigate, relieve, comfort, moderate, abate, appease, calm, still, lessen, reduce, diminish, lighten, disburden. AGGRAVATE
facilitate, assist, aid, simplify, smooth, expedite, speed up, advance, forward. HINDER
n, comfort, relief, peace, tranquillity, quiet, rest, repose, relaxation, content, contentment, serenity, complacency. DISQUIET
facility, readiness, easiness, dexterity, proficiency. DIFFICULTY
freedom, liberty, unconstraint, affluence, opulence, wealth, prosperity, luxury. CONSTRAINT

easily with ease, readily, effortlessly, simply, without difficulty.
by far, far and away, indisputably, undoubtedly, clearly, plainly, obviously, without a doubt. POSSIBLY

easy simple, effortless, straightforward, uncomplicated, facile, light, smooth, child's play (*inf*), a piece of cake (*inf*). DIFFICULT
tranquil, quiet, serene, untroubled, contented, comfortable, relaxed, secure. UNEASY
tolerant, lenient, indulgent, permissive, light, mild, gentle, easy-going, relaxed, casual, unaffected, natural. STRICT
compliant, tractable, yielding, submissive, docile, amenable, biddable, gullible, trusting. INTRACTABLE
leisurely, unhurried, moderate, gentle, undemanding, comfortable. STRENUOUS

easy-going relaxed, calm, carefree, nonchalant, happy-go-lucky, casual, easy, tolerant, flexible, amenable. STRICT

eat consume, devour, eat up, scoff (*inf*), chew, munch, masticate, swallow, ingest.
feed, dine, lunch, breakfast, feast.
erode, corrode, wear away, eat away, rot, decay, destroy, use up, eat into.

eatable edible, comestible, esculent, wholesome, palatable. UNEATABLE

eavesdrop listen in, overhear, pry, snoop (*inf*), spy, tap (*inf*), bug (*inf*).

ebb *v*, recede, retreat, retire, withdraw, flow back, go out. FLOW
subside, abate, sink, decline, fall, flag, fade, wane, decrease, diminish, dwindle, peter out. GROW
n, regression, recession, reflux, abatement, decline, fall, drop, wane, decrease, diminution, dwindling, weakening, degeneration. INCREASE

ebullience exuberance, enthusiasm, excitement, vivacity, exhilaration, buoyancy, high spirits. LETHARGY
boiling, ebullition, fermentation, effervescence.

ebullient exuberant, enthusiastic, excited, irrepressible, vivacious, effusive, exhilarated, buoyant, elated. LETHARGIC
boiling, seething, bubbling, effervescent.

ebullition boiling, seething, ebullience, effervescence.
outburst, explosion, fit, paroxysm, outbreak, storm, rage.

eccentric *adj*, irregular, abnormal, aberrant, strange, odd, peculiar, singular, bizarre, weird, freakish, whimsical, unconventional, idiosyncratic, wayward, capricious. NORMAL
n, character, oddity, original, weirdo (*inf*), freak (*inf*), crank (*inf*).

eccentricity irregularity, abnormality, oddity, peculiarity, singularity, weirdness, whimsicality, unconventionality, idiosyncrasy, quirk, caprice. NORMALITY

ecclesiastic *n*, clergyman, cleric, churchman, divine, priest, parson, minister. LAYMAN
adj, ecclesiastical, clerical, religious, holy, spiritual, divine. SECULAR

echo *v*, resound, reverberate, ring, repeat, reflect.
copy, imitate, ape, mimic, mirror, parallel, resemble.
n, resonance, reverberation, repetition, reflection.

copy, imitation, reproduction, replica, parallel, counterpart, semblance, likeness, reminder, repercussion.

éclat splendour, brilliance, lustre, pomp, pageantry, show, display, ostentation, effect.
glory, fame, renown, celebrity, acclaim, acclamation, applause. OBLOQUY

eclectic complex, multifarious, diverse, varied, heterogeneous, comprehensive, all-embracing, catholic, broad, wide-ranging, general.

eclipse *v*, obscure, blot out, block, hide, veil, shadow, darken, dim, extinguish.
surpass, transcend, excel, outstrip, outdo, overshadow, outshine.
n, obscuration, occultation, shading, darkening, concealment, obliteration, extinction.
decline, fall, loss, overshadowing.

economic monetary, financial, fiscal, pecuniary, budgetary, commercial, industrial, mercantile.
profitable, viable, productive, remunerative. UNECONOMIC
cheap, inexpensive, low-priced, reasonable. DEAR

economical thrifty, prudent, careful, frugal, sparing, saving. EXTRAVAGANT
cost-effective, efficient, money-saving. WASTEFUL

economize save, conserve, husband, scrimp, cut back, retrench, tighten one's belt. SQUANDER

economy thrift, thriftiness, husbandry, saving, frugality, parsimony, retrenchment, cutback. EXTRAVAGANCE

ecstasy rapture, transport, bliss, joy, delight, seventh heaven, elation, euphoria, felicity, exhilaration, thrill, exaltation, fervour. MISERY

ecstatic overjoyed, enraptured, blissful, euphoric, delirious, elated, delighted, on cloud nine (*inf*), rapturous, fervent, enthusiastic. INDIFFERENT

ecumenical universal, worldwide, general, catholic.

eddy whirlpool, vortex, swirl.

edge *n*, border, rim, lip, margin, periphery, fringe, verge, brink, threshold, side, outline, boundary, limit. CENTRE
sharpness, keenness, intensity, acuteness, bite, sting, force, zest. DULLNESS
on edge, nervous, tense, keyed up, on tenterhooks, eager, impatient, edgy, irritable. CALM
v, trim, bind, border, fringe.
creep, inch, steal, sidle, worm. DASH
sharpen, whet, hone. BLUNT

edging border, fringe, frill.

edgy nervous, tense, on edge, anxious, ill at ease, irritable, touchy, testy, sensitive. PLACID

edible eatable, comestible, esculent, good, wholesome, palatable. INEDIBLE

edict decree, ordinance, pronouncement, proclamation, mandate, command, order, statute, law.

edification improvement, uplifting, elevation, enlightenment, instruction, education, schooling, guidance, information. CORRUPTION

edifice building, structure, erection, construction, pile.

edify improve, uplift, elevate, enlighten, instruct, teach, educate, school, guide, inform. CORRUPT

edit correct, emend, revise, rewrite, modify, adapt, annotate, polish, redact, check, censor, compile, prepare, compose, assemble.

edition copy, volume, impression, printing, version, issue, number.

editor reviser, redactor, annotator, compiler, reader, writer, journalist.

educate school, instruct, teach, train, coach, tutor, exercise, drill, edify, enlighten, civilize, cultivate, develop, nurture, rear, discipline.

educated scholarly, learned, erudite, intellectual, literate, lettered, well-read, knowledgeable, versed, schooled, cultivated, cultured, refined, enlightened, informed. IGNORANT

education schooling, instruction, teaching, tuition, training, edification, enlightenment, development, civilization, culture, learning, knowledge, scholarship, erudition. IGNORANCE

educational educative, informative, instructive, edifying, didactic, heuristic.

educe elicit, evoke, bring out, draw forth, extract, derive, develop, evolve.

eerie weird, uncanny, strange, mysterious, frightening, unearthly, ghostly, creepy (*inf*), spooky (*inf*).

efface erase, rub out, obliterate, wipe out, eradicate, cancel, expunge, remove, delete, cross out, blot out, annihilate, destroy. IMPRINT

effect *n*, result, consequence, outcome, upshot, issue, event, conclusion, aftermath. CAUSE
efficacy, efficiency, power, force, strength, weight, influence, impact, validity.
action, operation, implementation, execution, performance.
meaning, significance, import, sense, drift.
in effect, in fact, actually, in reality, really, essentially, effectively, virtually.
v, cause, bring about, create, produce, make, procure, actuate, effectuate, achieve, accomplish, secure, perform, execute. PREVENT

effective efficient, effectual, efficacious, productive, competent, adequate, capable, able, useful. INEFFECTIVE
operative, functioning, active, current, in force, in effect, actual. INOPERATIVE
striking, impressive, cogent, forceful, telling, convincing, powerful. UNIMPRESSIVE

effects goods, chattels, movables, belongings, property, possessions.

effectual effective, efficient, efficacious, productive, powerful, influential, telling, cogent, useful, operative, functional. INEFFECTUAL
legal, lawful, binding, in force, valid, authoritative.

effectuate effect, cause, bring about, create, produce, make, procure, actuate, achieve, accomplish, secure, perform, execute. THWART

effeminate unmanly, womanish, feminine, soft, sissy, camp. VIRILE

effervesce bubble, foam, froth, fizz, sparkle, ferment, boil.

effervescent bubbling, bubbly, foaming, frothy, fizzy, sparkling, carbonated. FLAT
ebullient, vivacious, lively, gay, exuberant, animated, buoyant, excited, exhilarated. LISTLESS

effete weak, feeble, drained, spent, exhausted, worn out, enfeebled, decrepit, decadent, degenerate, dissipated. VIGOROUS
barren, sterile, infertile, unprolific, fruitless, unproductive. FERTILE

efficacious effective, effectual, productive, efficient, able, competent, potent, powerful, active, vigorous, useful, adequate. USELESS

efficacy effectiveness, efficiency, effect, power, force, potency, success, productivity, competence, ability, usefulness. INEFFICACY

efficiency effectiveness, efficacy, competence, proficiency, skill, expertise, ability, capability, success, productivity, power. INEFFICIENCY

efficient effective, effectual, efficacious, competent, proficient, skilled, skilful, expert, adept, able, capable, powerful, productive, economic, businesslike, successful. INEFFICIENT

effigy image, representation, likeness, icon, idol, figure, statue, portrait.

effloresce flower, bloom, blossom, blow.

effluence efflux, effluent, outflow, effusion, discharge, emission, emanation, exhalation. INFLUX

effluvium exhalation, emanation, vapour, gas, fumes, miasma, odour, smell, stench, reek, stink, pong (*inf*).

effort attempt, try, endeavour, essay, go (*inf*).
exertion, struggle, strain, application, labour, toil, pains. IDLENESS
achievement, exploit, feat, accomplishment, creation, product.

effortless easy, simple, facile, smooth, painless, undemanding. DIFFICULT

effrontery audacity, temerity, boldness, impudence, nerve, cheek (*inf*), impertinence, insolence, sauciness, shamelessness, presumption, assurance, brass (*inf*), gall (*inf*). TIMIDITY

effulgence brilliance, brightness, radiance, dazzle, blaze, shine, splendour, lustre, sheen, sparkle, glow, incandescence. DULLNESS

effulgent brilliant, radiant, bright, shining, dazzling, fiery, splendid, resplendent, lustrous, sparkling, luminous, incandescent, fluorescent. DULL

effuse pour out, spill, disembogue, emanate, issue, gush, diffuse.

effusion effluence, outflow, emission, discharge, outpouring, gush, stream.

effusive gushing, unreserved, expansive, lavish, fulsome, demonstrative, exuberant, ebullient, enthusiastic, profuse, unrestrained. RESERVED

egg on urge, press, push, goad, spur, incite, encourage, provoke, stimulate. DETER

egoism selfishness, self-interest, self-centredness, egomania, egotism, self-regard, self-esteem, self-importance, vanity, conceit, self-love. ALTRUISM

egoistic selfish, self-centred, egocentric, self-seeking, egotistic, self-important. ALTRUISTIC

egotism conceit, vanity, narcissism, self-love, self-centredness, self-esteem, self-importance, egoism. MODESTY

egotistic conceited, vain, self-centred, self-important, egocentric, self-admiring, boastful, narcissistic, egoistic. MODEST

egregious blatant, flagrant, glaring, striking, gross, scandalous, shocking, outrageous, notorious, infamous, heinous, monstrous.

egress exit, way out, outlet, emergence, issue, departure, exodus. ENTRANCE

ejaculate exclaim, cry, blurt out, utter, say.
discharge, emit, eject, spurt, spout.

ejaculation exclamation, cry, shout, utterance.
discharge, emission, ejection, release, spurt.

eject expel, emit, discharge, throw out, spout, spew, disgorge.
evict, throw out, dismiss, cashier, banish, exile, oust, drive out, remove, discharge, expel. RETAIN

ejection expulsion, emission, discharge, throwing out, eviction, dismissal, exile, ouster, removal.

eke out supplement, add to, increase, extend, stretch out, economize on, scrimp, be frugal with.

elaborate *adj*, detailed, thorough, minute, studied, laboured, intricate, complex, complicated, ornate, decorated, fancy, fussy, showy. SIMPLE
v, devise, work out, develop, amplify, expand, flesh out, improve, refine, enhance, embellish, decorate.

elapse lapse, intervene, transpire, pass by, slip away, go by, roll on.

elastic flexible, pliable, supple, yielding, resilient, springy, rubbery, ductile, extensible, stretchy. RIGID
adaptable, flexible, adjustable, accommodating, yielding, compliant. INFLEXIBLE

elasticity flexibility, suppleness, resilience, springiness, plasticity, ductility, stretch, give (*inf*). RIGIDITY
adaptability, flexibility, adjustability, compliance. INFLEXIBILITY

elated exhilarated, animated, excited, euphoric, ecstatic, jubilant, exultant, blissful, overjoyed, delighted, joyful, happy, proud. DEJECTED

elation exhilaration, animation, excitement, high spirits, euphoria, ecstasy, bliss, rapture, jubilation, joy, delight, happiness, glee. DEJECTION

elbow *n*, angle, corner, bend, turn, joint, flexure.
v, jostle, push, shove, nudge, knock, shoulder, hustle.

elder *adj*, older, senior, earlier, former, superior. YOUNGER
n, senior, superior, patriarch, chief, presbyter.

elect *v*, choose, select, prefer, pick, appoint, designate, vote for, decide on, opt for. REJECT
adj, elite, choice, select, hand-picked, appointed, chosen, selected.

election vote, voting, ballot, poll, appointment, selection, choice, preference. REJECTION

elector voter, constituent, selector, chooser.

electric exciting, thrilling, stirring, rousing, stimulating, charged, dynamic.

electrify thrill, excite, shock, startle, amaze, astound, stir, rouse, animate, galvanize.

elegance beauty, grace, refinement, polish, dignity, distinction, grandeur, luxury, style, taste, propriety, politeness, gentility. COARSENESS

elegant smart, stylish, chic, fashionable, neat, refined, cultivated, tasteful, fine, beautiful, classical, exquisite, choice, luxurious, sumptuous, graceful, genteel, sophisticated, polite, courtly, debonair. COARSE

elegiac plaintive, mournful, sorrowful, sad, melancholy, dirgeful, threnodic. MERRY

elegy dirge, lament, threnody, coronach, requiem.

element component, constituent, member, unit, part, section, ingredient, factor, feature, detail, particular. WHOLE
trace, hint, suggestion.

medium, habitat, domain, sphere, milieu, environment.

elementary basic, fundamental, elemental, rudimentary, primary, simple, uncomplicated, straightforward, introductory, preliminary. ADVANCED

elephantine huge, immense, gigantic, colossal, mammoth, enormous, ponderous, heavy, clumsy, hulking. TINY

elevate lift, raise, hoist, erect, heighten, magnify, boost, intensify. LOWER
exalt, advance, promote, ennoble, dignify, aggrandize. DOWNGRADE
elate, exhilarate, cheer, boost, uplift, hearten, rouse, animate, inspirit. DEPRESS

elevated lofty, high, raised, exalted, sublime, noble, dignified, grand, high-flown. BASE

elevation height, altitude, eminence, hill, rise, acclivity. DEPTH
exaltation, grandeur, loftiness, nobility, dignity.
lifting, raising, promotion, advancement, preferment, aggrandizement. LOWERING

elf imp, sprite, puck, pixie, brownie, leprechaun, fairy, gnome, dwarf.

elfin elfish, impish, puckish, mischievous, playful, arch, sprightly, elf-like, dainty.

elicit evoke, educe, bring forth, draw out, extract, derive, cause, give rise to.

eligible qualified, fit, appropriate, suitable, acceptable, worthy, desirable. INELIGIBLE

eliminate remove, take out, get rid of, discard, reject, dismiss, expel, oust, eject, throw out, exclude, omit, leave out, drop, eradicate, exterminate, annihilate, stamp out. INCLUDE

elimination removal, rejection, expulsion, ejection, exclusion, omission, eradication, extermination, annihilation. INCLUSION

elite *n*, best, cream, flower, aristocracy, nobility, gentry, upper class, *crème de la crème*. RABBLE
adj, select, exclusive, choice, first-class, aristocratic, noble, upper-class.

elliptical oval, egg-shaped.
concise, terse, laconic, succinct, ambiguous, obscure, circumlocutory.

elocution delivery, diction, articulation, eloquence, speech, oratory, rhetoric, declamation, public speaking.

elongate lengthen, extend, stretch, prolong, draw out, protract. CONDENSE

elope abscond, run away, slip off, flee, decamp, disappear, leave.

eloquence oratory, rhetoric, delivery, fluency, expressiveness, forcefulness, cogency, way with words.

eloquent fluent, glib, articulate, expressive, persuasive, cogent, forceful, impressive. INARTICULATE

else other, different, besides, more, in addition.

elucidate explain, expound, clarify, clear up, illuminate, shed light on, spell out, illustrate, unfold. MYSTIFY

elucidation explanation, clarification, illumination, illustration, exposition, commentary, annotation, gloss, footnote. MYSTIFICATION

elude evade, avoid, escape, dodge, duck, shun, shirk. FACE
baffle, confound, puzzle, frustrate, thwart.

elusive elusory, intangible, fugitive, fleeting, transient, indefinable.
slippery, shifty, tricky, deceptive, fallacious, equivocal, evasive.

Elysian blissful, happy, heavenly, celestial, blessed, paradisiacal, delightful, enchanting, charming, glorious. ABOMINABLE

emaciated lean, thin, gaunt, haggard, pinched, attenuated, scrawny, skinny, skeletal, wizened, wasted. OBESE

emaciation leanness, thinness, gauntness, haggardness, attenuation, scrawniness, wasting, marasmus. OBESITY

emanate proceed, originate, arise, issue, spring, flow, emerge. CULMINATE
emit, send forth, give off, radiate, exhale. ABSORB

emanation proceeding, origination, arising, flowing, springing, emergence. CULMINATION
emission, discharge, effusion, effluent, radiation, exhalation.

emancipate liberate, free, enfranchise, release, loose, unshackle, unfetter, unchain, manumit, disenthral. ENSLAVE

emancipation liberation, freeing, enfranchisement, release, deliverance, unshackling, manumission, freedom, liberty. ENSLAVEMENT

emasculate castrate, geld, unman.

weaken, debilitate, soften, enervate. STRENGTHEN

emasculation castration, gelding.
weakening, debilitation, enervation.

embalm mummify, preserve.
cherish, enshrine, consecrate, immortalize, treasure, store, keep, conserve. FORGET
perfume, scent.

embargo restraint, restriction, prohibition, ban, proscription, bar, barrier, stoppage, check, impediment, hindrance. LICENCE

embark board, get on, go aboard. DISEMBARK

embark on, begin, start, commence, set about, undertake, launch, broach, plunge into. COMPLETE

embarrass abash, shame, disconcert, discomfit, fluster, chagrin, mortify, confuse, confound, perplex, nonplus. EXTRICATE
encumber, burden, impede, hamper, trouble, plague. ASSIST

embarrassment abashment, shame, humiliation, awkwardness, self-consciousness, disconcertion, chagrin, mortification, confusion. EASE
predicament, plight, difficulty, scrape (*inf*), pickle (*inf*).

embed fix, implant, root, sink, set, drive in, hammer in.

embellish adorn, deck, ornament, decorate, garnish, beautify, enhance, enrich, gild, varnish, embroider, colour, elaborate. DISFIGURE

embellishment adornment, ornament, ornamentation, decoration, enhancement, enrichment, embroidery, exaggeration, elaboration. DISFIGUREMENT

embers cinders, ashes, remains.

embezzle steal, purloin, pilfer, appropriate, misappropriate, peculate, defalcate, defraud, cheat.

embezzlement stealing, pilfering, theft, appropriation, misappropriation, peculation, defalcation, fraud.

embitter sour, poison, envenom, anger, madden, irritate, exasperate, aggravate, exacerbate, disillusion, disaffect.

emblazon blazon, colour, illuminate, decorate, ornament, embellish.
proclaim, herald, trumpet, glorify, extol, praise.

emblem symbol, token, representation, sign, mark, badge, device, figure, insignia, logo.

embodiment incarnation, incorporation, personification, reification, expression, representation, symbol, example.
fusion, amalgamation, combination, unification, consolidation, inclusion, comprehension.

embody incarnate, incorporate, personify, reify, express, represent, symbolize, typify, exemplify.
embrace, encompass, include, comprise, comprehend, contain, collect, combine, unite.

embolden encourage, inspirit, hearten, rouse, animate, stimulate, spur, impel, rally, invigorate, cheer, reassure. DISCOURAGE

embowed bowed, arched, vaulted, arcuate, curved, bent. STRAIGHT

embrace *v*, clasp, hug, enfold, cuddle, squeeze.
adopt, take up, seize, grasp, accept, welcome. REJECT
include, comprise, encompass, comprehend, embody, cover, contain, encircle, enclose. EXCLUDE
n, clasp, hug, cuddle, squeeze, hold.

embroider embellish, exaggerate, colour, varnish, elaborate, dress up, fabricate.

embroil involve, implicate, compromise, incriminate, entangle, enmesh, complicate, confuse, disorder, perplex, muddle, disturb, discompose, trouble. EXTRICATE

embryo germ, nucleus, seed, root, beginning, rudiment.

embryonic rudimentary, undeveloped, early, elementary, primary, inchoate, incipient, beginning, immature. MATURE

emend correct, amend, improve, polish, rewrite, edit, redact, revise.

emendation correction, amendment, improvement, revision, alteration, editing, redaction.

emerge appear, come out, materialize, rise, surface, come up, proceed, issue, arise, emanate, come forth. DISAPPEAR

emergence appearance, apparition, materialization, rise, coming, advent, issue, emanation, evolution, development. DISAPPEARANCE

emergency crisis, exigency, urgency, juncture, extremity, pinch, necessity, contingency, predicament, difficulty, strait, plight, quandary.

emigrate migrate, move, relocate, depart, leave, quit. IMMIGRATE

emigration migration, relocation, expatriation, exodus, departure. IMMIGRATION

eminence distinction, celebrity, fame, renown, prominence, mark, note, notability, dignity, prestige, reputation, repute, esteem, greatness, loftiness, superiority. OBSCURITY
hill, mound, height, elevation.

eminent distinguished, illustrious, celebrated, well-known, famous, renowned, prominent, noted, notable, noteworthy, conspicuous, esteemed, revered, venerable, important, great, grand, lofty, superior, outstanding. UNKNOWN

emissary agent, ambassador, envoy, delegate, messenger, courier, herald, scout, spy.

emission discharge, issue, ejection, ejaculation, emanation, exhalation, diffusion, radiation, utterance.

emit discharge, issue, eject, ejaculate, expel, send forth, cast out, emanate, exhale, give off, radiate, diffuse, utter, give vent to.

emollient *adj*, soothing, lenitive, assuasive, palliative, balsamic, softening, relaxing. ASTRINGENT
n, ointment, balm, liniment, embrocation, lotion, salve.

emolument remuneration, pay, earnings, salary, wages, fee, stipend, profit, gain, income, living, compensation, benefit.

emotion feeling, passion, sensation, sentiment, ardour, fervour. INDIFFERENCE

emotional sensitive, susceptible, feeling, warm, tender, sentimental. EMOTIONLESS
passionate, ardent, fervent, zealous, enthusiastic, excitable, temperamental, heated, impassioned, fiery, melodramatic, hysterical, overwrought. CALM
emotive, touching, moving, stirring, poignant, pathetic.

emphasis weight, significance, importance, force, power, strength, stress, accent, insistence, pre-eminence, priority, attention, prominence, clarity.

emphasize stress, accentuate, accent, underline, highlight, point up, mark, press home, insist on. UNDERSTATE

emphatic positive, forceful, insistent, earnest, certain, definite, absolute, categorical, unequivocal, decided, marked, pointed, stressed, accented, pronounced, strong, energetic, important, significant.

empire domain, dominion, realm, commonwealth, province.
supremacy, sovereignty, sway, dominion, control, command, authority, power, rule, government.

empirical experimental, experiential, observed, practical, pragmatic. THEORETICAL

employ engage, hire, enlist, enrol, take on, commission. DISMISS
use, make use of, utilize, exercise, apply, wield.
occupy, keep busy, engage, engross.

employee worker, hand, wage-earner, staff member. EMPLOYER

employer boss, director, proprietor, owner, company, firm, business. EMPLOYEE

employment occupation, situation, job, work, trade, craft, business, profession, vocation, post, appointment. UNEMPLOYMENT
use, utilization, exercise, application.

emporium store, shop, market, mart, bazaar, fair.

empower authorize, warrant, license, commission, entitle, sanction, permit, allow, enable, qualify. DISQUALIFY

empty *adj*, void, unfilled, hollow, vacant, unoccupied, deserted, uninhabited, devoid, destitute, bare, blank, clear. FULL
futile, useless, vain, aimless, meaningless, worthless, senseless, insignificant, trivial, idle, hollow, insincere, unsubstantial. MEANINGFUL
expressionless, vacuous, blank, vacant, silly, inane.
v, drain, exhaust, deplete, void, evacuate, vacate, clear, discharge, unload, pour out, disembogue. FILL

empyreal empyrean, aerial, ethereal, celestial, heavenly, sublime, unworldly. EARTHLY

emulate imitate, copy, follow, take after, rival, compete with, vie with, equal, match.

emulation imitation, competition, rivalry, envy.

emulous imitative, competitive, competing, emulating, aspiring.

enable capacitate, qualify, arm, equip, empower, authorize, sanction, permit, allow, facilitate, assist. PREVENT

enact decree, ordain, pronounce, rule, establish, legislate, ratify, sanction, authorize. ABROGATE
perform, act out, play, act, represent, portray.

enactment decree, ordinance, edict, proclamation, law, statute, rule, act, legislation, ratification.
performance, acting, representation, portrayal.

enamour charm, captivate, enchant, bewitch, fascinate, endear, infatuate. REPEL

encamp camp, pitch camp, bivouac, lodge, settle.

encampment camp, campsite, bivouac, base, lodgment, quarters.

encase box, crate, pack, enclose, wrap, sheathe.

enchain shackle, fetter, manacle, bind, hold, rivet. LOOSE

enchant captivate, charm, beguile, win, fascinate, delight, enamour. REPEL
bewitch, spellbind, entrance, enthral, hypnotize, mesmerize, cast a spell on.

enchanting delightful, charming, captivating, winning, alluring, attractive, winsome, lovely, beguiling, fascinating, appealing, endearing. REPULSIVE

enchantment spell, charm, incantation, magic, sorcery, witchcraft.
delight, charm, fascination, allurement, bliss, rapture, captivation, mesmerism. REPULSION

encircle encompass, surround, gird, circumscribe, ring, environ, hem in, enclose.

enclose surround, encircle, encompass, fence, encase, envelop, wrap, hem in, confine, cage, hold, contain, include, embrace. EXCLUDE

enclosure pound, compound, paddock, pen, yard, arena, ring, close, cloister.
fence, railings, palisade, hedge, wall, barricade.

encomium eulogy, panegyric, laudation, homage, tribute, praise, acclaim. VITUPERATION

encompass encircle, surround, circumscribe, gird, environ, ring, enclose.
include, embrace, cover, comprise, contain, comprehend, embody. EXCLUDE

encounter *v*, meet, happen upon, come across, bump into (*inf*), accost, confront, face, experience, undergo. AVOID
fight, contend, grapple, struggle, clash with, do battle with.
n, meeting, confrontation, brush.
clash, conflict, combat, engagement, skirmish, battle, fight, contest, action.

encourage hearten, cheer, rally, buoy up, reassure, comfort, inspirit, rouse, animate, stimulate, embolden, incite, persuade, urge, exhort, egg on, spur. DISCOURAGE
support, advocate, back, help, aid, abet, foster, promote, advance, further, boost.

encroach intrude, invade, trespass, infringe, impinge, trench, overstep, arrogate, usurp.

encrust plaster, coat, cover, face, overlay.

encumber hamper, hinder, impede, obstruct, clog, burden, load, weigh down, oppress, saddle, cramp, trammel. RELIEVE

encumbrance hindrance, impediment, obstacle, handicap, inconvenience, burden, load, millstone, drag.

end *v*, finish, conclude, terminate, close, complete, cease, stop, wind up, culminate. START
kill, destroy, exterminate, annihilate, eradicate, abolish.
n, finish, conclusion, termination, close, completion, cessation, stoppage, ending, finale, denouement, culmination. BEGINNING
extremity, tip, limit, bound, boundary, edge, border, terminus.
aim, object, purpose, intention, reason, design, goal, objective.
scrap, fragment, remnant, stub, butt.
death, demise, ruin, destruction, annihilation, extinction, extermination. BIRTH
result, consequence, event, outcome, issue, upshot.

endanger imperil, jeopardize, hazard, risk, expose, commit, compromise. PROTECT

endear attract, charm, win, captivate, attach, engage. ALIENATE

endearing attractive, charming, winning, adorable, lovable, sweet, winsome. REPULSIVE

endearment affection, fondness, love, attachment. HATRED

loving word, sweet nothing, pet name, caress, hug, kiss.
endeavour *v*, try, attempt, strive, struggle, labour, essay, aspire, aim, do one's best, have a go (*inf*).
n, attempt, try, essay, go (*inf*), shot (*inf*), struggle, effort, venture, enterprise, undertaking, aim.
endemic local, indigenous, native, present, restricted, confined. UNIVERSAL
endless unending, boundless, unlimited, limitless, immeasurable, interminable, unceasing, ceaseless, incessant, constant, perpetual, continuous, uninterrupted, eternal, everlasting, infinite, immortal, undying. FINITE
endorse approve, sanction, ratify, confirm, authorize, support, back, second, advocate, champion, vouch for, sustain, uphold.
sign, countersign, superscribe.
endow bestow, bequeath, will, leave, give, present, supply, provide, furnish, grant, award, invest, endue. DIVEST
endowment bequest, legacy, grant, award, gift, benefaction, bounty, fund, provision, revenue, inheritance.
talent, gift, faculty, attribute, quality, property, aptitude, ability.
endue invest, endow, provide, supply, furnish. DIVEST
endurance fortitude, stamina, patience, resignation, stoicism, tolerance, perseverance, persistence, tenacity. WEAKNESS
permanence, durability, stability, immutability, duration, continuance. IMPERMANENCE
endure bear, stand, brook, tolerate, permit, allow, abide, stomach, swallow, put up with, suffer, undergo, experience, sustain, withstand.
last, persist, remain, continue, abide, prevail, survive. PERISH
enemy adversary, opponent, foe, rival, antagonist. ALLY
energetic vigorous, active, lively, dynamic, spirited, tireless, busy, strenuous, forceful, powerful, strong. LETHARGIC
energize invigorate, animate, enliven, stimulate, galvanize, activate. ENERVATE
energy vigour, activity, vitality, stamina, intensity, force, strength, power, drive, dynamism, animation, spirit, life, vivacity, zeal, ardour, fire. LETHARGY
enervate weaken, debilitate, enfeeble, unman, unnerve, sap, tire, exhaust, prostrate, disable, incapacitate, paralyse. INVIGORATE
enfeeble weaken, debilitate, enervate, devitalize, unman, unnerve, sap, tire, exhaust, wear out. STRENGTHEN
enfold envelop, wrap, swathe, shroud, enclose, encompass, embrace, clasp, hug.
enforce impose, apply, administer, implement, execute, carry out, force, compel, oblige, urge, constrain, require, insist on, exact. WAIVE
enfranchise emancipate, liberate, free, release, manumit, disenthral. ENSLAVE
engage hire, employ, take on, enlist, enrol, commission, appoint. DISMISS
engross, occupy, busy, absorb, involve, tie up.
attract, allure, draw, catch, win, captivate, charm. REPEL
pledge, promise, vow, undertake, agree, commit, bind, oblige.
participate, take part, embark on, take up, practise.
fight, battle, combat, attack, take on, encounter, meet. RETREAT
interlock, mesh, join, activate, apply. DISENGAGE
engaged betrothed, affianced, pledged, spoken for.
busy, occupied, in use, unavailable, tied up, involved, engrossed, absorbed. FREE
engagement betrothal, pledge, promise, vow, oath, assurance, contract, pact, covenant, bond, obligation, commitment.
appointment, meeting, rendezvous, date, assignation, arrangement, commitment.
employment, job, post, situation, work, business.
fight, battle, conflict, encounter, skirmish, action. RETREAT
engaging charming, delightful, enchanting, captivating, winning, appealing, attractive, pleasing, agreeable. REPULSIVE
engender produce, cause, occasion, bring about, create, generate, give rise to, provoke. SUPPRESS
beget, breed, procreate, propagate, sire, give birth to, spawn.
engine locomotive, motor, machine, mechanism, device, contrivance, implement, tool, instrument, agent, means.

engineer *n*, designer, architect, inventor, originator, planner, deviser.
v, plan, devise, contrive, manoeuvre, cause, bring about, direct, mastermind, orchestrate.

engorge devour, bolt, gulp, wolf, gobble, gorge, cram, stuff.

engrave inscribe, etch, cut, carve, chisel, chase.
imprint, impress, stamp, fix, lodge. ERASE

engraving print, impression, etching, woodcut, carving, inscription, plate, block.

engross absorb, immerse, occupy, engage, involve, preoccupy, grip, hold, fix, arrest, monopolize, corner. BORE

engulf consume, swallow up, overwhelm, swamp, flood, inundate, bury, immerse, submerge, plunge, absorb, engross.

enhance heighten, intensify, increase, swell, augment, raise, boost, improve, enrich, strengthen, reinforce. DEPRECIATE

enigma mystery, riddle, conundrum, puzzle. SOLUTION

enigmatic puzzling, perplexing, cryptic, mysterious, obscure, recondite, occult, esoteric, abstruse, incomprehensible, unfathomable, unintelligible, ambiguous, equivocal, inscrutable. PLAIN

enjoin order, command, direct, charge, instruct, require, bid, urge, advise, counsel, admonish, warn.
ban, prohibit, proscribe, disallow, forbid, interdict. PERMIT

enjoy like, love, relish, appreciate, take pleasure in, delight in, revel in. DETEST
possess, own, have, benefit from, experience, use. LOSE
enjoy oneself, have fun, have a good time, have a ball (*inf*).

enjoyable pleasant, agreeable, delightful, lovely, amusing, entertaining, delicious, delectable. ABOMINABLE

enjoyment delight, pleasure, gratification, amusement, entertainment, relish, joy, happiness, fun. DISPLEASURE
possession, ownership, use, benefit, advantage.

enkindle kindle, ignite, set fire to, light, fire. EXTINGUISH
arouse, stir, provoke, inflame, excite, stimulate. DAMP

enlarge expand, increase, augment, wax, swell, grow, amplify, magnify, extend, stretch, broaden, distend, dilate, inflate, heighten. DIMINISH
expatiate, descant, expound, develop, elaborate.

enlargement expansion, increase, augmentation, amplification, extension, magnification, dilation. CONTRACTION

enlighten instruct, edify, teach, educate, inform, apprise. CONFUSE

enlightened aware, informed, knowledgeable, educated, civilized, refined, sophisticated, broad-minded, liberal. IGNORANT

enlightenment understanding, awareness, insight, education, instruction, edification, information, learning, knowledge, wisdom, refinement, cultivation, broad-mindedness. IGNORANCE

enlist engage, enrol, sign up, register, recruit, secure, obtain, draft, conscript, volunteer, join up.

enliven animate, invigorate, stimulate, inspirit, excite, rouse, fire. DAMP
brighten, cheer up, perk up, gladden, hearten.

enmesh entangle, snarl, catch, ensnare, trap, embroil, involve. EXTRICATE

enmity hostility, animosity, strife, discord, hate, antagonism, bad blood, rancour, ill will, bitterness, spite, malice, malignity. FRIENDSHIP

ennoble elevate, raise, aggrandize, magnify, exalt, glorify, dignify, honour. DEGRADE

ennui boredom, tedium, languor, lassitude, listlessness, lethargy. ENERGY

enormity atrocity, outrage, scandal, horror, monstrosity, abomination, outrageousness, wickedness, villainy, heinousness, depravity, disgrace.

enormous huge, gigantic, massive, immense, colossal, vast, elephantine, gargantuan, mammoth, tremendous, prodigious, stupendous. TINY

enough *adj*, sufficient, adequate, ample, abundant, plentiful. INSUFFICIENT
n, sufficiency, adequacy, plenty, abundance. INSUFFICIENCY
adv, sufficiently, adequately, tolerably, passably, reasonably, moderately, abundantly, amply. INSUFFICIENTLY

enquire ask, question, interrogate, query, examine, inquire, investigate, look into, probe, explore.

enquiry question, query, interrogation, inquest, inquiry, investigation, survey, study.

enrage incense, infuriate, madden, exasperate, anger, rouse, provoke, inflame, irritate, annoy. PACIFY

enrapture delight, enchant, entrance, fascinate, captivate, bewitch, charm, ravish, transport. REPEL

enrich endow, make rich, enhance, improve, ameliorate, refine, augment, supplement, develop, aggrandize, uplift. IMPOVERISH
adorn, deck, decorate, ornament, embellish, beautify. DISFIGURE

enrol matriculate, register, enlist, sign up, join up, recruit, admit.
record, chronicle, list, note.

ensconce nestle, snuggle up, curl up, settle, lodge, install.
hide, screen, cover, shield, protect, shelter. EXPOSE

ensemble *n*, whole, totality, entirety, aggregate, assemblage, sum. ELEMENT
outfit, costume, attire, getup (*inf*).
group, company, troupe, band, choir, cast.
adv, together, en masse, as a group, in concert, at the same time, all at once. INDIVIDUALLY

enshrine dedicate, consecrate, hallow, sanctify, revere, immortalize, cherish, treasure, preserve, embalm.

ensign banner, standard, flag, pennant, colours, insignia, badge, emblem, device.

enslave subjugate, subject, master, dominate, bind, enchain, fetter. LIBERATE

ensnare snare, trap, entrap, catch, net, enmesh, entangle, inveigle, allure. LOOSE

ensue follow, come next, succeed, proceed, result, arise, issue, happen, occur, turn up. PRECEDE

ensure guarantee, assure, make sure, secure, confirm, certify.
guard, safeguard, protect. IMPERIL

entail involve, necessitate, call for, demand, require, occasion, cause, result in, bring about, impose.

entangle enmesh, embroil, involve, implicate, ensnare, entrap, catch, tangle, snarl, knot, ravel, muddle, confuse, perplex, puzzle, bewilder. EXTRICATE

entanglement tangle, knot, muddle, confusion, perplexity, bewilderment, complication, intricacy, involvement, difficulty.

enter go into, come into, arrive, penetrate, pierce, invade, introduce, insert. LEAVE
record, note, register, log, take down, inscribe. EXPUNGE
join, enrol, enlist, embark on, set about, begin, start, commence, participate in, engage in.

enterprise undertaking, venture, project, plan, effort, endeavour, attempt.
initiative, resourcefulness, gumption (*inf*), drive, energy, push (*inf*), get-up-and-go (*inf*), courage, boldness, daring, adventurousness, readiness, enthusiasm, zeal. TIMIDITY
business, company, firm, establishment, concern.

enterprising venturesome, adventurous, bold, daring, eager, ready, energetic, vigorous, strenuous, zealous, enthusiastic, spirited, active, alert, resourceful, inventive. APATHETIC

entertain amuse, divert, occupy, interest, please, charm, regale, cheer. BORE
receive, welcome, accommodate, lodge, host, have company, throw a party (*inf*).
harbour, foster, nurture, cherish, hold, consider, contemplate, ponder. BANISH

entertainment amusement, diversion, recreation, pastime, sport, play, fun, pleasure, enjoyment.
show, performance, carnival, festival, gala, spectacle.

enthral captivate, charm, fascinate, spellbind, entrance, enchant, beguile, thrill, hypnotize, rivet, transport, enrapture. BORE

enthrone crown, install, ennoble, exalt, glorify, honour, elevate, aggrandize, idolize. DETHRONE

enthusiasm zeal, ardour, fervour, passion, frenzy, vehemence, keenness, eagerness, avidity, earnestness, excitement, warmth, devotion, fanaticism, mania, craze. APATHY

enthusiast zealot, devotee, admirer, supporter, fanatic, fan, aficionado, buff (*inf*), fiend (*inf*).

enthusiastic keen, eager, avid, earnest, ardent, fervent, fervid, warm, whole-hearted, devoted, vehement, zealous, passionate, spirited, lively, exuberant, ebullient, excited. INDIFFERENT

entice tempt, lure, allure, attract, draw, seduce, inveigle, cajole, wheedle, coax, persuade. DETER

enticement bait, lure, decoy, temptation, allurement, attraction, seduction, cajolery, persuasion. DETERRENT

entire complete, whole, total, full, unbroken, undivided, intact, perfect, pure, unalloyed, unimpaired, thorough, absolute, unmitigated, unqualified, exhaustive, comprehensive. PARTIAL

entirely completely, wholly, totally, fully, perfectly, absolutely, utterly, in every respect, without reservation. PARTIALLY

entirety completeness, wholeness, totality, fullness, unity, aggregate, ensemble, sum total, whole. PART

entitle qualify, authorize, empower, permit, allow, enable, license. DISQUALIFY
name, style, call, dub, christen, designate, denominate, term.

entity thing, object, body, creature, being, existence, essence, quiddity.

entomb bury, inter, inhume, sepulchre. EXHUME

entourage attendants, staff, retinue, suite, train, cortege, escort, followers, companions.
surroundings, environment, milieu, ambience.

entrails intestines, bowels, guts, viscera, offal, insides, innards (*inf*).

entrance[1] *n*, entry, admission, admittance, entrée, access, way in, ingress, door, gate, portal, opening, inlet, passage, lobby, vestibule, foyer. EXIT
appearance, arrival, introduction, debut, beginning, start, commencement, outset. DEPARTURE

entrance[2] *v*, enrapture, charm, enchant, captivate, ravish, transport, delight, fascinate, enthral, spellbind, hypnotize, mesmerize. REPEL

entrant newcomer, novice, beginner, tyro, neophyte, new member, initiate, convert.
competitor, contestant, entry, candidate, applicant, player, participant.

entrap trap, snare, ensnare, catch, net, entangle, enmesh, involve, implicate, embroil, inveigle, lure, trick, lead on. LOOSE

entreat beg, implore, plead, crave, supplicate, petition, beseech, enjoin, pray, importune, ask, request. COMMAND

entreaty appeal, plea, prayer, suit, petition, supplication, cry, request. ORDER

entrench establish, fix, dig in, embed, root, implant, lodge, settle. MOVE
encroach, trespass, infringe, impinge, intrude.

entrust commit, confide, consign, hand over, deliver, commend, assign, delegate.

entry entrance, admission, admittance, entrée, access, way in, ingress, avenue, passage, door, gate, opening, inlet. EXIT
appearance, arrival, introduction, debut. DEPARTURE
item, note, record, minute, statement, memorandum.

entwine twine, weave, interweave, lace, interlace, twist, braid, plait, knit, splice, wind. SEPARATE

enumerate list, name, cite, detail, specify, itemize, recount, relate, tell, number, count, reckon, tally, calculate.

enumeration list, catalogue, listing, naming, recapitulation, specification, itemization, narration, counting, reckoning, calculation.

enunciate articulate, pronounce, intone, vocalize, voice, utter, say, speak, express. STAMMER
state, assert, declare, proclaim, announce, promulgate, publish. SUPPRESS

enunciation articulation, pronunciation, delivery, presentation, intonation, modulation, inflection, voice, utterance, speech.
statement, assertion, declaration, proclamation, announcement.

envelop wrap, enwrap, enfold, sheathe, encase, cover, enshroud, hide, conceal, cloak, veil, surround, encompass, encircle, enclose. EXPOSE

envelope wrapper, wrapping, case, casing, sheath, cover, skin, shell, capsule, coating, covering.

envenom poison, contaminate, pollute, taint.
embitter, sour, exacerbate, anger, enrage, incense, madden, provoke, inflame, irritate. APPEASE

enviable desirable, covetable, favoured, privileged, lucky, fortunate. UNENVIABLE

envious covetous, desirous, jealous, grudging, begrudging, resentful, dissatisfied. CONTENT

environ encircle, surround, encompass, gird, ring, circumscribe, enclose, envelop, hem in.

environment surroundings, milieu, circumstances, conditions, element, medium, habitat, background, setting, atmosphere, ambience.

environs vicinity, neighbourhood, district, locality, surroundings, suburbs, outskirts.

envisage visualize, imagine, picture, contemplate, conceive, envision, foresee, anticipate.

envoy agent, representative, diplomat, ambassador, minister, plenipotentiary, legate, emissary, messenger, courier.

envy *v*, covet, desire, resent, grudge, begrudge, be jealous of.

n, enviousness, covetousness, desire, jealousy, resentment, grudge, malice, spite, discontent. CONTENTEDNESS

ephemeral transitory, transient, fleeting, passing, brief, short, short-lived, fugacious, evanescent, momentary, temporary. PERMANENT

epic *adj*, heroic, impressive, great, grand, legendary, historic.

n, saga, épopée, narrative, story, legend.

epicure epicurean, gourmet, gastronome, *bon vivant*, voluptuary, sensualist, hedonist, sybarite, gourmand, glutton.

epidemic *adj*, widespread, extensive, prevalent, rampant, rife, pandemic.

n, plague, outbreak, upsurge, increase, wave, rash.

epigrammatic laconic, terse, concise, succinct, pithy, sharp, pointed, pungent, piquant, witty. VERBOSE

episode incident, event, occurrence, happening, occasion, circumstance, affair, matter, adventure, experience.

instalment, chapter, section, part, scene.

epistle letter, missive, communication, message, note.

epithet name, title, appellation, designation, nickname, sobriquet, label, tag.

epitome personification, embodiment, archetype, exemplar, representation, quintessence.

summary, digest, abstract, compendium, précis, résumé, conspectus, synopsis, abridgment. AMPLIFICATION

epitomize typify, represent, exemplify, embody, personify, symbolize.

summarize, abridge, condense, abstract, shorten, abbreviate, contract, précis. AMPLIFY

epoch age, era, period, time, date.

equable placid, serene, calm, even-tempered, unruffled, collected, composed, imperturbable. EXCITABLE

even, uniform, unvarying, stable, constant, steady, regular, consistent. VARIABLE

equal *adj*, identical, the same, like, alike, equivalent, commensurate, proportionate, tantamount. DIFFERENT

even, unvarying, uniform, steady, regular, constant, level, balanced, matched, symmetrical. UNEQUAL

adequate, suitable, fit, competent, capable, able. UNSUITABLE

n, peer, compeer, fellow, partner, mate, match, twin, counterpart, equivalent.

v, match, parallel, correspond, balance, come up to, rival, amount to.

equality uniformity, evenness, equivalence, parity, par, symmetry, balance, sameness, identity, correspondence, justice, fairness, impartiality, egalitarianism. INEQUALITY

equalize level, even up, square, make equal, match, balance, regularize, equate.

equanimity composure, self-possession, calmness, serenity, tranquillity, placidity, imperturbability, coolness, sang-froid, aplomb. AGITATION

equate compare, liken, parallel, pair, offset, balance, correspond, equalize.

equestrian rider, jockey, horseman, horsewoman, equestrienne, knight, cavalryman, dragoon. PEDESTRIAN

equilibrium balance, equipoise, stability, parity, symmetry.

equanimity, composure, calmness, sang-froid, aplomb, self-possession, coolness, poise. AGITATION

equip supply, furnish, provide, fit out, rig, prepare, stock, arm, dress, array, accoutre. DIVEST

equipage carriage, coach.

accoutrements, paraphernalia, belongings, effects, baggage, outfit, gear, equipment, stores, munitions, materiel.

equipment apparatus, tackle, rig, tools, accoutrements, furniture, outfit, gear, kit, supplies, belongings, effects, baggage, paraphernalia.

equipoise balance, equilibrium, counterbalance, counterpoise.

equitable just, fair, even-handed, impartial, unbiased, disinterested, right, rightful, proper, reasonable. UNJUST

equity justice, fairness, impartiality, objectivity, rightfulness, reasonableness, rectitude, honesty, integrity. INJUSTICE

equivalence parity, equality, identity, sameness, correlation, correspondence, similarity, analogy, parallel. DIFFERENCE

equivalent *adj*, equal, equipollent, commensurate, tantamount, synonymous, the same, interchangeable, comparable, correspondent, similar, alike. DIFFERENT
n, same, equivalence, match, twin, counterpart, equal, parallel.

equivocal ambiguous, ambivalent, vague, obscure, uncertain, indefinite, oblique, evasive, misleading, dubious, questionable, doubtful, suspicious. CLEAR

equivocate prevaricate, fence, hedge, dodge, evade, shuffle, shift, quibble, fudge, tergiversate, beat about the bush (*inf*).

equivocation prevarication, evasion, hedging, ambiguity, vagueness, tergiversation, waffle (*inf*).

era epoch, age, period, time, date, day, cycle, generation.

eradicate annihilate, extirpate, destroy, exterminate, efface, obliterate, stamp out, uproot, deracinate, remove, abolish, extinguish, eliminate. RESTORE

eradication annihilation, extirpation, destruction, extermination, obliteration, deracination, abolition, extinction, elimination. RESTORATION

erase expunge, rub out, eradicate, obliterate, efface, remove, delete, cancel, blot out. ENGRAVE

erasure rubbing out, eradication, obliteration, effacement, removal, deletion. ENGRAVING

erect *v*, build, construct, put up, set up, found, establish, raise, lift up, stand up, rear, elevate. DEMOLISH
adj, upright, vertical, straight, raised, standing, firm, stiff, rigid. FLAT

erection building, construction, structure, edifice.
raising, elevation, fabrication, construction, assembly. DEMOLITION

eremite recluse, hermit, solitary, anchorite.

ergo therefore, hence, consequently, so, thus.

eristic polemic, polemical, controversial, disputative, disputatious, argumentative.

erode wear, eat away, corrode, abrade, grind down, consume, devour, destroy, deteriorate.

erosion wear, attrition, corrosion, abrasion, eating away, consumption, destruction, deterioration.

erotic aphrodisiac, seductive, titillating, sexy (*inf*), carnal, sensual, voluptuous, amatory.

err miscalculate, misjudge, be wrong, make a mistake, blunder, slip up (*inf*).
sin, transgress, do wrong, go astray, lapse, fall, wander, stray, deviate.

errand commission, mission, assignment, task, charge, message.

errant erring, wrong, incorrect, straying, deviant, aberrant. RIGHT
wandering, roving, roaming, rambling, travelling, itinerant.

erratic changeable, capricious, variable, irregular, inconsistent, unstable, unreliable, unpredictable, aberrant, eccentric, abnormal, desultory, wandering. STEADY

erratum error, mistake, misprint, typo (*inf*), omission, corrigendum, correction.

erroneous wrong, incorrect, mistaken, untrue, false, inexact, inaccurate, unfounded, unsound, faulty. RIGHT

error mistake, inaccuracy, slip, blunder, oversight, omission, miscalculation, misapprehension, fault, flaw, fallacy. ACCURACY
offence, transgression, trespass, sin, wrong, wrongdoing, misdeed, fault, crime.

ersatz artificial, imitation, simulated, synthetic, sham, bogus, counterfeit, spurious. GENUINE

erudite learned, scholarly, knowledgeable, well-read, educated, literate, cultured, refined. ILLITERATE

erudition learning, scholarship, knowledge, lore, education, culture, refinement. ILLITERACY

erupt eject, emit, discharge, gush, spout, burst forth, break out, burst open, explode, blow up.

eruption ejection, emission, discharge, outburst, outbreak, explosion.
rash, inflammation.

escalate increase, grow, intensify, heighten, step up, raise, rise, mount, expand, magnify. DIMINISH

escapade adventure, scrape (*inf*), prank, caper, stunt, trick, romp, lark (*inf*).

escape *v*, get away, break free, flee, fly, run away, bolt, decamp, abscond. STAY
avoid, evade, dodge, elude. FACE
leak, seep, drain, flow, issue, gush, spurt.
n, getaway, flight, decampment, departure, break-out, release.
avoidance, evasion, elusion.
leak, leakage, seepage, discharge, emission, outflow, gush, spurt.

eschew shun, avoid, steer clear of, abstain from, forgo, refrain from, elude, shrink from.

escort *n*, companion, partner, chaperon, attendant, guide, protector, bodyguard.
entourage, cortege, retinue, company, convoy, guard, protection.
v, accompany, attend, conduct, guide, lead, usher, chaperon, protect, guard.

esculent edible, eatable, wholesome. INEDIBLE

escutcheon shield, scutcheon, arms.

esoteric abstruse, recondite, inscrutable, occult, cryptic, obscure, hidden, arcane, private, secret. EXOTERIC

especial special, exceptional, unusual, outstanding, marked, notable, remarkable, distinguished, signal, principal, chief. ORDINARY
particular, singular, individual, specific, distinctive, unique, personal, peculiar.

espousal adoption, support, advocacy, promotion, maintenance, defence, championship. REJECTION

espouse adopt, embrace, take up, support, uphold, maintain, defend, champion, advocate, promote. REJECT

espy notice, perceive, catch sight of, see, descry, make out, discern, detect, spot, glimpse, observe. MISS

essay *n*, composition, dissertation, treatise, article, paper, commentary, piece.
attempt, try, endeavour, effort, bid, go, shot, trial, test, experiment.
v, attempt, endeavour, try, have a go, strive, aim, test, try out.

essence quintessence, quiddity, principle, nature, entity, being, substance, pith, core, heart, spirit, life, significance, meaning.
concentrate, extract, distillate.

essential *adj*, vital, indispensable, crucial, important, necessary, requisite. DISPENSABLE
basic, fundamental, inherent, intrinsic, principal, main.
n, necessity, requisite, must, fundamental, rudiment, vital part.

establish found, start, form, set up, institute, organize, create, base, plant, settle, install, entrench, lodge, secure, fix. UPROOT
prove, substantiate, demonstrate, validate, confirm, certify, verify, ratify, support, corroborate. REFUTE

establishment foundation, institution, organization, creation, formation, setting up, installation.
business, concern, firm, company, corporation, house, organization, institute, institution, system.
household, house, home, abode, domicile, residence.

estate land, demesne, manor, lands, property, assets, effects, belongings, possessions, holdings, wealth.
status, standing, position, station, condition, rank, class.

esteem *v*, respect, admire, think highly of, value, prize, treasure, cherish, love, like, hold dear, honour, revere, venerate. SCORN
deem, consider, regard, judge, think, believe, reckon, hold.
n, respect, admiration, estimation, regard, consideration, honour, reverence, veneration, love. CONTEMPT

estimable admirable, respected, esteemed, valued, honourable, worthy, meritorious, deserving, good, excellent. DESPICABLE

estimate *v*, reckon, gauge, guess, assess, evaluate, value, appraise, rate, rank, judge.
n, reckoning, rough calculation, educated guess, approximation, guesstimate (*inf*).
assessment, evaluation, valuation, appraisal, judgment, opinion, estimation.

estimation judgment, opinion, belief, view, consideration, estimate, evaluation, assessment, reckoning.
esteem, respect, regard, honour, credit, admiration, reverence. CONTEMPT

estrange alienate, disaffect, antagonize, separate, divide, disunite, withdraw. RECONCILE

estuary inlet, mouth, firth, fiord, creek.

etch corrode, eat into, cut, engrave, carve, incise, impress, stamp, imprint.

etching print, impression, engraving, inscription.

eternal everlasting, enduring, abiding, immortal, undying, imperishable, unchanging, infinite, unending, endless, interminable, incessant, ceaseless, perpetual, continuous, perennial. TRANSIENT

eternity perpetuity, infinity, timelessness, evermore, forever, ages.
immortality, afterlife, hereafter, heaven.

ethereal light, airy, impalpable, delicate, fine, dainty, insubstantial, tenuous, subtle, rarefied, heavenly, celestial, empyreal, spiritual.

ethical moral, right, proper, just, fair, righteous, honest, upright, conscientious, honourable, decent, principled. UNETHICAL

ethnic racial, native, indigenous, national, traditional, cultural.

etiolate bleach, whiten, blanch, pale, fade, wash out, achromatize.

etiquette propriety, decorum, manners, politeness, protocol, form, convention, code, usage. IMPROPRIETY

Eucharist Communion, Lord's Supper, Mass.

eulogize praise, extol, laud, panegyrize, exalt, glorify, acclaim, commend. CENSURE

eulogy panegyric, encomium, praise, laudation, paean, accolade, plaudit, acclaim, commendation, exaltation, glorification. OBLOQUY

euphonious euphonic, melodious, harmonious, tuneful, dulcet, musical, mellifluous, mellow, clear, silvery. CACOPHONOUS

euphony harmony, melody, tunefulness, music, sweetness, smoothness, mellowness. HARSHNESS

euphoria elation, bliss, ecstasy, joy, rapture, jubilation, exhilaration, intoxication. DESPONDENCY

evacuate leave, depart, quit, withdraw, vacate, clear, abandon, desert, forsake. OCCUPY
empty, void, eject, expel, discharge, eliminate, excrete, defecate.

evacuation departure, exodus, withdrawal, retreat, emptying, clearance. OCCUPATION
ejection, expulsion, discharge, elimination, defecation, excretion.

evade avoid, circumvent, escape, get away from, dodge, elude, sidestep, shun, steer clear of. FACE
quibble, prevaricate, equivocate, fence, hedge.

evaluate appraise, assess, value, estimate, weigh, calculate, gauge, reckon, judge, rate.

evanesce fade, dissipate, disperse, evaporate, dissolve, melt, disappear, vanish. APPEAR

evanescent fading, vanishing, fleeting, passing, brief, ephemeral, transient, transitory. PERMANENT

evaporate vaporize, exhale, dry, dehydrate, desiccate. CONDENSE
disappear, vanish, dematerialize, fade, evanesce, dissolve, melt, dissipate, dispel. APPEAR

evaporation vaporization, exhalation, dehydration, desiccation. CONDENSATION
disappearance, dematerialization, evanescence, dissipation, dispersion. APPEARANCE

evasion avoidance, circumvention, escape, dodge, ruse, artifice, subterfuge, prevarication, equivocation, tergiversation, sophistry.

evasive prevaricating, equivocating, indirect, oblique, devious, misleading, deceptive, deceitful, tricky, slippery, elusive, cagey (*inf*). STRAIGHTFORWARD

even *adj*, level, smooth, flat, plane, uniform, regular, steady, constant, unvarying, equable, equal, parallel, abreast, symmetrical, balanced. UNEVEN
same, identical, equal, level, neck and neck, square, similar, like. UNEQUAL
calm, placid, serene, tranquil, even-tempered, composed, unruffled, imperturbable. AGITATED
balanced, even-handed, fair, just, equitable, impartial, unbiased. UNJUST
adv, notwithstanding, in spite of, although, even so, yet, still, nonetheless, all the more.
just, exactly, precisely, at the same time.
v, level, smooth, flatten, equalize, square, align, steady, balance.

evening dusk, twilight, nightfall, eventide, sunset. MORNING

event happening, occurrence, incident, affair, matter, occasion, episode, circumstance, fact.
consequence, result, outcome, upshot, issue, sequel. CAUSE
in any event, come what may, regardless, irrespective, at any rate, in any case, anyway.

eventful busy, full, lively, memorable, notable, remarkable, signal, momentous, significant, important, crucial, critical. UNEVENTFUL

eventual final, ultimate, resulting, consequent, prospective, future, inevitable.

eventually finally, ultimately, at last, in the end, in the long run, sooner or later.

eventuate result, issue, follow, ensue, happen, come about, end. BEGIN

ever always, continually, perpetually, constantly, relentlessly, at all times, forever, eternally, evermore, to the end of time. NEVER
at any time, on any occasion, by any chance, at all.

everlasting eternal, undying, imperishable, immortal, enduring, abiding, unchanging, infinite, endless, unending, perpetual, continuous, incessant, ceaseless, unremitting, interminable. PASSING

evermore always, ever, eternally, perpetually, forever.

every all, each. NO

everyday ordinary, common, commonplace, usual, habitual, routine, accustomed, customary, conventional, familiar, mundane, workaday, run-of-the-mill. UNUSUAL

evict expel, eject, turn out, kick out (*inf*), remove, oust, dispossess. HOUSE

evidence *n*, proof, verification, confirmation, substantiation, documentation, data, grounds, testimony, deposition, indication, sign, mark, demonstration.
v, evince, manifest, show, demonstrate, denote, indicate.

evident apparent, plain, clear, obvious, patent, manifest, visible, palpable, conspicuous, unmistakable, indisputable, incontrovertible.

evil *adj*, wrong, bad, sinful, wicked, iniquitous, base, vile, immoral, corrupt, villainous, vicious, malevolent, malignant, malicious, nefarious. GOOD
harmful, pernicious, injurious, baleful, baneful, noxious, deleterious, mischievous, hurtful, ruinous. BENEFICIAL
disastrous, calamitous, adverse, ill, unfortunate, unlucky, unpropitious, inauspicious. LUCKY
foul, vile, offensive, unpleasant, noxious, pestilential. PLEASANT
n, wrong, badness, sin, wickedness, iniquity, baseness, vice, immorality, depravity, corruption, malevolence, malignity, maleficence. GOODNESS
harm, ill, injury, hurt, mischief, affliction, suffering, pain, sorrow, misery, ruin, disaster, calamity.

evince evidence, show, display, exhibit, manifest, establish, indicate, demonstrate, betoken, reveal. CONCEAL

eviscerate disembowel, gut, draw.

evoke summon, call, elicit, educe, rouse, provoke, stimulate, stir, excite, awaken, rekindle, conjure up, call forth, invoke. STIFLE

evolution development, evolvement, unfolding, progression, growth, expansion, increase, ripening, maturation. RETROGRESSION

evolve develop, unfold, unroll, open, progress, grow, expand, increase, result, emerge. RETROGRESS

exacerbate aggravate, worsen, intensify, inflame, irritate, provoke, infuriate, exasperate, enrage, madden, embitter, envenom. SOOTHE

exacerbation aggravation, intensification, irritation, provocation, infuriation, exasperation. APPEASEMENT

exact *adj*, precise, accurate, correct, right, faultless, faithful, literal, strict, rigid, specific, explicit, definite. INEXACT
careful, meticulous, scrupulous, punctilious, particular, exacting, conscientious, painstaking, methodical, orderly, critical, rigorous, severe. LOOSE
v, extort, extract, wring, elicit, compel, impose, demand, require, call for, insist on, ask, request, claim.

exacting difficult, hard, demanding, taxing, critical, rigorous, severe, harsh, oppressive, tough, stern, imperious. EASY

exaction extortion, extraction, demand, imposition, requisition, tribute.

exactitude exactness, precision, accuracy, correctness, faultlessness, faithfulness, fidelity, carefulness, scrupulousness, strictness, rigour. INEXACTITUDE

exactly precisely, accurately, faithfully, literally, definitely, strictly, scrupulously.
just, quite, absolutely, indeed, truly, of course.

exaggerate magnify, inflate, overstate, overdo, stretch, embroider, embellish, amplify, emphasize, overemphasize, hyperbolize, overestimate. UNDERSTATE

exaggeration overstatement, hyperbole, magnification, inflation, embellishment, amplification, overestimation. UNDERSTATEMENT

exalt ennoble, elevate, raise, promote, advance, aggrandize, dignify, honour. DOWNGRADE
praise, extol, glorify, acclaim, applaud, commend. DISPARAGE
excite, stimulate, inspire, animate, exhilarate, thrill, elate. DAMP

exaltation ennoblement, elevation, promotion, advancement, aggrandizement, dignity, honour, grandeur, loftiness, eminence, prestige.
praise, laudation, extolment, glorification, acclaim, acclamation, tribute. DISPARAGEMENT
excitement, animation, elation, exhilaration, exultation, joy, rapture. DEPRESSION

examination inspection, scrutiny, inquiry, investigation, observation, study, survey, research, exploration, probe, analysis.
test, quiz, trial, interrogation.

examine inspect, investigate, scrutinize, study, analyse, explore, survey, research, look into, probe, sift, check out, observe. IGNORE
test, quiz, question, interrogate, cross-examine.

example sample, specimen, illustration, exemplification, instance, case, precedent, exemplar, model, pattern, standard, prototype, ideal, paragon.
warning, caution, lesson.

exasperate anger, incense, infuriate, enrage, vex, annoy, irritate, madden, irk, nettle, provoke, aggravate, exacerbate. APPEASE

exasperation anger, infuriation, fury, rage, vexation, annoyance, irritation, provocation, aggravation, exacerbation. APPEASEMENT

excavate dig, delve, burrow, tunnel, scoop, hollow, dig out, quarry, mine, dig up, unearth, disinter.

excavation hole, cavity, trench, trough, hollow, pit, mine, quarry, burrow, dugout, cutting, dig.

exceed surpass, outstrip, pass, outdo, beat, transcend, surmount, outshine, eclipse, excel, cap, top, go beyond, overstep.

exceedingly very, extremely, exceptionally, especially, greatly, vastly, tremendously, enormously, highly. SLIGHTLY

excel *vt*, surpass, outshine, eclipse, exceed, outstrip, outdo, outclass, beat, cap, top.
vi, shine, predominate, lead, be proficient, be talented, succeed.

excellent superior, first-rate, exceptional, outstanding, superlative, prime, capital, choice, select, first-class, supreme, matchless, sterling, fine, very good, admirable, estimable, worthy, eminent, great, splendid, wonderful, marvellous. INFERIOR

except *prep*, but, excepting, save, saving, other than, apart from, besides, excluding, barring. INCLUDING
v, omit, exclude, leave out, reject, bar, ban. INCLUDE

exception omission, exclusion, rejection, debarment. INCLUSION
anomaly, oddity, odd one out, freak, irregularity, peculiarity. RULE
take exception, object, demur, be offended, take offence.

exceptional anomalous, abnormal, aberrant, unusual, rare, uncommon, special, irregular, deviant, odd, strange, peculiar, extraordinary. NORMAL
outstanding, remarkable, excellent, prodigious, phenomenal, superior, above average. ORDINARY

excerpt *n*, extract, passage, section, citation, quotation, selection, pericope, fragment, piece.
v, extract, take, quote, cite, select, pick out.

excess *n*, surfeit, overabundance, glut, plethora, profusion, surplus, remainder, balance, superfluity. DEFICIENCY

overindulgence, immoderation, unrestraint, dissipation, debauchery, intemperance, extravagance. RESTRAINT
adj, extra, surplus, superfluous, spare, leftover. INSUFFICIENT

excessive immoderate, extreme, inordinate, undue, disproportionate, fulsome, unreasonable, needless, extravagant, exorbitant, too much, overmuch. MODERATE

exchange *v*, trade, barter, swap, change, interchange, commute, switch, substitute, reciprocate, bandy.
n, trade, barter, swap, change, interchange, commutation, switch, substitution, reciprocation.
market, fair, Bourse.

excise¹ *n*, duty, tax, impost, toll, customs.

excise² *v*, delete, expunge, cross out, cut out, remove.

excitable volatile, mercurial, nervous, highly-strung, emotional, passionate, sensitive, temperamental, quick-tempered, irascible, touchy. IMPERTURBABLE

excite rouse, arouse, awaken, stir up, animate, stimulate, kindle, evoke, raise, elicit, incite, provoke, spur, agitate, foment, disturb, inflame, inspire, galvanize, electrify, thrill, exhilarate. CALM

excitement animation, enthusiasm, passion, agitation, commotion, restlessness, fever, thrill, stimulation, exhilaration. CALMNESS
stimulus, provocation, incentive, motive, urge, impulse.

exclaim cry, shout, yell, vociferate, ejaculate, call, call out, declare.

exclamation cry, ejaculation, interjection, vociferation, call, shout, yell, clamour, outcry.

exclude ban, bar, debar, blackball, keep out, shut out, proscribe, prohibit, veto, disallow. ADMIT
omit, except, leave out, preclude, pass over, rule out, eliminate, reject, ignore. INCLUDE
expel, eject, throw out, oust, evict, remove.

exclusion omission, exception, elimination, rejection. INCLUSION
ban, bar, proscription, prohibition, veto, embargo. ADMISSION
expulsion, ejection, eviction, removal.

exclusive individual, sole, single, only, unique, unshared, undivided, total, full, complete. SHARED
limited, restricted, narrow, closed, cliquish, snobbish, select, choice, posh, elegant. COMMON
excluding, barring, excepting, omitting. INCLUSIVE

excogitate contrive, invent, devise, think up, coin, create, hatch, frame, conceive, imagine, contemplate, deliberate, ponder.

excommunicate exclude, remove, banish, expel, cast out, unchurch, anathematize, denounce, proscribe. ADMIT

excoriate skin, flay, strip, peel, scrape, abrade, gall, scarify.
denounce, condemn, censure, reprove, rebuke, reproach, upbraid, castigate, attack, scourge, vilify, defame. EXTOL

excrement excretion, excreta, faeces, stools, ordure, dung, droppings.

excrescence protuberance, lump, growth, swelling, tumour, protrusion, prominence, projection, outgrowth.

excrete discharge, eject, expel, eliminate, evacuate, void, defecate, urinate, egest, exude.

excruciate torment, torture, afflict, harrow, distress, agonize. SOOTHE

excruciating agonizing, painful, intense, severe, acute, unbearable, racking, harrowing, distressing. SOOTHING

exculpate exonerate, vindicate, clear, absolve, acquit, free, release, discharge, pardon. CHARGE

excursion trip, outing, jaunt, expedition, tour, ramble, drive, ride, journey.
digression, excursus, deviation, detour.

excursive discursive, digressive, rambling, wandering, roving, errant. DIRECT

excuse *v*, pardon, forgive, overlook, condone, tolerate, remit, absolve, exculpate, exonerate, acquit, clear, vindicate, justify, explain. CONDEMN
exempt, free, release, let off, spare, discharge, dismiss.
n, explanation, justification, defence, plea, apology, reason, grounds, pretext, pretence, feint, subterfuge, evasion, cop-out (*inf*).

execrable abominable, abhorrent, detestable, odious, hateful, horrible, vile, loathsome, obnoxious, repulsive, disgusting, damnable, accursed, bad, appalling, atrocious. DELIGHTFUL

execrate abominate, abhor, detest, loathe, hate, curse, damn, imprecate, revile, deplore, condemn, denounce. LOVE

execute perform, do, carry out, fulfil, complete, finish, accomplish, achieve, effect, enforce, enact, administer.
kill, put to death, behead, hang, electrocute, shoot.

execution performance, operation, discharge, fulfilment, completion, accomplishment, achievement, enforcement, implementation, administration.
killing, capital punishment, beheading, hanging, electrocution, shooting.
style, technique, manner, delivery, rendition, interpretation.

executive *n*, administration, management, government, leadership, administrator, manager, leader, director, official.
adj, administrative, managerial, directorial, governing, controlling.

exegetic explanatory, expository, explicative, interpretative.

exemplary model, admirable, estimable, commendable, praiseworthy, laudable, good, fine, excellent, worthy, honourable, perfect, ideal. DESPICABLE
admonitory, cautionary, warning.
typical, representative, illustrative.

exemplify illustrate, instance, show, demonstrate, exhibit, manifest, represent, embody.

exempt *v*, excuse, release, free, relieve, except, spare, let off, absolve, exonerate. COMPEL
adj, exempted, excused, released, free, spared, immune, not liable, excepted, privileged. LIABLE

exemption release, exception, exclusion, immunity, privilege, dispensation, freedom. LIABILITY

exercise *v*, use, utilize, employ, exert, bring to bear, apply, wield, practise.
drill, train, practise, limber up, work out, develop, discipline. RELAX
worry, trouble, disturb, afflict, annoy, vex.
n, effort, exertion, work, labour, workout, activity, drill, training, practice, task, lesson, discipline, development. REST
use, employment, exertion, application, practice, performance, operation, discharge.

exert use, utilize, employ, exercise, apply, bring to bear.

exert oneself, struggle, strive, toil, labour, make an effort, try hard, do one's best. IDLE

exertion effort, labour, toil, struggle, strain, endeavour, attempt. IDLENESS
use, employment, exercise, application.

exhalation breath, expiration, emission, emanation, evaporation, vapour, steam, mist, smoke, fume, effluvium.

exhale breathe out, respire, emit, expel, emanate, give off, evaporate, steam. ABSORB

exhaust consume, use up, drain, deplete, expend, spend, dissipate, squander, waste. REPLENISH
weary, tire out, fatigue, wear out, prostrate, weaken, debilitate, sap, drain. STRENGTHEN

exhausted weary, tired out, fatigued, worn out, drained, jaded, dead beat (*inf*), all in (*inf*), knackered (*inf*). REFRESHED
used up, spent, drained, depleted, empty, bare, gone, finished, at an end.

exhaustive comprehensive, all-embracing, wide-ranging, far-reaching, all-inclusive, full, thorough, extensive, in-depth. RESTRICTED

exhibit display, show, demonstrate, manifest, evince, evidence, indicate, betray, reveal, disclose, express, parade, flaunt, air, expose. CONCEAL

exhibition display, show, demonstration, manifestation, indication, expression, airing, presentation, exposition, fair, performance, spectacle.
scholarship, allowance, grant, bursary.

exhilarate elate, thrill, animate, enliven, invigorate, stimulate, inspirit, cheer, gladden, delight. DEPRESS

exhilaration elation, thrill, joy, glee, hilarity, mirth, gaiety, high spirits, exaltation, animation, excitement, gladness, cheerfulness, delight. DEPRESSION

exhort urge, enjoin, bid, persuade, prevail upon, induce, advise, counsel, entreat, beseech, encourage, incite, spur. DETER

exhortation urging, persuasion, advice, entreaty, encouragement, lecture, sermon, homily. DISCOURAGEMENT

exhume disinter, dig up, unearth, unbury, disentomb. INTER

exigency crisis, emergency, juncture, extremity, pinch, strait, pass, predicament, plight, quandary.

urgency, need, necessity, demand, requirement, pressure, constraint.

exigent urgent, pressing, critical, crucial, pivotal, imperative, importunate. UNIMPORTANT

demanding, taxing, exacting, arduous, difficult, hard, harsh, severe, rigorous. EASY

exiguous scanty, meagre, paltry, tiny, small, thin, slender, slight, bare, sparse. AMPLE

exile *v*, expel, banish, expatriate, deport, drive out, ostracize, proscribe, eject, oust. WELCOME

n, expulsion, banishment, expatriation, deportation, ostracism, proscription, ejection.

expatriate, refugee, émigré, outcast, displaced person.

exist be, live, breathe, subsist, survive, remain, endure, last, continue, abide, be present, prevail, occur, obtain.

existence being, life, breath, animation, subsistence, survival, continuance, duration, persistence, reality, actuality, presence. NONEXISTENCE

exit *n*, egress, way out, door, gate, outlet, vent. ENTRANCE

departure, going, withdrawal, retirement, exodus, demise, death. ARRIVAL

v, depart, leave, go, withdraw, retire, issue, go out. ENTER

exodus exit, departure, withdrawal, retreat, escape, flight, migration. ARRIVAL

exonerate absolve, acquit, clear, exculpate, vindicate, justify, excuse, pardon, discharge, free, release. CHARGE

exempt, relieve, release, spare, excuse, let off. COMPEL

exorbitant excessive, immoderate, unreasonable, inordinate, disproportionate, extreme, preposterous, outrageous, extortionate, prohibitive, extravagant. MODERATE

exorcism expulsion, casting out, deliverance, adjuration, incantation, invocation.

exordium preamble, introduction, preface, foreword, prologue, prelude, opening. EPILOGUE

exoteric public, open, communal, accessible, comprehensible, simple, plain, common, vulgar. ESOTERIC

external, outer, exterior, superficial. INNER

exotic foreign, alien, imported, extraneous, extrinsic. NATIVE

remarkable, striking, strange, unusual, extraordinary, outlandish, bizarre, glamorous, exciting, fascinating. ORDINARY

expand stretch, spread, enlarge, increase, amplify, magnify, swell, dilate, distend, inflate, open, unfold, prolong, extend, broaden, widen, grow, augment, multiply, develop, elaborate, flesh out. CONTRACT

expanse stretch, extent, area, space, spread, field, scope, range, breadth.

expansion enlargement, increase, amplification, dilation, inflation, spread, unfolding, extension, growth, augmentation, development, elaboration. CONTRACTION

expansive extensive, wide, broad, vast, comprehensive, far-reaching, wide-ranging, universal, global. NARROW

expanding, swelling, inflatable, extendable, elastic, stretchy, spreading.

talkative, loquacious, garrulous, outgoing, sociable, unreserved, communicative, affable, genial. RESERVED

expatiate enlarge, expand, elaborate, descant, dwell, dilate, amplify. SUMMARIZE

expatriate *v*, deport, exile, banish, expel, proscribe, ostracize.

n, exile, émigré, emigrant, displaced person.

expatriation exile, banishment, expulsion, deportation, emigration.

expect anticipate, await, look forward to, envisage, contemplate, foresee, hope, bargain for.

require, demand, insist on, call for, count on.

suppose, presume, surmise, believe, think, imagine, reckon.

expectant hopeful, awaiting, apprehensive, anxious, eager, ready, in suspense, on tenterhooks.

pregnant, expecting (*inf*), gravid, enceinte.

expectation anticipation, prospect, outlook, expectancy, contemplation, hope, apprehension, suspense, trust, reliance, assurance, belief, supposition, presumption, probability, likelihood, possibility.

expediency expedience, suitability, appropriateness, fitness, propriety, usefulness, desirability, advisability, wisdom, prudence, advantageousness, helpfulness, convenience, profit, gain, benefit, utility, practicality.

expedient *adj*, appropriate, suitable, fitting, seemly, proper, right, useful, desirable, advisable, wise, prudent, judicious, advantageous, helpful, worthwhile, valuable, profitable, convenient, practical. UNWISE
n, means, contrivance, device, shift, resource, resort, scheme, stratagem, makeshift, stopgap.

expedite accelerate, hasten, precipitate, speed, hurry, promote, advance, forward, assist, facilitate, dispatch. DELAY

expedition journey, voyage, trip, excursion, tour, safari, trek, exploration, mission, crusade, campaign, march.
haste, speed, dispatch, celerity, swiftness, alacrity, promptness. TARDINESS

expeditious prompt, instant, quick, rapid, speedy, fast, brisk, efficient, nimble. SLOW

expel eject, drive out, evict, exile, banish, expatriate, remove, oust, throw out, dismiss, proscribe, exclude. WELCOME
discharge, eject, void, evacuate, cast out, spew.

expend spend, disburse, pay out, fork out (*inf*). SAVE
consume, use up, exhaust, deplete, dissipate. CONSERVE

expenditure spending, disbursement, outlay, outgoings, expense, cost, charge, payment. INCOME

expense cost, charge, price, expenditure, disbursement, outlay, payment. RECEIPT
sacrifice, cost, loss, detriment.

expensive dear, costly, high-priced, steep (*inf*), exorbitant, extortionate, extravagant, rich, lavish, valuable. CHEAP

experience *v*, undergo, feel, suffer, go through, live through, endure, encounter, meet, face, try, know, perceive. MISS
n, incident, event, episode, adventure, encounter, ordeal, trial.
knowledge, familiarity, contact, involvement, participation, exposure, practice, understanding, observation. INEXPERIENCE

experienced practised, versed, familiar, knowledgeable, expert, proficient, skilled, trained, qualified, accomplished, able, competent, adept, professional, veteran. INEXPERIENCED

experiment *n*, trial, test, investigation, examination, research, experimentation, attempt, essay, venture.
v, try, test, investigate, examine, research, attempt, venture.

experimental empirical, tentative, speculative, exploratory, provisional, test, trial.

expert *n*, specialist, connoisseur, authority, professional, master, dab hand (*inf*), ace (*inf*), adept, past master, old hand. NOVICE
adj, proficient, adept, skilful, skilled, adroit, dexterous, practised, experienced, knowledgeable, versed, masterly.

expiate atone for, make amends for, redress, redeem, do penance for, pay for.

expiation atonement, amends, redress, reparation, satisfaction, redemption, penance.

expiration termination, end, finish, close, cessation, expiry, demise, decease, death. BEGINNING
exhalation, breathing out, respiration. INHALATION

expire end, finish, cease, close, terminate, stop, run out, lapse, die, perish. BEGIN
exhale, breathe out, respire. INHALE

explain interpret, expound, define, describe, explicate, clarify, make clear, elucidate, solve, unravel, unfold, illustrate, demonstrate. MYSTIFY
justify, account for, warrant, excuse.

explanation interpretation, exposition, definition, description, explication, clarification, elucidation, solution, theory, illustration, demonstration. MYSTIFICATION
justification, warrant, reason, motive, excuse, defence, account, meaning, key, answer.

explanatory explicative, descriptive, elucidative, illustrative, interpretative, expository, justificatory.

expletive *adj*, unnecessary, nonessential, superfluous, redundant. ESSENTIAL
n, oath, swearword, obscenity, curse, exclamation, ejaculation.

explication explanation, exposition, interpretation, illustration, clarification, elucidation, analysis, exegesis, commentary, formulation, development.

explicit plain, clear, distinct, unambiguous, precise, specific, express, definite, positive, categorical, absolute, full, detailed, straightforward, blunt, unreserved, open. IMPLIED

explode burst, blow up, blast, discharge, detonate, set off, go off.
discredit, invalidate, refute, repudiate, disprove, belie. CONFIRM

exploit *v*, use, utilize, capitalize on, profit from, take advantage of, misuse, abuse, manipulate.
n, feat, deed, act, achievement, accomplishment, adventure.

exploration examination, investigation, search, probe, research, study, analysis, inspection, scrutiny, survey, inquiry.

explore examine, investigate, probe, study, analyse, plumb, inspect, scrutinize, survey, inquire into, pry into.
travel, traverse, search, prospect, reconnoitre.

explosion blast, detonation, burst, discharge, bang, boom, crack, pop.
outburst, eruption, outbreak, increase.

exponent advocate, champion, defender, promoter, interpreter, expounder, expositor, presenter.
example, specimen, symbol, indication, representation, illustration.

export ship, send abroad, sell overseas. IMPORT

expose exhibit, display, show, reveal, disclose, divulge, air, make known, unmask, unveil, uncover, bare, unearth, bring to light, detect. HIDE
endanger, jeopardize, imperil, risk, hazard, venture. PROTECT

exposition explanation, interpretation, explication, description, account, commentary, critique, exegesis, presentation.
display, show, exhibition, demonstration, presentation, fair, market.

expostulate object, protest, argue, remonstrate, exhort, reason.

expostulation objection, protest, argument, remonstrance, exhortation.

exposure revelation, disclosure, exposé, unmasking, unveiling, airing, divulgence, publication, presentation, display, exhibition, baring. CONCEALMENT
jeopardy, peril, danger, risk, hazard, vulnerability. SAFETY

expound explain, elucidate, define, set forth, unfold, develop, describe, interpret.

express *v*, utter, say, voice, verbalize, articulate, phrase, communicate, put across, convey, state, declare, assert, announce. SUPPRESS
show, manifest, exhibit, evince, demonstrate, reveal, denote, depict, indicate, represent, symbolize, stand for.
adj, rapid, fast, quick, swift, direct, nonstop, high-speed. SLOW
explicit, specific, definite, precise, plain, clear, unambiguous, unmistakable, distinct, positive, categorical. VAGUE

expression look, countenance, face, air, aspect, mien, appearance.
utterance, verbalization, articulation, communication, statement, declaration, assertion, announcement. SUPPRESSION
phrase, locution, word, term, saying.
manifestation, exhibition, demonstration, indication, evidence, sign, symbol, token.
tone, feeling, modulation, intonation, delivery, execution.

expressive forceful, eloquent, meaningful, significant, pregnant, pointed, demonstrative, suggestive, indicative, telling, vivid, graphic, striking, strong, emphatic, moving, poignant, emotional.

expulsion ejection, eviction, exile, banishment, expatriation, dismissal, proscription, exclusion, discharge. WELCOME

expunge erase, delete, cross out, cancel, efface, blot out, obliterate, eradicate, extirpate, annihilate, wipe out, destroy, exterminate.

expurgate bowdlerize, censor, purge, clean up (*inf*), cut.

exquisite fine, delicate, dainty, beautiful, lovely, attractive, elegant. UGLY
choice, select, excellent, fine, rare, matchless, perfect, valuable, precious, splendid, outstanding, superb. ORDINARY
refined, cultivated, discriminating, selective, impeccable, fastidious, sensitive, appreciative. COARSE
intense, sharp, keen, acute. DULL

extant existing, existent, surviving, present, remaining, undestroyed.

extemporaneous extemporary, extempore, improvised, impromptu, ad-lib, spontaneous, unrehearsed, unprepared, off-the-cuff (*inf*). PREPARED

extempore extemporaneous, improvised, impromptu, ad lib, off the cuff (*inf*), spontaneously.

extend stretch, spread, reach, unfold, draw out, lengthen, prolong, elongate, protract, spin out, continue.
expand, enlarge, increase, amplify, widen, broaden, augment, add to. CONTRACT
offer, hold out, proffer, give, bestow, present, impart, confer. WITHHOLD

extension stretching, lengthening, prolongation, elongation, protraction, continuation, expansion, enlargement, increase, augmentation. CONTRACTION
delay, postponement, deferment.
addition, addendum, adjunct, supplement, appendix, appendage, annexe, wing, branch.

extensive broad, wide, large, huge, vast, spacious, capacious, widespread, universal, all-embracing, comprehensive, exhaustive, wide-ranging, long, lengthy, protracted. LIMITED

extent degree, amount, measure, quantity, size, magnitude, volume, length, breadth, width, height, depth, range, scope, limit, reach, compass, bounds.

extenuate mitigate, palliate, lessen, diminish, reduce, temper, moderate, qualify, play down, minimize, make light of, underestimate. EXAGGERATE

exterior *n*, outside, surface, face, shell, skin, covering, façade, appearance, aspect. INTERIOR
adj, outer, outside, external, outward, superficial, surface. INNER

exterminate annihilate, eradicate, extirpate, wipe out, destroy, kill, eliminate, abolish.

extermination annihilation, eradication, extirpation, destruction, extinction, elimination.

external outer, exterior, outside, outward, superficial, apparent, visible. INTERNAL

extinct dead, defunct, wiped out, vanished, gone, lost, finished, ended, obsolete, abolished, extinguished, quenched, inactive. LIVING

extinction annihilation, extermination, eradication, extirpation, destruction, abolition, death, dying out. SURVIVAL

extinguish quench, put out, snuff, douse, blow out, smother, stifle, suffocate, choke. LIGHT
annihilate, destroy, eradicate, extirpate, eliminate, kill, suppress, quash, erase, remove.

extirpate destroy, wipe out, annihilate, exterminate, eradicate, uproot, stamp out, abolish, extinguish. ESTABLISH

extirpation destruction, annihilation, extermination, eradication, abolition, extinction. ESTABLISHMENT

extol praise, laud, eulogize, panegyrize, exalt, glorify, acclaim, applaud, commend. DECRY

extort extract, wring, wrest, milk, squeeze, blackmail, bleed (*inf*), coerce, force, exact, elicit.

extortionate exorbitant, excessive, immoderate, unreasonable, outrageous, usurious, exacting, hard, severe, harsh, grasping, rapacious. MODERATE

extra *adj*, additional, supplementary, spare, reserve, accessory, ancillary, auxiliary, more, further, surplus, leftover, excess, superfluous.
n, addition, supplement, accessory, appurtenance, bonus.
adv, especially, exceptionally, particularly, unusually.

extract *v*, remove, pull out, draw out, take out, withdraw, exact, extort, wrest, uproot, tear out. INSERT
derive, draw, distil, squeeze out, get, obtain, elicit, educe, glean.
cite, quote, abstract, select.
n, excerpt, quotation, citation, abstract, passage, clipping, selection.
essence, concentrate, distillate, juice.

extraction removal, withdrawal, derivation, distillation, separation.
parentage, descent, ancestry, lineage, family, stock, blood, birth, origin.

extradition surrender, delivery, handing over.

extraneous extrinsic, external, alien, foreign, adventitious, incidental, additional, extra, nonessential, unnecessary, superfluous, redundant. INTRINSIC
irrelevant, immaterial, beside the point, unconnected, unrelated. RELEVANT

extraordinary strange, peculiar, singular, odd, curious, bizarre, weird, unusual, uncommon, rare, signal, remarkable, striking, outstanding, exceptional, surprising, amazing. ORDINARY

extravagance prodigality, lavishness, wastefulness, profligacy, overspending, recklessness, improvidence. ECONOMY
immoderation, unrestraint, excess, absurdity, wildness, folly, preposterousness, unreasonableness. MODERATION
extravagant prodigal, lavish, wasteful, profligate, spendthrift, reckless, improvident, thriftless. THRIFTY
immoderate, unrestrained, inordinate, excessive, exaggerated, outrageous, preposterous, wild, absurd, foolish. MODERATE
costly, dear, expensive, overpriced, exorbitant, extortionate. REASONABLE
extreme *adj*, great, intense, severe, acute, ultimate, maximum, greatest, highest, utmost, excessive, immoderate, unreasonable, utter, downright, out-and-out, exceptional, remarkable. REASONABLE
fanatical, radical, zealous, extremist. MODERATE
farthest, outermost, faraway, last, final, ultimate, endmost. NEAR
drastic, radical, uncompromising, rigid, severe, dire.
n, extremity, top, acme, apex, peak, height, depth, climax, end, termination, edge, limit, maximum, minimum. MEDIAN
extremity extreme, limit, boundary, border, edge, verge, brink, end, termination, height, depth, maximum, minimum.
emergency, crisis, exigency, plight, hardship, adversity.
extricate disentangle, disembarrass, disengage, clear, free, release, deliver, liberate, rescue, relieve, remove, withdraw, get out. INVOLVE
extrinsic extraneous, external, exterior, outside, foreign, alien, exotic, unrelated. INTRINSIC
extrude eject, force out, squeeze out, press out, expel, discharge.
exuberance liveliness, vivacity, ebullience, buoyancy, vitality, animation, vigour, enthusiasm. LETHARGY
abundance, profusion, plenty, copiousness, superabundance, richness, luxuriance, lavishness, prodigality. SCARCITY
exuberant lively, vivacious, ebullient, effervescent, buoyant, elated, animated, sparkling, enthusiastic. LETHARGIC
abundant, plentiful, copious, profuse, superabundant, rich, luxuriant, lavish, prodigal, extravagant. SCARCE
exudation sweating, sweat, perspiration, oozing, secretion, discharge, emanation. ABSORPTION
exude ooze, seep, leak, filter, trickle, drip, flow out, secrete, discharge, emanate, sweat, excrete. ABSORB
exult rejoice, triumph, jubilate, crow, gloat, be joyful, make merry, jump for joy. MOURN
exultant triumphant, jubilant, exulting, rejoicing, joyful, overjoyed, elated, delighted. MISERABLE
eye *n*, look, glimpse, glance, gaze.
appreciation, sensitivity, discernment, taste, discrimination.
viewpoint, opinion, judgment, mind.
watch, surveillance, observation, lookout.
v, look at, watch, observe, peruse, scrutinize, scan, survey, gaze at, stare at. IGNORE

F

fable allegory, parable, apologue, tale, story, myth, legend.
untruth, lie, falsehood, fib, fiction, fabrication, invention, romance, tall story (*inf*). TRUTH
fabric cloth, material, stuff, textile, texture, weave.
structure, framework, organization, makeup, constitution, construction.
fabricate build, construct, make, manufacture, produce, form, frame, assemble, erect. DESTROY
devise, invent, coin, formulate, make up, concoct, fake, forge, counterfeit, falsify.
fabrication building, construction, manufacture, production, assembly, erection. DESTRUCTION
invention, formulation, concoction, fake, forgery, fable, lie, falsehood, fiction.
fabulous legendary, mythical, fantastic, unreal, imaginary, fictitious, invented, incredible, unbelievable, amazing, astounding, marvellous, superb, wonderful.
façade front, appearance, exterior, mask, disguise, veneer, show, pretence, semblance, illusion.
face *n*, countenance, visage, physiognomy, features, mug (*inf*), phiz (*inf*).
appearance, look, expression, aspect, air, façade, front, surface, exterior, veneer, pretence, semblance.

dignity, honour, repute, prestige, standing, image.
boldness, audacity, effrontery, brass, gall, impudence, cheek (*inf*). TIMIDITY
v, confront, brave, beard, defy, oppose, meet, encounter, come up against, deal with, face up to. AVOID
overlook, front on, be opposite.
cover, coat, veneer, encrust, dress, line, finish, level, smooth.

facet face, surface, side, aspect, angle, slant, element, detail.

facetious joking, jesting, jocular, witty, droll, waggish, frivolous, flippant, tongue-in-cheek, funny, humorous, amusing, comical. SERIOUS

facile easy, simple, effortless, smooth, fluent, skilful, adept, dexterous, adroit, proficient. AWKWARD
glib, slick, superficial, shallow.
complaisant, easy-going, affable, mild, compliant, docile, yielding. OBDURATE

facilitate assist, aid, help, forward, advance, expedite, speed up, ease, make easy, simplify. HINDER

facility ease, easiness, effortlessness, smoothness, fluency, readiness, skill, dexterity, proficiency, ability, knack, talent, aptitude. AWKWARDNESS
convenience, advantage, resource, amenity, aid, means.

facsimile copy, reproduction, replica, duplicate, carbon, photocopy, transcript. ORIGINAL

fact truth, actuality, reality, certainty. FICTION
event, happening, occurrence, incident, circumstance, deed, act.
element, detail, point, particular, item, factor.
in fact, actually, in reality, indeed, really, truly.

faction group, party, gang, band, clique, set, junta, confederacy, cabal, contingent, division, splinter group, camp.
discord, dissension, strife, conflict, disagreement, rebellion, sedition, upheaval, tumult, division. UNANIMITY

factious discordant, disagreeing, at variance, quarrelsome, disputatious, warring, rebellious, seditious, dissident, divisive, disruptive.

factitious artificial, false, unnatural, contrived, affected, simulated, insincere, sham, mock, fake. GENUINE

factor element, part, component, detail, item, facet, point, aspect, circumstance, cause.
agent, middleman, intermediary, deputy, proxy, representative.

factory plant, shop, works, mill, foundry.

factual authentic, genuine, true, real, actual, accurate, precise, correct, unbiased, objective, literal. FALSE

faculty ability, aptitude, facility, gift, knack, talent, skill, dexterity, proficiency, power, capacity, capability. INABILITY
department, school, discipline, profession.
right, licence, power, authority, prerogative, privilege.

fad fashion, vogue, trend, craze, rage, mania, whim, fancy.

fade pale, dim, bleach, blanch, blench, discolour, etiolate, wash out. DARKEN
diminish, decrease, dwindle, wane, ebb, fall, decline, fail, languish, wither, perish, dissolve, disperse, evanesce, vanish, disappear. GROW

fag *v*, fatigue, weary, tire out, exhaust, jade, wear out, prostrate. REFRESH
n, chore, drag (*inf*), bother, nuisance, inconvenience, bind (*inf*).

fail miscarry, fall through, go wrong, be unsuccessful, flop (*inf*), founder, fall short, miss, be in vain, come to nothing, fizzle out (*inf*), disappoint, let down. SUCCEED
omit, neglect, forget, desert, forsake, abandon.
decline, decay, wane, dwindle, fade, sink, weaken, flag, collapse, crumble, cease, die, disappear, go bankrupt, go under, fold (*inf*). FLOURISH

failing flaw, fault, defect, weakness, frailty, imperfection, deficiency, shortcoming, drawback, foible, failure. STRENGTH

failure miscarriage, abortion, lack of success, frustration, defeat, breakdown, collapse, fiasco, washout (*inf*), disappointment, flop (*inf*), dud (*inf*), loser, also-ran (*inf*). SUCCESS
omission, neglect, negligence, dereliction, delinquency, default, nonperformance.
decline, decay, failing, deterioration, collapse, bankruptcy, insolvency, ruin.

faint *adj*, weak, feeble, dim, pale, faded, indistinct, imperceptible, soft, low, muffled, slight, little, remote. STRONG
dizzy, giddy, light-headed, weak, drooping, languid, exhausted, weary.
v, collapse, pass out, lose consciousness, black out, swoon, keel over (*inf*), flake out (*inf*).
n, blackout, collapse, unconsciousness, swoon, syncope.

faint-hearted timid, diffident, timorous, cowardly, fearful, chicken (*inf*), yellow (*inf*). BRAVE

fair[1] *adj*, just, equitable, impartial, dispassionate, objective, square, legitimate, right, proper, above board, honest, trustworthy, honourable, upright. UNFAIR
blond, blonde, flaxen, light, pale. DARK
attractive, beautiful, handsome, pretty, lovely, bonny, comely, good-looking. UGLY
passable, average, reasonable, moderate, middling, mediocre, so-so (*inf*), all right, OK (*inf*), not bad, adequate, satisfactory. EXCELLENT
sunny, clear, bright, cloudless, fine, favourable. STORMY

fair[2] fête, bazaar, show, exhibition, market, gala, festival, carnival.

fairy elf, sprite, pixie, brownie, leprechaun, fay, peri.

faith belief, credence, conviction, confidence, assurance, trust, reliance, dependence. DOUBT
religion, creed, doctrine, dogma, belief, persuasion, denomination, sect.
faithfulness, fidelity, loyalty, allegiance, steadfastness, constancy, truthfulness, truth. FAITHLESSNESS

faithful loyal, true, devoted, steadfast, constant, staunch, trusty, trustworthy, reliable, dependable. UNFAITHFUL
accurate, exact, precise, close, strict, just, true, literal, factual. INACCURATE

faithless unfaithful, disloyal, untrue, perfidious, treacherous, untrustworthy, unreliable, fickle, inconstant, false, dishonest. FAITHFUL
unbelieving, doubting, sceptical, agnostic.

fake *v*, counterfeit, forge, fabricate, falsify, pretend, feign, affect, put on, sham, dissemble.
n, counterfeit, forgery, imitation, copy, sham, hoax, fraud, impostor, charlatan.
adj, counterfeit, forged, false, bogus, spurious, phoney (*inf*), artificial, ersatz, synthetic, pseudo. GENUINE

fall drop, descend, sink, go down, slope, incline, plunge, dive, plummet, fall down, trip, tumble, come a cropper (*inf*), topple, slide, decline, subside, abate, decrease, lessen, fall off, dwindle, ebb, slump, crash, collapse, fall in. RISE
yield, surrender, submit, capitulate, be defeated, be taken. TRIUMPH
be killed, be slain, perish, die. SURVIVE
happen, occur, befall, chance, come to pass, take place.
lapse, err, sin, transgress, go astray.
fall apart, crumble, disintegrate, break up, fall to pieces.
fall on, fall upon, attack, assail, descend on, set upon, lay into.
fall out, quarrel, argue, disagree, fight, wrangle.
n, drop, descent, slope, declivity, incline, plunge, dive, trip, tumble, decline, abatement, decrease, ebb, slump, collapse. RISE
surrender, capitulation, failure, defeat, overthrow, capture, downfall, ruin, destruction, death. TRIUMPH
lapse, sin, transgression.

fallacious wrong, erroneous, mistaken, incorrect, misleading, deceptive, delusive, illusory, false, untrue, fictitious, spurious, illogical, unsound, invalid, sophistic. TRUE

fallacy misconception, misapprehension, mistake, error, illusion, delusion, chimera, falsehood, untruth, deception, sophistry, casuistry. TRUTH

fallible imperfect, erring, weak, frail, mortal, human, unreliable. INFALLIBLE

fallow uncultivated, untilled, unsown, undeveloped, dormant, inactive, idle, inert, resting. CULTIVATED

falls waterfall, cascade, cataract, rapids.

false untrue, unsound, misleading, fallacious, fictitious, inaccurate, erroneous, wrong, incorrect, mistaken, untruthful, unreliable, mendacious, lying, deceitful, deceptive, delusive. TRUE
treacherous, perfidious, disloyal, faithless, unfaithful, hypocritical, two-faced, untrustworthy, dishonest, dishonourable. FAITHFUL
counterfeit, forged, fake, imitation, spurious, ersatz, artificial, synthetic, unreal, mock, feigned, sham, bogus. GENUINE

falsehood lie, fib, untruth, fabrication, fiction, falsity, mendacity, untruthfulness, deceit, deception. TRUTH

falsify misrepresent, belie, distort, pervert, doctor, alter, cook (*inf*), adulterate, counterfeit, forge, fake.

falter hesitate, waver, vacillate, be unsure. DECIDE
stammer, stutter, speak haltingly.
stumble, totter, dodder, tremble, shake.

fame renown, celebrity, stardom, name, reputation, repute, credit, honour, glory, acclaim, eminence, illustriousness. OBLIVION

familiar well-known, recognizable, common, household, domestic, everyday, ordinary, customary, routine, frequent. UNFAMILIAR
intimate, close, confidential, friendly, amicable, sociable, informal, unceremonious, easy, relaxed, unconstrained, open, free. FORMAL
forward, bold, presumptuous, impudent, disrespectful.
familiar with, conversant with, acquainted with, versed in, conscious of, aware of, no stranger to.

familiarity knowledge, acquaintance, grasp, understanding, experience, awareness. IGNORANCE
intimacy, closeness, friendliness, sociability, informality, openness, ease. FORMALITY
boldness, presumption, liberty, impudence, disrespect.

familiarize acquaint, accustom, habituate, inure, acclimatize, break in, train, instruct, school.

family relatives, relations, kin, children, offspring, progeny, household, ménage.
ancestry, lineage, parentage, extraction, blood, race, stock, pedigree, clan, tribe, house, dynasty.
group, class, subdivision, genus, species, kind, type, system.

famine starvation, hunger, want, lack, dearth, scarcity. PLENTY

famished starving, ravenous, hungry, empty, voracious. FULL

famous well-known, renowned, celebrated, famed, illustrious, eminent, distinguished, noted, great, acclaimed, legendary, memorable. UNKNOWN

fan[1] *v*, agitate, excite, arouse, stimulate, stir up, whip up, inflame, provoke. QUELL
ventilate, air-condition, blow, cool, refresh.
n, ventilator, air conditioner, blower.

fan[2] *n*, devotee, enthusiast, aficionado, addict, freak (*inf*), buff (*inf*), admirer, follower, supporter, fanatic.

fanatic zealot, bigot, extremist, radical, militant, visionary, enthusiast, devotee, fan. MODERATE

fanatical zealous, bigoted, immoderate, extreme, radical, visionary, enthusiastic, fervent, frenzied, wild, mad, obsessive. RESTRAINED

fanciful capricious, flighty, whimsical, wild, fantastic, fabulous, chimerical, imaginary, unreal, visionary, extravagant, impractical, romantic, imaginative, inventive. REALISTIC

fancy *v*, imagine, conceive, think, reckon, believe, suppose, conjecture, guess, picture, visualize, envisage.
want, desire, wish for, crave, long for, feel like, hanker after, like, be attracted to, prefer, favour.
n, caprice, whim, vagary, crotchet, notion, idea, conception, image, picture, impression, vision, dream, fantasy.
desire, urge, impulse, hankering, inclination, tendency, liking, predilection, fondness, partiality. AVERSION
adj, ornate, ornamental, decorative, ornamented, decorated, elaborate, showy, ostentatious. PLAIN
capricious, whimsical, fanciful, extravagant, fantastic. PRACTICAL

fantastic fanciful, imaginary, unreal, weird, odd, strange, grotesque, chimerical, bizarre, outlandish, ridiculous, absurd, wild, extravagant, capricious, whimsical, far-fetched, unrealistic, preposterous, incredible, mad, crazy, irrational. REALISTIC
wonderful, splendid, marvellous, excellent, first-rate, great, tremendous.

fantasy fancy, imagination, invention, image, dream, nightmare, illusion, hallucination, mirage, phantom, vision, daydream, reverie. REALITY

far *adj*, distant, remote, removed, faraway, far-flung. NEAR
adv, afar, a long way, miles.
greatly, considerably, much, very much, extremely, decidedly.

farce comedy, burlesque, slapstick, buffoonery, satire. TRAGEDY
mockery, travesty, sham, absurdity, nonsense, joke.
farcical ludicrous, ridiculous, absurd, preposterous, laughable.
comic, funny, humorous, amusing, droll. TRAGIC
fare *n*, charge, fee, price, cost.
food, diet, meals, menu, provisions, victuals, nourishment, sustenance.
v, manage, get along, do, make out.
farewell *interj*, goodbye, adieu, so long (*inf*).
n, departure, leave-taking, valediction, goodbye, parting.
far-fetched improbable, implausible, unlikely, unbelievable, incredible, fantastic, doubtful, dubious. PROBABLE
farm *n*, farmstead, grange, homestead, smallholding, croft, ranch, plantation.
v, till, cultivate, work.
farming agriculture, agronomy, husbandry.
farrago hotchpotch, miscellany, jumble, mixture, medley, potpourri, mishmash, salmagundi.
farther further, beyond, past, longer, more, in addition. NEARER
farthest furthest, longest, last, utmost, remotest, most distant, extreme. NEAREST
fascinate charm, captivate, beguile, enchant, delight, attract, allure, entrance, spellbind, hypnotize, mesmerize, rivet, transfix, engross, absorb. BORE
fascination charm, appeal, allure, attraction, draw, pull, magnetism, enchantment, entrancement, captivation, hypnotism, mesmerism. REPULSION
fashion *n*, vogue, mode, look, style, trend, craze, fad, custom, convention, usage.
form, mould, shape, style, cut, stamp, cast, model, design, pattern.
way, method, manner, sort, kind, type.
v, make, form, mould, shape, design, create, forge, construct.
adapt, accommodate, suit, fit, adjust, tailor.
fashionable stylish, modish, in vogue, à la mode, chic, elegant, smart, trendy (*inf*), all the rage, modern, up-to-date, current, in (*inf*), popular. UNFASHIONABLE
fast *adj*, rapid, swift, quick, speedy, accelerated, brisk, fleet. SLOW
secure, fixed, firm, immovable, tight, fastened, loyal, staunch, constant, steadfast, sound, lasting. LOOSE
dissolute, dissipated, rakish, loose, wild, reckless, immoral, promiscuous, extravagant, self-indulgent. RESTRAINED
adv, rapidly, swiftly, quickly, speedily, briskly, in haste. SLOWLY
securely, firmly, tightly, immovably. LOOSELY
deeply, soundly.
wildly, recklessly, extravagantly, loosely, promiscuously, wantonly.
fasten secure, fix, make fast, bind, tie, tether, attach, join, unite, connect, bolt, chain, strap, lace, buckle, button, hook, pin, latch, lock. UNFASTEN
aim, direct, focus, point, bend, fix.
fastidious critical, hard to please, particular, fussy, finicky, pernickety, meticulous, dainty, delicate, squeamish.
fat plump, obese, flabby, podgy, chubby, rotund, tubby, portly, corpulent, stout, overweight, large, big, broad, wide, thick, heavy, gross. THIN
fatty, greasy, oily.
profitable, lucrative, rich, fertile, fruitful, productive, abundant, plentiful, wealthy, affluent. POOR
fatal deadly, lethal, mortal, destructive, ruinous, calamitous, disastrous, incurable, terminal, malignant, harmful, pernicious, baleful, baneful. BENEFICIAL
critical, crucial, decisive, fateful, inevitable, destined, fated.
fatality death, disaster, catastrophe, casualty, mortality, accident, fate, destiny.
fate destiny, providence, chance, fortune, lot, portion, doom, kismet, predestination, destination, future, end, death, destruction, ruin.
fated destined, doomed, predestined, preordained, foreordained, sure, certain, inevitable, inescapable.
fateful crucial, critical, decisive, pivotal, momentous, portentous, important, significant.
disastrous, ruinous, fatal, deadly.
father *n*, parent, progenitor, sire, ancestor, forefather, predecessor. OFFSPRING
pater, dad (*inf*), daddy (*inf*), papa, pa (*inf*), old man (*inf*). MOTHER

creator, maker, author, inventor, architect, founder, prime mover.
v, sire, beget, procreate, generate, engender.
create, make, invent, originate, found.
fatherly paternal, kind, benevolent, benign, caring, tender, affectionate, sympathetic, understanding, protective, supportive, parental.
fathom measure, sound, gauge, plumb, probe, penetrate, understand, comprehend, grasp, see, get to the bottom of.
fathomless unfathomable, impenetrable, incomprehensible, immeasurable, bottomless, abysmal, deep, profound. SHALLOW
fatigue *v*, exhaust, weary, tire out, jade, fag, drain, weaken, debilitate, prostrate. REFRESH
n, exhaustion, weariness, tiredness, lassitude, lethargy, listlessness, debility, prostration. VIGOUR
fatten stuff, cram, feed, build up, bloat, make fat, get fat, swell, broaden, spread, put on weight. SLIM
fatuity fatuousness, foolishness, folly, silliness, absurdity, inanity, stupidity, idiocy, imbecility, madness, lunacy. SENSE
fatuous foolish, silly, absurd, inane, stupid, idiotic, senseless, asinine, witless, vacuous, moronic. SENSIBLE
fault flaw, blemish, defect, imperfection, failing, weakness, frailty, shortcoming. VIRTUE
offence, misdeed, crime, wrong, sin, transgression, misdemeanour, error, mistake, slip, lapse, omission.
culpability, responsibility, accountability, blameworthiness.
at fault, culpable, responsible, guilty, to blame, in the wrong.
find fault, complain, carp, cavil, quibble, criticize.
faultless perfect, flawless, model, exemplary, impeccable, unblemished, immaculate, spotless, pure, blameless, guiltless, innocent. IMPERFECT
faulty defective, imperfect, broken, damaged, impaired, not working, out of order, unsound, weak, incorrect, erroneous, wrong, fallacious, invalid, flawed. PERFECT
favour *n*, approval, approbation, countenance, sanction, backing, support, patronage, preference, partiality, bias, favouritism, good will, kindness, friendliness, graciousness. DISAPPROVAL
good turn, good deed, benefaction, boon, service, courtesy, kindness.
gift, present, souvenir, memento, keepsake, token, badge, rosette, decoration.
in favour of, for, pro, approving, supporting, backing, on the side of, for the sake of.
v, approve, countenance, sanction, back, support, patronize, befriend, champion, advocate, encourage, oblige, help, assist, facilitate, ease, advance. OPPOSE
prefer, side with, choose, select, like, fancy, be partial to, esteem, value, indulge, spoil, pamper.
resemble, take after, look like.
favourable encouraging, promising, propitious, auspicious, advantageous, beneficial, helpful, suitable, fit, opportune, timely. UNFAVOURABLE
approving, agreeable, amicable, well-disposed, kind, friendly, understanding, sympathetic, congenial, encouraging, enthusiastic. DISAPPROVING
favourite *n*, pet, darling, dearest, beloved, preference, choice, blue-eyed boy (*inf*), apple of one's eye.
adj, dearest, best-loved, preferred, chosen, pet.
fawn grovel, cringe, crawl, creep, kowtow, bow and scrape, toady, truckle, flatter, court.
fawning servile, obsequious, sycophantic, bootlicking (*inf*), grovelling, cringing, crawling, flattering. INDEPENDENT
fealty loyalty, allegiance, fidelity, faithfulness, devotion, homage.
fear *n*, terror, horror, panic, alarm, fright, cowardice, timidity, dread, apprehension, trepidation, misgiving, qualm. BOLDNESS
anxiety, worry, distress, concern, solicitude, uneasiness, foreboding. REASSURANCE
phobia, bogey, bugbear, *bête noire*, nightmare.
awe, reverence, veneration, respect. DISRESPECT
v, dread, be afraid of, be frightened of, shudder at, apprehend, anticipate, expect, worry, be anxious, feel concern.
revere, venerate, respect.
fearful terrified, afraid, frightened, scared, alarmed, uneasy, apprehensive, anxious, nervous, jumpy, timid, timorous, diffident. BOLD

fearsome, dreadful, terrible, horrendous, awful, frightful, dire, grim, formidable, horrible, ghastly, hideous, shocking, appalling, atrocious. WONDERFUL

fearless bold, brave, courageous, dauntless, undaunted, intrepid, heroic, gallant, valiant, valorous, daring, unafraid. FEARFUL

feasible practicable, workable, viable, possible, likely, reasonable, practical, realistic, realizable, attainable. IMPOSSIBLE

feast *n*, banquet, spread (*inf*), dinner, barbecue, blowout (*inf*), slap-up meal (*inf*), repast, treat.
festival, celebration, holy day, saint's day, fête.
v, dine, banquet, eat one's fill, gorge, stuff, regale, treat, wine and dine, entertain.
delight, please, gladden, gratify, thrill.

feat deed, act, exploit, achievement, accomplishment, stroke, coup.

feature *n*, characteristic, peculiarity, trait, mark, hallmark, attribute, property, quality, aspect, facet.
highlight, speciality, main item, attraction, focal point.
article, story, item, piece, column, report.
v, highlight, emphasize, accentuate, play up, spotlight, give prominence to, promote, star.

features face, countenance, physiognomy, lineaments.

feculence scum, sediment, residue, dregs, lees, muck, filth, mud, dirt.

fecund fruitful, productive, fertile, rich, prolific, abundant. BARREN

federation confederation, confederacy, union, league, alliance, coalition, syndicate, combination, amalgamation.

fee payment, remuneration, reward, recompense, pay, hire, emolument, honorarium, allowance, charge, toll, bill, account.

feeble weak, frail, infirm, delicate, sickly, puny, debilitated, enervated, languid, drooping, failing, faint, slight, thin. STRONG
ineffectual, powerless, unavailing, inefficient, incompetent, inadequate, lame, flimsy, unconvincing. POWERFUL

feed *v*, nourish, sustain, satisfy, provide for, supply, cater for, provision. STARVE
eat, devour, dine, fare, subsist, graze.
n, fodder, forage, food.

feel touch, handle, finger, stroke, caress.
sense, experience, perceive, be aware of, know, undergo, suffer, enjoy.
fumble, grope, try, test.
seem, appear.

feel for, sympathize with, commiserate with, bleed for, be sorry for, grieve for.

feeling *n*, sense, sensation, impression, perception, consciousness, awareness, touch, contact, feel.
hunch, inkling, suspicion, idea, notion, premonition, presentiment, opinion, viewpoint, thought.
emotion, sentiment, sensibility, sensitivity, sympathy, compassion, affection, tenderness, passion, ardour, fervour. INSENSITIVITY
adj, sentient, sensible, sensitive, emotional, sympathetic, compassionate, tender, warm, passionate, ardent, fervent. UNFEELING

feign affect, put on, assume, pretend, act, sham, simulate, fake, counterfeit, forge, fabricate, copy, imitate, dissemble.

feint dodge, trick, stratagem, ruse, artifice, pretext, expedient, blind, bluff, sham, hoax, pretence, show.

felicitate congratulate, compliment.

felicitous apt, appropriate, well-chosen, suitable, pertinent, apposite, opportune, timely, propitious, seasonable, happy, fortunate, lucky, successful. INAPPROPRIATE

felicity happiness, joy, bliss, ecstasy, rapture, delight. MISERY
aptness, appropriateness, suitability, pertinence, propitiousness. INAPPROPRIATENESS

fell hew, cut down, knock down, prostrate, level, raze, demolish.

fellow man, boy, person, chap (*inf*), bloke (*inf*), guy (*inf*).
companion, comrade, friend, colleague, partner, associate, equal, peer, compeer, mate, counterpart, match, twin.

fellowship companionship, comradeship, camaraderie, friendship, amity, brotherhood, intimacy, familiarity, sociability, company, communion, intercourse. ENMITY
association, society, club, fraternity, guild, league.

felon criminal, offender, malefactor, wrongdoer, culprit, convict.

felony crime, offence, misdemeanour.

feminine womanly, girlish, ladylike, soft, gentle, tender, delicate, graceful. MASCULINE
effeminate, womanish, unmanly, sissy, weak, effete. MANLY

fen bog, marsh, swamp, morass, quagmire.

fence *n*, railing, paling, hedge, wall, barrier, barricade, defence, guard.
v, enclose, shut in, surround, encircle, circumscribe, bound, defend, protect, guard. EXPOSE
hedge, quibble, prevaricate, equivocate, fudge, evade, dodge, parry, shuffle, tergiversate.

fend **fend for,** provide for, support, look after, take care of.
fend off, ward off, avert, forestall, deflect, turn aside, parry, stave off, repulse, drive back.

feral ferine, wild, untamed, unbroken, uncultivated. DOMESTICATED
savage, fierce, ferocious, vicious, brutal, cruel. GENTLE

ferment *v*, foam, froth, bubble, effervesce, boil, seethe, brew, rise, leaven.
rouse, stir up, excite, inflame, agitate, foment, provoke. CALM
n, yeast, leaven, enzyme, bacteria.
excitement, commotion, tumult, uproar, turmoil, agitation, unrest, stew, heat, fever, frenzy. PEACE

ferocious fierce, savage, vicious, feral, bestial, cruel, brutal, barbarous, violent, inhuman, bloodthirsty, sanguinary, ruthless, merciless, pitiless, relentless, harsh, severe. GENTLE

fertile fecund, productive, fruitful, prolific, teeming, abundant, profuse, plentiful, rich, luxuriant. BARREN

fertilize fecundate, impregnate, inseminate, pollinate.
enrich, dress, feed, manure, marl, mulch, compost.

fervent fervid, ardent, passionate, eager, keen, earnest, zealous, animated, intense, vehement, burning, glowing, warm. APATHETIC

fervour ardour, passion, fervency, eagerness, keenness, earnestness, zeal, animation, intensity, vehemence. APATHY

fester *v*, suppurate, ulcerate, putrefy, rot, decay, corrupt.
rankle, irk, gall, rile, inflame, chafe, irritate.
n, abscess, ulcer, boil, pustule, gathering.

festival gala, carnival, celebration, commemoration, anniversary, jubilee, fair, fête, banquet, feast, saint's day, holiday.

festive festal, merry, jovial, jolly, convivial, hearty, joyful, joyous, mirthful, cheery, gay. MOURNFUL

festivity merriment, joviality, conviviality, joyfulness, mirth, gaiety, revelry, fun. MOURNING
festival, carnival, celebration, party, carousal.

festoon *v*, decorate, adorn, array, deck, wreathe, garland, drape, hang. STRIP
n, garland, wreath, chaplet.

fetch bring, carry, convey, deliver, get, obtain, retrieve, go for.
realize, yield, bring in, make, sell for.

fetching attractive, sweet, taking, fascinating, charming, enchanting, alluring. REPULSIVE

fête fair, bazaar, gala, festival, carnival, garden party.
holiday, feast day, saint's day, festival.

fetid foul, rank, malodorous, stinking, noisome, offensive, mephitic, rancid, corrupt, foul. FRAGRANT

fetish charm, talisman, amulet.
obsession, mania, fixation, compulsion.

fetter *v*, chain, shackle, manacle, tie, bind, trammel, encumber, hamper, restrain, restrict, confine. LOOSE
n, chain, shackle, manacle, bond, iron.

feud vendetta, hostility, antagonism, enmity, bad blood, discord, strife, conflict, dissension, contention, quarrel, row, argument, rupture, breach, faction. AGREEMENT

fever feverishness, pyrexia, high temperature.
agitation, excitement, heat, flush, passion, fervour, frenzy, ferment, turmoil. COMPOSURE

few rare, scarce, scanty, meagre, hardly any, not many, infrequent, sporadic. MANY

fiasco failure, disaster, catastrophe, mess, flop (*inf*), washout (*inf*), fizzle (*inf*). SUCCESS

fiat permission, sanction, authorization, warrant. BAN

order, command, decree, edict, proclamation, ordinance, law, dictum.

fib *n*, lie, untruth, falsehood, fabrication, story, whopper (*inf*). TRUTH
v, lie, misrepresent, falsify, prevaricate, equivocate.

fibre thread, strand, filament, fibril, staple, texture.
spirit, nature, constitution, disposition, strength, stamina, toughness.

fickle changeable, variable, capricious, mercurial, volatile, flighty, unpredictable, fitful, erratic, irresolute, vacillating, wavering, inconstant, unstable, unsteady, unreliable. CONSTANT

fiction story, tale, novel, fable, legend, fantasy, romance, invention, fabrication, fancy, imagination, lie, falsehood, untruth. FACT

fictitious false, untrue, invented, imaginary, fanciful, make-believe, mythical, unreal, bogus, spurious, counterfeit, artificial, feigned, assumed. TRUE

fiddle play, tinker, tamper, toy, trifle, mess around, idle, fidget.
swindle, cheat, falsify, cook (*inf*), manoeuvre, finagle (*inf*), wangle (*inf*).

fiddling trifling, trivial, small, insignificant, petty. IMPORTANT

fidelity faithfulness, loyalty, devotion, fealty, allegiance, staunchness, constancy, steadfastness, trustworthiness, dependability. INFIDELITY
closeness, faithfulness, exactness, accuracy, precision, correspondence, conformity, accordance.

fidget squirm, twitch, fiddle, twiddle, move about, jitter (*inf*), worry, fret.

fidgety restless, restive, impatient, nervous, fretful, uneasy, jumpy, jittery (*inf*). STILL

field meadow, pasture, green, common, ground, pitch.
domain, province, realm, sphere, department, discipline, speciality, territory, area, range, scope, extent, limits, bounds.

fiend demon, devil, evil spirit, monster, brute, beast, savage, ogre. ANGEL
addict, enthusiast, fan, devotee, maniac, fanatic.

fiendish demonic, devilish, diabolical, infernal, wicked, evil, malicious, malignant, malevolent, cruel, inhuman, savage, monstrous. ANGELIC

fierce savage, ferocious, vicious, dangerous, menacing, threatening, wild, feral, brutal, barbarous, bloodthirsty, sanguinary, cruel, ruthless. HARMLESS
violent, raging, furious, relentless, stormy, tempestuous, wild, intense, keen, powerful, strong, uncontrollable, passionate, ardent, fervent. GENTLE

fiery hot, burning, blazing, flaming, glowing, heated, ardent, fervent, vehement, passionate, excitable, temperamental, violent, fierce. COOL

fight *n*, battle, combat, strife, conflict, war, fighting, hostilities, action, engagement, encounter, bout, duel, scrap (*inf*), struggle, brawl, fray, fracas, riot, dispute, row, quarrel. PEACE
v, battle, combat, war, contend, strive, struggle, oppose, contest, resist, defy, attack, assault, grapple, wrestle, spar, box, brawl, dispute, argue, bicker, wrangle.

figment invention, fabrication, creation, illusion, fancy, notion, fiction, fable, story, falsehood. FACT

figurative metaphorical, emblematic, symbolic, allegorical, representative, typical, illustrative.

figure *n*, number, numeral, digit, cipher, symbol, character. LETTER
outline, shape, silhouette, form, configuration, body, build, physique, frame, structure.
diagram, drawing, picture, illustration, representation, effigy, image, design, pattern, device, motif, emblem.
personage, character, notable, celebrity, somebody, worthy. NOBODY
v, calculate, reckon, compute, work out, add up, count.
represent, symbolize, depict, portray, feature, appear.
decorate, adorn, ornament, embellish, mark, variegate.
imagine, picture, conceive.
figure out, understand, comprehend, grasp, see, fathom, work out, solve.

filament strand, thread, fibre, fibril, staple, hair, wire, string.

filch steal, pilfer, purloin, thieve, take, abstract, lift (*inf*), pinch (*inf*). RETURN

file[1] *v*, rasp, scrape, grind, abrade, rub down, smooth, polish, shape.

file[2] *n*, folder, portfolio, dossier, documents, information.

line, row, rank, queue, column, list, string, chain.
v, record, register, place, classify, arrange, pigeonhole.
march, troop, parade, pass.

fill stuff, cram, pack, fill up, satisfy, content, satiate, glut, sate, swell, inflate, fill out, stock, supply, furnish, replenish. EMPTY
pervade, suffuse, imbue, impregnate, infuse, overspread, cover.
plug, cork, bung, stop, close, block.
occupy, hold, discharge, execute, perform, carry out, do, fulfil.
fill in, complete, fill out, answer.
replace, substitute, stand in, deputize.
inform, apprise, acquaint, bring up to date.

film covering, coat, layer, sheet, skin, membrane, pellicle, veil, haze, blur, cloud, mist.
picture, motion picture, movie (*inf*), flick (*inf*), video.

filter *v*, strain, clarify, filtrate, purify, refine, screen, sift.
exude, ooze, transude, seep, leak, trickle, leach, percolate.
n, strainer, screen, sieve, riddle, net, mesh, gauze.

filth dirt, muck, grime, ordure, sewage, refuse, pollution, foulness, defilement, corruption, squalor, filthiness, uncleanness. CLEANNESS
obscenity, vulgarity, pornography, smut, grossness, indecency.

filthy dirty, mucky, grimy, grubby, unwashed, foul, unclean, polluted, defiled, corrupt, squalid. SPOTLESS
obscene, vulgar, pornographic, smutty, lewd, indecent, ribald, bawdy, blue.

final ultimate, last, terminal, concluding, closing, eventual. FIRST
conclusive, decisive, definitive, irrevocable.

finale end, conclusion, finish, close, termination, climax, culmination, finis. BEGINNING

finality conclusiveness, decisiveness, definitiveness, irrevocability, unavoidability, inevitability.

finally ultimately, eventually, at last, in the end, in the long run, lastly. INITIALLY
conclusively, decisively, irrevocably, definitely, absolutely, completely, once and for all.

finance *n*, banking, economics, commerce, investment, money, funds, accounts.
v, fund, pay for, back, support, subsidize, underwrite.

finances resources, assets, wealth, wherewithal, funds, money, cash, capital.

financial monetary, money, pecuniary, fiscal, economic.

find *v*, discover, come across, happen upon, uncover, unearth, locate, track down, ferret out, encounter, meet, notice, observe, descry, perceive, detect, realize, attain, obtain, acquire, get. LOSE
provide, supply, furnish, contribute.
find out, ascertain, learn, discover, determine, detect, expose, uncover, unmask.
n, discovery, finding, strike, catch, bargain.

finding verdict, judgment, decision, conclusion, award, sentence, decree, pronouncement.

fine[1] *adj*, excellent, choice, select, superior, outstanding, exceptional, first-rate, first-class, splendid, magnificent, ornate, showy, beautiful, lovely, exquisite, elegant, smart, stylish, tasteful. INFERIOR
thin, slender, attenuated, tenuous, slight, small, little, dainty, delicate, fragile, flimsy, sheer, light. COARSE
pure, clear, unadulterated, refined, subtle, keen, acute, sharp, precise, minute, nice.
sunny, cloudless, dry, bright, clear, fair, clement. CLOUDY
acceptable, satisfactory, all right, OK (*inf*).

fine[2] *n*, penalty, punishment, mulct, forfeit, damages.
v, penalize, punish, mulct.

finery trappings, trinkets, decorations, ornaments, splendour, frippery, Sunday best, glad rags (*inf*).

finesse subtlety, tact, diplomacy, delicacy, grace, polish, skill, adroitness, mastery, craft. CLUMSINESS
artifice, trick, ruse, wile, stratagem.

finicky fussy, particular, meticulous, fastidious, dainty, squeamish, choosy (*inf*), difficult, hard to please, critical.

finish *v*, complete, conclude, close, terminate, end, stop, cease, fulfil, achieve, accomplish, do discharge, execute, perform, settle, finalize, perfect, consummate, culminate, round off. START

consume, use up, drain, empty, dispatch, dispose of, get rid of, destroy, kill, ruin, defeat, overcome, finish off.
polish, varnish, face, dress, gild, veneer, glaze, coat.
n, completion, conclusion, close, termination, end, cessation, perfection, consummation, culmination. BEGINNING
surface, polish, varnish, lustre, shine, texture, veneer, appearance, coating.

finished complete, done, over, through, completed, ended, achieved, fulfilled. UNFINISHED
accomplished, masterly, proficient, expert, skilled, consummate, polished, refined, elegant, perfect, impeccable.
ruined, bankrupt, lost, gone, done for (*inf*), doomed, defeated.

finite limited, restricted, bounded, circumscribed, demarcated, terminable, measurable. INFINITE

fire *n*, burning, combustion, spark, flame, blaze, conflagration, inferno, holocaust.
ardour, fervour, heat, passion, enthusiasm, eagerness, spirit, élan, vigour, energy, force, intensity, animation, excitement, inspiration, life, vivacity. COLDNESS
light, radiance, lustre, splendour, glow, sparkle.
bombardment, barrage, salvo, volley, fusillade, cannonade, flak, shelling.
on fire, alight, ablaze, burning, blazing, in flames. EXTINGUISHED
v, discharge, shoot, detonate, explode, shell, hurl, launch.
ignite, kindle, light, set fire to, set on fire, set alight. EXTINGUISH
animate, rouse, stir, stimulate, inspire, invigorate, excite, arouse, inspirit, inflame. DAMP
dismiss, discharge, cashier, sack (*inf*). APPOINT

firm[1] *adj*, solid, hard, compact, dense, stiff, rigid, inflexible, unyielding, set, congealed, frozen. SOFT
secure, fixed, fast, immovable, rooted, anchored, steady, stable, constant, enduring, sturdy, strong. UNSTABLE
steadfast, staunch, unwavering, unshakable, dogged, tenacious, fixed, resolute, determined, obdurate, adamant, unyielding, inflexible, strict, unbending.

firm[2] *n*, company, business, concern, establishment, organization, corporation, house, partnership.

firmament sky, heavens, empyrean, vault, space, universe. EARTH

first *adj*, earliest, primeval, primordial, primitive, original, initial, introductory, primary, rudimentary, elementary, basic, fundamental. LAST
foremost, chief, leading, greatest, principal, head, highest, top, supreme. LOWEST
adv, beforehand, firstly, initially, to begin with, in the first place. LAST

fish angle, trawl, cast, net.
fish for, seek, solicit, invite, angle for, look for, search for.

fishy suspicious, suspect, dubious, doubtful, questionable, unlikely, improbable, odd, queer.

fission cleavage, splitting, parting, division, rupture.

fissure rift, cleft, crevice, cranny, chasm, crack, break, fracture, breach, rupture, split, gap, opening, interstice.

fit[1] *v*, adapt, adjust, accommodate, alter, modify, fashion, shape.
match, tally, correspond, conform, agree, suit, go, belong, dovetail, harmonize, meet.
equip, rig, furnish, supply, provide, arm, accoutre, prepare, clothe, dress. STRIP
adj, suitable, fitting, appropriate, well-suited, apt, right, correct, proper, seemly, becoming. INAPPROPRIATE
able, capable, competent, qualified, eligible, ready, prepared, adequate, worthy, deserving. INELIGIBLE
healthy, robust, sturdy, strong, hale, well. UNFIT

fit[2] *n*, convulsion, paroxysm, spasm, seizure, attack, bout, spell, outburst, outbreak.

fitful irregular, intermittent, spasmodic, erratic, variable, inconstant, unstable, fluctuating, broken, disturbed, desultory, impulsive. REGULAR

fitness suitability, appropriateness, aptness, propriety, seemliness. IMPROPRIETY
competence, qualifications, eligibility, readiness. INELIGIBILITY
health, vigour, strength, fine fettle, good shape, condition. UNFITNESS

fix *v*, secure, make fast, anchor, cement, root, plant, place, locate, install, position, fasten, attach, connect, join, tie, bind, stick, glue, rivet, nail, pin. MOVE

settle, resolve, establish, decide, determine, limit, define, specify, arrange, appoint, name, set.
mend, repair, patch up, restore, regulate, correct. DAMAGE
direct, focus, level, rivet.
n, dilemma, predicament, quandary, plight, mess, spot (*inf*), pickle (*inf*).

fixation obsession, *idée fixe*, compulsion, mania, fetish, preoccupation, thing (*inf*).

fixed established, stable, firm, secure, fast, steady, constant, unchanging, immovable, rooted, set, intent, resolute, unwavering.

fizz sparkle, effervesce, bubble, froth, ferment, fizzle, hiss.

flabbergasted amazed, astounded, dumbfounded, astonished, stunned, staggered, bowled over, speechless, nonplussed.

flabby flaccid, limp, drooping, floppy, loose, slack, yielding, soft. FIRM

flaccid limp, drooping, floppy, flabby, soft, yielding. FIRM

flag[1] *n*, standard, ensign, colours, banner, pennant, streamer, bunting, jack.

flag[2] *v*, droop, languish, faint, fail, tire, weary, weaken, wilt, sag, drop, sink, decline, fall.

flagellate scourge, flog, lash, whip, beat, thrash, cane, birch, castigate, chastise.

flagitious monstrous, atrocious, outrageous, scandalous, shocking, heinous, villainous, wicked, notorious, infamous. HONOURABLE

flagrant blatant, glaring, bold, barefaced, arrant, conspicuous, open, ostentatious, outrageous, scandalous, shocking, atrocious, egregious. DISGUISED

flair talent, gift, knack, faculty, aptitude, disposition, skill, ability, genius.
style, dash, panache, elegance, discernment, taste.

flake *n*, scale, chip, sliver, shaving, wafer.
v, scale, peel, desquamate, exfoliate, chip.

flake out, faint, pass out, collapse, swoon.

flamboyant showy, ostentatious, gaudy, flashy, dazzling, brilliant, resplendent, florid, ornate, elaborate, fancy, extravagant. PLAIN

flame *v*, burn, blaze, flare, flash, glow, shine.
n, fire, blaze, spark, flash, light, glow.
ardour, fervour, passion, zeal, eagerness, keenness, warmth, heat, intensity. COLDNESS
sweetheart, lover, beau, boyfriend, girlfriend.

flank *n*, side, wing, loin, haunch, thigh, hip.
v, border, edge, fringe, skirt, limit, bound.

flap *v*, wave, swing, wag, flutter, shake, agitate, vibrate, beat, flail, thresh.
n, fold, tab, overlap, fly, skirt, cover.
commotion, fuss, panic, agitation, tizzy (*inf*), state (*inf*).

flare blaze, flash, gleam, sparkle, flicker, flutter, glare.
widen, broaden, splay, spread out, expand. TAPER

flare up, explode, blow one's top (*inf*), lose control, boil over, fly off the handle (*inf*).

flash *v*, flare, flame, glare, blaze, sparkle, scintillate, coruscate, gleam, glint, twinkle, glitter, shimmer, glisten.
dart, dash, streak, fly, race, bolt, speed. CRAWL
show, display, flaunt, flourish. CONCEAL
n, beam, ray, flare, blaze, burst, glint, gleam, spark, streak, patch.
instant, moment, second, trice, twinkling, split second.
display, show, showing, demonstration, manifestation.

flashy showy, ostentatious, gaudy, flamboyant, flash (*inf*), loud, garish, cheap, tawdry.

flat[1] *adj*, level, even, smooth, unbroken, plane, low, horizontal, prostrate, recumbent, supine.
vapid, uninteresting, dull, insipid, bland, boring, tedious, monotonous, prosaic, lifeless, spiritless. EXCITING
direct, downright, out-and-out, positive, absolute, categorical, final, unconditional.
punctured, burst, deflated, collapsed.
n, lowland, plain, marsh, swamp, shallow, shoal, sandbank.

flat[2] *n*, apartment, rooms, penthouse.

flatten level, smooth, even out, iron, press, roll, crush, squash, demolish, raze.

flatter praise, compliment, fawn, court, butter up, humour, adulate, blandish, cajole, wheedle, coax, soft-soap (*inf*). INSULT

flattery praise, compliments, fawning, sycophancy, servility, adulation, blandishments, blarney, cajolery, soft-soap (*inf*), flannel (*inf*). ABUSE

flatulent windy, gassy.
wordy, verbose, long-winded, bombastic, pompous, pretentious, inflated, turgid. TERSE

flaunt display, show off, parade, sport, flash, brandish, flourish, vaunt, boast. HIDE

flavour taste, savour, tang, smack, zest, piquancy, relish, seasoning, flavouring.
essence, spirit, tone, character, quality, aspect, suggestion, style, touch.

flaw defect, fault, blemish, imperfection, spot, mark, weakness, failing.
crack, rift, cleft, fissure, split, rent, break, fracture, breach.

flawless perfect, faultless, unblemished, whole, intact, sound, undamaged, spotless, impeccable. FLAWED

flay skin, excoriate, peel, strip.
attack, criticize, pan (*inf*), castigate, berate, pull to pieces (*inf*). PRAISE

fleck *v*, streak, speckle, spot, dot, dapple, variegate, mottle, mark.
n, streak, spot, dot, speck, mark.

flee fly, run away, abscond, make off, escape, bolt, decamp, scarper (*inf*), take off (*inf*), leave, depart. STAY

fleece shear, clip, strip.
swindle, defraud, cheat, diddle (*inf*), overcharge, rip off (*inf*), rob, plunder, rifle.

fleet[1] *adj*, rapid, swift, fast, quick, speedy, nimble, agile. SLOW

fleet[2] *n*, armada, flotilla, argosy, squadron, task force, navy.

fleeting ephemeral, transitory, transient, evanescent, passing, brief, short-lived, momentary, temporary. LASTING

fleetness rapidity, swiftness, quickness, speed, velocity, celerity, nimbleness, agility. SLOWNESS

flesh tissue, fat, meat, body, carnality, physicality.
mankind, humanity, mortality, human race, stock, family, kin, kindred, blood.

fleshly carnal, sensual, lustful, lascivious, lecherous, animal, physical, bodily, corporeal, material, earthly, worldly. SPIRITUAL

fleshy fat, plump, corpulent, stout, rotund, podgy, chubby, tubby, obese, overweight. THIN

flexible pliable, pliant, bendable, ductile, elastic, tensile, malleable, plastic, supple, lithe, yielding. RIGID
adaptable, adjustable, variable, compliant, docile, biddable, amenable, tractable, complaisant. INFLEXIBLE

flexuous winding, serpentine, sinuous, tortuous, twisting, turning, bending, curving. STRAIGHT

flexure bending, flexing, incurvation, curvature, bend, turn, fold.

flick flip, rap, tap, dab, touch, snap, click, fillip.

flicker *v*, flash, twinkle, glimmer, shimmer, blink, flutter, waver, fluctuate, vibrate, quiver, tremble.
n, flash, gleam, glimmer, spark, trace, vestige.

flight flying, soaring, gliding, aviation, aeronautics.
journey, trip, run, shuttle.
cloud, swarm, flock, squadron, unit, formation.
fleeing, escape, getaway, stampede, exodus, departure, retreat, rout, migration. RETURN

flighty frivolous, capricious, fickle, volatile, mercurial, inconstant, changeable, irresponsible, scatterbrained, giddy, wild, impulsive, thoughtless, unstable, erratic. CONSTANT

flimsy frail, fragile, delicate, thin, sheer, light, insubstantial, slight, superficial, trivial, frivolous, poor, inadequate, weak, feeble, unsubstantial, rickety, shaky. STRONG

flinch wince, shrink, cower, quail, blench, recoil, draw back, shy away, withdraw, retreat, dodge, shirk, flee.

fling *v*, hurl, toss, throw, shy, pitch, cast, sling, lob (*inf*), chuck (*inf*).
n, toss, throw, pitch.
spree, binge, debauch, fun.

flip flick, jerk, toss, pitch, throw, spin, turn, twist, rap, tap, snap, fillip.

flip through, skim, flick through, thumb through, browse, glance at. STUDY

flippancy frivolity, levity, irreverence, impudence, pertness, impertinence, sauce (*inf*), cheek (*inf*). RESPECT

flippant frivolous, offhand, irreverent, disrespectful, rude, impudent, pert, impertinent, cheeky, saucy. SERIOUS

flirt *v*, philander, coquet, tease, lead on, make advances, ogle, chat up (*inf*), dally, toy, trifle.
n, philanderer, playboy, coquette, vamp, tease.

flit fly, dart, skim, flash, speed, dash, hop, flutter, flicker.

float sail, drift, waft, glide, slide, ride, swim, bob, hover, hang. SINK
launch, start, get going, establish, set up, promote.

flock *n*, herd, pack, flight, swarm, bevy, crowd, throng, mass, group, company, collection, gathering, assembly, congregation.
v, congregate, gather, collect, assemble, herd, swarm, throng, crowd, cluster. DISPERSE

flog whip, lash, beat, scourge, flagellate, thrash, castigate, chastise, cane.

flood *v*, inundate, deluge, submerge, drown, swamp, engulf, overwhelm, overflow, brim over, pour forth, gush, surge. DRAIN
n, inundation, deluge, overflow, outpouring, torrent, downpour, spate, freshet, flow, stream, abundance, profusion. DROUGHT

floor *n*, bottom, ground, level, storey, stage, flooring. CEILING
v, knock down, fell, overthrow, defeat, beat, confound, nonplus, disconcert, perplex, puzzle, baffle.

flop *v*, collapse, fall, slump, droop, sag, drop, hang, dangle.
fail, founder, fall flat. SUCCEED
n, failure, fiasco, disaster, washout (*inf*). SUCCESS

florid ruddy, rubicund, flushed, rosy. PALE
flowery, ornate, elaborate, fussy, flamboyant, showy, high-flown, euphuistic. PLAIN

flounce fling, toss, jerk, bounce, spring, stamp, storm.

flounder wallow, struggle, thrash, toss, stumble, blunder, grope, fumble.

flourish *v*, thrive, prosper, succeed, do well, get on, grow, increase, wax, boom, burgeon, blossom. DECLINE
brandish, wield, wave, swing, shake, flaunt, parade, vaunt, display.
n, show, display, ostentation, parade, wave, twirl, dash, fanfare.
ornament, decoration, embellishment, curlicue.

flout mock, jeer, scoff, deride, sneer, scorn, disdain, contemn, spurn, defy. RESPECT

flow *v*, run, pour, stream, course, roll, sweep, drift, glide, move, circulate, ooze, seep, surge, rush, gush, spurt, cascade, abound, teem. STOP
issue, proceed, arise, spring, emanate, result.
n, stream, course, drift, movement, circulation, progression, current, tide, surge, rush, outpouring, discharge, flood, deluge, abundance, plethora.

flower *n*, bloom, blossom.
prime, peak, height, cream, pick, best, finest, elite.
v, bloom, blossom, blow, effloresce, come out, open, unfold, develop, mature. WITHER

flowery florid, ornate, fancy, elaborate, high-flown, rhetorical, figurative, grandiloquent. PLAIN

flowing fluent, smooth, easy, graceful, unbroken, continuous. STILTED
rich, prolific, teeming, abounding. LACKING

fluctuate vacillate, waver, vary, change, alter, undulate, shift, veer, swing, oscillate. STABILIZE

fluctuation vacillation, wavering, instability, unsteadiness, inconstancy, change, variation, shift, undulation, oscillation. STABILITY

fluency smoothness, ease, facility, control, command, eloquence, articulateness, glibness, flow.

fluent smooth, flowing, fluid, easy, effortless, natural, articulate, eloquent, glib, ready, voluble. STILTED

fluffy furry, fuzzy, fleecy, woolly, downy, flossy, silky, soft, light.

fluid *n*, liquid, solution, gas, vapour. SOLID
adj, liquid, gaseous, molten, flowing, running, fluent.
changeable, shifting, mobile, flexible, protean.

fluke accident, chance, coincidence, stroke of luck, windfall, blessing, lucky break.

flummery nonsense, rubbish, trash, balderdash, humbug, poppycock, flattery, blandishments, adulation.

flunky footman, lackey, servant, valet, underling, menial, minion, drudge.
sycophant, toady, yes man, bootlicker (*inf*).
flurry *n*, bustle, stir, commotion, ado, excitement, agitation, to-do (*inf*), fuss, fluster, hurry, haste. CALM
squall, gust, outbreak, burst, spell.
v, fluster, agitate, ruffle, disconcert, perturb, confuse, bewilder, perplex, confound. COMPOSE
flush[1] *v*, blush, colour, redden, go red, glow, burn, suffuse. BLANCH
flood, drench, douse, cleanse, wash, clean out, rinse, drain, empty.
excite, elate, elevate, exhilarate, thrill, animate, stir, rouse, cheer, encourage. DAMP
n, blush, colour, redness, rosiness, bloom, glow, radiance. PALLOR
excitement, thrill, elation, exhilaration, animation.
flush[2] *adj*, even, level, flat, plane, smooth. UNEVEN
wealthy, rich, affluent, well-off. POOR
generous, liberal, prodigal, lavish, abundant. MEAN
fluster *v*, flurry, agitate, ruffle, disconcert, perturb, bother, disturb, upset, rattle (*inf*), excite, confuse, bustle, hurry. COMPOSE
agitation, flutter, flap (*inf*), bustle, flurry, turmoil, confusion. COMPOSURE
fluted grooved, furrowed, corrugated, channelled.
flutter *v*, flap, wave, vibrate, shake, quiver, tremble, ripple, waver, fluctuate, oscillate, flicker, bat, beat, palpitate.
n, vibration, quiver, shudder, tremble, tremor, palpitation.
fluster, flurry, stir, commotion, agitation, excitement, confusion, perturbation. COMPOSURE
flux flow, fluidity, motion, transition, change, alteration, mutation, fluctuation, instability. STAGNATION
fly *v*, mount, soar, wing, hover, flutter, flap, flit, glide, float, sail.
dash, dart, bolt, shoot, tear, rush, hurry, race, speed, career, hare (*inf*). AMBLE
escape, flee, abscond, decamp, run, take flight. REMAIN
pass, elapse, go by, slip away, glide, roll on.
pilot, aviate, control, manoeuvre.
foam *n*, froth, spume, spray, bubbles, suds, lather.
v, froth, lather, bubble, fizz, effervesce.
focus *n*, centre, core, heart, nucleus, focal point, centre of attention, cynosure.
v, aim, direct, fix, concentrate, centre, line up, converge, meet.
fodder feed, food, forage, silage, hay, provender, rations.
foe enemy, opponent, adversary, antagonist, rival, competitor. FRIEND
fog *n*, mist, haze, smog, peasouper (*inf*), gloom, murk, murkiness.
obscurity, vagueness, haziness, daze, stupor, confusion, perplexity, bewilderment.
v, cloud, obscure, veil, shroud, dim, darken, obfuscate, confuse, bewilder, perplex. CLARIFY
foggy misty, hazy, murky, cloudy, obscure, dim, vague, blurred, indistinct, confused, unclear. CLEAR
foible weakness, failing, infirmity, fault, defect, imperfection, quirk, peculiarity, idiosyncrasy. FORTE
foil[1] *v*, frustrate, thwart, baffle, balk, outwit, defeat, checkmate, counter, circumvent, hamper, impede. ASSIST
foil[2] *n*, contrast, antithesis, complement, background, setting.
leaf, lamina, sheet, film.
foist pass, palm, fob, unload, get rid of, impose, thrust, insert, interpolate.
fold *v*, bend, double, overlap, turn under, crease, pleat, tuck, gather. FLATTEN
enfold, envelop, wrap, enclose, clasp, embrace, entwine, intertwine.
collapse, fail, go under (*inf*), go bust (*inf*), close, shut down. PROSPER
n, crease, wrinkle, pleat, tuck, bend, turn, overlap, layer.
folk people, nation, race, tribe, clan, kin, kindred, family.
follow succeed, come next, go after, replace. PRECEDE
pursue, chase, run after, hound, hunt, track, stalk, trail.
ensue, result, arise, spring, issue, proceed.
obey, observe, note, heed, conform to, comply with. BREAK
attend, accompany, escort, go with. DESERT
copy, imitate, ape, emulate, adopt.
understand, comprehend, grasp, see, take in, keep up with.
follower disciple, adherent, partisan, convert, supporter, backer, pupil, student,

attendant, companion, devotee, fan, admirer, hanger-on.
following *adj*, next, subsequent, successive, ensuing, consequent, resulting, coming, later. PRECEDING
n, entourage, train, suite, clientele, circle, public, supporters, admirers.
folly foolishness, stupidity, silliness, absurdity, nonsense, madness, craziness, idiocy, lunacy, rashness, recklessness, indiscretion, imprudence. WISDOM
foment encourage, stimulate, instigate, incite, provoke, stir up, arouse, brew, agitate, excite, goad, spur, promote, foster. QUELL
fomentation encouragement, stimulation, instigation, incitement, provocation, arousal, agitation, excitement.
fond loving, tender, warm, affectionate, amorous, adoring, devoted, doting, caring. COLD
foolish, absurd, empty, vain, optimistic, naive, credulous. SENSIBLE
fond of, partial to, attached to, keen on, enamoured of, having a liking for. AVERSE
fondle caress, stroke, pet, pat, cuddle.
fondness liking, predilection, partiality, penchant, fancy, weakness. AVERSION
love, affection, tenderness, devotion, care. COLDNESS
food nourishment, sustenance, nutriment, aliment, fare, diet, meals, board, foodstuffs, provisions, victuals, comestibles, eats (*inf*), grub (*inf*), commons, rations.
fodder, feed, provender, forage.
fool *n*, blockhead, dunce, dolt, ninny, nincompoop, simpleton, idiot, halfwit, ass, donkey, chump (*inf*), twit (*inf*), clot (*inf*), dope (*inf*).
clown, jester, buffoon, harlequin, pierrot.
v, deceive, dupe, trick, hoodwink, beguile, cheat, delude, mislead, hoax, cozen, take in, con (*inf*).
jest, joke, pretend, play, trifle, toy, meddle, fiddle, tamper.
foolery antics, capers, mischief, pranks, tricks, buffoonery, tomfoolery, horseplay.
foolhardy reckless, rash, incautious, irresponsible, daredevil, madcap, temerarious, bold, daring, adventurous, impetuous, precipitate, desperate. CAUTIOUS
foolish silly, unwise, injudicious, imprudent, ill-advised, absurd, ridiculous, fatuous, senseless, unreasonable, irrational, brainless, witless, stupid, unintelligent, simple, puerile, mad, crazy, idiotic, daft (*inf*). SENSIBLE
foolishness folly, stupidity, imprudence, senselessness, absurdity, inanity, madness, craziness, foolery, nonsense. SENSE
foot *n*, paw, hoof, trotter, pad.
bottom, base, foundation, pedestal, support. TOP
v, pay, settle, discharge, meet.
footing basis, foundation, establishment, settlement, groundwork, foothold.
standing, status, position, condition, rank, grade, relationship, terms.
footstep footprint, footmark, track, trace.
footfall, step, tread.
fop dandy, coxcomb, beau, popinjay, swell (*inf*).
foppery foppishness, dandyism, vanity, affectation.
foppish dandyish, dandified, vain, conceited, affected, spruce, dapper. SLOVENLY
for *prep*, towards, to, in order to. FROM
belonging to, appropriate to, concerning.
during, through, throughout.
in favour of, pro, with, in support of, on behalf of. AGAINST
because of, owing to, due to.
conj, since, as, because.
forage *n*, fodder, food, feed, provender.
v, search, hunt, seek, scour, scavenge, rummage, ransack, plunder, pillage, raid.
foray raid, incursion, inroad, invasion, sally, sortie, attack, assault. RETREAT
forbear refrain, abstain, desist, cease, stop, pause, hold back, withhold, restrain oneself, avoid, shun, eschew, decline. INDULGE
forbearance abstinence, restraint, self-control, moderation, temperance, patience, tolerance, leniency, clemency.
forbid prohibit, ban, interdict, proscribe, outlaw, taboo, veto, disallow. PERMIT
impede, hinder, inhibit, prevent, exclude, rule out. ALLOW
forbidding menacing, threatening, ominous, sinister, hostile, unfriendly, grim, daunting, off-putting (*inf*), repulsive, repellent, unpleasant. ATTRACTIVE
force *v*, compel, constrain, oblige, make, drive, impel, coerce, press, urge. COAX

strain, wrench, break open, blast, push, thrust. EASE
n, compulsion, constraint, coercion, duress, pressure, violence.
power, might, strength, vigour, drive, energy, dynamism, potency, efficacy, cogency, impact, stress, emphasis, weight. WEAKNESS
army, host, legion, squadron, troop, regiment, unit, division, detachment, battalion.

forced compulsory, obligatory, mandatory, involuntary, enforced, compelled, constrained. VOLUNTARY
unnatural, strained, artificial, false, affected, mannered, laboured, stiff. NATURAL

forcible forceful, compelling, powerful, mighty, strong, potent, cogent, pithy, effective, weighty, impressive. WEAK
forced, compulsory, obligatory, violent, aggressive, coercive.

fore front, lead, head, top, bow, forefront, foreground. REAR

forebear ancestor, forefather, progenitor, predecessor, forerunner. DESCENDANT

forebode portend, augur, presage, foretell, predict, prophesy, foreshadow, betoken, indicate, promise, warn, forewarn.

foreboding premonition, presentiment, apprehension, misgiving, dread, fear, anxiety. REASSURANCE
omen, portent, token, augury, prediction, prophecy, warning.

forecast *v*, predict, augur, prophesy, divine, foresee, prognosticate, anticipate, speculate, estimate, calculate, plan, project.
n, prediction, augury, prophecy, divination, prognosis, anticipation, speculation, projection, outlook.

foreclose exclude, shut out, preclude, debar, block, hinder, prevent, stop.

forefather ancestor, forebear, progenitor, procreator, father. OFFSPRING

foregoing preceding, prior, previous, former, antecedent, anterior. FOLLOWING

foregone past, previous, former, earlier, bygone. FUTURE
predetermined, preordained, fixed, inevitable.

foreign alien, strange, unfamiliar, imported, exotic, outlandish, external, exterior, remote, distant. NATIVE
extrinsic, extraneous, irrelevant, unrelated. RELEVANT

foreigner alien, immigrant, stranger, outsider, newcomer. NATIVE

foreknowledge prescience, foresight, precognition, premonition, clairvoyance.

foreland cape, headland, promontory, spur, point.

foreman supervisor, overseer, superintendent, charge hand, manager, boss (*inf*).

foremost chief, leading, front, head, first, primary, principal, main, supreme, paramount, prime.

forerunner precursor, harbinger, herald, predecessor, ancestor, forebear, forefather. SUCCESSOR
omen, portent, sign, token, indication, forewarning, premonition.

foresee anticipate, expect, envisage, forecast, predict, prophesy, divine, foretell.

foreshadow augur, presage, predict, prophesy, prefigure, portend, forebode, betoken, indicate, signify.

foresight forethought, anticipation, provision, precaution, prudence, care, circumspection, far-sightedness. IMPROVIDENCE

forest wood, woodland, woods, grove, copse, plantation.

forestall anticipate, thwart, frustrate, intercept, ward off, fend off, parry, obviate, preclude, prevent, hinder.

foretell predict, prophesy, augur, divine, forecast, prognosticate, presage, foreshadow, forebode, prefigure, betoken.

forethought anticipation, foresight, provision, precaution, prudence, far-sightedness. IMPROVIDENCE

forever evermore, always, till the end of time, eternally, constantly, perpetually, incessantly, all the time. TEMPORARILY

forewarn warn, alert, put on guard, caution, admonish, advise.

foreword preface, introduction, preamble, prologue. EPILOGUE

forfeit *v*, lose, surrender, relinquish, give up, renounce. EARN
n, loss, penalty, fine, mulct, forfeiture. REWARD

forge *v*, make, shape, form, mould, work, hammer out, create, fabricate, devise, invent, frame, coin.
fake, counterfeit, falsify, copy, imitate.
n, smithy, foundry, furnace, hearth.

forged fake, counterfeit, false, fraudulent, imitation, sham, bogus, spurious. GENUINE

forgery fake, counterfeit, falsification, imitation, sham, fraud.

forget overlook, neglect, disregard, ignore, omit, pass over, let slip. REMEMBER

forgetful absent-minded, inattentive, negligent, neglectful, heedless, careless, oblivious, unmindful. MINDFUL

forgive pardon, absolve, excuse, acquit, exonerate, remit, condone, overlook, let off (*inf*). PUNISH

forgiveness pardon, absolution, acquittal, remission, clemency, mercy. PUNISHMENT

forgo surrender, relinquish, give up, yield, hand over, renounce, abandon, waive, do without, abstain from, shun.

forgotten unremembered, past, bygone, lost, irretrievable, neglected, overlooked. REMEMBERED

fork *v*, branch, bifurcate, divide, part, split, separate, diverge, divaricate. UNITE
n, bifurcation, divarication, separation, division, branch.

forlorn miserable, wretched, desolate, cheerless, comfortless, unhappy, woebegone, pathetic, pitiful, helpless, friendless, homeless, destitute, lost, abandoned, deserted, forsaken. HAPPY

form *n*, shape, configuration, figure, appearance, cast, mould, pattern, model, cut, structure, frame, outline, contour, build, body.
type, kind, sort, variety, style, design, description, nature, character, mode, manner, method, arrangement, system, order.
document, paper, blank.
convention, etiquette, protocol, formality, procedure, ritual, ceremony, practice, custom, conduct, behaviour.
condition, health, fitness, shape, fettle.
class, grade, group, stream, year.
bench, seat.
v, make, shape, mould, model, fashion, create, fabricate, build, construct, assemble, produce. DESTROY
frame, devise, invent, conceive, formulate, think up, design, plan, arrange, dispose, organize.
compose, make up, constitute, comprise.
take shape, materialize, crystallize, appear, develop. VANISH
contract, acquire, get, pick up. LOSE
train, educate, instruct, teach, school, discipline.

formal conventional, customary, regular, standard, approved, official, set, fixed, methodical, strict, precise, exact, correct, punctilious. UNCONVENTIONAL
ceremonious, stiff, starched, prim, solemn, dignified, ceremonial, stately, pompous, aloof, reserved. INFORMAL

formality convention, form, custom, usage, practice, procedure, ritual, ceremony, protocol, etiquette, decorum.

format design, layout, appearance, arrangement, organization, style, form, composition, plan.

formation forming, making, creation, generation, production, manufacture, construction, composition, constitution, establishment, development. DESTRUCTION
arrangement, grouping, pattern, design, layout, structure.

former previous, earlier, prior, preceding, foregoing, antecedent, past, bygone, foregone, anterior, one-time, erstwhile, late. FUTURE

formerly previously, heretofore, hitherto, once, at one time.

formidable alarming, terrifying, fearful, dreadful, frightful, menacing, threatening, horrible, awful, terrible, daunting, overwhelming, arduous, difficult. REASSURING
tremendous, colossal, terrific, great, strong, powerful, mighty, impressive, redoubtable, indomitable. CONTEMPTIBLE

formless amorphous, vague, indefinite, nebulous, shapeless, unformed, chaotic, disorganized.

formula rule, principle, prescription, recipe, procedure, method, ritual, formulary, equation.

formulate define, specify, detail, itemize, set down, articulate, express, state.
devise, invent, forge, coin, think up, conceive, plan, draw up.

forsake desert, leave, quit, abandon, cast off, give up, relinquish, forgo, surrender, yield, forswear, renounce. KEEP

forswear abjure, renounce, reject, forgo, relinquish, give up, forsake, abandon. RETAIN
disavow, retract, deny, recant, repudiate, disown. AFFIRM

fort fortress, stronghold, citadel, fastness, garrison, castle, defence, fortification.

forte strength, strong point, gift, talent, métier, speciality. FOIBLE

forth forward, onward, ahead, out, away, abroad.

forthcoming future, prospective, coming, approaching, expected, imminent, impending. PREVIOUS
communicative, open, sociable, expansive, chatty, talkative, responsive. RETICENT

forthright direct, straightforward, candid, frank, blunt, outspoken. EVASIVE

forthwith directly, immediately, at once, instantly, straightaway, without delay, right away. PRESENTLY

fortification defence, bastion, rampart, battlement, bulwark, fort, stronghold, citadel, fastness.

fortify strengthen, reinforce, stiffen, brace, buttress, support, protect, defend, garrison.
encourage, cheer, hearten, invigorate, revive, sustain.

fortitude endurance, patience, forbearance, hardihood, courage, bravery, backbone, strength, firmness, resolution, determination, perseverance. WEAKNESS

fortuitous accidental, unplanned, contingent, chance, unforeseen, casual, arbitrary, lucky, fortunate. PLANNED

fortunate lucky, happy, felicitous, fortuitous, blessed, favoured, prosperous, successful, auspicious, propitious, favourable, advantageous, opportune, timely. UNFORTUNATE

fortune wealth, riches, opulence, affluence, assets, possessions, property, estate. POVERTY
luck, chance, accident, contingency, fortuity, fate, destiny, lot, portion, doom, kismet, future, prospect, expectation.

forward *adj*, advanced, early, premature, precocious, progressive, onward. BACKWARD
front, leading, first, foremost, head, anterior, fore. BACK
bold, brazen, cheeky, pert, impertinent, impudent, presumptuous, assuming, familiar, fresh (*inf*), confident, cocky (*inf*). RESERVED
adv, forwards, on, onward, forth, ahead. BACKWARD
out, into view, into the open, to the fore, into prominence.
v, advance, further, promote, foster, support, aid, help, encourage, expedite, quicken, hasten, hurry, speed, accelerate, dispatch. HINDER
send, transmit, dispatch, mail, post, ship, send on.

foster promote, advance, further, encourage, stimulate, cultivate, support, maintain, cherish, nurture, nurse, harbour, sustain, nourish, raise, rear, bring up.

foul adj, dirty, filthy, soiled, unclean, impure, contaminated, polluted, tainted, sullied, offensive, disgusting, revolting, loathsome, putrid, fetid, stinking, rank, noisome. PURE
wicked, vile, ignoble, despicable, disgraceful, shameful, heinous, infamous, base, low, vulgar, coarse, gross, obscene, ribald, scurrilous, profane, blasphemous. NOBLE
unfair, dishonourable, dishonest, crooked, underhand, unsportsmanlike, unscrupulous. FAIR
rainy, wet, gloomy, murky, overcast, bad, stormy, rough, wild. FINE
v, soil, dirty, begrime, pollute, contaminate, taint, sully, defile.
block, clog, jam, choke, snarl, entangle. CLEAR

found establish, set up, institute, organize, originate, start, create, build, raise, erect. ABOLISH
base, ground, root, fix, set, rest, place.

foundation base, basis, footing, groundwork, bottom, substructure, root. SUPERSTRUCTURE
establishment, institution, organization, endowment, settlement.

founder[1] *v*, sink, go down, collapse, fail, abort, miscarry, fall through, break down, fall, trip, stumble, stagger.

founder[2] *n*, originator, creator, organizer, benefactor, architect, designer, builder, author, father.

fountain jet, spout, spray, fount, spring, well.
fountainhead, source, origin, cause, beginning.

foxy wily, artful, cunning, sly, crafty, subtle, shrewd, astute, tricky, guileful, scheming. ARTLESS

fracas quarrel, row, brawl, fight, disturbance, fray, uproar, commotion, rumpus.

fraction part, piece, fragment, bit, portion, section, segment, division. WHOLE
fractious irritable, peevish, testy, touchy, captious, cross, waspish, crabby, petulant, fretful. AFFABLE
unruly, refractory, recalcitrant, rebellious, awkward, contrary, perverse. DOCILE
fracture *v*, break, crack, split, rupture, tear. MEND
n, break, breach, crack, rift, division, split, fissure, cleft, rupture, rent.
fragile brittle, frangible, breakable, frail, delicate, dainty, flimsy, slight, weak, feeble. STRONG
fragility brittleness, frangibility, frailty, delicacy, flimsiness, weakness, feebleness. STRENGTH
fragment piece, portion, fraction, part, bit, morsel, scrap, remnant, chip, sliver. WHOLE
fragmentary broken, disconnected, disjointed, bitty, incomplete, partial, sketchy, unfinished, scattered, piecemeal.
fragrance perfume, scent, aroma, smell, odour, redolence, balm, bouquet. FETOR
fragrant perfumed, scented, ambrosial, balmy, aromatic, sweet-smelling, redolent, odoriferous. FETID
frail weak, feeble, infirm, fragile, delicate, slight, slender, thin, flimsy. STURDY
frailty weakness, feebleness, infirmity, fragility, delicacy, slenderness. STURDINESS
failing, faulty, defect, imperfection, foible, weakness, fallibility, susceptibility. STRENGTH
frame *v*, make, form, construct, build, fashion, model, forge, fabricate, devise, invent, concoct, compose, draw up, formulate, draft, sketch, outline, map out, plan.
enclose, surround, border, mount, encase.
n, structure, construction, framework, skeleton, shell, casing, support, substructure, form, shape, fabric, constitution, system.
mount, setting, border, case.
condition, state, mood, temper, humour, disposition.
franchise vote, suffrage, right, privilege, licence, authorization, exemption, immunity, freedom.
frank honest, straightforward, direct, forthright, candid, outspoken, unreserved, blunt, open, sincere, guileless, artless, ingenuous. DEVIOUS
indisguised, unconcealed, avowed, apparent, obvious, plain, clear, transparent. CONCEALED
frantic frenzied, wild, mad, delirious, hysterical, distraught, distracted, raging, furious, beside oneself, hectic, frenetic. CALM
fraternity brotherhood, fellowship, association, society, league, guild, union, circle, set, clan, company, companionship, camaraderie.
fraternize associate, league, unite, cooperate, sympathize, socialize, mix, mingle, go around, keep company, consort, hobnob.
fraud deception, deceit, trickery, cheating, fraudulence, imposture, duplicity, treachery. HONESTY
trick, artifice, swindle, hoax, wile, ruse, stratagem.
impostor, charlatan, quack, cheat, swindler, fake, phoney (*inf*).
fraudulent deceitful, tricky, crafty, wily, knavish, treacherous, dishonest, crooked, false, counterfeit, fake. HONEST
fraught filled, full, charged, loaded, laden, replete, abounding, attended, accompanied. DEVOID
fray[1] *n*, fight, battle, combat, conflict, quarrel, row, brawl, melee, riot, fracas. PEACE
fray[2] *v*, wear, unravel, shred, tatter, chafe, rub, fret.
freak monstrosity, monster, abnormality, anomaly, oddity, curiosity, mutant, teratism, malformation, deformity, abortion.
whim, caprice, fancy, notion, vagary, crotchet, quirk, humour.
freakish abnormal, aberrant, unnatural, bizarre, weird, strange, monstrous, malformed, grotesque. NORMAL
whimsical, capricious, fanciful, wayward, fitful, erratic, odd. CONSISTENT
free *adj*, independent, unconfined, loose, unattached, liberated, released, unfettered, unrestrained, unrestricted, unbridled, at large. CONFINED
gratis, gratuitous, on the house, complimentary, without charge, for nothing.
idle, at leisure, unoccupied, vacant, empty, available, spare. BUSY
clear, unobstructed, unimpeded, unhampered, open, permitted, allowed. BLOCKED

exempt, immune, not liable, devoid, without. LIABLE

informal, easy, relaxed, casual, unceremonious, familiar, uninhibited, natural, open, frank. CONSTRAINED

liberal, generous, prodigal, lavish, bountiful, extravagant, munificent. MEAN

voluntary, unforced, willing, spontaneous, unbidden. FORCED

v, liberate, release, loose, let go, set free, emancipate, manumit, unfetter, unchain, unbind, untie. BIND

deliver, rescue, relieve, rid, clear, extricate, disentangle, disengage, discharge, exempt, except. EMBROIL

freebooter pirate, buccaneer, bandit, brigand, robber, raider, marauder, highwayman.

freedom liberty, emancipation, independence, liberation, release, deliverance. CAPTIVITY

exemption, exception, immunity, privilege. LIABILITY

range, scope, play, latitude, leeway, licence, authority, carte blanche. RESTRICTION

informality, unconstraint, ease, familiarity, frankness, openness. CONSTRAINT

freeze solidify, congeal, harden, ice up, refrigerate, chill, benumb. MELT

stop, stand still, suspend, hold, fix, peg.

freezing icy, bitter, biting, raw, wintry, arctic, polar, glacial, frigid. HOT

freight transportation, conveyance, carriage, shipment, cargo, load, lading, burden, charge, consignment, goods, merchandise.

frenetic frantic, frenzied, wild, mad, demented, distraught. CALM

frenzy agitation, excitement, fury, rage, passion, madness, derangement, distraction, aberration, hysteria, delirium, fit, paroxysm, outburst. COMPOSURE

frequent *adj*, recurrent, repeated, incessant, continual, persistent, constant, many, numerous. RARE

common, everyday, familiar, customary, usual, habitual. UNUSUAL

v, visit, attend, patronize, haunt.

frequently often, repeatedly, again and again, over and over, many times, constantly, regularly, commonly, usually. SELDOM

fresh new, recent, latest, modern, up-to-date, novel, original, different, unfamiliar. OLD

additional, extra, more, further, renewed, other.

cool, refreshing, invigorating, bracing, brisk, crisp, clear, clean, pure, sweet. STALE

energetic, vigorous, lively, hearty, healthy, keen, alert, revived, refreshed, rested, strong, hardy, flourishing, blooming, glowing, fair. TIRED

inexperienced, green, raw, callow, youthful, artless, unsophisticated, untrained. EXPERIENCED

natural, unprocessed, uncured, raw, crude. PROCESSED

familiar, forward, presumptuous, bold, cheeky, saucy, impertinent, impudent, disrespectful.

freshen refresh, invigorate, revive, revitalize, enliven, renew, ventilate, air.

fret worry, brood, agonize, grieve, pine, distress, torment, irritate, annoy, vex, trouble, disturb, upset, bother, ruffle, harass, provoke, goad. SOOTHE

rub, chafe, wear, abrade, fray, erode, corrode, eat away.

fretful irritable, petulant, peevish, waspish, captious, testy, touchy, fractious, querulous, edgy, anxious, uneasy.

friable crumbly, powdery, brittle. TOUGH

friction attrition, abrasion, rubbing, grating, scraping, grinding.

discord, dissension, dispute, disagreement, conflict, strife, hostility, antagonism, animosity. AGREEMENT

friend companion, intimate, confidant, familiar, comrade, ally, associate, partner, crony, chum (*inf*), pal (*inf*), mate (*inf*), benefactor, patron, supporter. ENEMY

friendly amicable, kind, kindly, benevolent, neighbourly, brotherly, sisterly, cordial, amiable, genial, affable, sociable, outgoing, approachable, close, intimate, familiar, fond, affectionate, sympathetic, understanding. UNFRIENDLY

favourable, propitious, auspicious, advantageous, beneficial, helpful. HOSTILE

friendship amity, harmony, rapport, comradeship, companionship, friendliness, amicability, cordiality, kindness, benevolence, intimacy, familiarity, love, affection, fondness, attachment, regard. ENMITY

fright fear, alarm, scare, terror, shock, horror, panic, dismay, consternation, dread, trepidation, apprehension. REASSURANCE

frighten alarm, scare, terrify, shock, startle, horrify, dismay, daunt, intimidate, unnerve. REASSURE

frightful frightening, alarming, terrifying, fearsome, fearful, dreadful, terrible, awful, horrible, hideous, gruesome, ghastly, dire, distressing, horrifying, shocking, appalling, outrageous, monstrous. DELIGHTFUL

frigid cold, cool, icy, glacial, formal, stiff, rigid, prim, aloof, unapproachable, forbidding, unfriendly, unresponsive, unfeeling, passionless, passive, indifferent. WARM

frigidity coldness, coolness, formality, stiffness, aloofness, unapproachability, unfriendliness, impassivity, indifference, apathy. WARMTH

frill flounce, ruche, furbelow, ruff, ruffle, valance, purfle, border, trimming.
affectation, mannerism, ostentation, showiness, fuss, frippery.

fringe border, edging, trimming.
edge, periphery, outskirts, limits, border, margin, verge. CENTRE

frisk frolic, gambol, caper, skip, jump, leap, dance, play, sport, romp, cavort.

frisky frolicsome, sportive, playful, lively, full of beans (*inf*), coltish, high-spirited, gay, animated. SEDATE

fritter waste, squander, spend, dissipate, misspend, idle, dally. SAVE

frivolity frivolousness, levity, flippancy, light-heartedness, foolishness, silliness, puerility, childishness, triviality, superficiality. SERIOUSNESS

frivolous foolish, silly, puerile, childish, flippant, idle, light, trivial, petty, unimportant, paltry, superficial, shallow. SERIOUS

frolic *v*, gambol, caper, frisk, romp, cavort, play, sport.
n, gambol, caper, romp, game, sport, lark, antic, prank, fun, merriment, gaiety, jollity.

frolicsome playful, sportive, frisky, coltish, lively, merry, gay. SEDATE

front *n*, anterior, forepart, foreground, face, exterior, façade, frontage. BACK
fore, head, top, lead, vanguard, forefront, beginning. REAR
aspect, appearance, air, demeanour, bearing, mien, exterior, façade, mask, disguise, show.
in front, ahead, leading, first, before, in advance. BEHIND
adj, anterior, frontal, forward, foremost, leading, head, first. BACK
v, face, be opposite, look out on, overlook, confront, encounter.

frontier boundary, border, marches, limits, confines, bounds, edge.

frosty icy, glacial, freezing, frigid, cold, chilly, wintry. HOT
unenthusiastic, indifferent, cool, frigid, distant, aloof, unfriendly, unwelcoming. WARM

froth *n*, foam, spume, bubbles, effervescence, lather, suds, head, scum.
triviality, emptiness, idle talk, nonsense, humbug, flummery.
v, foam, lather, fizz, bubble, effervesce.

frown scowl, glower, glare, lower, pout, grimace. SMILE
frown on, disapprove of, dislike, disfavour, discountenance, take a dim view of. APPROVE

frowzy unkempt, untidy, slovenly, slatternly, shabby, sloppy, frumpish, dirty. NEAT
stale, musty, frowsty, fusty, ill-smelling.

frozen icy, frigid, arctic, glacial, chilled, frosted, numb. HOT

frugal thrifty, sparing, economical, careful, provident, temperate, abstemious, parsimonious, niggardly, meagre, scanty. EXTRAVAGANT

frugality thrift, economy, providence, temperance, parsimony, meagreness. EXTRAVAGANCE

fruit produce, crop, harvest, yield, product, result, consequence, issue, outcome, return, profit, reward, advantage.

fruitful productive, prolific, fecund, fertile, rich, teeming, plentiful, plenteous, abundant, profuse. BARREN
profitable, worthwhile, effective, successful, useful, productive, rewarding. FRUITLESS

fruition fulfilment, attainment, achievement, realization, completion, consummation, perfection, maturation, gratification, enjoyment. ABORTION

fruitless futile, vain, useless, bootless, ineffectual, unproductive, unprofitable, unsuccessful, abortive, idle, worthless, unavailing, barren, sterile. FRUITFUL

frustrate thwart, foil, dash, balk, confound, baffle, defeat, undo, circumvent, check, block, stymie, hinder, prevent, disappoint, discourage, upset, annoy, irritate. GRATIFY

frustration thwarting, balking, defeat, failure, circumvention, hindrance, prevention, disappointment, annoyance, irritation. GRATIFICATION

fuddled inebriated, intoxicated, drunk, tipsy, stupefied, muddled, confused. SOBER

fuel combustible, wood, coal, gas, oil, petrol.
food, nourishment, sustenance, incitement, provocation, encouragement.

fugacious fleeting, transitory, transient, fugitive, brief, short-lived, passing, ephemeral, evanescent. PERMANENT

fugitive *n*, runaway, escapee, deserter, refugee.
adj, fleeting, transitory, transient, fugacious, brief, short-lived, passing, ephemeral, evanescent. PERMANENT

fulcrum pivot, support, prop.

fulfil complete, accomplish, achieve, realize, perfect, consummate, effect, effectuate, perform, execute, discharge, do, carry out, satisfy, fill, meet, answer, obey, observe, keep.

fulfilment completion, accomplishment, achievement, realization, perfection, consummation, performance, execution, discharge, satisfaction, observance.

fuliginous sooty, smoky, dusky, dark.

full *adj*, filled, brimming, packed, replete, sated, gorged, satiated, saturated. EMPTY
complete, entire, whole, intact, integral, unabridged. PARTIAL
abundant, plentiful, plenteous, copious, ample, generous, capacious, voluminous, vast, extensive, large, broad, comprehensive, thorough, detailed, exhaustive. RESTRICTED
plump, rounded, curvaceous, buxom, puffy, baggy, loose.
occupied, taken, in use. VACANT
resonant, rich, deep, loud, clear, distinct. MUTED
adv, directly, straight, right, squarely, exactly, precisely.
completely, entirely, fully, wholly, quite, altogether. PARTLY

fully completely, entirely, wholly, totally, utterly, absolutely, altogether, quite, thoroughly, perfectly. PARTLY
sufficiently, adequately, enough, amply, abundantly. INADEQUATELY

fulminate denounce, condemn, decry, rail, inveigh, roar, thunder, rage, fume, censure, upbraid, berate, animadvert, remonstrate, protest. EXTOL
explode, detonate, blow up, burst.

fulmination denunciation, condemnation, censure, animadversion, tirade, diatribe, obloquy, philippic. EULOGY
explosion, detonation, blast.

fulsome excessive, extravagant, overdone, adulatory, fawning, sycophantic, insincere, sickening, nauseating. MEAGRE

fumble grope, feel, scrabble, search, flounder, stumble, bungle, botch, muff.

fume *v*, rage, storm, rant, rave, seethe, boil, chafe, fret.
smoke, emit, exhale, reek.
n, rage, storm, fury, passion, agitation, fret, stew (*inf*). CALM

fumes gas, vapour, smoke, effluvium, exhalation, pollution, reek.

fumigate smoke, disinfect, purify, cleanse, sterilize. INFECT

fun amusement, entertainment, diversion, recreation, sport, pleasure, enjoyment, merriment, jollity, joy, gaiety, cheer, mirth. MISERY
make fun of, mock, jeer, gibe, taunt, deride, scoff at, satirize, lampoon. RESPECT

function *n*, purpose, use, part, role, province, duty, charge, task, job, office, position, business, mission, occupation.
operation, performance, execution, exercise, activity.
ceremony, party, reception, gathering, affair, do (*inf*).
v, work, operate, act, behave, run, go, perform.

fund *n*, stock, supply, store, reserve, accumulation, hoard, reservoir, pool, kitty, treasury, capital, endowment, investment, savings, money, resources, funds, finance.
v, finance, pay for, subsidize, support, endow, capitalize.

fundamental *adj*, basic, primary, first, elementary, important, necessary, essential,

principal, key, vital, indispensable, cardinal, underlying, organic, constitutional, integral. SECONDARY
n, basic, rudiment, essential, principle, rule, foundation, basis, cornerstone.

funeral burial, interment, inhumation, cremation, obsequies, exequies.

funereal mournful, dirgeful, lugubrious, gloomy, dismal, sorrowful, woeful, sombre, dark, dreary, grave, solemn. JOYOUS

funk *n*, fear, panic, terror, fright, alarm, dread, trepidation, nervousness. COURAGE
v, flinch, recoil, quail, cower, take fright, chicken out (*inf*). FACE

funny amusing, comic, comical, humorous, droll, witty, facetious, entertaining, diverting, hilarious, hysterical (*inf*), farcical, laughable, ridiculous, ludicrous. SERIOUS
odd, strange, queer, weird, curious, peculiar, mysterious, suspicious, dubious. NORMAL

fur hair, coat, hide, skin, pelt.

furbish polish, rub, burnish, shine, brighten, clean up, renovate, restore. TARNISH

furcate furcated, forked, branched, divided, divaricate, bifurcate.

furious angry, enraged, fuming, incensed, irate, infuriated, wrathful, raging, mad, frantic, frenzied, wild, violent, agitated, turbulent, stormy, tempestuous, savage, fierce, intense, unrestrained. CALM

furl roll, wrap, fold, wind. UNFURL

furnish equip, rig, fit out, appoint, decorate, stock, supply, provide, give, grant, afford, bestow, endow, invest. DIVEST

furniture fixtures, appliances, fittings, movables, furnishings, appointments, effects, goods, belongings, possessions, apparatus, equipment.

furore outcry, uproar, commotion, stir, outburst, rage, fury, frenzy. APATHY
craze, mania, rage, enthusiasm, fad.

furrow *n*, trench, trough, channel, rut, hollow, groove, flute, wrinkle, crease, line, seam. RIDGE
v, wrinkle, crease, knit, pucker.

further *adj*, additional, more, extra, supplementary, new, fresh, other.
adv, furthermore, besides, moreover, in addition, what's more, also, yet.
farther, beyond, past, longer, more. NEARER
v, advance, promote, forward, assist, help, foster, encourage, support, expedite, hasten. HINDER

furtherance advancement, promotion, boost, assistance, help, aid, encouragement, support, backing. HINDRANCE

furthermore moreover, yet, in addition, besides, what's more, further, too, also, as well.

furthest farthest, utmost, extreme, ultimate, remotest, most distant. NEAREST

furtive secret, secretive, clandestine, hidden, covert, sly, stealthy, surreptitious, underhand. OPEN

fury rage, anger, wrath, ire, passion, temper, frenzy, madness, wildness, violence, force, intensity, fierceness, ferocity, severity, vehemence, tempestuousness, turbulence. CALM
shrew, vixen, termagant, virago, hellcat, spitfire.

fuse unite, join, combine, integrate, amalgamate, blend, intermix, commingle, intermingle, merge, coalesce. SEPARATE
melt, liquefy, smelt, weld, solder.

fusion union, amalgamation, coalescence, synthesis, blend, mixture, merger, amalgam, alloy.

fuss *n*, agitation, commotion, stir, to-do (*inf*), bustle, fluster, flurry, bother, ado, palaver, flap (*inf*), excitement. PEACE
complaint, objection, difficulty, trouble, argument, altercation, quarrel, dispute, row.
v, bustle, fret, worry, fidget, fume, gripe (*inf*), bother, pester.

fussy particular, finicky, faddy, pernickety, choosy (*inf*), difficult, hard to please, fastidious, dainty, discriminating, exacting. EASY-GOING
fidgety, restless, fretful, crotchety. PLACID
ornate, elaborate, busy, cluttered. SIMPLE

fustian *n*, bombast, rant, pomposity, grandiloquence, magniloquence, bluster.
adj, bombastic, pompous, high-flown, lofty, euphuistic. PLAIN

fusty musty, mouldy, mildewy, damp, frowsty, stale, rank, ill-smelling, stuffy. FRESH
old-fashioned, out-of-date, antiquated, archaic, passé. MODERN

futile useless, vain, fruitless, bootless, ineffectual, unavailing, idle, empty, profit-

less, worthless, abortive, unsuccessful, unproductive, pointless. FRUITFUL
trifling, trivial, minor, insignificant, unimportant. IMPORTANT
futility uselessness, vanity, fruitlessness, idleness, worthlessness, pointlessness. USEFULNESS
triviality, insignificance, unimportance. IMPORTANCE
future *adj*, forthcoming, coming, to come, prospective, expected, impending, approaching, eventual, ultimate, subsequent, later. PAST
n, prospect, outlook, expectation, offing, hereafter.
fuzzy fluffy, woolly, downy. SMOOTH
blurred, indistinct, unclear, out of focus, bleary, misty, vague, obscure, distorted. SHARP

G

gab *v*, chatter, gossip, prattle, blabber, babble.
n, chat, talk, small talk, chitchat, gossip, chatter, babble.
gabble *v*, jabber, gibber, spout, gush, chatter, babble, blather, prattle.
n, drivel, gibberish, chatter, babble, blather, prattle, jabber.
gadget device, contraption (*inf*), contrivance, appliance, tool, implement.
gag[1] *v*, muzzle, muffle, stifle, stop up, silence, quiet, suppress, curb.
throttle, choke, retch, heave, gasp.
gag[2] *n*, joke, quip, witticism, crack (*inf*), trick, hoax.
gage pledge, security, bond, guarantee, surety, deposit, pawn, token, earnest.
challenge, dare, glove, gauntlet.
gaiety joy, joyousness, glee, cheerfulness, hilarity, mirth, jollity, joviality, merriment, liveliness, animation, vivacity, buoyancy, high spirits, elation, jubilation. SADNESS
festivity, merrymaking, revelry, celebration. MOURNING
colour, brightness, brilliance, sparkle, showiness. DRABNESS
gain *v*, acquire, procure, obtain, get, secure, win, earn, capture, glean, gather, reap. LOSE
profit, benefit, make, yield, produce, net, clear, realize, bring in.
attain, reach, arrive at, get to.
gain on, catch up with, get nearer, approach, overtake, draw away from, leave behind.
n, profit, advantage, benefit, earnings, winnings, revenue, income, proceeds, return, yield. LOSS
increase, growth, rise, advance, progress, headway, improvement. DECLINE
gainful profitable, lucrative, remunerative, paying, rewarding, productive, fruitful, worthwhile, beneficial, advantageous. UNPROFITABLE
gainsay deny, contradict, controvert, dispute, oppose. AFFIRM
gait walk, step, pace, stride, tread, bearing, carriage.
gala celebration, festival, carnival, fête, jamboree, pageant.
galaxy assemblage, gathering, assembly, collection, bevy, host.
gale wind, hurricane, cyclone, tornado, blast, squall, storm, tempest. BREEZE
gall *n*, rancour, bitterness, spite, malice, acrimony, venom, spleen. CHARITY
impudence, insolence, effrontery, impertinence, cheek (*inf*), nerve (*inf*).
irritation, exasperation, vexation, annoyance, aggravation. APPEASEMENT
v, irritate, exasperate, vex, annoy, aggravate, irk, nettle, peeve (*inf*), rile (*inf*), bother, provoke, harass, plague. APPEASE
gallant *adj*, brave, courageous, valiant, valorous, heroic, intrepid, bold, daring, fearless, dauntless, dashing, noble, honourable. COWARDLY
polite, courteous, chivalrous, gracious, magnanimous, gentlemanly, courtly, obliging, considerate. CHURLISH
stately, dignified, majestic, august, imposing, grand, splendid, magnificent, glorious.
n, beau, suitor, admirer, lover, boyfriend, escort.
dandy, beau, ladies' man, man about town.
gallantry courage, bravery, valour, heroism, boldness, fearlessness, mettle, spirit, pluck. COWARDICE
courtesy, politeness, chivalry, graciousness, magnanimity, courtliness, nobility. CHURLISHNESS
gallery corridor, passage, hallway, cloister, loggia, veranda, balcony, platform.
gallivant gad about, rove, roam, range, wander, ramble.

gallop lope, canter, race, dash, speed, rush, hurry, fly, bolt, career, shoot. AMBLE

galvanize electrify, excite, stimulate, fire, rouse, animate, invigorate, startle, shock, jolt. DAMP

gamble *v*, bet, wager, game, punt, back, stake, speculate, risk, hazard, venture.
n, bet, wager, flutter (*inf*), speculation, risk, hazard, venture, chance, lottery. CERTAINTY

gambol frolic, frisk, romp, caper, leap, jump, play, sport, skip, prance.

game *n*, pastime, recreation, diversion, amusement, distraction, entertainment, sport, play, fun, frolic. WORK
match, contest, competition, meeting, event, fixture.
quarry, prey.
scheme, plan, plot, design, stratagem, device.
adj, brave, courageous, valiant, plucky, spirited, bold, intrepid, dauntless, fearless. COWARDLY
ready, willing, eager, inclined, disposed, prepared. RELUCTANT

gammon *v*, deceive, trick, hoax, dupe, beguile, hoodwink.
n, deception, trick, hoax, humbug.

gamut compass, range, scale, scope, series, sweep.

gang band, group, pack, crowd, mob, horde, company, party, ring, circle, set, coterie, clique, team, squad, troop.

gangway path, passage, aisle.

gap break, breach, rift, cleft, crack, crevice, chink, cranny, hole, opening, space, blank, void, interstice, interval, pause, hiatus, interruption.

gape stare, gaze, gawk, gawp (*inf*), goggle.
open, yawn, crack, split. CLOSE

garb dress, attire, clothes, clothing, garments, wear, apparel, outfit, costume, habit, uniform, livery, robes.

garbage rubbish, refuse, waste, trash, junk, litter, debris, scraps, leftovers.

garble confuse, mix up, jumble, misquote, misrepresent, falsify, corrupt, pervert, distort, twist, slant, colour.

gargantuan enormous, huge, immense, colossal, tremendous, prodigious, massive, mammoth, gigantic, elephantine, great, big, large. MINUTE

garish gaudy, flashy, showy, flamboyant, glaring, loud, bold, meretricious, tawdry, tasteless, vulgar. SUBDUED

garland wreath, festoon, coronal, chaplet, crown, laurels, bays.

garments clothes, clothing, wear, attire, apparel, dress, costume, garb, array, habit, wardrobe, outfit, togs (*inf*), gear (*inf*).

garner gather, collect, accumulate, amass, hoard, save, husband, store, lay in, put by, reserve, deposit. WASTE

garnish *v*, decorate, adorn, ornament, deck, beautify, embellish, trim, grace. STRIP
n, decoration, adornment, ornament, embellishment, trimming, garniture.

garniture decorations, ornaments, garnish, trimmings, adornment, embellishment.

garret attic, loft, mansard. BASEMENT

garrulity loquacity, talkativeness, garrulousness, volubility, chatter, babble, verbosity, prolixity, wordiness. TACITURNITY

garrulous loquacious, talkative, garrulous, voluble, chatty, babbling, verbose, prolix, wordy. TACITURN

gas vapour, fume, exhalation, effluvium, wind.

gash *n*, cut, incision, slash, slit, score, tear, rent, laceration, wound.
v, cut, incise, slash, slit, score, lacerate, wound.

gasp pant, puff, blow, choke, wheeze, gulp.

gate entrance, exit, access, opening, portal, door, barrier.

gather collect, assemble, muster, convene, congregate, accumulate, amass, hoard, garner, cluster, flock. DISPERSE
pick, pluck, glean, reap, harvest, cull.
conclude, assume, deduce, infer, understand, learn.
increase, grow, swell, rise, expand, heighten, intensify. DECREASE
pucker, ruffle, shirr, pleat, tuck, fold, crease, wrinkle, contract, knit.

gathering assembly, muster, meeting, rally, party, group, company, congregation, conclave, convention, concourse, crowd, throng.
collection, accumulation, mass, heap, pile, cluster.
pustule, abscess, ulcer, boil, carbuncle, pimple.

gaudy bright, colourful, gay, garish, flashy, showy, flamboyant, glaring, loud, bold, meretricious, tawdry, tasteless, vulgar. MUTED

gauge *v*, measure, weigh, determine, calculate, evaluate, appraise, judge, estimate, assess, check.

n, measure, standard, norm, criterion, yardstick, bench mark, touchstone, guideline, test.

gaunt thin, lean, lank, spare, meagre, skinny, scrawny, emaciated, bony, angular, pinched, haggard. PLUMP

bleak, desolate, dreary, bare, barren, harsh, grim, forbidding.

gawk *n*, boor, lout, churl, clod, oaf, dolt.

v, gape, gawp, goggle, stare, gaze.

gawky awkward, ungainly, clumsy, lumbering, oafish, loutish, clownish. GRACEFUL

gay merry, jolly, jovial, cheerful, blithe, carefree, bright, gleeful, happy, joyful, joyous, lively, animated, vivacious, sprightly, festive, convivial. SAD

bright, colourful, vivid, brilliant, gaudy, garish, flashy, flamboyant. SOMBRE

homosexual, lesbian, queer (*inf*), bent (*inf*).

gaze stare, look, gape, gawk, contemplate, watch. GLANCE

gazette journal, periodical, newspaper, paper.

gear wheel, cog, gearing, mechanism, machinery.

equipment, apparatus, appurtenances, trappings, accessories, paraphernalia, tools, instruments, kit, outfit, rig, supplies, material, harness, tackle, belongings, effects, things (*inf*).

clothes, clothing, wear, dress, attire, apparel, garments, togs (*inf*).

gelatinous viscous, glutinous, gummy, sticky, mucilaginous.

gelid icy, frigid, glacial, freezing, frozen, arctic, polar. WARM

gem jewel, stone, precious stone, pearl, treasure, prize, flower.

genealogy descent, pedigree, family tree, stemma, ancestry, extraction, derivation, lineage, stock, stirps.

general *adj*, widespread, extensive, broad, universal, catholic, public, common, collective, comprehensive, total, blanket, across-the-board, sweeping, overall. SPECIFIC

usual, regular, normal, customary, habitual, common, ordinary, conventional. RARE

vague, loose, indefinite, unspecified, ill-defined, inexact, approximate, miscellaneous. PRECISE

n, commander, leader, chief, head.

generally usually, as a rule, by and large, ordinarily, in general, mostly, mainly, chiefly, principally, on the whole, largely.

generate produce, create, make, form, engender, breed, beget, propagate, cause, bring about, originate. DESTROY

generation production, creation, formation, propagation, procreation, breeding, reproduction, origination, genesis. DESTRUCTION

era, age, epoch, day, time, lifetime.

breed, race, offspring, progeny, children, age group.

generic collective, general, common, sweeping, blanket, all-inclusive, universal. SPECIFIC

generosity liberality, munificence, charity, bounty, largess, beneficence, benevolence, magnanimity, unselfishness, goodness, nobleness. MEANNESS

generous liberal, lavish, open-handed, munificent, charitable, bountiful, benevolent, beneficent, magnanimous, philanthropic, unselfish, kind, good, noble, honourable. MEAN

abundant, plentiful, copious, rich, full, ample. SCANTY

genial hearty, cordial, warm, friendly, amiable, affable, jolly, jovial, happy, cheerful, cheery, pleasant, agreeable, good-natured, easy-going, kindly, sunny. COLD

genius prodigy, virtuoso, maestro, master, expert, adept. DUNCE

gift, talent, aptitude, faculty, flair, knack, ability, skill, power, inclination, bent, brilliance, cleverness, intelligence, brains, intellect. STUPIDITY

genre category, class, school, style, type, sort, kind, brand, species, genus.

genteel polite, civil, courteous, respectable, well-bred, mannerly, proper, gentlemanly, ladylike, cultured, refined, polished, aristocratic, fashionable, elegant, stylish. BOORISH

gentility politeness, civility, courtesy, respectability, breeding, manners, propriety, decorum, refinement, polish, elegance, urbanity. BOORISHNESS aristocracy, nobility, gentry, upper class, elite.

gentle tender, kind, kindly, compassionate, considerate, benign, mild, moderate, soft, merciful, clement, indulgent, lenient, humane. ROUGH

gradual, easy, slow, light, soft, bland, moderate, temperate, calm, quiet, tranquil. HARSH

meek, tame, tractable, biddable, docile, placid. WILD

gentlemanly genteel, well-bred, courteous, polite, civil, mannerly, courtly, gallant, chivalrous, noble, honourable, suave, urbane, refined, cultivated. CHURLISH

gentry aristocracy, upper class, elite, nobility, gentility.

genuine real, authentic, sterling, pure, unadulterated, true, veritable, actual, bona fide, legitimate, honest, sincere, earnest, unaffected, frank, candid. FALSE

genus order, class, species, breed, kind, sort, type, group, set, category, genre.

germ microbe, bacterium, virus, microorganism, bug (*inf*).

seed, embryo, bud, root, source, origin, beginning, start. FRUIT

germane relevant, pertinent, connected, cognate, allied, related, akin, apposite, apropos, appropriate, fitting, suitable, apt. IRRELEVANT

germinate sprout, shoot, grow, develop, vegetate, bud. WITHER

gesticulate gesture, signal, motion, wave, beckon, nod.

gesture *n*, gesticulation, signal, sign, indication, demonstration, action, motion, movement, wave, flourish.

v, gesticulate, motion, signal, wave, beckon.

get obtain, acquire, procure, secure, gain, earn, win, receive, come by, reap, glean, achieve, attain, realize. LOSE

fetch, pick up, collect, bring, carry.

catch, seize, capture, take. RELEASE

become, grow, turn, go.

understand, grasp, see, take in, perceive, hear, follow, fathom, work out, comprehend. MISS

persuade, induce, talk into, coax, prevail upon, influence, sway.

arrive, reach, come. LEAVE

affect, move, stir, irritate, annoy, vex.

get away, escape, flee, get out, break free, decamp, leave, depart.

get back, recover, retrieve, recoup, regain. LOSE

get by, cope, manage, get along, fare, survive, subsist.

get off, alight, disembark, dismount, get down, descend, leave, depart. EMBARK

get on, board, mount, ascend, embark. DISEMBARK

succeed, prosper, progress, advance, cope, get along.

get round, circumvent, bypass, evade, cajole, wheedle, win over.

get up, rise, stand, mount, ascend, climb.

gewgaw trinket, bauble, gaud, trifle, bagatelle, toy, plaything.

ghastly dreadful, frightful, terrible, awful, shocking, appalling, hideous, horrible, loathsome, repulsive, fearful, frightening, horrendous, grim, gruesome. PLEASANT

pale, ashen, cadaverous, livid, spectral, pallid, wan, pasty. RUDDY

ghost spectre, phantom, spirit, soul, apparition, revenant, shade, spook (*inf*), ghoul.

glimmer, trace, shadow, suggestion, hint.

ghostly eerie, weird, uncanny, unearthly, supernatural, spooky (*inf*), haunted, spectral, illusory, phantom, ghostlike.

giant *n*, colossus, titan, behemoth, leviathan, monster. DWARF

adj, gigantic, colossal, huge, immense, enormous, mammoth, elephantine, gargantuan, large, big. TINY

gibber gabble, jabber, prattle, babble, chatter, blather.

gibberish drivel, nonsense, rubbish, twaddle, prattle, chatter, gabble, blather, balderdash, humbug, gobbledegook (*inf*), mumbo jumbo, claptrap. SENSE

gibbous rounded, hunched, humpbacked, bulging, protuberant, convex, gibbose. CONCAVE

gibe jeer, scoff, mock, sneer, deride, taunt, rag, ridicule, make fun of. COMPLIMENT

giddy dizzy, vertiginous, faint, lightheaded, reeling, unsteady, woozy (*inf*).

flighty, fickle, capricious, volatile, inconstant, erratic, thoughtless, scatterbrained, frivolous, impulsive, wild, reckless. SENSIBLE

gift present, offering, benefaction, bounty, largess, donation, contribution, grant, allowance, endowment, bequest, legacy.
talent, faculty, aptitude, flair, knack, genius, skill, power, ability, turn, bent. INABILITY

gifted talented, skilled, accomplished, expert, masterly, able, capable, clever, intelligent. INEPT

gigantic huge, enormous, immense, colossal, giant, tremendous, vast, prodigious, gargantuan, titanic, elephantine, mammoth, great, big, large. MINUTE

giggle snigger, titter, laugh, cackle, chortle, chuckle.

gild adorn, decorate, embellish, beautify, enhance, enrich, brighten.

gimmick device, contrivance, gambit, manoeuvre, ploy, scheme, stratagem, trick.

gin trap, snare, noose, net, springe.

gingerly cautiously, warily, carefully, daintily, tenderly, gently, hesitantly, reluctantly, timidly, guardedly, suspiciously. BOLDLY

gird encircle, surround, ring, encompass, environ, hem in, enclose, confine.
girdle, belt, strap, bind.

girdle *n*, corset, foundation, stays, belt, sash, cummerbund, waistband.
v, gird, encircle, surround, ring, encompass.

girl maiden, lass, miss, young lady, wench, damsel, daughter, bird (*inf*). BOY

girth circumference, perimeter, size, bulk.

gist substance, essence, pith, core, kernel, point, idea, meaning, import.

give grant, bestow, present, award, confer, accord, administer, distribute, give out, donate, contribute, supply, provide, offer, proffer, commit, consign, entrust. WITHHOLD
yield, surrender, concede, give in, relinquish, give up, cede, hand over, sacrifice, devote. RETAIN
utter, emit, pronounce, announce, give out, publish, transmit, communicate, impart, convey, render.
produce, cause, occasion, make, do, perform.
collapse, give way, break, yield, bend, buckle, sag, sink, fall, recede, retire.

give away, betray, expose, divulge, reveal, disclose, let slip, leak.

give off, exhale, exude, emit, discharge, release.

give up, renounce, forgo, forswear, desist, stop, cease, abandon, surrender, yield, capitulate, submit, resign, despair. CONTINUE

given inclined, disposed, apt, wont, prone, addicted.
specified, stated, fixed, set, arranged, appointed.

glacial icy, frozen, freezing, frigid, gelid, arctic, polar, raw, bitter, wintry. HOT
cold, unfeeling, hostile, unfriendly. WARM

glad happy, pleased, contented, gratified, delighted, elated, overjoyed, ready, willing, cheerful, merry, gay, joyful, gleeful. SAD
pleasing, gratifying, cheering, encouraging, pleasant, joyous, delightful, gladsome. GLOOMY

gladden please, gratify, delight, elate, exhilarate, cheer, encourage, hearten, brighten, animate. GRIEVE

gladness pleasure, gratification, animation, cheer, cheerfulness, happiness, glee, joy, joyfulness, delight, elation, merriment, gaiety. SORROW

glamorous elegant, smart, attractive, beautiful, fascinating, captivating, appealing, alluring, exciting, thrilling, glossy, glittering. DULL

glamour fascination, enchantment, allure, attraction, appeal, charm, beauty, elegance, excitement, glitter, sparkle.

glance glimpse, peek, peep, scan, look. STARE
glint, gleam, flash, shine, glitter, sparkle.
ricochet, rebound, bounce, skim, graze, brush.

glare *v*, glower, scowl, frown, lower, look daggers. SMILE
dazzle, blind, blaze, flame, flare, beam, shine.
n, dazzle, blaze, brilliance, brightness, radiance, flare, beam. DULLNESS

glaring conspicuous, prominent, obvious, manifest, patent, overt, blatant, flagrant, egregious, open, undisguised. CONCEALED
garish, gaudy, flashy, showy, loud, bright, brilliant, dazzling, blazing, blinding. MUTED

glassy clear, crystalline, transparent, smooth, slippery, shiny, glossy.

expressionless, blank, vacant, glazed, dull, dazed, fixed.

glaze *v*, lacquer, varnish, gloss, enamel, polish, burnish, furbish.
n, lustre, patina, sheen, shine, gloss, coat, finish, polish, enamel, lacquer, varnish.

gleam glint, glimmer, glisten, flash, flare, glance, sparkle, glitter, twinkle, shimmer, shine, beam, glow.

glean gather, collect, pick up, cull, harvest, reap, garner, amass. SCATTER

glee merriment, hilarity, mirth, jollity, joviality, joy, joyfulness, delight, elation, exhilaration, gaiety, cheer, cheerfulness, liveliness, exuberance. SORROW

gleeful merry, jolly, joyful, joyous, elated, exhilarated, gay, cheerful, lively, exuberant, happy, pleased. SAD

glen valley, vale, dale, dell, dingle. MOUNTAIN

glib smooth, slick, fluent, easy, ready, voluble, talkative, suave, insincere. HESITANT

glide slide, slip, sail, float, skate, skim, drift, coast, roll, flow, fly, soar.

glimmer *v*, gleam, glitter, glisten, flicker, shimmer, sparkle, twinkle, glow, shine.
n, gleam, glitter, flicker, shimmer, sparkle, twinkle, glow.
trace, hint, suggestion, inkling, ray, gleam, flicker.

glimpse *n*, glance, peep, peek, look, sight, view. SCRUTINY
v, spot, descry, catch sight of, espy. SCRUTINIZE

glisten gleam, glint, glitter, shine, sparkle, flash, glance, shimmer, glimmer, twinkle, scintillate, coruscate.

glitter *v*, flash, sparkle, gleam, glint, glisten, shine, scintillate, twinkle, glimmer, shimmer.
n, flash, beam, sparkle, gleam, twinkle, shine, scintillation, brightness, radiance, brilliance, sheen, lustre. DULLNESS
glamour, splendour, pageantry, tinsel, gaudiness, show, showiness.

gloaming dusk, twilight, half-light, nightfall.

gloat exult, triumph, rejoice, revel, crow, boast, vaunt.

global world-wide, international, universal, wide-ranging, extensive, comprehensive, all-inclusive, exhaustive, thorough, encyclopedic, total, general. RESTRICTED

globe orb, sphere, ball, earth, world, planet.

globular globate, globulous, globose, globoid, round, spherical, spheroid.

globule drop, bead, pearl, spherule, ball, pellet.

gloom dark, darkness, shade, shadow, obscurity, dimness, murkiness, cloudiness, dusk twilight. BRIGHTNESS
melancholy, depression, dejection, despondency, despair, sadness, sorrow, misery, low spirits, blues. CHEERFULNESS

gloomy dark, shadowy, obscure, dim, murky, cloudy, dull, dismal, dreary. BRIGHT
depressing, cheerless, comfortless, saddening, disheartening, discouraging, dispiriting, sombre, dismal, sad. ENCOURAGING
depressed, despondent, dejected, crestfallen, melancholy, glum, saturnine, taciturn, downcast, dispirited, downhearted, sad, unhappy, miserable, morose, pessimistic. CHEERFUL

glorify exalt, aggrandize, elevate, ennoble, dignify, honour, venerate, adore, worship, praise, extol, acclaim, magnify, enhance, augment, adorn. DEFAME

glorious illustrious, renowned, celebrated, famous, noted, eminent, distinguished, noble, exalted, grand, supreme, triumphant. HUMBLE
splendid, magnificent, radiant, brilliant, resplendent, bright, dazzling, glittering. DULL
delightful, wonderful, marvellous, enjoyable, pleasurable, agreeable, pleasant. AWFUL

glory *n*, praise, exaltation, acclaim, kudos, credit, distinction, honour, fame, renown, celebrity, eminence, prestige. BLAME
magnificence, splendour, grandeur, majesty, dignity, nobility, pomp, stateliness, pageantry, parade, triumph, success. HUMILITY
brilliance, resplendence, brightness, radiance, effulgence, lustre, beauty. DULLNESS
worship, adoration, veneration, respect, homage, praise, thanksgiving.
v, triumph, exult, rejoice, revel, bask, boast, crow, gloat.

gloss *n*, lustre, sheen, polish, shine, brightness, glaze, varnish. DULLNESS
appearance, façade, front, veneer, show, semblance.

v, polish, burnish, shine, varnish, glaze, lacquer.
disguise, mask, hide, conceal, cover up, smooth over. EXPOSE

glossary gloss, index, vocabulary, dictionary, lexicon.

glossy smooth, sleek, shiny, lustrous, bright, glassy, polished. MATT

glow *v*, shine, radiate, glimmer, gleam, burn, redden, blush.
n, light, luminosity, incandescence, phosphorescence, shine, lustre, brightness, brilliance, radiance, effulgence, blaze, gleam. DARKNESS
warmth, passion, ardour, fervour, eagerness, enthusiasm, intensity, vehemence, excitement, thrill. APATHY

glower glare, scowl, frown, lower, look daggers. SMILE

glue *n*, gum, paste, adhesive, cement.
v, stick, paste, gum, fix, seal, adhere.

glum gloomy, despondent, dejected, downcast, low, crestfallen, pessimistic, morose, sullen, unsmiling, moody, grumpy, sour. CHEERFUL

glut *n*, surfeit, excess, surplus, superfluity, superabundance, plethora, repletion, saturation. DEARTH
v, cram, stuff, fill, sate, satiate, surfeit, cloy, flood, inundate, saturate, choke, clog.

glutinous sticky, gummy, gluey, adhesive, mucilaginous, viscous, viscid.

glutton gourmand, gormandizer, gobbler, pig (*inf*).

gluttony greed, greediness, voraciousness, voracity, gourmandism. TEMPERANCE

gnarled lumpy, nodular, knotty, knurled, twisted, contorted, bent, weather-beaten, rugged, wrinkled, rough, leathery.

gnaw bite, nibble, chew, munch, eat, erode, corrode, consume, fret, worry, trouble, bother.

go *v*, move, proceed, advance, pass, travel, journey, start, set out, leave, depart, withdraw, go away, vanish, disappear. STOP
work, operate, perform, function, run. FAIL
become, grow, get, turn.
extend, stretch, reach, run, spread.
fit, suit, match, harmonize, blend, correspond, belong. CLASH
result, turn out, eventuate, end up, develop, fare.
contribute, serve, avail, lead, conduce, tend, incline.
elapse, slip away, pass, go by, lapse, expire.
go for, attack, assail, assault, set about.
go off, explode, blow up, detonate.
leave, depart, go away.
rot, go bad, turn.
go on, continue, proceed, persist, last, endure, abide, remain, stay.
occur, happen, take place.
go through, undergo, endure, suffer, experience, brave, bear, tolerate, stand.
let go, release, free, liberate, drop. HOLD
n, try, attempt, essay, bid, stab, shot (*inf*), crack (*inf*), turn.
drive, energy, vigour, verve, dynamism, spirit, animation. LETHARGY

goad *v*, spur, prick, prod, provoke, incite, prompt, arouse, stimulate, impel, urge, drive, hound, plague, annoy, needle, harass. DETER
n, spur, incentive, stimulus, motivation, incitement, provocation. DETERRENT

go-ahead *n*, permission, consent, authorization, sanction, OK (*inf*), green light (*inf*). BAN
adj, ambitious, aspiring, enterprising, pushy (*inf*).

goal aim, objective, mark, target, intention, object, purpose, end, ambition, aspiration, destination.

gobble bolt, gulp, guzzle, wolf, devour, gorge, cram.

go-between intermediary, mediator, middleman, agent, broker, factor.

god deity, divinity, goddess, spirit, idol, image. DEVIL

God Godhead, Almighty, Father, Lord, Creator, Jehovah. SATAN

godless atheistic, agnostic, impious, ungodly, profane, irreligious, sinful, wicked, evil. GODLY

godly pious, devout, religious, holy, saintly, good, righteous, god-fearing. GODLESS

goggle stare, gape, gawp, gawk.

golden gold, yellow, flaxen, blond, fair, bright, shining, brilliant, splendid, resplendent, rich, precious, priceless, valuable.
happy, joyful, blissful, glorious, prosperous, successful, flourishing, halcyon, palmy.

favourable, propitious, excellent, auspicious, timely, opportune, promising, rosy, advantageous. UNFAVOURABLE

good *adj*, virtuous, righteous, moral, upright, honest, honourable, admirable, worthy, well-behaved, obedient. WICKED
acceptable, satisfactory, agreeable, pleasant, enjoyable, fine, excellent, first-rate, splendid. BAD
beneficial, advantageous, profitable, worthwhile, useful, helpful, wholesome, healthy, salutary, favourable, propitious, opportune, convenient.
proficient, competent, skilful, dexterous, adept, adroit, expert, accomplished, able, talented, gifted. INCOMPETENT
kind, kindly, benevolent, obliging, gracious, good-natured, humane, merciful, friendly, generous. UNKIND
suitable, appropriate, apt, fitting, proper, correct, right. UNSUITABLE
reliable, dependable, trustworthy, sound, secure. UNRELIABLE
sizable, considerable, goodly, substantial, large, ample, adequate, sufficient. SMALL
n, advantage, benefit, profit, gain, welfare, interest, behalf, use, avail. HARM
virtue, righteousness, goodness, rectitude, morality, worth, merit, excellence. EVIL

goodbye farewell, adieu, so long (*inf*), bye-bye (*inf*), cheerio (*inf*), see you later, *au revoir*, *ciao* (*inf*). HELLO

good-looking attractive, fair, comely, pretty, beautiful, handsome. UGLY

goodly sizable, considerable, substantial, large, ample, tidy (*inf*). SMALL
attractive, good-looking, fair, comely, beautiful, handsome, pleasing, pleasant, agreeable. UNATTRACTIVE

goodness virtue, righteousness, good, rectitude, uprightness, honesty, integrity, probity, morality, honour. EVIL
kindness, benevolence, kindliness, compassion, thoughtfulness, generosity, graciousness, friendliness, humanity, mercy. UNKINDNESS
excellence, superiority, worth, value, merit. INFERIORITY

goods belongings, possessions, effects, chattels, property, trappings, appurtenances, paraphernalia, gear.
merchandise, wares, stock, commodities.

goodwill benevolence, kindliness, goodness, graciousness, favour, friendliness, amity, willingness, acquiescence, heartiness, zeal. ENMITY

gore[1] *v*, pierce, stab, impale.

gore[2] *n*, blood, bloodshed, carnage, slaughter, butchery.

gorge *v*, stuff, cram, fill, gormandize, devour, bolt, wolf, guzzle, gobble, gulp, glut, sate, surfeit, overeat. FAST
n, ravine, canyon, defile, pass, gulch.

gorgeous magnificent, superb, fine, splendid, resplendent, sumptuous, rich, exquisite, beautiful, grand, glittering, dazzling, glorious, marvellous, wonderful, excellent, great. POOR

gormandize gorge, devour, guzzle, stuff, cram, bolt, wolf.

gory bloody, bloodstained, bloodthirsty, sanguinary, savage, fierce, murderous.

gospel truth, fact, certainty, verity. FALSEHOOD
doctrine, creed, credo, teaching, message, news, tidings.

gossip *n*, chat, talk, natter, chitchat, small talk, prattle, tittle-tattle, scandal, rumour, hearsay.
scandalmonger, gossipmonger, prattler, tattler, busybody, quidnunc, blabbermouth (*inf*).
v, chat, chatter, talk, natter, gab (*inf*), prattle, tattle, blab.

gouge scratch, claw, scoop, dig, chisel, cut, score, gash.

gourmet gastronome, epicure, connoisseur, *bon vivant*.

govern rule, reign, direct, manage, administer, control, guide, lead, conduct, supervise, oversee, command, regulate, restrain, check, curb, bridle, discipline, master, steer, pilot, influence, sway.

governable controllable, manageable, tractable, docile, submissive, obedient. WILD

government rule, dominion, direction, management, administration, control, guidance, conduct, supervision, command, leadership, authority, regulation, restraint, discipline.
ministry, cabinet, parliament, council, executive, state, regime.

governor ruler, president, director, manager, administrator, executive, head, chief, leader, commander, controller, supervisor, overseer, superintendent, boss (*inf*).

grab seize, snatch, pluck, take hold of, catch, nab (*inf*), grasp, grip, clutch, clasp.

grace *n*, elegance, poise, gracefulness, ease, beauty, loveliness, charm, refinement, polish, propriety, decorum. CLUMSINESS
favour, goodwill, kindness, benevolence, goodness, generosity, compassion, clemency, mercy, pardon, forgiveness. UNKINDNESS
blessing, benediction, thanksgiving, prayer.
v, adorn, embellish, decorate, ornament, enhance, honour, favour, distinguish, dignify. MAR

graceful elegant, supple, nimble, agile, easy, smooth, flowing, pleasing, charming, lovely, beautiful, fine. CLUMSY

graceless clumsy, awkward, ungainly, inelegant, uncouth, coarse, crude, boorish, unsophisticated, rude, shameless, unabashed. GRACEFUL

gracious kind, kindly, benevolent, benign, friendly, affable, obliging, courteous, civil, polite, amiable, cordial, compassionate, gentle, mild, merciful, indulgent, condescending, patronizing, charitable. CHURLISH

grade *n*, degree, stage, step, rung, level, position, rank, station, quality, rating, mark, score, brand, class, group, category, measure, size.
v, arrange, sort, group, classify, categorize, brand, rate, rank.

gradient slope, incline, hill, ramp, acclivity, declivity.

gradual slow, unhurried, moderate, gentle, regular, steady, even, continuous, progressive. SUDDEN

graduate grade, mark off, divide, calibrate, regulate, adjust, adapt.
arrange, sort, group, classify, grade, rank.

graft *v*, join, unite, splice, implant, insert, attach, affix, transplant. SEPARATE
n, scion, slip, sprout, shoot, transplant.

grain cereal, corn, seed, kernel, grist.
particle, speck, granule, crumb, morsel, piece, bit, iota, atom, jot, scrap, trace.
texture, pattern, weave, nap, fibre.

grand impressive, great, large, imposing, majestic, august, lofty, exalted, illustrious, distinguished, lordly, noble, regal, princely, dignified, stately, glorious, splendid, magnificent, fine, superb, sumptuous, luxurious, showy, pretentious, ostentatious. HUMBLE
excellent, wonderful, marvellous, very good, first-class, first-rate, super (*inf*). POOR
chief, principal, main, head, leading, supreme. MINOR

grandeur splendour, magnificence, glory, pomp, stateliness, majesty, nobility, dignity, greatness, importance, eminence, loftiness. HUMILITY

grandiloquent bombastic, pompous, magniloquent, orotund, fustian, high-flown, euphuistic, rhetorical, pretentious. SIMPLE

grandiose pretentious, ostentatious, showy, flamboyant, extravagant, pompous, bombastic. PLAIN
grand, impressive, imposing, lofty, majestic, ambitious. HUMBLE

grant *v*, give, bestow, award, present, confer, accord, allot. WITHHOLD
allow, permit, consent to, agree to, acknowledge, admit, concede, cede, yield.
n, award, gift, present, benefaction, bequest, endowment, concession, allowance, donation, contribution, subsidy.

graphic striking, telling, vivid, expressive, descriptive, illustrative, diagrammatic, pictorial, picturesque, detailed, clear, lucid, explicit. UNCLEAR

grapple grip, clasp, grasp, seize, grab, clutch, hold. RELEASE
struggle, wrestle, battle, contend, tackle, face, encounter.

grasp *v*, grip, clasp, hold, clutch, grapple, grab, seize, snatch. RELEASE
understand, comprehend, take in, realize, see, perceive, follow, get.
n, grip, clasp, hold, clutches, possession.
reach, compass, scope, range, capacity, power, control.
understanding, comprehension, realization, awareness, perception, knowledge.

grasping greedy, avaricious, covetous, acquisitive, rapacious, miserly, niggardly, parsimonious, mean, stingy. GENEROUS

grate shred, mince, comminute, triturate, grind, rasp, scrape, scratch, creak.
annoy, irritate, exasperate, vex, irk, nettle, jar, aggravate. SOOTHE

grateful thankful, appreciative, obliged, beholden, indebted. UNGRATEFUL pleasant, agreeable, gratifying, satisfying, acceptable, welcome, refreshing, relaxing.

gratification satisfaction, fulfilment, indulgence, contentment, pleasure, enjoyment, fun, joy, delight. FRUSTRATION

gratify satisfy, fulfil, indulge, humour, favour, please, gladden, delight. DISPLEASE

gratifying satisfying, fulfilling, rewarding, pleasing, pleasant, agreeable, enjoyable, pleasurable, delightful. UNPLEASANT

grating harsh, strident, raucous, rasping, hoarse, scraping, grinding, jarring, irritating, annoying, vexatious, irksome, unpleasant, disagreeable.

gratitude gratefulness, thankfulness, appreciation, obligation, indebtedness, thanks, acknowledgment, recognition. INGRATITUDE

gratuitous free, gratis, voluntary, spontaneous, complimentary.
groundless, baseless, unfounded, unwarranted, unjustified, uncalled-for, unnecessary, needless, superfluous.

gratuity tip, gift, present, reward, recompense, bonus, perquisite, donation, benefaction, largess, bounty.

grave[1] *adj*, serious, solemn, staid, sober, sedate, thoughtful, pensive, unsmiling, grim. FRIVOLOUS
important, weighty, momentous, vital, crucial, critical, dangerous, perilous, serious. TRIVIAL

grave[2] *n*, tomb, sepulchre, crypt, vault, mausoleum, burial place.

graveyard cemetery, churchyard, burial ground, necropolis, God's acre.

gravitate incline, lean, tend, move, be drawn.
descend, sink, drop, fall, precipitate, settle. RISE

gravity seriousness, solemnity, dignity, sobriety, sedateness, thoughtfulness, grimness. FRIVOLITY
importance, weight, moment, seriousness, severity, enormity, significance, consequence. TRIVIALITY

graze[1] scrape, scratch, skin, bark, abrade, rub, brush, shave, touch, skim, glance off.

graze[2] feed, browse, crop, pasture.

greasy oily, fatty, sebaceous, slimy, slippery, unctuous, smooth, slick, glib, fawning, ingratiating.

great big, large, huge, vast, immense, massive, enormous, colossal, tremendous, gigantic. SMALL
excessive, inordinate, decided, pronounced, extreme, considerable, prodigious, high, strong. SLIGHT
eminent, illustrious, distinguished, renowned, noted, famed, celebrated, prominent, outstanding, impressive, remarkable, noteworthy, grand, august, majestic, noble, exalted, superior, sublime, magnificent, glorious, fine, heroic, lofty. LOWLY
chief, main, principal, leading, major, important, significant, consequential, weighty, momentous, critical, serious. MINOR
absolute, utter, perfect, complete, thoroughgoing, out-and-out, arrant, flagrant, downright.
excellent, wonderful, marvellous, fine, first-rate, terrific (*inf*), fantastic (*inf*). AWFUL

greatness vastness, immensity, largeness, enormity, magnitude, bulk, mass, size. SMALLNESS
eminence, renown, fame, note, grandeur, majesty, nobility, dignity, magnificence, glory. LOWLINESS
importance, significance, gravity, seriousness. TRIVIALITY

greed greediness, gluttony, esurience, edacity, voracity, hunger, desire, craving, longing, covetousness, avarice, selfishness, rapacity, cupidity, avidity, eagerness. UNSELFISHNESS

greedy gluttonous, esurient, edacious, voracious, insatiable, ravenous, hungry, desirous, covetous, avaricious, selfish, rapacious, grasping, avid, eager. UNSELFISH

green *adj*, verdant, verdurous, grassy, leafy, emerald.
fresh, new, recent, raw, unripe, immature, unseasoned, young, vigorous, flourishing. DECAYING
inexperienced, callow, unsophisticated, naive, ingenuous, gullible, credulous, inexpert, unskilled, untrained. EXPERIENCED
envious, jealous, covetous, resentful.
n, lawn, sward, common, turf, verdure.

greet hail, salute, address, accost, welcome, receive, meet.

greeting salutation, address, hail, salute, welcome, reception. FAREWELL

greetings respects, compliments, regards, best wishes.

gregarious sociable, social, outgoing, friendly, affable, companionable, genial, cordial, convivial. RECLUSIVE

grey dull, drab, dismal, dreary, gloomy, sombre, dark, cloudy, overcast. BRIGHT
pale, colourless, neutral.
old, aged, elderly, hoary, venerable, ancient. YOUNG

grief sorrow, sadness, misery, woe, heartache, mourning, distress, anguish, affliction, agony, pain, suffering, trouble, trial, tribulation, regret, remorse. JOY

grievance injury, damage, wrong, injustice, complaint, grudge, resentment, indignation.

grieve *vi*, sorrow, lament, mourn, weep, bewail, bemoan. REJOICE
vt, sadden, afflict, distress, hurt, wound, pain, agonize. PLEASE

grievous painful, distressing, afflicting, intolerable, unbearable, sorrowful, mournful, damaging, injurious, hurtful, harmful, serious, severe, intense. MILD
heinous, outrageous, monstrous, egregious, flagrant, gross, atrocious, appalling, shocking, dreadful, shameful, deplorable, lamentable. COMMENDABLE

grim stern, severe, resolute, firm, relentless, harsh, formidable, dire, dreadful, frightful, terrible, horrible, hideous, ghastly, grisly, fierce, savage, cruel, merciless, menacing, forbidding, sinister. BENIGN

grimace *n*, frown, scowl, pout, sneer, smirk, wry face.
v, frown, scowl, pout, sneer, smirk, make a face.

grime *n*, dirt, filth, muck, smut, soot.
v, begrime, dirty, soil, befoul, sully, defile. CLEANSE

grimy dirty, filthy, mucky, begrimed, smutty, sooty, foul, unclean. CLEAN

grin smile, beam, smirk, leer.

grind pulverize, triturate, comminute, powder, crush, pound, mill, grate, rasp, scrape, abrade.
sharpen, whet, sand, file, smooth, polish.
oppress, tyrannize, persecute, plague, afflict, torment, trouble.

grip *v*, hold, clutch, clasp, grasp, seize. RELEASE
n, hold, clasp, purchase, clutches, possession, keeping, grasp, understanding, comprehension, control, mastery, command.

gripe *v*, complain, moan, grumble, grouse, carp, beef (*inf*).
hurt, pain, ache, cramp, pinch, twinge.
n, complaint, grievance, moan, grumble, beef (*inf*).
pain, ache, twinge, pang, cramp, colic.

grisly grim, gruesome, macabre, hideous, horrible, dreadful, frightful, awful, ghastly, appalling, shocking, sickening, repugnant. PLEASANT

grit gravel, sand, pebbles, dust, dirt.
courage, nerve, pluck, mettle, spirit, guts (*inf*), fortitude, tenacity, resolution, toughness, stamina. WEAKNESS

groan *v*, moan, sigh, cry, lament, complain, grumble, creak.
n, moan, sigh, cry, complaint, creak.

groom brush, curry, smooth, preen, tidy, arrange, smarten up, clean.
prepare, prime, train, coach, drill, school.

groove furrow, channel, rut, trench, hollow, indentation, cut, score. RIDGE

grope fumble, feel, search, fish, scrabble, grabble.

gross big, large, great, fat, obese, bulky, heavy, thick, dense. SLIGHT
coarse, vulgar, tasteless, crude, rude, indecent, ribald, earthy, indelicate, unsophisticated, unrefined, crass, boorish, dull, stupid. REFINED
flagrant, glaring, blatant, arrant, egregious, outrageous, plain, manifest, sheer, outright, rank, unmitigated, downright.
entire, total, whole, aggregate. NET

grotesque bizarre, strange, weird, odd, fantastic, whimsical, fanciful, absurd, ludicrous, freakish, outlandish, unnatural, deformed, misshapen, distorted, hideous, repugnant. NORMAL

ground *n*, earth, soil, clod, sod, turf, land, terrain, field, area, pitch.
v, base, found, establish, fix, set.
instruct, teach, train, coach, familiarize, acquaint.

groundless baseless, unfounded, unsupported, idle, empty, unjustified, unreasonable, unwarranted, gratuitous. JUSTIFIED

grounds estate, land, property, domain, territory, park, garden, yard.
basis, base, foundation, reason, motive, cause, call, excuse, justification, pretext, argument.
dregs, sediment, lees, deposit, grouts.

groundwork foundation, basis, footing, bottom, basics, fundamentals, preliminaries, preparation, background.

group *n*, cluster, clump, bunch, batch, set, class, category, party, company, body, gang, crowd, congregation, gathering, collection, assemblage. INDIVIDUAL
v, collect, assemble, gather, cluster, congregate. SEPARATE
sort, classify, organize, arrange, dispose. DISARRANGE

grove wood, copse, thicket, spinney, brake, covert.

grovel cower, cringe, fawn, toady, kowtow, bow and scrape, crawl, creep, sneak.

grovelling servile, obsequious, fawning, sycophantic, slavish, cringing, crawling, base, mean, low, abject.

grow increase, expand, enlarge, wax, swell, spread, extend, stretch, develop, multiply. SHRINK
originate, arise, spring up, germinate, sprout, shoot, bud, blossom, flower, thrive, flourish, prosper, advance, progress, improve. DECLINE
become, turn, go, get.
cultivate, produce, raise, nurture, breed, propagate, farm.

growl snarl, rumble, roar, murmur, complain, grumble.

growth increase, expansion, enlargement, extension, development, advance, advancement, progress, rise, improvement. DECLINE
germination, sprouting, vegetation, crop, produce, cultivation.
tumour, lump, excrescence, protuberance.

grubby dirty, soiled, grimy, filthy, messy, mucky, unwashed, scruffy, shabby, seedy, squalid, sordid. CLEAN

grudge *v*, begrudge, resent, envy, covet, mind, be reluctant.
n, resentment, envy, grievance, spite, malice, ill will, bitterness, rancour, hard feelings, animosity, hatred, enmity.

gruelling arduous, strenuous, hard, difficult, harsh, severe, exhausting, tiring, taxing, demanding, punishing. EASY

gruesome grim, grisly, macabre, ghastly, hideous, loathsome, repulsive, repugnant, horrible, terrible, awful, frightful, dreadful, abominable. ATTRACTIVE

gruff surly, churlish, curt, brusque, blunt, sour, grumpy, rough, rude, uncivil, ungracious, discourteous, impolite. AFFABLE
throaty, guttural, harsh, raucous, husky, hoarse.

grumble *v*, complain, moan, grouse, carp, gripe (*inf*), grouch (*inf*), beef (*inf*).
growl, rumble, roar, murmur, mutter.
n, complaint, grievance, protest, objection, moan, grouse, gripe (*inf*), beef (*inf*).

grumpy cantankerous, irascible, crabbed, crusty, testy, surly, crotchety (*inf*), cross, irritable, grouchy (*inf*), peevish, petulant, sulky, sullen.

guarantee *n*, warranty, guaranty, pledge, promise, bond, assurance, certainty, security, surety, collateral, earnest.
v, warrant, certify, pledge, promise, assure, ensure, secure, insure, protect.

guard *v*, protect, defend, watch over, mind, supervise, shield, screen, shelter, cover, patrol, police, save, preserve, safeguard. NEGLECT
n, protection, defence, shield, screen, bulwark, rampart, buffer, security, safeguard.
sentry, sentinel, watchman, warder, keeper, custodian, guardian, defender, protector, escort, convoy, patrol.
watchfulness, vigilance, wariness, caution, care, heed, attention.

guarded careful, cautious, circumspect, wary, suspicious, prudent, discreet, reticent, noncommittal, cagey (*inf*). RASH

guardian protector, defender, keeper, custodian, warden, warder.

guess *v*, conjecture, surmise, speculate, hypothesize, estimate, reckon, judge, think, believe, suspect, suppose, imagine, fancy. KNOW
solve, work out, fathom, penetrate.
n, conjecture, surmise, speculation, hypothesis, theory, estimate, reckoning, judgment, belief, opinion, supposition.

guest visitor, caller, company, lodger, boarder. HOST

guidance direction, instruction, clue, hint, advice, counsel, help, leadership, control, government, management.

guide *v*, lead, direct, pilot, steer, conduct, usher, escort, accompany, control, regulate, handle, manage, govern, rule, influence, teach, instruct, advise, counsel. FOLLOW

n, leader, director, pilot, usher, escort, courier, cicerone, conductor, controller, adviser, counsellor, mentor, teacher. FOLLOWER
clue, hint, key, pointer, sign, beacon, landmark, guidebook, handbook, manual, directory.
model, pattern, example, exemplar, ideal, standard, criterion.

guild fellowship, fraternity, brotherhood, union, society, association, organization, league, lodge, order.

guile deceit, deception, fraud, duplicity, artfulness, craft, craftiness, cunning, artifice, wiles, wiliness, trickery, treachery. HONESTY

guileful deceitful, artful, crafty, cunning, wily, foxy, tricky, treacherous, sly, shrewd, clever. HONEST

guileless artless, ingenuous, naive, innocent, unsophisticated, sincere, candid, frank, open, straightforward, honest. GUILEFUL

guilt guiltiness, culpability, criminality, sinfulness, wrongdoing, blame, responsibility. INNOCENCE
remorse, contrition, regret, self-reproach, self-accusation, guilty conscience. IMPENITENCE

guiltless innocent, blameless, unimpeachable, irreproachable, sinless, clear, pure, spotless, immaculate, unsullied, clean (*inf*). GUILTY

guilty culpable, criminal, at fault, blameworthy, reprehensible, responsible, wrong, sinful. INNOCENT
remorseful, contrite, regretful, sorry, conscience-stricken, sheepish, shamefaced. IMPENITENT

guise appearance, exterior, front, façade, semblance, pretence, show, behaviour, air, mien, demeanour, form, shape, fashion, manner, mode, dress, costume, disguise.

gulf chasm, abyss, rift, breach, separation, gap, opening.
bay, bight, inlet, sound.

gullible credulous, unsuspecting, trustful, trusting, naive, ingenuous, innocent, green, born yesterday, simple, foolish.

gulp *v*, swallow, quaff, swill, guzzle, gobble, bolt, devour, wolf.
n, swallow, draught, mouthful.

gumption common sense, initiative, enterprise, resourcefulness, sagacity, nous (*inf*), acumen, shrewdness, ability, cleverness, spirit, courage.

gun pistol, revolver, rifle, shotgun.

gurgle babble, burble, murmur, bubble, ripple, purl.

gush flow, pour, run, stream, spurt, spout, jet, rush, cascade, flood, burst. DRIP

gushing flowing, pouring, streaming, spouting, rushing. DRIPPING
gushy, effusive, fulsome, demonstrative, sentimental, mawkish.

gust blast, puff, flurry, squall, gale, storm, burst, outburst, fit, paroxysm.

gusto relish, zest, enjoyment, pleasure, zeal, enthusiasm, fervour.

guts intestines, bowels, viscera, entrails, insides, innards (*inf*).
courage, grit, mettle, spirit, pluck, nerve, boldness, audacity, daring, stamina, tenacity, willpower. WEAKNESS

gutter channel, conduit, duct, trough, trench, ditch, drain.

guttural hoarse, husky, gruff, throaty, thick, deep, low.

guy man, boy, lad, fellow, chap, bloke (*inf*).

guzzle gobble, bolt, wolf, devour, gorge, gulp, quaff, swill, knock back (*inf*).

gyration rotation, revolution, spinning, whirling, pirouette, twirl, spiral.

H

habiliments, clothes, clothing, dress, garb, attire, array, apparel, habit, costume, robes, regalia, uniform, livery.

habit *n*, practice, custom, usage, wont, routine, manner, way, tendency, disposition, propensity, inclination, bent.
addiction, dependence, weakness, compulsion, obsession.
clothing, garb, attire, apparel, dress, habiliments, vestments.
v, clothe, dress, garb, attire, array. STRIP

habitat environment, element, natural home, surroundings, territory, haunt, stamping ground.

habitation dwelling, abode, domicile, home, residence, lodgings, quarters, accommodation.
occupation, occupancy, inhabitance, residence, tenancy.

habitual customary, usual, wonted, accustomed, regular, routine, traditional, common, ordinary, familiar. UNUSUAL
chronic, inveterate, hardened, confirmed, fixed, set, established, frequent, recurrent, persistent. OCCASIONAL

habituate accustom, familiarize, condition, acclimatize, make used to, harden, inure, break in, train.

hack[1] *v*, cut, chop, hew, gash, slash, mutilate, mangle.

hack[2] *n*, jade, nag, workhorse, drudge, hireling, mercenary, scribbler.

hackneyed banal, commonplace, trite, clichéd, stale, tired, threadbare, worn-out, overworked, unoriginal, stock, stereotyped. ORIGINAL

hag crone, harridan, virago, vixen, shrew, nag, scold, witch.

haggard gaunt, drawn, worn, weary, pale, wan, pinched, wasted, shrunken, wrinkled. FRESH

haggle bargain, chaffer, barter, negotiate, wrangle, quarrel, bicker, quibble. AGREE

hail[1] *v*, greet, salute, address, welcome, receive, acknowledge, accost, signal, flag down, call, acclaim, cheer, exalt, glorify. IGNORE

hail[2] *n*, shower, rain, storm, volley, barrage, bombardment.

hair locks, tresses, mop, shock, mane, coat, fur.

hairy hirsute, shaggy, furry, woolly, fluffy, bearded, unshaven. HAIRLESS
difficult, dangerous, risky, exciting, frightening, scary (*inf*).

halcyon peaceful, tranquil, serene, placid, calm, still, quiet, mild, gentle. STORMY
happy, carefree, palmy, golden, prosperous.

hale healthy, hearty, robust, strong, hardy, sound, well, fit, in fine fettle, vigorous, energetic, lusty. FRAIL

half *n*, bisection, equal part, fifty per cent. WHOLE
adv, halfway, partly, partially, barely, incompletely, nearly. COMPLETELY

half-hearted indifferent, uncaring, apathetic, lukewarm, cool, unenthusiastic, languid, listless, careless, perfunctory. ENTHUSIASTIC

hall vestibule, lobby, foyer, corridor, passage, chamber, auditorium, amphitheatre.

hallow sanctify, consecrate, bless, dedicate, devote, venerate, revere, exalt, glorify. DESECRATE

hallowed holy, sacred, sanctified, consecrated, blessed, revered, sacrosanct. PROFANE

hallucination delusion, illusion, dream, fantasy, mirage, vision, apparition, phantasm, figment of the imagination. REALITY

halt[1] *v*, stop, cease, break off, rest, stand still, stay, wait, hold back, arrest, check, curb, impede, block, end, terminate. PROCEED
n, stop, standstill, rest, pause, break, interruption, end, termination.

halt[2] *v*, hesitate, falter, waver, pause, stammer, stutter, stumble, hobble.

halve bisect, divide, split, cut in half.

hammer beat, pound, batter, strike, hit, drive, drum, forge, shape, fashion.

hamper hinder, impede, obstruct, encumber, embarrass, handicap, cramp, shackle, restrain, restrict, confine, check, curb, prevent, thwart. ASSIST

hand *n*, palm, fist, paw (*inf*), mitt (*inf*). FOOT
agency, intervention, part, share, participation.
help, aid, assistance.
labourer, worker, operative, employee, assistant, helper, crew member.
handwriting, script, penmanship, calligraphy, chirography.
ovation, clap, round of applause.
at hand, nearby, close, handy, within reach, accessible, to hand, on hand, available, ready.
v, give, present, deliver, pass, transmit.
hand down, bequeath, will, transfer, pass on.
hand out, distribute, dispense, give out, deal out, mete. WITHHOLD
hand over, deliver, transfer, surrender, yield. RETAIN

handicap *n*, hindrance, disadvantage, drawback, disability, impediment, obstacle, barrier, restriction, limitation. ADVANTAGE
v, hinder, hamper, impede, encumber, restrict, disable, hold back. ASSIST

handicraft craft, art, skill, handiwork, craftsmanship, workmanship.

handiwork work, labour, creation, production, craft, handicraft.

handle *v*, feel, touch, finger, maul, pick up, hold.
manipulate, manage, wield, use, operate, control, direct, administer, treat, deal with, cope with.
n, knob, grip, haft, stock, hilt, shaft.

hands clutches, possession, keeping, custody, care, grip, power, control.

handsome good-looking, attractive, personable, fair, comely, elegant, fine, stately. UGLY
liberal, generous, ample, plentiful, large, considerable, magnanimous, gracious, noble. STINGY

handy nearby, near, close, at hand, on hand, available, ready, accessible, to hand, within reach, convenient, useful, practical, helpful. INCONVENIENT
adroit, dexterous, skilful, deft, adept, expert, proficient, clever. CLUMSY

hang suspend, hang up, drape, dangle, swing, droop, sag, drop, fall, trail, hang down. STAND
hover, float, drift, waft, linger, remain. DISPERSE
depend, hinge, turn, rest.
gibbet, string up (*inf*), execute, lynch.
hang on, cling, cleave, stick, adhere, hold fast, grip, grasp, clutch.
persevere, carry on, continue, persist, hold out, endure, remain, hold on, wait.

hanker long, yearn, itch, hunger, thirst, crave, desire, want, covet, lust.

hankering longing, yearning, yen (*inf*), itch, hunger, thirst, craving, desire, lust. AVERSION

haphazard random, chance, arbitrary, accidental. DELIBERATE
careless, slipshod, slapdash, disorderly, disorganized, unmethodical, aimless, casual. ORDERLY

hapless unfortunate, unlucky, luckless, ill-fated, ill-starred, wretched, miserable, unhappy. LUCKY

happen occur, take place, come about, come to pass, befall, betide, chance, arise, crop up, transpire, materialize, result, ensue, turn out.

happening event, occurrence, incident, episode, case, circumstance, chance, accident, phenomenon.

happiness joy, delight, bliss, ecstasy, elation, glee, felicity, gladness, contentment, pleasure, gaiety, merriment, cheerfulness, high spirits. SADNESS

happy joyful, joyous, delighted, overjoyed, thrilled, pleased, contented, satisfied, glad, gleeful, ecstatic, elated, blissful, blithe, cheerful, gay, merry, jolly. SAD
fortunate, lucky, favourable, felicitous, prosperous, successful, auspicious, seasonable, opportune, timely, appropriate, apt, befitting. UNFORTUNATE

harangue *v*, address, lecture, hold forth, rant, declaim, spout (*inf*).
n, address, speech, talk, oration, lecture, spiel (*inf*), sermon, declamation, tirade, diatribe, philippic.

harass plague, torment, persecute, harry, pester, nag, hector, badger, bother, trouble, annoy, vex, provoke, bait, tease, tire, weary, fatigue, exhaust.

harbinger precursor, forerunner, herald, messenger, announcer, sign, indication, omen, portent.

harbour *n*, port, anchorage, haven, shelter, refuge, sanctuary, asylum.
v, protect, shelter, lodge, house, hide, conceal, shield. EXPOSE
cherish, foster, nurture, nurse, hold, maintain, entertain. EXPEL

hard *adj*, solid, dense, compact, firm, rigid, stiff, unyielding, resistant, impenetrable, strong, tough, stony, steely. SOFT
difficult, arduous, laborious, gruelling, strenuous, rigorous, taxing, tiring, exhausting, fatiguing. EASY
puzzling, perplexing, intricate, complicated, complex, involved, knotty, thorny. SIMPLE
harsh, severe, stern, strict, cruel, ruthless, pitiless, unrelenting, obdurate, hard-hearted, callous, unfeeling, unsympathetic, cold, unkind. TENDER
painful, distressing, unpleasant, disagreeable, bad, grievous, calamitous, disastrous. PLEASANT
hard up, poor, short, penniless, bankrupt, broke (*inf*), skint (*inf*). RICH
adv, diligently, industriously, assiduously, conscientiously, earnestly, intently, vigorously, energetically, strenuously, laboriously, steadily, persistently.
violently, forcibly, forcefully, sharply, heavily, severely, harshly, badly, painfully. SOFTLY

harden solidify, compact, set, stiffen, petrify, freeze, bake. SOFTEN

strengthen, toughen, fortify, buttress, brace, steel, temper, anneal. WEAKEN
inure, season, habituate, accustom, acclimatize, break in, train, discipline.

hardened inveterate, confirmed, habitual, chronic, impenitent, incorrigible, set, fixed.

hard-headed shrewd, astute, keen, sharp, wise, level-headed, sensible, realistic, practical, cool, unsentimental, tough.

hard-hearted cold, callous, stony, obdurate, unfeeling, insensible, unkind, cruel, pitiless, merciless, implacable. SOFT-HEARTED

hardihood courage, bravery, pluck, mettle, intrepidity, boldness, audacity, daring, fearlessness, strength, hardiness, fortitude, determination, resolution. COWARDICE
assurance, effrontery, temerity, rashness, recklessness, foolhardiness. CAUTION

hardly scarcely, barely, narrowly, only just.

hardness solidity, firmness, rigidity, stiffness, resistance, strength, toughness. SOFTNESS
difficulty, arduousness, strenuousness, rigour, complexity, intricacy. EASINESS
harshness, severity, strictness, cruelty, callousness, coldness, unkindness. TENDERNESS

hardship trouble, difficulty, trial, tribulation, affliction, suffering, misfortune, adversity, privation, want, need, austerity, burden, oppression. PROSPERITY

hardy strong, tough, rugged, firm, sturdy, robust, hale, hearty, lusty, vigorous, sound, fit, healthy. WEAK
courageous, brave, plucky, valiant, intrepid, daring, bold, audacious, determined, resolute. COWARDLY
rash, reckless, foolhardy, headstrong, impetuous. CAUTIOUS

hark listen, give ear, hearken, pay attention, hear. IGNORE

hark back, revert, go back, regress, recall, recollect, think back.

harlot prostitute, whore, hussy, trollop, strumpet, scrubber (*inf*), tart (*inf*).

harm *v*, hurt, injure, damage, impair, mar, spoil, maltreat, abuse, molest. BENEFIT
n, hurt, injury, damage, abuse, detriment, mischief, ill, evil, wrong, sin, iniquity, wickedness. GOOD

harmful hurtful, injurious, damaging, deleterious, detrimental, pernicious, mischievous, baleful, baneful, noxious, dangerous, evil. BENEFICIAL

harmless innocuous, safe, inoffensive, innocent, innoxious, gentle, mild. PERNICIOUS

harmonious harmonic, tuneful, melodious, euphonious, mellifluous, dulcet, musical. CACOPHONOUS
concordant, consonant, congruous, consistent, correspondent, compatible, agreeable, amicable, friendly, congenial, cordial. DISCORDANT

harmonize agree, accord, correspond, coincide, match, coordinate, blend, adapt, attune. DIFFER

harmony accord, concord, accordance, concordance, consonance, congruity, correspondence, coordination, agreement, consensus, unanimity, unity, amity, friendship, peace, understanding, goodwill, rapport. DISCORD

harness *n*, equipment, tack, bridle, yoke, gear, tackle.
v, control, rein, yoke, utilize, exploit, channel.

harp dwell, go on, repeat, reiterate, press, push, persist, insist.

harrow distress, disturb, alarm, perturb, torment, torture, rack, agonize, wound, vex, frighten, terrify, chill. SOOTHE

harry harass, plague, torment, worry, fret, trouble, vex, annoy, exasperate, bother, disturb. APPEASE
ravage, devastate, raid, plunder, pillage, sack, rob, despoil.

harsh rough, coarse, raucous, guttural, strident, grating, cacophonous, discordant, jarring, glaring, acrid, bitter, sharp, sour. MELLOW
severe, hard, austere, bleak, Spartan, grim, stern, cruel, unkind, pitiless, ruthless, unfeeling, brutal, tough, stringent. GENTLE

harvest *n*, crop, yield, produce, fruits, result, consequence, outcome, issue, product, effect.
v, gather, reap, pick, pluck, glean, garner, collect.

hash *n*, mess, jumble, muddle, mix-up, confusion, medley, mishmash, hotchpotch.
v, chop, dice, mince, mangle, mutilate.

haste speed, rapidity, swiftness, quickness, fleetness, celerity, velocity, dispatch,

expedition, promptitude, alacrity, briskness, urgency. DELAY
hurry, rush, bustle, hustle, hastiness, precipitance, recklessness, rashness, impetuosity, impulsiveness, heedlessness. CAUTION

hasten *vt*, quicken, hurry, speed, accelerate, precipitate, expedite, dispatch, urge, press. RETARD
vi, hurry, rush, dash, race, fly, speed, run, bolt. DAWDLE

hasty quick, fast, rapid, speedy, swift, fleet, brisk, prompt, urgent. SLOW
hurried, rushed, superficial, cursory, perfunctory, fleeting, brief, slight. THOROUGH
reckless, rash, impetuous, impulsive, precipitate, headlong, heedless, thoughtless, indiscreet. CAUTIOUS
irascible, touchy, testy, short-tempered, irritable, peevish, petulant, waspish, impatient, excitable, fiery. PLACID

hatch incubate, brood, bring forth, emerge.
contrive, devise, concoct, brew, conceive, think up, plot, plan, scheme.

hate *v*, detest, loathe, abhor, abominate, execrate, dislike. LOVE
n, hatred, detestation, loathing, abhorrence, odium, abomination, execration, aversion, dislike, antipathy, hostility, enmity. LOVE

hateful detestable, loathsome, abhorrent, abominable, odious, execrable, horrible, obnoxious, vile, foul, offensive, repulsive, repugnant, revolting. DELIGHTFUL

hatred hate, detestation, loathing, abhorrence, odium, abomination, execration, aversion, dislike, antipathy, hostility, enmity, animosity, ill will, revulsion, repugnance. LOVE

haughtiness arrogance, self-importance, hauteur, loftiness, superciliousness, snobbishness, airs, pride, conceit, contempt, disdain. HUMILITY

haughty arrogant, self-important, lofty, vain, conceited, proud, supercilious, disdainful, contemptuous, snobbish, snooty (*inf*), stuck-up (*inf*), hoity-toity (*inf*), high and mighty (*inf*), imperious, lordly, aloof. HUMBLE

haul *v*, drag, lug, draw, pull, tow, tug, heave. PUSH
carry, convey, transport, cart.
n, catch, yield, takings, spoils, booty.

haunt *v*, visit, frequent.
obsess, beset, plague, torment, prey on, recur, come back.
n, retreat, refuge, den, meeting place, stamping ground.

hauteur arrogance, haughtiness, pride, conceit, superciliousness, contempt, disdain, loftiness, airs, snobbishness. HUMILITY

have own, possess, hold, keep, retain. LACK
get, obtain, gain, acquire, procure, receive, take, accept. LOSE
feel, experience, undergo, suffer, enjoy.
be obliged, be forced, be compelled, must.
entertain, consider, tolerate, allow, permit. FORBID
cheat, swindle, deceive, dupe, take in (*inf*), fool, outwit.
bear, give birth to, bring forth, deliver, beget.

haven harbour, port, anchorage.
shelter, refuge, sanctuary, asylum, retreat.

havoc destruction, devastation, desolation, waste, wreck, ruin, ravage, despoliation.
confusion, disorder, chaos, mayhem.

hawk peddle, sell, vend, cry, bark (*inf*).

hazard *n*, danger, risk, peril, jeopardy, threat.
chance, accident, fluke, gamble.
v, risk, venture, dare, gamble, stake, chance, endanger, imperil, expose.
advance, submit, offer, proffer, volunteer. WITHDRAW

hazardous dangerous, risky, perilous, hairy (*inf*), unsafe, insecure, precarious. SAFE
uncertain, unpredictable, random, haphazard, chancy (*inf*). CERTAIN

haze mist, fog, cloud, vapour, film, obscurity, dimness, haziness.

hazy misty, foggy, cloudy, nebulous, filmy, blurry, dim, obscure. CLEAR
vague, indistinct, unclear, ill-defined, muddled, confused. DEFINITE

head *n*, skull, cranium, pate, nut (*inf*). FOOT
top, summit, apex, crown, crest, peak, tip, vertex, acme, zenith, height. BASE
mind, brain, intellect, intelligence, thought, understanding, genius, aptitude, flair.

leader, chieftain, chief, principal, master, captain, commander, director, manager, superintendent. SUBORDINATE
front, vanguard, beginning, start, origin, source. END
climax, culmination, crisis, turning point.
section, division, category, class, department, heading.
v, lead, command, direct, control, guide, govern, rule, run, manage. FOLLOW
steer, turn, aim, direct, point, go, make.
head off, intercept, divert, deflect, avert, parry, forestall, prevent.
adj, leading, first, chief, principal, main, supreme, highest, top, front.

heading title, rubric, caption, headline.
section, division, head, category, class.

headland cape, promontory, foreland, spur, point, cliff, bluff.

headlong *adv*, headfirst, hastily, precipitately, pell-mell, helter-skelter, wildly, impetuously, recklessly, rashly, heedlessly. CAUTIOUSLY
adj, hasty, rash, precipitate, reckless, rash, heedless, thoughtless, impetuous, impulsive, foolhardy, breakneck. CAUTIOUS

headstrong wilful, self-willed, obstinate, stubborn, mulish, intractable, pig-headed, perverse, contrary, refractory, unruly, ungovernable, wayward. TRACTABLE
rash, reckless, imprudent, foolhardy, heedless. PRUDENT

headway progress, advance, improvement, progression, movement, motion. RETROGRESSION

heady intoxicating, exciting, thrilling, exhilarating, stimulating.
rash, reckless, headlong, precipitate, hasty, impulsive, impetuous, heedless, thoughtless. CAUTIOUS

heal cure, restore, repair, mend, remedy, treat, make well, get well, recover.
reconcile, conciliate, patch up, settle, compose, appease, assuage, soothe, alleviate. AGGRAVATE

healing curative, restorative, analeptic, remedial, medicinal, therapeutic, lenitive, soothing, comforting, gentle, mild. HARMFUL

health fitness, well-being, soundness, robustness, healthiness, haleness, strength, vigour, condition, state, shape, form, tone, fettle. ILLNESS

healthy fit, well, sound, robust, hale, hearty, sturdy, strong, vigorous, lusty. ILL
salubrious, salutary, healthful, wholesome, hygienic, beneficial, bracing, invigorating. UNHEALTHY

heap *n*, pile, mound, stack, mass, lot, hoard, store, accumulation, collection, abundance, plenty, great deal, load (*inf*).
v, pile, stack, amass, accumulate, gather, collect, hoard, store. SCATTER
load, burden, shower, pour, supply, bestow, assign.

hear listen to, attend, hark, hearken, catch, perceive, heed, eavesdrop, overhear. IGNORE
learn, be informed, be told, find out, gather.
try, examine, investigate, judge.

hearing ear, audition, audience, interview, examination, investigation, inquiry, trial.
earshot, range, sound.

hearsay rumour, gossip, talk, report, buzz, tittle-tattle.

heart core, centre, middle, kernel, nucleus, marrow, pith, essence, crux. SURFACE
soul, spirit, nature, character, disposition, temperament, passion, emotion, feeling, sentiment, sympathy, pity, compassion, love, tenderness, affection, humanity.
courage, bravery, fortitude, nerve, pluck, mettle, spirit, boldness, resolution. COWARDICE

heartache distress, anguish, grief, sorrow, woe, pain, agony, torment, suffering, affliction, despair, desolation, heartbreak. JOY

hearten cheer, buoy up, buck up (*inf*), comfort, console, assure, reassure, encourage, embolden, inspirit, inspire, animate, rouse, stimulate, invigorate. DEPRESS

heartfelt sincere, profound, deep, hearty, cordial, warm, earnest, fervent, wholehearted. INSINCERE

heartless cruel, unkind, unfeeling, uncaring, hard-hearted, cold, callous, harsh, brutal, pitiless, merciless, savage, coldblooded. KIND

hearty genial, cordial, jovial, amiable, affable, friendly, warm, unreserved, heartfelt, sincere, genuine, profound, earnest, wholehearted, enthusiastic. COOL

strong, hale, healthy, robust, sturdy, sound, vigorous, lusty, energetic. FEEBLE
nourishing, filling, substantial, ample, square, solid. MEAGRE

heat *n*, warmth, hotness, calefaction, high temperature, fever. COLD
passion, zeal, ardour, fervour, vehemence, intensity, violence, frenzy, rage, fury, excitement. COOLNESS
v, warm, cook, heat up, make hot. CHILL
excite, inflame, stir, rouse, stimulate, animate, impassion. COOL

heathen *n*, pagan, infidel, unbeliever, idolater, barbarian, philistine.
adj, pagan, idolatrous, godless, ungodly, barbarous, primitive, uncivilized. GODLY

heave haul, drag, pull, hoist, raise, lift.
throw, cast, fling, hurl, sling, pitch, toss.
surge, swell, rise, throb, billow, roll, pant, sigh.
retch, gag (*inf*), vomit, throw up (*inf*).

heaven paradise, hereafter, afterworld, Elysium, Valhalla, Zion, utopia. HELL
ecstasy, rapture, bliss, happiness, felicity, joy, delight. TORMENT

heavenly wonderful, delightful, lovely, beautiful, exquisite, sublime, glorious, blissful, rapturous. ABOMINABLE
holy, angelic, saintly, blessed, divine, celestial, extraterrestrial, supernatural, spiritual, unearthly. EARTHLY

heavens sky, ether, firmament, empyrean.

heaviness weight, heftiness, ponderousness, bulk, mass. LIGHTNESS
intensity, violence, severity, harshness, oppressiveness, laboriousness, difficulty.
sadness, sorrow, dejection, despondency, gloom, melancholy. CHEERFULNESS
seriousness, gravity, importance, profundity, complexity.
sluggishness, languor, listlessness, apathy, dullness, slowness, inactivity, inertia. ACTIVITY

heavy weighty, ponderous, hefty, bulky, massive, large, great, considerable, fat, stout. LIGHT
intense, violent, severe, hard, harsh, grievous, oppressive, burdensome, laborious, arduous, difficult. SLIGHT
sad, sorrowful, downcast, crestfallen, dejected, despondent, gloomy, melancholy. CHEERFUL
serious, grave, critical, important, profound, deep, complex. TRIVIAL
sluggish, torpid, languid, listless, apathetic, drowsy, sleepy, dull, slow, inactive, inert. ACTIVE
burdened, laden, loaded, encumbered, weighted.
overcast, cloudy, dull, gloomy, dark, leaden, lowering. BRIGHT

heckle interrupt, disrupt, barrack (*inf*), taunt, jeer, bait, badger, hector, harass.

hectic feverish, frenetic, frantic, frenzied, furious, excited, animated, heated, riotous, boisterous, wild, chaotic, unruly. CALM

hector *v*, bully, browbeat, intimidate, threaten, menace, torment, plague, harass, badger, harry, worry.
bluster, boast, brag, swagger, roister.
n, bully, braggart, blusterer, swaggerer.

hedge *n*, hedgerow, quickset, fence, barrier, guard, protection.
v, surround, enclose, fence, confine, restrict, obstruct, hinder, impede, block.
evade, dodge, equivocate, prevaricate, fudge.
protect, guard, shield, safeguard, cover. EXPOSE

heed *v*, mind, attend, pay attention to, listen to, take notice of, regard, note, mark, observe, obey, follow. IGNORE
n, attention, notice, regard, mind, thought, consideration, care, caution, heedfulness, watchfulness. DISREGARD

heedful mindful, attentive, regardful, thoughtful, prudent, careful, circumspect, cautious, chary, wary, watchful, observant. HEEDLESS

heedless unmindful, regardless, oblivious, thoughtless, unthinking, careless, inattentive, neglectful, negligent, rash, reckless. HEEDFUL

heel[1] *n*, remnant, remainder, stub, stump, butt, rump, crust.
scoundrel, blackguard, cad (*inf*), rotter (*inf*).

heel[2] *v*, lean, list, tilt, cant, incline.

hegemony supremacy, primacy, dominion, domination, ascendancy, rule, sway, command, mastery, control, leadership.

height altitude, elevation, loftiness, tallness, stature. DEPTH
top, summit, apex, peak, pinnacle, zenith, apogee, acme, climax, culmination, maximum, utmost, limit, extremity, extreme.
mountain, hill, eminence.

heighten increase, augment, amplify, intensify, aggravate, enhance, enrich, improve, strengthen. MODERATE
raise, elevate, uplift, exalt, ennoble. LOWER

heinous wicked, evil, nefarious, infamous, atrocious, scandalous, outrageous, monstrous, villainous, flagitious, abominable, odious, hateful, deplorable. ADMIRABLE

heir child, offspring, descendant, successor, inheritor, beneficiary, heiress.

hell underworld, perdition, inferno, Hades, Gehenna. HEAVEN
torment, anguish, agony, suffering, affliction, misery, nightmare. ECSTASY

hellish infernal, diabolical, fiendish, satanic, demonic, demoniacal, devilish, damnable, accursed, wicked, evil, nefarious, heinous, monstrous, cruel, savage, barbaric, inhuman. HEAVENLY

helm rudder, wheel, tiller.
control, command, direction, reins, saddle, driver's seat.

help *v*, assist, aid, lend a hand, abet, succour, back, support, encourage, promote, further, serve, avail, cooperate, collaborate. HINDER
relieve, alleviate, improve, ameliorate, ease, facilitate, remedy, restore. AGGRAVATE
avoid, refrain from, resist, withstand, stop, prevent, control.
n, assistance, aid, succour, backing, support, encouragement, service, avail, use, cooperation, collaboration. HINDRANCE
relief, remedy, cure, corrective, improvement. AGGRAVATION
helper, assistant, aider, abettor, mate.

helper assistant, aider, aide, auxiliary, help, supporter, backer, second, ally, colleague, partner, mate, helpmate, collaborator, adjutant. OPPONENT

helpful useful, serviceable, beneficial, advantageous, practical, constructive, profitable, valuable. USELESS
friendly, neighbourly, caring, sympathetic, kind, benevolent, supportive, obliging.

helpless impotent, powerless, incapable, incompetent, weak, feeble, infirm, unfit, dependent, defenceless, unprotected, vulnerable, abandoned, forsaken. STRONG

hem *n*, edge, border, margin, edging, trimming.
v, edge, border, bind, trim.

hem in, surround, encircle, environ, gird, enclose, confine, shut in.

hence therefore, thus, for this reason, ergo.
henceforth, henceforward, hereafter, from now on. HITHERTO

henchman attendant, servant, retainer, follower, supporter, aide, right-hand man, crony.

herald *n*, messenger, runner, announcer, crier, harbinger, forerunner, precursor, sign, indication, omen, portent.
v, announce, proclaim, trumpet, promulgate, broadcast, advertise, publish. SUPPRESS
precede, usher in, portend, presage, foretoken.

herbage grass, plants, vegetation, pasture, pasturage.

herculean laborious, arduous, strenuous, toilsome, heavy, hard, difficult, formidable, gruelling, demanding. EASY
strong, mighty, powerful, stalwart, robust, strapping, muscular, brawny, athletic. PUNY

herd *n*, drove, pack, flock, swarm, horde, crowd, throng, multitude, mob, rabble, populace.
v, gather, assemble, muster, flock, congregate, collect. DISPERSE
drive, lead, guide, shepherd.

hereditary inheritable, heritable, hereditable, genetic, transmissible. ACQUIRED
inherited, bequeathed, transmitted, handed down, ancestral, traditional.

heresy unorthodoxy, heterodoxy, nonconformism, dissent, schism, apostasy, iconoclasm. ORTHODOXY

heretical unorthodox, heterodox, nonconformist, schismatic, iconoclastic, idolatrous, heathen, pagan. ORTHODOX

heritage inheritance, patrimony, tradition, birthright, portion, legacy, bequest.

hermetic hermetical, sealed, airtight.

hermit solitary, recluse, anchorite, eremite.

heroic courageous, brave, valiant, valorous, intrepid, fearless, dauntless, bold, daring, gallant, noble. COWARDLY
legendary, classical, classic, epic, grand, grandiose, extravagant.

heroism courage, bravery, valour, fortitude, intrepidity, fearlessness, boldness, daring, gallantry, chivalry. COWARDICE

hesitate pause, wait, delay, hold back, waver, vacillate, doubt, be uncertain, demur, be reluctant, scruple, think twice, falter, stammer, stutter. PROCEED

hesitation pause, delay, hesitancy, wavering, vacillation, doubt, uncertainty, irresolution, indecision, qualm, scruple, reluctance, faltering. DECISION

heterodox unorthodox, heretical, schismatic, iconoclastic. ORTHODOX

heterodoxy unorthodoxy, heresy, schism, iconoclasm, dissent. ORTHODOXY

heterogeneous dissimilar, different, unlike, disparate, unrelated, varied, diverse, mixed, miscellaneous. HOMOGENEOUS

hew chop, hack, axe, lop, sever, cut down, fell.
carve, sculpt, shape, fashion, form.

hiatus gap, break, interruption, pause, interval, blank, void, space, opening, aperture, rift, cleft.

hidden concealed, latent, unseen, masked, veiled, covert, cryptic, secret, private, close, clandestine, dark, obscure, occult, abstruse, recondite, mystical. OPEN

hide[1] *v*, conceal, cloak, shroud, cover, screen, mask, veil, dissemble, disguise, camouflage, obscure, eclipse, suppress, bury, secrete, lie low. REVEAL

hide[2] skin, pelt, coat, leather.

hideous ugly, grotesque, unsightly, repulsive, revolting, ghastly, monstrous, gruesome, grisly, grim, horrible, horrid, frightful, dreadful, terrible, horrific, appalling, shocking, odious, abominable. BEAUTIFUL

hieratic hieratical, priestly, sacerdotal, clerical, ecclesiastical, holy.

higgledy-piggledy disorderly, jumbled, confused, muddled, topsy-turvy, haphazard, helter-skelter, pell-mell. ORDERLY

high tall, lofty, elevated, towering, soaring. LOW
great, intense, extreme, strong, violent, sharp, excessive, expensive, dear.
shrill, piercing, piping, high-pitched, treble. DEEP
eminent, prominent, important, exalted, distinguished, dignified, noble, august, influential, leading, chief, ruling. LOWLY
haughty, arrogant, proud, high and mighty (*inf*), lordly, overbearing, domineering, supercilious, disdainful, contemptuous.
happy, cheerful, elated, exhilarated, euphoric, intoxicated, stoned (*inf*). DEPRESSED

highlight *n*, climax, peak, best part, outstanding feature, high spot, focal point.
v, stress, emphasize, accent, accentuate, underline, point up, spotlight, feature.

highly greatly, extremely, very, immensely, vastly, tremendously, supremely, exceptionally, extraordinarily.
favourably, well, appreciatively, approvingly, warmly, respectfully. BADLY

hike *v*, walk, tramp, trek, ramble.
hitch, pull, lift, raise.
n, walk, tramp, trek, ramble.

hilarious funny, amusing, side-splitting, hysterical (*inf*), uproarious, noisy, boisterous, merry, jolly, jovial, mirthful, cheerful, gay, joyful, happy, elated, exhilarated. SERIOUS

hilarity merriment, jollity, mirth, laughter, gaiety, cheerfulness, joy, exhilaration, exuberance, high spirits, boisterousness. DESPONDENCY

hill mound, knoll, hillock, hummock, eminence, elevation, rise, incline, slope, acclivity. PLAIN

hind back, rear, posterior, hinder. FRONT

hinder impede, obstruct, block, hamper, thwart, frustrate, retard, delay, check, stop, arrest, prevent, oppose. HELP

hindrance impediment, encumbrance, handicap, obstacle, obstruction, block, barrier, hitch, snag, difficulty, delay, check, restriction, limitation. ASSISTANCE

hinge turn, hang, depend, rest, pivot, revolve around.

hint *n*, suggestion, intimation, implication, insinuation, innuendo, allusion, mention, inkling, clue, tip.
trace, suspicion, *soupçon*, dash, touch, whisper, taste.
v, suggest, intimate, imply, insinuate, allude, mention, tip off.

hire *v*, rent, charter, lease, let, engage, commission, appoint, employ, take on.
n, rental, rent, charge, fee, pay, payment, wages, cost, price.

hireling mercenary, tool, puppet, employee, servant, slave, menial.

hirsute hairy, shaggy, hispid, bristly, bearded, unshaven. SMOOTH

hiss *v*, sibilate, whistle, rasp, wheeze, whiz.

boo, hoot, catcall, jeer, mock, deride, decry, shout down. APPLAUD
n, sibilation, sibilance, whistle, hissing, buzz, whiz.
boo, hoot, catcall, raspberry, jeer, mockery, derision. APPLAUSE

historic famous, celebrated, noteworthy, memorable, remarkable, important, significant, consequential, momentous. INCONSEQUENTIAL

historical authentic, real, true, actual, factual, documented, chronicled. LEGENDARY

history chronicle, annals, record, account, story, narration, narrative, memoirs, biography.
antiquity, the past, olden days, yesteryear. FUTURE

histrionic theatrical, melodramatic, dramatic, affected, forced, insincere, unnatural, false, artificial.

hit *v*, strike, knock, beat, batter, smack, slap, whack, punch, thump, box, cuff, bash (*inf*), clout (*inf*).
bump, bang, crash into, smash into, collide with, clash with. MISS
reach, attain, achieve, arrive at, gain, touch.
hit upon, find, discover, come upon, light upon, chance upon, happen upon, think of, dream up.
n, stroke, blow, knock, smack, slap, thump, cuff, bump, crash, collision, clash, impact.
success, triumph, winner, sellout, sensation, smash (*inf*). FAILURE

hitch *v*, tie, fasten, attach, connect, unite, couple, tether, moor, harness. LOOSE
pull, tug, hike, jerk.
n, impediment, obstacle, hindrance, problem, difficulty, snag, catch, delay, hold-up.
jerk, tug, pull.

hoard *v*, gather, collect, amass, accumulate, garner, store, stockpile, save, husband, reserve, put by, lay up, stash away (*inf*). SQUANDER
n, collection, store, stockpile, reserve, fund, cache, accumulation, mass, heap, pile.

hoarse husky, raucous, throaty, croaky, guttural, gruff, harsh, rough, grating, rasping. MELLOW

hoary grey, silvery, frosty, white, grizzled, grey-haired, white-haired. DARK
venerable, aged, old, ancient.

hoax *n*, trick, practical joke, prank, deception, fraud, imposture, cheat, swindle.
v, trick, deceive, dupe, fool, hoodwink, bamboozle (*inf*), cheat, swindle.

hobble limp, stumble, totter, dodder, falter. RUN
fetter, shackle, tie, bind, fasten. UNFETTER

hobby pastime, recreation, amusement, diversion, leisure, activity, sideline. WORK

hobnob fraternize, socialize, mingle, mix, consort, keep company, go around.

hog *n*, pig, swine, porker, grunter.
glutton, gourmand.
v, monopolize, corner, keep for oneself. SHARE

hoggish piggish, swinish, selfish, greedy, grasping, rapacious, gluttonous, voracious, dirty, filthy, unclean, squalid, sordid.

hoist raise, lift, crane, winch, elevate, heave, erect, rear. LOWER

hold *v*, grip, grasp, clutch, clasp, seize, keep, retain, have, possess, own, occupy. DROP
support, sustain, bear, carry, take, contain, accommodate.
detain, arrest, imprison, confine, restrain, hold back, check, curb, stop. RELEASE
maintain, think, believe, consider, regard, judge, deem, reckon.
stick, adhere, cling, hold on, cleave, embrace, hug, cradle.
last, endure, abide, remain, stay, persist, continue, stand. PERISH
convene, call, conduct, run, preside over, engage in, carry on.
hold forth, speak, orate, preach, lecture, harangue, discourse, spout (*inf*).
hold out, offer, proffer, extend, present.
last, endure, stand firm, hang on, persevere.
hold up, delay, retard, slow down, hinder, impede. ADVANCE
support, sustain, brace, prop, buttress.
brandish, wave, flaunt, display, show, exhibit.
n, grip, grasp, clasp, embrace, foothold, purchase.
influence, control, power, sway, mastery, dominion, ascendancy.

hole aperture, opening, gap, break, breach, rift, cleft, fissure, split, tear, rent, puncture, perforation, fault, flaw.
cavity, hollow, depression, concavity, pit, cave, cavern, chamber, burrow, den, lair.
hovel, slum, dive (*inf*), dump (*inf*).

predicament, quandary, dilemma, plight, strait, fix (*inf*).

holiday leave, vacation, time off, break. festival, feast, saint's day, anniversary, celebration, gala, fête, carnival.

holiness devoutness, piety, religiousness, saintliness, godliness, sanctity, sacredness, divinity, purity, virtue. PROFANITY

hollow *adj*, empty, unfilled, vacant, concave, cavernous, sunken.
muffled, muted, low, deep, rumbling, reverberating, flat, dull.
meaningless, pointless, empty, vain, fruitless, unavailing, worthless, useless.
insincere, hypocritical, artificial, sham, false, deceitful. SINCERE
n, depression, dip, basin, bowl, cavity, pit, hole, crater, dent, dimple, indentation.
v, dig, excavate, scoop, gouge, pit, dent.

holy devout, pious, religious, saintly, godly, good, virtuous, righteous, pure, divine, spiritual, sacred, hallowed, consecrated, blessed. PROFANE

homage honour, respect, deference, worship, adoration, veneration, reverence, esteem, admiration. DISRESPECT
loyalty, allegiance, constancy, devotion, fidelity, fealty, duty, tribute.

home *n*, house, abode, dwelling, residence, domicile, habitation, habitat, territory, environment, element.
family, household, hearth, fireside, birthplace, native land.
adj, domestic, family, household, internal, interior, national, native. FOREIGN

homely simple, plain, unpretentious, ordinary, familiar, domestic, homelike, homy, comfortable, cosy, welcoming, informal. GRAND

homicide murder, manslaughter, killing, slaying, assassination.

homily sermon, discourse, lecture, harangue, address, speech.

homogeneous uniform, consistent, identical, alike, like, similar, akin. HETEROGENEOUS

hone sharpen, whet, grind, file, polish. BLUNT

honest trustworthy, trusty, reliable, upright, law-abiding, virtuous, honourable, conscientious, principled, truthful, veracious, sincere, candid, frank, straightforward, open, fair, just, equitable, lawful, legal, genuine, authentic, real, true. DISHONEST

honesty truthfulness, veracity, probity, integrity, honour, morality, rectitude, uprightness, sincerity, candour, frankness, fairness, justice, equity. DISHONESTY

honorary titular, nominal, ex officio, unofficial, unpaid.

honour *n*, distinction, eminence, fame, glory, repute, reputation, esteem, regard, dignity, prestige, standing, credit. DISGRACE
honesty, integrity, probity, rectitude, uprightness, morality, principles, justice, fairness, virtue, decency, sincerity. DISHONESTY
praise, acclaim, acclamation, tribute, homage, reverence, veneration, worship, adoration, respect, deference. CONTEMPT
privilege, pleasure, joy, pride, satisfaction.
virginity, chastity, purity, virtue.
v, respect, esteem, value, prize, admire, revere, reverence, venerate, worship, adore. DESPISE
glorify, dignify, exalt, ennoble, praise, acclaim, celebrate, commemorate. DISHONOUR
keep, observe, discharge, fulfil, accept, acknowledge, pay.

honourable honest, upright, moral, principled, right, proper, virtuous, trustworthy, respectable, reputable, creditable, true, just, fair. DISHONOURABLE
noble, distinguished, illustrious, noted, eminent, great, venerable, respected, esteemed. DESPISED

hoodwink dupe, deceive, delude, trick, hoax, fool, bamboozle (*inf*), cheat, swindle, cozen, con (*inf*).

hook *n*, hasp, clasp, catch, fastener.
snare, trap.
angle, crook, bend, curve, twist, loop.
v, catch, snare, ensnare, trap, entrap. RELEASE
fasten, clasp, join, link, connect. UNHOOK

hooked bent, curved, crooked, aquiline, hamate, uncinate, hooklike.
addicted, dependent, obsessed, enamoured.

hoop band, ring, circlet, wheel.

hoot *v*, screech, shriek, howl, yell, cry, shout, whoop, toot.
boo, catcall, hiss, decry, shout down, jeer, deride. CHEER
n, screech, shriek, call, cry, toot.

boo, catcall, hiss, jeer. CHEER
clown, card (*inf*), scream (*inf*), laugh (*inf*).

hop skip, caper, jump, leap, spring, bound, dance.

hope *n*, dream, ambition, aspiration, expectation, expectancy, anticipation, longing, yearning, desire, hopefulness, faith, trust, belief, confidence. DESPAIR
v, desire, long, yearn, wish, expect, anticipate, await, look forward to, count on, trust, believe.

hopeful optimistic, sanguine, expectant, confident, assured. DESPAIRING
promising, encouraging, favourable, auspicious, propitious, bright, rosy. DISCOURAGING

hopeless despairing, desperate, despondent, downcast, downhearted, disconsolate, dejected, forlorn. HOPEFUL
lost, irretrievable, irredeemable, irreparable, irremediable, incurable. PROMISING
impossible, impracticable, vain, futile, useless, worthless, pointless. WORTHWHILE
incompetent, inadequate, poor, inferior, no good. PROFICIENT

horde crowd, multitude, throng, mob, host, gang, pack, troop, band, company, swarm, flock, herd.

horizontal flat, level, plane, prone, supine. VERTICAL

horrible horrid, unpleasant, disagreeable, nasty, awful, dreadful, frightful, fearful, terrible, horrifying, horrific, horrendous, ghastly, grim, formidable, hideous, loathsome, abominable, revolting, disgusting, repulsive. WONDERFUL

horrid horrible, unpleasant, disagreeable, nasty, mean, unkind, beastly (*inf*). PLEASANT
frightening, alarming, terrifying, horrific, horrendous, ghastly, repulsive, hideous, dreadful, awful, frightful, terrible. WONDERFUL

horrific horrendous, horrifying, frightening, alarming, terrifying, shocking, appalling, dreadful, awful, frightful. REASSURING

horrify shock, appal, disgust, sicken, dismay, distress, outrage, alarm, frighten, scare, terrify, petrify. REASSURE

horror terror, fear, panic, fright, alarm, dread, dismay. REASSURANCE
loathing, hatred, detestation, abomination, abhorrence, repugnance, revulsion, disgust. LIKING

horse mount, steed, stallion, gelding, mare, filly, colt, foal, pony, cob, nag, jade.

hospitable welcoming, friendly, neighbourly, genial, amicable, cordial, convivial, sociable, warm, kind, benevolent, generous, liberal, amenable, receptive, approachable. INHOSPITABLE

hospitality welcome, hospitableness, kindness, geniality, cordiality, conviviality, sociability, warmth, kindness, benevolence, generosity, liberality. UNFRIENDLINESS

host[1] proprietor, landlord, landlady, innkeeper, hostess, entertainer, master of ceremonies, compere, presenter. GUEST

host[2] throng, multitude, horde, crowd, mob, drove, herd, swarm, pack.

hostage prisoner, captive, pawn, surety, security.

hostile opposed, anti (*inf*), contrary, antagonistic, adverse, unfavourable, inimical, unfriendly, inhospitable, aggressive, belligerent, bellicose, warlike. FRIENDLY

hostilities war, warfare, conflict, fighting. PEACE

hostility opposition, antagonism, enmity, unfriendliness, hatred, ill will, animosity, antipathy. FRIENDLINESS

hot warm, heated, fiery, burning, flaming, blazing, roasting, baking, scorching, scalding, blistering, sweltering, torrid, sultry. COLD
pungent, sharp, acrid, spicy, peppery, piquant. MILD
ardent, fervent, fervid, passionate, inflamed, irate, violent, intense, vehement, animated, excited, enthusiastic, eager, impetuous. APATHETIC
recent, latest, new, fresh.

hotel inn, motel, guest house, boarding house, pension, hostel.

hound chase, pursue, dog, hunt, harry, harass, persecute, provoke, goad, spur, drive, urge.

house *n*, dwelling, abode, residence, domicile, home, habitation, building, cottage, bungalow, villa, mansion.
household, family, pedigree, lineage, ancestry, race, tribe, clan, dynasty.
firm, business, company, partnership, concern, establishment, organization.

v, domicile, lodge, quarter, billet, accommodate, put up, contain, shelter, protect.

household *n*, family, ménage, house, home.
adj, domestic, family, home, ordinary, plain, common.

hovel hut, shack, shanty, cabin, shed. PALACE

hover hang, fly, float, drift, flutter, linger. waver, vacillate, fluctuate, oscillate, falter. DECIDE

however nevertheless, notwithstanding, but, still, yet, though.

howl bay, yowl, wail, hoot, bellow, roar, cry, shriek, yell.

hubbub noise, din, racket, uproar, tumult, commotion, hullabaloo, brouhaha, clamour, rumpus, riot, confusion, disorder. QUIET

huddle *v*, cluster, bunch, gather, crowd, throng, flock. DISPERSE
nestle, snuggle, curl up, crouch.
n, heap, mass, cluster, bunch, crowd, muddle, jumble, confusion, disorder.

hue colour, shade, tint, tinge, tone, cast, complexion.

huff temper, bad mood, pet, pique, rage, anger, passion, miff (*inf*).

huffish huffy, pettish, peevish, petulant, waspish, cross, irritable, touchy, testy, grumpy, angry, impatient, sullen, resentful. AFFABLE

hug embrace, enfold, clasp, squeeze, cuddle, hold, cling to, cherish.

huge enormous, tremendous, prodigious, vast, immense, colossal, gigantic, gargantuan, elephantine, mammoth, great, big, large, bulky. TINY

hull body, skeleton, frame, framework, casing, shell, husk, peel, rind, skin.

hullabaloo noise, din, racket, bedlam, outcry, uproar, hubbub, clamour, brouhaha, commotion, tumult, rumpus, disturbance, pandemonium. QUIET

hum drone, buzz, whirr, purr, murmur, thrum, vibrate.

human *adj*, anthropoid, manlike, mortal, physical, natural, vulnerable, fallible.
kind, humane, sensitive, compassionate, understanding. INHUMAN
n, person, individual, human being, mortal, man, woman, child. BEAST

humane kind, kindly, benevolent, benign, tender, compassionate, sympathetic, merciful, clement, mild, gentle, good, charitable, humanitarian. CRUEL

humanity mankind, humankind, human race, people, mortality, human nature. BESTIALITY
kindness, benevolence, tenderness, compassion, mercy, clemency, charity. INHUMANITY

humanize civilize, tame, educate, enlighten, cultivate, refine, soften, mellow. BRUTALIZE

humble *adj*, modest, unassuming, unpretentious, simple, plain, poor, mean, lowly, meek, submissive, docile, servile, obsequious, deferential, respectful, polite, courteous. HAUGHTY
v, lower, reduce, degrade, abase, demean, humiliate, abash, shame, mortify, chagrin, subdue, crush. EXALT

humbug trick, trickery, deception, deceit, hoax, fraud, imposture, pretence, sham, ruse, wile.
cheat, fraud, swindler, trickster, charlatan, quack, impostor.
nonsense, rubbish, flummery, bunkum, baloney (*inf*), bosh (*inf*).

humdrum monotonous, boring, tiresome, wearisome, dull, routine, uninteresting, prosaic, prosy, dry, dreary, mundane, commonplace, ordinary. INTERESTING

humid damp, moist, wet, dank, steamy, muggy, clammy, sticky, sultry. DRY

humiliate humble, shame, disgrace, abase, demean, degrade, lower, mortify, chagrin, embarrass, abash, crush, subdue. DIGNIFY

humiliation shame, disgrace, degradation, lowering, mortification, chagrin, embarrassment, abashment, indignity. DIGNITY

humility humbleness, modesty, diffidence, lowliness, meekness, submissiveness, servility. HAUTEUR

hummock knoll, hillock, hump, mound, ridge.

humorous funny, amusing, entertaining, comic, comical, droll, witty, waggish, facetious, farcical, laughable, ludicrous. SERIOUS

humour *n*, comedy, wit, drollery, facetiousness, amusement, fun, funniness, jocularity, pleasantry, jokes, farce. SERIOUSNESS

mood, temper, frame of mind, disposition, temperament, nature.
whim, caprice, fancy, vagary, crotchet, quirk, freak.
v, gratify, placate, indulge, pamper, cosset, spoil, accommodate.

hump *n*, protuberance, bulge, swelling, lump, bump, knob, mound, hunch.
v, arch, vault, hunch, curve. STRAIGHTEN
carry, lug, heave, hoist, shoulder.

hunch *n*, guess, intuition, feeling, notion, idea, premonition, suspicion.
v, crouch, stoop, hump, arch, bend. STRAIGHTEN

hunger *n*, hungriness, appetite, emptiness, famine, starvation.
longing, yearning, desire, craving, lust, thirst.
v, starve, long, yearn, desire, crave, hanker, lust, thirst.

hungry ravenous, starving, famished, hollow, empty, peckish (*inf*).
desirous, longing, yearning, craving, greedy, eager. CONTENTED

hunk chunk, lump, block, wedge, slab, piece, portion, slice.

hunt *v*, chase, pursue, hound, follow, stalk, trail, track.
seek, search, scour, look for, rummage, forage. FIND
n, chase, pursuit, hunting, stalking, tracking.
search, quest. DISCOVERY

hurdle barrier, obstacle, fence, wall, hedge.
impediment, hindrance, obstacle, barrier, snag, difficulty, stumbling block.

hurl throw, sling, fling, cast, pitch, chuck (*inf*), shy, launch, propel.

hurricane gale, storm, tempest, cyclone, typhoon, tornado. BREEZE

hurried quick, swift, hasty, cursory, superficial, perfunctory, brief, short, rushed, slapdash, careless. THOROUGH

hurry *v*, rush, hasten, race, dash, fly, scurry, bustle. DAWDLE
accelerate, quicken, speed up, hasten, precipitate, expedite, dispatch, drive, urge, goad, hustle. RETARD
n, rush, haste, bustle, hustle, flurry, speed, quickness, celerity, dispatch, expedition, promptitude, precipitation, urgency. LEISURE

hurt *v*, harm, injure, damage, impair, mar, wound, bruise, pain, afflict, grieve, distress, upset, offend, aggrieve. SOOTHE
ache, be sore, throb, sting.
n, pain, suffering, distress, affliction, wound, injury, harm, damage.
adj, injured, wounded, cut, bruised, upset, aggrieved, offended.

hurtful injurious, wounding, upsetting, distressing, unkind, cruel, spiteful, malicious, offensive, damaging, harmful, detrimental, deleterious, pernicious. HARMLESS

hurtle *vi*, rush, tear, fly, race, charge, plunge.
vt, fling, hurl, pitch, propel, impel.

husband *n*, married man, spouse, consort, bridegroom, old man (*inf*), lord and master, widower.
v, conserve, save, economize, store, hoard. WASTE

husbandry agriculture, agronomy, farming, tillage, cultivation.
frugality, thrift, economy, good housekeeping.

hush *v*, silence, quieten, shush, still, mute, muzzle.
soothe, calm, allay, appease, assuage.
hush up, suppress, smother, squash, keep dark, cover up.
interj, shush, quiet, silence, be quiet, shut up (*inf*).
n, quiet, silence, stillness, peace. NOISE

husk shell, hull, shuck, chaff, rind, covering, coating. KERNEL

husky hoarse, guttural, raucous, harsh, grating, rasping, croaky, throaty.
burly, brawny, muscular, strapping, sturdy, well-built, stocky. PUNY

hustle push, shove, jostle, elbow, bustle, hurry, hasten, rush, speed, force, impel.

hut shed, cabin, hovel, shanty, shack, shelter. PALACE

hutch cage, box, pen, coop, hut, shed.

hybrid cross, crossbreed, mongrel, mule, mixture, compound, composite, combination.

hygienic clean, sanitary, sterile, aseptic, disinfected, pure, healthy. UNHYGIENIC

hypercritical captious, carping, fussy, pernickety, finicky, overscrupulous, overcritical, pedantic.

hypnotic mesmeric, mesmerizing, fascinating, entrancing, spellbinding, soporific, somniferous, narcotic, opiate.

hypochondria hypochondriasis, valetudinarianism, depression, melancholy.

hypochondriac hypochondriacal, valetudinarian, depressed, melancholy.

hypocrisy insincerity, two-facedness, duplicity, deceit, deception, falseness, pretence, dissimulation, cant, sanctimoniousness, pharisaism. SINCERITY

hypocrite fraud, impostor, deceiver, charlatan, pretender, dissembler, whited sepulchre, pharisee.

hypocritical insincere, two-faced, duplicitous, deceitful, false, dissembling, hollow, canting, sanctimonious, pharisaic. SINCERE

hypothesis theory, postulate, premiss, assumption, supposition, conjecture, speculation. PROOF

hypothetical theoretical, academic, supposed, assumed, putative, conjectural, speculative. REAL

hysterical mad, crazed, raving, frenzied, wild, uncontrollable, berserk, frantic, distraught. CALM

hilarious, side-splitting, uproarious, very funny.

I

ice freeze, frost, chill, glaze. HEAT

icy frozen, freezing, glacial, arctic, ice-cold, gelid, bitter, cold, chilly, frosty, glassy, slippery. HOT

frigid, cold, frosty, glacial, aloof, distant, stony, steely, unfeeling, unfriendly. WARM

idea thought, conception, concept, abstraction, fancy, notion, belief, opinion, viewpoint, doctrine, impression, perception, understanding, inkling, clue, hint, suspicion, guess, theory, hypothesis, suggestion, plan, scheme, design, aim, intention, purpose, object. FACT

ideal *n*, model, exemplar, paragon, nonpareil, paradigm, example, pattern, standard, prototype, archetype, epitome.

aim, objective, goal, target.

adj, perfect, exemplary, model, supreme, classic, consummate. IMPERFECT

fanciful, imaginary, illusory, unreal, abstract, mental, intellectual, theoretical, idealistic. REAL

idealistic perfectionist, utopian, visionary, optimistic, romantic, quixotic, unrealistic, impractical, impracticable. REALISTIC

identical same, selfsame, indistinguishable, duplicate, twin, matching, equal, corresponding, congruous, tantamount, equivalent, like, alike. DIFFERENT

identification recognition, naming, perception, differentiation, designation.

credential, papers, ID, identity card.

rapport, empathy, sympathy, fellow feeling, association, involvement.

identify recognize, name, label, perceive, make out, detect, pick out, single out, classify.

relate, associate, ally, sympathize, empathize.

identity individuality, particularity, singularity, uniqueness, self, personality, name.

sameness, oneness, unity, correspondence, equality, likeness. DIFFERENCE

ideology ideas, beliefs, creed, doctrine, teachings, dogma, tenets, philosophy, theory.

idiocy imbecility, foolishness, asininity, stupidity, fatuity, lunacy, insanity, absurdity, inanity. SENSE

idiom locution, expression, set phrase.

language, talk, parlance, vernacular, jargon, argot, usage, style.

idiosyncrasy characteristic, peculiarity, quirk, eccentricity, singularity, mannerism, affectation, trait, speciality.

idiot imbecile, moron, cretin, halfwit, simpleton, dunce, fool, nincompoop, ass, donkey, dolt, blockhead.

idiotic foolish, asinine, stupid, fatuous, senseless, imbecilic, moronic, witless, crazy, daft (*inf*), insane, absurd, inane. WISE

idle *adj*, inactive, unemployed, jobless, unoccupied, vacant, empty, unused. ACTIVE

lazy, indolent, slothful, sluggish, lethargic, inert, shiftless. BUSY

trivial, frivolous, superficial, unimportant, foolish, vain, futile, useless, abortive, unprofitable, fruitless, unavailing, bootless, ineffectual, unproductive. FRUITFUL

v, loaf, lounge, laze, loiter, dawdle, waste time, drift, coast, mark time, do nothing, vegetate. WORK

idler loafer, lounger, lazybones, sluggard, sloth, laggard, dawdler, layabout, good-for-nothing, malingerer, shirker.

idol image, effigy, icon, god, hero, favourite, pet, darling, beloved.

idolize worship, revere, reverence, venerate, admire, adore, love, exalt, glorify, lionize, deify. DESPISE

idyllic charming, picturesque, heavenly, blissful, ideal, Arcadian, pastoral, rustic.

if provided, supposing, granting, though, whether.

ignite kindle, light, set fire to, catch fire, burn, inflame, fire. EXTINGUISH

ignoble low, base, vile, abject, contemptible, despicable, dishonourable, ignominious, shameful, disgraceful, heinous, infamous, mean, wretched, humble, common, vulgar, inferior. NOBLE

ignominious disgraceful, shameful, contemptible, despicable, ignoble, dishonourable, unworthy, base, low, mean, shabby, disreputable. HONOURABLE

ignominy disgrace, shame, dishonour, infamy, disrepute, discredit, contempt, obloquy, opprobrium, odium, stigma, humiliation. CREDIT

ignoramus dunce, dullard, dolt, simpleton, donkey, ass, blockhead, fool. GENIUS

ignorance unawareness, unenlightenment, darkness, blindness, nescience, innocence, illiteracy, unintelligence, inexperience. KNOWLEDGE

ignorant unaware, unenlightened, uninformed, benighted, in the dark, unknowing, unwitting, blind, oblivious, innocent, inexperienced. AWARE

illiterate, unlettered, unread, untaught, uneducated, unlearned, unschooled, unscholarly, thick, dense, crass. LEARNED

ignore disregard, neglect, overlook, wink at, skip, pass over, cut, snub, cold-shoulder. ACKNOWLEDGE

ill *adj*, sick, unwell, poorly (*inf*), out of sorts (*inf*), ailing, indisposed, laid up (*inf*), diseased, infirm, unhealthy. WELL

bad, evil, wicked, vile, sinful, iniquitous, wrong, unfavourable, unpropitious, adverse, hostile, harmful, pernicious, damaging, injurious, unlucky, unfortunate. GOOD

unfriendly, unkind, malevolent, malicious, harsh, surly, cross, crabbed, irritable.

adv, badly, poorly, insufficiently, improperly, unfortunately, unluckily, adversely, unfavourably. WELL

n, evil, harm, mischief, hurt, injury, affliction, pain, suffering, misery, trouble, misfortune, disaster, calamity. GOOD

ailment, illness, malady, complaint, disorder, sickness, indisposition, disease.

ill-advised incautious, imprudent, foolish, injudicious, unwise, impolitic, ill-judged, foolhardy, hasty, rash, reckless, thoughtless, ill-considered, misguided. WISE

ill-bred ill-mannered, rude, impolite, discourteous, uncivil, unmannerly, vulgar, coarse, unrefined, unladylike, ungentlemanly. POLITE

illegal unlawful, illicit, illegitimate, criminal, unauthorized, unlicensed, unofficial, unconstitutional, banned, prohibited, forbidden, contraband, black-market, lawless. LEGAL

illegible unreadable, undecipherable, indecipherable, hieroglyphic, crabbed, scrawly, scribbly.

illegitimate natural, bastard, fatherless, baseborn. LEGITIMATE

illegal, unlawful, illicit, unauthorized, forbidden. LAWFUL

ill-fated ill-starred, star-crossed, doomed, unfortunate, unlucky, luckless, hapless. LUCKY

illiberal narrow-minded, intolerant, bigoted, prejudiced, hidebound, reactionary. BROAD-MINDED

miserly, mean, stingy, parsimonious, close-fisted, tight-fisted, niggardly, ungenerous. LIBERAL

illicit illegal, unlawful, illegitimate, criminal, unauthorized, unlicensed, unofficial, unconstitutional, prohibited, banned, contraband, black-market, improper, wrong, immoral. LAWFUL

illimitable limitless, unlimited, boundless, unbounded, infinite, endless, unending, eternal, vast, immense, immeasurable. LIMITED

illiterate ignorant, uneducated, untaught, unlearned, unlettered, uncultured, benighted. LITERATE

ill-mannered bad-mannered, unmannerly, ill-bred, rude, impolite, discourteous, uncivil, uncouth, churlish, boorish. POLITE

illness ailment, sickness, disease, disorder, malady, complaint, indisposition, affliction. FITNESS

illogical unreasonable, irrational, unsound, invalid, sophistic, faulty, fallacious, inconsistent, absurd, senseless. LOGICAL

ill-treat maltreat, abuse, misuse, ill-use, mishandle, harm, injure, batter, persecute.

illuminate light, light up, brighten. DARKEN
clarify, elucidate, explain, shed light on, enlighten, inform. MYSTIFY
adorn, decorate, ornament, embellish, illustrate.

illusion delusion, hallucination, mirage, vision, dream, fantasy, phantasm, chimera, mockery, deception, error, fallacy, misconception, misapprehension, notion, fancy. REALITY

illusory illusive, imaginary, unreal, fanciful, chimerical, deceptive, misleading, delusive, false, fallacious. REAL

illustrate exemplify, instance, clarify, explain, illuminate, demonstrate, show. OBSCURE
adorn, decorate, embellish, ornament, draw, sketch, depict.

illustration example, instance, case, sample, specimen, analogy, explanation, clarification, elucidation, demonstration.
picture, plate, figure, drawing, photograph, diagram.

illustrative typical, representative, exemplary, explanatory, descriptive, graphic, pictorial, diagrammatic.

illustrious famous, renowned, famed, celebrated, distinguished, noted, eminent, notable, great, brilliant, glorious, splendid. INFAMOUS

ill will hostility, enmity, antagonism, animosity, hate, hatred, dislike, spite, malice, rancour, venom, acrimony, bitterness, bad blood, grudge, resentment, envy. GOODWILL

image likeness, representation, effigy, icon, picture, portrait, statue, figure, reflection.
copy, duplicate, replica, facsimile, reproduction, twin, double, Doppelgänger, dead ringer (*inf*), match, counterpart, conception, concept, idea, impression, perception, vision, notion.

imaginary unreal, fanciful, fancied, illusory, illusive, fictitious, made-up, invented, legendary, mythical, hypothetical, supposed, abstract, ideal, visionary, chimerical, shadowy, unsubstantial. REAL

imagination creativity, inventiveness, imaginativeness, ingenuity, resourcefulness, enterprise, originality, vision, insight, perception.
conception, impression, idea, notion, fancy, unreality, dream, illusion, fantasy, chimera. REALITY

imaginative creative, inventive, ingenious, resourceful, enterprising, clever, original, visionary, dreamy, fanciful. UNIMAGINATIVE

imagine conceive, picture, visualize, envisage, conjure up, invent, dream up, devise, create.
think, believe, fancy, guess, suppose, assume, deduce, infer. KNOW

imbecile *n*, idiot, moron, fool, dolt, dullard, simpleton, halfwit.
adj, imbecilic, idiotic, moronic, feeble-minded, simple, witless, foolish, stupid, asinine, inane, fatuous. CLEVER

imbecility idiocy, feeble-mindedness, incompetence, foolishness, stupidity, asininity, inanity, fatuity. CLEVERNESS

imbibe drink, quaff, swallow, tipple, tope.
absorb, assimilate, take in, acquire, gain.

imbue instil, inspire, infuse, pervade, permeate, impregnate, penetrate, steep, soak, bathe, saturate, dye, stain, colour, tint. PURGE

imitate copy, mimic, ape, impersonate, follow, emulate, repeat, echo, mirror, reflect, mock, burlesque, parody, take off (*inf*), simulate, forge, fake, counterfeit, duplicate, reproduce.

imitation *n*, copy, mimicry, impersonation, impression, emulation, echo, reflection, resemblance, mockery, burlesque, parody, travesty, takeoff (*inf*), simulation, forgery, fake, counterfeit, reproduction, replica. ORIGINAL
adj, simulated, artificial, synthetic, man-made, ersatz, fake, spurious, counterfeit. GENUINE

immaculate spotless, pure, pristine, unsullied, undefiled, unpolluted, stainless, untarnished, perfect, impeccable, faultless, flawless, unblemished, sinless, virtuous, irreproachable, clean, neat, spick-and-span. IMPURE

immanent innate, inborn, congenital, inherent, intrinsic, internal, indwelling, ingrained, natural. EXTRINSIC

immaterial unimportant, insignificant, inconsequential, trivial, trifling, minor, irrelevant. IMPORTANT
incorporeal, spiritual, metaphysical, disembodied, bodiless, ethereal, supernatural, intangible, unsubstantial. PHYSICAL

immature undeveloped, unripe, green, young, premature, untimely, imperfect, unfinished, incomplete, unformed, rudimentary.
inexperienced, raw, callow, unsophisticated, jejune, youthful, puerile, childish, infantile. MATURE

immaturity unripeness, greenness, imperfection, incompleteness, crudity, rawness, youth, childishness, puerility, inexperience. MATURITY

immeasurable illimitable, limitless, unlimited, boundless, unbounded, infinite, endless, unfathomable, incalculable, vast, immense. LIMITED

immediate instant, instantaneous, prompt, direct, next, nearest, closest, near, close, adjacent, contiguous, proximate. DISTANT
present, current, latest, actual, existing. FUTURE

immediately instantly, at once, now, without delay, right away, straightaway, forthwith, promptly, directly. LATER

immemorial ancient, age-old, olden, archaic, of yore, fixed, permanent, traditional, time-honoured. MODERN

immense huge, enormous, colossal, gigantic, elephantine, massive, mammoth, great, tremendous, prodigious, stupendous, vast, extensive, immeasurable, boundless, unbounded, illimitable, limitless, unlimited. SMALL

immerse dip, plunge, duck, dunk, submerge, sink, douse, souse, bathe, baptize.
involve, engross, absorb, engage, occupy.

imminent impending, forthcoming, coming, approaching, at hand, near, close, menacing, threatening, looming, in the offing. PAST

immobile motionless, stationary, still, unmoving, static, immovable, fixed, rooted, stiff, rigid, stable. MOBILE

immoderate extreme, excessive, inordinate, unreasonable, unwarranted, undue, uncalled-for, exorbitant, intemperate, extravagant, unrestrained, unbridled, wanton. MODERATE

immodest indecent, indecorous, improper, impure, unchaste, obscene, rude, coarse, gross, lewd, bawdy. DECOROUS
bold, brazen, shameless, forward, impudent. BASHFUL

immoral corrupt, depraved, degenerate, dissolute, profligate, licentious, lewd, obscene, indecent, impure, sinful, wicked, bad, wrong, unprincipled, unscrupulous, unethical. VIRTUOUS

immorality corruption, depravity, degeneracy, profligacy, licentiousness, obscenity, indecency, sin, wickedness, vice, wrong, unscrupulousness. VIRTUE

immortal deathless, undying, imperishable, indestructible, eternal, everlasting, unfading, perennial, endless, ceaseless, lasting, enduring, abiding, perpetual, constant, permanent. PERISHABLE

immortality deathlessness, indestructibility, eternity, everlasting life, endlessness, ceaselessness, perpetuity, constancy, permanence. DEATH
fame, renown, celebrity, glory, greatness.

immovable fixed, riveted, fast, secure, firm, stiff, rigid, stable, immobile, stationary, unalterable, unchangeable, unchanging, steadfast, staunch, inflexible, unyielding, unshakable, impassive. FLEXIBLE

immune safe, protected, resistant, insusceptible, invulnerable, unaffected, exempt, free, not liable. SUSCEPTIBLE

immunity protection, resistance, exemption, exoneration, freedom, release, liberty, charter, privilege, right. LIABILITY

immunize inoculate, vaccinate, protect.

immure imprison, incarcerate, confine, enclose, shut in, cage.

immutable constant, invariable, unalterable, unchangeable, unchanging, changeless, fixed, constant, permanent, stable, enduring, abiding, ageless, perpetual. CHANGEABLE

imp sprite, demon, devil, scamp, rascal, urchin, brat. CHERUB

impact collision, crash, bump, knock, bang, blow, shock, force, contact.
impression, effect, influence, bearing, repercussions, consequences.

impair damage, injure, harm, mar, spoil, weaken, lessen, reduce, enfeeble, enervate, vitiate, diminish, deteriorate. IMPROVE

impale pierce, transfix, stick, spear, spit, run through.

impalpable imperceptible, intangible, insubstantial, tenuous, shadowy, indistinct, airy. PALPABLE

impart communicate, tell, relate, transmit, pass on, disclose, reveal, divulge, make known. SUPPRESS
bestow, confer, give, grant, assign, contribute. WITHHOLD

impartial unbiased, unprejudiced, disinterested, objective, detached, dispassionate, neutral, just, fair, equitable. BIASED

impassable impenetrable, impervious, impermeable, pathless, unnavigable, blocked, closed. PENETRABLE

impassioned passionate, fervent, fervid, ardent, warm, vehement, zealous, excited, animated, eager, glowing, fiery, forceful, intense. COOL

impassive impassible, emotionless, unemotional, unmoved, unfeeling, cool, aloof, reserved, inscrutable, imperturbable, unruffled, composed, serene, indifferent, dispassionate, passionless, apathetic. SUSCEPTIBLE

impatient restless, fretful, jumpy, nervous, anxious, uneasy, excitable, eager, agog, impetuous, reckless, hasty, precipitate, headlong, vehement, violent. PATIENT
irritable, testy, edgy, irascible, waspish, short-tempered, brusque, curt, abrupt, intolerant.

impeach indict, accuse, araign, charge, incriminate, denounce, censure, blame. VINDICATE
challenge, question, impugn, discredit, disparage, malign.

impeccable faultless, flawless, perfect, immaculate, spotless, unblemished, pure, irreproachable, exemplary, innocent. IMPERFECT

impede obstruct, hinder, block, clog, encumber, hamper, hold up, delay, retard, thwart, prevent, restrain, check, curb, stop. ASSIST

impediment obstruction, hindrance, block, obstacle, bar, barrier, encumbrance, defect, snag, difficulty, stumbling block. AID

impel urge, press, drive, force, compel, constrain, oblige, spur, goad, incite, stimulate, motivate, move, push, inspire, influence, induce, persuade. DETER

impend approach, be imminent, come, hover, gather, loom, threaten, menace. PASS

impenetrable thick, dense, impervious, impermeable, solid, sealed, hermetic, impassable, pathless. PENETRABLE
incomprehensible, unintelligible, unfathomable, dark, obscure, abstruse, recondite, inscrutable, enigmatic. INTELLIGIBLE

impenitent unrepentant, uncontrite, unabashed, hardened, obdurate, incorrigible, unreformed. PENITENT

imperative urgent, pressing, exigent, essential, vital, crucial, necessary, compulsory, obligatory, binding. UNIMPORTANT
authoritative, dictatorial, peremptory, imperious, lordly, magisterial, commanding.

imperceptible indiscernible, impalpable, inaudible, invisible, microscopic, tiny, minute, slight, gradual, fine, subtle, faint, shadowy. NOTICEABLE

imperfect faulty, defective, flawed, impaired, damaged, broken, incomplete, unfinished, partial, undeveloped, rudimentary, inexact, crude, deficient. PERFECT

imperfection fault, defect, flaw, blemish, stain, scratch, tear, crack.
frailty, infirmity, weakness, foible, failing, shortcoming, inadequacy, deficiency.

imperial regal, royal, majestic, sovereign, supreme, grand, imposing, stately, august, imperious, lordly, magisterial, lofty, noble, great, magnificent. LOWLY

imperil endanger, jeopardize, risk, hazard, expose. PROTECT

imperious despotic, tyrannical, dictatorial, autocratic, authoritative, domineering, overbearing, lordly, magisterial, commanding, high-handed, arrogant, haughty. HUMBLE

imperishable undying, unfading, indestructible, incorruptible, perennial, lasting, enduring, abiding, eternal, everlasting, immortal. PERISHABLE

impersonal objective, dispassionate, detached, remote, cold, stiff, formal, businesslike. PERSONAL

impersonate mimic, ape, imitate, copy, mock, parody, burlesque, take off (*inf*).

impertinence impudence, insolence, rudeness, effrontery, pertness, sauce (*inf*), cheek (*inf*), nerve (*inf*), gall (*inf*), boldness, audacity, forwardness, assurance. POLITENESS
irrelevance, inapplicability, inappropriateness, inappositeness. PERTINENCE

impertinent impudent, insolent, rude, impolite, disrespectful, pert, saucy, cheeky, bold, audacious, forward, presumptuous. POLITE
irrelevant, inapplicable, inappropriate, inapposite. PERTINENT

imperturbable composed, collected, self-possessed, calm, serene, placid, tranquil, cool, unruffled, unmoved, impassive, sedate. AGITATED

impervious impermeable, impenetrable, impassable, sealed, hermetic, resistant, proof, tight. PERMEABLE
invulnerable, unreceptive, immune, insensitive, thick-skinned, unaffected. RECEPTIVE

impetuous hasty, precipitate, headlong, rash, reckless, impulsive, spontaneous, thoughtless, heedless, spur-of-the-moment, passionate, eager, vehement, violent, fierce, furious. CAUTIOUS

impetus force, energy, momentum, push, spur, goad, stimulus, incentive, motivation, impulse.

impiety ungodliness, godlessness, unholiness, irreligion, profanity, blasphemy, sacrilege, irreverence, disrespect, sin, iniquity, wickedness, vice. PIETY

impinge encroach, infringe, trespass, intrude, invade.
strike, hit, dash, clash, collide.

impious ungodly, godless, unholy, irreligious, profane, blasphemous, sacrilegious, irreverent, disrespectful, sinful, iniquitous, wicked, unrighteous. PIOUS

impish mischievous, elfin, elfish, arch, roguish, puckish, devilish.

implacable unbending, inflexible, unyielding, unappeasable, intractable, firm, adamant, inexorable, relentless, unrelenting, pitiless, merciless, harsh, cruel. MERCIFUL

implant inculcate, instil, infix, infuse, imbue.
plant, embed, root, insert, graft, sow. ERADICATE

implement *n*, tool, utensil, appliance, instrument, device, contrivance, gadget.
v, execute, carry out, perform, effect, fulfil, realize.

implicate incriminate, inculpate, involve, embroil, entangle, associate, concern, affect, imply.

implication suggestion, insinuation, innuendo, inference, meaning, signification, connotation.
incrimination, inculpation, involvement, association.

implicit implied, tacit, understood, inferred, unspoken, unexpressed. EXPLICIT
absolute, unreserved, unconditional, unqualified, complete, total, utter, unquestioning, unhesitating. RESERVED

implore beg, beseech, entreat, supplicate, petition, solicit, conjure, plead, pray, crave, ask. DEMAND

imply suggest, insinuate, intimate, hint, infer, connote, signify, mean, betoken, indicate, import, involve, entail. DECLARE

impolite rude, uncivil, discourteous, impudent, impertinent, insolent, bad-mannered, unmannerly, unladylike, ungentlemanly, churlish, boorish. POLITE

impolitic unwise, injudicious, unsagacious, imprudent, indiscreet, inexpedient, ill-advised, misguided. WISE

import *v*, introduce, bring in. EXPORT
mean, signify, denote, betoken, connote, imply.
n, significance, importance, consequence, moment, weight. INSIGNIFICANCE
meaning, signification, purport, sense, gist, intention, implication, connotation.

importance significance, import, consequence, moment, weight, concern, value, worth. UNIMPORTANCE
status, standing, prestige, esteem, regard, eminence, distinction, influence, power.

important significant, consequential, momentous, weighty, material, critical, crucial, urgent, serious, grave, primary, essential, valuable, considerable. UNIMPORTANT
influential, powerful, prominent, eminent, prestigious, distinguished, esteemed, leading, notable.

importunate persistent, dogged, insistent, demanding, exigent, pressing, urgent, clamorous, solicitous, troublesome, annoying.

importune harass, badger, pester, plague, beset, dun, press, urge, beseech, entreat, beg, solicit.

impose inflict, lay, place, set, put, establish, levy, exact, charge, prescribe, dictate, enforce, require, enjoin. LIFT
encroach, trespass, intrude, obtrude, inconvenience, bother, put out, abuse, exploit, take advantage.

imposing impressive, grand, majestic, stately, august, dignified, commanding, striking, effective. INSIGNIFICANT

imposition burden, charge, task, duty, tax, levy.
infliction, enforcement, prescription, injunction.
encroachment, intrusion, liberty, presumption.
imposture, trick, fraud, deception, hoax.

impossible impracticable, unfeasible, unworkable, unattainable, unobtainable, unachievable, unthinkable, inconceivable, absurd, ludicrous, outrageous, preposterous, illogical, unreasonable, inadmissible, unacceptable, out of the question. POSSIBLE

impost tax, levy, toll, duty, customs, excise, rates. REVENUE

impostor fraud, charlatan, quack, cheat, humbug, trickster, rogue, fake, pretender, dissembler, hypocrite, deceiver, con man (*inf*).

imposture deception, fraud, pretence, humbug, imposition, artifice, trick, hoax, wile, ruse, cheat, swindle. HONESTY

impotent powerless, weak, feeble, frail, helpless, infirm, disabled, incapacitated, incapable, unable, ineffective, inefficient, incompetent, inept, inadequate. POWERFUL

impound imprison, confine, cage, pen. FREE
seize, confiscate, appropriate, expropriate, distrain.

impoverish beggar, ruin, bankrupt, pauperize.
exhaust, deplete, drain, sap, use up. ENRICH

impoverished penniless, penurious, impecunious, indigent, destitute, poverty-stricken, poor, needy, ruined, bankrupt, broke (*inf*), hard up (*inf*). WEALTHY
barren, sterile, empty, exhausted, depleted, spent. RICH

impracticable impossible, unfeasible, unworkable, unattainable, unachievable, out of the question. POSSIBLE
unsuitable, inconvenient, impractical, useless, unserviceable. SERVICEABLE

impractical unrealistic, idealistic, visionary, wild, impracticable, impossible, unworkable, unserviceable, inapplicable. PRACTICAL

imprecate curse, swear, anathematize, execrate, denounce, damn, blaspheme. BLESS

imprecation curse, malediction, anathema, execration, denunciation, slander, blasphemy, profanity. BLESSING

impregnable invincible, unassailable, invulnerable, indestructible, impenetrable, inviolable, strong, secure, unshakable, irrefutable. WEAK

impregnate saturate, soak, steep, fill, suffuse, infuse, imbue, permeate, pervade, penetrate.
fertilize, fecundate, inseminate, make pregnant.

impress influence, sway, move, affect, touch, stir, strike.
imprint, stamp, mark, print, engrave, emboss, indent.
stress, emphasize, instil, inculcate, fix.

impression effect, influence, impact, mark, stamp, imprint, indentation, brand, impress.
feeling, sensation, sense, idea, notion, fancy, belief, concept, awareness, perception, recollection, remembrance.
edition, printing, issue.
impersonation, imitation, parody, take off (*inf*).

impressionable susceptible, receptive, open, suggestible, gullible, sensitive, vulnerable.

impressive imposing, striking, commanding, awe-inspiring, moving, stirring, powerful. UNIMPRESSIVE

imprint *n*, mark, impression, print, stamp, indentation.
v, impress, stamp, print, engrave, etch.

imprison jail, incarcerate, confine, intern, immure, detain, lock up, put away. RELEASE

imprisonment incarceration, confinement, internment, durance, duress, detention, custody. FREEDOM

improbable unlikely, doubtful, dubious, questionable, implausible, far-fetched, incredible, unbelievable, uncertain. LIKELY

improbity dishonesty, fraud, falseness, crookedness (*inf*), wickedness, villainy, knavery, unscrupulousness. PROBITY

impromptu extempore, extemporary, improvised, unrehearsed, unprepared, spontaneous, unpremeditated, off the cuff, ad lib, offhand. PREPARED

improper unseemly, indecorous, unbecoming, impolite, indecent, risqué, obscene, offensive, indelicate. PROPER
unsuitable, inappropriate, unfit, inapt, uncalled-for, unwarranted, unseasonable, untimely, inapplicable, impractical. APPROPRIATE
irregular, abnormal, wrong, incorrect, erroneous, false. CORRECT

improve better, ameliorate, amend, mend, reform, correct, rectify, put right, restore, touch up, polish, enhance. IMPAIR
develop, increase, rise, augment, advance, further, rally, pick up, recover, recuperate. WORSEN

improvement amelioration, amendment, correction, rectification, restoration, enhancement, development, increase, rise, advancement, progress, betterment, change, alteration, addition, rally, recovery. DETERIORATION

improvident thriftless, unthrifty, extravagant, lavish, prodigal, wasteful, spendthrift, imprudent, incautious, careless, heedless, reckless, rash. PROVIDENT

improvise ad-lib, extemporize, play by ear (*inf*), invent, devise, contrive, throw together.

imprudent unwise, injudicious, incautious, rash, hasty, heedless, careless, thoughtless, indiscreet, impolitic, ill-advised, foolish. PRUDENT

impudence impertinence, insolence, rudeness, disrespect, effrontery, audacity, boldness, shamelessness, assurance, presumption, cheek (*inf*), sauce (*inf*), lip (*inf*), face (*inf*). POLITENESS

impudent impertinent, insolent, rude, disrespectful, impolite, audacious, bold, shameless, forward, presumptuous, pert, fresh (*inf*), cheeky, saucy. POLITE

impugn dispute, challenge, question, oppose, gainsay, contradict, deny, criticize, attack, assail. SUPPORT

impulse impetus, thrust, boost, surge, force, momentum, push, spur, stimulus, incitement, motive.
urge, desire, yen (*inf*), drive, whim, caprice, notion, feeling, instinct, passion, inclination.

impulsive impetuous, rash, hasty, precipitate, heedless, passionate, emotional, spontaneous, unplanned, unpremeditated, instinctive, natural. DELIBERATE

impure contaminated, polluted, adulterated, mixed, unrefined, sullied, tainted, defiled, soiled, unclean, dirty, foul. PURE
unchaste, depraved, corrupt, immoral, indecent, obscene, lewd, licentious, coarse, gross. CHASTE

imputation ascription, attribution, accusation, charge, blame, censure, reproach, defamation, aspersion, slander, calumny.

impute ascribe, attribute, accredit, assign, charge, blame, put down.

in *prep*, within, inside, among, during, while, into.
adj, fashionable, modish, stylish, chic, all the rage (*inf*). OUT

inability incapacity, incapability, impotence, powerlessness, incompetence, ineptitude, disability. ABILITY

inaccurate inexact, imprecise, incorrect, wrong, erroneous, mistaken, faulty, unsound. ACCURATE

inactive inert, immobile, still, idle, dormant, quiescent, inoperative, unoccupied, unemployed, in abeyance. ACTIVE
indolent, slothful, lazy, lethargic, sluggish, torpid, slow, dull, passive. BUSY

inadequate insufficient, deficient, lacking, scanty, meagre, skimpy, sparse, short, incomplete, imperfect, defective, faulty, unsatisfactory. ADEQUATE
incompetent, incapable, inapt, inept, unfit, unequal, unqualified. COMPETENT

inadvertence oversight, blunder, error, mistake, slip, omission, negligence, neglect, heedlessness, inattention, carelessness, thoughtlessness. ATTENTION

inadvertent careless, thoughtless, unthinking, heedless, inattentive, unmindful, negligent. CAREFUL
chance, accidental, unintentional, unpremeditated, involuntary, unwitting. DELIBERATE

inane fatuous, foolish, silly, senseless, stupid, idiotic, asinine, absurd, unintelligent, puerile, frivolous, empty, vacuous, vain, worthless. SENSIBLE

inanimate lifeless, dead, inorganic, mineral. LIVING

inert, inactive, immobile, dormant, quiescent, sluggish, dull, vapid, soulless, spiritless. ACTIVE

inapplicable irrelevant, inapposite, impertinent, unsuitable, inappropriate, inapt, unfit. APPLICABLE

inapposite inappropriate, unsuitable, unfit, inapt, inapplicable, irrelevant, impertinent. APPOSITE

inappreciable imperceptible, microscopic, infinitesimal, minuscule, minute, slight, insignificant, negligible. APPRECIABLE

inappropriate unsuitable, unfit, ill-suited, unfitting, inapt, inapposite, incongruous, out of place, unseemly, unbecoming, improper, inapplicable, untimely, infelicitous, irrelevant. APPROPRIATE

inapt inappropriate, unsuitable, unfit, inapposite, infelicitous. SUITABLE

inept, incompetent, incapable, maladroit, clumsy, awkward, dull, slow. CLEVER

inattention inattentiveness, absent-mindedness, daydreaming, woolgathering, forgetfulness, oversight, inadvertence, negligence, neglect, carelessness, thoughtlessness, heedlessness, disregard, unconcern, indifference. CARE

inaudible imperceptible, silent, noiseless, quiet, muted, low, faint, indistinct, muffled, stifled. AUDIBLE

inaugurate commence, begin, start, initiate, institute, originate, launch, open, introduce. TERMINATE

induct, invest, install, ordain.

inauguration commencement, beginning, start, initiation, institution, origination, launch, opening, introduction. TERMINATION

induction, investiture, installation, ordination.

inauspicious unpromising, discouraging, unpropitious, ominous, black, dark, ill-omened, unfavourable, unlucky, unfortunate, untoward. AUSPICIOUS

inborn innate, congenital, inbred, inherent, natural, instinctive, inherited, hereditary. ACQUIRED

incalculable countless, innumerable, numberless, untold, inestimable, immeasurable, unfathomable, vast, immense, boundless, infinite.

incandescent glowing, phosphorescent, luminous, radiant, bright, brilliant, shining. DULL

incantation spell, charm, chant, invocation, conjuration, magic, sorcery, witchcraft.

incapable unable, powerless, impotent, helpless, weak, feeble, inadequate, unequal, incompetent, inept, unfit, unqualified. CAPABLE

incapacitate disable, cripple, immobilize, paralyse, debilitate, enervate, weaken, enfeeble, disenable, disqualify, scupper (*inf*). ENABLE

incarcerate imprison, jail, immure, cage, confine, intern, impound, lock up, put away. RELEASE

incarnation embodiment, archetype, personification, manifestation, avatar.

incautious imprudent, unwise, injudicious, impolitic, unwary, careless, thoughtless, unthinking, heedless, hasty, headlong, precipitate, rash, reckless, negligent, improvident, indiscreet. CAUTIOUS

incendiary *adj*, inflammatory, seditious, subversive, provocative, rabble-rousing.

combustible, flammable.

n, arsonist, pyromaniac, fire raiser.

agitator, rabble-rouser, firebrand, insurgent, rebel, revolutionary, troublemaker.

incense[1] *v*, enrage, infuriate, madden, anger, provoke, rouse, inflame, irk, irritate, annoy, exasperate. PACIFY

incense[2] *n*, perfume, fragrance, balm, scent, aroma.

incentive inducement, enticement, bait, lure, incitement, stimulus, spur, impulse, motivation, persuasion, encouragement, motive, cause. DETERRENT

inception beginning, start, commencement, inauguration, initiation, outset, birth, dawn. END

incessant unceasing, ceaseless, continual, continuous, unremitting, uninterrupted, perpetual, constant, persistent, relentless, eternal, everlasting, unending, endless, interminable. INTERMITTENT

inchoate incipient, inceptive, beginning, commencing, initial, elementary, rudimentary, embryonic, undeveloped, immature. FINISHED

incident occurrence, event, happening, occasion, circumstance, episode, scene, affair, matter.
disturbance, commotion, encounter, confrontation, clash, skirmish.

incidental chance, accidental, casual, fortuitous, random.
minor, unimportant, subsidiary, secondary, nonessential, occasional. ESSENTIAL
concomitant, related, attendant, accompanying, contingent.

incipient inchoate, inceptive, beginning, commencing, starting, initial, nascent, rudimentary, embryonic. COMPLETE

incision cut, gash, slit, slash, notch.

incisive sharp, keen, acute, piercing, penetrating, cutting, trenchant, mordant, biting, acid, caustic, sarcastic, satirical, sardonic. MILD

incite rouse, stir up, stimulate, animate, provoke, foment, prompt, goad, spur, urge, encourage, impel, excite, inflame. DETER

incitement stimulation, provocation, fomentation, agitation, encouragement, spur, goad, impulse, stimulus, motivation, incentive, inducement.

incivility impoliteness, rudeness, discourtesy, discourteousness, disrespect, unmannerliness, ill-breeding. CIVILITY

inclement stormy, tempestuous, windy, rainy, foul, bad, rough, intemperate, harsh, severe. MILD
cruel, unmerciful, merciless, pitiless, hardhearted, unfeeling, harsh, severe, rigorous, tyrannical. KIND

inclination tendency, leaning, bent, proclivity, propensity, disposition, predisposition, penchant, partiality, predilection, bias, preference, liking, fondness, taste, desire, wish. AVERSION
slope, slant, incline, gradient, angle, pitch.
bend, bow, nod.

incline *v*, slope, slant, lean, tilt, cant, bend, bow, lower.
tend, be disposed, predispose, sway, influence, bias, prejudice.
n, inclination, slope, slant, gradient, acclivity, declivity.

inclined disposed, prone, apt, likely, liable, given, willing. UNLIKELY

include contain, comprise, embrace, encompass, embody, incorporate, cover, involve. EXCLUDE
count, number, add, insert, subsume, group, categorize. OMIT

incognito disguised, in disguise, concealed, unrecognized, undercover, in secret.

incoherent disjointed, unconnected, rambling, discursive, confused, disordered, muddled, wild, loose, inconsistent, illogical, unintelligible, inarticulate. COHERENT

income revenue, receipts, takings, proceeds, yield, return, gains, profits, earnings, pay, wages, salary. EXPENDITURE

incommensurate unequal, disproportionate, insufficient, inadequate. COMMENSURATE

incommode inconvenience, bother, disturb, trouble, put out, hinder, upset, annoy. ASSIST

incommodious inconvenient, awkward, cramped, restricted, confined, narrow. COMMODIOUS

incomparable matchless, peerless, unequalled, unrivalled, unparalleled, transcendent, supreme, beyond compare, unique, inimitable. ORDINARY

incompatible conflicting, discordant, contrary, antagonistic, antipathetic, irreconcilable, unsuited, mismatched, incongruous, inconsistent, contradictory. COMPATIBLE

incompetent incapable, unfit, unable, inadequate, inefficient, unequal, useless, inept, bungling, inexpert, unskilful. COMPETENT

incomplete unfinished, imperfect, partial, deficient, lacking, wanting, short, abridged, undeveloped. COMPLETE

incomprehensible unintelligible, incoherent, unfathomable, impenetrable, obscure, enigmatic, mysterious, inexplicable, puzzling, inconceivable, unthinkable. PLAIN

inconceivable unthinkable, unimaginable, incomprehensible, impossible, incredible, unbelievable, unheard-of, preposterous, absurd. POSSIBLE

inconclusive indecisive, undecided, unsettled, uncertain, open, indeterminate, unconvincing. CONCLUSIVE

incongruous incompatible, inappropriate, inapt, unsuitable, improper, discrepant, discordant, conflicting, contradictory, inconsistent, out of place, absurd. CONGRUOUS

inconsequential insignificant, unimportant, negligible, paltry, trifling, trivial, petty, minor. IMPORTANT
inconsequent, disconnected, inconsistent, incongruous, illogical, irrelevant, immaterial.

inconsiderable small, slight, minor, inconsequential, negligible, insignificant, unimportant, immaterial, trivial, trifling, petty. CONSIDERABLE

inconsiderate thoughtless, unkind, uncharitable, unthinking, heedless, tactless, insensitive, rude, selfish. CONSIDERATE

inconsistent contradictory, conflicting, irreconcilable, incompatible, incongruous, discrepant, discordant, at odds, out of keeping. CONSISTENT
inconstant, irregular, changeable, variable, unsteady, unstable, erratic, fickle, capricious. CONSTANT

inconsolable disconsolate, comfortless, forlorn, desolate, heartbroken, brokenhearted, despairing, hopeless. CHEERFUL

inconstant variable, changeable, mutable, vacillating, wavering, uncertain, unsteady, unstable, unsettled, inconsistent, erratic, mercurial, volatile, fickle, capricious, unreliable. STEADY

incontestable indisputable, incontrovertible, unquestionable, indubitable, undeniable, irrefutable, unassailable, certain, sure. DUBIOUS

incontinent unrestrained, uncontrolled, unchecked, unbridled, ungovernable, uncontrollable. CONTROLLED
dissolute, debauched, licentious, lascivious, lecherous, lewd, lustful, wanton, profligate, promiscuous, unchaste, impure. CHASTE

incontrovertible indisputable, incontestable, undeniable, irrefutable, unquestionable, indubitable, certain, sure, positive. DUBIOUS

inconvenience *n*, trouble, bother, nuisance, annoyance, vexation, disturbance, disruption, difficulty, drawback, disadvantage, hindrance. HELP
awkwardness, unwieldiness, cumbersomeness, untimeliness, inopportuneness. CONVENIENCE
v, trouble, bother, put out, upset, disturb, disrupt, hinder. ASSIST

inconvenient awkward, troublesome, bothersome, annoying, inopportune, untimely, unseasonable, inappropriate, unsuitable, disadvantageous, difficult. CONVENIENT
unwieldy, cumbersome, awkward, incommodious.

incorporate include, comprise, embody, integrate, merge, blend, amalgamate, combine, unite, consolidate, assimilate. SEVER

incorporeal disembodied, bodiless, immaterial, insubstantial, metaphysical, spiritual. MATERIAL

incorrect wrong, erroneous, false, untrue, inexact, inaccurate, mistaken, faulty, unsound, flawed, fallacious. CORRECT
improper, unbecoming, unseemly, inappropriate, unsuitable. PROPER

incorrigible hardened, inveterate, incurable, irremediable, irredeemable, lost, hopeless, obdurate, intractable. REFORMABLE

incorruptible honest, upright, honourable, just, high-minded, unbribable, above suspicion. DISHONEST
imperishable, immortal, deathless, undying, everlasting, eternal, abiding, lasting, indestructible. PERISHABLE

increase *v*, enlarge, expand, swell, grow, spread, extend, prolong, lengthen, accrue, augment, add to, raise, rise, mount, escalate, intensify, heighten, enhance, amplify, boost, magnify, multiply, proliferate. DECREASE
n, enlargement, expansion, growth, extension, augmentation, addition, increment, rise, escalation, intensification, boost, upsurge. REDUCTION

incredible unbelievable, beyond belief, inconceivable, unthinkable, preposterous, absurd, improbable, unlikely, impossible. CREDIBLE
marvellous, wonderful, astonishing, amazing, fantastic, fabulous, great, tremendous, prodigious.

incredulity disbelief, unbelief, scepticism, distrust, mistrust, doubt, incredulousness. BELIEF

incredulous disbelieving, unbelieving, sceptical, distrustful, mistrustful, doubtful, dubious, suspicious. CREDULOUS

increment increase, addition, augmentation, rise, growth, enlargement, gain, accrual. DECREASE

incriminate accuse, charge, indict, arraign, impeach, blame, implicate, involve, inculpate. VINDICATE

inculcate instil, infuse, ingrain, implant, impress, drum, drill, indoctrinate.

inculpable innocent, guiltless, blameless, irreproachable, unimpeachable, above suspicion. GUILTY

inculpate incriminate, accuse, charge, blame, indict, arraign, impeach, involve, implicate. ACQUIT

incumbent binding, obligatory, necessary, mandatory, compulsory. OPTIONAL
resting, reclining, lying, leaning.

incur bring, draw, earn, gain, contract, meet with, provoke. AVOID

incurable irremediable, hopeless, terminal, inoperable. CURABLE
incorrigible, inveterate, hardened, dyed-in-the-wool.

incursion raid, invasion, attack, foray, sally, inroad, encroachment, infiltration, penetration. RETREAT

indebted obliged, obligated, owing, beholden, grateful, thankful.

indecent obscene, vulgar, coarse, gross, offensive, lewd, salacious, crude, foul, dirty, filthy, impure, unchaste, immodest, indelicate, improper, indecorous, unseemly, tasteless, outrageous, shocking. DECENT

indecipherable undecipherable, illegible, unreadable, unintelligible, crabbed, hieroglyphic. LEGIBLE

indecision indecisiveness, irresolution, hesitation, hesitancy, vacillation, wavering, uncertainly, doubt. RESOLUTION

indecisive irresolute, hesitant, wavering, vacillating, undecided, unresolved, uncertain, in two minds, open, inconclusive, unsettled. DECISIVE

indecorous improper, unseemly, unbecoming, ill-bred, uncouth, rude, vulgar, indecent, immodest. DECOROUS

indeed really, truly, in truth, in fact, certainly, positively, absolutely, actually, strictly, exactly.

indefatigable tireless, untiring, unwearied, unwearying, unflagging, indomitable, diligent, assiduous, sedulous, dogged, persistent, persevering, relentless, unremitting. INDOLENT

indefensible inexcusable, unjustifiable, unwarrantable, insupportable, unpardonable, unforgivable. JUSTIFIABLE
untenable, weak, flawed, unsound, faulty, wrong. TENABLE

indefinite undefined, undetermined, unlimited, indeterminate, indistinct, unclear, vague, loose, general, obscure, confused, unsettled, indecisive, uncertain, unknown, inexact, imprecise, ambiguous, equivocal, evasive. DEFINITE

indelible ineffaceable, ineradicable, indestructible, lasting, permanent, ingrained, fixed. ERASABLE

indelicate indecent, coarse, crude, rude, vulgar, gross, obscene, offensive, tasteless, improper, indecorous, unseemly, unbecoming, immodest.

indemnify secure, guarantee, endorse, underwrite, insure.
compensate, reimburse, repay, pay, remunerate, satisfy, requite.

indemnity insurance, protection, security, guarantee.
compensation, reimbursement, remuneration, reparation, restitution, satisfaction.
exemption, immunity, impunity, privilege.

indentation notch, nick, cut, dent, hollow, dimple, depression.

independence autonomy, freedom, liberty, self-rule, self-government, self-reliance, self-sufficiency. DEPENDENCE

independent autonomous, free, sovereign, self-governing, self-reliant, bold, self-confident, unaided, self-sufficient, self-supporting, separate, unconnected, unrestricted, unrestrained. DEPENDENT

indescribable inexpressible, ineffable, unutterable, beyond words. COMMONPLACE

indestructible durable, unbreakable, imperishable, incorruptible, indelible, permanent, lasting, abiding, enduring, everlasting. PERISHABLE

indeterminate indefinite, vague, undefined, undetermined, unsettled, unfixed, uncertain, unknown, inexact, imprecise, obscure, confused. DEFINITE

index catalogue, list, directory, file.
sign, indication, mark, token, clue, guide, pointer, needle, hand, forefinger.

indicate denote, betoken, show, mark, signify, mean, suggest, imply, evince, mani-

fest, exhibit, display, reveal, express, register, betray. CONCEAL
designate, point out, show.

indication sign, mark, token, symbol, signal, symptom, warning, omen, suggestion, hint, clue, evidence, manifestation.

indict charge, accuse, arraign, impeach, incriminate, inculpate, prosecute, summon. ACQUIT

indictment charge, accusation, allegation, arraignment, impeachment, incrimination, prosecution, summons. ACQUITTAL

indifference apathy, unconcern, lack of interest, disregard, negligence, inattention, coolness, aloofness, detachment, disinterest, neutrality, impartiality, objectivity, dispassion, insensibility, insensitivity. CONCERN
unimportance, insignificance, triviality, irrelevance. IMPORTANCE

indifferent apathetic, unconcerned, uninterested, heedless, regardless, nonchalant, uncaring, cool, aloof, detached, impassive, insensitive, unmoved. CONCERNED
impartial, disinterested, neutral, objective, dispassionate, unbiased, unprejudiced. BIASED
mediocre, fair, passable, average, middling, so-so (*inf*), moderate, ordinary. EXCELLENT
unimportant, insignificant, irrelevant, immaterial, inconsequential. IMPORTANT

indigenous native, aboriginal, autochthonous, home-grown. EXOTIC
inherent, innate, connate, congenital, inborn. ACQUIRED

indigent poor, needy, necessitous, destitute, penniless, impecunious, impoverished, poverty-stricken, penurious. RICH

indignant irate, angry, incensed, wrathful, furious, mad (*inf*), exasperated, annoyed, riled, irked, peeved (*inf*). CALM

indignation anger, ire, wrath, rage, fury, exasperation, annoyance, vexation, pique, umbrage, resentment. COMPOSURE

indignity slight, snub, insult, affront, outrage, abuse, obloquy, aspersion, reproach, disrespect, humiliation. RESPECT

indirect roundabout, circuitous, tortuous, meandering, oblique, circumlocutory, devious, evasive. STRAIGHT
secondary, ancillary, incidental, contingent, collateral. PRIMARY

indiscernible imperceptible, indistinguishable, invisible, slight, subtle, inconsiderable. VISIBLE

indiscreet unwise, injudicious, imprudent, incautious, heedless, rash, reckless, hasty, precipitate, unthinking, inconsiderate, tactless, undiplomatic. CAUTIOUS

indiscretion folly, imprudence, heedlessness, rashness, recklessness, tactlessness. CAUTION
gaffe, faux pas, blunder, slip, error, mistake.

indiscriminate random, haphazard, unsystematic, unmethodical, unselective, promiscuous, broad, wide, wholesale, general, desultory, confused, jumbled, mixed, assorted, miscellaneous, motley.

indispensable essential, vital, necessary, needed, required, requisite, key, crucial, basic, fundamental. NONESSENTIAL

indisposed unwell, ill, sick, ailing, poorly (*inf*), out of sorts (*inf*). WELL
disinclined, unwilling, reluctant, hesitant, loath, averse. EAGER

indisputable undeniable, irrefutable, unquestionable, indubitable, incontrovertible, incontestable, unassailable, certain, sure, positive, absolute. DUBIOUS

indissoluble indestructible, imperishable, incorruptible, indivisible, inseparable, permanent, lasting, abiding, enduring, fixed, binding. PERISHABLE

indistinct dim, faint, hazy, blurred, shadowy, weak, muffled, vague, indefinite, obscure, confused, doubtful, unclear, ambiguous, indistinguishable, imperceptible, indiscernible. DISTINCT

indistinguishable identical, twin, same, alike, like, similar. DIFFERENT
indiscernible, imperceptible, indistinct, indefinite, obscure, invisible. CONSPICUOUS

indite write, pen, compose, formulate, word, draft, frame.

individual *adj*, separate, distinct, particular, peculiar, characteristic, distinctive, singular, personal, own, exclusive, unique, special, single, solitary, sole. GENERAL
n, person, being, creature, mortal, human, personage, soul, body, head, character. GROUP

indocile intractable, ungovernable, uncontrollable, unruly, unmanageable, stubborn, obstinate, headstrong, wilful, perverse, recalcitrant, refractory, contumacious. DOCILE

indoctrinate inculcate, instil, infuse, imbue, brainwash, drill, school, instruct, teach, ground, initiate.

indolent idle, lazy, slothful, sluggish, lethargic, apathetic, listless, slow, inert, inactive. DILIGENT

indomitable invincible, unconquerable, unbeatable, unyielding, irrepressible, indefatigable, staunch, steadfast, unwavering. FEEBLE

indubitable unquestionable, undoubted, indisputable, undeniable, irrefutable, incontrovertible, incontestable, certain, sure. DUBIOUS

induce persuade, influence, move, encourage, urge, prevail upon, convince, impel, incite, prompt, spur, actuate, coax, entice. DETER
cause, bring about, effect, produce, lead to, generate. PREVENT

inducement incentive, motive, incitement, stimulus, impulse, spur, enticement, lure, attraction, bait, influence, encouragement, persuasion. DETERRENT

induct install, invest, inaugurate, initiate, introduce. OUST

indulge gratify, satisfy, yield to, cater to, humour, pander to, pamper, cosset, coddle, pet, spoil. DENY
luxuriate, revel, wallow, regale, treat.

indulgence dissipation, intemperance, self-indulgence, luxury, treat, extravagance, immoderation, excess. TEMPERANCE
gratification, satisfaction, fulfilment, humouring, pampering, spoiling. DENIAL
favour, privilege, kindness, leniency, tolerance, clemency, forbearance. SEVERITY

indulgent lenient, permissive, tolerant, liberal, forbearing, clement, mild, gentle, kind, tender, fond, obliging, compliant. STRICT

indurate harden, toughen, strengthen, temper, inure, accustom, season, habituate. SOFTEN

industrious diligent, assiduous, sedulous, hard-working, busy, active, energetic, laborious, tireless, persistent, persevering, conscientious. LAZY

industry manufacture, production, trade, commerce, business.
diligence, assiduity, sedulity, work, toil, labour, effort, activity, persistence, perseverance, application. IDLENESS

inebriated drunk, intoxicated, inebriate, tight (*inf*), plastered (*inf*), well-oiled (*inf*), blotto (*inf*). SOBER

inebriation inebriety, drunkenness, intoxication, insobriety, intemperance, crapulence, alcoholism, dipsomania. SOBRIETY

ineffable unutterable, unspeakable, inexpressible, indescribable, indefinable, beyond words. COMMONPLACE

ineffectual ineffective, inefficacious, unavailing, useless, futile, bootless, fruitless, unproductive, vain, idle, abortive, impotent, powerless, weak, effete, feeble, inefficient, incompetent, inadequate. EFFECTUAL

inefficacious ineffectual, ineffective, unavailing, useless, futile, bootless, fruitless, unproductive, barren, abortive, unsuccessful. EFFICACIOUS

inefficient incompetent, inept, incapable, ineffectual, weak, wasteful, careless. EFFICIENT

inelegant unrefined, unpolished, coarse, crude, rough, rude, uncouth, uncourtly, ungainly, clumsy, awkward, graceless. ELEGANT

ineligible unqualified, disqualified, unsuitable, unacceptable, undesirable, objectionable. ELIGIBLE

inept incompetent, inefficient, ineffectual, unskilful, inexpert, clumsy, awkward, bungling. COMPETENT
inapt, inappropriate, unsuitable, unseemly, unfit, improper, out of place, absurd, foolish, nonsensical, pointless, meaningless. APT

inequality disparity, imbalance, disproportion, unevenness, irregularity, difference, diversity, unfairness, injustice, inequity, prejudice, bias, discrimination. EQUALITY

inequitable unfair, unjust, biased, prejudiced, partial, partisan, discriminatory. EQUITABLE

inert immobile, static, motionless, still, inactive, inanimate, idle, indolent, lazy, slothful, sluggish, lethargic, torpid, slow, dull. ACTIVE

inertia immobility, stillness, inactivity, idleness, indolence, laziness, sloth, apathy, lethargy, torpor, dullness. ACTIVITY

inestimable invaluable, priceless, precious, incalculable, immeasurable.

inevitable unavoidable, inescapable, ineluctable, certain, sure, destined, ordained. AVOIDABLE

inexact inaccurate, incorrect, wrong, erroneous, imprecise, indefinite, loose. EXACT

inexcusable indefensible, unjustifiable, unwarrantable, unpardonable, unforgivable. EXCUSABLE

inexhaustible unlimited, limitless, boundless, infinite, endless. LIMITED
tireless, unwearying, indefatigable, unflagging, unfailing. INDOLENT

inexorable inflexible, unbending, unyielding, immovable, adamant, cruel, harsh, severe, pitiless, merciless, relentless, unrelenting, implacable, remorseless. INDULGENT

inexpedient imprudent, injudicious, unwise, impolitic, ill-advised, inadvisable, misguided, indiscreet, inappropriate, unsuitable, disadvantageous. JUDICIOUS

inexpensive cheap, reasonable, low-priced, economical, low-cost. EXPENSIVE

inexperienced green, raw, callow, fresh, new, untrained, unschooled, unpractised, unskilled, inexpert, unversed, ignorant, unfamiliar, unaccustomed. EXPERIENCED

inexpiable unpardonable, unforgivable, inexcusable, unjustifiable, irremissible. PARDONABLE

inexplicable unexplainable, unaccountable, insoluble, unfathomable, incomprehensible, enigmatic, mysterious, strange, puzzling, baffling. EXPLICABLE

inexpressible unutterable, ineffable, indescribable, incommunicable, unspeakable, beyond words. COMMONPLACE

inextricable involved, intricate, complicated, entangled, knotty, insoluble. EXTRICABLE

infallible sure, certain, dependable, reliable, foolproof, unfailing, unerring, faultless, perfect. FALLIBLE

infamous notorious, ignominious, disreputable, dishonourable, shameful, disgraceful, shocking, scandalous, outrageous, nefarious, egregious, heinous, vile, base, wicked, monstrous, atrocious, loathsome, detestable, abominable. ILLUSTRIOUS

infamy notoriety, ignominy, shame, disgrace, disrepute, obloquy, opprobrium, discredit, dishonour, scandal, wickedness, villainy, baseness. HONOUR

infant baby, babe, suckling, toddler, tot, child, minor. ADULT

infantile babyish, childish, puerile, immature, young, newborn. MATURE

infatuated enamoured, besotted, smitten (*inf*), crazy about (*inf*), captivated, fascinated, bewitched, beguiled, obsessed, possessed.

infatuation obsession, fixation, passion, crush (*inf*), madness, folly, captivation, beguilement.

infect contaminate, pollute, taint, blight, corrupt, defile, vitiate, poison. STERILIZE

infection contamination, pollution, taint, corruption, defilement, contagion, germ, virus, poison. ASEPSIS

infectious contagious, catching, spreading, communicable, transmittable, infective, virulent, pestilent.

infelicitous unfortunate, unlucky, inauspicious, unfavourable, unhappy, wretched, miserable. FELICITOUS
inapt, inappropriate, unsuitable, unfitting, unfit, incongruous. APPROPRIATE

infer conclude, deduce, derive, gather, presume, surmise, guess.

inference conclusion, deduction, corollary, presumption, assumption, surmise, guess, conjecture.

inferior lower, lesser, subordinate, minor, junior, secondary, subsidiary, insignificant, unimportant, lowly, menial, subservient. SUPERIOR
mediocre, poor, bad, shoddy, second-rate, second-class, indifferent, imperfect, substandard. EXCELLENT

infernal demoniacal, demonic, devilish, diabolical, satanic, fiendish, hellish, damnable, accursed, confounded (*inf*), abominable, execrable. HEAVENLY

infertile sterile, barren, infecund, unfruitful, unproductive. FERTILE

infest overrun, swarm, throng, crawl, pervade, penetrate, invade, beset, plague.

infidelity unfaithfulness, adultery, faithlessness, disloyalty, treachery, perfidy. FAITHFULNESS
disbelief, unbelief, scepticism, irreligion. BELIEF

infiltrate permeate, pervade, percolate, penetrate, insinuate oneself.

infinite limitless, unlimited, boundless, unbounded, endless, eternal, everlasting, interminable, immeasurable, unfathomable, bottomless, inexhaustible, inestimable, incalculable, vast, immense, all-embracing, total, absolute. LIMITED

infinitesimal microscopic, minuscule, minute, tiny, small, little, negligible, insignificant, inappreciable, imperceptible. VAST

infirm weak, feeble, frail, decrepit, debilitated, enfeebled, doddering, shaky, unsteady, unstable, unsound, insecure. STRONG
indecisive, irresolute, faltering, wavering, vacillating. RESOLUTE

infirmity weakness, feebleness, frailty, decrepitude, debility, ill health, disorder, ailment, disability, defect, failing. STRENGTH

infix implant, engraft, fix, fasten, set, place, ingrain, impress, instil, infuse, inculcate. EXTIRPATE

inflame arouse, excite, impassion, fire, kindle, stimulate, animate, incite, provoke, rouse, madden, enrage, incense, infuriate, anger, exasperate. PACIFY
aggravate, exacerbate, fan, increase, intensify. MITIGATE

inflammable flammable, combustible, ignitable, incendiary. NONFLAMMABLE
excitable, temperamental, volatile, fiery. PLACID

inflammation heat, burning, redness, rash, swelling, pain, soreness, tenderness.

inflate expand, swell, blow up, puff up, bloat, dilate, distend, increase, enlarge, amplify. DEFLATE

inflated swollen, bloated, distended, conceited, pompous, bombastic, high-flown, turgid, flatulent, tumid, grandiloquent, magniloquent.

inflect curve, bend, bow, crook, arch. STRAIGHTEN
modulate, intonate, intone, conjugate, decline.

inflection modulation, intonation, accent, stress, conjugation, declension, affix.
angle, bend, curve, arc, arch, flexure, curvature.

inflexible rigid, stiff, hard, firm, unbending, unyielding, stubborn, obstinate, intractable, obdurate, adamant, implacable, immovable, fixed, hard and fast, unchangeable, unalterable, inexorable, resolute, persevering, dogged, steadfast. FLEXIBLE

inflict impose, apply, administer, mete out, deal out, wreak, visit. SPARE

influence *n*, power, sway, hold, control, authority, effect, weight, pressure, guidance, direction, rule, mastery, spell, magnetism.
connections, good offices, prestige, importance, pull (*inf*), clout (*inf*).
v, affect, modify, move, persuade, induce, impress, control, guide, direct, lead, sway, incline, dispose, prompt, impel, incite, instigate.

influential powerful, potent, forceful, forcible, effective, cogent, persuasive, moving, controlling, guiding, authoritative, weighty, important, significant. INSIGNIFICANT

inform tell, apprise, advise, let know, notify, communicate, acquaint, enlighten, instruct.
betray, denounce, grass (*inf*), squeal (*inf*), tell on (*inf*), rat (*inf*).

informal casual, inceremonious, easy, relaxed, natural, simple, unofficial, familiar, colloquial, irregular, unconventional. FORMAL

information knowledge, intelligence, facts, data, gen (*inf*), news, word, message, report, notice, advice, instruction, lowdown (*inf*).

informer betrayer, stool pigeon, grass (*inf*), nark (*inf*), sneak.
informant, adviser, reporter, announcer, source.

infraction violation, breach, infringement, contravention, transgression, trespass. OBSERVANCE

infrequent rare, unusual, uncommon, occasional, sporadic, few, scarce. FREQUENT

infringe violate, break, disobey, contravene, infract, transgress. OBSERVE
encroach, trespass, intrude, impinge.

infringement violation, breach, contravention, infraction, transgression, trespass. OBSERVANCE

infuriate enrage, incense, madden, anger, provoke, exasperate, vex, irritate, rile. PACIFY

infuriated furious, enraged, raging, incensed, fuming, mad (*inf*), wrathful, irate, angry, indignant, exasperated. CALM
infuse instil, inculcate, engraft, implant, infix, ingrain, inspire, introduce, imbue, pervade, permeate, saturate, steep, soak, macerate, brew.
infusion instillation, inculcation, inspiration, introduction, saturation, soaking, maceration, brew.
ingenious clever, skilful, adroit, dexterous, talented, gifted, masterly, inventive, resourceful, creative, original, shrewd, subtle, crafty. STUPID
ingenuity ingeniousness, cleverness, skill, dexterity, talent, flair, inventiveness, resourcefulness, creativity, imagination, shrewdness. STUPIDITY
ingenuous artless, naive, unsophisticated, simple, innocent, guileless, open, sincere, honest, frank, candid, straightforward.
ingenuousness artlessness, naivety, simplicity, innocence, guilelessness, openness, sincerity, honesty, frankness, candour. ARTFULNESS
inglorious disgraceful, shameful, dishonourable, ignominious, infamous, ignoble, despicable, base, low, disreputable, discreditable, humiliating. GLORIOUS
unknown, obscure, unrenowned, humble, lowly. FAMOUS
ingrain instil, impress, implant, engraft, imprint, fix, imbue, infuse, impregnate. ERADICATE
ingrained fixed, rooted, deep-seated, inveterate, built-in, inherent, intrinsic, inbred, innate, fundamental.
ingratiate flatter, blandish, fawn, crawl, grovel, toady, curry favour, suck up to (*inf*).
ingredient constituent, component, part, element. WHOLE
ingress entrance, entry, way in, admission, admittance, access, entrée. EGRESS
inhabit occupy, live, dwell, reside, abide, populate, people, tenant. VACATE
inhabitant native, aborigine, indigene, citizen, denizen, resident, occupant, occupier, dweller, tenant. VISITOR
inhale breathe in, respire, inspire, sniff, gulp, gasp, puff, take in, suck in. EXHALE
inharmonious discordant, cacophonous, unharmonious, unmusical, atonal, clashing, jarring, grating, harsh, strident. HARMONIOUS
inherent intrinsic, built-in, inborn, innate, immanent, ingrained, natural, native, congenital, hereditary, basic, fundamental. EXTRANEOUS
inherit receive, get, acquire, come into, be left, succeed to, accede to, take over. BEQUEATH
inheritance heritage, legacy, bequest, patrimony, birthright.
inhibit restrain, suppress, repress, constrain, curb, hold back, hinder, impede, prevent, stop, arrest, check, discourage, prohibit, forbid, ban, bar. ENCOURAGE
inhibition restraint, repression, constraint, reserve, reticence, hang-up (*inf*), hindrance, impediment, arrest, check, prohibition, ban, embargo.
inhospitable unfriendly, cool, unwelcoming, unsociable, hostile, uncongenial, ungracious, unkind, ungenerous. FRIENDLY
barren, desolate, bleak, uninviting, forbidding, unfavourable, uninhabitable, wild. HOSPITABLE
inhuman inhumane, unkind, cruel, brutal, heartless, unfeeling, hard-hearted, callous, pitiless, merciless, ruthless, implacable, remorseless, savage, barbarous, barbaric, cold-blooded. HUMANE
inhume inter, bury, entomb, sepulchre. EXHUME
inimical hostile, antagonistic, adverse, unfavourable, opposed, contrary, unfriendly, harmful, pernicious, destructive. FAVOURABLE
inimitable unique, peerless, unmatched, matchless, unparalleled, incomparable, consummate, unequalled, unrivalled, unexampled. COMMONPLACE
iniquity sin, vice, wickedness, evil, wrong, crime, offence, misdeed, wrongdoing, sinfulness, unrighteousness, injustice, unfairness, inequity. RIGHTEOUSNESS
initial first, primary, opening, beginning, commencing, early, original, introductory, inaugural, incipient, inceptive, inchoate. FINAL
initiate begin, start, commence, open, originate, inaugurate, institute, found, set up, launch, pioneer. CLOSE
introduce, teach, instruct, coach, train, prime, ground, break in, indoctrinate, in-

culcate, induct, instate, invest, enrol, admit.

initiative lead, first move, beginning, commencement.
enterprise, drive, ambition, dynamism, get-up-and-go (*inf*), resourcefulness, inventiveness. APATHY

inject introduce, insert, vaccinate, inoculate, infuse, interject.

injection introduction, insertion, vaccination, inoculation, jab (*inf*), shot (*inf*), dose.

injudicious imprudent, unwise, ill-judged, ill-advised, impolitic, inexpedient, indiscreet, rash, hasty, foolish. JUDICIOUS

injunction instruction, order, command, mandate, ruling, precept, behest, exhortation, admonition.

injure hurt, wound, damage, harm, impair, abuse, maltreat, mar, spoil, deface, disfigure, disable, weaken, wrong, offend. BENEFIT

injurious hurtful, damaging, harmful, pernicious, deleterious, detrimental, bad, noxious, baneful, mischievous, disadvantageous, unfavourable, adverse, ruinous, destructive, abusive, offensive, slanderous, libellous. BENEFICIAL

injury hurt, wound, harm, damage, impairment, ill, evil, wrong, mischief, detriment, loss, prejudice, injustice, grievance, abuse, offence. REPARATION

injustice unfairness, inequity, inequality, discrimination, prejudice, bias, favouritism, partiality, iniquity, wrong, grievance, injury. JUSTICE

inkling intimation, suggestion, hint, clue, whisper, suspicion, idea, notion, glimmering.

inland internal, interior, upcountry, home, domestic. FOREIGN

inlet bay, bight, cove, creek, arm, firth, opening, entrance, passage.

inmate prisoner, convict, patient, resident, inhabitant.

inn pub, public house, tavern, hotel.

innate inborn, inbred, connate, congenital, native, natural, instinctive, inherent, intrinsic, immanent, ingrained. ACQUIRED

inner interior, internal, inward, inside, innermost, central, private, intimate, secret, hidden. OUTER

innermost inmost, deepest, central, private, intimate, secret, basic, fundamental, essential. OUTERMOST

innocent guiltless, blameless, inculpable, clear, not guilty, above suspicion, irreproachable. GUILTY
pure, chaste, virginal, sinless, virtuous, upright, unsullied, spotless, immaculate, clean, faultless, impeccable. IMPURE
harmless, innocuous, innoxious, inoffensive, safe. INJURIOUS
naive, unsophisticated, artless, ingenuous, simple, guileless, credulous.

innocuous harmless, innoxious, innocent, inoffensive, safe. HARMFUL

innovation novelty, change, alteration, modernism. CONSERVATISM

innoxious harmless, innocuous, innocent, inoffensive, safe. NOXIOUS

innuendo insinuation, allusion, implication, suggestion, hint, intimation, whisper.

innumerable countless, untold, many, numerous, myriad, incalculable, numberless. FEW

inoculate vaccinate, immunize, protect, inject, imbue.

inoffensive unobjectionable, innocent, harmless, innocuous, innoxious, mild, quiet. OFFENSIVE

inoperative ineffectual, ineffective, inefficacious, inefficient, useless, worthless, broken, out of order, unserviceable, invalid, null and void. OPERATIVE

inopportune untimely, unseasonable, ill-timed, inconvenient, unsuitable, inappropriate, inauspicious, unfavourable. TIMELY

inordinate excessive, immoderate, extreme, exorbitant, disproportionate, unwarranted, undue, uncalled-for, unreasonable, extravagant, intemperate, unrestrained. MODERATE

inorganic inanimate, mineral, chemical, artificial, man-made. ORGANIC

inquietude uneasiness, anxiety, nervousness, restlessness, disquiet, disquietude, discomposure. EASE

inquire investigate, look into, inspect, study, examine, probe, explore, enquire, ask, question, interrogate.

inquiry investigation, inquest, inquisition, hearing, study, examination, scrutiny, survey, research, probe, exploration, interrogation, enquiry, question, query.

inquisitive inquiring, questioning, curious, nosy (*inf*), prying, intrusive, meddlesome. UNINTERESTED

inroad incursion, raid, foray, irruption, invasion, intrusion, encroachment. RETREAT

insalubrious unhealthy, unwholesome, noxious, insanitary, unhygienic, dirty, unclean. SALUBRIOUS

insane mad, crazy (*inf*), deranged, demented, lunatic (*inf*), unbalanced, *non compos mentis*, mentally ill, nuts (*inf*), bonkers (*inf*), barmy (*inf*), crackers (*inf*). SANE
foolish, stupid, senseless, idiotic, irresponsible, irrational, absurd. SENSIBLE

insanity madness, craziness (*inf*), derangement, dementia, mental disorder, mental illness, aberration. SANITY
folly, foolishness, stupidity, idiocy, lunacy, irresponsibility, absurdity. SENSE

insatiable rapacious, voracious, ravenous, greedy, gluttonous, omnivorous, unappeasable, unquenchable, insatiate.

inscribe engrave, carve, cut, etch, impress, imprint, write, pen. ERASE
enter, record, register, enrol, enlist. DELETE
sign, autograph, dedicate, address.

inscription engraving, legend, words, lettering, epitaph, dedication, autograph.

inscrutable mysterious, inexplicable, unfathomable, incomprehensible, hidden, impenetrable, enigmatic, deadpan, poker-faced, sphinxlike. OBVIOUS

insecure uncertain, unsure, hesitant, anxious, nervous, afraid. CONFIDENT
unsafe, risky, perilous, dangerous, hazardous, exposed, vulnerable, unprotected, defenceless. SAFE
unstable, unsteady, shaky, wobbly, loose, infirm, unsound, weak, frail. STABLE

insensate insensible, insentient, numb, anaesthetized, unfeeling, unconscious, inanimate, lifeless, dead. SENTIENT
insensitive, unfeeling, hard, callous, thick-skinned, impassive, indifferent, apathetic, blind, unperceiving. SENSITIVE
senseless, foolish, stupid, witless, brainless. SENSIBLE

insensible insensate, insentient, numb, unfeeling, unconscious. SENTIENT
indifferent, impervious, oblivious, unaware, unaffected, unmoved, blind, deaf, callous, hard. SUSCEPTIBLE

insensitive unfeeling, insensate, insensible, hard, callous, uncaring, indifferent, unsympathetic. CARING
immune, proof, unsusceptible, unaffected. SENSITIVE

inseparable indissoluble, indivisible, devoted, close.

insert introduce, put in, enter, interpolate, intercalate, inject, interject, inset, infix, imbue, infuse. EXTRACT

inside *n*, interior, contents. SURFACE
adj, interior, inner, internal, innermost, inward. EXTERNAL
adv, indoors, within. OUTSIDE

insidious stealthy, subtle, slick, crafty, artful, sly, wily, cunning, guileful, tricky, deceitful, deceptive, treacherous. STRAIGHTFORWARD

insight penetration, perception, intuition, perspicacity, acumen, discernment, shrewdness, awareness, realization, understanding, comprehension, knowledge, vision.

insignificant unimportant, trivial, trifling, nugatory, immaterial, irrelevant, negligible, minor, paltry, petty, meaningless, of no account. SIGNIFICANT

insincere hypocritical, dissembling, two-faced, deceitful, dishonest, untruthful, false, untrue, hollow, empty, faithless, perfidious, disingenuous, evasive, shifty. SINCERE

insinuate intimate, hint, suggest, imply, allude, refer. STATE
introduce, infuse, instil, infiltrate, ingratiate, fawn, curry favour, worm.

insinuation intimation, hint, suggestion, implication, innuendo, allusion. STATEMENT
introduction, infusion, instillation, infiltration, ingratiation.

insipid bland, tasteless, watery, colourless, anaemic, vapid, dull, boring, uninteresting, tedious, flat, lifeless, spiritless, jejune, banal, trite, prosaic, stale, tame, characterless, wishy-washy (*inf*).

insist demand, require, command, urge, stand firm, stress, emphasize. WAIVE
maintain, assert, aver, vow, contend, claim. DENY

insistent demanding, persistent, tenacious, repeated, incessant, urgent, pressing, forceful, emphatic, dogmatic.

insobriety drunkenness, intoxication, inebriety, intemperance, crapulence. SOBRIETY

insolence impudence, impertinence, rudeness, sauce (*inf*), cheek (*inf*), pertness, boldness, audacity, effrontery, disrespect, contumely, arrogance. DEFERENCE

insolent impudent, impertinent, rude, saucy, cheeky, pert, fresh (*inf*), bold, disrespectful, offensive, insulting, presumptuous, arrogant, contemptuous. DEFERENTIAL

insolvent bankrupt, ruined, beggared, bust (*inf*), penniless, broke (*inf*). RICH

inspect examine, scrutinize, scan, peruse, study, check, vet, investigate, view, review, survey, observe.

inspection examination, scrutiny, perusal, checkup, once-over (*inf*), investigation, review, survey.

inspector examiner, scrutineer, censor, checker, investigator, observer.

inspiration stimulation, arousal, awakening, exaltation, exhilaration, elevation, passion, enthusiasm, genius, creativity.
stimulus, incentive, spur, influence, encouragement, muse, afflatus, revelation, enlightenment, idea.

inspire inspirit, enliven, animate, invigorate, stimulate, arouse, excite, stir, exalt, exhilarate, elevate, cheer, hearten, encourage, imbue, infuse, instil, prompt, spark off, inflame.

inspirit enliven, animate, invigorate, inspire, stimulate, arouse, excite, stir, rouse, fire, cheer, hearten. DEPRESS

install place, put in, fix, lodge, ensconce, settle, position, establish, set up.
invest, induct, instate, introduce, inaugurate, initiate. OUST

installation placing, establishment, fitting, fixture, machinery, equipment.
investiture, induction, instatement, introduction, inauguration, initiation. EJECTION

instalment portion, part, section, episode, chapter, payment.

instance *n*, example, case, illustration, precedent, occasion, time, situation, place, stage, step.
request, demand, entreaty, solicitation, suggestion, prompting, instigation.
v, cite, quote, adduce, mention, specify.

instant *n*, moment, second, minute, twinkling, trice, flash, jiffy (*inf*).
adj, immediate, instantaneous, quick, prompt, direct. SLOW
urgent, pressing, imperative, importunate, exigent, critical.

instantaneous instant, immediate, quick, prompt, direct, on-the-spot, sudden, abrupt. SLOW

instantly immediately, at once, now, without delay, forthwith, directly, straightaway, instantaneously. LATER

instead in lieu, preferably, rather, in place of, as an alternative.

instigate incite, provoke, spur, goad, actuate, start, initiate, bring about, prompt, urge, impel, encourage, influence, persuade, foment, rouse, stir up. SUPPRESS

instigation incitement, provocation, actuation, initiation, prompting, urging, impulse, encouragement, influence, persuasion, fomentation, agitation. SUPPRESSION

instil infuse, imbue, implant, engraft, inculcate, impress, infix, introduce. ERADICATE

instinct intuition, feeling, sixth sense, prompting, impulse, inclination, tendency, proclivity, predisposition. REASON
aptitude, knack, flair, talent, gift, faculty.

instinctive intuitive, automatic, spontaneous, impulsive, involuntary, reflex, unpremeditated, natural, inborn, innate. RATIONAL

institute *v*, found, establish, set up, organize, start, begin, commence, originate, initiate, inaugurate, introduce, launch, pioneer, enact, appoint, install, induct. TERMINATE
n, institution, school, college, academy, seminary, conservatory, society, association, organization, foundation.

institution introduction, initiation, inauguration, origination, launch, appointment, installation, induction. TERMINATION
institute, school, college, hospital, asylum, establishment, organization, foundation, society, association, business, company.
custom, tradition, usage, convention, rule, law, principle, practice.

instruct tell, order, command, direct, bid, enjoin.
teach, educate, school, edify, enlighten, train, coach, drill, indoctrinate.

inform, notify, apprise, acquaint, brief.

instruction order, command, mandate, direction, ruling, directive, briefing, recommendation, advice, guideline, rule.
teaching, education, tuition, training, coaching, guidance, enlightenment, indoctrination.

instructor teacher, coach, trainer, tutor, pedagogue, schoolmaster, schoolmistress, adviser, guide, demonstrator. PUPIL

instrument implement, tool, utensil, device, contrivance, gadget, appliance, mechanism.
agency, means, vehicle, medium, agent, factor, pawn, puppet.
document, paper, contract, charter.

instrumental helpful, serviceable, useful, contributory, conducive, important, significant, influential, active, involved.

instrumentality helpfulness, usefulness, service, utility, importance, influence, action, help.
intervention, mediation, medium, agency, means, vehicle, instrument.

insubordinate recalcitrant, refractory, disobedient, contumacious, defiant, rebellious, mutinous, seditious, intractable, ungovernable, unruly, disorderly, riotous, turbulent. DOCILE

insubordination recalcitrance, disobedience, defiance, rebellion, mutiny, sedition, revolt, insurrection, disorder, riot, unruliness. COMPLIANCE

insufferable unbearable, intolerable, unendurable, insupportable, too much, impossible, outrageous, detestable, dreadful. TOLERABLE

insufficient deficient, lacking, wanting, short, scanty, scarce, inadequate, incapable, incompetent. SUFFICIENT

insular narrow-minded, illiberal, parochial, provincial, petty, limited, restricted, circumscribed, isolated, detached, remote, aloof.

insulate isolate, separate, detach, cut off, sever, part.
protect, shield, cover, wrap, pad, cushion.

insult *v*, abuse, affront, offend, outrage, hurt, injure, snub, slight, slander, call names, mock, humiliate. FLATTER
n, abuse, affront, offence, outrage, rudeness, disrespect, insolence, snub, slight, slander, aspersion, contumely, contempt, scorn, humiliation, indignity. RESPECT

insuperable insurmountable, impassable, unconquerable, invincible, overpowering, overwhelming.

insurance assurance, protection, cover, security, indemnity, guarantee, warranty, provision, safeguard, providence. JEOPARDY

insure protect, cover, indemnify, underwrite, guarantee, warrant, assure, safeguard. IMPERIL

insurgent *n*, rebel, revolutionary, insurrectionist, rioter, mutineer.
adj, rebellious, revolutionary, insurrectionary, riotous, mutinous, seditious, insubordinate, disobedient. OBEDIENT

insurmountable insuperable, impassable, unconquerable, invincible, overpowering, overwhelming.

insurrection rebellion, revolt, revolution, coup, uprising, mutiny, sedition, insurgency, insubordination, riot. SUBJUGATION

insusceptible insensible, insensitive, indifferent, unmoved, unresponsive, immune, unimpressible. SUSCEPTIBLE

intact whole, entire, complete, integral, perfect, unbroken, sound, unhurt, uninjured, unharmed, undamaged, unimpaired, unscathed, untouched, inviolate. BROKEN

intangible impalpable, insubstantial, airy, vague, indefinite, shadowy, evanescent, incoporeal, unreal, imperceptible. TANGIBLE

integral intact, whole, entire, complete, individed, total. PARTIAL
intrinsic, inherent, essential, indispensable, basic, fundamental, component, constituent. NONESSENTIAL

integrate incorporate, combine, amalgamate, mix, mingle, blend, merge, unite, join. SEGREGATE

integrity honesty, uprightness, rectitude, probity, honour, principle, morality, virtue, goodness, purity. DISHONESTY
unity, wholeness, completeness, soundness.

intellect mind, intelligence, brains, sense, reason, understanding, judgment.

intellectual *adj*, mental, cerebral, learned, erudite, academic, scholarly, highbrow, intelligent, thoughtful, rational.
n, scholar, academic, thinker, genius, egghead (*inf*). DUNCE

intelligence intellect, mind, brains, aptitude, cleverness, understanding, comprehension, perception, discernment, acumen, quickness, alertness, brightness, sharpness, reason, sense, nous (*inf*). STUPIDITY
information, knowledge, facts, data, news, word, report, notification.

intelligent clever, brainy (*inf*), smart, bright, quick, sharp, alert, astute, perceptive, discerning, perspicacious, knowledgeable, wise, sensible, rational. STUPID

intelligible comprehensible, understandable, clear, plain, distinct, explicit. UNINTELLIGIBLE

intemperate excessive, immoderate, inordinate, extreme, wild, uncontrolled, unrestrained, unbridled, extravagant, self-indulgent, profligate, incontinent. MODERATE
drunken, intoxicated, bibulous, crapulent, alcoholic. TEMPERATE

intend mean, propose, have in mind, contemplate, plan, design, purpose, aim, destine, resolve, determine.

intense great, extreme, concentrated, strong, powerful, forceful, acute, fierce, harsh, deep, profound, intensive, vigorous, energetic. MILD
earnest, eager, ardent, fervent, vehement, zealous, passionate. APATHETIC

intensify heighten, enhance, deepen, strengthen, reinforce, sharpen, concentrate, magnify, increase, boost, escalate, raise, aggravate, exaggerate. MODERATE

intensity greatness, extremity, concentration, depth, strength, power, force, vigour, energy, ardour, fervour, vehemence, passion. MILDNESS

intent *adj*, set, determined, resolute, bent, fixed, steadfast, concentrated, intense, eager, earnest, absorbed, engrossed, rapt, alert, attentive. INDIFFERENT
n, intention, aim, goal, object, end, purpose, design, plan.

intention aim, goal, object, objective, target, end, intention, plan, design, purpose, meaning.

intentional intended, premeditated, planned, deliberate, calculated, wilful, voluntary, studied, purposeful. ACCIDENTAL

inter bury, inhume, entomb, sepulchre. EXHUME

intercede mediate, arbitrate, intervene, interpose, step in, plead, advocate.

intercept interrupt, stop, check, arrest, obstruct, block, deflect, head off, cut off, catch, seize.

intercession mediation, arbitration, intervention, advocacy, plea, prayer, entreaty, petition, supplication.

interchange *v*, exchange, alternate, switch, swap, trade, barter, replace, substitute, change places, reciprocate.
n, exchange, alternation, swap, trade, reciprocation, give and take.

intercourse communication, dealings, commerce, trade, traffic, communion, liaison, contact.
copulation, coitus, sexual intercourse, sex (*inf*), carnal knowledge.

interdict *v*, prohibit, ban, forbid, disallow, veto, bar, proscribe. ALLOW
n, interdiction, prohibition, ban, veto, taboo, proscription.

interest *n*, curiosity, attention, notice, regard, concern, care, importance, consequence, moment, weight. INDIFFERENCE
hobby, pastime, diversion, activity, pursuit.
benefit, advantage, good, profit, gain, avail, use, worth, behalf, sake.
share, stake, portion, part, right, claim, involvement, business, affair, concern, matter.
premium, dividend, percentage. PRINCIPAL
v, engage, absorb, captivate, fascinate, intrigue, attract, amuse, move, excite, arouse. BORE
affect, concern, touch, involve.

interested curious, inquisitive, intrigued, attracted, drawn, attentive, held, engaged, absorbed, fascinated. UNINTERESTED
concerned, involved, prejudiced, biased, partial. DISINTERESTED

interesting intriguing, engaging, absorbing, fascinating, amusing, entertaining, stimulating, exciting, gripping, appealing, attractive, pleasing. BORING

interfere interpose, intervene, meddle, tamper, intrude, butt in.
hinder, impede, hamper, obstruct, restrain, cramp, thwart, clash, conflict, oppose.

interim *n*, interval, meantime, meanwhile.
adj, temporary, provisional, makeshift.

interior *adj*, internal, inner, inside, inward. EXTERIOR

inland, upcountry, home, domestic.
n, inside, contents, heart, core, centre. SURFACE

interject interpose, interpolate, intercalate, insert, put in, throw in.

interjection exclamation, ejaculation, cry, remark, interpolation, intercalation.

interlace interweave, twine, intertwine, plait, braid, interlock, twist, cross, reticulate. UNRAVEL

interlock join, lock, interconnect, interlink.

interlocution conversation, dialogue, colloquy, discussion, discourse, confabulation.

interloper meddler, interferer, intruder, trespasser, gate-crasher.

intermediate intervening, intermediary, mean, middle, halfway, in-between, transitional.

interminable endless, unending, never-ending, incessant, ceaseless, perpetual, eternal, everlasting, infinite, boundless, limitless, unlimited, illimitable, long, protracted, long-winded, monotonous, boring. BRIEF

intermingle intermix, mingle, mix, commingle, commix, blend, merge, combine, amalgamate. SEPARATE

intermission interlude, interval, entr'acte, break, pause, stop, rest, respite, lull, recess, suspension, interruption. CONTINUANCE

intermittent spasmodic, fitful, sporadic, periodic, recurrent, occasional, broken, discontinuous, interrupted. CONTINUOUS

internal inner, interior, inside, inward. EXTERNAL
domestic, home, civil, in-house.

international global, worldwide, universal, cosmopolitan. NATIONAL

internecine destructive, ruinous, deadly, mortal, bloody, sanguinary.
internal, civil, domestic.

interpolate insert, introduce, interpose, interject, intercalate, add. DELETE

interpose intervene, intercede, come between, mediate, interfere, meddle, introduce, insert, interpolate, intercalate, interject.

interpret explain, expound, elucidate, clarify, define, construe, understand, read, solve, decode, decipher, unravel, render, translate. MYSTIFY

interpretation explanation, exposition, elucidation, clarification, construction, reading, analysis, exegesis, rendition, version, translation.

interrogate question, catechize, quiz, grill (*inf*), pump, cross-examine, examine, ask, enquire.

interrupt discontinue, suspend, stop, break off, disjoin, sever, cut. CONTINUE
intrude, break in, butt in, interpose, interfere, disturb, hinder, obstruct.

interruption disturbance, disruption, intrusion, break, pause, stoppage, cessation, suspension, discontinuance, hindrance, obstacle. CONTINUANCE

intersect divide, cut, cross, meet.

intersperse scatter, sprinkle, pepper, dot, interlard, intermix.

interstice gap, opening, chink, cranny, crevice, cleft, fissure, crack, space, interval.

intertwine twine, entwine, twist, intertwist, interweave, interlace, interwind, reticulate. UNRAVEL

interval space, gap, interstice, interspace, opening, distance.
interim, meantime, spell, period, interlude, intermission, break, pause, rest, hiatus.

intervene interpose, step in, intercede, mediate, arbitrate, intrude, interfere.
happen, occur, take place, befall, ensue.

interview *n*, meeting, dialogue, discussion, conference, consultation, audience.
v, examine, question, interrogate.

interweave inweave, interlace, intertwine, entwine, braid, mesh, blend, mix, intermingle. UNRAVEL

intestines bowels, guts, entrails, viscera, innards (*inf*), insides (*inf*).

intimate[1] *adj*, close, dear, bosom, familiar, confidential, personal, private, secret, warm, cosy, friendly.
deep, profound, thorough, exhaustive, detailed, personal, first-hand, direct. SUPERFICIAL
n, friend, confidant, familiar, crony.

intimate[2] *v*, suggest, imply, insinuate, hint, allude, indicate, communicate, make known. CONCEAL

intimation suggestion, implication, insinuation, innuendo, hint, allusion, inkling, indication, communication, notice.

intimidate frighten, scare, alarm, appal, daunt, cow, overawe, dismay, dishearten, dispirit, discourage, deter, bully, browbeat, coerce, threaten, terrorize. ENCOURAGE

intolerable unbearable, insufferable, unendurable, too much, insupportable. BEARABLE

intolerant narrow-minded, illiberal, bigoted, biased, prejudiced, chauvinistic, dogmatic, self-opinionated, small-minded, insular. TOLERANT

intonation modulation, tone, pitch, accentuation, cadence, inflection.

intoxicate inebriate, make drunk, addle, fuddle, stupefy, exhilarate, elate, excite, stimulate, invigorate.

intoxication drunkenness, inebriation, inebriety, insobriety, crapulence. SOBRIETY

euphoria, exhilaration, elation, excitement, delirium.

intractable stubborn, obstinate, obdurate, headstrong, wilful, intransigent, perverse, contrary, indocile, refractory, contumacious, insubordinate, unmanageable, ungovernable, unruly, wayward, difficult. TRACTABLE

intransigent uncompromising, unbending, unyielding, intractable, stubborn, obstinate, obdurate, tough, rigid, immovable. AMENABLE

intrepid fearless, dauntless, unafraid, daring, brave, courageous, valiant, valorous, bold, heroic, lion-hearted, doughty, stalwart, indomitable, plucky, spirited. COWARDLY

intricate involved, complicated, complex, obscure, difficult, puzzling, perplexing, tortuous, labyrinthine, entangled, knotty, convoluted, ornate, fancy. SIMPLE

intrigue *v*, attract, interest, fascinate, charm, tantalize, arouse, stir, puzzle, baffle. BORE

conspire, plot, scheme, connive, machinate.

n, conspiracy, plot, scheme, machination, cabal, ruse, wile, stratagem.

affair, liaison, amour, romance.

intrinsic inherent, essential, basic, fundamental, built-in, inborn, inate, immanent, natural, native, real, true, genuine. EXTRINSIC

introduce present, acquaint, familiarize, bring together, begin, start, commence, initiate, inaugurate, launch, establish, found, bring in, announce, herald, usher in. END

propose, suggest, submit, offer, advance, put forward, broach, bring up. WITHDRAW

insert, inject, interpose, interpolate, interject. REMOVE

introduction presentation, announcement, debut, induction, initiation, inauguration, launch, opening, beginning, establishment.

preface, foreword, preamble, prologue, preliminary, prelude, overture. EPILOGUE

intrude obtrude, push in, butt in, break in, interrupt, interpose, interfere, meddle, trespass, encroach, infringe. WITHDRAW

intruder interloper, trespasser, invader, raider, burglar, prowler, snooper (*inf*), meddler, gate-crasher (*inf*).

intrusion encroachment, infringement, invasion, trespass, violation, interruption, obtrusion, meddling, interference, interposition.

intuition insight, instinct, clairvoyance, divination, sixth sense, presentiment, hunch, perception, discernment, knowledge, understanding. REASON

intumescence swelling, tumefaction, turgescence, tumidity, distension.

inundate flood, deluge, swamp, submerge, drown, engulf, overwhelm, overflow. DRAIN

inure harden, toughen, indurate, temper, accustom, make used to, habituate, familiarize, acclimatize.

invade attack, assault, raid, storm, enter, penetrate, occupy, overrun, infest, pervade. EVACUATE

intrude, encroach, infringe, trespass, violate.

invalid[1] *n*, patient, convalescent, valetudinarian.

adj, ill, sick, weak, feeble, frail, infirm, bedridden, valetudinarian, disabled, handicapped. HALE

invalid[2] *adj*, null, void, inoperative, unsound, fallacious, untrue, illogical, irrational, baseless, unfounded. VALID

invalidate annul, nullify, abrogate, repeal, rescind, quash, cancel, overthrow, refute, undermine, weaken. VALIDATE

invaluable priceless, inestimable, precious, valuable, indispensable. WORTHLESS

invariable changeless, unchanging, unchangeable, immutable, unalterable, unvarying, constant, fixed, set, uniform, regular, consistent, unfailing. VARIABLE

invariably always, without exception, every time, inevitably, habitually, regularly, perpetually. SOMETIMES

invasion attack, assault, raid, foray, irruption, inroad, incursion, aggression, offensive. RETREAT
intrusion, encroachment, infringement, trespass, violation, breach, infraction.

invective vituperation, revilement, censure, condemnation, denunciation, reproach, abuse, obloquy, diatribe, philippic, tirade, castigation, contumely, sarcasm. EULOGY

inveigh rail, vituperate, revile, denounce, condemn, censure, blame, abuse, reproach, berate, expostulate, protest. PRAISE

inveigle entrap, ensnare, entice, lure, tempt, beguile, coax, cajole, persuade, bamboozle (*inf*).

invent originate, create, discover, design, think up, conceive, imagine, devise, contrive, concoct, coin, formulate, fabricate, make up, cook up (*inf*).

invention origination, formulation, creation, discovery, design, device, contrivance, gadget, concoction.
inventiveness, originality, resourcefulness, creativity, imagination, inspiration, genius.
fabrication, lie, fib (*inf*), untruth, falsehood, fiction, story, fantasy, romance. TRUTH

inventory list, catalogue, register, roll, record, account, schedule, enumeration.

inverse opposite, contrary, converse, counter, reversed, transposed, inverted.

inversion reversal, transposition, opposite, contrary, antithesis, reverse, converse.

invert reverse, transpose, turn upside down, overturn, capsize, introvert, turn inside out.

invest spend, lay out, put in, advance, fund, supply, provide, endow, give, devote. WITHDRAW
install, induct, instate, inaugurate, enthrone.
clothe, dress, robe, deck, array, adorn, cover. STRIP

investigate explore, examine, probe, sift, scrutinize, study, inspect, inquire into, look into, check out. IGNORE

investigation exploration, search, examination, probe, scrutiny, study, review, analysis, inspection, inquiry, inquest, inquisition.

investiture installation, induction, instatement, inauguration, enthronement, coronation, ordination.

investment asset, venture, speculation, stake, contribution.

inveterate ingrained, deep-seated, deep-rooted, entrenched, set, established, hardened, chronic, habitual, confirmed, incurable, dyed-in-the-wool.

invidious unpopular, undesirable, objectionable, offensive, hateful, odious, unfair, malignant.

invigorate enliven, animate, stimulate, quicken, brace, refresh, energize, fortify, strengthen, revitalize, pep up, exhilarate. ENERVATE

invincible unconquerable, indomitable, unbeatable, invulnerable, unassailable, impregnable, insuperable, insurmountable, indestructible. VULNERABLE

inviolate intact, whole, undamaged, unimpaired, unharmed, uninjured, unhurt, unsullied, undefiled, pure, virginal, untouched, stainless, unpolluted. DEFILED
inviolable, sacred, sacrosanct, hallowed, holy.

invisible unseen, hidden, concealed, out of sight, imperceptible, indiscernible, unapparent, inconspicuous. VISIBLE

invitation summons, call, invite (*inf*), request, bidding, solicitation, challenge, dare, proposition, offer.
attraction, allurement, lure, enticement, temptation, come-on (*inf*). REPULSION

invite summon, call, ask, request, bid, solicit, beg.
attract, welcome, provoke, bring on, encourage, court, tempt, entice, allure. REPULSE

inviting attractive, pleasing, welcoming, tempting, alluring, seductive, appealing, engaging, fascinating, captivating, irresistible. REPULSIVE

invocation prayer, supplication, entreaty, solicitation, petition, appeal.

invoice bill, statement, list, schedule, record.

invoke adjure, call on, appeal to, implore, entreat, supplicate, beg, beseech, pray.
summon, call forth, conjure up, raise.

involuntary automatic, mechanical, reflex, spontaneous, instinctive, unintentional, unconscious, unthinking, blind, uncontrolled. VOLUNTARY
compulsory, obligatory, forced, reluctant, unwilling. WILLING

involve entail, require, imply, signify, mean, include, contain, comprise, embrace, cover. EXCLUDE
implicate, incriminate, inculpate, embroil, entangle, complicate, confuse, mix up. EXTRICATE
absorb, engross, preoccupy, engage, commit, concern, affect.

involvement connection, association, participation, concern, interest, responsibility, commitment, implication.
complexity, intricacy, complication, convolution, entanglement, imbroglio, confusion.

invulnerable safe, secure, unassailable, invincible, indestructible, insusceptible. VULNERABLE

inward inner, internal, interior, inside, innermost, private, personal, confidential, secret, mental, spiritual. OUTWARD
ingoing, incoming. OUTGOING

inweave weave, interweave, interlace, intertwine, entwine, mesh, reticulate. UNRAVEL

iota atom, jot, tittle, whit, bit, scrap, mite, grain, trace, glimmer, shadow, touch, hint.

irascible irritable, touchy, testy, short-tempered, cross, waspish, snappish, peppery, cantankerous, crabbed, peevish, petulant. AFFABLE

irate angry, furious, incensed, enraged, fuming, ireful, wrathful, indignant, annoyed, exasperated, riled, piqued. CALM

ire anger, rage, fury, choler, wrath, indignation, exasperation, annoyance, irritation. COMPOSURE

iridescent shimmering, pearly, nacreous, opalescent, opaline, multicoloured, polychromatic, prismatic, rainbow-like. DULL

irk irritate, annoy, vex, nettle, rile, peeve (*inf*), aggravate. PLEASE

irksome tiresome, wearisome, annoying, irritating, aggravating, vexatious, troublesome, bothersome, tedious, boring, monotonous. PLEASANT

ironic ironical, sarcastic, sardonic, satirical, mocking, derisive, contemptuous.
paradoxical, incongruous, coincidental.

irony sarcasm, satire, ridicule, derision, mockery.
paradox, incongruity, contrariety.

irradiate brighten, illuminate, illumine, light up, enlighten. DARKEN

irrational illogical, unreasonable, absurd, preposterous, ridiculous, ludicrous, nonsensical, meaningless, foolish, crazy, stupid, senseless, idiotic, insane, demented, raving, brainless, unwise, injudicious. RATIONAL

irreclaimable irrecoverable, irretrievable, lost, irredeemable, incurable, irremediable, irreparable, hopeless, incorrigible.

irreconcilable incompatible, conflicting, opposed, at variance, incongruous. COMPATIBLE
implacable, inexorable, uncompromising, intransigent, inflexible. APPEASABLE

irrecoverable irretrievable, lost, irreclaimable, irredeemable. RECOVERABLE

irrefutable incontrovertible, undeniable, incontestable, indisputable, unquestionable, irrefragable, unassailable, invincible, conclusive, sure, certain. QUESTIONABLE

irregular uneven, rough, bumpy, crooked, unsymmetrical, asymmetric, unequal. LEVEL
fitful, spasmodic, changeable, variable, unsettled, erratic, inconstant, capricious, desultory, unmethodical, unsystematic, disorderly, random, haphazard. REGULAR
unusual, uncommon, exceptional, anomalous, aberrant, abnormal, eccentric, unconventional, unorthodox, odd, peculiar. NORMAL

irrelevant inapplicable, impertinent, immaterial, inapposite, inappropriate, inapt, beside the point, unrelated, unconnected, foreign, extraneous. RELEVANT

irreligious impious, ungodly, godless, pagan, heathen, unbelieving, agnostic, atheistic, irreverent, sacrilegious, profane. RELIGIOUS

irremediable incurable, irreparable, hopeless, remediless, irrecoverable. REMEDIABLE

irreparable irreclaimable, irrecoverable, irreversible, beyond repair, irremediable, uncurable. REPARABLE

irrepressible uncontrollable, unrestrainable, insuppressible, ebullient, buoyant. REPRESSIBLE

irreproachable blameless, faultless, impeccable, immaculate, spotless, perfect, pure, innocent, guiltless, inculpable, beyond reproach. REPROACHABLE

irresistible overwhelming, overpowering, compelling, powerful, imperative, indomitable, invincible, irrepressible, unsuppressible, unavoidable, inescapable, ineluctable. RESISTIBLE
tempting, seductive, alluring, fascinating, enchanting, charming. REPULSIVE

irresolute undecided, unresolved, undetermined, uncertain, in two minds, hesitant, vacillating, wavering, faltering, unstable, inconstant, weak, feeble, half-hearted. RESOLUTE

irrespective regardless, despite, in spite of, notwithstanding, apart from, independent.

irresponsible unreliable, untrustworthy, thoughtless, careless, reckless, rash, devil-may-care. RESPONSIBLE

irretrievable irrecoverable, irreclaimable, lost, irredeemable. RETRIEVABLE

irreverent disrespectful, discourteous, impolite, impudent, impertinent, cheeky (*inf*), impious, irreligious, sacrilegious, profane. REVERENT

irreversible unalterable, unchangeable, irrevocable, incurable, irremediable, irreparable. REVERSIBLE

irrevocable irreversible, unalterable, unchangeable, immutable, irreclaimable, irrecoverable. REVOCABLE

irrigate water, wet, moisten, soak, flood, wash, bathe. DRAIN

irritable touchy, testy, irascible, waspish, snappish, peppery, peevish, petulant, captious, hasty, fiery, short-tempered, quick-tempered, excitable, prickly, cross, crabbed, crusty, grumpy, cantankerous, ill-humoured, bad-tempered. AFFABLE

irritate annoy, vex, nettle, needle, rattle, chafe, fret, pique, aggravate, exasperate, anger, enrage, incense, infuriate, provoke, bother, pester, harass.
rub, chafe, inflame, exacerbate. SOOTHE

irruption invasion, incursion, inroad, raid, foray, sally. RETREAT

isolate separate, set apart, segregate, quarantine, insulate, cut off, detach, sever, disconnect, dissociate. UNITE

isolated solitary, alone, lonely, remote, detached, separate, single, unique.

isolation separation, segregation, quarantine, insulation, detachment, disconnection, dissociation, solitude, seclusion, exile, loneliness.

issue *n*, issuance, supply, delivery, distribution, circulation, dissemination, promulgation, publication. SUPPRESSION
edition, impression, copy, number.
outflow, outlet, egress, exit. INFLUX
offspring, progeny, children, descendants, posterity.
topic, subject, point, question, problem, matter, affair, concern.
result, consequence, outcome, upshot, effect, end, conclusion.
v, emerge, appear, come forth, emit, discharge, flow, proceed, spring, arise, originate, emanate.
deliver, supply, give out, distribute, send out, circulate, disseminate, promulgate, publish, announce, broadcast, put out, release. WITHHOLD

itch *v*, tingle, prickle, tickle, crawl.
yearn, long, crave, hunger, thirst, hanker, lust.
n, itchiness, irritation, tingling, prickling.
yearning, longing, craving, hunger, thirst, hankering, yen (*inf*).

item article, thing, point, aspect, particular, detail, entry, note.

iterate repeat, reiterate, restate, recapitulate.

itinerant wandering, roving, roaming, strolling, travelling, peripatetic, nomadic, unsettled, vagrant.

itinerary route, schedule, programme, circuit, course, guide, guidebook.

J

jab poke, prod, thrust, stab, dig, nudge.

jabber chatter, prattle, prate, gibber, babble, gabble, rabbit (*inf*).

jacket coat, covering, casing, case, sheath, wrapping, wrapper, skin.

jade *n*, hack, nag, shrew, harridan, hag, crone, hussy, trollop.
v, exhaust, weary, tire, fatigue, wear out, fag (*inf*). REFRESH

jagged notched, serrated, indented, uneven, rough, ragged, ridged.

jail *n*, gaol, prison, lockup, nick (*inf*), jug (*inf*), clink (*inf*), cooler (*inf*), inside (*inf*).

v, imprison, incarcerate, lock up, confine, intern, detain. RELEASE

jam[1] *v*, wedge, cram, pack, crowd, press, squeeze, stuff, ram, force.
block, obstruct, congest, clog, stick, stall, stop.
n, crowd, press, crush, congestion, pack, mob, throng.
predicament, plight, trouble, dilemma, quandary, fix (*inf*), pickle (*inf*).

jam[2] *n*, preserve, conserve.

jangle *v*, clash, jar, clang, clank, rattle.
n, clash, clang, clank, rattle, clangour, din, racket, cacophony, dissonance, discord.

jar[1] *n*, pot, vessel, container, receptacle, vase, jug, crock.

jar[2] *v*, jolt, jerk, jog, rattle, vibrate, shake, agitate, disturb.
clash, jangle, grate, rasp, disagree, quarrel. AGREE
n, jolt, jerk, shock, vibration, agitation.
clash, disagreement, discord, jangle, cacophony, grating, rasping. HARMONY

jargon vocabulary, phraseology, language, usage, idiom, parlance, cant, argot, lingo (*inf*).
nonsense, gibberish, drivel, balderdash, mumbo jumbo.

jaunt excursion, outing, trip, ramble, stroll, airing, spin (*inf*).

jaunty brisk, sprightly, lively, breezy, airy, buoyant, blithe, gay, spruce, trim, smart, dapper.

jealous envious, covetous, grudging, resentful, green. CONTENT
suspicious, distrustful, mistrustful, anxious, watchful, attentive, possessive.

jeer *v*, scoff, mock, deride, taunt, gibe, ridicule, sneer, scorn, contemn, heckle, boo, hiss. ACCLAIM
n, mockery, derision, ridicule, gibe, taunt, sneer, catcall, boo, hiss. ACCLAMATION

jejune naive, unsophisticated, inexperienced, simple, childish, puerile, juvenile.
insipid, tasteless, dull, vapid, dry, tame, uninteresting, banal. EXCITING
meagre, scanty, insubstantial, barren, sterile. RICH

jeopardize risk, venture, gamble, hazard, endanger, imperil. PROTECT

jerk jolt, jar, bump, pull, tug, yank, twitch, tweak, lurch, start.

jest *n*, joke, quip, crack (*inf*), banter, raillery, prank, jape, fun, sport, play.
v, joke, quip, tease, banter, chaff, gibe, jeer, mock, scoff.

jester clown, harlequin, fool, buffoon, joker.

jet gush, stream, spurt, squirt, spout, spring, spray.

jetty breakwater, groyne, mole, pier, dock, wharf, quay.

jewel gem, gemstone, precious stone, rock (*inf*), trinket, ornament, bauble, pearl, diamond, treasure.

jilt abandon, forsake, desert, leave, throw over, discard, reject, drop, ditch (*inf*).

jingle ring, tinkle, chime, clink, chink, rattle.

jinx *n*, curse, voodoo, black magic, evil eye, hex.
v, curse, bewitch, hex.

job work, employment, position, situation, post, occupation, profession, business, calling, vocation, trade, craft, métier.
task, chore, duty, responsibility, charge, office, role, function, concern, affair, venture, undertaking.

jockey *n*, rider, horseman, horsewoman, equestrian.
v, manoeuvre, manipulate, engineer, negotiate, cajole, wheedle, finagle (*inf*).
trick, cheat, deceive, delude, bamboozle, hoodwink, dupe.

jocose jocund, merry, jovial, jolly, blithe, cheerful, jocular, jesting, joking, playful, sportive, witty, droll, funny, humorous, comical. MELANCHOLY

jocular jesting, joking, waggish, facetious, witty, droll, comical, funny, humorous, jocose, merry, playful. SERIOUS

jog jolt, jar, nudge, prod, shake, jerk, jostle, joggle, jiggle, bounce.
prompt, arouse, stir, stimulate, remind.
trot, run, plod, trudge.

join unite, connect, link, conjoin, adjoin, meet, attach, fasten, couple, tie, splice, combine, amalgamate, ally, affiliate, add, append, enrol, enlist, sign up, join up, contribute, participate, join in. SEPARATE

joint *n*, junction, connection, union, join, link, knot, seam, hinge, articulation.
adj, common, communal, shared, mutual, combined, collective, concerted, united, joined. INDIVIDUAL

joke *n*, jest, quip, witticism, pun, crack (*inf*), gag (*inf*), anecdote, jape, lark, prank, trick.

v, jest, quip, banter, chaff, tease, kid (*inf*).

joker comedian, comic, wag, wit, humorist, clown, prankster.

jollity merriment, fun, mirth, hilarity, gaiety, joviality, jocundity, jocosity, jocularity. MELANCHOLY

jolly jovial, jocund, jocose, mirthful, merry, happy, joyful, joyous, cheerful, cheery, blithe, gay, playful, sportive, frolicsome, lively, genial, convivial, festive, spirited. SOMBRE

jolt jar, jerk, jog, jostle, push, shove, bump, knock, shake, shock, start, lurch.

jostle push, shove, hustle, elbow, crowd, jolt, jog, bump, shake.

jot *n*, iota, atom, whit, tittle, bit, scrap, grain, mite.

v, write, note, record, list, scribble.

journal newspaper, paper, periodical, magazine, review, gazette, chronicle, record, diary, log, daybook.

journalist reporter, newspaperman, hack (*inf*), newspaperwoman, pressman, correspondent, columnist, editor, broadcaster, commentator.

journey *n*, voyage, trip, travel, passage, expedition, trek, safari, excursion, jaunt, outing, tour, drive, ride, flight, sail.

v, travel, voyage, go, proceed, roam, rove, trek, tour.

jovial jolly, genial, convivial, jocose, jocund, jocular, blithe, cheerful, cheery, merry, gay, mirthful, hearty, cordial.

joy happiness, pleasure, gladness, glee, delight, rapture, ecstasy, bliss, felicity, elation, joyfulness, joyousness, gaiety, cheerfulness. SORROW

joyful happy, pleased, glad, gleeful, jubilant, delighted, elated, joyous, gay, merry, jolly, jocose, jocund, cheerful, blithe, buoyant. SAD

jubilant joyful, joyous, ecstatic, overjoyed, thrilled, elated, triumphant, exultant, rejoicing. MOURNFUL

jubilation triumph, exultation, joy, ecstasy, elation, celebration, festivity. MOURNING

judge *v*, adjudicate, referee, umpire, arbitrate, try, find, sentence, condemn, decree, rule.

determine, ascertain, decide, conclude, appraise, evaluate, assess, estimate, reckon, deem, consider, think, believe.

n, justice, magistrate, adjudicator, referee, umpire, arbiter.

connoisseur, authority, expert, critic, reviewer.

judgment verdict, sentence, decree, ruling, award, finding, decision, adjudication, arbitration. PLEADING

discernment, perspicacity, discrimination, taste, perception, insight, penetration, understanding, wisdom, sagacity, prudence, discretion, sense, acumen, intelligence.

assessment, evaluation, appraisal, view, opinion, belief, estimation.

judicious wise, prudent, sagacious, politic, provident, discreet, careful, cautious, circumspect, sober, sensible, rational, sound, shrewd, astute, clever, intelligent, informed. INJUDICIOUS

jug pitcher, ewer, urn, carafe, flagon, vessel, container.

juggle manipulate, alter, change, falsify, tamper with, rig, fix (*inf*).

juice liquid, fluid, extract, secretion, sap.

juicy succulent, lush, moist, wet, dripping. DRY

racy, risqué, spicy, sensational, vivid, colourful, exciting, provocative.

jumble *v*, disorder, disarrange, disorganize, mix, muddle, confuse. ARRANGE

n, disorder, disarray, muddle, confusion, chaos, mess, mixture, medley, hotchpotch. ORDER

jump *v*, leap, spring, bound, vault, clear, skip, hop, caper, gambol, frolic.

start, jerk, flinch, recoil.

miss, omit, skip, leave out. INCLUDE

n, leap, spring, bound, vault, skip, hop.

hurdle, fence, obstacle.

start, jerk, jolt, lurch.

rise, increase, boost, escalation, upsurge. DROP

jumpy nervous, anxious, fretful, agitated, jittery, fidgety, restless, on edge, tense, apprehensive. CALM

junction joint, connection, seam, union, alliance, link, intersection, combination. DIVISION

juncture point, stage, time, moment, crux, crisis, emergency, exigency.

junior younger, minor, lesser, lower, inferior, subordinate. SENIOR

junk rubbish, refuse, trash, garbage, scrap, waste, litter.

jurisdiction judicature, power, authority, control, sway, rule, dominion, domain, province, sphere, field, area.

just *adj*, fair, equitable, impartial, unbiased, objective, right, lawful, honest, conscientious, good, sound, valid. UNJUST
deserved, merited, rightful, proper, reasonable, due, fitting, appropriate, suitable, condign. UNMERITED
true, exact, precise, accurate, correct. INACCURATE
adv, exactly, precisely, absolutely, perfectly.
barely, hardly, scarcely, only, merely, simply.

justice fairness, equity, justness, impartiality, objectivity, honesty, integrity, right, propriety, legality, legitimacy, lawfulness. INJUSTICE
judge, magistrate. DEFENDANT

justifiable warrantable, defensible, reasonable, acceptable, right, proper, fit, lawful, legitimate, vindicable, excusable. UNJUSTIFIABLE

justification defence, plea, apology, explanation, reason, grounds, excuse, vindication, exculpation, exoneration. CONDEMNATION

justify vindicate, exculpate, exonerate, acquit, warrant, substantiate, support, uphold, maintain, defend, excuse, explain. CONDEMN

jut project, protrude, stick out, overhang.

juvenile *adj*, young, youthful, boyish, girlish, adolescent, immature, inexperienced, puerile, infantile, childish. ADULT
n, child, minor, youth, adolescent, boy, girl. ADULT

juxtaposition contiguity, contact, adjacency, proximity, nearness, closeness.

K

keel over overturn, capsize, upset, turn turtle.
faint, collapse, pass out, black out (*inf*).

keen eager, avid, enthusiastic, ardent, fervent, fervid, zealous, earnest, diligent, ambitious. APATHETIC
sharp, acute, penetrating, piercing, cutting, incisive, pointed, biting, caustic, trenchant, mordant, tart, acid, pungent. DULL
shrewd, astute, quick, clever, perceptive, discerning, sensitive. STUPID
intense, strong, deep, profound. MILD
keen on, fond of, devoted to.

keep *v*, retain, hold, preserve, conserve, maintain, support, protect, defend, guard, possess, control. DISCARD
continue, carry on, persist, keep on, keep up, remain, last, endure. CEASE
store, amass, accumulate, put, place, deposit, save. USE
detain, delay, retard, hold back, restrain, check, curb, prevent, hinder, keep back, withhold.
tend, look after, sustain, support, maintain, subsidize, provide for, board. NEGLECT
observe, obey, comply with, fulfil, respect, honour, celebrate, commemorate, solemnize. BREAK
n, board, subsistence, maintenance, support, living, livelihood.
dungeon, stronghold, castle, fort.

keeper custodian, curator, guard, warden, jailer, guardian, steward, proprietor.

keeping custody, charge, care, aegis, auspices, hands, possession, protection, guardianship.
conformity, agreement, harmony, accord, correspondence, consistency, congruity, compliance, observance.

ken knowledge, acquaintance, cognizance, awareness, perception, comprehension, view, sight, vision, range, field.

kernel seed, grain, core, nucleus, heart, centre, substance, essence. SHELL

key solution, answer, explanation, guide, clue, means.
style, mood, tone, scale, tonic.

kick *v*, boot, punt, strike, hit, drive.
recoil, kick back, resist, oppose, object, protest.
give up, abandon, stop.
kick out, eject, expel, oust, throw out, dismiss, discharge, get rid of.
n, boot, punt, blow.
zest, vitality, energy, sparkle, excitement, thrill, pleasure, enjoyment, fun.

kid *n*, child, youngster, baby, son, daughter, boy, girl, youth. ADULT
v, tease, rib (*inf*), joke, jest, trick, dupe, deceive, delude.

kidnap abduct, carry off, seize, capture, hijack, hold to ransom. FREE

kill slaughter, slay, murder, assassinate, execute, do in (*inf*), bump off (*inf*), dispatch, destroy, annihilate, exterminate, liquidate, butcher, massacre.
deaden, stifle, quash, negate, neutralize, cancel, delete, obliterate, stop.

killing *n*, slaughter, butchery, massacre, carnage, murder, manslaughter, homicide, assassination, execution.
coup, success, gain, profit, stroke of luck, windfall.
adj, deadly, fatal, lethal, mortal, murderous, homicidal. HARMLESS
tiring, exhausting, taxing, punishing, hard, arduous.
hilarious, side-splitting, uproarious, funny, comical.

kin *n*, kindred, relations, relatives, family, kinsfolk, people.
kinship, consanguinity, relationship, connection, blood, extraction, descent.
adj, consanguineous, related, kindred, akin, allied, cognate. UNRELATED

kind[1] *adj*, benign, benevolent, beneficent, kindly, charitable, philanthropic, generous, bounteous, gracious, humane, gentle, tender, kind-hearted, warm, affectionate, compassionate, sympathetic, understanding, indulgent, lenient, clement, mild, good, friendly, amiable, obliging, considerate, thoughtful. UNKIND

kind[2] *n*, sort, type, class, group, genre, set, variety, species, genus, breed, race, family, ilk, style, nature, character, manner, make, brand.

kindle ignite, light, set on fire. EXTINGUISH
fire, inflame, arouse, stimulate, excite, rouse, provoke, incite, foment, agitate, stir. QUELL

kindly *adj*, kind, warm, sympathetic, compassionate, benign, benevolent, genial, cordial. CRUEL
adv, gently, mildly, well, tenderly, warmly, graciously, considerately, thoughtfully, sympathetically. UNKINDLY

kindness benevolence, kindliness, charity, philanthropy, generosity, graciousness, humanity, tenderness, warmth, affection, compassion, clemency, mildness, goodness, friendliness, consideration, thoughtfulness. UNKINDNESS
favour, service, good turn, aid, assistance, help. DISSERVICE

kindred *n*, kinship, consanguinity, relationship, blood.
kin, kinsfolk, relations, relatives, family, connections.
adj, related, akin, allied, cognate, similar, like, matching, corresponding. UNRELATED

king monarch, ruler, sovereign, prince, overlord, chief. SUBJECT

kingdom monarchy, sovereignty, principality, empire, realm, dominion, country, nation, state, land, territory, province, domain.

kingly royal, regal, sovereign, princely, imperial, majestic, stately, imposing, grand, august, noble, splendid. LOWLY

kink *n*, curl, twist, bend, coil, crimp, wrinkle, knot.
crick, twinge, spasm.
flaw, fault, quirk, whim, vagary, crotchet, fetish.
v, curl, twist, bend, coil, frizz. STRAIGHTEN

kiosk booth, stall, stand.

kiss *v*, greet, embrace, osculate, buss, peck (*inf*), neck (*inf*).
touch, brush, graze, glance.
n, osculation, peck (*inf*), smack.

kit *n*, set, parts, tools, implements, equipment, apparatus, outfit, gear, tackle, supplies, provisions.
v, **kit out**, equip, supply, provide, fit, arm.

knack flair, faculty, aptitude, ability, skill, talent, gift, forte, genius, trick, dexterity, adroitness, expertise. INABILITY

knavery deceit, deception, dishonesty, trickery, fraud, duplicity, chicanery, villainy, roguery, rascality. HONESTY

knavish rascally, roguish, villainous, dishonest, fraudulent, deceitful, tricky, unscrupulous, unprincipled. HONEST

knell toll, ring, chime, peal, sound.

knickers pants, panties, drawers, briefs, smalls (*inf*), undies (*inf*).

knit join, unite, connect, bind, tie, interlace, interweave, intertwine, heal, mend. SEPARATE
furrow, wrinkle, crease.

knob lump, boss, protuberance, projection, bump, swelling, knot, handle.

knock *v*, hit, strike, tap, rap, bump, buffet, thump, pound, hammer, beat, smack, slap.

carp, cavil, find fault, criticize, run down, belittle, deprecate, pan (*inf*), slam (*inf*). PRAISE

knock down, fell, floor, level, raze, demolish, destroy. RAISE

n, blow, hit, tap, rap, bump, thump, smack, slap.

knoll hill, hillock, hummock, mound.

knot *v*, tie, secure, bind, twist, knit, entangle, ravel. UNTIE

n, tie, bond, connection, fastening, loop, bow.

bunch, clump, cluster, group, company, set, circle, crowd, mob.

protuberance, node, swelling.

problem, difficulty, complication, complexity, intricacy, tangle.

knotty gnarled, nodular, lumpy, rough. SMOOTH

complicated, complex, intricate, difficult, thorny, puzzling, perplexing. SIMPLE

know understand, comprehend, perceive, apprehend, realize, see, be aware, experience, undergo.

recognize, identify, be familiar with, be acquainted with, fraternize with.

differentiate, distinguish, discriminate, discern, tell.

knowing shrewd, astute, sagacious, sharp, smart, clever, subtle, cunning, perceptive, discerning, aware. ARTLESS

meaningful, significant, eloquent, expressive.

deliberate, intentional, wilful, conscious. UNCONSCIOUS

knowledge erudition, learning, scholarship, education, instruction, enlightenment, information, facts, data.

acquaintance, familiarity, cognizance, ken, experience, awareness, consciousness, realization. IGNORANCE

understanding, comprehension, perception, apprehension, cognition, grasp, recognition, judgment, discernment, wisdom.

kowtow bow, kneel, grovel, fawn, cringe, truckle, toady, curry favour, suck up (*inf*).

kudos glory, prestige, fame, renown, acclaim, praise, credit. DISGRACE

L

label *n*, tag, ticket, sticker, marker, mark, brand, epithet, name, description.

v, mark, stamp, tag, brand, call, name, describe, classify.

laborious hard, arduous, strenuous, tiring, fatiguing, wearisome, toilsome, burdensome, difficult, tough, uphill. EASY

diligent, industrious, assiduous, sedulous, painstaking, thorough, tireless, indefatigable, persevering. INDOLENT

labour *n*, work, toil, drudgery, industry, effort, exertion, pains. IDLENESS

workers, labourers, employees, work-force. MANAGEMENT

job, task, chore.

childbirth, parturition, delivery, confinement, travail.

v, work, toil, drudge, slave, struggle, strive. REST

labyrinthine labyrinthian, mazelike, mazy, circuitous, tortuous, involved, intricate, complex, complicated, convoluted, tangled, knotty, confused, confusing, perplexing, puzzling. SIMPLE

lace *n*, netting, web, filigree, openwork, tatting.

string, cord, thong, tie.

v, tie, fasten, bind, thread, interlace, interweave, intertwine. UNRAVEL

mix, fortify, spike (*inf*).

lacerate tear, rip, rend, claw, gash, slash, cut, wound, mangle, mutilate, hurt, pain, harrow. MEND

lack *n*, need, want, shortage, deficiency, insufficiency, dearth, scarcity, absence. ABUNDANCE

v, need, want, require, be short of, be without. HAVE

lackey sycophant, toady, fawner, yes man, parasite, hanger-on, minion, pawn, tool, puppet.

servant, valet, attendant, flunky, underling, menial. MASTER

laconic terse, succinct, concise, brief, short, pithy, curt. VERBOSE

lad boy, youngster, youth, stripling, young man, fellow, chap (*inf*). LASS

laden loaded, burdened, encumbered, weighed down, full, fraught, charged.

lading cargo, freight, load, burden, charge.

ladylike refined, genteel, elegant, courtly, proper, decorous, well-bred, mannerly, polite. UNSEEMLY

lag dawdle, saunter, loiter, linger, dally, idle, fall behind, trail, straggle, hang back, tarry, delay. HURRY

laggard dawdler, loiterer, idler, loafer, straggler, sluggard, slowcoach (*inf*).

lair den, hole, cave, burrow, nest, hideaway, retreat.

lambent flickering, twinkling, dancing, fluttering, licking, glowing, shimmering, sparkling, brilliant.

lame crippled, disabled, handicapped, hobbling, limping.
weak, feeble, flimsy, unconvincing, inadequate, unsatisfactory, poor, ineffectual. STRONG

lament *v*, mourn, bewail, bemoan, sorrow, grieve, repine, cry, weep, wail, moan, regret, rue, deplore. REJOICE
n, lamentation, complaint, moan, wail.
dirge, requiem, elegy, threnody, coronach.

lamentable deplorable, regrettable, unfortunate, pitiful, miserable, wretched, sorry, poor, mean, sad, sorrowful, tragic, grievous, distressing.

lamentation lament, mourning, sorrow, grief, weeping, wailing, ululation. REJOICING

lampoon *n*, satire, parody, burlesque, skit, caricature.
v, satirize, ridicule, mock, parody, burlesque, send up (*inf*).

land *n*, earth, ground, terra firma, soil, dirt, sod.
estate, property, demesne, realty, grounds, acres.
country, nation, state, province, region, area, territory, realm, empire.
v, alight, disembark, dock, touch down, arrive, settle, come down.

landscape scene, panorama, view, prospect, vista.

language speech, tongue, dialect, idiom, parlance, vernacular, slang, lingo (*inf*), jargon, vocabulary, terminology, phraseology, wording, style, expression, diction, talk, conversation, communication.

languid weak, feeble, faint, drooping, flagging, languishing, tired, weary, exhausted. STRONG
listless, lethargic, languorous, sluggish, torpid, heavy, inactive, inert, lazy, slothful, apathetic, spiritless, unenthusiastic, uninterested, indifferent. SPIRITED

languish droop, flag, fail, fade, wither, decline, weaken, faint. FLOURISH
pine, long, yearn, hanker, desire, want.

languor weakness, feebleness, debility, enervation, tiredness, weariness, exhaustion, fatigue. ENERGY
listlessness, lassitude, lethargy, apathy, sluggishness, torpor, heaviness, laziness, sloth, sleepiness, drowsiness. ENTHUSIASM
stillness, tranquillity, calm, lull, silence.

lank limp, lifeless, dull, straight, long.
gangling, lanky, tall, thin, slim, slender, skinny, scrawny, bony, gaunt, angular. DUMPY

lap *n*, circuit, round, tour, loop, circle, orbit, stage, part.
v, fold, wrap, envelop, cover, overlap.

lapse *n*, drop, fall, decline, deterioration. IMPROVEMENT
slip, error, mistake, fault, failing, oversight, omission, negligence.
break, gap, interval, lull, pause. CONTINUATION
v, drop, fall, sink, decline, slip, slide, drift.
expire, terminate, discontinue, end, stop. CONTINUE

larceny theft, stealing, robbery, burglary.

large *adj*, big, great, massive, immense, enormous, huge, vast, considerable, substantial, extensive, broad, wide, full, ample, abundant, copious, generous, bulky, heavy, stout. SMALL
n, **at large,** free, loose, at liberty, unconfined, on the run. CAPTIVE

largely chiefly, mainly, principally, in general, as a whole, by and large, mostly, greatly, considerably. PARTLY

largess generosity, liberality, bounty, charity, beneficence, philanthropy. MEANNESS
gift, present, donation, benefaction, bequest, endowment.

lascivious lecherous, lustful, lewd, libidinous, concupiscent, prurient, salacious, licentious, unchaste, incontinent, randy (*inf*), voluptuous, sensual. CHASTE
obscene, indecent, dirty, pornographic, blue, ribald, bawdy, crude.

lash[1] *n*, whip, scourge, stroke, blow, stripe.
v, whip, flog, beat, scourge, flagellate, cane, birch. CARESS
hit, beat, pound, hammer, buffet, dash, strike.

attack, criticize, satirize, ridicule, castigate, scold, berate, censure. PRAISE

lash[2] *v*, tie, bind, fasten, secure, join, attach. UNTIE

lass girl, miss, young woman, bird (*inf*), maiden, damsel.

lassitude languor, lethargy, listlessness, apathy, tiredness, weariness, heaviness, sluggishness, torpor, drowsiness. VIGOUR

last[1] *adj*, ultimate, final, closing, concluding, terminal, utmost, extreme, hindmost, rearmost, latest, most recent. FIRST
n, end, finish, termination, conclusion, close. BEGINNING
at last, finally, eventually, in the end, at length.

last[2] *v*, continue, persist, remain, stay, abide, endure, survive, hold out, wear, keep. PERISH

lasting abiding, enduring, continuing, persisting, permanent, eternal, everlasting, constant, durable, strong. TRANSIENT

late delayed, tardy, belated, overdue, unpunctual, behind, slow. EARLY
recent, up-to-the-minute, current, latest, fresh, new, advanced.
dead, deceased, former, previous, past, old.

lately recently, latterly, of late.

latent potential, dormant, quiescent, unrealized, undeveloped, hidden, concealed, veiled, unseen, invisible, secret, tacit, implicit. CONSPICUOUS

lateral side, sideways, sideward, indirect, oblique.

lather *n*, suds, foam, froth, bubbles.
fuss, fluster, state (*inf*), flap (*inf*).
v, foam, froth.

latitude freedom, liberty, laxity, indulgence, licence, leeway, scope, range, room, space, extent, compass. RESTRICTION

latter later, last, closing, second, last-mentioned, latest, recent, modern. FORMER

latterly recently, lately, of late. FORMERLY

laud praise, extol, glorify, honour, acclaim. DECRY

laudable praiseworthy, commendable, meritorious, admirable, estimable, creditable, worthy. BLAMEWORTHY

laugh *v*, giggle, chuckle, snigger, titter, chortle, guffaw, roar with laughter. CRY
laugh at, mock, deride, jeer, scoff, make fun of.
n, giggle, chuckle, chortle, guffaw. SOB

laughable ludicrous, ridiculous, absurd, preposterous, derisory. REASONABLE
funny, comical, amusing, droll, humorous, farcical, risible. SERIOUS

laughter laughing, giggling, chuckling, tittering, chortling. CRYING
fun, amusement, glee, mirth, merriment, hilarity. GLOOM

launch propel, send off, dispatch, move, set in motion, set afloat, fire, hurl, cast, throw.
begin, start, commence, initiate, inaugurate, establish, found. TERMINATE

lavatory toilet, WC, loo (*inf*), bathroom, cloakroom, Ladies, Gents, public convenience, bog (*inf*).

lavish *adj*, abundant, plentiful, profuse, copious, lush, luxuriant, sumptuous, effusive, fulsome. SCANT
extravagant, prodigal, wasteful, improvident, thriftless, immoderate, intemperate, excessive. THRIFTY
generous, liberal, unstinting, open-handed, bountiful. MEAN
v, shower, pour, heap, waste, squander, dissipate.

law statute, rule, regulation, decree, edict, enactment, ordinance, order, command, act, code, charter, constitution.
principle, formula, canon, standard, criterion.
jurisprudence, legislation, litigation, police.

lawful legal, licit, legitimate, constitutional, rightful, right, proper, just, valid, permissible, allowable. UNLAWFUL

lawless rebellious, mutinous, seditious, insurgent, insubordinate, unruly, disorderly, riotous, chaotic, anarchic, wild, unbridled, unrestrained. LAW-ABIDING

lawsuit litigation, suit, action, case, proceedings, cause, dispute, prosecution, trial.

lawyer solicitor, barrister, counsel, advocate, attorney.

lax loose, slack, negligent, neglectful, remiss, permissive, lenient, tolerant, indulgent, easy-going. STRICT
imprecise, inexact, inaccurate, broad, general, vague. EXACT

laxative purgative, cathartic, aperient.

laxity laxness, looseness, slackness, negligence, neglect, freedom, latitude, permissiveness, indulgence, licence. STRICTNESS imprecision, inexactitude, inaccuracy, vagueness, generality. PRECISION

lay[1] *v*, put, place, set down, deposit, establish, spread, rest. REMOVE
arrange, dispose, position, locate, set out, lay out, prepare, devise, work out, plan, plot.
present, put forward, submit, lodge. WITHDRAW
attribute, ascribe, assign, impute, charge.
bet, wager, gamble, stake, risk, hazard.
suppress, allay, quiet, still, appease, pacify. AROUSE
lay off, discharge, dismiss, let go, make redundant, sack (*inf*), fire (*inf*).

lay[2] *adj*, laic, laical, secular, nonclerical, amateur, nonprofessional.

layer stratum, seam, bed, thickness, tier, cover, covering, coat, coating, film, blanket.

laze loaf, idle, lounge, kill time, waste time, fritter away. WORK

lazy slothful, idle, indolent, slack, inactive, inert, sluggish, torpid, slow, languid. INDUSTRIOUS

lead *v*, guide, conduct, precede, escort, convoy, marshal, usher, pilot, steer. FOLLOW
head, rule, govern, command, direct.
influence, induce, persuade, incline, dispose.
surpass, excel, outstrip, transcend.
pass, spend, live, have.
lead on, entice, lure, tempt, seduce, deceive, delude.
lead to, cause, produce, result in, bring on, contribute to, tend to, serve to.
n, priority, first place, precedence, supremacy, front, vanguard, advantage, initiative.
leadership, direction, guidance, example, model.
clue, hint, tip, guide, indication, pointer.

leader head, chief, ruler, director, commander, captain, principal, superior, boss (*inf*), guide, pioneer. FOLLOWER

leading principal, main, chief, primary, first, foremost, supreme, best, greatest, highest, ruling, governing, commanding. MINOR

league *n*, association, confederation, confederacy, union, guild, alliance, coalition, combination, fellowship, partnership, consortium.
class, category, group.
v, associate, confederate, unite, ally, combine, collaborate. PART

leak *v*, seep, ooze, drip, trickle, escape.
disclose, divulge, reveal, expose, give away, let slip. CONCEAL
n, crack, split, chink, hole, opening, puncture.
leakage, seepage, drip, escape.

lean[1] *v*, rest, recline, repose.
bend, slant, slope, tilt, list, incline, tend.
depend, rely, count, trust, have faith.

lean[2] *adj*, thin, spare, slender, slim, lank, skinny, scrawny, bony, angular, gaunt, emaciated. FAT
meagre, scanty, sparse, poor, barren, unproductive. RICH

leaning tendency, inclination, propensity, disposition, bent, bias, prejudice, partiality, liking, proclivity.

leap *v*, jump, bound, spring, vault, clear, hop, skip, caper, gambol, frisk, frolic.
surge, rocket, soar, rise, increase, escalate. DROP
n, jump, bound, spring, vault, hop, skip, caper, frolic.
upsurge, rise, increase, escalation. DROP

learn master, grasp, comprehend, pick up, acquire, glean, gather.
memorize, commit to memory. FORGET
discover, find out, hear, ascertain, detect, determine.

learned scholarly, erudite, versed, lettered, literate, well-read, well-informed, academic, intellectual. IGNORANT

learner novice, beginner, tyro, neophyte, apprentice, trainee, pupil, student. EXPERT

learning scholarship, erudition, letters, education, schooling, instruction, knowledge, information, lore, study, research. IGNORANCE

lease let, rent, hire, charter.

least smallest, lowest, slightest, fewest, minimum, poorest, meanest. MOST

leave[1] *v*, depart, go, set out, quit, retire, withdraw, disappear. ARRIVE
abandon, desert, forsake, renounce, relinquish, give up, vacate, evacuate. KEEP
bequeath, will, devise, consign, commit, entrust.
leave off, stop, cease, discontinue, desist, refrain. CONTINUE
leave out, omit, exclude, overlook, ignore, disregard, reject. INCLUDE

leave[2] *n*, permission, allowance, sanction, consent, liberty, freedom, licence. PROHIBITION
holiday, vacation, time off.
farewell, adieu, goodbye, parting, leave-taking, departure, retirement, withdrawal. GREETING

leavings scraps, leftovers, remnants, remains, residue, dregs, waste, refuse.

lecherous lustful, lewd, lascivious, libidinous, concupiscent, prurient, salacious, licentious, unchaste, wanton, incontinent, randy (*inf*). CHASTE

lecture *n*, discourse, address, speech, talk, harangue, sermon, homily.
reprimand, rebuke, reproof, scolding, lesson, telling-off (*inf*), dressing-down (*inf*).
v, discourse, speak, talk, hold forth.
reprimand, rebuke, reprove, scold, chide, berate, upbraid, tell off (*inf*).

ledge shelf, mantelpiece, sill, step, ridge.

lees dregs, residue, grounds, sediment, deposit, precipitate.

legacy bequest, gift, devise, inheritance, heritage, patrimony.

legal legitimate, licit, lawful, constitutional, permissible, allowable, proper, rightful, valid. ILLEGAL

legalize legitimize, legitimatize, warrant, authorize, sanction, license, permit, allow. VETO

legate envoy, ambassador, emissary, plenipotentiary, delegate, deputy.

legend myth, tale, story, fable, fiction. HISTORY
inscription, device, motto, caption.

legendary mythical, fictitious, fabled, storied, fabulous, fanciful, make-believe. HISTORICAL
famous, renowned, celebrated, illustrious, great. UNKNOWN

legible readable, decipherable, clear, plain, neat, tidy. ILLEGIBLE

legion army, brigade, troop, division, unit.
host, multitude, throng, horde, mass, myriad.

legislation lawmaking, codification, enactment.
law, statute, ruling, act.

legitimate legal, lawful, licit, constitutional, authorized, proper, rightful, permissible, allowable. ILLEGAL
reasonable, logical, sound, valid, correct. INVALID

leisure rest, relaxation, ease, convenience, recreation, freedom, liberty, spare time, time off, holiday, vacation, break, respite, peace, quiet. WORK

leisurely unhurried, slow, relaxed, comfortable, easy, gentle. HASTY

lend loan, advance. BORROW
give, grant, bestow, provide, furnish, contribute, impart.

length extent, reach, span, stretch, distance, duration. BREADTH
piece, portion, section, measure.
at length, in detail, in depth, in full, fully, thoroughly, interminably, for ages. BRIEFLY
eventually, finally, at last, in the end.

lengthen stretch, extend, elongate, prolong, protract, draw out, continue, increase. SHORTEN

lengthy long, extended, prolonged, protracted, interminable, long-winded, verbose, wordy, prolix. SHORT

lenient tolerant, indulgent, clement, merciful, mild, gentle, moderate, soft, tender, compassionate. STRICT

lenitive soothing, palliative, mitigative, emollient, balmy, alleviating, easing. IRRITANT

less smaller, slighter, fewer, lower, inferior, lesser, minor, secondary. MORE

lessen reduce, diminish, decrease, lower, abate, ease, decline, dwindle, shorten, curtail, abridge, contract, shrink. INCREASE

lesser lower, inferior, minor, secondary, less, smaller, slighter. GREATER

lesson class, period, lecture, tutorial, seminar, teaching, instruction.
assignment, task, exercise, drill, practice, homework.
example, model, deterrent, punishment, warning, correction, reprimand, rebuke, reproof, scolding, admonition.

let[1] *v*, permit, allow, grant, sanction, authorize, enable.
lease, rent, hire, charter.
let down, disappoint, disenchant, disillusion, fail, leave in the lurch.
let off, excuse, exempt, pardon, forgive, absolve, exonerate, acquit.
let up, abate, subside, ease, lessen, diminish, moderate.

let² *n*, hindrance, obstruction, impediment, obstacle, restriction, constraint.

lethal fatal, deadly, mortal, murderous, destructive, dangerous, noxious, poisonous. SAFE

lethargic sluggish, torpid, dull, slow, heavy, sleepy, drowsy, stupefied, inactive, inert, idle, lazy, apathetic. ENERGETIC

lethargy sluggishness, torpor, dullness, slowness, heaviness, sleepiness, drowsiness, stupor, inactivity, inertia, idleness, laziness, apathy. VITALITY

letter note, line, message, communication, missive, epistle, reply, answer, acknowledgment.
charter, symbol.

lettered learned, scholarly, erudite, educated, well-read, cultured, cultivated, literate. IGNORANT

level *adj*, horizontal, plane, flat, even, smooth, uniform. UNEVEN
equal, even, balanced, on a par, neck and neck. UNEQUAL
v, flatten, smooth, plane.
demolish, raze, destroy, devastate, pull down, knock down, bulldoze. BUILD
direct, aim, point, focus, train.
n, height, altitude, elevation.
position, rank, status, degree, grade, stage, floor, layer.

lever *n*, bar, crowbar, jemmy, handle.
v, force, prise, jemmy.

levity frivolity, flippancy, facetiousness, light-heartedness, triviality, silliness, giddiness, flightiness, fickleness, inconstancy. SERIOUSNESS

levy *v*, impose, exact, charge, tax, raise, collect, gather, muster.
n, imposition, exaction, charge, fee, tax, duty, toll, tariff, collection, gathering.

lewd obscene, pornographic, blue, coarse, vulgar, dirty, smutty, bawdy, ribald, indecent, salacious, lascivious, lecherous, lustful, libidinous. DECOROUS

lexicon dictionary, wordbook, glossary, vocabulary, thesaurus.

liabilities debts, obligations, responsibilities, duties. ASSETS

liable responsible, answerable, accountable, amenable.
subject, susceptible, exposed, open, vulnerable. INSUSCEPTIBLE
likely, probable, apt, inclined, disposed. UNLIKELY

liaison communication, contact, connection, link, bond, tie, alliance, relationship.
affair, romance, amour, intrigue.

libel *n*, defamation, calumny, slander, aspersion, slur, obloquy, denigration, vilification. EULOGY
v, defame, calumniate, slander, traduce, denigrate, vilify, malign. PRAISE

liberal progressive, reformist, enlightened, broad-minded, permissive, tolerant, indulgent, open-minded, unbiased, unbigoted, catholic. NARROW-MINDED
generous, charitable, bounteous, munificent, unstinting, unselfish, philanthropic, kind, princely, handsome, ample, abundant, lavish, profuse, plentiful, bountiful. MEAN

liberality broad-mindedness, permissiveness, tolerance, indulgence, latitude, open-mindedness, catholicity. NARROW-MINDEDNESS
generosity, charity, bounty, munificence, unselfishness, philanthropy, kindness, abundance, profusion, plenty. MEANNESS

liberate free, loose, emancipate, manumit, disenthral, release, discharge, deliver, rescue. CONFINE

libertine *n*, profligate, debauchee, lecher, rake, roué, playboy, womanizer, philanderer. ASCETIC
adj, dissolute, profligate, debauched, depraved, corrupt, loose, wanton, abandoned, rakish, licentious, immoral. CHASTE

liberty freedom, independence, autonomy, liberation, emancipation, release. SERVITUDE
privilege, right, exemption, immunity, authorization, permission, leave, licence, latitude, carte blanche.
familiarity, impertinence, impudence, disrespect, presumptuousness, forwardness. RESPECT

libidinous lecherous, lustful, lascivious, randy (*inf*), concupiscent, incontinent, carnal, sensual, prurient, salacious, unchaste. CHASTE

licence certificate, permit, warrant, authority, authorization, permission, leave, charter, right, privilege, exemption, immunity, liberty, freedom, latitude, carte blanche. PROHIBITION
abandon, immoderation, unrestraint, anarchy, disorder, laxity, indulgence, licen-

tiousness, dissipation, debauchery. RESTRAINT

license allow, permit, authorize, warrant, sanction, empower, commission, certify, charter. PROHIBIT

licentious dissolute, debauched, profligate, abandoned, loose, wanton, promiscuous, unchaste, immoral, libidinous, lecherous, lustful, lascivious, lewd. CHASTE

lick tongue, touch, brush, taste, lap, flicker, dart.
defeat, beat, conquer, vanquish, trounce.
flog, thrash, beat, spank.

lid top, cap, cover.

lie¹ *v*, fib, fabricate, invent, equivocate, prevaricate, falsify, misrepresent.
n, untruth, falsehood, fib, fiction, invention, fabrication, equivocation, prevarication, mendacity. TRUTH

lie² *v*, rest, repose, recline, be prostrate, sprawl, stretch, extend.
be, be situated, be found, remain, exist, consist.

liege lord, master, chief, leader, sovereign, superior. VASSAL

lieu place, stead.

life being, existence, viability, animation. DEATH
lifetime, duration, span, days.
biography, autobiography, memoir, memoirs, history.
energy, vitality, vigour, verve, sparkle, animation, liveliness, vivacity, spirit, enthusiasm. LETHARGY

lifeless dead, deceased, defunct, cold, inanimate, inorganic. LIVING
lethargic, sluggish, torpid, spiritless, listless, inactive, inert, dull, flat, insipid. LIVELY

lift *vt*, raise, elevate, hoist, jack, pick up, pull up. DROP
uplift, exalt, boost, enhance, improve, advance, promote. LOWER
revoke, rescind, cancel, stop, terminate, remove. IMPOSE
vi, rise, mount, ascend, disperse, dissipate. FALL

ligature bond, tie, link, connection, ligament, band.

light¹ *n*, illumination, brightness, brilliance, radiance, luminosity, ray, beam, glow, flash. DARKNESS
lamp, lantern, bulb, candle, torch.
daylight, sunshine, dawn, daybreak. NIGHT
enlightenment, elucidation, explanation, understanding, comprehension, insight, knowledge. MYSTIFICATION
adj, bright, clear, illuminated, luminous, well-lit. DARK
pale, pastel, whitish, faded, bleached, fair, blond.
v, ignite, kindle, fire, inflame. EXTINGUISH
illuminate, brighten, lighten, light up. DARKEN

light² *adj*, weightless, insubstantial, feathery, flimsy, delicate, airy, buoyant, easy, simple, effortless. HEAVY
trivial, trifling, slight, small, inconsiderable, insignificant, superficial. WEIGHTY
amusing, entertaining, humorous, funny, frivolous. SERIOUS
agile, nimble, sprightly, lithe, supple, deft, dexterous. CLUMSY
cheerful, blithe, gay, merry, jolly, happy, joyful, carefree, fickle, capricious, mercurial, volatile, flighty.
v, land, settle, alight.

light on, come across, find, discover, happen upon.

lighten¹ illuminate, brighten, light, light up, shine, flash. DARKEN
bleach, whiten, pale, fade.

lighten² disburden, disencumber, unload, ease, lessen, reduce, relieve, alleviate. ENCUMBER
cheer, brighten, hearten, encourage, gladden, perk up, uplift. DEPRESS

light-headed dizzy, giddy, faint, vertiginous, woozy (*inf*).
flighty, fickle, capricious, silly, foolish, scatterbrained, frivolous, superficial, trifling. SOBER

light-hearted cheerful, blithe, bright, gay, merry, jolly, happy, joyful, carefree, happy-go-lucky. SERIOUS

like¹ *adj*, similar, alike, resembling, same, identical, allied, akin, related, cognate, corresponding, parallel, analogous, equivalent. DIFFERENT
n, equal, peer, match, counterpart.

like² *v*, enjoy, delight in, relish, appreciate, be partial to, be fond of, love, admire, esteem, prize, fancy, take to, care for, approve. DISLIKE
prefer, choose, select, wish, want, desire, care.

n, liking, preference, partiality, predilection. DISLIKE

likely probable, possible, liable, apt, inclined, disposed, prone. IMPROBABLE
plausible, credible, believable, reasonable, conceivable, imaginable. IMPLAUSIBLE
promising, hopeful, appropriate, suitable, acceptable, pleasing, agreeable. UNSUITABLE

likeness similarity, resemblance, similitude, sameness, corresponding. DISSIMILARITY
image, representation, portrait, effigy, copy, replica, facsimile, reproduction, counterpart.
semblance, guise, appearance, form.

likewise moreover, furthermore, also, too, in addition, besides.
similarly, the same. OTHERWISE

liking fondness, love, affection, attraction, affinity, partiality, preference, predilection, taste, appreciation, fancy, inclination, tendency. AVERSION

Lilliputian tiny, diminutive, miniature, petite, small, little, short, dwarfish, pygmy, undersized. COLOSSAL

limber *adj*, lithe, lissom, supple, pliant, flexible, elastic. STIFF
v, **limber up,** warm up. loosen up, exercise, prepare, get ready.

limit *n*, boundary, frontier, confine, precinct, border, edge, extent, bound, end, termination, extreme, utmost.
restriction, restraint, check, curb, limitation, maximum, ceiling.
v, restrict, confine, curb, check, restrain, bound, circumscribe, delimit, demarcate.

limitless unlimited, illimitable, boundless, unbounded, infinite, endless, unending, vast, immense, incalculable, immeasurable. LIMITED

limp[1] *v*, hobble, falter, stumble, stagger, shuffle.
n, hobble, lameness.

limp[2] flaccid, flabby, soft, flexible, pliant, slack, loose, relaxed. STIFF

limpid clear, transparent, translucent, pellucid, crystalline. OPAQUE
plain, lucid, clear, intelligible, comprehensible. INCOMPREHENSIBLE
calm, peaceful, serene, tranquil, still, quiet. AGITATED

line *n*, row, rank, file, queue, column, series, sequence.
stroke, mark, streak, stripe, band, strip, bar, rule, dash.
string, rope, cord, thread, wire, cable.
crease, wrinkle, furrow.
limit, boundary, border, edge, frontier.
course, path, track, direction, route, way, method, policy.
occupation, business, profession, trade, field, area, activity, interest.
ancestry, descent, extraction, lineage, family, house, race.
v, mark, rule, score, streak, draw, trace, crease, wrinkle.

line up, align, range, straighten, arrange, array, order, queue up, fall in.

lineage ancestry, descent, extraction, birth, family, house, line, race, stock, pedigree, genealogy, offspring, progeny, succession.

linger loiter, tarry, wait, remain, stay, persist, endure, hang around, lag, dawdle, dally, saunter, delay, procrastinate.

link *v*, connect, join, couple, tie, fasten, unite, associate, relate. SEPARATE
n, connection, joint, coupling, tie, bond, association, relationship.
part, piece, member, element, division.

lion-hearted brave, courageous, bold, fearless, intrepid, daring, heroic, valiant, valorous, dauntless. COWARDLY

lip edge, brim, rim, brink, border, margin.
impudence, impertinence, insolence, cheek (*inf*), sauce (*inf*), rudeness, backchat (*inf*). POLITENESS

liquefy liquidize, liquesce, melt, thaw, fuse, condense, dissolve, deliquesce. SOLIDIFY

liquid *n*, liquor, fluid, juice. SOLID
adj, fluid, flowing, running, runny, watery, wet, liquefied, molten.
fluent, smooth, dulcet, sweet, pure, clear.

liquidate pay, settle, discharge, clear, sell, cash, realize.
terminate, dissolve, break up, abolish, annihilate, exterminate, kill.

list *n*, catalogue, inventory, roll, register, schedule, enumeration, series, file, index, directory.
v, enumerate, catalogue, file, index, tabulate, record, register, enter, write down.

listen hark, pay attention, concentrate, attend, hear, give ear, heed, mind, eavesdrop, overhear. IGNORE

listless lethargic, languid, sluggish, torpid, enervated, weary, spiritless, inactive, inert, apathetic, indifferent. ENERGETIC

literal verbatim, word-for-word, strict, close, exact, precise, accurate, faithful, true, actual, genuine. LOOSE

literary scholarly, erudite, learned, lettered, literate, well-read. ILLITERATE

literature letters, writings, literary works, books, publications, lore, information.

lithe lissom, limber, supple, pliant, pliable, flexible, elastic, agile, nimble, graceful.

litigation lawsuit, action, case, proceedings, dispute, contest.

litigious quarrelsome, argumentative, disputatious, contentious, belligerent, pugnacious, combative. GENIAL

litter *n*, rubbish, refuse, waste, debris, clutter, mess, disorder, jumble, confusion. TIDINESS
brood, young, progeny, offspring.
bedding, straw, hay.
v, strew, scatter, clutter, mess up, disarrange, disorder. TIDY

little *adj*, small, short, wee, tiny, minute, petite, diminutive, Lilliputian, dwarfish, pygmy, young, baby. BIG
brief, short, fleeting, passing, limited. LENGTHY
trivial, trifling, paltry, inconsiderable, slight, insignificant. CONSIDERABLE
insufficient, meagre, scant, skimpy. AMPLE
adv, barely, hardly, not much. MUCH
rarely, seldom, not often. OFTEN
n, bit, dash, pinch, drop, trace, spot, touch, trifle. LOT

live[1] *vi*, be, exist, be alive, breathe, subsist, survive, remain, endure, persist, continue, last. DIE
reside, dwell, occupy, inhabit, lodge, abide.
vt, pass, spend, lead.

live[2] *adj*, alive, living, breathing, animate, existent. DEAD
controversial, topical, current, active, connected, loaded, burning, unrecorded.
lively, brisk, energetic, vigorous, dynamic, spirited, alert.

livelihood occupation, job, employment, work, living, maintenance, support, subsistence, sustenance.

lively vivacious, animated, spirited, active, brisk, nimble, spry, agile, frisky, energetic, vigorous, dynamic, alert, keen, eager, quick, busy, bustling, astir, stimulating, exciting, buoyant, gay, vivid. DULL

livery uniform, costume, dress, attire, regalia.

livid greyish, leaden, ashen, pale, pallid, wan.
discoloured, bruised, purple, black-and-blue.
angry, furious, enraged, incensed, fuming. CALM

living *adj*, alive, live, breathing, animate, existent, extant, current, active, operative. DEAD
n, livelihood, maintenance, support, subsistence, sustenance, income, work, job, occupation.
being, existence, animation, life. DEATH

load *n*, burden, onus, encumbrance, weight, charge, cargo, freight, lading, shipment, consignment, worry, trouble, affliction, oppression.
v, burden, encumber, oppress, weigh down, weight, charge, fill, pack, lade, freight, heap, pile. UNLOAD

loaf lounge, idle, laze, loll, loiter, waste time, fritter away.

loafer idler, sluggard, lounger, shirker, layabout, good-for-nothing, ne'er-do-well, drone. WORKER

loan *n*, advance, credit, usury.
v, lead, advance. BORROW

loath loth, unwilling, reluctant, disinclined, indisposed, averse. EAGER

loathe detest, abhor, abominate, execrate, hate, dislike. ADORE

loathing detestation, abhorrence, abomination, execration, odium, hate, hatred, dislike, aversion, antipathy, repugnance, revulsion, disgust. LOVE

loathsome detestable, abhorrent, abominable, execrable, odious, hateful, repugnant, repulsive, disgusting, revolting, obnoxious, vile, nasty, offensive. DELIGHTFUL

lobby *n*, vestibule, foyer, hall, hallway, corridor, passage.
v, urge, press, influence, persuade.

local regional, provincial, parochial, neighbourhood, community, home, native, nearby, limited, restricted. GENERAL

locality neighbourhood, vicinity, district, area, region, location, place, spot, site, locale.

locate find, discover, unearth, come across, ferret out, track down, detect, pinpoint.
situate, place, put, set, fix, establish, settle. REMOVE

location position, situation, whereabouts, place, spot, site, locality, locale.

lock[1] *v*, fasten, secure, bolt, latch. UNLOCK
join, unite, link, engage, interlock, entangle.
clasp, embrace, hug, hold, clutch, grapple.
lock up, jail, imprison, incarcerate, confine. RELEASE
n, fastening, bolt, latch, hasp, padlock.

lock[2] *n*, tress, curl, ringlet, bunch, tuft, wisp, strand.

locomotion movement, motion, moving, progress, travel.

lodge *v*, live, reside, dwell, stay, sojourn, room, board, put up, accommodate, house, billet, quarter, take in, shelter, harbour, entertain.
fix, implant, embed, stick, put, place, deposit, lay, set. REMOVE
n, cottage, hut, cabin, chalet, retreat, den, lair.

lodger boarder, paying guest, tenant. LANDLORD

lodgings accommodation, digs (*inf*), rooms, quarters, abode, residence, dwelling, habitation.

lofty high, tall, towering, elevated, exalted, stately, imposing, majestic, august, dignified, noble, grand, eminent, illustrious. LOWLY
arrogant, proud, haughty, high-and-mighty (*inf*), lordly, overbearing, supercilious, disdainful, condescending. HUMBLE

logic reasoning, argumentation, deduction, dialectics, rationale, reason, sense, coherence.

logical reasonable, rational, sound, valid, clear, coherent, consistent, sensible, wise, judicious. ILLOGICAL

loiter loaf, idle, stand around, tarry, linger, dally, dilly-dally (*inf*), dawdle, saunter, lag. HURRY

loll lounge, sprawl, slouch, slump, flop, lie, rest, recline, repose, lean.
hang, dangle, droop, sag, flop.

lone single, isolated, separate, sole, only, solitary, unaccompanied, alone, lonely, lonesome.

lonely lonesome, friendless, abandoned, forsaken, forlorn, bereft, solitary, unaccompanied, by oneself, isolated, withdrawn, sequestered, reclusive, outcast.
remote, secluded, isolated, out-of-the-way, deserted, uninhabited, unfrequented.

long[1] *adj*, lengthy, extensive, extended, stretched, elongated, protracted, prolonged, long-winded, sustained, interminable. SHORT

long[2] *v*, yearn, desire, wish, crave, hunger, thirst, pine, hanker.

longing yearning, desire, wish, craving, hunger, thirst, hankering, yen (*inf*), aspiration.

long-winded long, lengthy, overlong, long-drawn-out, interminable, wordy, verbose, prolix, diffuse, discursive. TERSE

look *v*, watch, observe, contemplate, survey, view, regard, see, notice, scrutinize, study, examine, scan, gaze, stare, peer, glance, glimpse, peep. IGNORE
seem, appear.
search, hunt, seek. FIND
look after, mind, take care of, attend to, tend, nurse, supervise, protect, guard. NEGLECT
look down on, despise, scorn, disdain, contemn, misprize, disparage. RESPECT
look into, investigate, probe, explore, examine, study, research, inquire, check out.
look up to, admire, esteem, respect, revere. DESPISE
n, gaze, stare, glance, glimpse, view, sight, observation, examination, inspection, scrutiny.
appearance, aspect, air, demeanour, manner, expression, guise, semblance.

loom appear, bulk, hover, impend, be imminent, threaten, menace. RECEDE
overhang, tower, rise, soar, overshadow, dominate.

loop *n*, circle, ring, hoop, noose, bend, curve, curl, coil, twist.
v, encircle, ring, roll, turn, bend, curve, curl, coil, twist.

loose *adj*, slack, lax, relaxed, baggy, sloppy, hanging, drooping. TIGHT
free, unconfined, untied, unfastened, undone, detached, floating, movable, wobbly. SECURE
vague, indefinite, broad, imprecise, inexact, random. PRECISE

dissolute, debauched, immoral, unchaste, wanton, promiscuous, libertine, licentious. CHASTE

v, free, set free, release, let go, liberate, unfasten, undo, untie, unleash, detach, disengage. SECURE

loosen slacken, ease, relax, unbind, untie, undo, loose, free, release, liberate. TIGHTEN

loot *n*, spoils, booty, plunder.

v, pillage, plunder, despoil, ravage, sack, ransack, rifle, raid, rob, steal.

lop cut, chop, cut off, sever, detach, crop, dock, prune, truncate, shorten, curtail.

loquacious talkative, voluble, garrulous, babbling, chatty, gossipy. TACITURN

lord peer, nobleman, earl, baron. COMMONER

master, ruler, governor, monarch, sovereign, king, prince, commander, leader, chief, superior.

lordly haughty, arrogant, proud, overbearing, domineering, imperious, lofty, condescending, patronizing, supercilious, snooty (*inf*). HUMBLE

noble, dignified, lofty, exalted, regal, kingly, princely, majestic, imperial, grand, stately. LOWLY

lore knowledge, wisdom, learning, erudition, scholarship, traditions, beliefs, sayings.

lose mislay, misplace, drop, forget, miss, forfeit, fail, be defeated. GAIN

waste, squander, dissipate, expend, use up, exhaust. KEEP

elude, dodge, escape, evade, outrun, outstrip, leave behind.

loss deprivation, disadvantage, detriment, harm, damage, destruction, ruin, death, bereavement, sacrifice, forfeiture, failure, defeat. GAIN

waste, depletion, deficit, deficiency, shrinkage.

at a loss, bewildered, confused, perplexed, baffled, puzzled, helpless, lost.

lost missing, mislaid, misplaced, disappeared, vanished, gone, forgotten, irretrievable, irrecoverable, irreclaimable. FOUND

wasted, squandered, misused, misspent, forfeited, wrecked, ruined, destroyed, dead.

bewildered, perplexed, confused, baffled, puzzled, astray, adrift.

depraved, corrupt, abandoned, fallen, loose, wanton, unchaste, hardened, incorrigible, damned. VIRTUOUS

abstracted, absorbed, preoccupied, engrossed, rapt, absent.

lot collection, assortment, batch, set, group, band.

fate, destiny, fortune, luck, chance, hazard, doom, plight.

share, portion, part, allowance, ration.

heap, pile, stack, mass, great deal, abundance, plenty, lots.

lotion ointment, cream, balm, salve, embrocation, liniment.

loud noisy, deafening, ear-splitting, booming, thundering, blaring, resounding, sonorous, stentorian, piercing, strident, clamorous, vociferous, rowdy, boisterous. QUIET

garish, glaring, gaudy, lurid, flashy, showy, ostentatious, tasteless, vulgar. SUBDUED

lounge *v*, rest, relax, recline, repose, loll, lie, loaf, idle, laze. WORK

n, saloon, waiting room, living room, sitting room.

lout boor, churl, oaf, dolt, lubber, bumpkin, brute.

lovable adorable, endearing, winning, charming, sweet, attractive, likable. DETESTABLE

love *v*, adore, cherish, hold dear, treasure, be fond of, care for, desire, like, worship, idolize. HATE

n, affection, attachment, fondness, tenderness, warmth, devotion, adoration, passion, infatuation, ardour, rapture, liking, delight, enjoyment, partiality, inclination, weakness, taste. HATRED

lovely beautiful, attractive, pretty, comely, handsome, graceful, sweet, charming, enchanting, adorable, exquisite, delightful, pleasing, agreeable, enjoyable, pleasant, nice. HORRIBLE

lover boyfriend, fiancé, paramour, philanderer, mistress, girlfriend, fiancée.

low[1] *adj*, short, small, squat, stunted, shallow, flat, depressed, sunken, deep. HIGH

insufficient, inadequate, paltry, meagre, poor, inferior.

coarse, vulgar, rude, base, mean, vile, abject, contemptible, despicable, nasty, malicious, ignoble, unworthy. HONOURABLE

cheap, inexpensive, modest, moderate, reasonable. EXORBITANT
subdued, muted, soft, gentle, quiet, hushed. LOUD
depressed, dejected, blue, melancholy, gloomy, glum, miserable, sad, despondent, downcast. HAPPY

low² *v*, moo, bellow.

lower¹ *v*, drop, fall, sink, descend, depress, let down. RAISE
reduce, cut, decrease, diminish, lessen, soften, moderate, abate, subside, dwindle, decline. INCREASE
abase, degrade, humble, humiliate, demean, belittle, debase, devalue.
adj, inferior, lesser, subordinate, minor, junior. SUPERIOR

lower² *v*, lour, darken, threaten, menace, loom, impend. BRIGHTEN
frown, scowl, glower, glare. SMILE

lowering dark, black, grey, overcast, cloudy, murky, threatening, menacing, ominous. BRIGHT

lowly humble, lowborn, plebeian, poor, simple, plain, unpretentious, modest, unassuming, meek, docile, submissive. LOFTY

loyal true, faithful, constant, devoted, patriotic, staunch, trusty, dependable, reliable, trustworthy. PERFIDIOUS

loyalty allegiance, faithfulness, fidelity, constancy, devotion, patriotism, staunchness, dependability, reliability. INFIDELITY

lubberly awkward, clumsy, maladroit, bungling, ungainly, gawky, clownish, oafish, loutish, churlish, boorish, uncouth.

lubricate oil, grease, smooth.

lucent bright, brilliant, effulgent, shining, luminous, radiant, translucent. DARK

lucid clear, plain, intelligible, comprehensible, distinct, explicit, obvious, sane, rational, sound. UNINTELLIGIBLE
bright, shining, radiant, clear, transparent, translucent, pellucid, crystalline, limpid, pure. OPAQUE

luck chance, fortune, hazard, accident, fortuity, destiny, fate, lot. DESIGN
success, prosperity, fluke, godsend, blessing, windfall. MISFORTUNE

luckless unlucky, unfortunate, hapless, unhappy, unsuccessful, ill-fated, ill-starred, disastrous, calamitous, doomed, fated. LUCKY

lucky fortunate, fortuitous, happy, blessed, charmed, successful, prosperous, favourable, propitious, auspicious, timely, opportune. UNLUCKY

lucrative paying, well-paid, remunerative, gainful, profitable, rewarding, productive, fruitful, advantageous. UNPROFITABLE

lucre wealth, riches, money, profit, gain.

lucubration study, brainwork, cogitation, meditation.
dissertation, thesis, treatise, work.

ludicrous absurd, ridiculous, preposterous, comical, farcical, laughable, droll, funny, crazy, nonsensical, illogical, incongruous, outlandish.

lug pull, drag, heave, tug, tow, haul, carry.

luggage baggage, suitcases, bags, things, belongings, effects, paraphernalia, impedimenta.

lugubrious mournful, sombre, gloomy, dismal, dreary, melancholy, sad, sorrowful, doleful, miserable, depressing. CHEERFUL

lukewarm tepid, warm. COLD
indifferent, uninterested, apathetic, unresponsive, cool, unenthusiastic, half-hearted. ENTHUSIASTIC

lull *v*, soothe, assuage, allay, calm, still, quiet, hush, quell, appease, pacify. DISTURB
abate, subside, diminish, wane, decrease, lessen, cease. INCREASE
n, calm, peace, quiet, hush, stillness, tranquillity, pause, break, respite.

lumber jumble, rubbish, trash, clutter, junk, refuse.

lumbering awkward, clumsy, lumpish, lubberly, ungainly, oafish, heavy, ponderous, unwieldy. DAINTY

luminous glowing, luminescent, phosphorescent, fluorescent, incandescent, bright, shining, brilliant, radiant, effulgent, resplendent, lit, illuminated. DARK
lucid, clear, plain, intelligible, comprehensible, explicit, obvious. UNINTELLIGIBLE

lump *n*, mass, clump, cluster, bunch, ball, piece, chunk.
bump, boss, swelling, growth, tumour, protuberance, bulge.
v, collect, gather, cluster, mass, conglomerate, aggregate, accumulate, combine, unite, group.

lumpish clumsy, awkward, dull, stupid, bovine, heavy, oafish, loutish.

lunacy madness, insanity, derangement, dementia, mania, craziness, aberration, idiocy, stupidity, foolishness, folly, absurdity. SANITY

lunatic *adj*, mad, insane, deranged, demented, crazy, idiotic, stupid, foolish, senseless, absurd. SANE
n, madman, maniac, psychopath, nutter (*inf*), loony (*inf*).

lunge thrust, pass, stab, jab, plunge, pounce.

lurch pitch, roll, toss, rock, sway, stagger.

lure *v*, tempt, entice, attract, draw, allure, decoy, seduce, inveigle. REPEL
n, temptation, enticement, attraction, allurement, bait, decoy. REPULSION

lurid vivid, graphic, exaggerated, melodramatic, sensational, grisly, gruesome, shocking, appalling, violent, intense, dazzling, glaring.

lurk skulk, prowl, sneak, slink, hide, lie in wait. EMERGE

luscious delicious, delectable, appetizing, tasty, mouthwatering, succulent, juicy, ambrosial, fragrant, aromatic, delightful, pleasurable, attractive, gorgeous. REVOLTING

lush succulent, juicy, moist, watery, fresh, tender, fleshy. DRY
luxuriant, dense, prolific, rank, abundant, flourishing, green, verdant. SPARSE

lust *n*, libido, sensuality, carnality, lechery, lasciviousness, lewdness, concupiscence, prurience. FRIGIDITY
desire, longing, craving, appetite, greed, passion. INDIFFERENCE
v, desire, covet, long, yearn, crave, hunger, thirst.

lustful libidinous, lecherous, lascivious, lewd, salacious, licentious, carnal, sensual, concupiscent, prurient, randy (*inf*). CHASTE

lustre sheen, gloss, shine, glow, brightness, brilliance, radiance, effulgence, dazzle, resplendence, splendour, sparkle, glitter. DULLNESS
glory, honour, distinction, fame, renown, illustriousness.

lusty strong, robust, sturdy, hardy, healthy, hale, vigorous, energetic, stout, stalwart, rugged, strapping. WEAK

luxuriant lush, dense, profuse, abundant, plentiful, plenteous, exuberant, rank, prolific, copious, rich, fertile, productive. SPARSE
elaborate, ornate, fancy, flowery, rococo, baroque, flamboyant. SIMPLE

luxuriate bask, revel, wallow, indulge, enjoy, delight, relish.
flourish, thrive, prosper, mushroom, boom, burgeon. WITHER

luxurious sumptuous, opulent, rich, expensive, extravagant, lavish, grand, splendid, magnificent, plush (*inf*), comfortable. AUSTERE
voluptuous, sensual, self-indulgent, epicurean, sybaritic. ASCETIC

luxury opulence, sumptuousness, richness, affluence, grandeur, splendour, magnificence, comfort, pleasure, delight, enjoyment, gratification, self-indulgence, voluptuousness, indulgence, extravagance, treat. AUSTERITY

lying *n*, deceit, fibbing, falsity, untruthfulness, mendacity, dishonesty, duplicity. HONESTY
adj, deceitful, untruthful, mendacious, false, dishonest. TRUTHFUL

M

macabre gruesome, grim, grisly, morbid, horrible, frightful, ghastly, eerie, ghostly, frightening.

macerate soak, steep, soften, pulp, mash.

machiavellian crafty, artful, cunning, sly, wily, tricky, devious, shrewd, astute, deceitful, unscrupulous, opportunist, scheming, designing, intriguing.

machinate plot, plan, scheme, devise, contrive, design, intrigue, conspire.

machination plot, plan, scheme, design, intrigue, conspiracy, trick, ruse, stratagem.

machine instrument, tool, device, contrivance, mechanism, engine, apparatus, appliance.
agency, organization, structure, system, machinery.

mad insane, deranged, demented, unbalanced, unhinged, crazy, lunatic, daft (*inf*), bonkers (*inf*), nuts (*inf*), barmy (*inf*), crackers (*inf*), mental (*inf*). SANE

absurd, ridiculous, foolish, silly, idiotic, senseless, irrational, foolhardy, reckless, unwise. SENSIBLE
frenzied, frenetic, frantic, hysterical, delirious, excited, wild, riotous. CALM
angry, enraged, furious, incensed, infuriated, raging, fuming, irate, wrathful, exasperated, irritated, annoyed. PLEASED
ardent, fanatical, enthusiastic, avid, impassioned, infatuated. INDIFFERENT

madden anger, enrage, incense, infuriate, exasperate, irritate, annoy, vex, inflame, provoke, craze, unhinge, derange. PACIFY

madness insanity, derangement, dementia, mania, aberration, lunacy, craziness, frenzy, hysteria, delirium. SANITY
absurdity, foolishness, folly, stupidity, idiocy, foolhardiness, recklessness. SENSE
anger, rage, fury, ire, wrath, exasperation. COMPOSURE

magazine journal, periodical, review, publication, paper, pamphlet, brochure.
arsenal, storehouse, warehouse, depot.

magic *n*, sorcery, witchcraft, necromancy, theurgy, enchantment, spell.
conjuring, prestidigitation, legerdemain, sleight of hand, illusion.
charm, fascination, power.
adj, magical, miraculous, mystical, occult, supernatural, enchanting, charming, fascinating, bewitching, spellbinding.

magician conjurer, illusionist, wizard, warlock, sorcerer, witch, sorceress, enchantress, miracle-worker.

magisterial authoritative, commanding, imperative, peremptory, dictatorial, despotic, domineering, overbearing, imperious, lordly, lofty, haughty, arrogant. HUMBLE

magnanimity generosity, tolerance, forbearance, kindness, benevolence, charity, bounty, munificence. MEANNESS

magnanimous generous, liberal, openhanded, unselfish, philanthropic, charitable, kind, benevolent, clement, tolerant, forbearing, big, big-hearted, noble, highminded. MEAN

magnate tycoon, industrialist, entrepreneur, baron, mogul, personage, VIP, big shot (*inf*). NOBODY

magnetic hypnotic, fascinating, enchanting, entrancing, attractive, alluring, seductive, irresistible, compelling, charismatic.

magnificent splendid, imposing, impressive, noble, august, grand, stately, majestic, regal, superb, glorious, sublime, excellent, fine, exquisite, gorgeous, sumptuous, rich, lavish, luxurious. POOR

magnify enlarge, increase, amplify, expand, inflate, blow up (*inf*), aggrandize, exaggerate, overstate, overemphasize, deepen, heighten, intensify, exacerbate. REDUCE

magniloquent bombastic, pompous, turgid, tumid, inflated, grandiloquent, high-flown, lofty, declamatory, rhetorical. SIMPLE

magnitude importance, significance, consequence, greatness, immensity, weight, moment, note. INSIGNIFICANCE
size, extent, measure, dimensions, proportion, volume, mass, amplitude, expanse.

maid servant, domestic, housemaid.

maiden *n*, girl, lass, miss, damsel, virgin. LAD
adj, first, initial, inaugural, fresh, new.

maidenly modest, decorous, demure, pure, chaste, virginal, gentle, girlish.

mail *n*, post, correspondence, letters, parcels.
v, post, send, dispatch, forward.

maim disable, incapacitate, cripple, lame, mutilate, injure, hurt, harm, mar, impair.

main *adj*, chief, principal, leading, first, foremost, primary, cardinal, capital, supreme, paramount, essential, vital, indispensable, necessary, critical, crucial. MINOR
sheer, pure, downright, utter, absolute, direct, brute.
n, pipe, conduit, duct, channel, line, cable.
bulk, mass, majority, preponderance, body. PART
strength, might, power, force.

mainly chiefly, principally, primarily, mostly, in the main, on the whole, largely, essentially, generally, usually, above all. PARTLY

maintain keep, retain, conserve, preserve, sustain, support, keep up, continue, perpetuate, look after, care for. ABANDON
state, assert, aver, affirm, asseverate, declare, allege, contend, claim, hold. DENY
defend, uphold, champion, advocate, back, justify, vindicate. ATTACK

maintenance conservation, preservation, upkeep, repairs, care, support, subsistence, living, livelihood, keep, allowance, alimony. NEGLECT
perpetuation, continuance, continuation, prolongation.

majestic grand, august, dignified, noble, regal, royal, kingly, princely, imperial, lofty, exalted, stately, pompous, magnificent, splendid, impressive, imposing. LOWLY

majesty grandeur, dignity, nobility, loftiness, stateliness, pomp, magnificence, splendour. HUMILITY

major larger, greater, chief, main, leading, supreme, important, significant. MINOR

majority bulk, mass, preponderance, body, greater part, greater number, more, most. MINORITY
adulthood, maturity, manhood, womanhood.

make create, fabricate, manufacture, produce, build, construct, fashion, form, shape, invent, originate, devise, contrive. DESTROY
cause, effect, bring about, occasion, generate, produce, render, do, perform, execute, accomplish. UNDO
force, oblige, require, compel, constrain, coerce, drive, urge, impel, induce. PREVENT
constitute, compose, comprise, form, amount to, add up to.
appoint, elect, nominate, assign, invest, install.
earn, clear, net, gross, gain, get, obtain, acquire. SPEND
make believe, pretend, imagine, fantasize, dream.
make do, cope, manage, get by, survive.
make for, head for, aim for, be bound for.
make out, discern, perceive, descry, espy, detect, recognize, see, understand, comprehend, ascertain, distinguish.
draw up, write out, fill in, complete.
make up, invent, fabricate, concoct, hatch, coin, formulate, create, originate, compose, write.
recompense, requite, make amends, make good, compensate, offset.
n, brand, type, sort, kind, shape, form, build, construction, composition.

maker creator, manufacturer, producer, builder, constructor.

makeshift temporary, provisional, improvised, rough-and-ready, emergency.

maladministration mismanagement, misgovernment, misrule, corruption, malpractice, inefficiency, incompetence, bungling.

maladroit clumsy, awkward, bungling, ham-fisted, inapt, inept, inexpert, unskilful, incompetent. DEXTEROUS

malady illness, sickness, ailment, complaint, disorder, disease, indisposition, affliction. FITNESS

malcontent *adj*, discontented, disgruntled, dissatisfied, displeased, uneasy, restive, factious, rebellious. CONTENTED
n, grumbler, complainer, fault-finder, agitator, troublemaker, rebel.

malediction curse, anathema, imprecation, execration, damnation, denunciation, condemnation, slander, calumny. BLESSING

malefactor criminal, felon, lawbreaker, wrongdoer, sinner, offender, miscreant, culprit.

maleficent harmful, hurtful, injurious, baleful, pernicious, noxious, deleterious, detrimental, malignant. HARMLESS

malevolent malicious, malignant, malign, ill-disposed, spiteful, vindictive, revengeful, bitter, rancorous, resentful. BENEVOLENT

malice malevolence, malignity, maliciousness, enmity, hostility, animosity, hate, ill will, spite, vindictiveness, bitterness, rancour, resentment, grudge, spleen, venom. LOVE

malicious malevolent, malignant, malign, ill-disposed, spiteful, vindictive, bitter, rancorous, maleficent, injurious, mischievous, pernicious, vicious. KIND

malign *v*, defame, slander, calumniate, traduce, vilify, denigrate, blacken, revile, disparage, derogate, run down. PRAISE
adj, malignant, malevolent, evil, bad, harmful, injurious, pernicious. GOOD

malignant malevolent, malign, malicious, spiteful, venomous, vindictive, bitter, rancorous, hostile, baleful, injurious, pernicious, harmful, destructive.
deadly, fatal, incurable, irremediable, uncontrollable, virulent. BENIGN

malpractice malversation, misconduct, misbehaviour, negligence, dereliction, mismanagement, misdeed, offence, transgression.

maltreat mistreat, ill-treat, abuse, injure, hurt, harm.

mammon riches, wealth, opulence, affluence, money, lucre, possessions, property.

mammoth huge, enormous, colossal, elephantine, gigantic, gargantuan, vast, immense, massive, titanic. TINY

man male, gentleman, fellow, chap (*inf*), bloke (*inf*), guy (*inf*). WOMAN
person, human being, adult, individual, body, soul. BEAST
mankind, humanity, human race.
employee, worker, hand, soldier, servant, attendant, follower, subject, dependant. MASTER

manacle *v*, handcuff, shackle, fetter, chain, bind, restrain, confine, curb, check. FREE
n, handcuff, shackle, fetter, iron, chain, bond.

manage administer, direct, command, rule, govern, run, conduct, supervise, superintend. MISMANAGE
contrive, succeed, engineer, manoeuvre, bring about, effect. FAIL
cope, fare, get by, make do, survive.
control, influence, guide, steer, pilot, manipulate, operate, handle, wield.

manageable tractable, governable, amenable, docile, compliant, submissive, controllable, handy, convenient, easy. UNMANAGEABLE

management administration, executive, board, directorate, directors, employers, managers. LABOUR
direction, administration, control, regulation, rule, government, command, supervision, conduct, running, handling, operation, care, charge. MISMANAGEMENT

manager director, administrator, executive, controller, overseer, supervisor, superintendent, governor, boss (*inf*), gaffer (*inf*).

mandate command, order, precept, edict, decree, injunction, charge, commission, authorization, authority, warrant, sanction.

mandatory obligatory, binding, compulsory, necessary, requisite, essential. OPTIONAL

mangle mutilate, disfigure, mar, spoil, maim, cripple, cut, lacerate, tear, crush, ruin, destroy.

manhood adulthood, maturity. BOYHOOD
virility, masculinity, manliness, strength, fortitude, hardihood, stamina, bravery, courage, valour, determination, resolution. WOMANHOOD

mania madness, insanity, derangement, dementia, aberration, lunacy, craziness, frenzy, delirium. SANITY
passion, obsession, fixation, craze, rage, urge, desire, craving. PHOBIA

maniac madman, lunatic, psychopath, nutter (*inf*), loony (*inf*).
enthusiast, fanatic, fiend (*inf*), freak (*inf*).

maniacal manic, mad, insane, deranged, unbalanced, lunatic, crazy, demented, crazed, frenzied, hysterical, delirious, wild, raving. SANE

manifest *v*, exhibit, show, display, prove, demonstrate, evince, reveal, expose, declare, make known. HIDE
adj, obvious, evident, plain, clear, visible, apparent, conspicuous, noticeable, glaring, unmistakable, patent, palpable, open, overt. QUESTIONABLE

manifestation display, demonstration, show, exhibition, revelation, exposure, proof, declaration, expression, sign, indication. CONCEALMENT

manifesto statement, declaration, pronouncement, proclamation.

manifold numerous, many, multiple, varied, diverse, assorted, multifarious. FEW

manipulate handle, wield, use, operate, work, manage, control, influence, direct, guide, engineer, exploit.

mankind man, humanity, human race.

manly virile, masculine, strong, mighty, hardy, robust, brave, courageous, valiant, bold, intrepid, resolute, firm, gallant, chivalrous. WOMANLY

manner way, method, means, style, fashion, mode, wont, custom, habit, practice, procedure, routine.
behaviour, conduct, bearing, carriage, deportment, demeanour, mien, air, aspect, appearance, guise, look.
kind, sort, type, variety, make, brand.

mannerism idiosyncrasy, peculiarity, quirk, trait, habit, gesture.

mannerly polite, courteous, well-mannered, civil, respectful, deferential, well-behaved, well-bred, refined, genteel, gentlemanly, ladylike. RUDE

manners behaviour, conduct, comportment, bearing, demeanour, etiquette, decorum, protocol, politeness, courtesy, breeding.

manoeuvre *v*, contrive, engineer, wangle (*inf*), plot, plan, scheme, intrigue, manage, manipulate, handle, steer, pilot, move, deploy.
n, move, movement, action, operation, plot, plan, scheme, intrigue, ruse, artifice, stratagem, tactic.

mansion palace, castle, villa, hall, manor house, stately home, country seat. HOVEL

mantle cloak, cover, blanket, shroud, veil, screen.

manual *n*, handbook, guide, guidebook, vade mecum.
adj, physical, human, hand-operated. AUTOMATIC

manufacture *v*, make, produce, fabricate, build, construct, assemble, turn out, mass-produce, process.
invent, make up, concoct, fabricate, think up.
n, making, production, fabrication, construction, assembly.

manumission liberation, emancipation, enfranchisement, release, deliverance. SERVITUDE

manumit liberate, free, set free, emancipate, enfranchise, release, deliver. ENSLAVE

manure fertilizer, compost, dressing, muck, dung, ordure.

many *adj*, numerous, manifold, myriad, countless, innumerable, umpteen (*inf*), abundant, copious, several, divers, sundry. FEW
n, plenty, a lot, hundreds, lots (*inf*), heaps (*inf*).

map *n*, chart, plan, diagram, graph.
v, plot, plan, map out, chart, delineate.

mar spoil, damage, impair, taint, sully, blight, disfigure, deface, mutilate, injure, hurt, harm, ruin. IMPROVE

marauder robber, bandit, brigand, raider, plunderer, pillager, looter, freebooter, pirate, corsair, buccaneer.

march *v*, walk, stride, step, pace, parade, file, tramp, tread, advance, proceed. HALT
n, parade, procession, file, column, demonstration.
trek, tramp, walk, hike.
step, pace, stride.
advance, progression, progress, development. RETROGRESSION

margin border, edge, periphery, rim, lip, brim, brink, verge, bound, limit, boundary.
allowance, extra, surplus, leeway, latitude, freedom, scope, space, room.

marginal borderline, peripheral, minimal, slight, negligible.

marine sea, maritime, oceanic, pelagic, nautical, naval, seafaring, ocean-going. LAND

mariner sailor, seaman, seafarer, bluejacket, tar (*inf*), matelot (*inf*).

marital conjugal, connubial, matrimonial, nuptial, wedded, married. CELIBATE

maritime marine, seafaring, nautical, naval, sea, oceanic, coastal, littoral. LAND

mark *n*, spot, stain, blemish, bruise, dent, impression, scar, line, scratch.
sign, symbol, indication, brand, stamp, badge, emblem, token, proof, characteristic, feature.
target, objective, goal, aim, purpose.
trace, track, trail, footprint, footmark.
distinction, eminence, fame, renown, note, importance, consequence, influence.
v, stain, blemish, bruise, dent, scar, scratch.
brand, stamp, label, identify, characterize, distinguish, designate, indicate.
note, heed, mind, pay attention, regard, observe, notice.
correct, assess, grade. IGNORE

marked noticeable, obvious, evident, conspicuous, pronounced, prominent, striking, outstanding, remarkable.

market *n*, mart, bazaar, fair, exchange.
trade, commerce, demand, call.
v, sell, retail, deal, trade.

maroon abandon, desert, forsake, leave, strand, isolate, cut off.

marriage wedlock, matrimony, match, wedding, nuptials. DIVORCE
alliance, union, merger, amalgamation, association. SEPARATION

marrow essence, substance, pith, core, kernel, heart, soul, spirit.

marry wed, espouse, get hitched (*inf*), get spliced (*inf*), join, unite, link, connect, ally, associate. SEPARATE

marsh bog, swamp, fen, quagmire, morass, slough.

marshal arrange, dispose, array, order, rank, line up, organize, assemble, gather. DISARRANGE lead, guide, conduct, usher, escort, shepherd.

martial warlike, bellicose, belligerent, military, soldierly, brave, courageous. PACIFIC

marvel *v*, wonder, gape, goggle, be amazed.
n, wonder, prodigy, miracle, phenomenon.

marvellous wonderful, splendid, magnificent, excellent, superb, smashing (*inf*), super (*inf*), fantastic (*inf*), terrific (*inf*). DREADFUL
wondrous, miraculous, astonishing, amazing, remarkable, extraordinary, stupendous, prodigious, incredible, unbelievable. ORDINARY

masculine male, manlike, manly, virile, mannish. FEMININE
strong, mighty, robust, hardy, brave, bold, gallant.

mash crush, pulp, beat, pound, bruise.

mask *n*, disguise, camouflage, front, façade, blind, screen, cover, veil, shield, protection.
v, cover, disguise, camouflage, hide, conceal, screen, veil, shield, protect. EXPOSE

masquerade *n*, masque, masked ball, fancy dress party, revel.
disguise, costume, mask, cloak, guise, pretence, subterfuge, dissimulation, imposture, deception.
v, disguise, impersonate, pose, pretend, dissimulate, dissemble.

mass *n*, lump, chunk, block, heap, pile, stack, load, lot, bunch, collection, group, crowd, throng, mob, host, number, quantity.
size, bulk, dimension, magnitude, body, majority, whole, aggregate, total, sum.
adj, large-scale, widespread, general, popular. LIMITED
v, collect, gather, assemble, muster, swarm, throng, cluster, amass, accumulate. DISPERSE

massacre *n*, slaughter, butchery, carnage, murder, killing, extermination, genocide.
v, slaughter, butcher, mow down, kill, slay, murder, exterminate, wipe out.

massage rub, knead, manipulate.

massive huge, enormous, colossal, immense, gigantic, big, large, imposing, bulky, solid, substantial, heavy, weighty, ponderous. TINY

master *n*, lord, ruler, governor, director, manager, controller, chief, head, leader, commander, owner, proprietor, holder, keeper, employer, boss (*inf*). SERVANT
expert, ace (*inf*), dab hand (*inf*), genius, maestro, virtuoso, adept, pro (*inf*). NOVICE
teacher, instructor, tutor, pedagogue, guide. PUPIL
adj, chief, principal, main, major, great, leading, controlling. MINOR
expert, masterly, adept, proficient, skilled, skilful. INEPT
v, conquer, vanquish, defeat, beat, overpower, overcome, crush, quell, subdue, subjugate. YIELD
rule, govern, dominate, control, command.
learn, grasp, acquire, become proficient.

masterly expert, ace (*inf*), skilful, skilled, adept, proficient, first-rate, excellent, supreme, consummate, polished, finished. INEPT

masterpiece masterwork, *chef-d'oeuvre*, magnum opus, classic.

mastery command, control, domination, upper hand, supremacy, ascendancy, sway, rule, dominion, power, conquest, victory. SERVITUDE
knowledge, command, grasp, understanding, acquisition.
skill, ability, proficiency, expertise, prowess, dexterity, virtuosity. INCOMPETENCE

masticate chew, munch, champ, eat.

mat *n*, rug, pad, cover, mesh.
v, tangle, ravel, interweave, interlace, intertwine, twist. UNRAVEL

match *n*, competition, contest, trial, bout, game.
equal, peer, fellow, mate, twin, counterpart, equivalent, rival, competitor.
marriage, alliance, union, partnership.
v, fit, adapt, suit, accord, agree, correspond, tally, harmonize, coordinate, blend, go with. CLASH
join, unite, marry, mate, couple, pair. SEPARATE
equal, compare, resemble, rival, compete, vie, pit, oppose.

matchless peerless, unrivalled, unmatched, unequalled, unparalleled, incomparable, inimitable, unique, ideal, superlative, consummate, perfect. ORDINARY

mate *n*, partner, spouse, friend, companion, comrade, compeer, colleague, associate, assistant, helper.
match, counterpart, fellow, twin.

v, pair, couple, copulate, breed.
join, match, marry, wed. SEPARATE
material *n*, substance, matter, stuff, fabric, cloth.
information, facts, data, notes, papers.
adj, physical, corporeal, bodily, worldly, earthly, concrete, substantial, tangible, palpable. SPIRITUAL
relevant, important, significant, essential, vital, momentous, weighty, grave, serious. IMMATERIAL
materially considerably, greatly, much, significantly, substantially, essentially.
maternal motherly, protective, caring.
mathematical exact, precise, accurate, strict, rigid.
arithmetic, geometric, algebraic.
matrimonial marital, nuptial, connubial, conjugal, married, wedded.
matrimony marriage, wedlock, wedding, nuptials.
matronly maternal, motherly, middle-aged, staid, sober, sedate, dignified, portly, plump.
matter *v*, signify, count, be important, carry weight, make a difference.
n, substance, material, stuff, body.
subject, topic, question, issue, business, affair, concern, thing, circumstance, event.
trouble, problem, difficulty, distress, worry.
importance, significance, consequence, note, moment, weight.
discharge, secretion, pus.
mature *adj*, ripe, mellow, seasoned, full-grown, grown-up, adult, of age, complete, perfect, fully developed, ready, prepared. IMMATURE
v, ripen, mellow, season, age, develop, grow up.
maudlin sentimental, emotional, mawkish, soppy (*inf*), tearful, weepy (*inf*).
maul paw, manhandle, batter, beat, claw, lacerate, ill-treat, abuse, injure, hurt, harm, damage.
mawkish maudlin, sentimental, emotional, soppy (*inf*), weak, feeble.
nauseating, sickly, foul, insipid, tasteless, stale, flat, vapid.
maxim saying, proverb, adage, aphorism, axiom, dictum, saw.
maximum *n*, height, peak, top, climax, limit, ceiling, extreme, utmost. MINIMUM
adj, maximal, greatest, highest, most, utmost, supreme. MINIMAL
maybe perhaps, possibly, perchance, peradventure. DEFINITELY
maze labyrinth, network, tangle, web, confusion, perplexity, bewilderment, complexity, intricacy.
meadow field, grassland, pasture, lea.
meagre scanty, scant, sparse, skimpy, short, deficient, inadequate, insufficient, poor, paltry, small, little, slight. AMPLE
thin, lean, skinny, scrawny, bony, emaciated. FAT
barren, sterile, infertile, unproductive, unfruitful. RICH
meal repast, feast, banquet, snack, breakfast, lunch, tea, dinner, supper. FAST
mean[1] *v*, signify, denote, betoken, represent, symbolize, stand for, indicate, portend, presage, imply, suggest, connote, purport.
intend, aim, purpose, contemplate, have in mind, propose, plan.
destine, design, make, predestine, preordain.
cause, bring about, produce, result in, involve, entail.
mean[2] *adj*, miserly, niggardly, stingy, parsimonious, close, tight-fisted, tight, selfish, ungenerous. GENEROUS
unkind, nasty, unpleasant, malicious, callous, cruel, base, low, despicable, contemptible, abject, shabby, shameful, disgraceful, dishonourable, ignoble, petty, small-minded. HONOURABLE
poor, lowly, humble, miserable, wretched, shabby, seedy, squalid, vulgar, common, ordinary, inferior, second-rate. MAGNIFICENT
mean[3] *n*, average, norm, median, mid-point, middle, compromise, happy medium. EXTREME
adj, medium, average, normal, middle, intermediate.
meander wind, zigzag, snake, twist, turn, bend.
wander, ramble, drift, stray.
meaning significance, signification, sense, import, purport, connotation, implication, gist, drift, interpretation, explanation.
aim, intention, idea, object, end, purpose, plan, design.
value, worth, point, use, effect.

means method, way, mode, medium, vehicle, instrument, agency, course, channel, resource, measure, expedient. END
resources, funds, income, revenue, property, estate, money, riches, wealth, substance. POVERTY
by all means, certainly, of course, definitely, absolutely.

measure *v*, weigh, sound, quantify, gauge, assess, rate, value, evaluate, appraise, estimate, calculate, compute, determine.
n, size, magnitude, quantity, amount, extent, degree, scope, range.
rule, meter, gauge, scale, standard, norm, criterion, yardstick, touchstone.
portion, share, ration, division, piece, part. WHOLE
limit, bounds, control, limitation.
step, action, course, procedure.

measured slow, leisurely, unhurried, deliberate, planned, studied, calculated, steady, regular, even, uniform, regulated, precise, exact.

measureless immeasurable, incalculable, limitless, unlimited, illimitable, boundless, unbounded, infinite, endless, interminable, vast, immense. FINITE

measurement dimension, size, extent, amount, height, depth, length, breadth, area, volume, capacity, weight.
mensuration, metage, assessment, evaluation, estimation, calculation.

mechanical automatic, involuntary, instinctive, unconscious, unthinking, habitual, routine, cold, unfeeling, emotionless, spiritless, lifeless.

mechanism machine, motor, engine, appliance, device, contrivance, instrument, tool, workings, machinery.
means, agency, system, procedure, process, method, technique.

meddle interfere, intermeddle, pry, snoop (*inf*), interpose, intervene, intrude, butt in.

meddlesome meddling, intrusive, interfering, officious, obtrusive, prying, inquisitive, nosy (*inf*).

medial middle, central, intermediate, median. EXTREME
average, mean, ordinary.

mediate arbitrate, referee, umpire, intercede, intervene, interpose, reconcile, conciliate.

mediation arbitration, good offices, intercession, intervention, reconciliation, conciliation.

medicinal therapeutic, healing, curative, remedial, restorative, medical.

medicine medicament, medication, remedy, cure, drug.

mediocre average, middling, passable, tolerable, so-so (*inf*), ordinary, commonplace, run-of-the-mill, indifferent, undistinguished, inferior, second-rate. EXCELLENT

meditate ruminate, contemplate, reflect, ponder, muse, brood, cogitate, deliberate, consider, think.
plan, scheme, intend, purpose, devise, contrive, design.

meditation rumination, contemplation, reflection, cogitation, deliberation, thought, cerebration, concentration, brown study.

medium *adj*, average, mean, medial, median, middle, intermediate, middling, mediocre. EXTREME
n, average, mean, midpoint, middle.
means, vehicle, agency, instrumentality, avenue, channel, way.
element, environment, milieu, surroundings, conditions.

medley mixture, assortment, miscellany, hotchpotch, pot-pourri, jumble, confusion.

meek patient, long-suffering, forbearing, mild, gentle, modest, unassuming, humble, lowly, deferential, compliant, submissive, yielding, docile, acquiescent, resigned, spiritless, tame.

meet encounter, come across, happen upon, run into, bump into, face, confront. MISS
join, converge, come together, touch, cross, intersect. DIVERGE
fulfil, satisfy, answer, match, measure up, discharge, carry out, handle, cope with, settle.
gather, collect, assemble, congregate, convene, muster. DISPERSE

meeting encounter, confrontation, rendezvous, tryst, assignation, introduction, presentation. PARTING
gathering, assembly, congregation, convention, conference, concourse, rally, reunion, get-together (*inf*), session, meet.
convergence, confluence, junction, intersection, crossing. DIVERGENCE

melancholy *n*, gloominess, gloom, depression, dejection, despondency, low spirits, blues, sadness, sorrow, unhappiness, misery. ELATION
adj, gloomy, glum, depressed, dejected, downcast, downhearted, dispirited, disconsolate, despondent, low-spirited, blue, doleful, dismal, mournful, sad, sorrowful, unhappy, miserable, woebegone. ELATED

melee fight, brawl, scuffle, fray, fracas, free-for-all.

mellifluous mellifluent, mellow, smooth, flowing, euphonious, melodious, harmonious, soft, sweet, honeyed, dulcet, silvery. HARSH

mellow ripe, mature, soft, tender, sweet, full-flavoured, rich, full, resonant, mellifluous, melodious, smooth.
genial, affable, amiable, jovial, cheerful.
v, age, develop, improve, mature, season, ripen, soften.

melodious tuneful, melodic, musical, concordant, harmonious, euphonious, sweet, dulcet, silvery. DISCORDANT

melodramatic histrionic, theatrical, stagy, exaggerated, overdramatic, hammy (*inf*), sensational, extravagant.

melody tune, music, theme, strain, air, song.
melodiousness, tunefulness, harmony, euphony. DISCORD

melt liquefy, thaw, fuse, dissolve, deliquesce, soften. FREEZE
fade, disappear, vanish, evanesce, disperse, dissipate.

member adherent, associate, fellow, subscriber.
part, component, constituent, element, limb, organ, appendage.

memento keepsake, souvenir, relic, reminder, memorial, remembrance.

memoir biography, life, history, record, account, essay, monograph.

memoirs reminiscences, recollections, experiences, autobiography, journal, diary.

memorable unforgettable, remarkable, striking, extraordinary, noteworthy, historic, important, significant, momentous, great, famous, illustrious, celebrated. INSIGNIFICANT

memorandum memo, note, message, record, statement, minute, reminder.

memorial remembrance, memento, monument, statue, plaque, inscription, commemoration.

memorize learn, learn by heart, commit to memory, remember. FORGET

memory recall, retention, recollection, remembrance, reminiscence, retrospection. FORGETFULNESS
commemoration, honour, glory, fame, renown, regard, repute. OBLIVION

menace *v*, threaten, alarm, scare, frighten, intimidate, terrorize, lower, impend, loom. REASSURE
n, threat, intimidation, warning. REASSURANCE
danger, peril, hazard, risk, jeopardy.
nuisance, pest, annoyance, vexation, pain (*inf*).

mend repair, fix, darn, patch, restore, renovate, remedy, cure, heal. DAMAGE
amend, emend, correct, rectify, reform, improve, ameliorate. DETERIORATE
recover, get better, recuperate, convalesce.

mendacious lying, untruthful, deceitful, dishonest, insincere, false, untrue, fraudulent. HONEST

mendacity lying, untruthfulness, deceit, dishonesty, insincerity, falsity, duplicity, deception, fraudulence. HONESTY
lie, fib, untruth, falsehood. TRUTH

menial *adj*, humble, lowly, low, base, mean, ignoble, degrading, demeaning, servile, obsequious, fawning, grovelling, sycophantic, subservient.
n, servant, domestic, attendant, lackey, flunky, slave, drudge, skivvy (*inf*). MASTER

mensuration measurement, measuring, survey, surveying, calculation, computation.

mental intellectual, cerebral, psychological, abstract. PHYSICAL
deranged, unbalanced, mentally ill, insane, mad. SANE

mention *v*, name, cite, quote, refer to, speak of, touch on, bring up, broach, point out, say, utter, declare, tell, communicate, disclose, divulge, make known, acknowledge. OMIT
n, reference, allusion, remark, observation, declaration, announcement, tribute, citation, acknowledgment, recognition.

mentor advisor, counsellor, guide, confidant, guru, master, teacher, instructor, tutor.

mephitic foul, putrid, rank, stinking, malodorous, fetid, noisome, noxious, poisonous, pestilential, miasmatic, unwholesome. SALUBRIOUS

mercantile commercial, trading, marketable, saleable.

mercenary greedy, avaricious, covetous, grasping, acquisitive, selfish, sordid. LIBERAL
hired, paid, bought, venal. VOLUNTARY

merchandise goods, ware, commodities, stock, produce.

merchant trader, dealer, broker, tradesman, shopkeeper, retailer, wholesaler, seller, vendor, salesman.

merciful compassionate, forgiving, forbearing, clement, lenient, kind, benignant, mild, humane, tender-hearted, sympathetic, gracious, magnanimous, generous. MERCILESS

merciless pitiless, unforgiving, unmerciful, cruel, unkind, harsh, hard, callous, heartless, unfeeling, ruthless, implacable, relentless, unrelenting, inhuman, savage, barbarous. MERCIFUL

mercurial lively, vivacious, active, energetic, spirited, volatile, capricious, fickle, changeable, variable, inconstant, impulsive.

mercy clemency, leniency, pardon, grace, forgiveness, forbearance, pity, compassion, kindness, tenderness, mildness, magnanimity, benevolence. CRUELTY

mere bare, sheer, simple, plain, pure, unadulterated, unmitigated, utter, absolute, entire, complete.

merely only, just, simply, solely, purely, utterly, entirely.

meretricious showy, flashy, gaudy, garish, tawdry, cheap.
sham, bogus, false, insincere, spurious, counterfeit. GENUINE

merge join, unite, meet, converge, combine, amalgamate, blend, mingle, mix, fuse. SEPARATE

merger amalgamation, combination, incorporation, coalition, union. SEPARATION

meridian zenith, peak, apex, summit, pinnacle, acme, height, climax, culmination. NADIR

merit *v*, deserve, be worthy of, earn, incur, be entitled to, have a right to.
n, worth, worthiness, excellence, quality, value, good, virtue, asset, credit, desert, due. FAULT

meritorious worthy, deserving, creditable, praiseworthy, commendable, admirable, excellent, good, honourable, virtuous. DESPICABLE

merriment mirth, hilarity, laughter, levity, jollity, gaiety, glee, joy, cheer, fun, pleasure, sport, revelry, merrymaking, festivity, conviviality. GLOOM

merry jolly, jovial, jocund, mirthful, hilarious, cheerful, blithe, happy, joyful, gleeful, gay, festive, convivial. GLOOMY
tipsy, tiddly (*inf*), squiffy (*inf*). SOBER

mesh *n*, net, netting, network, web, snare, trap, tangle, entanglement.
v, catch, net, snare, trap, entangle. FREE
engage, interlock, coordinate.

mesmerize hypnotize, fascinate, captivate, enthral, entrance, spellbind.

mess *n*, untidiness, dirtiness, disorder, disarray, clutter, litter, jumble, muddle, confusion, perplexity. ORDER
difficulty, trouble, plight, predicament, quandary, dilemma, fix (*inf*), pickle (*inf*).
v, untidy, dirty, disorder, disarrange, mess up, botch, bungle, muddle, confuse. CLEAR

message communication, intimation, missive, dispatch, bulletin, note, letter, memorandum, word, news.

messenger courier, runner, bearer, carrier, envoy, emissary, go-between, harbinger, herald.

messy untidy, unkempt, slovenly, sloppy, dirty, grubby, disordered, cluttered, muddled, confused. NEAT

metamorphosis change, alteration, modification, transformation, transfiguration, mutation, transmutation, conversion, regeneration.

metaphor allegory, image, symbol, figure of speech, analogy.

metaphysical abstract, theoretical, intangible, immaterial, supernatural, spiritual, intellectual, philosophical, ideal, speculative, abstruse, esoteric. MATERIAL

mete distribute, dispense, deal, administer, allot, assign, allocate, apportion. WITHHOLD

method way, manner, mode, procedure, process, means, approach, style, technique, system, routine, course.

order, orderliness, organization, planning, structure, regularity. DISORDER

methodical systematic, organized, orderly, neat, tidy, businesslike, efficient, structured, planned, exact, precise, meticulous. DISORGANIZED

meticulous precise, exact, scrupulous, punctilious, fastidious, particular, fussy, finicky, painstaking, thorough. SLAPDASH

metropolis capital, city.

mettle character, temperament, disposition, nature, make-up, temper, humour.
spirit, vigour, energy, animation, ardour, fervour, fire, pluck, nerve, grit, courage, bravery, valour, boldness, fortitude, resolution.

miasmatic miasmal, miasmic, mephitic, foul, putrid, rank, fetid, stinking, malodorous, noisome, noxious, poisonous, unwholesome. SALUBRIOUS

microscopic minute, tiny, minuscule, infinitesimal, imperceptible, negligible. HUGE

middle *n*, centre, midpoint, mean, midst, heart, core. EDGE
adj, central, halfway, intermediate, medium, mean, medial. EXTREME

middling mediocre, fair, average, medium, moderate, passable, tolerable, so-so (*inf*), OK (*inf*).

midst middle, centre, heart, thick. EDGE

mien bearing, carriage, deportment, manner, demeanour, air, appearance, look, aspect, aura.

might power, force, strength, vigour, energy, potency, ability, capability. WEAKNESS

mighty powerful, forceful, strong, robust, hardy, sturdy, stalwart, strapping, lusty, hearty, vigorous. WEAK
huge, enormous, gigantic, colossal, massive, immense. TINY

migrate move, relocate, resettle, emigrate, immigrate, travel, journey, wander, roam. REMAIN

migratory migrant, wandering, roving, nomadic, itinerant, peripatetic, travelling, displaced, unsettled.

mild bland, gentle, tender, soft, moderate, meek, docile, kind, compassionate, merciful, clement, lenient, amiable, genial, pacific, calm, placid, serene, equable, mellow, temperate, balmy, pleasant, soothing. HARSH

mildew mould, fungus, blight, rust, blast, smut, must, mustiness.

militant *adj*, aggressive, belligerent, bellicose, combative, warring, fighting, contending. PACIFIC
n, activist, combatant, fighter, warrior.

military soldierly, armed, martial, warlike. CIVIL

militate oppose, counter, conflict with, go against, contend, war.

mill *n*, factory, plant, works.
grinder, crusher, roller.
v, grind, pulverize, powder, comminute, triturate, crush, pound.

mimic *v*, imitate, ape, copy, impersonate, take off (*inf*), mock, simulate, mirror, echo. resemble.
n, mimicker, imitator, copycat (*inf*), impersonator, impressionist.
adj, imitative, mimetic, simulated, mock, sham. GENUINE

minatory minatorial, minacious, threatening, menacing.

mince chop, hash, dice, grind, crumble.
pose, attitudinize, put on airs.

mind *n*, intellect, brain, intelligence, mentality, sense, wits, reason, understanding, soul, spirit, attention, thoughts, imagination, head, sanity, rationality.
memory, recollection, remembrance.
opinion, view, attitude, feeling, sentiment, thought, belief, idea, judgment.
inclination, disposition, tendency, desire, wish, urge, notion, fancy, will, purpose, intention.
v, care, object, take offence, disapprove, dislike.
regard, heed, pay attention, attend, mark, note, obey, watch, observe, be careful. IGNORE
look after, tend, take care of, watch over. NEGLECT

mindful aware, conscious, alert, attentive, regardful, heedful, thoughtful, careful, wary, chary.

mindless thoughtless, unthinking, heedless, foolish, witless, senseless, stupid, careless, negligent, inattentive, oblivious. MINDFUL

mine *n*, pit, colliery, shaft, excavation, vein, seam, deposit.
source, supply, fund, reserve, treasury, wealth, abundance.

v, dig, bore, excavate, tunnel, quarry, extract.
undermine, sap, weaken. PROP

mingle mix, commingle, intermingle, intermix, merge, blend, combine, amalgamate, join, unite. SEPARATE
associate, fraternize, consort, hobnob, socialize, circulate.

miniature tiny, small, little, wee, minute, diminutive, mini, pygmy, dwarf, midget, baby, toy. LARGE

minimum *n*, least, lowest, bottom, nadir. MAXIMUM
adj, minimal, least, lowest, smallest, slightest. MAXIMAL

minion favourite, darling, pet, follower, dependant, parasite, hanger-on, underling, subordinate, flunky, lackey, bootlicker (*inf*), sycophant, toady, yes man. MASTER

minister *n*, clergyman, cleric, churchman, ecclesiastic, vicar, parson, rector, pastor, curate, preacher. LAYMAN
official, dignitary, administrator, executive, ambassador, diplomat, plenipotentiary, envoy, agent, servant.
v, attend, wait on, serve, take care of, tend, oblige, accommodate, help, aid, assist.

ministration help, aid, assistance, support, service, relief, care.

ministry church, clergy, priesthood, holy orders, religion.
government, cabinet, administration, department, office.

minor lesser, smaller, secondary, subsidiary, subordinate, inferior, junior, slight, trivial, petty, insignificant, unimportant, inconsiderable, small. MAJOR

minstrel musician, singer, troubadour, bard, performer, entertainer.

mint *v*, coin, stamp, strike, punch.
make, product, forge, create, fabricate, invent, coin, formulate, think up, devise.
adj, perfect, excellent, brand-new, unused.

minus less, lacking, without. PLUS

minute[1] *n*, moment, second, instant, flash, twinkling, trice, jiffy (*inf*).
note, memorandum, memo (*inf*), record, transcript.

minute[2] *adj*, tiny, minuscule, microscopic, infinitesimal, diminutive, small, little, wee, fine. HUGE
detailed, exact, precise, meticulous, painstaking, scrupulous, punctilious. CURSORY

miracle wonder, marvel, prodigy, phenomenon.

miraculous wonderful, marvellous, extraordinary, phenomenal, amazing, astonishing, incredible, unbelievable, inexplicable, supernatural, preternatural, superhuman, divine. ORDINARY

mire marsh, bog, swamp, quagmire, morass, fen, mud, dirt.

mirror *n*, glass, looking-glass, reflector.
reflection, copy, replica, representation, likeness, paragon, exemplar, model, pattern.
v, reflect, echo, imitate, copy, represent, depict.

mirth merriment, gaiety, glee, joy, happiness, cheerfulness, jollity, levity, hilarity, laughter, amusement, fun, sport, pleasure, revelry, festivity, merrymaking. MELANCHOLY

mirthful merry, gay, joyful, happy, blithe, cheerful, jolly, jovial, jocund, lighthearted, playful, sportive, festive, lively, vivacious. GLOOMY

misadventure misfortune, mischance, mishap, bad luck, accident, calamity, disaster, reverse, setback.

misanthropy cynicism, egoism, selfishness, malevolence, inhumanity. PHILANTHROPY

misapprehend misunderstand, misconceive, misconstrue, misinterpret, misread, mistake.

misappropriate steal, embezzle, peculate, defalcate, misuse, misspend.

misbehaviour misconduct, naughtiness, indiscipline, insubordination, disobedience, impropriety, rudeness, misdemeanour, delinquency.

miscalculate miscount, misjudge, overestimate, underestimate, err, go wrong, slip up, make a mistake.

miscarriage abortion, failure, defeat, frustration, mismanagement, misfortune, misadventure, mishap, mischance. SUCCESS

miscarry abort, fail, go wrong, misfire, fall through. SUCCEED

miscellaneous mixed, varied, various, diverse, sundry, assorted, heterogeneous, motley, multiform, multifarious.

miscellany mixture, variety, diversity, assortment, medley, hotchpotch, pot-pourri, jumble, collection, anthology.

mischance misadventure, mishap, bad luck, ill luck, misfortune, accident, calamity, disaster.

mischief naughtiness, misconduct, misbehaviour, roguery, rascality, impishness, devilment.
trouble, ill, harm, hurt, injury, damage, annoyance, nuisance. GOOD

mischievous naughty, roguish, rascally, impish, puckish, arch, playful, teasing, annoying, exasperating. GOOD
harmful, hurtful, injurious, damaging, detrimental, pernicious, bad, evil, wicked. BENEFICIAL

misconceive misunderstand, misapprehend, misinterpret, misconstrue, misread, mistake, misjudge, miscalculate.

misconduct misbehaviour, wrongdoing, delinquency, misdemeanour, misdeed, transgression, malpractice, negligence, impropriety, mismanagement.

misconstrue misinterpret, misread, misunderstand, misapprehend, misconceive, mistake, misjudge.

miscreant wrongdoer, malefactor, criminal, villain, rogue, rascal, scoundrel, blackguard, reprobate, sinner.

misdeed misdemeanour, felony, crime, offence, wrong, fault, sin, transgression, trespass, misdoing.

misdemeanour misdeed, offence, violation, infringement, peccadillo, transgression, trespass, misconduct, misbehaviour.

miser niggard, skinflint, churl, curmudgeon, Scrooge, hoarder, penny-pincher (*inf*), cheapskate (*inf*). SPENDTHRIFT

miserable unhappy, sad, sorrowful, forlorn, wretched, woebegone, doleful, depressed, dejected, downcast, despondent, gloomy, melancholy, distressed, disconsolate, heartbroken. HAPPY
contemptible, despicable, base, mean, low, abject, sordid, squalid, wretched, sorry, pathetic, pitiful, pitiable. NOBLE
poor, penniless, impoverished, poverty-stricken, destitute, indigent, needy. RICH

miserly niggardly, mean, stingy, close, tight, tight-fisted, parsimonious, penurious, avaricious, covetous, selfish, ungenerous, penny-pinching (*inf*), cheeseparing. GENEROUS

misery unhappiness, sadness, sorrow, woe, grief, wretchedness, depression, dejection, despondency, gloom, melancholy, distress, affliction, hardship, suffering, anguish, torment, despair, desolation. JOY
poverty, need, want, privation, indigence, destitution. AFFLUENCE

misfortune mischance, bad luck, ill luck, mishap, misadventure, accident, tragedy, calamity, disaster, adversity, affliction, hardship, trouble, trial, tribulation, blow, reverse, setback.

misgiving doubt, hesitation, uncertainty, suspicion, mistrust, distrust, qualm, scruple, reservation, anxiety, apprehension. ASSURANCE

misguided misled, misinformed, deluded, imprudent, ill-advised, injudicious, foolish, erroneous, mistaken, wrong.

mishap accident, misfortune, misadventure, mischance, bad luck, ill luck, calamity, disaster, contretemps.

misinterpret misconstrue, misread, misconceive, misunderstand, misapprehend, mistake, misjudge, misrepresent, distort, garble.

misjudge miscalculate, underestimate, underrate, overestimate, overrate, misinterpret, misconstrue, misunderstand.

mislay lose, misplace. FIND

mislead misguide, misdirect, misinform, deceive, delude, fool, trick, hoodwink, lead astray.

mismanage mishandle, botch, bungle, mess up, maladminister, misgovern, misdirect, misconduct.

misprint mistake, error, erratum, corrigendum, literal, typo (*inf*).

misprize underrate, undervalue, underestimate, despise, scorn, disparage, belittle, slight. VALUE

misrepresent falsify, distort, twist, pervert, garble, misinterpret, misstate, belie.

misrule maladministration, misgovernment, mismanagement, anarchy, lawlessness, chaos, disorder, confusion, tumult, turmoil. ORDER

miss¹ *v*, fail, miscarry, lose, omit, overlook, skip, escape, avoid, dodge.
want, need, long for, yearn for, desiderate. HAVE
n, failure, miscarriage, mistake, error, slip, blunder, oversight, omission, loss.

miss² *n*, girl, lass, young lady, damsel, maiden.

misshapen deformed, malformed, unshapely, twisted, warped, distorted, crooked, grotesque, ugly. SHAPELY

missile projectile, shot, arrow, rocket, weapon.

missing absent, lost, mislaid, lacking, wanting, gone. FOUND

mission duty, task, job, office, business, assignment, commission, charge, trust, errand, quest, goal, objective, aim, purpose, work, vocation, calling.

embassy, commission, delegation, deputation, legation, ministry.

missive letter, epistle, dispatch, communication, message.

misspend misuse, misapply, squander, waste, dissipate, throw away.

misstate misquote, misreport, misrepresent, falsify, distort, pervert, garble.

mist haze, fog, cloud, vapour, steam, condensation, film, drizzle, spray.

mistake *n*, error, slip, inaccuracy, fault, oversight, blunder, howler (*inf*), miscalculation, misunderstanding, misapprehension, misconception, gaffe, faux pas.

v, misinterpret, misconstrue, misconceive, misunderstand, misapprehend, misjudge, confuse, mix up, get wrong.

err, be wrong, miscalculate, slip up (*inf*).

mistaken wrong, erroneous, incorrect, inaccurate, inexact, imprecise, false, untrue, fallacious, unsound, faulty, misguided, misled, misinformed. CORRECT

mistreat maltreat, ill-treat, misuse, ill-use, abuse, molest, harm, injure, manhandle, batter.

mistress paramour, courtesan, concubine, kept woman, lover, girlfriend, inamorata.

head, proprietor, owner, teacher, governess.

mistrust *v*, distrust, doubt, suspect, disbelieve, be wary of, fear. TRUST

n, distrust, doubt, scepticism, suspicion, wariness, qualm, misgiving. CONFIDENCE

misty hazy, foggy, cloudy, murky, bleary, fuzzy, blurred, obscure, dim, vague, indistinct. CLEAR

misunderstand misapprehend, misinterpret, misconstrue, misconceive, mistake, misjudge, misread, mishear. UNDERSTAND

misunderstanding mistake, error, misapprehension, misinterpretation, misconstruction, misconception, misjudgment. UNDERSTANDING

disagreement, discord, dissension, clash, conflict, variance, difference, quarrel, argument. AGREEMENT

misuse *v*, misemploy, misapply, squander, waste, profane, pervert, abuse, mistreat, maltreat, ill-treat, ill-use, exploit.

n, misemployment, misapplication, waste, abuse, maltreatment, ill-use, exploitation.

mitigate moderate, lessen, reduce, diminish, abate, alleviate, allay, assuage, ease, relieve, soften, lighten, calm, appease, mollify, pacify, dull, blunt, subdue. AGGRAVATE

mix combine, blend, mingle, commingle, intermingle, intermix, compound, alloy, amalgamate, join, cross. SEPARATE

associate, fraternize, consort, hobnob, socialize, mingle.

mix up, confuse, muddle, confound, mistake, jumble, garble, scramble, bewilder, puzzle, entangle, involve.

mixture mix, combination, blend, compound, alloy, amalgamation, union, cross, hybrid, medley, miscellany, pot-pourri, hotchpotch, jumble, assortment, variety.

moan *v*, complain, grumble, lament, bewail, bemoan, mourn, grieve, sorrow, deplore, groan, sigh. REJOICE

n, complaint, grumble, lament, wail, cry, sob, groan, sigh.

mob crowd, throng, multitude, mass, horde, host, herd, pack, flock, swarm, gang. INDIVIDUAL

rabble, populace, hoi polloi, masses, commonalty.

mobile movable, portable, travelling, itinerant, peripatetic, moving, motile, changeable, variable, animated. IMMOBILE

mock ridicule, jeer, scoff, laugh at, make fun of, tease, taunt, deceive, delude, deride, sneer, scorn, flout, defy. RESPECT

mimic, ape, simulate, counterfeit, imitate, impersonate, take off (*inf*), lampoon, parody, burlesque, satirize.

adj, counterfeit, fake, bogus, spurious, false, sham, imitation, simulated, artificial, feigned, pretended. GENUINE

mockery ridicule, jeering, scoffing, gibe, taunt, derision, scorn, contempt. RESPECT

imitation, travesty, lampoon, parody, burlesque, send-up (*inf*), sham, pretence.

mode manner, way, method, approach, technique, style, fashion, form, custom, practice.

model *n*, example, pattern, template, mould, standard, norm, type, archetype, prototype, original, exemplar, paragon, epitome, ideal.
copy, replica, facsimile, representation, imitation, miniature.
dummy, mannequin, sitter, poser, subject.
design, style, version, mark.
v, make, mould, shape, form, fashion, sculpt, carve, cast, plan, design.
wear, show, display, sit, pose.

moderate *adj*, reasonable, restrained, controlled, temperate, equable, mild, gentle, steady, calm, middle-of-the-road. EXTREME
average, medium, modest, mediocre, middling, fair, passable, so-so (*inf*).
v, temper, control, regulate, lessen, reduce, diminish, mitigate, soften, abate, allay, assuage, appease, pacify, calm, subdue, repress, restrain. AGGRAVATE
arbitrate, judge, umpire, referee, preside, chair.

moderation temperance, restraint, control, regulation, reduction, diminution, mitigation, calm, composure, equanimity, fairness, justice. IMMODERATION

modern contemporary, current, present, new, novel, fresh, recent, latest, up-to-date, up-to-the-minute, stylish, fashionable. OUT-OF-DATE

modest humble, unassuming, unpretentious, self-effacing, retiring, quiet, shy, bashful, reticent, reserved, coy, diffident, meek, demure, discreet, decent, decorous. IMMODEST
moderate, medium, limited, fair, middling, ordinary, simple. EXCESSIVE

modicum bit, iota, atom, grain, pinch, drop, scrap, shred, ounce. LOT

modification change, alteration, variation, mutation, adjustment, modulation, revision, limitation, restriction, qualification.

modify change, alter, vary, adjust, adapt, remodel, revise, transform, convert.
moderate, temper, lower, lessen, limit, restrict, qualify.

modulate change, modify, adjust, regulate, vary, inflect, attune, tune, harmonize.

moiety half, fifty per cent, part, piece, fragment, portion, share. WHOLE

moist damp, clammy, dank, humid, muggy, dewy, wet. DRY

moisture liquid, water, damp, dampness, wetness, humidity, vapour, condensation, dew. DRYNESS

mole breakwater, groyne, pier, jetty, sea wall, embankment, dyke.

molest disturb, bother, pester, plague, harass, badger, harry, worry, annoy, vex, irritate, torment, tease.
accost, assault, attack, mistreat, maltreat, ill-use, abuse, hurt, injure.

mollify soothe, calm, pacify, appease, placate, compose, tranquillize, still, quiet. PROVOKE
abate, lessen, reduce, mitigate, moderate, temper, allay, assuage, alleviate, ease, soften. AGGRAVATE

mollycoddle pamper, cosset, coddle, spoil, ruin, indulge, pet, baby. DISCIPLINE

moment second, minute, instant, twinkling, flash, trice, jiffy (*inf*). AGE
point, juncture, stage, time, hour.
importance, significance, consequence, import, weight, gravity, worth, value, note, concern. INSIGNIFICANCE

momentary brief, short, temporary, transitory, transient, fleeting, passing, ephemeral, short-lived. LENGTHY

momentous important, significant, consequential, weighty, grave, serious, crucial, critical, vital, major, historic. TRIVIAL

momentum impetus, impulse, force, thrust, drive, push, power, strength.

monarch ruler, sovereign, crowned head, king, queen, emperor, empress. SUBJECT

monarchal monarchical, royal, regal, kingly, queenly.

monastery friary, abbey, priory, cloister, religious community.

monastic reclusive, solitary, sequestered, cloistered, ascetic, celibate, conventual, monkish, coenobitic, eremitic. SECULAR

monetary financial, pecuniary, fiscal.

money currency, legal tender, cash, coin, specie, bread (*inf*), dough (*inf*), lucre, wealth, riches, funds, capital, wherewithal, means.

moneyed rich, wealthy, affluent, prosperous, well-off, flush (*inf*), loaded (*inf*). POOR

monitor *n*, supervisor, overseer, prefect, guide.
v, check, observe, watch, supervise, oversee, record.

monomania fixation, obsession, *idée fixe*, bee in one's bonnet.

monopolize appropriate, take over, control, dominate, corner, hog (*inf*), engross, absorb.

monopoly control, domination, exclusiveness, corner, trust, cartel. COMPETITION

monotonous boring, tedious, dull, uninteresting, humdrum, repetitive, unvaried, unchanging, uniform, tiresome, wearisome. INTERESTING

monotony tedium, dullness, routine, sameness, uniformity.

monster freak, mutant, teratism, monstrosity, abortion.
brute, beast, fiend, demon, devil, ogre, villain, savage, barbarian.
giant, colossus, titan, behemoth. MIDGET

monstrous hideous, grotesque, horrible, horrendous, dreadful, awful, frightful, terrible, shocking, scandalous, outrageous, atrocious, heinous, fiendish, diabolical, infamous, villainous, odious, loathsome. WONDERFUL
abnormal, unnatural, freakish, deformed, misshapen. NORMAL
huge, colossal, gigantic, enormous, massive, immense, prodigious, gargantuan, titanic. TINY

monument memorial, cenotaph, shrine, tombstone, pillar, obelisk, statue, commemoration, remembrance, reminder, memento.

monumental enormous, colossal, immense, massive, significant, important, historic, classic, memorable, lasting, awe-inspiring, impressive, striking, majestic, grand. TRIVIAL

mood temper, humour, disposition, frame of mind, feeling, vein, spirit.

moody sullen, sulky, glum, gloomy, morose, melancholy, broody, peevish, petulant, fretful, irritable, irascible, crabbed, testy, touchy, temperamental, huffish, hurt, offended, cross, angry. EQUABLE
capricious, fickle, changeable, mercurial, volatile, impulsive, fitful, erratic.

moor[1] *n*, heath, moorland, fell, wasteland, common.

moor[2] *v*, fasten, secure, tie up, berth, anchor. UNTIE

moot *adj*, debatable, disputable, arguable, controversial, at issue, open, unresolved, unsettled, doubtful, questionable. INDISPUTABLE
v, broach, put forward, propose, introduce, bring up, discuss, debate, ventilate.

mop *v*, swab, wash, clean, wipe, sponge, soak up.
n, shock, mane, tangle.

mope brood, fret, sulk, pout, be gloomy, be dejected, grieve, pine, languish, moon.

moral *adj*, ethical, good, virtuous, pure, right, proper, just, fair, honest, upright, honourable, noble, high-minded, principled. IMMORAL
n, lesson, message, maxim, adage, proverb, saying, aphorism, saw.

morale confidence, spirit, heart, mood, humour, will.

morals morality, integrity, ethics, principles, scruples, ideals, standards, mores, customs, habits, manners, behaviour, conduct.

morass swamp, marsh, bog, fen, quagmire, slough.

morbid unhealthy, unwholesome, sick, ghoulish, macabre, gruesome, grisly, grim, sombre, melancholy, morose, gloomy, pessimistic.
pathological, diseased, infected, unsound, unhealthy, sick, sickly. HEALTHY

mordant mordacious, caustic, biting, cutting, trenchant, incisive, sarcastic, stinging, sharp, acid, acerbic, bitter, pungent. SOOTHING

more *adj*, further, additional, added, extra, fresh, new, other. FEWER
adv, further, longer, again, besides, in addition. LESS

moreover furthermore, further, besides, in addition, too, as well, also.

morning daybreak, sunrise, dawn, morn, forenoon.

moron idiot, imbecile, cretin, halfwit, simpleton, fool, ass, donkey, dolt, nincompoop, blockhead, dunce, ignoramus, dope (*inf*). GENIUS

morose gloomy, glum, melancholy, depressed, moody, sullen, sulky, sour, surly, crabbed, gruff, crusty, crotchety, ill-tempered. GENIAL

morsel bit, piece, fragment, crumb, scrap, grain, bite, mouthful, titbit, nibble, taste.

mortal *adj*, worldly, earthly, human, physical, corporeal, temporal, ephemeral. IMMORTAL
deadly, fatal, lethal, destructive, murderous, killing.
great, extreme, intense, terrible, awful, dire, severe, grave.
n, human being, man, person, individual, earthling. GOD

mortality humanity, temporality, ephemerality, death, fatality, destruction. IMMORTALITY

mortification humiliation, shame, chagrin, embarrassment, discomfiture, discomposure, abashment, confusion, annoyance, vexation, dissatisfaction, displeasure. DELIGHT

mortify humiliate, humble, abase, shame, chagrin, embarrass, discomfit, discompose, abash, confound, chasten, crush, annoy, vex, displease. PLEASE
discipline, control, subdue, subjugate. INDULGE
fester, putrefy, gangrene, necrose, rot, corrupt.

mortuary morgue, funeral parlour, chapel of rest.

most *adj*, greatest, utmost, extreme, nearly all. FEWEST
n, majority, greater part, greater number, nearly all, utmost. LEAST

mostly mainly, chiefly, principally, on the whole, largely, generally, usually, as a rule.

mother *n*, parent, mater, mum (*inf*), mummy (*inf*), mama, ma (*inf*). FATHER
v, bear, give birth to, nurture, rear, nurse, care for, protect, pamper, indulge.

motherly maternal, kind, loving, tender, affectionate, caring, protective, gentle, warm, parental.

motion *n*, movement, action, activity, mobility, locomotion, travel, passage, flow, drift. REST
gesture, gesticulation, signal, sign.
proposal, proposition, suggestion, recommendation.
v, signal, gesticulate, gesture, wave, beckon, nod.

motionless stationary, immobile, still, unmoving, paralysed, transfixed, fixed, immovable, static, inanimate, inert. MOVING

motivate incite, prompt, move, lead, spur, impel, drive, stimulate, provoke, persuade, induce, cause, instigate, actuate. DETER

motive reason, cause, ground, object, purpose, intention, stimulus, spur, incentive, inducement, motivation, drive, impulse, inspiration.

motley mixed, varied, assorted, miscellaneous, diverse, heterogeneous, dissimilar. UNIFORM
multicoloured, polychromatic, chequered, variegated.

mottled speckled, dappled, piebald, brindled, tabby, streaked, flecked, spotted, blotchy, motley, chequered, variegated.

motto slogan, watchword, legend, inscription, saying, maxim, proverb, adage, aphorism, saw.

mould[1] *n*, die, matrix, pattern, cast, form, shape, style, fashion, design, frame, structure, format, build, brand, make, stamp, type, sort, kind, nature, character.
v, shape, form, model, fashion, cast, forge, stamp, make, influence, affect.

mould[2] *n*, mildew, fungus, blight, mustiness, mouldiness.

moulder rot, decay, decompose, crumble, disintegrate, perish.

mouldy mildewed, blighted, musty, fusty, stale, rotting, decaying, rotten, bad. FRESH

mound hill, hillock, knoll, hummock, heap, pile, stack, bank, rampart, bulwark, earthwork, barrow, tumulus.

mount *v*, climb, ascend, go up, rise, soar, scale, board, get on. DESCEND
increase, grow, multiply, accummulate, escalate, intensify, swell. DECREASE
prepare, set up, exhibit, display, produce, stage.
n, mounting, backing, setting, frame, stand, base, support.
horse, steed, charger.

mountebank charlatan, quack, impostor, pretender, fraud, fake, cheat, con man (*inf*).

mourn lament, grieve, sorrow, bewail, bemoan, deplore, regret, miss, weep, wail. REJOICE

mournful sad, sorrowful, unhappy, woeful, distressing, tragic, grievous, lamentable, deplorable, piteous, plaintive, depressing, sombre, lugubrious, funereal, gloomy, melancholy, depressed, downcast, doleful, disconsolate, heartbroken. JOYFUL

mourning grief, sorrow, woe, lamentation, bereavement.

mouth jaws, lips, gob (*inf*), trap (*inf*).
orifice, opening, aperture, entrance, inlet.
impudence, insolence, cheek (*inf*), sauce (*inf*), lip (*inf*).

movable mobile, portable, transportable, transferable, changeable. FIXED

movables furniture, goods, chattels, belongings, possessions, effects, property. IMMOVABLES

move *v*, stir, budge, shift, go, advance, progress, proceed, carry, transport, change, transfer.
relocate, remove, migrate, leave, quit. STAY
push, shove, propel, drive, impel.
prompt, stimulate, urge, impel, induce, persuade, incite, provoke, actuate, instigate, motivate, inspire, cause, lead. DETER
touch, affect, impress, influence, stir, excite.
propose, suggest, recommend, advocate.
n, movement, motion, action, step, manoeuvre, stratagem.
relocation, removal, migration.

movement motion, move, action, gesture, activity, stir, shift, change, advance, progress, course, drift, trend.
campaign, crusade, drive, faction, party, group, organization.
rhythm, beat, tempo, lilt, swing, pace, metre.
part, passage, section, division.
works, workings, mechanism, machinery.

moving touching, affecting, emotive, poignant, pathetic, stirring, inspiring, impressive, stimulating.
mobile, movable, active, running, in motion. STILL

mow cut, trim, clip, shear, prune, crop.
mow down, slaughter, massacre, butcher.

much *adj*, abundant, plentiful, plenteous, ample, considerable, great, a lot of. LITTLE
adv, greatly, considerably, a lot, a great deal, often, frequently.
nearly, almost, practically.
n, plenty, a lot, lots (*inf*), loads (*inf*), heaps (*inf*).

mucilaginous sticky, gummy, viscous, glutinous, mucous, slimy, viscid, gelatinous.

muck dung, ordure, manure, sewage, sludge, dirt, filth, mud, mire.

mucky dirty, filthy, grimy, grubby, soiled, muddy. CLEAN

mud clay, dirt, muck, mire, sludge.

muddle *v*, confuse, mix up, jumble, scramble, disorder, disarrange, mess up.
perplex, bewilder, confuse, confound, befuddle, stupefy.
n, confusion, mix-up, jumble, disorder, disarray, mess, chaos. ORDER
perplexity, bewilderment, confusion, stupefaction, daze, disorientation.

muddy mucky, miry, boggy, swampy, marshy, dirty, grimy. CLEAN
cloudy, turbid, murky, dingy, dull, opaque, obscure, vague, unclear. CLEAR

muffle envelop, wrap, swathe, cover, cloak, conceal, mask, disguise. EXPOSE
deaden, damp, mute, stifle, gag, muzzle, silence, suppress.

muffled muted, subdued, stifled, suppressed, soft, faint, dull. LOUD

muggy humid, clammy, sticky, damp, dank, moist, sultry, oppressive, close. FRESH

mulct *v*, cheat, defraud, swindle.
fine, penalize, punish.
n, fine, penalty, damages, forfeiture.

mulish stubborn, obstinate, headstrong, wilful, obdurate, intransigent, inflexible, perverse, contrary, intractable, refractory, recalcitrant. AMENABLE

multifarious manifold, many, numerous, multitudinous, multiple, multiform, varied, diverse, miscellaneous, sundry, motley, variegated, diversified.

multiply increase, augment, grow, build up, intensify, expand, extend, spread, breed, reproduce, propagate, proliferate. DECREASE

multitude crowd, throng, horde, flock, swarm, mob, assembly, congregation, army, legion, host, mass, myriad, lot. FEW

mum quiet, silent, dumb, mute, speechless, uncommunicative, taciturn. TALKATIVE

mumble mutter, murmur. EXCLAIM

munch chew, masticate, champ, crunch.

mundane banal, ordinary, everyday, commonplace, trite, humdrum, routine. UNUSUAL
worldly, earthly, terrestrial, temporal, secular, physical, material. SPIRITUAL

municipal civil, civic, urban, town, city, borough, local, public, community.

munificent generous, bountiful, bounteous, open-handed, liberal, unstinting, lavish, princely, beneficent, magnanimous, charitable, philanthropic. MEAN

munitions ammunition, weapons, arms, materiel, stores, supplies, equipment, gear.

murder *v*, kill, slay, assassinate, dispatch, bump off (*inf*), do in (*inf*), slaughter, butcher, massacre, destroy.
n, homicide, manslaughter, killing, assassination, slaughter, butchery, massacre, destruction.

murderer killer, slayer, assassin, slaughterer, butcher.

murderous homicidal, savage, barbarous, cruel, brutal, ferocious, bloodthirsty, sanguinary, deadly, lethal.
difficult, arduous, rigorous, strenuous, exhausting, dangerous, perilous. EASY

murky dark, gloomy, dismal, dusky, dull, dim, cloudy, overcast, grey, misty, foggy, obscure. CLEAR

murmur *v*, mutter, mumble, whisper, babble, rumble, hum.
complain, grumble, grouse, carp.
n, mutter, mumble, whisper, undertone, babble, rumble, hum, drone.
complaint, grumble, grouse.

muscular brawny, sinewy, beefy (*inf*), husky (*inf*), strapping, stalwart, burly, lusty, strong, robust, vigorous, energetic, athletic. PUNY

muse ruminate, reflect, ponder, contemplate, meditate, brood, mull over, cogitate, consider, deliberate, think over.

mushroom increase, grow, expand, boom, spring up, burgeon, flourish, prosper, thrive. DECLINE

music tune, melody, harmony, composition, opus, score.

musical tuneful, melodious, melodic, harmonious, euphonious, mellifluous, dulcet, lyrical. DISCORDANT

musician player, instrumantalist, composer, singer, performer, artiste, minstrel.

muster *v*, convene, convoke, assemble, congregate, rally, meet, collect, gather, summon, marshal, round up. DISPERSE
n, meeting, rally, assembly, congregation, gathering, collection, convention, convocation.

musty mouldy, mildewy, stale, fusty, frowsty, rank, ill-smelling, stuffy, old, ancient. FRESH

mutable changeable, variable, alterable, changing, inconstant, unstable, unsteady, uncertain, irresolute, unsettled, vacillating, fluctuating, wavering, fickle, capricious. CONSTANT

mutation change, alteration, modification, variation, transformation, metamorphosis.

mute *adj*, silent, dumb, voiceless, speechless, mum, taciturn, uncommunicative, still, quiet, unexpressed, unspoken. LOUD
v, soften, lower, subdue, damp, deaden, muffle, stifle.

mutilate maim, cripple, disable, disfigure, deface, mar, damage, injure, mangle, butcher, dismember, amputate. MEND

mutinous rebellious, seditious, insurgent, revolutionary, riotous, unruly, turbulent, insubordinate, disobedient, refractory, contumacious, ungovernable. OBEDIENT

mutiny *n*, rebellion, sedition, insurrection, revolution, revolt, uprising, riot, insubordination, defiance, disobedience. OBEDIENCE
v, rebel, revolt, rise up, resist, disobey. OBEY

mutter mumble, murmur, complain, grumble. EXCLAIM

mutual reciprocal, interchangeable, interactive, joint, shared, common, communal.

myopic short-sighted, near-sighted. LONG-SIGHTED

myriad *adj*, innumerable, countless, untold, incalculable, many, numerous. FEW
n, host, mass, multitude, thousands, millions.

mysterious unexplainable, inexplicable, enigmatic, cryptic, puzzling, baffling, incomprehensible, unfathomable, strange, curious, weird, uncanny, dark, obscure, hidden, veiled, secret, secretive, inscrutable. PLAIN

mystery enigma, riddle, conundrum, puzzle, question, secret.

mystical occult, esoteric, cabalistic, abstruse, arcane, metaphysical, supernatural, transcendental, mysterious, enigmatic, cryptic.

mystify puzzle, baffle, perplex, nonplus, bewilder, confuse, confound, stump. ENLIGHTEN

myth legend, saga, tale, story, fable, parable, allegory, tradition. HISTORY
lie, fib, falsehood, untruth, fabrication, fiction, fantasy, illusion. FACT

mythical mythological, legendary, fabled, storied, traditional, fabulous, fantastic. HISTORICAL
fictitious, make-believe, made-up, invented, fanciful, imaginary, unreal, false, untrue. REAL

N

nab seize, grab, snatch, catch, capture, arrest. RELEASE

nag *v*, scold, berate, henpeck, carp, cavil, pester, plague, badger, hector, harass, vex, irritate, annoy, worry, bother, torment.
n, shrew, termagant, virago, scold.

naive ingenuous, artless, guileless, unsophisticated, simple, innocent, trusting, credulous, gullible, open, frank, candid. ARTFUL

naked nude, unclothed, undressed, uncovered, exposed, bare, stripped, denuded, starkers (*inf*), in the altogether (*inf*). CLOTHED
unvarnished, unadorned, undisguised, open, stark, obvious, evident, manifest, plain, simple. CONCEALED

name *n*, title, appellation, denomination, designation, term, label, epithet, cognomen, nickname, sobriquet, handle (*inf*), moniker (*inf*).
reputation, character, credit, esteem, honour, distinction, note, fame, renown, eminence, celebrity.
v, call, baptize, christen, dub, style, term, label, entitle, denominate.
designate, nominate, appoint, select, choose, specify, mention, cite.

nap doze, slumber, drowse, snooze (*inf*), sleep, rest.

narcotic *n*, drug, opiate, sedative, tranquillizer, anodyne, analgesic, painkiller, anaesthetic. STIMULANT
adj, soporific, hypnotic, sedative, calming, numbing, analgesic.

narrate tell, relate, recount, rehearse, report, chronicle, detail, describe.

narration narrative, account, story, tale, report, chronicle, history, recital, description, relation.

narrow *adj*, thin, slender, attenuated, fine. WIDE
tight, cramped, pinched, constricted, confined, restricted, limited, straitened, close, meagre, scanty. BROAD
v, taper, attenuate, constrict, confine, restrict, limit, straiten, tighten. BROADEN

narrow-minded biased, prejudiced, bigoted, illiberal, intolerant, insular, parochial, provincial, limited. BROAD-MINDED

nascent beginning, incipient, budding, developing, young, embryonic. MATURE

nasty unpleasant, disagreeable, offensive, repulsive, revolting, disgusting, nauseating, odious, loathsome, objectionable, obnoxious, horrible, vile, foul, polluted, dirty, filthy, indecent, obscene. PLEASANT
spiteful, malicious, mean, vicious, malevolent, ill-tempered, ill-natured, wicked, evil, villainous. BENEVOLENT

nation people, race, country, land, realm, empire, commonwealth, state, population, society, community.

national civil, state, nationwide, general, domestic, internal. LOCAL

native *n*, inhabitant, resident, dweller, citizen, national, aborigine, autochthon, indigene. FOREIGNER
adj, inborn, inbred, innate, connate, congenital, hereditary, natural, inherent, immanent, intrinsic. ACQUIRED
local, vernacular, domestic, home, mother, indigenous, aboriginal, autochthonous, original. FOREIGN

natural normal, typical, regular, usual, ordinary, common, logical, reasonable. ABNORMAL
inborn, inbred, innate, congenital, inherent, intrinsic, native, indigenous, basic, fundamental, instinctive, intuitive. ACQUIRED
artless, guileless, ingenuous, naive, unsophisticated, simple, frank, open, candid,

sincere, unaffected, spontaneous, impulsive. ARTFUL
genuine, real, authentic, pure, unmixed, raw, unrefined. ARTIFICIAL

naturalize habituate, familiarize, domesticate, accustom, acclimatize, adapt, adopt, introduce.

nature essence, character, identity, constitution, make-up, quality.
disposition, temper, humour, mood, temperament, character, personality.
kind, sort, type, class, category, style, brand, variety.
creation, earth, world, universe, cosmos.

naughty bad, wicked, mischievous, disobedient, defiant, wayward, unruly, impish, roguish, vexatious, exasperating. GOOD
bawdy, ribald, risqué, titillating, smutty, vulgar, rude, improper, indecent.

nausea biliousness, queasiness, sickness, vomiting.
disgust, revulsion, repugnance, loathing, aversion, dislike. RELISH

nauseate sicken, disgust, revolt, repel, offend, appal.

nauseous nauseating, sickening, disgusting, revolting, repulsive, loathsome, offensive, distasteful. PLEASANT

nautical naval, marine, maritime, seafaring, seagoing, sailing.

navigate direct, guide, pilot, steer, drive, plot, plan, cross, sail, cruise, voyage.

navy fleet, flotilla, armada, marine.

near *adj*, close, nearby, neighbouring, adjacent, adjoining, contiguous. FAR
imminent, impending, forthcoming, approaching, next. DISTANT
dear, intimate, familiar, close, related, akin. REMOTE
mean, niggardly, parsimonious, stingy, miserly, tight-fisted, close-fisted, ungenerous. GENEROUS
adv, close, close by, nigh, nearby.
v, approach, draw near, border on, come close.

nearly almost, practically, all but, virtually, well-nigh, just about, approximately, roughly, more or less.

neat tidy, orderly, trim, smart, spruce, clean, spick-and-span, fastidious, methodical. UNTIDY
clever, dexterous, adroit, deft, adept, apt, skilful, expert. CLUMSY
pure, unadulterated, unmixed, undiluted, straight.

neaten tidy, straighten, spruce up, clean, groom, arrange, order. DISARRANGE

nebulous vague, indeterminate, obscure, indistinct, hazy, misty, cloudy, shapeless, amorphous. CLEAR

necessary needed, required, needful, requisite, essential, vital, indispensable, imperative, compulsory, obligatory, unavoidable, inescapable, inevitable, certain. UNNECESSARY

necessitate cause, require, entail, demand, call for, oblige, force, compel, impel, constrain, coerce.

necessitous needy, poor, impoverished, poverty-stricken, indigent, impecunious, penurious, penniless, destitute, distressed. RICH

necessity essential, fundamental, requisite, prerequisite, need, want, requirement, demand, exigency, indispensability, needfulness, compulsion, obligation, inevitability.
poverty, indigence, penury, destitution, need. WEALTH

necromancy magic, black magic, sorcery, witchcraft, wizardry, voodoo, divination.

need *v*, lack, miss, want, require, demand, call for, necessitate. HAVE
n, necessity, lack, want, desideratum, requirement, demand, requisite, obligation, exigency, urgency, emergency.
poverty, indigence, penury, destitution, distress, extremity, privation. WEALTH

needful needed, necessary, required, requisite, essential, vital, indispensable. UNNECESSARY

needless unnecessary, gratuitous, redundant, superfluous, unwanted, uncalled-for, excessive, dispensable, nonessential, expendable, useless. NEEDFUL

needy poor, necessitous, indigent, impecunious, impoverished, poverty-stricken, penniless, destitute, deprived, underprivileged. WEALTHY

nefarious wicked, evil, bad, sinful, iniquitous, heinous, flagitious, villainous, infamous, vile, odious, abominable, execrable horrible, dreadful, atrocious, outrageous scandalous, monstrous. ADMIRABLE

negate nullify, annul, cancel, invalidate, revoke, repeal, rescind, abrogate, countermand.
deny, contradict, gainsay, refute, disprove, oppose. AFFIRM

negation opposite, reverse, contrary, antithesis.
denial, contradiction, disavowal, disclaimer, retraction, repudiation, refusal, rejection, renunciation.
nothing, nullity, nonentity, void, vacuity.

negative *adj*, denying, contradictory, opposing, contrary, nullifying, invalidating. POSITIVE
pessimistic, cynical, unhelpful, uncooperative, contrary, antagonistic.
n, contradiction, denial, negation, refusal, no.

neglect *v*, disregard, ignore, overlook, pass over, omit, miss, skip, forget, shirk, skimp, spurn, slight, abandon, leave alone.
n, negligence, disregard, oversight, omission, remissness, forgetfulness, default, dereliction, carelessness, inattention, laxity. ATTENTION

neglectful negligent, remiss, careless, heedless, regardless, disregardful, inattentive, unmindful, thoughtless, forgetful. ATTENTIVE

negligence neglect, disregard, oversight, omission, dereliction, default, remissness, forgetfulness, inattention, carelessness, heedlessness, thoughtlessness, indifference, laxity, slackness. ATTENTION

negligent neglectful, remiss, careless, heedless, inattentive, unmindful, forgetful, slack, lax, indifferent, offhand, nonchalant. ATTENTIVE

negligible unimportant, insignificant, inconsequential, trifling, trivial, minor, small, imperceptible. IMPORTANT

negotiate bargain, deal, debate, discuss, arrange, work out, mediate, arbitrate, conciliate, settle, compromise, transact, manage, get through, clear, pass.

neighbourhood vicinity, environs, surroundings, district, quarter, locality, community.
nearness, proximity, propinquity, region.

neighbouring adjoining, adjacent, contiguous, connecting, proximate, near, close, nearby, nigh. DISTANT

neighbourly sociable, friendly, amiable, cordial, hospitable, kind, generous, obliging, attentive, helpful, civil. UNFRIENDLY

neophyte convert, proselyte, novice, beginner, tyro, learner, student, pupil, apprentice, trainee. MASTER

nerve *n*, courage, bravery, valour, mettle, pluck, guts (*inf*), fortitude, endurance, will, firmness, determination, resolution, steadfastness, power, might, strength, vigour. WEAKNESS
audacity, boldness, effrontery, impudence, impertinence, insolence, gall, cheek (*inf*). TIMIDITY
v, steel, brace, strengthen, fortify, embolden, invigorate, hearten, encourage. WEAKEN

nervous excitable, highly strung, tense, agitated, shaky, anxious, worried, apprehensive, fearful, fidgety, jumpy, jittery (*inf*), nervy (*inf*), edgy, on edge, uneasy, hesitant, timid. CALM

nestle snuggle, cuddle, huddle, settle, lodge, shelter.

net *n*, mesh, web, netting, network, reticulum, lace.
v, catch, capture, bag, trap, ensnare, enmesh. RELEASE

nether lower, under, bottom, inferior. UPPER

nettle vex, annoy, irritate, irk, pique, chafe, provoke, ruffle, exasperate, bother, harass, incense, enrage. SOOTHE

network system, organization, complex, maze, labyrinth, grid, mesh, net, web.

neutral impartial, nonpartisan, unbiased, unprejudiced, disinterested, indifferent, dispassionate, objective, aloof, uninvolved, uncommitted, nonaligned. PARTISAN
bland, dull, drab, colourless, achromatic, indeterminate, indistinguishable.

neutralize counteract, counterbalance, offset, compensate for, cancel, negate, nullify, annul, undo. INTENSIFY

nevertheless nonetheless, notwithstanding, however, yet, but, still.

new recent, latest, modern, contemporary, current, novel, original, newfangled, unknown, unfamiliar, fresh, unused, other, additional, renewed, improved, changed. OLD

news report, account, information, intelligence, word, advice, tidings, dispatch, communiqué, bulletin.

next following, succeeding, subsequent, later, consequent. LAST
neighbouring, adjacent, adjoining, nearest, closest.

nibble *v*, bite, gnaw, peck at, eat.
n, bite, morsel, titbit, taste.

nice pleasant, agreeable, enjoyable, delightful, charming, attractive, pleasing, likable, friendly, kind, good, polite. NASTY
fine, subtle, delicate, fastidious, particular, discriminating, exact, precise, accurate, strict, scrupulous, minute.

nicety delicacy, subtlety, refinement, distinction, nuance.
precision, accuracy, exactitude, fastidiousness, scrupulousness.

niche recess, alcove, nook, cranny, corner.

nick *n*, notch, indentation, cut, chip, scratch, dent, groove.
v, notch, cut, chip, scratch, dent.

niggardly mean, miserly, stingy, parsimonious, close-fisted, tight, tight-fisted, ungenerous, frugal, sparing. GENEROUS
meagre, scanty, paltry, inadequate, insufficient. AMPLE

nigh *adj*, near, close, nearby, proximate, adjacent, next, imminent, impending. DISTANT
adv, nearly, almost, practically, about, approximately.

night dark, darkness, night-time. DAY

nightfall sunset, dusk, twilight, evening. DAYBREAK

nil nothing, nought, zero, love.

nimble agile, sprightly, spry, active, lively, smart, quick, brisk, prompt, ready, alert, deft, dexterous. CLUMSY

nip[1] *v*, bite, pinch, squeeze, compress, tweak, snip, clip, catch, grip.

nip[2] *n*, dram, draught, drop, sip, swig (*inf*), shot (*inf*).

nipple teat, tit, mamilla, papilla, dug, pap.

nobility gentry, aristocracy, upper class, peerage, lords, nobles. COMMONALTY
nobleness, dignity, exaltation, eminence, loftiness, greatness, distinction, grandeur, magnificence, honour, virtue, goodness, integrity. LOWLINESS

noble *n*, nobleman, noblewoman, aristocrat, patrician, peer, peeress, lord, lady. COMMONER
adj, aristocratic, patrician, highborn, blue-blooded, titled. LOWBORN
magnanimous, generous, worthy, honourable, virtuous, good, great, dignified, distinguished, eminent, lofty, elevated, lordly, stately, grand, magnificent, superior, fine, excellent. BASE

nobody no-one, nonentity, nothing, cipher. SOMEBODY

nocturnal night, nightly, crepuscular. DIURNAL

nod bow, indicate, acknowledge, agree, assent.
drowse, nap, doze, sleep. WAKE

node protuberance, nodule, knob, knot, swelling, lump, bump.

noise sound, din, row, racket, clamour, outcry, uproar, hubbub, tumult, commotion, pandemonium, talk, cry. SILENCE

noiseless silent, inaudible, quiet, still, mute. LOUD

noisome offensive, foul, fetid, putrid, malodorous, mephitic, noxious, poisonous, pestilential, unhealthy, unwholesome, harmful, pernicious, deleterious, detrimental, mischievous, injurious, hurtful. WHOLESOME

noisy loud, clamorous, boisterous, obstreperous, riotous, uproarious, turbulent, tumultuous, vociferous, cacophonous, strident, blaring, deafening, ear-splitting. QUIET

nomadic wandering, roving, vagrant, travelling, itinerant, peripatetic, migrant, migratory.

nominal titular, formal, theoretical, so-called, supposed, would-be, self-styled. ACTUAL
token, minimal, small, inconsiderable. EXCESSIVE

nominate propose, suggest, present, name, choose, select, elect, appoint, assign, designate.

nonchalant unconcerned, dispassionate, indifferent, apathetic, careless, blasé, insouciant, carefree, cool, calm, easy, casual, offhand. CONCERNED

nondescript unclassifiable, indefinite, indeterminate, unremarkable, unexceptional, characterless, dull, bland, ordinary, commonplace. DISTINCTIVE

nonentity nothing, nobody, cipher. SOMEBODY
nonesuch paragon, nonpareil, ideal, exemplar, model, pattern.
nonpareil *adj*, peerless, matchless, unmatched, unequalled, unparalleled, incomparable, unique, unrivalled, supreme. ORDINARY
n, paragon, nonesuch, ideal, exemplar.
nonplus confound, perplex, bewilder, confuse, puzzle, baffle, mystify, stump, disconcert, take aback, dumbfound, astonish, astound. ENLIGHTEN
nonsense rubbish, trash, rot, balderdash, humbug, twaddle, drivel, bosh, gibberish, senselessness, absurdity, silliness, stupidity, foolishness, folly, fatuity. SENSE
nonsensical senseless, meaningless, ridiculous, ludicrous, absurd, crazy, silly, foolish. SENSIBLE
nook corner, recess, niche, alcove, cranny, cubbyhole, retreat.
norm average, mean, rule, standard, measure, criterion, yardstick, type, model.
normal usual, common, general, ordinary, conventional, customary, habitual, routine, regular, standard, typical, natural, rational, sane, well-adjusted. ABNORMAL
nosegay posy, bouquet, bunch, spray, corsage.
nostalgia yearning, longing, reminiscence, remembrance, wistfulness, regret, homesickness.
nosy inquisitive, curious, prying, meddlesome, interfering.
notable *adj*, remarkable, noteworthy, signal, noticeable, conspicuous, marked, striking, memorable, unusual, distinctive, noted, distinguished, celebrated, eminent, famous. INSIGNIFICANT
n, personage, celebrity, VIP, dignitary, somebody. NOBODY
notch *n*, cut, nick, incision, identation, groove, score.
v, cut, nick, indent, serrate.
note *n*, memorandum, memo, record, minute, jotting, annotation, comment, remark, message, letter, communication.
fame, renown, celebrity, distinction, prestige, eminence, regard, esteem, significance, importance, consequence. INSIGNIFICANCE
heed, attention, regard, notice, observation.
v, notice, perceive, remark, observe, heed, mark, register, record, jot down. IGNORE
noted famous, renowned, celebrated, well-known, illustrious, distinguished, eminent, notable. UNKNOWN
noteworthy remarkable, notable, signal, outstanding, memorable, exceptional, unusual, extraordinary, important, significant. ORDINARY
nothing nought, nil, zero, cipher, nonentity, nobody, void, nothingness, nihility, nullity, nonexistence. SOMETHING
notice *n*, attention, observation, note, heed, regard, consideration, respect.
information, notification, advice, warning, announcement, declaration, intimation, news.
poster, placard, sign, bill, advertisement.
review, criticism, comment.
v, note, perceive, remark, observe, see, detect, mark, heed. MISS
noticeable perceptible, appreciable, conspicuous, distinct, clear, plain, evident, obvious, manifest, visible, apparent. INCONSPICUOUS
notification announcement, declaration, notice, warning, advice, intimation, information, intelligence, statement, message, communication.
notify inform, tell, advise, warn, acquaint, apprise, announce, declare, disclose, reveal. SUPPRESS
notion idea, impression, concept, sentiment, thought, opinion, view, belief, theory, conception, apprehension, understanding.
whim, caprice, fancy, inclination.
notoriety infamy, disrepute, obloquy, opprobrium, disgrace, dishonour. ILLUSTRIOUSNESS
notorious infamous, disreputable, ignominious, dishonourable, disgraceful, scandalous. ILLUSTRIOUS
notwithstanding despite, although, though, nevertheless, however, yet.
nought zero, nil, nothing, naught, nothingness.
nourish feed, sustain, nurture, nurse, tend, maintain, support, harbour, cherish, foster, encourage, promote. STARVE
nourishing nutritive, nutritious, alimentary, alimentative, healthy, wholesome, beneficial. UNHEALTHY

nourishment nutrition, nutriment, food, sustenance, aliment, alimentation.

novel *adj*, new, fresh, original, innovative, different, uncommon, unusual, unfamiliar, strange. STALE
n, story, tale, narrative, romance, fiction, book.

novelty newness, freshness, originality, innovation, difference, unfamiliarity. STALENESS
trifle, bagatelle, trinket, knick-knack, toy, gadget.

novice beginner, tyro, neophyte, learner, pupil, student, apprentice, probationer, trainee, amateur. MASTER

now immediately, at once, straightaway, right away. LATER
nowadays, today, at the moment, at present. THEN

noxious poisonous, toxic, pernicious, harmful, hurtful, injurious, baleful, deleterious, detrimental, deadly, destructive, noisome, unwholesome, unhealthy, pestilential, foul. BENEFICIAL

nuance shade, gradation, distinction, subtlety, refinement, trace, touch, hint, suggestion.

nucleus centre, focus, core, kernel, heart, nub, essence.

nude naked, bare, unclothed, undressed, uncovered, exposed, starkers (*inf*), in the altogether (*inf*), *au naturel*. CLOTHED

nudge push, shove, poke, prod, dig, elbow, jog.

nugatory worthless, trifling, frivolous, insignificant, ineffective, futile, useless, vain, bootless, unavailing. VALUABLE

nuisance annoyance, vexation, bother, pest, pain (*inf*), bore, trouble, inconvenience. PLEASURE

null void, invalid, worthless, nugatory, useless, futile, ineffectual, characterless, nonexistent. VALID

nullify annul, abrogate, revoke, rescind, repeal, quash, invalidate, cancel, negate, abolish.

numb dead, deadened, benumbed, insensible, insensate, frozen, paralysed, immobile, unfeeling, insensitive. SENSITIVE

number *n*, figure, numeral, digit, integer.
sum, total, aggregate, collection, amount, quantity, crowd, multitude, host, throng, many.
copy, issue, edition.
v, count, enumerate, calculate, compute, reckon, total, add, include.

numberless countless, innumerable, infinite, incalculable, untold, many, myriad, multitudinous. FEW

numeral number, figure, digit, integer, character, symbol.

numerous many, manifold, several, multiple, abundant, plentiful, innumerable, numberless. FEW

nuptial conjugal, connubial, matrimonial, marital, bridal, wedding.

nurse tend, look after, care for, minister to, treat. NEGLECT
suckle, feed, nurture, rear.
harbour, preserve, keep, cherish, foster, encourage, promote. BANISH

nurture nourish, feed, sustain, support, nurse, tend, rear, bring up, raise, train, discipline, educate, school, instruct, cultivate, develop, foster.

nutriment nutrition, nourishment, food, aliment, alimentation, sustenance, subsistence.

nutritious nutritive, nourishing, alimentary, alimentative, wholesome, healthy, benficial. UNHEALTHY

nymph sylph, dryad, naiad, oread, damsel, maiden, girl, lass.

O

oaf dolt, dunce, dullard, blockhead, idiot, fool, wally (*inf*), simpleton, lout, clod.

oath vow, pledge, promise, word, statement, asseveration, affirmation.
curse, imprecation, malediction, expletive, swearword, obscenity, profanity.

obdurate hard, hard-hearted, cold, callous, unfeeling, insensitive, relentless, unrelenting, harsh, inflexible, unyielding, adamant, firm, stubborn, obstinate, mulish, pig-headed, headstrong, wilful, unshakable, immovable. AMENABLE

obedient compliant, acquiescent, yielding, submissive, deferential, respectful, dutiful, law-abiding, docile, biddable, tractable, subservient. DISOBEDIENT

obeisance homage, deference, respect, reverence, worship, salutation, bow, curtsy, genuflection, salaam. DISRESPECT

obese fat, stout, overweight, corpulent, rotund, portly, plump, tubby, podgy, fleshy. THIN

obey comply, observe, keep, heed, mind, follow, abide by, conform, submit, yield, discharge, fulfil, carry out, perform. DISOBEY

obfuscate obscure, darken, cloud, befog, confuse, bewilder, muddle, perplex. CLEAR

object *n*, thing, article, entity, body. CONCEPT
aim, purpose, objective, goal, end, motive, intent, intention, design, mark, butt, target.
v, protest, disapprove, demur, mind, take exception, expostulate, oppose. AGREE

objection protest, disapproval, demur, opposition, dissent, scruple, qualm, complaint, grievance, exception, remonstrance, expostulation. ASSENT

objectionable unpleasant, disagreeable, offensive, repulsive, repugnant, obnoxious, abominable, loathsome, detestable, odious, vile, insufferable, intolerable, unacceptable. AGREEABLE

objective *adj*, impartial, unbiased, unprejudiced, neutral, detached, disinterested, fair, just, dispassionate. SUBJECTIVE
n, aim, purpose, goal, end, target, object, intention, design, ambition, aspiration.

objurgate scold, chide, rebuke, reprove, reprimand, upbraid, berate. PRAISE

oblation offering, sacrifice, gift, present, donation, contribution.

obligation duty, responsibility, charge, onus, liability, accountability, necessity, requirement, compulsion, contract, bond, agreement, commitment, debt.

obligatory compulsory, mandatory, binding, required, necessary, essential, imperative. OPTIONAL

oblige obligate, compel, constrain, force, bind, necessitate, require, coerce, make. RELEASE
accommodate, favour, serve, help, please, gratify.

obliged beholden, indebted, grateful, thankful, appreciative.

obliging accommodating, amenable, willing, agreeable, kind, friendly, cooperative, helpful, civil, gracious. UNOBLIGING

oblique slanting, aslant, sloping, inclined, tilted. VERTICAL
indirect, evasive, devious, circuitous, roundabout, backhanded, furtive, sidelong. DIRECT

obliterate eradicate, destroy, annihilate, wipe out, expunge, erase, cancel, delete, efface, blot out. RESTORE

oblivion darkness, obscurity, extinction, abeyance, neglect, forgetfulness, obliviousness, blankness, unconsciousness. AWARENESS

oblivious unaware, unconscious, insensible, unmindful, blind, deaf, heedless, careless, forgetful, absent-minded. AWARE

obloquy censure, criticism, denunciation, invective, abuse, aspersion, defamation, vilification, slander, calumny, reproach, reproof, blame, opprobrium, dishonour, shame, disgrace, infamy, ignominy. PRAISE

obnoxious objectionable, unpleasant, disagreeable, nasty, offensive, repulsive, repugnant, odious, vile, horrid, hateful, loathsome, detestable, intolerable, insufferable. DELIGHTFUL

obscene indecent, immoral, improper, offensive, disgusting, foul, dirty, filthy, smutty, blue, pornographic, salacious, lewd, bawdy, ribald, coarse, vulgar, rude, gross, outrageous, shocking, shameless, immodest, impure, unchaste. DECENT

obscure *adj*, unclear, indistinct, vague, indefinite, uncertain, doubtful, abstruse, arcane, recondite, hidden, concealed, cryptic, enigmatic, mysterious, impenetrable, unfathomable, incomprehensible, intricate, involved. CLEAR
faint, dim, hazy, blurred, dark, gloomy, murky, cloudy, shadowy. BRIGHT
unknown, inconspicuous, insignificant, undistinguished, inglorious, unheard-of, unsung, nameless, minor, humble. FAMOUS
v, obfuscate, cloud, befog, hide, conceal, cover, mask, screen, veil, shroud, eclipse, darken, dim, shade, shadow.

obsequious servile, flattering, fawning, sycophantic, ingratiating, grovelling, cringing, slavish, subservient, submissive. INDEPENDENT

observance adherence, compliance, discharge, fulfilment, performance, execution, attention, heed, regard, respect. DISREGARD rite, ritual, ceremony, service, celebration, custom, practice, convention, fashion, form, usage, tradition.

observant attentive, alert, vigilant, watchful, heedful, mindful, aware, perceptive. UNOBSERVANT

observation notice, attention, examination, scrutiny, inspection, surveillance, study, consideration, cognition. INATTENTION

comment, remark, statement, finding, discovery, note, annotation, reflection, thought, opinion.

observe watch, study, monitor, contemplate, regard, look at, view, espy, witness, see, perceive, notice, descry, discern, detect, discover, note, mark. MISS

remark, comment, say, utter, state, declare, mention, reflect.

keep, honour, heed, mind, follow, abide by, comply with, fulfil, perform, discharge, execute, respect, celebrate, commemorate. IGNORE

observer watcher, viewer, spectator, onlooker, witness, bystander, beholder.

obsess preoccupy, dominate, rule, monopolize, possess, grip, bedevil, plague, haunt.

obsession preoccupation, fixation, *idée fixe*, passion, mania, compulsion, fetish, complex, phobia.

obsolete discontinued, disused,outmoded, antiquated, dated, superannuated, passé, old-fashioned, archaic, old, ancient. MODERN

obstacle barrier, hurdle, obstruction, impediment, hindrance, check, snag, difficulty, stumbling block. ASSISTANCE

obstinate stubborn, mulish, pig-headed, opinionated, headstrong, wilful, self-willed, dogged, persistent, firm, adamant, immovable, unshakable, obdurate, inflexible, unyielding, contrary, perverse, refractory, contumacious. AMENABLE

obstreperous boisterous, rowdy, uproarious, clamorous, noisy, loud, unruly, disorderly, wild, tumultuous, turbulent, unmanageable, out of hand. QUIET

obstruct block, clog, choke, bar, barricade, hinder, impede, hamper, prevent, stop, arrest, check, curb, retard, inhibit, frustrate, thwart, interrupt, interfere. ASSIST

obstruction blockage, obstacle, barricade, blockade, barrier, bar, hindrance, impediment, block, stop, check, snag, difficulty. CLEARANCE

obtain get, acquire, procure, come by, secure, gain, win, earn, attain, achieve. LOSE

prevail, exist, stand, be in force.

obtrude push, thrust, impose, intrude, interfere. WITHDRAW

obtrusive conspicuous, obvious, noticeable, prominent, protruding, protuberant. UNOBTRUSIVE

intrusive, interfering, officious, importunate, forward, pushy (*inf*). RETIRING

obtuse slow, dull, stupid, thick, dense, stolid, insensitive, thick-skinned. SHARP

blunt, rounded. POINTED

obviate preclude, forestall, avert, prevent, counter, get rid of, do away with. NECESSITATE

obvious evident, manifest, patent, clear, plain, distinct, apparent, visible, palpable, overt, unconcealed, conspicuous, pronounced, unmistakable. HIDDEN

occasion *n*, time, occurrence, incident, event, opportunity, chance, opening.

affair, function, party, celebration.

reason, cause, motive, ground, excuse, justification.

v, cause, bring about, prompt, elicit, provoke, generate, produce, create, originate. PREVENT

occasional periodic, intermittent, sporadic, irregular, infrequent, rare, casual, incidental. CONSTANT

occasionally sometimes, periodically, intermittently, rarely, seldom, now and then, every so often, from time to time. OFTEN

occult mystical, supernatural, magical, abstruse, arcane, esoteric, recondite, mysterious, obscure, hidden, concealed, secret.

occupant holder, owner, occupier, tenant, resident, inhabitant, inmate, incumbent.

occupation job, profession, work, employment, craft, trade, business, vocation, calling, career, activity, pursuit.

occupancy, tenure, possession, holding, tenancy, residence. EVICTION

conquest, defeat, seizure, invasion, control, rule.

occupy fill, take up, use, hold, keep, own, possess, inhabit, live in, seize, capture, invade. VACATE
absorb, engross, preoccupy, engage, employ, busy, tie up, monopolize, entertain, amuse.
occur happen, take place, come about, chance, befall, betide, transpire, supervene, arise, result, appear, materialize, be present, exist.
occurrence happening, event, incident, episode, occasion, instance, affair, proceeding.
ocean sea, main, deep, briny (*inf*).
odd unusual, uncommon, strange, peculiar, curious, queer, eccentric, unconventional, weird, bizarre, singular, rare, extraordinary, unique. ORDINARY
occasional, incidental, casual, random, irregular, diverse. REGULAR
unmatched, single, sole, solitary, lone, spare, surplus, leftover, uneven.
odds probability, likelihood, chances.
advantage, lead, edge, superiority.
difference, disparity, inequality, distinction.
odious obnoxious, objectionable, offensive, repugnant, repulsive, disgusting, detestable, loathsome, abominable, execrable, hateful, horrid, nasty, unpleasant, vile. PLEASANT
odium dislike, disfavour, hate, hatred, antipathy, loathing, detestation, abhorrence, repugnance, obloquy, opprobrium, censure, shame, dishonour. LIKING
odour smell, scent, redolence, aroma, fragrance, perfume, stench.
air, aura, spirit, quality, emanation, flavour.
off *adv*, away, out, aside, apart. ON
prep, from, away from.
adj, cancelled, postponed, finished, gone, absent, free, poor, substandard, bad, rotten, mouldy, sour, rancid.
offence violation, infringement, crime, misdemeanour, wrong, fault, sin, trespass, transgression, misdeed, peccadillo. RIGHT
affront, insult, snub, slight, injury, hurt, outrage, indignity.
resentment, umbrage, pique, huff, indignation, displeasure, annoyance, anger.
attack, assault, offensive. DEFENCE
offend hurt, wound, injure, wrong, insult, affront, snub, slight, humiliate, outrage, upset, displease, annoy, vex, irritate, anger. PLEASE
disgust, repel, sicken, nauseate.
sin, transgress, trespass, err, go astray.
offender culprit, criminal, lawbreaker, miscreant, malefactor, wrongdoer, sinner, transgressor.
offensive *adj*, unpleasant, disagreeable, nasty, obnoxious, objectionable, repugnant, disgusting, revolting, vile, odious, loathsome, detestable, abominable, execrable. PLEASANT
insulting, abusive, rude, disrespectful, insolent, impertinent, irritating, annoying. POLITE
aggressive, attacking, invading. DEFENSIVE
n, attack, assault, aggression, onset, onslaught, invasion, incursion. DEFENCE
offer *v*, present, hold out, proffer, tender, bid, propose, put forward, submit, advance, extend, give, provide, furnish, volunteer. WITHDRAW
n, bid, tender, proposal, proposition, suggestion, advance, overture.
offering present, gift, donation, contribution, oblation, sacrifice.
offhand impromptu, extempore, ad lib, off the cuff (*inf*).
casual, informal, unceremonious, abrupt, curt, brusque, cavalier, careless, nonchalant.
office post, position, situation, appointment, commission, role, capacity, function, duty, responsibility, trust, charge, work, employment, service, place, station.
official *adj*, authoritative, formal, ceremonial, authorized, legitimate, sanctioned, licensed, proper, authentic, bona fide. UNOFFICIAL
n, officer, office bearer, functionary, bureaucrat, executive, agent, representative.
officiate preside, chair, conduct, run, direct, manage, oversee, supervise.
officious obtrusive, importunate, interfering, meddlesome, intrusive, pragmatic, forward, pushy (*inf*), overzealous.
offset *v*, counterbalance, countervail, compensate for, cancel out, counteract, neutralize.
n, counterbalance, counterpoise, compensation, equalizer.
offshoot branch, outgrowth, development, derivative, by-product, spin-off.

offspring child, children, young, progeny, issue, descendant, descendants, seed, posterity. PARENT

often frequently, repeatedly, oft, generally, time after time, again and again. OCCASIONALLY

ogre giant, monster, brute, fiend, demon, devil, bogeyman.

oily greasy, fatty, oleaginous.
smooth, unctuous, glib, flattering, servile, obsequious.

ointment balm, salve, lotion, liniment, embrocation, cream, unguent.

OK okay, satisfactory, acceptable, passable, tolerable, fair, all right, so-so (*inf*), good, fine, correct, approved, permitted. UNACCEPTABLE

old ancient, antique, early, primitive, original, archaic, antiquated, outmoded, outdated, obsolete, worn out, dilapidated, decrepit. NEW
aged, elderly, grey, hoary, senile. YOUNG
former, erstwhile, quondam, previous, one-time. CURRENT

old-fashioned outmoded, outdated, out-of-date, dated, unfashionable, passé, obsolete, antiquated, superannuated, old hat. MODERN

omen portent, sign, indication, foretoken, warning, premonition, presage, augury, prediction, prognostic, forecast.

ominous portentous, foreboding, unpropitious, inauspicious, threatening, menacing, premonitory.

omission exclusion, exception, gap, oversight, neglect, disregard, default, failure.

omit exclude, leave out, drop, miss, skip, pass over, overlook, ignore, disregard, neglect, forget, fail. INCLUDE

omnipotent almighty, all-powerful, supreme, sovereign. FEEBLE

omniscient all-knowing, all-wise, all-seeing. IGNORANT

on *prep*, upon, by. OFF
adv, onward, forward, ahead. BACK
continually, unceasingly.

once formerly, previously, at one time, long ago. NOW
at once, immediately, instantly, straightaway, right away, directly, forthwith, now. LATER
together, simultaneously, at the same time.

one single, individual, lone, sole, only, unique. MANY

onerous burdensome, oppressive, heavy, laborious, arduous, toilsome, difficult, hard, taxing. LIGHT

one-sided unfair, unjust, inequitable, partial, partisan, biased, prejudiced. IMPARTIAL

onlooker bystander, observer, spectator, watcher, viewer, witness.

only *adj*, sole, solitary, lone, single, individual, exclusive, unique.
adv, just, merely, simply, purely, at most, alone.

onset beginning, start, inception, commencement, outbreak. END
onslaught, onrush, attack, assault, charge. RETREAT

onus burden, load, responsibility, obligation.

onward onwards, forward, ahead, on. BACKWARD

ooze seep, exude, percolate, filter, leak, escape, drip, drop, secrete, discharge, emit.

opalescent opaline, iridescent, pearly, nacreous, prismatic.

opaque cloudy, hazy, murky, turbid, dull, lustreless. TRANSPARENT
obscure, unclear, unfathomable, unintelligible. CLEAR
thick, dense, unintelligent, stupid, obtuse. CLEVER

open *adj*, unclosed, gaping, ajar, unlocked, unfastened, unsealed, unfolded, extended. CLOSED
clear, unobstructed, free, unrestricted, public, accessible, available, vacant, bare, exposed, uncovered, wide, extensive. RESTRICTED
overt, plain, obvious, evident, manifest, undisguised, unconcealed, apparent, visible. HIDDEN
undecided, unsettled, unresolved, debatable, moot. SETTLED
frank, candid, unreserved, honest, sincere, artless, ingenuous, natural. SECRETIVE
liable, prone, susceptible, vulnerable, exposed, unprotected, undefended. SAFE
v, unfasten, unlock, undo, unwrap, uncover, expose, unblock, clear. CLOSE
spread, expand, extend, unfold, unfurl, split, part, separate.
begin, start, launch, inaugurate, commence. END
disclose, reveal, show, exhibit. HIDE

opening *n*, gap, breach, aperture, orifice, hole, cleft, split, rift, crack, fissure, crevice, chasm.
beginning, start, launch, inauguration, initiation, commencement, inception, dawn. CLOSE
opportunity, chance, occasion, break (*inf*), vacancy, place.
adj, beginning, starting, commencing, first, initial, introductory, inaugural. CLOSING

open-minded receptive, tolerant, catholic, broad-minded, liberal, fair, just, reasonable, unbiased, unprejudiced, impartial, dispassionate. BIGOTED

operate function, work, act, perform, go, run, manage, use, handle, manipulate, manoeuvre.

operation performance, working, action, motion, handling, manipulation.
procedure, process, exercise, manoeuvre, affair, business, undertaking, venture.

operative *adj*, operational, in operation, functioning, working, active, in force, effective. INOPERATIVE
influential, important, significant, key, crucial, relevant.
n, worker, hand, employee, labourer, artisan, mechanic, operator.

opiate narcotic, sedative, tranquillizer, soporific, anodyne. STIMULANT

opine believe, think, feel, consider, reckon, judge, deem, suppose, conclude, say, declare.

opinion belief, judgment, view, point of view, idea, notion, fancy, thought, impression, feeling, sentiment, theory, conjecture, estimation, assessment. KNOWLEDGE

opinionated opinionative, dogmatic, dictatorial, doctrinaire, overconfident, cocksure, arrogant, overbearing, pig-headed, obdurate, prejudiced, biased, bigoted. MEEK

opponent adversary, antagonist, foe, enemy, rival, competitor, contestant, opposer. ALLY

opportune timely, seasonable, convenient, appropriate, apt, suitable, fitting, fit, favourable, auspicious, propitious, lucky, fortunate. INOPPORTUNE

opportunity chance, occasion, time, moment, opening, break (*inf*).

oppose resist, withstand, counter, fight, contest, combat, attack, face, confront, defy, hinder, obstruct, block, bar, check, prevent, thwart. AID
contrast, compare, match, counterbalance, offset.

opposite *adj*, facing, corresponding.
opposed, opposing, conflicting, antagonistic, hostile, inimical, contrary, reverse, contrasting, different, antithetical, contradictory, incompatible, irreconcilable. SAME
n, converse, inverse, reverse, contrary, antithesis.

opposition antagonism, hostility, defiance, resistance, counteraction, obstruction, hindrance, prevention, disapproval, conflict, confrontation, competition. AGREEMENT

oppress burden, encumber, trouble, afflict, torment, sadden, depress. RELIEVE
subjugate, subdue, crush, suppress, overwhelm, overpower, tyrannize, persecute. FREE

oppression tyranny, despotism, subjection, persecution, cruelty, severity, harshness, injustice, suffering, misery, hardship. LIBERTY

oppressive tyrannical, despotic, overbearing, harsh, severe, cruel, unjust. MILD
burdensome, onerous, heavy, overwhelming, overpowering, close, sultry, stuffy, stifling, uncomfortable.

opprobrious shameful, disgraceful, dishonourable, infamous, ignominious, reprehensible, despicable, contemptible, odious, disreputable. HONOURABLE
scornful, contemptuous, reproachful, derogatory, defamatory, vituperative, slanderous, calumniatory, unfavourable, offensive, insulting. LAUDATORY

oppugn dispute, contest, question, oppose, resist, attack, assail.

opt choose, select, decide, elect, prefer.

optimistic hopeful, confident, assured, sanguine, cheerful, positive, idealistic, utopian. PESSIMISTIC

option choice, alternative, selection, election, preference, wish, will, discretion.

optional voluntary, unforced, discretionary, elective. COMPULSORY

opulent rich, wealthy, affluent, moneyed, prosperous, well-off. POOR
sumptuous, luxurious, lavish, exuberant, luxuriant, abundant, profuse, copious, plentiful. MEAGRE

oracular prophetic, sibylline, vatic, fatidic, mantic, augural, divinatory, prognostic, predictive, portentous, ominous, foreboding.
wise, sage, venerable, grave, authoritative, positive, dogmatic.
allegorical, figurative, obscure, arcane, mysterious, cryptic, ambiguous.

oral verbal, spoken, vocal, unwritten. WRITTEN

oration speech, discourse, declamation, harangue, address, lecture.

orb ball, sphere, globe, round.

orbit *n*, revolution, cycle, circle, circuit, path, course, trajectory.
range, scope, field, compass, sphere, domain.
v, revolve, circle.

ordain consecrate, anoint, frock, induct, invest, call, appoint. UNFROCK
destine, predestine, fate, doom, foreordain.
order, command, decree, rule, enact, establish, bid, enjoin, prescribe.

ordeal trial, test, tribulation, trouble, affliction, suffering, hardship, nightmare.

order *n*, arrangement, disposition, sequence, progression, grouping, classification, structure, organization, system, method, plan, neatness, tidiness, orderliness. DISORDER
command, injunction, instruction, direction, decree, mandate, edict, ordinance, regulation, rule, law, precept.
peace, quiet, calm, tranquillity, discipline, law and order. ANARCHY
association, society, fraternity, community, lodge, league, guild, sect, denomination.
kind, sort, type, class, species, genus, family, rank, degree.
requisition, request, commission, booking, reservation.
out of order, broken, inoperative, not working, kaput (*inf*), on the blink (*inf*).
wrong, unseemly, indecorous, improper, not done.
v, command, instruct, direct, bid, enjoin, decree, ordain, prescribe, demand, require. BESEECH
request, book, reserve, apply for, send for. RECEIVE
arrange, dispose, organize, marshal, classify, group, sort, neaten, tidy. DISARRANGE

orderly neat, tidy, shipshape, systematic, methodical, regular, well-organized. UNTIDY
well-behaved, disciplined, law-abiding, peaceable, quiet, restrained. DISORDERLY

ordinance decree, edict, order, command, precept, rule, regulation, law, statute.
ceremony, rite, ritual, sacrament, observance.

ordinarily usually, generally, as a rule, normally, customarily, habitually, commonly.

ordinary common, commonplace, everyday, familiar, unexceptional, run-of-the-mill, plain, simple, conventional, normal, standard, typical, usual, customary, habitual, wonted, accustomed, regular, routine, humdrum, average, medium, mediocre, indifferent. UNUSUAL

organic natural, biological, living, animate. INORGANIC
basic, fundamental, structural, integral, constitutional, inherent, intrinsic. EXTRANEOUS
systematic, methodical, organized, ordered, structured. UNSYSTEMATIC

organization arrangement, order, classification, system, structure, construction, method, plan, design, constitution, composition.
association, institution, company, group, league, guild, consortium, confederation, union, syndicate.

organize coordinate, marshal, order, systematize, arrange, dispose, classify, sort, shape, form, constitute, establish, set up. DISRUPT

orgy debauch, revel, carousal, bacchanalia, spree, binge (*inf*).

orientate orient, direct, position, align, adjust, adapt, familiarize, acclimatize, get one's bearings. DISORIENTATE

orifice opening, aperture, hole, mouth, vent.

origin source, root, fount, spring, cause, derivation, provenance, base, foundation. RESULT
beginning, start, commencement, genesis, dawn, inception, outset. END
ancestry, extraction, lineage, family, stock, pedigree, birth, descent.

original *adj*, first, initial, primary, earliest, primordial, primeval, primitive, aboriginal, autochthonous. LATEST
fresh, new, novel, innovative, creative, inventive, imaginative, unconventional, different. HACKNEYED
n, master, prototype, archetype, model, pattern, standard. COPY

originate *vt*, begin, start, initiate, inaugurate, commence, create, invent, formulate, conceive, launch, introduce, found, institute. ABOLISH
vi, rise, spring, issue, proceed, flow, emanate, come, derive, stem. END

ornament *n*, adornment, decoration, embellishment, garnish, trimming, frill, accessory, bauble, trinket, knick-knack, gewgaw.
v, adorn, decorate, embellish, garnish, trim, deck, festoon, beautify, prettify. STRIP

ornate elaborate, fancy, baroque, rococo, florid, flowery, ornamented, adorned, decorated, embellished, elegant, beautiful. PLAIN

orotund resonant, sonorous, rich, full, ringing, booming. SOFT
pompous, bombastic, grandiloquent, magniloquent, turgid, inflated. SIMPLE

orthodox conventional, conformist, accepted, approved, official, usual, customary, traditional, sound, correct, true. UNORTHODOX

oscillate swing, sway, vibrate, vacillate, fluctuate, vary, waver, hesitate, falter.

ostensible outward, superficial, pretended, alleged, supposed, professed, avowed, apparent, seeming, manifest. REAL

ostentation display, show, parade, pageantry, pomp, flourish, flamboyance, affectation, pretentiousness, window dressing. RESERVE

ostentatious showy, flashy, flamboyant, loud, vulgar, affected, mannered, pretentious, pompous, vain, boastful. SUBDUED

ostracize exclude, banish, exile, excommunicate, blacklist, blackball, reject, shun, cold-shoulder (*inf*), ignore, send to Coventry. ACCEPT

other different, unlike, dissimilar, separate, distinct, diverse. SAME
further, more, extra, additional, supplementary, spare, alternative.

oust eject, expel, throw out, evict, dispossess, dislodge, depose, unseat. INSTALL

out away, absent, abroad, elsewhere, outside. IN
unfashionable, passé, antiquated, dated, old-fashioned.
exposed, revealed, disclosed, published, broadcast.
extinguished, dead, finished, exhausted.
impossible, unacceptable, not allowed.
wrong, incorrect, inaccurate, erroneous.

outbreak outburst, eruption, explosion, flare-up, burst, fit, rush, surge, epidemic.

outburst outbreak, eruption, explosion, flare-up, tantrum, fit, spasm, attack, outpouring, burst.

outcast castaway, pariah, exile, expatriate, refugee, wanderer, vagabond.

outcome consequence, result, issue, upshot, sequel, aftermath. CAUSE

outcry protest, complaint, uproar, clamour, hullaballoo, hue and cry, vociferation, exclamation, shout, yell.

outdo surpass, exceed, beat, top, excel, transcend, outshine, eclipse, outclass, outstrip, outdistance, outrun, outwit.

outer external, exterior, outward, outside, peripheral, superficial. INNER

outfit clothes, garb, ensemble, costume, get-up (*inf*), rigout (*inf*), kit, set, gear, equipment.

outing excursion, trip, jaunt, airing.

outlandish unconventional, bizarre, eccentric, weird, odd, strange, unfamiliar, exotic, foreign, alien, freakish, grotesque. CONVENTIONAL

outlaw bandit, brigand, robber, marauder, pirate, freebooter, fugitive, criminal, outcast, pariah.

outlay expenditure, disbursement, cost, expense, spending, outgoings. INCOME

outlet vent, release, escape, exit, egress, way out, opening, channel.
market, mart, store, shop.

outline *n*, draft, sketch, plan, skeleton, framework, drawing, tracing, delineation, contour, silhouette, shape, form.
summary, synopsis, résumé, précis, recapitulation, thumbnail, sketch.
v, draft, sketch, delineate, summarize, recapitulate.

outlook attitude, viewpoint, perspective, frame of mind, slant, angle.
prospect, expectation, future.
view, vista, panorama, scene.

outlying distant, remote, outer, peripheral. INNER

outrage *n*, atrocity, enormity, wrong, injury, harm, violation, desecration, abuse, offence, affront, insult, indignity.
anger, rage, fury, wrath, indignation, shock.
v, anger, enrage, infuriate, madden, offend, insult, disgust, shock, horrify.
abuse, injure, violate, desecrate.

outrageous shocking, scandalous, atrocious, abominable, unspeakable, vile, horrible, monstrous, heinous, disgraceful, offensive, intolerable, insufferable.
immoderate, excessive, extravagant, unreasonable, preposterous. REASONABLE

outright *adj*, total, complete, utter, absolute, sheer, perfect, consummate, unconditional, downright, unmitigated, unqualified, direct, straightforward.
adv, totally, completely, utterly, absolutely, openly, unreservedly, directly, instantly, immediately, at once.

outrun outstrip, outpace, outdistance, pass, overtake, behind, escape, beat, surpass, excel, outdo.

outset start, beginning, commencement, inception, opening, inauguration. END

outshine eclipse, overshadow, surpass, excel, transcend, outclass, outrival, outdo, outstrip.

outside *n*, exterior, surface, edge, border, appearance, façade.
adj, exterior, external, outer, outward, superficial, peripheral, extraneous. INSIDE
distant, remote, unlikely, slim, marginal.

outsider stranger, alien, foreigner, newcomer, intruder, interloper, visitor, nonmember, gate-crasher (*inf*).

outskirts suburbs, environs, precincts, periphery, edge, border, boundary. CENTRE

outspoken candid, frank, blunt, explicit, open, free, unreserved, direct, straightforward, forthright. RESERVED

outspread outstretched, open, unfolded, unfurled, extended, expanded, spread out. CLOSED

outstanding excellent, superb, superior, exceptional, great, distinguished, eminent, notable, striking, impressive, prominent, salient, signal, noticeable, conspicuous, memorable. INSIGNIFICANT
owing, due, unpaid, unsettled, remaining. PAID

outstretch outspread, extend, stretch out, expand, spread out, open, unfold, unfurl. CLOSE

outstrip outrun, outpace, outdistance, outdo, surpass, exceed, excel, beat, outclass, outshine, eclipse.

outward outer, external, exterior, outside, superficial, apparent, visible, ostensible. INWARD

outweigh override, overcome, prevail over, outbalance, overbalance, preponderate, surpass, exceed.

outwit cheat, defraud, trick, dupe, deceive, outjockey, outfox, outsmart (*inf*), get the better of, outthink, overreach, circumvent.

ovation applause, plaudits, clapping, cheering, acclaim, acclamation, laudation, praise.

over *prep*, above, on, upon, on top of, higher than. UNDER
across, through, during.
exceeding, in excess of, more than, greater than.
adv, above, overhead, out, beyond, across, through.
extra, surplus, remaining, left over, in excess, in addition. SHORT
adj, finished, ended, concluded, completed, done, gone, past.

overall general, universal, global, comprehensive, all-embracing, inclusive, complete, total, sweeping.

overawe intimidate, cow, daunt, abash, frighten, scare, domineer, browbeat. REASSURE

overbearing domineering, imperious, lordly, high-handed, haughty, arrogant, autocratic, dictatorial, tyrannical, oppressive. HUMBLE

overcast cloudy, grey, dull, gloomy, dreary, dismal, sombre, murky, dark, lowering, leaden. CLEAR

overcharge surcharge, cheat, shortchange, rook (*inf*), rip off (*inf*), do (*inf*), diddle (*inf*). UNDERCHARGE
overload, overburden, strain, overtax.

overcome conquer, vanquish, defeat, beat, best, worst, overpower, overwhelm, crush, quell, subdue, master, surmount, triumph over, rise above. SUBMIT

overdo exaggerate, go overboard (*inf*), overact, overplay, overstate, overindulge, overwork, overtax, overcook.
overdue late, tardy, behind, behindhand, delayed, belated, owing, in arrears, due, payable. PUNCTUAL
overestimate overrate, overvalue, overpraise, exaggerate. UNDERESTIMATE
overflow overrun, overspill, run over, spill over, surge, pour forth, flood, inundate, deluge, swamp, overspread, cover, abound, teem. SUBSIDE
overhaul inspect, examine, check, service, repair.
catch up, overtake, pass, outstrip.
overjoyed delighted, ecstatic, elated, jubilant, thrilled, over the moon (*inf*). UPSET
overload overcharge, overburden, strain, overtax, oppress, burden, encumber. RELIEVE
overlook miss, neglect, omit, leave out, skip, pass over, disregard, ignore, forget. NOTE
forgive, pardon, excuse, condone, blink at, wink at. PUNISH
overpower overwhelm, overcome, conquer, vanquish, defeat, beat, master, surmount, crush, quell, subdue, best, worst. SUBMIT
overpowering overwhelming, strong, powerful, forceful, weighty, irresistible, uncontrollable. WEAK
overrate overestimate, overvalue, overpraise, exaggerate. UNDERRATE
overreach outwit, outsmart (*inf*), cheat, defraud, swindle, trick, dupe, deceive, circumvent.
override disregard, ignore, supersede, outweigh, prevail over, quash, annul, reverse, cancel, overrule.
overrule disallow, reject, override, supersede, annul, rescind, abrogate, countermand, revoke, repeal, cancel, nullify.
rule, govern, dominate, prevail over, influence, sway, control, direct.
overrun attack, invade, overwhelm, ravage, devastate, infest, inundate, swarm, spread, overflow.
exceed, go beyond, overshoot, overreach.
overseer supervisor, superintendent, manager, foreman, boss (*inf*).
overshadow eclipse, outshine, surpass, excel, dwarf, dominate, tower over, rise above.
cloud, darken, dim, obscure, veil, spoil, blight.
oversight omission, fault, lapse, slip, blunder, mistake, error, neglect, inattention. ATTENTION
supervision, surveillance, administration, management, direction, control, care, custody.
overt plain, clear, manifest, patent, apparent, visible, open, public, unconcealed, undisguised, blatant, deliberate. SECRET
overtake pass, leave behind, outrun, outstrip, catch up, overhaul.
overthrow *v*, oust, depose, unseat, dethrone, conquer, vanquish, defeat, beat, overcome, overpower, subvert, overturn, upset, bring down, demolish, raze, ruin, destroy, abolish. RESTORE
n, deposition, dethronement, defeat, fall, subversion, demolition, downfall, ruin, destruction, abolition. RESTORATION
overture advance, approach, offer, proposal, proposition, invitation. REJECTION
introduction, prelude, opening, preface, prologue. FINALE
overturn upset, capsize, keel over, tip over, upend, invert, topple, spill.
overthrow, subvert, bring down, destroy, abolish, reverse.
overweening arrogant, haughty, supercilious, proud, vain, lordly, high and mighty (*inf*), pompous, opinionated, cocky, cocksure. MEEK
excessive, immoderate, extravagant, exaggerated.
overweight obese, fat, plump, stout, portly, heavy, outsize, flabby, fleshy. SKINNY
overwhelm overcome, devastate, stagger, bowl over (*inf*), engulf, submerge, inundate, flood, deluge, swamp, bury.
overpower, overthrow, conquer, vanquish, defeat, master, crush. SUBMIT
overwrought agitated, frantic, tense, on edge, keyed up, worked up (*inf*), excited, overexcited. CALM
elaborate, fancy, ornate, flowery, overdone, overworked. PLAIN
owing due, unpaid, payable, owed, outstanding, unsettled, overdue, in arrears. PAID
own *adj*, personal, private, individual, particular.

on one's own, alone, by oneself, singly, independently, unaided.
v, possess, have, hold, keep.
recognize, grant, concede, avow, acknowledge, admit, confess, own up. DENY
owner possessor, holder, proprietor, proprietress, master, mistress.

P

pace *n*, step, stride, gait, walk.
speed, velocity, rate, tempo, progress, rapidity, swiftness.
v, walk, stride, step, measure.
pacific conciliatory, placatory, peacemaking, irenic, peaceable, peace-loving, mild, gentle, nonviolent. BELLIGERENT
peaceful, calm, serene, tranquil, quiet, still. TURBULENT
pacify appease, conciliate, propitiate, placate, mollify, calm, compose, lull, quiet, soothe, tranquillize, allay, assuage, moderate, mitigate, quell, subdue. AGGRAVATE
pack *n*, bundle, package, parcel, packet, load, burden.
herd, flock, crowd, throng, mob, group, band, gang, company, lot, set, collection, assortment.
v, cram, stuff, jam, wedge, press, ram, compact, compress, fill, crowd.
load, stow, store.
package *n*, bundle, pack, parcel, packet, box, carton, wrapper, wrapping.
v, pack, box, wrap.
packet pack, package, parcel, box, carton, container, receptacle.
pact agreement, compact, covenant, concordat, bond, contract, treaty, entente, league, alliance, bargain, deal, arrangement.
pad *n*, cushion, bolster, wad, buffer, stuffing, padding, filling, wadding.
block, tablet, jotter, notepad.
v, cushion, stuff, fill, pack.
pagan *n*, heathen, unbeliever, infidel, idolater, atheist, agnostic. BELIEVER
adj, heathen, idolatrous, irreligious, godless, atheistic, agnostic.
page[1] *n*, leaf, sheet, folio, side.
episode, chapter, period, era, point, stage.
page[2] *n*, pageboy, bellboy, servant, attendant.
v, call, summon, send for, announce.
pageant parade, procession, tableau, spectacle, show, display, exhibition, extravaganza.
pageantry pomp, ceremony, state, magnificence, splendour, glamour, grandeur, show, display, showiness, ostentation.
pain *n*, hurt, discomfort, suffering, agony, ache, throb, pang, twinge, soreness, tenderness. RELIEF
distress, anguish, trouble, affliction, torment, torture, misery, sorrow, grief, woe. JOY
v, hurt, ache, throb, sting, smart, chafe, injure, wound. EASE
distress, trouble, afflict, torment, torture, agonize, grieve, sorrow, vex, annoy. COMFORT
painful sore, tender, hurting, aching, throbbing, stinging, smarting, agonizing, excruciating.
distressing, harrowing, unpleasant, disagreeable, grievous, unhappy. PLEASANT
hard, difficult, arduous, laborious, toilsome, troublesome, vexatious. EASY
painstaking careful, scrupulous, punctilious, meticulous, conscientious, diligent, assiduous, sedulous, thorough. CARELESS
paint *n*, colour, colouring, pigment, stain, dye, tint.
v, colour, tint, coat, cover, decorate.
portray, depict, picture, represent, delineate, draw, sketch.
pair *n*, couple, brace, twosome, duo, doublet.
v, match, couple, mate, twin, partner, join, yoke, marry, wed. SEPARATE
palatable tasty, toothsome, savoury, delicious, appetizing, mouthwatering, luscious, delectable.
pleasant, agreeable, acceptable, satisfactory. UNPLEASANT
palatial grand, stately, majestic, imposing, splendid, magnificent, sumptuous, luxurious, opulent. MEAN
palaver rigmarole, procedure, business, affair, fuss, carry-on (*inf*).
chatter, babble, prattle, blather.
conference, colloquy, discussion, confabulation, conversation.
pale *adj*, colourless, whitish, wan, pallid, pasty, ashen, sallow, white, bleached, faded, light. DARK
dim, faint, feeble, weak.

v, blanch, whiten, fade, dim, lessen, diminish.

pall[1] *n*, shroud, mantle, shadow, damper, gloom, melancholy.

pall[2] *v*, cloy, satiate, glut, surfeit, bore, tire.

palliate alleviate, mitigate, allay, assuage, soothe, ease, relieve, abate, soften. AGGRAVATE

extenuate, excuse, minimize, lessen, diminish, varnish, gloss over, whitewash (*inf*), conceal, cover up. EXPOSE

palliative analgesic, anodyne, sedative, lenitive, demulcent.

pallid pale, wan, ashen, pasty, sallow, white, whitish, colourless, vapid, insipid.

pallor paleness, pallidness, pallidity, wanness, whiteness. RUDDINESS

palmy prosperous, thriving, flourishing, halcyon, golden, glorious, triumphant, happy, fortunate. UNFORTUNATE

palpable obvious, evident, manifest, patent, clear, plain, overt, blatant, perceptible, visible, apparent, conspicuous, unmistakable.

tangible, real, concrete, solid, substantial, material, corporeal. IMPALPABLE

palpitate pulsate, beat, throb, pound, flutter, tremble, quiver, vibrate.

palter equivocate, fudge, hedge, shuffle, quibble, prevaricate, tergiversate.

haggle, bargain, chaffer.

paltry trivial, trifling, minor, petty, small, little, slight, insignificant, inconsiderable, meagre, derisory, worthless, wretched, miserable, poor, contemptible, despicable, abject, mean, base, low. CONSIDERABLE

pamper indulge, humour, spoil, ruin, coddle, mollycoddle, cosset, baby, pet. DISCIPLINE

pamphlet booklet, leaflet, brochure, circular, hand-out, tract, treatise.

panacea cure-all, elixir, nostrum, universal, remedy.

pandemonium chaos, confusion, disorder, tumult, turmoil, riot, uproar, commotion, hullaballoo. PEACE

pander to gratify, satisfy, indulge, humour, please, cater to.

panegyric eulogy, encomium, praise, commendation, paean, accolade, tribute. TIRADE

panegyrize eulogize, praise, commend, extol, laud, glorify, acclaim. DECRY

panel sheet, board, section.

board, council, committee, jury.

pang pain, stab, prick, twinge, spasm.

panic *n*, terror, alarm, fright, fear, consternation, dismay, confusion, turmoil. COMPOSURE

v, be alarmed, overreact, go to pieces (*inf*).

terrify, alarm, frighten, scare.

pant puff, blow, gasp, wheeze, pulsate, throb, heave.

paper newspaper, journal, gazette, daily, rag (*inf*).

document, certificate, credential, instrument, deed.

article, report, monograph, treatise, essay, composition, dissertation, thesis.

par level, standard, norm, average, mean.

parity, equality, balance, equilibrium.

above par, excellent, first-rate, superior, exceptional, outstanding. INFERIOR

below par, substandard, inferior, second-rate, poor. EXCELLENT

on a par, equal, the same, well-matched. UNEQUAL

up to par, acceptable, satisfactory, passable, adequate. UNACCEPTABLE

parable fable, allegory, tale, story, lesson.

parabolic allegorical, figurative, symbolic, metaphorical.

parade *n*, procession, train, column, file, review, march, cavalcade, pageant, array.

show, display, exhibition, spectacle, ostentation, pomp. MODESTY

v, march, file, process.

flaunt, vaunt, show off, display, exhibit, air, swagger, strut. HIDE

paradise heaven, Elysium, Eden, utopia, bliss. PURGATORY

paradox contradiction, incongruity, inconsistency, absurdity, puzzle, riddle, enigma, mystery. TRUISM

paragon model, pattern, paradigm, ideal, exemplar, archetype, prototype, nonesuch, nonpareil, standard, norm, criterion.

paragraph section, subdivision, clause, passage.

parallel *adj*, equidistant, aligned, even, equal, corresponding, similar, like, analogous, equivalent. DIVERGENT

n, counterpart, equivalent, match, twin. CONVERSE

analogy, correspondence, similarity, likeness, resemblance, comparison. DIFFERENCE
v, equal, match, correspond, resemble, compare. DIFFER

paralyse deaden, numb, anaesthetize, freeze, transfix, immobilize, incapacitate, disable, cripple.

paramount pre-eminent, supreme, chief, cardinal, principal, leading, dominant, prime, primary, first, foremost. MINOR

parapet wall, railing, breastwork, battlement.

paraphernalia belongings, effects, things, stuff, baggage, impedimenta, gear, equipment, tackle, accoutrements, appurtenances, trappings.

paraphrase *n*, explanation, interpretation, translation, rewording, restatement, rehash.
v, reword, restate, explain, interpret.

parasite hanger-on, leech, sponger (*inf*), scrounger (*inf*), sycophant, toady.

parcel *n*, package, bundle, pack, packet, lot, batch, bunch, group, collection.
piece, part, portion, plot, tract, patch.
v, package, wrap, pack. UNDO
divide, share, apportion, allot, mete, dole, deal, distribute. WITHHOLD

parched dry, arid, waterless, scorched, roasted, withered, shrivelled, dehydrated, thirsty. FLOODED

pardon *v*, forgive, excuse, condone, overlook, remit, absolve, acquit, clear, exonerate, discharge, release. PUNISH
n, forgiveness, excuse, clemency, mercy, grace, amnesty, remission, absolution, acquittal, exoneration, discharge, release. PUNISHMENT

pare peel, skin, shave, clip, trim, cut, crop, prune, dock, reduce, decrease, diminish, lessen.

parentage ancestry, lineage, descent, extraction, birth, origin, family, race, stock, pedigree.

pariah outcast, leper, untouchable, exile, outlaw.

parity equality, par, equivalence, parallelism, evenness, uniformity, identity, sameness, correspondence, analogy. DISPARITY

parlance idiom, vernacular, tongue, language, jargon, lingo (*inf*), speech, talk.

parley *v*, talk, discuss, negotiate, confer, converse, confabulate.
n, talk, discussion, meeting, conference, colloquy, dialogue, conversation, confabulation.

parliament legislature, assembly, council, congress, senate, diet.

parochial provincial, insular, small-minded, narrow-minded, restricted, limited, illiberal, petty.

parody *n*, burlesque, lampoon, caricature, satire, spoof, skit, send-up (*inf*), mockery, travesty, imitation, mimicry.
v, burlesque, lampoon, caricature, satirize, take off (*inf*), mock, imitate.

paroxysm fit, seizure, attack, spasm, convulsion, outburst, eruption.

parry deflect, ward off, fend off, stave off, repulse, avert, avoid, evade, dodge, sidestep, circumvent.

parsimonious mean, stingy, miserly, niggardly, close-fisted, tight-fisted, ungenerous, grasping, frugal, sparing. GENEROUS

parson clergyman, cleric, churchman, ecclesiastic, priest, minister, rector, vicar, pastor, preacher. LAYMAN

part *n*, piece, portion, share, section, division, segment, fraction, fragment, bit, scrap, ingredient, constituent, element, component, branch, member. WHOLE
character, role, function, office, duty, responsibility, participation, interest, concern, behalf, side, party, faction.
in part, partly, partially, to some extent, somewhat, moderately. ENTIRELY
v, divide, separate, split, break, sever, disunite, disjoin, disconnect, detach. JOIN
go, depart, quit, leave, withdraw, retire.
part with, relinquish, give up, renounce, abandon, surrender, yield. RETAIN

partial incomplete, fragmentary, unfinished, imperfect, restricted, limited. TOTAL
biased, prejudiced, partisan, one-sided, unfair, unjust, discriminatory. IMPARTIAL
be partial to, like, be fond of, care for. DISLIKE

participate share, partake, take part, join in, be involved, help, contribute.

particle grain, speck, atom, iota, whit, jot, tittle, bit, scrap, shred, crumb.

particular *adj*, special, specific, exact, distinct, separate, peculiar, individual. GENERAL

notable, remarkable, marked, especial, exceptional, unusual, uncommon. ORDINARY
fussy, finicky, fastidious, dainty, choosy (*inf*), discriminating, critical, difficult, exacting, careful, meticulous, painstaking, thorough, detailed, minute, strict.
n, particularity, detail, point, feature, item.
in particular, particularly, especially, specifically, exactly. GENERALLY

particularize specify, spell out, detail, itemize, enumerate. GENERALIZE

parting *n*, farewell, goodbye, valediction, leave-taking, departure, going.
division, separation, partition, cleavage, rift, split, break, rupture, severance, disunion. UNION
adj, farewell, valedictory, departing, final, last. OPENING

partisan *n*, adherent, follower, disciple, votary, champion, supporter, enthusiast, devotee.
adj, biased, prejudiced, partial, one-sided, factional, sectarian. NEUTRAL

partition *n*, division, separation, parting, severance. UNION
screen, barrier, wall, divider, separator.
share, portion, allotment, allocation, distribution.
v, divide, separate, split, apportion, share.

partner companion, comrade, ally, colleague, associate, copartner, confederate, collaborator, accomplice, helper, mate, consort, spouse. RIVAL

partnership association, collaboration, cooperation, sharing, participation, companionship, fellowship, union, alliance, corporation, company, firm, house.

parts region, area, district, locality, neighbourhood, vicinity.
ability, calibre, talents, gifts, attributes, faculties, intelligence, intellect, accomplishments.

parturition childbirth, confinement, *accouchement*, labour, delivery.

party social, soirée, celebration, gathering, get-together (*inf*), reception, at-home.
group, band, gang, team, crew, squad, troop, body, company.
side, faction, coterie, set, clique, circle, ring, league, alliance, association.
person, individual, participant, litigant, plaintiff, defendant.

pass *v*, go, move, proceed, flow, run, go by, elapse, go past, overtake. STOP
surpass, exceed, transcend, go beyond, outdo, outstrip.
succeed, get through, qualify, come up to scratch (*inf*), do. FAIL
spend, fill, occupy, employ, while away.
spread, circulate, transfer, exchange, convey, transmit, hand, give. WITHHOLD
enact, legislate, sanction, approve, ratify, accept, adopt, ordain, decree. REJECT
ignore, disregard, pass over, overlook, pass by, skip, miss, omit, neglect. NOTE
depart, leave, go, end, cease, die, pass on, pass away, fade, vanish, disappear. REMAIN
discharge, eliminate, void, evacuate, excrete.
pass out, faint, collapse, swoon, black out, flake out (*inf*), keel over (*inf*).
n, passage, way, gap, col, defile, gorge, ravine, canyon.
passport, visa, ticket, licence, warrant, permit, authorization, permission.
advance, overture, move, thrust, lunge, throw, kick, transfer.
plight, predicament, situation, condition, state of affairs.

passable fair, middling, all right, OK (*inf*), so-so (*inf*), acceptable, adequate, tolerable, admissible, allowable, ordinary, unexceptional. EXCELLENT
clear, unobstructed, open, traversable, navigable. IMPASSABLE

passage route, course, path, road, way, pass, thoroughfare, channel, avenue, access, opening, entrance, exit.
passageway, corridor, hall, hallway, lobby, vestibule, aisle, alley, alleyway.
section, piece, excerpt, extract, paragraph, verse, quotation, text.
journey, voyage, trip, crossing.
transition, passing, flow, movement, progression, motion, progress, transit. HALT
enactment, legislation, sanction, approval, ratification. REJECTION

passenger fare, rider, traveller, voyager, tourist.

passing transitory, transient, fleeting, momentary, ephemeral, brief, short, hasty, cursory, superficial, slight, casual.

passion emotion, feeling, ardour, fervour, zeal, enthusiasm, eagerness, excitement, animation, warmth, fire, intensity, vehemence, spirit, rapture. APATHY

desire, craving, lust, love, affection, fondness, adoration, infatuation, mania, obsession. LOATHING
rage, fury, anger, wrath, storm, outburst. COMPOSURE

passionate vehement, impassioned, ardent, fervent, warm, heartfelt, zealous, enthusiastic, eager, excited, animated, fierce, intense, strong, impulsive, impetuous. APATHETIC
loving, amorous, lustful, erotic, sensual, sexy (*inf*). FRIGID
hot, fiery, excitable, temperamental, stormy, violent, furious, irate, enraged, incensed. CALM

passive submissive, unresisting, docile, acquiescent, compliant, patient, resigned, indifferent, uninvolved, inert, still, inactive, lifeless. ACTIVE

past *adj*, over, finished, ended, done, gone, spent, elapsed, forgotten. AHEAD
ancient, old, bygone, obsolete, previous, former, prior, preceding, recent, late. FUTURE
n, history, antiquity, long ago, olden days, yesteryear, yesterday. PRESENT
life, background, experience, youth, memories.
adv, by, on, over, across, ago.
prep, beyond, over, above, after.

paste *n*, adhesive, glue, gum, mucilage.
v, stick, glue, gum, fix.

pastime hobby, recreation, activity, sport, game, entertainment, diversion, amusement. WORK

pastor clergyman, cleric, churchman, ecclesiastic, priest, minister, rector, parson, vicar, preacher. LAYMAN

pastoral rural, rustic, country, bucolic, idyllic.
clerical, ecclesiastical, ministerial.

pasture pasturage, grazing, grassland, meadow, herbage, grass.

pat tap, dab, hit, slap, rap, stroke, caress.

patch *n*, piece, scrap, area, tract, plot.
v, mend, repair, fix, reinforce, cover.

patent *adj*, obvious, plain, clear, manifest, evident, apparent, open, unconcealed, undisguised, unmistakable, conspicuous, blatant, glaring. HIDDEN
n, copyright, right, privilege, licence, grant, invention.

paternal fatherly, protective, solicitous, benevolent.

path track, trail, pathway, footpath, walk, way, road, passage, route, course, avenue.

pathetic moving, touching, affecting, poignant, plaintive, piteous, pitiable, sad, distressing, tender, emotional.
paltry, meagre, inadequate, pitiful, lamentable, feeble, contemptible, worthless, useless.

patience tolerance, forbearance, restraint, leniency, calmness, composure, equanimity, imperturbability, self-control, self-possession.
endurance, sufferance, stoicism, resignation, submission, perseverance, persistence, constancy, fortitude. IMPATIENCE

patient *adj*, tolerant, forbearing, clement, forgiving, lenient, indulgent, calm, composed, imperturbable, self-possessed.
enduring, long-suffering, uncomplaining, stoical, philosophical, resigned, submissive, passive, persevering, persistent. IMPATIENT
n, invalid, sufferer, case, inmate.

patrician *n*, aristocrat, noble, peer. COMMONER
adj, aristocratic, noble, highborn, blue-blooded. PLEBEIAN

patrimony heritage, birthright, inheritance, legacy, bequest.

patrol *v*, guard, protect, police, keep watch, inspect.
n, guard, garrison, sentry, sentinel, watch, watchman.
protection, vigilance, round, beat.

patron sponsor, promoter, backer, supporter, advocate, benefactor, guardian, protector, defender, helper, friend.
customer, client, regular, habitué, buyer, shopper.

patronize frequent, buy from, deal with, sponsor, promote, back, support, help, befriend.
condescend, stoop, talk down to, look down on, contemn, disdain. RESPECT

pattern design, style, motif, figure, decoration, ornamentation.
method, system, plan, arrangement, order.
model, exemplar, paragon, standard, norm, original, archetype, prototype, mould, stencil, template, diagram, blueprint, sample, specimen. COPY

paucity dearth, lack, scarcity, scantiness, sparseness, fewness, shortage, deficiency, inadequacy, insuffiency. ABUNDANCE

pauper beggar, mendicant, indigent, down-and-out, poor person, bankrupt, insolvent.

pause *v*, stop, halt, cease, desist, break, rest, interrupt, discontinue, wait, delay, hesitate. PROCEED

n, stop, halt, cessation, suspension, break, rest, interval, intermission, interruption, wait, delay, hesitation. CONTINUANCE

pave flag, cobble, tile, floor, concrete, asphalt, tar, macadamize, surface, cover.

prepare, smooth, facilitate. IMPEDE

pawn[1] *v*, deposit, pledge, hock (*inf*), stake, wager. REDEEM

n, deposit, pledge, security, surety, gage, earnest, assurance, guarantee.

pawn[2] *n*, instrument, tool, puppet, cat's-paw.

pay *v*, remunerate, reward, recompense, requite, repay, pay back, refund, reimburse, compensate, remit, defray, settle, clear, discharge, pay off, liquidate, meet, satisfy, honour. OWE

spend, disburse, pay out, fork out (*inf*), cough up (*inf*).

yield, return, profit, benefit, be advantageous, be profitable, be lucrative.

give, offer, proffer, afford, bestow, render. WITHHOLD

suffer, answer, atone, make amends.

n, salary, wages, remuneration, earnings, payment, hire, fee, stipend, emolument, reward, compensation.

payment settlement, discharge, liquidation, defrayal, remittance, advance, premium, deposit, instalment, expenditure, outlay.

recompense, compensation, reward, remuneration, fee, pay, wage.

peace concord, harmony, amity, pacification, conciliation, truce, armistice. WAR

calm, calmness, tranquillity, serenity, rest, repose, quiet, silence, hush, stillness, peacefulness. DISTURBANCE

peaceable pacific, peace-loving, nonviolent, mild, gentle, amicable, friendly, peaceful, peacemaking, irenic, conciliatory, placatory. WARLIKE

peaceful calm, tranquil, serene, quiet, still, restful, placid, unruffled. AGITATED

peaceable, nonviolent, peace-loving, peacemaking, irenic, pacific. BELLIGERENT

peak top, summit, pinnacle, apex, point, tip, crest, crown, acme, apogee, zenith, climax, culmination, maximum. BASE

peal *v*, ring, chime, toll, tintinnabulate, sound, resound, resonate, reverberate, roar, thunder.

n, carillon, chime, toll, tintinnabulation, ringing, sound, reverberation, clap, rumble, roar, burst.

peasant countryman, rustic, provincial, bumpkin, yokel, boor, churl. CITIZEN

peccant sinful, bad, wicked, corrupt, criminal, culpable, guilty, wrong, faulty, morbid, unhealthy. RIGHTEOUS

peck tap, rap, hit, strike, kiss, bite, nibble, pick.

peculate embezzle, defalcate, appropriate, misappropriate, steal, purloin, defraud, swindle.

peculiar strange, odd, queer, curious, weird, bizarre, unusual, uncommon, rare, singular, exceptional, extraordinary. ORDINARY

distinct, special, specific, particular, characteristic, distinctive, unique, individual, personal. GENERAL

peculiarity idiosyncrasy, quirk, mannerism, eccentricity, oddity, curiosity, singularity, individuality, particularity, characteristic, trait, feature, mark.

pecuniary monetary, financial.

pedagogue teacher, educator, tutor, instructor, schoolmaster, schoolmistress. PUPIL

pedantic precise, exact, punctilious, fussy, finicky, particular, hairsplitting, nitpicking (*inf*), formal, puristic, bookish, academic, erudite, pompous, dogmatic.

peddle hawk, vend, sell, push (*inf*). BUY

pedigree *n*, descent, line, lineage, ancestry, parentage, family, extraction, race, stirps, stock, breed, genealogy, background, derivation.

adj, pedigreed, purebred, thoroughbred. HYBRID

pedlar hawker, vendor, seller, salesman, dealer, peddler, pusher (*inf*). BUYER

peel *v*, pare, skin, decorticate, scale, flake, desquamate, strip, excoriate. COVER

n, peeling, skin, rind.

peep[1] peek, glimpse, glance, spy, peer, squint, look.

peep[2] squeak, chirp, tweet, twitter.

peer[1] *n*, noble, nobleman, aristocrat, lord, duke, marquess, earl, viscount, baron. COMMONER
equal, compeer, match, like, mate, fellow.

peer[2] *v*, squint, gaze, scrutinize, peep, peek.

peerless matchless, unmatched, unequalled, unparalleled, unrivalled, unsurpassed, second to none, nonpareil, superlative, excellent, unique, incomparable. ORDINARY

peevish irritable, fretful, fractious, crotchety, cross, touchy, testy, waspish, snappish, petulant, crabbed, cantankerous, grumpy, sullen, sulky, moody, surly, churlish, captious, querulous, sour, acrimonious. GENIAL

pelf lucre, money, wealth, riches, mammon.

pellucid transparent, translucent, clear, limpid, crystalline. OPAQUE
lucid, coherent, comprehensible, intelligible, clear, plain. UNINTELLIGIBLE

pelt[1] *v*, bombard, pepper, shower, assail, belabour, batter, beat, strike, throw, hurl, cast, sling.
dash, race, rush, hurry, speed, tear. AMBLE
pour, teem, rain hard. DRIZZLE

pelt[2] *n*, skin, hide, fell, fur, coat.

pen[1] *n*, ballpoint, felt-tip, fountain pen, quill.
v, write, jot down, draft, compose.

pen[2] *n*, enclosure, pound, fold, sty, cage, coop.
v, enclose, confine, coop up, fence in, cage. FREE

penal punitive, disciplinary, corrective, retributive.

penalize punish, discipline, correct, handicap, disadvantage. REWARD

penalty punishment, retribution, forfeiture, forfeit, fine, mulct, handicap, disadvantage. REWARD

penance punishment, penalty, atonement, reparation, contrition, mortification, humilation.

penchant inclination, tendency, proclivity, propensity, leaning, bent, liking, predilection, partiality, fondness, taste. AVERSION

pendent hanging, suspended, dangling, swinging, pendulous, overhanging, projecting, jutting out, beetling. ERECT

pending *prep*, until, awaiting, during.
adj, unsettled, undecided, in abeyance, hanging fire, imminent, impending.

penetrable pervious, permeable, porous, accessible, passable, comprehensible, fathomable, vulnerable. IMPENETRABLE

penetrate pierce, pass through, enter, bore, perforate, prick.
permeate, pervade, percolate, impregnate, infiltrate, invade.
understand, comprehend, grasp, fathom, perceive, see, decipher, unravel, sink in, register (*inf*).

penetrating piercing, shrill, sharp, acute, keen, perceptive, discerning, discriminating, intelligent, clever, shrewd, astute, incisive, biting. DULL

penitence contrition, repentance, regret, remorse, compunction, sorrow, shame. IMPENITENCE

penitent contrite, repentant, regretful, remorseful, sorrowful, abject, sorry, apologetic. IMPENITENT

penniless poor, impecunious, penurious, broke (*inf*), skint (*inf*), bankrupt, indigent, destitute, needy, necessitous, impoverished, poverty-stricken. RICH

pennon pennant, streamer, banner, banderole, jack, flag, ensign, standard, colours.

pension annuity, allowance, grant.

pensive thoughtful, reflective, musing, meditative, ruminative, dreamy, wistful, brooding, melancholy, mournful, sad, sober, solemn, serious, grave. CAREFREE

pent-up repressed, suppressed, held back, restrained, bridled, confined, bottled up. RELEASED

penurious niggardly, miserly, mean, stingy, cheeseparing, penny-pinching (*inf*), parsimonious, tight-fisted, close-fisted. GENEROUS
poor, penniless, impecunious, impoverished, poverty-stricken, destitute, indigent. RICH
scanty, meagre, inadequate, deficient, poor, paltry. ABUNDANT

penury poverty, destitution, indigence, need, want, beggary, pauperism. AFFLUENCE
death, scarcity, deficiency, shortage, lack, paucity. ABUNDANCE

people *n*, persons, humans, human beings, men, women, children, mankind, humanity.
nation, race, tribe, community, society, population, inhabitants, public, folk.
populace, crowd, mob, general public, masses, commonalty, rabble, hoi polloi. NOBILITY
v, populate, inhabit, settle, colonize.

peppery hot, spicy, pungent, piquant, sharp, incisive, biting, caustic, trenchant. MILD
irritable, irascible, quick-tempered, hot-tempered, fiery, choleric, testy, touchy, snappish, waspish. AFFABLE

per each, every, a, by, through.

perceive sense, feel, be aware of, see, observe, notice, discern, make out, distinguish, recognize.
understand, comprehend, grasp, fathom, realize, learn, know, conclude, deduce.

perceptible perceivable, discernible, appreciable, recognizable, apparent, visible, noticeable, distinct, evident, obvious, palpable. IMPERCEPTIBLE

perception understanding, comprehension, apprehension, awareness, recognition, discernment, knowledge, percipience, sense, feeling, intuition, insight, idea, notion, conception. IGNORANCE

perceptive percipient, perspicacious, discerning, aware, observant, alert, sensitive, intuitive, sharp, penetrating, astute, shrewd. SLOW

perch *n*, pole, bar, branch, roost.
v, alight, land, settle, rest, sit, roost.

percolate strain, filter, drip, seep, ooze, exude, permeate, penetrate.

percussion impact, crash, collision, knock, bump, shock, concussion.

perdition damnation, destruction, ruin, downfall, hell. SALVATION

peregrination journey, voyage, trip, expedition, travel, globetrotting, wandering, roaming.

peremptory commanding, imperative, obligatory, mandatory, binding, absolute, categorical, decisive, final, arbitrary, imperious, dictatorial, dogmatic, assertive, positive.

perennial lasting, enduring, permanent, constant, incessant, continual, perpetual, everlasting, eternal, immortal, undying, imperishable, endless, ceaseless. EPHEMERAL

perfect *adj*, pure, unblemished, flawless, immaculate, spotless, faultless, impeccable, blameless, exemplary, ideal, excellent, superb. IMPERFECT
complete, finished, consummate, entire, full, whole, total, utter, absolute, sheer. INCOMPLETE
accurate, precise, exact, correct, right, true. INACCURATE
accomplished, practised, polished, expert, masterly, skilled, skilful.
v, finish, complete, consummate, realize, achieve, accomplish. COMMENCE
polish, elaborate, improve, ameliorate, rectify. SPOIL

perfection completion, consummation, realization, achievement, accomplishment.
perfectness, purity, spotlessness, flawlessness, faultlessness, excellence. IMPERFECTION
ideal, paragon, quintessence.

perfectly completely, totally, entirely, fully, altogether, quite, thoroughly, utterly, absolutely. PARTLY
flawlessly, faultlessly, superbly, admirably, ideally, exactly, precisely. BADLY

perfidious treacherous, traitorous, false, faithless, unfaithful, disloyal, dishonest, deceitful, untrustworthy, two-faced, double-dealing. LOYAL

perforate puncture, pierce, penetrate, punch, bore, drill, prick.

perforce necessarily, by necessity, unavoidably, inevitably.

perform do, carry out, discharge, execute, transact, effect, achieve, accomplish, complete, fulfil, comply with, observe, act, function, work. FAIL
play, act, stage, put on, enact, represent.

performance show, entertainment, production, presentation, appearance, gig (*inf*), play, exhibition.
accomplishment, achievement, completion, execution, discharge, act, deed, exploit, feat, action, operation, conduct, behaviour.

performer entertainer, player, actor, actress, artiste.

perfume scent, fragrance, essence, cologne, aroma, bouquet, balminess, redolence, odour, smell. STENCH

perfunctory cursory, superficial, sketchy, hasty, careless, slipshod, mechanical, routine, indifferent, offhand, negligent, headless, thoughtless. THOROUGH

perhaps maybe, possibly, perchance, peradventure. DEFINITELY

peril danger, jeopardy, risk, hazard, menace, vulnerability, exposure, insecurity, uncertainty. SAFETY

perilous dangerous, unsafe, risky, hazardous, vulnerable, exposed, precarious, insecure. SAFE

perimeter circumference, boundary, border, edge, margin, periphery. CENTRE

period time, age, era, epoch, term, spell, stretch, interval, season, generation, days, years, course, cycle.

periodic intermittent, recurrent, cyclic, regular, occasional, infrequent, sporadic, spasmodic. CONTINUOUS

periodical magazine, review, journal, paper, weekly, monthly.

peripatetic itinerant, wandering, roaming, travelling, mobile, nomadic, migratory.

periphery boundary, circumference, perimeter, ambit, edge, margin, fringe, border, outside, surface. CENTRE

periphrastic circumlocutory, verbose, wordy, prolix, circuitous, roundabout. DIRECT

perish die, expire, decease, pass away, be killed, rot, decay, waste, wither, fade, fail, decline, vanish, disappear. LAST

perishable destructible, frail, fragile, temporary, impermanent, transitory, fleeting. IMPERISHABLE

perk up cheer up, liven up, buck up (*inf*), brighten, take heart, rally, recover, recuperate, revive.

perky jaunty, sprightly, lively, vivacious, bouncy, animated, spirited, sparkling. LETHARGIC

permanent lasting, enduring, abiding, durable, indestructible, imperishable, eternal, everlasting, perpetual, constant, fixed, stable, changeless, unchanging, immutable, invariable. TEMPORARY

permeable pervious, porous, penetrable. IMPERMEABLE

permeate penetrate, infiltrate, pervade, percolate, impregnate, suffuse, imbue, saturate, fill.

permissible allowable, allowed, permitted, lawful, legal, licit, legitimate, right, proper, acceptable, admissible, all right, OK (*inf*). PROHIBITED

permission authorization, sanction, approval, warrant, licence, freedom, liberty, leave, consent, assent, allowance, tolerance, toleration, dispensation, go-ahead. PROHIBITION

permit *v*, allow, let, sanction, authorize, warrant, license, enable, empower, consent, assent, grant, tolerate, countenance. FORBID

n, permission, authorization, licence, warrant, pass, passport.

permutation alteration, transformation, change, shift, transposition, rearrangement.

pernicious deadly, fatal, lethal, mortal, ruinous, destructive, injurious, hurtful, harmful, damaging, deleterious, detrimental, noxious, noisome. BENEFICIAL

perorate discourse, expatiate, harangue, speechify, summarize, sum up, recapitulate, recap (*inf*).

perpendicular upright, vertical, straight, plumb, erect, standing, on end. OBLIQUE

perpetrate commit, do, execute, perform, carry out, effect, bring about.

perpetual continual, incessant, endless, unending, ceaseless, unceasing, constant, continuous, uninterrupted, interminable, never-ending, eternal, everlasting, permanent, perennial, lasting, enduring. TEMPORARY

perpetuate continue, keep up, maintain, sustain, preserve, keep alive, immortalize, eternalize. END

perplex puzzle, baffle, mystify, nonplus, flummox, bewilder, confuse, confound, muddle. ENLIGHTEN

complicate, involve, embroil, entangle, jumble, mix up. SIMPLIFY

perplexity bewilderment, confusion, puzzlement, bafflement, mystification, incomprehension, stupefaction. ENLIGHTENMENT

complication, involvement, entanglement, complexity, intricacy. SIMPLICATION

puzzle, mystery, enigma, quandary, dilemma, difficulty, muddle.

persecute harass, hound, torment, torture, martyr, molest, maltreat, ill-treat, victimize, oppress, plague, pester, badger, bother, worry, vex, annoy.

perseverance persistence, tenacity, dedication, diligence, sedulity, zeal, steadfastness, constancy, determination, resolution, doggedness, stamina, endurance, indefatigability.

persevere persist, continue, carry on, stand firm, hold fast, pursue, maintain. WAVER

persiflage banter, badinage, wit, repartee, frivolity, pleasantry, teasing, raillery.

persist continue, carry on, persevere, stand firm, insist. DESIST
last, endure, abide, remain, survive, continue, carry on. STOP

persistent persevering, tenacious, diligent, assiduous, determined, resolute, dogged, unflagging, indefatigable, stubborn, obstinate, obdurate, unshakable, immovable, fixed. WAVERING
constant, steady, incessant, interminable, continual, perpetual, unrelenting. INTERMITTENT

person individual, body, soul, human, human being, man, woman, child, someone, somebody.

personal private, intimate, secret, confidential, individual, own, particular, exclusive, special. COMMUNAL

personality character, nature, disposition, temperament, individuality, identity.
charisma, magnetism, attraction, charm.
personage, notable, VIP, public figure, celebrity, star, famous person, household name.

personate portray, play, act, represent, impersonate, imitate.

personify embody, incarnate, exemplify, epitomize, represent, symbolize, typify.

perspective viewpoint, outlook, angle, aspect, proportion, objectivity, view, vista, prospect, scene, panorama.

perspicacious perceptive, percipient, astute, shrewd, sharp, keen, acute, penetrating, discerning, sagacious, wise, intelligent, clever. DULL

perspicacity perception, percipience, astuteness, shrewdness, sharpness, keenness, penetration, discernment, insight, acumen, sagacity, wisdom. DULLNESS

perspicuity lucidity, clarity, clearness, plainness, intelligibility, comprehensibility. OBSCURITY

perspicuous lucid, clear, plain, distinct, intelligible, comprehensible, explicit, unambiguous, obvious, apparent. OBSCURE

perspiration sweat, sweating, diaphoresis, exudation, secretion, moisture, wetness.

persuade induce, urge, impel, influence, sway, prevail upon, incline, dispose, move, prompt, entice, coax, advise, counsel, convince, convert. DETER

persuasion inducement, enticement, temptation, cajolery, exhortation, advice. DISSUASION
power, potency, force, cogency, influence.
belief, faith, creed, credo, sect, cult, denomination, school.

persuasive convincing, cogent, telling, effective, forceful, influential, impressive, plausible, sound, valid, compelling, winning. UNCONVINCING

pert impudent, impertinent, insolent, rude, cheeky, saucy, bold, forward. BASHFUL
jaunty, perky, lively, sprightly, smart, dapper.

pertain appertain, relate, refer, regard, concern, belong.

pertinacious tenacious, dogged, persistent, persevering, determined, resolute, steadfast, constant, firm, unshakable, stubborn, obstinate, mulish, pig-headed, inflexible, unyielding, headstrong, wilful. IRRESOLUTE

pertinent relevant, germane, apposite, apropos, apt, appropriate, fit, fitting, suitable, proper, seemly. IRRELEVANT

perturb trouble, disturb, upset, worry, disquiet, alarm, agitate, discompose, ruffle, fluster, unsettle, disconcert, vex, confuse, muddle, disorder, disarrange. COMPOSE

peruse study, scrutinize, examine, inspect, read, browse, scan, survey.

pervade permeate, spread, diffuse, fill, saturate, impregnate, penetrate, percolate, imbue, suffuse.

perverse contrary, contumacious, refractory, wayward, headstrong, wilful, stubborn, obstinate, mulish, obdurate, intransigent, awkward, difficult, troublesome, deviant, abnormal. DOCILE
cantankerous, cross, peevish, petulant, ill-tempered, irascible, crabbed, surly. AFFABLE

perversion aberration, deviation, abnormality, irregularity, corruption, depravity, misuse, prostitution, debasement, vitiation, distortion, misinterpretation, misrepresentation, falsification.

pervert misuse, abuse, corrupt, deprave, subvert, lead astray, debase, vitiate, distort, twist, warp, misinterpret, misrepresent, falsify.

pervious permeable, porous, penetrable, passable, accessible, receptive. IMPERVIOUS

pessimistic cynical, gloomy, glum, depressed, despondent, hopeless, despairing, negative. OPTIMISTIC

pest nuisance, bother, annoyance, vexation, pain (*inf*), curse, bane, scourge, blight, plague, pestilence. BLESSING

pester plague, torment, trouble, worry, bother, disturb, harass, hound, badger, nag, annoy, irritate, vex, irk.

pestilence epidemic, plague, disease, scourge, curse, bane, blight.

pestilent annoying, irritating, vexatious, irksome, troublesome.
pernicious, dangerous, destructive, ruinous, deadly, fatal, deleterious, detrimental, harmful, injurious, noxious, corrupting. BENEFICIAL
pestiferous, pestilential, infectious, contagious, diseased, infected, contaminated, unhealthy, insalubrious, poisonous, venomous. PURE

pet *n*, favourite, darling, apple of one's eye, blue-eyed boy (*inf*).
adj, tame, domestic, house-trained. WILD
favourite, dearest, beloved, cherished, prized, treasured.
v, pamper, cosset, coddle, mollycoddle, indulge, spoil. DISCIPLINE
fondle, stroke, caress, pat, cuddle.

petition *n*, request, appeal, entreaty, plea, supplication, invocation, solicitation, application, suit.
v, ask, request, appeal, beg, beseech, plead, entreat, supplicate, solicit, apply, sue.

petrify calcify, fossilize, harden, solidify, turn to stone.
stupefy, stun, daze, paralyse, dumbfound, stagger, astonish, astound, amaze, appal, horrify, terrify. REASSURE

pettish peevish, petulant, touchy, testy, waspish, cross, irritable, querulous, fractious, fretful. GENIAL

petty trivial, minor, unimportant, insignificant, trifling, paltry, slight, small, little, inconsiderable. IMPORTANT
small-minded, narrow-minded, mean, stingy, niggardly, grudging. GENEROUS

petulant peevish, pettish, cross, grumpy, touchy, testy, irascible, irritable, waspish, snappish, fretful, querulous, impatient, sullen, moody. GENIAL

phantasm phantom, apparition, spectre, ghost, illusion, hallucination, chimera, figment, dream, vision.

phantom *n*, ghost, spectre, apparition, spirit, spook (*inf*), phantasm, chimera, illusion, hallucination, vision.
adj, phantasmal, phantasmagoric, unreal, illusory, spectral, ghostly. REAL

pharisaic pharisaical, sanctimonious, self-righteous, goody-goody, holier-than-thou, hypocritical, insincere.

phase period, stage, aspect, appearance, side, angle, state, condition.

phenomenal marvellous, wonderful, extraordinary, prodigious, remarkable, exceptional, outstanding, fantastic, miraculous. ORDINARY

phenomenon marvel, wonder, prodigy, miracle, sensation, spectacle.
fact, circumstance, occurrence, event, happening, incident.

philander flirt, coquet, dally, trifle, womanize (*inf*).

philanthropic charitable, benevolent, beneficent, munificent, liberal, generous, altruistic, humanitarian, kind, humane, benign, benignant, public-spirited. SELFISH

philistine *n*, boor, lout, barbarian, yahoo, lowbrow, bourgeois, vulgarian. AESTHETE
adj, uncultured, unrefined, uncultivated, uneducated, boorish, loutish, lowbrow, bourgeois. CULTURED

philosopher thinker, theorist, metaphysician, logician, sage.

philosophical wise, learned, erudite, thinking, logical, rational, theoretical, metaphysical.
calm, composed, cool, unruffled, tranquil, serene, stoical, resigned, imperturbable. AGITATED

philosophy logic, reasoning, metaphysics, knowledge, wisdom, thought, thinking.
viewpoint, attitude, ideology, beliefs, values.

calmness, composure, equanimity, self-possession, serenity, stoicism, resignation. AGITATION

phlegmatic sluggish, lethargic, apathetic, indifferent, uninterested, stolid, unemotional, impassive, unfeeling, cold, dull, placid, imperturbable, philosophical. EMOTIONAL

phobia fear, terror, horror, dread, dislike, aversion, hatred, loathing. MANIA

phosphorescent luminous, radiant, fluorescent, bright.

photograph *n*, picture, photo (*inf*), snapshot, shot, snap (*inf*), print, slide, transparency.
v, shoot, film, take, snap (*inf*).

phrase *n*, expression, locution, idiom, saying, utterance, clause.
v, express, put, word, style, couch, frame, say, utter, voice, deliver.

phraseology phrasing, wording, syntax, style, diction, language, parlance, idiom.

physical bodily, corporeal, corporal, carnal, fleshly, earthly, mortal, natural, material, substantial, tangible, concrete, real, visible, external. SPIRITUAL

physician doctor, medical practitioner, GP, specialist, consultant.

physiognomy features, lineaments, face, countenance, visage, look, aspect, appearance.

physique build, frame, figure, body, shape, form, constitution, make-up.

pick *v*, choose, select, single out, decide on, opt for. REJECT
pluck, cull, glean, harvest, gather, collect. LEAVE
open, crack, jemmy, force, rob, steal.
pick out, choose, select, single out.
distinguish, discriminate, tell apart, discern, perceive, make out.
pick up, lift, raise, grasp, gather. DROP
improve, get better, mend, recover, gain, advance.
n, choice, selection, option, preference.
best, cream, flower, prize, elite. REJECT

pickle *v*, marinade, preserve, cure.
n, plight, predicament, quandary, dilemma, fix (*inf*), jam (*inf*).

pictorial graphic, illustrative, vivid, expressive, illustrated.

picture *n*, image, representation, likeness, portrait, sketch, drawing, painting, etching, engraving, photograph, print, illustration.
description, portrayal, depiction, account.
epitome, archetype, embodiment, personification.
v, imagine, visualize, conceive of, envisage.
depict, portray, draw, paint, photograph, illustrate, show, represent, describe.

picturesque scenic, quaint, attractive, beautiful, charming, delightful, colourful, vivid, graphic, pictorial, artistic, aesthetic. UGLY

piece *n*, part, section, division, bit, fragment, portion, share, slice, chunk, length, quantity, scrap, morsel, shred, element, component. WHOLE
example, specimen, case, instance.
composition, creation, production, work.
v, join, unite, connect, fit, assemble, fix, mend, repair, patch. SEPARATE

pied piebald, mottled, dappled, speckled, brindled, spotted, flecked, motley, variegated, multicoloured. PLAIN

pierce penetrate, enter, puncture, perforate, stab, prick, bore, drill.
touch, move, affect, strike, stir, rouse, excite, thrill.

piercing shrill, high-pitched, ear-splitting, loud, sharp, penetrating, probing, searching, keen, biting, bitter, fierce, acute, stabbing, excruciating. DULL

piety piousness, devoutness, godliness, saintliness, holiness, sanctity, devotion, reverence, faith, religion. IMPIETY

pigeonhole *n*, compartment, section, place, slot (*inf*), cubbyhole, niche, category, class.
v, classify, categorize, label, catalogue, sort.
shelve, postpone, defer, put off.

piggish hoggish, swinish, dirty, filthy, boorish, rude, greedy, gluttonous, mean, selfish, obstinate, stubborn, pig-headed.

pigment colour, colouring, tint, dye, paint, stain, colorant.

pile *n*, heap, mound, stack, mass, store, hoard, accumulation, collection.
lot, great deal, load, quantity. FEW
building, edifice, structure.
v, heap, stack, amass, store, hoard, accumulate, collect, gather. SCATTER

pilfer steal, purloin, filch, pinch (*inf*), nick (*inf*), thieve, rob, peculate, embezzle. RETURN

pilgrim crusader, palmer, devotee, wanderer, traveller, wayfarer.

pilgrimage expedition, excursion, tour, journey, trip, voyage, peregrination, crusade, mission.

pill tablet, capsule, pellet, bolus.

pillage *v*, ransack, rifle, rob, plunder, loot, maraud, raid, sack, despoil, ravage.
n, plunder, looting, marauding, depredation, spoliation, devastation, spoils, loot, booty.

pillar column, shaft, post, pier, upright, prop, support, mainstay.

pilot *n*, aviator, airman, aeronaut, flier, helmsman, steersman, navigator, guide, leader, director, conductor.
v, fly, steer, control, drive, navigate, guide, direct, lead, conduct, shepherd, usher.

pimple spot, pustule, boil, eruption.

pin *n*, peg, bolt, nail, tack, clip, brooch.
v, fasten, secure, fix, attach, hold.

pin down, constrain, force, press, confine, restrain, bind, tie, hold, immobilize. RELEASE
pinpoint, locate, identify, specify, determine.

pinch *v*, squeeze, press, crush, compress, grip, grasp, tweak, nip, hurt, constrict, cramp.
steal, filch, pilfer, purloin, nick (*inf*). RETURN
n, squeeze, nip.
bit, dash, trace, *soupçon*.
emergency, exigency, urgency, crisis, stress, pressure, difficulty, predicament.

pine long, yearn, thirst, hunger, hanker, crave, wish, desire. HAVE
languish, droop, flag, wilt, wither, decline, fade, fail, waste. REVIVE

pinguid fat, fatty, greasy, oily, oleaginous. DRY

pinion bind, tie, chain, shackle, fetter, confine, restrain.

pinnacle peak, summit, top, height, crown, apex, apogee, acme, zenith, meridian, climax, culmination. BASE

pioneer *n*, settler, colonist, explorer, trailblazer, leader, innovator.
v, launch, introduce, initiate, originate, inaugurate, institute, found, establish, lead.

pious devout, godly, saintly, holy, religious, reverent, good, righteous, sanctimonious, self-righteous, goody-goody, holier-than-thou. IMPIOUS

pipe *n*, tube, duct, conduit, passage, line.
v, squeak, tweet, chirp, peep, whistle, warble.

piquant pungent, sharp, tart, tangy, spicy, hot, peppery. BLAND
interesting, stimulating, intriguing, titillating, racy, lively, spirited, sparkling, scintillating. DULL

pique *v*, wound, hurt, sting, offend, affront, upset, put out, annoy, irritate, irk, vex. PLEASE
excite, arouse, stimulate, provoke, stir, rouse.
n, offence, umbrage, resentment, indignation, annoyance, irritation, vexation, displeasure. PLEASURE

pirate *n*, corsair, buccaneer, rover, freebooter, robber, plunderer, marauder.
v, plagiarize, copy, crib (*inf*), lift (*inf*), steal, appropriate.

pit *n*, hole, cavity, crater, mine, excavation, ditch, trench, shaft, well, abyss, chasm, hollow, depression, dent, indentation, pockmark, scar.
v, match, oppose, set against.
dent, indent, pockmark, scar, nick, notch.

pitch *v*, hurl, fling, throw, cast, toss, sling, heave. CATCH
erect, raise, set up, establish, fix, settle, locate, place. STRIKE
roll, reel, lurch, wallow, plunge, dive, fall, drop.
n, degree, height, depth, level, point, extent, range.
slope, gradient, incline, angle, tilt, slant, inclination.
tone, timbre, modulation.
throw, toss, plunge, roll.
field, ground, area, station.

pitcher jug, ewer, urn, vessel, container.

piteous pitiable, pitiful, pathetic, plaintive, mournful, sad, sorrowful, doleful, sorry, wretched, lamentable, deplorable, poignant, moving, touching, affecting, distressing, heart-rending.

pitfall trap, snare, catch, hazard, danger, snag, drawback.

pith essence, quintessence, substance, gist, crux, nub, core, heart, kernel, marrow.
importance, significance, consequence, moment, weight, force, power, strength, vigour.

pithy terse, succinct, concise, compact, brief, short, laconic, pointed, cogent, forceful, meaningful, weighty. VERBOSE

pitiable pitiful, pathetic, poor, sorry, wretched, miserable, piteous, lamentable, deplorable, distressing. ENVIABLE

pitiful pathetic, pitiable, sorry, wretched, miserable, piteous, poignant, heart-rending, distressing, poor, lamentable.
deplorable, contemptible, despicable, mean, meagre, worthless. ADMIRABLE

pitiless merciless, unmerciful, unsparing, harsh, hard-hearted, callous, cold, unfeeling, unsympathetic, heartless, unkind, inhuman, cruel, ruthless, relentless, unrelenting, implacable, inexorable. COMPASSIONATE

pittance allowance, ration, modicum, trifle, peanuts (*inf*), chicken feed (*inf*).

pity *n*, compassion, tenderness, mercy, clemency, grace, charity, humanity, kindness, sympathy, commiseration, condolence. CRUELTY
shame, regret, misfortune, bad luck.
take pity on, forgive, pardon, have mercy on, spare, relent, melt.
v, commiserate with, sympathize with, feel for, feel sorry for.

pivot *n*, fulcrum, axis, axle, spindle, pin, hinge, hub, centre, focal point.
v, revolve, rotate, spin, turn, hinge.

placable appeasable, reconcilable, mild, forgiving, merciful, magnanimous. IMPLACABLE

placard notice, advertisement, poster, bill, sign, billboard.

placate pacify, appease, mollify, conciliate, soothe, calm, reconcile, win over. INCENSE

place *n*, spot, location, scene, site, position, situation, point, whereabouts.
area, region, district, locality, town, city, village.
status, rank, standing, station, state, condition.
post, appointment, job, employment.
duty, responsibility, role, function, right, prerogative, affair, concern.
space, room, stead, lieu.
house, flat, home, abode, dwelling, residence, domicile, accommodation, quarters, lodgings.
take place, happen, occur, come about, come to pass, befall, betide, transpire.
v, put, lay, set, deposit, position, locate, situate, install, appoint. REMOVE
arrange, dispose, order, group, classify, sort. DISARRANGE
identify, recognize, know.

placid calm, serene, peaceful, tranquil, quiet, undisturbed, unmoved, unruffled, unperturbed, composed, collected, equable, imperturbable.

plagiarize pirate, borrow, crib (*inf*), lift (*inf*), steal, appropriate, copy, forge.

plague *n*, epidemic, pestilence, disease, contagion.
curse, scourge, affliction, torment, trouble, trial.
pest, nuisance, annoyance, vexation, bother, pain (*inf*), problem, trouble. BLESSING
v, torment, torture, distress, trouble, afflict, harass, badger, hound, pester, annoy, irritate, vex, irk, bother, worry.

plain *adj*, clear, distinct, apparent, visible, patent, obvious, evident, manifest, open, blatant, palpable, unmistakable, intelligible, understandable, comprehensible, lucid. OBSCURE
simple, unadorned, pure, basic, Spartan, austere, unpretentious, ordinary, everyday, homely. FANCY
unattractive, ugly. ATTRACTIVE
frank, candid, open, blunt, direct, straightforward, forthright, plain-spoken, honest, sincere, guileless, artless, ingenuous. DEVIOUS
flat, level, even, smooth, plane. UNEVEN
n, plateau, tableland, lowland, grassland, prairie.

plaintiff accuser, prosecutor, suitor, petitioner. DEFENDANT

plaintive mournful, doleful, sad, melancholy, sorrowful, woeful, piteous, heart-rending. JOYOUS

plait *v*, braid, weave, interweave, interlace, twist, twine, intertwine. UNRAVEL
n, braid, pigtail.

plan *n*, scheme, design, arrangement, programme, project, idea, proposal, proposition, plot, device, method, procedure, system, strategy.
diagram, chart, map, blueprint, drawing, sketch, draft.
v, scheme, plot, devise, design, formulate, work out, arrange, organize, prepåre, outline, draft.

intend, purpose, mean, aim, envisage, contemplate.

plane *adj*, flat, level, even, smooth, regular, uniform, plain. UNEVEN
n, level, stratum, position, status, degree.
aeroplane, aircraft.

plant *n*, flower, herb, vegetable, weed, shrub, bush, tree.
factory, mill, works, machinery, equipment, apparatus.
v, sow, seed. UPROOT
set, place, insert, fix, establish, settle, lodge, root, implant, embed. REMOVE

plaster *n*, mortar, cement, stucco, gypsum.
dressing, bandage.
v, daub, smear, spread, cover, coat.

plastic soft, ductile, mouldable, malleable, pliable, pliant, supple, flexible, yielding, tractable, receptive, impressionable.

plate *n*, dish, platter.
sheet, pane, panel, slab, layer, coating.
illustration, print.
v, coat, cover, face, overlay, laminate, veneer, anodize, gild, silver.

platform stage, dais, podium, rostrum.
plan, programme, policy, principles.

platitude truism, commonplace, cliché, bromide (*inf*).
banality, triteness, insipidity, vapidity, flatness, dullness.

plaudits applause, ovation, acclaim, acclamation, praise, commendation, approval, approbation. DENUNCIATION

plausible reasonable, likely, probable, possible, conceivable, credible, believable. IMPLAUSIBLE
specious, smooth, glib.

play *v*, sport, revel, amuse oneself, have fun, romp, frolic, caper, gambol, clown, fool, toy, trifle, fiddle. WORK
contend, compete, participate, take part, challenge, oppose, take on.
perform, act, portray, represent, impersonate.
execute, discharge, fulfil, do, perform, carry out. NEGLECT
bet, wager, gamble, speculate, risk.
play down, minimize, make light of, underrate, underestimate, belittle, disparage. EMPHASIZE
play on, exploit, capitalize on, take advantage of, abuse, impose on.
play up, emphasize, stress, accentuate, highlight, underline, point up.
misbehave, irritate, bother, trouble, malfunction.
n, drama, piece, show, performance, comedy, tragedy, farce, melodrama.
recreation, amusement, entertainment, diversion, pastime, game, sport, fun, jest. WORK
action, movement, motion, function, operation, latitude, leeway, scope, range, sweep, swing, margin, room.

player competitor, contestant, contender, participant, sportsman, sportswoman.
performer, entertainer, artiste, actor, actress, musician, instrumentalist.

playful sportive, frolicsome, frisky, coltish, high spirited, gay, merry, cheerful, jolly, impish, mischievous, arch, waggish, humorous, joking, jesting. SERIOUS

plea request, entreaty, appeal, petition, suit, prayer, supplication.
excuse, pretext, apology, extenuation, vindication, justification, defence, claim, allegation. ACCUSATION

plead appeal, entreat, beg, beseech, implore, supplicate, petition, ask, request.
argue, reason, declare, assert, allege, maintain, put forward, present.

pleasant agreeable, pleasing, delightful, enjoyable, pleasurable, gratifying, nice, lovely, fine, acceptable, satisfactory, fair, charming, amiable, likable, affable, friendly, courteous. UNPLEASANT

pleasantry banter, badinage, persiflage, witticism, joke, jest.

please gratify, humour, delight, gladden, cheer, content, satisfy, amuse, entertain, charm. OFFEND
like, wish, want, desire, choose, prefer, will, see fit.

pleased glad, happy, contented, satisfied, delighted, thrilled, overjoyed, elated. UPSET

pleasing agreeable, pleasant, delightful, pleasurable, gratifying, nice, lovely, attractive, charming, likable, winning. OBNOXIOUS

pleasure gratification, contentment, satisfaction, enjoyment, delectation, delight, happiness, gladness, joy, comfort, amusement, recreation, fun. PAIN
choice, preference, wish, desire, will.

plebian *adj*, common, vulgar, coarse, unrefined, base, low, mean, ignoble, working-class, proletarian. ARISTOCRATIC
n, commoner, proletarian, peasant, pleb (*inf*). ARISTOCRAT

pledge *n*, promise, vow, oath, agreement, undertaking, assurance, word.
surety, security, collateral, deposit, earnest, gage, pawn, bond, guarantee, warranty.
v, promise, plight, vow, swear, engage, bind, guarantee, vouch.
toast, drink to.

plenary full, complete, entire, whole, thorough, absolute, unqualified, unconditional, unrestricted, unlimited. RESTRICTED

plenipotentiary ambassador, envoy, emissary, legate.

plenitude abundance, plenty, profusion, copiousness, fullness, repletion, completeness. SCANTNESS

plentiful plenteous, abundant, bountiful, copious, ample, profuse, lavish, generous, full, replete, bumper, prolific, fruitful. SCANTY

plenty plenitude, abundance, bounty, profusion, wealth, fund, mine, mass, great deal, lot, enough, sufficiency, excess, superfluity, plethora, glut, copiousness, plentifulness, amplitude, fullness, exuberance, fruitfulness, prosperity, affluence. LACK

pleonastic superfluous, redundant, tautological, repetitious, circumlocutory, periphrastic, verbose, wordy, prolix, diffuse, circuitous, roundabout. CONCISE

plethora superfluity, excess, surplus, surfeit, glut, overabundance, superabundance. SCARCITY

pliant pliable, flexible, bendy, supple, lithe, ductile, malleable, plastic, mouldable. STIFF
adaptable, amenable, yielding, tractable, compliant, docile, impressionable, susceptible, receptive. INTRACTABLE

plight[1] *n*, predicament, quandary, dilemma, fix (*inf*), jam (*inf*), difficulty, trouble, state, condition, position, situation.

plight[2] *v*, pledge, promise, vow, swear, engage, guarantee.

plod trudge, stump, tramp, lumber, drudge, toil, labour, slog, persevere, soldier on.

plot[1] *n*, plan, scheme, conspiracy, intrigue, cabal, machination, strategem.
story, narrative, theme, thread, action, scenario.
v, plan, scheme, conspire, intrigue, cabal, machinate, hatch, brew, concoct, frame, contrive, devise.

plot[2] *n*, patch, allotment, parcel, tract, area.

ploy manoeuvre, tactic, stratagem, gambit, ruse, wile, dodge, game, trick.

pluck *v*, pull out, draw, pick, gather, collect, tug, tweak, jerk, yank, snatch.
strum, thrum, plunk, twang.
n, courage, bravery, valour, mettle, spirit, nerve, grit, guts (*inf*), boldness, daring, heroism, fortitude, determination, resolution. COWARDICE

plucky courageous, brave, valiant, valorous, mettlesome, spirited, game (*inf*), bold, daring, heroic, intrepid, fearless, undaunted. COWARDLY

plug *n*, bung, stopper, cork.
publicity, promotion, mention, advertisement, puff, hype (*inf*).
v, stop, block, clog, choke, obstruct, bung, cork, seal. OPEN
publicize, promote, mention, advertise.

plumb *adv*, vertically, perpendicularly, straight, exactly, precisely. OBLIQUELY
v, sound, fathom, gauge, measure, probe, penetrate, explore, investigate.

plump fat, obese, stout, portly, rotund, fleshy, chubby, podgy, tubby, full, ample. THIN

plunder *v*, rob, steal, loot, pillage, rifle, ransack, sack, despoil, ravage, devastate, raid, maraud.
n, booty, spoils, loot, pillage, rapine, sack.

plunge *v*, dive, plummet, drop, fall, sink, descend, go down, swoop, pitch, jump. SOAR
immerse, submerge, dip, duck. EMERGE
dash, rush, race, tear, hurry, hasten, precipitate. AMBLE
n, dive, jump, drop, fall, dip.

plus *prep*, and, with, added to. MINUS
n, bonus, extra, perk (*inf*), benefit, advantage, gain, surplus.

ply[1] *v*, practise, exercise, carry on, pursue, follow, work at.
manipulate, wield, apply, utilize, use, employ.
provide, supply, shower, bombard, assail, beset, importune, press, urge.

ply[2] *n*, layer, thickness, fold, sheet, strand.

poach trespass, encroach, infringe, steal, appropriate, plunder.

pocket *n*, bag, pouch, receptacle, compartment, cavity, hollow.
adj, small, miniature, abridged, compact, portable.
v, take, appropriate, steal, purloin, filch, pilfer. RETURN

poem verse, rhyme, ode, sonnet, lyric, ballad.

poetic lyric, lyrical, metrical, rhythmical, rhyming. PROSAIC

poetry poems, verse, metre, rhyme. PROSE

poignant moving, touching, distressing, heart-rending, painful, agonizing, pathetic, piteous, plaintive, sad.
piercing, cutting, biting, caustic, sharp, keen, acute, intense, pungent, piquant. DULL

point *n*, dot, mark, speck.
spot, place, site, location, position, stage, phase, period, time, moment, instant, juncture, degree, extent.
tip, end, apex, spike, prong, nib.
cape, headland, foreland, promontory.
verge, brink.
aim, purpose, end, object, objective, goal, intent, intention, reason, motive.
gist, crux, heart, core, essence, substance, question, matter, subject, meaning, import, drift.
detail, item, feature, aspect, attribute, property, part, element.
v, direct, aim, level, train.
show, indicate, point to, point at, designate, specify, point out, denote, signify.
sharpen, whet, taper. BLUNT

pointed sharp, incisive, cutting, biting, trenchant, keen, acute, penetrating, cogent, telling. BLUNT
barbed, peaked, cuspidate, tapering.

pointer guide, indicator, needle, arrow.
tip, hint, advice, warning, recommendation, suggestion.

pointless meaningless, irrelevant, absurd, senseless, aimless, vain, futile, useless, fruitless, unproductive, unavailing, ineffectual, worthless. WORTHWHILE

poise *n*, composure, self-possession, aplomb, assurance, confidence, coolness, sang-froid, calmness, equanimity, dignity, grace.
balance, equilibrium, steadiness, stability. INSTABILITY
v, balance, hover, hang, hold.

poison *n*, venom, toxin, bane, contagion, contamination, corruption, blight, canker, virus.
v, envenom, infect, pollute, contaminate, taint, corrupt, vitiate, subvert. CLEANSE

poisonous venomous, toxic, deadly, fatal, lethal, mortal, virulent, infectious, contagious, pestiferous, pestilent, noxious, pernicious. HARMLESS

poke prod, jab, punch, dig, nudge, elbow, shove, push, thrust, stick, stab.

polar Arctic, Antarctic, frozen, extreme. TROPICAL
pivotal, central, guiding, leading.
opposite, contradictory, diametrically opposed, antagonistic, antipodal, antithetical.

pole shaft, post, rod, stick, staff, mast.

polemic *adj*, polemical, controversial, disputatious, contentious, argumentative.
n, controversy, debate, dispute, argument.

policy plan, programme, strategy, tactic, course, line, approach, system, procedure, action, code, protocol, rules, guidelines.
wisdom, sagacity, prudence, shrewdness. FOLLY

polish *v*, burnish, furbish, buff, wax, smooth, rub, clean, shine, brighten. TARNISH
refine, finish, perfect, improve.
n, shine, lustre, sheen, gloss, smoothness, finish, brilliance, brightness. DULLNESS
wax, varnish.
refinement, cultivation, sophistication, elegance, grace, style. COARSENESS

polished shiny, glossy, lustrous, smooth, glassy, bright, brilliant. DULL
refined, cultivated, sophisticated, elegant, courtly, genteel. COARSE
accomplished, masterly, expert, skilful, perfect, impeccable, excellent, outstanding. INCOMPETENT

polite courteous, civil, respectful, deferential, mannerly, charming, obliging, well-bred, courtly, genteel, refined, cultivated, polished, civilized, urbane, elegant. RUDE

politic artful, ingenious, shrewd, astute, crafty, cunning, wily, sly, subtle. ARTLESS
wise, sagacious, judicious, prudent, discreet, diplomatic, wary, cautious, advisable, expedient. RASH

political civil, civic, public, state, governmental, administrative.

poll vote, voting, ballot, survey, census, count, enumeration.

pollute contaminate, taint, corrupt, deprave, defile, desecrate, vitiate, adulterate, poison, infect, dirty, soil, foul, mar, spoil. PURIFY

poltroon coward, craven, dastard, chicken (*inf*), yellow-belly (*inf*). HERO

pomp show, display, state, ceremony, pageantry, parade, flourish, grandeur, splendour, magnificence, ostentation, pomposity. SIMPLICITY

pompous pretentious, self-important, vainglorious, arrogant, lofty, pontifical, imperious, magisterial, supercilious, affected, ostentatious, showy, bombastic, inflated, turgid, orotund, grandiloquent, magniloquent. HUMBLE

ponder think, consider, deliberate, meditate, ruminate, cogitate, muse, wonder, reflect, study, examine, weigh.

ponderous huge, massive, bulky, hefty, heavy, weighty, cumbersome, unwieldy, awkward, clumsy. LIGHT
dull, tedious, dreary, dry, laboured, stilted, pedestrian, pedantic.

pool[1] *n*, pond, lake, tarn, puddle.

pool[2] *n*, fund, reserve, kitty, bank.
syndicate, combine, consortium, trust, cartel, collective.
v, combine, merge, amalgamate, league. DISTRIBUTE

poor needy, necessitous, penniless, penurious, impecunious, impoverished, poverty-stricken, indigent, destitute, hard-up (*inf*), broke (*inf*), skint (*inf*). RICH
meagre, scanty, deficient, inadequate, insufficient, lacking, short, scant, slight. AMPLE
inferior, second-rate, substandard, shoddy, unsatisfactory, weak, feeble, mediocre, bad, worthless, useless. GOOD
barren, infertile, sterile, unproductive, unfruitful, depleted, impoverished. FERTILE
luckless, unlucky, unfortunate, hapless, wretched, miserable, sorry, pitiable. FORTUNATE

pop *v*, burst, explode, go off, bang, snap, crack.
put, insert, slip, tuck, push, stick.
n, burst, explosion, report, bang, snap, crack.

populace inhabitants, population, people, crowd, mob, rabble, hoi polloi, masses, commonalty, general public.

popular favoured, favourite, liked, well-liked, accepted, approved, admired, in demand, sought-after, famous, renowned, celebrated, acclaimed. UNPOPULAR
common, familiar, public, general, universal, prevailing, prevalent, current. EXCLUSIVE

populate inhabit, people, colonize, settle.

population inhabitants, residents, natives, populace, people, folk, society.

populous crowded, packed, teeming, swarming. DESERTED

pore[1] *v*, study, examine, scrutinize, peruse, brood, dwell, ponder, meditate.

pore[2] *n*, opening, orifice, aperture, hole, outlet, stoma.

porous permeable, pervious, penetrable, absorbent, spongy. IMPERMEABLE

port harbour, haven, anchorage, roadstead.

portable light, compact, handy, convenient, manageable, movable, transportable. PONDEROUS

portend forebode, foretoken, foretell, predict, prognosticate, foreshadow, augur, presage, indicate, betoken, herald, warn, forewarn.

portent omen, sign, indication, token, harbinger, augury, prognostication, prophecy, prediction, presage, premonition, foreboding, warning.
phenomenon, marvel, wonder, prodigy, miracle.

portentous ominous, minatory, threatening, menacing, inauspicious, unpropitious, momentous, weighty, consequential, significant, crucial, pivotal. INSIGNIFICANT
phenomenal, prodigious, miraculous, remarkable, extraordinary, amazing, astounding. ORDINARY

portion *n*, share, lot, allotment, allocation, quota, ration.
part, section, segment, division, fraction, piece, fragment, bit, scrap, morsel. WHOLE
helping, serving.
v, apportion, allot, allocate, share, divide, distribute, deal out.

portly stout, corpulent, rotund, fat, plump, obese, burly, well-built, large, heavy. SLIM

portrait picture, image, likeness, representation, painting, drawing, photograph.

portray depict, picture, represent, draw, paint, delineate, describe, characterize.

pose *v*, model, sit, arrange, dispose, position, stand.
feign, pretend, impersonate, masquerade, act, posture, attitudinize, put on airs, affect, assume.
ask, put, advance, present, assert, state.
n, posture, attitude, position, stance.
pretence, masquerade, act, airs, affectation.

poser riddle, enigma, mystery, puzzle, conundrum, brain-teaser (*inf*).

posh smart, elegant, stylish, fashionable, exclusive, classy (*inf*), rich, luxurious, ritzy (*inf*), upper-class, genteel. VULGAR

position *n*, place, situation, location, bearings, spot, point, locality, site, station, post.
arrangement, disposition, pose, attitude, posture, stance.
condition, state, circumstances, situation, plight, predicament.
job, post, situation, appointment, place, office, role, duty.
status, standing, station, rank, class.
viewpoint, attitude, stand, angle, outlook, view, feeling, opinion, belief.
v, place, pose, arrange, dispose, put, locate.

positive certain, sure, assured, confident, convinced. UNCERTAIN
clear, direct, precise, explicit, express, definite, categorical, unequivocal, indisputable, incontrovertible, unmistakable, conclusive, decisive, emphatic, firm, assertive, dogmatic, affirmative. VAGUE
real, actual, substantial, true, genuine, veritable, absolute. NEGATIVE
constructive, practical, helpful, useful, beneficial, optimistic, hopeful. ADVERSE
utter, complete, perfect, absolute, downright, out-and-out, unqualified.

possess own, have, hold, enjoy, acquire, take, occupy, control, influence, dominate, consume, obsess. LOSE

possession ownership, tenure, occupancy, title, custody, control.

possessions belongings, property, effects, things, wealth, assets, estate.

possible conceivable, imaginable, credible, likely, probable, potential, hopeful, feasible, practicable. IMPOSSIBLE

possibly perhaps, maybe, perchance, peradventure. CERTAINLY

post[1] *n*, pole, shaft, stake, picket, prop, support, upright, pillar, column.
v, affix, put up, announce, made known, publish, advertise.

post[2] *n*, position, situation, job, employment, assignment, appointment, place, station.
v, assign, appoint, station, place, position, locate, situate.

post[3] *n*, mail, correspondence, letters, parcels, collection, delivery.
v, mail, send, dispatch, forward.
enter, record, inform, notify.

poster placard, bill, notice, advertisement, sticker.

posterior rear, back, hind, hinder. FRONT
after, later, following, succeeding, ensuing, subsequent. ANTERIOR

posterity descendants, heirs, progeny, offspring, issue, children, family, future generations. ANCESTRY

postpone delay, defer, shelve, table, suspend, adjourn, procrastinate, put off. ADVANCE

postscript PS, afterthought, appendix, supplement, addition. PREFACE

postulate *v*, assume, suppose, presuppose, take for granted, posit. PROVE
claim, demand, ask, beg, solicit.
n, assumption, supposition, theory, hypothesis, axiom, principle, condition, prerequisite.

posture position, attitude, pose, stance, bearing, carriage, deportment.
disposition, frame of mind, attitude, point of view, feeling, opinion.
condition, state, situation, position.

posy bouquet, nosegay, bunch, spray, corsage.

pot container, receptacle, vessel, pan, casserole, bowl, jar, glass, mug, tankard, jug.

potent powerful, mighty, strong, forceful, influential, cogent, persuasive, convincing, effective, efficacious, effectual, authoritative, commanding. WEAK

potentate ruler, sovereign, monarch, emperor, mogul.

potential *adj*, possible, likely, future, prospective, budding, undeveloped, latent, dormant, hidden. ACTUAL *n*, capacity, capability, ability, potentiality, possibility, promise.

pother commotion, turmoil, tumult, uproar, hullabaloo, pandemonium, confusion, fuss, to-do. QUIET

potion drink, beverage, draught, dose, brew, concoction.

pottery ceramics, earthenware, crockery, china.

pouch bag, sack, purse, satchel, pocket, sac.

pounce swoop, descend, spring, jump, surprise, ambush.

pound strike, beat, batter, pummel, hammer, thump. CARESS
pulverize, comminute, levigate, triturate, powder, crush, bruise, mash.
throb, pulsate, palpitate, beat.

pour flow, stream, run, rush, gush, spout, emit, discharge, issue, emerge.
decant, serve.
rain, teem, pelt. DRIZZLE

pout frown, scowl, glower, grimace, sulk, mope, brood. SMILE

poverty want, need, impoverishment, indigence, destitution, beggary, pauperism, pennilessness, penury, impecuniousness, privation, distress, hardship. WEALTH
scarcity, dearth, paucity, lack, shortage, deficiency, insufficiency. PLENTY

powder *n*, dust, pounce, talc, grains, particles.
v, pulverize, comminute, levigate, triturate, pound, crush, grind.
dust, dredge, sprinkle, scatter, cover, coat.

power ability, capability, capacity, potential, aptitude, faculty, competence. INABILITY
potency, might, strength, force, intensity, energy, vigour. WEAKNESS
command, rule, sovereignty, mastery, control, dominion, domination, sway, authority, influence, ascendancy, supremacy. SUBJECTION
right, perogative, privilege, authority, warrant, licence.

powerful potent, strong, mighty, forceful, intense, energetic, vigorous, robust, sturdy. WEAK
effective, efficacious, telling, cogent, persuasive, convincing, influential, weighty, effectual, authoritative, commanding, supreme. INEFFECTIVE

powerless impotent, ineffectual, ineffective, weak, feeble, helpless, incapable, defenceless, vulnerable. POWERFUL

practicable possible, feasible, attainable, achievable, workable, viable. IMPRACTICABLE

practical actual, applied, pragmatic, useful, utilitarian, practicable, workable, efficient, businesslike, realistic, sensible, down-to-earth, ordinary, everyday. IMPRACTICAL
skilled, proficient, competent, qualified, trained, practised, experienced. INEXPERIENCED

practically virtually, in effect, almost, nearly, well-nigh, basically, fundamentally.

practice custom, habit, wont, use, usage, convention, tradition, way, method, system, procedure.
exercise, drill, training, study, repetition, rehearsal.
application, action, effect, operation, performance. THEORY

practise do, perform, carry out, apply, observe, follow, pursue, work at.
exercise, drill, train, study, repeat, rehearse, go over, run through.

practised expert, proficient, accomplished, skilled, versed, experienced, trained, qualified. INEXPERIENCED

pragmatic practical, practicable, realistic, sensible, down-to-earth, businesslike.
meddlesome, interfering, intrusive, officious, dogmatic, opinionated.

praise *v*, commend, extol, laud, eulogize, panegyrize, applaud, cheer, acclaim, congratulate, compliment, flatter, admire, approve, exalt, glorify, honour, worship. CENSURE
n, commendation, laudation, eulogy, panegyric, encomium, accolade, applause, plaudits, acclaim, acclamation, congratulation, compliment, flattery, admiration, approval, approbation, tribute, homage, glory, honour, worship. CRITICISM

praiseworthy commendable, laudable, meritorious, admirable, estimable, worthy, creditable, fine, excellent. REPREHENSIBLE

prance leap, spring, gambol, frolic, caper, romp, frisk, cavort, swagger, strut.

prank trick, practical joke, caper, lark (*inf*), mischief, antics, escapade.

prattle prate, babble, chatter, jabber, blather, gab (*inf*), witter (*inf*).

pray beg, beseech, entreat, implore, adjure, petition, supplicate, ask, request, crave, plead, invoke, call on, urge, importune.

prayer communion, devotion, litany, invocation, supplication, entreaty, adjuration, petition, appeal, plea, request.

preach evangelize, sermonize, proclaim, declare, promulgate, spread, disseminate, teach, exhort, urge, advocate, orate, lecture, harangue.

preacher evangelist, missionary, clergyman, churchman, minister, parson. LAYMAN

preamble exordium, introduction, preface, prolegomenon, prologue, proem, foreword, prelude. EPILOGUE

precarious uncertain, unsure, doubtful, dubious, shakey, unsteady, unstable, insecure, unsafe, dangerous, perilous, risky, hazardous, hairy (*inf*), dicey (*inf*). SAFE

precaution safeguard, protection, insurance, provision, anticipation, foresight, forethought, prudence, circumspection, caution, care.

precede antecede, go before, lead, head, herald, usher in, introduce, preface, come first, antedate, predate. FOLLOW

precedence antecedence, precession, lead, priority, preference, seniority, superiority, supremacy, pre-eminence. SUBORDINATION

precedent antecedent, instance, example, lead, model, pattern, standard, criterion, authority.

preceding precedent, antecedent, prevenient, anterior, previous, foregoing, earlier, prior, former, aforesaid, above-mentioned. SUBSEQUENT

precept rule, principle, canon, motto, maxim, adage, axiom, guideline, instruction, direction, order, command, injunction, mandate, edict, decree, ordinance, regulation, law.

precincts region, area, environs, purlieus, district, neighbourhood, limits, bounds, ambit, confines.

precious dear, cherished, beloved, prized, treasured, favourite, valued, esteemed.
valuable, expensive, costly, dear, priceless, invaluable, inestimable. WORTHLESS
affected, pretentious, flowery, artificial, overrefined, overnice, twee (*inf*). NATURAL

precipitate *v*, hasten, hurry, accelerate, quicken, speed, advance, further, bring on, trigger, expedite, dispatch. RETARD
throw, hurl, fling, cast, propel, launch.
adj, rapid, swift, headlong, hurried, hasty, rash, reckless, heedless, thoughtless, careless, abrupt, sudden, impetuous, impulsive. CAUTIOUS

precipitous steep, sheer, perpendicular, abrupt. GRADUAL
hasty, rash, reckless, precipitate. CAUTIOUS

precise exact, explicit, distinct, clear, unambiguous, definite, express, specific, accurate, correct, strict, literal, nice, particular, finicky, meticulous, scrupulous, punctilious, rigid, severe, inflexible, formal. VAGUE

precision exactitude, exactness, accuracy, correctness, fidelity, strictness, nicety, meticulousness, scrupulousness. VAGUENESS

preclude debar, exclude, rule out, prohibit, obviate, prevent, hinder, stop, check, inhibit, restrain. ENCOURAGE

precocious forward, advanced, bright, clever, smart, quick, premature, early. BACKWARD

preconception prejudgment, predetermination, preconceived idea, presumption, presupposition, bias, prejudice.

precursor harbinger, herald, usher, messenger, pioneer, forerunner, antecedent, predecessor, ancestor. FOLLOWER

precursory antecedent, precedent, previous, prior, preparatory, preliminary, introductory, prefatory. FINAL

predatory predacious, raptorial, rapacious, voracious, ravenous, greedy, ravaging, plundering, pillaging, marauding.

predecessor forerunner, precursor, antecedent, ancestor, forefather, forebear. SUCCESSOR

predestination predetermination, preordination, foreordination, foreordainment, fate, destiny, lot, doom.

predetermined predestined, preordained, foreordained, fated, destined, doomed.
prearranged, set, fixed, foregone, cut and dried (*inf*). OPEN

predicament plight, quandary, dilemma, fix (*inf*), jam (*inf*), pickle (*inf*), scrape (*inf*), spot (*inf*), hole (*inf*), difficulty, mess, state, situation, extremity, emergency.

predicate assert, aver, asseverate, affirm, maintain, proclaim, declare, state, contend, argue. DENY

predict prophesy, prognosticate, foretell, augur, divine, foresee, forecast, foreshadow, presage, portend, forebode.

prediction prophesy, prognostication, augury, divination, forecast.

predilection inclination, leaning, tendency, bent, predisposition, proclivity, propensity, bias, preference, partiality, liking, fondness, weakness, taste, fancy. AVERSION

predispose bias, prejudice, sway, influence, affect, incline, dispose, prepare, prime.

predisposition inclination, tendency, predilection, proclivity, propensity, bias, preference, proneness, susceptibility, vulnerability, likelihood.

predominant ruling, sovereign, pre-eminent, dominant, ascendant, controlling, prevailing, prevalent, principal, chief, supreme, paramount. MINOR

predominate prevail, preponderate, outweigh, override, dominate, rule.

pre-eminent supreme, transcendent, paramount, outstanding, peerless, matchless, unequalled, unrivalled, unsurpassed, incomparable, superior, distinguished, predominant, prevailing, main, chief. INFERIOR

preen groom, dress, primp, prink, spruce up, titivate.

preface *n*, introduction, foreword, prelude, prologue, proem, preamble, exordium. EPILOGUE

v, introduce, open, begin, prefix, precede. CLOSE

prefatory introductory, opening, preliminary, preparatory, precursory, antecedent, prelusive, prelusory, proemial. FINAL

prefer favour, like better, choose, select, opt for, elect, pick, single out, adopt, fancy, desire. REJECT

advance, promote, elevate, raise. DOWNGRADE

lodge, file, place, put forward. WITHDRAW

preferable better, superior, more desirable, favoured, chosen.

preference choice, selection, pick, option, favourite, desire, fancy, liking, partiality, bias, prejudice, favouritism, advantage, priority, precedence.

preferment advancement, promotion, elevation, rise. DEMOTION

pregnable assailable, open to attack, vulnerable, exposed, defenceless, unprotected. FORTIFIED

pregnant gravid, enceinte, with child, expectant, expecting (*inf*), in the club (*inf*), in the family way (*inf*).

meaningful, significant, loaded, charged, eloquent, expressive, suggestive.

inventive, imaginative, creative, original.

fraught, full, replete, teeming, prolific, fruitful, fertile, fecund. BARREN

prejudice *v*, bias, warp, predispose, sway, influence, dispose, incline, jaundice.

harm, damage, impair, hurt, injure, mar, hinder. AID

n, bias, predisposition, prepossession, prejudgment, preconception, partiality, favouritism, discrimination, bigotry, intolerance, unfairness, injustice. IMPARTIALITY

harm, damage, impairment, hurt, injury, mischief, detriment, disadvantage. BENEFIT

prejudiced biased, warped, predisposed, jaundiced, bigoted, intolerant, partial, one-sided, partisan, unfair, unjust, discriminatory. IMPARTIAL

prejudicial harmful, damaging, hurtful, injurious, mischievous, pernicious, detrimental, deleterious, disadvantageous. BENEFICIAL

prelate cardinal, archbishop, metropolitan, primate, pontiff, pope, bishop.

preliminary *adj*, introductory, opening, initial, preparatory, prefatory, proemial, prelusive, precursory, antecedent, prior. FINAL

n, preparation, groundwork, foundation, introduction, opening, beginning, preface, preamble, prelude.

prelude introduction, overture, preliminary, opening, beginning, start, preamble, exordium, preface, proem, prologue. FINALE

premature early, untimely, unseasonable, hasty, precipitate, advanced, forward, immature, unripe, green, undeveloped, incomplete, embryonic. LATE

premeditate plot, plan, scheme, calculate, intend, prearrange, precontrive, predesign, preplan. IMPROVISE

premise *v*, postulate, posit, predicate, assert, state, preface, introduce. CONCLUDE
n, premiss, postulate, proposition, hypothesis, assumption, presupposition, assertion, argument, basis, ground.

premises property, building, establishment, grounds.

premium bonus, extra, tip, commission, perk (*inf*), prize, reward, bounty, recompense, remuneration, fee, incentive, discount.
value, regard, esteem, appreciation.

premonition foreboding, presentiment, feeling, hunch, intuition, apprehension, misgiving, presage, portent, omen, forewarning.

preoccupied engrossed, absorbed, immersed, lost, rapt, abstracted, oblivious, unaware, distracted, inattentive, absent-minded, pensive. ATTENTIVE

preordain foreordain, predestine, predetermine, fate, doom.

preparation groundwork, foundation, background, experience, provision, measure, plan, arrangement.
readiness, preparedness, precaution, anticipation, expectation.
mixture, compound, concoction, medicine.

preparatory preliminary, introductory, opening, prefatory, basic, elementary, primary, precursory, prior. FINAL

prepare get ready, prime, arrange, order, adjust, adapt, fit, equip, provide, supply, plan, anticipate, practice, warm up, brief, train, make, produce, compose, draw up, concoct, put together, assemble. DESTROY

preponderant predominant, prevailing, prevalent, dominant, ascendant, supreme, paramount, chief, leading, major, greater. INSIGNIFICANT

preponderate predominate, prevail, outweigh, outnumber.

prepossessing attractive, fetching, good-looking, charming, engaging, taking, winning, appealing, pleasing, delightful, likable, fascinating, captivating, alluring, inviting, enchanting. REPULSIVE

prepossession preoccupation, absorption, abstraction, inattention. ATTENTION
bias, prejudice, predisposition, partiality, predilection, liking. INDIFFERENCE

preposterous ridiculous, ludicrous, absurd, foolish, laughable, farcical, crazy, irrational, illogical, unreasonable, senseless, nonsensical, outrageous, excessive, extravagant, incredible, impossible. REASONABLE

prerogative privilege, right, liberty, choice, authority, due, claim, advantage, exemption, immunity.

presage *v*, predict, forecast, prophesy, prognosticate, foretell, augur, portend, forebode, foresee, feel, sense.
n, omen, portent, sign, warning, prediction, forecast, prophecy, prognostication, augury, foreboding, presentiment, premonition, feeling, intuition.

prescience foreknowledge, precognition, clairvoyance, second sight, foresight, prevision.

prescribe direct, bid, enjoin, order, command, rule, ordain, decree, dictate, impose, lay down, urge, recommend. PROHIBIT

prescription direction, instruction, formula, recipe, medicine, drug, remedy.
directive, injunction, order, command, decree, ordinance, edict, mandate, ruling, prescript, rule, law.

presence attendance, company, being, existence, residence, habitation. ABSENCE
nearness, closeness, proximity, vicinity, neighbourhood.
air, appearance, demeanour, carriage, bearing, poise, personality.

present¹ *adj*, existing, existent, current, present-day, immediate.
here, in attendance, to hand, at hand, near, nearby. ABSENT
n, now, today, this day and age. FUTURE

present² *v*, introduce, show, display, exhibit, demonstrate, stage, put on.
give, donate, bestow, award, confer, grant, hand over, offer, proffer, hold out. WITHHOLD
n, gift, benefaction, donation, offering, tip, gratuity, largess.

presentation award, grant, conferral, bestowal, gift, present, donation, offering.
introduction, debut, launch, demonstration, exhibition, display, show, performance, representation, appearance, delivery.

presentiment premonition, foreboding, intuition, hunch, anticipation, apprehension, foreknowledge, prescience.

presently soon, shortly, in a minute, in a while, by and by, later.

preservation protection, defence, conservation, keeping, maintenance, support, prepetuation, continuation, safeguarding, safekeeping, storage. DESTRUCTION

preserve *v*, protect, defend, guard, safeguard, care for, save, conserve, keep, maintain, uphold, perpetuate, continue. DESTROY
store, can, bottle, cure, pickle, dry, freeze.
n, jam, jelly, marmalade, conserve, confection, sweetmeat.
domain, sphere, realm, field, area.

preside officiate, chair, lead, direct, control, manage, supervise, head, govern.

president chief, head, leader, director, executive, principal, chairman.

press *v*, push, squeeze, compress, crush, pinch, force, drive, cram, stuff, crowd, throng, mill.
iron, smooth, flatten, calender, mangle. CRUMPLE
hug, embrace, clasp.
urge, beg, plead, petition, importune, harass, worry, plague, torment, besiege, demand, constrain, compel.
hurry, hasten, rush, move, advance.
n, journalism, fourth estate, newspapers, journalists, reporters, photographers.
crowd, throng, multitude, mob, crush.
hurry, bustle, urgency, pressure, stress.

pressing urgent, exigent, crucial, vital, imperative, demanding, importunate, important, serious. TRIVIAL

pressure force, weight, compression, crushing, squeezing.
constraint, compulsion, coercion, obligation, insistence, urgency, power, influence.
stress, strain, tension, burden, load, harassment, oppression. RELAXATION

prestige authority, influence, eminence, distinction, stature, status, reputation, fame, renown, celebrity.

presume assume, take for granted, suppose, surmise, guess, conjecture, believe, think, conclude, infer, take it. KNOW
venture, dare, make so bold.

presumption assumption, supposition, surmise, guess, conjecture, belief, opinion, hypothesis, inference. KNOWLEDGE
boldness, audacity, temerity, effrontery, impertinence, cheek (*inf*), nerve (*inf*), gall (*inf*), forwardness, assurance, arrogance. MODESTY

presumptive probable, likely, believable, credible, plausible, reasonable, assumed, supposed, believed, inferred.

presumptuous bold, audacious, impertinent, impudent, disrespectful, fresh (*inf*), forward, brazen, pushy (*inf*), arrogant, overconfident, cocksure, assured. MODEST

presuppose assume, take for granted, suppose, presume, postulate, posit, imply.

pretence simulation, fabrication, make-believe, invention, semblance, appearance, guise, masquerade, mask, cloak, veneer, façade, show, affectation, pretension, sham, deception, deceit, falsehood, pretext, excuse. TRUTH

pretend imagine, make believe, fabricate, invent, simulate, sham, counterfeit, fake, feign, dissemble, affect, put on, assume, claim, allege, purport, profess.

pretentious ostentatious, showy, flamboyant, theatrical, affected, mannered, vain, conceited, arrogant, puffed-up, pompous, bombastic, inflated, high-flown. UNPRETENTIOUS

preternatural unnatural, anomalous, abnormal, irregular, unusual, exceptional, extraordinary, strange, weird, mysterious, inexplicable, unearthly, supernatural. NORMAL

pretext excuse, reason, claim, allegation, pretence, guise, semblance, appearance, show, cloak, mask, cover.

pretty attractive, good-looking, beautiful, fair, comely, appealing, cute, pleasing, charming, lovely, nice, dainty, delicate, neat, trim. UGLY

prevail predominate, preponderate, reign, rule, hold sway, persist, obtain.
succeed, win, triumph, be victorious, overcome. LOSE

prevail upon, persuade, induce, influence, sway, convince, win over.

prevailing prevalent, widespread, universal, general, common, usual, accepted, established, current, popular, fashionable. RARE
predominant, preponderant, dominant, ruling, chief, main, principal, superior, powerful. SUBORDINATE

prevaricate equivocate, tergiversate, evade, dodge, hedge, shift, shuffle, quibble, cavil, lie, deceive.

prevent stop, check, preclude, hinder, impede, obstruct, hamper, deter, restrain, inhibit, thwart, frustrate, foil, forestall, anticipate, avert, avoid, ward off. AID

prevention stoppage, check, preclusion, hindrance, impediment, obstruction, obstacle, deterrence, determent, inhibition, avoidance. ASSISTANCE

preventive preventative, prophylactic, deterrent, protective, counteractive.

previous prior, preceding, antecedent, anterior, earlier, former, erstwhile, foregoing. LATER

prey *n*, quarry, game, victim, target.
v, hunt, seize, devour, feed on.
victimize, intimidate, bully, terrorize, exploit, take advantage of.
oppress, weigh, burden, trouble, worry.

price *n*, cost, expense, fee, rate, charge, value, worth, amount, figure, expenditure, outlay, valuation, assessment, estimate, quotation, bounty, reward.
penalty, loss, sacrifice, consequence, cost.
v, value, assess, appraise, evaluate.

priceless invaluable, inestimable, beyond price, precious, treasured, dear, expensive, unique, irreplaceable. CHEAP

prick *v*, pierce, puncture, perforate, punch, stab, lance, cut, wound, pain, hurt, move, touch, affect.
prick up, raise, erect, rise, stand up.
n, puncture, perforation, hole, pinhole, cut, wound, pain, pang, twinge.

prickle *v*, sting, smart, tingle, itch, prick.
n, point, barb, thorn, needle, spine.

pride vanity, conceit, egotism, self-love, boastfulness, self-praise, smugness, complacency, arrogance, hauteur, loftiness, self-importance, presumption, pretension. MODESTY
dignity, self-respect, self-esteem, *amour-propre*. SHAME
treasure, jewel, prize, boast, cream, pick.
pleasure, delight, satisfaction, gratification.

priest ecclesiastic, divine, churchman, clergyman, cleric, minister, vicar, parson, rector, pastor. LAYMAN

priggish prim, strait-laced, prudish, puritanical, smug, self-righteous, sanctimonious, goody-goody (*inf*), stuffy, starchy (*inf*).

prim formal, proper, demure, stiff, staid, starchy (*inf*), strait-laced, priggish, prudish, puritanical, fussy, fastidious, precise. EASY-GOING

primary first, initial, primal, earliest, original, primeval, primordial, primitive, aboriginal. LAST
prime, principal, chief, main, leading. MINOR
basic, fundamental, elementary, rudimentary, introductory, preparatory. SECONDARY

prime *adj*, first, primary, original, fundamental, basic, principal, chief, main.
first-rate, excellent, superior, choice, select, supreme, best, top. INFERIOR
n, zenith, peak, height, flower, bloom, heyday, maturity. DECLINE
v, prepare, make ready, break in, train, brief, inform, notify, tell.

primeval primordial, original, aboriginal, primitive, primal, primary, first, pristine, early, ancient, prehistoric. MODERN

primitive primeval, primordial, pristine, early, first, primary, original, ancient, archaic. MODERN
crude, rough, rudimentary, simple, uncivilized, savage, unsophisticated, naive. SOPHISTICATED

primordial primeval, original, primitive, primal, primary, first, earliest, pristine. MODERN
basic, fundamental, radical, elementary.

prince monarch, sovereign, ruler, potentate, lord. SUBJECT

princely generous, liberal, bounteous, munificent, magnanimous, gracious, lavish, rich, ample, bountiful. MEAN
noble, royal, regal, majestic, stately, august, imposing, grand, lofty, dignified. LOWLY

principal *adj*, chief, main, leading, first, foremost, primary, prime, paramount, cardinal, major, key, essential. MINOR
n, head, chief, leader, ruler, master, boss (*inf*), director, headmaster, headmistress. SUBORDINATE
capital, assets.

principle rule, law, standard, criterion, formula, precept, dictum, tenet, axiom, maxim, truth, doctrine, belief, credo, code. PRACTICE
morals, ethics, conscience, scruples, probity, integrity, virtue, goodness, honesty, uprightness, rectitude. UNSCRUPULOUSNESS

print *v*, reproduce, copy, stamp, impress, imprint, engrave, publish, issue.
n, impression, imprint, mark, indentation.
type, lettering, typescript, newsprint, publication.
reproduction, copy, duplicate, picture, photograph, engraving.

prior preceding, antecedent, earlier, anterior, previous, former, foregoing. SUBSEQUENT

priority precedence, antecedence, preference, prerogative, superiority, supremacy, seniority, rank.

prison jail, lockup, nick (*inf*), jug (*inf*), clink (*inf*), cooler (*inf*), inside (*inf*), confinement, captivity.

pristine original, earliest, first, primary, primal, primeval, primordial. LATER
pure, immaculate, spotless, unspoiled, untouched, new, virgin, undefiled, uncorrupted. DEFILED

privacy seclusion, retirement, retreat, solitude, isolation, secrecy, concealment. PUBLICITY

private secret, confidential, hush-hush (*inf*), unofficial, off the record, concealed, hidden, clandestine. PUBLIC
personal, intimate, individual, own, particular, special, exclusive. COMMUNAL
secluded, retired, solitary, isolated, independent.
in private, privately, secretly, confidentially, in camera, behind closed doors. PUBLICLY

privation want, need, lack, loss, hardship, distress, poverty, penury, indigence, destitution, beggary, pauperism. WEALTH

privilege right, prerogative, due, entitlement, benefit, advantage, liberty, freedom, immunity, exemption, concession, favour, indulgence.

privy *adj*, informed, aware, cognizant, in on.
private, personal, secret, confidential. PUBLIC
n, lavatory, toilet, latrine, bog (*inf*).

prize[1] *n*, reward, recompense, premium, award, trophy, honour, accolade, jackpot, windfall, winnings, spoils, loot, booty. PENALTY

prize[2] *v*, value, esteem, appreciate, treasure, cherish, hold dear. UNDERRATE

probable likely, odds-on, presumable, apparent, ostensible, credible, believable, plausible, reasonable. UNLIKELY

probably likely, doubtless, in all probability, possibly, maybe, perhaps.

probation test, trial, apprenticeship, novitiate.

probe *v*, search, investigate, look into, scrutinize, examine, sift, explore, sound, question, inquire.
n, investigation, inquiry, scrutiny, examination, study, search, exploration.

probity integrity, uprightness, rectitude, honesty, truthfulness, honour, worth, virtue, goodness, morality, principle, justice, equity. DISHONESTY

problem difficulty, trouble, predicament, quandary, dilemma, complication.
question, poser, riddle, enigma, puzzle, conundrum. SOLUTION

problematic dubious, doubtful, questionable, debatable, moot, uncertain, unsettled, puzzling, enigmatic. CERTAIN

procedure process, method, system, course, plan of action, policy, approach, custom, practice, rule, formula, routine, rigmarole, operation, performance.

proceed advance, progress, go ahead, move on, go on, continue, carry on. RETREAT
arise, originate, spring, stem, emanate, issue, flow, derive, come, result, ensue.

proceeding act, deed, action, process, step, measure, undertaking, move.

proceedings affairs, matters, concerns, dealings, transactions, doings, goings-on (*inf*), minutes, record.

proceeds profit, gain, receipts, returns, income, earnings, yield, result. EXPENSES

process *n*, procedure, method, system, course, routine, practice, operation, performance.
step, move, action, stage, advance, progression, development.
v, handle, deal with, treat, prepare.

procession parade, march, train, cavalcade, file, column, string, series, sequence, succession, course, cycle.

proclaim declare, announce, promulgate, advertise, publish, broadcast, herald, blazon, cry, trumpet. SUPPRESS

proclamation declaration, announcement, notice, statement, manifesto, pronouncement, edict, decree.

proclivity bent, leaning, inclination, tendency, propensity, proneness, disposition, penchant, predilection, liking, fondness, partiality, bias. AVERSION

procrastinate defer, put off, postpone, adjourn, delay, stall, temporize, prolong, retard. EXPEDITE

procreate beget, engender, propagate, breed, sire, generate, produce.

procure obtain, get, acquire, secure, gain, come by, pick up, buy, win, effect, contrive, manage. LOSE

prod poke, jab, dig, nudge, push, shove, goad, spur.

prodigal extravagant, wasteful, spendthrift, thriftless, improvident, reckless, generous, lavish. ECONOMICAL

prodigious huge, immense, massive, enormous, colossal, gigantic, vast, tremendous, stupendous. SMALL
wonderful, marvellous, phenomenal, extraordinary, amazing, astounding, astonishing, staggering, striking, remarkable. ORDINARY

prodigy genius, wonder child, wunderkind, whiz kid (*inf*). DUNCE
marvel, wonder, phenomenon, miracle.
freak, monster, mutation, curiosity.

produce *v*, make, create, invent, formulate, compose, construct, fabricate, manufacture, generate, engender, occasion, cause, bring about. DESTROY
bear, bring forth, beget, yield, give, render, afford, furnish, supply, provide. WITHHOLD
show, exhibit, present, bring out, stage, direct.
n, product, yield, crop, harvest, fruit, vegetables.

product yield, fruit, result, consequence, effect, outcome, issue. CAUSE
commodity, merchandise, goods, produce, work, creation.

production making, creation, fabrication, manufacture, construction, assembly, preparation. DESTRUCTION
output, work, presentation, show, direction.

productive fertile, rich, fruitful, profitable, worthwhile, valuable, constructive, creative, inventive. UNPRODUCTIVE

profane *adj*, blasphemous, sacrilegious, irreverent, irreligious, impious, ungodly, godless, wicked, heathen, pagan. REVERENT
secular, lay, unconsecrated, unhallowed, unholy, unsanctified, worldly, temporal. SACRED
v, desecrate, violate, abuse, defile, corrupt, pollute, vitiate. HALLOW

profanity blasphemy, sacrilege, irreverence, irreligion, impiety, ungodliness, curse, malediction, imprecation, obscenity. REVERENCE

profess claim, allege, pretend, feign, assert, aver, proclaim, declare, affirm, avow, acknowledge, own, confess, admit. REPUDIATE

profession calling, vocation, career, métier, occupation, business, line, sphere, office, position.
declaration, assertion, affirmation, avowal, acknowledgment, confession. REPUDIATION

professional *adj*, skilled, proficient, expert, masterly, experienced, trained, qualified, paid. AMATEUR
n, expert, master, pro (*inf*), dab hand (*inf*), specialist, authority.

proffer offer, tender, extend, hold out, present, propose, suggest, volunteer. WITHHOLD

proficient skilled, skilful, expert, masterly, adept, polished, practised, experienced, capable, able, competent, trained, qualified, accomplished, talented, good. INCOMPETENT

profile side view, outline, silhouette, shape, form, contour, sketch, study, analysis.

profit *n*, gain, return, yield, proceeds, earnings, income, revenue, surplus. LOSS
advantage, benefit, good, avail, use, value, advancement, improvement.
v, gain, benefit, help, aid, serve, avail, improve, advance, exploit, take advantage of, use. LOSE

profitable lucrative, paying, remunerative, gainful, cost-effective, productive, fruitful, rewarding, worthwhile, valuable, useful, beneficial, advantageous. UNPROFITABLE

profitless unprofitable, worthless, unproductive, fruitless, unavailing, vain, useless, futile, bootless. PROFITABLE

profligate *adj*, dissolute, dissipated, debauched, abandoned, loose, wanton, im-

moral, degenerate, depraved, corrupt, unprincipled, shameless. VIRTUOUS
extravagant, prodigal, wasteful, spendthrift, thriftless, improvident. THRIFTY
n, rake, roué, libertine, debauchee, degenerate, reprobate, wastrel, spendthrift.

profound deep, bottomless, fathomless, abysmal, cavernous. SHALLOW
sagacious, wise, learned, erudite, intellectual, knowledgeable, thoughtful, philosophical, penetrating, abstruse, recondite, esoteric. SUPERFICIAL
intense, keen, acute, extreme, complete, utter, absolute, thorough. MILD

profuse copious, ample, plentiful, abundant, exuberant, bountiful, generous, liberal, lavish, extravagant, prodigal. SCANTY

profusion plenty, plenitude, abundance, bounty, exuberance, excess, surplus, surfeit, glut, plethora, lavishness, extravagance, prodigality. LACK

progeny descendants, issue, posterity, offspring, young, children, family. ANCESTRY

prognostic *adj*, predictive, prophetic, diagnostic.
n, sign, symptom, indication, warning, omen, portent, token, presage, foreboding, prediction, forecast, prophecy, prognostication, augury.

prognosticate foretell, prophesy, predict, forecast, presage, augur, betoken, portend, foreshadow.

programme list, schedule, agenda, syllabus, curriculum, plan, scheme.
show, production, performance, broadcast.

progress *n*, advance, advancement, movement, progression, growth, development, improvement, amelioration, furtherance, promotion, headway, breakthrough. RETROGRESSION
v, advance, proceed, continue, go forward, move on, make headway, gain ground, travel, grow, develop, improve, ameliorate. RETROGRESS

prohibit forbid, disallow, ban, interdict, proscribe, veto, debar, stop, prevent, rule out, hinder, impede, obstruct. PERMIT

prohibitive restrictive, preventive, repressive, proscriptive, prohibitory, forbidding. PERMISSIVE
exorbitant, extortionate, excessive, steep (*inf*).

project *n*, proposal, plan, scheme, design, purpose, idea, undertaking, venture, task, assignment, activity, work. ACHIEVEMENT
v, propose, intend, plan, scheme, devise, contrive, design, calculate, estimate, extrapolate, predict.
cast, throw, hurl, fling, propel, shoot, eject, launch, discharge. RETAIN
jut, protrude, stick out, overhang, beetle, bulge, extend.

projection protrusion, protuberance, bulge, overhang, prominence, extension, ledge.
scheme, plan, programme, proposal, estimate, prediction, blueprint, diagram, representation.

proletariat working class, commonalty, masses, rabble, hoi polloi, common people. ARISTOCRACY

proliferate increase, expand, spread, reproduce, breed, multiply, escalate, burgeon, mushroom, snowball.

prolific productive, fertile, fruitful, copious, profuse, abundant, teeming, rich. UNPRODUCTIVE

prolix verbose, wordy, long-winded, rambling, discursive, lengthy, protracted, long-drawn-out, tedious, boring, prosaic. TERSE

prologue introduction, preface, foreword, preamble, exordium, prolegomenon, proem, prelude. EPILOGUE

prolong extend, lengthen, protract, draw out, spin out, stretch, elongate, continue, sustain, keep up. CURTAIL

prominent conspicuous, noticeable, marked, pronounced, striking, unmistakable, obvious, evident. INCONSPICUOUS
eminent, distinguished, notable, noted, famous, celebrated, well-known, important, leading. MINOR
projecting, jutting, protruding, protuberant.

promiscuous loose, wanton, abandoned, licentious, libertine, profligate, dissolute, immoral, debauched. VIRTUOUS
indiscriminate, unselective, careless, heedless, casual, indifferent, diverse, miscellaneous, mixed, mingled, disorderly, confused. SELECTIVE

promise *v*, pledge, vow, swear, give one's word, engage, contract, covenant, assure, guarantee.

augur, betoken, suggest, indicate, look like, give hope of.
n, pledge, vow, oath, word, assurance, guarantee, engagement, contract, covenant, bond, agreement.
potential, capacity, ability, capability.

promising hopeful, likely, encouraging, reassuring, optimistic, bright, rosy, favourable, auspicious. HOPELESS

promontory headland, foreland, cape, point.

promote further, advance, forward, help, assist, aid, support, back, boost, encourage, foster, cultivate. HINDER
upgrade, raise, elevate, prefer, exalt, aggrandize, move up, kick upstairs (*inf*). DEMOTE
advertise, publicize, push, plug (*inf*), hype (*inf*), advocate, champion, endorse, sponsor.

promotion advancement, preferment, rise, elevation, aggrandizement, exaltation. DEMOTION
support, backing, encouragement, furtherance, publicity, advertising. HINDRANCE

prompt *adj*, immediate, instant, direct, quick, swift, rapid, fast, punctual, timely, ready, eager, alert, sharp, brisk, smart. SLOW
v, urge, encourage, induce, impel, move, goad, spur, incite, stimulate, motivate, inspire. DETER
remind, cue, assist, help, hint, suggest.

promulgate proclaim, declare, announce, decree, advertise, broadcast, disseminate, publish, circulate, cry, trumpet, blazon, divulge, make known. SUPPRESS

prone apt, inclined, disposed, liable, given, subject, likely, susceptible. UNLIKELY
prostrate, procumbent, face down, recumbent, supine, flat, horizontal. UPRIGHT

pronounce utter, articulate, enunciate, voice, say.
proclaim, declare, announce, decree, affirm, assert. SUPPRESS

pronounced marked, distinct, definite, clear, plain, noticeable, conspicuous, striking, unmistakable. VAGUE

proof *n*, evidence, confirmation, substantiation, corroboration, testimony, demonstration. CONJECTURE
trial, test, assay, examination, inspection.
print, impression, galley.
adj, resistant, repellant, impervious, impenetrable, strong.

prop *v*, support, hold up, shore up, brace, bolster, uphold, sustain, maintain.
lean, rest, stand, place.
n, support, brace, buttress, bolster, stay, pillar, upright, shore, mainstay.

propaganda publicity, promotion, advertising, advertisement, information, indoctrination, brainwashing.

propagate reproduce, breed, procreate, beget, generate, engender, produce, increase, multiply, proliferate. DESTROY
disseminate, spread, diffuse, promulgate, circulate, publish, advertise, broadcast, publicize, promote. SUPPRESS

propel drive, impel, urge, push, thrust, force, move, launch, project, shoot, throw. STOP

propensity tendency, disposition, inclination, proneness, proclivity, bent, leaning, aptness, liability, susceptibility, penchant, predisposition.

proper correct, right, accurate, exact, precise, accepted, usual, customary, conventional, just, real, actual. WRONG
appropriate, apt, suitable, fit, fitting, seemly, becoming, decorous, decent, polite, respectable, genteel, refined. IMPROPER
personal, own, individual, characteristic, peculiar, special. COMMON

property possessions, effects, belongings, goods, chattels, assets, capital, wealth, fortune, estate, land, building.
attribute, quality, mark, characteristic, feature, trait, peculiarity, idiosyncrasy.

prophecy prediction, forecast, prognostication, augury, divination, clairvoyance, second sight.

prophesy predict, foresee, foretell, divine, prognosticate, forecast, augur, presage.

prophet soothsayer, diviner, clairvoyant, seer, fortune-teller, augur, oracle, forecaster.

prophetic predictive, prognostic, oracular, augural, divinatory, sibylline, mantic, portentous, ominous.

propinquity nearness, closeness, proximity, vicinity, neighbourhood, contiguity, adjacency. DISTANCE
affinity, kinship, kindred, consanguinity, relationship.

propitiate pacify, placate, appease, conciliate, reconcile. OFFEND

propitious auspicious, favourable, advantageous, promising, encouraging, timely, opportune, lucky, fortunate, happy. UNFAVOURABLE

well-disposed, benign, benevolent, gracious, kind, friendly. HOSTILE

proportion *n*, ratio, relationship, distribution, balance, symmetry, uniformity, harmony, agreement, correspondence, congruity, conformity. DISPROPORTION

share, portion, division, lot, quota, ration, part, fraction, percentage. WHOLE

dimension, measurement, size, magnitude, extent, capacity.

v, adjust, arrange, regulate, balance, harmonize, fit.

proportional proportionate, balanced, symmetrical, corresponding, consistent, commensurate, equivalent. DISPROPORTIONATE

proposal proposition, suggestion, recommendation, offer, proffer, tender, bid, overture, plan, scheme, project, idea.

propose suggest, recommend, move, advance, put forward, submit, present, offer, proffer, tender, nominate, name. WITHDRAW

plan, intend, purpose, design, mean, have in mind.

propound suggest, propose, put forward, advance, submit, advocate, postulate, state, declare.

proprietor owner, possessor, holder, landowner, freeholder, master, mistress, landlord, landlady.

propriety correctness, seemliness, fitness, appropriateness, decorum, decency, etiquette, protocol, good manners, politeness, breeding, refinement, modesty, delicacy. IMPROPRIETY

prorogue adjourn, postpone, defer, suspend, discontinue. RECONVENE

prosaic prosy, dry, unimaginative, flat, tame, commonplace, ordinary, bland, uninteresting, uninspiring, vapid, dull, tedious, boring, monotonous, pedestrian, trite, hackneyed, banal, humdrum. IMAGINATIVE

proscribe condemn, denounce, censure, interdict, prohibit, forbid, ban, outlaw, exile, banish, expel, deport, excommunicate, exclude, reject, blackball, ostracize.

prosecute sue, take to court, summon, prefer charges, arraign, indict, accuse, try. DEFEND

practise, carry on, conduct, perform, pursue, follow, continue, persist. ABANDON

proselyte convert, catechumen, neophyte, novice, disciple.

prospect *n*, chance, possibility, likelihood, probability.

outlook, future, expectation, hope, anticipation, contemplation, calculation, plan.

view, vista, scene, landscape, panorama, spectacle, vision, outlook, perspective.

v, explore, survey, search, seek.

prospective future, coming, approaching, expected, anticipated, planned, intended, imminent, impending, likely, probable, possible, potential, eventual.

prospectus syllabus, outline, programme, plan, scheme, announcement, notice, catalogue, brochure.

prosper thrive, flourish, succeed, make good, advance, progress. FAIL

prosperous thriving, flourishing, successful, booming, lucky, fortunate, favourable, auspicious, promising, rich, wealthy, affluent, well-off. UNSUCCESSFUL

prostitute *n*, whore, harlot, fallen woman, strumpet, trollop, courtesan, call girl, streetwalker, tart (*inf*), hooker (*inf*).

v, devalue, cheapen, debase, degrade, demean, abuse, misuse, misapply.

prostrate *v*, bow, kneel, kowtow, grovel, submit.

overcome, overthrow, overpower, overwhelm, disarm, paralyse, crush, flatten, exhaust, weary, tire, fatigue. RESTORE

adj, flat, horizontal, prone, procumbent, recumbent, supine, grovelling, abject. ERECT

overcome, overwhelmed, disarmed, paralysed, helpless, defenceless, impotent. POWERFUL

exhausted, jaded, weary, tired, disconsolate, heartbroken.

prosy prosaic, unimaginative, uninspiring, pedestrian, commonplace, dull, tedious, boring, wearisome, tiresome, long-winded, wordy, prolix. LIVELY

protagonist hero, heroine, principal, lead, central character.

supporter, advocate, champion, defender, leader, prime mover.

protean variable, changeable, mutable, inconstant, mercurial, volatile, polymorphous, many-sided, versatile. CONSTANT

protect defend, guard, safeguard, secure, screen, cover, shield, shelter, harbour, save, preserve, keep, look after, care for, mind, foster. EXPOSE

protection defence, guard, safeguard, precaution, security, safety, shield, cover, shelter, refuge, preservation, safekeeping, care, custody, aegis, patronage, support, aid. EXPOSURE

protective defensive, protecting, guarding, shielding, covering, preventive, watchful, vigilant, possessive, jealous.

protest *v*, object, complain, oppose, take exception, demur, expostulate, remonstrate, demonstrate, disapprove. AGREE
maintain, contend, argue, assert, avow, aver, asseverate, attest, affirm, declare. DENY
n, objection, complaint, opposition, demurral, protestation, expostulation, remonstrance, outcry, demonstration. AGREEMENT

protocol etiquette, customs, conventions, formalities, manners, decorum.

prototype original, model, pattern, precedent, example, type, archetype, standard, norm, exemplar, ideal. COPY

protract prolong, draw out, spin out, extend, lengthen, elongate, stretch, continue, sustain. CURTAIL

protrude project, stick out, jut, extend, bulge, thrust out.

protuberance bulge, swelling, lump, bump, knob, excrescence, protrusion, projection. CAVITY

proud satisfied, content, pleased, glad, self-satisfied, smug, complacent, vain, conceited, egotistic, self-important, boastful, big-headed (*inf*), arrogant, haughty, imperious, lordly, overbearing, presumptuous, supercilious, stuck-up (*inf*). MODEST
self-respecting, dignified, high-minded, honourable, noble, majestic, stately, grand, magnificent, splendid, glorious, great, exalted, eminent, distinguished, illustrious. HUMBLE

prove demonstrate, show, manifest, evidence, evince, verify, confirm, corroborate, substantiate, uphold, sustain, establish. REFUTE
test, try, assay, examine, analyse, check.

proverb saying, maxim, aphorism, adage, apophthegm, saw, dictum, byword.

proverbial acknowledged, accepted, famous, well-known, notorious, legendary, traditional, axiomatic, self-evident.

provide supply, furnish, equip, stock, contribute, give, afford, yield, produce, present.
prepare, get ready, take precautions, anticipate, allow, plan, cater, arrange.
stipulate, specify, lay down, state, determine.

provide for, maintain, support, sustain, keep, look after, take care of. NEGLECT

provided providing, given, on condition that, subject to, if.

providence fate, destiny, fortune, divine intervention.
prudence, discretion, foresight, care, caution, economy, thrift.

provident judicious, far-sighted, prudent, sagacious, careful, cautious, wary, vigilant, economical, thrifty. RECKLESS

province territory, district, region, division, zone, realm, domain, colony, dependency, county, department. CAPITAL
field, discipline, line, sphere, orbit, role, function, duty, responsibility, business.

provision preparation, precaution, measure, step, arrangement, plan.
providing, supply, furnishing, equipment, catering.
proviso, condition, stipulation, specification, clause, term, reservation, qualification.

provisional temporary, interim, makeshift, conditional, contingent, provisory. ABSOLUTE

provisions food, sustenance, provender, victuals, comestibles, eatables, groceries, rations, stores, supplies.

provocation incitement, encouragement, instigation, agitation, motive, cause, insult, affront, offence, annoyance, irritation. APPEASEMENT

provocative provoking, inciting, stimulating, offensive, insulting, annoying, irritating, vexatious, exasperating. PACIFIC
alluring, tempting, inviting, tantalizing, seductive, sexy (*inf*). REPULSIVE

provoke anger, enrage, infuriate, incense, madden, exasperate, vex, irk, rile, annoy, irritate, insult, offend. APPEASE incite, encourage, foment, agitate, goad, spur, stimulate, stir, rouse, move, inspire, motivate, instigate, cause, occasion, bring about, elicit, evoke, prompt, promote, produce. DETER

prowess skill, ability, expertise, mastery, genius, talent, dexterity, adroitness, proficiency. INCOMPETENCE
strength, might, bravery, valour, courage, fearlessness. COWARDICE

prowl roam, rove, wander, range, steal, sneak, slink, skulk, lurk, scavenge, forage, hunt, stalk.

proximity nearness, closeness, propinquity, vicinity, neighbourhood, contiguity, adjacency. DISTANCE

proxy substitute, agent, representative, delegate, deputy, surrogate.

prudent judicious, sagacious, discreet, circumspect, sensible, wise, shrewd, careful, cautious, wary, vigilant, canny, politic, thoughtful, considerate, practical, provident, economical, thrifty, frugal. RASH

prudish prim, demure, modest, strait-laced, starchy (*inf*), proper, priggish, stuffy, puritanical, strict, narrow-minded, squeamish. BROAD-MINDED

prune trim, clip, snip, lop, dock, cut, shorten, reduce.

prurient lustful, lecherous, lewd, salacious, libidinous, concupiscent, erotic, obscene, pornographic, dirty. CHASTE

pry meddle, interfere, question, inquire, nose, snoop (*inf*), spy, peep, peer.

prying meddlesome, interfering, inquisitive, curious, nosy, snoopy (*inf*).

pseudonym alias, assumed name, pen name, nom de plume, stage name.

psychic clairvoyant, telepathic, extrasensory, supernatural, mystic, occult, spiritual, psychological, mental. NATURAL

psychological mental, cerebral, intellectual. PHYSICAL
emotional, irrational, subjective, imaginary.

public *adj*, open, unrestricted, communal, common, general, national, universal, civic, civil, popular. PRIVATE
known, acknowledged, published, overt, plain, exposed, unconcealed, obvious, patent. SECRET
n, population, people, community, society, populace, commonalty, hoi polloi, masses.
clientele, customers, followers, supporters, fans, admirers, audience.

publication publishing, issuance, appearance, announcement, proclamation, advertisement, broadcast, promulgation, dissemination, revelation, disclosure. SUPPRESSION
edition, issue, book, magazine, periodical, newspaper, pamphlet, booklet, leaflet, brochure.

publicity promotion, advertising, advertisement, puff, plug (*inf*), hype (*inf*), attention, spotlight. OBSCURITY

publish issue, bring out, distribute, circulate, disseminate, promulgate, announce, proclaim, advertise, publicize, trumpet, blazon, disclose, reveal, divulge, expose, tell, impart. SUPPRESS

pucker wrinkle, crinkle, crease, corrugate, furrow, purse, knit, tighten, contract, gather, ruck. SMOOTH

puerile childish, infantile, immature, silly, foolish, irresponsible, petty, trivial, frivolous. ADULT

puff *n*, gust, blast, whiff, breath, flurry.
praise, commendation, advertisement, publicity, plug (*inf*).
v, blow, pant, gasp, breathe, exhale.
smoke, draw, pull, drag (*inf*), inhale.
swell, inflate, bloat, distend, puff up. DEFLATE
praise, flatter, advertise, promote, push, plug (*inf*), hype (*inf*). DISPARAGE

pugnacious belligerent, bellicose, combative, aggressive, quarrelsome, argumentative, contentious, disputatious. PEACEABLE

pull *v*, draw, drag, haul, tow, trail, tug, yank. PUSH
pluck, pick, extract, remove, detach, rip, tear, wrench, sprain, stretch.
attract, draw, pull in, entice, lure. REPEL
pull off, succeed, accomplish, achieve. FAIL
pull out, leave, depart, quit, withdraw, retreat. ARRIVE
pull through, recover, get over, survive, weather.
n, drag, tow, tug, yank, jerk. PUSH
effort, exertion, force, power, magnetism, attraction, lure, appeal, influence, weight.

pulpy fleshy, succulent, soft, squashy, mushy. HARD

pulsate beat, throb, pulse, pound, palpitate, vibrate, quiver.

pulse *n*, beat, throb, rhythm, pulsation, vibration.
v, beat, throb, pulsate.

pulverize powder, pound, crush, grind, comminute, triturate, levigate.
destroy, annihilate, demolish, wreck, smash.

pummel batter, beat, thump, pound, hammer, punch, belabour, thrash.

pump drive, force, push, draw.
interrogate, question, quiz, cross-examine, grill (*inf*).

pump up, inflate, blow up. DEFLATE

pun play on words, double entendre, witticism, quip.

punch[1] *v*, strike, hit, box, thump, pummel, beat, bash (*inf*), clout (*inf*).
n, blow, hit, knock, thump, bash (*inf*) clout (*inf*).

punch[2] *v*, pierce, puncture, perforate, bore, drill.

punctilious strict, exact, precise, correct, proper, formal, meticulous, scrupulous, conscientious, careful, particular, fussy, nice, minute. LAX

punctual prompt, on time, timely, seasonable, punctilious, exact, precise, regular. LATE

puncture *v*, pierce, prick, perforate, punch, bore, deflate.
n, hole, perforation, opening, leak, flat tyre.

pungent acrid, bitter, biting, sour, tart, acid, burning, stinging, hot, piquant, strong, harsh, sharp, keen, pointed, cutting, incisive, caustic, trenchant, mordant, piercing, penetrating. MILD

punish discipline, correct, chastise, chasten, reprove, scold, castigate, spank, beat, flog, scourge, penalize, sentence. REWARD

punitive penal, disciplinary, corrective, retaliatory, revengeful, punishing, harsh.

puny weak, feeble, frail, delicate, stunted, undersized, dwarfish, pygmy, small, tiny, trivial, petty, paltry, insignificant. STURDY

pupil student, scholar, schoolboy, schoolgirl, learner, beginner, novice, neophyte, tyro, apprentice, trainee, disciple, follower. MASTER

puppet marionette, dummy, doll.
pawn, cat's-paw, tool, instrument, figurehead.

purchase *v*, buy, procure, acquire, obtain, get, pay for, invest in. SELL
n, acquisition, buy, investment, possession.
grasp, grip, hold, foothold, leverage, advantage.

pure unmixed, unadulterated, neat, undiluted, real, genuine, natural, simple, perfect, flawless. IMPURE
clear, clean, unpolluted, uncontaminated, spotless, immaculate, sterilized, disinfected. POLLUTED
chaste, virginal, undefiled, uncorrupted, unsullied, impeccable, virtuous, innocent, honest, upright. CORRUPT
sheer, downright, utter, mere, thorough, absolute. PARTIAL

purely only, solely, exclusively, merely, simply, completely, totally, entirely, wholly, utterly, absolutely.

purgative laxative, cathartic, aperient, evacuant.

purge *v*, cleanse, purify, deterge, clean out, wash, clear, absolve, rid, free, expel, eject, oust, remove, eradicate, eliminate.
n, enema, purgative, laxative, cathartic, aperient, evacuant.
purgation, purification, ejection, expulsion, removal, eradication, elimination.

purify cleanse, purge, clean, wash, disinfect, sanitize, clarify, refine, distil, filter. BEFOUL

puritanical puritan, prim, strait-laced, strict, austere, ascetic, severe, rigid, stiff, prudish, narrow-minded. IMMORAL

purity pureness, clearness, clarity, cleanness, spotlessness, flawlessness, perfection, simplicity. IMPURITY
chastity, virginity, virtue, innocence, honesty, integrity, honour, piety. CORRUPTION

purlieus outskirts, periphery, borders, limits, suburbs, precincts, environs, vicinity, neighbourhood.

purloin steal, pilfer, filch, thieve, rob, nick (*inf*), embezzle, appropriate. RESTORE

purport *v*, claim, profess, pretend, allege, maintain, assert, declare.
mean, signify, denote, betoken, imply, suggest.
n, meaning, significance, signification, import, implication, drift, gist.
purpose, intention, object, aim, design, plan.

purpose *n*, reason, point, idea, design, function, use.
aim, intention, intent, object, objective, end, goal, aspiration, hope, plan, design.
resolution, resolve, determination, will, drive, persistence, tenacity. INDECISION
avail, effect, good, use, advantage, benefit, gain, profit.
on purpose, purposely, deliberately, intentionally, wilfully, wittingly, knowingly, by design. ACCIDENTALLY
v, mean, intend, plan, design, propose, aim, aspire, resolve, determine.
purposeful determined, decided, resolved, resolute, firm, set, fixed, persistent, dogged, tenacious. INDECISIVE
pursue follow, chase, go after, hunt, trail, track, hound, dog, harass, harry, attend, accompany.
practise, engage in, conduct, prosecute, ply, work at, perform, see through, persist in, continue, carry on, proceed, maintain, hold to. ABANDON
seek, desire, aspire to, aim for, strive for.
pursuit chase, hunt, search, quest.
occupation, business, profession, vocation, hobby, pastime, activity, recreation.
purvey sell, provide, supply, furnish, cater, provision, retail.
purview scope, field, range, compass, sphere, orbit, province, limit, extent, reach.
push *v*, shove, thrust, drive, propel, move, force, press, squeeze, ram, crowd, jostle, elbow. PULL
urge, encourage, egg on, impel, spur, prompt, persuade, coerce, expedite, advocate, promote, advertise, publicize. DETER
n, shove, thrust, propulsion, nudge, prod.
effort, endeavour, attack, charge, drive, force, ambition, enterprise, energy, vigour, spirit, gumption (*inf*).
pushy pushing, ambitious, enterprising, go-ahead, dynamic, forceful, assertive, self-assertive, presumptuous, bumptious, aggressive, officious, intrusive. MEEK
pusillanimous timid, timorous, fearful, cowardly, faint-hearted, lily-livered, spineless, weak, feeble. BRAVE
pustule abscess, ulcer, fester, gathering, blister, pimple, boil.
put place, set, lay, deposit, situate, locate, position, stand, plant, fix. REMOVE
impose, inflict, levy, exact, enjoin, subject, condemn, commit.
say, express, utter, word, phrase, state, declare, advance, put forward, propose, present, offer, tender. WITHDRAW
assign, attribute, attach, impute, put down.
put across, communicate, convey, make clear, explain, spell out.
put away, replace, put back, tidy up.
save, keep, put aside, put by, store, lay in, lay up. USE
consume, devour, eat, drink, swallow, bolt, wolf, gobble.
lock up, confine, commit. RELEASE
put down, enter, inscribe, log, record, jot down.
suppress, repress, quash, quell, crush.
kill, destroy, put to sleep.
disparage, belittle, criticize, knock (*inf*), humiliate, mortify, shame. PRAISE
put off, postpone, defer, delay, shelve, adjourn. ADVANCE
repel, disgust, disconcert, unsettle, discourage. ENCOURAGE
put on, don, change into, wear, dress, clothe.
feign, fake, simulate, pretend, assume, affect.
present, produce, mount, stage, perform, do.
put out, extinguish, douse, quench, snuff out, blow out. LIGHT
annoy, irritate, vex, irk, confuse, disturb, bother, inconvenience, upset, trouble.
put up, erect, built, construct, raise. DEMOLISH
accommodate, house, lodge, board.
put up with, tolerate, suffer, bear, endure, stand, abide, take, swallow, stomach, brook.
putative accepted, recognized, imputed, alleged, reputed, supposed, assumed, presumed. PROVEN
putrefy rot, decompose, decay, go bad, spoil, corrupt, taint. PRESERVE
putrid rotten, decomposed, decayed, bad, off, rancid, fetid, rank, mephitic, foul, offensive, corrupt, tainted. FRESH
puzzle *v*, perplex, baffle, mystify, confuse, confound, nonplus, bewilder, stump. ENLIGHTEN
ponder, study, reflect, meditate, brood, muse, wonder, think.
puzzle out, solve, resolve, work out, figure out, decipher, crack, unravel, clear up.

n, riddle, conundrum, enigma, mystery, poser, question, problem, dilemma. SOLUTION
perplexity, bafflement, confusion, bewilderment. ENLIGHTENMENT

pygmy *n*, dwarf, midget, manikin, homunculus. GIANT
adj, miniature, diminutive, dwarfish, midget, undersized, stunted, small, little, tiny, Lilliputian. GIGANTIC

Q

quack mountebank, impostor, fraud, charlatan, fake, pretender, humbug.

quaff drink, imbibe, gulp, swallow, swig (*inf*).

quagmire swamp, bog, marsh, fen, morass, slough.

quail shrink, recoil, blench, flinch, cower, falter, tremble, shake, quake.

quaint picturesque, old-world, old-fashioned, antiquated. MODERN
strange, unusual, uncommon, extraordinary, curious, odd, peculiar, bizarre, eccentric, singular, unique, fantastic, fanciful, whimsical. ORDINARY

quake tremble, shake, quiver, vibrate, shudder, shiver, quail, waver, falter, wobble, totter, rock, throb, pulsate.

qualification suitability, fitness, eligibility, competence, proficiency, experience, skill, ability, capability, capacity, aptitude, attribute, quality, accomplishment, achievement, attainment. DISQUALIFICATION
restriction, limitation, modification, condition, proviso, stipulation, requirement, criterion.

qualify fit, equip, endow, prepare, train, capacitate, empower, permit, certify, license. DISQUALIFY
restrict, limit, regulate, restrain, moderate, mitigate, temper, reduce, diminish, lessen, abate, soften, assuage, modify, alter, change, adapt.

quality characteristic, property, attribute, feature, trait, peculiarity, idiosyncrasy, condition, character, nature, kind, sort.
grade, rank, status, value, worth, distinction, excellence, superiority.

qualm scruple, compunction, remorse, contrition, regret, doubt, hesitation, misgiving, uneasiness, apprehension, trepidation, anxiety. EASE
pang, twinge, spasm, attack, nausea, sickness, queasiness.

quandary dilemma, predicament, difficulty, trouble, plight, puzzle, perplexity, doubt, uncertainty.

quantity amount, number, extent, measure, size, magnitude, volume, capacity, weight, mass, sum, total, lot, portion.

quarrel *v*, argue, disagree, dispute, squabble, altercate, wrangle, bicker, differ, contend, clash, row, fight, brawl. AGREE
n, argument, disagreement, dispute, tiff, squabble, altercation, wrangle, dissension, difference of opinion, contention, clash, row, fight, brawl, feud, vendetta. AGREEMENT

quarrelsome argumentative, contentious, disputatious, pugnacious, combative, belligerent, quick-tempered, choleric, irritable, irascible, peevish, petulant, touchy, testy, cross. GENIAL

quarry[1] *n*, pit, mine, excavation.
v, mine, extract.

quarry[2] *n*, game, prey, victim, object.

quarter *n*, fourth, three months.
district, region, neighbourhood, locality, place, part, area, zone, province, territory, point, direction.
mercy, clemency, forgiveness, compassion, pity, leniency.
v, accommodate, house, put up, lodge, board, billet, station, post.

quarters lodgings, digs (*inf*), accommodation, housing, residence, domicile, abode, dwelling, habitation, billet, station, post.

quash suppress, subdue, squash, crush, put down, quell, repress, overthrow.
annul, nullify, invalidate, cancel, repeal, revoke, rescind, abolish, overrule.

quaver tremble, shake, quake, quiver, vibrate, flicker, flutter, waver, twitter, trill, warble.

quay wharf, landing stage, dock.

queasy bilious, nauseous, sick, ill, squeamish, uncomfortable, uneasy.

queer odd, curious, strange, unusual, uncommon, weird, bizarre, extraordinary, peculiar, singular, irregular, abnormal, funny. ORDINARY
dubious, questionable, suspicious, shady (*inf*), fishy (*inf*).

dizzy, giddy, faint, queasy.
homosexual, lesbian, gay (*inf*), bent (*inf*).

quell suppress, subdue, put down, quash, crush, squelch, squash, stamp out, extinguish, conquer, overcome.
allay, assuage, mitigate, alleviate, moderate, soothe, mollify, dull, deaden, blunt, calm, pacify, quiet. AGGRAVATE

quench slake, satisfy, sate, satiate, allay, appease.
extinguish, douse, put out, snuff out. LIGHT
quell, quash, suppress, subdue, crush, put down.

querulous peevish, petulant, whining, grumbling, complaining, discontented, fretful, irritable, fractious, captious, cross, irascible, testy, touchy. CONTENTED

query *n*, question, enquiry, problem, issue, doubt, scepticism, reservation, objection. ANSWER
v, question, dispute, challenge, doubt, disbelieve, mistrust, distrust, suspect, ask, enquire. ACCEPT

quest search, pursuit, expedition, journey, crusade, mission, goal, objective, aim, target.

question *n*, query, enquiry, interrogation, examination, investigation. REPLY
problem, difficulty, doubt, uncertainty, issue, subject, point, matter.
v, interrogate, examine, quiz, catechize, grill (*inf*), pump (*inf*), ask, enquire. ANSWER
query, challenge, dispute, doubt, disbelieve, mistrust, distrust, suspect. ACCEPT

questionable debatable, dubious, doubtful, uncertain, moot, problematical, controversial, disputable, controvertible, equivocal, suspicious.

queue line, file, train, string, chain, series, succession.

quibble *v*, equivocate, prevaricate, palter, hedge, shift, shuffle, evade, cavil, carp, split hairs.
n, equivocation, prevarication, evasion, criticism, objection, protest.

quick fast, swift, rapid, speedy, fleet, express, expeditious, prompt, ready, sudden, hasty, hurried, cursory, perfunctory, brisk, brief, fleeting. SLOW
nimble, agile, spry, sprightly, alert, active, lively, vivacious, animated, spirited. SLUGGISH
sharp, keen, acute, quick-witted, shrewd, astute, smart, clever, intelligent, adroit, deft, dexterous, skilful. DULL
touchy, testy, quick-tempered, irascible, irritable, impatient, excitable, temperamental, waspish, peppery, petulant, choleric. AFFABLE

quicken accelerate, speed up, expedite, precipitate, hasten, hurry. RETARD
stimulate, rouse, kindle, inspire, whet, excite, animate, revive, vivify, resuscitate, refresh, energize, enliven, vitalize, invigorate. DEADEN

quickly fast, swiftly, rapidly, speedily, hastily, posthaste, apace, promptly, immediately, instantly, forthwith, soon. SLOWLY

quiescent still, motionless, inactive, dormant, quiet, calm, tranquil, serene, placid, unruffled, peaceful, restful. ACTIVE

quiet *adj*, silent, noiseless, inaudible, hushed, low, soft. LOUD
calm, quiescent, serene, tranquil, placid, unruffled, peaceful, restful, untroubled, undisturbed, smooth, still, motionless, mild, gentle, docile, subdued, sober.
private, secret, isolated, secluded, unfrequented. PUBLIC
n, quietness, silence, hush, peace, quiescence, calm, calmness, tranquillity, serenity, rest, repose, ease. DISTURBANCE

quieten quiet, silence, hush, mute, still, calm, lull, tranquillize, soothe, pacify, appease, allay, assuage, mitigate, soften, mollify, dull, blunt, quell, subdue. DISTURB

quilt bedspread, counterpane, eiderdown, duvet.

quintessence quiddity, essence, extract, pith, marrow, heart, core, kernel, spirit, embodiment, personification.

quip joke, jest, gag (*inf*), gibe, wisecrack (*inf*), witticism, bon mot, sally, riposte, retort, repartee, pleasantry, badinage.

quirk mannerism, habit, idiosyncrasy, characteristic, trait, peculiarity, oddity, eccentricity, whim, caprice, vagary, foible.

quit stop, desist, discontinue, cease, abandon, give up, resign, abdicate, relinquish, surrender, renounce.
leave, depart, go, decamp, retire, withdraw. ENTER

quite completely, totally, entirely, wholly, fully, altogether, utterly, absolutely, positively, perfectly, thoroughly. PARTLY

fairly, moderately, pretty (*inf*), rather, somewhat. VERY
really, truly, indeed.

quiver tremble, shake, quake, quaver, vibrate, shiver, shudder.

quixotic impractical, impracticable, unrealistic, idealistic, utopian, fanciful, visionary, romantic, fantastic, imaginary, wild, mad. PRACTICAL

quiz *n*, test, examination, investigation, interrogation, questioning.
v, interrogate, question, examine, catechize, grill (*inf*), pump (*inf*).

quondam former, one-time, past, previous, late, earlier. PRESENT

quota share, portion, allotment, allocation, allowance, ration, part, proportion.

quotation extract, excerpt, passage, line, reference, citation, quote (*inf*).
estimate, tender, cost, price, rate, charge.

quote cite, adduce, instance, repeat, recite, extract, excerpt, refer to, mention.

R

rabble mob, crowd, horde, herd, masses, commonalty, populace, proletariat, hoi polloi, riffraff, *canaille*. ARISTOCRACY

rabid mad, wild, raging, raving, frantic, frenetic, frenzied, berserk, furious, violent, maniacal, fanatical, extreme, fervent, zealous. RATIONAL

race [1] *n*, contest, competition, chase, pursuit, dash, sprint, marathon, steeplechase.
flow, rush, stream, course, channel.
v, run, dash, sprint, tear, fly, career, speed, hurry, rush. AMBLE
compete, contend.

race [2] *n*, people, nation, tribe, clan, breed, family, line, descent, extraction, blood, stock, ancestry, lineage, house.

racial ethnic, ethnological, tribal, national.

rack *n*, frame, framework, stand, holder.
torture, torment, pain, agony, anguish, suffering, affliction.
v, torture, torment, excruciate, agonize, pain, afflict, distress, plague, harass. SOOTHE

racket din, noise, uproar, clamour, hubbub, hullabaloo, commotion, pandemonium, tumult, turmoil, disturbance, row. QUIET
scheme, confidence trick, fraud, swindle, business, line.

racy lively, spirited, animated, buoyant, interesting, entertaining, exciting, stimulating, piquant, pungent, sharp, spicy, distinctive, strong. DULL
risqué, suggestive, bawdy, ribald, blue, smutty, immodest, indecent.

radiant bright, shining, brilliant, resplendent, beaming, dazzling, effulgent, sparkling, glittering, gleaming, shiny, lustrous, glowing, luminous, lambent, glorious, splendid. DARK
happy, joyful, delighted, elated, ecstatic, overjoyed, beaming, glowing, sparkling. MISERABLE

radiate emit, emanate, diffuse, shed, disseminate, scatter, spread, diverge, branch out.
shine, beam, glow, glitter, sparkle.

radical *adj*, basic, fundamental, constitutional, essential, inherent, intrinsic, natural, organic, ingrained, deep-seated. SUPERFICIAL
complete, total, thorough, sweeping, drastic, severe, extreme, excessive, fanatical, revolutionary.
n, extremist, fanatic, militant, revolutionary, rebel. MODERATE

radio wireless, transistor, receiver, transmitter.

raffle lottery, draw, sweepstake.

rage *n*, anger, fury, wrath, ire, passion, mania, madness, frenzy, violence, vehemence. CALMNESS
craze, fad, fashion, mode, vogue, style.
v, rant, rave, seethe, fume, storm, rampage.

ragged tattered, torn, frayed, worn, threadbare, shabby, unkempt. SMART
rough, uneven, jagged, rugged, notched, serrated. SMOOTH

raging angry, furious, incensed, infuriated, enraged, fuming, ranting, raving, rabid, mad, wild, violent. CALM

raid *n*, attack, assault, incursion, invasion, irruption, inroad, foray, sally, seizure, pillage.
v, attack, assault, invade, descend on, plunder, pillage, sack, rifle.

rail [1] *n*, bar, balustrade, fence, barrier, railing.

rail [2] *v*, complain, criticize, denounce, fulminate, inveigh, attack, censure, upbraid, vituperate, revile, abuse.

railing fence, barrier, paling, palisade, rail, balustrade.

raillery banter, badinage, pleasantry, persiflage, joking, jesting, teasing, satire, ridicule, mockery.

rain *n*, precipitation, rainfall, drizzle, shower, downpour, cloudburst.
v, drizzle, spit, fall, shower, pour, teem.

raise lift, elevate, uplift, hoist, heave, jack up, erect, put up, build, construct. LOWER
increase, augment, heighten, intensify, amplify, magnify, strengthen, boost, escalate. DECREASE
promote, prefer, upgrade, advance, exalt, aggrandize. DEMOTE
arouse, awaken, stir, rouse, excite, provoke, stimulate, activate, cause, occasion, produce.
rear, bring up, breed, cultivate, grow, develop.
broach, introduce, present, put forward.
collect, gather, assemble, muster, levy, obtain, get.

rake[1] *v*, scrape, scratch, collect, gather, remove, comb, scour, hunt, search.

rake[2] *n*, debauchee, libertine, roué, profligate, playboy, womanizer (*inf*).

rally *v*, muster, assemble, unite, gather, collect, reassemble, regroup, mobilize, round up, meet, convene. DISPERSE
recover, recuperate, perk up, revive, improve, get better, mend, pull through. DETERIORATE
n, gathering, meeting, assembly, convention.
recovery, recuperation, renewal, revival, improvement, comeback (*inf*).

ram force, drive, cram, stuff, pack, crowd, hammer, pound, hit, strike, collide, crash, bump, butt.

ramble *v*, walk, hike, stroll, amble, saunter, wander, roam, rove, range, meander, stray.
digress, expatiate, maunder, babble, chatter, witter (*inf*), rabbit (*inf*).
n, walk, hike, stroll, amble, trip, excursion.

ramification branching, forking, divergence, divarication, branch, offshoot, development, consequence, result, sequel, complication.

ramp slope, incline, gradient, acclivity, declivity.

rampage *v*, rage, storm, go berserk, run riot, rush, tear.
n, rage, fury, frenzy, violence.
on the rampage, violent, destructive, amok, berserk, out of control, wild.

rampant unrestrained, uncontrolled, unchecked, unbridled, wild, raging, violent, riotous, uncontrollable, ungovernable, excessive, wanton, rife, rank, profuse, exuberant, luxuriant. CONTROLLED
erect, upright, standing, rearing. COUCHANT

rampart bulwark, fortification, defence, guard, security, embankment, earthwork, breastwork, parapet, barricade, fence, wall.

ramshackle tumbledown, dilapidated, derelict, rickety, shaky, decrepit. STURDY

rancid sour, off, stale, musty, rank, fetid, foul, offensive, bad, rotten, putrid. FRESH

rancour malice, spite, venom, ill will, malignity, malevolence, animosity, antipathy, enmity, hostility, hatred, hate, resentment, grudge, spleen, bitterness. BENEVOLENCE

random haphazard, casual, hit or miss, arbitrary, chance, fortuitous, unsystematic, unplanned, indiscriminate, irregular, aimless, stray, accidental, incidental. DELIBERATE

range *n*, scope, reach, extent, sweep, compass, limit, distance, span, gamut, area, field.
line, row, rank, tier, file, string, chain, series.
sort, kind, variety, assortment, class, order.
v, align, line up, order, dispose, array, arrange, classify, categorize, group, bracket.
extend, stretch, reach, run, vary, fluctuate.
roam, rove, wander, stray, stroll, ramble, traverse, travel.

rank[1] *n*, position, standing, station, status, class, grade, echelon, level, stratum, order, degree, division, group, dignity, nobility.
line, row, range, tier, file, column, string, series.
v, align, line up, arrange, range, class, group, classify, sort, grade, position.

rank[2] *adj*, exuberant, luxuriant, lush, dense, profuse, abundant, prolific, rampant. SCANTY
foul, offensive, fetid, malodorous, stinking, smelly, rancid, putrid, rotten, stale, disgusting, revolting. FRESH
complete, utter, sheer, absolute, downright, thorough, unmitigated, blatant, glaring.

rankle fester, annoy, irritate, chafe, vex, irk, rile, gall.

ransack search, scour, comb, rake, rummage, rifle, sack, loot, strip, raid, plunder, pillage, rob.

ransom *n*, release, deliverance, rescue, redemption.
price, payment.
v, redeem, rescue, deliver, release, free, liberate.

rant *v*, declaim, hold forth, shout, bluster, rave, vociferate.
n, bombast, rhetoric, bluster, vociferation, declamation, tirade, diatribe.

rap *v*, tap, knock, hit, strike, crack.
n, tap, knock, blow, hit, stroke.
blame, responsibility, punishment, sentence.

rapacious greedy, grasping, avaricious, ravenous, voracious, insatiable, predatory, predacious, marauding, plundering.

rape *v*, ravish, violate, deflower, defile, molest, abuse, assault, seduce.
plunder, pillage, despoil, spoliate, loot, sack.
n, ravishment, violation, molestation, assault.
plunder, pillage, rapine, spoliation.

rapid fast, quick, swift, speedy, fleet, express, expeditious, hurried, hasty, precipitate, brisk, prompt. SLOW

rapidity rapidness, speed, velocity, celerity, quickness, swiftness, fleetness, haste, hurry, rush, dispatch, expedition, briskness, promptness, alacrity. SLOWNESS

rapine plunder, pillage, spoliation, depredation, rape, robbery, theft, looting, marauding, raid, seizure.

rapport sympathy, empathy, understanding, harmony, affinity, bond, link, tie, relationship.

rapt absorbed, engrossed, preoccupied, lost, enthralled, entranced, fascinated, spellbound, transported, enchanted, delighted, charmed, thrilled, rapturous, ecstatic. BORED

rapture ecstasy, bliss, transport, ravishment, euphoria, elation, joy, happiness, delight, delectation, felicity, beatitude. SORROW

rapturous ecstatic, blissful, transported, ravished, euphoric, elated, thrilled, enthusiastic, delighted, overjoyed, joyful, happy. SAD

rare uncommon, unusual, unfamiliar, singular, exceptional, infrequent, scarce, sparse, scant, few. COMMON
excellent, fine, choice, superior, outstanding, incomparable, peerless, priceless, invaluable, precious. INFERIOR

rarely seldom, infrequently, hardly ever, once in a blue moon. OFTEN

rascal scoundrel, rogue, rapscallion, scamp, knave, blackguard, villain, reprobate, miscreant, wretch, imp, devil.

rash[1] *adj*, hasty, precipitate, reckless, thoughtless, heedless, careless, incautious, indiscreet, unwary, impetuous, impulsive, foolhardy, madcap, headlong, audacious. CAUTIOUS

rash[2] *n*, eruption, outbreak, epidemic, spate, flood, series, succession.

rasp *v*, scrape, scratch, rub, abrade, grate, grind, file, sand.
n, scraping, scratching, grating, grinding.
file, grater.

rate[1] *n*, speed, velocity, pace, tempo.
charge, price, cost, fee, tax, duty.
ratio, proportion, grade, class, degree, value, worth, rank.
v, value, evaluate, appraise, assess, estimate, reckon, esteem, regard, deem, consider, rank, grade, class, classify.

rate[2] *v*, scold, chide, upbraid, rebuke, reprove, reprimand, berate, chastise, castigate, censure. PRAISE

rather somewhat, fairly, moderately, relatively, slightly, quite. VERY
sooner, preferably, instead.

ratify authorize, sanction, warrant, approve, consent, endorse, confirm, corroborate, substantiate, establish, settle, seal, bind. REPUDIATE

ratio proportion, rate, percentage, fraction, relationship, correspondence.

ration *n*, quota, allowance, share, portion, allotment, part, measure, helping.
v, distribute, dole, divide, apportion, allot, allocate. WITHHOLD
restrict, control, conserve, save. SQUANDER

rational reasonable, logical, sensible, practical, realistic, right, proper, wise, intelligent, sagacious, judicious, prudent, discreet, sane, sound, lucid, normal, *compos mentis*, reasoning, thinking. IRRATIONAL

rattle clatter, knock, bang, jangle, tinkle, shake, jiggle, bounce, bump.
disconcert, confuse, fluster, disturb, perturb, upset, frighten. REASSURE

raucous hoarse, harsh, grating, rasping, rough, noisy, strident. SOFT

ravage *v*, spoil, mar, ruin, wreck, destroy, demolish, devastate, desolate, pillage, plunder, loot, sack. PRESERVE
n, damage, ruin, havoc, destruction, demolition, devastation, plunder, pillage, rape, rapine.

rave rage, storm, roar, rant, ramble, babble.
praise, extol, gush, enthuse.

ravel tangle, entangle, involve, complicate, interweave, intertwine. DISENTANGLE
disentangle, unravel, undo, resolve, elucidate, explain. ENTANGLE

ravenous starving, famished, hungry, greedy, gluttonous, rapacious, voracious, insatiable. SATED

ravine gorge, canyon, chasm, abyss, gully, defile, pass.

raving mad, crazy, insane, frantic, frenzied, delirious, hysterical, raging, rabid, wild, furious. COMPOSED

ravish charm, delight, transport, enrapture, captivate, enchant, fascinate. REPEL
rape, violate, deflower, molest, assault, abuse.

ravishing charming, delightful, lovely, beautiful, enchanting, bewitching, entrancing, captivating, fascinating, dazzling. REPULSIVE

raw uncooked, fresh. COOKED
natural, unprocessed, untreated, crude, unrefined, unfinished. PROCESSED
green, immature, callow, inexperienced, naive, unsophisticated, untried, new, unskilled, untrained, unpractised, ignorant. EXPERIENCED
tender, sore, painful, sensitive, scratched, grazed, open, exposed. HEALED
cold, chilly, wet, damp, bleak, bitter, biting, piercing. TORRID

ray beam, shaft, flash, gleam, glint, glimmer, flicker, spark, hint, trace.

raze demolish, destroy, level, flatten, bulldoze, pull down, knock down. BUILD
erase, efface, obliterate, expunge, delete, strike out, extirpate, annihilate.

reach *v*, stretch, extend, touch, grasp.
get to, arrive at, come to, attain.
contact, get hold of, communicate with, get through to.
n, extent, distance, sweep, range, scope, compass, stretch, extension, grasp, hold, control, influence.

react act, behave, function, operate, respond, reply, answer, retaliate, reciprocate, counteract, counterbalance, recoil, rebound.

read peruse, study, decipher, interpret, understand, comprehend.
recite, deliver, present, declaim.
indicate, show, record, register.

readable legible, decipherable, clear, intelligible, comprehensible. ILLEGIBLE
interesting, entertaining, pleasant, enjoyable, absorbing, gripping. TEDIOUS

readily promptly, quickly, at once, right away, easily, effortlessly, willingly, gladly, cheerfully, eagerly. RELUCTANTLY

reading perusal, study, interpretation, version, understanding, comprehension.
rendering, rendition, recital, recitation, lecture, lesson, sermon.
knowledge, learning, erudition, scholarship.

ready prepared, set, primed, fit, arranged, organized, done, completed.
willing, game (*inf*), eager, keen, happy, cheerful, inclined, disposed. RELUCTANT
prompt, quick, swift, speedy, sharp, acute, nimble, agile, deft, adroit, dexterous, skilful, clever, astute. SLOW
handy, convenient, accessible, available, near, at hand. INACCESSIBLE

real true, actual, genuine, authentic, veritable, legitimate, positive, factual, existent, substantial, tangible, natural, sincere, heartfelt, honest. FALSE

realistic practical, pragmatic, down-to-earth, matter-of-fact, sensible, rational, businesslike, hard-headed. IDEALISTIC
natural, lifelike, true-to-life, faithful, graphic, real, authentic, genuine, truthful. UNREALISTIC

reality actuality, truth, verity, fact, realism, existence, corporeality. IMAGINATION

realize understand, comprehend, be aware of, take in, grasp, perceive, recognize, appreciate. MISUNDERSTAND
accomplish, achieve, fulfil, carry out, actualize, effect, bring off, make happen.

make, produce, sell for, bring in, get, obtain, acquire, gain.

really actually, in reality, in fact, indeed, truly, verily, genuinely, certainly, assuredly, positively, absolutely, unquestionably, undoubtedly.

realm kingdom, empire, principality, domain, dominion, province, department, branch, field, area, region, territory.

reap cut, crop, harvest, glean, gather, get, obtain, acquire, gain, win. SOW

rear[1] *n*, back, end, stern, tail, rump, buttocks, posterior. FRONT

adj, back, hind.

rear[2] *v*, raise, bring up, nurse, nurture, foster, train, instruct, educate, breed, cultivate, grow.

erect, build, construct, put up. DEMOLISH

raise, elevate, lift, hoist. LOWER

rise, tower, loom, soar.

reason *n*, mind, intellect, intelligence, understanding, sense, rationality, judgment, wisdom, sanity, reasoning, logic. FOLLY

motive, cause, ground, basis, aim, object, intention, purpose, excuse, justification, defence, explanation.

v, think, ponder, ratiocinate, analyse, conclude, deduce, infer, work out, solve.

argue, debate, discuss, talk over, prevail upon, urge, persuade, dissuade.

reasonable rational, sensible, logical, practical, sane, sober, wise, intelligent, judicious, sagacious, advisable, well-advised, justifiable, arguable, credible, plausible. MAD

equitable, fair, just, right, proper, moderate, within reason, tolerable, acceptable, modest, inexpensive, cheap, low-priced. UNREASONABLE

reassure comfort, encourage, hearten, cheer, buoy up, embolden, inspirit. PERTURB

rebate refund, discount, reduction, deduction, allowance. SURCHARGE

rebel *v*, revolt, rise up, mutiny, resist, defy, dissent. CONFORM

n, revolutionary, insurgent, mutineer, traitor, dissenter, nonconformist.

rebellion revolt, revolution, insurgence, insurrection, uprising, mutiny, sedition, resistance, defiance, insubordination, dissent.

rebellious revolutionary, rebel, insurgent, insurrectionary, seditious, mutinous, unruly, contumacious, defiant, insubordinate, disobedient, intractable, refractory, recalcitrant. SUBMISSIVE

rebound *v*, bounce, ricochet, recoil, spring back, return, resound, reverberate, boomerang, backfire.

n, bounce, ricochet, recoil, return, reaction, repercussion.

rebuff *v*, snub, reject, repel, check, resist, spurn, refuse, turn down, slight, cut. ACCEPT

n, snub, rejection, check, refusal, slight, cut, cold shoulder, brushoff (*inf*). ACCEPTANCE

rebuke *v*, scold, chide, upbraid, berate, castigate, reprove, reprehend, reproach, reprimand, admonish, tell off (*inf*), censure, blame. COMMEND

n, scolding, dressing-down (*inf*), castigation, reproof, reproach, reprimand, admonition, telling-off (*inf*), censure, blame. PRAISE

rebut refute, disprove, negate, invalidate, confute, contradict, defeat, overturn. SUPPORT

recalcitrant refractory, contumacious, disobedient, insubordinate, intractable, ungovernable, unmanageable, uncontrollable, wilful, wayward, perverse, stubborn. AMENABLE

recall *v*, remember, recollect, reminisce, look back, think back, call to mind, evoke, commemorate. FORGET

summon, call back, revoke, retract, withdraw, take back, repeal, rescind, overrule, annul, nullify, cancel, recant, abjure.

n, memory, remembrance, recollection, reminiscence.

revocation, retraction, withdrawal, repeal, annulment, cancellation.

recant withdraw, retract, revoke, recall, deny, disavow, disclaim, disown, repudiate, abjure, take back, unsay. MAINTAIN

recapitulate restate, repeat, reiterate, review, go over, summarize, sum up, recap (*inf*).

recede retreat, withdraw, retire, go back, return, retrogress, retrocede, ebb, subside, abate, lessen, diminish, dwindle, wane. ADVANCE

receipt acknowledgment, quittance, voucher, ticket, stub, counterfoil, reception, acceptance.

receive take, accept, get, obtain, acquire, derive. GIVE
suffer, undergo, experience, bear, endure, sustain.
admit, greet, welcome, entertain.

recent modern, late, latter, new, novel, fresh, current, up-to-date, contemporary. OLD

receptacle container, vessel, holder, repository.

reception acceptance, admission, receipt, response, greeting, welcome, entertainment, party, function.

recess alcove, niche, nook, corner, bay, hollow, indentation, cavity. PROJECTION
break, interval, rest, respite, holiday, vacation.

recipe directions, instructions, formula, prescription, method, process, procedure, technique.

recipient receiver, beneficiary. DONOR

reciprocal mutual, exchanged, reciprocative, reciprocatory, interchangeable, alternate, complementary, corresponding. ONE-SIDED

reciprocate return, give back, requite, exchange, swap, interchange, alternate, correspond, equal.

recital solo, concert, performance, show.
recitation, reading, rehearsal, repetition, account, narration, narrative, description, relation, recapitulation, chronicle, history, tale, story.

recite repeat, rehearse, declaim, deliver, relate, tell, narrate, recount, detail, enumerate, itemize, list.

reckless rash, heedless, thoughtless, careless, imprudent, injudicious, unwise, foolish, hasty, impetuous, impulsive, foolhardy, madcap, daredevil, headlong, wild, irresponsible. CAUTIOUS

reckon calculate, compute, add up, total, count, enumerate, number, figure.
consider, regard, deem, judge, esteem, rate, estimate, value.
think, believe, imagine, fancy, suppose, assume, presume, guess.
rely, depend, count, bank.

reckon with, anticipate, expect, foresee, bargain for, take into account, bear in mind.
cope with, deal with, handle, face.

reckoning calculation, computation, addition, count, estimate.
settlement, account, bill, charge.

reclaim recover, regain, redeem, rescue, save, salvage, recycle, convert, reform, restore, regenerate.

recline lean, lie, rest, repose, loll, lounge, sprawl. STAND

recluse hermit, solitary, anchorite, anchoress, eremite, ascetic, monk, nun.

recognize identify, know, place, remember, recall, recollect.
acknowledge, admit, own, grant, concede, confess, accept, respect, see, perceive, realize, understand. DENY
honour, salute, greet, appreciate. IGNORE

recoil rebound, spring back, kick, react.
shy, draw back, shrink, flinch, quail, falter.

recollect remember, recall, reminisce, call to mind. FORGET

recommend advise, counsel, suggest, prescribe, urge, advocate. DISCOURAGE
praise, commend, promote, approve, endorse, vouch for. DISAPPROVE

recompense *v*, pay, reward, remunerate, repay, reimburse, indemnify, compensate, redress, requite, make amends.
n, compensation, indemnity, amends, redress, reparation, remuneration, reward, payment, repayment, reimbursement.

reconcile reunite, conciliate, propitiate, appease, pacify, placate, settle, resolve, adjust, harmonize, mend, patch up. ALIENATE
accept, resign, submit, yield. OPPOSE

recondite abstruse, esoteric, profound, deep, mystical, hidden, concealed, secret, cryptic, occult, arcane, mysterious, dark, obscure, difficult. PATENT

reconnoitre survey, spy out, scout, explore, inspect, examine, view, scan.

reconstruct rebuild, reassemble, remake, remodel, restore, renovate, regenerate, recreate. DESTROY

record *n*, journal, diary, chronicle, memoir, annals, archives, log, register, document, minute, memorandum, note, account, report.
evidence, testimony, reputation, performance, history, career.
recording, disc, album, LP, single.
v, enter, note, write down, register, log, minute, document, chronicle, tape.

recount narrate, relate, tell, report, recite, repeat, rehearse, detail, specify, enumerate, list, describe, depict.

recourse resort, refuge, resource, remedy, appeal.

recover *vt*, regain, recoup, get back, retrieve, reclaim, repossess, recapture, redeem, rescue, save, salvage. LOSE
vi, get better, get well, pull through, improve, mend, heal, rally, revive, recuperate, convalesce. DETERIORATE

recovery recuperation, convalescence, rally, revival, improvement, amelioration, cure, healing. RELAPSE
retrieval, reclamation, repossession, recapture, redemption, restoration. LOSS

recreation relaxation, refreshment, hobby, pastime, amusement, diversion, distraction, entertainment, pleasure, enjoyment, fun, play, sport, exercise. WORK

recrimination countercharge, retaliation, retort, accusation.

recruit *v*, enlist, draft, call up, mobilize, muster, round up, enrol, sign up, engage, take on. DISMISS
renew, replenish, reinforce, strengthen, supply, furnish.
n, novice, rookie (*inf*), beginner, tyro, neophyte, initiate, learner, trainee, apprentice, helper, supporter. VETERAN

rectify correct, put right, redress, reform, remedy, fix, mend, repair, improve, ameliorate, amend, emend, adjust, straighten, regulate.

rectitude uprightness, righteousness, virtue, goodness, integrity, probity, morality, honour, justice, equity, correctness, accuracy, precision, exactitude. CORRUPTION

rector cleric, clergyman, churchman, ecclesiastic, parson, vicar, minister, pastor. LAYMAN

recumbent lying, reclining, leaning, resting, prostrate, flat, horizontal, supine, prone. ERECT

recuperate recover, convalesce, improve, get better, get well, mend, heal. DECLINE

recur repeat, happen again, return, come back, reappear, persist, come and go.

recurrent recurring, repeated, frequent, regular, periodic, cyclical, intermittent, persistent. SOLITARY

red crimson, carmine, scarlet, ruby, cherry, vermilion, .maroon, coral, auburn, chestnut.
rosy, ruddy, florid, glowing, blooming, blushing, flushed. PALLID

redeem recover, regain, reclaim, repossess, buy back, ransom, rescue, save, deliver, free, liberate, emancipate. SURRENDER
exchange, cash, trade in.
discharge, fulfil, perform, carry out, meet, satisfy.
reinstate, rehabilitate, absolve, expiate, make amends for, atone for, redress, offset, compensate.

redemption recovery, reclamation, repossession, ransom, salvation, deliverance.
rehabilitation, absolution, expiation, atonement, reparation, compensation.

redolent fragrant, scented, perfumed, aromatic, odoriferous, sweet-smelling. MALODOROUS
reminiscent, remindful, suggestive, evocative.

redouble intensify, increase, augment, multiply. REDUCE

redoubtable formidable, awe-inspiring, fearsome, terrible, dreadful, awful. DERISIBLE

redound conduce, contribute, lead, tend, result, recoil, rebound.

redress *v*, rectify, put right, correct, remedy, compensate for, make amends for, repair, fix, amend, improve, adjust, regulate.
n, rectification, correction, remedy, cure, compensation, recompense, amends, atonement, reparation. WRONG

reduce lessen, diminish, decrease, shrink, contract, shorten, cut, abridge, curtail, abate, attenuate, moderate, lower, weaken, impair. INCREASE
degrade, debase, demote, downgrade, ruin, impoverish, humble, humiliate. EXALT
subdue, quell, crush, conquer, vanquish, overcome, overpower, overwhelm, master, subjugate.
discount, mark down, cut, slash. RAISE

redundant superfluous, unnecessary, *de trop*, surplus, extra, excessive. ESSENTIAL
verbose, wordy, prolix, diffuse, repetitious, tautological. TERSE

re-echo resound, resonate, reverberate, echo, repeat.

reek *v*, smell, stink.
steam, smoke, fumigate.
n, smell, odour, stink, stench, fetor, effluvium, pong (*inf*). PERFUME

reel[1] *n*, bobbin, spool.

reel[2] *v*, stagger, totter, falter, stumble, lurch, pitch, rock, sway, spin, whirl.

refer mention, allude, speak of, bring up, quote, cite, advert, touch on.
direct, point, guide, send, hand over, deliver, consign, commit.
relate, pertain, apply, concern, mean, indicate, signify, suggest.
consult, turn, apply, appeal, have recourse.
assign, attribute, ascribe, put down, impute, credit.

referee umpire, arbiter, judge, adjudicator, arbitrator.

reference mention, allusion, quotation, citation, note, remark, hint, intimation, suggestion, insinuation.
regard, respect, consideration, concern, bearing, connection, relation, relevance.
testimonial, character, recommendation, endorsement.

refine purify, rarefy, clarify, cleanse, filter, sift, process. POLLUTE
polish, cultivate, civilize, elevate, improve, ameliorate, hone, perfect. BARBARIZE

refined cultivated, cultured, civilized, polished, genteel, courtly, polite, well-bred, gentlemanly, ladylike, elegant, sophisticated. COARSE
pure, purified, clear, clarified, clean, distilled, processed. CRUDE

reflect mirror, throw back, return, give back, echo, imitate, copy, reproduce.
show, exhibit, demonstrate, manifest, indicate, betray. CONCEAL
meditate, contemplate, cogitate, ruminate, ponder, muse, think, deliberate, consider, wonder.

reflection image, echo, shadow, likeness.
thought, idea, opinion, view, impression, feeling, meditation, contemplation, cogitation, rumination, deliberation, consideration.
censure, blame, criticism, reproach, aspersion, slur.

reflex automatic, mechanical, involuntary, spontaneous, immediate. VOLUNTARY

reform *v*, improve, better, ameliorate, mend, repair, amend, emend, correct, rectify, change, revolutionize, remodel, rebuild, restore, renovate, rehabilitate, reclaim. DETERIORATE
n, reformation, improvement, amelioration, amendment, correction, rectification, change, progress, renovation, rehabilitation, reclamation. CORRUPTION

refractory recalcitrant, contumacious, obstinate, stubborn, intractable, perverse, wilful, wayward, unruly, unmanageable, ungovernable, uncontrollable. DOCILE

refrain[1] *v*, abstain, forbear, desist, stop, give up, renounce, forgo, do without. INDULGE

refrain[2] *n*, chorus, burden, melody, tune. VERSE

refresh freshen, cool, revive, reanimate, invigorate, revitalize, brace, fortify, rejuvenate, exhilarate, cheer, enliven, stimulate, regenerate, renew, restore, repair, renovate. WEARY

refreshment food, drink, sustenance, snack.
revival, reanimation, invigoration, revitalization, rejuvenation, regeneration, renewal, restoration. FATIGUE

refrigerate cool, chill, freeze. HEAT

refuge shelter, protection, safety, security, sanctuary, asylum, haven, harbour, retreat, hide-out, resort, recourse. EXPOSURE

refulgent radiant, brilliant, bright, shining, effulgent, resplendent, lambent, lustrous. DULL

refund *v*, repay, pay back, return, give back, restore, reimburse, recompense, make good. WITHHOLD
n, repayment, reimbursement, rebate.

refuse[1] *v*, decline, turn down, reject, spurn, repudiate, deny, withhold, rebuff, repel. ACCEPT

refuse[2] *n*, rubbish, waste, garbage, trash, junk, litter, dregs, dross, scraps, leftovers.

refute disprove, rebut, negate, confute, deny, discredit. CONFIRM

regain recover, get back, retrieve, recoup, recapture, repossess. LOSE

regal royal, kingly, queenly, princely, imperial, sovereign, majestic, stately, august, noble, magnificent, grand. LOWLY

regale entertain, amuse, delight, feast, banquet, fête, treat.

regalia emblems, insignia, robes, finery.

regard *v*, watch, observe, notice, remark, note, mark, heed, look at, eye. IGNORE
consider, deem, rate, judge, think, believe, see, view, look upon, esteem, value, honour, respect.
concern, relate to, pertain to, refer to, apply to.

n, notice, attention, heed, thought, consideration, care, concern. NEGLECT

esteem, respect, estimation, admiration, honour, deference, liking, fondness, affection, love. CONTEMPT

reference, relation, respect, concern, bearing, connection.

look, gaze, stare, observation.

regardful mindful, heedful, attentive, careful, thoughtful, considerate, watchful, vigilant, observant, aware. HEEDLESS

regarding about, re, concerning, respecting, as regards, with reference to, apropos of.

regardless *adj*, heedless, mindless, unmindful, inattentive, reckless, careless, neglectful, negligent, disregarding, thoughtless, inconsiderate, indifferent, unconcerned. MINDFUL

adv, anyway, notwithstanding, in any case, nevertheless.

regenerate renew, restore, renovate, revive, invigorate, rejuvenate, uplift, reform, convert, change, reconstruct, remodel.

regime government, administration, system, reign, rule, direction, management.

region area, zone, territory, district, quarter, province, department, place, spot, country, land, tract, part, section, division, realm, domain, sphere, orbit, field, range, scope, vicinity, neighbourhood, locality.

register *v*, record, enter, write down, inscribe, note, list, catalogue, chronicle, minute.

enrol, enlist, sign up, sign on.

show, indicate, read, express, display, manifest, exhibit, reveal.

n, record, roll, list, catalogue, journal, diary, log, schedule, minutes, annals, archives, chronicle.

regnant reigning, ruling, ascendant, predominant, prevalent, prevailing.

regress *v*, return, go back, retreat, ebb, recede, retrocede, retrogress, revert, relapse, backslide, degenerate, decline, retrograde. PROGRESS

n, regression, return, reversion, relapse, retrogression, retreat, retrocession, recession. PROGRESSION

regret *v*, deplore, bemoan, bewail, lament, rue, repent, repine, mourn, grieve, miss.

n, sorrow, grief, remorse, repentance, penitence, contrition, compunction, lamentation, disappointment. SATISFACTION

regular normal, usual, customary, habitual, routine, typical, standard, familiar, conventional, ordinary, commonplace, everyday, formal, official, orthodox, correct, traditional. ABNORMAL

steady, rhythmic, constant, unchanging, unvarying, fixed, set, established, periodic, recurrent, orderly, methodical, systematic, uniform, even, level, symmetrical. IRREGULAR

regulate adjust, control, rule, govern, direct, manage, run, administer, handle, guide, arrange, organize, establish, fix, set, systematize, methodize, order.

regulation *n*, adjustment, control, government, direction, management, administration.

rule, law, statute, ordinance, edict, decree, order, commandment, directive, direction.

adj, formal, official, standard, regular, usual, normal. UNORTHODOX

regurgitate vomit, throw up (*inf*), disgorge, bring back.

rehabilitate reform, improve, adapt, adjust, reintegrate, redeem, save.

restore, reinstate, reclaim, renovate, renew, revive, repair, mend, reconstruct.

rehearse practise, drill, exercise, train, prepare, run through, repeat, recite.

recount, relate, review, recapitulate, detail, list, enumerate, narrate, describe, depict.

reign *v*, rule, govern, command, hold sway, predominate, prevail. SUBMIT

n, rule, government, regime, command, control, sway, power, sovereignty, empire, dominion.

reimburse repay, pay back, refund, recompense, compensate, indemnify.

rein *n*, bridle, harness, curb, check, restraint, control.

v, restrain, check, curb, bridle, hold back, control, guide. INDULGE

reinforce strengthen, fortify, support, brace, buttress, harden, stiffen, augment, supplement, increase, redouble. WEAKEN

reinstate restore, replace, return, rehabilitate. REMOVE

reiterate repeat, iterate, restate, recapitulate.

reject refuse, turn down, decline, deny, disallow, spurn, rebuff, repel, cast aside, discard, throw away, scrap, renounce, repudiate, jilt, eliminate, exclude, eject, expel. ACCEPT

rejoice exult, triumph, glory, revel, celebrate, make merry, delight, joy. MOURN

rejoinder reply, answer, response, riposte, retort.

relapse *v*, revert, slip back, lapse, backslide, regress, retrogress, degenerate, deteriorate, decline, weaken. IMPROVE
n, reversion, lapse, regression, retrogression, deterioration, setback. IMPROVEMENT

relate narrate, tell, recount, recite, rehearse, describe, detail, report, communicate, impart, mention. SUPPRESS
connect, link, associate, ally, couple.
refer, apply, regard, respect, concern, pertain.

relation relationship, connection, link, bond, association, affiliation, affinity, interdependence, similarity, propinquity.
relative, kinsman, kinswoman, kin, kindred, kinship, consanguinity.
reference, respect, regard, concern, bearing, relevance, pertinence.
account, narrative, narration, report, story, tale, recital, description.

relative *n*, relation, kinsman, kinswoman, kin, family.
adj, comparative, proportionate, respective, corresponding, analogous, comparable, connected, related, allied, associated, contingent, dependent. ABSOLUTE
relevant, pertinent, germane, apropos, applicable, appropriate.

relax loosen, slacken, ease, let up, moderate, reduce, lessen, lower, diminish, abate, weaken. TIGHTEN
rest, unwind, laze, take it easy (*inf*), calm, tranquillize, unbend.

relaxation rest, leisure, recreation, amusement, diversion, entertainment, hobby, pastime, fun, pleasure. WORK
loosening, slackening, easing, moderation, reduction, diminution.

relay *n*, relief, shift.
broadcast, transmission, communication.
v, broadcast, transmit, communicate, spread, pass on.

release *v*, free, set free, loose, turn loose, let out, let go, drop, liberate, emancipate, unshackle, untie, clear, acquit, discharge, let off, exempt. HOLD
publish, issue, circulate, disseminate, announce, make known. SUPPRESS
n, freedom, liberation, emancipation, acquittal, discharge, exemption. IMPRISONMENT
publication, issue, circulation, dissemination, announcement, proclamation.

relegate demote, downgrade. PROMOTE
assign, delegate, consign, transfer, entrust.
banish, exile, deport, expatriate, oust, eject. REINSTATE

relent unbend, yield, give way, soften, relax, slacken. HARDEN

relentless unrelenting, unyielding, implacable, inexorable, remorseless, ruthless, hard, harsh, cruel, merciless, pitiless, unremitting, unflagging, persistent. MILD

relevant pertinent, germane, apropos, applicable, to the point, apposite, appropriate, apt, proper, related. IRRELEVANT

reliable trustworthy, dependable, trusty, unfailing, sure, certain, sound, stable, honest, truthful, true, faithful. UNRELIABLE

reliance trust, dependence, confidence, faith, belief.

relic keepsake, memento, souvenir, token, trace, vestige, remnant, fragment.

relief comfort, solace, consolation, reassurance, ease, alleviation, mitigation, palliation, assuagement, remedy, cure. AGGRAVATION
help, aid, assistance, support, rescue, deliverance.
lull, remission, break, respite.

relieve ease, alleviate, mitigate, palliate, assuage, allay, soothe, diminish, lessen, comfort, solace, console, reassure. AGGRAVATE
help, aid, assist, support, free, deliver, release, replace, take over from, stand in for.
break, interrupt, vary, relax.

religious pious, godly, devout, reverent, good, pure, righteous, saintly, holy, sacred, divine, spiritual, theological. PROFANE
strict, rigid, rigorous, exact, scrupulous, conscientious, faithful. LAX

relinquish abandon, give up, surrender, renounce, abdicate, resign, quit, leave, desert, forsake, repudiate, yield, waive, forgo, drop, let go, release. RETAIN

relish *v*, enjoy, delight in, savour, appreciate, look forward to. LOATH

n, enjoyment, pleasure, delight, gusto, zest, liking, appreciation, fondness, fancy, partiality, predilection. AVERSION
taste, flavour, savour, tang, appetizer, sauce, condiment, seasoning. INSIPIDITY

reluctant loath, loth, unwilling, disinclined, indisposed, averse, hesitant. EAGER

rely depend, count, bank, lean, trust, swear by, have confidence in, be sure of. DISTRUST

remain stay, continue, abide, last, endure, persist, survive, be left, linger, tarry, wait, rest. GO

remainder rest, remains, remnant, residue, balance, surplus, excess.

remains relics, remnants, remainder, residue, dregs, fragments, scraps, leavings, leftovers, oddments, odds and ends.

remark *v*, comment, observe, mention, say, state, declare.
notice, note, see, perceive, observe, regard, heed, mark. MISS
n, comment, observation, mention, utterance, statement, declaration, opinion, thought, attention, heed, regard, notice.

remarkable notable, noteworthy, outstanding, striking, noticeable, conspicuous, extraordinary, unusual, uncommon, exceptional, rare, singular, peculiar, strange, surprising, wonderful. ORDINARY

remedy *n*, cure, antidote, restorative, specific, treatment, medicine, therapy, panacea, solution.
v, cure, heal, restore, treat, relieve, ease, alleviate, palliate, mitigate, assuage.
rectify, correct, redress, put right, fix, repair, improve, solve. AGGRAVATE

remember recall, recollect, call to mind, recognize, reminisce, commemorate, memorize. FORGET

remembrance memory, recollection, reminiscence, retrospect, thought, regard.
souvenir, memento, keepsake, token, reminder, commemoration, memorial.

remind prompt, jog the memory, bring back, call up, put in mind.

reminiscence memory, recollection, remembrance, reflection, retrospection, memoir, anecdote.

reminiscent evocative, suggestive, remindful, redolent, nostalgic.

remiss negligent, neglectful, careless, inattentive, heedless, thoughtless, unmindful, forgetful, derelict, delinquent, dilatory, slack, lax, slow, tardy, indolent, slothful. DILIGENT

remission forgiveness, pardon, amnesty, reprieve, release, discharge, acquittal, exoneration, absolution. PUNISHMENT
diminution, reduction, lessening, abatement, ebb, decrease, moderation, relaxation, respite, let-up (*inf*). INCREASE

remit send, dispatch, mail, post, forward, pay.
halt, stop, desist, forbear, reprieve, release, cancel.
relax, slacken, mitigate, alleviate, moderate, weaken, abate, ebb, decrease, diminish, lessen, reduce. INCREASE
postpone, defer, put off, delay.

remnant remainder, rest, remains, residue, scrap, fragment, bit, piece, trace, vestige.

remonstrate protest, object, expostulate, argue, dissent, take issue. ACQUIESCE

remorse regret, sorrow, grief, contrition, penitence, repentance, guilt, shame, compunction. SATISFACTION

remorseful sorry, apologetic, regretful, contrite, penitent, repentant, guilty, ashamed, sorrowful, sad. IMPENITENT

remorseless relentless, unrelenting, inexorable, implacable, merciless, pitiless, cruel, hard, harsh, callous, ruthless. MERCIFUL

remote distant, far, removed, sequestered, secluded, isolated, lonely, inaccessible, out-of-the-way. NEAR
foreign, alien, extraneous, extrinsic, irrelevant, unconnected, unrelated.
slight, slender, slim, faint, inconsiderable, negligible, unlikely. CONSIDERABLE
detached, stand-offish, distant, aloof, indifferent, cool, frigid. FRIENDLY

remove take off, detach, doff, shed, take away, withdraw, abstract, dislodge, displace, move, transport, transfer, eliminate, eradicate, abolish, obliterate, efface, expunge, erase, delete, oust, depose, dismiss, discharge, expel, eject. REPLACE

remunerate pay, reward, recompense, reimburse, indemnify, repay, requite, redress.

remuneration payment, reward, recompense, reimbursement, pay, wages, salary, emolument, stipend, fee.

remunerative profitable, gainful, lucrative, rewarding, paying, advantageous, worthwhile. UNPROFITABLE

renaissance renascence, rebirth, revival, renewal, reappearance, resurgence, re-emergence, awakening.

rend tear, rip, cleave, sever, sunder, rive, split, divide, rupture, fracture, break, crack. MEND
pierce, stab, lacerate, wound, pain, afflict, distress, harrow.

render give, supply, provide, furnish, present, submit, offer, tender, deliver, yield. WITHHOLD
show, exhibit, manifest, display, represent, depict, portray, do.
make, cause to be.
translate, transcribe, construe, interpret, explain.

rendition rendering, performance, execution, presentation, delivery, arrangement, version, interpretation, construction, transcription, translation.

renegade traitor, apostate, backslider, recreant, turncoat, defector, deserter, rat (*inf*), mutineer, outlaw, rebel.

renew recommence, resume, repeat, reiterate, revive, restore, replenish, restock, refresh, regenerate, rejuvenate, reinvigorate, revitalize, repair, renovate, refurbish, refit, recondition.

renounce give up, forgo, forswear, eschew, abandon, forsake, desert, abdicate, resign, relinquish, let go, yield, surrender, cede. RETAIN
disown, disinherit, repudiate, reject, decline, turn down, deny, disclaim, disavow, recant. ACKNOWLEDGE

renovate restore, renew, repair, do up (*inf*), recondition, refurbish, refit, rehabilitate, revive, refresh.

renown fame, celebrity, illustriousness, note, eminence, repute, distinction, honour, glory, acclaim. NOTORIETY

rent[1] *v*, lease, let, hire, charter.
n, rental, hire, lease, payment, tariff.

rent[2] *n*, tear, rip, slit, gash, opening, gap, crevice, cleft, fissure, crack, split, rift, break, rupture, breach, division, schism.

repair[1] *v*, mend, fix, patch up, restore, renovate, renew, correct, rectify, put right, adjust, redress, make good. DAMAGE
n, mend, patch, restoration, renovation, correction, adjustment, overhaul, service.

repair[2] *v*, go, betake oneself, leave for, head for, resort, have recourse.

reparation amends, atonement, redress, requital, satisfaction, recompense, compensation, indemnity, damages, repair, restoration. INJURY

repartee banter, badinage, raillery, persiflage, pleasantry, riposte, rejoinder, quip, witticism.

repast meal, feast, banquet, food.

repay refund, return, pay back, reimburse, requite, recompense, reward, square.
reciprocate, retaliate, revenge, avenge.

repeal *v*, rescind, revoke, abrogate, annul, nullify, abolish, invalidate, countermand, overrule, reverse, cancel. ENACT
n, revocation, abrogation, annulment, abolition, reversal, cancellation.

repeat reiterate, iterate, restate, recapitulate, rehearse, recite, quote, recount, retell, redo, rerun, reproduce, duplicate, echo, renew.

repel repulse, drive back, ward off, check, resist, parry, reject, spurn, rebuff. WELCOME
disgust, nauseate, sicken, revolt, put off, offend. ATTRACT

repent regret, rue, lament, deplore, be penitent, be contrite, feel remorse.

repentance penitence, contrition, regret, remorse, compunction, sorrow, grief, guilt, shame. SATISFACTION

repentant penitent, contrite, regretful, remorseful, sorry, apologetic. UNREPENTANT

repercussion result, consequence, aftermath, backlash, recoil, rebound, echo, reverberation.

repetition repeat, reiteration, iteration, tautology, redundancy, restatement, recapitulation, rehearsal, recital, reproduction, duplication, echo, renewal, return, recurrence. ORIGINALITY

repine grumble, complain, moan, lament, fret, mope, brood, sulk. REJOICE

replace supersede, take the place of, succeed, follow, supplant, take over, substitute.
return, put back, restore, reinstate. REMOVE

replenish refill, restock, recharge, reload, renew, stock, supply, furnish, provide, fill. EXHAUST

replete full, filled, well-stocked, packed, stuffed, bursting, overflowing, abounding, gorged, sated, satiated. EMPTY

replica copy, duplicate, reproduction, facsimile, model, imitation. ORIGINAL

reply *v*, answer, respond, acknowledge, rejoin, retort, riposte, return, echo. ASK

n, answer, response, acknowledgment, reaction, rejoinder, retort, riposte, echo. QUESTION

report *n*, account, statement, description, narrative, narration, relation, recital, article, story, review, write-up, paper, study, record, minute, announcement, declaration, news, tidings, word, communication, message, communiqué, dispatch, bulletin, rumour, hearsay.

reputation, repute, fame, renown, esteem, regard, character, performance.

bang, crack, boom, shot, blast, explosion, detonation, discharge, noise, sound, reverberation.

v, tell, relate, recount, narrate, describe, relay, communicate, announce, broadcast, state, declare, record, write up. SUPPRESS

reporter journalist, correspondent, columnist, newsman, newswoman, newscaster.

repose[1] *n*, rest, ease, relaxation, sleep, slumber, peace, quiet, tranquillity, stillness, inactivity, inertia. ACTIVITY

composure, calmness, poise, aplomb, self-possession, equanimity. AGITATION

v, rest, relax, lie, recline, sleep. WORK

repose[2] *v*, place, put, lodge, deposit, store.

reprehend blame, censure, criticize, find fault with, reprove, rebuke, reprimand, reproach, chide, berate, upbraid, scold, admonish. PRAISE

reprehensible blameworthy, censurable, culpable, disgraceful, shameful, opprobrious, ignoble, objectionable. COMMENDABLE

represent symbolize, stand for, epitomize, exemplify, typify, personify, embody, express, illustrate, depict, describe, reproduce, show.

act for, stand for, speak for, substitute for.

portray, impersonate, mimic, pose as, pretend to be, act, perform, produce, stage.

representative *n*, agent, deputy, delegate, spokesman, spokeswoman, proxy, substitute, stand-in.

salesman, commercial traveller, agent, rep.

adj, typical, characteristic, illustrative, symbolic, emblematic.

repress suppress, restrain, control, check, curb, hold back, bottle up, inhibit, stifle, smother, muffle, quash, quell, subdue, crush, overcome, overpower, master, subjugate. RELEASE

reprieve *v*, pardon, remit, postpone, relieve, allay, alleviate, mitigate, palliate.

n, remission, stay of execution, pardon, amnesty, respite, relief, alleviation, mitigation.

reprimand *v*, admonish, reprehend, scold, tell off (*inf*), rebuke, reprove, reproach, chide, upbraid, berate, castigate, censure, criticize. COMMEND

n, rebuke, reproof, reproach, admonition, reprehension, telling-off (*inf*), dressing-down (*inf*), castigation, censure. PRAISE

reprisal retaliation, retribution, revenge, vengeance.

reproach *v*, blame, censure, criticize, find fault with, rebuke, reprove, reprehend, reprimand, scold, chide, upbraid, admonish. APPROVE

n, blame, censure, criticism, disapproval, rebuke, reproof, reprimand, admonition. APPROVAL

shame, disgrace, dishonour, discredit, ignominy, odium, opprobrium, obloquy, slur, stigma. HONOUR

reprobate *adj*, corrupt, depraved, degenerate, immoral, abandoned, shameless, profligate, irredeemable, hardened, wicked, evil, vile, base. VIRTUOUS

n, villain, miscreant, wretch, rogue, scoundrel, rascal, sinner, wrongdoer. PARAGON

v, condemn, denounce, criticize, disapprove, censure, blame, reproach, reprehend. APPROVE

reproduce duplicate, replicate, copy, imitate, emulate, parallel, mirror, echo, repeat, represent, re-create.

propagate, multiply, breed, procreate, produce, generate.

reproduction propagation, breeding, procreation, generation.

duplicate, copy, replica, facsimile, print.

reproof reproval, reproach, rebuke, reprimand, reprehension, admonition, censure, blame. PRAISE

reprove rebuke, scold, tell off (*inf*), reproach, reprehend, reprimand, admonish, chide, upbraid, berate, blame, censure, condemn. PRAISE

repudiate reject, renounce, disavow, abjure, disclaim, forswear, retract, deny, disown, abandon, cast off, discard. ACKNOWLEDGE

repugnant repellent, repulsive, revolting, disgusting, offensive, objectionable, distasteful, obnoxious, odious, loathsome, abhorrent.
hostile, inimical, adverse, antagonistic, contrary, opposed, conflicting, incompatible.

repulse repel, drive back, ward off, check, reject, rebuff, spurn, turn down. WELCOME

repulsive repellent, repugnant, revolting, disgusting, nauseating, sickening, offensive, objectionable, obnoxious, odious, loathsome, abhorrent, detestable, hateful, hideous, ugly, foul, horrid. DELIGHTFUL

reputation repute, name, character, standing, status, respect, esteem, estimation, regard, fame, renown, celebrity, distinction, honour.

reputed supposed, putative, apparent, ostensible, seeming, alleged, believed, considered, reckoned, deemed, held.

request *v*, ask, beg, beseech, supplicate, entreat, appeal, petition, solicit, demand.
n, entreaty, supplication, appeal, petition, prayer, desire, demand, requisition.

require need, lack, want, desire, necessitate, involve, call for, demand.
ask, request, bid, enjoin, instruct, direct, order, command, oblige, compel.

requisite *adj*, required, needed, necessary, needful, essential, indispensable, vital, imperative, obligatory, compulsory, mandatory. NONESSENTIAL
n, requirement, need, necessity, must, essential, condition, prerequisite, stipulation, provision.

requite repay, reciprocate, return, reimburse, recompense, redress, make good, reward, retaliate, avenge.

rescind repeal, revoke, abrogate, reverse, annul, nullify, quash, invalidate, countermand, cancel. CONFIRM

rescue *v*, save, deliver, redeem, ransom, free, liberate, release, extricate, recover, salvage. ENDANGER
n, salvation, deliverance, redemption, ransom, liberation, release, recovery, salvage.

research *n*, investigation, inquiry, study, analysis, examination, scrutiny, groundwork, documentation.
v, investigate, look into, study, analyse, examine, scrutinize, experiment.

resemblance likeness, similarity, semblance, similitude, analogy, parity, correspondence, comparison, closeness, affinity. DISSIMILARITY

resemble look like, take after, favour, mirror, echo, duplicate, match, parallel.

resent begrudge, take offence, take umbrage, object to, dislike.

resentful bitter, embittered, indignant, angry, irate, wrathful, miffed (*inf*), peeved (*inf*), grudging, jealous, envious, aggrieved, wounded. CONTENTED

resentment bitterness, ill will, animosity, hatred, indignation, offence, umbrage, pique, anger, rage, ire, wrath, displeasure, grudge, jealousy, envy. SATISFACTION

reservation qualification, condition, proviso, qualm, scruple, demur.
reserve, preserve, sanctuary, territory, area, plot.

reserve *v*, withhold, hold, keep, keep back, save, conserve, husband, retain, set aside, put by. USE
book, engage, secure, retain.
n, stock, supply, store, stockpile, fund, reservoir.
park, sanctuary, reservation, tract.
reticence, taciturnity, shyness, restraint, modesty, formality, aloofness, detachment, coolness. FRANKNESS
adj, substitute, auxiliary, spare, extra.

reserved booked, engaged, taken, retained, held, kept, set aside. FREE
reticent, taciturn, shy, retiring, unsociable, uncommunicative, aloof, distant, standoffish, formal, restrained, prim, modest, demure, constrained, cool. FRANK

reservoir lake, tank, basin, receptacle, container.
stock, supply, reserve, store, fund, pool.

reside live, dwell, abide, sojourn, stay, lodge, inhabit, settle.
lie, rest, exist, abide, dwell, inhere.

residence house, home, abode, dwelling, habitation, quarters, lodging, accommodation.
mansion, palace, villa, castle, hall, manor.
sojourn, stay, occupancy, inhabitancy.

resident inhabitant, citizen, denizen, occupier, householder, inmate, lodger, tenant. VISITOR

residue residuum, remainder, remains, rest, balance, surplus, excess, remnant, leavings, leftovers, dregs.

resign abdicate, give up, renounce, relinquish, hand over, surrender, yield, leave, quit. RETAIN

resignation abdication, renunciation, relinquishment, surrender, departure, retirement, notice.
acquiescence, submission, compliance, nonresistance, passivity, acceptance, endurance, patience, forbearance. REBELLION

resilient springy, bouncy, elastic, rubbery, flexible, pliable, supple, buoyant, irrepressible.

resist withstand, repel, repulse, rebuff, stand firm, hold out, oppose, counteract, face, confront, fight, battle, contend with, check, curb, stop, block, hinder, thwart. YIELD
refrain from, abstain from, refuse, desist.

resolute steadfast, firm, set, intent, determined, resolved, decided, staunch, unwavering, unflinching, unyielding, obdurate, dogged, constant, steady, relentless, persistent, persevering, undaunted, unshaken. IRRESOLUTE

resolution firmness, determination, resolve, resoluteness, steadfastness, constancy, perseverance, tenacity, zeal, earnestness. IRRESOLUTION
decision, resolve, objective, intention, aim, purpose, verdict, judgment, declaration, statement.

resolve *v*, determine, decide, fix, settle, intend, purpose. WAVER
solve, explain, answer, fathom, clear up.
dispel, unravel, disentangle. EMBROIL
separate, dissect, anatomize, analyse, break down, reduce, dissolve.
n, decision, resolution, intention, purpose.
firmness, determination, resoluteness, resolution, steadfastness, constancy, persistence, doggedness, perseverance, tenacity, fortitude, willpower. IRRESOLUTION

resonant resounding, reverberant, ringing, booming, loud, sonorous, full, rich. QUIET

resort *v*, turn, have recourse, use, employ, utilize, exercise.
go, repair, frequent, haunt.
n, retreat, refuge, haunt, rendezvous, spot, place, holiday centre, spa.
recourse, expedient, alternative, possibility, chance, hope.

resound resonate, reverberate, ring, echo, re-echo.

resource ingenuity, enterprise, ability, inventiveness, resourcefulness, initiative.
device, expedient, resort, recourse.
source, store, hoard, stockpile.

resources wealth, capital, money, funds, assets, property, supplies, reserves, means.

respect *v*, honour, esteem, admire, revere, venerate, think highly of, look up to, appreciate, prize, value. DESPISE
notice, heed, observe, comply with, abide by, adhere to, obey, defer to, be polite to, regard, consider.
n, honour, esteem, admiration, reverence, veneration, appreciation, deference, regard, consideration, politeness, courtesy. DISRESPECT
reference, connection, relation, regard, point, detail, particular, feature.

respectable worthy, estimable, laudable, commendable, praiseworthy, admirable, honourable, venerable, reputable, honest, upright, proper, decent. DISREPUTABLE
acceptable, passable, tolerable, fair, goodly, considerable.

respectful courteous, polite, mannerly, civil, gracious, deferential, considerate, thoughtful, dutiful, obedient, submissive, humble. DISRESPECTFUL

respective individual, separate, several, specific, particular, own, corresponding.

respite pause, lull, rest, break, interval, breather (*inf*), recess, adjournment, postponement, delay, reprieve, remission.

resplendent splendid, glorious, bright, brilliant, radiant, shining, dazzling, effulgent, glittering, sparkling. DULL

respond reply, answer, rejoin, retort, react, acknowledge, reciprocate, return.

response reply, answer, rejoinder, retort, riposte, reaction, feedback, acknowledgment.

responsibility duty, obligation, onus, burden, charge, care, trust.
accountability, liability, culpability, guilt, fault, blame.

responsible accountable, answerable, liable, bound, culpable, guilty.

dependable, reliable, trustworthy, honest, upright, stable, sound, sensible, rational. IRRESPONSIBLE

responsive sensitive, reactive, susceptible, impressionable, sympathetic, receptive. INSENSITIVE

rest[1] *n*, relaxation, ease, leisure, inactivity, repose, sleep, slumber, nap, stillness, quiet, calm, tranquillity, motionlessness, inertia, standstill. TUMULT
pause, respite, break, breather (*inf*), recess, holiday, vacation, intermission, halt, cessation. CONTINUATION
support, prop, brace, stand.
v, relax, take it easy (*inf*), laze, lounge, sleep, slumber, repose, recline. WORK
stop, cease, desist, halt, pause, stay. CONTINUE
support, prop, stand, lean, lay, lie, hinge, hang, depend, rely.

rest[2] *n*, remainder, remains, residue, balance, surplus, excess, remnants, leftovers, others.

restful relaxing, soothing, calm, tranquil, serene, quiet, still, peaceful. TUMULTUOUS

restitution restoration, return, reparation, amends, redress, requital, satisfaction, compensation, indemnity, indemnification, recompense, remuneration, repayment, refund, reimbursement. INJURY

restive restless, uneasy, nervous, fretful, impatient, fidgety, refractory, recalcitrant, stubborn, obstinate, wilful, unruly. DOCILE

restless moving, active, unsettled, unstable, changeable, inconstant, wandering, roving, nomadic, migrant. STILL
uneasy, restive, unquiet, fidgety, jumpy, edgy, fretful, nervous, anxious, agitated, disturbed, sleepless, wakeful. RESTFUL

restoration renovation, repair, reconstruction, rehabilitation, renewal, revival, refreshment, rejuvenation. DECLINE
return, restitution, replacement, reinstatement, recovery, compensation. REMOVAL

restore return, give back, replace, put back, bring back, reintroduce, reinstate, reestablish. REMOVE
renovate, repair, fix, mend, recondition, reconstruct.
renew, revive, refresh, reinvigorate, strengthen, cure.

restrain hold back, constrain, curb, check, bridle, inhibit, contain, repress, suppress, subdue, moderate, control, restrict, limit, confine, imprison. RELEASE

restraint control, self-control, self-restraint, inhibition, reserve, moderation, repression, suppression, constraint, check, curb, restriction.

restrict limit, bound, demarcate, cramp, constrict, hamper, impede, confine, circumscribe, restrain, regulate.

restriction limitation, condition, stipulation, qualification, regulation, control, check, curb, confinement, demarcation. FREEDOM

result *n*, consequence, outcome, issue, effect, upshot, end, conclusion, sequel, aftermath, product, fruit, development, score. CAUSE
v, ensue, follow, eventuate, issue, proceed, arise, spring, happen, end, culminate. BEGIN

resume renew, recommence, restart, continue, proceed, carry on, go on. STOP

résumé summary, précis, abstract, synopsis, epitome, digest, compendium. AMPLIFICATION

resurrection resuscitation, revival, reappearance, comeback (*inf*), regeneration, rebirth, renaissance, resurgence, restoration, return. EXTINCTION

resuscitate revive, revivify, restore, bring round, reanimate, quicken, resurrect.

retain keep, hold, reserve, save, preserve, maintain, detain, hold back. RELINQUISH
remember, recall, recollect, memorize. FORGET
engage, employ, hire, pay.

retainer servant, domestic, attendant, valet, lackey, dependant.
fee, payment, deposit, advance.

retaliate return, repay, strike back, revenge, avenge, requite. FORGIVE

retard delay, slow down, hold back, detain, check, restrain, hinder, impede, hamper, handicap, arrest, halt. ACCELERATE

reticent reserved, taciturn, quiet, uncommunicative, tight-lipped, mum. GARRULOUS

retinue suite, train, entourage, attendants, escort, bodyguard.

retire withdraw, go away, leave, depart, retreat, recede, ebb, resign, go to bed.

retiring shy, reserved, diffident, bashful, timid, coy, modest, demure, meek, humble, unassuming, self-effacing. FORWARD

retort *v*, answer, reply, respond, riposte, rejoin.
n, answer, reply, response, riposte, rejoinder.

retract disavow, recant, withdraw, take back, unsay, deny, abjure, disclaim, repudiate, disown, revoke, cancel, recall, reverse, go back on, renege. CONFIRM
draw back, pull in, sheathe.

retreat *v*, retire, withdraw, depart, leave, fall back, recoil, turn tail, flee, recede, ebb. ADVANCE
n, retirement, withdrawal, departure, flight.
refuge, haven, asylum, sanctuary, shelter, privacy, seclusion.

retrench curtail, reduce, decrease, lessen, diminish, cut, shorten, abridge, abbreviate, crop, clip, trim, prune, limit, restrict, economize, cut back.

retribution punishment, just deserts, revenge, vengeance, retaliation, reprisal, requital, redress, satisfaction, recompense. PARDON

retrieve recover, regain, get back, recoup, recapture, salvage, rescue, save, redeem, restore, bring back, fetch. LOSE

retrocede recede, go back, retire, withdraw, retreat, retrograde, retrogress. ADVANCE

retrograde *adj*, backward, inverse, retreating, retrogressive, declining, waning, degenerate. FORWARD
v, recede, retrocede, retrogress, regress, revert, decline, deteriorate. ADVANCE

retrogress decline, deteriorate, worsen, degenerate, regress, revert, retrograde, recede, retrocede. PROGRESS

retrospect review, reminiscence, remembrance, recollection, hindsight, afterthought. SPECULATION

return *v*, go back, revert, retreat, come back, recur, reappear, recoil, rebound. DEPART
restore, replace, put back, give back, reinstate, re-establish. REMOVE
reciprocate, requite, refund, repay.
retort, rejoin, riposte, answer, reply, respond, come back.
n, reversion, retreat, recurrence, reappearance, recoil, rebound.
restoration, replacement, restitution, reinstatement, reciprocation, requital, reparation, recompense.
profit, gain, income, revenue, yield, interest, benefit, advantage. LOSS
retort, rejoinder, riposte, answer, reply, response, comeback (*inf*).

reveal disclose, divulge, expose, uncover, unfold, bare, unmask, unveil, show, exhibit, display, bring to light, make known, tell, impart, communicate, broadcast, betray, leak, give away. CONCEAL

revel *v*, wallow, bask, luxuriate, indulge, relish, savour, rejoice, delight.
carouse, make merry, celebrate, roister. MOURN
n, carousal, spree, debauch, orgy, party, celebration, gala, festival, carnival, revelry, festivity.

revelation disclosure, exposure, exposition, manifestation, unmasking, discovery, broadcast, publication, announcement, proclamation, betrayal, leak. CONCEALMENT

revelry merriment, jollification, merrymaking, carousal, revel, debauch, orgy, saturnalia. MOURNING

revenge *n*, vengeance, retribution, reprisal, retaliation, requital, satisfaction. FORGIVENESS
v, avenge, requite, retaliate, return, repay. FORGIVE

revengeful vengeful, vindictive, malevolent, spiteful, malicious, malignant, bitter, resentful, unforgiving, merciless, pitiless, implacable, cruel, harsh. MERCIFUL

revenue income, receipts, return, yield, profit, gain, proceeds, takings. EXPENDITURE

reverberate echo, re-echo, resound, resonate, ring, rebound, recoil.

revere reverence, venerate, worship, adore, admire, respect, think highly of, look up to. DESPISE

reverence veneration, worship, honour, adoration, devotion, homage, respect, deference, awe. CONTEMPT

reverent reverential, solemn, respectful, deferential, humble, submissive. DISRESPECTFUL

reverie dream, fantasy, daydream, trance, abstraction, woolgathering, daydreaming, preoccupation, brown study. ATTENTION

reverse *v*, invert, transpose, turn round, upend, upset, overturn. RIGHT
change, alter, negate, invalidate, cancel, quash, overrule, countermand, revoke, annul, rescind, repeal, undo, overthrow.
retreat, backtrack, back up, go backwards. ADVANCE
n, opposite, contrary, converse, antithesis.
back, rear, other side.
setback, reversal, check, defeat, misfortune, mishap, misadventure, mischance, adversity, hardship, trial, affliction. SUCCESS
adj, opposite, contrary, converse, inverse, backward, upside-down.

revert return, go back, relapse, backslide, regress, recur, come back.

review *v*, reconsider, re-examine, reassess, recall, recollect, remember, look back on.
inspect, examine, survey, study, revise, edit, assess, evaluate, criticize, discuss.
n, notice, criticism, critique, commentary, assessment, evaluation.
magazine, periodical, journal, newspaper.
inspection, examination, survey, report, re-examination, reconsideration, revision, study, analysis.
parade, procession, display, inspection.

revile abuse, vituperate, upbraid, reproach, vilify, asperse, traduce, malign, denigrate, defame, slander, calumniate. EXTOL

revise change, alter, amend, correct, review, reconsider, rework, rewrite, edit, update.
study, swot (*inf*), reread, go over, learn, memorize.

revive renew, restore, refresh, resuscitate, revivify, reanimate, reinvigorate, revitalize, rejuvenate, regenerate, rekindle, cheer, hearten, animate, invigorate, quicken, rouse, awaken, rally, recover.

revoke retract, withdraw, recant, take back, disavow, repudiate, rescind, renege, repeal, abrogate, annul, nullify, abolish, cancel, quash, reverse, countermand. CONFIRM

revolt *n*, rebellion, rising, uprising, insurrection, insurgence, mutiny, revolution. LOYALTY
v, rebel, rise up, mutiny. SUBMIT
disgust, repel, nauseate, sicken, offend, appal. ATTRACT

revolting repulsive, repellent, repugnant, offensive, obnoxious, disgusting, nauseating, sickening, foul, horrid, loathsome, abominable, shocking, appalling, nasty, horrible, hideous, obscene. ATTRACTIVE

revolution revolt, rebellion, rising, uprising, insurrection, insurgence, mutiny, sedition, putsch, coup de'état.
change, alteration, transformation, metamorphosis, innovation, upheaval. CONSERVATISM
rotation, turn, whirl, spin, circle, cycle, round, lap.

revolve rotate, turn, wheel, whirl, spin, gyrate, circle, orbit.

revulsion repugnance, repulsion, disgust, nausea, loathing, abomination, abhorrence, detestation, aversion, distaste, shrinking, recoil. ATTRACTION

reward *n*, payment, recompense, return, requital, compensation, remuneration, pay, prize, award, honour, premium, bonus, tip, gratuity. PUNISHMENT
punishment, retribution, just deserts, comeuppance (*inf*).
v, pay, recompense, repay, requite, compensate, remunerate. PUNISH

rhetorical oratorical, declamatory, eloquent, silver-tongued, flowery, florid, ornate, flamboyant, bombastic, orotund, pretentious, pompous, magniloquent, grandiloquent. SIMPLE

rhyme poetry, verse, poem, ode, limerick, jingle.

rhythm beat, pulse, tempo, cadence, measure, metre, accent, lilt, swing.

ribald bawdy, risqué, racy, naughty, smutty, dirty, rude, vulgar, obscene, indecent, lewd, licentious, gross, coarse. PURE

rich wealthy, affluent, opulent, moneyed, prosperous, well-off, flush (*inf*), loaded (*inf*). POOR
fertile, fecund, fruitful, productive, prolific, ample, abundant, plentiful, plenteous, copious, replete, full, well-stocked, abounding, profuse, exuberant. BARREN
valuable, precious, expensive, costly, dear, sumptuous, luxurious, splendid, gorgeous, fine, exquisite. CHEAP
juicy, succulent, luscious, delicious, spicy, piquant, creamy, heavy. TASTELESS
bright, vivid, intense, deep, sonorous, resonant, mellifluous, dulcet. SOFT

riches wealth, affluence, opulence, money, fortune, treasure, assets, funds, means, resources. POVERTY

rickety shaky, unstable, unsteady, tottering, infirm, frail, feeble, weak, decrepit, ramshackle, dilapidated, broken-down. STURDY

rid clear, free, relieve, disencumber, deliver, release.

get rid of, discard, throw away, dispose of, eject, eliminate, dispense with. RETAIN

riddle puzzle, conundrum, enigma, mystery, problem, poser, brain-teaser (*inf*). SOLUTION

ride *v*, travel, journey, move, go, sit on, control, handle, manage, propel.

n, journey, trip, excursion, jaunt, outing, drive, spin (*inf*), lift. WALK

ridge ledge, crest, summit, peak, chain, range, fold, corrugation, spine, chine.

ridicule *n*, mockery, derision, scorn, satire, sarcasm, irony, raillery, banter, taunt, jeer. RESPECT

v, mock, deride, burlesque, lampoon, parody, caricature, satirize, laugh at, make fun of, scoff, taunt, jeer. ADMIRE

ridiculous absurd, ludicrous, laughable, risible, comical, farcical, preposterous, outrageous, fantastic, unbelievable, nonsensical, foolish, contemptible, derisory. SERIOUS

rife prevalent, prevailing, current, rampant, widespread, general, universal, plentiful, abundant. RARE

rifle ransack, loot, sack, strip, rob, steal, plunder, pillage.

rift split, cleft, fissure, crevice, chink, crack, breach, gap, opening, space.

difference, disagreement, quarrel, schism, separation, division, alienation, estrangement. RECONCILIATION

rig *v*, equip, supply, furnish, fit, outfit, kit out, accoutre, deck, array, clothe, dress, rig out, turn out.

manipulate, falsify, fake, trump up, doctor, tamper with, fix, engineer, manoeuvre.

n, gear, equipment, outfit, accoutrements, apparatus, tackle, rigging, kit.

right *adj*, just, fair, equitable, lawful, good, virtuous, righteous, upright, moral, ethical, honourable, honest. WRONG

true, factual, actual, real, correct, accurate, precise, exact. INCORRECT

proper, seemly, becoming, fit, fitting, apt, appropriate, suitable, advantageous, convenient, opportune, desirable, favourable. INAPPROPRIATE

healthy, well, sound, normal, sane.

adv, properly, suitable, justly, fairly, well, correctly, accurately, precisely, exactly, straight, directly, immediately, promptly.

n, claim, title, privilege, prerogative, authority, power, due.

justice, fairness, equity, legality, lawfulness, goodness, virtue, rectitude, uprightness, honesty, truth, integrity, honour, morality, propriety. WRONG

v, straighten, adjust, rectify, correct, redress, fix, put right.

righteous good, virtuous, moral, upright, honest, honourable, holy, saintly, pure, innocent, just, fair, equitable. WICKED

rightful legal, lawful, licit, legitimate, proper, right, true, real, genuine, valid, just, fair. WRONGFUL

rigid stiff, inflexible, unbending, unyielding, unswerving, fixed, set, firm, strict, stern, severe, harsh, austere, tough, rigorous, stringent, exact, precise. FLEXIBLE

rigorous strict, stern, severe, harsh, austere, tough, stringent, firm, rigid, inflexible, demanding, exacting, meticulous, painstaking, conscientious, thorough, scrupulous, punctilious, exact, precise. LAX

rigour strictness, sternness, severity, harshness, austerity, hardship, privation, suffering, accuracy, precision, exactitude, meticulousness, conscientiousness, scrupulousness. LAXITY

rile annoy, irritate, vex, irk, nettle, exasperate, anger, incense. PACIFY

rim edge, border, lip, brim, brink, verge, margin. CENTRE

rind skin, peel, husk, shell, crust.

ring[1] *n*, band, circle, round, loop, hoop.

gang, mob, syndicate, combine, cartel, trust, clique, coterie, league, association.

v, encircle, surround, gird, girdle, circle, encompass, enclose.

ring[2] *v*, resound, resonate, reverberate, peal, chime, toll, tinkle, clang.

phone, telephone, call, summon.

rinse wash, clean, bathe, dip, flush, wet. DRY

riot *n*, uproar, commotion, tumult, turbulence, disturbance, rumpus, brawl, fray,

fracas, anarchy, lawlessness, disorder, confusion. ORDER
revelry, carousal, merrymaking, jollification, boisterousness, high jinks. SOBRIETY
display, show, splash, flourish.
v, rampage, run riot, fight, brawl, rebel, revolt.
revel, carouse, make merry, roister.

rip tear, rend, split, burst, lacerate, slash. MEND

ripe mature, seasoned, mellow, fully developed, fully grown, advanced, ready, prepared, set, fit, full, perfect, finished, complete. UNRIPE

ripple *v*, wave, undulate, lap, splash, babble, gurgle, ruffle, wrinkle.
n, wave, undulation, splash, gurgle.

rise *v*, arise, get up, stand up.
ascend, mount, climb, soar, go up, increase, grow, swell, intensify. FALL
advance, progress, improve, prosper, thrive, get on.
appear, emerge, spring, flow, stem, originate, occur, happen, eventuate.
rebel, revolt, mutiny, resist. SUBMIT
n, ascent, climb, slope, incline, elevation, increase, growth, advance, progress, improvement, upturn, upsurge, rising, uprising. FALL
appearance, emergence, origin, source, beginning, commencement.

risible ridiculous, ludicrous, absurd, laughable, farcical, comical, funny, amusing, humorous, droll. SERIOUS

risk *n*, hazard, peril, danger, jeopardy, chance, uncertainty, gamble, speculation. SAFETY
v, chance, venture, dare, gamble, hazard, imperil, endanger, jeopardize.

risky hazardous, perilous, dangerous, unsafe, precarious, dicey (*inf*). SAFE

ritual *n*, rite, ceremony, ceremonial, service, sacrament, observance, custom, practice, form, convention, usage, formality, habit, routine.
adj, ceremonial, ceremonious, formal, customary, conventional, routine.

rival *n*, competitor, opponent, antagonist, adversary, contender, contestant, challenger, emulator. ALLY
adj, competitive, competing, emulous, opposing, conflicting.
v, compete, vie, contend, oppose, challenge, emulate, equal, match.

road thoroughfare, street, highway, motorway, avenue, lane, route, path, way, course.

roam rove, range, wander, stray, drift, meander, ramble, stroll, saunter, prowl.

roar bellow, yell, shout, cry, howl, growl, rumble, thunder, guffaw. MURMUR

rob burgle, hold up, mug (*inf*), plunder, pillage, raid, rifle, ransack, strip, fleece, swindle, defraud, deprive. ENDOW

robber burglar, thief, bandit, brigand, pirate, highwayman, plunderer, marauder, raider, swindler.

robbery burglary, hold-up, theft, larceny, embezzlement, piracy, plunder, pillage, rapine, spoliation, swindle, fraud, rip-off (*inf*).

robe *n*, gown, vestment, habit, dress.
v, clothe, dress, garb, attire, drape, invest. STRIP

robust strong, hardy, hale, hearty, vigorous, lusty, sound, firm, stout, sturdy, powerful, stalwart, rugged, sinewy, muscular, brawny, strapping, athletic, boisterous, rough. DELICATE

rock[1] *n*, stone, boulder, crag, reef.
foundation, cornerstone, anchor, mainstay, support, protection.

rock[2] *v*, sway, reel, roll, pitch, swing, wobble, totter, stagger.

rod stick, wand, baton, staff, cane, switch, birch, bar, shaft, pole, dowel.

rogue rascal, scoundrel, scamp, blackguard, knave, villain, reprobate, charlatan, fraud, swindler, cheat, con man (*inf*), crook (*inf*). GENTLEMAN

roguish rascally, knavish, villainous, unscrupulous, unprincipled, dishonest, deceitful, crooked. HONEST
mischievous, impish, puckish, waggish, arch, sportive, playful, frolicsome.

roister revel, carouse, make merry, paint the town red (*inf*). MOURN
bluster, swagger, boast, brag.

role part, character, portrayal, impersonation.
function, purpose, use, job, task, position, capacity.

roll *v*, revolve, rotate, turn, whirl, twirl, spin, gyrate, wheel, swing, rock, sway, reel, pitch, toss, lurch, wallow.
flow, run, go, move, pass, elapse, undulate, trundle.

wrap, enfold, envelop, swathe, wind, twist, curl, coil, furl, entwine.
flatten, level, smooth, press.
rumble, thunder, roar, boom, resound, reverberate.
n, revolution, rotation, turn, twirl, spin, gyration, twist, coil, curl, undulation, wave.
cylinder, roller, reel, spool, bobbin, ball, scroll.
register, roster, list, inventory, catalogue, schedule, record, chronicle, index, directory.
rumble, thunder, roar, boom, resonance, reverberation.
bun, bread, cake, pastry.

rollicking boisterous, spirited, hearty, lively, playful, frisky, sportive, frolicsome, jolly, merry, gay, carefree. STAID

romance love, passion, affair, liaison, intrigue, amour.
story, tale, novel, fiction, love story, fairy tale, legend, fantasy, invention, fabrication, exaggeration, falsehood, lie. FACT

romantic sentimental, tender, loving, fond, passionate, amorous. COLD
unrealistic, idealistic, visionary, quixotic, fanciful, fantastic, imaginary, fictitious, wild, extravagant, impractical. REALISTIC

romp frolic, caper, frisk, gambol, sport, rollick, revel, carouse, make merry.

roof cover, top, ceiling, canopy, shelter. FLOOR

rook swindle, defraud, cheat, mulct, diddle (*inf*), rip off (*inf*).

room chamber, apartment.
space, expanse, extent, scope, range, compass, latitude, leeway, margin, play, capacity. RESTRICTION

roomy spacious, capacious, commodious, ample, large, broad, wide, extensive. NARROW

root[1] *n*, radix, radicle, rhizome, tuber.
base, foundation, source, origin, derivation, cause, motive, ground, bottom, germ, seed, crux, essence.
v, fix, plant, implant, embed, establish, set. UPROOT

root[2] *v*, dig, delve, burrow, rummage, ferret, hunt, search, poke, pry, nose.

rooted fixed, set, firm, rigid, ingrained, deep-seated, inveterate, confirmed, radical, fundamental. SUPERFICIAL

rope *n*, cable, cord, line, string.
v, tie, bind, fasten, secure, moor, tether. LOOSE

roster rota, list, roll, register, catalogue, table, schedule, agenda.

rostrum platform, dais, stage, stand, pulpit, lectern.

rosy pink, roseate, red, reddish, rubicund, ruddy, blushing, flushed, blooming, glowing. PALE
optimistic, hopeful, bright, cheerful, encouraging, promising, auspicious, favourable. HOPELESS

rot *v*, decay, decompose, putrefy, go bad, spoil, moulder, crumble, disintegrate, perish, corrode, corrupt, taint. PRESERVE
n, decay, decomposition, putrefaction, mould, mildew, blight.
nonsense, rubbish, twaddle, balderdash. SENSE

rotate revolve, turn, twirl, whirl, spin, wheel, pivot, swivel, gyrate, reel.
alternate, take turns, interchange, switch.

rotation revolution, turn, spin, gyration, cycle, alternation, sequence, succession.

rotten rotting, decayed, decaying, decomposed, decomposing, putrid, putrescent, bad, mouldy, rancid, rank, fetid, foul, tainted, spoiled. FRESH
despicable, contemptible, mean, low, base, vile, nasty, unpleasant, wicked, immoral, corrupt, degenerate.

rotund round, rounded, spherical, bulbous, globular. ANGULAR
plump, corpulent, portly, stout, podgy, tubby, fat, obese. SLIM
full, rich, sonorous, resonant, orotund, magniloquent.

rough uneven, irregular, bumpy, rugged, jagged, coarse, unkempt, bristly, unshaven, shaggy, hairy, bushy. SMOOTH
stormy, tempestuous, choppy, agitated, turbulent, wild, violent, boisterous. CALM
rude, impolite, discourteous, uncivil, unmannerly, churlish, uncouth, coarse, vulgar, unrefined, uncultured. REFINED
hard, harsh, sharp, severe, cruel, brutal, drastic, extreme, tough, austere. GENTLE
crude, unfinished, incomplete, shapeless, preliminary, rudimentary, cursory, sketchy, vague, approximate. FINISHED

round *adj*, circular, annular, curved, rounded, rotund, spherical, globular, cylindrical. ANGULAR

complete, entire, whole, full, ample.
candid, frank, blunt, plain, direct, straightforward. EVASIVE
rough, approximate. EXACT
n, circle, disc, ring, band, sphere, ball, orb, globe.
cycle, series, succession, sequence, bout, period, session, turn.
circuit, lap, compass, ambit, beat, course, route, routine, tour.
prep, around, about, surrounding, encircling.
adv, around, near, nearby, throughout.
v, curve, bow, turn, circle, encircle, surround.
round off, complete, finish, conclude, close, crown, cap. BEGIN
round up, gather, collect, assemble, marshal, muster, herd. DISPERSE
roundabout tortuous, circuitous, indirect, circumlocutory, periphrastic, longwinded. DIRECT
rouse wake, awaken, rise, get up, arouse, call, stimulate, whet, animate, stir, move, provoke, incite, foment, excite, agitate, enkindle, inflame, startle, disturb. SOOTHE
rout *n*, defeat, beating, overthrow, debacle, flight, retreat. VICTORY
v, defeat, vanquish, conquer, beat, overthrow, overpower, crush, thrash, disperse, scatter.
route way, road, path, course, itinerary, circuit, round, beat.
routine *n*, system, method, pattern, order, convention, custom, practice, habit, wont, procedure, course, way.
adj, customary, habitual, regular, usual, ordinary, everyday, humdrum, boring. UNUSUAL
rove wander, roam, range, stray, drift, meander, ramble, stroll, gallivant, travel. SETTLE
rover wanderer, roamer, drifter, rambler, nomad, gypsy, itinerant, vagrant, gadabout (*inf*), traveller.
row[1] *n*, line, rank, tier, file, column, queue, string, series, sequence, succession.
row[2] *n*, quarrel, dispute, argument, tiff, fight, brawl. HARMONY
noise, din, disturbance, commotion, fuss, tumult, turmoil, uproar. QUIET
v, quarrel, argue, squabble, wrangle, fight, brawl. AGREE
rowdy noisy, loud, boisterous, rough, unruly, disorderly. QUIET
royal regal, kingly, queenly, princely, imperial, sovereign, majestic, august, noble, stately, grand, magnificent. LOWLY
rub *v*, chafe, abrade, scour, scrape, grate, polish, smooth, wipe, clean, brush, graze, stroke, caress, knead, massage, apply, smear.
rub out, erase, efface, wipe out, obliterate, expunge, delete, cancel.
n, friction, polish, wipe, stroke, caress, massage.
difficulty, problem, obstacle, impediment, hindrance, hitch, snag.
rubbish waste, refuse, garbage, litter, trash, junk, debris, dross.
nonsense, rot, twaddle, balderdash, humbug, bunkum, codswallop (*inf*), bosh (*inf*), drivel, claptrap. SENSE
rubicund red, reddish, ruddy, florid, rosy, roseate, flushed, blushing. PALE
ruddy red, reddish, rubicund, florid, glowing, blooming, flushed, blushing, pink, rosy, roseate, sanguine. PALE
rude impolite, discourteous, uncivil, unmannerly, disrespectful, insolent, impudent, impertinent, cheeky, saucy, curt, abrupt, brusque, sharp, insulting, abusive, offensive, obscene, indecent. POLITE
coarse, vulgar, boorish, barbarous, uncouth, unrefined, uncultured, unpolished, uncivilized, untutored, uneducated, ignorant, rough, crude. REFINED
rudimentary rudimental, basic, fundamental, elementary, primary, initial, undeveloped, embryonic. ADVANCED
rudiments basics, fundamentals, essentials, principles, elements, foundation, beginning, commencement.
rue regret, repent, lament, deplore, bewail, bemoan, mourn, grieve, sorrow.
ruffian thug, tough, hooligan, rowdy, bully, brute, villain, scoundrel, rogue, rascal, wretch. GENTLEMAN
ruffle rumple, derange, disarrange, disorder, mess up, tousle, dishevel, crease, wrinkle. SMOOTH
agitate, disturb, upset, rattle (*inf*), unsettle, disconcert, fluster, perturb, annoy, irritate, vex, nettle, trouble. COMPOSE
rug carpet, mat, blanket.
rugged rough, uneven, irregular, bumpy, rocky, craggy, jagged, ragged, lined, wrin-

kled, gnarled, leathery, weather-beaten. SMOOTH
harsh, severe, stern, austere, difficult, hard, tough, strong, hardy, robust, rude, uncouth, churlish, blunt.
ruin *v*, destroy, devastate, desolate, lay waste, demolish, raze, wreck, shatter, break, smash, crush, defeat, overthrow, overturn. RESTORE
bankrupt, impoverish, pauperize.
spoil, mar, damage, mess up, botch. FIX
n, destruction, devastation, desolation, havoc, ruination, wreck, disrepair, dilapidation, decay, deterioration, disintegration, defeat, overthrow. RESTORATION
fall, downfall, collapse, failure, undoing, bankruptcy, insolvency, impoverishment, destitution. PROSPERITY
ruinous destructive, devastating, disastrous, calamitous, catastrophic, pernicious, deleterious, baneful, mischievous, injurious, baleful, noxious. BENEFICIAL
rule *n*, regulation, statute, ordinance, law, principle, precept, tenet, maxim, order, directive, direction, guide, guideline, standard, criterion, canon. EXCEPTION
government, direction, reign, regime, dominion, domination, control, command, authority, sway, mastery, supremacy.
habit, routine, wont, custom, practice.
as a rule, generally, usually, ordinarily, normally, mainly, on the whole. RARELY
v, reign, govern, direct, manage, administer, lead, command, control, regulate. SUBMIT
prevail, predominate, preponderate, thrive.
decree, judge, decide, settle.
ruler monarch, sovereign, king, queen, emperor, empress, potentate, lord, chief, leader, commander, governor. SUBJECT
measure, rule.
ruling *adj*, reigning, governing, controlling, chief, principal, main, dominant, predominant, prevailing, prevalent, current. SUBORDINATE
n, decree, judgment, decision, finding, verdict.
rumble thunder, roll, roar, growl, resound, reverberate.
ruminate meditate, cogitate, muse, ponder, think, reflect, consider, brood, mull over.
rummage search, hunt, ransack, explore, root, forage.
rumour *n*, gossip, hearsay, talk, word, report, story, information, news, tidings. TRUTH
v, circulate, publish, tell, report, gossip.
rumple ruffle, tousle, dishevel, wrinkle, crease, crumple, pucker. SMOOTH
rumpus commotion, uproar, disturbance, noise, row, brouhaha, tumult. PEACE
run *v*, sprint, race, dash, dart, tear, bolt, career, hare (*inf*), speed, hasten, hurry, rush, scamper, gallop, lope, jog. SAUNTER
go, proceed, move, pass, roll, glide, work, function, operate, perform. STOP
flow, stream, spill, pour, gush, leak, melt, dissolve.
spread, stretch, extend, reach, continue, last.
manage, direct, govern, control, command, lead, head, supervise.
drive, propel, convey, transport, ship, smuggle.
compete, contend, challenge, stand.
run away, run off, flee, abscond, escape, take flight, decamp, elope. RETURN
run down, hit, strike, knock down, run over.
reduce, decrease, decline, weaken, debilitate, tire, weary, exhaust.
criticize, knock (*inf*), disparage, belittle, denigrate, defame, vilify. PRAISE
find, locate, discover, track, hunt, catch, capture, seize.
run out, finish, terminate, end, expire, exhaust, consume, use up.
n, sprint, race, dash, rush, gallop, jog. WALK
trip, journey, excursion, outing, jaunt, ride, drive, spin (*inf*).
series, sequence, succession, string, chain, stream, course, spell, period.
rupture *v*, break, burst, crack, split, fracture, tear, cleave, separate, divide. MEND
n, break, burst, crack, split, breach, rift, cleft, tear.
quarrel, altercation, dispute, disagreement, feud, schism, division, hostility, estrangement. RECONCILIATION
rural country, rustic, bucolic, pastoral, agricultural, agrarian. URBAN
ruse wile, trick, artifice, stratagem, contrivance, device, subterfuge, deceit, deception, manoeuvre, ploy.
rush *v*, hurry, hasten, race, run, dash, speed, press, hustle, accelerate, quicken, dispatch, expedite. DAWDLE
charge, attack, assault, storm.

n, hurry, haste, run, dash, scramble, stampede, speed, quickness, dispatch, expedition.
charge, attack, assault, onslaught.

rust *n*, corrosion, oxidation, mould, mildew, blight.
v, corrode, oxidize, deteriorate, decline.

rustic *adj*, rural, country, countrified, provincial, pastoral, bucolic, sylvan, Arcadian. URBAN
simple, plain, homely, unsophisticated, artless, coarse, rough, uncouth, churlish, awkward, loutish. SOPHISTICATED
n, peasant, countryman, bumpkin, yokel.

rustle *v*, whisper, swish, susurrate, crinkle, crackle, crepitate.
n, rustling, whisper, susurration, crackle, crepitation.

rut groove, furrow, track, groove, hollow, indentation.
routine, habit, pattern, system.

ruthless pitiless, unpitying, merciless, unmerciful, hard, harsh, severe, cruel, brutal, savage, heartless, unfeeling, callous, hard-hearted, relentless, unrelenting, implacable, inexorable. COMPASSIONATE

S

sable black, jet, raven, ebony, dark, dusky, sombre. WHITE

sabotage *n*, destruction, damage, subversion, treachery, treason.
v, destroy, damage, disable, wreck, undermine, subvert.

sack[1] *n*, bag, pouch.
dismissal, discharge, boot (*inf*).
v, dismiss, discharge, fire (*inf*). APPOINT

sack[2] *v*, plunder, pillage, despoil, ravage, maraud, ransack, loot, rifle, devastate, lay waste.
n, plunder, pillage, despoliation, rape, rapine, looting, devastation.

sacred holy, consecrated, hallowed, sanctified, blessed, divine, venerable, sacrosanct, inviolable, untouchable. PROFANE

sacrifice *n*, offering, oblation, immolation, slaughter, surrender, renunciation, loss, destruction. GAIN
v, offer, immolate, surrender, give up, forgo, let go, lose, destroy.

sacrilege desecration, profanation, violation, profanity, blasphemy, impiety, irreverence, disrespect, mockery. REVERENCE

sad unhappy, sorrowful, downcast, dejected, depressed, despondent, low, blue, melancholy, glum, gloomy, mournful, miserable, woebegone, heartbroken, disconsolate. HAPPY
distressing, depressing, heartbreaking, tragic, regrettable, grievous, lamentable, deplorable, unfortunate, sorry, pitiful, poignant, pathetic, wretched, cheerless, dismal, sombre, grave. JOYFUL

sadden upset, distress, grieve, deject, depress, dispirit, dishearten. CHEER

saddle burden, encumber, load, charge, tax, lumber (*inf*). RELIEVE

safe secure, protected, guarded, invulnerable, impregnable, sound, intact, unhurt, unharmed, undamaged, unscathed. EXPOSED
sure, certain, dependable, reliable, trustworthy, cautious, circumspect, conservative. RISKY
harmless, innocuous, tame, nonpoisonous. DANGEROUS

safeguard *v*, protect, guard, defend, shield, look after, watch over. IMPERIL
n, protection, guard, defence, shield, security, precaution, escort, convoy, bodyguard.

sag droop, dip, sink, drop, fall, slump, flag, weaken, decline. RISE

sagacious wise, sage, judicious, shrewd, astute, sharp, acute, discerning, penetrating, percipient, perspicacious, clever, intelligent, apt, quick-witted, far-sighted, knowing. STUPID

sage *n*, philosopher, savant, wise man, guru, master, expert, authority. FOOL
adj, wise, sagacious, sapient, judicious, sensible, learned. FOOLISH

sail *v*, embark, set sail, travel, journey, boat, yacht, cruise, drift, float, glide, pilot, steer, captain, navigate.
n, cruise, trip, journey, voyage, crossing.

sailor mariner, seaman, seafarer, bluejacket, salt, tar (*inf*), matelot (*inf*).

saintly godly, holy, pious, devout, reverent, religious, spiritual, righteous, virtuous, angelic, blessed. GODLESS

sake account, interest, behalf, welfare, benefit, good, regard, respect, consideration.
purpose, end, reason, motive, end, cause.

salacious lecherous, lascivious, licentious, lewd, lustful, libidinous, concupiscent, prurient, bawdy, ribald, smutty, dirty, obscene, pornographic. PURE

salary pay, wage, remuneration, earnings, emolument, stipend.

sale selling, vendition, trade, traffic, auction, market, demand, outlet, deal, transaction, bargain, reduction, discount, clearance. PURCHASE

salient prominent, striking, conspicuous, outstanding, noticeable, remarkable, marked, pronounced, projecting, jutting, protruding. INCONSPICUOUS

sallow yellow, yellowish, pale, pallid, wan, anaemic, pasty. RUDDY

sally *n*, sortie, charge, foray, offensive, raid, onslaught, rush, outburst.
excursion, trip, jaunt, outing.
retort, riposte, repartee, joke, jest, quip, crack (*inf*), witticism, bon mot.
v, rush, surge, charge, storm, issue, erupt.

salt *n*, flavour, savour, taste, relish, seasoning, spice, pungency, piquancy, bite, punch, zest, liveliness, wit.
sailor, seaman, seafarer, mariner.
adj, salty, saline, salted, briny, brackish. SWEET
v, preserve, cure, season, flavour.

salubrious wholesome, healthy, healthful, salutary. UNHEALTHY

salutary beneficial, advantageous, useful, helpful, valuable, profitable, good, wholesome, salubrious. HARMFUL

salute *v*, greet, hail, address, accost, welcome, receive, acknowledge, recognize, honour. IGNORE
n, greeting, salutation, address, welcome, homage, tribute.

salvage save, rescue, redeem, reclaim, recover, retrieve, restore. DESTROY

salvation saving, rescue, deliverance, redemption, restoration, preservation. DESTRUCTION

salve *n*, balm, lotion, cream, ointment, liniment, embrocation.
remedy, cure, antidote.
v, remedy, heal, soothe, alleviate, mitigate, palliate, ease, comfort. AGGRAVATE

salvo fusillade, broadside, volley, outburst.

same identical, selfsame, twin, duplicate, corresponding, equivalent, similar, like, alike, changeless, unvarying, consistent. DIFFERENT

all the same, . nonetheless, nevertheless, anyway, still, yet.
immaterial, unimportant, of no consequence.

sample *n*, specimen, example, instance, illustration, model, pattern, cross section, sampling.
v, try, test, inspect, taste.

sanctify hallow, consecrate, bless, anoint, purify, cleanse. PROFANE

sanctimonious self-righteous, self-satisfied, smug, holier-than-thou, goody-goody (*inf*), pharisaical, pietistic, hypocritical, unctuous.

sanction *n*, permission, consent, allowance, authorization, warrant, approval, endorsement, support, ratification. PROHIBITION
ban, embargo, boycott, penalty.
v, permit, allow, authorize, warrant, approve, countenance, endorse, support, ratify. PROHIBIT

sanctity holiness, saintliness, godliness, sanctitude, sacredness, inviolability, piety, righteousness, goodness, purity. PROFANITY

sanctuary shrine, sanctum, church, temple.
refuge, asylum, haven, retreat, shelter, reserve.

sane rational, normal, *compos mentis*, lucid, sound, sober, sensible, intelligent, reasonable, judicious. INSANE

sang-froid composure, calmness, coolness, self-possession, poise, aplomb, imperturbability. AGITATION

sanguinary bloody, gory, bloodthirsty, murderous, brutal, cruel, savage, ruthless.

sanguine hopeful, optimistic, assured, confident, cheerful, buoyant, lively, spirited, animated. PESSIMISTIC
ruddy, rubicund, reddish, red, florid. PALE

sanitary hygienic, clean, germ-free, salubrious, healthy, wholesome. INSANITARY

sanity saneness, reason, sense, normality, rationality, lucidity, wisdom, sagacity, judiciousness, common sense. INSANITY

sap¹ *n*, juice, lifeblood.
fool, dupe, idiot, simpleton, jerk (*inf*), sucker (*inf*).

sap² *v*, undermine, weaken, deplete, drain, enervate, exhaust. STRENGTHEN

sapient wise, sagacious, sage, discerning, perspicacious, discriminating, judicious, knowing, intelligent, clever, shrewd, astute, sharp, keen, acute. STUPID

sarcasm irony, satire, cynicism, ridicule, mockery, scorn, derision, contempt.

sarcastic ironical, sardonic, satirical, cynical, mocking, scornful, derisive, contemptuous, sneering, taunting, mordant, caustic, cutting, trenchant, bitter, acrimonious.

sardonic sarcastic, ironical, cynical, scornful, mocking, derisive, contemptuous, bitter, malicious, malignant, malevolent. PLEASANT

satanic devilish, diabolic, fiendish, demonic, demoniacal, hellish, infernal, wicked, evil, malevolent, black. ANGELIC

sate satisfy, fill, slake, satiate, surfeit, cloy, glut, overfill, stuff, gorge. STARVE

satellite moon, sputnik.
follower, disciple, minion, subordinate, attendant, dependant, retainer, vassal, parasite, hanger-on, sycophant. LEADER

satiate surfeit, cloy, glut, overfill, stuff, gorge, sate, satisfy, fill, slake. STARVE

satire irony, ridicule, sarcasm, lampoon, burlesque, parody, caricature, travesty, skit, spoof (*inf*), send-up (*inf*), take-off (*inf*).

satirical ironical, sarcastic, sardonic, burlesque, trenchant, biting, cutting, mordant, caustic, incisive, mocking, derisive.

satirize mock, deride, ridicule, lampoon, burlesque, parody, send up (*inf*), take off (*inf*), attack.

satisfaction gratification, fulfilment, contentment, content, pleasure, happiness, enjoyment, comfort, ease. DISSATISFACTION
reparation, compensation, indemnification, recompense, amends, atonement, redress, settlement, payment. INJURY

satisfactory adequate, sufficient, suitable, passable, acceptable, all right, fair, good. UNSATISFACTORY

satisfy gratify, indulge, content, please, appease, pacify, fill, sate, satiate. DISSATISFY
meet, fulfil, discharge, settle, answer, match, suffice, serve.
convince, persuade, assure, reassure.
atone, requite, compensate, recompense.

saturate soak, drench, waterlog, steep, sate, satiate, imbue, pervade, infuse, impregnate. DRAIN

saturnine gloomy, morose, dismal, glum, sombre, grave, phlegmatic, dour, taciturn, uncommunicative. JOVIAL

sauce condiment, relish, dressing, ketchup, seasoning.
impertinence, impudence, insolence, rudeness, cheek (*inf*), brass (*inf*), nerve (*inf*), lip (*inf*). RESPECT

saucy impertinent, pert, impudent, insolent, rude, disrespectful, bold, presumptuous, forward, fresh (*inf*), cheeky (*inf*), flippant. RESPECTFUL

saunter stroll, amble, ramble, wander, loiter, dawdle, dally, linger. HASTEN

savage *adj*, fierce, ferocious, vicious, cruel, brutal, brutish, inhuman, barbaric, barbarous, murderous, bloodthirsty, sadistic, diabolical, merciless, pitiless, ruthless, relentless, harsh. GENTLE
wild, untamed, undomesticated, feral, uncivilized, barbarian, primitive, rough, rude. CIVILIZED
n, barbarian, primitive, native, aborigine, beast, brute, boor, yahoo.

savant sage, philosopher, scholar, intellectual, master, expert, authority. FOOL

save rescue, free, liberate, deliver, redeem, salvage. ABANDON
keep, reserve, hoard, store, husband, economize, set aside, put by. SQUANDER
preserve, conserve, protect, guard, safeguard, shield. EXPOSE
spare, prevent, obviate, preclude, rule out.

saviour redeemer, deliverer, liberator, rescuer, protector, defender, guardian.

savour *n*, flavour, taste, relish, tang, piquancy, smack, smell, odour, scent, aroma, bouquet.
v, relish, enjoy, appreciate, revel, bask, wallow, luxuriate.

savoury tasty, delicious, delectable, appetizing, luscious, ambrosial, palatable, toothsome, piquant, pungent, spicy, tangy. INSIPID

saw[1] *n*, saying, adage, dictum, proverb, axiom, maxim, aphorism, apophthegm.

saw[2] *v*, cut, divide, sever, cleave, hack.

say *v*, utter, speak, pronounce, articulate, voice, answer, reply, remark, mention, state, declare, affirm, assert, tell, reveal, disclose, recite, deliver. SUPPRESS

allege, claim, report, rumour.
assume, suppose, conjecture, speculate, estimate.
n, utterance, expression, statement, declaration, assertion, speech.
turn, chance, vote, influence, weight.

saying saw, adage, dictum, proverb, axiom, maxim, aphorism, apophthegm.

scaffold scaffolding, frame, framework, platform, stage, gallows, gibbet.

scale[1] *n*, flake, squama, plate, layer, lamina.

scale[2] *n*, gradation, graduation, series, sequence, progression, hierarchy, ladder, spectrum, gamut, range, scope, extent, degree.
ration, proportion, measure.
v, climb, mount, ascend, escalade. DESCEND

scamp scallywag, rascal, rogue, scapegrace, imp, devil, knave, blackguard, villain, wretch.

scamper scurry, scoot, scuttle, run, speed, hasten, hurry, dash, dart, fly. AMBLE

scan examine, scrutinize, study, investigate, search.
skim, browse, look over, glance through.

scandal crime, sin, offence, outrage, disgrace, shame, dishonour, disrepute, reproach, infamy, ignominy, opprobrium, condemnation, censure, discredit. HONOUR
gossip, talk, backbiting, slander, calumny, aspersion, abuse.

scandalize horrify, appal, shock, outrage, offend, affront, repel, disgust.

scandalous shocking, outrageous, disgraceful, shameful, dishonourable, infamous, ignominious, opprobrious, atrocious, discreditable, disreputable, improper, unseemly. CREDITABLE
slanderous, libellous, scurrilous, defamatory.

scanty meagre, skimpy, exiguous, scant, limited, insufficient, inadequate, short, little, small, narrow, thin, sparse, poor, paltry. AMPLE

scar cicatrix, mark, disfigurement, blemish, wound, injury, trauma.

scarce rare, infrequent, uncommon, few, sparse, scanty, insufficient, deficient, short. PLENTIFUL

scarcely barely, hardly, only just.

scarcity dearth, paucity, lack, want, shortage, insufficiency, deficiency, rarity, infrequency. ABUNDANCE

scare *v*, frighten, affright, alarm, startle, shock, daunt, terrify, horrify, appal, dismay, intimidate. REASSURE
n, fright, alarm, start, shock, terror, panic. REASSURANCE

scathing caustic, mordant, biting, cutting, incisive, trenchant, critical, sarcastic, scornful, withering. PLEASANT

scatter sprinkle, strew, broadcast, disseminate, spread, diffuse. GATHER
disperse, dispel, dissipate, disband, separate. COLLECT

scene place, spot, locality, site, location, setting, background, milieu.
incident, episode, event, chapter.
view, vista, prospect, landscape, panorama, scenery.
display, show, exhibition, spectacle, sight, representation, tableau, pageant.
fuss, commotion, outburst, tantrum.

scenery landscape, panorama, view, vista, scene, setting.
set, backdrop, flats.

scent *n*, smell, odour, aroma, redolence, perfume, fragrance.
trail, track, spoor.
v, sniff, smell, detect, discern, recognize.
perfume, aromatize.

sceptical doubting, doubtful, dubious, questioning, suspicious, distrustful, mistrustful, unbelieving, incredulous, unconvinced, cynical. CREDULOUS

scepticism doubt, suspicion, distrust, mistrust, disbelief, incredulity, cynicism, Pyrrhonism, unbelief, agnosticism. FAITH

schedule plan, programme, agenda, calendar, timetable, itinerary, list, inventory, catalogue, record, register.

scheme *n*, plan, system, programme, schedule, project, design, proposal, idea, outline, diagram, arrangement, strategy, device, contrivance, wile, ruse, stratagem, ploy, plot, intrigue, conspiracy.
v, plan, project, devise, contrive, formulate, frame, design, imagine, plot, intrigue, machinate, conspire.

schism disunion, separation, division, split, breach, rift, rupture, faction. UNITY

scholar schoolboy, schoolgirl, student, pupil, learner. TEACHER savant, intellectual, academic, egghead (*inf*). DUNCE

scholarship erudition, learning, letters, schooling, education, knowledge, lore, accomplishments, attainments, achievements. IGNORANCE
grant, bursary, fellowship, exhibition.

school *n*, college, academy, seminary, institute, institution, faculty, department.
denomination, sect, faction, persuasion, creed, class, set, group, followers, disciples, pupils, adherents, devotees, admirers.
v, teach, educate, instruct, tutor, coach, train, discipline, drill, prepare, prime.

scientific natural, physical, technical, logical, systematic, methodical, mathematical, accurate, exact, precise. UNSCIENTIFIC

scintilla spark, glimmer, trace, hint, *soupçon*, iota, atom, jot, tittle, speck, particle.

scintillate sparkle, twinkle, gleam, coruscate, glitter, glint, glisten, flash.

scintillating lively, stimulating, spirited, animated, sparkling, brilliant, dazzling, exciting. DULL

scion descendant, heir, successor, offspring, child, issue, progeny.
offshoot, shoot, twig, branch, cutting, graft. STOCK

scoff[1] mock, jeer, sneer, gibe, make fun of, laugh at, ridicule, deride, taunt, scorn, flout. RESPECT

scoff[2] devour, wolf, bolt, guzzle, gobble, cram, stuff, gorge.

scold upbraid, berate, reprimand, reprehend, rebuke, reprove, reproach, chide, castigate, tell off (*inf*), blame, censure, nag. PRAISE

scoop *n*, ladle, spoon, shovel.
exclusive, sensation, inside story.
v, dig, excavate, hollow, gouge, ladle, shovel, gather, pick up, remove.

scope opportunity, freedom, liberty, latitude, space, room, range, extent, reach, span, area, sphere.

scorch burn, singe, char, toast, blister, scald, roast, bake, parch, sear, wither.

score *n*, record, tally, reckoning, sum, total, account, bill, points, result, mark.
twenty, lot, mass, crowd, legion, hundred, thousand, million.
reason, cause, basis, grounds, account.
grievance, grudge, wrong, injury, debt, obligation.
v, gain, achieve, win, earn, get, make, tally, count, record, register.
cut, gouge, nick, mark, scratch, scrape.

scorn *n*, contempt, disdain, contumely, scornfulness, derision, mockery, ridicule. RESPECT
v, disdain, contemn, reject, spurn, look down on, despise, slight, disregard, deride, mock, scoff at, sneer at.

scornful contemptuous, disdainful, supercilious, haughty, contumelious, sneering, derisive, mocking, sarcastic, sardonic. RESPECTFUL

scoundrel rogue, rascal, villain, miscreant, scapegrace, knave, blackguard, wretch, reprobate, ne'er-do-well. GENTLEMAN

scour[1] rub, abrade, scrub, clean, wash, polish, burnish, buff, cleanse, purge, clear, flush. SOIL

scour[2] search, hunt, ransack, comb, rake, range.

scourge *n*, whip, lash, strap, thong, switch, rod.
punishment, penalty, torment, torture, plague, affliction, bane, curse, misfortune, hardship, visitation. BLESSING
v, whip, lash, beat, flog, punish, chastise, castigate, correct. INDULGE

scout *n*, spy, lookout, outrider, vanguard.
v, reconnoitre, inspect, investigate, check out, spy, watch, observe, search, hunt, seek.

scowl *v*, frown, glower, glare, lower. SMILE
n, frown, glower, grimace, dirty look.

scraggy scrawny, lean, thin, skinny, bony, angular, gaunt, spare, lanky. FAT

scramble *v*, clamber, climb, struggle, strive, contend, compete, vie, contest, hasten, hurry, rush, bustle, scurry, scamper. DAWDLE
mix, blend, combine, jumble, disorder, confuse.
n, struggle, competition, race, rush, muddle, confusion.

scrap[1] *n*, piece, bit, fragment, part, morsel, crumb, iota, mite, atom, particle, trace. MASS
waste, leftovers, remains, remnants.
v, discard, throw away, reject, abandon, drop, get rid of. KEEP

scrap[2] *n*, fight, scuffle, brawl, row, quarrel, argument.

scrape *v*, grate, grind, rasp, file, rub, abrade, scrub, scour, scratch, graze, bark, scuff.
n, predicament, plight, dilemma, quandary, difficulty, fix (*inf*), trouble, pickle (*inf*).

scratch *v*, scrape, claw, cut, mark, score, scuff, graze, bark, rub, chafe.
erase, delete, cross out, expunge, obliterate, eliminate.
n, scrape, scuff, mark, scar, cut, laceration, graze, abrasion.
up to scratch, satisfactory, adequate, acceptable, capable. UNACCEPTABLE

scream screech, shriek, cry, yell, shout, bawl, wail, squeal, howl, squall. WHISPER

screen *n*, partition, divider, curtain, net, shade, blind, cover, shelter, protection, guard, shield, veil, cloak, shroud.
v, shelter, cover, protect, guard, shield, defend, hide, conceal, shroud, cloak, veil, mask. EXPOSE
sieve, sift, sort, pick, select, evaluate, examine, vet.

screw twist, turn, distort, contort, wrench, wrest, squeeze, press, force, coerce.

scribble scrawl, scratch, jot, write, doodle.

scribe copyist, amanuensis, secretary, clerk, pen-pusher, writer.

scrimmage scuffle, brawl, affray, melee, riot, rumpus, row, fight, struggle, scramble.

scrimp stint, pinch, restrict, limit, straiten, reduce, economize, skimp. LAVISH

script handwriting, penmanship, calligraphy, writing, hand.
manuscript, text, lines, libretto.

scrounge forage, hunt, beg, cadge, sponge (*inf*).

scrub rub, scour, wash, clean, cleanse. SOIL
cancel, drop, give up, scrap.

scrubby insignificant, puny, diminutive, small, dwarfish, stunted, undersized, underdeveloped. IMMENSE

scruffy untidy, messy, unkempt, disreputable, shabby, ragged, slovenly, seedy. SMART

scrunch crumple, crush, squash, crunch.

scruple *n*, qualm, misgiving, conscience, compunction, doubt, hesitation, uneasiness, reluctance. ASSURANCE
v, hesitate, falter, waver, think twice about, demur, doubt, be loath.

scrupulous punctilious, strict, exact, precise, meticulous, painstaking, fastidious, minute, nice, careful, cautious, conscientious, moral, ethical, principled. LAX

scrutinize examine, study, peruse, pore over, scan, probe, search, investigate, inspect, analyse, sift. IGNORE

scrutiny examination, study, perusal, probe, search, investigation, inquiry, inspection, analysis.

scud run, race, speed, fly, sail, skim.

scuffle *v*, fight, struggle, contend, grapple, tussle, brawl.
n, fight, struggle, tussle, brawl, riot, fray, melee, rumpus. PEACE

scum froth, dregs, deposit, residue, dross.

scurrilous abusive, offensive, insulting, vituperative, defamatory, gross, foul, coarse, vulgar, rude, obscene, dirty, indecent, ribald. COMPLIMENTARY

scurry scamper, scuttle, scoot, dash, dart, run, race, hurry, hasten, fly. AMBLE

scurvy low, base, mean, despicable, contemptible, abject, vile, rotten, shabby, worthless, dishonourable. HONOURABLE

scuttle scamper, scurry, scoot, dash, dart, run, race, hurry, hasten, fly. AMBLE

sea ocean, main, deep, briny (*inf*), swell, surge, wave, billow. LAND
at sea, adrift, astray, lost, disorientated, bewildered, baffled, perplexed, confused.

seal *v*, fasten, secure, close, shut, plug, cork, stop. OPEN
stamp, validate, sanction, endorse, confirm, settle, clinch.
n, stamp, cachet, insignia, pledge, assurance, confirmation.

seam joint, suture, line, furrow, ridge, wrinkle, scar.
stratum, vein, layer, lode.

seaman sailor, mariner, seaman, seafarer, bluejacket, tar (*inf*), matelot (*inf*).

seamy unpleasant, unattractive, disagreeable, nasty, repulsive, sordid, dark, low, rough. PLEASANT

sear burn, scorch, cauterize, brand, wither, dry, parch, desiccate.

search *v*, seek, look, hunt, rummage, sift, comb, examine, scrutinize, scour, probe, explore, inspect, check, frisk (*inf*).

n, hunt, pursuit, quest, examination, scrutiny, exploration, probe, inspection, investigation, inquiry. DISCOVERY

searching penetrating, piercing, keen, sharp, intent, thorough, close, inquiring, probing.

season *n*, time, period, spell, interval, term, quarter.
v, flavour, spice, enliven.
mature, prepare, harden, toughen, anneal, inure, habituate, accustom, acclimatize, train.
temper, moderate, qualify, mitigate.

seasonable opportune, timely, well-timed, suitable, appropriate, fit, convenient, auspicious, welcome. UNTIMELY

seasoning flavouring, spice, salt, pepper, relish, condiment, sauce, dressing.

seat *n*, chair, bench, stool, sofa, pew, stall.
situation, site, location, place, centre, cradle, base, foundation.
residence, abode, house, mansion.
v, accommodate, hold, contain, take.
install, establish, fix, settle, deposit, place, set, put, sit.

secede withdraw, retire, leave, pull out, break with, apostatize. AFFILIATE

secluded isolated, remote, solitary, sequestered, cloistered, withdrawn, retired, sheltered, private, hidden, screened. PUBLIC

second[1] *adj*, next, following, subsequent, alternate, other, further, extra, additional. FIRST
secondary, subordinate, inferior, minor. PRINCIPAL
n, attendant, assistant, helper, supporter, backer. OPPONENT
v, back, support, help, aid, assist, further, forward, advance, promote, encourage, endorse. OPPOSE

second[2] *n*, instant, moment, trice, twinkling, flash, jiffy (*inf*).

secondary subordinate, subsidiary, ancillary, auxiliary, extra, inferior, minor, lesser, lower, unimportant. PRIMARY

secret *adj*, hidden, concealed, disguised, camouflaged, unseen, covert, surreptitious, clandestine, undercover, stealthy, sly, underhand, secretive, reticent. OPEN
private, confidential, intimate, unknown, secluded, retired, isolated, out-of-the-way. PUBLIC
mysterious, cryptic, occult, arcane, esoteric, recondite, abstruse.
n, confidence, mystery, enigma, code, formula, recipe.

secretary clerk, typist, scribe, amanuensis, assistant, aide.

secrete[1] discharge, emit, exude, emanate, give off. ABSORB

secrete[2] hide, conceal, veil, screen, camouflage, disguise, stow, stash (*inf*). EXPOSE

sect faction, schism, group, party, school, denomination.

sectarian factional, denominational, partisan, bigoted, intolerant, insular, narrow-minded, narrow, limited, doctrinaire, fanatical. BROAD-MINDED

section part, segment, division, subdivision, piece, portion, slice, fragment, fraction. WHOLE

secular lay, profane, temporal, worldly, state, civil. RELIGIOUS

secure *adj*, safe, protected, defended, fortified, sheltered, immune, invulnerable, impregnable. VULNERABLE
firm, stable, steady, sound, fast, tight, dependable, reliable, fixed, settled, sure, certain, confident, assured. INSECURE
v, obtain, get, procure, acquire. LOSE
tie, fix, attach, fasten, lock, bind, fortify, defend, guard, protect. RELEASE
guarantee, assure, ensure, insure.

security safety, protection, precaution, safeguard, immunity, asylum, shelter, refuge, sanctuary. DANGER
confidence, assurance, conviction, certainty, sureness, reliance. INSECURITY
guarantee, warranty, surety, pledge, assurance, insurance.

sedate calm, composed, serene, tranquil, placid, cool, quiet, demure, staid, dignified, proper, decorous, sober, grave.

sedative *n*, tranquillizer, narcotic, opiate, anodyne. STIMULANT
adj, calming, soothing, assuasive, lenitive, anodyne, soporific.

sedentary seated, sitting, inactive, motionless, idle. ACTIVE

sediment precipitate, dregs, lees, grounds, deposit, residue, residuum, dross, scum.

sedition insurrection, rebellion, mutiny, subversion, incitement, agitation, treason. LOYALTY

seditious seditionary, rebellious, mutinous, insurgent, insurrectionary, revolutionary, refractory, insubordinate, subversive. OBEDIENT

seduce tempt, lure, lead astray, inveigle, ensnare, entice, beguile, attract, allure, corrupt, deprave, debauch, deflower. REPEL

seductive tempting, alluring, inviting, appealing, attractive, exciting, provocative, sexy (*inf*). REPULSIVE

sedulous assiduous, diligent, conscientious, scrupulous, painstaking, industrious, laborious, persevering, persistent, constant, unremitting, tireless, unflagging, energetic, active, busy. IDLE

see[1] *v*, perceive, discern, look at, behold, notice, observe, regard, watch, view, witness, note, mark, spot, make out, descry, espy, examine, inspect. MISS
comprehend, understand, grasp, know, feel, appreciate, realize, recognize.
ascertain, determine, learn, find out, discover.
envisage, visualize, imagine, conceive, foresee, anticipate.
consider, deliberate, think, reflect, ponder. DECIDE
meet, encounter, receive, speak to, escort, accompany, usher, lead.
see to, arrange, organize, see about, attend to, take care of, look after.

see[2] *n*, diocese, bishopric, episcopate.

seed germ, embryo, ovule, spore, grain.
source, origin, beginning, start, cause.

seedy shabby, scruffy, unkempt, rundown, squalid. SMART
ill, unwell, ailing, poorly (*inf*), sickly. WELL

seek hunt, look for, search for, pursue, follow. FIND
try, attempt, endeavour, aim, aspire. FAIL
want, desire, ask, beg, entreat, solicit.

seem look, appear, sound, pretend. BE

seemingly apparently, ostensibly, outwardly, on the face of it. ACTUALLY

seemly proper, decent, fit, fitting, suitable, appropriate, becoming, decorous. UNSEEMLY

seep ooze, trickle, leak, percolate, leach, bleed.

seer prophet, soothsayer, augur, clairvoyant.

seethe boil, foam, froth, ferment.
rage, fume, smoulder, simmer, be furious.

segment section, portion, part, division, piece, fragment, slice, wedge. WHOLE

segregate separate, dissociate, isolate, set apart. UNITE

seize grab, snatch, take, grasp, grip, clasp, clutch. DROP
capture, apprehend, arrest, confiscate, impound, sequestrate, usurp, commandeer, appropriate. RELEASE

seizure capture, apprehension, confiscation, sequestration. RELEASE
convulsion, fit, spasm, paroxysm, attack.

seldom rarely, infrequently, hardly ever, occasionally. OFTEN

select *v*, pick, choose, single out, opt for, prefer.
adj, selected, picked, preferred, choice, prime, excellent, first-class, chosen, elect, elite, exclusive. INFERIOR

selection pick, choice, option, preference.
collection, assortment, variety, range.

self-centred egotistic, egoistic, egocentric, narcissistic, selfish.

self-conscious shy, bashful, coy, diffident, embarrassed, sheepish, awkward, uncomfortable.

selfish self-centred, egotistic, egoistic, self-seeking, greedy, miserly, mean, ungenerous, mercenary. ALTRUISTIC

self-possessed cool, collected, composed, unruffled, poised, self-assured, imperturbable. NERVOUS

self-righteous sanctimonious, holier-than-thou, goody-goody (*inf*), pietistic, pharisaic, smug, complacent.

sell vend, exchange, barter, trade, traffic in, deal in, hawk, peddle, retail, market. BUY

semblance appearance, look, aspect, air, demeanour, mien, guise, pretence, show, façade, likeness, similarity, resemblance.

seminary academy, college, institute, school.

send forward, dispatch, remit, consign, transmit, convey, mail, post. RETAIN
hurl, propel, fling, cast, shoot.
emit, discharge, exude, give off.
send for, summon, call for, order.

senile aged, old, doting, gaga (*inf*), failing, doddering, decrepit. YOUNG

senior older, elder, superior, higher, major. JUNIOR

sensation feeling, sense, impression, awareness, perception.
excitement, thrill, stir, commotion, fuss, ado, agitation. APATHY

sensational exciting, thrilling, electrifying, hair-raising, shocking, scandalous, melodramatic, lurid, amazing, astounding, breathtaking, staggering, marvellous, superb, impressive, spectacular.

sense *n*, feeling, sensation, impression, sentiment, awareness, consciousness, perception, sensibility, faculty.
understanding, mind, intellect, brains, intelligence, discernment, discrimination, judgment, common sense, wisdom, sagacity, reason, sanity. FOLLY
meaning, gist, substance, import, significance, signification, connotation, implication.
v, feel, perceive, discern, apprehend, understand, appreciate.

senseless foolish, stupid, silly, asinine, crazy, mad, brainless, mindless, ridiculous, nonsensical, absurd, irrational, meaningless, pointless. SENSIBLE
unconscious, insensible, numb, deadened, insensate, unfeeling. SENSITIVE

sensible wise, sagacious, judicious, prudent, discreet, politic, sound, sane, rational, reasonable, practical, realistic, shrewd, intelligent. STUPID
aware, conscious, cognizant, mindful, observant. UNCONSCIOUS
tangible, palpable, appreciable, perceptible, visible. IMPERCEPTIBLE

sensitive susceptible, impressionable, receptive, responsive, conscious, sentient, delicate, fine, keen, tender, irritable, touchy. INSENSITIVE

sensual carnal, fleshly, voluptuous, bodily, physical, sexual, erotic, lascivious, libidinous, lecherous, licentious, lewd, salacious. SPIRITUAL

sensuous sensory, sumptuous, luxurious, rich, aesthetic, sybaritic.

sentence *n*, condemnation, judgment, ruling, decree, verdict, decision.
v, condemn, doom, penalize, pass judgment. ACQUIT

sententious terse, pithy, succinct, concise, pointed, laconic, aphoristic, axiomatic, pompous, moralistic.

sentiment feeling, emotion, sensibility, sentimentality. REASON
attitude, view, opinion, thought, idea, notion.

sentimental emotional, tender, romantic, maudlin, mawkish, sloppy (*inf*), nostalgic, corny (*inf*). REALISTIC

sentinel sentry, guard, picket, patrol, watch, lookout, watchman, guardian.

separate *v*, divide, part, split, sunder, cleave, sever, disjoin, disconnect, disunite, break up, come between, estrange, divorce, diverge, bifurcate. JOIN
sort, segregate, isolate, keep apart. MIX
adj, independent, individual, different, disparate, discrete, detached, unconnected, distinct, apart, isolated, unattached, divided, separated, divorced. CONNECTED

separation division, partition, break, split, severance, cleavage, disjunction, dissociation, disconnection, estrangement, divorce, isolation, segregation.

sepulchral funereal, lugubrious, mournful, woeful, sombre, grave, sad, melancholy, dismal, gloomy, hollow, deep. CHEERFUL

sequel development, continuation, follow-up, result, consequence, outcome, upshot, issue, end, aftermath. BEGINNING

sequence order, arrangement, series, progression, chain, succession, continuity. DISORDER

sequestered withdrawn, retired, cloistered, reclusive, solitary, isolated, remote, secluded. PUBLIC

seraphic angelic, cherubic, holy, divine, heavenly, celestial, pure, sublime, beatific, blissful. DIABOLIC

serene tranquil, calm, peaceful, quiet, placid, cool, composed, unruffled, undisturbed, imperturbable. AGITATED
clear, cloudless, bright, fair. MURKY

series sequence, succession, run, concatenation, chain, string, progression, set.

serious grave, solemn, thoughtful, pensive, sober, sedate, stern, unsmiling. JOCOSE
earnest, resolute, sincere, genuine.
weighty, momentous, important, significant, vital, crucial, critical, dangerous. TRIVIAL

sermon address, discourse, homily, exhortation, lecture, harangue.

serpentine snaky, sinuous, winding, meandering, twisting, tortuous, crooked, coiled, spiral. STRAIGHT

serrated serrate, serrulate, notched, jagged, sawlike, toothed. SMOOTH

serried close, compact, dense, massed.

servant domestic, maid, valet, retainer, attendant, assistant, helper, hireling, menial, lackey, drudge, slave. EMPLOYER

serve attend, wait on, minister to, oblige, help, aid, assist, benefit, work for, obey. COMMAND
function, perform, act, do, suffice, suit, answer, satisfy, fulfil.
present, distribute, dish up, provide, supply.

service help, aid, assistance, benefit, advantage, use, avail. USELESSNESS
maintenance, overhaul.
work, employment, duty, function, business, department, bureau.
ceremony, rite, ritual, sacrament, observance, worship.

servile obsequious, slavish, menial, submissive, cringing, grovelling, fawning, sycophantic, abject, humble, mean, base. INDEPENDENT

servitude bondage, slavery, serfdom, vassalage, captivity, enslavement, thrall, subjection, subjugation. COMMAND

session meeting, sitting, gathering, assembly, period, term.

set[1] *v*, place, put, position, locate, situate, plant, deposit, rest, stick, lodge, fix, establish, arrange, prepare, lay, apply. MOVE
determine, fix, establish, appoint, name, designate, settle, decide, resolve, decree, ordain. CHANGE
adjust, regulate, synchronize, coordinate, direct, aim.
solidify, harden, stiffen, congeal, jell, thicken, cake, crystallize. MELT
sink, go down, dip, drop, decline, disappear. RISE

set about, start, begin, tackle, undertake, get down to (*inf*). FINISH

set back, retard, delay, hold up, hinder, impede. ADVANCE

set off, set out, set forth, start out, begin, embark, leave, depart, go. ARRIVE
detonate, explode, light, ignite.

set up, build, erect, construct, raise, establish, found, inaugurate, institute, arrange, prepare. ABOLISH
n, bearing, carriage, posture, hang, tendency, drift.
scene, scenery, setting, *mise en scène*.
adj, fixed, established, prescribed, ordained, appointed, agreed, decided, settled, regular, usual. VARIABLE
rigid, firm, entrenched, hardened, inflexible, immovable, stubborn, determined, resolute, intent. FLEXIBLE

set[2] *n*, collection, assortment, group, series, batch, outfit, kit.
band, gang, crowd, company, party, faction, sect, circle, clique, coterie.

setting scene, set, scenery, background, surroundings, location, framework, mounting.

settle arrange, order, regulate, adjust, clear up, resolve, reconcile, conclude.
appoint, set, fix, establish, determine, agree on, decide, choose.
land, alight, perch, lodge, repose, rest.
dwell, live, reside, inhabit, populate, colonize. MIGRATE
pay, discharge, liquidate, clear. OWE
sink, drop, fall, descend, subside, abate. RISE

settlement arrangement, regulation, adjustment, reconciliation, resolution, conclusion, decision, agreement.
payment, discharge, liquidation, defrayal.
colonization, colony, community, encampment.

sever part, divide, separate, cut, split, cleave, sunder, disjoin, disunite, dissociate, break off, dissolve. JOIN

several some, a few, sundry, various, assorted, different, separate, distinct, own, individual, particular, respective.

severe strict, harsh, rigid, inflexible, relentless, unrelenting, inexorable, cruel, tough, hard, difficult, rigorous, exacting, stern, dour, grim, serious, grave, sober. MILD
plain, simple, unadorned, restrained, austere, ascetic, Spartan.
violent, fierce, intense, extreme, bitter, acute, critical, dangerous.

shabby ragged, tattered, worn, threadbare, faded, scruffy, dilapidated, rundown, seedy. SMART
mean, base, low, despicable, contemptible, ignoble, dishonourable, rotten. HONOURABLE

shackle *v*, bind, tie, chain, fetter, trammel, manacle. LOOSE
restrict, restrain, impede, hinder, hamper, obstruct. FREE

n, bond, chain, fetter, manacle, handcuff, iron.

shade *n*, shadow, darkness, dusk, gloom, obscurity. LIGHT
screen, shutter, blind, veil, cover, shelter, shield, protection.
degree, nuance, hint, trace, suspicion, suggestion, dash, touch.
colour, hue, tint, tinge.
v, shadow, eclipse, darken, dim, obscure, cloud.
screen, veil, cover, hide, shield, protect. EXPOSE

shadow *n*, shade, darkness, dusk, gloom, cloud, shelter, protection. BRIGHTNESS
image, adumbration, silhouette, phantom, spectre.
trace, vestige, hint, suggestion.
v, shade, eclipse, darken, screen, shield. EXPOSE
follow, trail, track, stalk, dog, hound.

shadowy shady, shaded, dark, murky, gloomy, tenebrous, dim, obscure, indistinct, vague. BRIGHT
imaginary, illusory, unreal, unsubstantial, impalpable, ghostly, spectral. REAL

shady shaded, shadowy, umbrageous, dark. LIGHT
dubious, questionable, suspicious, shifty, dishonest, crooked. HONEST

shaft pole, rod, bar, shank, handle.
ray, nbeam, streak.

shaggy hairy, hirsute, unkempt, dishevelled, rough, coarse. SMOOTH

shake *v*, vibrate, tremble, quiver, quake, shudder, shiver, waver, vacillate, oscillate, swing, rock, sway, totter, wobble, convulse, churn, rattle, jar, jolt, bump.
brandish, wave, flourish.
stir, agitate, disturb, upset, unsettle, unnerve, frighten, shock, weaken, impair, undermine.
n, vibration, tremor, shudder, shiver, oscillation, convulsion, rattle, jolt, wave, agitation.

shaky shaking, trembling, tremulous, shivery, wobbly, rickety, unstable, unsteady, tottering, doddering, weak. FIRM
unsound, unsupported, unreliable, dubious, questionable, uncertain. SOUND

shallow superficial, empty, meaningless, slight, trivial, trifling, petty, unimportant, frivolous, silly, foolish. DEEP

sham *n*, counterfeit, forgery, fake, imitation, pretence, feint, imposture, impostor, fraud.
adj, false, counterfeit, forged, fake, phoney (*inf*), bogus, spurious, mock, ersatz, artificial, simulated, pretended, feigned. GENUINE
v, pretend, feign, simulate, assume, affect, put on, fake, counterfeit.

shame *n*, mortification, humiliation, embarrassment, abashment, chagrin, guilt, remorse. PRIDE
disgrace, dishonour, scandal, ignominy, infamy, opprobrium, discredit, disrepute, obloquy, reproach. HONOUR
v, mortify, humiliate, humble, embarrass, abash, confound, disgrace, dishonour, reproach.

shameful disgraceful, dishonourable, scandalous, ignominious, infamous, opprobrious, discreditable, disreputable, despicable, contemptible, heinous, atrocious, outrageous, nefarious, vile, low, base. HONOURABLE

shameless brazen, bold, audacious, brash, barefaced, impudent, insolent, unabashed, unashamed, immodest, indecent, hardened, unprincipled, corrupt, depraved, abandoned, wanton. ASHAMED

shanty shack, hut, cabin, shed, hovel.

shape *n*, form, figure, outline, silhouette, cut, model, pattern, mould, cast, structure, build.
guise, appearance, aspect, likeness, semblance, phantom, apparition.
condition, state, fettle, health.
v, mould, model, form , fashion, make, produce, create, devise, adapt, modify.

shapeless amorphous, nebulous, unstructured, formless, misshapen, asymmetrical.

shapely neat, trim, attractive, comely, elegant, curvaceous. UGLY

share *n*, portion, part, division, lot, ration, quota, allocation, allotment, allowance, contribution. WHOLE
v, apportion, allocate, allot, divide, split, ration, parcel out, participate, partake.

sharp keen, acute, pointed, edged, thin, fine, cutting, jagged, serrated. BLUNT
sudden, abrupt, extreme, violent, fierce, intense, severe, acute, piercing, excruciating, stabbing. GENTLE

biting, cutting, caustic, trenchant, bitter, acrimonious, scathing, harsh, shrill, tart, acrid, piquant, pungent. MILD
clever, intelligent, shrewd, astute, sharp-witted, quick-witted, perspicacious, discerning, penetrating, knowing, smart, alert, bright, subtle, crafty, cunning, artful, sly. STUPID

sharpen hone, grind, strop, whet, edge, point. BLUNT

shatter break, smash, splinter, shiver, split, crack, burst, crush. MEND
demolish, wreck, ruin, destroy, devastate. RESTORE

shave shear, cut, pare, trim, clip, crop, plane, scrape, graze, brush, touch, skim.

shear fleece, poll, clip, trim, cut, shave.

shed[1] *n*, outhouse, lean-to, hut, shack, shelter.

shed[2] *v*, spill, pour forth, drop, emit, radiate, diffuse, scatter, spread, cast, slough, moult, discard. RETAIN

sheen lustre, gloss, polish, burnish, shine, gleam, brightness, brilliance. DULLNESS

sheepish abashed, ashamed, shamefaced, embarrassed, bashful, timid, diffident, self-conscious.

sheer steep, precipitous, abrupt, perpendicular, vertical. GENTLE
utter, complete, out-and-out, downright, absolute, unqualified, unmitigated, unadulterated, pure, simple. PARTIAL
thin, fine, transparent, diaphanous, gossamer. THICK

sheet layer, covering, coating, blanket, veneer, film, panel, plate, pane, slab, piece, leaf, expanse, stretch.

shell *n*, case, casing, capsule, cartridge, carapace, husk, pod.
skeleton, framework, frame, structure.
v, bomb, bombard, strafe, barrage, blitz.

shelter *n*, refuge, haven, harbour, sanctuary, asylum, retreat, covert, cover, protection, safety, security, defence, guard, screen, shield.
v, cover, protect, defend, guard, shield, screen, hide, harbour. EXPOSE

shelve postpone, defer, put aside, put off, pigeonhole, mothball.

shield *n*, buckler, escutcheon, aegis, protection, defence, guard, safeguard, cover, shelter, screen, rampart, bulwark.
v, protect, guard, defend, shelter, screen, cover, hide. EXPOSE

shift *v*, move, budge, change, alter, vary, fluctuate, relocate, transfer, switch, exchange, remove. FIX
manage, fend, get by, get along, contrive, devise.
n, move, swerve, change, alteration, transfer, switch.
device, contrivance, expedient, resort, resource, scheme, stratagem, artifice, trick, wile, ruse, dodge, subterfuge.

shifty crafty, artful, wily, tricky, slippery, evasive, furtive, underhand, dishonest, crooked, deceitful. HONEST

shimmer *v*, glimmer, glisten, gleam, flash, shine, twinkle, scintillate, phosphoresce.
n, glow, phosphorescence, incandescence, iridescence, lustre, shine, glimmer, glistening, gleam, flash. DULLNESS

shine *v*, gleam, beam, flash, glow, radiate, glisten, glimmer, sparkle, twinkle, glitter, shimmer.
polish, burnish, buff, rub.
excel, stand out.
v, lustre, sheen, gloss, polish, brightness, radiance, brilliance, effulgence, splendour, resplendence. DULLNESS

shiny bright, shining, radiant, gleaming, glossy, lustrous, polished. DULL

ship vessel, craft, liner, steamer, boat.

shipshape neat, tidy, orderly, trim. UNTIDY

shirk *v*, evade, avoid, dodge, sidestep, get out of, malinger, neglect. DISCHARGE
n, shirker, idler, slacker, dodger, malingerer.

shiver[1] *v*, shudder, tremble, shake, quiver, quake, palpitate, vibrate.
n, shudder, tremor, quiver, vibration.

shiver[2] *v*, shatter, splinter, smash, break, fragment. MEND

shock *v*, horrify, appal, revolt, disgust, offend, scandalize, outrage, disturb, stagger, stupefy, astound, stun, shake, jar, jolt. DELIGHT
n, blow, jolt, impact, collision, upset, disturbance, bombshell, horror, astonishment, stupefaction, trauma.

shocking horrifying, appalling, outrageous, scandalous, disgraceful, shameful, disgusting, sickening, offensive, revolting, repulsive, terrible, abominable, dreadful, ghastly, monstrous, atrocious, loathsome, detestable, foul. DELIGHTFUL

shoe footwear, sandal, boot, clog, plimsoll, slipper.

shoot *v*, fire, discharge, propel, project, launch, fling, hurl.
hit, wound, kill, bag, snipe. MISS
dart, dash, tear, rush, race, speed, scoot, fly, spring. AMBLE
germinate, sprout, bud, burgeon.
n, sprout, bud, burgeon, offshoot, scion, branch, twig.

shop store, supermarket, boutique.

shore[1] *n*, beach, strand, seaside, coast, land.

shore[2] *n*, support, prop, brace, buttress, strut, stay.
v, support, prop, hold up, strengthen, reinforce, underpin. UNDERMINE

short little, small, diminutive, petite, squat. TALL
brief, concise, succinct, terse, laconic, pithy, sententious, condensed, abridged, abbreviated, curtailed. LENGTHY
fleeting, momentary, transient, transitory, ephemeral, temporary, short-lived, brief. LONG
scant, scanty, deficient, insufficient, inadequate, lacking, wanting, meagre, sparse, limited. AMPLE
abrupt, curt, sharp, blunt, brusque, gruff, impolite, discourteous, rude, short-tempered, irascible. AFFABLE

shortage dearth, paucity, lack, want, need, scarcity, deficiency, deficit, insufficiency, inadequacy. GLUT

shorten cut, curtail, reduce, lessen, dock, trim, abbreviate, abridge. LENGTHEN

shortly soon, presently, before long. LATER
briefly, succinctly, concisely, tersely, abruptly, curtly, sharply.

shot report, discharge.
ball, pellet, bullet, slug, projectile, missile.
try, attempt, go, crack (*inf*), effort, endeavour.

shout *v*, cry, call, vociferate, exclaim, yell, bellow, roar, scream, holler (*inf*). WHISPER
n, cry, vociferation, exclamation, yell, roar, scream.

shove push, thrust, move, propel, drive, jostle, elbow, press, crowd. PULL

show *v*, display, exhibit, present, demonstrate, manifest, indicate, register, reveal, expose, evince, evidence, prove, explain, elucidate, point out, teach, instruct. CONCEAL
usher, escort, accompany, guide, lead, direct.
appear, be visible, stand out.
show off, parade, flaunt, swagger, boast.
show up, reveal, give away, expose, highlight.
outshine, upstage, shame, embarrass.
appear, turn up, arrive, come. LEAVE
n, display, exhibition, exposition, presentation, production, demonstration, parade, pageant, spectacle.
affectation, ostentation, pretence, illusion, appearance, semblance, indication, evidence.

shower *n*, cloudburst, torrent, flood, deluge, barrage, volley.
v, spray, sprinkle, pour, inundate, deluge, lavish.

showy flamboyant, flashy, gaudy, garish, loud, ostentatious, pretentious. SUBDUED

shred scrap, bit, fragment, piece, sliver, strip, rag, tatter, atom, iota, grain, particle, jot, whit. WHOLE

shrew nag, scold, termagant, virago, harridan, fury, vixen, spitfire. ANGEL

shrewd astute, sharp, keen, acute, smart, clever, intelligent, wise, sagacious, discriminating, discerning, knowing, artful, crafty, cunning, sly, wily. STUPID

shriek screech, scream, squeal, yell, cry, shout.

shrill sharp, acute, piercing, ear-splitting, high, high-pitched. LOW

shrink contract, shorten, narrow, shrivel, wither, decrease, reduce, diminish, dwindle. EXPAND
recoil, draw back, shy away, flinch, wince, quail, withdraw, retire. VENTURE

shrivel wither, wilt, wrinkle, shrink, contract, dry up, desiccate. SWELL

shroud *n*, cerecloth, cerement, winding sheet.
mantle, cloud, pall, veil, cover, covering.
v, wrap, swathe, envelop, cover, hide, conceal, mask, veil, screen, cloak. EXPOSE

shudder *v*, shiver, shake, tremble, quiver, quake.
n, shiver, tremor, quiver, spasm, convulsion.

shuffle shamble, falter, hobble, drag, scrape.

mix, intermix, jumble, muddle, confuse, disarrange, disorder, shift. SORT
equivocate, hedge, evade, dodge, quibble, cavil, prevaricate.
shun avoid, eschew, spurn, steer clear of, evade, elude, shirk, shrink from. COURT
shut *v*, close, lock, seal, fasten. OPEN
shut in, confine, imprison, enclose. RELEASE
shut out, exclude, bar, debar, ostracize. ADMIT
shut up, coop up, box in, cage, imprison, incarcerate, intern. RELEASE
silence, hush, be quiet, keep mum.
adj, closed, locked, sealed, fastened. OPEN
shy bashful, retiring, reserved, reticent, backward, diffident, coy, modest, self-conscious, timid, nervous, wary, chary, cautious, distrustful, suspicious. BOLD
sibyl prophetess, oracle, fortune-teller, witch, sorceress.
sick ill, unwell, ailing, poorly (*inf*), indisposed, laid up (*inf*), weak, sickly, queasy, nauseated. WELL
tired, weary, jaded, satiated, fed up.
morbid, sadistic, ghoulish, macabre, black.
sicken nauseate, disgust, revolt, repel, tire, weary. PLEASE
sickly unhealthy, delicate, infirm, weak, feeble, faint, languid, pale, wan, peaky, ailing. HEALTHY
sickness illness, ailment, disorder, complaint, malady, affliction, indisposition, disease, nausea, vomiting. HEALTH
side *n*, edge, border, margin, verge, flank, face, facet, surface. CENTRE
aspect, angle, view, viewpoint, standpoint.
team, party, faction, sect, camp, interest, cause.
adj, lateral, oblique, indirect.
subordinate, secondary, incidental, minor, unimportant. MAIN
v, support, join, ally, associate. OPPOSE
sieve *n*, colander, strainer, sifter, riddle.
v, sift, strain, filter, riddle, bolt, screen.
sift sieve, filter, riddle, bolt, screen, separate, sort, analyse, examine, scrutinize, investigate, probe.
sigh breathe, exhale, moan, lament, mourn, grieve, long, pine.
sight *n*, vision, eyesight, eyes, seeing. BLINDNESS
view, eyeshot, ken, perception, glimpse, look.
spectacle, scene, show, display, eyesore.
v, see, view, glimpse, catch sight of, perceive, observe. MISS
sign *n*, symbol, representation, token, indication, symptom, mark, emblem, device, password, countersign, signal, gesture, proof, evidence, trace, vestige, hint, suggestion, omen, portent, presage, warning, notice, placard.
v, initial, autograph, write, endorse, subscribe.
signal, gesture, gesticulate, beckon, wave.
sign on, sign up, enlist, enrol, register, join. LEAVE
recruit, hire, employ, engage, appoint, take on. DISMISS
signal *n*, sign, beacon, flag, siren, gesture, cue, token, indication.
adj, conspicuous, noteworthy, remarkable, notable, memorable, significant, striking, exceptional. ORDINARY
v, communicate, gesture, gesticulate, beckon, wave, sign.
significant important, consequential, weighty, momentous, crucial, vital, critical. TRIVIAL
meaningful, suggestive, indicative, expressive, telling. MEANINGLESS
signify *vt*, mean, denote, indicate, show, symbolize, represent, betoken, augur, portend, imply, suggest, impart, convey, utter, express, tell, proclaim, declare.
vi, matter, count, be significant, carry weight.
silence *n*, quiet, hush, peace, stillness, calm. NOISE
muteness, dumbness, speechlessness, taciturnity, reticence. GARRULITY
v, quieten, hush, still, suppress, quell, subdue, muffle, gag, stifle, smother.
silent quiet, still, soundless, noiseless, inaudible, hushed, calm, peaceful.
dumb, mute, speechless, voiceless, mum, taciturn, reticent, uncommunicative. TALKATIVE
tacit, unspoken, understood, implicit, implied.
silly absurd, foolish, senseless, nonsensical, ridiculous, fatuous, asinine, childish, puerile, frivolous, simple, stupid, unintelligent, brainless, witless, mad, insane, unwise, imprudent, foolhardy, indiscreet. SENSIBLE
silt deposit, sediment, alluvium, ooze, sludge.

silvery silver, white, bright, clear, dulcet, sweet.

similar like, alike, resembling, akin, allied, corresponding, analogous, uniform. DIFFERENT

similarity similitude, likeness, resemblance, correspondence, congruity, analogy, uniformity. DIFFERENCE

simmer boil, seethe, bubble, stew, fume, rage.

simmer down, calm down, control oneself, cool off.

simper smile, smirk, grimace, giggle, snigger, titter.

simple easy, effortless, clear, lucid, understandable, uncomplicated, uninvolved, straightforward, elementary, pure, single, natural, plain, unadorned, bare, unpretentious, homely, humble, lowly. COMPLEX
artless, guileless, ingenuous, naive, innocent, green, frank, candid, open, direct, sincere, credulous, silly, foolish, stupid, unintelligent, witless, feeble-minded, retarded. CLEVER

simply merely, only, just, purely, solely, absolutely, utterly, totally, altogether, really.

simulate pretend, feign, sham, counterfeit, reproduce, imitate, copy, assume, affect.

simultaneous concurrent, concomitant, coincident, synchronous, contemporaneous. SEPARATE

sin *n*, trespass, transgression, offence, crime, misdeed, wrong, iniquity, evil, wickedness, vice, guilt. VIRTUE
v, transgress, err, offend, lapse, go astray.

since as, because, seeing that.

sincere honest, truthful, guileless, artless, frank, candid, open, straightforward, direct, forthright, plain, unaffected, natural, genuine, true, heartfelt, wholehearted, earnest. INSINCERE

sinewy strong, powerful, muscular, brawny, strapping, robust, sturdy, stalwart, vigorous, lusty. PUNY

sinful bad, wicked, evil, wrong, iniquitous, criminal, guilty, immoral, corrupt, unholy, ungodly, irreligious. VIRTUOUS

sing trill, warble, carol, croon, pipe, chirp, chant.

singe burn, scorch, char, sear.

single *adj*, sole, only, one, lone, solitary, isolated, separate, distinct, individual, particular, singular, unique. NUMEROUS
unmarried, unwed, unattached. MARRIED

single out, *v*, choose, select, pick, prefer, separate, set apart, cull. REJECT

singular remarkable, outstanding, exceptional, unparalleled, noteworthy, notable, eminent, conspicuous, rare, unique, extraordinary, odd, curious, peculiar, queer, strange, eccentric, unusual, uncommon, particular, individual, single, sole. ORDINARY

sinister ominous, portentous, inauspicious, menacing, threatening, evil, wicked, bad, malign, malevolent, maleficent, baleful, injurious, treacherous.

sink fall, drop, descend, sag, droop, subside, ebb, recede, dip, plunge, submerge, immerse, abate, decrease, diminish, decline, fail, weaken, lapse. RISE
bore, drill, dig, excavate.

sink in, penetrate, register (*inf*), be understood.

sinless innocent, guiltless, faultless, perfect, spotless, pure, immaculate, undefiled, unsullied, virtuous. SINFUL

sinner transgressor, offender, wrongdoer, evildoer, delinquent, criminal. SAINT

sinuous serpentine, winding, tortuous, flexuous, crooked, curved, anfractuous, convoluted, intricate, devious, supple, lithe. STRAIGHT

sip *v*, taste, sup, drink.
n, taste, drink, swallow, drop.

sit be seated, rest, squat, perch, settle, seat. STAND
meet, assemble, convene, preside, officiate.

site location, place, position, situation, spot, plot, ground.

situation position, place, location, site, spot, locality, locale, setting, scene.
state, circumstances, condition, case, plight, predicament.
post, job, employment, place, position, status, rank.

size dimensions, measurements, proportions, magnitude, bulk, mass, volume, greatness, bigness, extent, amount, range, scope.

skeleton bones, structure, framework, frame, shell, outline, sketch, draft.

sketch *n*, drawing, delineation, draft, outline, skeleton, plan, design.

v, draw, delineate, represent, depict, portray, draft, outline.

sketchy rough, crude, unfinished, incomplete, imperfect, slight, superficial, cursory, skimpy, inadequate, vague. THOROUGH

skilful skilled, adept, proficient, expert, masterly, adroit, dexterous, gifted, clever, apt, able, competent, versed, experienced, practised, accomplished. CLUMSY

skill skilfulness, proficiency, expertise, mastery, dexterity, facility, adroitness, gift, talent, faculty, ability, cleverness, aptitude, art, technique, knack, address, finesse. INEPTITUDE

skim glide, coast, fly, skate, graze, touch, brush. PENETRATE
glance, scan, flip through. PORE

skin *n*, epidermis, cuticle, integument, hide, pelt, covering, coating, peel, rind, shell, outside.
v, peel, pare, flay, excoriate, graze, bark.

skinny thin, lean, lank, scrawny, scraggy, gaunt, emaciated. PLUMP

skip hop, spring, jump, leap, bound, caper, frisk, gambol, prance, dance, bounce.
omit, exclude, leave out, miss out, pass over, neglect.

skirmish battle, fight, conflict, tussle, scrap (*inf*), fray, combat, brush, encounter, engagement.

skirt edge, border, flank, circle, avoid, evade.

skit burlesque, parody, take-off (*inf*), send-up (*inf*), spoof (*inf*), sketch, satire.

skittish nervous, jumpy, excitable, highly strung, restive, fidgety, lively, playful, fickle, capricious. STEADY

skulk lurk, lie in wait, prowl, slink, sneak, steal, creep.

sky heaven, heavens, firmament, empyrean, ether, azure, upper atmosphere, outer space. EARTH

slab block, piece, chunk, lump, hunk, slice.

slack *adj*, loose, lax, limp, relaxed. TAUT
negligent, remiss, careless, lazy, indolent, idle, dilatory, sluggish, slow, inactive, quiet. BUSY
v, shirk, skive (*inf*), dodge, evade, neglect, idle.

slacken loosen, relax, ease, lessen, moderate, abate, reduce, diminish, let up. TIGHTEN

slake quench, satisfy, sate, satiate, allay, assuage.

slam bang, crash, smash, dash, hurl, fling, close, shut.

slander *n*, defamation, detraction, obloquy, scandal, calumny, libel, abuse, aspersion, slur, smear. EULOGY
v, defame, vilify, malign, disparage, decry, calumniate, libel, traduce, asperse, smear, abuse, backbite. PRAISE

slant *v*, slope, incline, lean, tilt, list, shelve.
angle, bias, twist, distort, colour.
n, slope, incline, ramp, gradient, pitch, angle.
viewpoint, approach, attitude, angle, bias, prejudice.

slanting oblique, aslant, sloping, slanted, inclined, tilted, diagonal. PERPENDICULAR

slap *v*, hit, strike, smack, spank, whack, cuff, clip (*inf*).
n, blow, hit, smack, whack, cuff.

slash cut, gash, score, slit, rip, lacerate. MEND
reduce, cut, drop, lower. RAISE

slaughter *n*, killing, slaying, butchery, murder, bloodshed, carnage, massacre, extermination.
v, kill, slay, butcher, massacre, murder, assassinate, exterminate, destroy.

slave *n*, bondservant, serf, helot, vassal, drudge, skivvy. MASTER
v, toil, labour, work, drudge.

slavery bondage, thraldom, serfdom, vassalage, servitude, enslavement, captivity. FREEDOM
toil, labour, drudgery.

slavish servile, obsequious, submissive, abject, sycophantic, fawning, grovelling, cringing, base, mean, low, menial. INDEPENDENT

slay kill, murder, assassinate, execute, dispatch, slaughter, butcher, massacre, exterminate, destroy. SAVE

sleek smooth, shiny, glossy, lustrous, silky, well-groomed. ROUGH

sleep *v*, slumber, doze, drowse, nap, snooze (*inf*), nod off (*inf*), drop off (*inf*), rest, repose, hibernate. WAKE
n, slumber, nap, catnap, siesta, snooze (*inf*), forty winks (*inf*), rest, repose, dormancy, hibernation. WAKEFULNESS

sleepless insomniac, wakeful, restless, disturbed, watchful, vigilant, alert, awake.

sleepy drowsy, somnolent, tired, weary, lazy, sluggish, torpid, lethargic, dormant, inactive. ALERT
soporific, sleep-inducing, hypnotic.

slender slim, thin, lean, spare, willowy, svelte, slight, narrow, frail, flimsy, fine, weak, feeble, faint, small, inconsiderable, trivial, meagre, scanty, inadequate, insufficient. AMPLE

slice *n*, piece, slab, wedge, sliver, portion, share.
v, cut, carve, split, divide.

slide slip, glide, skate, skim, slither, skid.
let slide, neglect, forget, ignore, let ride.

slight *adj*, small, little, inconsiderable, slim, slender, light, minor, petty, insignificant, unimportant, trivial, trifling, paltry, superficial, flimsy, frail, feeble, weak, faint. CONSIDERABLE
v, snub, cut (*inf*), ignore, disregard, cold-shoulder (*inf*), rebuff, insult, affront, scorn, disdain, disparage. ACKNOWLEDGE
n, snub, rebuff, cold shoulder (*inf*), disregard, indifference, neglect, scorn, contempt, insult, affront, disrespect, disparagement. RESPECT

slim slender, thin, lean, spare, willowy, svelte, slight, small, inconsiderable, poor. FAT

slime mud, mire, ooze, sludge, muck, mucus.

slimy muddy, miry, oozy, mucous, mucilaginous, viscous, glutinous.

sling throw, fling, hurl, toss, cast, chuck (*inf*).
suspend, hang, dangle, swing.

slink sneak, steal, creep, prowl, skulk.

slip[1] *v*, slide, glide, slither, skid, trip, fall.
err, blunder, slip up, go wrong.
sneak, steal, creep, slink.
let slip, disclose, reveal, divulge, blurt out, leak, give away.
n, error, mistake, blunder, boob (*inf*), oversight, omission, indiscretion, fault.

slip[2] *n*, scion, cutting, offshoot, sprout, twig.
strip, sliver, note, chit.

slippery smooth, glassy, icy, greasy, lubricated, perilous, unsafe.
treacherous, perfidious, faithless, unreliable, untrustworthy, shifty, tricky, crafty, cunning, dishonest. TRUSTWORTHY

slipshod negligent, careless, slapdash, disorderly, untidy, messy, slovenly, slatternly. CAREFUL

slit *v*, cut, slash, gash, split, rip, tear. MEND
n, cut, incision, slash, gash, split, opening, rip, tear. SEAM

slope *v*, incline, slant, lean, tilt, list, shelve.
n, incline, inclination, ramp, gradient, pitch, cant, slant, tilt, acclivity, declivity. LEVEL

sloping oblique, slanting, slanted, inclined.

sloppy wet, watery, slushy, muddy. DRY
careless, loose, slapdash, slipshod, messy, untidy.
sentimental, emotional, mawkish, maudlin, mushy (*inf*), soppy (*inf*).

slot opening, aperture, hole, slit, crack, groove.

sloth slothfulness, laziness, indolence, idleness, inertia, inactivity, torpor, sluggishness. INDUSTRY

slothful lazy, indolent, idle, sluggardly, inert, inactive, torpid, sluggish. INDUSTRIOUS

slouch stoop, droop, slump, shuffle, shamble, lumber.

slough bog, morass, swamp, quagmire.

slovenly slatternly, sluttish, untidy, unkempt, sloppy (*inf*), careless, slipshod, slapdash, disorderly, negligent, loose.

slow *adj*, leisurely, unhurried, easy, gradual, deliberate, measured, sluggish, lazy, dawdling, plodding, crawling, creeping, slack, inactive, protracted, lingering. FAST
late, behindhand, tardy, backward, dilatory. PROMPT
unintelligent, stupid, thick, dense, dull, obtuse, blockish, bovine. SMART
tedious, boring, uninteresting, dull, tiresome, wearisome. LIVELY
reluctant, hesitant, unwilling, loath, disinclined.
v, brake, decelerate, delay, retard, hold up, hold back, check. SPEED

sluggish slow, torpid, inert, inactive, heavy, dull, lethargic, lazy, slothful, indolent, idle, sleepy, drowsy. QUICK

slumber sleep, rest, repose, doze, drowse, nap, snooze (*inf*).

slump *v*, sink, fall, drop, plunge, decrease, decline, collapse, sag, droop, bend, slouch. RISE
n, recession, depression, decline, fall, collapse, failure. BOOM

slur slight, insult, aspersion, innuendo, insinuation, slander, calumny, stigma, brand, smear, stain, disgrace.

slut slattern, sloven, trollop, frump.

sly artful, cunning, crafty, wily, foxy, subtle, shrewd, astute, sharp, knowing, guileful, scheming, insidious, devious, underhand, furtive, clandestine, stealthy, roguish, impish, arch, mischievous. ARTLESS

smack[1] *n*, flavour, taste, savour, tang, smell, aroma, trace, hint, tinge, touch, dash.
v, **smack of**, resemble, be like, suggest, smell of.

smack[2] *v*, slap, hit, strike, cuff, box, spank, pat.
n, blow, hit, slap, pat.

small little, tiny, short, slight, diminutive, miniature, minute, microscopic. BIG
insignificant, unimportant, minor, trifling, trivial, paltry, petty, mean, small-minded, narrow-minded.
limited, meagre, scanty, insufficient, inadequate. AMPLE
humble, modest, unpretentious, simple, low, base. GRAND

smart *adj*, spruce, trim, neat, dapper, elegant, fashionable, chic, stylish, modish. UNTIDY
bright, clever, intelligent, witty, shrewd, astute, sharp, acute, quick-witted, ready, prompt, alert, apt, adept, active, agile, quick, lively, spirited, brisk. SLOW
keen, sharp, poignant, stinging, painful, severe. DULL
v, sting, prick, burn, tingle, throb, pain, hurt.
n, sting, prick, pain, pang.

smash *v*, break, shatter, splinter, shiver, dash, crash, pulverize, crush, demolish, destroy, wreck, ruin, defeat.
n, crash, collision, wreck, ruin, destruction, defeat, collapse, failure.

smear *v*, besmear, daub, bedaub, rub, spread, plaster, coat, cover, soil, dirty, smudge. SCOUR
slander, libel, calumniate, slur, vilify, sully, tarnish, blacken.
n, smudge, patch, spot, smear, blot.
slander, libel, calumny, defamation, slur, aspersion.

smell *v*, sniff, inhale, scent, detect.
stink, reek, pong (*inf*).
n, odour, scent, aroma, perfume, fragrance, redolence, bouquet, whiff, stink, stench, fetor.

smile grin, beam, smirk, simper. FROWN

smirk simper, grimace, grin, smile.

smoke *n*, fumes, gas, vapour, mist, fog, smog.
v, fume, smoulder, exhale, puff, draw, inhale, fumigate, cure.

smooth *adj*, level, even, flush, plane, horizontal, flat, uniform, regular. UNEVEN
glossy, shiny, polished, silky, sleek, glassy, calm, still, peaceful, unruffled, mild, bland. ROUGH
flowing, fluent, easy, facile, glib, slick, oily, unctuous, suave, urbane.
v, level, plane, flatten, iron, press.
polish, lubricate, ease, facilitate, calm, soothe, appease, pacify, assuage, allay, mitigate, alleviate.

smother suffocate, stifle, asphyxiate, choke, strangle, extinguish, snuff out. REVIVE
suppress, repress, hold back, conceal, hide, muffle, stifle.
envelop, cover, shroud, surround, heap, shower.

smoulder burn, smoke, fume, simmer, seethe, boil.

smudge *v*, smear, blur, soil, dirty, smirch, stain.
n, smear, blur, blot, spot, blotch, smut, streak.

smug complacent, self-satisfied, content, conceited, proud, self-righteous.

smut smudge, smear, spot, stain, streak, soot, dirt.

smutty dirty, filthy, obscene, indecent, risqué, racy, ribald, bawdy, vulgar, crude, coarse, earthy, blue, pornographic. CLEAN

snag drawback, disadvantage, difficulty, problem, catch, hitch, hindrance, impediment, obstacle, stumbling block. ADVANTAGE

snap *v*, break, crack, pop, come apart.
bite, nip, growl, bark, flash, sparkle.
snap up, grab, seize, take, nab (*inf*).
n, crack, pop, click, bite, nip, grab.
catch, clasp, fastener.

snapshot, photograph, photo (*inf*).
snappy snappish, waspish, testy, touchy, irritable, irascible, peevish, petulant, peppery, grumpy, crabbed, crusty, cross, ill-tempered. AFFABLE
brisk, quick, sharp, abrupt, brusque, curt.
smart, fashionable, chic, stylish, elegant. SHABBY
snare *n*, trap, gin, springe, noose, net.
v, catch, net, trap, entrap, ensnare. FREE
snarl[1] growl, bark, snap, threaten, grumble. PURR
snarl[2] tangle, entangle, ravel, confuse, complicate, embroil. DISENTANGLE
snatch *v*, grab, seize, grasp, clutch, clasp, grip, pluck, pull, take, wrest, rescue, save. RELEASE
n, bit, fragment, scrap, snippet, spell.
sneak steal, creep, slip, sidle, slink, skulk, prowl, lurk.
inform, grass (*inf*), tell tales.
sneer *v*, jeer, scoff, gibe, mock, scorn, deride, disdain. ADMIRE
n, jeer, gibe, taunt, mockery, scorn, derision, contempt, disdain. RESPECT
sniff inhale, breathe in, snuff, snuffle, smell.
snigger laugh, titter, giggle, chuckle, smirk, sneer.
snip *v*, cut, clip, trim, crop, nick, slit.
n, cut, nick, bit, piece, scrap, shred, fragment, snippet, cutting, clipping, bargain.
snivel cry, weep, sob, blubber, whine, whimper, sniffle, snuffle. LAUGH
snobbish condescending, patronizing, stuck-up (*inf*), snooty (*inf*), arrogant, supercilious, high and mighty. HUMBLE
snub *v*, slight, cut (*inf*), cold-shoulder (*inf*), rebuff, ignore, insult, humiliate, mortify.
n, slight, rebuff, insult, affront, humiliation, mortification. FLATTERY
snug cosy, comfortable, comfy (*inf*), intimate, homely, warm, sheltered, protected, safe, secure. EXPOSED
small, compact, trim, neat, tight, close-fitting.
snuggle nestle, cuddle, nuzzle, curl up.
so thus, therefore, hence.
also, too, likewise, similarly.
very, extremely.
soak wet, drench, saturate, steep, immerse, damp, moisten, permeate, infuse, penetrate, absorb. DRY
soar rise, mount, ascend, climb, tower, fly. SINK
sob cry, weep, blubber, bawl. LAUGH
sober temperate, moderate, teetotal, abstemious, abstinent. DRUNK
rational, reasonable, level-headed, calm, composed, cool, staid, sedate, solemn, serious, grave, sombre, dark, drab, subdued, plain, quiet, cold, realistic, practical, sound.
sobriety temperance, moderation, self-restraint, abstinence, soberness, teetotalism. DRUNKENNESS
calmness, composure, staidness, solemnity, seriousness, gravity.
sociable friendly, genial, cordial, neighbourly, amiable, affable, communicative, companionable, gregarious, outgoing, social. UNSOCIABLE
social communal, community, group, collective, common, public, civil, civic. PERSONAL
sociable, friendly, genial, amiable, affable, companionable, gregarious, convivial. ASOCIAL
society association, organization, club, circle, group, league, guild, union, fraternity, fellowship, body, community.
company, companionship, fellowship, camaraderie. PRIVACY
humanity, mankind, community, public, people, civilization.
elite, upper classes, high society, gentry, aristocracy, nobility. COMMONALTY
sodden soaked, saturated, drenched, waterlogged, sopping, dripping, wet, soggy, flooded, boggy, marshy. DRY
soft spongy, squashy, mushy, pulpy, yielding, elastic, pliable, malleable, flexible, plastic. HARD
silky, smooth, velvety, furry. COARSE
quiet, low, faint, dim, muted, subdued, light, pale, delicate, bland, mellow, sweet, dulcet, gentle, mild, moderate, temperate. HARSH
tender, kind, compassionate, soft-hearted, sympathetic, sensitive, sentimental, lenient, clement, indulgent, permissive, lax. SEVERE
soften melt, mellow, moderate, temper, cushion, lighten, ease, relax, lessen, diminish, weaken, abate, mitigate, allay, assuage, soothe, calm, pacify, appease, subdue, mute, muffle, lower.

soil¹ *v*, dirty, begrime, besmirch, stain, spot, sully, foul, defile, taint, pollute, tarnish, smear. CLEAN

soil² *n*, earth, ground, dirt, dust, clay, loam.

sojourn *v*, stay, stop, tarry, rest, abide, dwell, lodge, reside. TRAVEL
n, stay, visit, rest, holiday.

solace *n*, consolation, comfort, relief, cheer. DISTRESS
v, console, comfort, cheer, relieve, alleviate. AFFLICT

sole only, single, one, lone, solitary, unique, exclusive, individual. NUMEROUS

solecism mistake, error, slip, blunder, gaffe, faux pas, impropriety, indiscretion, incongruity, absurdity.

solemn serious, earnest, sincere, grave, sober, staid, sedate, sombre, glum, gloomy. FRIVOLOUS
grand, stately, august, imposing, majestic, impressive, dignified, formal, ceremonial, ceremonious, ritual. INFORMAL
sacred, holy, religious, devotional. PROFANE

solemnize observe, keep, celebrate, commemorate, honour.

solicit ask, request, seek, crave, beg, beseech, implore, entreat, pray, petition, canvass, urge, importune, accost.

solicitous concerned, anxious, worried, uneasy, apprehensive, troubled, disturbed, earnest, eager, zealous, careful, thoughtful, attentive. INDIFFERENT

solid hard, dense, compact, firm, solidified, frozen, congealed, set, substantial, strong, sound, stable.
reliable, dependable, trustworthy, sure, sensible, level-headed, reasonable, logical.
genuine, real, pure, unalloyed, complete, whole, united, undivided.

solidarity unity, concordance, accord, union, fellowship, camaraderie, unanimity, stability. DISSENT

solidify harden, set, congeal, coagulate, jell, consolidate, unite. MELT

solitary alone, lone, sole, single, one, only, lonely, companionless, separate, reclusive, unsociable.
unfrequented, secluded, private, isolated, lonely, remote, out-of-the-way, cut off, desolate, deserted.

solitude loneliness, isolation, remoteness, seclusion, privacy, retirement. SOCIETY

solution answer, explanation, key, elucidation, clarification, resolution. PROBLEM
mixture, compound, blend, emulsion, suspension.

solve answer, work out, resolve, crack, unravel, disentangle, fathom, explain, interpret, clear up, elucidate, unfold. COMPLICATE

sombre dark, shadowy, dim, dull, drab, dreary, dismal, gloomy, melancholy, doleful, sad, mournful, lugubrious, funereal, sober, grave. BRIGHT

somebody someone, personage, notable, dignitary, VIP, celebrity, star, luminary, bigwig (*inf*), household name, public figure. NOBODY

sometimes occasionally, at times, now and then, from time to time, every so often. NEVER

somnolent drowsy, sleepy, dozy, slumberous, soporific. ALERT

song carol, hymn, psalm, anthem, ballad, lay, ditty, air, tune, melody, lyric, ode, sonnet.

sonorous resonant, resounding, loud, deep, rich, full, rounded, ringing, orotund, grandiloquent. SOFT

soon shortly, before long, anon, presently, in a minute, promptly, quickly. LATER

soothe calm, compose, still, quieten, pacify, tranquillize, ease, relieve, comfort, moderate, temper, mitigate, assuage, allay, alleviate, palliate, appease, soften, mollify. IRRITATE

soothsayer prophet, seer, augur, diviner, sibyl.

sophisticated refined, cultured, educated, worldly-wise, cosmopolitan, urbane, elegant, jet-set, seasoned, blasé. UNCOUTH
complex, complicated, intricate, advanced. PRIMITIVE

sophistry sophism, casuistry, fallacy, paralogism, quibble. TRUTH

soporific soporiferous, somniferous, somnific, sleep-inducing, sedative, narcotic, hypnotic, somnolent, sleepy. STIMULANT

sorcery magic, black magic, witchcraft, wizardry, necromancy, spell, charm, enchantment. EXORCISM

sordid dirty, filthy, foul, unclean, squalid, seedy, seamy, poor, wretched, shabby, mean, ignoble, base, low, vile, shameful, disgraceful. RESPECTABLE
greedy, avaricious, grasping, selfish, miserly, niggardly, parsimonious, ungenerous, mercenary, venal. GENEROUS

sore *adj*, tender, painful, raw, sensitive, inflamed, irritated, hurting, injured.
annoying, irritating, vexing, irksome, distressing, harrowing, grievous, afflictive, troublesome, sharp, acute, severe, dire.
annoyed, vexed, irked, irritated, aggrieved, hurt, upset, distressed. PLEASED
n, wound, injury, inflammation, ulcer, abscess, boil, gathering.

sorrow *n*, sadness, grief, woe, heartache, misery, anguish, mourning, unhappiness, distress, affliction, trouble, worry, regret. JOY
v, mourn, grieve, weep, lament, bemoan, bewail, despair. REJOICE

sorrowful sad, unhappy, depressed, dejected, miserable, woebegone, melancholy, disconsolate, heartbroken, mournful, doleful, weeping, tearful, sorry. JOYFUL

sorry apologetic, penitent, repentant, contrite, remorseful, regretful, compunctious, sheepish, shamefaced. IMPENITENT
sad, distressed, sorrowful, unhappy, moved, sympathetic. GLAD
wretched, miserable, pitiful, pitiable, piteous, pathetic, abject, poor, mean, shabby, paltry. SPLENDID

sort *n*, kind, class, category, order, group, genus, species, variety, type, character, nature, description, denomination, make, brand, style, breed, race, family.
v, arrange, order, categorize, classify, class, group, separate, divide, sort out, select, assort, organize, systematize, catalogue, file. MUDDLE

soul spirit, mind, reason, intellect, life, heart, essence, embodiment.
person, being, individual, man, woman, body, mortal, creature.
energy, vitality, animation, ardour, fervour, feeling, emotion.

sound[1] *n*, noise, report, din, racket, voice, utterance, tone, resonance. SILENCE
earshot, hearing, range.
v, utter, voice, pronounce, articulate, declare, announce.
resound, echo, reverberate, resonate, ring.
seem, appear.

sound[2] *adj*, fit, healthy, hale, hearty, vigorous, robust, sturdy, firm, solid, strong, whole, intact, undamaged, unimpaired, uninjured, unhurt, unbroken, perfect. FAULTY
sensible, reasonable, logical, rational, valid, good, reliable, dependable, correct, right, proper, fair, wise, sane, responsible, level-headed, stable, secure, safe. UNRELIABLE

sound[3] *v*, fathom, measure, plumb, probe, test, examine.

sound[4] *n*, channel, strait, passage, inlet.

soundless noiseless, quiet, silent, still, inaudible, muffled. NOISY

sour *adj*, tart, acid, acerbic, bitter, sharp, pungent, bad, rancid, unpleasant, offensive. SWEET
acrimonious, embittered, surly, ill-tempered, cross, snappy, testy, touchy, peevish, petulant, waspish, crabbed, sullen, morose, nasty, disagreeable. GENIAL
v, embitter, envenom, disenchant, disillusion.
ferment, turn, curdle, go off.

source origin, beginning, commencement, derivation, rise, spring, fountainhead, cause. ISSUE

souse plunge, immerse, submerge, dip, duck, drench, soak, steep, pickle, marinate.

souvenir keepsake, memento, reminder, token, relic.

sovereign *n*, ruler, monarch, king, queen, emperor, empress, tsar, autocrat, potentate, lord. SUBJECT
adj, royal, regal, majestic, kingly, queenly, imperial, ruling, supreme, predominant, chief, principal, excellent, efficacious.

sow plant, scatter, strew, broadcast, disseminate, propagate. REAP

space room, area, expanse, extension, capacity, volume, scope, range, margin, latitude, seat, place, accommodation.
gap, blank, break, pause, hiatus, lacuna, interval, period, time, distance, span.
universe, cosmos, sky, infinity. EARTH

spacious capacious, ample, roomy, commodious, big, large, vast, huge, broad, wide, extensive. SMALL

span *n*, extent, stretch, reach, spread, distance, space, interval, period, spell, duration.
v, bridge, cross, traverse, extend across, reach across.

spank smack, slap, beat, thrash.

spare *v*, save, rescue, pardon, release, relieve, protect, withhold, forbear. PUNISH
afford, give, part with, relinquish, manage without. KEEP
adj, extra, additional, superfluous, surplus, over, unwanted, free, unoccupied, reserve, emergency.
thin, lean, gaunt, skinny, meagre, scanty, frugal, sparing. AMPLE

sparing economical, thrifty, frugal, saving, careful, chary, mean, parsimonious. LAVISH

spark *n*, flash, sparkle, gleam, flicker, scintilla, trace, hint, atom, jot.
v, excite, stimulate, kindle, animate, inspire, activate, stir, start.

sparkle *v*, glitter, glisten, twinkle, shine, gleam, beam, flash, coruscate, shimmer, scintillate.
fizz, effervesce, bubble.
n, twinkle, spark, glint, gleam, flash, shine, brilliance, radiance. DULLNESS
liveliness, vivacity, spirit, élan, gaiety, animation, ebullience, effervescence.

sparse scattered, scanty, meagre, thin, few, scarce. DENSE

Spartan austere, harsh, strict, severe, rigorous, disciplined, ascetic, abstemious. INDULGENT
brave, courageous, heroic, valiant, bold, hardy, fearless, intrepid. COWARDLY

spasm convulsion, paroxysm, fit, attack, seizure, cramp, contraction, twitch, outburst, eruption.

spasmodic fitful, irregular, sporadic, intermittent, jerky, convulsive. REGULAR

spatter splash, scatter, strew, sprinkle, spray, bespatter, spot, daub.

speak talk, converse, say, utter, express, voice, articulate, enunciate, pronounce, state, tell, communicate.
discourse, address, lecture, orate, hold forth, harangue.

special especial, specific, definite, express, particular, certain, distinct, distinctive, individual, peculiar, unique, different, uncommon, unusual, exceptional, extraordinary, memorable, momentous, important, significant, distinguished, noteworthy. ORDINARY

specialist expert, connoisseur, authority, master, professional, consultant.

species group, sort, class, kind, type, variety, category, genus, description.

specific particular, definite, express, explicit, exact, precise, clear, distinct, special, especial, characteristic, peculiar. GENERAL

specification particular, item, detail, condition, stipulation, qualification, requirement, description.

specify state, name, mention, itemize, enumerate, designate, indicate, detail, spell out, stipulate, particularize, describe, define.

specimen sample, example, exemplar, illustration, case, instance, pattern, model, type.

specious misleading, deceptive, fallacious, sophistic, casuistic, plausible.

speck spot, dot, mark, stain, blemish, flaw, fleck, speckle, bit, jot, iota, atom, whit, mite, grain, particle.

spectacle sight, show, display, exhibition, scene, phenomenon, curiosity, marvel, wonder, vision, picture, parade, pageant, extravaganza, performance.

spectacular impressive, striking, breathtaking, staggering, grand, magnificent, remarkable, sensational, dramatic. ORDINARY

spectator onlooker, bystander, watcher, viewer, observer, witness.

spectre ghost, apparition, phantom, spook (*inf*), spirit, wraith, image, vision.

speculate conjecture, guess, surmise, suppose, theorize, hypothesize, consider, think, meditate, cogitate, reflect, deliberate, contemplate, ponder, muse, ruminate. KNOW

speculation conjecture, guess, surmise, supposition, theory, hypothesis, opinion, view, thought, deliberation, contemplation, rumination. REALITY

speech talk, address, oration, lecture, discourse, harangue, conversation, dialogue, communication, language, tongue, dialect, idiom, diction, articulation, enunciation, utterance.

speechless mute, dumb, silent, voiceless, inarticulate, tongue-tied, wordless, dumbfounded, amazed, astounded, shocked, thunderstruck. TALKATIVE

speed *n*, velocity, celerity, rapidity, swiftness, quickness, haste, hurry, acceleration, pace, rate. SLOWNESS *v*, hasten, hurry, rush, race, tear, accelerate, quicken, expedite, advance, further, boost, aid, assist. DELAY

speedy hasty, hurried, precipitate, expeditious, fast, quick, rapid, swift, prompt, early. SLOW

spell[1] charm, incantation, enchantment, bewitchment, fascination, allure, magic, sorcery.

spell[2] period, time, stretch, interval, term, stint, bout, turn.

spend disburse, pay out, expend, fork out (*inf*), squander, dissipate, waste, fritter away, use up, consume. SAVE
employ, use, apply, devote, pass, occupy, while away.

spendthrift *n*, wastrel, prodigal, profligate, squanderer, spender. MISER
adj, extravagant, prodigal, improvident, thriftless. THRIFTY

spent exhausted, worn out, weary, tired, fagged out (*inf*), dead beat (*inf*), all in (*inf*), drained, consumed, used up.

sphere ball, globe, orb, round. CUBE
field, domain, realm, province, department, territory, beat, range, order, rank, class, station.

spice flavour, savour, relish, tang, zest, piquancy, seasoning, flavouring.

spicy piquant, pungent, aromatic, fragrant, tangy, hot, seasoned, savoury. INSIPID
racy, bawdy, ribald, indelicate, risqué, scandalous, sensational.

spike point, prong, nail, pin.

spill upset, overturn, overflow, run over, pour out, disgorge, shed, scatter.

spin *v*, rotate, revolve, turn, twirl, whirl, wheel, pirouette, gyrate, reel.
tell, recount, relate, narrate, unfold, develop, invent.

spin out, protract, prolong, lengthen, extend, drag out, draw out, amplify, pad out. ABRIDGE
n, ride, drive, jaunt, outing, whirl.

spine backbone, vertebrae, vertebral column, spinal column.
point, spike, barb, quill, needle, ridge.

spineless weak, feeble, weak-willed, irresolute, timid, pusillanimous, cowardly, faint-hearted, lily-livered. BOLD

spinney copse, coppice, thicket, grove, wood.

spiral *n*, helix, coil, corkscrew, whorl.
adj, helical, coiled, winding, twisting. STRAIGHT

spirit soul, life, breath, mind, will. BODY
mood, humour, temper, feeling, temperament, disposition, outlook, attitude.
liveliness, vivacity, animation, enthusiasm, zeal, ardour, fervour, vigour, energy, enterprise, dash, zest, valour, courage, mettle. APATHY
essence, quintessence, substance, character, nature, sense, drift, gist, tenor, significance, meaning, purport, intent.
ghost, apparition, spectre, phantom, fairy, sprite, imp, goblin, angel, demon.

spirited lively, vivacious, animated, active, energetic, vigorous, enthusiastic, ardent, fervent, courageous, brave, mettlesome. APATHETIC

spiritless listless, languid, torpid, sluggish, lethargic, lifeless, apathetic, melancholic, depressed, dejected, dispirited. SPIRITED

spiritual incorporeal, immaterial, intangible, ethereal, ghostly, supernatural. PHYSICAL
holy, sacred, religious, pious, devout, pure. PROFANE

spite *n*, malice, maliciousness, malevolence, malignity, venom, ill will, animosity, resentment, grudge, hate, gall, spleen, rancour, pique. BENEVOLENCE

in spite of, despite, notwithstanding, regardless of, in defiance of.
v, annoy, vex, offend, pique, nettle, provoke, hurt, injure. PLEASE

spiteful malicious, malevolent, malign, malignant, vindictive, rancorous, venomous, cruel. BENEVOLENT

splash *v*, spatter, bespatter, sprinkle, spray, shower, strew, dash, buffet, wash.
n, spot, splodge, daub, patch, dash, touch.
ostentation, display, spectacle, sensation.

spleen spite, spitefulness, malice, maliciousness, bitterness, acrimony, venom, gall, bile, pique, peevishness, petulance, ill will, irascibility, anger, wrath. BENEVOLENCE

splendid brilliant, resplendent, magnificent, fine, grand, stately, gorgeous, sumptuous, luxurious, showy, glorious, illustrious, superb, supreme, outstanding, admirable, excellent, first-class, marvellous, wonderful, super (*inf*). POOR

splendour brilliance, resplendence, magnificence, grandeur, pomp, display, parade, show, stateliness, majesty, glory.

splenetic spiteful, malicious, peevish, petulant, irritable, choleric, testy, touchy, surly, crabbed, crusty, churlish. GENIAL

splice join, unite, connect, bind, braid, plait, knit, interweave, intertwine, interlace. SEVER

splinter *v*, shatter, shiver, split, break up. *n*, piece, fragment, sliver, shard, chip.

split *v*, separate, divide, part, break, sever, cleave, cut, crack, rupture, burst, rip, tear, branch, fork, disband, divorce, split up. UNITE
share, divide, apportion, partition, parcel out.
n, crack, fissure, rip, tear, rift, rupture, break, breach, separation, division, partition, schism, disunion. UNION

spoil mar, harm, damage, injure, hurt, impair, disfigure, deface, blemish, ruin, wreck, destroy. IMPROVE
indulge, pamper, coddle, cosset, baby.
decay, go bad, go off, turn, addle, rot, putrefy.

spoils booty, loot, plunder, pillage, pickings, prize.

sponge wipe, mop, rub, clean, rub out, efface, expunge.
cadge, scrounge (*inf*), live off.

spongy porous, absorbent, soft, light, springy.

sponsor *n*, patron, backer, supporter, promoter, guarantor, godparent.
v, back, support, finance, subsidize, promote, guarantee.

spontaneous instinctive, natural, impulsive, impetuous, free, voluntary, willing, unforced, unprompted, gratuitous, unpremeditated, unplanned, extempore, impromptu. STUDIED

sporadic irregular, random, occasional, intermittent, fitful, spasmodic, infrequent, scattered, dispersed, isolated, separate. CONTINUOUS

sport *n*, game, exercise, play, recreation, amusement, diversion, entertainment, pastime, fun. WORK
jest, joke, mirth, fun, banter, badinage, raillery, mockery, ridicule.
v, frolic, gambol, frisk, romp, caper, play, disport, amuse oneself.
wear, display, show off.

sportive playful, gamesome, frolicsome, frisky, coltish, skittish, lively, sprightly, gay, merry. SEDATE

spot *n*, mark, dot, speckle, speck, stain, blot, blemish, flaw, patch, blotch, pimple.
place, site, locality, location, scene, area.
v, discern, make out, espy, descry, see, recognize, identify. MISS
mark, dot, speckle, stain, blot, taint, tarnish, soil, sully, dirty. CLEAN

spotless unspotted, immaculate, clean, pure, unsullied, unblemished, stainless, untarnished, perfect, flawless. IMPURE

spouse husband, wife, consort, companion, partner, mate, better half (*inf*).

spout gush, spurt, squirt, jet, spray, surge, stream, flow, pour, discharge.
orate, declaim, hold forth, speechify.

sprain wrench, twist, strain, rick.

sprawl loll, lounge, slouch, slump, spread, straggle.

spray[1] *n*, mist, drizzle, spindrift, foam, spume.
sprinkler, atomizer, aerosol.
v, sprinkle, spatter, splash, shower, scatter, atomize.

spray[2] *n*, sprig, shoot, bough, branch, posy, nosegay, corsage.

spread *v*, stretch, extend, widen, expand, dilate, swell, escalate, unfold, unfurl, unroll, open, sprawl. FOLD
disseminate, distribute, circulate, broadcast, promulgate, propagate, publicize, advertise, scatter, strew, sow, disperse, shed, radiate, diffuse. SUPPRESS
apply, daub, smear, plaster, cover, lay.
n, extent, expanse, stretch, reach, compass, range.
dissemination, dispersion, diffusion, radiation, transmission, escalation, development, increase, growth, expansion.
feast, banquet, repast, meal.

spree fling, revel, binge (*inf*), bender (*inf*), orgy, debauch, romp, lark (*inf*).

sprightly spry, agile, nimble, brisk, active, jaunty, airy, lively, animated, vivacious, gay, bouyant, jocose, jolly, blithe, cheerful, playful, frolicsome. LIFELESS

spring *v*, jump, leap, bound, vault, hop, skip, rebound, recoil.
start, begin, commence, rise, arise, issue, emanate, flow, emerge, proceed, originate, derive, stem. END

spring up, appear, develop, sprout, burgeon, shoot up. DISAPPEAR
n, jump, leap, bound, vault, hop, skip.
elasticity, resilience, springiness, bounce, give (*inf*).
well, fountainhead, wellspring, fount, source, origin, root, cause.

sprinkle scatter, strew, spray, shower, dust, dredge.

sprite elf, brownie, fairy, pixie, goblin, leprechaun, nymph, dryad.

sprout bud, burgeon, germinate, shoot, spring, grow, develop. WITHER

spruce smart, trim, natty (*inf*), dapper, neat, tidy. UNTIDY

spry brisk, nimble, agile, active, lively, sprightly, quick, alert. SLUGGISH

spur *n*, goad, prick, stimulus, motive, incentive, inducement, incitement, encouragement. DETERRENT
v, goad, prick, prod, prompt, push, press, drive, impel, stimulate, animate, incite, provoke, urge, encourage. DETER

spurious false, unreal, counterfeit, fake, phoney (*inf*), bogus, mock, sham, simulated, feigned, pretended, artificial, specious. GENUINE

spurn reject, rebuff, snub, disregard, scorn, despise, contemn, disdain. RESPECT

spurt gush, spout, squirt, jet, burst, surge.

spy *n*, agent, secret agent, double agent, informer, detective, scout.
v, watch, observe, see, espy, descry, discern, make out, spot, detect, notice. MISS

squabble *v*, quarrel, row, altercate, contend, bicker, wrangle, argue, dispute, fight, brawl. AGREE
n, quarrel, row, altercation, contention, disagreement, argument, dispute, wrangle, fight, tiff. AGREEMENT

squad band, gang, crew, team, company, troop, unit, group.

squalid foul, filthy, unclean, dirty, repulsive, nasty, sordid, seedy, run-down, decayed. CLEAN

squall *n*, gust, blast, gale, hurricane, storm, tempest.
v, cry, bawl, yell, shriek, scream, howl.

squander waste, dissipate, spend, blow (*inf*), fritter away, throw away, lavish, splurge, misuse, misspend. SAVE

square *n*, quadrate, rectangle, quadrilateral, cube. CIRCLE
place, plaza, piazza, quadrangle.
adj, rectangular, quadrilateral, right-angled, perpendicular, straight, true, level, even, equal, balanced. UNEVEN
fair, just, honest, straightforward. DISHONEST
conservative, conventional, strait-laced, old-fashioned. AVANT-GARDE
v, straighten, set, regulate, adjust, align, tailor, fit, adapt, accord, suit, accommodate, balance, harmonize, conform, reconcile.
settle, pay, discharge, liquidate, satisfy.

squash crush, squeeze, press, mash, pulp, compress, flatten.
suppress, quash, quell, silence, humiliate.

squat *v*, crouch, sit, cower. STAND
adj, short, squab, dumpy, stubby, stout, stocky, thickset, broad, tubby, fat. LANKY

squeak creak, whine, squeal, yelp, peep, pipe.

squeal cry, wail, yell, squall, squeak, yelp, shriek, scream.

squeamish queasy, qualmish, delicate, dainty, finicky, particular, fastidious, prudish.

squeeze press, compress, squash, crush, wring, pinch, constrict, grip, clasp, hug, embrace, crowd, jam, pack, cram, stuff, force.

squirm writhe, wriggle, twist, turn, shift, move.

squirt spout, spurt, gush, jet, eject, discharge.

stab *v*, pierce, stick, knife, spear, gore, transfix, cut, wound, hurt, injure, jab, thrust.
n, wound, injury, cut, gash, jab, thrust, pang, twinge, pain, ache.
try, attempt, effort, go (*inf*), shot (*inf*).

stable firm, steady, fast, fixed, established, sound, sturdy, solid, secure, constant, durable, lasting, abiding, permanent, unchanging, immutable, invariable, unalterable, perpetual, steadfast, sure, reliable. UNSTABLE

stack *n*, pile, heap, mass, load, hoard, store, mound, mountain.
v, pile, heap, amass, accumulate, hoard, load.

staff employees, personnel, workers, work force, teachers, officers, team, crew.
stick, cane, rod, pole, stave, club, crook, mace, baton, wand, prop, support.

stage *n*, point, juncture, period, phase, leg, step, level.

platform, dais, rostrum, podium, theatre, boards, scene, setting.
v, produce, present, put on, mount, perform, organize.

stagger totter, wobble, reel, sway, lurch, falter, hesitate, waver, vacillate.
astound, astonish, amaze, flabbergast (*inf*), bowl over (*inf*), dumbfound, stupefy, nonplus, confound, bewilder, stun, shock.
alternate, zigzag.

stagnant still, quiet, motionless, static, inert, standing, brackish, foul, stale, dull, sluggish. FLOWING

staid sedate, sober, serious, grave, solemn, quiet, settled, steady, demure, prim. FRIVOLOUS

stain *v*, mark, spot, dye, colour, discolour, soil, dirty, sully, blot, blemish, tarnish, blacken, taint, contaminate, defile, disgrace.
n, mark, spot, dye, tint, discoloration, blot, blemish, taint, stigma, slur, shame, disgrace.

stake[1] *n*, pale, picket, palisade, stick, post, pole.
v, tether, tie, fasten, secure, prop, support.
stake out, demarcate, mark out, outline, define, delimit, claim.

stake[2] *n*, bet, wager, ante, pledge, venture, risk, hazard, chance.
interest, concern, share, involvement, investment.
v, bet, wager, gamble, hazard, risk, venture, imperil, jeopardize.

stale old, musty, fusty, hard, dry, flat, insipid, tasteless, mouldy. FRESH
trite, banal, hackneyed, commonplace, unoriginal, dull.

stalk hunt, track, trail, shadow, follow, pursue, chase.
strut, stride, pace, march, flounce. SLINK

stall *n*, stand, booth, compartment, cubicle, pen, stable.
v, stop, halt, stick, get stuck.
delay, hedge, equivocate, prevaricate, play for time.

stalwart sturdy, stout, rugged, athletic, robust, lusty, hardy, strong, brave, valiant, intrepid, courageous, bold, daring, staunch, steadfast, firm, resolute. WEAK

stamina strength, vitality, energy, vigour, fortitude, endurance, resistance, resilience, power, force. WEAKNESS

stammer stutter, falter, hesitate, pause, stumble.

stamp *v*, tread, step, tramp, stomp (*inf*), trample, crush, beat, pound.
mark, brand, label, characterize, impress, imprint, print, engrave.
stamp out, quell, suppress, crush, put down, eliminate, eradicate, extirpate, extinguish.
n, mark, brand, print, impression, hallmark, seal, die, mould, cast, sort, kind, type, variety, character, description.

stampede rush, charge, flight, rout.

stand *v*, rise, get up, place, put, set.
stop, halt, pause, rest, stay, abide, remain, hold, continue, persist.
bear, tolerate, endure, suffer, abide, brook, withstand, resist.
stand by, defend, uphold, support, stick up for (*inf*). ABANDON
stand for, represent, symbolize, exemplify, betoken, denote, mean.
permit, allow, countenance, tolerate, brook, put up with (*inf*). OPPOSE
stand out, be prominent, be conspicuous, project, stick out.
n, stance, standpoint, position, attitude, opinion, point of view.
stop, halt, standstill, rest, stay. MOTION
station, post, place, platform, stall, rack, frame, support.
opposition, resistance, defiance. SUBMISSION

standard *n*, model, pattern, example, type, gauge, measure, criterion, yardstick, scale, rule, principle, norm, average.
flag, banner, ensign, pennant, pennon, colours.
adj, typical, regular, normal, usual, customary, orthodox, official, approved, accepted, recognized, classic, basic, universal. IRREGULAR

standing *n*, rank, status, position, station, reputation, repute, credit, estimation.
adj, upright, vertical, perpendicular, erect. HORIZONTAL
fixed, set, lasting, permanent, regular, static.

staple principal, chief, main, primary, basic, fundamental, essential, vital. MINOR

starchy stiff, formal, prim, conventional, precise, punctilious. LIBERAL

stare gaze, gape, goggle, gawk, look, watch. IGNORE

stark *adj*, absolute, sheer, arrant, downright, utter, unmitigated, pure, mere, outright, flagrant, blunt, bald.
bare, barren, bleak, grim, dreary, harsh, severe, austere, plain, simple.
adv, absolutely, utterly, quite, altogether, totally, entirely, completely, wholly, fully. PARTIALLY

start *v*, begin, commence, depart, set off, appear, arise, issue, originate, inaugurate, found, establish, institute, initiate, pioneer, open, launch, instigate, set in motion. FINISH
jump, flinch, wince, twitch, jerk, shy, recoil.
n, beginning, commencement, outset, dawn, birth, inception, origin, source, foundation, initiation. END
lead, advantage, head start, chance, opportunity, break (*inf*), opening.
jump, twitch, jerk, surprise.

startle surprise, take aback, alarm, scare, frighten, shock, amaze, astound, astonish. COMPOSE

starve die, perish, fast, hunger, be famished, be ravenous. GORGE

state *n*, condition, situation, circumstances, shape, form, phase, plight, predicament, case, status, rank.
pomp, ceremony, grandeur, magnificence, splendour, glory, majesty, dignity.
nation, country, republic, commonwealth, realm, kingdom, body politic, government.
v, say, utter, express, articulate, declare, assert, asseverate, aver, affirm, avow, maintain, profess, announce, proclaim. SUPPRESS

stately pompous, grand, magnificent, splendid, august, dignified, imposing, lofty, majestic, regal, royal, noble. LOWLY

statement declaration, announcement, proclamation, utterance, assertion, asseveration, averment, avowal, testimony, account, report, record.

station *n*, depot, terminus, headquarters, base, post, location, place, position, situation.
status, standing, rank, class, condition, degree.
v, post, assign, place, locate, fix, establish. MOVE

stationary static, immobile, immovable, fixed, motionless, still, inert. MOBILE

stature height, tallness, size, eminence, prominence, prestige, rank, standing.

status standing, station, position, condition, rank, degree, grade, prestige.

statute decree, edict, act, enactment, law, ordinance, rule, regulation.

staunch loyal, faithful, constant, true, reliable, dependable, steady, steadfast, firm, unwavering, stout, resolute. WAVERING

stave off avert, evade, dodge, ward off, fend off, avoid, parry, deflect, keep at bay.

stay[1] *v*, remain, keep, continue, abide, endure, persist, last.
stop, halt, pause, wait, delay, tarry, linger, loiter, rest, settle, live, reside, lodge, sojourn. MOVE
check, curb, prevent, obstruct, hinder, impede, adjourn, suspend, put off, defer. HASTEN
n, sojourn, visit, holiday, rest, stop, halt, pause, wait, delay, reprieve.

stay[2] *n*, prop, support, brace, buttress.

steadfast steady, fixed, intent, firm, unwavering, resolute, constant, loyal, faithful, staunch, dependable, stable. WAVERING

steady stable, firm, safe, sound, solid, balanced, fixed, steadfast, reliable, sensible, rational, calm, imperturbable. UNSTEADY
even, regular, rhythmic, uniform, unvarying, continuous, continual, perpetual, ceaseless, unremitting, constant, habitual. IRREGULAR

steal take, pilfer, purloin, filch, thieve, rob, shoplift, nick (*inf*), pinch (*inf*), embezzle, peculate, appropriate, plagiarize, poach. RETURN
creep, tiptoe, slip, slink, sneak.

stealthy furtive, sly, sneaky, underhand, clandestine, surreptitious, covert, secret. OPEN

steam vapour, mist, fog, condensation, smoke, fume, exhalation.

steel brace, fortify, toughen, harden. RELAX

steep[1] *adj*, sheer, abrupt, precipitous, sudden. GRADUAL
unreasonable, extreme, excessive, exorbitant. MODERATE

steep[2] *v*, soak, marinate, souse, drench, immerse, submerge, saturate, imbue, impregnate, infuse, pervade, permeate. DRY

steer pilot, guide, direct, control, conduct, lead.
steer clear of, shun, eschew, avoid, evade.
stem[1] *n*, stalk, trunk, peduncle, shaft, stock.
v, arise, come, issue, emanate, originate, derive.
stem[2] *v*, stop, stay, check, curb, hold back, restrain, dam, stanch.
stench stink, fetor, mephitis, effluvium, reek, pong (*inf*). PERFUME
stentorian loud, thundering, booming, deafening, powerful, sonorous. SOFT
step *n*, pace, stride, footstep, footfall, footprint, track, gait, walk.
proceeding, measure, move, action, act, deed, phase, stage.
stair, rung, rank, degree, grade, level.
v, move, walk, stride, pace, tread.
step up, increase, raise, augment, boost, accelerate, intensify. REDUCE
sterile barren, infertile, infecund, unprolific, unfruitful, fruitless, unproductive, abortive, empty, bare. FRUITFUL
sterilized, disinfected, germ-free, aseptic.
sterling genuine, true, real, sound, solid, pure, excellent, first-class. SPECIOUS
stern strict, severe, harsh, hard, rigid, firm, adamant, inflexible, unyielding, uncompromising, relentless, inexorable, grim, forbidding, dour, austere. LENIENT
stew simmer, boil, seethe.
stick[1] *n*, rod, staff, wand, baton, pole, cane, twig, switch, birch, club.
stick[2] *v*, stab, pierce, puncture, penetrate, spear, transfix, impale, gore, jab, thrust.
fasten, attach, join, fix, set, glue, paste.
cement, weld, adhere, cling, cleave, hold. SEPARATE
put, place, lay, plant, drop, deposit.
stay, remain, persist, abide.
stick out, protrude, project, jut out, poke out, extend, bulge.
stick up for, support, champion, defend, stand up for. OPPOSE
sticky adhesive, gummy, gluey, glutinous, viscid, viscous, tacky. DRY
muggy, close, humid, sultry. FRESH
difficult, awkward, tricky, delicate, unpleasant.
stiff rigid, inflexible, unbending, unyielding, firm, hard, solid, thick, tight, taut, tense. LIMP
harsh, severe, stringent, unsparing, pitiless, merciless, cruel, oppressive, excessive, extreme. LENIENT
difficult, hard, arduous, laborious, strenuous, fatiguing, exacting, rigorous, tough, trying. EASY
formal, starchy (*inf*), strait-laced, prim, priggish, strict, precise, punctilious, ceremonious, pompous, chilly, cold, aloof, standoffish, constrained, unrelaxed, awkward, clumsy, graceless, inelegant.
strong, potent, powerful, vigorous, fresh, brisk, keen. LIGHT
stifle suffocate, asphyxiate, choke, smother, strangle, restrain, check, curb, suppress, repress, silence, hush, quell, extinguish.
stigma mark, spot, blot, stain, blemish, brand, slur, defamation, shame, disgrace, dishonour.
still *adj*, motionless, immobile, inert, stationary, static, stagnant, calm, tranquil, serene, sedate, placid, peaceful, pacific, unruffled, undisturbed, smooth, quiet, silent, noiseless. AGITATED
n, stillness, silence, quiet, hush, calm, tranquillity, peace, peacefulness. NOISE
v, hush, quieten, silence, lull, calm, tranquillize, appease, pacify, compose, soothe, allay, assuage, alleviate, settle, subdue, check, stop. AGITATE
adv, yet, even, however, nevertheless, notwithstanding, but.
stilted bombastic, pompous, turgid, inflated, high-flown, grandiloquent, formal, stiff, wooden, laboured, forced. SIMPLE
stimulate arouse, rouse, excite, foment, fire, kindle, inflame, goad, spur, prick, prompt, urge, incite, instigate, provoke, motivate, animate, invigorate, inspirit, encourage, impel. DETER
stimulus incentive, fillip, provocation, motive, spur, goad, impulse, urge, incitement, inducement, encouragement. DETERRENT
sting prick, bite, burn, smart, tingle, pain, hurt, injure, wound, afflict, distress. SOOTHE
stingy mean, parsimonious, niggardly, miserly, penurious, tight-fisted, close-fisted, ungenerous. GENEROUS
meagre, scanty, small, measly (*inf*), insufficient, inadequate. AMPLE
stink *n*, stench, fetor, mephitis, effluvium, reek, pong (*inf*). PERFUME

v, reek, smell, pong (*inf*).

stint *v*, limit, restrict, confine, restrain, scrimp, economize, save, skimp, begrudge. LAVISH
n, period, spell, shift, turn, share, ration, quota, part, duty, assignment, task, work.

stipend pay, salary, wages, remuneration, emolument, allowance, honorarium.

stipulate specify, insist, require, demand, agree, contract, guarantee, promise, pledge, engage.

stipulation condition, specification, prerequisite, requirement, demand, provision, proviso, qualification, clause, term, obligation, agreement, contract.

stir *v*, move, budge, exert oneself, shift, go. STAY
mix, blend, beat, whip, disturb, agitate, rustle, shake.
rouse, awaken, arouse, stimulate, provoke, spur, goad, incite, instigate, prompt, excite, thrill, animate, galvanize, inspire, inflame, affect, touch, move.
n, excitement, commotion, disorder, confusion, ado, to-do, fuss, bother, uproar, tumult, activity, movement, hustle, bustle, flurry, agitation. TRANQUILLITY

stirring rousing, stimulating, moving, exciting, thrilling, exhilarating, impassioned, dramatic, animated, spirited, lively, active, busy. DULL

stock *n*, store, supply, hoard, reserve, reservoir, fund, accumulation, collection, assortment, range, variety, goods, wares, commodities, capital.
cattle, sheep, horses, pigs, animals, livestock.
trunk, stalk, stem, shaft, butt, handle.
type, species, breed, race, family, house, lineage, descent, pedigree, ancestry, parentage, extraction.
adj, standard, staple, basic, usual, normal, customary, traditional, commonplace, hackneyed, trite, state. NOVEL
v, keep, deal in, sell, supply, provision, equip, store, amass, accumulate, hoard, save, reserve.

stoical philosophical, patient, long-suffering, resigned, indifferent, apathetic, impassive, dispassionate, cool, calm, imperturbable, phlegmatic. EXCITABLE

stolid dull, obtuse, bovine, stupid, slow, indifferent, apathetic, impassive, phlegmatic.

stomach *n*, abdomen, belly, tummy (*inf*), gut, paunch.
appetite, hunger, relish, liking, desire, inclination, leaning, proclivity. AVERSION
v, tolerate, bear, endure, suffer, abide, stand, put up with (*inf*), swallow.

stone pebble, rock, boulder, cobble, gem, jewel, seed, pip.

stony hard, flinty, impenetrable, adamant, unfeeling, callous, cold, pitiless, merciless, cruel, rigid, inflexible, obdurate, expressionless, blank.

stoop bend, lean, incline, bow, hunch, crouch, squat, kneel, slouch, droop, duck.
condescend, deign, submit, yield, acquiesce, descend, lower oneself.

stop *v*, halt, pause, cease, discontinue, quit, desist, finish, complete, conclude, end, terminate, arrest, check, curb, restrain, repress, suppress, stall, delay, hinder, hamper, impede, thwart, prevent, obstruct, block, stem, close, plug, seal.
visit, sojourn, stay, remain, rest, tarry, wait, linger. DEPART
n, halt, standstill, pause, break, interruption, intermission, cessation, end, finish, conclusion, termination, arrest, stoppage. CONTINUATION
visit, sojourn, stay, rest.
impediment, block, obstacle, hindrance, bar, plug, stopper.

store *v*, amass, accumulate, stockpile, garner, save, reserve, put aside, hoard, keep, preserve, husband. CONSUME
n, stock, stockpile, supply, fund, hoard, reserve, accumulation, mass, abundance, plenty.
warehouse, storehouse, depot, depository, repository.
shop, market, mart, emporium.

storm *n*, tempest, squall, gale, hurricane, tornado, blizzard. CALM
assault, attack, onslaught, onset, rush, raid, blitz.
disturbance, outbreak, disorder, commotion, tumult, turmoil, furore, riot, outburst, tantrum. PEACE
v, rage, roar, thunder, rant, rave, fume.
assail, assault, attack, raid, charge, rush.

stormy tempestuous, wild, violent, rough, turbulent, squally, windy, gusty, blustery, raging, furious. STILL

story tale, romance, novel, narrative, narration, account, recital, history, legend, myth, fable, anecdote, yarn (*inf*), fiction, lie, fib, falsehood. FACT

stout fat, obese, overweight, corpulent, portly, rotund, plump, heavy, large, big. THIN

sturdy, strong, substantial, robust, lusty, brawny, strapping, athletic, rugged, tough, hardy, brave, courageous, valiant, bold, fearless, intrepid, stout-hearted, resolute, firm, staunch, stalwart. WEAK

stow pack, stuff, cram, load, store, hoard, hide, secrete.

straggle stray, digress, deviate, ramble, wander, roam, rove, range, drift, lag, trail.

straight *adj*, direct, undeviating, unswerving, level, even, horizontal, vertical, upright, erect, right, true. CROOKED

honest, honourable, upright, respectable, just, fair, reliable, trustworthy, straightforward. DISHONEST

neat, tidy, orderly, shipshape. UNTIDY

adv, directly, immediately, instantly, frankly, candidly, honestly.

straightaway immediately, instantly, at once, right away, forthwith, directly, now. LATER

straightforward frank, candid, forthright, plain, open, sincere, genuine, honest, truthful, direct, straight. DECEITFUL

simple, easy, uncomplicated. COMPLICATED

strain[1] *v*, tighten, stretch, extend, pull, wrench, sprain, injure, exert, tax, force, drive, overexert, overtax, exhaust, fatigue, tire, weaken, strive, struggle, labour, overwork. RELAX

filter, percolate, screen, sieve, sift, purify.

n, stretch, pull, wrench, sprain, injury, effort, struggle, force, exertion, fatigue, tension, stress, pressure. RELAXATION

tune, melody, air, theme, song, lay.

strain[2] *n*, family, race, stock, ancestry, descent, lineage, extraction, pedigree, breed.

trace, streak, vein, tendency.

strait channel, sound, narrows.

dilemma, quandary, predicament, plight, difficulty, problem, trouble, distress, hardship.

straitened distressed, embarrassed, pinched, reduced, limited, restricted, impoverished, destitute.

strand[1] *v*, maroon, cast away, shipwreck, beach, ground, run aground, abandon, desert, leave. RESCUE

n, shore, coast, beach.

strand[2] thread, fibre, filament, string, hair.

strange odd, peculiar, curious, queer, uncommon, unusual, rare, singular, exceptional, remarkable, extraordinary, irregular, abnormal, weird, bizarre, eccentric, unaccountable, inexplicable. NORMAL

unfamiliar, unknown, untried, exotic, foreign, alien, new, novel, unaccustomed, inexperienced. FAMILIAR

stranger alien, foreigner, visitor, guest, newcomer, outsider. ACQUAINTANCE

strangle throttle, choke, suffocate, smother, asphyxiate, stifle, gag, repress, suppress.

strap *n*, belt, thong, strip, band.

v, tie, bind, truss, lash, fasten, secure. LOOSE

beat, flog, whip, lash, scourge, belt.

stratagem ruse, artifice, trick, wile, scheme, plot, plan, ploy, gambit, manoeuvre, machination, device.

strategy tactics, approach, policy, plan, programme, scheme.

stratum layer, bed, seam, vein.

level, grade, degree, rank, station, class.

stray *v*, wander, roam, rove, ramble, range, drift, straggle, meander, digress, deviate, swerve, go astray, err.

adj, lost, abandoned, homeless, vagrant, wandering.

scattered, random, accidental, chance, isolated.

streak strip, stripe, line, band, bar, stroke.

strain, vein, trace, element.

stream *n*, brook, beck, burn, river, freshet, rivulet, rill, run, tributary, current, race, drift, course, flow, tide, rush, gush, torrent, outpouring.

v, flow, issue, pour, cascade, run, course, rush, gush, spout. HALT

streamer pennon, pennant, flag, ensign, standard, banner, ribbon.

street thoroughfare, road, avenue, boulevard.

strength power, might, force, vigour, energy, sinew, muscle, brawn, hardiness, robustness, sturdiness, toughness, durability, fortitude, backbone. WEAKNESS

intensity, vehemence, potency, efficacy, cogency, validity, soundness.

strengthen fortify, reinforce, invigorate, energize, hearten, encourage, nerve, steel, brace, harden, toughen. WEAKEN
support, back up, confirm, substantiate, intensify, heighten.

strenuous energetic, vigorous, active, forceful, ardent, zealous, persistent, tireless, determined, resolute. FEEBLE
arduous, hard, difficult, laborious, toilsome, tough, tiring, taxing.

stress *n*, emphasis, accent, accentuation, weight, importance, significance, urgency.
strain, tension, force, pressure, worry, anxiety. RELAXATION
v, emphasize, accentuate, accent, underline, point up, harp on, dwell on, repeat.

stretch *v*, extend, lengthen, elongate, pull, draw out, expand, distend, tighten, strain, reach, spread, cover. CONTRACT
n, extent, reach, range, scope, compass.
expanse, area, space, spell, period, time.

strew scatter, spread, diffuse, disperse, sow, sprinkle, broadcast. GATHER

stricken afflicted, smitten, hit, struck, wounded, laid low.

strict rigorous, stringent, harsh, rigid, inflexible, stern, severe, austere. LENIENT
exact, precise, accurate, faithful, close, careful, particular, punctilious, scrupulous. LOOSE
complete, total, utter, absolute.

stricture censure, blame, criticism, animadversion. PRAISE

stride pace, step, walk, march.

strident harsh, grating, raucous, jarring, discordant, loud, clamorous, vociferous. SOFT

strife conflict, discord, dissension, friction, animosity, disagreement, contention, quarrel, row, dispute, brawl, battle, fight, struggle, contest, rivalry. PEACE

strike hit, tap, knock, buffet, cuff, box, punch, slap, smack, beat, pound, thump. CARESS
collide, crash, hit, bump, touch.
attack, assail, assault, set upon, afflict.
impress, affect, dawn on, occur to, reach.
walk out, down tools, mutiny, revolt.
strike out, delete, cross out, erase, efface, cancel.

striking impressive, stunning (*inf*), wonderful, extraordinary, noticeable, conspicuous. COMMONPLACE

string *n*, cord, twine, rope, thread.
series, chain, row, line, file, queue, procession.
v, hang, suspend, festoon, loop, join, link.
string along, deceive, fool, dupe, bluff.
string out, stretch, extend, lengthen, space out, spread out, straggle.

stringent strict, severe, harsh, rigorous, exacting, demanding, tough, tight, rigid, inflexible. LAX

strip[1] *v*, peel, skin, remove, deprive, divest, denude, bare, uncover, undress, disrobe, unclothe. COVER
rob, plunder, despoil, pillage, sack, loot, ransack, gut.

strip[2] *n*, band, stripe, belt, ribbon, fillet, piece, shred.

stripe band, bar, line, streak, strip.

stripling youth, youngster, lad, boy.

strive struggle, labour, toil, strain, try, attempt, exert, endeavour, aim, aspire, compete, contend, fight.

stroke *n*, blow, hit, knock, tap, rap, slap, cuff, thump.
feat, accomplishment, achievement, action.
apoplexy, paralysis, attack, fit, seizure, collapse.
v, caress, rub, pat, fondle, pet.

stroll *v*, walk, amble, saunter, ramble, wander. RUN
n, walk, constitutional, promenade, amble, saunter, airing, excursion, ramble.

strong powerful, mighty, muscular, sinewy, brawny, athletic, strapping, rugged, stalwart, lusty, hale, hearty, healthy, robust, hardy, tough, stout, sound, solid, sturdy, durable, substantial, firm, resolute. WEAK
intense, deep, bright, vivid, concentrated, potent, fierce, violent, vehement, vigorous, fervent, zealous, eager, keen, sharp, hot, spicy, piquant, pungent.
weighty, effective, forceful, cogent, convincing, persuasive.

stronghold fortress, fort, citadel, bastion, bulwark, keep.

structure building, edifice, erection, construction, fabric, form, formation, framework, arrangement, organization, composition, make-up.

struggle *v*, strive, fight, battle, contend, wrestle, compete, labour, endeavour, try, work. YIELD

n, fight, battle, skirmish, clash, conflict, strife, contention, contest. PEACE
effort, exertion, strain, trouble, labour, toil, work, endeavour.

strut swagger, prance, parade, stalk, flounce.

stub butt, end, tail, stump, counterfoil.

stubborn obstinate, mulish, pig-headed, headstrong, wilful, perverse, contrary, refractory, recalcitrant, contumacious, ungovernable, unmanageable, inflexible, unbending, unyielding, intractable, persistent, dogged, obdurate. AMENABLE

stubby short, squat, stumpy, dumpy, stocky, thickset. LONG
rough, stubbly, bristly. SMOOTH

stuck fixed, fast, lodged, jammed, embedded. FREE
baffled, mystified, stumped, nonplussed, puzzled, perplexed.

student pupil, scholar, learner, apprentice, trainee, undergraduate. MASTER

studied deliberate, wilful, premeditated, calculated, contrived, forced, planned, intentional, considered. SPONTANEOUS

studious scholarly, academic, intellectual, bookish, diligent, industrious, sedulous, assiduous, careful, attentive, thoughtful, reflective, serious, earnest. LAZY

study *v*, learn, swot (*inf*), work, read, peruse, pore over, scan, scrutinize, examine, investigate, research, consider, weigh, ponder, meditate, muse, reflect, cogitate, ruminate. IGNORE
n, learning, reading, work, application, thought, reflection, contemplation, meditation, attention, consideration, research, investigation, analysis, examination, scrutiny, inquiry, survey.

stuff *v*, fill, pack, cram, crowd, jam, press, squeeze, force, thrust, shove, ram.
n, cloth, fabric, material, matter, substance, essence.
belongings, effects, things, gear, paraphernalia, trappings, goods, chattels, possessions.
rubbish, nonsense, humbug, bunkum, balderdash, rot.

stuffing padding, packing, wadding, filling.
forcemeat, dressing.

stuffy close, airless, sultry, oppressive, musty, fusty, stale. FRESH
dull, uninteresting, stodgy, old-fashioned, square (*inf*), strait-laced, staid, prim, priggish, conservative, pompous.

stumble trip, fall, lurch, stagger, flounder, blunder, err, falter.

stumble upon, happen upon, chance upon, come across, find, discover. MISS

stump *n*, trunk, remnant, stub, butt, end.
v, baffle, mystify, nonplus, puzzle, perplex, confuse, confound. ENLIGHTEN
stamp, stomp (*inf*), trudge, plot, lumber, clump, clomp.

stun stupefy, daze, knock out, shock, amaze, astound, astonish, overwhelm, flabbergast (*inf*), bowl over (*inf*), stagger, dumbfound.

stunt feat, exploit, trick, act, deed.

stunted undersized, dwarfish, pygmy, diminutive, short, small, little, tiny. GIANT

stupefy benumb, stun, daze, bemuse, shock, amaze, astound, astonish, stagger, dumbfound, confound, confuse.

stupendous astounding, astonishing, amazing, staggering, wonderful, marvellous, extraordinary, phenomenal, fantastic, fabulous, tremendous, immense, vast, colossal, prodigious, massive, enormous, huge, gigantic. ORDINARY

stupid unintelligent, dull, slow, thick, dense, brainless, witless, dim-witted, simple, feeble-minded, foolish, silly, idiotic, asinine, inane, absurd, ridiculous, ludicrous, senseless, pointless, imprudent, unwise, rash, irresponsible. INTELLIGENT
stupefied, stunned, dazed, groggy, sluggish, torpid.

stupor coma, unconsciousness, daze, trance, numbness, stupefaction, torpor, lethargy, sluggishness.

sturdy strong, powerful, brawny, muscular, strapping, stalwart, robust, hardy, lusty, hale, hearty, healthy, vigorous, sound, solid, stout, tough, substantial, durable, firm, staunch. WEAK

stutter stammer, hesitate, pause, falter, stumble.

style *n*, manner, mode, method, way, approach, fashion, design, cut, shape, form, kind, type, sort, tone, tenor.
vogue, mode, fashion, trend, chic, elegance, smartness, taste, refinement, culture, sophistication, urbanity.
v, design, fashion, cut, shape, tailor, adapt.

name, call, designate, denominate, dub, label.

stylish fashionable, modish, chic, smart, elegant, classy (*inf*), suave, urbane, sophisticated. DOWDY

suave urbane, sophisticated, smooth, polite, courteous, civil, agreeable, pleasant, charming, gracious, affable. RUDE

subconscious inner, innermost, deep, hidden, latent, repressed, suppressed, unconscious, subliminal.

subdue conquer, vanquish, subjugate, rout, crush, defeat, overwhelm, overpower, overcome, master, control, discipline, humble, quell, check, curb, restrain, suppress, repress, reduce, moderate, soften, tone down, mute.

subject *n*, topic, theme, substance, point, object, matter, affair, issue, question.
patient, client, case, victim, guinea pig (*inf*), dependant, subordinate, citizen.
adj, subordinate, dependent, subservient, inferior, subjugated, obedient. RULING
exposed, vulnerable, open, susceptible, liable, prone. IMMUNE
conditional, dependent, depending, contingent.
v, expose, lay open, put through, treat, submit.
subdue, subjugate, quell, conquer, vanquish, crush, master, subordinate.

subjection subjugation, mastery, conquest, defeat, enslavement, servitude, subordination, dependence. INDEPENDENCE

subjective internal, mental, nonobjective, personal, biased, prejudiced, idiosyncratic. OBJECTIVE

subjugate conquer, vanquish, rout, defeat, overwhelm, overpower, overcome, master, crush, quell, subdue, humble, tame, discipline, subject, enslave, oppress. LIBERATE

sublimate refine, purify, exalt, uplift, heighten, elevate. DEGRADE
divert, redirect, transfer, channel.

sublime exalted, noble, dignified, eminent, lofty, elevated, glorious, superb, magnificent, grand, august, stately, majestic, imposing. RIDICULOUS

submerge submerse, immerse, plunge, dive, dip, duck, sink, drown, inundate, flood, deluge, engulf, overwhelm. SURFACE

submissive docile, tractable, yielding, compliant, acquiescent, amenable, accommodating, obliging, obedient, deferential, humble, meek, patient, resigned, passive, subservient, servile, obsequious. OBSTINATE

submit yield, surrender, capitulate, succumb, acquiesce, resign oneself, bow, bend, stoop, defer, obey, comply, conform. RESIST
refer, present, hand in, tender, offer, proffer, propose, advance, put forward, suggest. WITHDRAW

subordinate *adj*, inferior, lesser, lower, minor, junior, subaltern, subservient, dependent, subject, secondary, subsidiary, ancillary, auxiliary. CHIEF
n, inferior, junior, subaltern, hireling, assistant, dependant, subject. SUPERIOR

subscribe pledge, promise, pay, contribute, donate, chip in (*inf*).
endorse, support, assent, consent, agree, approve, countenance.

subsequent succeeding, following, ensuing, future, successive, consequent, later, next. PREVIOUS

subservient obsequious, servile, submissive, deferential, slavish, sycophantic, subordinate, inferior, dependent, subject. INDEPENDENT
instrumental, useful, helpful, ancillary, subsidiary, auxiliary.

subside abate, let up, moderate, lessen, diminish, lull, quieten, wane, ebb, dwindle, peter out. INCREASE
sink, descend, decline, lower, settle, fall, drop, cave in, collapse. RISE

subsidence sinking, descent, settling, fall, diminution, abatement.

subsidiary auxiliary, supplementary, ancillary, accessory, aiding, assistant, helpful, instrumental, subservient, inferior, lesser, subordinate. PRIMARY

subsidy aid, grant, allowance, contribution, assistance, help, support.

subsist exist, be, live, survive, last, continue, endure, remain, maintain, keep going, cope, make ends meet. DIE

subsistence food, nourishment, sustenance, upkeep, maintenance, keep, support, living, existence, being.

substance matter, material, stuff, fabric, body, element, solidity, reality, actuality, substantiality.

essence, gist, meaning, significance, sense, drift, import, point, subject, theme.
wealth, means, resources, property, estate.
substantial large, big, considerable, sizable, important, significant. SMALL
firm, strong, solid, stout, sound, durable. FLIMSY
real, actual, material, corporeal, genuine, true, valid, positive. IMAGINARY
wealthy, rich, prosperous, well-to-do, powerful, influential. POOR
substantiate prove, establish, confirm, verify, validate, authenticate, corroborate, bear out. REFUTE
substitute *v*, replace, exchange, change, interchange, commute, swap (*inf*), deputize, stand in, cover, relieve.
n, replacement, relief, surrogate, agent, deputy, proxy, understudy, stand-in, equivalent.
subterfuge artifice, stratagem, wile, ruse, trick, device, dodge, evasion, shift, manoeuvre, deception, excuse, pretext.
subtle faint, delicate, nice, refined, slight, implied, indirect. OBVIOUS
astute, shrewd, keen, acute, penetrating, discerning, discriminating, deep. STUPID
sly, cunning, crafty, wily, artful, designing, Machiavellian, clever, smart. ARTLESS
subtract deduct, take away, remove, withdraw. ADD
suburbs outskirts, environs, precincts, purlieus, neighbourhood, suburbia, edge, periphery. CENTRE
subversive *adj*, revolutionary, insurrectionary, seditious, disruptive, riotous, destructive.
n, rebel, revolutionary, insurrectionary, saboteur, traitor, seditionary.
subvert overthrow, overturn, upset, disrupt, demolish, destroy, undermine. CONSERVE
corrupt, deprave, pervert, vitiate, contaminate, poison.
succeed thrive, prosper, flourish, make good, triumph, prevail, work. FAIL
follow, ensue, supervene, come next, inherit, accede, replace, take over. PRECEDE
success prosperity, luck, fortune, triumph, victory, achievement, attainment, accomplishment, fame, celebrity, hit (*inf*). FAILURE
successful prosperous, thriving, flourishing, lucky, fortunate, triumphant, victorious, famous, wealthy, profitable, rewarding, paying, lucrative, favourable. UNSUCCESSFUL
succession chain, run, course, train, series, procession, cycle, concatenation, sequence, progression, order, consecution, continuity.
accession, inheritance, promotion.
descendants, posterity, lineage, descent.
succinct brief, short, concise, terse, pithy, laconic, curt, compact, condensed, compendious, summary. PROLIX
succour *n*, help, aid, assistance, support, relief, comfort.
v, help, aid, assist, support, relieve, comfort, nurse, minister to.
succulent juicy, sappy, fleshy, moist, luscious, lush, rich. DRY
succumb surrender, yield, give way, give in, submit, capitulate, die. RESIST
such like, similar, so, so much.
suck absorb, draw in, take in, extract.
suck up to, fawn on, truckle, toady, curry favour, flatter.
sudden abrupt, hasty, quick, rapid, swift, unexpected, unanticipated, unforeseen, brief, momentary. GRADUAL
sue prosecute, summon, take to court, prefer charges, indict, charge. DEFEND
solicit, petition, appeal, beg, plead, implore, entreat, beseech.
suffer undergo, experience, feel, endure, go through, sustain, bear, tolerate, brook, stand, put up with (*inf*), support.
ache, hurt, be in pain, grieve.
suffering pain, agony, affliction, torment, torture, discomfort, distress, anguish, misery, grief, ordeal. EASE
sufficient enough, adequate, ample, abundant, plentiful, satisfactory. DEFICIENT
suffocate asphyxiate, smother, stifle, choke, strangle.
suffrage franchise, ballot, vote, voice.
suffuse cover, overspread, colour, bathe, imbue, permeate, transfuse, infuse, steep. DRAIN
suggest propose, submit, put forward, advance, advise, recommend.
hint, intimate, imply, insinuate, evoke.
suggestion proposal, proposition, plan, idea, advice, recommendation.
implication, insinuation, intimation, indication, hint, trace, touch, suspicion.

suggestive evocative, reminiscent, redolent, indicative.
ribald, bawdy, dirty, smutty, obscene, indecent, risqué, racy, crude, vulgar.
suit *v*, befit, become, conform, harmonize, match, fit, correspond, accord, agree, satisfy, gratify, please.
adapt, fashion, proportion, adjust, accommodate, fit.
n, outfit, ensemble, costume, clothing.
lawsuit, case, action, trial, cause, proceeding, litigation.
petition, appeal, plea, prayer, request, entreaty, solicitation, addresses, courtship.
suitable appropriate, apt, apposite, fit, fitting, right, proper, seemly, becoming, relevant, pertinent, convenient, opportune, acceptable, agreeable. UNSUITABLE
suite set, series, collection, apartment.
retinue, train, entourage, attendants, followers, escort, bodyguard.
suitor beau, gallant, admirer, lover, wooer.
sulk pout, mope, brood, be put out.
sullen sulky, morose, scowling, glowering, cross, peevish, petulant, moody, surly, sour, bitter, resentful, put out, gloomy, sombre. CHEERFUL
sully soil, dirty, spot, stain, blemish, pollute, contaminate, taint, tarnish, defile, disgrace, dishonour, defame. CLEAN
sultry close, oppressive, muggy, humid, hot, sticky, stuffy, stifling. COOL
sum *n*, total, aggregate, tally, score, amount, quantity, whole, entirety, totality. PART
v, add, add up, total, tot up, count, tally, reckon, calculate.
sum up, summarize, epitomize, recapitulate, review.
summarize sum up, epitomize, encapsulate, outline, recapitulate, review, condense, abridge. AMPLIFY
summary *n*, abstract, synopsis, précis, compendium, conspectus, digest, epitome, outline, résumé, recapitulation, review. AMPLIFICATION
adj, quick, rapid, hasty, cursory, short, brief, concise, succinct, pithy, terse, curt, laconic, condensed, compendious, compact. LENGTHY
summit top, crown, cap, peak, pinnacle, apex, vertex, apogee, height, zenith, acme, culmination. BASE
summon call, invite, bid, send for, convoke, convene, muster, assemble. DISMISS
sumptuous costly, expensive, dear, extravagant, lavish, luxurious, rich, opulent, magnificent, splendid, gorgeous, grand, superb, plush (*inf*), de luxe. POOR
sundry various, diverse, assorted, miscellaneous, different, several.
sunless dark, black, grey, cloudy, murky, gloomy, dismal, bleak, sombre, dreary, depressing, cheerless. SUNNY
sunny bright, sunshiny, sunlit, shining, radiant, clear, cloudless, fine, summery. DULL
cheerful, cheery, blithe, jolly, genial, happy, joyful, buoyant, optimistic. GLOOMY
super wonderful, marvellous, excellent, outstanding, glorious, magnificent, splendid, superb, sensational, smashing (*inf*). AWFUL
superannuated old, aged, senile, decrepit, antiquated, passé, obsolete, retired, pensioned off.
superb excellent, first-rate, matchless, peerless, outstanding, superior, marvellous, wonderful, magnificent, splendid, glorious, gorgeous, sumptuous, fine, exquisite, grand. POOR
supercilious arrogant, haughty, insolent, contemptuous, scornful, disdainful, lofty, lordly, proud, vain, domineering, overbearing, patronizing, condescending. HUMBLE
superficial surface, exterior, external, outer, shallow, slight, trivial, frivolous, empty. DEEP
apparent, seeming, ostensible, outward. ACTUAL
hasty, cursory, slapdash, perfunctory. THOROUGH
superfluity superabundance, surfeit, surplus, excess, glut, plethora. LACK
superfluous superabundant, supererogatory, redundant, excessive, extra, surplus, unnecessary, needless. DEFICIENT
superhuman supernatural, preternatural, paranormal, divine, herculean, prodigious, phenomenal, miraculous. NATURAL
superintend supervise, manage, run, administer, oversee, direct, control.
superintendent supervisor, overseer, inspector, director, manager, administrator, chief, boss (*inf*).

superior *adj*, better, higher, greater, excellent, first-rate, exceptional, outstanding, superlative, supreme, matchless, peerless, choice, fine. INFERIOR
n, chief, boss (*inf*), manager, director, supervisor, senior. JUNIOR

superlative supreme, transcendent, superior, peerless, matchless, incomparable, unrivalled, excellent, first-class, first-rate, outstanding. POOR

supernatural preternatural, unnatural, abnormal, paranormal, unearthly, spiritual, mystical, occult, mysterious, miraculous. NORMAL

supernumerary extra, superfluous, redundant, surplus, excess, spare, odd.

supersede supplant, displace, oust, usurp, replace, succeed, discard, set aside, override, overrule.

supervene ensue, follow, succeed, occur, happen, transpire.

supervise oversee, superintend, administer, direct, manage, run, handle, control, watch over.

supervision direction, management, oversight, superintendence, control, guidance, surveillance, care, charge.

supine recumbent, prostrate, prone, flat, horizontal. UPRIGHT
lethargic, apathetic, indifferent, sluggish, torpid, languid, listless, lifeless, inactive, inert, lazy, idle, indolent, otiose, slothful. ENERGETIC

supple pliable, pliant, flexible, elastic, plastic, yielding, lithe, lissom, limber. STIFF

supplement *n*, addition, addendum, appendix, postscript, extension, complement.
v, add, augment, extend, top up, complement. REDUCE

supplementary additional, complementary, extra, ancillary, auxiliary, secondary, subsidiary.

suppliant *adj*, supplicant, supplicating, petitioning, entreating, beseeching, praying, imploring, asking, begging.
n, supplicant, petitioner, suitor, applicant.

supplicate petition, solicit, beg, plead, crave, beseech, ask, pray, implore, entreat, importune. DEMAND

supplication petition, solicitation, invocation, prayer, plea, entreaty, appeal, request.

supply *v*, provide, furnish, equip, stock, replenish, give, contribute, afford, yield, grant, bestow, satisfy. WITHHOLD
n, provision, stock, store, hoard, reserve, quantity, fund.

support *v*, bear, carry, hold up, uphold, sustain, maintain, prop, brace, buttress, bolster. DROP
back, second, further, forward, encourage, abet, help, assist, aid, promote, advocate, champion, defend, finance, subsidize, fund, foster, nurture. OPPOSE
endorse, verify, confirm, corroborate, substantiate. REFUTE
tolerate, put up with (*inf*), stomach, brook, bear, endure.
n, prop, brace, stay, base, foundation, stanchion, upright.
sustenance, subsistence, maintenance, keep, upkeep.
backing, encouragement, furtherance, help, assistance, aid, patronage, sponsorship, protection, friendship. OPPOSITION

supporter backer, patron, sponsor, advocate, champion, adherent, follower, admirer, fan, well-wisher, ally, colleague. OPPONENT

suppose presume, assume, presuppose, postulate, surmise, conjecture, guess, suspect, imagine, fancy, believe, opine, think, conclude, judge, imply. KNOW

supposed hypothetical, assumed, accepted, so-called, alleged.

supposition assumption, presumption, presupposition, postulate, hypothesis, theory, surmise, conjecture, guess, speculation, idea, notion. KNOWLEDGE

suppress restrain, curb, check, repress, smother, stifle, silence, conceal, withhold, censor, quash, quell, crush, overpower, conquer, stamp out, extinguish.

supremacy ascendancy, superiority, pre-eminence, primacy, sovereignty, rule, mastery, dominion, power, authority. SUBJECTION

supreme highest, greatest, utmost, extreme, best, superlative, top, paramount, pre-eminent, first, foremost, leading, principal, chief, main, sovereign, predominant. LOWEST

sure certain, positive, definite, convinced, persuaded, satisfied, confident, assured, decided. DOUBTFUL

reliable, dependable, trustworthy, trusty, guaranteed, unfailing, infallible, foolproof, unquestionable, indisputable, steady, firm, stable, secure, safe. PRECARIOUS
bound, destined, inevitable, unavoidable, inescapable.

surety security, guarantee, warranty, indemnity, insurance, pledge, bond, bail, deposit, hostage, guarantor, sponsor.

surface exterior, outside, façade, veneer, appearance, covering, coating, top. INTERIOR

surfeit *n*, excess, surplus, glut, superabundance, superfluity, plethora, satiety. DEFICIENCY
v, sate, satiate, glut, cloy, gorge, overfeed, stuff, cram. STARVE

surge *n*, rush, gush, flow, outpouring, rise, increase, swell, billow, wave.
v, rush, gush, rise, swell, billow, roll, heave, undulate.

surly sullen, sulky, cross, irritable, testy, touchy, irascible, crabbed, crusty, ill-tempered, gruff, brusque, curt, churlish, uncivil, rude. AFFABLE

surmise *v*, infer, guess, conjecture, suppose, imagine, suspect, presume, assume, conclude, deduce, opine. KNOW
n, inference, assumption, presumption, supposition, guess, conjecture, hypothesis, idea, thought. KNOWLEDGE

surmount overcome, conquer, vanquish, triumph over, scale, climb, ascend, top. SUCCUMB

surpass exceed, pass, transcend, excel, outstrip, outdo, beat, overshadow, eclipse.

surplus *n*, excess, surfeit, superabundance, plethora, residue, remainder, rest, balance. DEFICIT
adj, extra, spare, excess, superfluous, remaining.

surprise *v*, amaze, astound, astonish, stun, stagger, flabbergast (*inf*), bowl over (*inf*), startle, catch.
n, amazement, astonishment, wonder, shock, start, bolt from the blue.

surprising amazing, astounding, astonishing, staggering, startling, unexpected, incredible, extraordinary, remarkable. ORDINARY

surrender *v*, relinquish, part with, yield, hand over, give up, renounce, forgo, resign, abdicate, cede, capitulate, submit, give in, succumb. HOLD
n, capitulation, submission, yielding, relinquishment, renunciation, abdication, resignation.

surreptitious clandestine, stealthy, covert, underhand, furtive, sly, secret, hidden, unauthorized. OPEN

surrogate substitute, stand-in, proxy, deputy, agent, representative.

surround encircle, circle, encompass, environ, enclose, gird, girdle, hem in, fence in, besiege.

surroundings environment, milieu, setting, background, environs, neighbourhood.

surveillance supervision, watch, observation, inspection, scrutiny, care, control, superintendence, direction. FREEDOM

survey *v*, view, scan, scrutinize, observe, contemplate, review, study, examine, inspect, reconnoitre. IGNORE
assess, appraise, take stock of, size up, estimate, calculate, measure, plot.
n, review, study, examination, inspection, scrutiny, investigation, inquiry, assessment.

survive outlive, outlast, live, persist, last, continue, abide, remain, endure, subsist. DIE

susceptible vulnerable, subject, given, liable, disposed, inclined, prone, open, receptive, sensitive, impressionable.

suspect *v*, doubt, mistrust, distrust, disbelieve. BELIEVE
surmise, guess, conjecture, think, believe, imagine, fancy, suppose, assume, presume. KNOW
adj, suspicious, questionable, doubtful, dubious.

suspend hang, dangle, swing.
postpone, defer, delay, put off, withhold, shelve, adjourn, stop, stay, interrupt, discontinue, arrest, debar, expel. CONTINUE

suspense uncertainty, doubt, indecision, irresolution, hesitation, vacillation, insecurity, anxiety, expectation, anticipation, excitement.

suspicion doubt, distrust, mistrust, scepticism, misgiving, wariness. TRUST
surmise, guess, conjecture, supposition, thought, idea.
trace, hint, touch, suggestion, *soupçon*.

suspicious distrustful, mistrustful, sceptical, unbelieving, wary, apprehensive. TRUSTFUL doubtful, dubious, questionable, suspect, shady (*inf*), strange, queer.

sustain support, uphold, hold up, carry, bear. DROP
suffer, undergo, experience, endure, withstand.
maintain, keep up, continue, prolong, nurture, nourish, feed, strengthen, foster, help, aid, assist, relieve, comfort.
uphold, endorse, verify, validate, justify, confirm, establish, ratify, sanction, approve. OVERRULE

sustenance nourishment, nutrition, nutriment, food, subsistence, maintenance, livelihood, upkeep, keep, support. STARVATION

swagger strut, prance, parade, show off (*inf*), vaunt, boast, brag, bluster.

swallow gulp, down (*inf*), eat, drink, consume, devour, absorb, assimilate, engulf, overwhelm. VOMIT
believe, fall for, buy (*inf*), accept, take, tolerate, suffer, endure.

swamp *n*, marsh, bog, morass, fen, slough, quagmire.
v, flood, inundate, deluge, drench, soak, saturate, overwhelm, engulf, swallow up, submerge, immerse, sink.

swap exchange, barter, trade, switch, interchange.

swarm *n*, throng, crowd, multitude, mob, horde, host, herd, drove, flock, bevy, shoal, mass, concourse.
v, throng, crowd, cluster, flock, mass, teem, abound, crawl, overrun, infest. SCATTER

swarthy dark, dusky, dark-skinned, dark-complexioned, black, brown. PALE

swathe swaddle, bandage, bind, wrap, enwrap, envelop, fold, enfold, drape, clothe. UNWRAP

sway *v*, swing, rock, oscillate, wave, totter, reel, lean, incline, fluctuate, vacillate.
influence, move, persuade, win over, control, guide, direct, govern.
n, influence, control, command, power, authority, dominion, rule, sovereignty, ascendancy. SUBJECTION

swear affirm, avow, aver, asseverate, assert, declare, vow, promise, testify, depose. DENY
blaspheme, curse.

sweat *v*, perspire, exude, secrete.
n, perspiration, diaphoresis, sweating, exudation, secretion.

sweep *v*, brush, clean, clear.
n, arc, curve, bend, stroke, swing, compass, scope, range, stretch, extent, reach, span, spread.

sweeping comprehensive, wide-ranging, all-inclusive, all-embracing, broad, wide, extensive, global, universal, general, blanket, indiscriminate, wholesale. SPECIFIC

sweet sugary, sweetened, honeyed, saccharine, syrupy, tasty, toothsome, luscious, delicious. SOUR
fragrant, aromatic, balmy, redolent, perfumed, scented, sweet-smelling, fresh, clean, pure, wholesome. FOUL
dulcet, mellifluous, melodious, musical, tuneful, harmonious, euphonious, mellow, soft, silvery. DISCORDANT
attractive, appealing, charming, pleasant, agreeable, amiable, lovable, kind, gentle, dear, beloved, precious. NASTY

swell expand, dilate, spread, extend, inflate, distend, bloat, puff up, bulge, billow, balloon, enlarge, increase, augment, amplify, intensify. SHRINK

swelling bulge, bump, lump, protuberance, tumefaction, tumescence, distension, inflation, dilation, enlargement.

swerve turn, veer, stray, drift, wander, deviate, diverge, deflect.

swift fast, rapid, quick, speedy, fleet, expeditious, brisk, nimble, prompt, sudden, hurried, hasty. SLOW

swimmingly easily, effortlessly, smoothly, successfully.

swindle *v*, defraud, cheat, fleece, rook (*inf*), deceive, trick, overcharge, diddle (*inf*), do (*inf*), con (*inf*).
n, fraud, trickery, deception, sharp practice, racket (*inf*), con trick (*inf*), rip-off (*inf*). HONESTY

swindler fraud, con man (*inf*), crook (*inf*), trickster, cheat, sharper, impostor, charlatan, mountebank, rogue, scoundrel.

swing *v*, sway, oscillate, rock, vacillate, waver, wave, hang, dangle, veer, turn, whirl, spin, pivot, wheel, rotate.
n, oscillation, vacillation, fluctuation, sway, rock, sweep, rhythm.

swirl whirl, eddy, turn, gyrate, twist, spin.

switch *n*, rod, stick, birch, cane, twig.
change, shift, about-turn, reversal, exchange, swap (*inf*).
v, change, shift, turn, interchange, exchange, swap (*inf*), substitute, replace.

swivel turn, spin, pivot, rotate, revolve.

swoop *v*, descend, dive, plunge, sweep, rush, pounce, seize, snatch.
n, descent, dive, plunge, rush, pounce, snatch.

sybarite sensualist, voluptuary, epicure, hedonist. ASCETIC

sycophant flatterer, fawner, toady, truckler, yes man, lickspittle, bootlicker (*inf*), cringer, groveller, parasite, hanger-on.

sycophantic flattering, fawning, ingratiating, servile, obsequious, slavish, grovelling, cringing. INDEPENDENT

syllabus summary, synopsis, abstract, digest, conspectus, résumé, précis, outline, prospectus, curriculum.

symbol token, emblem, sign, representation, character, figure, letter, badge, logo.

symbolic representative, emblematic, typical, allegorical, figurative, metaphorical.

symbolize represent, stand for, signify, mean, denote, betoken, exemplify, typify, embody, personify.

symmetry balance, proportion, harmony, congruity, regularity, evenness, similarity, correspondence. ASYMMETRY

sympathetic compassionate, caring, concerned, supportive, affectionate, kind, warm, tender, considerate, understanding. UNSYMPATHETIC

sympathize pity, feel for, commiserate, condole, console, comfort, understand.
side with, back, support, agree.

sympathy compassion, concern, pity, commiseration, condolence, tenderness, thoughtfulness, understanding, empathy. INDIFFERENCE
agreement, accord, harmony, rapport, affinity. ANTIPATHY

symptom sign, indication, mark, symbol, token, warning, characteristic, manifestation, syndrome.

synchronous simultaneous, coincident, concurrent, contemporaneous.

syndicate trust, cartel, combine, alliance, federation, union.

synonymous equivalent, equal, tantamount, similar, identical, interchangeable. OPPOSITE

synopsis outline, précis, résumé, abstract, digest, epitome, condensation, abridgment, conspectus, compendium, summary.

synthesis combination, amalgamation, union, fusion, amalgam, compound, composite, blend. ANALYSIS

synthetic artificial, man-made, imitation, mock, ersatz, fake. GENUINE

system method, procedure, technique, approach, way, practice, plan, scheme, order, structure, arrangement, organization. CHAOS

systematic methodical, businesslike, regular, orderly, organized, planned. UNSYSTEMATIC

T

table board, slab, counter, stand, bench, desk.
diagram, chart, graph, plan, index, tabulation, inventory, list, catalogue, register, schedule.

tableau representation, picture, scene, spectacle, pageant.

taboo prohibited, banned, forbidden, not allowed. PERMITTED

tacit implied, implicit, understood, inferred, unstated, unexpressed, unspoken, silent. AVOWED

taciturn silent, quiet, reserved, reticent, uncommunicative, tight-lipped, mum, mute. TALKATIVE

tack *n*, nail, pin, stitch.
direction, bearing, course, way, path, approach, method, procedure, line.
v, nail, pin, fasten, fix, attach, affix, append, annex, add.
stitch, baste.

tackle *n*, gear, equipment, rig, outfit, apparatus, trappings, impedimenta, paraphernalia, tools, implements.
v, undertake, attempt, try, begin, set about, embark on, turn one's hand to, deal with, take on, face, confront.
challenge, intercept, obstruct, stop, seize, grab, throw, bring down.

tact diplomacy, discretion, sensitivity, perception, discernment, finesse, savoir-faire, skill, dexterity, adroitness, judgment, sense. TACTLESSNESS

tactful diplomatic, discreet, prudent, politic, judicious, sensitive, perceptive, skilful, thoughtful, considerate, careful. TACTLESS

tactics strategy, plan, scheme, method, approach, policy, campaign, manoeuvres.

tactless undiplomatic, indiscreet, impolitic, imprudent, gauche, maladroit, clumsy, inept, thoughtless, inconsiderate, rude, impolite. TACTFUL

tag *n*, label, sticker, ticket, flap, tab.
v, label, mark, name, call, identify.
add, append, affix, attach, tack, trail, shadow, follow.

tail end, tip, extremity, conclusion, rear, rump. HEAD

taint *v*, contaminate, infect, poison, pollute, defile, befoul, begrime, dirty, soil, sully, tarnish, stain, besmirch, smear, spoil, ruin, blemish, blacken, vitiate, corrupt, brand, stigmatize, shame, disgrace. PURIFY
n, spot, stain, blot, blemish, flaw, defect, fault, stigma, shame, disgrace, infection, contamination, contagion, pollution.

take get, obtain, acquire, secure, gain, win, capture, catch, seize, grasp, clasp, grip, receive, accept, adopt, assume, have, hold, accommodate, pick, select, choose. LEAVE
subtract, deduct, take away, remove, carry off, appropriate, steal, purloin, pinch (*inf*), nick (*inf*). REPLACE
stand, put up with (*inf*), tolerate, brook, abide, bear, suffer, endure.
carry, bear, convey, transport, bring, escort, accompany, lead, conduct, guide, usher.
require, need, call for, demand.
attract, charm, captivate, fascinate, enchant, delight. REPEL

take after, resemble, favour (*inf*), be like, copy.

take back, retract, recant, unsay, disavow, withdraw.
regain, repossess, reclaim, recapture.

take in, understand, comprehend, grasp, absorb, assimilate.
include, embrace, encompass, cover, comprise, contain. EXCLUDE
accommodate, lodge, admit, let in.
deceive, trick, cheat, defraud, swindle, dupe, hoodwink.

take on, employ, hire, engage, retain, enlist. DISMISS
undertake, adopt, assume, tackle, face, challenge, contend with, compete with, oppose.

take up, occupy, cover, fill, use up, consume.
start, begin, continue, go on, resume, recommence. STOP

tale story, narration, account, narrative, novel, romance, fable, myth, legend, anecdote, yarn (*inf*), fiction, lie, fib, rumour.

talent gift, endowment, faculty, flair, knack, turn, bent, forte, genius, aptitude, ability, capacity, skill. INABILITY

talk *v*, speak, articulate, utter, express, say, communicate, converse, confer, parley, discuss, confabulate, gossip, chat, chatter, prattle, prate, natter.
n, speech, lecture, oration, address, discourse, harangue.
conversation, dialogue, confabulation, discussion, conference, chat, chatter, prattle, gossip, rumour, scandal.

talkative garrulous, loquacious, voluble, chatty, verbose, wordy, prolix. TACITURN

tall high, lofty, towering, elevated, big, giant. SHORT

tally *v*, agree, correspond, accord, coincide, match, harmonize, suit, fit, square. CLASH
n, score, total, count, record.
ticket, label, stub, counterfoil, mark, notch.

tame *adj*, domesticated, broken, fearless, unafraid, gentle, docile, tractable, submissive, subdued, meek, obedient. WILD
dull, flat, uninteresting, boring, tedious, insipid, vapid. EXCITING
v, domesticate, break, train, discipline, master, curb, subdue, moderate, soften, temper.

tamper meddle, interfere, mess about, fool around (*inf*), tinker, fiddle (*inf*), rig, corrupt.

tang flavour, taste, savour, relish, piquancy, pungency, odour, smell, smack, hint, trace, touch.

tangible palpable, tactile, perceptible, material, substantial, physical, corporeal, real, actual, positive, solid, concrete, evident, plain. INTANGIBLE

tangle *v*, entangle, ravel, snarl, mat, knot, twist, intertwine, interlace, interweave, confuse, complicate, involve, embroil, enmesh, ensnare, entrap. UNTANGLE
n, knot, snarl, mass, mess, jumble, muddle, confusion, complication, mix-up.

tantalize torment, torture, disappoint, frustrate, tease, taunt, titillate, provoke, tempt, entice. SATISFY

tantamount equivalent, equal, synonymous, commensurate, the same.

tantrum outburst, temper, rage, fit, paddy (*inf*).

tap *v*, rap, pat, touch, knock, hit, strike.
n, rap, pat, touch, knock, blow.

taper narrow, thin, diminish, decrease, dwindle, fade, lessen, die away.

tardy late, belated, overdue, delayed, retarded, slow, leisurely, sluggish, dilatory. PROMPT

target mark, objective, object, aim, goal, butt, victim.

tariff tax, impost, levy, duty, excise, toll, rate, charge, schedule, price list.

tarnish discolour, rust, dull, dim, stain, sully, soil, taint, blemish, spot, blot, besmirch, blacken. POLISH

tarry linger, loiter, dally, dawdle, delay, remain, stay, sojourn, abide, stop, rest, wait. MOVE

tart sour, acid, sharp, bitter, pungent, piquant. SWEET
biting, cutting, caustic, mordant, trenchant, incisive, acrimonious, sharp, barbed, curt, waspish, testy. MILD

task job, chore, duty, assignment, exercise, mission, undertaking, work, labour, toil, drudgery. LEISURE

taste *v*, smack, savour, relish, try, sample, sip, nibble.
experience, undergo, encounter, meet, know, feel.
n, flavour, savour, relish, tang, smack.
bit, morsel, mouthful, sample, bite, sip.
liking, fondness, predilection, penchant, appetite, longing, relish. AVERSION
perception, discernment, discrimination, judgment, appreciation, culture, cultivation, refinement, polish, elegance, style, delicacy, propriety.

tasteful refined, polished, cultured, cultivated, elegant, stylish, artistic, aesthetic, harmonious, restrained. TAWDRY

tasteless insipid, vapid, flavourless, bland, flat, stale, weak, watery, dull, tame, uninteresting, boring. TASTY
vulgar, coarse, crude, gross, tawdry, gaudy, flashy, showy, unrefined, inelegant, improper, indelicate. TASTEFUL

tasty savoury, sapid, palatable, toothsome, appetizing, delicious, delectable, luscious, scrumptious (*inf*). INSIPID

tattle *v*, gossip, tittle-tattle, gab (*inf*), chatter, prattle, prate, natter, blab, tell tales.
n, gossip, tittle-tattle, idle talk, chitchat, chatter, prattle.

taunt *v*, tease, torment, twit, mock, make fun of, jeer, sneer, ridicule, deride, insult, reproach, upbraid. RESPECT
n, gibe, jeer, sneer, insult, ridicule, derision, mockery.

taut tight, tense, stretched, strained. SLACK

tautology repetition, iteration, reiteration, verbosity, redundancy, pleonasm. CONCISENESS

tawdry flashy, showy, meretricious, loud, gaudy, garish, brummagem, cheap, vulgar. TASTEFUL

tax *n*, impost, levy, duty, excise, customs, toll, rate, charge, tariff, tribute.
v, assess, rate, charge, impose, exact, demand.
load, burden, encumber, strain, task, overload, overburden, wear out, exhaust, weary, tire. RELIEVE

teach educate, school, instruct, tutor, coach, train, ground, drill, discipline, tell, inform, enlighten, edify, explain, show, demonstrate, advise, guide, direct, warn.

teacher instructor, tutor, coach, trainer, educator, pedagogue, schoolmaster, schoolmistress, lecturer, professor.

team group, band, gang, crew, squad, side.

tear *v*, rip, rend, rive, split, divide, pull apart, rupture, shred, lacerate. MEND
race, speed, sprint, run, fly, shoot, dash, dart. AMBLE
n, rip, rent, split, rupture, laceration.

tearful weeping, crying, sobbing, in tears, lachrymose, weepy (*inf*), maudlin, sad, sorrowful, distressing, pathetic, pitiful, poignant. HAPPY

tease torment, plague, harass, pester, bother, worry, annoy, irritate, vex, provoke, tantalize, taunt, twit, rag (*inf*), rib (*inf*), mock, make fun of. PACIFY

technique manner, style, method, way, approach, system, procedure, line, course.
skill, art, facility, knack, know-how (*inf*), proficiency, expertise.

tedious boring, monotonous, dull, tiresome, wearisome, long-drawn-out, prosaic, banal, uninteresting, dreary, humdrum, routine, flat, vapid. INTERESTING

teeming swarming, bristling, crawling, alive, full, overflowing, prolific, abundant. EMPTY

teeter sway, rock, stagger, totter, wobble, waver, seesaw.

telephone *n*, phone, blower (*inf*).
v, phone, call, ring, buzz (*inf*), dial.

tell relate, narrate, report, recount, recite, rehearse, describe.
notify, let know, inform, impart, communicate, make known, disclose, reveal, divulge, publish, confess, blab, utter, declare. SUPPRESS
command, order, instruct, direct, require, bid.
distinguish, differentiate, discriminate, discern, make out, discover.
count, enumerate, reckon, compute, calculate, tally.

tell off, reprimand, tick off (*inf*), scold, chide, berate, upbraid, reprove, rebuke, reproach, censure.

telling striking, forceful, effective, cogent, influential, powerful, potent. WEAK

temerity rashness, recklessness, foolhardiness, heedlessness, boldness, audacity, nerve (*inf*), gall (*inf*), impudence, effrontery. TIMIDITY

temper *n*, mood, humour, frame of mind, disposition, temperament, constitution, nature, character, tone.
tantrum, paddy (*inf*), rage, fury, anger, passion, pique, irritation, annoyance, irritability, peevishness, petulance. CALMNESS
calmness, composure, cool (*inf*), self-control, equanimity. RAGE
v, moderate, mitigate, abate, lessen, palliate, allay, assuage, mollify, soften, tone down, modify, qualify. INTENSIFY
toughen, harden, anneal.

temperament character, nature, disposition, temper, mood, humour, frame of mind, spirit, constitution.

temperamental excitable, volatile, mercurial, capricious, highly-strung, sensitive, moody, irritable, touchy, impatient. PLACID
erratic, unpredictable, unreliable, inconsistent. RELIABLE

temperate mild, fair, clement, balmy, cool, calm.
moderate, self-controlled, self-restrained, calm, composed, sensible, reasonable, abstinent, abstemious, continent, sober, teetotal. INTEMPERATE

tempest storm, squall, hurricane, tornado, typhoon, cyclone. CALM
commotion, furore, upheaval, tumult, turmoil, disturbance. PEACE

tempestuous stormy, squally, windy, blustery, turbulent, violent, wild, intense, impassioned, furious, boisterous. CALM

temporal secular, lay, profane, mundane, earthly, worldly, terrestrial, mortal, carnal, material. SPIRITUAL
passing, transient, transitory, fleeting, ephemeral, evanescent, momentary, temporary, impermanent. PERMANENT

temporary impermanent, passing, transient, transitory, fleeting, ephemeral, evanescent, brief, short, short-lived, momentary. LASTING
provisional, makeshift, stopgap. PERMANENT

temporize delay, procrastinate, fence, hedge, equivocate, tergiversate, play for time, stall.

tempt allure, lure, entice, seduce, tantalize, invite, court, bait, provoke, inveigle, persuade, coax, attract, draw. REPEL

tempting attractive, alluring, inviting, appealing, seductive, appetizing. REPULSIVE

tenable sound, rational, reasonable, plausible, believable, maintainable, defensible. UNTENABLE

tenacious stubborn, obstinate, dogged, persistent, pertinacious, determined, resolute, steadfast, set, firm, adamant.
retentive, cohesive, tough, strong, forceful, adhesive, clinging.

tenant lodger, renter, lessee, leaseholder, holder, occupant, occupier, resident. LANDLORD

tend[1] incline, gravitate, lean, trend, be inclined, be disposed, head, aim, point, bear, lead, influence, contribute, conduce. DIVERGE

tend[2] care for, attend to, minister to, wait on, serve, watch over, protect, guard, take care of, nurse, nurture. NEGLECT

tendency leaning, bent, turn, inclination, disposition, propensity, proclivity, penchant, partiality, predilection, bias, proneness, susceptibility, gravitation, bearing, drift, trend. AVERSION

tender¹ *adj*, soft, delicate, fragile, feeble, weak. TOUGH
gentle, kind, humane, merciful, compassionate, sympathetic, caring, thoughtful, tender-hearted, soft-hearted, sensitive, warm, affectionate, loving, fond, emotional. HARSH
callow, immature, inexperienced, raw, green, young, youthful, impressionable, vulnerable.
sore, painful, sensitive, inflamed.

tender² *v*, proffer, offer, present, extend, propose, suggest, volunteer, submit. WITHHOLD
n, offer, proposal, suggestion, bid.
currency, money.

tenebrous dark, gloomy, sombre, shady, shadowy, unlit, murky, obscure, dusky. LIGHT

tenet dogma, doctrine, principle, precept, maxim, canon, creed, belief, conviction, opinion, view.

tenor meaning, purport, intent, sense, gist, aim, direction, drift, trend, course.

tense *adj*, tight, taut, rigid, stiff, stretched, strained, nervous, keyed up, wound up (*inf*), worked up, jumpy, edgy, stressful, nerve-racking. SLACK
v, brace, tighten, strain, stretch. RELAX

tension tightness, tautness, rigidity, stiffness, stretch, strain, stress, pressure, nervousness, anxiety, agitation, excitement, suspense, apprehension. RELAXATION

tentative experimental, exploratory, probative, probatory, trial, speculative, provisional, hesitant, unsure, uncertain, faltering. SURE

tenuous flimsy, insubstantial, insignificant, slight, slender, slim, thin, attenuated, fine, delicate. SUBSTANTIAL

tenure holding, possession, occupancy, occupation, residence, tenancy, incumbency, term.

tepid lukewarm, warm, cool, half-hearted, apathetic.

tergiversate apostatize, change sides, desert, defect, renege.
vacillate, shift, fence, hedge, equivocate, prevaricate.

term *n*, name, title, denomination, designation, word, phrase, expression.
time, period, spell, space, span, interval, duration, stretch, season, session.
v, call, name, designate, denominate, style, dub, christen, entitle.

termagant shrew, scold, virago, harridan, vixen.

terminal *adj*, bounding, limiting, closing, concluding, final, ultimate, fatal, lethal, deadly, mortal, incurable.
n, end, termination, terminus, boundary, bound, limit, extremity.

terminate end, conclude, complete, finish, close, stop, cease, discontinue, abort, expire, lapse. BEGIN

termination end, conclusion, completion, close, finish, ending, issue, result, consequence. BEGINNING

terminus end, extremity, terminal, depot, station, limit, boundary, goal, target.

terms conditions, provisions, stipulations, qualifications.
price, charges, rates, fees.
language, terminology, phraseology.
footing, standing, relations, relationship.

terrestrial earthly, tellurian, terrene, sublunary, worldly, mundane, temporal. CELESTIAL

terrible extreme, severe, awful, dreadful, dire, frightful, fearful, terrifying, horrifying, shocking, horrible, horrendous, hideous, gruesome, abominable, detestable, loathsome, vile, repulsive. WONDERFUL

terrific extreme, intense, tremendous, great, excellent, superb, marvellous, wonderful, smashing (*inf*), super (*inf*). ORDINARY

terrify frighten, scare, shock, horrify, appal, alarm, dismay, petrify, terrorize. REASSURE

territory district, zone, area, region, realm, domain, province, state, land.

terror fear, fright, horror, dread, awe, panic, alarm, consternation, dismay. REASSURANCE

terrorize intimidate, threaten, menace, bully, terrify.

terse concise, succinct, compact, pithy, sententious, laconic, brief, short, curt, abrupt, brusque. PROLIX

test *v*, try, assay, prove, check, examine, analyse, assess, evaluate.
n, trial, experiment, attempt, essay, analysis, examination, exam, quiz, assessment, evaluation, proof, ordeal.

testify swear, state, depose, certify, witness, evidence, attest, assert, declare, affirm, avow. DENY

testimonial recommendation, reference, credential, endorsement.

testimony evidence, statement, deposition, affidavit, witness, declaration, asseveration, affirmation, avowal, proof, confirmation, corroboration, verification.

testy irritable, touchy, tetchy, irascible, petulant, peevish, waspish, peppery, grumpy, cantankerous, crabbed, splenetic, cross, crusty, quick-tempered, captious. GENIAL

tether *n*, rope, chain, lead, leash.
v, tie, fasten, secure, chain. LOOSE

text words, wording, contents, matter, subject, theme, topic, passage, book.

texture surface, feel, grain, weave, fabric, structure, composition, constitution.

thankful grateful, appreciative, obliged, indebted, beholden. UNGRATEFUL

thankless unthankful, ungrateful, unappreciative. GRATEFUL
unappreciated, unrewarding, unprofitable, vain, useless. REWARDING

thanks gratitude, gratefulness, thankfulness, appreciation, acknowledgment, recognition, credit, thanksgiving. INGRATITUDE

thanks to, because of, owing to, due to, through.

thaw melt, liquefy, dissolve, soften, defrost, unfreeze. FREEZE

theatre playhouse, auditorium, hall, arena, stage, drama.

theatrical dramatic, Thespian, histrionic, hammy (*inf*), stagy, melodramatic, overdone, affected, artificial.

theft thievery, stealing, pilfering, robbery, burglary, larceny, embezzlement, peculation, shoplifting, fraud.

theme subject, topic, matter, argument, text, idea, thesis.
motif, leitmotiv, melody, tune.

theoretical hypothetical, conjectural, speculative, abstract, impractical, academic, ideal. PRACTICAL

theory hypothesis, conjecture, speculation, thesis, postulate, presumption, assumption, supposition, idea, philosophy. PRACTICE

therapeutic curative, healing, remedial, corrective, restorative, beneficial, salutary, good.

therefore consequently, hence, whence, thence, then, so, thus, ergo, accordingly. BECAUSE

thesaurus dictionary, lexicon, wordbook, encyclopedia, treasury, repository.

thesis dissertation, essay, treatise, disquisition, monograph, paper.
theory, hypothesis, idea, postulate, supposition, proposition, subject, theme, topic.

thews strength, brawn, muscles, sinews.

thick broad, wide, fat, deep, solid, dense, close, crowded, heavy, impenetrable, condensed, compact, viscous. THIN
abundant, plentiful, numerous, full, packed, bristling, teeming, crawling, swarming. SPARSE
stupid, unintelligent, slow, dull, stolid, obtuse, brainless, dim-witted (*inf*). CLEVER
throaty, guttural, hoarse, husky, indistinct, inarticulate. CLEAR
friendly, close, familiar, intimate, matey (*inf*), pally (*inf*), chummy (*inf*). DISTANT

thicken condense, congeal, jell, set, solidify, harden, coagulate, clot, deepen, intensify. THIN

thicket coppice, copse, spinney, grove, wood. CLEARING

thief robber, burglar, housebreaker, shoplifter, pickpocket, swindler, embezzler, crook (*inf*).

thieve steal, rob, purloin, pilfer, filch, nick (*inf*), pinch (*inf*), peculate, embezzle, cheat, swindle.

thievery theft, stealing, robbery, burglary, larceny, shoplifting, peculation, embezzlement.

thin *adj*, narrow, fine, attenuated, slim, slender, lean, spare, skinny, scraggy, scrawny, lank, lanky, underweight, emaciated, gaunt, bony. FAT
sparse, scattered, scarce, scanty, deficient, poor, meagre. ABUNDANT
delicate, fine, gossamer, light, sheer, diaphanous, transparent, flimsy, weak, watery, diluted. THICK
v, attenuate, rarefy, weaken, dilute, water down, prune, trim, reduce. THICKEN

thing object, article, something, being, entity, body, substance, gadget, device, contrivance, item, point, factor, detail, particular, feature, aspect, deed, act, incident, occurrence, phenomenon.

think believe, consider, conceive, imagine, fancy, judge, deem, regard, reckon, suppose, presume, surmise, hold, maintain, feel, conclude, deduce, visualize, envisage, expect.
ponder, meditate, deliberate, reason, reflect, muse, mull over, cerebrate, cogitate, ruminate, weigh up, think over, contemplate, consider.
think up, devise, contrive, invent, create, dream up.

thinking *n*, reasoning, thought, judgment, opinion, view, meditation, rumination, contemplation, deliberation.
adj, rational, reasoning, sensible, logical, intelligent, philosophical, reflective, contemplative, thoughtful.

thirst *n*, thirstiness, dryness, dehydration, drought.
craving, desire, lust, hunger, appetite, yearning, longing, hankering, yen (*inf*).
v, crave, desire, hunger, yearn, long, hanker.

thirsty dry, dehydrated, parched, arid.
eager, avid, desirous, longing, yearning, greedy, hungry. SATISFIED

thorn prickle, spine, barb, point, spike.
nuisance, bother, vexation, irritation, annoyance, trouble, plague, scourge, curse.

thorny prickly, spiny, spinous, barbed, spiky, pointed, sharp. SMOOTH
difficult, hard, tough, trying, troublesome, vexatious, awkward, delicate.

thorough meticulous, painstaking, scrupulous, careful, exhaustive, in-depth, comprehensive, all-embracing. SUPERFICIAL
complete, total, entire, perfect, downright, out-and-out, unmitigated, unqualified, absolute, utter, thoroughgoing.

though *conj*, although, albeit, notwithstanding, despite the fact that, allowing, admitting, granting.
adv, nevertheless, still, yet, however.

thought idea, concept, conception, fancy, notion, view, opinion, belief, sentiment, judgment, assessment, conclusion.
thinking, brainwork, cerebration, concentration, reflection, cogitation, meditation, contemplation, speculation, consideration, deliberation, rumination.
thoughtfulness, care, concern, regard, attention, kindness, compassion. THOUGHTLESSNESS
hope, anticipation, dream, aspiration, plan, design, aim, intention, purpose.

thoughtful considerate, kind, regardful, concerned, solicitous, mindful, heedful, attentive, careful, cautious, wary, prudent, discreet. THOUGHTLESS
pensive, thinking, absorbed, lost in thought, reflective, ruminative, contemplative, meditative, quiet, serious.

thoughtless inconsiderate, unkind, insensitive, tactless, undiplomatic, indiscreet, unthinking, unmindful, heedless, careless, regardless, inattentive, negligent, neglectful, remiss, rash, reckless, imprudent, improvident. CAREFUL

thraldom thrall, servitude, slavery, enslavement, subjection, subjugation, bondage, captivity. FREEDOM

thrash beat, whip, flog, lash, cane, smack, spank, thresh, flail, defeat, trounce, conquer, overwhelm.

thread line, string, cord, yarn, cotton, fibre, filament, strand.
theme, motif, plot, story line, train of thought, drift, course.

threadbare worn, worn out, ragged, frayed, tatty, shabby, old, thin, poor. NEW
trite, hackneyed, commonplace, conventional, stale, stock.

threat intimidation, commination, warning, caution, menace, danger, peril, hazard, risk, omen, portent.

threaten intimidate, cow, warn, caution, menace, endanger, imperil, impend, loom, portend, forebode. REASSURE

threshold sill, doorstep, doorway, door, entrance.
start, beginning, outset, brink, verge, dawn. END

thrift economy, frugality, thriftiness, saving, parsimony. EXTRAVAGANCE

thriftless extravagant, lavish, prodigal, wasteful, spendthrift, improvident, unthrifty, imprudent. THRIFTY

thrifty economical, frugal, saving, sparing, parsimonious, provident, prudent, careful. THRIFTLESS

thrill *n*, excitement, stimulation, titillation, sensation, tingle, tremor, kick (*inf*).

v, excite, stimulate, galvanize, electrify, touch, move, stir, rouse, titillate, agitate. BORE

thrilling exciting, gripping, hair-raising, electrifying, stirring, rousing, stimulating, moving. BORING

thrive prosper, succeed, do well, make good, advance, get on, flourish, boom, grow, wax, bloom, blossom. FAIL

thriving prosperous, successful, flourishing, booming, growing, blooming, wealthy, rich.

throb *v*, beat, pulsate, pulse, palpitate, pound.
n, beat, pulsation, palpitation, throbbing.

throes pangs, pain, agony, anguish, suffering.

throng *n*, crowd, multitude, mob, horde, host, mass, swarm.
v, crowd, flock, swarm, herd, pack, cram, press.

throttle strangle, choke, suffocate, asphyxiate, smother, stifle.

through past, by, between, across, during, throughout.
finished, done.
via, by way of, by means of, because of.

throw *v*, cast, fling, toss, hurl, sling, pitch, lob (*inf*), chuck (*inf*), launch, propel, project, deliver. CATCH
floor, fell, bring down, prostrate, overturn, upset.
throw away, discard, reject, get rid of, scrap, dispose of, waste. KEEP
throw out, expel, eject, evict, dismiss, discard, get rid of. ADMIT
disconcert, confuse, bewilder, mislead, deceive, upset.
n, cast, fling, toss, sling, pitch. CATCH

thrust *v*, drive, propel, impel, urge, push, shove, force, press, ram, poke, stick, stab, jab, lunge. WITHDRAW
n, drive, push, shove, force, impetus, momentum, lunge, stab, poke, prod, attack, assault.

thud thump, knock, smack, crash, clonk, clunk.

thug ruffian, hooligan, tough, gangster, robber, murderer.

thump *v*, hit, strike, smack, whack, beat, batter, pummel, pound, thud.
n, blow, rap, knock, thud.

thunder *v*, resound, reverberate, rumble, roll, boom, crash, crack, blast, detonate, roar, bellow.
n, reverberation, rumble, roll, boom, roar, crash, peal.

thus so, in this way, like this.
therefore, consequently, hence, ergo, then.

thwart frustrate, balk, foil, check, stop, cross, oppose, contravene, defeat, hinder, impede, obstruct, prevent. AID

tick *v*, click, tap.
mark, check.
tick off, tell off, scold, reprimand, reprove, rebuke, chide, berate, upbraid. PRAISE
n, ticktock, click, tap.
moment, instant, minute, second, flash, trice, jiffy (*inf*).

ticket pass, certificate, token, coupon, voucher, card, slip, label, tag.

tickle titillate, gratify, please, delight, amuse, entertain, divert, thrill, excite.

ticklish sensitive, touchy, delicate, awkward, difficult, complex, thorny, risky, unstable, unsteady, uncertain.

tide ebb, flow, stream, current, drift, direction, movement, course.

tidings news, word, advice, information, message, report.

tidy *adj*, neat, orderly, trim, spruce, shipshape, spick-and-span, organized, systematic, methodical. UNTIDY
considerable, sizable, goodly, large, big, substantial, ample. SMALL
v, neaten, straighten, spruce up, clean, groom, arrange, order. DISORDER

tie *v*, bind, truss, knot, fasten, join, connect, unite, link, attach, secure, tether, moor, lash. UNTIE
restrict, confine, limit, curb, restrain, tie up, hinder, hamper. FREE
n, bond, link, connection, liaison, relationship, obligation, duty, responsibility, restriction, restraint.
knot, bow, string, rope, fastening.
draw, dead heat.

tier row, rank, line, band, layer, stratum, level, storey.

tiff quarrel, row, dispute, squabble, disagreement, argument. HARMONY
bad mood, ill humour, huff, pet, tantrum, temper.

tight taut, stretched, tense, stiff, rigid, firm, stable, fixed, fast, secure, snug, close, compact, cramped. LOOSE

mean, miserly, stingy, niggardly, tight-fisted, close-fisted. GENEROUS
sealed, hermetic, proof, impervious.
drunk, inebriated, intoxicated, tipsy, tiddly (*inf*). SOBER

till farm, cultivate, work, dig, plough.

tilt *v*, slope, slant, incline, lean, tip, list, cant. STRAIGHTEN
n, slope, slant, inclination, angle.
joust, tournament, contest, encounter.

timbre tone, tonality, tone colour, tone quality, ring, resonance.

time *n*, duration, period, span, spell, stretch, while, term, interval, season, era, epoch, age, date, hour, juncture, point, occasion.
tempo, beat, rhythm, metre, measure.
v, count, measure, clock, regulate, control, adjust, set, schedule.

timely opportune, seasonable, well-timed, propitious, auspicious, favourable, convenient. INOPPORTUNE

timid timorous, shy, bashful, coy, diffident, retiring, shrinking, fearful, afraid, pusillanimous, cowardly. BOLD

tinge *n*, tincture, stain, dye, tint, colour, hue, shade, touch, trace, hint, suggestion, *soupçon*, dash, smack.
v, tincture, dye, stain, tint, colour.

tingle *v*, prickle, sting, smart, itch, tickle, shiver.
n, itch, shiver, quiver, thrill.

tinkle jingle, ring, peal, chime.

tint *n*, colour, hue, shade, tone, tinge, tincture, dye, stain.
v, colour, stain, dye, tinge, tincture, affect, influence.

tiny minute, minuscule, infinitesimal, microscopic, miniature, diminutive, small, little, wee, dwarfish, pygmy, Lilliputian. ENORMOUS

tip[1] *n*, point, end, extremity, head, top, apex, summit, peak, pinnacle. BASE

tip[2] *v*, tilt, incline, lean, list, cant, upset, overturn, topple.

tip[3] *n*, gratuity, baksheesh, gift, perquisite, reward.
hint, suggestion, clue, tip-off (*inf*), warning.

tip off, *v*, warn, forewarn, caution, advise, tell, inform.

tipsy drunk, intoxicated, inebriated, tight (*inf*), tiddly (*inf*), merry (*inf*). SOBER

tirade diatribe, philippic, invective, denunciation, harangue, abuse. EULOGY

tire weary, fatigue, exhaust, drain, wear out, jade, fag (*inf*). REFRESH
bore, annoy, irritate, exasperate.
flag, droop, weaken, fail.

tired weary, fatigued, exhausted, drained, worn out, jaded, fagged (*inf*), dead beat (*inf*), knackered (*inf*), all in (*inf*), sleepy, drowsy. REFRESHED
bored, sick, fed up (*inf*).

tiresome wearisome, boring, tedious, monotonous, dull, annoying, irritating, irksome, vexatious, exasperating, trying, troublesome. PLEASANT

tissue fabric, paper, mesh, net, network, web, combination, collection, set, mass, accumulation, conglomeration.

titanic huge, gigantic, colossal, enormous, massive, immense, vast, herculean, elephantine, monstrous, stupendous. SMALL

titillate tickle, excite, thrill, arouse, stimulate, please.

title name, heading, caption, inscription, label, designation, denomination, appellation, epithet, nickname, sobriquet.
claim, right, due, privilege, prerogative, ownership, possession.

titter snigger, chuckle, chortle (*inf*), giggle, laugh. WEEP

together collectively, jointly, side by side, closely, in unison, en masse, all at once, simultaneously, concurrently, contemporaneously, mutually, reciprocally. SEPARATELY

toil *v*, work, labour, travail, slog, drudge, slave. RELAX
n, hard work, labour, travail, drudgery, slavery, effort, exertion, industry. REST

toilet lavatory, latrine, urinal, bathroom, washroom, powder room, cloakroom, water closet, WC, privy, public convenience, ladies, gents, loo (*inf*), bog (*inf*).

toilsome laborious, arduous, hard, difficult, tough, strenuous, taxing, tiring, fatiguing, exhausting, tiresome, wearisome. EASY

token *n*, symbol, sign, representation, emblem, mark, indication, evidence, proof, expression, manifestation, reminder, remembrance, memorial, keepsake, souvenir, memento.

adj, nominal, minimal, superficial, perfunctory, symbolic.

tolerable bearable, endurable, sufferable, supportable, acceptable, allowable, permissible. INTOLERABLE
passable, fair, indifferent, middling, mediocre, average, so-so (*inf*), not bad (*inf*). EXCEPTIONAL

tolerant broad-minded, open-minded, liberal, catholic, unprejudiced, unbigoted, patient, forbearing, long-suffering, benevolent, magnanimous, indulgent, lenient, permissive, easy-going. INTOLERANT

tolerate bear, suffer, endure, brook, abide, stand, put up with (*inf*), stomach, swallow, permit, allow, admit, countenance, sanction, indulge, condone.

toll[1] *v*, ring, knell, peal, chime, sound, strike.

toll[2] *n*, levy, tax, impost, duty, tariff, rate, charge.

tomb vault, crypt, sepulchre, grave.

tome volume, book.

tomfoolery antics, shenanigans (*inf*), horseplay, skylarking (*inf*), clowning, buffoonery, foolishness, folly, silliness, stupidity, nonsense.

tone *n*, sound, noise, note, pitch, tonality, timbre, intonation, inflection, modulation, cadence, accent, stress, emphasis.
colour, cast, tinge, tint, shade, hue.
tenor, quality, spirit, mood, temper, vein, style, manner, approach, drift, air.
v, harmonize, blend, fit, adapt.

tone down, moderate, temper, subdue, soften, dampen. ENHANCE

tonic *n*, stimulant, refresher, pick-me-up (*inf*), boost, shot in the arm (*inf*), restorative, analeptic.
adj, stimulating, invigorating, bracing, restorative.

too also, as well, in addition, besides, moreover, furthermore.
excessively, inordinately, immoderately, unduly, overly, extremely.

tool implement, instrument, gadget, device, contrivance, utensil, apparatus, appliance, machine.
vehicle, means, medium, agent, pawn, cat's-paw, puppet, hireling.

toothsome tasty, palatable, savoury, appetizing, delicious, luscious, scrumptious (*inf*), delectable, agreeable, attractive. NASTY

top *n*, summit, apex, vertex, apogee, peak, pinnacle, crown, acme, zenith, height, head, lead. BOTTOM
cap, lid, cover.
adj, highest, topmost, uppermost, upper, best, greatest, supreme, ruling, principal, chief, main, leading, first, foremost. LOWEST
v, cap, crown, tip, cover.
exceed, transcend, surpass, excel, eclipse, outshine, outdo, outstrip, beat, better, best.

topic subject, theme, matter, issue, question, point.

topical current, up-to-date, popular, familiar, local, regional.

topple totter, fall, tumble, fall over, collapse, tip over, knock down, upset, overturn, overthrow.

torment *v*, torture, agonize, rack, excruciate, pain, persecute, distress, harrow, afflict, plague, pester, bother, harass, harry, badger, annoy, vex, irritate, exasperate, provoke, tease, worry. SOOTHE
n, torture, agony, pain, suffering, anguish, distress, misery, affliction, plague, scourge, vexation, irritation, nuisance, pest. RELIEF

tornado cyclone, hurricane, typhoon, whirlwind, gale, squall, storm, tempest. CALM

torpid sluggish, slow, lethargic, languid, dull, listless, apathetic, lazy, indolent, dormant, inactive, inert, lifeless, inanimate. ACTIVE

torpor torpidity, torpidness, sluggishness, lethargy, listlessness, apathy, inactivity, inertia. ACTIVITY

torrent flood, deluge, cascade, downpour, stream, flow, rush, gush, outburst. TRICKLE

torrid hot, scorching, blistering, roasting, burning, fiery, tropical, sultry, parched, arid, dry. ARCTIC
passionate, ardent, fervent, erotic, lustful, steamy (*inf*).

tortuous sinuous, serpentine, twisting, winding, zigzag, meandering, curved, bent, crooked, twisted, mazy, labyrinthine, involved, complicated, indirect, circuitous, roundabout, devious. STRAIGHT

torture *v*, agonize, rack, excruciate, crucify, martyr, persecute, torment, pain, distress. SOOTHE
n, torment, persecution, martyrdom, agony, suffering, pain, anguish. EASE

toss *v*, throw, pitch, fling, chuck (*inf*), cast, hurl, sling, propel, project, flip.
roll, rock, shake, jolt, agitate, disturb, wriggle, writhe, turn.
n, throw, fling, cast, pitch, shake, movement.

total *n*, sum, all, totality, entirety, whole, aggregate, mass, amount. PART
adj, entire, whole, integral, complete, full, aggregate, absolute, utter, sheer, thorough, out-and-out, downright, unqualified, unmitigated. PARTIAL
v, amount to, come to, sum up, add up, tot up.

totter stagger, reel, sway, rock, teeter, wobble, waver, falter, tremble, shake.

touch *v*, feel, finger, handle, palpate, fondle, caress, stroke, pat, tap, hit, strike, meet, adjoin, brush, graze.
affect, influence, impress, inspire, move, stir, soften, melt, upset, disturb.
reach, arrive at, attain, match, equal, rival.
concern, regard, relate to, pertain to.
touch on, deal with, cover, refer to, mention.
touch up, enhance, improve, perfect, brush up, polish up, patch up, repair, retouch, renovate.
n, feel, feeling, contact, stroke, caress, pat, tap.
trace, hint, suggestion, suspicion, *soupçon*, dash, smack, tinge, tincture.
skill, knack, flair, talent, ability, art, facility, technique, approach, style, manner.

touching *adj*, moving, affecting, stirring, tender, poignant, pathetic, pitiable, pitiful, sad.
prep, regarding, respecting, apropos, with reference to, concerning, about, relating to.

touchstone standard, criterion, norm, measure, gauge, yardstick, test, proof.

touchy testy, irritable, irascible, petulant, peevish, waspish, peppery, grumpy, cantankerous, splenetic, choleric, cross, crusty, crabbed, fractious, captious, sensitive, thin-skinned. GENIAL

tough strong, durable, resilient, resistant, firm, solid, hard, rigid, stiff, inflexible, leathery, chewy, fibrous, stringy. TENDER
hardy, sturdy, rugged, stalwart, robust, strapping, brawny, muscular, rough, vicious. WEAK
obstinate, stubborn, obdurate, unyielding, stern, unfeeling, callous, hard-boiled (*inf*).
difficult, hard, arduous, laborious, exacting, thorny, knotty, baffling, puzzling, perplexing. SIMPLE

tour *n*, voyage, journey, excursion, trip, expedition, outing, jaunt, circuit, round, course.
v, travel, journey, voyage, visit, sightsee (*inf*).

tournament competition, contest, match, meeting.

tousle ruffle, rumple, dishevel, mess up, disarrange, disarray, disorder. GROOM

tow pull, draw, drag, haul, tug, lug, trail. PUSH

towards to, for, in the direction of.
nearly, almost, about, just before.
respecting, regarding, concerning, touching.

tower *n*, steeple, turret, spire, minaret, belfry, column, pillar.
citadel, fortress, castle, stronghold, refuge, keep.
v, rise, ascend, soar, mount, surpass, transcend, exceed, top, dominate, overlook. SINK

town borough, municipality, settlement, village, city, metropolis.

toxic poisonous, pestilent, pernicious, noxious, harmful, deadly, lethal. HARMLESS

toy *n*, plaything, game, trifle, trinket, bauble, knickknack.
v, play, sport, trifle, tinker, fiddle, dally, flirt.

trace *n*, mark, token, sign, indication, vestige, remains, evidence, clue, hint, suggestion, touch, tinge, dash, bit, jot, iota.
track, trail, spoor, footprint, footmark, footstep.
v, follow, pursue, trail, track, stalk, hunt, find, discover, ascertain, detect.
sketch, draw, outline, delineate, copy, depict, map, chart.

track *n*, trail, trace, scent, spoor, footprint, footstep, footmark, wake, path, line, route, course, way, road, rail.
v, trace, trail, follow, pursue, hunt, chase. CATCH
track down, find, discover, ferret out, sniff out, run to earth. MISS

tract[1] area, region, stretch, expanse, strip, patch, plot, lot, zone, district, territory.

tract[2] treatise, dissertation, disquisition, essay, sermon, homily, discourse, pamphlet, booklet, leaflet, brochure.

tractable amenable, complaisant, willing, yielding, submissive, docile, manageable, governable, malleable, pliable, pliant, ductile. INTRACTABLE

trade *n*, business, commerce, traffic, barter, exchange, transaction, deal.
occupation, profession, calling, vocation, job, employment, craft, métier.
v, deal, transact, buy and sell, traffic, bargain, barter, exchange, swap.

tradition custom, practice, way, habit, convention, usage, folklore, unwritten law.

traditional oral, unwritten, old, accustomed, customary, habitual, usual, regular, conventional.

traduce calumniate, slander, libel, misrepresent, defame, malign, vilify, asperse, denigrate, revile, vituperate, decry, denounce, disparage, depreciate. EULOGIZE

traffic vehicles, transport, transportation, freight.
trade, commerce, business, dealings, barter, exchange.

tragedy disaster, catastrophe, calamity, adversity, misfortune.

tragic disastrous, catastrophic, calamitous, dreadful, terrible, awful, dire, shocking, appalling, unfortunate, ill-fated, lamentable, deplorable, pathetic, pitiful, sad, sorrowful, unhappy, miserable. COMIC

trail *v*, drag, draw, pull, haul, tow, dangle, hang, droop, lag, linger, fall behind, straggle.
track, trace, follow, pursue, stalk, hunt. CATCH
n, track, trace, scent, spoor, footprint, footstep, footmark, path, way, road, wake, tail, stream, train.

train *v*, teach, instruct, school, educate, coach, drill, exercise, discipline, ground, prepare, rear, guide.
direct, aim, point, focus, level.
n, line, file, column, convoy, procession, chain, series, succession, sequence, order, progression, course.
retinue, suite, entourage, cortege, attendance, staff, following, followers.

trait characteristic, attribute, feature, quality, idiosyncrasy, peculiarity, quirk, mark.

traitor betrayer, Judas, quisling, informer, renegade, apostate, turncoat, defector, deserter, rebel. LOYALIST

trammel *n*, restraint, check, curb, obstacle, hindrance, impediment, fetter, bond. FREEDOM
v, restrict, restrain, hinder, impede, block, obstruct, fetter, chain, ensnare, entrap, enmesh, net, catch. RELEASE

tramp *v*, trudge, plod, stump, stomp (*inf*), stamp, trample, march, walk, hike, traipse (*inf*), trek, rove, range, ramble, wander.
n, vagrant, vagabond, drifter, down-and-out.
walk, ramble, hike, trek, march, footfall, tread, stamp.

trample crush, squash, stamp, tread, tramp.
encroach, infringe, violate, defy.

trance daze, stupor, dream, abstraction, coma, rapture, ecstasy.

tranquil peaceful, calm, still, quiet, smooth, undisturbed, serene, placid, composed, unruffled, unmoved, unperturbed, untroubled, sedate. AGITATED

tranquillize calm, compose, soothe, allay, still, hush, smooth, settle, relax, sedate. EXCITE

transact conduct, carry on, do, perform, execute, dispatch, negotiate, manage.

transaction deal, bargain, negotiation, settlement, business, performance, execution, action, proceeding, matter, affair.

transcend surpass, exceed, rise above, go beyond, excel, outrival, outvie, outstrip, outdo, eclipse, outshine.

transcendent surpassing, exceeding, matchless, peerless, unrivalled, unparalleled, unequalled, incomparable, supreme, consummate. ORDINARY
transcendental, supernatural, mystical, abstract, metaphysical.

transcribe copy, write out, translate, transliterate.

transcript transcription, copy, reproduction, duplicate, translation, transliteration.

transfer *v*, move, remove, transport, convey, carry, transmit, change, shift, relocate, transplant, hand over, pass on.
n, transference, move, transmission, change, shift, relocation.

transfigure transform, change, transmute, metamorphose, exalt, glorify, idealize, apotheosize.

transfix rivet, stun, captivate, fascinate, hypnotize, mesmerize.
pierce, impale, perforate, penetrate, spear, skewer.

transform change, convert, translate, transmogrify, transmute, metamorphose, transfigure, alter, modify, revolutionize.

transgress break, disobey, violate, infringe, contravene, exceed, overstep, go beyond, trespass, sin, err, go astray, offend. OBEY

transgression offence, crime, sin, wrong, fault, error, misdeed, misdemeanour, trespass, contravention, breach, infringement, infraction, violation.

transgressor sinner, wrongdoer, malefactor, culprit, offender, delinquent, criminal, felon.

transient transitory, temporary, impermanent, brief, short, ephemeral, evanescent, passing, fleeting, momentary, short-lived, fugitive, fugacious. PERMANENT

transit passage, crossing, movement, motion, change, transition, transport, transportation, conveyance, carriage, shipment.

transition change, conversion, transformation, alteration, passage, passing, movement, shift.

transitory transient, temporary, impermanent, brief, short, ephemeral, evanescent, passing, fleeting, momentary, short-lived, fugitive, fugacious. PERMANENT

translate render, interpret, transliterate, transcribe, decode, decipher, explain, elucidate.
transform, transmute, convert, change, transfer, transport.

translucent pellucid, diaphanous, limpid, transparent, clear. OPAQUE

transmission transmittal, transmittance, conveyance, transport, sending, transfer, transference, communication. RECEPTION
broadcast, programme.

transmit transfer, transport, carry, take, convey, send, forward, remit, communicate, pass on, hand down, spread, diffuse, disseminate, broadcast. RECEIVE

transmute change, transform, convert, alter, metamorphose, transfigure.

transparent clear, limpid, pellucid, lucid, crystalline, diaphanous, sheer, see-through, translucent. OPAQUE
obvious, patent, evident, apparent, clear, plain, distinct, manifest. UNCLEAR

transpire happen, occur, take place, come about, become known, come to light.

transplant move, remove, transfer, relocate, shift, displace.

transport *v*, convey, carry, bear, ship, take, transfer, shift, move.
banish, deport, exile, expatriate.
entrance, enrapture, enchant, captivate, delight, ravish. REPEL
n, transportation, conveyance, carriage, shipment, transit.
ecstasy, rapture, happiness, joy, delight, bliss, euphoria, enchantment. ANGUISH

transpose interchange, exchange, switch, swap (*inf*), change, move, shift, transfer.

transude ooze, seep, exude, percolate, filter, strain.

transverse crossways, crosswise, athwart, oblique, diagonal. PARALLEL

trap *n*, snare, gin, springe, net, pitfall, ambush, trick, ruse, wile, artifice, stratagem.
v, catch, net, snare, ensnare, entrap, trick, take in, dupe, deceive.

trappings appurtenances, accoutrements, gear, equipment, adornments, ornaments, finery, fixtures, fittings, paraphernalia.

trash rubbish, refuse, garbage, waste, litter.
nonsense, balderdash, rubbish, rot. SENSE

trauma shock, blow, upset, disturbance, ordeal, suffering, anguish, pain, injury, wound.

travel *v*, journey, voyage, tour, cross, traverse, trek, roam, rove, ramble, wander, go, move, proceed. SETTLE
n, journey, voyage, tour, trip, excursion, expedition, movement, passage.

traveller voyager, wayfarer, passenger, tourist, explorer, nomad, wanderer, salesman, representative.

traverse cross, cover, pass over, travel over, range, roam, wander, bridge, span.
obstruct, impede, thwart, frustrate, oppose, contravene. ASSIST

travesty parody, caricature, lampoon, burlesque, mockery, ridicule, distortion, perversion.

treacherous traitorous, perfidious, disloyal, faithless, unfaithful, false, untrue, deceitful, dishonest, untrustworthy, unreliable, treasonable. LOYAL dangerous, perilous, risky, hazardous, unsafe, precarious, deceptive. SAFE

treachery betrayal, perfidy, perfidiousness, treason, disloyalty, faithlessness, unfaithfulness, infidelity. LOYALTY

tread *v*, walk, step, pace, stride, march, tramp, trudge, plod, stump, stamp, trample, crush, squash.
n, step, pace, footfall, walk.

treason treachery, betrayal, disloyalty, sedition, subversion, mutiny, insurrection. ALLEGIANCE

treasure *n*, riches, wealth, fortune, cash, money, gold, silver, bullion, jewels, gems, valuables. RUBBISH
v, prize, value, hold dear, esteem, cherish, love, revere, worship. SCORN
hoard, store, save, accumulate.

treat *n*, party, entertainment, feast, banquet, gift, surprise, delight, pleasure, fun.
v, handle, deal with, regard, use, manage, negotiate, attend, minister to, nurse, doctor, medicate, heal. NEGLECT
entertain, regale, feast, wine and dine, pay for, stand (*inf*).

treatise discourse, disquisition, dissertation, essay, tract, thesis, paper, monograph, article, pamphlet.

treatment handling, use, usage, manipulation, dealing, management, care, nursing, medication, therapy, cure, remedy.

treaty agreement, compact, convenant, bargain, contract, pact, bond, convention, concordat, entente, alliance.

trek *n*, journey, voyage, expedition, odyssey, march, hike.
v, travel, journey, tramp, trudge, march, hike.

tremble *v*, shake, quiver, quaver, quake, shiver, shudder, vibrate, oscillate, rock, wobble.
n, tremor, shake, quiver, quake, shiver, shudder, vibration, oscillation.

tremendous huge, great, vast, immense, massive, enormous, colossal, gigantic, prodigious, monstrous, formidable, awful, terrible, dreadful. SMALL
wonderful, marvellous, remarkable, extraordinary, fantastic (*inf*), fabulous (*inf*), terrific (*inf*), super (*inf*). ORDINARY

tremor shudder, shiver, quiver, tremble, vibration, oscillation, agitation, palpitation.

tremulous trembling, quavering, quaking, quivering, shivering, shuddering, fearful, frightened, scared, afraid, anxious, nervous, jumpy, jittery (*inf*). STEADY

trench furrow, ditch, cut, channel, gutter, trough, earthwork, fosse.

trenchant keen, acute, sharp, pointed, incisive, cutting, caustic, biting, mordant, acid, tart, bitter, sarcastic, severe. MILD
effective, effectual, vigorous, energetic, powerful, potent, forceful, strong. INEFFECTUAL

trend *n*, tendency, course, drift, inclination, bearing, direction.
fashion, vogue, mode, style, craze, rage.
v, tend, lean, incline, drift, veer, turn.

trepidation fear, terror, fright, alarm, perturbation, consternation, dread, apprehension, anxiety, nervousness, agitation, trembling, shaking, quaking, tremor. COMPOSURE

trespass *v*, intrude, invade, encroach, infringe, poach.
n, intrusion, invasion, encroachment, infringement, poaching.
sin, offence, transgression, infraction, crime, misdemeanour, misdeed, error.

trespasser intruder, invader, interloper, gate-crasher (*inf*), poacher.

trial *n*, test, experiment, assay, analysis, examination, proof, probation, audition.
hearing, inquiry, tribunal, litigation.
try, attempt, effort, endeavour, go (*inf*), shot (*inf*).
hardship, adversity, trouble, tribulation, pain, distress, suffering, grief, affliction, ordeal, nuisance, pest, annoyance, vexation. RELIEF
adj, experimental, tentative, exploratory, pilot, provisional.

tribe clan, family, sept, race, stock, class, division, group, people.

tribulation trial, hardship, adversity, trouble, pain, distress, suffering, affliction, grief, misery, sorrow, woe, misfortune, bad luck, blow, burden. JOY

tribunal court, bar, bench, judicature, trial, hearing, assizes, session.

tribute acclaim, acclamation, recognition, acknowledgment, honour, homage, praise, commendation, eulogy, panegyric, testimonial. CENSURE gift, offering, donation, contribution, impost, duty, tax, levy, toll, charge, customs, excise.

trice moment, second, minute, instant, twinkling, flash, jiffy (*inf*). AGE

trick *n*, wile, stratagem, artifice, ruse, finesse, deceit, deception, feint, dodge, contrivance, device, subterfuge, hoax, fraud, imposture, swindle.
caper, prank, practical joke, jest, sleight of hand, legerdemain, knack, technique, art, craft.
trait, characteristic, idiosyncrasy, quirk, mannerism, habit.
v, dupe, cheat, defraud, deceive, delude, fool, hoodwink, bamboozle (*inf*), take in (*inf*), overreach, swindle, con (*inf*).

trickle drip, drop, dribble, ooze, seep, exude, percolate. GUSH

tricky difficult, problematic, complicated, knotty, delicate, ticklish. SIMPLE
crafty, cunning, artful, sly, wily, foxy, subtle, clever, deceitful, dishonest. ARTLESS

trifle *n*, toy, plaything, bauble, trinket, knickknack, bagatelle, triviality, nothing.
bit, drop, dash, pinch, touch, trace, jot, tittle, iota, particle.
v, toy, play, dally, tinker, fiddle, fritter, waste.

trifling trivial, unimportant, insignificant, inconsequential, inconsiderable, small, paltry, petty, worthless, valueless, frivolous, idle, silly. IMPORTANT

trim *adj*, neat, spruce, tidy, orderly, shipshape, smart, dapper, compact, slim, slender, sleek, fit. DISORDERLY
v, clip, prune, cut, crop, shave, shear, dock, lop, shorten, curtail, neaten, shape.
decorate, adorn, ornament, embellish, garnish, festoon, deck, beautify. STRIP
adjust, modify, amend, balance, arrange, order.
n, order, condition, state, shape, fitness, fettle.
trimming, decoration, adornment, ornament, embellishment, garnish, frill, fringe, edging, border.

trinket jewel, bijou, bauble, trifle, bagatelle, gewgaw, knickknack, ornament.

trip *n*, journey, excursion, tour, jaunt, outing, expedition, voyage.
stumble, fall, blunder, mistake, error, slip, lapse.
v, stumble, fall, tumble, slip, err, blunder, bungle.
hop, skip, dance, gambol, bound, spring.

trite hackneyed, corny (*inf*), stale, tired, thin, threadbare, old, unoriginal, stock, stereotyped, commonplace, ordinary, dull, banal. ORIGINAL

triturate pound, pulverize, comminute, levigate, bray, grind, crush, bruise.

triumph *n*, victory, win, conquest, mastery, coup, feat, accomplishment, achievement, attainment, success. FAILURE
jubilation, exultation, joy, pride. REGRET
v, win, prevail, conquer, vanquish, succeed. LOSE
rejoice, jubilate, exult, glory, celebrate, revel, gloat, swagger. LAMENT

triumphant winning, conquering, victorious, successful, unbeaten, undefeated, exultant, jubilant, proud, boastful. BEATEN

trivial trifling, unimportant, insignificant, inconsequential, negligible, inconsiderable, small, minor, immaterial, paltry, petty, frivolous, trite. IMPORTANT

trollop slut, slattern, sloven, whore, prostitute, tart (*inf*).

troop *n*, group, band, company, crew, team, squad, gang, crowd, throng, multitude, horde, herd, flock, pack.
v, flock, gather, collect, muster, throng, crowd, swarm, march, parade. DISPERSE

trophy prize, award, cup, medal, laurels, bays, spoils, booty, souvenir, memento.

trot canter, lope, run, jog.

trouble *n*, worry, concern, anxiety, agitation, distress, suffering, pain, grief, anguish, adversity, misfortune, trial, tribulation, affliction, burden, difficulty, problem, nuisance, pest, bother, inconvenience, vexation, irritation, annoyance. RELIEF
unrest, disturbance, disorder, commotion, tumult, strife, anarchy, mischief. ORDER
effort, exertion, pains, care, attention.
ailment, illness, disorder, complaint.
v, worry, agitate, alarm, concern, upset, distress, disturb, perturb, confuse, perplex, bother, inconvenience, pester, harass, plague, torment, vex, annoy, irk, irritate, grieve, afflict. SOOTHE

troublesome annoying, irksome, vexatious, bothersome, worrying, nagging, burdensome, oppressive, difficult, hard, laborious, arduous. EASY

trough ditch, trench, channel, gutter, furrow, groove, depression.

trousers pants, slacks, jeans, flannels.

truant *n*, absentee, dodger, shirker, malingerer, deserter, skiver (*inf*).
adj, absent, missing, AWOL, skiving (*inf*). PRESENT

truce armistice, cease-fire, peace, rest, break, intermission, lull, respite, treaty, pact. WAR

truck[1] *n*, lorry, van, wagon.

truck[2] *n*, dealings, business, commerce, trade, traffic, barter, exchange.
v, exchange, barter, swap, trade, traffic, deal, bargain, negotiate.

truckle yield, submit, give in, knuckle under, cower, cringe, grovel, crawl, kowtow, bow and scrape, fawn, toady. RESIST

truculent aggressive, hostile, belligerent, bellicose, pugnacious, combative, fierce, ferocious, cruel, brutal, savage, grim. GENTLE

trudge plod, tramp, stump, lumber, traipse (*inf*), march, walk.

true actual, real, factual, veritable, genuine, authentic, valid, veracious, truthful, honest, sincere, legitimate, rightful, proper, correct, accurate, precise, exact. FALSE
faithful, loyal, staunch, steadfast, trusty, trustworthy, reliable, dependable. FAITHLESS

truism platitude, commonplace, cliché, bromide, axiom, truth. PARADOX

truly really, indeed, in fact, actually, assuredly, positively, undoubtedly, genuinely, sincerely, exactly, precisely, rightly, legitimately.

trumpery *n*, rubbish, trash, nonsense, balderdash, rot, humbug, trinket, bauble.
adj, rubbishy, trashy, worthless, tawdry, flashy, showy, cheap, meretricious, trivial, trifling. VALUABLE

trumpet *n*, bugle, horn, clarion.
v, proclaim, announce, promulgate, advertise. SUPPRESS

truncate shorten, cut, lop, crop, dock, abbreviate.

truncheon club, cudgel, baton, staff.

trunk stem, stalk, bole.
body, torso.
chest, coffer, box, crate.

truss *v*, tie, bind, fasten, secure. LOOSE
n, support, prop, brace, buttress, strut.
bundle, package, packet.

trust *n*, faith, belief, conviction, certitude, confidence, assurance, reliance, dependence, hope, expectation, credit.
duty, responsibility, charge, custody, care, protection, safekeeping.
v, believe, have faith in, have confidence in, rely on, depend on, hope, expect. DOUBT
commit, entrust, consign, turn over, assign, delegate.

trustworthy trusty, dependable, reliable, loyal, faithful, true, constant, staunch, steadfast, firm, honest, truthful, honourable, upright. UNRELIABLE

truth verity, reality, actuality, fact, authenticity, genuineness, validity, accuracy, precision, exactness. FALSENESS
veracity, truthfulness, honesty, integrity, sincerity, candour, frankness. DECEIT
truism, platitude, axiom, maxim, principle, law.

truthful honest, veracious, sincere, frank, candid, straightforward, open, trustworthy, reliable. DECEITFUL
accurate, exact, precise, correct, faithful, literal, realistic, factual, true. FALSE

try *v*, attempt, endeavour, essay, undertake, seek, aim, strive, struggle, have a go, make an effort.
test, assay, experiment with, prove, examine, assess, analyse, sample.
tire, weary, strain, tax, bother, pester, annoy, irritate, vex, irk.
n, attempt, endeavour, effort, go (*inf*), shot (*inf*), crack (*inf*), stab (*inf*), trial, test, experiment, sample.

trying hard, difficult, arduous, tough, taxing, tiring, troublesome, bothersome, irksome, annoying, exasperating, infuriating. EASY

tube pipe, hose, line, passage, channel, conduit, duct.

tuck fold, pleat, gather, pucker, insert, put, push, thrust.

tuft bunch, clump, cluster, knot.

tug pull, jerk, wrench, yank, heave, haul, drag, draw, tow, lug. PUSH

tuition instruction, teaching, schooling, education, training, coaching.

tumble fall, slip, trip, stumble, sprawl, pitch, toss, roll, drop, plunge, topple, collapse.

tumble-down ramshackle, dilapidated, ruined, broken-down, crumbling, decrepit, rickety, shaky.

tumefy swell, puff up, distend, bloat, inflate.

tumid swollen, puffy, distended, bloated, inflated, enlarged, turgid, tumescent, bulging, protuberant. SHRUNKEN
pompous, bombastic, orotund, fustian, magniloquent, grandiloquent, rhetorical, flowery.

tumour swelling, lump, growth, neoplasm, sarcoma.

tumult commotion, uproar, turmoil, turbulence, disorder, ferment, hubbub, ado, racket, din, noise, clamour, confusion, pandemonium, riot, brawl, disturbance, agitation. PEACE

tumultuous uproarious, turbulent, stormy, tempestuous, wild, disorderly, boisterous, obstreperous, noisy, clamorous, riotous, excited, restless, agitated. QUIET

tune melody, air, song, strain, harmony, euphony. DISCORD

tuneful melodious, melodic, harmonious, euphonious, musical, sweet, dulcet, mellifluous. DISCORDANT

turbid muddy, cloudy, murky, opaque, foul, impure, thick, dense, foggy, hazy, muddled, confused. CLEAR

turbulent agitated, disturbed, restless, confused, disordered, choppy, rough, stormy, tempestuous, tumultuous, violent, wild, unruly, disorderly, boisterous, obstreperous, noisy, clamorous, uproarious, riotous. CALM

turf grass, sod, sward, green.

turgid swollen, puffy, distended, bloated, inflated, enlarged, tumid, tumescent, bulging, protuberant. SHRUNKEN
pompous, bombastic, orotund, fustian, magniloquent, grandiloquent, rhetorical, flowery.

turmoil tumult, turbulence, uproar, commotion, noise, din, racket, clamour, hubbub, stir, unrest, agitation, disturbance, disorder, confusion, fuss, ado, trouble. PEACE

turn *v*, rotate, revolve, spin, roll, twirl, wheel, whirl, pivot, gyrate, circle, go round.
change, move, shift, diverge, veer, swerve, bend, curve, twist, reverse, invert.
alter, modify, change, convert, transform, metamorphose, adjust, adapt, fit, suit, shape, form, apply, use, direct.
curdle, sour, go off, go bad, spoil.
become, go, grow, get.
hinge, hang, rest, depend.

turn down, lower, reduce, lessen, diminish, decrease. RAISE
reject, refuse, decline, spurn, repudiate. ACCEPT

turn out, expel, evict, dismiss, discharge, fire (*inf*), sack (*inf*). ADMIT
make, manufacture, fabricate, produce.
switch off, turn off, put out, unplug.
result, ensue, become, end up. BEGIN

turn up, arrive, appear, show up (*inf*), come.
raise, increase, amplify, intensify. LOWER

n, rotation, revolution, circle, cycle, round, gyration, spin, twirl, bend, curve, twist, turning, reversal, inversion.
change, alteration, variation, vicissitude, deviation, divergence, shift, adjustment.
shift, stint, spell, period, go (*inf*), shot (*inf*), chance, opportunity.
shape, form, style, manner, mode, fashion, mould, cast.
deed, act, action, service.
inclination, tendency, bent, aptitude, flair, gift, talent, knack, genius, faculty. DISINCLINATION
stroll, walk, drive, ride, airing, jaunt.

turpitude baseness, vileness, wickedness, evil, corruption, depravity, sin, iniquity, crime, vice. NOBILITY

tussle fight, wrestle, scuffle, struggle, brawl, scrap (*inf*).

tutelage guardianship, charge, care, protection, supervision, guidance, instruction, tuition, schooling, education.

tutor *n*, teacher, instructor, coach, preceptor, schoolmaster, schoolmistress, professor. PUPIL
v, teach, instruct, coach, train, educate, school, discipline, drill.

twaddle nonsense, rubbish, rot, drivel, balderdash, humbug, babble, prattle, chatter, gibberish. SENSE

tweak pinch, squeeze, twist, twitch, pull, jerk.

twiddle fiddle, play, toy, twirl, twist, turn.

twig stick, branch, shoot, offshoot, spray, sprig. LOG

twin *n*, double, duplicate, match, mate, counterpart.
adj, similar, like, corresponding, parallel, double, duplicate, paired, matching. SINGLE

twine *n*, string, rope, cord, yarn, thread, cotton.
v, twist, wind, turn, meander, wreathe, coil. interlace, interweave, entwine, knit, splice, braid, plait. UNRAVEL

twinge pang, spasm, twitch, tic, throb, pain, stab, prick.

twinkle *v*, sparkle, shine, glisten, glitter, glint, gleam, flash, coruscate, scintillate, flicker, blink, wink.
n, sparkle, shine, glint, gleam, flash, coruscation, blink, wink.
twinkling, instant, moment, second, trice, jiffy (*inf*).

twirl revolve, rotate, spin, wheel, whirl, pirouette, pivot, turn, twist, twiddle.

twist *v*, coil, curl, wind, turn, twirl, spin, twine, entwine, weave.
sprain, wrench, rick, contort, distort, warp, pervert, garble, falsify, misrepresent, misinterpret.
n, coil, curl, roll, spin, turn, bend, curve, meander, zigzag.
sprain, wrench, distortion, perversion.

twit[1] *v*, tease, taunt, chaff, mock, reproach, upbraid, rebuke, censure. PRAISE

twit[2] *n*, idiot, fool, simpleton, halfwit, nincompoop, ass.

twitch *v*, jerk, jump, snatch, pull, tug, yank.
n, spasm, tic, tremor, twinge, jerk, pull.

twitter chirp, chirrup, cheep, tweet, warble, trill, whistle, chatter, prattle.

tycoon magnate, industrialist, mogul, baron, big cheese (*inf*).

type kind, sort, stamp, class, order, genre, form, species, variety.
specimen, sample, example, exemplar, model, pattern, standard, archetype, prototype, epitome, paradigm.
print, face, font, fount, characters, letters.

typical representative, illustrative, classic, exemplary, characteristic, indicative, symbolic, emblematic, normal, regular, standard, stock, usual, conventional. ABNORMAL

typify represent, exemplify, epitomize, embody, personify, illustrate, characterize, symbolize, denote, indicate.

tyrannical tyrannous, autocratic, despotic, dictatorial, arbitrary, absolute, domineering, overbearing, authoritarian, imperious, oppressive, harsh, severe, cruel, brutal, savage, inhuman. DEMOCRATIC

tyranny autocracy, absolutism, totalitarianism, despotism, dictatorship, oppression, harshness, severity, cruelty, inhumanity. DEMOCRACY

tyrant autocrat, despot, dictator, oppressor, martinet, slave-driver.

tyro novice, neophyte, beginner, learner, student, pupil, apprentice. MASTER

U

ugly unsightly, plain, unattractive, unlovely, ill-favoured, hideous. BEAUTIFUL
unpleasant, disagreeable, nasty, revolting, repulsive, loathsome, vile, horrible, ominous, menacing, threatening, spiteful, bad-tempered. PLEASANT

ulcer sore, fester, gathering, abscess, boil, pustule.

ulterior hidden, concealed, secret, undisclosed, unrevealed. AVOWED

ultimate final, last, terminal, endmost, furthest, extreme, conclusive, decisive, eventual. FIRST
utmost, extreme, maximum, most, supreme, greatest, highest, top. LOWEST
basic, fundamental, elementary, primary.

ultra extreme, radical, immoderate, inordinate, excessive, fanatical. MODERATE

umbrage offence, resentment, grudge, indignation, huff, pique, annoyance, irritation, displeasure.

umpire *n*, referee, arbiter, adjudicator, judge, moderator, arbitrator.
v, referee, arbitrate, adjudicate, judge.

unabashed undaunted, undismayed, unblushing, brazen, bold, confident. ABASHED

unable incapable, powerless, impotent, incompetent, unfit, not able, not up to. ABLE

unacceptable unwelcome, undesirable, unpopular, disagreeable, objectionable, inadmissible. ACCEPTABLE

unaccompanied solitary, alone, lone, solo, unattended, unescorted. ACCOMPANIED

unaccountable inexplicable, unexplainable, incomprehensible, unfathomable, mysterious, odd, peculiar, strange, extraordinary, remarkable. UNDERSTANDABLE

unaccustomed unfamiliar, unexpected, strange, remarkable, unusual, uncommon, unused, inexperienced. FAMILIAR
unadorned plain, simple, stark, unvarnished, unembellished, unornamented, undecorated. ORNATE
unadulterated pure, unmixed, real, genuine, undiluted. MIXED
unaffected[1] artless, ingenuous, naive, unsophisticated, simple, plain, natural, unpretentious, sincere, honest, genuine, open. ARTIFICIAL
unaffected[2] unchanged, unaltered, untouched, unmoved, unfeeling, aloof. CHANGED
unaided unassisted, single-handed, alone. ASSISTED
unanimity agreement, accord, concord, unison, concert, harmony, unity, consensus. DISSENT
unanimous agreed, agreeing, accordant, concordant, concerted, united, solid, harmonious. DISAGREEING
unanswerable irrefutable, incontestable, undeniable, unarguable, incontrovertible, indisputable, conclusive, absolute. WEAK
unappetizing unappealing, unattractive, unpleasant, unsavoury, unpalatable, tasteless, insipid, vapid. APPETIZING
unapproachable aloof, standoffish, reserved, withdrawn, cool, frigid, unsociable, unfriendly. FRIENDLY
remote, distant, inaccessible, out-of-the-way. ACCESSIBLE
unarmed defenceless, vulnerable, unprotected, unguarded, exposed, open, helpless, weak. PROTECTED
unassailable impregnable, invulnerable, strong, secure. VULNERABLE
undeniable, indisputable, incontestable, irrefutable, incontrovertible, absolute, certain, sure. WEAK
unassuming modest, self-effacing, humble, retiring, reserved, diffident, unpretentious, unaffected, unobtrusive, unassertive. OSTENTATIOUS
unattached free, loose, detached, separate, at liberty, independent, autonomous, uncommitted, single, unmarried. ATTACHED
unattended alone, unaccompanied, unescorted, solitary, untended, unwatched, ignored, disregarded, neglected, abandoned. ATTENDED
unattractive unprepossessing, unappealing, uninviting, unappetizing, undesirable, plain, ugly, unlovely. ATTRACTIVE
unauthorized illegal, unlawful, illicit, unlicensed, unapproved, unofficial, unwarranted, forbidden. AUTHORIZED
unavailing vain, futile, useless, ineffectual, ineffective, bootless, fruitless, abortive, unproductive. SUCCESSFUL
unavoidable inevitable, necessary, inescapable, ineluctable, inexorable, irresistible, compulsory, obligatory, fated, destined, certain, sure. AVOIDABLE
unaware ignorant, unknowing, unacquainted, incognizant, unenlightened, uninformed, unconscious, oblivious, unmindful, heedless, unsuspecting, unprepared. AWARE
unawares suddenly, unexpectedly, abruptly, by surprise, off guard.
accidentally, unintentionally, by mistake, inadvertently, unwittingly, unknowingly. DELIBERATELY
unbalanced asymmetrical, lopsided, uneven, unequal, disproportionate, unstable. EVEN
unsound, irrational, deranged, insane, mad, crazy, lunatic, demented, unhinged, touched. SANE
biased, prejudiced, partisan, bigoted, unfair, unjust, one-sided, partial. UNBIASED
unbearable insufferable, insupportable, intolerable, unendurable, too much (*inf*). BEARABLE
unbecoming unseemly, indecorous, improper, indelicate, inappropriate, unsuitable, unfit, unbefitting, unattractive, unflattering. BECOMING
unbelief disbelief, incredulity, doubt, scepticism, distrust, mistrust, infidelity, atheism. BELIEF
unbending inflexible, unyielding, stiff, rigid, formal, severe, firm, resolute, intractable, stubborn. FLEXIBLE
unbiased fair, impartial, unprejudiced, unbigoted, disinterested, dispassionate, objective, neutral, just, equitable. BIASED
unbidden spontaneous, voluntary, willing, free, unforced. FORCED
uninvited, unasked, unwelcome, unwanted, unsolicited. WELCOME
unbind loose, free, release, let go, untie, unfetter, unchain, unshackle, unfasten, undo. BIND

unblemished perfect, flawless, faultless, immaculate, spotless, clean, pure, unsullied, untarnished, stainless. FLAWED

unblinking fearless, unafraid, unflinching, steady, unfaltering, unwavering, cool, calm, unemotional.

unblushing shameless, immodest, bold, brazen, unabashed, unashamed. ASHAMED

unbosom reveal, disclose, divulge, lay bare, unburden, admit, confess, confide. SUPPRESS

unbounded boundless, unlimited, limitless, illimitable, vast, immense, immeasurable, infinite, interminable, endless, unrestricted, unconfined, unrestrained, uncontrolled, unchecked, unbridled, immoderate. LIMITED

unbridled unrestrained, uncontrolled, unchecked, uninhibited, wild, unruly, rampant, immoderate, intemperate, wanton. RESTRAINED

unbroken whole, complete, sound, intact, integral, entire. BROKEN
uninterrupted, continuous, endless, ceaseless, incessant, constant.

uncalled-for unnecessary, needless, unjustified, unwarranted, gratuitous, undeserved, unfair, unjust, unsolicited, unwelcome, unwanted.

uncanny weird, strange, mysterious, odd, queer, eerie, ghostly, unnatural, extraordinary, remarkable, astonishing, amazing, exceptional, incredible. ORDINARY

unceasing incessant, ceaseless, endless, unending, constant, nonstop, unremitting, perpetual, eternal, everlasting, uninterrupted, continuous. INTERMITTENT

unceremonious informal, casual, natural, simple, abrupt, curt, brusque, blunt, gruff, rough, churlish, rude. FORMAL

uncertain doubtful, dubious, ambiguous, questionable, ambivalent, unsure, irresolute, undecided, unresolved, unsettled, undetermined, indefinite, unconfirmed, speculative, conjectural, indistinct, unclear, vague, chancy, risky, precarious, unreliable, unpredictable, capricious, changeable, variable, erratic, fitful, inconstant. SURE

unchangeable unalterable, invariable, immutable, changeless, fixed, permanent, stable, steady. CHANGEABLE

unchanging lasting, abiding, enduring, eternal, perpetual, constant, changeless, unvarying. TRANSITORY

uncharitable unkind, unfeeling, insensitive, unchristian, mean, selfish, cruel, harsh. CHARITABLE

unchaste impure, loose, wanton, depraved, indecent, immoral, dissolute, lewd, lascivious. CHASTE

uncivil rude, discourteous, impolite, unmannerly, ill-mannered, ill-bred, impudent, disrespectful, bearish, churlish. CIVIL

uncivilized uncouth, coarse, vulgar, unrefined, uncultured, uncultivated, uneducated, primitive, barbarian, barbarous, barbaric, savage. CIVILIZED

unclean dirty, filthy, soiled, foul, sullied, defiled, contaminated, impure. PURE

uncomfortable uneasy, ill-at-ease, disturbed, troubled, distressed, upset, restless, anxious, nervous, awkward, embarrassed. RELAXED
disagreeable, unpleasant, hard, rough, cramped, painful, irritating, troublesome. COMFORTABLE

uncommon rare, unusual, unfamiliar, scarce, infrequent, unique, singular, strange, odd, curious, queer, extraordinary, remarkable, exceptional, noteworthy, outstanding. ORDINARY

uncommunicative reserved, taciturn, reticent, shy, quiet, tight-lipped, unsociable, withdrawn, secretive, unforthcoming. TALKATIVE

uncompromising inflexible, unyielding, unbending, rigid, firm, obstinate, stubborn, obdurate, inexorable, implacable, determined, dogged. PLIANT

unconcerned indifferent, uninterested, apathetic, uninvolved, remote, aloof, dispassionate, detached, nonchalant, carefree, blithe, oblivious, untroubled, unworried, uncaring, unsympathetic, unmoved, unaffected. CONCERNED

unconditional total, complete, full, utter, downright, out-and-out, absolute, categorical, positive, unqualified, unreserved, unrestricted, unlimited. UNCONDITIONAL

uncongenial disagreeable, unpleasant, discordant, antagonistic, antipathetic, unsympathetic, uninviting. CONGENIAL

unconnected separate, detached, independent, unrelated, disconnected, disjointed, incoherent, illogical. CONNECTED

unconquerable invincible, indomitable, insuperable, insurmountable, overpowering, overwhelming, unbeatable, undefeatable. WEAK
unconscionable unscrupulous, unprincipled, amoral, unethical. PRINCIPLED
excessive, immoderate, unreasonable, inordinate, extreme, outrageous, preposterous. REASONABLE
unconscious insensible, senseless, out, asleep, comatose. CONSCIOUS
unaware, oblivious, blind, deaf, insensitive, unmindful, ignorant, unknowing. AWARE
automatic, involuntary, reflex, instinctive, subliminal, subconscious, unwitting, unthinking, inadvertent, accidental.
uncontrollable ungovernable, unmanageable, wild, unruly, intractable, irrepressible, mad, carried away, frantic, violent. CONTROLLABLE
unconventional unorthodox, unusual, uncommon, unfamiliar, irregular, abnormal, atypical, original, eccentric, offbeat, bizarre, odd, peculiar, informal. CONVENTIONAL
unconvincing weak, feeble, flimsy, thin, dubious, questionable, inconclusive, improbable, unlikely. CONVINCING
uncouth clumsy, awkward, ungainly, inelegant, graceless, crude, vulgar, coarse, rude, rough, rugged, churlish, impolite, discourteous, ill-bred, ill-mannered, uncivilized, uncultivated, unrefined, unpolished. REFINED
uncover bare, expose, unveil, unmask, unwrap, open, strip, show, discover, reveal, disclose, divulge. COVER
unction unguent, oil, lotion, ointment, salve, balm.
passion, feeling, fervour, ardour, enthusiasm, zest, spirit, verve, power, force.
unctuous smooth, suave, glib, sycophantic, fawning, ingratiating, flattering, insincere. SINCERE
oily, greasy, slippery.
undaunted undismayed, undeterred, unflinching, unfaltering, steadfast, resolute, intrepid, bold, brave, courageous, dauntless, fearless. AFRAID
undeceive enlighten, disabuse, disillusion, disenchant, correct, set straight. DECEIVE
undecided uncertain, unsure, doubtful, dubious, ambivalent, irresolute, indecisive, hesitant, wavering, torn. SURE
unsettled, unresolved, pending, up in the air, open, moot, undetermined, indefinite. SETTLED
undefiled pure, chaste, clean, immaculate, spotless, unspotted, stainless, untarnished, unblemished, unsullied, unpolluted, uncontaminated. DEFILED
undemonstrative reserved, unresponsive, uncommunicative, reticent, aloof, distant, unemotional, unexcitable, sedate, formal. DEMONSTRATIVE
undeniable unquestionable, indisputable, incontrovertible, irrefutable, incontestable, indubitable, definite, positive, certain, sure, proven, obvious, evident. QUESTIONABLE
under beneath, below, down, underneath, lower, inferior, subordinate, secondary, subservient. ABOVE
undercover secret, hidden, concealed, private, confidential, covert, surreptitious, clandestine, underground. PUBLIC
underestimate underrate, undervalue, misprize, miscalculate, misjudge, disparage, belittle, minimize. OVERESTIMATE
undergo suffer, endure, sustain, bear, experience, go through.
underhand underhanded, clandestine, surreptitious, furtive, stealthy, covert, undercover, secret, sly, crafty, unscrupulous, dishonest. OPEN
underline underscore, italicize, stress, emphasize, accent, accentuate, point up, highlight.
underling menial, lackey, flunky, servant, hireling, minion, subordinate, inferior. MASTER
undermine sap, subvert, sabotage, weaken, impair, ruin. STRENGTHEN
tunnel, burrow, dig, excavate, mine.
underneath *prep*, under, beneath, below. ABOVE
n, bottom, underside. TOP
underprivileged deprived, disadvantaged, poor, needy, impoverished, destitute. WEALTHY
underrate underestimate, undervalue, misprize, belittle, disparage. OVERRATE
understand comprehend, apprehend, perceive, discern, make out, fathom, follow, grasp, catch on (*inf*), recognize, see,

gather, hear, learn, take in, assimilate, appreciate, realize, believe, suppose, assume, presume.
sympathize, pity, commiserate, tolerate.

understanding *n*, intelligence, intellect, mind, brains, reason, sense, knowledge, comprehension, awareness, interpretation, view, opinion, judgment, insight, perception, discernment. IGNORANCE
agreement, bargain, pact, arrangement.
adj, compassionate, tender, kind, considerate, sympathetic, patient, tolerant, forgiving. INTOLERANT

undertake attempt, try, endeavour, essay, tackle, take on, venture, embark on, begin, start, commence, set about. ACHIEVE
promise, pledge, agree, vow, swear, guarantee, engage, contract.

undertaking venture, project, enterprise, affair, business, task, effort, endeavour.
promise, pledge, assurance, guarantee, word, vow.

undertone murmur, whisper, low voice. SHOUT
undercurrent, suggestion, connotation, nuance, trace, touch, tinge, flavour.

undervalue underestimate, underrate, misprize, disparage, depreciate, belittle, minimize. OVERESTIMATE

underwear underclothes, underclothing, undergarments, lingerie, undies (*inf*), smalls (*inf*).

underwrite endorse, sign, countersign, subscribe, approve, sanction, guarantee, back, support, sponsor, fund, finance.

undesigned unintentional, accidental, inadvertent, unpremeditated. INTENTIONAL

undesirable unpleasant, disagreeable, unattractive, uninviting, objectionable, obnoxious, unwelcome, unwanted, unacceptable, unsuitable, inappropriate. DESIRABLE

undeveloped immature, embryonic, latent, potential, primordial, rudimentary. MATURE

undignified unseemly, unbecoming, indecorous, improper, inelegant, infra dig (*inf*), inappropriate, unsuitable. DIGNIFIED

undisciplined wild, unruly, unrestrained, uncontrolled, wayward, erratic, untrained, unschooled. DISCIPLINED

undisguised open, overt, evident, manifest, plain, unconcealed, genuine, sincere. VEILED

undisputed undoubted, unquestioned, unchallenged, uncontested, recognized, acknowledged, accepted, certain, sure, indisputable, unquestionable, incontrovertible, undeniable. DEBATABLE

undistinguished ordinary, commonplace, everyday, run-of-the-mill, unexceptional, indifferent, mediocre, so-so (*inf*). EXCEPTIONAL

undisturbed tranquil, serene, placid, calm, composed, collected, unruffled, unperturbed, untroubled. AGITATED

undivided full, complete, entire, whole, intact, unbroken, solid, united. DIVIDED

undo untie, unfasten, release, loose, disengage, disentangle, open, unwrap. FASTEN
nullify, annul, reverse, invalidate, neutralize, counteract.
ruin, destroy, wreck, shatter, defeat, crush.

undoubted certain, sure, obvious, evident, undisputed, unquestioned, indisputable, unquestionable, indubitable, undeniable, accepted, acknowledged. DOUBTFUL

undress *v*, disrobe, unclothe, divest, strip. DRESS
n, nakedness, nudity, dishabille, informality.

undue excessive, immoderate, inordinate, extreme, disproportionate, unnecessary, uncalled-for, unwarranted, unjustified, undeserved, improper. MODERATE

undulate roll, ripple, heave, surge, swell, billow, wave.

unduly excessively, immoderately, inordinately, disproportionately, overmuch, overly. MODERATELY

undying immortal, deathless, eternal, everlasting, unending, endless, imperishable, indestructible, permanent, lasting. TRANSIENT

unearth excavate, dig up, exhume, disinter, find, discover, uncover, expose, reveal, disclose. BURY

unearthly weird, strange, eerie, uncanny, ghostly, spectral, spooky (*inf*), supernatural, preternatural, extraterrestrial.
unreasonable, ungodly, outrageous, ridiculous, abnormal, unheard-of. REASONABLE

uneasy uncomfortable, ill-at-ease, disturbed, perturbed, restless, restive, edgy, nervous, anxious, apprehensive, upset, agitated, worried, troubled. RELAXED

uneducated ignorant, illiterate, untaught, untutored, unschooled, uncultured, uncultivated, unenlightened, unread. EDUCATED

unemployed jobless, workless, out of work, on the dole (*inf*), laid off, redundant, idle, unoccupied. EMPLOYED

unending endless, interminable, never-ending, perpetual, ceaseless, unceasing, incessant, nonstop, continual, constant, eternal, everlasting. BRIEF

unequal uneven, unbalanced, asymmetrical, disproportionate, different, disparate, unlike, dissimilar. EQUAL

inadequate, insufficient, not up to, found wanting, incapable, unable. ADEQUATE

unequalled peerless, matchless, unmatched, unparalleled, unrivalled, unsurpassed, inimitable, incomparable, transcendent, supreme, paramount. INFERIOR

unequivocal clear, plain, obvious, evident, manifest, explicit, unambiguous, unmistakable, unquestionable, undeniable, indisputable, indubitable, sure, certain, absolute, categorical. AMBIGUOUS

unerring sure, certain, exact, accurate, precise, true, perfect, unfailing, infallible. FAULTY

uneven rough, rugged, lumpy, bumpy, hilly, undulating. FLAT

unequal, odd, different, disparate, unbalanced, asymmetrical, unfair, one-sided. EQUAL

irregular, variable, fitful, spasmodic, jerky, intermittent. REGULAR

uneventful ordinary, commonplace, dull, boring, monotonous, tedious, routine, humdrum, unexciting, uninteresting, exceptional, normal. EVENTFUL

unexpected unanticipated, unforeseen, sudden, abrupt, startling, surprising, unpredictable, fortuitous. EXPECTED

unfailing certain, sure, reliable, dependable, constant, staunch, steadfast, unflagging, inexhaustible, limitless, infallible, unerring. UNRELIABLE

unfair unjust, inequitable, uneven, one-sided, biased, prejudiced, partial, partisan. FAIR

wrongful, undue, unwarranted, unreasonable, dishonest, dishonourable, foul, unsporting.

unfaithful faithless, disloyal, false, perfidious, traitorous, treacherous, unreliable, untrustworthy, fickle, deceitful, adulterous, two-timing (*inf*). FAITHFUL

inaccurate, inexact, imprecise, incorrect, wrong, erroneous, faulty, imperfect. ACCURATE

unfaltering unflagging, untiring, tireless, indefatigable, unswerving, unwavering, steady, constant, staunch, steadfast, resolute, firm, determined, resolved. WAVERING

unfamiliar unusual, uncommon, unaccustomed, strange, odd, new, novel. FAMILIAR

unacquainted, unversed, unskilled, inexperienced. VERSED

unfashionable out-of-date, old-fashioned, dated, outmoded, obsolete, old hat (*inf*), passé, antiquated. FASHIONABLE

unfasten undo, detach, open, let go, untie, unlock, unbutton, unzip. FASTEN

unfathomable deep, bottomless, unplumbed, immeasurable. SHALLOW

incomprehensible, impenetrable, inscrutable, deep, profound, abstruse, mysterious, inexplicable.

unfavourable adverse, contrary, hostile, inimical, inauspicious, unpropitious, unpromising, discouraging, bad, threatening, ominous, untimely, unseasonable, unfortunate, unlucky, disadvantageous, detrimental. FAVOURABLE

unfeeling cold, callous, hard-hearted, unsympathetic, insensitive, uncaring, harsh, cruel, pitiless, inhuman. COMPASSIONATE

numb, dead, insensible, insensate.

unfeigned genuine, real, sincere, honest, heartfelt, pure, natural, unaffected. FEIGNED

unfetter unshackle, unchain, unbind, untie, loose, free, liberate, release. FETTER

unfinished incomplete, imperfect, lacking, wanting, deficient, sketchy, rough, raw, crude, unaccomplished, undone. FINISHED

unfit unsuitable, inappropriate, inadequate, unqualified, ineligible, ill-equipped, unprepared, incompetent, incapable, ineffectual, inept, useless, no good.

weak, feeble, frail, delicate, unhealthy, out of condition. FIT

unflagging indefatigable, tireless, untiring, unfailing, unwavering, unfaltering, unremitting, constant, persistent, steady.

unfledged undeveloped, immature, raw, green, callow, inexperienced. EXPERIENCED

unflinching unfaltering, unwavering, unshrinking, firm, resolute, brave, dauntless, undaunted, fearless, bold.

unfold open, unfurl, unroll, undo, spread out, extend, display, show, reveal, disclose, explain, unravel, expand, develop.

unforeseen unexpected, unanticipated, sudden, abrupt, surprising, startling. EXPECTED

unforgivable inexcusable, unpardonable, unjustifiable, unwarrantable, indefensible, reprehensible, deplorable, disgraceful. FORGIVABLE

unfortunate unlucky, luckless, hapless, cursed, unsuccessful, poor, wretched, unhappy, ill-fated, ill-starred, adverse, unfavourable, disastrous, calamitous, tragic, regrettable, lamentable, deplorable. FORTUNATE

unfounded baseless, groundless, idle, vain, unproven, unsubstantiated.

unfrequented deserted, uninhabited, remote, isolated, solitary, lonely.

unfriendly hostile, antagonistic, unsociable, inhospitable, unneighbourly, uncongenial, aloof, distant, cold, surly, inimical, unfavourable. FRIENDLY

unfruitful fruitless, barren, sterile, infertile, infecund, unproductive, unprofitable, unrewarding. FRUITFUL

unfurl open, unroll, unfold, spread out. FURL

ungainly awkward, clumsy, ungraceful, inelegant, lumbering, gangling, uncouth, unwieldy. GRACEFUL

ungenerous mean, stingy, parsimonious, penurious, tight-fisted, niggardly, penny-pinching (*inf*), cheeseparing, selfish. GENEROUS

ungodly impious, irreverent, irreligious, godless, profane, sacrilegious, wicked, sinful, corrupt, depraved, immoral, evil. PIOUS

ungovernable refractory, recalcitrant, intractable, unruly, wild, uncontrollable, unmanageable. MILD

ungracious discourteous, impolite, uncivil, rude, unmannerly, ill-bred, churlish, rough. GRACIOUS

ungrateful thankless, unthankful, unappreciative. GRATEFUL

unguarded unprotected, undefended, defenceless, vulnerable. PROTECTED
careless, incautious, unmindful, heedless, unthinking, thoughtless, indiscreet, imprudent, foolhardy, unwary. CAUTIOUS
artless, guileless, ingenuous, open, frank, candid. ARTFUL

unhandy clumsy, awkward, maladroit, bungling, unskilful, inexpert, incompetent. DEXTEROUS
unwieldy, unmanageable, awkward, inconvenient. HANDY

unhappy miserable, sad, depressed, dejected, despondent, disconsolate, downcast, crestfallen, glum, sorrowful, mournful, melancholy. HAPPY
wretched, unfortunate, unlucky, luckless, hapless, ill-fated, ill-starred. FORTUNATE

unharmed safe, sound, unhurt, uninjured, unscathed, undamaged, whole, intact. HURT

unhealthy sick, ill, unwell, ailing, poorly (*inf*), diseased, invalid, sickly, delicate, frail, feeble, weak, infirm. HEALTHY
morbid, unwholesome, insalubrious, noxious, unhygienic, insanitary, detrimental, deleterious. SALUBRIOUS

unheard-of unknown, unfamiliar, obscure, unsung. FAMOUS
unprecedented, new, novel, unusual, unique. CONVENTIONAL

unheeded ignored, disregarded, overlooked, neglected, unobserved, unnoticed. HEEDED

unhesitating unwavering, unfaltering, unswerving, unquestioning, unreserved, wholehearted, ready, prompt, immediate, instant. WAVERING

unhinge derange, unbalance, craze, madden, confuse, discompose, unsettle, disorder.

unholy impious, irreligious, ungodly, irreverent, profane, wicked, sinful, evil. DEVOUT
outrageous, shocking, appalling, dreadful, awful.

unhurried slow, leisurely, easy, easy-going.

unidentified anonymous, unrevealed, unnamed, nameless, unknown, unfamiliar, strange, mysterious. KNOWN

uniform *n*, outfit, costume, dress, livery. *adj*, regular, even, equable, unvarying, unchanging, constant, consistent, steady, same, identical, similar, alike. IRREGULAR

unify unite, join, merge, amalgamate, confederate, combine. SEPARATE

unimaginative dull, uninspired, unoriginal, ordinary, everyday, commonplace, trite, pedestrian, prosaic, unromantic. IMAGINATIVE

unimpaired undamaged, unharmed, uninjured, unhurt, unscathed, sound. IMPAIRED

unimpassioned cool, calm, composed, controlled, impassive, sedate, unemotional, dispassionate, rational, moderate. IMPASSIONED

unimpeachable blameless, irreproachable, faultless, impeccable, perfect, above reproach, unquestionable, unexceptionable. BLAMEWORTHY

unimportant insignificant, inconsequential, inconsiderable, slight, little, trivial, trifling, petty, minor, immaterial, nugatory. IMPORTANT

uninhabited deserted, abandoned, empty, vacant, unoccupied, unpopulated, unsettled, unfrequented. INHABITED

uninhibited free, unconstrained, unreserved, informal, casual, relaxed, open, frank, candid, uncontrolled, unrestrained, unbridled. INHIBITED

unintelligent stupid, foolish, dull, slow, brainless, dim-witted (*inf*), gormless (*inf*), thick, dense, obtuse, unthinking. INTELLIGENT

unintelligible incomprehensible, indecipherable, incoherent, inarticulate, meaningless, unfathomable. CLEAR

unintentional accidental, inadvertent, undesigned, unpremeditated, involuntary, unconscious, unwitting, fortuitous. INTENTIONAL

uninteresting boring, dull, unexciting, wearisome, tiresome, tedious, monotonous, uneventful, flat, stale, dreary. EXCITING

uninterrupted continuous, continual, unbroken, ceaseless, incessant, constant, perpetual, unending, nonstop. BROKEN

uninviting unappealing, undesirable, unattractive, repulsive, unpleasant, disagreeable, unappetizing, unwelcoming. INVITING

union conjunction, fusion, amalgamation, combination, blend, junction, connection. SEPARATION
league, alliance, coalition, association, confederacy, federation, society, guild.
unity, agreement, accord, concord, concert, harmony, unison, unanimity. DISCORD
marriage, matrimony, wedlock, copulation, coitus, intercourse.

unique single, sole, only, solitary, lone.
matchless, peerless, unequalled, unparalleled, incomparable, inimitable, unexampled, unrivalled, exceptional, peculiar, singular, rare. COMMON

unison agreement, harmony, accord, concord, unity, unanimity. DISCORD

unit whole, entity, group, system.
part, component, element, constituent, item, piece, section, module, measure, quantity.

unite join, unify, fuse, bind, connect, link, combine, amalgamate, marry, wed, ally, associate, league, band, cooperate, join forces. SEPARATE

unity oneness, singleness, wholeness, union.
agreement, harmony, accord, concord, unison, unanimity. DISCORD

universal general, comprehensive, all-embracing, all-inclusive, widespread, worldwide, ecumenical, catholic, total, whole, entire, unlimited. NARROW

unjust unfair, inequitable, biased, prejudiced, partial, one-sided, wrongful, undue, unmerited, undeserved. JUST

unjustifiable indefensible, unwarrantable, inexcusable, unforgivable, unpardonable, wrong. JUSTIFIABLE

unkempt dishevelled, tousled, uncombed, messy, untidy, disordered, disarranged, ungroomed, slovenly, slatternly, sluttish, scruffy. NEAT

unkind cruel, nasty, uncharitable, unfriendly, mean, spiteful, unfeeling, unsympathetic, thoughtless, inconsiderate, insensitive, callous, harsh, inhuman. KIND

unknown unfamiliar, strange, new, novel, unexplored, undiscovered, unheard-of, obscure, anonymous, nameless, unnamed, unidentified, unrevealed, secret, hidden, mysterious. KNOWN

unlawful illegal, illicit, illegitimate, unauthorized, criminal, banned, prohibited, forbidden. LAWFUL

unlike different, dissimilar, diverse, divergent, disparate, distinct, incompatible, unequal. SIMILAR

unlikely improbable, doubtful, dubious, implausible, incredible, unbelievable, remote, faint, slight, questionable, unpromising. LIKELY

unlimited infinite, limitless, illimitable, boundless, unbounded, immense, vast, great, immeasurable, incalculable, countless, endless, unrestricted, unfettered, absolute, full, unconditional, unqualified. LIMITED

unload disburden, unburden, unlade, empty, unpack, discharge, relieve, disencumber. LOAD

unlock open, unlatch, unbolt, unfasten, undo, free, release. LOCK

unlucky unfortunate, luckless, hapless, cursed, doomed, ill-fated, ill-starred, poor, wretched, unfavourable, adverse, inauspicious, ominous. LUCKY

unman demoralize, dishearten, discourage, dispirit, weaken, enfeeble, enervate, unnerve, daunt, intimidate.

unmanageable uncontrollable, ungovernable, difficult, unruly, refractory, recalcitrant, intractable, wild. DOCILE
unwieldy, inconvenient, unhandy, awkward, cumbersome, bulky. HANDY

unmanly effeminate, womanish, sissy, weak, feeble, cowardly, timid, timorous. MANLY

unmannerly rude, impolite, discourteous, uncivil, ungracious, bad-mannered, ill-bred, uncouth, boorish, churlish. POLITE

unmask expose, uncover, unveil, uncloak, show up, disclose, reveal. MASK

unmatched matchless, peerless, unequalled, unparalleled, unrivalled, unsurpassed, incomparable, supreme, consummate. INFERIOR

unmentionable unspeakable, unutterable, disgraceful, shameful, scandalous, shocking, indecent, immodest.

unmerciful merciless, pitiless, unpitying, cruel, harsh, hard, heartless, relentless, unrelenting, inexorable, implacable, ruthless, remorseless, unsparing, inhuman. MERCIFUL

unmethodical immethodical, unsystematic, disorganized, unorganized, disorderly, desultory, haphazard, irregular. METHODICAL

unmindful oblivious, unaware, unconscious, careless, negligent, neglectful, remiss, inattentive, heedless, mindless, unthinking. MINDFUL

unmistakable clear, distinct, plain, patent, obvious, evident, manifest, conspicuous, glaring, certain, sure, positive, unquestionable, indisputable. DOUBTFUL

unmitigated absolute, categorical, unqualified, thorough, utter, perfect, complete, total, downright, out-and-out. PARTIAL
undiminished, unmodified, intense, harsh, oppressive, relentless.

unmoved impassive, unfeeling, indifferent, uncaring, untouched, unaffected, cold, cool. MOVED
unshaken, unwavering, steadfast, firm, resolute, determined. SHAKEN

unnatural abnormal, aberrant, anomalous, irregular, unusual, odd, strange, uncanny, bizarre, extraordinary. NORMAL
cruel, inhuman, brutal, heartless, unfeeling, callous. HUMANE
artificial, forced, affected, mannered, stilted, stiff, assumed, feigned, insincere, self-conscious. SINCERE

unnecessary needless, unneeded, uncalled-for, nonessential, inessential, expendable, useless, superfluous, redundant. NECESSARY

unnerve daunt, dismay, intimidate, unman, discourage, dishearten, dispirit, demoralize, disconcert, fluster, rattle (*inf*), shake.

unnoticed unseen, unobserved, unheeded, ignored, disregarded, overlooked.

unobtrusive unpretentious, unassuming, restrained, low-key, inconspicuous, unostentatious, humble, modest, simple, quiet, reserved, retiring, meek, self-effacing. PRETENTIOUS

unoccupied empty, vacant, deserted, uninhabited, untenanted. OCCUPIED
idle, inactive, at leisure, unemployed. BUSY

unorthodox heterodox, heretical, unconventional, unusual, abnormal, irregular. ORTHODOX

unpaid due, overdue, outstanding, unsettled, owing, payable. PAID

unpalatable unpleasant, disagreeable, distasteful, unsavoury, unappetizing, inedible, uneatable, nasty, disgusting, offensive, repulsive. PALATABLE

unparalleled peerless, matchless, unmatched, unequalled, unrivalled, incomparable, inimitable, unprecedented, unexampled, unique, singular, supreme, consummate. ORDINARY

unpardonable unforgivable, inexcusable, unjustifiable, indefensible, reprehensible, deplorable, disgraceful, shameful. PARDONABLE

unperturbed calm, composed, serene, tranquil, unruffled, untroubled, placid, cool, poised, self-possessed, imperturbable. AGITATED

unpleasant disagreeable, obnoxious, offensive, nasty, repulsive, unattractive, objectionable, detestable, annoying, irksome, troublesome. PLEASANT

unpolished rough, coarse, rude, crude, unfinished, unrefined, uncultured, uncultivated, uncivilized, unsophisticated. POLISHED

unpopular disliked, unloved, unwelcome, rejected, undesirable, objectionable. POPULAR

unprecedented new, novel, unheard-of, unexampled, unparalleled, unequalled, original, unconventional.

unpredictable unforeseeable, doubtful, questionable, uncertain, unsure, erratic, capricious, fickle, changeable, unreliable, undependable, chance, accidental. PREDICTABLE

unprejudiced unbiased, impartial, disinterested, objective, detached, fair, just, neutral, indifferent. PREJUDICED

unpremeditated spontaneous, impulsive, spur-of-the-moment, impromptu, extempore, unprepared, unplanned. DELIBERATE

unprepossessing unattractive, unlovely, plain, ugly. ATTRACTIVE

unpretentious modest, humble, simple, plain, unaffected, unassuming, unostentatious, unobtrusive. PRETENTIOUS

unprincipled unscrupulous, dishonest, deceitful, crooked, unethical, amoral, immoral, unprofessional, dishonourable, corrupt. HONEST

unproductive fruitless, unfruitful, unprolific, sterile, barren, abortive, useless, futile, vain, unavailing, ineffective, unprofitable, worthless, unsuccessful. PRODUCTIVE

unprofitable unremunerative, unrewarding, worthless, valueless, unproductive, fruitless, bootless, useless, vain, unavailing. PROFITABLE

unpromising unpropitious, unfavourable, inauspicious, gloomy, ominous, discouraging, adverse, doubtful. PROMISING

unprotected unguarded, unarmed, undefended, defenceless, vulnerable, open, exposed, unsheltered. PROTECTED

unqualified incompetent, unfit, unsuited, ineligible, incapable. QUALIFIED
unmitigated, unconditional, categorical, unreserved, absolute, utter, complete, thorough, downright, out-and-out, perfect, consummate. PARTIAL

unquestionable indisputable, indubitable, irrefutable, undeniable, uncontestable, incontrovertible, certain, sure, clear, plain, evident, obvious, patent, manifest, conclusive, definite. QUESTIONABLE

unravel untangle, disentangle, undo, untwist, unwind, separate, solve, work out, clear up, explain, decipher, interpret. ENTANGLE

unreal imaginary, fanciful, illusory, visionary, intangible, nonexistent, fictitious, make-believe, false, artificial. REAL

unreasonable excessive, immoderate, extravagant, exorbitant, undue, unfair, unjust, uncalled-for. REASONABLE
irrational, illogical, senseless, foolish, silly, stupid, mad, crazy, absurd, preposterous. SENSIBLE

unrelenting relentless, implacable, inexorable, merciless, pitiless, cruel, ruthless, remorseless, unsparing. MERCIFUL
continuous, continual, constant, unbroken, unremitting, unabating, perpetual, incessant, ceaseless, endless. INTERMITTENT

unreliable undependable, untrustworthy, irresponsible, uncertain, fickle, changeable, capricious, erratic. RELIABLE

unremitting incessant, ceaseless, unceasing, perpetual, constant, continual, continuous, unrelenting, relentless, assiduous, diligent. INTERMITTENT

unrepentant impenitent, unregenerate, unreformed, incorrigible, inveterate, hardened. REPENTANT

unreserved unqualified, unrestricted, unlimited, unconditional, total, entire, full, wholehearted, open, frank, outspoken, uninhibited. RESERVED

unrest disquiet, uneasiness, restlessness, worry, anxiety, distress, agitation, turmoil, rebellion, strife, discord, discontent, dissatisfaction. PEACE

unrestrained unchecked, unhindered, unbridled, uncontrolled, unrestricted, unlimited, free, natural, uninhibited, unrepressed, wild, immoderate. RESTRAINED

unrestricted unlimited, limitless, unbounded, boundless, free, open, unhindered, unobstructed, unrestrained. RESTRICTED

unrighteous wicked, sinful, iniquitous, evil, bad, heinous, nefarious. GOOD
unfair, unjust, inequitable, wrongful. FAIR

unripe green, raw, immature, undeveloped, unready. RIPE

unrivalled matchless, unmatched, peerless, nonpareil, unequalled, unparalleled, incomparable, inimitable, unsurpassed, supreme. INFERIOR

unroll open, unfold, unfurl, unwind. ROLL

unruffled calm, composed, cool, collected, poised, self-possessed, unmoved, unperturbed, imperturbable, placid, serene, tranquil, peaceful, flat, smooth. AGITATED

unruly ungovernable, unmanageable, intractable, uncontrollable, refractory, recalcitrant, disobedient, insubordinate, mutinous, riotous, rebellious, restive, wild, disorderly, turbulent, lawless. ORDERLY

unsafe dangerous, hazardous, perilous, treacherous, risky, uncertain, precarious, insecure, unsound. SAFE

unsatisfactory inadequate, insufficient, deficient, poor, inferior, mediocre, unacceptable, unsuitable, not good enough. EXCELLENT

unsavoury insipid, vapid, tasteless, flat, unpalatable, unappetizing, nauseating, distasteful, unpleasant, disagreeable, objectionable, offensive, sordid, seamy, repulsive, revolting, nasty, obnoxious.

unscathed unharmed, unhurt, uninjured, undamaged, unimpaired, safe, sound, whole. HURT

unscrupulous unprincipled, unethical, amoral, unconscionable, shameless, corrupt, dishonest, dishonourable. HONEST

unseasonable untimely, ill-timed, inopportune, inappropriate, unsuitable. SEASONABLE

unseat unsaddle, unhorse, throw, depose, oust, dethrone, remove, dismiss, overthrow.

unseemly unbecoming, improper, indecorous, indecent, unbefitting, inappropriate. PROPER

unselfish charitable, selfless, altruistic, magnanimous, generous, liberal. SELFISH

unsettle upset, perturb, trouble, disturb, bother, fluster, rattle (*inf*), ruffle, agitate, disconcert, confuse, throw (*inf*).

unsettled disorderly, disorganized, unstable, shaky, unsteady, insecure, inconstant, changeable, variable, unpredictable. SETTLED
uneasy, tense, anxious, restless, flustered, ruffled, agitated, shaken, confused. CALM
unresolved, undecided, moot, debatable, open, pending, payable, owing, outstanding, due.

unsheltered unshielded, unprotected, open, exposed. SHELTERED

unshrinking unflinching, unfaltering, unwavering, firm, resolute, dauntless, undaunted, unblenching.

unsightly ugly, hideous, repulsive, unpleasant, disagreeable, unattractive, unprepossessing. BEAUTIFUL

unskilful clumsy, awkward, maladroit, unhandy, inexpert, inept, bungling, incompetent. SKILFUL

unskilled inexperienced, untrained, unqualified, inexpert, unprofessional, amateurish. SKILLED

unsociable unfriendly, uncongenial, unneighbourly, hostile, uncommunicative, reticent, retiring, withdrawn, aloof, distant. SOCIABLE

unsolicited unsought, unrequested, uncalled-for, uninvited, unwanted, unwelcome, voluntary, free. REQUESTED

unsophisticated innocent, childlike, naive, unworldly, inexperienced, guileless, artless, ingenuous, natural, simple, plain, unaffected, unrefined, unpolished, unadulterated, pure, genuine. SOPHISTICATED

unsound weak, feeble, infirm, unhealthy, unwell, diseased, deranged, unhinged, impaired, imperfect, defective, rotten, decayed. SOUND

fallacious, faulty, flawed, illogical, false, erroneous, wrong, invalid. VALID

unstable, shaky, rickety, unsteady, flimsy, unsafe. STABLE

unsparing profuse, lavish, abundant, bountiful, liberal, generous, unstinting, ungrudging. MEAN

merciless, unmerciful, pitiless, unpitying, relentless, unrelenting, inexorable, implacable, ruthless, cruel, harsh, severe, stern, unforgiving. MERCIFUL

unspeakable unutterable, ineffable, inexpressible, indescribable, unimaginable, unbelievable.

loathsome, odious, abominable, horrible, awful, unmentionable.

unspoiled unspoilt, perfect, unharmed, undamaged, preserved, unchanged, untouched, unaffected, natural, pure, simple, innocent.

unspoken tacit, understood, assumed, implied, implicit, unstated, unexpressed, unsaid, unuttered, silent, mute, wordless, voiceless. STATED

unstable unsteady, insecure, unsettled, shaky, wobbly, rickety, precarious, risky. STEADY

unpredictable, changeable, variable, inconstant, fickle, capricious, wavering, vacillating, fluctuating, erratic, irregular. STABLE

unsteady unstable, unsafe, insecure, precarious, wobbly, shaky, rickety, tottering, staggering. STABLE

irregular, erratic, wavering, vacillating, fluctuating, changeable, variable. STEADY

unstinted generous, liberal, lavish, profuse, ample, abundant, plentiful, bountiful. MEAGRE

unstudied natural, unaffected, unpremeditated, spontaneous, impromptu, casual.

unsubstantial insubstantial, fanciful, imaginary, unreal, visionary, illusory, airy, light, slight, thin, frail, fragile, flimsy, weak, tenuous, unsound. SOLID

unsuccessful futile, vain, unavailing, bootless, useless, ineffectual, worthless, fruitless, unproductive, abortive. FRUITFUL

unfortunate, unlucky, luckless, hapless, ill-fated, ill-starred, foiled, frustrated, defeated, losing. SUCCESSFUL

unsuitable inappropriate, inapt, unfitting, unfit, unsuited, incompatible, incongruous, out of place, out of keeping, impractical, unseemly, unbecoming, improper. SUITABLE

unsullied clean, pure, spotless, unspotted, immaculate, unsoiled, unblemished, stainless, unstained, untainted, untarnished, untouched, undefiled, unpolluted, uncontaminated. SULLIED

unsung unacclaimed, uncelebrated, unacknowledged, unrecognized, unrenowned, anonymous, unnamed, unknown. FAMOUS

unsure uncertain, doubtful, dubious, sceptical, suspicious, undecided, irresolute, hesitant, insecure. SURE

unsurpassed unexcelled, supreme, paramount, transcendent, unrivalled, unparalleled, unequalled, unmatched, matchless, peerless, nonpareil, incomparable. INFERIOR

unsuspecting unsuspicious, trusting, trustful, credulous, gullible, naive, ingenuous, unwary, off guard. SUSPICIOUS

unswerving straight, direct, undeviating, constant, steadfast, unfaltering, unwavering, untiring, unflagging.

unsympathetic unmoved, unconcerned, uncaring, unfeeling, unpitying, insensitive, callous, heartless, cold, cruel, unkind, inconsiderate. SYMPATHETIC

unsystematic unmethodical, unorganized, disorganized, disorderly, confused, muddled, random, haphazard, irregular. SYSTEMATIC

untarnished bright, shining, polished, clean, spotless, immaculate, pure, unstained, stainless, unblemished, untainted, unsullied. TARNISHED

untaught uneducated, unschooled, ignorant, illiterate, unlearned. EDUCATED

untenable indefensible, unsound, weak, flawed, faulty, fallacious, groundless, unreasonable, illogical. SOUND

unthinkable unimaginable, inconceivable, incredible, unbelievable, impossible, out of the question, unlikely, improbable, preposterous, absurd. CONCEIVABLE

unthinking thoughtless, inconsiderate, tactless, rude, senseless, witless, mindless, unmindful, heedless, regardless, neglectful, negligent, rash, careless, impulsive, automatic, mechanical, instinctive. THOUGHTFUL

untidy disorderly, messy, sloppy (*inf*), slovenly, unkempt, scruffy, bedraggled, littered, muddled, jumbled, chaotic. TIDY

untie undo, unfasten, unknot, unlace, release, loose, free, let go. TIE

untimely premature, early, unseasonable, ill-timed, inopportune, inconvenient, inappropriate, unsuitable. TIMELY

untiring tireless, indefatigable, unflagging, unwearying, unfaltering, unwavering, unremitting, determined, steady, constant, persistent, dogged. WAVERING

untold unspeakable, unutterable, indescribable, inexpressible, unimaginable, unthinkable.
countless, innumerable, numberless, myriad, incalculable, immeasurable.
secret, private, hidden, unknown, undisclosed, unrevealed.

untouched unused, new, pristine, intact, whole, undamaged, unharmed, unhurt, uninjured, unscathed. DAMAGED
unmoved, unaffected, dry-eyed, indifferent, apathetic, unconcerned. MOVED

untoward adverse, unfavourable, contrary, bad, inopportune, untimely, unseasonable, inauspicious, unfortunate, unlucky.
unseemly, unbecoming, indecorous, improper, unsuitable, inappropriate.

untroubled calm, composed, collected, cool, poised, self-possessed, unruffled, unperturbed, placid, tranquil, serene, peaceful. AGITATED

untrue false, untruthful, wrong, mistaken, erroneous, fallacious, incorrect, inaccurate, inexact, imprecise. CORRECT
unfaithful, faithless, disloyal, traitorous, perfidious, treacherous, false, untrustworthy. FAITHFUL

untrustworthy unreliable, undependable, dishonest, deceitful, false, untrue, disloyal, faithless, unfaithful, treacherous. TRUSTWORTHY

untruth falsehood, lie, fib, fabrication, fiction, story, tale. TRUTH
lying, mendacity, untruthfulness, falsity, deceit, deceitfulness. TRUTHFULNESS

untruthful lying, mendacious, deceitful, dishonest, insincere, hypocritical, false, untrue. TRUTHFUL

unused new, pristine, untouched, intact, leftover, surplus. USED
unaccustomed, unfamiliar, inexperienced. ACCUSTOMED

unusual uncommon, extraordinary, remarkable, odd, strange, queer, peculiar, curious, rare, singular, unfamiliar, unexpected, unwanted, unconventional. USUAL

unutterable ineffable, unspeakable, indescribable, inexpressible, beyond words.

unvarnished plain, simple, bare, naked, unembellished, unadorned, pure, direct, honest, frank.

unvarying unchanging, changeless, constant, steady, invariable, unchangeable. CHANGING

unveil reveal, expose, uncover, lay bare, disclose, divulge. VEIL

unwanted unsolicited, unsought, unasked, uninvited, unwelcome, undesirable, uncalled-for, unneeded, superfluous, rejected. WANTED

unwarranted unwarrantable, unjustified, uncalled-for, gratuitous, unjust, unfair, undeserved, unmerited, wrong, unjustifiable, indefensible, inexcusable. JUSTIFIED

unwary incautious, careless, heedless, thoughtless, unthinking, hasty, rash, reckless, indiscreet, imprudent, unwise, unguarded, unwatchful. WARY

unwavering unfaltering, unswerving, staunch, steadfast, constant, steady, unflagging, untiring, resolute, resolved, determined, firm. WAVERING

unwelcome unwanted, rejected, uninvited, unacceptable, unpopular, undesirable, unpleasant, disagreeable. WELCOME

unwell ill, sick, ailing, indisposed, poorly (*inf*), under the weather (*inf*), off colour, out of sorts. WELL

unwieldy bulky, large, heavy, weighty, ponderous, cumbersome, ungainly, clumsy, awkward, unmanageable, unhandy, inconvenient. HANDY

unwilling reluctant, averse, loath, indisposed, disinclined, opposed. WILLING

unwind unroll, uncoil, untwist, unravel, undo, slacken, loosen.
relax, calm down, slow down, take it easy (*inf*).

unwise injudicious, indiscreet, imprudent, incautious, impolitic, ill-advised, foolhardy, rash, reckless, irresponsible, foolish, senseless, silly, stupid. WISE

unwitting unknowing, unaware, ignorant, oblivious, unconscious, unsuspecting, accidental, inadvertent, unintentional, involuntary. CONSCIOUS

unwonted unusual, uncommon, uncustomary, unfamiliar, rare, exceptional, atypical, unheard-of, extraordinary, peculiar. USUAL

unworthy unseemly, unbecoming, unsuitable, inappropriate, unfitting, unbefitting, out of character, out of place, undeserving, ineligible. WORTHY
dishonourable, ignoble, discreditable, shameful, contemptible, base, worthless, paltry.

unwrap undo, open, uncover. WRAP

unyielding inflexible, unbending, stiff, rigid, firm, hard, adamant, steady, staunch, steadfast, resolute, determined, obstinate, stubborn, obdurate, intractable. FLEXIBLE

upbraid scold, chide, reprimand, reprove, reproach, rebuke, castigate, tell off (*inf*), berate, condemn, censure, blame. PRAISE

upheaval cataclysm, disruption, disturbance, disorder.

uphill hard, difficult, strenuous, toilsome, arduous, laborious, gruelling, punishing. EASY
rising, ascending, climbing, mounting. DOWNHILL

uphold sustain, maintain, support, back, endorse, aid, advocate, promote, champion, defend. OPPOSE

upkeep maintenance, conservation, preservation, subsistence, sustenance, expenses, costs.

uplift raise, elevate, lift up, hoist, heave. LOWER
improve, ameliorate, better, enhance, enrich, edify, advance, exalt, ennoble.

upper higher, top, superior, greater. LOWER

upright vertical, perpendicular, straight, erect. HORIZONTAL
just, fair, honest, honourable, ethical, principled, righteous, virtuous, good, decent. DISHONEST

uprising rebellion, revolt, revolution, insurrection, mutiny, riot.

uproar turmoil, tumult, clamour, brouhaha, hubbub, din, commotion, disturbance, disorder, riot, pandemonium, rumpus. PEACE

uproarious turbulent, tumultuous, riotous, disorderly, wild, noisy, clamorous, boisterous. QUIET
hilarious, hysterical, side-splitting, very funny.

uproot pull up, root out, extirpate, deracinate, displace, remove, eradicate, destroy, eliminate, wipe out.

upset *v*, overturn, knock over, tip over, capsize, topple, spill.
sadden, grieve, distress, dismay, worry, trouble, bother, disturb, perturb, discompose, agitate, ruffle, fluster, confuse, mix up, spoil, mess up.
adj, overturned, capsized, upside down, topsy-turvy, disordered, confused.
sad, distressed, worried, troubled, disturbed, perturbed, agitated, ruffled. CALM

upshot result, consequence, outcome, issue, effect, end, conclusion. BEGINNING

up-to-date modern, fashionable, stylish, trendy (*inf*), current, latest, new, up-to-the-minute. OLD

urban civic, municipal, metropolitan, town, city.

urbane elegant, refined, polished, suave, debonair, courteous, polite, civil, civilized, sophisticated. UNCOUTH

urge *v*, push, drive, force, propel, impel, press, constrain, incite, provoke, goad, spur, encourage, induce, persuade. DETER
plead, implore, beseech, supplicate, beg, entreat, exhort, advise, advocate, recommend.
n, desire, wish, itch, yearning, drive, impulse.

urgent pressing, instant, important, serious, grave, imperative, crucial, critical. UNIMPORTANT
insistent, importunate, earnest, persistent.

usage custom, practice, habit, tradition, convention, form, method, procedure, routine, rule, wont, fashion, mode.
use, employment, treatment, handling, management, operation, running, control.

use *v*, employ, utilize, apply, make use of, practise, exercise, operate, wield, handle, treat, manipulate, exploit, abuse, misuse.
consume, spend, expend, use up, exhaust, drain, waste, squander. SAVE

used to, accustomed to, familiar with, inured to, hardened to.

n, employment, utilization, application, practice, exercise, operation, treatment, usage, wear and tear.
utility, usefulness, advantage, benefit, profit, good, help, avail, service. FUTILITY
need, call, cause, occasion, purpose, reason, point.
custom, practice, habit, usage.
useful helpful, serviceable, advantageous, beneficial, valuable, profitable, worthwhile, effective, practical, handy. USELESS
useless futile, vain, idle, bootless, unavailing, ineffective, fruitless, abortive, unproductive, worthless, impractical, no good. USEFUL
usher *n*, guide, escort, usherette, doorkeeper.
v, guide, escort, pilot, steer, lead, direct, conduct, show.
usual customary, accustomed, habitual, wonted, routine, normal, stock, standard, typical, conventional, general, familiar, common, everyday, ordinary. UNUSUAL
usurp seize, take over, commandeer, appropriate, arrogate, assume, infringe, encroach.
utensil implement, instrument, tool, device, contrivance, apparatus, gadget.
utility usefulness, serviceability, use, advantage, benefit, profit, service, avail. FUTILITY
utilize use, employ, make use of, avail oneself of.
utmost uttermost, most, maximum, greatest, supreme, paramount, highest, top, extreme, farthest, last, final. MINIMUM
utter[1] *v*, say, speak, express, pronounce, articulate, voice, verbalize, enunciate, declare, proclaim, announce, promulgate. SUPPRESS
utter[2] *adj*, complete, total, thorough, absolute, downright, out-and-out, sheer, arrant, unqualified, unmitigated. PARTIAL

V

vacancy opportunity, job, position, room.
emptiness, void, gap, space, blankness, inanity.
vacant empty, void, unfilled, unoccupied, free, not in use. OCCUPIED
blank, expressionless, vacuous, inane, thoughtless, unthinking.
vacate evacuate, abandon, desert, quit, leave, depart.
vacation holiday, recess, rest, break, intermission. TERM
vaccinate inoculate, immunize, protect.
vacillate fluctuate, oscillate, waver, falter, hesitate, dither, be indecisive, sway, rock.
vacillating indecisive, irresolute, uncertain, wavering, hesitant, fickle. FIRM
vacuous empty, vacant, void, unfilled. FULL
blank, expressionless, inane, stupid, unintelligent, mindless. INTELLIGENT
vacuum void, emptiness, vacuity.
vagabond vagrant, tramp, nomad, itinerant, wayfarer, wanderer, rogue, rascal.
vagary whim, fancy, humour, crotchet, caprice, notion.
vagrant *n*, tramp, vagabond, down-and-out, beggar, nomad, itinerant.
adj, nomadic, itinerant, peripatetic, wandering, roaming, roving, homeless, down and out. SETTLED
vague indistinct, indeterminate, unclear, obscure, nebulous, hazy, blurred, dim, faint, imprecise, ambiguous, loose, indefinite, uncertain. CLEAR
vain conceited, boastful, proud, arrogant, inflated, stuck-up (*inf*), overweening, cocky, egotistical, big-headed (*inf*). MODEST
worthless, trivial, unimportant, idle, hollow, empty, futile, useless, bootless, unavailing, ineffective, ineffectual, fruitless, abortive. WORTHWHILE
valediction farewell, goodbye, adieu. GREETING
valiant valorous, brave, courageous, heroic, intrepid, fearless, dauntless, undaunted, bold, daring, gallant, plucky, doughty, indomitable. COWARDLY
valid sound, good, well-founded, logical, cogent, convincing, powerful, efficacious, conclusive, just. WEAK
official, legal, lawful, legitimate, genuine, authentic, real, true, binding, effective. INVALID
valley dale, dell, vale, glen, hollow, depression. HILL

valour bravery, courage, heroism, intrepidity, fearlessness, dauntlessness, boldness, daring, gallantry, pluck, spirit, mettle. COWARDICE

valuable precious, costly, expensive, priceless, rare, prized, valued, cherished, dear, estimable, worthy, worthwhile, useful, important, beneficial. WORTHLESS

value *n*, worth, merit, importance, significance, use, usefulness, advantage, benefit, profit, gain.
cost, price, valuation, assessment.
v, prize, esteem, appreciate, respect, cherish, hold dear, treasure. SCORN
evaluate, assess, appraise, estimate, rate, price.

vandalism destruction, ruin, damage, mutilation.

vanish disappear, fade, evanesce, dissolve, melt, evaporate, go away. APPEAR

vanity conceit, egotism, self-love, narcissism, pride, arrogance, boastfulness, bigheadedness. MODESTY
worthlessness, emptiness, hollowness, uselessness, futility, pointlessness, frivolity, triviality, unreality.

vanquish defeat, conquer, subjugate, subdue, rout, overwhelm, overcome, overpower, overthrow, crush, quell, beat, master. SURRENDER

vapid insipid, flat, flavourless, tasteless, bland, tame, dull, boring, uninteresting. PIQUANT

vapour steam, smoke, fog, mist, haze, breath, exhalation.

variable changeable, mutable, protean, chameleonic, vacillating, wavering, fluctuating, capricious, mercurial, fickle, inconstant, unsteady, unstable, shifting. CONSTANT

variance discrepancy, disparity, divergence, difference, disagreement, discord, conflict, strife, dissent, dissension. AGREEMENT

variation diversity, variety, difference, departure, deviation, change, alteration, modification, variant, innovation, novelty.

variegated mottled, speckled, dappled, pied, motley, streaked, varicoloured, multicoloured. PLAIN

variety difference, dissimilarity, discrepancy, disparity, variation, change, diversity, multiplicity. UNIFORMITY
miscellany, assortment, mixture, medley, collection, range.
class, kind, type, sort, order, group, species, brand.

various different, diverse, assorted, miscellaneous, mixed, motley, varied, sundry, many, numerous, several, manifold. IDENTICAL

varnish glaze, lacquer, polish, gild, adorn, embellish, ornament, decorate.

vary change, alter, modify, diversify, transform, permutate, alternate, fluctuate, swerve, deviate, diverge, depart, differ, disagree.

vast immense, broad, wide, extensive, expansive, massive, huge, enormous, great, tremendous, colossal, gigantic, boundless, unbounded, limitless, illimitable, immeasurable, measureless. TINY

vault[1] *n*, arch, span, cellar, strongroom, tomb, crypt, mausoleum.

vault[2] *v*, leap, spring, jump, bound, hurdle, clear.

vaunt boast, brag, crow, trumpet, parade, show off. BELITTLE

veer change, swing, shift, turn, sheer, swerve, deviate, diverge.

vegetate sprout, grow, shoot, burgeon, germinate, swell. WITHER
idle, do nothing, waste time, stagnate. WORK

vehement ardent, fervent, impassioned, passionate, earnest, enthusiastic, intense, forceful, furious, violent, burning, fierce, strong, powerful. SUBDUED

vehicle conveyance, transport.
means, agency, instrument, medium, organ, channel.

veil *n*, cover, screen, cloak, mantle, shroud, mask, disguise, blind.
v, cover, screen, cloak, muffle, dim, obscure, conceal, hide, mask, disguise. EXPOSE

vein streak, stripe, line, lode, seam, stratum.
strain, tendency, bent, character, mood, humour.

velocity speed, rate, swiftness, rapidity, quickness, celerity. SLOWNESS

velvety velvet, velutinous, smooth, soft. COARSE

venal corrupt, corruptible, bribable, mercenary, grasping, rapacious, sordid. INCORRUPTIBLE

vendetta feud, quarrel, enmity, bad blood.

veneer coat, layer, covering, facing, front, façade, show, appearance.

venerate revere, reverence, honour, esteem, adore, worship. DESPISE

vengeance revenge, retribution, requital, retaliation, reprisal. FORGIVENESS

vengeful revengeful, vindictive, spiteful, unforgiving, avenging, retaliatory. FORGIVING

venial excusable, pardonable, forgivable, allowable, slight, minor, insignificant, trivial. UNFORGIVABLE

venom poison, toxin.
rancour, spite, spitefulness, ill will, bitterness, acrimony, malice, malignity, malevolence, hate, gall, spleen, grudge. BENEVOLENCE

venomous poisonous, toxic, virulent, envenomed, noxious, harmful. HARMLESS
spiteful, malicious, hostile, malevolent, malignant, rancorous. BENEVOLENT

vent *n*, hole, aperture, opening, outlet, spiracle, orifice, passage, duct.
v, air, express, utter, emit, discharge, release.

ventilate air, aerate, oxygenate, fan, air-condition, cool, freshen, purify.
discuss, talk about, go over, review, examine, scrutinize, broadcast, make known.

venture *v*, risk, hazard, endanger, imperil, jeopardize, speculate, stake, wager, chance, dare, presume, advance, put forward.
n, undertaking, enterprise, project, adventure, chance, gamble, speculation, risk, hazard.

venturesome daring, bold, adventurous, enterprising, brave, courageous, doughty, dauntless, fearless, intrepid, plucky, spirited, reckless, foolhardy. COWARDLY

veracious truthful, honest, frank, candid, trustworthy, reliable, true, factual, accurate, precise.

verbal spoken, oral, unwritten, verbatim, literal. WRITTEN

verbiage verbosity, prolixity, wordiness, long-windedness, loquacity, circumlocution, periphrasis, pleonasm, tautology, repetition, redundancy. TERSENESS

verbose prolix, wordy, long-winded, loquacious, garrulous, talkative, circumlocutory, roundabout, periphrastic, tautological. TERSE

verdant green, grassy, leafy, fresh.

verdict decision, judgment, conclusion, finding, opinion, sentence.

verge *n*, edge, border, margin, lip, rim, brim, brink, limit, boundary, threshold.
v, approach, border, incline, tend, bear, lean.

verify confirm, substantiate, corroborate, bear out, prove, establish, attest, affirm, authenticate, validate. REFUTE

verisimilitude probability, likelihood, credibility, plausibility, realism, authenticity. IMPROBABILITY

veritable real, actual, genuine, authentic, positive, absolute.

verity truth, reality, actuality, fact. FALSITY

vernacular *adj*, native, indigenous, local, informal, colloquial, popular, common, vulgar. FOREIGN
n, native language, mother tongue, dialect, patois, jargon, slang.

versatile adaptable, all-round, multifaceted, many-sided, flexible, all-purpose, variable, changeable, inconstant, fickle.

verse stanza, poem, poetry, metre.

versed skilled, proficient, accomplished, practised, experienced, acquainted, familiar, conversant, knowledgeable. INEXPERIENCED

version rendering, interpretation, account, translation, reading.
type, model, form, variant.

vertex apex, apogee, peak, summit, point, tip, top, crown, acme, zenith, pinnacle, height. BASE

vertical upright, perpendicular, erect. HORIZONTAL

vertigo giddiness, dizziness, light-headedness.

verve vigour, energy, force, enthusiasm, spirit, life, dash, élan, vivacity, liveliness, animation, vitality, gusto. APATHY

very *adv*, extremely, exceedingly, terribly (*inf*), awfully (*inf*), remarkably, exceptionally, highly, greatly, really, truly. SLIGHTLY
adj, actual, real, true, genuine, perfect, exact, same, identical.

vessel boat, ship, craft.
container, receptacle, pot.

vest endow, bestow, confer, invest.
clothe, dress, robe, garb. STRIP
vestal virginal, chaste, pure, virtuous.
vestibule lobby, foyer, anteroom, antechamber, hall, porch.
vestige trace, mark, sign, indication, relics, remains, hint, touch, suggestion, suspicion.
vestment robe, habit, garment, clothes, clothing, apparel.
veteran *n*, old hand, past master, master, expert. NOVICE
adj, experienced, expert, proficient, seasoned, old.
veto *n*, prohibition, interdiction, ban, embargo, refusal, rejection. APPROVAL
v, reject, turn down, prohibit, forbid, disallow, ban. CONSENT
vex annoy, irritate, provoke, pique, nettle, chafe, exasperate, infuriate, irk, anger, bother, pester, harass, bug (*inf*), torment, tease, plague, trouble, worry, fret. SOOTHE
vexation annoyance, irritation, exasperation, anger, bother, nuisance, problem, trouble.
vexatious annoying, irritating, exasperating, infuriating, irksome, bothersome, troublesome, worrying.
vexed annoyed, irritated, nettled, peeved (*inf*), angry, irate, bothered, harassed, agitated, disturbed, troubled, worried.
contested, disputed, moot, controversial.
vibrate oscillate, swing, sway, wave, undulate, vacillate, fluctuate, shake, tremble, quiver, shiver, palpitate, pulse, pulsate, throb, resonate, reverberate.
vicarious indirect, second-hand, sympathetic, empathetic, surrogate, substitutive, delegated, deputed. PERSONAL
vice sin, wickedness, wrong, iniquity, evil, immorality, corruption, depravity.
fault, flaw, imperfection, defect, failing, shortcoming, weakness, foible. VIRTUE
vicinity neighbourhood, area, district, locality, precincts, environs, proximity, propinquity. DISTANCE
vicious savage, ferocious, fierce, violent, cruel, barbarous, harsh, severe, wicked, evil, bad, sinful, immoral, corrupt, depraved, mean, spiteful, malicious, bitter, rancorous, venomous. KIND
vicissitude variation, change, mutation, shift, alternation, fluctuation. STABILITY
victim sufferer, casualty, prey, scapegoat, sacrifice, martyr, dupe, sucker (*inf*), fall guy (*inf*), butt, target.
victimize persecute, discriminate against, pick on, exploit, use, deceive, fool, dupe, swindle, cheat, defraud.
victor winner, champion, conqueror, hero. LOSER
victorious winning, conquering, triumphant, successful. LOSING
victory win, conquest, triumph, success, superiority, mastery. DEFEAT
victuals food, provisions, rations, viands, eatables, edibles, grub (*inf*).
vie strive, struggle, compete, contend, contest.
view *n*, sight, vision, scene, vista, prospect, aspect, outlook, panorama, landscape.
survey, examination, inspection, scrutiny, study, observation.
opinion, judgment, belief, impression, idea, notion, estimation, sentiment, feeling.
aim, intention, purpose, design, object, end.
v, watch, observe, see, behold, look at, regard, survey, scan, examine, inspect, scrutinize, eye. IGNORE
consider, contemplate, think about, regard, deem, judge.
viewpoint attitude, angle, position, standpoint, stance, point of view.
vigilant watchful, observant, attentive, awake, alert, sleepless, unsleeping, wary, cautious, careful, circumspect. CARELESS
vigorous energetic, strenuous, active, dynamic, brisk, lively, strong, robust, lusty, hardy, hale, hearty, sound, sturdy, powerful, forceful. WEAK
vigour energy, vitality, activity, liveliness, strength, power, force, might, stamina, health, robustness, sturdiness, spirit, verve, vehemence, intensity. WEAKNESS
vile base, low, mean, bad, wicked, evil, sinful, immoral, depraved, corrupt, ignoble, villainous, heinous, nefarious, contemptible, despicable, odious, loathsome, wretched, miserable, abject, menial, degrading, humiliating, worthless, paltry, foul, disgusting, repulsive, revolting, nasty, offensive, obnoxious, objectionable, unpleasant, disagreeable. GOOD

vilify vituperate, defame, denigrate, revile, malign, slander, libel, calumniate, traduce, asperse, slur, disparage, decry. PRAISE
villain scoundrel, blackguard, reprobate, wretch, rogue, rascal, miscreant, evildoer, baddy (*inf*). HERO
villainous wicked, evil, sinful, bad, vile, base, mean, ignoble, nefarious, heinous, infamous, notorious, criminal, depraved. GOOD
vindicate clear, acquit, exculpate, exonerate, absolve, justify, defend, support, uphold, maintain, assert, advocate.
vindictive vengeful, revengeful, spiteful, malicious, rancorous, venomous, malevolent, malignant, unforgiving, implacable. FORGIVING
violate break, contravene, transgress, infringe, disobey, disregard. OBSERVE
rape, ravish, debauch, molest, defile, outrage, profane, desecrate, invade, disturb. RESPECT
violent strong, powerful, forceful, mighty, savage, brutal, cruel, bloodthirsty, wild, uncontrollable, boisterous, turbulent, stormy, tempestuous, raging, furious, fierce, vehement, ardent, fervent, impassioned, passionate, fiery, hot, harsh, severe, acute, sharp, extreme, intense. GENTLE
virago termagant, shrew, harridan, battle-axe (*inf*), fury, vixen, scold, nag. ANGEL
virgin *n*, maid, maiden, vestal, virgo intacta.
adj, virginal, vestal, chaste, pure, untouched, undefiled, unsullied, immaculate, spotless, celibate.
virile manly, masculine, potent, powerful, strong, lusty, robust, hardy, vigorous, forceful. EFFEMINATE
virtual practical, essential, effective, potential, implied, implicit. ACTUAL
virtually practically, as good as, in essence, in effect, almost, nearly. ACTUALLY
virtue goodness, righteousness, morality, rectitude, uprightness, probity, integrity, excellence, quality, credit, merit, worth, worthiness, chastity, purity, virginity, honour. VICE
virtuoso master, expert, maestro, genius, connoisseur.
virtuous good, righteous, moral, ethical, upright, excellent, exemplary, blameless, worthy, pure, chaste, virginal. WICKED
virulent poisonous, venomous, toxic, infective, deadly, lethal, noxious, pernicious. HARMLESS
bitter, acrimonious, hostile, resentful, spiteful, malicious, malevolent, malignant, rancorous, vicious. MILD
visage face, countenance, physiognomy, aspect, appearance.
viscera intestines, bowels, entrails, guts, innards (*inf*), insides (*inf*).
viscous viscid, thick, sticky, adhesive, gluey, mucilaginous, glutinous, syrupy, gelatinous, gooey (*inf*).
visible perceptible, discernible, apparent, evident, noticeable, observable, manifest, clear, plain, obvious, patent, conspicuous, distinct. INVISIBLE
vision sight, eyesight, seeing, view, perception, insight, discernment, penetration. BLINDNESS
apparition, spectre, phantom, ghost, mirage, hallucination, illusion, figment of the imagination, chimera, dream, conception, image.
visionary *adj*, romantic, idealistic, quixotic, utopian, impractical, impracticable, unreal, imaginary, illusory, fanciful, chimerical. REAL
n, romantic, idealist, dreamer, daydreamer, seer, prophet. CYNIC
visit *v*, call on, look up, stop by, drop in (*inf*), stay with, inspect, examine.
assail, attack, afflict, inflict, wreak.
n, call, stay, stop, sojourn, inspection, examination, visitation.
visitor caller, guest, company, visitant.
vista view, scene, prospect, outlook, panorama.
visualize picture, conjure up, envisage, imagine, conceive.
vital critical, crucial, key, important, essential, requisite, necessary, indispensable, imperative, urgent. UNIMPORTANT
living, alive, animate, life-giving, invigorative, lively, vivacious, animated, spirited, vigorous, forceful, dynamic. DEAD
vitality vigour, energy, life, animation, strength, power, stamina, spirit, liveliness, vivacity. WEAKNESS
vitiate impair, harm, mar, spoil, blight, debase, corrupt, deprave, pervert, defile, pollute, contaminate, adulterate, deteriorate. IMPROVE

vituperate censure, reproach, reprove, slate (*inf*), condemn, denounce, revile, rail against, berate, upbraid, vilify, denigrate, slander, abuse. PRAISE

vivacious lively, animated, spirited, sprightly, gay, merry, cheerful, jolly, sportive, bubbly, ebullient, effervescent. TORPID

vivacity liveliness, animation, high spirits, gaiety, energy, vigour, ebullience, effervescence. TORPOR

vivid bright, intense, brilliant, dazzling, colourful. DULL
graphic, striking, telling, dramatic, realistic, true to life, lifelike, clear, distinct, memorable.

vivify animate, vitalize, quicken, invigorate, stimulate, enliven.

vocabulary words, language, lexicon, glossary, dictionary, wordbook.

vocal oral, spoken, uttered, voiced.
noisy, vociferous, outspoken, articulate, eloquent. SILENT

vocation calling, career, profession, occupation, métier, trade, business, job, employment, pursuit.

vociferate shout, yell, bellow, bawl, scream, cry, roar, clamour. WHISPER

vociferous noisy, loud, clamorous, uproarious, loud-mouthed (*inf*), obstreperous. QUIET

vogue fashion, mode, style, trend, rage, craze, custom, practice, usage, use, favour, popularity, prevalence, currency.

voice *n*, speech, language, sound, tone, accent, articulation, expression, utterance. SILENCE
vote, say, preference, choice, option, wish, view, opinion.
v, express, state, utter, say, declare, proclaim, air, ventilate. SUPPRESS

void *adj*, empty, unfilled, vacant, unoccupied, blank, clear, free. FULL
devoid, destitute, lacking, wanting, without.
invalid, null, ineffectual, inoperative, worthless, useless, vain, nugatory. VALID
n, emptiness, vacuity, vacuum, space, blank, gap, hole, opening.

volatile changeable, variable, fickle, inconstant, capricious, whimsical, flighty, mercurial, unstable, unsteady, giddy, frivolous. STABLE

volition will, free will, discretion, determination, purpose, resolution, decision, choice, option, preference, wish. COMPULSION

volley barrage, bombardment, fusillade, salvo, report, discharge, explosion, blast, shower, storm, emission.

voluble fluent, glib, talkative, loquacious, garrulous. TACITURN

volume bulk, capacity, size, dimensions, mass, total, quantity, amount.
tome, book.

voluminous spacious, roomy, capacious, big, large, vast, ample, copious. SMALL

voluntary free, gratuitous, unasked, unsolicited, unconstrained, unforced, spontaneous, willing, intentional, deliberate, optional, unpaid. COMPULSORY

volunteer offer, proffer, tender, present, give, propose, put forward, step forward. WITHHOLD

voluptuous sensual, carnal, fleshly, licentious, hedonistic, self-indulgent, sybaritic, voluptuary. ASCETIC
seductive, provocative, erotic, sexy (*inf*), buxom, well-endowed, shapely, curvaceous (*inf*).

vomit disgorge, spew, puke (*inf*), bring up, throw up (*inf*), be sick, heave, retch, eject.

voracious greedy, ravenous, gluttonous, omnivorous, insatiable, rapacious, avid, hungry.

vortex whirlpool, maelstrom, eddy.

votary devotee, adherent, disciple, follower, zealot, fanatic, enthusiast, aficionado.

vote *n*, ballot, poll, election, referendum, suffrage, franchise, voice, say.
v, ballot, elect, appoint, opt.

vouch guarantee, assure, asseverate, attest, affirm, assert, certify, confirm, uphold, support, answer for. REPUDIATE

voucher receipt, chit, slip, note, document, paper, coupon, token.

vouchsafe grant, give, confer, accord, deign, condescend, yield, concede. REFUSE

vow *n*, promise, pledge, word, oath.
v, promise, pledge, swear, dedicate, devote, consecrate.

voyage journey, trip, expedition, cruise, passage, crossing.

vulgar coarse, rough, crude, rude, boorish, uncouth, unmannerly, ill-bred, unrefined, uncultivated, indecorous, indecent, obscene, dirty, tasteless, common, low, base. REFINED
ordinary, general, popular, colloquial, vernacular.

vulnerable unprotected, assailable, defenceless, exposed, weak, tender, sensitive, susceptible. TOUGH

W

wad lump, mass, ball, hunk, chunk, block, roll, bundle.

waft drift, float, blow, puff, carry, bear, convey, transport.

wag[1] *v*, wave, swing, wiggle, waggle, flutter, nod, shake, quiver.

wag[2] *n*, humorist, comic, comedian, wit, joker, jester.

wage *n*, pay, emolument, salary, earnings, remuneration, compensation, hire, fee, stipend, payment, recompense, reward.
v, engage in, carry on, undertake, conduct, practise.

wager *n*, bet, gamble, stake, pledge, venture.
v, bet, gamble, stake, risk, hazard, speculate.

waggish impish, puckish, roguish, mischievous, arch, playful, sportive, witty, droll, humorous, comical, funny, jocular, merry. SERIOUS

wail *v*, cry, moan, lament, bewail, bemoan, mourn, weep, keen, ululate, howl. REJOICE
n, cry, moan, lament, lamentation, ululation, howl.

wait *v*, stay, remain, abide, rest, linger, tarry, pause, hesitate. PROCEED
wait for, await, expect, anticipate, look forward to, be ready for, be in store for.
wait on, serve, attend, minister to.
n, delay, stop, halt, pause, rest.

waiter attendant, servant, steward, stewardess, maid, waitress.

waive renounce, relinquish, give up, abandon, surrender, yield, forgo, dispense with, defer, postpone. ASSERT

wake[1] *v*, waken, come to, awake, awaken, rouse, arouse, stir, animate, stimulate, activate, enliven, kindle, fire, excite, quicken.
n, vigil, watch.

wake[2] *n*, trail, track, path, wash.

wakeful awake, sleepless, restless, insomniac. ASLEEP
alert, watchful, vigilant, wary, attentive, observant. UNWARY

waken wake, come to, awake, awaken, rouse, arouse, stir, animate, stimulate, activate, kindle, excite.

walk *v*, step, stride, pace, march, perambulate, saunter, amble, stroll, ramble, hike, tramp, trudge, go, move, advance, proceed. RUN
n, stroll, amble, saunter, promenade, ramble, hike, tramp, march, perambulation, constitutional. RIDE
step, pace, gait, carriage.
path, footpath, pathway, pavement, esplanade, promenade.
field, sphere, province, course, trade, profession, career, vocation.

wall divider, partition, screen, fence, enclosure, embankment, rampart, bulwark, barricade, barrier, block, obstacle, obstruction.

wallow roll, splash, welter, flounder, stagger, lurch.
bask, luxuriate, revel, delight, relish, savour.

wan pale, pallid, ashen, colourless, sallow, pasty, white, bloodless, ghastly, sickly, haggard, gaunt, tired, weary, worn, weak, faint, dim. RUDDY

wand stick, twig, rod, baton, staff, mace.

wander stray, roam, rove, meander, straggle, range, drift, ramble, stroll. SETTLE
deviate, swerve, veer, go astray, digress, rave, ramble.

wandering roaming, roving, itinerant, peripatetic, migratory, nomadic, vagrant, vagabond, wayfaring, travelling. SETTLED

wane *v*, diminish, decline, decrease, ebb, subside, abate, fade, peter out, dwindle, weaken, droop, sink. WAX
n, diminution, decline, decrease, ebb, subsidence, abatement, drop, fall.

wangle fix, arrange, manoeuvre, finagle (*inf*), bring off, pull off.

want *v*, need, require, demand, call for, lack, miss, wish, desire, long, yearn, hanker after, covet, crave, hunger, thirst. POSSESS
n, need, necessity, requirement, demand, wish, desire, longing, yearning, craving, appetite. POSSESSION
lack, absence, dearth, default, deficiency, inadequacy, insufficiency, shortage, paucity, scarcity. ABUNDANCE
poverty, privation, indigence, penury, destitution, neediness. WEALTH

wanting missing, absent, lacking, short, deficient, imperfect, defective, inferior.

wanton *adj*, lewd, lecherous, libidinous, prurient, licentious, loose, abandoned, dissolute, dissipated, promiscuous, impure, unchaste. CHASTE
needless, unnecessary, motiveless, groundless, unjustifiable, gratuitous, uncalled-for, wilful, deliberate, arbitrary, cruel, vicious, malicious, malevolent.
playful, sportive, capricious, irresponsible, careless, unrestrained, wild, lavish, extravagant, luxuriant.
n, whore, prostitute, loose woman, hussy, profligate, libertine, rake, roué.
v, dissipate, debauch, sleep around (*inf*).
waste, squander, misspend, fritter away. SAVE

war *n*, warfare, hostilities, fighting, combat, conflict, strife, contention, battle. PEACE
v, wage war, fight, battle, contend, combat.

warble trill, sing, chirp, pipe.

ward *n*, district, precinct, division, zone, quarter, area.
room, apartment.
minor, dependant, charge, protégé. GUARDIAN
guardianship, custody, charge, care, protection, safekeeping.

ward off, *v*, avert, deflect, parry, fend off, stave off, repel.

warden guardian, keeper, custodian, protector, guard, warder, curator, steward, janitor, caretaker.

warehouse depot, depository, store, storehouse, storeroom, stockroom.

wares goods, commodities, merchandise, produce, stock.

warfare war, hostilities, fighting, combat, strife, conflict, contention, battle. PEACE

warlike belligerent, bellicose, pugnacious, combative, hostile, militant, aggressive, martial, military. PACIFIC

warm *adj*, tepid, lukewarm, heated, hot, thermal. COOL
ardent, fervent, vehement, passionate, emotional, earnest, heartfelt, enthusiastic, animated, lively, energetic, vigorous. APATHETIC
friendly, affable, cordial, genial, hearty, amiable, affectionate, tender, kindly, warm-hearted, sympathetic. COLD
v, heat, reheat, animate, rouse, stir, awaken. COOL

warmth heat, warmness. COOLNESS
ardour, fervour, vehemence, passion, zeal, enthusiasm. APATHY
friendliness, cordiality, affection, tenderness. COLDNESS

warn caution, alert, forewarn, give notice, admonish, advise, notify, inform, apprise, tip off.

warning caution, admonition, advice, alert, alarm, notice, notification, tip, tip-off, threat, omen, portent, premonition, augury.

warp twist, bend, turn, contort, misshape, deform, distort, pervert, bias. STRAIGHTEN

warrant *n*, authorization, authority, permission, permit, sanction, licence, carte blanche, commission, warranty, guarantee.
v, guarantee, pledge, assure, declare, affirm, vouch for, endorse, support, uphold. REPUDIATE
authorize, entitle, empower, commission, license, sanction, approve, permit, allow, justify, excuse, require, call for.

warrantable permissible, allowable, lawful, acceptable, justifiable, defensible, reasonable, right. UNJUSTIFIABLE

wary cautious, careful, chary, circumspect, prudent, heedful, guarded, suspicious, distrustful, watchful, vigilant, attentive, alert. RASH

wash *v*, clean, cleanse, bath, bathe, launder, shampoo, scrub, rinse. SOIL
n, washing, bath, bathe, ablution, cleaning, cleansing, scrub, rinse.

washy watery, weak, thin, insipid, wishy-washy (*inf*).

waspish irritable, irascible, cross, cantankerous, peppery, crabbed, peevish, petulant, touchy, testy. GENIAL

waste *v*, squander, fritter away, misspend, dissipate, lose, use up, consume, throw away, blow (*inf*), lavish. SAVE
erode, wear, gnaw, eat away, dwindle, decrease, diminish, decline, decay, wither, shrivel, wilt, emaciate, weaken, wane, fade. FLOURISH
n, dissipation, prodigality, misuse, squandering, consumption, loss, extravagance, wastefulness. ECONOMY
destruction, devastation, ruin, desolation, havoc, ravage.
rubbish, refuse, trash, garbage, leftovers, scraps, litter, dross, dregs, debris.
wasteland, desert, wilderness, wild.
adj, useless, worthless, superfluous, leftover, unused, unwanted.
desolate, desert, wild, barren, bare, uninhabited, deserted, empty, dreary, bleak. CULTIVATED

wasteful extravagant, prodigal, lavish, spendthrift, thriftless, improvident, uneconomical. ECONOMICAL

watch *v*, observe, view, see, regard, look at, look on, contemplate, notice, note, mark. IGNORE
guard, protect, watch over, keep, mind, tend, look after, take care of. NEGLECT
be careful, pay attention, watch out, look out.
n, timepiece, chronometer, wristwatch, clock.
vigil, lookout, vigilance, watchfulness, attention, alertness, surveillance, observation.

watchful vigilant, alert, attentive, observant, guarded, cautious, chary, wary, heedful, careful, circumspect. HEEDLESS

watchword password, countersign, catchword, catch phrase, slogan, motto, byword.

water damp, moisten, wet, sprinkle, spray, hose, irrigate, flood. PARCH
water down, dilute, weaken, thin, adulterate.

waterfall cascade, cataract, fall, chute.

watery liquid, fluid, aqueous, wet, damp, moist. DRY
thin, runny, weak, diluted, adulterated, insipid, tasteless, washy, wishy-washy (*inf*).

wave *v*, flourish, brandish, shake, flap, flutter, wag, sway, rock, swing, oscillate, undulate, ripple.
beckon, gesture, gesticulate, signal.
n, undulation, ripple, roller, breaker, billow, swell, surge, rush, stream, drift, trend, current.

waver oscillate, vacillate, fluctuate, falter, hesitate, shillyshally (*inf*), dither, sway, wobble, flicker, quiver. DECIDE

wax grow, increase, develop, enlarge, expand, swell, rise. WANE

way method, manner, fashion, mode, means, procedure, system, technique, approach.
direction, route, course, path, road, track, lane, avenue, channel, passage, journey, advance.
custom, practice, wont, usage, habit, trait, idiosyncrasy, characteristic.
by the way, incidentally, in passing, en passant, by the bye.
give way, collapse, cave in, yield, acquiesce, accede, surrender.
under way, moving, going, in progress, begun.

wayward wilful, perverse, contrary, refractory, recalcitrant, contumacious, headstrong, stubborn, obstinate, unruly, intractable, ungovernable, unmanageable, capricious, fickle, flighty, inconstant. DOCILE

weak feeble, frail, fragile, delicate, flimsy, puny, enervated, sickly, unhealthy, debilitated, infirm, vulnerable. STRONG
powerless, impotent, ineffectual, lacking, wanting, poor, lame, unconvincing, inconclusive, timorous, spineless, irresolute, indecisive. POWERFUL
faint, low, muffled, imperceptible, dim, pale, dull, soft, slight, small.
watery, diluted, thin, runny, insipid, tasteless.

weaken enervate, debilitate, enfeeble, exhaust, sap, undermine, impair, dilute, adulterate, diminish, lessen, reduce, lower, droop, languish, flag, tire. STRENGTHEN

weakness feebleness, frailty, debility, infirmity, impotence, powerlessness, vulnerability. STRENGTH
fault, flaw, Achilles heel, deficiency, shortcoming, failing, foible.
liking, fondness, soft spot, partiality, predilection, inclination, penchant. AVERSION

wealth money, cash, capital, riches, assets, resources, means, fortune, affluence, opulence, prosperity, richness. POVERTY
abundance, plenty, profusion, bounty, plenitude, copiousness. SCARCITY

wealthy rich, prosperous, affluent, well-off, well-to-do, moneyed, loaded (*inf*). POOR
wear *v*, carry, bear, put on, don, have on, sport, show, display.
erode, waste, consume, eat away, corrode, abrade, rub, fray, impair, deteriorate. REINFORCE
last, endure.
tire, weary, fatigue, irritate, annoy, bore, tax, weaken, enervate, sap, exhaust, wear out. INVIGORATE
n, use, employment, utility, service.
clothes, clothing, attire, dress, garb, garments.
erosion, corrosion, abrasion, friction, wear and tear, deterioration.
wearisome tiring, fatiguing, wearing, exhausting, boring, tedious, monotonous, dull, flat, humdrum, routine, uninteresting. EXCITING
weary *adj*, tired, fatigued, worn out, exhausted, spent, jaded, fagged (*inf*), all in (*inf*), dead beat (*inf*), knackered (*inf*), bored, fed up. REFRESHED
wearisome, tiresome, boring, tedious, arduous, laborious, tiring.
v, tire, fatigue, exhaust, wear out, sap, drain, jade, bore, irk, vex. REFRESH
weather *n*, climate, conditions, temperature.
v, endure, withstand, resist, bear up, survive, pull through, surmount, rise above. SUCCUMB
weave interlace, lace, intertwine, twine, interweave, braid, plait, knit, join. UNRAVEL
make, create, build, construct, fabricate, spin. DESTROY
web cobweb, mesh, net, network, lattice.
wed marry, espouse, get hitched (*inf*), join, unite, fuse, blend, combine, ally. DIVORCE
wedding marriage, nuptials, matrimony, wedlock. DIVORCE
wedge *n*, lump, chunk, block, chock.
v, cram, pack, squeeze, stuff, block, jam, lodge.
weep cry, sob, wail, keen, moan, mourn, lament, grieve. REJOICE
weigh measure, balance, consider, contemplate, mull over, ponder, deliberate, reflect upon, examine, think about.
tell, count, carry weight, have influence.
load, weight, weigh down, encumber, burden, oppress. RELIEVE
weight *n*, heaviness, gravity, pressure, mass, load, burden.
importance, consequence, significance, moment, substance, power, influence, effect, impact.
v, load, weigh down, burden, oppress, bias.
weighty heavy, hefty (*inf*), ponderous, massive, burdensome, onerous. LIGHT
important, significant, consequential, momentous, grave, serious, crucial, critical. TRIVIAL
weird uncanny, eerie, supernatural, preternatural, unnatural, unearthly, ghostly, spooky (*inf*), mysterious, strange, bizarre, odd, queer, peculiar. ORDINARY
welcome *adj*, agreeable, pleasant, pleasing, desirable, acceptable, refreshing. UNWELCOME
n, greeting, salutation, reception, acceptance, hospitality.
v, greet, salute, hail, receive, meet.
welfare well-being, prosperity, health, happiness, comfort, advantage, benefit, good, interest.
well[1] *n*, spring, fountainhead, fount, wellspring, source, mine.
v, flow, gush, run, stream, ooze, spring, surge, pour, spout, jet.
well[2] *adv*, satisfactorily, adequately, sufficiently, considerably, highly, thoroughly, fully, completely, personally, intimately, properly, rightly, correctly, accurately, carefully, closely, skilfully, excellently, splendidly, smoothly, nicely, comfortably. BADLY
adj, healthy, fit, sound, hale, hearty, robust. ILL
satisfactory, good, fine, thriving, flourishing, lucky, fortunate, advisable. BAD
well-bred well-mannered, mannerly, civil, polite, courteous, gentlemanly, ladylike, refined, cultivated, polished, genteel. ILL-BRED
well-known famous, celebrated, renowned, illustrious, eminent, notable, popular, familiar. UNKNOWN
welter *v*, wallow, flounder, writhe, tumble, toss, roll, billow, swell, surge, heave.
n, jumble, muddle, hotchpotch, mess.
wend go, move, proceed, travel.
wet *adj*, damp, moist, soaked, drenched, saturated, dripping, sopping, sodden, sog-

gy, dank, humid, clammy, misty, showery, rainy, pouring. DRY
weak, feeble, spineless, timorous, soft, namby-pamby.
n, wetness, moisture, damp, dampness, water, rain.
v, damp, dampen, moisten, soak, drench, saturate, spray, sprinkle, irrigate. DRY

wharf dock, quay, pier, jetty.

wheedle cajole, coax, inveigle, charm, persuade, entice, entreat, implore, flatter, butter up, humour, court.

wheel *n*, disc, round, circle, ring, hoop, caster.
turn, revolution, rotation, roll, twirl, whirl, spin.
v, turn, spin, rotate, revolve, pivot, swivel, twirl, whirl, roll, swing.

whereabouts location, place, position, situation.

wherewithal means, resources, supplies, funds, cash, money.

whet sharpen, hone, edge, strop, file, grind. BLUNT
stimulate, arouse, rouse, stir, awaken, kindle, excite, provoke, incite, increase.

whiff *n*, breath, puff, gust, blast, trace, hint, smell, odour.
v, waft, blow, puff, breathe, inhale, sniff, smell.

whim fancy, crotchet, caprice, notion, idea, impulse, whimsy, humour, quirk, vagary, freak.

whimper cry, snivel, sob, weep, blubber, whine, moan. LAUGH

whimsical fanciful, capricious, impulsive, playful, freakish, eccentric, weird, odd, curious, quaint, funny, droll.

whine *v*, cry, sob, whimper, whinge (*inf*), wail, moan, complain, grumble, grouse, gripe (*inf*).
n, cry, whimper, wail, moan, complaint, grumble.

whip *v*, beat, lash, flog, scourge, flagellate, birch, cane, spank, thrash, punish, castigate, discipline, chastise. CARESS
pull, jerk, whisk, snatch, flash, show.
drive, push, spur, provoke, urge, encourage.
n, lash, scourge, cat-o'-nine-tails, birch, cane, crop.

whirl *v*, spin, twirl, pivot, pirouette, gyrate, reel, rotate, revolve, turn, wheel.
n, spin, twirl, pirouette, gyration, rotation, revolution, turn.
attempt, try, go, shot (*inf*), crack (*inf*), stab.

whisk beat, whip, snatch, seize, flap, flick, brush, sweep.
dart, dash, tear, fly, race, rush, hurry, speed. AMBLE

whisper *v*, murmur, mutter, mumble, breathe, sigh, hiss, rustle. SHOUT
hint, intimate, insinuate, reveal, disclose, divulge.
n, undertone, murmur, sigh, hiss, rustle.

whit iota, jot, tittle, particle, bit, scrap, grain, speck, mite, atom, trace, scintilla.

white pale, pallid, wan, ashen, pasty. RUDDY
light, snowy, silvery, hoary, grey. DARK
pure, clean, spotless, immaculate, unsullied, stainless. FOUL

whiten bleach, blanch, etiolate, fade, blench, pale. COLOUR

whittle cut, carve, shave, pare, trim, reduce.

whole *adj*, entire, complete, total, full, integral, undivided. PARTIAL
perfect, flawless, intact, sound, unbroken, in one piece, unimpaired, undamaged, unharmed, unscathed, fit, well, healthy, recovered.
n, aggregate, total, sum total, all, entirety, totality, ensemble, unit. PART

wholehearted hearty, unreserved, heartfelt, sincere, genuine, real, earnest, enthusiastic, dedicated, devoted. HALF-HEARTED

wholesome healthy, sanitary, hygienic, salubrious, salutary, beneficial, good, nourishing, nutritious, bracing, invigorating. DELETERIOUS

wholly entirely, purely, completely, totally, fully, perfectly, altogether, thoroughly, utterly, absolutely, exclusively. PARTLY

whore prostitute, harlot, fallen woman, strumpet, trollop, courtesan, call girl, streetwalker, tart (*inf*), hooker (*inf*).

wicked evil, bad, wrong, sinful, iniquitous, vile, villainous, heinous, nefarious, flagitious, atrocious, abominable, criminal, unprincipled, godless, profane, immoral, abandoned, depraved, corrupt. VIRTUOUS
naughty, mischievous, impish, roguish. GOOD

wide broad, extensive, large, thick, roomy, spacious, capacious, ample, full, vast, immense, comprehensive, catholic, encyclopedic, inclusive, general. NARROW

widen broaden, extend, expand, spread, stretch, enlarge, open. NARROW

widespread rife, prevalent, extensive, general, universal, sweeping, far-reaching, wide-ranging. RESTRICTED

width breadth, thickness, diameter, span, reach, scope, range, compass, extent, measure.

wield handle, manipulate, brandish, flourish, control, manage, hold, have, use, exercise, employ, exert.

wild untamed, undomesticated, feral, ferine, savage, ferocious, fierce, barbarous, primitive, uncivilized, natural, uncultivated, desolate, waste, desert, uninhabited. TAME

violent, furious, stormy, tempestuous, turbulent, riotous, boisterous, rowdy, rough, lawless, unruly, undisciplined, intractable, unmanageable, unbridled, unrestrained. RESTRAINED

rash, reckless, madcap, foolhardy, imprudent, foolish, outrageous, preposterous, extravagant, impracticable. SENSIBLE

disorderly, untidy, messy, dishevelled, tousled, unkempt. TIDY

wile stratagem, artifice, device, contrivance, subterfuge, trick, ruse, manoeuvre.

cunning, artfulness, slyness, craft, guile, trickery, chicanery, deceit, fraud. ARTLESSNESS

wilful headstrong, obstinate, stubborn, mulish, pig-headed, obdurate, adamant, intransigent, unyielding, perverse, contrary, wayward, self-willed. DOCILE

intentional, deliberate, premeditated, voluntary. ACCIDENTAL

will *n*, volition, option, choice, discretion, decision.

wish, desire, fancy, inclination, preference, pleasure.

purpose, determination, resolution, resolve, firmness, willpower.

v, ordain, decree, order, command, cause, determine, decide, choose, see fit, want, wish, desire.

leave, bequeath, pass on, hand down.

willing disposed, inclined, ready, game (*inf*), desirous, nothing loath, eager, enthusiastic, happy, pleased, agreeable, compliant, consenting, amenable. RELUCTANT

willingly freely, voluntarily, happily, gladly, cheerfully, readily, eagerly. RELUCTANTLY

wilt wither, shrivel, droop, sag, weaken, languish, fade, flag, dwindle, ebb, diminish, fail. THRIVE

wily artful, crafty, cunning, sly, foxy, subtle, shrewd, astute, tricky, shifty, scheming, designing, underhand, deceitful. ARTLESS

win *v*, triumph, succeed, conquer, vanquish, prevail, overcome, come first. LOSE

achieve, attain, accomplish, gain, get, obtain, acquire, procure, secure, earn, take, catch, net.

win over, persuade, convince, sway, influence, convert, carry, bring round, prevail upon.

n, victory, triumph, success, conquest. DEFEAT

wince flinch, start, blench, quail, shrink, recoil, draw back, cringe.

wind[1] *n*, air, draught, breeze, zephyr, puff, breath, blast, gust, gale, hurricane, typhoon, tornado, cyclone.

babble, idle talk, hot air, humbug.

gas, flatus, flatulence.

hint, suggestion, intimation, inkling, report, rumour.

wind[2] *v*, coil, curl, wreathe, twine, twist, turn, loop, bend, curve, zigzag, meander, snake.

winding twisting, turning, sinuous, serpentine, tortuous, circuitous, indirect, roundabout, meandering, flexuous, spiral, crooked. STRAIGHT

windy breezy, blowy, blustery, gusty, stormy, squally. STILL

verbose, wordy, prolix, loquacious, bombastic, empty.

wing arm, branch, group, set, faction, side, extension, annexe.

wink blink, flutter, twinkle, sparkle, flash, gleam.

wink at, ignore, disregard, overlook, tolerate, condone, connive at.

winner victor, champion, conqueror, hero. LOSER

winnow sift, screen, separate, sort out, select, cull.

winsome winning, engaging, charming, pleasing, delightful, agreeable, sweet, pretty, attractive, fetching (*inf*), alluring, captivating, fascinating, enchanting. REPULSIVE

wintry brumal, hibernal, cold, freezing, icy, frosty, bleak, desolate, cheerless, dismal. SUMMERY

wipe rub, clean, mop, sponge, dust, brush, dry.

wipe out, destroy, obliterate, erase, eradicate, exterminate, annihilate.

wisdom sagacity, sapience, discernment, penetration, sense, reason, judgment, judiciousness, perspicacity, acumen, understanding, intelligence, prudence, foresight, knowledge, learning, erudition, enlightenment. FOLLY

wise sage, sagacious, sapient, perceptive, discerning, judicious, prudent, politic, reasonable, rational, sensible, intelligent, smart, shrewd, astute, erudite, knowledgeable, learned, informed, aware. FOOLISH

wish *v*, desire, want, long, yearn, hanker after, covet, crave, hunger, thirst, prefer.
bid, ask, order, command.
n, desire, want, longing, yearning, hope, aspiration, hankering, craving, liking, preference.
bidding, request, command, order, will.

wishful desirous, longing, wishing, hopeful, optimistic, expectant.

wistful pensive, thoughtful, reflective, meditative, musing, dreaming, longing, yearning, melancholy, sad.

wit humour, drollery, facetiousness, wittiness, repartee, badinage, banter, raillery.
humorist, comic, comedian, wag.
intelligence, brains, understanding, wisdom, discernment, acumen, insight, perception, sense, common sense, cleverness, ingenuity. STUPIDITY

witch sorceress, enchantress, necromancer, magician, soothsayer.

witchcraft witchery, sorcery, magic, necromancy, wizardry, voodoo, occultism, incantation, spell, charm, enchantment.

with using, accompanying, among, having, possessing, concerning, regarding. WITHOUT

withdraw retract, recoil, draw back, remove, pull out, take back, recall, recant, disavow, unsay, disclaim, revoke, rescind. PRESENT
retire, retreat, pull out, secede, drop out, leave, depart, go. REMAIN

withdrawn shy, reserved, retiring, introverted, aloof, distant, quiet, taciturn, uncommunicative. EXTROVERT

wither shrivel, shrink, droop, wilt, fade, languish, waste, decay, dry, blast, blight. FLOURISH

withering scornful, humiliating, mortifying, devastating.

withhold retain, keep, keep back, hold back, restrain, check, suppress, repress, hide, conceal, reserve, refrain. GIVE

without lacking, short of, free from, excluding. WITH

withstand oppose, resist, stand up to, defy, confront, face, brave, weather, take, bear, endure, tolerate. YIELD

witness *n*, eyewitness, onlooker, spectator, viewer, observer, bystander.
testifier, deponent, attestant.
testimony, attestation, deposition, statement, evidence, proof.
v, see, observe, view, watch, look on, mark, note, notice, attend. MISS
testify, bear witness, give evidence, depose, confirm, corroborate, attest, endorse.

witty humorous, droll, funny, amusing, waggish, jocular, clever, original. DULL

wizard sorcerer, warlock, necromancer, magician, enchanter, conjurer.
expert, adept, ace (*inf*), master, virtuoso, genius.

wizened shrivelled, shrunken, dried up, withered, wrinkled.

wobble shake, tremble, quake, quiver, rock, totter, teeter, sway.

woe grief, misery, sorrow, sadness, unhappiness, heartache, depression, melancholy, anguish, distress, suffering, affliction, adversity, misfortune, trial, tribulation, disaster, calamity. JOY

woeful woebegone, sad, unhappy, sorrowful, miserable, wretched, depressed, dejected, disconsolate, despondent, tragic, grievous, disastrous, calamitous, piteous, pitiable, pitiful, pathetic, deplorable, lamentable. JOYFUL

woman female, lady, girl, lass, miss, bird (*inf*). MAN
maid, domestic, housekeeper, charwoman, lady-in-waiting.

womanly feminine, gentle, tender, motherly, ladylike, womanish.

wonder *n*, awe, wonderment, admiration, amazement, astonishment, surprise, bewilderment, curiosity. INDIFFERENCE
marvel, phenomenon, miracle, prodigy, curiosity, rarity, sight, spectacle.

v, meditate, ponder, muse, think, speculate, conjecture, question, query, puzzle, ask oneself.
marvel, gape, stare.

wonderful marvellous, extraordinary, remarkable, prodigious, phenomenal, amazing, astonishing, astounding, surprising, wondrous, awe-inspiring, incredible, miraculous, fantastic, super (*inf*), splendid, magnificent, superb, excellent, great (*inf*), smashing (*inf*). ORDINARY

wont habit, routine, practice, custom, use.

wonted habitual, customary, familiar, usual, regular, accustomed. UNUSUAL

woo court, make love to, chase, pursue, importune.

wood forest, woodland, thicket, copse, coppice, grove. CLEARING

word *n*, term, name, expression, utterance.
chat, talk, discussion, conversation.
news, tidings, communication, report, notice, message, information, intelligence.
promise, pledge, assurance, guarantee, oath, vow.
command, order, instruction, signal.
v, phrase, put, express, utter, say.

wordy verbose, prolix, garrulous, loquacious, windy, long-winded, rambling, discursive. TERSE

work *n*, toil, labour, effort, exertion, drudgery, industry. IDLENESS
task, job, chore, duty, assignment, commission.
occupation, employment, job, business, profession, vocation, calling, career, trade, craft.
product, creation, opus, composition, production, achievement.
v, toil, labour, drudge, slave, exert oneself, be busy. REST
be employed, have a job, earn a living, ply one's trade, do business.
operate, function, go, run, perform, act. FAIL
handle, manipulate, wield, ply, use, manage, control, operate.
accomplish, achieve, effect, cause, bring about, produce.

work out, solve, resolve, clear up, figure out, calculate.
plan, arrange, devise, contrive, formulate, elaborate.

work up, rouse, excite, stir, move, stimulate, animate, arouse, foment.

worker employee, workman, labourer, hand, tradesman, operative, artisan, craftsman.

works factory, mill, plant, workshop.
machinery, mechanism, movement, action, workings, parts.

world earth, globe, planet, star, universe, cosmos, creation.
mankind, humankind, humanity, human race, everybody, everyone.
sphere, realm, kingdom, domain, province, field.

worldly temporal, earthly, terrestrial, mundane, physical, material, secular, profane. SPIRITUAL
materialistic, greedy, avaricious, covetous.
cosmopolitan, urbane, sophisticated, worldly-wise. UNSOPHISTICATED

worried anxious, troubled, concerned, disturbed, uneasy, ill at ease, tense, on edge, nervous, apprehensive, fearful, afraid. CALM

worry *vi*, fret, be anxious, agonize, brood.
vt, disturb, bother, trouble, harass, plague, torment, tease, pester, badger, vex, irritate, annoy, distress, upset. REASSURE
n, anxiety, uneasiness, concern, trouble, problem, care, nervousness, apprehension, fear, annoyance, vexation, irritation, bother, pest, plague, torment. DELIGHT

worsen deteriorate, degenerate, decline, get worse, aggravate, exacerbate. IMPROVE

worship *v*, venerate, revere, reverence, honour, esteem, adore, idolize, deify, adulate, praise, exalt, glorify. SCORN
n, veneration, reverence, homage, adoration, honour, esteem, adulation, praise, glorification, exaltation. CONTEMPT

worst defeat, beat, conquer, vanquish, best, crush, overcome, overpower, overwhelm, rout.

worth worthiness, merit, quality, virtue, usefulness, utility, advantage, good, help, avail, cost, price, value, estimation.

worthless valueless, nugatory, trivial, insignificant, paltry, trashy, useless, unavailing, vain, futile, vile, base, abject, contemptible, despicable. WORTHY

worthy deserving, meritorious, laudable, praiseworthy, estimable, admirable, worthwhile, valuable, good, decent, honest, upright, noble, excellent, exemplary, reputable. UNWORTHY

wound *n*, injury, hurt, harm, damage, cut, gash, laceration, lesion, trauma, shock.
v, injure, hurt, harm, damage, cut, gash, lacerate, pierce, grieve, offend. HEAL

wrangle *v*, argue, quarrel, bicker, squabble, row, brawl, differ, disagree. AGREE
n, argument, quarrel, squabble, tiff, row, brawl, dispute, controversy. AGREEMENT

wrap envelop, enfold, encase, sheathe, enclose, cover, shroud, cloak, muffle, swathe, wind, fold, parcel, package. UNWRAP

wrath anger, ire, rage, fury, passion, indignation, resentment, exasperation. COMPOSURE

wrathful angry, irate, incensed, enraged, raging, furious, passionate, indignant, displeased, exasperated. PLEASED

wreak inflict, execute, carry out, cause, bring about, vent, indulge, gratify.

wreath garland, festoon, chaplet, coronal.

wreathe festoon, adorn, twist, wind, coil, twine, encircle, surround, envelop, enfold.

wreck *v*, ruin, destroy, demolish, devastate, smash, shatter, spoil, upset. BUILD
n, ruin, mess, destruction, devastation, desolation, demolition, wreckage, debris, remains, fragments.

wrench strain, sprain, rick, twist, jerk, pull, tug, force.

wrest seize, take, pull, twist, wrench, force.

wrestle fight, grapple, scuffle, tussle, battle, strive, struggle, contend.

wretch rogue, scoundrel, rascal, blackguard, ruffian, villain, miscreant, rotter (*inf*), vagabond, outcast, beggar, unfortunate.

wretched miserable, poor, sorry, pitiable, pitiful, pathetic, unfortunate, hapless, forlorn, woebegone, sad, unhappy, abject, contemptible, despicable, base, vile, worthless. FINE

wriggle squirm, writhe, twist, wiggle, worm, snake, slink, crawl.

wring squeeze, extract, twist, wrench, wrest, force, extort.

wrinkle *v*, crease, fold, crumple, crinkle, pucker, gather, furrow, corrugate. SMOOTH
n, crease, fold, crumple, pucker, line, ridge, furrow, corrugation.

write pen, inscribe, scribble, scrawl, record, jot down, draft, compose.

writhe wriggle, squirm, twist, turn, contort, distort.

writing handwriting, penmanship, script, calligraphy, scribble, scrawl.
book, publication, opus, work, composition, letter.

wrong *adj*, incorrect, inaccurate, imprecise, inexact, erroneous, mistaken, false, untrue. CORRECT
bad, sinful, iniquitous, immoral, wicked, evil, wrongful, unlawful, illegal, illicit, criminal, crooked, dishonest, dishonourable. GOOD
inappropriate, unsuitable, inapt, improper, unseemly, indecorous. RIGHT
adv, amiss, awry, astray, badly, wrongly, incorrectly. PROPERLY
n, sin, misdeed, trespass, transgression, offence, crime, error, mistake, wickedness, iniquity, unfairness, injustice. RIGHT
v, abuse, mistreat, maltreat, ill-treat, oppress, exploit, cheat, hurt, injure, malign.

wrongful unjust, unfair, improper, illegal, unlawful, criminal, immoral, wrong. RIGHTFUL

wrought-up worked up, excited, aroused, inflamed, animated, keyed up, overwrought, agitated. CALM

wry awry, askew, crooked, lopsided, twisted, distorted, contorted, deformed. STRAIGHT
droll, witty, dry, ironic. SERIOUS

X

Xmas Christmas, Noel, Yule, Yuletide.

x-ray radiograph, shadowgraph, roentgenograph, roentgenogram.

Y

yank pull, jerk, tug, snatch.

yap yelp, bark, yammer (*inf*), chatter, jabber.

yard quadrangle, courtyard, enclosure, compound.

yardstick measure, gauge, standard, criterion, touchstone, benchmark.

yarn tale, story, anecdote.
thread, fibre.

yearn desire, long, pine, hanker after, covet, crave, hunger, thirst, lust.
yell shout, scream, cry, shriek, bellow, roar, howl, bawl. WHISPER
yelp yap, bark, cry, yell.
yet still, but, nevertheless, however.
so far, until now, up to now, as yet.
moreover, besides, as well, in addition.
yield *v*, produce, bear, give, supply, furnish, afford, bring in, earn.
surrender, part with, relinquish, forgo, renounce, resign, cede, give up, quit, abandon, submit, capitulate, succumb, give in, acquiesce, comply, concede, agree, consent, allow. RESIST
n, crop, produce, harvest, return.
yielding submissive, docile, tractable, obedient, manageable, compliant, amenable, obliging, complaisant, accommodating. STUBBORN
flexible, pliant, pliable, supple, soft, elastic. RIGID
yoke *n*, collar, harness, link, tie, bond, coupling.
oppression, servitude, slavery, bondage. FREEDOM
v, couple, link, unite, join, connect, fasten, hitch, harness. RELEASE
yokel rustic, peasant, bumpkin, clodhopper (*inf*), boor.
young youthful, adolescent, juvenile, childish, immature, green, callow, inexperienced, fresh, new, early, recent. OLD
youngster child, kid (*inf*), boy, girl, youth, teenager. ADULT
youth childhood, early life, adolescence, immaturity. AGE
adolescent, teenager, youngster, boy, lad, stripling. MAN
youthful young, boyish, girlish, childish, immature, fresh, vigorous, active. OLD

Z

zany comical, funny, clownish, crazy, loony (*inf*). SERIOUS
zeal fervour, ardour, passion, fire, warmth, enthusiasm, eagerness, keenness, earnestness, intensity, vigour, energy, vehemence, devotion, fanaticism. APATHY
zealot fanatic, enthusiast, partisan, bigot, extremist.
zealous fervent, ardent, passionate, enthusiastic, eager, keen, earnest, intense, vehement, devoted, fanatical. APATHETIC
zenith height, peak, summit, pinnacle, apex, vertex, top, acme, climax, culmination. NADIR
zero nought, nothing, nil, cipher, bottom, nadir.
zest relish, spice, tang, savour, flavour, taste, pungency, piquancy. INSIPIDITY
gusto, relish, appetite, enjoyment, keenness, enthusiasm.
zigzag crooked, tortuous, serpentine, meandering, twisting, winding. STRAIGHT
zone area, region, district, section, sector, territory, domain, sphere.
zoom shoot, fly, speed, race, rush, tear, buzz, whizz.